THE NEW YORK IRISH

WITHDRAWN

THE
NEW YORK
IRISH

Edited by

Ronald H. Bayor and

Timothy J. Meagher

The Johns Hopkins University Press

Baltimore and London

This book has been brought to publication with the generous
assistance of the Irish Institute of New York, Inc.

© 1996 The Johns Hopkins University Press
All rights reserved. Published 1996
Printed in the United States of America on acid-free paper

Johns Hopkins Paperbacks edition, 1997
9 8 7 6 5 4 3 2

The Johns Hopkins University Press
2715 North Charles Street, Baltimore, Maryland 21218-4363
The Johns Hopkins Press Ltd., London
www.press.jhu.edu

Library of Congress Cataloging-in-Publication Data will be found at the end of this book.
A catalog record for this book is available from the British Library.

ISBN 0-8018-5764-3 (pbk.)

In honor of the members

of the

Irish Institute of New York,

both living and deceased,

and

in memory of

Dennis J. Clark

who reminded us of our obligation

★

The past is prologue.

Contents

List of Illustrations and Tables xi

Foreword   xv
Paul O'Dwyer

Preface   xvii

Acknowledgments   xxi

Introduction   1

PART I   COLONIAL AND EARLY NATIONAL AMERICA

Overview   The Irish and the Emerging City: Settlement
to 1844   11
Leo Hershkowitz

Chapter 1   "Upon a bunch of straw": The Irish in Colonial
New York City   35
Joyce D. Goodfriend

Chapter 2   Religion, Ethnicity, and History: Clues to the
             Cultural Construction of Law   48
             Walter J. Walsh

Chapter 3   The Development of an Irish American Community
             in New York City before the Great Migration   70
             Paul A. Gilje

PART II   THE GREAT MIGRATION: 1844 to 1877

Overview   "The Most Irish City in the Union": The Era of the
             Great Migration, 1844–1877   87
             Hasia R. Diner

Chapter 4   "Desirable Companions and Lovers": Irish and
             African Americans in the Sixth Ward, 1830–1870
             107
             Graham Hodges

Chapter 5   Quimbo Appo's Fear of Fenians: Chinese-Irish-
             Anglo Relations in New York City   125
             John Kuo Wei Tchen

Chapter 6   Illness and Medical Care among Irish
             Immigrants in Antebellum New York   153
             Alan M. Kraut

Chapter 7   Shrewd Irishmen: Irish Entrepreneurs and
             Artisans in New York's Clothing Industry,
             1830–1880   169
             William E. Devlin

Chapter 8   Union Green: The Irish Community and the
             Civil War   193
             Edward K. Spann

PART III   THE TURN OF THE CENTURY: 1877 to 1914

Overview   Forging Forward and Looking Back   213
             Lawrence J. McCaffrey

Chapter 9   Going to the Ladies' Fair: Irish Catholics in New
             York City, 1870–1900   234
             Colleen McDannell

Chapter 10 The Irish Language in New York, 1850–1900
252
Kenneth E. Nilsen

Chapter 11 Irish County Societies in New York, 1880–1914
275
John T. Ridge

Chapter 12 The Irish American Worker in Transition,
1877–1914: New York City as a Test Case 301
John R. McKivigan and Thomas J. Robertson

Chapter 13 "In Time of Peace, Prepare for War": Key Themes in
the Social Thought of New York's Irish
Nationalists, 1890–1916 321
David Brundage

PART IV   THE EARLY TWENTIETH CENTURY:
1914 to 1945

Overview When New York Was Irish, and After 337
Chris McNickle

Chapter 14 Striking for Ireland on the New York Docks 357
Joe Doyle

Chapter 15 Of "Mornin' Glories" and "Fine Old Oaks": John
Purroy Mitchel, Al Smith, and Reform as an
Expression of Irish American Aspiration 374
John F. McClymer

Chapter 16 "From the East Side to the Seaside": Irish
Americans on the Move in New York City 395
Marion R. Casey

PART V   THE MODERN ERA: 1945 to 1992

Overview An End and a Beginning 419
David M. Reimers

Chapter 17 The Neighborhood Changed: The Irish of
Washington Heights and Inwood since 1945 439
Robert W. Snyder

Chapter 18 Emigrants, *Eirepreneurs*, and Opportunists:
A Social Profile of Recent Irish Immigration in New
York City   461
Mary P. Corcoran

Chapter 19 Irish Traditional and Popular Music in New York
City: Identity and Social Change, 1930–1975   481
Rebecca S. Miller

Chapter 20 The Heart's Speech No Longer Stifled: New York
Irish Writing since the 1960s   508
Charles Fanning

Conclusion   533

Appendix 1 Statistical Tables   551

Appendix 2 Maps   565

Notes   575

Select Bibliography   703

Contributors   709

Index   715

List of Illustrations
and Tables

Illustrations

The O'Connell Brothers' milk wagon	9
Manhattan from Brooklyn Heights, 1834	33
William Sampson	55
St. Patrick's Day parade, 1871	85
Irish Emigrant Society office	92
July 12, 1871 Orange-Green riot	98
Sixth Ward, 1846 (map)	111
"How the Chinaman Might Gain Favor"	133
Devlin & Co. billhead	184
Interior of Knox Hats	187
Departure of the Sixty-ninth Regiment, 1861	196
"The Tiger's Share"	211
St. Vincent's Nursery	220
25th Precinct station house	230
St. Patrick's Cathedral Grand Fair	242
The Gael, November 1900	269
County Monaghan Men's Society dance class	293
Laying street railway tracks, c. 1891	302
St. Columcille Branch, FOIF	333
First grade class, St. Patrick's School	335
Freshman class, St. Francis College	343

IRT motormen, c. 1929   354
St. Simon Stock baseball player, 1939   404
Football players, Gaelic Park, c. 1980   417
Paul O'Dwyer and John F. Kennedy   430
County Antrim Society Banner   434
Michael Flannery   435
Stouffer's restaurant, Pershing Square   474
Presentation of UICA *Feis* poster   503
Manhattan neighborhoods and parishes (map)   566
Brooklyn neighborhoods and parishes (map)   567
Bronx neighborhoods and parishes (map)   568
Queens neighborhoods and parishes (map)   569
Staten Island neighborhoods and parishes (map)   570
Manhattan, Annexed District, Brooklyn and Kings County,
    Irish stock, 1890 (map)   571
Irish-born, New York City, 1920 (map)   572
Irish-born, New York City, 1970 (map)   573

Tables

Irish and African American Populations of New York City and Sixth
    Ward, 1830–1870   110
Sixth Ward Groceries and Porterhouses   119
Population of Ireland by Province, 1881, and Irish Immigrant Arrivals
    to All Destinations and New York City, May 6 to July 29, 1882   286
Irish Immigrants to New York City, May 6 to July 29, 1882   288
Immigrants to Manhattan and Brooklyn   289
Number of Irish-born by New York City Borough, 1910–50   396
Irish Stock, New York City, 1910–60   396
Comparison of City Population by Borough with Irish-born Population,
    1910 and 1930   402
Net Irish Emigration, 1980–90   462
Immigrants Admitted to the United States from Ireland, 1980–90   463
Irish-born Population, New York City, by Decade, 1860–1990   551
Irish-born, Manhattan and Annexed District, 1855, 1865, 1875, by Ward   552
Irish-born, Brooklyn and Kings County, 1855, 1865, 1875, by Town or
    Ward   554
Irish-born, Queens County, 1855, 1865, 1875, by Town or Ward   556
Irish-born, Staten Island, 1855, 1865, 1875, by Area   557
Irish Stock, Manhattan, Annexed District and Brooklyn (Kings County)
    1890, by Ward   558
Percentage of Irish-born Naturalizations, New York City, 1910–1930   560
Percentage of Irish-born Population, New York City, 1930, by Year
    of Emigration and Borough   560
Family Size by Foreign-born Group, New York City, 1930   561

Percentage of Gainfully Employed Workers in Foreign-born Families,
New York City, 1930   561

Percentage of Foreign-born Home Ownership, New York City, 1930,
by Borough, Value, and Monthly Rental (Nonfarm Homes)   562

Number of Persons Claiming Single or Multiple Irish Ancestry,
New York City, 1980   563

Number of Persons Claiming Irish Ancestry, New York City, 1980
and 1990   563

Irish-born Population, New York City, 1990, by Year of Emigration   564

Foreword

WHEN I looked through my library several years ago, it struck me that books had been written about the Irish in Boston, Butte, Chicago, Cleveland, Detroit, Lowell, New Orleans, Philadelphia, San Francisco, and St. Louis. Why wasn't there a history of the Irish in New York City? We certainly have been in the city longer than any other ethnic group. With 300 years of continuous emigration from Ireland, New York has been a port of entry, temporary stopping point, and place of settlement for millions of Irish women and men. During those centuries, the city has undergone massive changes, and the Irish have played a crucial part in its history.

The incredible complexity of the subject was no doubt a challenge, yet not since the days of Michael O'Brien in the 1930s have the New York Irish had a historian to take up their tale. O'Brien is now dismissed—some say his work lacks analysis—but at least he had enthusiasm and the diligence needed to tackle primary sources. With the year 2000 swiftly approaching, there was an urgent need for the Irish community to encourage professional historians to follow O'Brien's lead and document the Irish role in New York's history.

In the 1980s certain events came to pass that allowed a financial and administrative collaboration between the Irish Institute of New York, Inc., and the New York Irish History Roundtable. Together we had the means necessary to commission the best scholars in the country to undertake primary research. We asked them to examine our relationship to New York City honestly and to give us no credit but that which we deserved.

This volume is the result. It is only a start—a collection of essays to help us better understand our history in this city. Its publication would not have been possible without the support of the members of the Irish Institute. It is their legacy.

Paul O'Dwyer

Preface

I N HIS essay for this collection, Charles Fanning recounts a story by Elizabeth Cullinan called "Commuting." Cullinan's story traces an Irish Catholic woman's journey to Manhattan after being let go from a Catholic college in one of the outer boroughs. It is a journey through time as well as space, a recollection at each stop of her family's sometimes painful odyssey through different homes and neighborhoods. At the end of her commute, she ponders the larger meaning of this simple bus trip: "I've reenacted in spirit the journey that has given my life its substance and shape, color and brightness."

This book is an attempt, if not to reenact, then to remember the far longer journey the Irish people of New York have taken over the past 300 or more years. The idea for the book was born in the Irish community of New York, in the shared conviction of the New York Irish History Roundtable and the Irish Institute that the Irish people of New York and their neighbors needed to know more about New York's Irish history. It was not a paean to past glories that the Roundtable and Institute sought, but a probing, scholarly examination of Celtic experience in America's largest city. The Roundtable, with support from the Irish Institute, thus recruited a number of scholars to advise it on how such a book might be written. Those scholars included Jay Dolan, Kerby Miller, Sean Wilentz, James Donnelly, David Reimers, Leo Hershkowitz, Hasia Diner, William Griffin, John Ridge,

Kenneth Jackson, the late Dennis Clark, and the coeditors. Those scholars, along with Marion Casey and Angela Carter from the Roundtable and Paul O'Dwyer and Kevin Morrissey from the Institute, became the editorial advisory board for the project.

The board met in January 1990 to discuss the nature and format of the book. Although the advisers recognized the need for a general synthesis of New York Irish history, they did not believe enough scholarship existed for such a work. They therefore agreed that the book should consist of essays summarizing what is already known about the history of the New York Irish in successive chronological periods, followed by original essays focusing on specific events, trends, movements, or persons that illuminate the Irish experience in each period. The editors solicited topical essays from more than 40 scholars and invited submissions at important conferences. Sixty proposals were submitted, and in August 1990 the advisers met again to consider these submissions.

The essays in this book were chosen not because they fill in any grand narrative or fit into broad thematic categories, but because they represent the best current, original research on the history of the New York Irish. Indeed, they move the study of the New York Irish into entirely new areas or bring fresh perspectives to older topics. Joe Doyle's essay, for example, departs from the usual treatment of Irish nationalist movements by considering the role of women in such movements, and Colleen McDannell's investigates the critically important but largely ignored fund-raising mechanism, the Ladies' Fair, in the building of an Irish Catholic subsociety. Perhaps an even more radical departure is taken in John Kuo Wei Tchen's piece on relations between the Irish and Chinese as seen through the eyes of Quimbo Appo, a Chinese immmigrant who was ultimately confined in a lunatic asylum, suffering, he believed, for Ireland until it won its independence.

Together, these specific essays and the introductory overviews in each section present an intriguing chronicle of the life of the New York Irish since the seventeenth century and almost the very beginning of the city itself. Their colonial history is not easy to recover, for it is overshadowed in public memory by the experience of the Famine migrants who came after the first Irish settlers. The overview of the early period by Leo Hershkowitz and the specific essays by Joyce Goodfriend, Walter Walsh, and Paul Gilje thus help to fill in a story that until now has remained sketchy. They tell of an economically, religiously, and even ethnically divided Irish people in eighteenth-century New York. (The New York "Irish" in those days included French Huguenots and German Palatines who had fled wars in their own country to settle in Ireland before remigrating shortly thereafter to New York.) That gave way slowly in the early nineteenth century to a more cohesive, working- or lower-class Catholic community. A remarkable trio of men—Thomas Addis Emmet, William MacNeven, and William Sampson— presided over this transition and helped crack open a monocultural Protestant New York to make space for the Catholic Irish.

The population of the new Catholic community exploded when the potato crop failed in Ireland and hundreds of thousands of Irish men and women, including skilled artisans as well as impoverished peasants, were cast out upon the Atlantic to seek survival in New York and other cities. The Irish of this era seem more familiar to us today than their predecessors of the seventeenth or eighteenth century. The Famine, a tragedy of immense proportions, and the massive tide of refugees it generated continue to figure strongly in the public imagination. The essays covering this period—Hasia Diner's overview and pieces by William Devlin, Graham Hodges, John Kuo Wei Tchen, Alan Kraut, and Edward Spann—flesh out this familiar story but also revise and extend it. They discuss the poverty, degradation, illness, wartime casualties, and prejudice suffered by these migrants. They analyze as well the bitter antipathy of the new Irish immigrants to the African and Asian Americans who shared their neighborhoods in the slums of the Lower East Side, pointing out also that the Irish intermarried and sometimes cooperated with these neighbors.

In the years after the Civil War up to the turn of the century, the New York Irish community changed dramatically. It became much more diverse, as a "lace curtain" population grew up alongside the "shanty" one and the immigrant Irish were joined by their American-born offspring. Upward mobility and an expanding population helped make the Irish community politically powerful and institutionally rich, as explained in Lawrence McCaffrey's overview and the essays by Colleen McDannell, John McKivigan, and Thomas Robertson, Kenneth Nilsen, and John Ridge. They trace the increasing conservatism of Irish workers on their way up the city's economic ladder, reveal the vital role played by women in Catholic institutional growth, and analyze Irish efforts to maintain old country allegiances through the Irish language, nationalist movements, and the founding of Irish county societies.

By the 1910s and 1920s, the Irish community forged in the early nineteenth century and centered on the Catholic church, the Democratic Party, and the nationalist movement had reached its peak. Irish Americans moved up the occupational ladder with considerable speed in the twentieth century. The Catholic Church reigned supreme among New York City's religious denominations, and the nationalist movement reached its apogee there and throughout America, as it provided massive support to help Ireland win the first real measure of autonomy since the seventeenth century. In this era of triumph, the Irish also came to dominate city politics, as Charlie Murphy, a taciturn saloon-keeper from the Gashouse district, emerged as Tammany's greatest boss. The overview by Christopher McNickle and essays by Joe Doyle, Marion Casey, and John McClymer document rising living standards as Irish of all generations began to move to the outer boroughs, the roles of women in the mass revival of Irish nationalism, and the complexity of Irish political perspectives, ranging from that of blue blood "wannabe," John Purroy Mitchel, to that of Alfred E. Smith, the symbol of a new, street-tough, urban liberalism.

In 1945 William O'Dwyer, not only Irish but an immigrant no less, was elected mayor of New York. Two years later the St. Patrick's Day parade attracted more than a million spectators. Neither of these events, however, gave even a hint of the decline in Irish political power and institutional strength that was well under way by then. By the 1960s Irish men had almost disappeared from the top ranks of the city's political leadership. Although nationalism revived in the next few years, it failed to hold substantial support outside New York's immigrant Irish population. The church, which under the leadership of Cardinal Spellman had been the one remaining Irish bastion through the 1940s and 1950s, was now wracked by internal conflicts and suffering a decline in lay allegiance and in clerical vocations. The overview by David Reimers and essays by Rebecca Miller, Mary Corcoran, Robert Snyder, and Charlie Fanning probe the dramatic changes in Irish life during this period: the transformation of old Irish neighborhoods, such as Inwood and Washington Heights in northern Manhattan; the struggles of new Irish immigrants in both the 1950s and 1980s to adapt their cultures to American circumstances; and the effort by a new breed of New York Irish novelists and poets to define what it means to be Irish in America's greatest city.

In his treatment of Elizabeth Cullinan, Fanning notes her envy of historians: "There is no such thing as the whole truth with respect to the living which is why history appeals to me. I like the finality." This book is history, but it is hardly the final say on the New York Irish. Cullinan may have envied the historian's distance, which makes it possible to assess the race after the course is run, the life after it is over, but that distance imposes problems too. Cullinan's heroine could retrace her childhood through neighborhoods that were at least still vaguely familiar and a memory still fresh with its incidents. The New York of the colonial Irish is buried under concrete and glass. The people of that era are only remembered when the dead rise up to reassert their claims to memory through the discovery of some long-forgotten cemetery. More remains of the mid-nineteenth-century Irish settlements in areas like the Lower East Side, but the traces of O'Donovan Rossa, John Devoy, and the many less famous Irish are hard to detect beneath the subsequent settlements of Italians, Jews, and now the Chinese. Even the vestiges of the late-nineteenth-century Irish are sadly fading away. St. Stephen's Church, further north on the East Side, was the parish of the great nationalist and labor reformer, Father Edward McGlynn, and the site of many rallies in his behalf. It still stands, but it is far too big for its current small congregation, who have had to alter its vast interior spaces to fit their own needs. The altered buildings are but a visible symbol of so much that is lost and that historians seek in order to understand the past: letters, diaries, records, and worst of all, the thoughts and impressions of people who never could or would write them down. Histories, then, are never final because some historical conclusions must always be speculations built on mere patches of evidence.

Histories are also tentative because there is too much to know. This is certainly true for this book. Rather than a final say to the story of the Irish in New York, this collection of essays—as big as it is—represents but a first attempt to tell that vast, complex, and fascinating tale.

Acknowledgments

THIS BOOK, more than most, has been a collaborative effort, and there are many to thank for their support, guidance, and interest.

The Irish Institute recognized the need for a one-volume history of the Irish in New York City back in 1988. With the enthusiastic approval of Paul O'Dwyer, who had founded the Institute in 1948, president Kevin Morrissey took the first steps toward making this book a reality. He contacted the sagacious Angela Carter, who put him in touch with the New York Irish History Roundtable. The two organizations soon began the collaboration that has resulted in the publication of this volume. It is clear that without Kevin Morrissey's long-term commitment to the project, a history of the Irish in New York might forever have remained the product of wistful imagining.

In consultation with a distinguished board of advisers, the Institute and the Roundtable brought us on as editors. Together, we commissioned over two dozen scholars with expertise in a variety of fields to focus their skills on telling the story of the Irish. In various meetings and through personal communications, the advisers offered help in conceptualizing and developing this book and in reading drafts of individual chapters. Their involvement was crucial to the book's initiation and completion. Our sincere thanks go to Angela M. Carter, Dennis J. Clark, Hasia R. Diner, Jay P. Dolan, James S. Donnelly, William D.

Griffin, Leo Hershkowitz, Kenneth T. Jackson, Kerby A. Miller, David M. Reimers, John T. Ridge, and Sean Wilentz. Special thanks go to Marion R. Casey, our liaison with the institute and the roundtable, who worked diligently with us during every stage of the project, offering helpful advice and caring as much as we did about producing a significant contribution to urban, ethnic, and social history. In numerous ways, she was the third editor of this book.

The book also benefited from the patience of a group of dedicated men and women who, over the past seven years, have unfailingly supported the original vision. We are grateful to all the members of the Irish Institute and the New York Irish History Roundtable, especially those who individually helped us to realize this book. We acknowledge the major and generous financial contribution of the Irish Institute, which was made in the belief that scholarship is a pursuit eminently worthy of remuneration. Additional support was provided by the Irish American Cultural Institute through their Irish Research Fund, and we thank them for their assistance, which helped defray the expenses of those scholars who needed to travel to New York City in order to complete their research.

During the evolution of this book, several of the chapters were presented as works-in-progress at meetings of the Organization of American Historians, the American Conference for Irish Studies, the Columbia University Seminar on Irish Studies, and the New York Irish History Roundtable. The input of colleagues on these occasions is sincerely appreciated.

Our thanks are also extended to Georgia Tech for providing mailing, photocopying, and secretarial support. LaDonna Bowen was faced with the difficult task of consolidating twenty-five diverse text files into one and also with various typing tasks. She completed this often maddening assignment with great skill and effort, and we appreciate her good work. We are grateful to Francis P. Vardy, John T. Ridge, Ty Ahmad-Taylor, and Marion Casey for helping to create detailed maps from the confusion of neighborhoods, parishes, and census categories that represent New York; to John T. Ridge, Angela Carter, and Jackie Cavalla for the statistical tables in the appendix; and to Sr. Eleanor Nishio, R.S.M., Bro. Emmett Corry, O.S.F., and several roundtable members for sharing photographs from their collections.

Leslie Bayor proofread the entire first draft of the manuscript and, through her usual perceptive and careful work, found many errors. We are grateful for her help; and for the proofreading skills of Denise O'Meara and Ann M. Shea.

Thanks also to Robert J. Brugger, our editor at the Johns Hopkins University Press, who recognized the uniqueness of this work and provided encouragement as well as useful advice. He was ever sensitive to the Irish Institute's wish that the book's production values reflect the quality of its scholarship. Our appreciation is also extended to his assistant, Robert J. Anthony.

Finally, our thanks to the many authors represented in this collection, for their enthusiasm for the subject matter, their cooperation in accepting suggestions, and their diligence in maintaining our publication schedule.

THE NEW YORK IRISH

Introduction

AROUND THE turn of this century, the people of western County Kerry along the Atlantic Coast of Ireland liked to tell a story about Sean Palmer from Rineen Bán whose craving for tobacco led him on a wild adventure. One night, desperate for a smoke, Sean was enticed aboard a boat with the promise of a fresh pipe by some men he had met near the village quay. They then whisked him away across the ocean to New York, where he saw his brother, best friend, and childhood sweetheart, all of whom had emigrated there. After visiting with his friends and relatives and taking a short tour of the city, Sean returned home on the magic boat of his mysterious new companions as quickly as he had come. It turned out to be a highly profitable trip for Sean, for his American relatives and friends had been so happy to see him that they gave him substantial sums of money, a new "Yankee" suit, and a half year's supply of his favorite weed.[1]

Sean Palmer's tale subtly suggests several important themes in the history of Irish emigration to America. Three are worth noting here: migration to America became so pervasive, so integral to Irish life, that one was as likely to meet one's brother, best friend, and old sweetheart on the streets of Manhattan or Brooklyn as in Rineen Bán; most Irish immigrants, like Sean, never intended to go, felt that they had been carried there against their will, and always believed that Ireland was their real home; and when they did leave, Irish immigrants were more likely to wind up in New York than anywhere else in America.

Irish men and women, as Kerby Miller has pointed out, clung to their little island; they could not conceive of leaving it voluntarily. Yet the economic revolutions that had transformed the West and then the rest of the world since the end of the Middle Ages would not let them remain there. The legendary Galwaymen on Columbus's ship or in every other famous explorer's crew are symbols less of Irish enterprise than of Irish necessity and desperation. The Irish migrated to America by the hundreds of thousands in the seventeenth and eighteenth centuries, and by the millions in the nineteenth and twentieth. From the time of Columbus to the age of steamships, Cormac O'Grada points out, the Irish may have made up close to one-seventh of all voluntary migrants from the Old World to the Americas. By 1980, about one in seven Americans claimed some Irish ancestors.[2]

Irish migration to New York City is almost as old as the city itself. As Leo Hershkowitz notes in the book's opening essay, the famous Jesuit missionary Isaac Jogues, in New Amsterdam in 1643 while in transit from Canada to France, heard the confession of a young Irishman who had recently arrived in the city. By the late eighteenth century, Joyce Goodfriend points out in chapter 1, thousands of Irish immigrants were arriving in New York every year. The great migrations of the nineteenth century made that river a flood. By the 1880s more than 200,000 Irish-born men and women and about as many of their American-born children lived in New York. A century later, in 1980, about one in six people living in the New York metropolitan area reported some Irish roots to their family tree, and in the decade that followed Irish immigrants began again to pour into the city by the thousands.[3]

Even a simple roster of names can show how much the Irish have contributed to the city's history: John McGraw, manager of the baseball Giants; William F. Buckley, conservative intellectual; Mike Quill, radical head of the Transport Workers Union; DeWitt Clinton, U.S. senator, governor, mayor, and candidate for president; John Quinn, lawyer and art impresario; Francis Cardinal Spellman, archbishop of New York and sometimes called the "American Pope"; Margaret Higgins Sanger, birth control advocate; Owney Madden, gangster; Charlie Murphy, Tammany boss; Timothy Sweeney, head of the Gay Men's Health Crisis; George M. Cohan, vaudevillian; "Fighting Father" Duffy, liberal theologian and World War I hero; and Frank O'Hara, the "poet of the city."

These prominent individuals are joined by countless others without whom the city's history would not have been the same. Can anyone imagine New York today without groups as large, culturally distinctive, and ethnically self-conscious as the Irish once were, groups such as the Jews or, more recent arrivals, such as the Hispanics? Counterfactual speculation is a tricky business, as Hasia Diner warns us in her essay, but clearly the city, and every other group that lived in it, would have developed in a radically different way if there had been no Irish in New York.

Simply as strong backs and dexterous fingers, the cheap labor offered by 150,000 Irish immigrants in the middle of the nineteenth century was essential to the city's skyrocketing economic growth and the shift to labor-intensive manufacture. By 1860 one of every four New Yorkers was an Irish immigrant. If they had not been there, would the city have grown as fast or as big, or would its economy have taken the same shape? And who would have replaced them? If the Irish had not come in such great numbers, what would that have meant to the city's labor movement, relations between whites and blacks, neighborhood development, or even the blend of saloons, songs, prizefighting, and "New Yawkese" dialect that emerged as a distinct, New York, working-class culture in the antebellum era?

In time the Irish became the leaders of some of New York's most important organizations, such as the Catholic Church. What would the church have been like without the Irish? Did they save it from the leadership of the "monarchical" French and thus perhaps rescue it from permanent alienation and irrelevance in a republican America? Did they prevent its balkanization into a host of German, Italian, Polish, and other ethnic churches? Or did they bury forever a native-born American Catholic effort, emerging during and after the Revolution, to create a "republican" church?

The Irish were nearly as prominent and influential in the city's politics as in the church. Indeed, they are so enmeshed in the city's political history that it is hard to conceive of it without them. Nevertheless, they did not invent machine politics, which, as Hasia Diner suggests, would in all likelihood have emerged in New York without them. It is also not clear whether city government would have been more or less "clean" without the Irish in charge. George Washington Plunkitt, the "sage" of Tammany Hall and expert on "white graft," took great delight in Lincoln Steffens's conclusion that "Philadelphia ruled almost entirely by Americans was more corrupt than New York where the Irish do almost all the governin'." Yet it is difficult to believe that New York's politics would have followed the same course without the Irish. Somebody else would have dominated the city's politics during those crucial decades around the turn of the century, the lines of division and conflict among the city's groups and classes would have shaken out differently, and, some historians suggest, the city's politics might even have had a more ideological cast.[4]

The New York Irish are important not only in terms of their long-time critical role in the city's history but also in the broad context of Irish American history. The New York Irish have always stood for Irish American communities writ large: not just a political machine but Tammany Hall; not just a cathedral but St. Patrick's; not just a St. Patrick's Day parade but a march up Fifth Avenue by thousands upon thousands.

This was at least in part because New York's Irish population was the largest of any city in America. Even though only a fraction of the Irish debarking in New York in the nineteenth or twentieth centuries stayed there, the sheer volume of the city's immigrant traffic almost guaranteed that New York would become the nation's largest Irish city. From 1855 to 1860, for example, more than 40 percent of the 650,000 immigrants who landed at New York declared their intention of settling in New York State. As time passed, New York City became more attractive to Irish immigrants, not less. In 1860 one-sixth of all Irish immigrants in the United States lived in New York City; by 1920 it was close to one in five, and by 1960 nearly one in three. Although the numbers of illegal Irish immigrants are by necessity hard to count, most experts would agree that New York has remained the principal destination of Irish immigrants, legal and illegal, in recent times as well. This constant flow produced the mammoth numbers claiming pure or predominant Irish ancestry in the New York metropolitan area in 1980: twice as many people as claimed Irish ancestry in Boston; three times as many as in Chicago.[5]

Some New York Irish politicians or churchmen have mobilized their community's vast numbers and riches to make it, and them, national powers. Charlie Murphy extended Tammany's power from City Hall to the State House in Albany and into national politics in the late 1910s and 1920s, eventually making Alfred E. Smith a viable candidate for president of the United States. Francis Cardinal Spellman also showed how to take advantage of New York's potential in the middle decades of the twentieth century. Sedulously cultivating connections in Rome and Washington, and exploiting fully the financial resources of New York's Catholics, Spellman made the New York chancery an American as well as a New York "powerhouse."[6]

New York also became the center of Irish American publishing, communications, and the arts. By the end of the nineteenth century most of the influential Irish newspapers were located in New York: Patrick Meehan's *Irish American* and John Devoy's *Irish Nation* and later *Gaelic American*, and Patrick Ford's *Irish World*. By 1882 Ford's *Irish World* had a readership of 60,000, which included subscribers from all across America; by the early 1900s the *World*'s circulation had more than doubled. Major Irish Catholic publishing houses like Sadlier's and P. J. Kenedy's also thrived in New York, and, as Kenneth Nilsen chronicles in chapter 10, New York was also the center of American efforts to publish in the Irish language. A steady flow of immigrant musicians and the city's early primacy in the recording industry helped New York surpass Chicago as the capital of Irish music in America. Indeed, recordings of New York fiddlers filtered back to Ireland and had a significant influence on the evolution of music in the old country in the 1920s and 1930s.[7]

The story of the New York Irish is worth telling not only because of their contribution to the life of the city or the nation; it is worth telling because it consists of a rich mosaic of experiences that reflect broad patterns in human history. The story of the Irish is in part the story of the migrant. In the 1800s and early 1900s, it was the story of the rural migrant gone to the city, of the traditional, often bewildered, peasant encountering the modern world. That story would be repeated many times in New York's history and is being repeated today on its streets and the streets of cities all over the globe. Thus it is just as much the story of sunburned Chinese country boys gawking at shop windows in Shanghai, of young Guatemalans making their way tentatively and awkwardly along the streets of Los Angeles, and of today's Irish immigrants gathering in the bars of Woodside or Norwood in New York. Whatever their knowledge of urban culture, all of these people, like their predecessors, are at the mercy of a changing world economy that continues to cast millions onto the roads or seas to find new lives far from home.

The story of the New York Irish is also the story of trying to make it in a new economy, a story of peasants and their children and grandchildren wrestling with the constraints and opportunities of an urban industrial economy. That struggle has been a central theme in the West for centuries, is now common throughout the world, and shows little sign of subsiding. That story has sparked a sharp debate over the relative importance of culture, opportunity, and even genes in determining the economic success or failure of people from different groups. Since the Irish were among the first peasant peoples to confront the new industrial order and try to wring a living or even some modest prosperity from it, their experience should offer a useful measuring stick or test case of how values, strategies, opportunities, or heredity shape economic success. The trouble is, few scholars can agree about how well the Irish did, much less why they succeeded or failed. Were the Celts successful because most worked their way out of degrading poverty, or were they failures because too many of them seemed to get stuck in the lower middle class too long? What held them back or thrust them forward? Were the values preached by the church a bulwark against demoralization or a barrier to capitalist risk taking and intellectual experimentation? Was carving a niche in public employment a useful strategy for a people with few skills, or was it a dead end that trapped the Irish in a morass of clerkships?[8]

Perhaps the most intriguing and instructive part of this story is not even the values and strategies of the Irish but the opportunities that New York and other northern cities provided for immigrants and their children. By all accounts, in the early to middle 1800s Irish Protestants appear to have had all the advantages of cultural preparation, capital, and skills over their Catholic fellow countrymen. (And, if it matters, Thomas Sowell reports, Irish Protestants in Ulster today have higher IQ test scores than their Catholic neighbors). Yet in late-twentieth-century America Irish Catholics appear to have higher occupational status and incomes than Irish Protestants. That is less a testament to strategy or culture than to the luck of landing in the right place: the Appalachian backcountry may have seemed the land of opportunity for the Irish Protestants who settled there in the eighteenth century, but it has been a torpid, economically stunted backwater ever since. Conversely, New York's slums may have seemed sinkholes of despair in the mid–nineteenth century when Irish Catholics crowded into them, but the city's dynamic economy gave some of them and more of their descendants (and the descendants of most white immigrants) a chance to improve themselves and escape the horrors of the Five Points or Hell's Kitchen.[9]

The story of the Irish is in addition the story of the problems and paradoxes of ethnically diverse or plural societies. It the complicated story of a people who have fought to push out the boundaries of American nationality to encompass their ethnic and religious beliefs and in so doing sometimes helped to reinforce the boundaries of race that kept African and Asian Americans from full participation in the city's or the nation's life. Throughout their history in New York, the Irish have been at the border of the ins and outs, interpreting one to the other, mediating, sometimes including, sometimes excluding. They have been both victim and victimizer, "other" and definer of the "other," and, paradoxically, sometimes played both roles simultaneously. In Peter Quinn's recent novel about nineteenth-century New York, *Banished Children of Eve*, one character, Jack Mulcahey, wins great fame as a minstrel in black face manipulating and ridiculing the image of blacks before white audiences; he got his start in "show business" in the old country as a boy named Sean, dancing jigs for his Donegal landlord who delighted in demonstrations of the "primitive" culture of the Irish peasantry.[10]

The New York Irish story is also about the meaning of social or cultural identities and communities. Few white groups in America have been more fiercely combative about their identity and more conscious of group boundaries and borders than the Irish—a legacy, perhaps, of their island's tragic history of invasion and resistance and persistent, bitter, sectarian conflict. Yet the Irish identity has changed over time. For many immigrants America was exile. Think of the Fenian leader John O'Mahony plotting revolution or poring lovingly over his Irish language manuscripts in his lower Manhattan garret. Ireland was the real focus of identity for him and his kind. They were "Irish" and "Catholic," which were treated as synonymous terms. For their children and grandchildren, Ireland grew distant, but Catholicism remained, perhaps even grew in importance as a focus of identity. In groups popular among the American-born, such as the Knights of Columbus, militant Catholicism was blended with a fierce American patriotism. Today, some observers suggest, even religion and ethnicity have begun to disappear as important markers of identity. This is the case not only for the Irish but for other white ethnic groups, which as a result are merging into a broad white or European American group. The cultural substance of that new white identity, however, is something of a mystery: what myths, heroes, customs, do these northern white ethnics share? As an Italian police officer from Canarsie asked Jonathan Rieder, "What the hell does white mean?"[11]

Such observations suggest that Irish ethnicity has become an anachronism, but, like Tim Finnegan, Irish ethnicity in New York may not be ready to be waked just yet. For one thing, stock images of the Irish are clearly still alive today in our written and visual language. New York's Irish cops continue to figure prominently in American popular culture as rugged and courageous in Tom Wolfe's *Bonfire of the Vanities,* sinister and corrupt in Caleb Carr's *The Alienist,* and tough but vulnerable in the television series *NYPD Blue.* Irish women, long symbols of strong-willed women in American popular culture, continue to play that role as television writers seek images of resolute and independent women in the wake of the feminist revival. Some of these characters, like "Murphy" Brown or Nurse McMurphy, inhabit, or have inhabited, TV homes far from New York, but others, like Cagney and Lacey or Rosie O'Neill, still walk New York's streets today—at least in reruns.[12]

More quintessentially New York is the fictional depiction of romance between Jewish boys and Irish girls. Intermarriage between the two groups has actually been quite low in New York or elsewhere in America for religious reasons, but the image of Jewish-Irish romance has been very popular for more than six decades. *Abie's Irish Rose* ran for more than 2,000 performances on Broadway in the mid-1920s and no fewer than 22 films were made about the relations between Irish and Jews in that decade. The juxtaposition, however, has remained intriguing to television writers and producers in the late twentieth century: *Bridget loves Bernie* from the 1970s, *Chicken Soup* in the 1980s (in which Jackie Mason played the liberal), and *Brooklyn Bridge* in the 1990s were all set in New York and all paired Jewish men or boys with Irish women or girls. The legacy of *Abie's Irish Rose* has, improbably, been most fully realized today in the television setting of Cicely, Alaska, where Joel Fleishman, representative of all the Jewish urban smarts of New York City, meets Maggie O'Connell, the complementary embodiment of the physical toughness and resolute independence that Irish girls have personified in America for the past century and a half. Set in Alaska it might be, but the roots of that frontier romance are in New York.[13]

Yet there is far more to the Irish presence in contemporary New York than the persistence of older images. In 1980 nearly one million people in the metropolitan area claimed predominately Irish ancestry. Irish immigration, dormant through the 1960s and 1970s, revived in the 1980s and sent tens of thousands of Irish men and women to New York. Although Irish political power has declined there, Irish men and women still fulfill their roles as interpreters of the city and mediators among its groups, either as newspaper reporters and columnists (Jimmy Breslin, Pete Hamill, Anna Quindlen, Jim Dwyer) or policemen (Raymond Kelly, William Brattan). There are fewer Irish athletes (though Paul O'Neill and Pat Kelly have emerged as mainstays of the Yankees), but Irishmen seem to have found success as coaches (Pat Riley of the Knicks or Mike Keenan of the Rangers). The church, still heavily Irish, is no longer as big or powerful as it once was, but it still retains a great deal of clout. Finally, the furor over gay marchers in the St. Patrick's Day parade suggests that contested definitions of Irish identity are central to broader battles over the entire city's vision of itself.[14]

This volume explores the history of the New York Irish community from all these perspectives. The Irish have certainly figured in mountains of books and articles on New York and New Yorkers, but only as a part of larger studies of the city's workers, women, partisan politics, neighborhood development, or religious history. Thus far, no comprehensive history of the Irish in New York from the colonial era to the present has been attempted. Daniel Patrick Moynihan's wide-ranging, witty, and insightful essay in *Beyond the Melting Pot*, remains, perhaps, the best single summary of their experiences. Historians have studied in depth New York's other ethnic groups or examined the Irish in other cities. The New York Irish may not have been ignored entirely, but, given the size and importance of their community, they have been neglected, until now.[15]

The Milk Man

Settlement to 1844

PART I

COLONIAL AND EARLY NATIONAL AMERICA

The O'Connell Brothers' milk wagon was painted by Nicolino Calyo for a series of New York street scenes, c. 1830s. Irish-born men and women made up 40 percent of the city's peddlers as late as 1855, mainly selling farm produce such as milk, vegetables, and fruit. New York's corner grocery stores were Irish until German immigration at midcentury brought competition. (Museum of the City of New York.Gift of Mrs. Francis P. Garvan.)

Leo Hershkowitz

OVERVIEW
The Irish and the Emerging City: Settlement to 1844

SEVERAL MAJOR themes emerge from the story of the Irish in early New York. One has to do with the perseverance of the Irish population, which started out with but a handful but by the mid–nineteenth century, at the time of Hasia Diner's study, accounted for about one-third of the city's population of almost one million. Many arrived following Ireland's "Great Hunger" of the 1840s, but some immigration had occurred two decades earlier, also spurred to a great extent by poverty. In 1835 three-quarters of the laborers in Ireland—more than two million people—were without employment of any kind.[1]

Most Irish immigrants during the colonial and early national periods were Protestant, many from Northern Ireland, although as Joyce Goodfriend writes, in chapter 1, "The largest number of Irish immigrants to New York came from Dublin." This was a relatively small migration not stirred by any great catastrophe. Catholic Irish began arriving after the end of the Napoleonic Wars and soon, as Walter J. Walsh relates in chapter 2, became predominant and "with their alien ways . . . posed an undeniable threat to the relatively homogenous metropolitan social structure that had existed during the Jeffersonian years." Protestant Irish, on the whole financially more secure, were generally welcomed and met few social and economic barriers. Later, in Jacksonian New York, the welcome mat was withdrawn, and the largely Catholic and poorer farmdwellers found a hostile climate of violent anti-Catholicism and chauvin-istic nativism. The sharp rivalry for jobs and space, resulting from economic inequities as well as new opportunities of an emerging industrial capitalism, ruffled raw nerves. Although rising democratic vistas brought universal suffrage for men, free expression was accompanied by a lack of responsibility and restraint.

In chapter 3, Paul A. Gilje points out that the hostility was clearly evident well before the "Hungry Forties" and that Irish Catholics and Protestants found it increasingly difficult to accommodate one another. Threatened with growing resentment among the general population, many Irish Catholics, especially in the lowerclass, sought "to reject the multiethnic and nonsectarian approach of the middle-class émigré." It would take decades, but gradually, haltingly, a new ethnicity would emerge. Barriers slowly lifted, and scorn and hostility were replaced by acceptance as jobs became available in municipal offices, schools, industry, and commerce. Progress was creeping and painful but in the end successful. If there is a single theme in this history it is that through their work, courage, and perseverance the Irish people overcame huge obstacles to help write definitive pages in history: from a "bunch of straw" they helped make a city.

A few Irish were in New York from almost its beginning. While visiting the settlement (then New Amsterdam) in 1643, Father Isaac Joques, a Jesuit from Canada, heard the confession of a young Irish traveler from Virginia or Maryland. Dr. William Hays of Barry's Court, Ireland, was in the Dutch town in 1647. He had been a surgeon in Curaçao. Through the following decades others arrived. Among them was Thomas Dongan, Irish born, and the only Catholic governor of New York until the twentieth century.

Significant numbers of Irish were not present in New York until 1700, when four companies of soldiers, 400 in strength, with 150 from Ireland, arrived. Governor Richard Coote (Earl of Bellomont), of County Sligo, remarked that the "recruits that came from Ireland are a parcel of the vilest fellows that ever wore the King's livery, the very scum of the army in Ireland and several Irish Papists amongst [them]." Something of a riot occurred and several citizens were wounded. Two "mutineers" were executed. It was not a pleasant beginning. What happened to the rest of the "recruits" is not known, though many surely remained in the colony.[2]

In 1706 mention is made of probably the first Presbyterian clergyman in New York, Irish-born Francis Makemie, said to be "a malicious man" and "a disturber of the peace and quiet of all places he comes into; he is Jack of all Trades, he is a Preacher, a Doctor of Physick, a Merchant, an Attorney, or Councillor at Law, and, which is worse of all, a Disturber of Governments." The minister was arrested for preaching without a license but set free. The incident reflected the early discord, established a degree of freedom of religion, and gave settlers further reason to separate church and state. Presbyterianism attracted many, especially those from northern Ireland. The Irish were, as Joyce Good-friend notes in chapter 1, "a vital element in that denomination."[3]

This small presence gradually expanded in the eighteenth century as vast numbers left their troubled homeland, some because of religious persecution, others because of land appropriations by the English, the lure of economic opportunity, or simply depressions. Ireland lost more than a million exiles to various parts of the world between 1712 and 1785. The destruction of the linen and woolen trades alone reduced the population of Ulster by an estimated half a million people before 1776. According to one historian, possibly one-quarter of all immigrants to the colonies between 1700 and the Revolution were Irish Catholics, but apparently few of these Catholics came to New York.[4]

Subsequently, however, thousands of colonists, mostly Protestants, were drawn to New York as a result of the city's extensive commerce with Ireland. The usual exchange was flaxseed and lumber in return for linen and "Rose Cork butter," but Irish beef and pork were sometimes imported "if the local supply was low." In 1772, 1,600 tons of general cargo left New York for Ireland and 915 tons came in from Ireland.[5] No other colony, with the possible exception of Pennsylvania, had such a regular and important trade with Hibernia.

Many immigrants during this period achieved fame and fortune. The Duanes and Clintons became outstanding political leaders. Christopher Colles designed New York's first reservoir (1774) and later suggested building canals to aid transportation. There were also printers like Hugh Gaine and merchants like David Matthews, Robert Ross Waddell, Hugh and Alexander Wallace, and the firm of Greg and Cunningham, which was "largely in the Irish trade."[6] Thomas Roach was a wine merchant, while William Edgar engaged in many activities, including real estate. Dr. Samuel Clossey, professor of anatomy at New York Hospital (1771), like Dr. John Charlton, was prominent in medicine, as was James Duane in law. The majority, however, were unheralded laborers and farmers who became part of a diverse community dominated by an Anglo-Dutch aristocracy. Through their labor and skill in trade and commerce they contributed to the growth and prosperity of the general community. The Irish were often linked socially, and through the Friendly Sons of St. Patrick (1784) maintained bonds with each other.[7]

Colonial New York was an extension of England in language, custom, and tradition, and anti-Irish attitudes were prevalent. Guy Fawkes Day was celebrated by almost as much revelry as it was in London, and the view that the Irish were "troublesome" was just as prevalent. But without large numbers of people (about 20,000 lived in the city just before the Revolution) and without entrenched political machines, there was little organized bigotry, although in 1712 and 1741 the fear of a supposed Catholic-led slave revolt produced anti-Catholic, antiblack hysteria. But with so few Catholics around, there was little opportunity to bloody noses or worse.

In September 1776 the city was occupied by the British, who remained there until November 25, 1783. Many New Yorkers, including Irish citizens, stayed behind British lines. Some fled to neutral territory, some joined Washington's army. Edward Hand from Clyduff commanded a regiment during the Battle of Long Island in August 1776. General Richard Montgomery of County Donegal was killed in December 1775 during an assault on Quebec.

Some joined the British army and served in regiments such as the Volunteers of Ireland.[8] Colonel Guy Johnson, for example, was an active member of His Majesty's forces. He was a son of Sir William Johnson, one of the most noted figures in colonial history chiefly because of his remarkable relationship with the Iroquois. For a time during the war the colonel was one of the managers of the John Street Theatre and was described as "short and pussy, hair powder'd, of stern countenance and haughty demeanor; his voice was harsh and his tongue bore evidence of his Irish extraction."[9] General Henry Clinton wrote that he had "recourse to those sources from whence the rebels themselves drew most of their best soldiers. I mean the Irish and other Europeans who had settled in America."[10]

The Revolution promised all men life, liberty, and happiness, but did all men include the Irish? Catholics? What was happiness? The right to possess property or the right to vote? For postwar New York—whose population was decimated, many of its buildings dilapidated or fire-ravaged, and trade and commerce almost at a standstill—such gallant ideals seemed vague promises for a distant time. The dominant Anglo-Dutch aristocracy, still by and large intact after the war, was not anxious to open its doors to the Irish or any outsider. Even so, the Revolution had begun a process of change.

Emigration slowed during the war but resumed once again after the conflict ended, as Irishmen fled the suppression of Gratton's volunteers, the failed rebellion of 1798, and their island's political unrest, including the dissolution of the Irish Parliament in 1800. Some fled police batons and others foreclosures, unemployment, and hunger. Postwar New York offered a more attractive alternative. The city was becoming increasingly accessible, productive, democratic, and also urban. Theater, arts, literature, new attitudes and opportunities were to be found there, but so were slums, crime, social degradation, and bigotry.

Probably the first Catholic to be elected to public office from the city was Francis Cooper, sent to the state assembly in 1806, but few others followed. The federal period also fostered its share of hatred, more bitter and dangerous than in earlier times. The state constitution of 1777 separated church and state and prevented any minister or priest from holding civil or military office. John Jay, principal author of the constitution, also had the ratifying convention adopt stronger anti-Catholic measures, including the denial of naturalization to Catholics or to those not renouncing allegiance to "every foreign king, prince or potentate, which by definition would include the Papacy."[11]

Most Federalists, strong law and order advocates, saw a dismal future if hordes of ignorant, Catholic Irish immigrants were allowed to chase hard-working Protestant Americans from their jobs. By contrast, liberal Jeffersonians saw the Federalists as a new breed of English royalists seeking to maintain their authority even at the cost of liberty and justice. The two groups had one of their first confrontations in 1795, when two immigrant ferrymen, Thomas Burke and Timothy Crady, seemingly Catholics, became involved in a fight with Federalist Alderman Gabriel Furman, who charged the pair with "improper, disrespectful" behavior. This led to their arrest and trial. Found guilty, both were jailed. Crady, who was also whipped, died soon after. The affair caused alarm. Democrats saw the event as a brutal example of Federalist elitism, while Federalists held the opposition to be a party that supported Irish ruffians and social disorder.[12] These views intensified over the years, especially as immigration increased, and gave rise to ethnic conflict and political controversy.

Still, New York was an American city in which the ideals of equality, liberty, freedom of expression, and freedom of religion were praised, if not always honored. Voicing those ideals, Jefferson welcomed newcomers: "Shall we whose forefathers received hospitality from the savage of the wilderness, deny it to our brethren in distress? Shall there be no where an asylum on the earth for a persecuted humanity?"[13] In this spirit, Governor George Clinton (later vice president) and his nephew, DeWitt, both of Irish extraction, extended a warm welcome to attorney Thomas Addis Emmet, Dr. William MacNeven, and William Sampson, participants in the failed rebellion of 1798.

DeWitt Clinton used his Irish background and his association with groups like the Shamrock Friendly Association (1816) to gain the vote of the newly arrived. However, Tammany Hall was at odds with Clinton, partly because he did not support the regular Jefferson–Madison ticket, and as usual Democrats split into several angry factions. Neither the Federalists nor the Democrats really sought to be identified with the Irish since both were nativists, but Tammany, while it attacked Clinton, made a greater show of support for the Irish and in this way shattered the Clinton–Irish alliance. It was at best a temporary accord, but one that would be solidified by midcentury.[14]

In 1821 the New York Constitutional Convention eliminated property qualifications for voting and provided universal suffrage for men, except blacks. This momentous step was the underpinning of a rising democracy and for the Irish represented empowerment. Numbers would now count. Politics became a vocation, a consuming passion. The day of the professional politician had arrived. Society now heard more and more strange voices, often producing a bitter, violent clamor. Partly as a result of the rapid development of capitalism, banking, and large-scale industry (which threatened the livelihood of traditional craftsmen and small entrepreneurs), the specter of widespread unemployment haunted laboring and middle classes for the first time. Riots between Orangemen and Catholics, between blacks and whites, between laborers and employers were frequent. The economic panics of 1819, 1837, and 1857 underscored the vulnerability of the middle class. This mix of democracy and the hazards of free enterprise produced religious antagonisms, fueled by traditional Protestant-

Catholic hatred. Added was a surge of emotional nationalism, which when mixed with religious suspicion fed a growing xenophobia. Hatred expressed in loud vocal and violent resentment, along with a more subtle discrimination, could be found in literature, newspapers, and the living room. Former mayor and diarist Philip Hone chronicled the "dreadful" election riots of 1834 when bands of "lowest class" Irishmen attacked Americans. In December 1835 he saw the "low Irishmen again threatening order. Ignorance and vice go together. . . . These Irishmen, strangers among us without feeling of patriotism . . . cry down with the natives."

By 1835, such sentiments helped form the Native Americans Democratic Association, an odd mixture of restless middle-class citizens fearing Irish competition, Protestant moralists seeking to maintain a society free from the threat of an "expansionist" Papacy, and various "patriotic" political opportunists. They formed themselves into a party to battle for "American" rights. Samuel F. B. Morse, artist and inventor, was one of the leaders of the organization. Another was Mordecai Noah, a native-born Jew, formerly an anti-Clinton, anti-Democratic politician, now a rabid Whig patriot who used his paper the *Evening Star* to stir up opposition to Catholic Irish. He and others, like James W. Webb, publisher of the *Courier and Enquirer,* called for strong registry laws to keep out those "depraved foreigners" who were flooding American shores. They saw "Popery" and "despotism" as synonymous terms. Noah, like Philip Hone and many others, thought the Irish "could not understand or appreciate the excellence of this [American] form of government."[15]

A number of incidents further fanned the flame. The Mexican attack on the Alamo in 1836 was seen as an example of what Catholics meant to do to Protestants. The recently invented rotary press provided the means to mass-produce printed material, a good deal of it anti-Catholic and anti-Irish. Books like the salacious and fictional *Six Months in a Convent* (1835) and newspapers like the *Evening Star* added to the explosive atmosphere.

In February 1838 two Irish refugees, John and James Bamber, were arrested in the city on the order of Governor William L. Marcy in response to a request of the British consul. A grand jury in England had indicted them for the murder of a police officer in Ireland some ten years before. Marcy, a Democrat, was ironically accused by the nativist *Evening Star* of "surrender" and of committing an act "reprehensible to the highest degree." Democrats were saved from further embarrassment when the brothers were released after a hearing. Obviously, politics in New York was not clear-cut: positions often changed and party affiliation was frequently tested.[16]

Although as a third party the nativists never dominated the scene, they made Democrats and the opposition Whigs, reborn Federalists, aware of antialien issues. Both major parties sought some accommodation with the Irish, while never fully supporting them. Always active, Morse helped form the American Protestant Union in 1841 to defend the "spirit of our ancestors." The Mexican

War of 1845–48 further stirred anti-Catholic bitterness. Patriotism was the order of the day and many immigrant Irish also became ardent flag wavers. The Protestant newspapermen John O'Sullivan and Michael "Mike" Walsh were superpatriots and jingoists. It was an angry time for a city clearly divided between Catholic and Protestant. Violence and social dislocation were increasingly evident.[17]

In May 1849 a riot at the Astor Place Theatre, near present-day Cooper Union, epitomized bigotry stirred up by a mix of nativism and chauvinism, now directed against the British. English actor William Macready, who had seemingly slighted his popular American rival Edwin Forrest, was attacked on stage by a small organized group of local toughs. The affair spilled out into the streets, troops were called, shots were fired, and some twenty-five people lay dead. Dozens were jailed. Most of those killed and arrested were Irish. Members of the community like Mike Walsh, editor of the *Subterranean* (1843) and soon-to-be assemblyman and congressman, denounced the murder of "innocent bystanders," whereas Horace Greeley's *Tribune* justified the actions as necessary to maintain law and order. Newspapers placed the blame on lawlessness, drink, poverty, and the inpouring of more immigrants. The image of the "drunken Irish mob" was now deeply engraved in the popular mind. Politics and time would erase some but not all of the sharp edges. Later, archconservatives like lawyer George T. Strong held that the gorilla was superior to the "Celt in muscle and hardly their inferior in moral sense." He went on, "Poor ould Ireland is in a low state because the majority of Irishmen are Jackasses." Strong, a noted diarist, also hated Jews, "niggers," Wagner, and Berlioz, among others, with equal passion.[18] Confrontation was only part of the story.

For most of the newcomers, opportunities lay in carting, hauling, digging, and low-paying manual labor jobs, but even those did not come easily. For the more educated, by midcentury there were limited openings in public schools and municipal government. Gradually, skilled workers could be found in shipyards, in newspapers, the small Irish press, or at the head of their own enterprise. There were grocery stores, theaters, for some the Church, and increasingly politics, though very few achieved dominant positions. Political power was not readily shared. None became a mayor and only a few were found in higher office.

Most of the early immigrants were people of some means—primarily artisans, merchants, some professionals, but also domestic servants—anxious to discover "a free country, where a man is allowed to thrive and flourish without a penny taken by government," as bookseller John Doyle, living in New York City in 1818 thought. A visiting lecturer remarked in 1835 that "the distinguished Irish citizen who had so hospitably welcomed me to America was a hack car man who I had often hired in Dublin and who now rejoiced in the possession of a two-horse coach."[19] Here also thrived an Irish mercantile aristocracy. Later in the century, however, it was not so much the lure or promise of

America that attracted the immigrant as it was the spur of further suffering in the old country. After the 1830s Irish immigrants were mainly poorer people, many from southern or western Ireland. From the end of the eighteenth century, a landlord class of foreign birth and religion dominated Ireland. The bulk of farmers were rent-paying tenants. The vast majority of the population consisted of cottiers, or landless farm laborers, living in grinding poverty, usually next to a small potato patch, and virtually giving away their labor to the landlord. Farms were always being reduced in size so that by 1841, 560,000 of Ireland's 690,000 holdings amounted to less than 15 acres. About 400,000 Irish-born migrated permanently to England and Scotland.[20] Following the Napoleonic Wars, grain prices fell and there was more profit in eviction. The Irish Poor Law of 1838 put additional economic pressure on farmers, many of whom were forced to give up their holdings and decided to risk the dangers of a long and hazardous sea voyage to find a better life in a new, if not-so-welcoming country.

They left from Sligo, Cork, Dublin, Londonderry (Derry), and Liverpool. They left sadly, often to unhappy songs like the *Lament of the Irish Emigrant:*

> I'm bidding you a long farewell,
> My Mary kind and true,
> But I'll not forget you, darling,
> In the land I'm going to:
> They say there's bread and work for all,
> And the sun shines always there;
> But I'll not forget old Ireland,
> Were it fifty times as fair.

The voyage cost about $15 a head in steerage, "tween decks." The food and space were meager, the sanitary conditions poor. For many it was a miserable, if not fatal experience. Death came to thousands from such diseases as dysentery and typhus; countless children were left without parents. It was not at all like the promises of fame and easy fortune made by the shipping lines.[21] Most ended their trip in New York, not so much because it was their intended destination but because the shipping concerns deposited them there. The Black Ball, Dramatic, and Red lines, their offices overlooking the forest of masts fronting on the East River, were all headquartered in New York. The city was also a national port of entry for much of the trade from the United Kingdom, this country's principal customer, especially in textiles. In 1825, 54 percent of imported linen and flax was still coming from Ireland. Such trade no doubt had a strong impact on immigration.[22]

Initially, the number of immigrants grew slowly. In 1817 all arrivals totaled 7,654. Of this number, 3,131 were from England and 1,703 from Ireland. By 1845 there were 371,000 immigrants living in the city, of whom 97,000 were Irish. In 1851, 163,000 Irish arrived. This was the peak year before the Civil War. By 1855, of the general population of 630,000, there were 176,000 Irish or 28% of the total. There were 96,000 Germans.[23]

Once past customs and quarantine officials, many of the human freight found themselves alone, helpless, if not hopeless, ready victims of boarding house "runners," "Cheap Johns," extortionists and ticket agents who often took what little was available. They sought the company of fellow aliens in crowded, slum-like neighborhoods, the comfort of parish churches and of the 2,000 saloons, "shebeens," found in Irish neighborhoods by 1840. For the more well-to-do there was Malachi Fallon's "Ivy Green Tavern," a rendezvous for politicians, or David Sweeney's "House of Refreshment." Slowly, some gravitated to the local political clubs like Tammany Hall, but until the 1850s few found ready acceptance. A congenial people, but moved by fear and bewilderment, as much as the desire for good company, newcomers went whereever there were kindred folk with whom to share memories of home. They tended, at least initially, to remain together in the port city, though some moved quickly into the interior. Groups like the Irish Emigrant Society (1841), as well as other smaller benevolent organizations extended help. The Shamrock Friendly Association was active after the War of 1812. By 1817 it had found employment for 1200 individuals. The Society for the Encouragement of Faithful Domestic Servants (1825), and the Irish Emigrant Association (1817) sought to advise and aid those in need.[24] Social cooperation helped offset an always ever-present indifference, if not open hostility.

Protestant employers were leery of what they saw as a "Catholic menace," with its "forwardness and impertinence" and "free drinking" and "riotous" ways. "Woman Wanted—to do general housework . . . English, Scotch, Welsh, German or any country or color except Irish" was typical of advertisements and attitudes.[25] This prejudice, as seen in George T. Strong's and Philip Hone's diaries, was more apparent after 1825. The unskilled Irish had to compete with blacks, who were traditionally waiters, servants, cooks, and laborers. This competition aggravated the growing social antagonism, although there was some intermarriage among the poor blacks and Irish women. Cheap Irish labor was a greater threat to Protestant mechanics and craftsmen already at the mercy of increasing industrialization.

Rapidly changing market conditions, however, gave rise to a labor movement having an important Irish component. John Commerford helped organize the Workingman's Party of 1829 and the General Trades Union of 1835. Organized labor even in an infant stage helped the immigrant gain a foothold.[26]

Corporate positions and the professions were still beyond the pale, however. Banking, shipping, transportation, shipbuilding, insurance, and real estate were all held in a tight grip by a Protestant aristocracy. There were but a few openings here, a legacy of early New York. Michael Hogan from County Clare arrived in the city in 1804, perhaps the only Hogan on record with a "dark skinned Indian princess and £400,000 in gold sovereigns." "This remarkable Irishman" went into the shipping business, mainly in West Indian trade, and established himself as a "prince of a merchant." Also active in the early century were Dominick

Lynch, George Barnswell, and Cornelius Heeney, all importing merchants. Joseph Moleneaux, "late from Dublin," was a watch and clockmaker. Among the Irish born or the first generation were Charles O'Conor, John McCunn, Charles P. Daly, John McKeon, Thomas Addis Emmet,William Sampson, and Dennis McCarthy in law. But they were among the few Irish in the professions. At midcentury some 2 percent of New York's 600 physicians and 1 percent or so of its lawyers were Irish. There were four Bradys, but no Kellys. The founding of the long sought-after St. Vincent's Hospital by the Sisters of Charity occurred in 1849 and provided some further opportunity. Even fewer Irish were members of the administration or the faculty (or for that matter, the student body) at Columbia College or New York University. The situation was no different at the Chamber of Commerce, the influential General Society of Mechanics and Tradesmen, the Horticultural Society, or the New-York Historical Society. Even the militia and city government appeared impenetrable; in 1844, not one of the City Council's thirty-four members appear to have been Irish.[27]

Most jobs were to be found not in government, big business, or the professions, but in the unskilled market. Even there the former cottiers found resistance. In 1818, the City Council proposed that Irishmen be allowed to "cart dirt and nothing else," thus hoping to calm fearful licensed cartmen. The "nothing else," however, was gradually expanded to include work on city streets and docks. By 1855, they were largest group of cartmen. Interestingly, those immigrants who had found work or had arrived a short time earlier now attempted to prevent newcomers from competing in the marketplace.[28]

By the mid–nineteenth century, the Irish accounted for 87 percent of foreign-born unskilled laborers, but only 9 percent of some 14,000 engaged in the building trades and but 11 percent of some 20,000 in the clothing industry.[29] These rather dismal figures complemented housing conditions in the "Bloody Ould Sixth" Ward, site of the notorious Five Points at the corner of Worth, Baxter, and Park Streets (then Anthony, Orange, and Cross Streets), a slum Charles Dickens described in 1843 as "loathsome, drooping and decayed."[30] Here immigrants usually lived in dilapidated, crowded wooden tenements, while children played in and around slaughterhouses, stables, packing houses, and foundries. Horses, cattle, dogs, pigs were all about. Sweeney's Shambles in the Fourth Ward housed 400 Irish residents in 1857, whereas a few years earlier there had been only 120 families. On Park Street near City Hall there were 50 families in a seven-story tenement filled with sickening smells, garbage, and filth. There were no indoor water closets and no sewerage. Conditions were as bad or worse than the warrens that many had endured in Liverpool or on the crowded ships that took them to New York. Bishop John Hughes remarked that the slum dwellers were "the poorest and most wretched population that can be found in the world—the scattered debris of the Irish nation."[31]

Trapped in the city's worst slums, toiling at its worst jobs, struggling to maintain fragile families, many Irish slipped into alcoholism, insanity, chronic welfare dependency, or crime. The notorious Holy Ground around Murray Street and near Columbia College expanded, as did prostitution. One minister estimated that New York had 6,000 to 8,000 prostitutes in 1816. By 1839, the estimate had grown to 11,000, and by 1849 to 50,000. The largest number of "nymphs of the pave" were from Ireland, with most under 23 years of age. Of some 3,100 patients at Bellevue Hospital in 1839, 2,052 were from Ireland, whereas only 618 were from America, 138 from England, and 193 from Germany. In 1850, 2,742 persons died of cholera; 1,086 were Irish. Common diseases were cholera, typhus, dysentery, and consumption. In 1849 the Lunatic Asylum admitted 228 natives of Ireland, compared with 84 from New York. In 1849 there were 341 foreigners in the Work House: 252 were from Ireland and 33 from Germany. In the same year, there were 1,006 Irish in the Alms House, but only 89 from Germany. Interestingly, suicide was less common among the Irish than any other foreign-born group, possibly because of the church's influence.[32]

Death was ever present. In the Sixth Ward, 1 out of every 17 persons died in 1854. In Sweeney's Shambles the rate was 1 of 5 adults during a 22-month period. The death rate among Irish families in 1850–59, now usually of consumption, was 21 percent, while among non-Irish it was perhaps 3 percent. Bishop Hughes thought the disease "the natural death of the Irish emigrants."[33]

Although Irish families moved from one place to another, it was seldom beyond their parish or beyond Fourteenth Street, that is, until after the Civil War. Two of every five people who lived in Irish (or German) neighborhoods in 1850 had left by 1860. These were replaced by new arrivals and the neighborhood remained.[34]

Perhaps, the most bitter adjustment the cottiers faced was the disintegration of the family unit. "In Ireland," wrote Thomas D'Arcy McGee, editor of the *Nation* and an exile because of his part in the revolution of 1848, "every son was a boy and a daughter was a girl 'til he or she was married. . . . They were considered subject to their parents till they became parents themselves. . . . In America . . . boys are men at sixteen. . . . They either live with the 'boss governor' or 'old man,' or elsewhere, as they please. . . . If . . . family tie is snapt . . . our children become our opponents, and sometimes our worst enemies." McGee noted with considerable frustration and concern, as did many Americans, this failure of family discipline. The lack of stable relationships endangered the future of the community. McGee blamed this problem on the loss of contact with the soil, the process of uprooting, and the newness of the American experience with its blatant materialism. He established the American Irish Society to educate immigrant adults to these dangers, believing that ignorance must be overcome. He was an outspoken opponent of Bishop Hughes and the dominant role of the church, especially in education. He decried clerical opposition to the Young Ireland movement.[35]

For all the great numbers that remained mired in the city's worst jobs and slums, there were at least a few glimpses of hope, signs of potential change and upward movement. Some Irish men, as already mentioned, discovered or carved out niches for themselves in small business, publishing, the theater, or municipal politics and government. Such occupations seldom produced riches, but for at least a few offered a modicum of wealth, status, and security. Efforts to help kinsmen in Ireland or to establish institutions, particularly churches and schools, also suggested that many had not been broken by their burdens and were attempting to forge a coherent community amid their problems and often surrounding squalor.

Some found opportunities in small business where low capital investment provided attractive possibilities. In addition to the taverns, there were Irish-run hotels and boardinghouses like Patrick Garrick's Sixth Ward Hotel (1850) or John McDermott's (1832) hotel of the same name. Some were highly successful. P. L. Rogers arrived in New York from County Tyrone at the age of eighteen, engaged himself to a tailor, opened a small store, and by 1850 ran a huge six-story business at Fulton and Nassau Streets. Wine merchant Dominick Lynch Jr. and shipowner John Flack were also successful in business. James Leary & Co. made hats in the "most fashionable shop" in Chatham Square and later in Hanover Square. In the 1830s, John L. Dillon's Old Established Ready Made Coffin Warehouse at 496 Pearl Street provided everything in the "English Style" to meet any solemn occasion. By the 1840s, Dillon and his brother Christopher had a major part of the funeral trade. Henry McCadden, at 511 Pearl, provided the same "ready made" service.[36]

Many of these people made use of their expertise with horses and carriages. In 1817 John Carroll and one Byrnes advertised in the *Exile* as carriage makers and repairers. James Murphy & Co. was in 1847 the owner of the largest coach line, four separate routes, having twenty-nine two-horse omnibuses and one four-horse vehicle running between various parts of lower Manhattan to South Ferry. Thomas Murphy ran three of his two-horse coaches between Chatham Street and Hellgate Ferry. But the non-Irish Kipp and Brown line, though smaller, achieved greater historical fame.[37]

Groceries, found mostly at street corners, "were as a practice occupied by the Irish," wrote a long-time New Yorker, though with the mass arrival of more Germans in the late 1840s they replaced the Irish grocer, many of whom now opened "absurdly termed saloons."[38] Grocers in the early part of the century sold "Yankee rum" and oil, in addition to food. One English visitor commented in 1818 with some anger that "the Irish have got the greater part of this business; and they will if possible, prevent an English journeyman from having employment."[39] They were more than grocers. Many were fish, oyster, and produce dealers. Germans were usually butchers and dairymen. Only 2 percent of the Irish were so engaged.[40]

In 1844 there were 48 licensed secondhand dealers, 15 of which appear to have been Irish. Three years later, there were 71 licensed secondhand dealers, but only 11—including Ann Mayo at 101 Chatham Street (Park Row), Hugh

McCaffrey at 78, and Ann McCaffrey at 30 Chatham Street—were Gaelic. These three had been in business three years earlier. The trade centered in poorer neighborhoods in or about Chatham Square and Five Points. Most interestingly, about 95–98 percent of the licensed junk shopkeepers were Irish. There were 78 in 1844 and about 100 three years later. A license cost $20.00, a fair sum at a time when an average working man earned a dollar to a dollar and a half a day. Dealers included James Boyle, 90 Sheriff Street, and John McCabe, 57 Sheriff Street. Ann Regan was at 428 Cherry Street. Most were in the Lower East Side in the heavily Irish Fourth and Sixth Wards. Of 35 pawnbrokers, four had Irish surnames, including Mary Murphy at 68 Chatham Street. The ratios were the same by 1860. In that year approximately 95 percent of junk dealers were still Irish, but there were now 651 licenses.[41]

By the Civil War the ubiquitous junk dealers had multiplied. Henry Callaghan was at 120 West 40th Street, while Martin McAleer was at 45 West 135th Street. There were none on Chatham Street. Perhaps they went into the peddling business because, as Italian and Eastern European immigrants would also discover, there was little overhead and less worry about unemployment. In New York, most of the fruit and vegetable peddlers were Irish women. The junk trade, however, was not indicative of the whole, only one-half of 1 percent of the total foreign-born merchants were Irish, the fewest of any national group.[42]

There were several Irish booksellers in antebellum New York. By the 1830s, Caleb Bartlett at 76 Bowery had a general assortment of books for school and for recreation, along with playing cards. James Ryan, publisher and bookseller at his Classical and Mathematical Bookstand, 322 Broadway, sold and published any number of math and science books, including some used at West Point.[43]

In 1830 Denis Sadlier arrived in New York from Tipperary. Sadlier had learned the bookbinding trade and entered the business in 1836 with his brother James, on Carmine Street. Here he printed numerous religious books, including Alban Butler's *Lives of the Saints*. His sister-in-law Mary Ann was a voluminous writer of short stories and some sixty novels. She was a favorite of Catholic readers, advocating pride in old country values, including those of religion, but also seeking compromise with those of the new country. She helped bridge the cultural gap for many of her readers, and her novels about growing up in New York provided considerable insight into tensions between two societies.[44]

Some work was available in special trades. A small press provided a little opportunity. The *Shamrock, or Hibernian Chronicle*, printed in 1810, was the first such example and concerned itself largely with relating the new country to Irish nationalism. The *Exile* (1817), *Globe & Emerald* (1824), the popular *Truth Teller* (1825), the *Irish Shield* (1828), *Old Countryman* (1833) and *Freeman's Journal* (1840) were examples of generally short-lived papers. Often torn between supporting Catholic and secular views, they nevertheless served an eager constituency. The *Truth Teller* had a readership of 4,500 by 1846.[45] Leading journals remained staunchly Protestant, however, and provided little opportunity for the Irish immigrant. Indeed, many of the city's largest papers, like the *Herald, Tribune, Evening Star,* and later *New York Times,* adopted anti-Irish attitudes.

Characteristic of the nineteenth-century social world were many clubs, social circles, athletic activities, political organizations, lecture halls, and libraries. Many of these groups were founded by young men, in particular, some with a passionate interest in art and literature. Sons of Erin was founded in 1854, the Irving and Moore Literary Association in 1834, the Carroll Club in 1841, and the Thomas Davis Club in 1853. Non-Irish clubs like the prestigious Century Club (1847), a socially important literary and arts establishment, admitted few Irish Americans unless they had attained considerable social status. Charles P. Daly and Charles O'Conor were members along with the Astors and Roosevelts. The elite Union Club (1836) seems to have had only native-born Peter B. Sweeny (anglicized spelling), an influential New Yorker, included with the Griswolds and Grinnells. The doors were opened only so wide.

In 1842 and in 1856 the New York Catholic Library Association succeeded in attracting forty young members of the community. The library movement, despite its name, was basically Irish rather than Catholic. There was some interest in the publication of Gaelic manuscripts.[46]

Among the more eminent Irish artists were John Ramage, a miniaturist who painted George Washington, and William Guy Wall, known for his New York landscapes. Others had more moderate reputations. One such artist was John W. Orr, born in Ireland in 1815, who came to the city as a child. Having studied wood engraving, he worked for *Harper's* and other journals, providing carefully drawn views and scenes, mostly of New York. Another was Thomas Kelly, born in Ireland about 1795. He was an excellent engraver and worked in various cities, including New York, between 1834 and 1841. Unfortunately, he died in a New York almshouse in 1841 after "contracting bad habits." Dubliner Charles C. Ingham studied art there and then settled in New York in 1817, where he became one of the founders of the National Academy of Design, serving as vice president between 1845 and 1850. Basically a portrait painter, he was well known for his renderings of women and children.[47]

Active in Ireland and England, many well-known actors received a hearty welcome on the stage or in the concert hall. Music and theater, deeply rooted in Ireland, were brought to New York. John Collins, Barney Williams, and Redmond Ryan, however, too often won applause by playing hackneyed stereotypes, acting frequently as drunken buffoons. Although Irish plays were popular and eagerly received, criticism later caused Collins to portray Irishmen with dignity and to avoid the "blundering stupidity" meant to please the unthinking, if not bigoted.[48] Tyrone Power, whom mayor and diarist Philip Hone called "the best Irish man I ever saw particularly in low farce" appeared at the well-known Park Theatre in August 1833 as a much admired Sir Patrick O'Flaherty in *The Irish*

Ambassador. For the next decade he was a star attraction in the playhouse. Born in Waterford in 1797, he played in various London theaters before coming to New York. Power drowned at sea in 1841.[49]

A native of Tipperary, John Hamburg Dwyer came to New York in 1810 fresh from Drury Lane. Critics thought him to be an excellent comedian. Said one, he is "one of the greatest acquisitions that it [Drury Lane] has ever had to boast of. . . . Light dashing comedy is his forte and it is always faultless." Dwyer, born O'Dwyer, wrote a well-circulated work, *Essay on Elocution.*[50] Dion Boucicault, also of Dublin, born in 1820, was already well known in Europe as an actor and playwright when he arrived in New York late in 1853. There he enjoyed considerable success, especially with his play about slavery, *The Octoroon* (1859). His *Colleen Bawn* (1860) was the first of a long series of Irish comedy dramas. Boucicault was particularly famed for his high spirits and dash.

The concert stage received the talented violinist Master Joseph Burke, the "wonder and admiration of two continents." He first appeared on the London stage at the age of seven and in 1830 came to New York, where he appeared at the Park Theatre, leading the orchestra as well as performing on stage. The "Boy Phenomenon" played with the New York Philharmonic in 1846. He also taught and composed music and moved in the highest circles of New York society, "honored and respected by all who knew him." In 1872 a critic reflected that Burke, still unmarried, was a "good catch."

For others, fame came via strong arms and legs. One of the more colorful figures was "Old Smoke," John Morrissey, who was born in County Tipperary in 1831. He came with his family via Canada and Troy, New York. He was good with his fists and his feet. As a "runner" and gang leader, he literally fought his way to a high position. In 1853 he won a championship prize fight before a huge, riotous crowd but was defeated the next year by "Big Bill" Poole. Members of Morrissey's gang allegedly killed Poole, who became a martyr for the nativists' cause. In 1858 Morrissey beat John J. Heenan, "Bonicia Boy," also from County Tipperary, for the heavyweight championship. Morrissey brought gambling to Saratoga Springs and gained a seat in Congress. There were other Irish sports figures, especially in boxing, including "Yankee Sullivan," born in Ireland as James Ambrose. Sports not only provided a sense of accomplishment and pride for many, but was a means to achieve a voice in the political arena.[51]

By the 1840s, Irishmen began to seek, and were slowly being admitted to, public service. Until that time, public schools had been run by the private, Protestant-controlled Public School Society (1805), which hired few Irish Catholic teachers. By 1844, however, in School No. 5 on Mott Street, near Old St. Patrick's Cathedral, the teachers included Joseph McKeen and Margaret F. Henratty, while M. J. O'Donnell and Elizabeth Ann Crawford were at School No. 11 on Wooster Street. Francis McNally taught at School No. 17 on Thirteenth Street. Not an impressive number, but they continued a long tradition of Irish teachers. Increased resentment directed against the Public School

Society by Catholics and a growing city rapidly assuming a role as the custodian of public interest, led, in 1842, to the creation of the Common School System directed by the Board of Education. Those schools had a much stronger Irish presence. Boys at Ward School No. 8 were taught by John Toumey, P. Conelly, Jeremiah Mahoney, J. P. Brody, and William Mullaney, while girls were instructed by Catherine O'Rourke, Margaret Kevney, Catherine Murphy, and Maria Belton. One could find Lyons, Carrigans, or Gallaghers throughout the system. By the mid-1840s about one-third to one-half of the staff were Irish, and by 1860 the number was 40 to 50 percent. Also by 1860, there were forty-four commissioners of common schools, eleven of whom seem to have been Irish.[52]

The Police Department, part of an expanding city bureaucracy, also provided some employment, but again reluctantly. In 1800 there were very few, if any, recognizable Irish policemen, but great changes occurred in the next decades, especially after 1840, although administrative appointments remained difficult to obtain. In 1844 there were six district watchmen, none seemingly Irish; but in the lower police section they were perhaps 6 of 31 constables. Of the mayor's 50 marshalls, about 12 were Irish. In 1847 31 of 66 policemen were apparently Irish in the Sixth Ward. In 1855, when newly elected mayor Fernando Wood, partly to curtail crime and partly to gain votes, appointed 246 officers, half had Irish surnames. There were then 800 on the force, of whom approximately 400 were probably from Ireland.[53]

The Fire Department, a voluntary group from the colonial period until 1865, prided itself on its elitism. It had even fewer Irish than the police, and none became chief engineer before the Civil War. However, some gained considerable fame, notably John Brice, born in Belfast in 1823, who arrived in New York a year later with his family. One of four sons, he and each of his brothers joined Hose Company No. 42. He was first elected foreman of the company in 1853 and then elected city councilman in 1860 and alderman in 1865. In 1863, during the Draft Riots, Engineer Brice saw a mob trying to set fire to a house occupied by "colored people." In defending the property, he ordered his company to "kill any man who resists you." The home and a whole block of buildings were saved. Thomas Cleery, whose father was "an arch rebel to British domination," became a foreman with Washington Engine Company No. 20. Thomas P. Walsh, born in 1834, arrived in New York in 1838. He became assistant foreman of Engine Company No. 20 and later was elected an alderman.[54] Relatively few numbers in the department were Irish born, however, perhaps because there was no salary attached to the position or perhaps because of the inbred hierarchy of the department. Still, membership did provide some access to politics and society.

There were other areas of employment in the city government. John Clancy was a clerk in the County Clerk's Office in 1860, and Lawrence Clancy a recording clerk. John Kelly was sheriff and Hugh Kelly deputy sheriff. Many departments, however, like the Bureau of City Revenue or the Croton

Aqueduct, had few Irish. In 1830 there were eighty-eight notary publics, four of whom appear to have been Irish, and in 1849 there were possibly only five out of ninety-nine. In 1847 only two Irishmen were working in the Custom House out of a staff of seventy-three. By 1860, the numbers had increased only slightly. For the most part, the remaining city agencies only offered a token presence.[55] Quasi-public institutions such as the Roman Catholic Female Orphan Asylum or the Roman Catholic Orphan Asylum provided a little employment, but philanthropic organizations like the Society for the Reformation of Juvenile Delinquents or the Institution for the Deaf and Dumb were dominated by the Protestant cultural establishment, and thus doors remained closed to the newcomers.[56]

Still, the political landscape was changing rapidly by midcentury. John McKeon, Irish born, was named district attorney in 1850. The *Irish American* (1849), founded by Patrick Lynch, used McKeon's career as a model for others. "What he was, you are: . . . what he is, any of you may be. Be honest, faithful, industrious and energetic, and the highest honors of the land are open to you."[57] A Democrat in the turbulent politics of the 1850s, McKeon managed to have a long and varied career. There were a few second- or third-generation Irish in important city and state positions, including historian Henry C. Murphy, Peter B. Sweeny, and jurist Charles O'Conor, but again the Irish presence was limited. In 1867, 4 of the 32 state senators were Irish born or first-generation Irish, and 18 of the 126 assemblymen were members of the first generation. In 1860, at least 4 of the 17 members of the Board of Aldermen, were Irish, including Terence Farley and John R. Brady, and 6 of the 23 Board of Councilmen, including Joseph Shannon and Charles McCarthy, were so. In 1800, none of the 14 city councilmen appeared to be of immediate Irish decent. The same applied to members of the state legislature.

Ties of family and community, although stretched tight by so many burdens, nonetheless bound together many poor and not-so-poor immigrants. Perhaps the best evidence was the help they gave relatives and friends in the old country. There was a spirit of self-help and self-improvement. Money was raised to bring family members to America. More than half of the immigrants who arrived in 1838 had tickets purchased by friends or relatives. During the next decade, more than a million dollars a year was sent back to Ireland to pay the passage of kin. These were hard-earned dollars, back-breaking dollars, often raised in the most menial of jobs. But it was worth the effort to escape famine, tax collectors, rent agents, and civil strife. Many thought not only of their own families back home but of the fate of the old country as a whole. An English visitor in the early 1840s, Charles Lyell, noted a "grand Repeal demonstration" seeking an end to the Act of Union (1800) and "an endless procession of Irish parading the streets with portraits of O'Connell emblazoned on their banners." For Lyell, Irish thoughts were of British, not American politics. He, like Philip Hone, disapproved of candidates appealing to Irish sympathizers and their "ignorant prejudices."[58] Hostility remained, as did other social and economic obstacles, but a people had been successfully transformed.

Ties of community were also manifest in the growth and development of the Catholic Church in New York. By 1808, New York had a population of about 80,000; some 13,000 were Catholics, and most of these were Irish. In 1810, there was one church (St. Peter's), one school, and three priests.[59] Pope Pius VII created four Suffragan Sees, one of which was New York, and Reverend Richard Luke Concanen, a Dominican, was named first bishop. In 1809 a cornerstone for a new church was laid on Mott and Mulberry Streets. Known as St. Patrick's Cathedral, it was completed in 1815 and became the seat of the diocese, which included the state of New York and part of New Jersey. The impressive dedication service was witnessed by some 4,000 persons, including former Mayor DeWitt Clinton.

Quickly joining St. Peter's in the first decades of the century, in addition to St. Patrick's, was the Transfiguration Church (1836) on Mott Street (both Mott Street churches served the needs of Sixth Ward Irish) and St. James on James Street. By 1840 Transfiguration was the largest parish in New York, estimated to have 10,000 parishioners. St. Patrick's ministered to almost the same number.[60] Various problems plagued church administrators. Money was always in short supply. Pew rental, not often used in Ireland, became more common in New York. Loans were resorted to, but not always with success. Somehow, revenues were still obtained.

Devotional life also posed questions. Practicing Catholics, or at least a "great body" of them, received Communion at least once or twice a year, according to Bishop John Hughes, but attendance at Mass was often overlooked, especially in prefamine New York. A lack of priests and churches was, in part, responsible, along with a general lack of information about religion. A New York priest observed that "half of our Irish population here is Catholic merely because Catholicity was the religion of the land of their birth."[61] There were changes to attract churchgoers. Music and song enlivened services. Richard L. Burtsell, a young priest, decried the fact that the liturgy was in Latin and believed English would be more "effective of good." Still, Latin held sway. The wake, celebrated as a social and religious event, gradually disappeared from the home and was adopted as a church function. Issues such as confession and salary also arose and were more or less settled, and by the mid–nineteenth century the Irish parish was an established institution in the city. Gaelic as a language was rarely used in church services or elsewhere. Bishop Hughes believed it was something of the past, and its use would further separate newcomers from the general society. An exception was Father Joseph Burke who preached in Irish at St. Columba's on West 25th Street.[62]

With the founding of St. Peter's, the first halting steps were taken to provide at least a minimal religious education for the few children who were part of a very small congregation. There was a "free school" at St. Peter's by 1800 and in

1803 a building was constructed next to the church, especially for educational purposes. There were no public schools, as first attempts to form them in the colonial period had failed. Children were expected to be taught by parents, and if they had money, by tutors and church schools, or not taught at all. The need for schools grew as the population increased. New York's second bishop, John Connolly, arrived in November 1815 after a long voyage from Dublin, and in 1817 St. Patrick's Charity or Free School was opened in the basement of the church. Priests and lay teachers were in charge. It is possible that Mother Elizabeth Seton and the Sisters of Charity in the same year opened New York's first orphanage in the Diocese and also conducted a free school. In 1814 there were 486 Catholic students in free schools and 500 a year later. Twenty years later, a new two-story brick building, also on Mulberry Street, was erected. Boys occupied the first floor, girls, the second, where the Sisters of Charity were in charge.[63]

The role of public funding, as well as the competition for money and educational control with the Public School Society, founded in 1805, became increasingly important. The Public School Society, led by Quakers Thomas Eddy and John Murray Jr. and dominated by the Protestant hierarchy, sought to instill values of the ruling gentry. Many Catholics eagerly sought an alternative school. In 1806 the state legislature passed an act authorizing the distribution of public money to all free schools in New York City. This included the school run by St. Peter's. Funds were administered by the mayor and City Council. St. Peter's received a first grant of $1,565.78 in May 1806.[64] Awards were continued until 1826, when such aid to the Catholic free schools was ended, despite their great need and the controversy surrounding the action. In 1830 St. Peter's had 150 boys and 120 girls in attendance, while St. Patrick's had 250 boys and, interestingly, 600 girls. In contrast, 6,000 pupils were in the society's public schools, while 15,320 were in 430 private schools and 2,544 in charity schools.[65] Obviously, New Yorkers still believed education was a private responsibility. A visitor from England, Henry Fearon, noted that "day schools are numerous. Some of them respectable, none large. A teacher, that is, an usher, at any of these establishments, is a situation not worth the attention of the poorest man. No species of correction is allowed. . . . The emigrant proprietors of seminaries are Scotch and Irish." Fearon observed no "respectable " English school master was to be seen here, "subordination being foreign to the comprehension of the youth as well as aged of the country."[66] Still, education was a means of gaining a livelihood.

The independence noted by Fearon was a growing problem facing a community threatened with assimilation, at least in the view of many church officials. The simmering controversy over school policy between Catholics and the Public School Society became more heated. By 1826 there were 35,000 Catholics in New York, with three churches and five Catholic schools. The stakes expanded accordingly.[67] Reverend John Dubois, New York's third bishop, anxious not to stir up popular resentment, tried to have the society hire a Catholic teacher at Public School No. 5 on Mott Street, in addition to possibly having the society sell one of its discontinued buildings to St. Patrick's. The society turned down both suggestions, hoping more Catholic children would attend public schools.[68] Dubois, elderly and ill, did not press the issue. His assistant did, and more.

John Hughes, son of a poor farmer, born in County Tyrone in 1797, arrived in the United States in 1817, became a friend of Dubois, and was ordained in 1826 in Philadelphia. Hughes became coadjudicator bishop and New York's fourth bishop in 1839. He was a militant leader, forceful, uncompromising and unrelenting, especially with regard to what he saw as Protestant bigotry, whether in school rooms or in the streets. At one point in his defense of Catholics during the 1840s, he informed city officials, at a time of angry and violent nativism, "if a single Catholic church were burned in New York, the city would become a Moscow." Earlier in 1831, St. Mary's had been set afire, but not destroyed.[69] In talking to nativist Mayor James Harper in 1844, he was asked if he was frightened about the fate of his churches. Hughes replied, "No, sir; but I am afraid that some of yours will be burned."[70] In fact, no churches of any denomination were destroyed by mobs in New York, though it did happen in Boston and Philadelphia.

Hughes did not shy away from the school question. There were about 60,000 Catholics in New York in 1839, seven churches, 1,200 students at three free church schools.[71] These schools, he felt strongly, should be financed by the government. Hughes, at odds with Tammany Hall, obtained an ally in Whig governor William H. Seward. Aware that thousands of poor Irish as well as other immigrant children were growing up without proper education or care, the governor proposed in 1840 the "establishment of schools in which they may be instructed by teachers speaking the same language with themselves and professing the same faith."[72] Although the move may have been a political ploy to gain immigrant votes, Seward seemed to believe strongly in promoting equal educational opportunity as a means of ending social inequality.

The school issue came at a particularly troubled and disjointed time in the city's history. When Bishop Hughes and other militant Catholics spoke of church schools supported by public money, part of which came from taxes paid by Catholics, and offering to teach Catholic children, rabid nativists such as publisher and mayor James Harper, saw a dangerous conspiracy. Bishop Hughes found the Public School Society and the idea of a common education profoundly anti-Catholic and believed it would destroy religious freedom in the state. Why, for example, would Catholics who were forbidden by the church to use the King James Bible, have to hear it read every day in public schools? Surely another reason to have separate schools was the American Protestant Society, founded in 1843 in New York to convert Catholic immigrants, thereby continuing a long-established program established in Ireland.

Hughes's arguments along with those of Seward were printed in a new newspaper, the *Freeman's Journal*, first issued in 1840. For many immigrants such arguments were persuasive, partly because of their dislike for the entrenched Protestant establishment that ran the School Society. Hughes's position, however, was not favorably received by the general public, the press, or the city government. Even for some Irish, as Walter Walsh explains in chapter 2, the idea of a common education, with their children sitting next to other ethnic groups and Irish lay teachers being employed, seemed a viable alternative to the church's position. In some respects, the argument continued the bitter fight in Ireland, where the more radical, secular Young Ireland movement was in opposition to O'Connell's more church-oriented Repeal Party. William Denman's the *Truth Teller*, part of the Irish-Catholic press, founded in 1825, at this point ardently opposed Seward on the school issue. He felt religion belonged at home and opposed any discriminatory legislation. Only Jews, some 12,000 out of a population of 312,000 in 1840, supported Hughes on the issue. Though Jewish–Irish relationships are rarely commented on, both groups were equally hated by elitists, but there seems to have been an undercurrent of resentment between poor Irish and the rising Jewish middle class. The Civil War Draft Riots of 1863 saw Irish rioting in Jewish neighborhoods. The school issue, however, was an example of mutual interest and cooperation.[73]

The Public School Society was willing to expunge anti-Catholic material, but insisted on the separation of church and state and cited state laws specifically prohibiting the use of the common school fund by religious societies. Seward continued to hold Hughes's position. Supporters carried 7,000 signatures to Albany in 1841 in an effort to sway the legislature. Meetings, handbills, and speeches added to the furor. Whigs and Democrats were caught up in a storm that they feared they could not control. Even as Seward clung to his position, many Whigs moved to support common education. The Democrats, caught on a fragile fence, carefully measured the political winds. Hughes responded late in 1841 with a proposal to form a separate political entity, the Carroll Hall faction. For nativists like Hone, this was proof, if such was needed, that Catholics really intended to rule the country.

As is usual in city elections, the fall election of 1841 ended in a narrow victory. The Hall's 2,000 votes gave Hughes a balance of power, much beyond his actual influence. A bill introduced in the legislature gave city wards the same rights as towns with regard to schools, making each ward responsible for the administration and distribution of school money. After furious campaigning, the bill barely passed and was immediately signed by Seward. On election day, April 11, 1842, however, many voted with their fists. Bishop Hughes's residence was stoned and partly ransacked by a mob of nativists. Cathedral windows were smashed. Hughes was not home at the time.[74] Victory even in the form of the Ward bill carried a price. Many New Yorkers found Hughes threatening and dangerous.

The bill was not enforced and Catholic schools did not receive public money, but the Public School Society did not survive the crisis either. In 1842 the first Board of Education was elected, controlled by non-Catholics. Daily Bible reading persisted, despite Catholic protests. In 1853 the society became part of the Board of Education. Hughes, who became archbishop in 1850, continued his struggle for a strong but separate Catholic school system, although the common school system provided education for most Irish children and opportunities for teachers. Hughes's dream of Irish Catholic teachers for young Catholics was now partly realized in the common school system, especially in heavily Irish wards.[75]

By midcentury the issue of slavery had come to the fore and become intertwined with the always present concern with Irish nationalism. This issue was a special component of continuing education as the Irish community became more an integral part of American society. American foreign policy, particularly America's role in helping Irish revolutionaries imprisoned by Britain, also stoked the fires of mutual antipathy between the Irish and their nativist opponents. The jailing of leaders of the Young Ireland revolt of 1848, including Thomas F. Meagher, John Mitchel, and John Martin, now martyrs to the "cause," further stirred sympathy as well as action. The movement developed after a split with Daniel O'Connell's less militant National Repeal Association. Public meetings were held and petitions sent to Congress to try to persuade the American government to bring pressure on the British to free the group. In February 1852 William H. Seward, now a senator but still a Whig, paid tribute to the Irish on behalf of the prisoners. Southern senators objected to the proposal, fearing repercussions among their slave population. Freedom for Ireland could translate into freedom for slaves.

The debate became unnecessary when Mitchel and others escaped from the British penal colony in Van Diemen's Land (Tasmania). Mitchel arrived in New York in November 1853. He was warmly greeted at City Hall, but in a curious, heavy-handed way, he missed an opportunity to become an effective leader of the Irish community. He seemingly assumed that the tributes given to him were meant not as personal accolades, but as insults to the British government. Further, at a banquet he criticized Secretary of State William L. Marcy and American foreign policy, proclaiming himself "a professed revolutionist" who wanted America to become a "stamping ground" for revolution. In 1854 he committed another error by stating he found no crime in slavery: "We, for our part, wish we had a good plantation, well stocked with healthy negroes in Alabama." For many New Yorkers, including the editor of the *Tribune*, Mitchel's views weakened support for those struggling to free Ireland. Next Mitchel angered popular Archbishop Hughes and his large constituency by supporting the seizure of Rome by Italian republicans and their creation of a new civil government. Mitchel also was willing to support the repressive Czarist government if it would lead to a free Ireland.[76] In October 1854 William Smith O'Brien, another exile from Tasmania, arrived in New York and also received an enthusiastic reception, including official greeting and a dinner. O'Brien was willing to accept these plaudits with little comment, realizing the influence of Irish voters in the city should be used to embarrass the British, not the American government. He did not take on Hughes or the slave issue.

The slavery issue remained a contentious one. Distressed by a statement of Daniel O'Connell and a papal bull of Pope Gregory XVI, both condemning the "peculiar institution," many, including the *Citizen,* founded by Mitchel in 1854, thought it was a "bad Irishman" who would jeopardize "the present freedom of a nation of white men for the vague forlorn hope of elevating blacks." The *Irish American* saw Republicans raising a banner inscribed, "Death to and down with Popery, Slavery, and Rum."[77] As a group, the Irish voted Democratic, partly because of their fear of opposition Republicans, popularly thought to be related to Know-Nothings, and partly because of job opportunities offered by

Manhattan in 1834 as seen from Brooklyn Heights. Painting New York from this prospect was a tradition first popularized by the Dublin-born artist William Guy Wall (1792–c. 1862). Wall's "The Bay of New York taken from Brooklyn Heights" was reproduced for sale as an engraved aqua tint and on a plate by Staffordshire (England) in the 1820s. It was widely imitated, with variations, as the city's skyline changed. (From the collection of Leo Hershkowitz.)

the entrenched, though divided Tammany Hall. Politics was largely put aside as the Civil War began, and most of the Irish marched in support of the Union. They were no small part of the conflict. Immigrant or not, they were citizens of the nation.

The road from colonist to citizen had been a long and difficult one. It was not easy for immigrants arriving from farm or town during the colonial and antebellum period to adjust to foreign surroundings, new customs, conditions, and language. Wherever they turned, they met resentment and prejudice. There were no official welcoming committees at the dock. Yet, slowly, often painfully, the Irish found a new life for themselves, as the following chapters attest. Slowly, doors of opportunity to professions, trades, labor, and government were pushed open by hard effort and enterprise. The costs were high. Disease, squalor, hatred took a dreadful toll of human lives. Yet, with spirit and determination, the Irish gained a foothold and then secured at least a grudging acceptance. The next generations would have a firm foundation upon which to build. New York offered a pleasing prospect. The climb was and would be arduous, but the view from the summit would be worth the effort.

Joyce D. Goodfriend

CHAPTER 1

"Upon a bunch of Straw"

THE IRISH IN COLONIAL

NEW YORK CITY

WHO WERE the Irish of colonial New York City? For nearly a century, the men and women who emigrated from Ireland to New York and other ports in British America have been pawns in a war of words between partisans of the Scots-Irish (those residents of Ireland whose ancestors originated in Scotland) and the Catholic Irish natives of the land.[1] Exaggerated claims have been advanced on both sides, but the enduring legacy of the debate has been the adoption by the historical profession of the Scots-Irish interpretation placing immigrants from Ulster, most of whom were Presbyterian, at center stage in accounts of the Irish in colonial America.

The tendency to conflate the Scots-Irish experience with the Irish experience in early America has not been challenged by historians of colonial New York despite the prodigious efforts of early-twentieth-century researchers to document the presence in the city and countryside of Irish immigrants whose roots were not in Scotland. Brimming with informative detail, though imperfect in conceptualization, the works of John D. Crimmins, Michael J. O'Brien, Richard J. Purcell, and Richard Doyle have been virtually ignored by the authors of the major studies of seventeenth- and eighteenth-century New York.[2] Indeed, what is striking about the historical literature on early New York, especially in light of the critical part played by ethnicity in the colony's development, is the failure of writers to discuss the Irish in New York before the Revolution in more than a perfunctory way.[3]

The biases of historians alone cannot explain why a numerically considerable population has remained historically invisible for so long. Efforts to reconstruct the history of early Irish New Yorkers are also complicated by the lack of uniformity among those who emigrated from Ireland to New York in the seventeenth and eighteenth centuries. At this time, Ireland was culturally and religiously diverse, encompassing individuals of Irish, English, Scottish, French, and German ancestry, as well as Roman Catholics, Anglicans, Presbyterians, Quakers, Huguenots, and Methodists.[4] Additionally, the problem of identifying city dwellers who were Irish is thorny, since using nomenclature as an indicator of Irish identity has been called into question as a research method.[5] In view of the fact that certain surnames were not unique to the Irish but were shared by other British people, for the purposes of this study I have categorized as Irish only those people who were identified as such in contemporary records, even though this procedure undoubtedly leads to an underestimate of the number of Irish in eighteenth-century New York City.

Irish men and women had found their way to the shores of Manhattan even before England captured the colony from the Dutch in 1664. But in the late seventeenth and early eighteenth centuries, the Irish constituted a minuscule proportion of the city's population. Only with the advent of a regularized emigrant trade from Ireland in the late 1720s did the numbers of Irish in New York begin to climb.[6] Ships that brought cargoes of flaxseed to Ireland for use in the linen industry used their return journeys to American ports to transport indentured servants and paying passengers. The human traffic that developed alongside Irish-American commerce in the eighteenth century augmented the profits of merchants on both sides of the Atlantic while furnishing workers and entrepreneurs for the colony. By the 1770s people of Irish descent had become a substantial presence in the city.

Ships carried hundreds of immigrants from ports in northern and southern Ireland to New York City during the eighteenth century, but the majority of these passengers moved to other parts of New York colony or to other colonies. "There is plenty of room and employ for them in the back countries, where many of them are gone," Scottish visitor Patrick McRobert put it in 1774.[7] Moreover, the paths of some Irish newcomers were convoluted, as they traveled to the city by way of England or Philadelphia. Bricklayer Patrick Blanchville, for example, noted in a 1768 advertisement that he was "lately from Kilkenny in Ireland, and just arrived with Capt. Gifford from Bristol."[8]

Nevertheless, the overall pattern of Irish immigration to New York, which resembled that to Philadelphia in timing if not in volume, provides a rough gauge to the pace at which the city's Irish population grew.[9] From the late seventeenth century until the American Revolution, ships regularly transported immigrants from Ireland to New York. At two points in time, however, there were sharp increases in the number of ships reaching the city.

A cluster of vessels carrying indentured servants from Ireland docked in the city between 1728 and 1732. The six ships for which statistics are available held 388 men and women, many of whom were skilled workers.[10] Over the next few decades, a variety of brigantines, schooners, scows, and sloops made their way from Dublin, Cork, Belfast, Londonderry, and other Irish ports to New York, conveying human cargoes in assorted quantities.

With the conclusion of the French and Indian War, however, there was an upsurge in immigration from Ireland. Between 1763 and 1774 at least 39 ships embarked from Irish ports headed for New York.[11] Immigrants streamed into New York City in the early 1770s, a good portion of them from Ireland. In August 1773 David Colden noted, "I find many settlers are comeing in this Year from Britain and Ireland."[12] John Watts, a prominent city merchant, echoed Colden in 1774, observing that "many Scots and Irish are come here."[13] That same year Patrick McRobert commented on "the arrival of so many adventurers from Britain and Ireland; they tell me that no less than twenty two vessels have arrived at New York with passengers within three twelvemonths."[14] The veracity of these observations is substantiated by a report published in *Gentleman's Magazine* in July 1774 stating that 1,611 Irish passengers had landed in New York between August 3 and November 29, 1773.[15] This flood of immigrants, reflected in the 74 percent increase in New York's white population from 10,768 in 1756 to 18,726 in 1771, undoubtedly swelled the city's Irish population.

Those who left Ireland for the American colonies in the eighteenth century did so in four ways: as indentured servants, as paying passengers, as members of the British army, and as convicts. Few, if any, Irish convicts were transported to New York, but it is probable that a good number of the soldiers stationed in the colony were natives of Ireland.[16] Enlisting in the British army offered Irish men a means of getting to America, where they could assess their prospects for future success. Once his term of service in New York's garrison had ended, Thomas Scurlock, whose sister lived in Dublin, became a vintner.[17] William Gilliland, who established himself as a merchant in the city prior to promoting a settlement in the Champlain valley, left his home near Armagh in northern Ireland by enlisting in His Majesty's 35th Regiment of Foot. Following his discharge in Philadelphia in 1758, he moved to New York City, where a fortuitous marriage to the daughter of a well-to-do merchant launched him on his career.[18]

Whether impatient to test their skills in the new labor market or just fed up with military discipline, a number of Irish soldiers stationed in New York during the years of the French and Indian War deserted, and some undoubtedly blended into the city's population of workingmen. Deserters from His Majesty's 22nd Regiment of Foot at New York City between March 30 and April 27, 1761, included James Carson, a laborer born in the county of Fermanagh, aged 25; David Herron, also a laborer, from the county of Down, aged 23; and two natives of the County of Tyrone, 22-year-old James Gallagher, a weaver, and 23-year-old Robert Smith, a laborer.[19]

The majority of Irish immigrants to colonial New York came as either paying passengers or indentured servants, though in what proportions cannot be determined from available evidence. Advertisements for servants were commonplace in the New York press from the 1720s on. *Rivington's New-York Gazeteer* carried one in March 1774 that read, "A few Irish Servants just arrived from Cork, on board the Gallway Packet, to be sold by Mrs. Lynch in Broad Street, near the Exchange."[20]

Indentured servants have loomed large in accounts of Irish migration to the American colonies, but those Irish who possessed the means to transplant themselves or members of their families to New York, though less visible, must not be overlooked. Visits home by migrants, as well as letters, kindled the interest of people still in Ireland. Impressed by the good fortune of a kinsman who had prospered as a merchant in New York, Robert Neilson, of Maddybenny, County Derry, Ireland, wrote his brother in Massachusetts in 1764: "William Neilson is now here and sold a large Cargo of flaxseed this season in Dublin, he sets out from home tomorrow on his way to London and from that to Newyorke; . . . I have five Children alive and Intend to send my oldest Son to Newyork this Summer."[21] In some instances, men who had already made good in New York allocated funds for relatives to travel there. Innkeeper David Young, one of whose brothers lived in County Tyrone, provided in his 1769 will that "the sons of my brother John and the sons of my sisters, Jane and Mary, such as choose to come to this city, shall have their passage paid . . . if they come within three years."[22]

Although the distribution of workers cannot be plotted as precisely as one would wish, the occupational profile of New York City's Irish in the half-century before the Revolution reveals a full range of occupations, including merchants and professionals who belonged to the city's elite, skilled craftsmen, mariners, and unskilled workers.

Heading the Irish occupational hierarchy were the merchants. After 1750, men of Irish antecedents engrossed the lion's share of New York's important trade to Ireland. "The typical firm," states Thomas Truxes, "was a flaxseed house that gathered, cleaned, and packaged seed and shipped it to Ireland in exchange for linens, salted provisions, and a few minor imports, such as potatoes, coal, and shoes. Most of the city's Irish merchants operated retail stores through which they marketed a wide variety of British manufactures, along with West India goods and articles they took directly from home."[23]

Estimated to number 30 at its peak, the city's Irish merchant community included overseas merchants of the first and second rank, men who were involved in intercolonial trade, and retail shopkeepers.[24] Waddell Cunningham, in partnership with Thomas Greg of Belfast in the firm of Greg, Cunningham and Company, towered above most of his competitors in New York as he engaged in complex trading operations. Counted among the city's principal merchants as well were Hugh Wallace, the son of a prominent Waterford merchant, and George Folliot, who embarked on his career in New York under the watchful eye of his uncle, a merchant in Londonderry. Lesser merchants such as James and Acheson Thompson, who imported linen from Newry, also capitalized on their connections in Ireland.

The business of other Irish men was on a more modest scale. Hercules Mulligan, whose father was a perukemaker and whose brother Hugh was a partner in the firm of Kortright and Company, which traded to the West Indies, ran a shop specializing in men's clothing. The city's Irish entrepreneurs also numbered some tavernkeepers, among them John Hill of the town of Omagh who gave notice in 1774 that he had opened the New Beef Steak and Oyster House.[25]

Several professional men of Irish birth made their mark in late-eighteenth-century New York City, among them physicians John Charlton and Samuel Clossy. A Dublin native and graduate of Trinity College, Charlton came to New York as a surgeon in the British Army in 1762 and, after resigning his commission, embarked on the private practice of medicine. Clossy, also a graduate of Trinity College, Dublin, as well as a fellow of Ireland's College of Physicians, was invited to join the faculty of King's College soon after his arrival in New York. One of his colleagues there was Irish-born Robert Harpur, a professor of natural philosophy and mathematics, who had studied at the University of Glasgow. Attorney Joseph Murray, an Irish immigrant whose distinguished career spanned the middle years of the eighteenth century, was a major benefactor of King's College. John Wilson, who noted that he was late of the Kingdom of Ireland when he made his will in 1749, was a schoolmaster.[26]

Irish immigrants who worked with their hands undoubtedly outnumbered those of more genteel status. Printer Hugh Gaine, a Belfast native who achieved fame as the publisher of the *New-York Mercury*, stands out among the city's craftsmen.[27] The Irish artisan community also included Philip Brooks, a bookbinder; Thomas Dunn, a combmaker; Richard Lightfoot, a pinmaker; Nesbett Deane, a hatter; John Hickey, a silk dyer and scowerer; and coachmakers Jeremiah Field and Elkanah Deane.[28] Advertising his skills in 1768, Thomas Vallentine boasted that he had "conducted the Gardening Business for the Right Hon. The Earl of Belvedere, a Nobleman remarkable for elegant taste, extensive Gardens and Plantations."[29] Greater numbers of Irish skilled workers, however, could be found as tailors, breeches makers, and weavers.

Scores of Irish New Yorkers were men of the sea. For them, the host of privateers who sailed from New York harbor during the French and Indian War proved a bonanza.[30] In the will he drafted in 1758, Michael Dunn, "of Ireland, but now of New York, mariner," left to a friend "all my Prize money that may be owing, or coming to me by the Privateer 'Royal Hunter,' Captain Harrison, Commander, now bound on a cruise."[31] When opportunities for signing on to privateers diminished as the theater of war shifted to the Caribbean, Irish mariners faced hard times. For many, the munificent bounties offered for enlistment in provincial units proved irresistible. Of the 177 Irish volunteeers who gave their occupations to recruiters, 66 (37%) identified themselves as mariners. For enterprising ship captains such as Thomas Randall from County Limerick, successful privateering ventures during the war were the springboard to mercantile careers.[32]

A host of Irish men earned their livelihood in New York City as laborers. Forty-one percent of the volunteer soldiers (72 out of 177) were laborers.[33] Shortly after the midpoint of the eighteenth century, Irish laborers began to enter the ranks of the city's cartmen, the men who were licensed to transport goods in the city. In the years betweeen 1756 and 1765, in Graham Hodges's estimate, Irish men accounted for about 5 percent of the 386 cartmen enrolled as freemen.[34]

Irish indentured servants bulked large in New York City's economy in the decades leading up to the Revolution. They filled a variety of jobs, ranging from barber to chimney sweep to tobacconist. But the majority probably worked in the cloth trades.[35]

As a rule, colonial New Yorkers did not differentiate among immigrants from Ireland. Perhaps influenced by stereotypes perpetuated in theatrical productions such as *The Committee or The Faithful Irishman,* presented in New York in 1762, or literary works such as David Garrick's play *The Irish Widow,* published in New York in 1773, they tended to use the term "Irish" indiscriminately.[36] Yet the impression of homogeneity fostered by convention is misleading because the city's Irish population not only was drawn from both the north and south of Ireland, but was comprised of people whose ancestry was Irish, English, Scottish, and German, and whose religious loyalties were divided between Protestant and Catholic.

Pinpointing any pattern in the geography of Irish migration to New York is hazardous, given the fact that information on place of birth in Ireland is available for only 19 percent (87 of 453) of a sample of the city's Irish population in the eighteenth century. Nonetheless, it is suggestive that little more than a third (37%) of these individuals came from locations in northern Ireland, where the Scots-Irish were concentrated.

Although Governor Robert Hunter informed English authorities in 1720 that "the Inhabitants increase day [daily] chiefly from New England & of late from the North of Ireland," the subsequent flow of immigration to New York from Ulster never matched that to colonies to the south.[37] Among the city's northern Irish immigrants were James Cochran, a pedlar born in the parish of Coleraine, County Derry, and perukemaker Hugh Mulligan and his family from County Antrim; and in 1764 Thomas Carroll from Newry advertised that he planned to open a school in New York City.[38] Immigrants from Belfast included printer Hugh Gaine, merchants Hamilton Young and Robert Ross Waddell, and tallow chandler Alexander Wallace, who in his 1772 will left £7 to "my honored father, James Wallace, of Belfast."[39]

The largest number of Irish immigrants to New York came from Dublin. Skilled craftsmen emphasized their Dublin origins in newspaper advertisements of the 1760s and 1770s. In his 1768 will, merchant Hugh Kennedy Hoy left 15 guineas to his mother, Zerviah Hoy, now residing in Dublin, Ireland. Immigrants from other places in southern Ireland included merchant Robert Pillson from Drogheda, mariner Charles Burns from Kilkenny, and coachmaker Jeremiah Field, whose brother John was a carpenter in Tipperary.[40]

Recent scholarship has cautioned that place of birth cannot be taken as a foolproof sign of ethnicity in eighteenth-century Ireland.[41] Anglo-Irish lived in Dublin alongside Gaelic Irish, and Scots-Irish, though concentrated in Ulster, did not form the entire population of that region. Nevertheless, the modest dimensions of immigration from the north of Ireland, the center of Scots-Irish strength, imply that Presbyterians were not the most influential group in New York City's Irish population.

Historians have emphasized the distinctiveness of Scots-Irish immigration to the North American colonies, pointing to the strength of family and communal ties among these Presbyterians from Ulster. Readily identifiable when they settled in separate communities on the frontier, they were less visible in pluralistic urban settings. This was particularly true in New York.

Though the term was not commonly used in eighteenth century New York City, in a handful of cases individuals were referred to as Scots-Irish. Hugh Brady, a 26-year-old mariner who formerly had lived with New York City merchant Jacob Franks, was called a "Scotch Irishman" when he deserted from a company of Foot at Albany in 1746.[42] Sixteen-year-old Michael Daugherty was described as a Scotch-Irish servant when he ran away from James McHugh in 1750.[43] In a 1755 letter, Catharine Pemberton, whose husband Ebenezer had resigned his post as minister of New York City's First Presbyterian Church, attributed the disruptions in the church that had precipitated his action to "a party of the begotted [bigoted?] Scots Irish Presbyterians."[44]

The search for New York City's Scots-Irish logically leads to its Presbyterian church. Contemporaries as well as later denominational historians recognized that Scots-Irish were a vital element in the mixture of peoples in the city's Presbyterian church. When they petitioned for a charter in 1766, Presbyterian leaders noted that the founders of the church included "sundry Protestants of their perswasion who came over into the Province from Great Britain and Ireland."[45] The congregation's earliest historian, Samuel Miller, working from documents prepared by Reverend John Rodgers, who had begun his ministry in 1765, noted that around 1750, "a large and respectable portion of the congregation consisted of emigrants from Scotland and the north of Ireland."[46] When the new Brick Presbyterian Church was constructed on Beekman Street in 1768 to house the overflow from the Wall Street church, "either by accident or, more probably, by the drawing together of congenial persons, the strong Scotch and Irish element of the Presbyterian membership remained for the most part in the older church."[47]

Determining how numerous Scots-Irish were in the congregation or, for that matter, distinguishing them from Scots is not possible except in the few instances when a family's history is known. Therefore, the Scottish ancestry of Irish New Yorkers must be inferred from their allegiance to the city's Presbyterian church. One of the church's founders, merchant Patrick MacKnight, came from northern Ireland.[48] Robert Harpur, the King's College professor, was the son of Scottish parents who had moved to Ireland. Samuel Johnson, the college's Anglican president believed that Professor Harpur would "do very well," even though he was a Presbyterian.[49] Harpur's name appears on a 1769 list of communicants of the city's Presbyterian church, along with that of William Gilliland, the entrepreneur who planned to settle immigrants in the Champlain valley.[50]

A few other New Yorkers from Ireland were associated with New York's Presbyterian church. Daniel McCormick, a merchant who settled in New York City in 1766, was a trustee of Brick Church.[51] Mariner John Neilson, whose 1762 will mentions relatives in Bangor, County Down, Ireland, left "the sum of £100 to be paid towards the purchase of a house for the residence of the Minister of the Presbyterian Congregation in New York." His Presbyterian values were evident in his instructions that his nephew would receive a large legacy only "provided he practices no immoralities of Gaming, Drinking, and other vices."[52]

Though sufficient evidence exists to disprove James Leyburn's claim that few Scots-Irish settled in New York during the colonial period, it remains true that only a minority of Irish newcomers to New York were of Scottish origin. In this respect, New York City offers a marked contrast to Philadelphia, where Scots-Irish formed a significant segment of the population.[53] In New York City, the dominant group among immigrants from Ireland were the Anglo-Irish.

Anglicans, who made up approximately one-fifth of the Irish immigrants to colonial America between 1700 and 1776, comprised descendants of those who were involved in the conquest of Ireland as well as more recent converts to the Church of Ireland.[54] Heirs to power and privilege in their homeland, they also took advantage of lucrative opportunities in the American colonies.

In New York, Anglo-Irish immigrants gravitated to Trinity Church. Not every Irish person who affiliated with Trinity Church boasted English lineage; printer Hugh Gaine had Scottish roots but became a loyal Anglican in his adopted city.[55] Nor, for that matter, did all Irish immigrants with English forebears adhere to the Anglican Church. Quakers, the vast majority of whom settled in Pennsylvania and New Jersey, may have numbered a few among New York's Anglo-Irish.[56] But the correspondence between English ethnicity and Anglicanism was strong and therefore association with Trinity Church provides the best index of this important segment of New York City's Irish population.

Anglo-Irish men were represented in the highest echelons of New York's government and society by Governor William Cosby and Sir Peter Warren, a British naval officer with extensive property holdings on Manhattan.[57] Attorney Joseph Murray defended the Crown's interests in New York courts and became the second husband of Grace Cosby, the governor's daughter.[58] A staunch Anglican, he worshiped in Trinity Church along with wealthy merchants such as Hugh Wallace and Anthony Duane, who served on the vestry. Duane, a native of County Galway, had been raised by his uncle, the Anglican vicar general of Tuam.[59] Oliver Templeton, whose 1774 marriage was performed by Dr. Miles Cooper, the Anglican president of King's College, was a partner in the firm of Templeton and Stewart.[60] Other Anglo-Irishman active in the mercantile world were Robert Pillson and Hercules Mulligan. New York's Irish Anglicans also included sea captains Thomas Randall and Thomas Roach, a native of County Cork who married in Trinity Church in 1778 and was buried there in 1795.[61] Among New York's Irish immigrants, Anglicans were the most visible and successful.

The German Irish formed an anomalous but historically significant segment of colonial New York City's Irish population. Descended from families that had been transplanted to the estates of Lord Southwell in County Limerick in 1709, when their homes in the Palatinate were ravaged by the armies of Louis XIV, they sought relief in New York from their travail as farmers in Ireland.[62] Before leaving Ireland, some of them had been converted to John Wesley's form of religion when Methodist missionaries visited their home towns in County Limerick.

When Philip Embury, a Wesleyan preacher in Ireland, and several other Palatines migrated to New York in 1760, they found no Methodist society established and worshipped instead at the Lutheran church of their ancestors. But after another party of Palatines arrived from Ireland in 1765, Embury, at the instigation of his cousin Barbara Heck, began to preach again and soon attracted a body of followers that quickly was organized into New York City's first Methodist society. The small number of German Irish who came to New York City in the 1760s are regarded as the pioneers of Methodism in the city.

The Gaelic Irish, with their rich culture and history of oppression, formed the majority of Ireland's population, but constituted a minority in the transatlantic migration. Nevertheless, their presence among Irish immigrants to colonial America can no longer be ignored, nor can their Catholic faith. In Kerby Miller's estimate, one-fifth to one-fourth of emigrants between 1700 and 1776 were Catholics. Most traveled to British America as indentured servants, while some arrived as soldiers.[63]

Catholic worship was banned in all but Pennsylvania and parts of Maryland during the colonial period and incentives to assimilate were strong, leading the great majority of Irish Catholic immigrants to abandon their accustomed faith.[64] New York's rigid penal laws constrained Catholic newcomers from practicing their religion and ultimately promoted their conversion to Protestantism.[65] Faced with a host of negative sanctions, immigrants raised as Catholics turned to the city's Protestant churches when they married and baptized their children. The scattering of men and women with Irish birthplaces among the brides and grooms listed in the marriage records of the Dutch Reformed Church offers mute testimony of the pressures placed on Catholic Irish immigrants to New York.[66] The supposition that New York had a dearth of Catholics is given added credence by the comments of Anglican observers. In 1745 "Robert Janney thought that Philadelphia, unlike New York was 'very much infested with Popery.'"[67] An Anglican minister living north of the city declared in 1748 that "there is not in New York the least face of popery."[68]

Few in number and forced to remain concealed, colonial New York City's Irish Catholics were drawn from the ranks of soldiers stationed in the fort and servants indentured to artisans and merchants. In 1700 Governor Bellomont railed against "the recruits that came from Ireland . . . a parcel of the vilest fellows that ever wore the King's livery, the very scum of the army in Ireland and several Irish Papists amongst 'em."[69] A later generation of British soldiers also included Irish Catholics, a fact brought out by the investigation of the 1741 "Negro conspiracy."[70] The probability that more than a few of the Irish indentured servants who labored in New York City had been raised in the Catholic faith in Ireland is strengthened by Cadwallader Colden's report to a correspondent in 1742 of "the Irish servants of which we have several in this part of the country [Ulster and Orange counties] & the greatest number of them roman Catholics."[71]

Andrew Burnaby, who visited New York in 1759, remarked that "besides the religion of the church of England there is a variety of others: dissenters of all denominations, particularly presbyterians, abound in great numbers, and there are some few Roman Catholics."[72] Just before the Revolution, a Jesuit priest regularly traveled from Maryland to New York to celebrate mass in the private homes of the city's Catholics.[73]

Despite the paucity of direct evidence of an Irish Catholic presence in the city during the half-century before the Revolution, it is difficult to believe that New York City, one of the two major ports for ships bearing immigrants from Ireland, sheltered no Catholics at a time when their number was spiraling in Philadelphia. William Penn's policy of toleration permitted Catholic worship in Pennsylvania, and a Roman Catholic chapel was opened in Philadelphia by the early 1730s, when there were probably no more than three dozen Catholics in the city.[74] By 1757 Philadelphia's Catholic population had multiplied tenfold to 378, "of whom 150 were said to be Irish or English," and the remainder German.[75]

Did the group loosely labeled "Irish" by outsiders have a common core of belief or a shared history that could serve as a foundation for the development of an Irish community in colonial New York City? As early as 1741, natives of

Ireland gathered on St. Patrick's Day in celebration of their verdant homeland.[76] Accounts of St. Patrick's Day festivities appeared in the New York press in succeeding years, including an extended description of the 1766 celebration that noted, "Monday last being the Anniversary of St. Patrick, tutelar Saint of Ireland, was ushered in at the dawn, with Fife and Drums, which produced a very agreeable Harmony before the Doors of many Gentlemen of that Nation and others. Many of them Assembled and spent a joyous though orderly Evening at the House of Mr. Bardin, in this city where the following Healths were drank." A list of 20 toasts followed, one of which was "The Protestant Interest."[77]

Some Irishmen in New York City belonged to a secret fraternal society brought to New York in 1767 by Irish officers in the British Army. This marching knot of the Ancient and Most Benevolent Order of the Friendly Brothers of St. Patrick in the Sixteenth Regiment of Foot grew from the original 10 members to about 60 members in 1769. "It included not only Irish officers in the Sixteenth Regiment of Foot but also other army and naval officers as well as several civilians, the most notable of whom was Sir Henry Moore, the governor of New York."[78] Announcements of dinners, theater parties, breakfasts, and concerts for the members of the organization were printed in New York newspapers between 1769 and 1775.[79]

The society also engaged in benevolent activities. Presumably distressed by the fact that some of their countrymen were languishing in the city's jail, members of the organization opened their pockets in 1771. On March 25 of that year, the *New-York Mercury* reported that "poor debtors in prison thanked the 'friendly brothers of St. Patrick' for their contribution sent to Mr. Coxon this day 'to be laid out on necessaries for their relief.'"[80]

A better indication that New York City's Irish immigrants had begun to coalesce into a unified bloc comes from their power at the polls. During the heated political contest of 1769, a story surfaced of an alleged insult to the city's Irish voters during the previous year's election. In the words of Peter van Schaack, "It was said, during the last election, that T. Smith had said that the Irish were poor beggars, and had come over here upon a bunch of straw. The whole body of Irishmen immediately joined and appeared with straws in their hats."[81] Lawyer Thomas Smith, the object of this rumor, was associated with the Livingston faction, whose leaders undoubtedly suspected that the rival De Lancey faction was seeking to discredit one of their members.[82] Keenly aware of the political cost if Irish voters remained alienated from their side, Livingston's partisans rushed to Thomas Smith's defense. On January 23, 1769, the first day of polling, they published a broadside intended to prove that Smith had not cast aspersions on the city's Irish.

> Whereas a Report prevails in this City, that Mr. Thomas Smith, during the last Election, did reflect on the Irish People, by saying, *That they came into this Country floating upon Straws.* We the Subscribers, as friends to Truth, and in Justice to Mr. Smith, Do HEREBY CERTIFY, That we were present with Mr.

Smith, on the Stairs of the City Hall, during the last Election, when some Person came down the Stairs, and complained that the *Irish* People had been abused, by the speaking of the above Words; upon which Mr. *Smith* immediately endeavoured to find out the Man that had spoke the Words; and was so far from abusing or reflecting upon the *Irish* People, that he expressed his Disapprobation of such Conduct, and endeavoured to put a Stop to the Report, by having the Matter cleared up.[83]

Another broadside circulated in the same year provides further evidence of ethnic cohesion among the city's Irish. Entitled "The Irishmen's Petition" and signed by Patrick O'Connor, Blaney O'Bryan, Carney MacGuire, and Lawrence Sweeney, the broadside appears to be a satire of the provincial patronage system composed by representatives of the Irish men who were routinely excluded from its favors.[84]

But as the number of Irish in the city multiplied, the divisions among them became more visible. The deepest chasm existed between native Irish of Catholic origins, who were primarily men low on the social scale, and the Protestant majority.[85] Compelled to disguise their beliefs so as not to imperil themselves in New York City's hostile climate, Catholic workers, servants, and soldiers may have secretly nourished elements of Gaelic culture such as the Gaelic language. From the testimony of Elizabeth Ashbridge, an English woman who traveled from Dublin to New York in 1732 with a group of Irish indentured servants, it is known that Irish was the first language of at least some servants.[86] Occasionally, advertisements for runaway servants mention the fact that individuals knew the Irish language or displayed an Irish accent.[87] Dr. Alexander Hamilton, socializing at a New York tavern in 1744, encountered "one Dr. McGraa, a pretended Scotsman, but by brogue a Teague."[88] Though immigrants were increasingly fluent in English as a result of the spread of Anglicization in Ireland during the eighteenth century, they may not have been willing to relinquish their traditional values.

The Protestant majority of New York City's Irish was far from homogeneous. Religious differences rooted in ethnic identity separated Anglicans of English ancestry from Scottish Presbyterians. With the city's political factions divided along similar lines after midcentury, Old World antagonisms may have been reinforced in the new environment. Though Irish-born merchants of differing religious affiliations likely acted in unison when their economic interests warranted it, the barriers between segments of the Irish population remained high.

The dissimilar backgrounds of colonial New York's Irish people hindered the formation of one Irish ethnic community in the city before the Revolution. Immigrants might unite annually to pay homage to St. Patrick, but their religious and cultural diversity, coupled with the sharp contrast in status between indentured servants and freemen, precluded the elaboration of ethnic bonds. Unlike other immigrant groups, the Irish lacked the resources to construct an ethnic church or any other ethnic institution. Marriages, business dealings, or social contact might narrow the distance between the Anglo-Irish and the Presbyterian Irish, but the Catholic Irish stood on the other side of an unbridgeable divide. To weave the disparate elements of colonial New York City's Irish population into a viable ethnic community would have required rewriting the history of Ireland.

Walter J. Walsh

CHAPTER 2

Religion, Ethnicity, and History

CLUES TO THE CULTURAL

CONSTRUCTION OF LAW

AS THE two-hundredth deathday of the 1798 Rebellion nears, it makes sense to ask "What was the original meaning of Irish Republicanism?" Antebellum New York City might seem an odd place to look for an answer to that incendiary question, but it is actually a great place to start. The bustling, burgeoning metropolis of the newly liberated colonies offered a safe haven to many exiled United Irishmen. In the 1790s, hard on the heels of the American and French revolutions, the United Irishmen cobbled together the first modern political theory of Irish Republican nationalism. By piecing together the banished lives and forbidden thoughts of those determined outcasts, we recover fragments of a strikingly antisectarian, egalitarian, and inclusive political philosophy. Today, the original tenets of Irish Republicanism often seem ignorantly forgotten or cynically ignored, both on the mainland and among the Irish diaspora. Even so, two full centuries later and a thousand leagues across the ocean, this distinctive political philosophy continues to echo from the rowdy immigrant streets of New York City's earliest visible non-African ethnic community.

Law, Culture, and Irish Republicanism

A single act of attainder banished the four most prominent United Irish exiles in New York City: the advocates William Sampson and Thomas Addis Emmet, the doctor William James MacNeven, and the printer John Chambers (all Anglicans except for MacNeven, the only Catholic member of the United Irish Directorate).[1] After their imprisonment and a sojourn in Napoleonic France, these exiles of 1798 joined a growing number of their lesser-known Gaelic compatriots who were gathering together in New York City. These United Irish leaders wielded unusual influence both inside and outside their ethnic subculture.

From a Hibernian perspective, the experience of the United Irish in a brand-new republic offers fascinating clues to what might have been had their ill-starred rebellion succeeded. The revolutionary ideology of their early Irish immigrant community made an important contribution to an emerging United States, particularly in heralding a multicultural society through their bold assertion of their ethnic identity and insistent demands for religious, cultural, and political equality. The exiles of 1798 introduced the advanced political theory of the United Irish into the New World.

If there was one tenet on which the United Irish agreed, it was that religious inequality had no place in any modern polity. During the Jeffersonian era, the New York Irish succeeded in establishing that ideal in American law by winning the first constitutional victory for the free exercise of religion in the United States. On that occasion, the impassioned rhetoric of their United Irish advocate, William Sampson, embodied the fiercely antisectarian ideals of those original Irish Republicans and made their political philosophy a part of the new republic's evolving constitutional structure.

Whatever its novelty to ethnic, religious, and cultural historians, this story may come as something of a surprise to many legal scholars. Recently, that initial courtroom victory for free exercise has gained new significance because of the U.S. Supreme Court's controversial ruling (in a case involving the spiritual use of Peyote by Native Americans) that the government can enforce unintended burdens on religious exercise even absent any compelling social interest. After heavy lobbying, Congress has since restored the constitutional standard introduced in the United Irish exiles' courtroom triumph for free exercise.[2] Yet, in the intense constitutional debate over this very history, the turbulent ethnic politics that won that first free exercise exemption have remained hidden from view.

Perhaps this is because American constitutional historians habitually trace free exercise of religion to such dominant intellects as John Locke in Carolina, William Penn in Pennsylvania and Delaware, Roger Williams in Rhode Island, the Calverts in Maryland, and Thomas Jefferson and James Madison during the founding period. In America's first free exercise case, only Penn was mentioned, and then in passing. Rather, the court was moved by a passionate firsthand account of systematic religious persecution in Ireland. Along with Emmet, MacNeven, and Chambers, Sampson was imprisoned and banished for trying to dismantle the religious apartheid that excluded three-quarters of the Irish population from that country's political and economic life. Under the infamous Penal Laws, the Catholic, ethnically distinct Gaelic masses paid tithes to the established church and were denied the rights to own property, educate their children, celebrate their religion, hold government office, vote in elections, sit in Parliament, serve on juries, or act as judges or lawyers.[3] The early American republic's first constitutional victory for free religious exercise did not flow from cold textual analysis but was a gut response to an appalling and skillful United Irish rhetorical portrait of ethnic persecution against the native Irish. In its inception, its argumentation, and its resolution, the first free exercise case turned on the religion, ethnicity, and history of New York City's early Irish immigrants. It offers important clues to the cultural construction of law.[4]

An Hibernocentric History of Religious Freedom in New York

In the colonies, with few exceptions, Roman Catholics did not enjoy the guarantees of religious liberty that were gradually extended to other sects. In 1691, a couple of years after Leisler's Rebellion sought to drive Romanists from New York, the elective assembly added this proviso to the colonial charter of broad religious freedom for Christian persuasions: "Allwayes provided that noething herein mentioned or Contained shall extend to give Liberty for any persons of the Romish Religion to exercise their worship Contrary to the Laws and Statutes of their Majesties Kingdom of England."[5] Similarly, when the Crown instructed Governor Henry Sloughter to establish the Church of England, it required him "to permit a liberty of Conscience to all Persons (except Papists)."[6] By 1701, the New York Penal Laws emulated their transatlantic counterparts by forbidding Catholic missionary priests from entering the colony under penalty of life imprisonment and barring Roman Catholics from voting or holding public office.[7] Some of these legal restrictions against Roman Catholics can be attributed to the commonly held belief that the papacy was a worldly power.[8] Because of their supposed civil allegiance to a foreign prince, for example, Locke denied Catholics the sweeping tolerance he advocated for all other believers, including Jews.[9] Even in Maryland, founded by the Calverts as a haven for English Catholics, formal freedom to worship lasted only half a century before being replaced by some of the harshest anti-Catholic laws in the colonies.[10]

The American Revolution signaled a shift in popular thinking.[11] In its immediate aftermath, although the principle of an established religion was by no means extinguished, the Church of England rapidly lost favor. Largely on account of its links to the Crown and the loyalist sympathies of its clergy, the Anglican Church was disestablished in every state where it formerly held sway, including the four metropolitan counties of New York City.[12] Yet at the state constitutional convention in 1777, a strong anti-Catholic faction was led by John Jay, later joint author of the *Federalist* papers and first chief justice of the

United States. In the debates over religious freedom, Jay unsuccessfully fought to deny civil rights to Catholics until they renounced the authority of the Pope and declared "false and wicked, the dangerous and damnable doctrine, that the pope, or any other earthly authority, have power to absolve men from sins."[13] Nevertheless, through the continuance of its Test Oath, New York remained one of four states that barred Catholics from public office, and by the same means it constitutionally forbade Catholic immigration until state naturalization procedures were preempted by the new national government. In a more enlightened spirit, and an implicit acknowledgment of Locke's influence, Jews suffered no such exclusions.[14]

These remnants of formal discrimination aside, increasing religious diversity during the colonial period had already led to a large practical measure of religious toleration in New York City.[15] At the dawn of the republic, Catholics were still a small and powerless minority. They were far outweighed by Congregationalists, Presbyterians, Baptists, and Anglicans, in that order. Four decades later, signs of change were readily apparent: close to 100,000 Catholics worshiped in the United States, 15,000 of them in New York City, making up about one-eighth of the city's residents. The earliest Catholics were generally Spanish or French, but by Jefferson's time the congregation was mainly Irish, with German immigrants soon to follow.[16] They joined the oppressed Africans as cultural outsiders in an anglicized Protestant society.

These demographics were heavily influenced by a shift in Irish emigration patterns. Before the American Revolution, the Gaelic Irish emigrated less, and seldom to Protestant America. A steady flow of Catholic emigration started with the 1798 Rebellion.[17]

Despite or maybe because of their minority ethnic status, the Irish Catholics were quick to defend their honor on American soil. Sometimes blood was spilt.

One taunt against them revived the anti-Catholic colonial symbols of Pope Day. From the 1790s intemperate nativist youths insulted St. Patrick's Day by parading with their Paddies, crude straw effigies designed to ridicule Catholics in general and the immigrant Irish in particular. After the 1798 exodus, nativist religious and ethnic hostility mounted and was met by the Irish in equal measure with collective resistance and internal solidarity. Following several outbreaks of violence between nativist gangs and Irish immigrants, the city council passed an ordinance in 1802 that outlawed the flaunting of Paddies or other insulting effigies.[18]

A few years later, the Irish Catholics demanded of the state assembly in Albany that they be put on the same formal footing of religious freedom and political equality. The infamous Test Oath flagrantly discriminated by excluding Catholics from public office. In 1806 Francis Cooper became the first New York Catholic to be elected to the state assembly. He was duly required to renounce all foreign authority "in all matters ecclesiastical" as well as civil, a declaration plainly contrary to the teachings of his church.[19]

At that time, New York City's only Catholic parish was St. Peter's in Barclay Street, founded in 1786. Naturally, it was a social, cultural, political, and religious gathering point for Irish immigrants.[20] On January 6, 1806, the congregation of St. Peter's held a general meeting at which they adopted a petition to the state legislature on Cooper's behalf. Within days, the petition carried more than 1,300 signatures. It pointed out that the Catholics composed a considerable portion of the population of New York City, but were denied the opportunity to discharge their social and civil duties. The Catholics were deprived of "the benefits of the free and equal participation of all the rights and privileges of Citizens" that were guaranteed to them by the state and federal constitutions. Especially in light of these solemn guarantees, the Catholics complained, it was frustrating "to have the cup of equalized rights dashed from their lips, by a subsequent determination, and an invidious barrier, surmountable only by perjury or apostacy, placed between them and those rights, tho' yielding, to none of their fellow-citizens in attachment to the prosperity and independence of the state." The petition prompted state senator and city mayor DeWitt Clinton to sponsor a bill to abolish the Test Oath in New York State. In the face of vigorous Federalist opposition, the emancipation bill comfortably passed both houses of the state legislature, and Cooper took his seat in the assembly. The Jeffersonian *American Citizen* applauded the outcome, saying that "religion is most prosperous when it is most free."[21]

Only the previous year, the Catholic majority in Ireland had failed in their essentially identical petition to gain admittance to the British Parliament in ruling Westminster.[22] Daniel O'Connell and his peasant horde would take another generation to achieve at home what the Irish exiles had already accomplished. In the meantime, as Catholic immigrants became more numerous, religious passions in New York City increased rather than dissipated. Less than a year after the Irish Catholics' successful petition to the legislature on behalf of Assemblyman Cooper, a gang of about 50 anti-Irish, anti-Catholic nativists known as the Highbinders surrounded St. Peter's Church. A spirited Irish defense against this threat sparked off two days of rioting, leaving hundreds injured and one guardian of the peace stabbed to death by the Irish.[23]

For the immigrant Irish, an expansive and nonsectarian ethnic identity was as much at stake as religious beliefs. A few months later, in the spring of 1807, the United Irish flexed their muscles at the polls. Their target was Rufus King, who had assumed the leadership of the Hibernophobic Federalists after Alexander Hamilton was killed in his duel with Aaron Burr. The irony was delicious. King had been the Adams administration's minister in London during the 1798 Rebellion. During it he described the radical ideals of the imprisoned United Irishmen as "so false and so utterly inconsistent with any practicable or settled form of Government."[24] Alarmed at the prospect that the Irish state prisoners might be banished to the United States, he fatefully warned Timothy Pickering, the American secretary of state, that "their Principles and Habits would be pernicious to the Order and Industry of our People, and I cannot persuade myself that the Malcontents of any character or country will ever become useful Citizens of ours."[25] King presciently added that nowhere would the United Irish leaders be more mischievous than in the United States, "where from the sameness of language and the similarity of Laws and Institutions they have greater opportunities of propagating their principles than in any other country."[26]

In the aftermath of the 1798 Rebellion, King persuaded the Adams administration to exclude the state prisoners from the United States.[27] As an Irish government official drily explained to the captives, "Mr. King does not like to have republicans in America."[28] Prematurely, King bragged that his decisive action had won him the "cordial and distinguished Hatred" of the United Irish leaders.[29] Because no other neutral country was available, about 20 state prisoners spent the next four years incarcerated in Fort George off the Scottish coast. On account of his poor health, Sampson enjoyed the privilege of being transported to a Portuguese dungeon before eventually joining his comrades in Napoleonic Paris, where the Irish Jacobins were greeted with a hero's welcome. After Thomas Jefferson's ascension to the U.S. presidency, Emmet, MacNeven, Sampson, and Chambers trickled one by one into New York City (as did Thomas O'Connor, Joseph Cuthbert, Thomas Traynor, and the radical publisher Samuel Neilson, who died soon afterward). There they joined a religiously diverse and rapidly growing Irish community.

In New York, the United Irish exiles delighted in fulfilling King's political prophecy. In the April 1807 elections, King led the so-called American Ticket for the Federalists against the Clintonians, who embraced the immigrant vote. King's treatment of the Irish state prisoners came back to haunt him. In letters to the *American Citizen*, Thomas Addis Emmet depicted gubernatorial candidate King as a "royalist" and an acknowledged enemy of liberty who had been the "political dupe" of the British and who had conspired "to torture oppressed Ireland and keep her bleeding patriots in dungeons."[30] Sampson described the controversy as "a hinge of the election."[31] Yet King, who had lost to Jefferson in the previous presidential election, aloofly chose "to enter into no explanations, leaving the Public to decide between me and these foreigners."[32] The public did just that and sided emphatically with the United Irish. "It was a complete political triumph," reported Sampson.[33] King's treatment of the exiles of 1798 proved equally damaging when he ran for governor again almost a decade later. "Federalists of our age," he acknowledged ruefully after his second defeat at the hands of the Irish immigrants, "must be content with the past."[34]

The First Free Exercise Case

During the War of 1812, the Irish immigrants won the first victory for free religious exercise in American constitutional law.[35] Compared with earlier riots, the controversy at first seemed mundane. James Keating, an Irish coppersmith and a parishioner of St. Peter's, reported a theft of some jewelry. Later, Keating mysteriously sought to withdraw his complaint. Upon questioning by the justices of the peace, it emerged that Keating had got his property back, but he refused to say who returned it. Only when threatened with jail did Keating reveal that the intermediary was his parish priest, Father Anthony Kohlmann, the rector of St. Peter's, which served a heavily Irish congregation. On other evidence, immigrants Daniel and Mary Philips were indicted as receivers by a grand jury, and the Alsatian Jesuit was subpoenaed to identify those whose repentance had led to the restitution. But Father Kohlmann shut up tight as a clam. He would not reveal even the color or the sex of the penitent who had come to him with a remorseful spirit and for whom he had made return of the stolen goods a condition of forgiveness.[36]

Father Kohlmann begged to be excused from testifying on the ground that his religious scruples would not permit him to reveal anything that had reached his ears in the darkness of the confessional. He vowed that he was bound both by the laws of God and the canons of the Catholic Church to a perpetual and inviolable secrecy. Knowledge he had obtained during the sacrament of penance could not be disclosed to anyone in the world without violating his religious tenets with the greatest impiety. Much worse than any worldly misfortune that his civil disobedience could bring down upon him, Father Kohlmann feared sinning in the eyes of God, becoming an outcast from his religious community, and risking the fires of hell. "If called upon to testify in quality of a minister of a sacrament, in which my God himself has enjoined on me a perpetual and inviolable secrecy, I must declare to this honorable Court, that I cannot, I must not answer any question that has a bearing upon the restitution in question; and that it would be my duty to prefer instantaneous death or any temporal misfortune, rather than disclose the name of the penitent in question. For, were I to act otherwise," Father Kohlmann continued, "I should become a traitor to my church, to my sacred ministry and to my God. In fine, I should render myself guilty of eternal damnation."[37]

Despite the conscientious nature of Father Kohlmann's objection, the English common law recognized no evidentiary exemption that would relieve him from his obligation to testify. On account of its importance, the case made its way to the Court of General Sessions, presided over by Mayor DeWitt Clinton sitting in his judicial capacity.[38] Suddenly, the radical United Irish lawyer William Sampson leapt to his feet and interrupted as a friend of the court. Compulsion to break the solemn and inviolable secrecy of sacramental confession, declared Sampson, would offend the most basic principles of the young republic. The court granted an adjournment so that this novel and important point could be fully argued.[39]

While the argument was pending, the newly appointed district attorney generously offered to drop the prosecution out of consideration for the religious sentiments of the Catholics. Significantly, after taking Sampson's advice, St. Peter's mostly Irish Board of Trustees said no. They were alarmed that any doubt should exist as to the existence of an exemption upon which rested the free toleration of their Catholic religion. Illustrating the more democratic origins of American Catholicism, the trustees apparently charted the course of their church even in deciding what was owed to God and what to Caesar. Gotham City's Irish immigrants boldly requested an early trial so that they could secure for all Catholics, as well as the rest of mankind, a judicial determination that would protect them in the "free exercise and enjoyment of their religious profession and worship."[40] The event ranks as perhaps the earliest recorded instance of impact litigation in American constitutional history—a test case in which an insular minority deliberately sought to appropriate the power of the courts to transform the political structure of American society.

William Sampson, as published in the frontispiece to the second edition of his *Memoirs* in 1817. Sampson, a lawyer, was one of several Irish political exiles banished in the aftermath of the 1798 rebellion who had influential careers in New York. His arguments in favor of the free exercise of religion are still cited today. (Engraving by F. Grimbede. General Research Division, The New York Public Library, Astor, Lenox and Tilden Foundations.)

The first free exercise case was argued in the summer of 1813 in a crowded courtroom in Irish architect John McComb's magnificent new City Hall, which had opened only the previous year. Thomas Addis Emmet, a member of the United Irish Directorate and elder brother of the nationalist martyr Robert Emmet, was supposed to join Sampson, but was called to another court. The prosecution's argument was simple: religious equality was not at stake. To the contrary, to exempt a Roman Catholic clergyman from his civic duty to testify would be to confer upon that religion a privilege enjoyed by none other.[41] The logic of this contention conceals its doubtful premise. Minority religious believers—typically immigrants—cannot lightly assume that the goodwill or foresight of the legislature will protect them from conflict with positive law.[42]

To counter the prosecution's argument, the Protestant Sampson painted a vivid portrait, drawn from his own experience as a United Irish lawyer, of the horrors of religious persecution in Ireland.[43] He was well-qualified to do so, having like Emmet been imprisoned, disbarred, and banished for his defense of the indigenous Irish Catholics and his defiance of the colonial Anglo-Irish Protestant ascendancy to which he belonged. In Ireland, Sampson had learned his trade defending a hundred or more political trials alongside the renowned John Philpot Curran, with the United Irish advocates tirelessly trying to turn the tables by accusing the government of treason.[44] "Alas! the advocates of the poor are few, and their reward is ruin," Sampson lamented after his banishment.[45] His experience in the Irish courts enabled Sampson to emerge as America's first career civil rights lawyer, preceding Clarence Darrow by almost a century. It also inspired his jurisprudentially radical antebellum codification movement.[46]

Sampson's rhetoric in the first free exercise case occupies an important place in the United Irish exiles' ongoing effort to create an Irish nationalist and republican historiography.[47] He pioneered the principal aim of political resistance in the courtroom: to portray the lawmaker as unlawful, and the lawbreaker as lawful. Sampson appropriated the New York courtroom both to put Irish history on trial and to inject his United Irish ideology into American law. The most damaging precedent against Father Kohlmann involved an Irish priest jailed for refusing to disclose the dying beliefs of Lord Dunboyne, whose will had been challenged on the ground that he had relapsed into popery.[48] Right from the start, Sampson warned the American court to reject this Irish decision because it came from a land "where the people were catholic, and the law anti-catholic; where the few trample upon the many, and where no concessions were made to the feelings of the proscribed, or the dictates of humanity or piety." According to Sampson, "if there be any country on the habitable globe, where we should not go to look for a pure and sound decision, upon the rights of Roman Catholics, it is surely that one . . . that Island, where for centuries past, a code has existed, and been in full and vigorous activity, which shames humanity." Irish law had been corrupted by its history. "Every where else," he said, "though there may be madness, superstition, or idolatry, there may be some chance of impartiality; but in Ireland there can be none!" Sampson argued that "we should never look to Ireland for a precedent, where the rights of catholics were concerned."[49]

At the heart of the first free exercise case was Sampson's United Irish historiography. "The rights, lives, liberties, and feelings of the catholics had been assailed through successive ages, in every wanton form that avarice, vengeance and malignity could devise," he railed. Bigotry and fanaticism had denied them even an education on their native soil. In such circumstances, it was hardly surprising that Protestant judges had rendered bad decisions. "The system under which they acted; the barbarous code with which they were familiar, was enough to taint their judgement. No judge, no legislator, historian, poet or philosopher, but what has been tinctured, with the follies or superstitions of his age." More probably, "may we not well suspect those Irish judges to have imbibed the poison of their cruel code, and to have eaten of the insane root that taketh the reason prisoner."

For Sampson, it was better to ground legal protections on reason, progress, and the rights of man. He observed that "it is easier to excite wickedness than it is to subdue it" and noted how "dangerous it is to give the reins to cruel prejudice." He pointed to the sufferings of the Quakers at the hands of the American colonists. "Thus did those who fled from persecution in England, become through ignorance most intolerant persecutors in America," maintained Sampson. "Such is the nature of that fiendlike spirit," be sighed, "which it requires but a moment to raise and centuries to lay. Thank heaven it is laid in this land, and I trust forever."

In the same breath, Sampson claimed that only greed could fully account for the persecution of the Irish Catholics by colonial settlers who included his own ancestors. "Mistaken conscience had nothing to do with the matter, nor religion nothing; but that the love of plunder, power, and confiscation was the sole and only motive." Continuing this attack, he bluntly declared that "it was their interest. They lived upon it. They had no living else than plots and forfeitures! They were not simple bigots, acting from mistaken conscience. They were pirates determined to hold what they had got, and rather than lose it scatter law and justice to the winds and waves."

The United States must learn from Ireland. "Were there rebellions? Were there massacres? Aye, to be sure, there were! They were the natural crop. For he that sows must reap!" Indeed, in later times, added Sampson, "the continuance of the catholic oppressions has taken the character of downright folly." After setting forth abundant examples of the civil rights denied to Irish Catholics, Sampson offered his grim but inspiring account of the Irish union of 1798:

> Then came the organized banditti. Then the no popery and peep of day men. Then the recall of faithless promises. And that government that refused to tolerate catholics, tolerated, instigated, and indemnified a faction, whose deeds will never be forgotten. Then came hangings, half hangings, conflagrations,

plunder, and torture. Rape, murder and indemnity went hand in hand. And then it was, that a spectacle new and appalling, for the first time, presented itself; and presbyterian, churchman, and catholic were seen to ascend the same scaffold, and die in the cause of an indissoluble union.

Although the United Irish rising had ended in bloody tragedy, Sampson noted that the great cause of human emancipation still proceeded in Ireland as the first free exercise case was being argued.

Why not contrast these histories and barbarous codes with Article 38 of the New York state constitution, which protected its citizens against religious persecution? Like a beacon on a rock, this principle was established to be a light and guide to all the world. To Sampson, it seemed "as if providence had decreed this land, to be the grave of persecution, and the cradle of tolerance." If anybody could not see the wisdom of this enactment, said Sampson, "let him open the page of history, and read of the bloody religious wars of Europe, of which the wounds are still fresh and bleeding. Let him reflect who his own fathers were, and he will find the cogency and wisdom of the act." In this country, according to the United Irish advocate, Catholic persecution received its death blow from the American Revolution. Although it was true, as the district attorney had pointed out, that the United States was formed by Protestants, "in establishing a constitutional code, different from that of England, they did nothing but unshackle themselves and the catholics together."

Exempting Father Kohlmann from testifying would not grant Roman Catholics any preference over other religions. "We claim no supremacy," insisted Sampson. "We seek nothing but pure and perfect equality. From the bottom of our hearts we sincerely tolerate you all. We will lay hands on none of you, for your worship or profession; and for ourselves, we claim neither more nor less. Hands off on all sides. And if any of you are aggrieved we will invoke the constitution in your favour, as we do in our own." Sampson's sudden flip from the third person into the first person is a stunning stroke of revolutionary political rhetoric. Like Emmet, Sampson had once sworn the United Irish oath in an Irish courtroom to display solidarity with his Catholic clients. This symbolic act rewrites Irish history. By inverting Ireland's past, Sampson stands Ireland's future on its head. In the New Republic, argued Sampson, "every citizen here is in his own country To the protestant it is a protestant country; to the catholic, a catholic country; and the jew, if he pleases, may establish in it his New Jerusalem."

Sampson's argument for the Irish Catholics was undoubtedly strengthened by his own Anglican upbringing. "I have been educated in that church," he pointed out. "I am no bigot, I see in it no certain token of *exclusive grace*, and yet I claim the right to love it above all others, if so I am disposed; and I turn to it with the more affection because those nearest and dearest to me, by every mortal tie, have been, and are its ministers, and have been good and virtuous men. I challenge for the catholic the self same right, and I should despise him as I should myself, if force or violence should make him swerve from any tenet of a religion, which he held as sacred." More puckishly, Sampson asked, "If my neighbour cleaves to his own wife, shall I quarrel that he does not prefer mine, and love her better; and if he loves his own religion better, is that a ground of enmity?"

It was an argument of extraordinary passion. "I am a friend to catholics," explained Sampson, recalling his own struggles as a United Irish advocate challenging an oppressive legal regime. "Amongst the friends I have had," he added, "none have been more true, more loyal, or more noble hearted, than catholics have proved. Without being a confessor, I have had occasions of knowing their inmost thoughts, in the hour of trial and sincerity." The importance of religious freedom he had seen at first hand. "The peculiar reasons I have had to dread and abhor every colour and shade of religious persecution, has communicated to my argument, perhaps, an over earnestness," explained Sampson. "Those who have not seen and felt as I have done, may think it common place." He closed with the great Christian commandment: "Thou shalt love thy neighbour as thyself."

DeWitt Clinton, the mayor of New York, delivered the court's unanimous decision. Mayor Clinton came from Irish Protestant stock and his uncle had risen to governor of New York and vice president of the United States. Only the previous year, the younger Clinton had lost the federal presidential race to James Madison, drafter of the First Amendment; he later rebounded to follow his uncle as governor of New York, building the Erie Canal with Irish sweat. The Clintonian political dynasty was always sensitive to the Irish, no doubt partly because it needed their growing vote.[50]

In the first free exercise case, Mayor Clinton bought Sampson's United Irish historiography lock, stock, and barrel. "With those who have turned their attention to the history of Ireland," said the mayor, "the decisions of Irish courts, respecting Roman Catholics, can have little or no weight." Republican America had no need for Irish legal authority. "That unfortunate country," declared Mayor Clinton, "has been divided into two great parties, the oppressors and the oppressed. The Catholic has been disfranchised of his civil rights, deprived of his inheritance, and excluded from the common rights of man; statute has been passed upon statute, and adjudication has been piled upon adjudication in prejudice of his religious freedom." That system of discrimination would surely collapse in time. "The benign spirit of toleration, and the maxims of an enlightened policy, have recently ameliorated his condition, and will undoubtedly, in process of time, place him on the same footing with his Protestant brethren; but until he stands upon the broad pedestal of equal rights, emancipated from the most unjust thraldom, we cannot but look with a jealous eye upon all decisions which fetter him or rivet his claims."[51]

Invoking the social compact, civil and religious liberty, and the republican principles of American government, the court construed the New York state constitution and the First Amendment to exclude forever calamities that had deluged Ireland and other countries with tears and with blood. The state had failed to establish that Father Kohlmann's conscientious refusal to testify was inconsistent with the peace or safety of the state. Even before a Protestant court,

Mayor Clinton held, the fundamental religious liberty of American Roman Catholics was safe. "They are protected by the laws and constitution of this country, in the full and free exercise of their religion, and this court can never countenance or authorize the application of insult to their faith, or of torture to their consciences." In the face of Father Kohlmann's impenetrable silence, the defendants were immediately acquitted.[52]

As well as being a historic new constitutional departure for religious freedom, *People* v. *Philips* was the jurisgenerative origin of the priest–penitent evidentiary privilege and its progeny.[53] The substance of Sampson's United Irish argument and DeWitt Clinton's resulting opinion should confound American constitutional historians who trace the legal doctrine of free exercise primarily to philosophical strides. Rather, the archaeology of the first free exercise case offers fascinating clues to the ethnocultural and biographical construction of law.[54]

In New York, Sampson promptly published his account of the first free exercise case under the name *The Catholic Question in America*. The printer was Edward Gillespy, who often serialized Sampson's works in *The Shamrock*, Gotham's earliest Irish newspaper.[55] To the advocates' arguments and the court's opinion, Sampson added his scathing abridgment of the anti-Catholic Penal Laws of Ireland.[56] Sampson's book also included Father Kohlmann's equally carefully documented theological defense of the sacrament of penance and his refutation of Protestant attacks upon it. Father Kohlmann's treatise provoked a nativist, anti-Catholic reaction, in a small way presaging the theological wars of the 1830s.[57]

Fully aware of the power of the word, Sampson expressed his pride in making the report public; he believed that "the general satisfaction given to every religious denomination, by the decision of this interesting question, is well calculated to dissipate antiquated prejudices, and religious jealousies." He added that "when this adjudication shall be compared with the baneful statutes and judgments in Europe, upon similar subjects, the superior equity and wisdom of American jurisprudence and civil probity will be felt." Sampson rightly predicted that the report would constitute "a document of history, precious and instructive to the present and future generations"![58]

Sufficiently edited to avoid Ireland's unforgiving seditious libel laws, Sampson republished his *The Catholic Question in America* the following year in Dublin. It was presumably seen by the aspiring Daniel O'Connell, who had joined the Irish bar as one of the earliest Catholics shortly before the United Irishmen were banished. The work was part of Sampson's lifelong effort to portray Irish history from the perspective of the vanquished. A tireless underground pamphleteer, political satirist, historian, and reporter of political trials, Sampson was banished for his radical pen. In his *Memoirs*, his expanded edition of William Cooke Taylor's *History of Ireland* and his other writings, Sampson recounted the events that led to 1798. But he gradually sought to extend the implications of the new United Irish historiography into every area of republican political theory and practice. Most of all, he turned his mind to the inherently antidemocratic nature of the English common law that he so frequently battled against.[59]

In like vein, MacNeven and Emmet brought out their *Pieces of Irish History*, an account of the 1798 Rebellion that sought to locate it firmly within the tradition of the American Revolution.[60] The single most influential Irish American work came from the pen of Sampson's son-in-law and former apprentice, William Tone. The younger Tone edited and published the revolutionary diaries of his father, the romantic nationalist martyr, who was captured in 1798 at the head of a French fleet.[61] Theobold Wolfe Tone's autobiography, filled with dark humor, gripped the Irish popular imagination. Its cultish following made it a central element of modern Irish nationalism.[62] Today, Tone's autobiography is most remarkable for its romantic antisectarian republicanism. The maverick authorship, literary skill, and intellectual nerve of such works gained New York's exiled United Irish historians an enduring influence upon public perception.

The Greenwich Village Riot

After the first free exercise case came another dramatic shift in the pattern of Irish immigration into New York City. With the lifting of the embargo in 1815 after the Treaty of Ghent, as many as one million Irish newcomers landed in America even before the great exodus unleashed in midcentury by the Potato Famine. In New York, the immigrants were soon predominantly Catholic and, reflecting worsening conditions in their homeland, drawn more and more from the laboring classes.[63]

Their daily increasing numbers magnified their visibility. With their alien ways, Papist religion, frequent destitution, and sometimes even their foreign language, the Irish ethnic village posed an undeniable threat to the relatively homogeneous metropolitan social structure that had existed during the Jeffersonian years.

Within the Irish community, the change was equally great, and it resulted in a gradual transformation of the meaning of Irish republicanism similar to that which was taking place on their native soil. While the inclusive ideals of the United Irish exiles continued to influence the public rhetoric of the immigrant leaders, that community turned inward as it crowded into the increasingly African and Irish tenements of the notorious Sixth Ward. The efforts of Sampson, Emmet, MacNeven, and the quietly influential Chambers to maintain the tolerant ideals of 1798 met with growing indifference among the most recent arrivals. The choice between the older integrationist yet socially transformative ideology and an impatient new ethnic separatism was vividly shown when the hitherto United Irish immigrant community went to war with itself.

A turning point in Irish history, Orange Day marks the anniversary of the Battle of the Boyne, when the Protestant armies of King William routed the

Catholic troops of King James II. By the early nineteenth century, the celebration of Orange Day was deeply symbolic, with sectarian animosities much in evidence on both sides. Imported into the United States by the newer immigrants, these harsh feelings erupted into serious violence on July 12, 1824. On that day, the eve of General LaFayette's jubilant return to the city, Irish Presbyterian laborers marched proudly through Greenwich Village where they confronted an equally determined band of Irish Catholic weavers. The fighting began when the Catholics demanded that the Protestants lower their orange flag. Each side accused the other of throwing the first punch. Probably both were guilty. By the end of the day, countless rioters fell to clubs and brickbats, including a pregnant Catholic woman who fearlessly charged into the fray.[64]

True to form, Sampson took the side of the Catholics. On this occasion he was joined by Emmet, another disbarred, imprisoned, and banished Protestant hero of 1798. The rhetoric of Sampson and Emmet constitutes another appeal for acceptance of the inclusive United Irish political philosophy in a republican democracy. Sampson insisted that "there is holiness in the cause of Ireland: posterity will discriminate between him that seeks blood, and the friend of mankind." Arguing for the Catholics, he urged the jury to "put these illegal associations down; you must avert the arm of the sanguinary bigot who would drench your country in blood." As in the first free exercise case a decade earlier, Sampson used a relatively mundane event to put all of Irish history on trial. Again, the courtroom became the crucible for the public adoption of a republican, egalitarian, and anticolonial political philosophy true to the original ideals of the 1798 rebellion.[65]

At the outset, Sampson sought to read from Plowden's *History of Ireland.* After accepting his commission from the British government, the English historian Plowden had found his sympathies on the side of the Irish peasantry, and for this had been harshly condemned by partisan English reviewers. Although Plowden fell far short of the United Irish effort to place the 1798 Rebellion within the eighteenth-century tradition of lawful revolution against unjust tyranny, he was a great favorite of the United Irish Republicans. On that ground, counsel for the Irish Protestants strenuously protested against the use of Plowden as evidence. In the end, after vigorous historical debate, counsel on both sides relied heavily on sharply divergent interpretations of Ireland's past to justify the conduct of their respective clients, and to discredit the bigotry and intolerance of the opposing rioters. In contrast to the first free exercise case, the Greenwich Village trial reveals not one account of Irish history, but two, and they cannot be reconciled.[66]

Curiously, the judge was Richard Riker, who had joined Sampson in arguing for Father Kohlmann a decade earlier (switching from prosecution to defense after deciding that the exemption was legal!). Like DeWitt Clinton before him, Recorder Riker fused the United Irish political vision with that of the Jeffersonian Republicans. In equal measure, he condemned the conduct of all the rioters. In the September trial of the Protestants, he charged the jury by their verdict to put a stop "to such open violations of the hospitality and laws of the American people." Freedom of conscience was constitutionally guaranteed, but such freedom could never lead to anarchy and blood. "The equality and liberty of our laws are known throughout the world. This happy country is an asylum to the oppressed of every nation on the face of the earth—here they find security and protection. What do we ask of them in return? Do we ask them to change their religious opinions—to renounce their political creed—to abandon the forms and ceremonies of their former life? No. All we ask in return for all the privileges they enjoy, is that they will be good and peaceable citizens, and obey the laws."[67]

A fellow Presbyterian, Recorder Riker chastised the Orangemen for the folly of their attempting to introduce into the United States "those dangerous and unbecoming practices, which had caused so much disorder and misery in their own [country]." He attributed their errors to "the recency of their sojourn here." Recorder Riker observed that religious persecution was the deadliest scourge that had ever been inflicted upon man, and that, wherever a religion arrogated the right of dictation, persecution was the natural consequence. Like Mayor DeWitt Clinton in the first free exercise case, Recorder Riker feared that "cruel persecutions . . . existed in the afflicted country from whence they came, but that it should be transplanted to this land of freedom was subject of equal astonishment and regret, and could scarcely be believed did not history furnish so many melancholy proofs of this infirmity in human nature, which nothing but the best institutions and the light of reason and experience could subdue."[68]

But the Irish Catholics were equally to blame. In sentencing them a month after the Protestants, Recorder Riker described the Catholics as valuable accessions to the national strength, and ornaments to society, but lamented that they had allowed themselves to be provoked into acts that had caused them so much difficulty. He reminded them of the trouble and vexation these broils had brought them into, and pointed out the advantage of forgetting all party feelings which had their origin in sorry Ireland. Now being settled in the United States, it was the civic responsibility of all the Irish immigrants to bury the hatchet and live in harmony with each other. Although the Protestants had every right to celebrate Orange Day peacefully, "it was irrational for Irishmen to go back so far into history for causes to perpetuate quarrels and bloody affrays with each other." Binding all the rioters on both sides to the peace, he hoped that time, a lenient sentence, and their own reflections "would have the happy effect of healing the divisions and allaying those animosities which had been productive of so much wretchedness to unhappy Ireland."[69]

Through the 1820s, Sampson, MacNeven, Emmet, and Chambers continued to insist that this socially transformative United Irish political vision opened the way for immigrants to advance in their adopted republic. The issue of religious freedom remained a live one with mounting pressure for Catholic emancipation in Ireland. The agitation led by Daniel O'Connell, perhaps the earliest modern instance of nonviolent mass protest, kept Ireland in the public mind. In the past, New York City's United Irish leaders had rallied their fellow exiles behind the Jeffersonians, called on them to volunteer for the War of 1812, published hints for emigrants, formed an emigrants' aid society, lobbied Congress for land to form an Irish colony in the West, helped newcomers find jobs, and donated their professional skills to indigent countrymen. In 1828, Mac-Neven and Sampson reached outside the immigrant community by launching the Society for Civil and Religious Liberties, devoted to Irish Catholic emancipation, which for a couple of years drew together an impressively ecumenical collection of New York public figures—including the mayor and numerous prominent judges and lawyers. In the same year, spurred by Sampson's simultaneous codification campaign, the clergy privilege was endorsed by the state legislature (and has since been endorsed throughout the United States, thus overthrowing the English common law nationwide). Together with Thomas O'Connor the exiles of 1798 also organized the Association of the Friends of Ireland in New-York, which raised money from the Irish immigrant community to contribute to the penny-rent O'Connell collected outside Irish churches.[70] According to the Catholic Association's contemporary historian, the New York exiles' fiery United Irish rhetoric sparked a radical resurgence at home, which the normally conciliatory O'Connell contained only by adopting the uncompromising stance in Westminster that ultimately yielded Catholic emancipation in 1829.[71]

The Decline of the United Irish Political Vision in New York City

Ironically, Catholic emancipation split the New York Irish. O'Connell's victory allowed Catholics to sit in the British Parliament that governed Ireland. This recognition of religious if not political equality in their homeland began the gradual eclipse of the United Irish political ideal in New York City. This is evident from the controversy over a memorial to Thomas Addis Emmet, who had died the previous year. Since his disbarment in Ireland, Emmet had risen to such professional prominence that he was considered the foremost advocate in New York and was ranked along with Daniel Webster and Charles Pinckney as perhaps the three finest in the nation. His funeral was by some accounts the largest public spectacle ever seen in the rapidly growing city. His pallbearers included Governor Clinton, two U.S. senators (including future president Martin Van Buren), several important judges (including one from the U.S. Supreme Court), Sampson, Chambers, and other well-known figures.[72]

The passage of Catholic emancipation left some unused funds in the hands of the Association of the Friends of Ireland, led by MacNeven, Sampson, Dennis McCarthy, and other well-heeled Irish professional and merchant leaders. At the time, these men were raising money for a monument to the memory of

Emmet. Rashly, they decided to divert to the Emmet memorial the unused funds that had been collected for O'Connell's successful political movement.[73]

This provoked a sharp response from the *Irish Shield*, which heard murmurs of discontent and dissatisfaction from every quarter. It was true that Emmet, like Sampson and MacNeven, was a devoted patriot who had suffered the inflictions of despotism in his country's cause. But it was preposterous to compare his contribution to Ireland with that of O'Connell, who had achieved more without spilling a single drop of patriot blood. According to the *Irish Shield*, the diversion of unused funds to the Emmet memorial was presumptuous and oligarchical. It would be denounced and decried by considerate and intelligent Irishmen, and censured by posterity.[74] Despite the fuss, a 30-foot-high obelisk was completed with inscriptions in Irish, Latin, and English. Together with an equally impressive monument dedicated to the Catholic MacNeven, the Emmet memorial symbolically flanks St. Paul's Episcopalian Church at Broadway and Fulton in Lower Manhattan, the burial ground of city notables. Strangely, it was in the same graveyard that Sampson had prepared his argument for the first free exercise case barely more than a decade earlier.[75]

In the wake of the Greenwich Village riot, the Emmet memorial controversy provides telling evidence that New York City's hitherto United Irish community was fragmenting. The incident was a metaphorical marker of the shift from exiles to emigrants.[76] After three decades, the message of 1798 seemed far removed from the stark needs of the newest arrivals. This is further suggested by the 1830s' competing array of St. Patrick's Day dinners—apparently all strongly nationalist, but attended by different classes of Irish immigrants. Some attracted politically well-connected United Irish exiles, who were joined by prominent New Yorkers. Other celebrations were exclusively attended by Irish Catholics, to judge by their Gaelic names.[77]

Sampson's last great blow for his lifelong cause of religious and cultural equality came in 1831. His friend Matthew Carey and other Philadelphia Irish leaders invited him to defend Irish Catholic immigrants after another bloody July 12 riot in which the Irish Protestants were ominously joined by American nativists. Once more, Sampson put his United Irish historiography—at once anti-imperial and postcolonial—at the heart of the case. Bigotry against the new Irish immigrants was on the rise. Pointing out that his own ancestors had fought for King William at the Battle of the Boyne, Sampson accused the Orangemen of raising a dangerous pretext. "I believe there is very little to be apprehended by the people here," declared Sampson, "that the Pope will come to this country to afflict us with either wooden shoes or brass money; but here they would revive the same miserable feelings again that then existed, and disregarding the peace and happiness of this glorious constitution, smother the steady lights which the generous founders of this hallowed country, with such generosity of soul and purpose, established."[78] After the trial, at a dinner held in his honor,

Sampson warned Carey and the Philadelphia Irish that "Divide and conquer is the tyrant's maxim—Unite and conquer, is the patriot's creed."[79]

In 1834 the city elections poignantly revealed the widening gap between integrationist United Irish ideals and the separatist tendencies of the most recent immigrants. As we have seen, the United Irish embraced the Jeffersonian Republicans, and the Jeffersonians embraced the United Irish. In Jacksonian America, it was much harder to see where United Irish Republicanism fitted in. After the Jeffersonian era, the shifting and confusing party politics of New York City defied summary; it will do to say that the forebears of today's parties were already taking embryonic shape as the Jacksonian Democrats (branded Tories by their rivals) and the National Republicans (commonly called Whigs).

The ideals of the United Irish movement did not fall comfortably into this new dichotomy. As had the Jeffersonians before them, the Jacksonians embraced immigrants and in that sense were obviously attractive. But the Jacksonian version of democracy was very different from that proposed by the original Irish Republicans. The United Irish saw society as a holistic, organic whole with common interests (such as freedom and equality) that human reason could discern. This Englightenment conception justified their American appeals for civic responsibility in the pursuit of a shared republican vision. They accurately perceived the Jacksonian democratic appeal as essentially populist, not principled.[80]

With Emmet gone, MacNeven and Sampson supported President Andrew Jackson until he launched his controversial attack on the national bank as a bastion of big money and centralized private power. An Irish Catholic, MacNeven was unusually literate and cosmopolitan, having obtained in Vienna and Prague the education he was denied at home. In New York, he was a successful doctor and a pioneer in American chemistry. Like many of the better-educated, more prosperous Jacksonians, MacNeven regarded Jackson's decision as an irresponsible sop to public sentiment and a perversion of sound economic principle. MacNeven predicted that without a central money supply, the economy would collapse.[81] This position put him at odds with his own immigrant community, a prime target of Jacksonian populist reasoning. Not only did Sampson defend his United Irish friend's integrity, but even ran as a Whig congressional candidate on the bank issue.[82]

At that time, before the 1834 spring elections for the mayor and the city council, the ethnic configuration of the emerging party system was far from clear, and both sides competed for the coveted Irish vote.[83] For the first time, the Irish poll split sharply, with the poorer immigrants choosing the Jacksonians and the professional and merchant leaders going with the Whigs.[84] In the fall congressional elections, the contest for the Irish vote continued with Sampson running as a candidate.[85] The returns from the heavily Irish Sixth Ward represent documentary evidence of a new, inward-looking Irish ethnic community, breaking along class lines that had not been evident in the past. The new

Irish immigrants did not see themselves as sharing common interest with the metropolitan establishment—in which, when it came time to choose, they were willing to place MacNeven and Sampson. In keeping with his lifelong suspicion of parties, Sampson was a reluctant politician, standing on high principle rather than the modern Jacksonian art of pragmatic campaigning. He was encumbered by the fact that one of his running mates was the son of Rufus King, ironically enough, since Sampson was among the United Irish exiles themselves who had suffered at the elder King's hands almost two score years earlier.[86] Sampson lost even in the heavily Irish Sixth Ward.[87]

Many of the new Irish Catholics evidently felt that the older immigrants had betrayed their factional allegience. The Whigs' more progressive attitude toward an emerging industrial economy may have appealed to the United Irish exiles, but the Whigs also harbored within their ranks a growing contingent who had nothing but contempt for the new shanty Irish. It is an odd historical fact that while the Whigs eagerly embraced the new cause of abolitionism, they increasingly spoke of the poorer Irish immigrants in the same racist tone that Southern slaveholders used for their human chattels.[88]

At the polls, nativist against ethnic politics exploded into full view. Four days of rioting between Whig nativists and Irish immigrants broke out around the polling booths causing widespread injury and destruction.[89] The 1834 riots were the worst yet seen in the city. They mark a true watershed in the history of the New York Irish. The elections were contested at precisely the time that American nativist parties began to emerge as a major force in nineteenth-century urban politics. With the luxury of hindsight, it is evident that Mac-Neven and Sampson were whistling in the dark. Shortly before the fall election, the Ursuline Convent near Boston was burned to the ground. The next year a riot broke out at a meeting in Broadway Hall to discuss whether Popery was compatible with civil liberty. Numerous scurrilous "disclosures" of convent life described nuns as baby-killers. The no-Popery press sprang to life. Samuel F. B. Morse, artist, snob, inventor of the telegraph, and wayward Democrat politician, explicitly linked no-Popery and Hibernophobia in his *Foreign Conspiracy against the Liberties of the United States* (New York, 1835) and *Imminent Dangers to the Free Institutions of the United States through Foreign Immigration* (New York, 1835). The Know-Nothing movement was in the making.[90]

In their opposition to Jackson on the bank question, MacNeven and Sampson foresaw the Panic of 1837 in which the Irish of the Sixth Ward were among those hit hardest.[91] None could imagine the full horror of the impending Irish Famine that would bring veritable hordes of destitute Irish refugees to the city barely a decade later. Whatever the merits of their eighteenth-century Irish Republicanism, the 1834 elections symbolized the passing of the United Irish political influence within New York City's Irish ethnic enclave. Emmet was gone; MacNeven berated in the heat of party; and Sampson rejected at the polls.

Including Chambers, by the early 1840s all had passed on to a fond but fading folk memory in the deteriorating Irish ghetto.

Their United Irish dream of an inclusive and egalitarian Irish republican nationalism was no longer the mood of the day. From that time onward, Irish politics was ethnic politics, class politics, and machine politics. Gone was the rhetoric of commonality and unity in which society was understood to be larger than the sum of its parts. Ethnic politics became brutal, intense, and unforgiving. The Irish Protestants continued to pursue the assimilationist ideal, while the Irish Catholics were driven into a countercultural separatism. By the mid-1840s almost all Irish Catholics voted Democrat and almost all Irish Protestants voted Whig.[92] By abandoning the original ideals of Irish Republicanism, the United Irish immigrant community became a closed Irish Catholic enclave, with the Irish Protestants being absorbed into the larger American society. With increasingly rare exceptions, Irish Republican nationalism became Irish Catholic nationalism. The cultural diversity offered by the radical Protestant leaders was replaced by a narrower—maybe more pragmatic—ethnic identity.

Conclusion: The Forgotten Legacy of 1798

By midcentury, the antisectarian republican ideals of Sampson, MacNeven, Emmet, and Chambers were seldom heard. The New York Irish faced open and organized nativist hostility and resisted it without the cultural and ideological diversity contributed by the radical Protestant dissidents of 1798. The new immigrants gave up their effort to separate their Catholicism, their Irishness, and their individual politics. The reins of Irish ethnic politics passed into the hands of hard-line Catholic churchmen such as Archbishop John Hughes, who led the fight against Protestant and nativist instruction in the city schools and demanded equal public funding for parochial education. The Irish immigrant community found itself on the outside looking in. Their religion, their ethnicity, and their history constituted their social identity. Not for several decades did Irish immigrants attain comparable professional success and exert such immediate political influence as had the exiles of 1798.

But the story I have told here is about more than a couple of generations of New York Irish immigrants. It tells a great deal about the cultural and biographical construction of law, specifically, the American constitutional doctrine of free exercise of religion. State intrusion into the secrecy of the confessional threatened an important part of the Irish ethnic identity, just as outlawing spiritual Peyote use further attacks today's beleaguered Native American culture.[93] Far from being an inexorable application of constitutional guarantees, religious freedom in New York City emerged as the product of ethnic struggle, a continuing clash between the United Irish immigrants and the Protestant, anglicized society into which they had come. Law emerges from power and resistance. By rhetorically converting their political demands into legal claims, the Irish opened the door for those who followed, doing much to establish our complex, demanding multicultural society of today. The story of the immigrant Irish influence on postcolonial legal structure promises rich insights akin to such current legal methodologies as critical race theory and feminist jurisprudence. It suggests the historical, ethnocultural, and biographical dimensions of jurisprudence.

Perhaps most important at this critical moment, the story of the United Irish exiles in New York City tells volumes about the original meaning of Irish Republicanism. As we enter the third millennium exactly 200 years after the 1798 Rebellion, that historical inquiry assumes infinite importance. For the original authors of Irish republican nationalism, creed and ethnicity were immaterial to a common political identity. Today, the United Irish leaders confuse Irish Republicans because they were Protestant, and equally confuse Irish Protestants because they were Republican. At stake here is the vital question of whether a modern version of Irish republican nationalism can be founded on inclusion, not exclusion. The United Irish exiles of 1798 added religious diversity and cultural difference to their immigrant community. They rewrote Irish history to create a shared national ethnic identity. Their privileged birth into a fractured society made the Protestant exiles of 1798 especially powerful advocates for the cause of Irish Catholic equality in New York City. For a time, they served as a strong shield against American nativism and religious intolerance precisely because they stood between two worlds: that of the Irish Catholic minority and the larger Protestant population. In the young republic of the United States, they found a second chance to realize the political and social ideals that had met with such miserable failure in Ireland. They proposed a new image of republican society rid of barriers based on creed, caste, and ethnicity. Cultural difference was no excuse for bigotry. With the passing of New York City's exiles of 1798, something very important was lost to Irish republican nationalism.

Paul A. Gilje

CHAPTER 3

The Development of an Irish American Community in New York City before the Great Migration

T HE GREAT FAMINE migration that began in 1844–45 marks an important watershed in Irish American history. The flood of immigrants driven out of Ireland in the wake of the potato blight dramatically altered the demographic profile of the United States. Confronted with this rising tide of Irish immigrants, most of whom were Catholic, American society entered a period of great adjustment, which was difficult for the newcomers and more established Americans alike. Many Irish men and women found comfort in settling with their own countryfolk. Distinct Irish American communities trying to preserve their own identity emerged in city after city. These Irish American communities played a vital role in New York City in that they acted as halfway houses for immigrants on their way toward assimilation. Perhaps more important, they exerted considerable influence, however unwittingly, on non-Irish society. The postfamine Irish American community stood as a great testament to the new polyglot democracy that was developing in America.[1]

The prototype of these communities had already appeared in several cities by the 1840s. For well over a century the Irish had streamed into North America. In the eighteenth century most of these immigrants were Protestants, although by the 1790s more Catholics had begun to arrive. In the years after 1815 thousands of Irish Catholics emigrated every year. Many of these people settled in cities. In few places was the nascent Irish American community more apparent than in the City of New York. As early as 1816 at least one overoptimistic estimate put the Irish American component of the city population at 25,000, or approximately one-fourth of New York's total inhabitants. The development of New York's Irish American community cannot be fully understood without considering how these prefamine Irish Americans interacted with one another and with the larger society.[2]

The New York Irish American community did not appear overnight, and the direction of the definition of this community was not fixed. Initially middle-class businessmen, lawyers, and professionals—Protestant and Catholic—attempted to mold the Irish American community in their own image; they also wanted to assimilate into the mainstream of society while retaining some elements of their Irish identity. This group was heavily influenced by the republican movement in Ireland, and, following the lead of the United Irishmen, hoped to put aside religious and sectarian differences. They feared the worst effects of too large an influx of poorer countrymen and therefore sought to help immigrants, as well as limit the number of impoverished Irish who settled in New York City. Countering these middle-class efforts were the bonds that developed among the mass of largely Catholic Irish who arrived in growing numbers in the nineteenth century. This group pursued a less conscious policy yet ultimately had the most influence on the final shape of the Irish American community. Although poor Protestants and Catholics increasingly distanced themselves from one another, special ties developed among the Irish through neighborhood, workplace, and politics. Middle-class efforts at times merged with the concerns of the poorer Irish Catholics, but for the most part their notions about respectability would pit them against the Irish American community of the lower class that had developed by the 1830s and 1840s.

For a time, the middle class dominated the Irish American community, in voluntary organizations, the church, and the press. In 1784 some of the city's most affluent Protestant and Catholic Irish Americans organized the Friendly Sons of St. Patrick, a fraternal lodge typical of many associations that sprang up in the early republic. Similar Irish organizations appeared in subsequent decades. Several of these associations were influenced by the Irish Republican movement. The impact of the political émigrés after the failed revolution of 1798–99 can be seen in the toasts to an independent Ireland offered by the Hibernian Society on March 17, 1801, which saluted both the United Irishmen and American liberty. By the following year this group had written its own constitution and called itself the Hibernian Provident Society.[3]

Some of these organizations continued to represent middle-class values. One of these groups, the Shamrock Friendly Association of New York, formed around 1816, brought together the city's leading Irish Protestants and Catholics in an effort to aid the growing number of immigrants. They widely distributed a pamphlet that sent mixed signals to the poor in Ireland and reveals the middle-class effort to mold the Irish American community. It encouraged artisans to emigrate, suggesting that trained men would find plenty of work and contribute to the nation as independent mechanics and potential members of the middle class. They did not want too many poor Irish to come to New York and therefore indicated that unskilled laborers would have to find employment in the countryside. Members of the Shamrock Friendly Association feared that the poor might pose a threat to the American republic because their dire condition would lead them to succumb to the evils of alcohol, which was cheap and plentiful in the United States. Drink would destroy one's sense of self-worth, prevent independent judgment, and corrupt the individual. These middle-class Irish Americans declared that "Civil liberty every where rests on self-respect," which would quickly disappear once intemperance took hold and dragged one down into "degradation or voluntary debasement" and eventually "despotism." The pamphlet praised the political system in America, declaring that immigrants had great opportunity, freedom, and equal treatment under law, as long as he or she was willing to work and be industrious. Reading between the lines, one can detect the middle-class apprehension over the growing number of Irish filling the city's poorer neighborhoods and creating an Irish American community alien to both Irish and American middle-class values.[4]

In the 1820s and 1830s groups like the Shamrock Friendly Association gave way to associations whose interests were closer to those of the mass of immigrants coming to the city. Organizations such as the Hibernian Universal Benevolent Society celebrated St. Patrick's Day with a public parade, special religious services, and festivities at plebeian establishments like the Sixth Ward Hotel. Although the membership of the Hibernians probably consisted of small businessmen and artisans, the openness of their celebration allowed the community to develop an identity that contrasted sharply with the more exclusive dinners held by the Friendly Sons of St. Patrick at Banks Coffee House or Niblio's Garden. Since this was a period of growing Irish American antipathy toward the English, the Friendly Sons of St. Patrick endeavored to improve relations by making the British Consul a guest of honor. The Hibernians associated with a different level of society. Their Fourth of July parades included mechanic groups like painters, coopers, tailors, and cordwainers. On such occasions the Hibernians displayed their ethnic insignias and made all Irish Americans feel proud.[5]

The middle-class difficulty in dictating the shape of the Irish American community can be seen in developments concerning the Catholic Church. During the 1780s organizers of St. Peter's, the city's first Catholic congregation, wanted to avoid any sign of ethnicity. The leaders of St. Peter's, including Irish American businessman Dominick Lynch, prided themselves in their commitment to a universal church. This open-minded approach was not to last. In the early 1800s the Irish began to dominate the parish.[6]

Worse, from the middle-class perspective, poorer Irish Americans became very possessive of St. Peter's. In 1806, when a group of rowdy Protestants called the Highbinders threatened to disrupt St. Peter's on Christmas Eve, the poorer

Irish retaliated the following night with a battle on Augustus Street in their own neighborhood against Highbinders and the city watch that left one policeman dead.[7]

Such clashes along class lines also occurred within the church. On April 4, 1820, a large crowd of mostly Irish Catholics confronted an ethnically mixed group of trustees at St. Peter's that included Charles D'Eshinville, Lewis Larue, James Lynch, and Matthew Carroll. The rioters opposed the continued selling of pews in the church—probably because it violated their egalitarian sensibilities—and determined to make their views known. In this instance the middle-class trustees had to face the disorder of the Irish immigrant head on. The trustees backed down that day, but continued the sale later on. Although the trustees won out in the end, this confrontation was an indication of the assertiveness and growing predominance of lower-class Irish in the Catholic community.[8]

As the numbers of Catholic Irish swelled in the 1820s and 1830s, the Catholic Church became an important focal point of the community. In the old country the Catholic Church had been a bastion of Irish nationality in the face of English persecution. In America, where Catholics were set apart from the rest of society, it was only natural for the Irish to view the church as a refuge and a reflection of their own identity.[9] Thus, even within the Catholic Church, ethnic divisions intensified. By the 1830s most of the parishioners of St. Patrick's, opened in 1815, were lower-class Irish.[10] In the same decade the Church of the Transfiguration opened its doors in the Sixth Ward. The parishioners of this church were almost exclusively Irish. Recognizing their separateness and afraid of being engulfed by the sea of Protestantism and non-Irish, many Catholic Irish began to reject the multiethnic and nonsectarian attitude of the middle-class émigré.[11]

This shift toward lower-class values can also be seen in the Irish American press. Two Irish American newspapers appeared in the early nineteenth century, both of which strived to shape the identity of the community, asserting Irish nationalism, adhering to republican principles, and expressing a concern for new immigrants. There was, however, a subtle difference between the two. The *Shamrock* or *Hibernian Chronicle*, which operated from 1810 to 1817, reflected to a large extent the values of the middle-class émigrés. While claiming allegiance to the United States, the editor, Edward Gillespy, quickly spoke out against the sectarian activities of the Protestant Orange societies in his native land and defended Catholic emancipation in Great Britain in the interests of the freedom of religion. Both causes were fervently espoused by Protestant and Catholic middle-class émigrés. The *Shamrock* also took note of Irish immigration, occasionally listing new arrivals. To assist immigrants, and probably to make a little money, Gillespy ran an intelligence office that farmed out agricultural laborers. Its purpose was to keep the immigrants out of the hands of "designing speculators" and sinister agents and funnel as many Irishmen into the countryside as possible.[12]

The city's second Irish American newspaper, the *Truth Teller*, began publication in 1825 and appealed more directly to the lower-class Irish; it was fervently pro-Catholic—the founder was an Irish-born priest—and anti-English. Like its predecessor it focused many of its stories on Anglo-Irish relations. At the same time, it devoted a great deal of column space to domestic issues, particularly in defense of the Irish in urban and rural America. Occasionally the *Shamrock* included some national news and certainly complained when commentators assumed that any unidentified criminal was Irish.[13] The *Truth Teller* took an activist stand as a mouthpiece for the Catholic Irish American community. In its first year, for instance, it ran a series of bold essays attacking the Protestant Bible societies for advocating religious principles that challenged the Catholic Church.[14] The poor immigrant also found a defender in the *Truth Teller*. One article, "A Switch for Libellers," decried the disrespect that many Americans held for the Irish, who were widely "viewed with the most determined hostility, hatred and contempt." For the author this "uncharitableness, ignorance, and illiberality" was especially galling since the Irishman in his native country was subject to tyranny because of his religion. By the 1830s the *Truth Teller* had become embroiled in partisan Democratic politics and controversies even on the ward level.[15]

The middle class failed in its effort to mold the Irish American community through voluntary associations, the church, and the press because its ideas and values did not reflect the day-to-day experience of the majority of New York's Irish Americans. That experience took place in the streets and alleyways of New York, where invisible bonds developed to tie the Irish Americans together. It was in these neighborhoods that the true outlines of the nineteenth-century Irish American urban community began to take shape.

As New York City's Irish Americans grew in number, certain areas came to be identified as particularly Irish. These neighborhoods often contained the worst and most crowded housing, but offered their residents important bonds and support mechanisms that came to form the very lineaments of the Irish American community. In the 1790s the Irish tended to settle not too far from the East River docks, near Bancker and Harmon Streets. In the early nineteenth century, they expanded inland to cover most of the Sixth Ward. The center of this ward was the Five Points, formed by the intersection of Orange, Anthony, and Cross Streets. By the 1820s the area had become the worst slum in the city, if not the country. The cheapest housing was often on the northern edge of the city, so, as the city expanded uptown, the Irish moved with it. In the 1820s and 1830s many Irish lived in and above Greenwich Village.[16]

Tax assessment records, jury lists, and other sources provide some insight into the Irish pattern of settlement in this area. Since residential segregation had not reached the levels it would later in the century, individuals with Gaelic-sounding names could be found in every ward.[17] Interestingly, certain streets had clusters of houses with a larger percentage of Irish than others. In numbers 250, 252, and 252 1/2 William Street in the Fourth Ward, for instance, half of the twelve names in the 1819 jury census appeared to be Irish and 46 out of 65 residents were listed as "alien" (non-U.S. citizens). Similar concentrated pockets of Irish can be found elsewhere: on Ferry, Rose, and Hague Streets in the Fourth Ward; Lombardy, Bancker, and Henry Streets in the Seventh Ward; and Elizabeth, Mulberry, Orange, Greenwich, and Prince Streets in the Eighth Ward. In the Ninth Ward many Irish lived next to each other on Greenwich Street and shared the same occupation, weaving.[18]

Only in the Sixth Ward did the Irish begin to break out of this pattern and dominate a whole neighborhood. With a quarter of its 15,000 residents listed as aliens, the Sixth Ward in 1819 had the highest number of foreigners of any ward in the city. Many of these aliens, as well as the citizens, were Irish Americans. Even in the Sixth Ward some streets had almost no Irish, whereas others were packed with Irish. Only a small part of Chambers Street was in the Sixth Ward: 212 people lived on this short section, including 15 aliens. None had an Irish-sounding name. Of the 643 residents on Anthony Street, however, 254 were aliens. Many of these were probably Irish. The census book listed 92 heads of household on the street, 32 with Irish names. One of the most notorious tenements in the city, owned by grocer Paul Healy was 122 Anthony Street. It housed 83 residents. Most of the heads of households (total 15) had Irish names. Similar densities of Irish could be found elsewhere in the Sixth Ward, on Catherine Lane, Orange, Mulberry, Cross, Augustus, Duane, and Elm Streets.[19]

The census record reveals that grocer Patrick Mehan, laborer Terence McGowan, bottling porter Denis Mehan, waiter Drake Fitch, and rigger John Hoyt all lived at 21 Orange Street. In addition, 17 males and 17 females lived with them. It is not difficult to imagine what conditions were like there. This building was probably crowded and the walls separating one apartment from another thin enough to hear every argument and intimate exchange between family members. These individuals no doubt saw each other every day, but whether they talked to each other's, drank together, and shared each other's secrets we can never know.[20]

The city census record does, however, indicate the variety of occupations filled by the Irish and thus provides some important information about the Irish American community. Up and down Orange Street and the other heavily Irish avenues surrounding it in 1819, one would find not only the occupations listed above, but also carpenters, fruit sellers, machine makers, masons, tanners, sawyers, tailors, painters, bootmakers, sailmakers, and a variety of other tradesmen. In other words, Irish immigrants during this period might have worked at any number of jobs. Some arrived with specific skills, others obtained some training in the United States, and still others remained unskilled and worked as day laborers.[21]

Many journeymen born in America complained that immigrants who were hastily trained took their positions or lowered the going wage. These complaints were echoed by city cartmen during the 1810s and 1820s as the number of Irish who made their living as carters increased sharply. During the War of 1812 the City Corporation issued licenses to Irish immigrants because of the shortage of labor. It was also a good way of ensuring political support. After the war, American-born cartmen petitioned the Common Council complaining that "aliens" were making it difficult for patriotic citizens to earn a living and pointedly reminded city officials of their own sacrifices as soldiers while the aliens stayed in New York and made money.[22] In response, the city government limited aliens to carting dirt. Irishmen quickly dominated this area of the trade and still continued to challenge American citizens in other areas. By the 1820s, the heavily Irish Sixth Ward was commonly referred to as the cartman's ward.[23]

The Gaelic clannishness that non-Irish workers objected to on the job actually helped solidify the bonds of the Irish American community. In 1826 Isaac Anderson found himself confronted by a group of hostile cartmen asking him if he were an Orangeman and announcing that only Roman Catholics were allowed to remove dirt from a particular construction sight. Anderson had aroused suspicion by working faster than everyone else. The year before Irish cartmen had attacked some of their Connecticut counterparts during another construction job because the Connecticut men had loaded their carts too high.[24] Labor crews in the city were frequently organized by ethnicity, and the Irish guarded their jobs against all comers.[25]

Clannishness did not affect individual initiative. Like other immigrant groups before or since, many Irish were determined to make good despite the odds. Often this called for a high degree of job flexibility. In 1818 John Doyle wrote to tell his wife in Ireland that he had put aside his training as a printer after arriving in New York and became a street vendor, earning a nice profit selling picture prints. These entrepreneurial activities eventually led John to open his own store and to become a successful bookseller.[26] Robert Brunt's career shows a similar opportunism. In 1833 Brunt was thirty-five years old and had been in the United States for sixteen years. Although brought up as a farmer in Ireland, he at one time had learned the weaving trade. In 1833, however, he employed a great many people, all Irish, and worked as a contractor removing dirt for construction on the northern edge of the city. Not only did this position offer him a modicum of success, but it probably enabled him to exert some influence over his countrymen.[27]

Like contracting, the grocery business created opportunities for ambitious Irish Americans and allowed the nascent entrepreneur to develop a small-scale patronage network within the immediate neighborhood. Although information about grocers is hard to come by, it is known that they sold food, items for the household, and any other product that the grocer believed he could make a profit on. Groceries were an adaptable institution and varied from location to location. In many areas they sold liquor, combining the function of grocery and grog shop. Groceries were also arenas of entertainment and conviviality. Some groceries served as the neighborhood gossip mill by day and offered fiddling and dancing at night. In either case, they were a place to drink and further cement community bonds among the Irish. As a result the grocer became a central figure in the neighborhood. He often dispensed credit and may have even helped some individuals find a job. Groceries dotted every section of the city and were not a uniquely Irish American institution. Yet they may have been more important among the Irish than among other groups.[28]

One measure of the grocer's significance in the Irish American community can be determined from bail bonds. When the city police arrested and formally charged an individual, that person had the opportunity to pay a bond to get out of jail until the trial. In the early nineteenth century there were no bail bond offices, as there are today. Instead, the accused person needed to raise the cash and find someone else to post bond and swear surety for good behavior. Given the poverty of many of the accused and the lack of personal connections with those further up the social and economic scale, that task was not always easy. In a random sample of bail bonds from 1810, approximately one-third, whether they had Irish names or not, had grocers listed as surety. Among those who had Irish names, the total proportion with grocers signing surety increased to forty percent, while the percentage of the remaining non-Irish names dropped to less than 30 percent.[29] Although these figures no doubt underrepresent the number of Irish involved, they do suggest that the grocer played a more significant role as a patron and protector within the Irish American community than he did within the larger New York society.

Not every grocer, and certainly not every immigrant, could enjoy economic success. For many Irish Americans it was not easy to earn a living. Yet in this period an important pattern of working and saving was established in order to fund the immigration of relatives left behind.[30] Because of this staggered pattern of migration, the demographic profile of the Irish American community was slightly skewed. In most wards the total number of women outnumbered the men. In 1819, for instance, there were 5,644 women and 5,290 men in the Fourth Ward. But among the 1,831 aliens listed, there were almost 300 fewer women than men. These same trends persisted in the Sixth Ward, which had almost 400 fewer alien women than men out of a total of 3,875 aliens.[31]

A few of these women headed their own household. In 1819 Mrs. McMurray was a 56-year-old grocer living at 1 Mulberry Street, while across the street Widow McGee ran a boardinghouse. A perusal of the census and assessment records indicates that these women householders, while relatively rare, were not unique. In 1819 on Mulberry Street in the Sixth Ward, for example, there were 56 household heads with Irish-sounding names; 9 of these were female.[32]

Most women, therefore, lived in households headed by men. Younger women immigrants often became domestic servants at first, and thus found themselves dispersed throughout the city. Like their male counterparts, these women saved money, helped their families come to New York, and even continued to contribute to the family once it arrived. Younger women also formed bonds with one another, holding their own parties and attending church, but probably had to await marriage before they became fully integrated into Irish American neighborhoods.[33]

Whether they were domestic servants, married or widowed, the archives give only a small glimpse into women's lives. On a lonely March night in 1820 Bridget McGlone left her infant daughter on the steps of Bishop Connoly's house. She wanted to relieve herself of her infant burden, but feared for its future. In the letter that she penned and attached to the child she explained that she had not taken the baby to the Alms House—she had three other children there already—because she did not want the infant exposed to the Protestant teachings of that public institution.[34] Faced with a similar situation, the widow Mary Erwin took a different tack: she petitioned the city for money to return to Ireland in 1810 and had the rector of St. Peter's testify as to her character.[35] Women sometimes were the victims of violence. Betsy Dougherty ran a tavern on Bloomingdale Road and reported that five or six people came smashing in on the night of November 12, 1824, breaking her furniture and kicking her in the belly even though she was in the advanced stages of pregnancy.[36] Women could also be the perpetrators of violence. Bridget Doyle attacked Ann Yates in February 1827. Yates had a long-standing complaint against Bridget and her husband. She declared that the Doyle grocery was really "a mere rendezvous of Riot and Dissipation, disturbing the peace of all their neighbors" both night and day and was "a disgrace to the Neighborhood as well as the Society at large."[37]

Piecing together these small snapshots of the lives of ordinary people, combined with the residential proximity of the urban landscape, one can begin to understand some of the key elements of the Irish American community as it defined itself before the famine migration. The hopes and ideals of the middle class meant little to these people. What counted was, the day-to-day experience of living in crowded neighborhoods, close to one's countrymen, but close, too, to others who were often openly hostile to the Irish. Driven to depend on each other, Irish Americans sustained and built upon their ties to one another.

The solidarity among Irish Americans had a great impact on urban politics. In turn, political participation influenced the development of the Irish American community. The Irish became important to New York politics at a very early date. During the 1790s the mistreatment of two Irish ferrymen by a Federalist magistrate led to a major political controversy. Although the Alien Acts were intended to limit the political input of immigrants, the Irish vote helped strengthen the Jeffersonian Party and set the stage for electoral victory in 1800.[38] In the opening decades of the nineteenth century the voting patterns of the Irish were of intense interest to the Anglophile Federalists. In June 1807 the Federalist *New York Evening Post* ridiculed a Democratic procession, noting the green jackets worn by some of the marchers "in compliment to the new made citizens" who had been responsible for a recent Jeffersonian political victory. Before that election, the same newspaper had denied that there were any parallels between the failed Irish rebellion of 1798–99 and the American Revolution and had cast disparaging comments on the character of the Irish.[39]

If Federalist politicians refused to see a relationship between the Irish and American situation, this was not true for the middle-class émigrés who came to New York. In fact there was a close affiliation between the middle-class Irish who were attempting to mold the Irish American community and the Jeffersonian Democrats. Not only did several of these men take an active part in the politics of the day through electioneering, editing newspapers, and even running for office, but some of their fraternal organizations became overtly political. When one member of the Hibernian Provident Society voted Federalist in 1809, the whole association became gripped in a debate over whether to reprimand him.[40]

What really counted politically, however, was what the mass of immigrants did. The political émigrés had joined with the Jeffersonian Democrats because of their shared republican sympathies. By the late 1810s, Irish involvement in politics, while still retaining an ideological component, was moving closer to machine politics. In 1816, as the *New York Evening Post* repeated its attacks on immigrant voting, the *Shamrock* proudly declared the Sixth Ward Irish territory and cleverly reported that the voters there had struck a blow against monarchy by voting down Rufus King. The watchword for all Irishmen at the polls had been "Refuse King."[41]

During the first two decades of the nineteenth century there was a close association between the republicanism of the middle-class Irish émigrés and the emerging street politics of the lower-class Irish. Indeed, men like Protestant Thomas Addis Emmet, remained a hero for almost all Irish. On April 24, 1817, about 200 Irishmen rioted at Tammany Hall, destroying furniture and injuring several people because the Tammany regulars had refused to nominate Emmet for a seat in the assembly.[42] Emmet won special recognition from Catholic Irish seven years later when he aided William Sampson in the defense of a group of Catholics that had been arrested after a confrontation with Protestant Orangemen in Greenwich Village. With a great deal of rhetorical flourish he had developed as a lawyer in both America and Ireland, Emmet seized upon the occasion to lecture the court on the historic mistreatment of the Irish in their native land.[43]

Eventually the political significance of the middle-class émigrés waned as the Irish American community relied increasingly on the rough and tumble street tactics of machine politics. Men like Emmet participated in this endeavor to a certain extent, but working the wards and watching the polls was a job for those with less ideology and a stronger arm. It was in the years before the 1840s that the nonethnic fraternal association of the Tammany Society began to take on its political trappings and started to become associated with the Irish.

Although Tammany remained in the hands of the non-Irish, by the early 1830s it could count on Irish politicians regularly delivering the vote of the Sixth Ward as well as on the Irish supporting other sections of the city. Any opposition to this control was likely to bring violence.[44]

When the Whig politicians decided to contest the Democratic control of the Sixth Ward, serious rioting broke out in April 1834. This riot demonstrates the close association between neighborhood, politics, and the Irish in the development of the Irish American community. Whig political hacks, whom the Democratic papers said came from the First and Second Wards, appeared at the Sixth Ward poll on April 8 and attempted to intimidate voters. During the acrimonious exchanges that followed, some of the Whigs were quoted as saying, "We should get along well enough if it was not for the Irish." These heated words, and others, led to a pushing match and the exchange of blows. Without too much difficulty, the Whigs were driven from the area. On the second day of the election the Whigs formed a procession and marched "in military order" along Duane Street and through the heart of the Sixth Ward. During this parade the Whigs shouted out terms like "low Irish" and "the damned Irish." After the parade, the Irish retaliated by attacking Whig headquarters on Broadway at the edge of the Sixth Ward. The battle there was brutal, with many on both sides injured. A few shots were exchanged, but further violence was avoided when the mayor persuaded the Whigs, who had rushed to a nearby arsenal to seize weapons, to disperse. By the third day only minor scuffles were occurring. The Irish had shown their political colors and successfully defended their neighborhood and their party.[45]

When their interests seemed threatened, many Irish Americans in early-nineteenth-century New York were willing to disregard their middle-class leaders' notions of propriety and order and meet suspected enemies quickly and directly with force. While this characteristic—evident in politics, religion, and other areas—marks an important divergence from the goals of the middle-class émigrés, the exact nature of this violence bears closer examination. The willingness of both the nativist Whigs and the Democratic Irish to resort to rioting in the 1834 election indicates that this violence was a result of American conditions. It was the nativists who entered the Sixth Ward, insulted, and antagonized the Irish, and quickly turned to violence when the Irish objected. In the contentious world of Jacksonian America one interest group after another scrambled for power and, denying the legitimacy of its opposition, eagerly turned to blows to establish supremacy.[46]

Despite the mutual culpability in creating disorder, many Anglo-Americans blamed the Irish for being too eager to join the fray. One Whig judge in 1832 was reported to have declared that the Irish took the idea of liberty too far: the Irish, according to the judge, believed that they had the liberty to use the shillelagh on any one.[47] In November 1814, a Federalist paper sarcastically commented on the riots at the Downpatrick Fair in Ireland, proclaiming that "we all know that an Irish fair is nothing without a fight."[48] New York magistrates repeatedly lectured Irishmen on their rights and obligations as Americans. In July 1830 a judge told one such group that although they may have had reason to oppose the law in their native land, "in this country where all can receive justice—where the laws are made by the authority of the whole people, and for the people's benefit, no excuse, no palliation can be offered by persons of self government for resisting the due execution of them."[49]

Such comments were hardly disinterested observations and often built upon blatantly racist assumptions about the Celts and their lack of control. Ireland, however, was a stormy and rugged country in the early nineteenth century. This was not because of any genetic predisposition of the mercurial Celts. Indeed, although some English contemporaries argued that this was the case, others thought the Irish docile and amiable and attributed high rates of violence in counties like Tipperary to local inbreeding with the many descendants of Cromwell's troopers and other "robust" Anglo-Saxons. Rather than genes, Irish violence was rooted in heated religious rivalry, nationalist frustrations, and the severe strains placed on the island's limited resources of land and industry by an expanding population. In 1798, for instance, a rebellion, fiercely fought and cruelly suppressed, left 30,000 Irish dead. Through the next three decades, Protestant Orange lodges and Catholic secret Ribbon societies sprouted up throughout the mixed religious areas of southern Ulster and northern Connacht and Leinster, where they preyed upon each other through acts of covert terrorism. Further south, running through the middle of the country, the rapid pace of economic change and competition nourished more violent secret societies split along economic lines: renters organized against landlords, peasants against agricultural laborers, and laborers against peasants. Violence often cut through class and occupational lines, as groups of kin or "factions" fought for the few meager rewards Ireland could offer its impoverished masses. Rife with resentment of authority, bitter religious antipathy, and desperation born of poverty and hopelessness, Ireland was a fertile breeding ground for mob action and physical force in the early nineteenth century.[50]

Where the opponents and protagonists of New York's Irish made their mistake was to assume the conditions that had encouraged the violence in Ireland had evaporated in the "democratic" atmosphere of America. The values that the Irish brought with them made them suspicious of those in authority and quick to resort to violence. In the United States these tendencies were reinforced by experiences that led to rioting and thus helped to articulate the boundaries of New York's Anglo-American community.

Before the 1840s New York's police force was poorly organized, divided between the night watch, sheriffs, and constables. Few Irishmen served as peace officers, and antagonism between the police and the Irish persisted throughout the period.[51] After Protestant and Catholic Irish fought in Greenwich Village in July 1824, for instance, the police arrested dozens of Catholics, but did not detain even one Protestant. Long before that date, Catholic Irish had become suspicious of every New York peace officer. In the Christmas riot in 1806 on Augustus Street, the appearance of the watch, combined with some high-handed tactics, led to an all-out onslaught by the Irish in defense of their religion and neighborhood.[52] Some twenty years later that same street was still a center of the Irish American community. In late May 1829, two officers attempted to serve legal papers in a suit against the property of an Irishman on Augustus Street. This act provoked a "general turn out of his countrymen" that could only be quelled by police reinforcements.[53] During the 1820s and 1830s the Irish were strongly opposed to antihog laws. The magistrates wanted to clean up the city and remove all pigs from the streets. The Irish, and other lower-class New Yorkers, objected since the pigs provided a cheap source of food. From the Irish perspective, rioter Dennis Dougherty eloquently explained, "the corporation [the city government], the police and their officers . . . were a damned set of thieves" who "were stealing their hogs."[54]

The Irish found plenty of reason to resent the wealthy in New York as well. Most Irish immigrants, as already mentioned, were packed into crowded housing in areas like the Sixth Ward, or, especially in the late 1820s and early 1830s, pushed to the periphery of the city to live on the outskirts. This newly settled area was an odd mixture of housing. Interspersed between streets of cheaply produced wooden buildings were some fenced and hedged estates of the wealthy. This situation must have reminded many an Irishman of his homeland. Antagonism between the landed and impoverished occasionally broke out into acts of vandalism and collective violence. In one of the largest of these disturbances, focused against Stuyvesant property, the rallying cry was that the rioters "would have the satisfaction of the Irish."[55] Resentment of wealth also appeared in other circumstances. When a gig driven by a merchant came too close to a line of Irish cartmen on Third Avenue and 18th Street in August 1833, a disturbance quickly erupted. Some of the cartmen grabbed the horse of the offending gig and forced it onto the sidewalk. Enraged by this affront to his dignity, the merchant lashed out with his buggy whip. That opened the floodgates for more violence. Irishmen came pouring out of the Third Avenue groceries, where many were drinking after a day's work, and attacked the merchant and some of his friends in other buggies. By the time the police arrived and made arrests—only the Irish were taken—the merchants had been badly beaten.[56]

In what must have often seemed a hostile environment, the Irish found other causes for resorting to violence. On more than one occasion, Irish workers attacked individuals who they believed threatened their jobs. Ancient resentment also explains some of the battles between Catholics and Protestants, such as the fight between Greenwich Village weavers on July 12, 1824, the anniversary of the seventeenth-century Orange victory at the Battle of the Boyne. There is also some evidence to suggest a recurrence of conflict between various factions during the 1820s. The Irish also became involved in a number of racial incidents in which they attacked blacks, who shared some of the same neighborhoods and competed for some of the same jobs.[57]

Irish women seemed to take a more direct part in the violent world of the street than did other New York women. This activity suggests that Irish women operated from somewhat different values and felt possessive about their neighborhood and strongly about their Irish identity. As early as the Augustus Street riot of Christmas 1806, commentators mentioned that women were encouraging their men to fight and were supplying them with weapons.

Similarly, the *Gazette* reported a July 4 riot on Anthony Street committed by the "low Irish" and declared that the women supplied the men with shillelaghs and that some of the women, "amazon like," joined in the fray.[58] During the Protestant and Catholic Irish clash in Greenwich Village in 1824, one pregnant woman was knocked down and another woman charged into the melee swinging a stick at all who stood in her way.[59]

This violence reveals a complex set of values reflecting a mixture of class awareness and ethnicity that gave the Irish American community its shape and form. The Irish defended their neighborhoods, their jobs, and their church, while expressing a strain of antiauthoritarianism and a resentment of wealth. Moreover, they demonstrated a persistent faith in the roughhouse democracy of the streets and asserted their equal rights despite poverty and nationality. They developed a special Irish identity, increasingly associated with the Catholic Church, and thus perceived of themselves as a distinct group, as did others. It is this sense of identity that created the New York Irish American community.

In the opening decades of the nineteenth century, middle-class Irish Americans wanted to meld into the larger society while celebrating their ethnicity and republican ideals; this vision for the Irish American community excluded many of their poorer countrymen. By the 1830s this effort, as seen in voluntary associations, the church, the press, and even in politics, had failed. Poorer immigrants joined elements of the Irish and American cultures to create a hybrid identity. The mass of Irishmen understood that their new home had much to offer, but they also knew that even in the United States they remained besieged by prejudice. They therefore clung to one another, secure in the knowledge that they retained something unique and special that revolved around the bonds that tied them to their fellow Irish Americans. In the process they left an indelible mark on American history.

1844 to 1877

PART II

THE GREAT MIGRATION

The St. Patrick's Day parade of 1871, with thirty thousand
marchers and fifty bands, was the largest ever seen in New York
up to that time. Gallowglasses, the soldiers of ancient Ireland,
provided a very rare element of pageantry. Standing over 6 feet
4 inches tall and dressed in red, green, saffron, and gold
costumes, the long-haired warriors escorted a "triumphal car"
bearing a bust of Daniel O'Connell, the leader of the Catholic
Emancipation movement in Ireland. (Museum of the City of
New York. J. Clarence Davies Collection.)

Hasia R. Diner

OVERVIEW
"The Most Irish City in the Union"
THE ERA OF THE GREAT MIGRATION, 1844–1877

T HE MOMENTOUS YEARS of the mid–nineteenth century shaped the histories of both the Irish in America and the city of New York. Commencing with the Famine of the 1840s, a great migration transformed the small Irish community already there and facilitated the metropolis's massive expansion. In turn, spectacular physical and economic growth spurred on even more transatlantic migration. In these years the destinies of New York and the Irish became inseparable. Although the speaker at an 1844 Irish meeting who trumpeted New York as America's "most Irish city" may have been a bit premature, he was prophetic.[1]

Three decades later New York could legitimately claim that distinction. It not only housed America's largest Irish community but stood at the center of Irish American political, cultural, and social activism. Opinions would have been mixed, however, on whether this distinctiveness constituted a blessing or a curse.

The New York Scene

Without the Irish, New York might have evolved from a large city to America's largest city; it might have expanded beyond Lower Manhattan; it might have produced a volume of goods and services unequaled in the nation; it might have developed a complex political machinery and network of public services; and its relations with the state government might have been equally contentious. But when all is said and done, it would be difficult to imagine nineteenth-century New York without the Irish.

Some characteristics of New York life that later had an impact on the Irish began well before 1844 and the large-scale Irish migration. New York had in fact been growing rapidly for some time. It became the largest American city in 1825 with the completion of the Erie Canal, linking the port of New York with the resource-rich hinterlands of the Midwest. With this coup, New York became the center for national and international commerce and transportation and overtook Philadelphia as the chief commercial entrepôt in the United States. Between 1825 and 1845 the city's population grew from 166,000 to 371,000. By 1830 it was the center of the nation's ready-made clothing industry.[2]

Well before the arrival of hundreds of thousands of daughters and sons of Erin needing a place to live, New Yorkers pushed out from Lower Manhattan and expanded the city's physical space. In 1816 Houston Street and Greenwich Village constituted the city's northern rim. By the mid-1840s residential and commercial development stretched along Fifth Avenue up to Twentieth Street, with a smattering of houses sprouting up all the way to Forty-second Street.[3]

New York saw more than its share of poverty's devastation long before the Irish came to symbolize the horrors of urban life. Even before the 1840s observers had commented on the extent of poverty, the shabbiness of working-class housing, and the dirt, crime, and disorder on the sidewalks of New York. In 1834 the city government opened the nation's first municipal mental hospital, the New York City Lunatic Asylum, drawing its inmates from the poor.[4] Riotous behavior had punctuated the "tranquility" of civic life before the tidal wave of Irish immigration.[5]

The urban political machine, the complex power organism that dispensed favors to the masses in exchange for political fealty, existed in New York decades before Ireland experienced the Famine and sent forth legions of its women and men to the New World. According to political scientist Amy Bridges and other political historians, the machine predated the Irish and had nothing to do with their purported naiveté, subservience, ignorance, or corruption. The Society of St. Tammany existed before the Irish migration and indeed before the drafting of the U.S. Constitution.[6]

Americans in New York City and the state, were already reacting to the growing immigrant and Catholic presence in their midst before the floodgates from Ireland opened in earnest. Numbers alone were not the issue. Starting in the 1820s, tension mounted over the allocation of state resources and power. Nativism as a political and ideological issue surfaced in New York politics in the 1830s, and in the municipal elections held in the spring of 1835, two wards sported avowedly nativist tickets.[7] In the years immediately preceding the large-scale migration, controversy flared over Bible reading in the common schools, and the relationship between the common schools and the Public School Society, a self-proclaimed Protestant organization. Anti-Catholics dominated the first elected School Board (1842), and in the last mayoral election before the great migration, nativists enjoyed a landslide victory in municipal elections, capturing City Hall and the Common Council.[8]

Urban growth, economic expansion, the recognition of the human cost of industrial development, political machine-building, and intergroup conflict—all of these issues became increasingly important as the migration from Ireland was transformed from a steady stream into a deluge.

The Isle of Saints and Scholars

Few single natural events in modern history transformed as many women and men as did the Great Famine, which hit Ireland in the summer of 1845 and then savaged the island for the next few years. It transformed the country's basic patterns of existence, and its repercussions were felt on other continents.

Irish life, economic and social, had centered on the cultivation of potatoes since the mid–eighteenth century. The potato was the staff of life, the basic staple consumed at every meal and burned for fuel. It enabled the poor—that is, the majority of the population—to keep subdividing leases on tiny plots of land, since potatoes could be grown anywhere. The potato also played a key role in the astronomical increase in the Irish population, particularly in the western part of the island, ever since its importation to Ireland in the early eighteenth century. It enabled the poor to marry at a much younger age, and therefore increase their fertility. But with a larger population, they descended into even greater poverty.

The impact of the potato needs to be seen alongside British imperial policy. In the eighteenth century England began relying on Ireland to produce much of the basic foodstuff it needed to undergird urbanization and industrialization at home, as well as to support imperialism and wars around the globe. The mother country, not the colony, reaped the profits of any agricultural exports, notably grain, that flowed into the coffers of English owners of Irish land. In order to make this possible, England had to appropriate the common lands on which the poor depended. As a result, the energies of the Irish peasantry went toward the commercial cultivation of crops for England and English landowners. The ordinary people thus came to depend on the only available noncommercial crop: the potato. As one observer noted in 1804, "The poor Irish have to furnish other countries with such vast quantities of that which they themselves are starving for want of."[9]

In addition, over the course of the nineteenth century the number of acres devoted to tillage increased, whereas those for pasturage went down as absentee landlords grew increasingly concerned about profits. Although Ireland's eastern counties experienced some economic modernization and successful commercialization in the eighteenth and early nineteenth centuries, the western ones did not. Indeed, the dependence on the potato started first with the poorest communities in the west, where its cultivation set the standards for daily life.[10]

Thus when *Phytophthora infestans* destroyed the tubular staple, it unleashed a series of forces that proved devastating to the fundamental way of life in Ireland. Starvation obviously resulted from the infestation. Every year it worsened, and by 1846 almost the entire crop rotted. The crisis stretched into the 1850s. Relief efforts, hampered by primitive methods of distribution, British antipathy to the Irish, and Irish distrust of their British rulers, made little difference.[11]

After four years of continuous blight, close to one million people had vanished. Hundreds of thousand had died because of starvation, typhus, and dysentery; others had fled the country. One historian puts the number of dead due directly to starvation or the diseases attendant to malnutrition at 1.1 to 1.5 million.[12] Commentators at the time of the Famine wrote in harrowing terms of starving beggars streaming through the countryside, of the dead and the dying lying along the sides of the roads, of "little children . . . their limbs fleshless . . . their faces bloated yet wrinkled and of a pale greenish hue, . . . who would never, it was too plain, grow up to be men and women."[13]

The Famine itself contributed to a massive exodus to escape starvation: 1.5 million Irish people left for North America between 1845 and 1855.[14] The Famine also changed the composition of the stream of emigrants that had been steadily flowing out of Ireland since the beginning of the nineteenth century. In general, those who left Ireland in the decade after the Famine came from the poorer classes, and the Irish migrated in family units rather than as single men.

The Famine also changed the basic structure of marriage and landholding in Ireland. Previously, because of the nature of potato cultivation, the poor married young. After the 1850s, the Irish deferred marriage or just eschewed it, with only one son and one daughter in a family marrying and therefore inheriting the lease (or increasingly, ownership) on the family holding.[15]

This evolving system of nonpartible inheritance, coupled with a strikingly low rate of marriage, created an excess population of unmarried men and women. With no economic opportunities at home, since no urban or industrial development could absorb those passed over for marriage and inheritance, Ireland exported its young. The forces at work pushed out more women than men, and Irish migration to the United States, as well as to Canada, Australia, and New Zealand, became a heavily female-oriented trend, facilitated along female kin and friendship networks.[16]

America's Most Irish City

From 1844 on, New York and its Irish population grew rapidly. New York became an increasingly Irish city and the Irish increasingly New Yorkers. As a result of shipping patterns and economic developments unconnected to the nature of Irish society or the devastation of the Famine, New York emerged in the 1840s as the premier port of entry for immigrants from Ireland, as well as from other sending societies.

Few newcomers had the resources to go beyond New York and therefore stayed for negative reasons: most, although certainly not all, had no other options.[17] Yet, as more and more Irish settled there, creating within the metropolis dense, throbbing Irish enclaves, replete with formal and informal institutions that sustained communal life, New York became an increasingly attractive destination. A French visitor to New York summarized it best perhaps when he commented, "Emigration will soon cause it to be said that Ireland is no longer where flows the Shannon, but rather besides the banks of the Hudson River."[18]

Between 1847 and 1851 a total of 1.8 million immigrants disembarked in New York, of whom 848,000 were Irish women and men and the rest mainly German. Between May and December of 1847, the number from Ireland who landed in New York totaled 52,946, which was more than from any other place. In the same months of the following year, the number rose to 91,061, and the year after that it went up again, to 112,591.[19] In 1851 the Irish influx peaked, with 163,000 arrivals.[20] It should be remembered, however, that individuals who landed in New York, Irish or otherwise, may not have stayed there or may not have stayed very long. Given the explosion in work opportunities for unskilled men on railroad or canal building projects, Irish male newcomers in particular who disembarked in New York may have left immediately. Others, women as well as men, could easily have only landed in New York, going on to join other family members in Albany, Buffalo, Rochester, or any of the hundreds of Irish communities sprouting around the country. It is indeed possible that the best capitalized Irish immigrants were those who did *not* linger in New York (or Boston or the other east coast ports) but went elsewhere, making New York and the other harbor cities somewhat atypical of the rest of Irish America.

But even with these caveats in mind, it is clear that New York evolved into a heavily Irish city, and America's premier one. Between 1845 and 1851 New York housed 12 percent of America's Irish population.[21] The U.S. census of 1850 counted 133,730 people (26% of the city's total population) born in Ireland, while the New York State census of 1855 reported 175,735 (27.9% of the city's population) born there. (These figures exclude the American-born children of Irish parents, which would surely push the "Irish" total up higher.)[22]

The pressure of the Irish (and German) influx into New York led to the state supervision of the immigration process. Despite the disapproval of the city's Common Council, in 1847 the state legislature created the Board of Commissioners of Emigration. Of the board's 10 original members, 6 were Irish and belonged to the Friendly Sons of St. Patrick, an Irish benevolent organization. Under the new law, ships' captains had to report the names and port of embarkation of all immigrants and confirm that all individuals could support themselves. Another state law of 1848 set aside a separate pier for ships carrying immigrants, and in 1855 the legislature designated Castle Garden a reception point for the new arrivals. It hoped thereby to protect the hordes of newcomers from unscrupulous "runners" and others eager to fleece the survivors of the ocean voyage.[23]

By 1860 New York had more than 200,000 Irish-born individuals out of a total population of about 800,000, which made the Irish New York City's largest immigrant bloc. These Irish accounted for 13 percent of all the Irish in the United States and thus formed America's largest Hibernian enclave.[24] By 1870 the Irish percentage of Gotham's population had climbed to 21.4 percent of the city's total, but Boston and Jersey City, New Jersey, registered somewhat larger Irish concentrations, at 22.7 percent and 21.5 percent of their populations,

The Irish Emigrant Society held its first meeting on March 30, 1841. Through its office, men and women could obtain advice and information, jobs and lodgings, as well as file complaints against swindlers and protest conditions on board ships. The society also remitted money and prepaid passage tickets back to Ireland in such volume that in 1850 it established a thrift institution, the Emigrant Industrial Savings Bank. (Bettmann.)

respectively. Nevertheless, the Irish priest Stephen Byrne, who visited his
countrymen in the United States in the early 1870s, claimed that New York
deserved to be called America's most Irish city.[25] The 1880 U.S. census, which
finally began to count both place of birth and parents' place of birth, estimated
that a whopping one-third of all New York stemmed from Irish parentage, truly
making New York an extension of Ireland.[26]

Pockets of Irish settlement of varying sizes dotted most of developed—and
undeveloped—New York. Equally important, the Irish, like nineteenth-century
Americans in general, moved a great deal in their constant search for better, less
costly housing. They moved when jobs took them to other neighborhoods or
out of New York entirely. A New York Irish newspaper noted with regret in
1859 that "the immense majority are as yet but a mere floating population,
migrating from place to place wherever they may find a market for their
labor."[27]

With this transience in mind, it is still possible to pinpoint pockets of Irish
life in mid-nineteenth-century New York. A substantial number made their
homes in Brooklyn, New York's rival across the East River (to be incorporated
into a greater New York by the end of the century). The Irish constituted
Brooklyn's largest foreign-born group as early as 1855, when they numbered
56,753 out of a total population of 205,250. The number of Irish in Brooklyn
jumped to 57,143 in 1865, 73,985 in 1870, and then 78,880 in 1875. In each of
these years the Irish outnumbered all other nonnative Americans. Within
Brooklyn, the largest Irish enclave sprouted around the Navy Yard, in an area
dubbed "Irish Town."[28] As early as the 1840s small Irish areas formed in the
Bronx clustering around such hubs of employment as the Harlem Railroad, the
Hudson River Railroad, and the Croton Aqueduct.

The poorest Irish settled or squatted in shanty towns on the city's rims,
preceding the juggernaut of urban development. The most destitute Irish,
numbering about 20,000 in 1864, found themselves in the sparsely settled
northern parts of the city. They occupied the vast area that in the 1860s would
be carved into Central Park and lived under the shadow of the slowly constructed St. Patrick's Cathedral on Fifth Avenue. Here, in their jerry-built
shacks, the Irish newcomers raised pigs and goats as they had in Ireland,
scavenged for food and hired themselves out as day-laborers, finding work as
best they could.[29]

The Irish made their homes almost everywhere in the city in the 1840s
through the 1870s. Most young Irish women went into domestic service, living
with employers. Thus, Irish women in particular, lived in some of the city's
most affluent and "American" wards and therefore accounted for an Irish
presence in unlikely places. In addition, those who became economically
mobile sought out better housing in nicer neighborhoods. Even when they
moved "up," however, they continued to live predominantly among their own
kind. The area around Grammar School 14, on Twenty-seventh Street between

Second and Third Avenue, represented an area of second settlement for the Irish, and Irish boys accounted for 41.8 percent of eligible students. Thus, even among the nonpoor, non-"green" Irish, residence and ethnicity went hand in hand.[30]

But as of the 1855 New York State census, the heaviest Irish concentrations were in the First, Fourth, and Sixth Wards, as well as the adjoining Fourteenth, all of which were nearly one-half Irish in their ethnic makeup. The more easterly Second and Seventh Wards, those facing the East River, also registered large numbers of Irish residents in the 1850s, accounting for about 38 percent of their totals. According to the 1855 count, the Irish made up 20 to 35.5 percent of 7 of the city's 22 wards and more than 35.5 percent of an additional 9.[31] In general, the Irish gravitated to Lower Manhattan, because this zone contained the oldest and most dilapidated housing stock, the cheapest rents, and the lion's share of available jobs for unskilled and semiskilled laborers.

Occupation and class shaped the symbiotic relationship of the Irish and the city. In Ireland the vast majority lived in rural areas. Peasants of various ranks had command of the skills appropriate to an agricultural way of life. They then found themselves in America's most urban of locations, where the skills that had sustained their lives in the Old World served them poorly in the New. They found themselves on the bottom of America's, and New York's, occupational hierarchy.

The literature on the Irish in the United States has dwelt at length, indeed perhaps obsessively, on this connection between the Irish and poverty. Scholars have attributed such developments as Irish–black tension, the Irish connection to the political machine, the devotion of the Irish to Catholicism, and labor radicalism to their impoverishment. In the usual telling of the story of the Irish in America, they are for the most part relegated to the economic bottom until well into the last decade of the nineteenth century.

This picture certainly requires some adjustment. The Irish community in New York always contained many economic layers. They ranged from recent immigrants, unskilled laborers in the main, to more settled, more affluent descendants of earlier Irish immigrants. They included merchants, large and small, and a small professional class of physicians, lawyers, teachers constituted its elite. These successful and longer-term New York Irish created benevolent associations to help their distressed countrypeople, both in Ireland and in New York. They made up the backbone of organizations like the Friendly Sons of Saint Patrick, the Irish Emigrant Society, and other such groups.[32] When Jeremiah O'Donovan, a Philadelphia Hibernian came to New York in 1854 to sell a history of Ireland that he had written, he encountered his country-men in comfortable positions of all kinds. He met a "Mrs. O'Doherty . . . a widow, young, handsome, modest . . . she is both a milliner and dressmaker; and has a house full of young ladies sewing for her." His recollections of his journey contain flattering portraits of Irish women and men who "made it," successful entrepreneurs, master artisans, professionals, and buyers of his book![33]

The usual portrait of the Irish as an impoverished group trapped on the lowest rung of the class structure can be refined by looking at the Irish concern with the education of their children. Although few Americans living in the nineteenth century experienced rapid movement out of poverty through education, the Irish and their leaders did recognize that schooling was an antidote to enduring poverty. The New York, Irish Catholic community leadership, beginning with Bishop John Hughes, put tremendous emphasis on creating parochial schools, first at the elementary and then at the secondary level. They wanted to ward off Protestant and secular influences, since they assumed that a portion of the Irish population would and should go to school. Irish politicians maintained rigid control over the ward schools under their jurisdiction, making public schools in Irish neighborhoods community institutions.[34] By 1870 Irish women constituted some 20 percent of all New York City public school teachers.[35] Scattered evidence indicates that a sizable percentage of New York's Irish children attended school with success, at least as measured by completion data. Irish boys who made up 41.8 percent of the potential pupils of Grammar School 14 showed up as 40.8 percent of the attendees in 1855 and 25 percent of the graduates. The hefty dropout rate was balanced by the number who actually completed their education.[36]

Even so, the harsh reality for the Irish throughout the nineteenth century was that their primary source of work lay in the least skilled, lowest-paying jobs that New York City offered. This applied to both men and women. The years 1844–77, in particular, brought severe economic distress to the residents of New York City, and the poor were the hardest hit. Depressions in 1854–55, 1857, and 1873 impeded the occupational mobility of the Irish in New York. These large-scale economic debacles shaped the fortunes of the Irish just as dramatically as did the primitive skills they brought with them, the social problems they faced, and the antagonism they met.

In mid-nineteenth-century New York, Irish women predominated in several areas of employment. As already mentioned, they served, particularly if they were young and unmarried, as domestic workers in private homes and in hotels, usually living with their employer and saving their money. A good number sewed in establishments of all sizes, although older Irish women, married or widowed with children, found themselves often plying a needle in their own homes for contractors. Many married Irish women in New York took in boarders to compensate for the income that they lost upon marriage. Irish women could also be found on the streets of mid-nineteenth-century New York selling fruit and vegetables, and the more successful ones became owners of small grocery and liquor stores.[37]

Men labored on the docks as longshoremen, in the factories as unskilled hands, as porters, coachmen, boatmen, ferrymen, omnibus and stage drivers, carters, needle workers, printers, and as undifferentiated "laborers." In the building trades, they made a living as hod-carriers, brickmakers, masons, plasterers, bricklayers, glaziers, and carpenters and performed just about every task necessary for the continued expansion of the city. They basically performed those jobs that required physical strength and occupational flexibility. Irish men, it seems, worked foremost in ganglike situations. They tended to work with other Irish men, cementing the bonds of work and ethnicity. The Irish tended to cluster in those occupations that no longer functioned on the craft system. Finally, Irish men who were unmarried and therefore did not support a family had a degree of freedom in the workplace. They could leave New York either for good or for awhile to take advantage of work projects upstate or out-of-state.[38]

Wage demands in times of labor strife give some indication of what these people earned. In 1846 the 500 Irish laborers on Brooklyn's Atlantic Dock struck for 87 cents a day and for a workday of 10 hours. In 1853 the Irish men who made up the vast majority of the workers of the Erie Railroad went out on strike for $1.25 a day, also hoping to secure a 10-hour day.[39]

In some ways Irish male occupations resembled those of Irish females. "Laborer" for a man functioned much as did "domestic" for a woman. For both, marriage constrained job flexibility. Both were catch-all kinds of jobs and both fell along a wide spectrum in terms of pay, work conditions, and real skill level. In the main, neither earned an impressive income, although Irish female domestics enjoyed the advantage of being able to save much more of their earnings than laborers could. Like their sisters, some Irish men engaged in petty business, running liquor stores, saloons, oyster parlors, grocery stores, hotels, and other kinds of small enterprises. Many of these shops served Irish neighborhoods, making the proprietor, particularly the saloon-keeper, a well-known community figure. And, just as Irish women hawked goods from carts and baskets on the streets of New York, so too did Irish men.[40]

The work taken up by Irish men differed from that of Irish women in some respects, however. Irish men were heavily tied up with the political machine. They could secure employment in municipal services, with the machine a powerful intermediary. This is not to say that Irish women had no connection with the machine in their search for bread. Some Irish women, usually American-born daughters of Irish immigrants, were able to teach school through the help of the machine, and as the city expanded its educational services, these women benefited. Furthermore, shopkeepers of all kinds, male or female, needed licenses to ply their trade, and peddlers also were required to secure permission from municipal authorities to sell on the streets.

But for men, connections to politicians, the ability to trade a vote for a job, helped them secure employment on large-scale construction projects, a labor sector that supported many New York Irish families. When in 1865 the New York State Supreme Court building was being constructed, Irish men made up the vast majority of those drawing a paycheck.[41] Other heavily Irish male occupations also depended on the machine and on the governmental process.

As early as 1855 Irish men were the largest group of the cartmen of New York, including those that specialized in doing city work on sanitation, landfill, road projects, and the like. To be a private cartman one required a license; to work for the municipal government in particular one needed good connections.[42] Even before the massive influx of famine Irish in 1843, the Democrat-dominated Common Council gave a large number of market licenses to Irish men, much to the chagrin of native American entrepreneurs.[43]

Being a policeman may have been the most visible job associated with Irish men, and it may have been the one most connected to politics. The machine dispensed positions on the police force directly at the neighborhood or ward level. By 1855 men born in Ireland accounted for 27 percent of the New York city police force, which roughly equaled the percentage of Irish in the population. Since police served the wards of their residence, the predominantly Irish wards had the largest number of immigrant policemen.[44] In 1869 no police captains had been born in Germany (Germans made up New York's second immigrant bloc), but 32 hailed from Ireland.[45] As of 1860, some 309 New Yorkers of Irish birth listed their occupation in the census as "police," while only 84 were born in Germany.[46] After the Civil War, as the city increased the number of policemen and the Irish held firmer control on the machinery of municipal government, the Irish came to be even more prominent in this highly political job.[47]

How did Irish men function as defenders of municipal "law and order"? How did these relative newcomers with a sharp sense of "otherness" serve this American city? Being a police officer may have put an Irish man in somewhat of a bind. The vast majority of those whom he had to arrest were fellow Hibernians. Did this cause emotional conflict? According to New York police historian Wilbur Miller, officers with Irish surnames made as many arrests of Irish male offenders as did native-born officers, presumably Protestants of English background. Despite the Irish reputation in America for violence and brawling, citizens filed no more complaints against Irish police than against native-born police. During the violent confrontations between Irish-dominated mobs—such as the Astor Place Riot of 1849, the Dead Rabbits Riot of 1857, the Draft Riots of 1863, and the Orange Riots of 1870 and 1871—the Irish police did not enforce the law any less punctiliously than did their American-born co-workers. During New York's frequent Irish street riots of the nineteenth century, neither the Irish-born police nor their American-born children were ever accused of treating the rioters with ethnic favoritism or "kid gloves."[48] Furthermore, the Irish policemen represented something of an elite within their own community and as such did not exactly come from the same ranks as the offenders. They earned the income of skilled workers, while the masses in the community still found themselves in the ranks of unskilled laborers. Most police officers were married men, although those arrested were typically single.[49]

The economic adjustment of the Irish to the realities of New York life did not proceed smoothly or evenly. Poverty remained a grinding and long ordeal. Irish laborers in every enterprise found themselves at the mercy of the vagaries of the economy, with its constant cycles of boom and bust. They suffered low wages, erratic employment, and the constant influx of newer immigrants, who were also willing to accept almost any wage. Indeed, by 1880 the Irish economic situation had not improved substantially. As of that year 20 percent of all the Irish still found themselves in the category of "laborer," as opposed to 4 percent of native-born Americans.[50]

The shakiness of Irish economic adjustment can certainly be measured by the intense activism of the Irish in New York's labor movement. No passive workers, the Irish frequently banded together and struck for better wages and better conditions. Their unionism was not motivated by an ideological opposition to capitalism or support for some other economic arrangement. Unlike

On July 12, 1871, Irish longshoremen assembled outside Hibernian Hall on Prince Street before heading north to Lamartine Hall, where three Orange Lodges were housed on the top floor. The July 12 parading tradition commemorated a seventeeth-century Protestant victory over Catholics in Ireland. It led to periodic confrontations between "Orange" (Protestant Irish) and "Green" (Catholic Irish) on the streets of New York. The 1870 and 1871 Orange parades resulted in 76 deaths, no less than 165 injuries, and 92 arrests. Most of the casualties were inflicted in 1871 when the Eighty-fourth Regiment, NYSM, fired indiscriminately on the crowd in what the *Irish World* called "Slaughter on 8th Avenue." The causes of one of the worst examples of urban violence lay in the turbulent New York City political climate, where nativism and Anglo-centrism polarized issues of race and class, exacerbating ethnic tensions with roots in Ireland. (*Harper's Weekly.* Courtesy of John T. Ridge.)

some of the Germans who gravitated to socialism, the Irish offered a pragmatic, "bread-and-butter" resistance to poor wages.

Throughout these four decades Irish laborers found themselves in strident conflict with their employers. In the 1840s Irish dockworkers had already begun to organize, while in the 1850s Irish railroad workers went out on strike.[51] The Irish in the 1850s found themselves prominent in the unions or labor organizations of longshoremen, blacksmiths, cigar makers, boilermakers, shoemakers, printers, and in the construction field.[52] Groups like the Operative Masons, the Quarrymen's United Protective Society, and the Laborers United Benevolent Society marched proudly in the Saint Patrick's Day parades starting in the 1850s, blending class and ethnicity, while in the 1860s Irish laborers protested the war's effect on the struggling poor.[53]

Beginning in the 1850s the New York Irish press reported in glowing terms the heroic organization of laborers against oppressive conditions, and editorials in these newspapers championed the right of workers to extract a living wage from their employers. The *Irish World,* founded in 1870 by Patrick Ford, vigorously endorsed labor activism among the Irish and others and came out in favor of the Greenback-Labor Party in 1876. The rival *Irish American* also expressed solidarity with trade unions but counseled the Irish to stick with their well-proven friend and ally, the Democratic Party.[54]

Labor activism among the Irish immigrants reflected the relatively poor economic position they occupied. Contemporary observers noted, often exaggerated, the poverty, destitution, disease, and wretchedness of much of New York Irish life. The commissioner of New York's Almshouse, which had more than its share of "exiles" from Ireland, remarked that "many of [the Famine Irish] had far better been cast into the deep sea, than linger in the pangs of hunger, sickness and pain, to draw their last agonized breath in the streets of New York."[55] George G. Foster, a journalist, described the Irish Five-Points neighborhood of the Sixth Ward, as "the great . . . ulcer of wretchedness—the very rotting skeleton of civilization."[56]

Although such an assessment clearly overstated the case, life was not easy for the rural Irish struggling to adjust to urban America. Statistics on Irish housing find them living in New York's most overcrowded neighborhoods. Figures on income put them more often among the city's paupers than anyone else. Arrest records put them either among the criminals or victims of the police in regard to police brutality and false arrests. Legions of destitute Irish women and men on the one hand offended New Yorkers' sense of civility, but on the other became the objects of Catholic charity. In 1846 Bishop Hughes asked the Irish-based Sisters of Mercy to come in and serve Irish women in New York who had no home, no work, and no prospects, while the St. Vincent de Paul Society emerged as a alternative to Protestant charity.[57] The Irish entered lunatic asylums, charity hospitals, prisons, and almshouses more than any other group. They had the city's highest rates of typhus, typhoid fever, cholera, and all the other diseases that accompany hunger, poverty, and congestion.[58]

The Irish newcomers to New York faced not only a mountain of social problems growing out of their poverty but also a metropolis full of hostile "neighbors." Even before the Irish arrived in large number on the heels of the Famine, anti-Irish, anti-Catholic sentiment ran rampant in New York, both city and state. Irish Catholic newcomers were blasted from the politicians' stump, in the columns of the city's press, and on the pages of popular pulp fiction, which screamed about the Irish threat to American liberty. The state legislature debated a plan to dismiss all foreign-born—a code for "Irish"—from public service employment. In the 1850s Reverend Daniel Parsons and the "Angel Gabriel" (John S. Orr) ranted to crowds of up to 10,000 from the steps of City Hall about the evils of the Irish and their Catholic Church. Such militant and popular organizations as the Order of the Star Spangled Banner actually went into Irish neighborhoods picking fights, and the Know-Nothings in 1855 stood at the zenith of their political power. During the Civil War, despite the large number of Irish volunteers in all-Irish or mixed regiments, nativists condemned them as disloyal, cowardly, and unpatriotic southern sympathizers. In addition, New York housed a large Irish Protestant population. This group shared with their Catholic countrymen a long history of enmity and conflict that was reinforced by class differences and clashes on this side of the Atlantic. Street fights and outbursts of rioting between the "green" and the "orange" punctuated New York's urban order. The notorious Orange Riot of 1871 offered just one example of intra-Irish fighting that non-Irish New Yorkers came to consider a major social problem, a serious disruption of the social order.[59]

When Irish workers went on strike, employers brought in others, usually native-born whites, Germans, and blacks, as strikebreakers.[60] Of the three groups, the Irish considered blacks to be a serious threat to their thin thread of economic security. The Irish responded to their competitors with venom and antipathy. New York's Irish and New York's blacks jostled with each for a place on the lowest rung of the economic ladder. When the Irish first entered the New York economy in large numbers, they depressed black wages and thus pushed blacks out of their particular niche in the labor force.

Friction between Irish and black workers flared often, particularly on the waterfront and in factories, as the two groups of poor struggled for economic survival. It is therefore not so surprising that New York's Irish did not greet the abolitionist movement with enthusiasm, did not celebrate the 1863 Emancipation Proclamation, or participate in other efforts on behalf of free blacks. In addition, many Irish, although by no means all, believed that those who supported blacks were precisely their own enemies. That is, they associated abolitionism with anti-Catholicism and nativism. In that context the causes of the Draft Riots of July 1863 seem clear. Economic and cultural competition provided the context for the Irish mob attacks on black people and their institutions, which left in their wake hundreds dead, injured, and arrested.[61]

But not all of Irish life in New York in the nineteenth century could be described under the heading of "social pathology." Many Irish moved from poverty to small business. It was not unheard of to capitalize on Old World skills in the New York setting. Unmarried women who could take advantage of opportunities in domestic service found New York a treasure trove of unimagined possibilities. As one young woman wrote to her father from Gotham in 1850: "I must only say that this is a good place . . . any man or woman without a family are fools that would not venture and come to this plentyful country."[62]

The New York setting and the thick clustering of the Irish in massive numbers made it possible for the Irish to create institutions to ease the difficulties of migration and to help sustain the movement of some, slowly for sure, out of poverty. The political machine and the machinery of urban government, the Roman Catholic Church, the social and cultural organizations of the community, and the nationalist movements all helped define Irish ethnicity and a New York urban life that transcended the pathos of poverty.

These institutions—the political machine, the Catholic Church, the panoply of social and cultural organizations, and the nationalist movement—did not lift the Irish masses in New York out of poverty's grip. Rather, they anchored the Irish into the urban structure and defined the identity of the New York Irish as a group. They bridged the chasm between being immigrants from Ireland to being Irish Americans.

The political machine and the Irish involvement in it, has long intrigued historians. Why, historians have asked, did the Irish become so adept at politics? How much of their political prowess came from Ireland and how much was a response to American conditions? Why did they, of all groups, jump into the political fray in urban America and learn with such savvy how to manipulate the machine for their own ends? Although no consensus has yet developed, historians have agreed on a few general points about the affinity of the Irish for politics.

The Irish arrived in New York at a time when conflict between a rural-dominated, upstate-tilted legislature sought to dominate and control the affairs of the city. As New York City became increasingly Irish and Democratic, tensions between the legislature and the municipal government became more acerbic and issues of ethnicity and religion charged already contentious intergovernmental relations. A critique of the city amounted to a critique of the Irish and their influence on urban life. A defense of New York City became synonymous with a defense of the Irish.

After the late 1840s it was by and large the Democrats who controlled municipal government, while the Whigs and their Republican successors held power in the legislature. The Democrats increasingly articulated a pro-Irish, pro-immigrant position, while the Whig-Republicans owed much of their strength to nativists, in the city and around the state. These battle lines drawn in the 1840s and 1850s played themselves out for decades until the end of the century.[63]

The story of the Irish in New York City politics revolved around their relationship to the Democratic Party and their almost visceral reaction against the Whig-Republicans. As the Democrats splintered among an ever-changing set of factions, the Irish shifted among them, calculating who could give them the best deal and who was most likely to win. Thus although the Irish may have aligned themselves overwhelmingly with one party—one scholar puts it at 90 percent—they did not box themselves into a single niche within it.[64] The Irish shunned ideologies and jockeyed between factions in search of favors and recognition. As the Democratic Party grew more dependent on the Irish vote in New York City, its various factions catered to the Irish, offering favors, both concrete and symbolic, posturing as their friends regardless of real feelings, condemning nativism, and developing strategies to get their considerable votes.[65]

In the 1840s Tammany Hall devised a plan to bring in volunteer fire companies, saloon keepers, and police, all heavily Irish constituencies.[66] The enigmatic William "Boss" Tweed (not Irish) who dominated New York City politics in the half decade after the Civil War dispensed patronage galore to the Irish to lock them in to his faction. According to the *New York Times* of September 17, 1869, his "Ring" had given a total of 46 jobs in the city government to Germans and 754 to Irish New Yorkers.[67]

The Irish began their political career in New York as the pawns of the urban Democratic machine. They exchanged their votes for unskilled jobs, petty licenses, and other relatively low-cost benefits. These "crumbs" represented the absolutely highest these impoverished rural newcomers expected. But as they grew in number, they became more American and experienced a modest degree of economic mobility, their demands increased, their appetites were whetted, and the Democratic factions responded. The crumbs grew into substantial slices, and by the 1860s, the time of Tweed's hegemony, the Irish garnered the most jobs, the best patronage, and increasingly significant positions, even key leadership roles. As a reporter for the London *Times* noted in 1861, "In New York there is scarcely a situation of honour or distinction from the chief magistrate down to the police, that is not filled by the descendant of some Irishman who lived in savage hatred of England beyond the pale!"[68] After Tweed's fall in 1871, the Irish stepped into the leadership of the Democratic Party. "Honest" John Kelly, a former volunteer firefighter and businessman, elected first in 1854 to an alderman's seat, took over the helm of Tammany. Now instead of crumbs and slices, the Irish had the whole loaf of New York City politics.[69]

Where the political system was inherited from someone else's and over time manipulated by the Irish, the Catholic Church represented their own key institution, which they made, sustained, and dominated. Before the Irish arrived, New York had a small Catholic community, predominantly English, respectable, and middle-class, and it maintained a low public profile. Even the Irish immigrants earlier in the nineteenth century fit comfortably into this picture.[70] But the tidal wave of Catholic Irish immigrants of the 1840s and beyond transformed the church into an immigrant institution that served the poor. It strove to make itself a visible and powerful institution in the New York landscape.

On the eve of the Famine immigration, in 1842 John Hughes became the bishop of New York. Until his death in 1864 Hughes staked out a Catholic and Irish position within the church and without. He aggressively called on New York's Catholics to defend themselves, symbolically and physically, against attacks from Protestant nativists. He called for the creation of separate Catholic institutions, including schools, hospitals, orphanages, banks, and benevolent associations to incubate an Irish American culture, blending Catholic piety, love of the Irish homeland, and American patriotism.[71] Internally, he made the Catholic Church more responsive to the needs of the poor Irish masses. He vigorously increased the number of parishes to make the church more accessible to the masses. Before 1844, there were 14 Catholic churches serving New York, and of these 1 consisted of French parishioners and 2 of German. By 1844 the rest were Irish. Of those built between 1844 and 1863, 6 were German while the other 13 ministered exclusively to Irish women and men. According to Hughes, even this growth had not kept pace with the influx of Catholic Irish immigrants and he wanted to build more.[72] Hughes also felt the need to increase the number of clergy, priests and nuns. In 1846 he invited the Sisters of Mercy from Ireland to create a whole infrastructure of services for Irish women in New York.[73]

Hughes recognized that Irish immigrants came to New York relatively unchurched, and he hoped to transform them into avid churchgoers. The array of Catholic institutions that Hughes and other clergy created, particularly parochial schools, cemented the bonds between the laity and the church. Parochial schools developed slowly but became significant community institutions in the 1860s and 1870s, as they nurtured both Catholic piety and Irish ethnic identity.[74]

Hughes, and his successor John McCloskey, enjoyed immense success, making the Irish devout Catholics and the parish the central institution in Irish neighborhoods. By 1877 the Irish of New York became a churched people: ardent worshippers at Mass, participants in parish devotionals, students at parochial schools, their sons and daughters joining the religious orders, and participating in multifarious church societies. But perhaps the efforts of clerics alone may not have caused this transformation.

The shrill anti-Catholicism heard in New York may have heightened the Irish immigrant's latent devotion to the church. In Ireland Catholicism functioned as a folk rather than an ecclesiastical institution. In New York, Catholicism elicited a more formal, strident, affirmative involvement. Here, religion offered a vehicle for expressing ethnic identity. It helped forge bonds between the Irish in America and their memories of home, while expressing patriotism and loyalty to America.[75]

These same goals, often unstated but palpable, nonetheless suffused the various benevolent associations, volunteer fire companies, military societies, and social clubs that mushroomed in the Irish neighborhoods. Limited primarily to men, these organizations emphasized sociability. Much of neighborhood Irish life centered around saloons and grocery stores, places where Irish men, in particular, enjoyed some recreation after grueling hours of physical labor. Irish women tended to spend their social life on the stoops of their apartment buildings and on the sidewalks of their streets, blending gender solidarity with ethnic familiarity.

On a formal level, the New York Irish press combined Irish ethnicity with integration into America and helped the Irish define themselves. From 1848 on, editors tried to mold Irish communal public opinion and stake out an Irish position on public affairs.[76] The annual St. Patrick's Day parade became a visible symbol of the bonds of Irish communal solidarity, and for that one day at least, the Irish took over the streets of New York and announced to its non-Irish residents that they were a force to be contended with. American conditions produced and gave shape to the parades, the press, and the organizations. Irish ethnicity gave them their distinctive character.[77]

Like the church, the press, and the voluntary societies, the Irish nationalist activities of New York defined Irish communal life and in effect an Irish American identity. Connections between the New York Irish and the Irish back home remained strong despite great distances. Irish New Yorkers sent hundreds of thousands of dollars to their families in Ireland through the Irish Emigrant Society, which in 1850 created the Emigrant Industrial Savings Bank. A constant flow of new immigrants, kin, and friends kept the images of Ireland vivid for settled New York Irish women and men, and the political "troubles" in Ireland were sharply etched in the consciousness of the Irish in New York.[78]

Irish immigrants brought to New York, along with their meager possessions, a deep and unshakable hatred of their British overlords, whom they saw as the root of all Irish misfortune and evil. That hatred carried over to their civic lives in America, and not a few of the Irish-dominated riots of mid-nineteenth-century New York drew upon that antagonism.[79] Old World sentiments became issues in New York City politics, and Irish New Yorkers expected local Democratic politicians, regardless of their own origin, to stand behind efforts on behalf of Irish liberation from England. Democratic politicians frequently came out to greet heroes of the struggle, attend banquets in their honor, and chair mass meetings of nationalist societies.[80]

New York Irish life reflected the factionalism and internal disputes of the nationalist movement. Every faction had its ideologues, advocates, organizations, and publications in New York. Support for one faction or another divided the Irish in New York from each other, causing rifts within the church, press, societies, and benevolent associations. Whereas non-Irish New Yorkers saw the Irish as a kind of undifferentiated mass, internally the politics of Ireland divided them and helped create a panoply of community institutions.[81]

New York became the American headquarters for the Repealers, the Young Ireland group, the Fenians, and other organizations concerned with aiding the cause back home. Political refugees from Ireland like John O'Mahony, John Devoy, John Mitchel, O'Donovan Rossa, and numerous other heroes of the struggle, flocked to New York and used the New York Irish community as the springboard for their political causes. Conversely, Irish nationalism became an issue in New York City politics, and groups like the Fenians galvanized local political campaigns into battles in the struggle for Irish independence. By virtue of New York's position as the center of American journalism and letters, by virtue of its strategic location as the chief port of entry, and because of the throbbing size of its Irish community, it became a valued prize in the struggle between factions and transformed New York from an American city with a large Irish community into *the* Irish city of nineteenth-century America.

Support for the struggles back home gave Irish New Yorkers a concrete cause to bring to American politics. It gave them a distinct agenda that differentiated them from all other immigrants and from native-born Americans. It became a palpable measure of group loyalty and a sine qua non of "being" Irish, as the American-born children of Irish parents increasingly predominated.

By the end of the 1870s, although the Irish were still clustered in low-paying jobs, they had began to dominate the city's political apparatus and command the resources of a mighty church structure. The leadership of the increasingly respectable trade union movement rested primarily in their hands, and some highly visible jobs, including teaching, police work, and firefighting, had become almost synonymous with being Irish. The Irish had a political cause they could offer as a litmus test to non-Irish politicians and developed a hybrid culture that organically blended Irish and American motifs. This was true all over America, but more so in New York, because it was New York. Its size made it sui generis.

———

This brief overview of the history of the Irish in New York, spanning the middle decades of the nineteenth century, gives some idea of the general contours of that period. The five essays that follow fill in some of the gaps. In chapters 4 and 5 Graham Hodges and John Kuo Wei Tchen accomplish at least two notable ends. They demonstrate, first, that studies of the Irish need to ask more sophisticated questions about adaptation to America. The Irish confronted a multiethnic society and interacted with all sorts of new people, including African Americans and Chinese. Second, these two essays venture well beyond the stereotypes that show the Irish becoming Americanized through the acceptance of racism. The Irish who emerge in these two essays responded in complicated ways to the American racial mosaic. Alan Kraut's discussion of illness and medical care among the Irish in chapter 6 fits into a new scholarly paradigm that posits immigrants not as victims of discrimination and poverty but as active agents of their own destiny. The Irish who came to New York did indeed suffer a whole host of medical problems, but solutions lay firmly in the hands of their middle-class women and men, within and without the church, who shaped Irish American culture. The presence of a successful cadre of Irish New Yorkers is further confirmed in chapter 7 by William Devlin's "Shrewd Irishmen." The Irish tailors and hatters, skilled artisans and competent entrepreneurs, force one to think of the Irish in broader class terms than usual. And in chapter 8 Edward Spann questions the traditional retelling of the story about the Irish and the Civil War in which historians have emphasized Irish antipathy for abolitionism, Unionism, and conscription. For sure, Spann notes, some Irish New Yorkers did oppose the Civil War, but this complex, diverse community responded in multiple ways. Patriotic calls and high levels of military participation need to be factored in, too.

These essays tell a dramatic story of grand changes in the histories of the city of New York and its Irish residents during the mid–nineteenth century. They also point to the need for further research, particularly a comparative analysis of New York, the mega-city, and the smaller, inland Irish communities. What difference did size and geography make in shaping the Irish community? The New York Irish need to be studied in the context of other immigrants of the time and their process of identity formation. Jay Dolan first raised this point in *The Immigrant Church*, and his model should be employed in studies of other institutions. Irish women's history remains an open field for further exploration and refinement. Did patterns described in Hasia Diner's *Erin's Daughters in America* hold for New York? How did the size of the city and of the Irish community modify that portrait? Cultural and social patterns of the New York Irish represent the most unexplored aspect of the community's past. The internal dynamics of Irish households, the entry of Irish women in public school teaching, the experience of Irish children in those schools, male and female leisure patterns, the role of small businesses in the life of the Irish enclave, Irish street life on the "sidewalks of New York," efforts by the New York Irish to forge a self-conscious ethnic culture, and myriad other subjects have not yet been taken up by historians. There is still much to learn about the New York Irish in the decades flanking the Civil War.

CHAPTER 4

"Desirable Companions and Lovers"

IRISH AND AFRICAN AMERICANS IN THE

SIXTH WARD, 1830–1870

I N 1850 GEORGE FOSTER, while guiding his readers through a midnight tour of the infamous Five Points, reflected on the frequency of intermarriage among African American males and Irish women, who, Foster believed, regarded their husbands as "desirable companions and lovers."[1] Foster's observations fall sharply apart from historical perceptions of the relationships between Irish and African Americans in antebellum New York City. Pointing to an Irish embrace of pro-slavery ideology, opposition to black suffrage, antagonism over work, and periodic Irish violence toward blacks, historians have constructed a paradigm of irreconcilable racial conflict.[2] A second, related approach emphasizes Irish acculturation through embrace of American racism. Designed to explain the role of race in working-class culture, this perspective, emphasizing the environmental and historical context of racial conflict, explains how the Irish earned "the wages of whiteness" to grasp a tenuous foothold in the American working class.[3]

In numbers and commonality of experience, the lives of Irish and African Americans epitomize the experiences of ordinary New Yorkers in the burgeoning nineteenth-century metropolis. By adding consideration of the gender and racial contexts of their relationships, it is possible to move beyond the fractured paradigm of class that pervades historical discussion of the antebellum working class in New York. Despite the extraordinary importance of the semiskilled

Irish and black laborers in New York during the antebellum years, historians have little close description or succinct analysis of their work or culture.[4] One reason is that historians of the antebellum working class have studied industrial laborers primarily as prototypes of the modern, class-conscious proletarian or as pursuers of the American dream, seekers of middle-class fortunes inaccessible in Ireland.[5]

There is, it should be admitted, evidence of racial animosity over work even before the notorious Draft Riots of 1863. In one incident, in 1855, after white stevedores struck for higher wages, blacks replaced them. Fighting soon erupted between the discharged Irish and blacks. After the strike was settled, white longshoremen supplanted the blacks.[6] However many disturbing examples one may find of contention between the Irish and African Americans, there are some countervailing examples of cooperation. In 1853 black waiters agitated for higher wages and won pay of $16 a month to the white waiter's $12. A black man attending a later meeting of white waiters advised them to go for even higher wages. On March 31, 1853, the *New York Times* reported that black and Irish waiters had formed a union and gone on strike. On this occasion, the Irish and African Americans, often portrayed as irreconcilably hostile in the work-place, shared goals including wage protection and reduction of hours.[7]

There are additional problems, beyond those tantalizing fragments, to historical visions of irreconcilable racism. Scant attention is given to variations within the Irish populace itself, which, by virtue of more than 1.1 million immigrants arriving at the port of New York between 1847 and 1860, amounted to one in four New Yorkers by the onset of the Civil War. Some of the divisions among the Irish dated back to their home towns. Within the Sixth Ward, County Sligo men and women gravitated to upper Mulberry Street, Corkonians to the lower part of Mulberry, and Kerryonians to nearby Orange (later Baxter) Street.[8] Although the growth of the Irish populace dwarfed the African American population of the city, concentrations of blacks in certain wards ensured daily contact between the two groups.

This chapter is about the complexity of Irish and African American relations in the New York City's turbulent Sixth Ward between 1830 and 1870. This ward was the crucible of Irish-black relations. African Americans had lived in the area since the 1640s and later shared it with republican-minded journeymen and carters. The remnants of the Negro Burying Ground was near, sustaining a spiritual sense of place among blacks, a trait noticed by George Foster in 1850. Known for decades as the Cartman's Ward, the neighborhood boasted a powerful tradition of assertive trade solidarity. Another force was immigration. By 1810, immigrants and blacks attracted by cheap rents accounted for one-fourth of the ward's population, the highest such percentage in the city. The ward was home for 31 percent of all aliens in the city, primarily the Irish.[9]

Although conflict was present, so was a surprising degree of community, shared work experience, affection, and family building. In many ways, the relationships of Irish and African Americans resembled the spontaneous "communitas" described by Victor Turner in which daily relationships shaped their lives and added symbolic meaning to pedestrian occurrences. This relationship becomes clearer when one examines the demographics of the ward, the effects of rioting and crime on the ward, of race and gender within racially integrated occupations, and of occupation and neighborhood on laborers' culture in the Sixth Ward. In a significant departure from other scholars, I have deemphasized industrial occupations, which included very few blacks, concentrating instead on three groups: laborers and domestics; city-licensed, semiskilled wage earners, comprised of cartmen, porters, grocers, tavern and porterhouse keepers, butchers, junk and rag dealers; and the "useless trades" of prostitutes and petty criminals.[10] These three groups of workers provide considerable insight into the daily interplay of gender, class, and race among Irish and African Americans.

Each of these occupational groups was extremely important in the Irish experience in New York City. In 1855 the two largest occupations for Irish immigrants were laborers and domestic servants, with 17,426 in the former category and 23,386 in the latter. Together, these 40,812 workers constituted 46 percent of the 88,480 Irish immigrants gainfully employed in the city. These citywide patterns were amplified in the Sixth Ward, where 53 percent of Irish workers were unskilled laborers or service workers. About 12 percent had a permanent status as a carter, porter, or hackman.[11]

Other laborers sustained a tenuous relationship within the skilled trades in New York. As craft skills declined, small shops still dominated the industrial sector in the antebellum period. Although journeymen and unskilled workers made occasional efforts to join forces, laborers generally formed their own unions.[12] Laborers' unions were the largest in the city and the Irish made up the largest portions of the memberships. In the early 1850s, the 3,000-man Laborers' Union used strikes and closed shops to protect standard wages of $1.50 per day and push for a 10-hour work day. The Laborers' Union also boasted successful benevolent societies, associations, and cooperatives.[13]

Irish women crowded into domestic work, an arena once controlled exclusively by blacks. By 1855, over 45 percent of Irish females under the age of 50 in the Sixth Ward worked as domestics: as hotel maids, waitresses, and cooks, as well as personal servants, housekeepers, nurses, and washerwomen. Older Irish women took in boarders, an ancillary occupation to domestic work. Seniority did not insulate a woman from domestic service. Almost 30 percent of Irish females over the age of 50 in the ward worked as domestics.[14]

The semiskilled trades were also open to Irish and black men and women. For example, tavernkeepers and grocers opened their doors to all. Similarly, crime had no gender or racial boundaries. The fleeting nature of prostitution and other minor crime hampers any exact count of these occupations, though census takers did visit the Tombs to list inmates.

TABLE 4.1. Irish and African American Populations of New York City and Sixth Ward, 1830–1870

	New York City			Sixth Ward		
Year	Total	Irish	African American	Total	Irish	African American
1830	197,112	17,773[a]	13,976	13,570	2,306[a]	1,878
1835	268,089	27,669[a]	15,061	14,827	2,026[a]	1,797
1840	312,710	—	16,358	17,198	2,026	1,812
1845	371,223	96,581	12,913	19,343	7,552	1,073
1850	515,547	133,730[b]	13,815	24,698	—	991
1855	629,547	175,735	11,840	25,562	10,845	545
1860	813,669	203,740	12,574	26,696	—	334
1865	726,386	—	9,943	19,754	7,211	289
1870	942,292	201,999	13,093	21,153	11,709[a]	203

Sources: *Fifth Census, or, Enumeration of the Inhabitants of the United States, as Corrected at the Department of State in 1830* (Washington. D.C., 1830); *Census of the State of New York for 1835* (Albany, 1837); *Sixth Census, or, Enumeration of the Inhabitants of the United States, as Corrected at the Department of State in 1840* (Washington, D.C., 1840); *Census of the State of New York for 1845* (Albany, 1847); J. D. Debow, *The Seventh Census of the United States: 1850* (Washington, D.C., 1850); *Census of the State of New York for 1855* (Albany, 1857); Joseph C. G. Kennedy, *Population of the United* States *in 1860 . . . The Eighth Census* (Washington, D.C., 1864); Franklin B. Hough, ed., *Census of the State of New York for 1865* (Albany, 1867); Francis A. Walker, ed., *Ninth Census*, Vol. 1, *The Statistics of the Population of the United States* (Washington, D.C., 1872).
[a]All aliens.
[b]Includes Great Britain and all possessions.

As table 4.1 indicates, the proportion of Irish and African Americans in the population of the Sixth Ward was about equal until 1845, accounting for 44 percent in that census. After that the Irish proportion soared while the African American declined precipitously. Although the numbers in the Sixth Ward did not increase dramatically between 1830 and 1870—rising to a zenith of 25,000 in 1855, then falling back to 21,000 by 1870—the size of the Irish population jumped fivefold. The decline of African Americans in the neighborhood may be construed as evidence that the beleaguered minority fled under the oppression of hostile immigrants. Although the Irish eventually accounted for one in four residents of the ward, they still shared the neighborhood with African Americans, Germans, Italians, Chinese, and multinational sailors. Furthermore, although the number of blacks dropped precipitously after the Fugitive Slave Act of 1850, black churches and schools remained in the ward until much later and local blacks held prominent, not furtive roles in the district's picaresque street life.

A tour around the ward in 1850 reveals several distinct neighborhoods. Its southern border was City Hall, with its adjacent row of lawyers' offices on City Hall Place. To the west was Broadway, studded by commercial buildings packed with small businesses ranging from fancy and dry goods to daguerrotypists and book dealers. The ward's northern perimeter was Canal Street, a composite of stables, porterhouses, pawnbrokers, and boardinghouses. This ambiance flowed into the Bowery, the eastern limits of the ward, where oysterhouses, taverns, and working-class theaters vied for attention with dentists, blacksmiths, junk dealers, and assorted small manufactories. One tabulator found more than 240 trades in a few blocks of lower Bowery.[15] On the side streets between Broadway and the Bowery were clusters of boardinghouses that varied greatly in quality and purpose, produced by a combination of soaring property values and a transient, immigrant work force. Operated by a keeper of either gender, on property usually owned by a businessman, boardinghouses were older homes chopped into single rooms, or, tenements of four and five stories crammed with sailors, laborers, cartmen, domestics, and seamstresses.[16]

A number of institutions anchored the ward. On the east was the Bowery Theater, the home of working-class melodrama. The St. Andrew's and Transfigu-

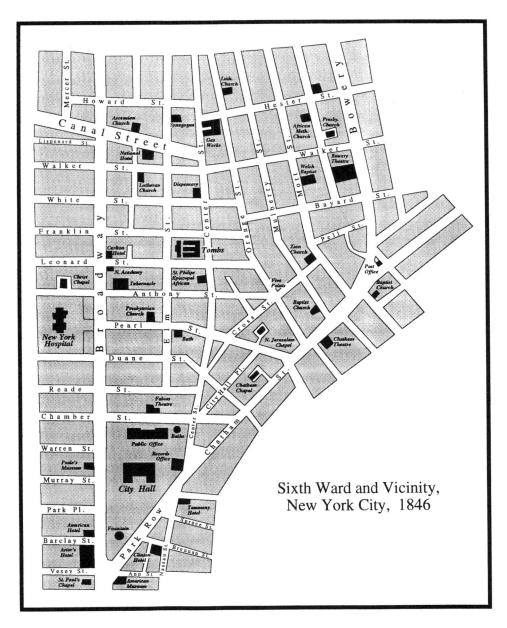

Sixth Ward, 1846.

111

Irish and African Americans in the Sixth Ward, 1830–1870

ration churches served Irish Roman Catholics. A map of the ward in 1847 clearly shows the Abyssinian Baptist Church at 44 Anthony and St. Philip's African Episcopal Church at 85 Centre, both repaired after the 1834 riots. Public schools for whites were located at Mott near Cross and Elm near Leonard; nearby were schools for blacks at 145 Mulberry and 161 Duane. The Tombs glowered over the neighborhood on a block bordered by Franklin, Leonard, Centre and Elm Streets. By 1851 the Five Points Mission had replaced the Old Brewery with a House of Industry.[17]

What accounts for the ward's notoriety was the carnivalesque Five Points, which excited and appalled moralistic New Yorkers. The triangular Paradise Square, the center of the Five Points, was located a scant fifth of a mile from City Hall. Here Little Water, Cross, Anthony, Orange, and Mulberry Streets entered, like rivers emptying themselves into a bay. Early in the century, Mulberry and Orange Streets became centers for laboring and immigrant boardinghouses, surrounded by dozens of groceries selling liquor and by porterhouses and dancing halls.[18]

George Foster's midnight tour at the Five Points highlighted local landmarks. Standing under a gaslamp next to a policeman, Foster drew attention first to the Old Brewery, erected in 1797, and transformed into a residence in 1837, into which were crammed several hundred black and Irish men, women, and children. The Old Brewery, as Foster informed his breathless readers, housed countless prostitutes, many of whom, Foster claimed, practiced their trade in rooms shared with their children. Crowded around the brewery, demolished soon after Foster's description, were taverns, oyster cellars, and brothels. Patrons of the bars were "mostly sailors, negroes, and the worst of loafers and vaga-bonds." Every saloon employed a black fiddler, "ready to tune up his villainous squeaking for sixpence a piece and a treat at the end." The oyster saloons were open all night and served a motley clientele of pickpockets, card-sharps, coun-terfeiters, gamblers, and thugs.

According to Foster, the brothels employed young, rural women, who, repressed by severe parents, came to the city with desperation in their hearts. Arrival proved their undoing when "either murdering their infants" upon birth, or abandoning them on a doorstep, they prepared for "any course of crime that will procure a living." Foster romanticized the reality of their origins, but was correct about the prevalence of prostitution and pornography in the ward. Middle-class tourists found all the vices ready in another hot spot. Peter Williams' dance hall, immortalized by Charles Dickens, had become a successful tourist attraction. Gleanings from contemporary observers suggest that the Five Points was an early version of the Black and Tan bars in Harlem in the 1920s, around Times Square in the 1950s, and later in the East Village. Like their descendants, the Five Pointers were ripe for casual violence, carousing, and open love-making. Many of the players in these daily human melodramas were black and Irish men and women.[19]

In a neighborhood where shared experiences surmounted racial differences and people were identified more by work than ethnicity, blacks and Irish brushed regularly against each other. By 1820, the greatest concentrations of blacks and Irish in the city lived along Cross Street between Augustus and Duane, in the heart of the Five Points.[20] Thirty years later, blacks and whites still coexisted. Moving up Orange Street, a main street of the Sixth Ward, Doggett's 1851 Street Directory points out Gilbert Palmer, an Irish liquor dealer; then Levi Marks, a Jewish used-clothing dealer; and Anaste Plete, a black barber from Trinidad. Plete's neighbor was Edward McDaniel, an Irish shoemaker, followed by Henry Mathews, a black porter from Maryland. Such random ethnicity continued throughout the principal streets of the ward.[21] Since most activities were public, it is not surprising to read in John D. Vose's tour of New York after dark of "gangs of negroes, Irish, and sailors," standing around "discussing matters . . . [in] their line of conversation." Unrelated Irish and blacks lived together. In the early nineteenth century, a black recorded living in the home of a white was invariably a servant or a slave. By midcentury, around the Five Points, necessity obliterated racial differences. George Washington, one of three black men in the city named after the first president, lived with his black wife, Adelaide, another black woman, Harriet Morris, and an Irish woman, Joanna Cosgrove. The 1860 census reveals Moses Downey, a 43-year-old black musician renting space in his home to James and Mary Gallagher, an Irish printer and his wife.[22]

Often these ties developed early in life as the agencies of social reform pressed many Irish and blacks together. Through fiction, song, melodrama, and folk tale, a secularized version of *Pilgrim's Progress* chronicled the lives of local Irish and African Americans. Sadly, unlike John Bunyan's hero, few of the residents of the Sixth Ward achieved any earthly sanction and were dubious candidates for immortal bliss. Still, missionary and charitable organizations labored to reform the Five Pointers. For troubled Irish and black children, reformation began with enforced training at the House of Refuge, New York's juvenile reform school. Irish and African American teenage boys and girls were commonly taken into the school after committing a petty crime in New York or for simply being poor and orphaned. Irish children constituted 40 percent of the inmates at the House of Refuge while 11 percent were black. After a period of education and training, Irish and black youths were bound out together. Boys were most frequently sent to work on farms or to the sea; girls invariably were sent "into service."[23] Even then, their lives seldom improved. After returning to the neighborhood, some must have felt nostalgia for the rural institutions. Health officials noted that Sixth Ward blacks and Irish lived in disease-ridden, overcrowded hovels. In a letter published in 1845, Dr. B. W. McCready described conditions for typhus patients in "a covered alleyway" on Elizabeth Street just off the Five Points. The three-story building stood in the center of a yard surrounded by pig sties and stables. Animal filth made the ground impassable, so boards covered the yard. The part decayed boards, when pushed, yielded up a "thick greenish fluid" through the crevices.[24]

As adults, African Americans and Irish in New York City suffered under the implacable hands of charity and correction. The Five Points Mission House of Industry tore down the Old Brewery in 1851 and offered shelter and hope in the form of schools and references. The numbers of needy were sufficiently great to garner a clientele, but the Catholic Irish and the Protestant missionary women were fundamentally opposed. With the loss of temporal salvation, Irish and black New Yorkers suffered from earthly purgatories. In New York City in the 1850s, the Irish accounted for 60 percent of the almshouse population, 70 percent of the recipients of charity, and more than half of those arrested for drunkenness. The "Bloody Ould Sixth" represented the deadly effects of poverty on Irish and African American New Yorkers. By 1855 the Sixth Ward had the highest death rate in the city. Pulmonary diseases including tuberculosis, pleurisy, pneumonia, and hemorrhage of the lungs were the leading causes of death among the young. Intemperance devastated the Irish and black populations equally. Laudanum and opium were favored drugs for suicide for black and Irish women. Children died from neglect, convulsions, and suffocation. Such abysmal statistics reveal shared hardship.[25]

To contemporaries, the Sixth Ward, and the Five Points in particular, epitomized crime. By modern standards, individual attacks on persons were rare. There were only 13 convictions for murder in the entire city between 1838 and 1851, a figure matched in the next three years. Many New Yorkers blamed the increase on conditions in the Five Points.[26] This perception of a violent Sixth Ward was enhanced by the rise of Irish gangs, immortalized by historians in their chronicles of the Forty Thieves, the Kerryonians, the Chichesters, Roach Guards, Plug Uglies, Shirt Tails, and Dead Rabbits. The stalwarts of the gangs were the clientele for the bars and brothels around the Five Points, bringing them into everyday contact with black men and women.

Fist-fights often elevated into riots. Historians cite Irish participation in street battles as overwhelming proof of their hatred of the city's African Americans. In the 1830s, rioting changed from an acceptable mode of political discourse to an unruly, dangerous expression of class, ethnic, and racial antagonism. The government's inability to control rioters deepened the widespread despair about the city's future and heightened the calls for a professional police force.[27]

The July 1834 riots were the largest single action against African Americans before the Civil War years. Rioters, angered by reports of interracial marriage and assertions of racial equality, rampaged through the Sixth Ward for three days and demolished the venerable St. Philip's African Episcopal Church on Centre Street. The riots went beyond past harassment of black churches with frightening intensity and marked an attempt to drive the established black community out of the city. The *Commercial Advertiser*, blaming abolitionists for the riots, reported that "whenever a colored person appeared, it was a signal of combat, fight, and riot." The rioters included professional and commercial men, skilled laborers and tradesmen, and a scattering of semiskilled and unskilled workers. Sixteen percent of those arrested came from the Sixth Ward, while others came from wards with equal concentrations of African Americans. Significantly, most rioters came from established New York families, and only a few of those detained were Irish. On the third day, rioters targeted both the Irish and the abolitionists. As the mob charged down the streets of the ward, it attacked in random sequence black homes and churches and Irish bars. Although African Americans were the chief victims, the Irish were not exempt from the rage of the mob.[28]

This animosity became plain a year later when the Irish battled "Americans" for five days around the Sixth Ward. Stemming from a dispute between an Irish man and a native-born apple vendor, a riot quickly roiled the streets of the Five Points. Newspapers reported an ethnic texture to the fighting. During an initial night of fisticuffs between "citizens and foreigners," bystanders exhorted the brawlers by shouting, "Well-done Americans," or "Irishmen." The danger in these melees can be seen in one report of policemen arresting Irishman Edward Lynch for wielding a "wooden pallisade" studded with nails. Newspapers circulated rumors that Irish gangs were organizing an Irish guerrilla militia. The ethnic nature of the conflict continued in the next few days as squads of native-born rioters ransacked the homes of Irish Five Pointers, destroyed brothels frequented by Irishmen, and wrecked a Bowery tavern, the Green Dragon, also attacked in the riots a year before. Two people were killed, an English piano forte maker and a doctor. Virtually all of those arrested were Irish residents of the Sixth Ward.[29]

In the aftermath, the *New York Sun* blamed its fellow newspapers for the riot, contending the city was suffering from irresponsible journalism practiced the year before by the *Courier and Enquirer*, the *Times*, and the *Commercial Advertiser*. Maintaining that civic authorities neglected to condemn mob violence, allowing the "spirit" of riot to remain respectable, the paper pronounced the city would now "reap the whirlwind." What is significant here is that a popular newspaper equated treatment of the Irish in 1835 with the attack on African Americans the previous year. Reflecting this mutual insecurity, radical Democrat Gilbert Vale editorialized in 1840 that rioters in the Sixth Ward attacked blacks "for no other reason except the incitation of a brutal editor of a party newspaper." Vale added that in 1835 a mob attacked the Irish "because they were Irish."[30]

Although the ward was the scene of innumerable riots in subsequent years, strikingly little violence occurred between Irish and blacks. Even though interracial lovers, black churches, and abolitionists remained in the ward amidst an escalating Irish population, its residents did not participate in future riots against blacks. In 1849 the *Irish-American* congratulated the Sixth Ward for not brawling during the elections. In the worst incident of rioting before the Draft Riots, at least seven Irish laborers were among the 22 people killed in the bloody fighting at Astor Place in May 1849. In the greatest battle between the gangs, the Dead Rabbit Riots of 1857, there was no mention of abuse of African Americans or their institutions. And while the rest of the city was aflame, during the infamous Draft Riots of 1863, the ward was quiet.[31]

As the Irish battled against perceived grievances, African Americans displayed open hostility against slavery. In 1837 blacks formed a committee of vigilance that confronted slave catchers in the streets. Tugs of war over fugitives often broke into violence. Policeman William H. Bell recorded one such confrontation in early 1851. Angered by the city marshall's determination to return a fugitive slave to his master in Virginia, a crowd of blacks and whites surrounded a "Southern Gentleman" in City Hall Park in the lower part of the ward. Before the police could get to him, the angry mob beat the Southerner in retaliation for the forced return of the fugitive. Such black assertiveness did not provoke violence among Irish residents.[32]

Perhaps the Irish were content with their enormous political superiority. Organized political behavior clearly favored the Irish, who participated in the emerging working-class politics of the 1840s in two ways. They shared with blacks the opprobrium of nativist politics and evangelical crusading. On occasion, Irish newspapers even showed glimmers of sympathy for the slave. Early in the century, the Federalist *Political Bulletin and Miscellaneous Repository*, aimed at an Irish audience, published a number of abolitionist articles. Gilbert Vale, the radical equal rights editor of the *Diamond* in the early 1840s, promoted opposition to slavery, though he argued that wage slavery was much worse. The *Irish-American* disavowed any support for slavery and commended Irish reformer priest Father Theobald Mathew for his abolitionist efforts, but condemned black activist Frederick Douglass as a "sworn enemy of republican institutions" and offered support to the American Colonization Society.[33]

In truth, the Irish had nothing to fear politically from African Americans. Emancipation from slavery in 1827 in the state of New York brought a long-awaited, but very limited, civil freedom to blacks. The end of slavery did not offer economic, political, or social equality to blacks. Their declining numbers and the unshakable racism of the political parties doomed the valiant efforts of black clergy and activists to regain the vote for blacks. New York remained intransigent toward black citizenship. Voting restrictions limited the ballot to blacks worth more than $250 under the constitution of 1821. There were six qualified black voters in a population of 1,073 in the Sixth Ward in 1845. Full black male suffrage did not arrive in New York until the passage of the Reconstruction Amendments in the middle 1860s.[34]

Unlike African Americans, however, the Irish reaped many gains from political allegiance. Two major legislative drives propelled Irish citizenship and with it, access to government patronage and work in the licensed trades. Nativism spurred the initial reform that emanated from a dispute between native-born carters and butchers and the mayor over licenses awarded to "aliens" during the War of 1812. This fractious quarrel culminated in legislation in 1826 restricting permits to citizens. Although this legislation applied primarily to cartmen, it soon extended to all licensed workers. Unintentionally, the legislation greatly increased the value of citizenship to Irish aliens.[35]

Believing erroneously that their monopolies were spared, the nativist-licensed trades faced more opposition in 1829 from the Workingmen's Movement, which attacked their privileges as authoritarian relics of English rule. The Workingmen's Petition sought abolition of all licenses, a position supported by the Irish and blacks. After the initial hubbub, the issue lay dormant for several years. In 1836 the Loco-Foco movement, a radical spur of the Democratic Party, made equal access to licenses its chief political goal. As the Democratic Party gradually accepted Loco-Foco reforms, it massively enfranchised the Irish, qualifying them for licenses. Swapping licenses for votes enabled the Democratic Party to sweep the Sixth Ward for decades. This neat exchange further encouraged municipal reformers to loosen regulations in the 1840s, creating structures mixing mercantile and capitalist allotments of patronage. Politically, this meant that the Democratic Party could advertise itself as the "true home of the working classes" while favoring the Irish. The Democrats adapted the rhetoric of the American Revolution to fit the rise of symbolic leaders like Mike Walsh, and, most importantly, the spread of patronage throughout the burgeoning public sector. In addition, the Democratic Party rewarded Irish support with appointments to the ranks of police, fire, sanitation, and minor city officials.[36] The explosion in patronage intensified the political weaknesses of blacks. The Democrats refused blacks access to patronage and Whigs rarely mounted sincere efforts for their African American constituents. In short, Irish adoption of what has been called the "wages of whiteness" came not from any innate prejudice, but rather from cooperation with the existing political system.[37]

To gain a toehold in society, Sixth Ward Irishmen poured into carting. Thomas Mooney, in his famous guide for arriving Irish immigrants, described the conditions of carting to aspiring immigrants as the "road to success . . . common to all." The task always earned "advanced wages," provided good connections for future mobility, and was a good "business connection." Carting, noted Mooney, cost little to set up; a horse, cart, and harness cost about $150. Upkeep was minimal. Empty lots served as stables; horses could be fed for $1.50 per week, the carter for $2.50; "cab-tax, horse-shoes, and wear and tear" amounted to half a dollar for a total of $5 per week, an outlay costing little compared with the benefits of the trade.[38]

Mooney misled his compatriots somewhat. When licensed carters gained the right to "horse-hire" their carts, by employing day laborers as drivers in 1844, they expanded their holdings into fleets. Such growth required more stableroom. Virtually all the owners of cart fleets listed in the superintendent's roster of licensed drivers in the 1850s lived in the northern wards of the city. Few of the nearly six hundred Irish cartmen living in the Sixth Ward owned their carts.

These transformations instituted a class division among carters. Ownership of a fleet, or even a good wagon placed one carter above another.[39]

This division resolved the issue of race within the trade. There had been periodic African American attempts to integrate the trade before 1840, but mayors cited custom and law as excuses to decline licenses to blacks. By 1850 black carters are listed in the census, although they could not obtain licenses until the mayorality of Fernando Wood. The few black carters working in the 1850s were harbingers of future changes. By 1900, more than 1,400 blacks drove public carts in the city. The class divisions and racial integration of carting meant that Irish and black carters as wage laborers had more in common than the monopolistic master carters. In addition, both Irish and blacks worked as porters, the simplest form of transport worker. In both trades, black and Irish laborers shared work experiences and philosophies.[40]

Loosened government control allowed Irish and blacks access to other licensed trades. The minor trades of pawnbrokers, intelligence officers (job referral services), and rag and junk dealers lining the blocks of the Bowery and Orange and Centre Streets were of mixed ethnicity. Equal rights logic demanded licenses for all, and the city awarded individual franchises to a host of Irish and black petty entrepreneurs. By 1854 there were 32 licensed junk shop dealers on Orange Street alone. Although displaying gratuitous anti-Semitism, George Foster slurred these entrepreneurs as "jews of course," the diary of William Bell, a policeman patrolling the Sixth Ward in 1850, lists many unlicensed Irish and black peddlers. Dealing in clothing, furniture, junk, and jobs, these brokers reflected the surface of an underground economy. Bell's diary is filled with citations to Irish and black residents of Orange Street for selling goods without licenses or for fencing stolen property.[41] A number of smaller trades were interracial. For example, hairdressers, whom Mooney advised arriving Irishmen were "generally black, or copper coloured men," was an interracial occupation by 1860; of 29 listed barbers in the Sixth Ward, 12 were Irish, 9 were African American, and 8 were from France, Italy, or Germany. Irish and black men shared the labors of public waiters and scavengers.[42]

All of these trades were fairly low in status. In contrast, a more lucrative trade remained segregated. Butchers were another licensed occupation losing their exclusive monopolies. Once famous for their solidarity, the butchers found their earning power and potential now tied to ownership of a stall or, in the new setup, stores. Stall owners remained ensconced at older markets downtown. Stores became the venue for ethnic butchers, especially German ones, who operated beyond the scope of the butcher's downtown monopoly. Many of the younger butchers living in the downtown wards were journeymen without shops or stalls. These changes were not as apparent as in other trades. Possessed of political strength, stronger trade unity, a bank, and a boisterous culture, butchers resisted industrialism until after the Civil War. While class differences were a distant threat, meat cutting remained a preserve for New Yorkers of

TABLE 4.2. Sixth Ward Groceries and Porterhouses

	1846		1851		1860	
	Groceries	Porterhouses	Groceries	Porterhouses	Groceries	Porterhouses
North (Anthony)	11	15	17	25	7	9
Centre	10	15	2	12	8	37
Cross	7	9	16	13		
Elm	7	4	24	13	10	11
Leonard	4	2	9	12	8	2
Mulberry	42	7	28	25	33	37
Mott	29	19	26	12	46	25
Orange (Baxter)	33	6	40	28	24	31
Bowery					18	50
Walker					24	
Other	43	6	46	19	19	44

Sources: *Doggett's New-York Directory of 1846 & 1847* (New York, 1846); *Doggett's New York Street Directory for 1851* (New York, 1851); *Wilson's Business Directory of New York City* (New York, 1860).

European descent. As the Irish shared opportunities with Anglo-Americans, Dutch, and Germans, the door was closed to women and to blacks. There were no women of any race or black men listed among 1,208 butchers in the 1860 directory. Although they seldom worked with blacks, butchers were steady customers at Five Points and Bowery dives.[43]

Perhaps the most public mixing occurred at porterhouses and groceries, which the Sixth Ward housed in abundance. Table 4.2 indicates the number of grocers and porterhouses by street. In 1850 the ward had a population of 24,000, 204 groceries, and 169 licensed porterhouses, which meant that 1 out of every 60 residents of the ward was selling liquor to the rest. Although every street in the ward had a few groceries and porterhouses, the majority were bunched along Mulberry, Mott, and Orange (Baxter). The nature of the two businesses meant that generally all races and genders were acceptable customers. In one example, Michael Crown, a grocer working at the corner of Anthony and Little Water Street in the heart of the Five Points, was about to close at two o'clock in the morning when someone asked for admission to his shop. In his subsequent testimony, Crown noted that he "knew the person calling to be one Alexander Davis, who was in the practice of coming about the store." After drinking some whiskey at the grocery, Davis and a second black man, Samuel Daily, attempted to rob Crown. Crown called for help and a mob of whites chased the pair down the street. Was this an example of racial violence? Perhaps, but the testimony also attested to easy familiarity between the grocer and his black customers.[44]

Grocers catered to the laboring class of the ward, selling items in infinitesimal quantities and remaining open 18 hours a day. Credit was necessary to secure return customers. Grocers gained their greatest profits not from food but from the sale of alcohol, legal after 1841. Despite attempts to curb liquor sales in 1836 and 1856, which temporarily reduced the numbers of groceries and ale-houses, their numbers steadily increased. The huge increase in porterhouses and grocers did not mean a broader base of wealth because the hundreds of ale and food vendors in the Sixth Ward were usually employees of a distant landlord.[45]

The previous examples have emphasized public interaction among African Americans and Irish. Inside New York's homes, gender and racial equality were common. In the Sixth Ward, Irish women dominated the boardinghouse trade, with 10 entries in the 1860 directory to 7 for Irish males, and scattered German, Italian, and English keepers. Black boardinghouses were known by word of mouth rather than print. George Thompson maintained a house sheltering seven sailors and three dressmakers. Next door Andrew Coleman, a black carter, rented part of his house to an Irish cigar maker and his wife.[46]

Similar shared experiences took place among domestics working in the middle-class houses of the city. Although a few males worked in the field, domestic service seemed the most promising opportunity for Irish and black women. During the colonial and early national period, African Americans were the largest body of domestics. Attitudes toward servants became interwined with racial hatred, which later influenced ethnophobic attitudes toward the Irish.[47] Domestic service expanded exponentially between 1830 and 1870. Two factors fueled this transformation. First, growing racism after the final extinction of slavery in New York State in 1827 and the ensuing social disintegration of the African American community pushed the black population out of the city. Second, as slavery ended, newly freed black women asserted their independence by constant shuttling between domestic employments. Third, as married women of New York's growing middle class discarded postrevolutionary antipathies against household work and sought relief from the unending chores, vast if ill-paid opportunities opened. As early as 1826 the Society for the Encouragement of Faithful Domestic Servants noted the growing significance of Irish women in the occupation. By 1855 Irish women accounted for 92 percent of the domestic work force.[48]

Domestic work had few rewards. The work was unceasing and drab. Domestics hauled water and firewood, disposed of human and other waste, washed, cleaned floors, and minded children in an atmosphere of hostility and exploitation, at the beck and call of their mistresses. Nonetheless, young Irish women arriving in New York preferred the $4 to $7 per month plus room and board they received for domestic work to the harsh, unhealthy, and insecure conditions of factory labor. Like laborers, domestics moved readily from job to job. The exploitative nature of the work negated any feelings of loyalty, and female domestics quickly learned to bargain for their value. Mooney asserted that domestics who quickly learned American modes of housewifery and who displayed loyalty and hard work could expect up to $7 a month plus board in a comfortable home, "where she will be treated nearly as an equal by the Lady of House." Despite his cheery words, Irish women were less sanguine and displayed what Mooney called their Irish spirit by frequently changing masters and mistresses.[49] At the bottom of domestic work, blacks and Irish women worked together as washerwomen. The 1860 directory lists eight Irish and eight black washerwomen living in the Sixth Ward.[50]

Boredom, poor conditions and wages, and shrill mistresses produced a rapid turnover. Yet the occupation remained attractive because black and Irish domestics shared equally poor chances for marriage and family life. The demand for domestics in the colonial period and after the American Revolution caused a gender imbalance in the city's black population. With many black men employed as sailors, the numbers of black families with female-headed households far exceeded those of whites. Among blacks between the ages of 15 and 40 in 1860, females outnumbered males in New York County by 4,267 to 2,672. Females accounted for 56 percent of the black population. Similarly, 58 percent of the city's Irish were female in 1855. Irish and black female domestics shared a second demographic trait. Few had children. In 1860, there were ten percentage points fewer black women with children than white females. Domestic work also lowered the Irish birth rate. As poverty, drinking, fighting, and desertion undermined marital relations, matrimony became devalued, and Irish female-headed families became common.[51]

The decline of family life produced an advantage for a few women. Delayed marital patterns, access to education, and cultural influences trickling down from the mistress enabled black and Irish domestics to move up in society. As modern forms of education and medicine blossomed, single or late-marrying women found opportunity and class mobility in school teaching and nursing.[52] Irish women and a few blacks gained employment as typists in emerging businesses. Sadly, such successes were rare. For those who did not marry, illness and old age presented problems of support. Lacking children to look after them, cut off from their communities and support networks, the single Irish and black women who inhabited the prisons, asylums, and the poorhouse were invariably spent domestics.[53]

A look at the census taken in the Tombs in 1860 dispels any illusions about the conditions for women in the Sixth Ward. As might be expected, Irish prostitutes were the greatest perpetrators of minor crimes of intoxication, public lewdness, petty larceny, and, sadly, pauperism. Reflecting the troubles of their status, however, there are significant numbers of servants, housekeepers (domestics), day laborers, and washerwomen whose crimes commonly included petty larceny and intoxication.

Weary of their poverty and the exploitative routine of factory piecework or the relentless harassment of domestic service, and with the gender imbalance for black and Irish women, many of these women either flirted with prostitution or embraced it. Love for sale could be an avenue of mobility for women. To the despair of moralists, prostitutes frequently earned more than their factory and domestic sisters. Despite their lives of desperation, prostitutes had career paths to follow and successes were folk heroes. Although prominent families actually owned many brothels, the most common individual female property owners in the ward were madams. The center of love markets was the Five Points. Here, historian Timothy Gilfoyle has charted at least 17 domiciles for sex at the crossroads of Anthony, Leonard, Orange, and Center in each of the four decades from 1820 to 1859.[54]

Five Pointers articulated their tough, raucous lives through a special night speech known as "flash talk," used to describe fast food places, drinking holes, dance halls, gambling halls, pawnshops, lodging houses, prostitutes, scams, and sports. "Going the rounds" or "on a bender" meant a drinking spree. Professional thieves were known as "crossmen," while burglars were called "crackmen," who worked together "on the dub . . . to crack a can" or break into a house. Streets had slang names. Anthony Street from Centre Street to the Five Points was Cat Hollow; Little Water, the southern edge of Paradise Square, occupied by two black and two Irish taverns, was called Dandy Lane.[55]

Language became song and dance at the markets, hotspots in the public economy, where black and Irish hucksters sold many varieties of food and filled the air with their poignant cries and songs while Irish butchers watched as blacks "danced for eels" at the nearby Catherine Market. Black and white female fruit and corn sellers shared territories on the streets, respecting each other's monopoly over favored corners. Originally a black tradition dating back into the eighteenth century, hot corn girls became universal during tough times in the 1840s. Legends grew about beautiful young women of indeterminate ethnicity selling corn and being the beloved of gang leaders.[56]

Tavern life, a staple since the earliest colonial days, shook races, classes, and genders in a rum punch. In Five Points bars, Irish and black revelers danced, sang, and courted to popular melodies composed from European and African rhythms. One visitor to a black tavern noted the mingling of black and white musical styles: "In the negro melodies you catch a strain of what has been metamorphosed from such Scotch or Irish tune, into somewhat of a chiming jiggish air." One Irishman is said to have "commenced humming, in a low tone, the popular negro melody of 'Mary Blane,'" but it seems "there was nothing in this to arrest particular attention." Walt Whitman argued in his Daybooks and Notebooks, that such mixing of cultures presaged a "native grand opera in America."[57]

Dance halls, attended by local blacks, Irish, and sailors, created a racial blend. George Foster described the hot music played at Peter Williams': "That red-faced trumpeter . . . looks precisely as if he were blowing glass, which needles [of sound] penetrating the tympanum, pierce through and through the brain without remorse . . . the bass drummer . . . sweats and deals his blows on every side, in all violation of the laws of rhythm." Another attraction was the fabled dancer, Juba, whom Dickens described dancing as Williams, performing the "single shuffle, double shuffle, cut and cross cut . . . spinning about on his toes and heels like nothing but the man's fingers on the tambourine." Juba and Peter Williams became so well known by 1850 that local sports regarded them as tame, preferring a dark cellar known as the Diving Bell. Located in a remote cellar on the Bowery, here "blacks mixed in freely with the gang" as interracial rowdies danced.[58]

Equally shocking to the middle classes was the neighborhood's predilection for what the nineteenth century termed amalgamation. Interracial love was sparked in such bordellos as the Diving Bell, Swimming Bath, and Arcade on Orange Street, and in the nearby Yankee Kitchen, Cow Bay, and Squeeze Gut Alley. Recording his visit of the early 1840s, Charles Dickens beckoned to his readers, "Let us go on again . . . and plunge into the Five Points." Accompanied by two policemen on a visit to Peter Williams' tavern, Dickens gaped as Irish and black men and women drank, danced, and made love. After Dickens, no popular construction of the Five Points was complete without a description of a love affair between a black man and an Irish woman.[59]

Brothels and dance halls were not the only venues for interracial love. Although Irish kinship ties in the Sixth Ward were very strong, occasionally Irish men and women took partners from other ethnic groups. A few brave Irish defied social sanctions and even married blacks. In the years after the 1834 riot, mixed couples appeared regularly in the Sixth Ward. One early indication of such unions was the children who fell into the clutches of the House of Refuge after 1840.[60] Peter Williams, a fifty-three year old Danish seaman, lived openly with his wife Deborah, a black woman from Maryland. Another union was blessed with young children. William Moore, a black male laborer, married an Irish woman, Winnifred. They lived with a 12-year-old son and a 2-year-old daughter at 228 Mulberry Street. Perhaps the bravest was John Baker, a black carter married to an Irish woman named Julia. Baker faced burly opposition on the street while living in a marriage which could provoke assault from thugs.[61] In 1860, 10 years after the Fugitive Slave Act, which sent hundreds of New Yorkers fleeing to Canada, Stephen Sanders, a black chimney sweep from Virginia, his wife Mary, from Ireland, hosted assorted boarders from Germany, Ireland, and New York City. One home sheltered two interracial couples. John DePoyster, a black laborer and his wife, Bridget, from Ireland, shared a house with John Francis of Virginia and his Irish wife Susan.[62]

Even in the late 1860s, several years after the fierce attacks on blacks during the Draft Riots, assaults that often took on a psychosexual tenor, interracial couples thrived in the Sixth Ward. When only 203 blacks lived in the entire ward, surrounded by almost 12,000 Irish, the presence of 11 interracial couples stands out. The men worked as laborer, seaman, boardinghouse keeper, carter, porter, servant, sweep, and liquor dealer.[63] These marriages are not significant numerically but have great symbolic importance. Irish men and women, from a people not known for intermarriage, wedded African Americans and defied the racist conventions of their times to build genuine relationships and at times families. Although popular commentators generally sneered at such marriages, the men's occupations suggest serious commitment rather than casual romance.[64]

In sum, the relations of Irish and African Americans were polyvalent, but there is no easy explanation for them. Although they competed economically and lived closely together, Irish and black coexisted far more peacefully than historians have suggested. Day-to-day contact was as harmonious as could be in a tough, urban slum, while nighttime leisure produced a syncretic culture. A few brave souls intermarried. The example of the Sixth Ward contrasts with James O. Horton's interesting findings on relations between blacks and Germans in Buffalo, New York, in the nineteenth century.[65] Blacks and whites in Buffalo apparently got along when there was little competition for work or housing; blacks and Irish in the Sixth Ward cohabited in a slum where work was scarce and casual. Daily contact created a toleration not present in wards of greater segregation, which produced, for example, the draft rioters of 1863 and their racial terrorism.[66] Although disharmony and conflict abounded, there were also many points of cooperation and exchange. In their mutual experiences in the crowded Sixth Ward, black and Irish found common ground and affection.

John Kuo Wei Tchen

CHAPTER 5

Quimbo Appo's Fear of Fenians

CHINESE-IRISH-ANGLO RELATIONS IN
NEW YORK CITY

IN A locked antiseptic room, the man whom the New York City newspapers dubbed "the Chinese devil man" was screaming that he was being harassed by the "Fenian party" and that for political reasons, the Democrats had conspired with the governor to delay his release from prison. The year was 1883, a year after the passage of the Chinese Exclusion Law. A doctor's typed notes documented the regularly drugged patient's statements over the years.

Mar. 30, 1885. Has delusion that he has been, and is now, suffering for the cause of Ireland and that he must suffer until she is free. . . .

Feb. 26, 1890. Is at times irritable and always preserves a sense of his own importance. . . . He believes that he has grand hotels, palaces, servants and horses outside of the asylum; says he is King of the World and has power over the sun, the wind, and over day and night, and that he is omnipotent. Often he is very happy in his delusions and says he is a Second God.

Nov. 7, 1893. Claims to have power of taking away votes.

Sept. 9, 1895. Imagines that he owns ten hotels and all the laundries in the country.

Jan. 4, 1899. Imagines that he owns Madison Square Garden. . . . Says he was the first Chinaman that ever came to America and while in China he ran the largest tea trade of any man in that country.

Jan. 2, 1907. He says that he is the World Law and has immense sums of money, has a number of hotels in New York City where his National Palace is located. Says that he has many gun boats on the Hudson River and that soon 400,000 [B]oxers are coming to this institution, raze it to the ground and release him.[1]

Such a sampling of this deluded man's purported statements are all the more startling when one learns who this man used to be.

Five days into 1878, Quimbo Appo, who two decades earlier had been cited by the *New York Times* as the "exemplary Chinaman," was incarcerated in the Matteawan State Hospital for the Criminally Insane. His "certificate of insanity" stated that the once prominent tea merchant married to an Irish woman had no known trade, was widowed, had two previous convictions, and was most recently convicted of manslaughter. His "form of Insanity" was described as "mania with delusions" and its cause hypothesized to be "probably [from] confinement?—." Although he had a living son named George Washington Appo, the once popular leader of the community had "none" filled in for "Name and address of nearest relative or friend." The prison physician signed a statement explaining his reasons for committing Appo to the insane asylum: "He imagines and believes that great numbers of persons visit him in his cell and also the Holy Virgin and numerous other personages—with a variety of other delusions. His general condition is such as not to be trusted out of close confinement." He was to remain at Matteawan until his death in 1912.[2]

How can Quimbo Appo's variegated, cross-cultural delusions be understood? Conspiring political parties, Fenians, Ireland, Madison Square Garden, laundries, Boxers on the Hudson? Should they simply be dismissed as the rantings of a crazed man? Perhaps. Yet, Appo's paranoia was not without basis. His life's story bears reconstruction and examination because it offers a glimpse into the experiences of the Chinese in lower Manhattan, especially in relation to the neighborhood's large Irish population and the metropolis's well-established Anglo-Protestant political culture. Mr. Quimbo Appo's fall from grace embodied the profound shift of attitude New Yorkers had toward Chinese in their midst. What happened to Appo over his life in Gotham? And what was the social and historical context of his "insanity"?

An "Exemplary Chinaman"

While conducting a survey of the Chinese in lower Manhattan in 1854, the British missionary Edward Syle was directed to Quimbo Appo, an English-speaking tea seller who seemed to have been the single best-known Chinese in New York. In contrast to the "heathens" Syle visited in their tenements, the missionary was favorably impressed with Appo and his business acumen. "I saw a veritable Chinaman," Syle wrote in a somewhat surprised tone, "playing his part as a salesman with an alacrity of movement and flourish of manner that was quite exemplary." In contrast to a troupe of stranded and now-begging

Chinese actors on Broadway, New Yorkers viewed Appo as one who knew how to operate in the commercial environs of New York and as an independent, rational individual. From Syle's admiring vantage, Appo "wanted nobody to take care of him but was abundantly able to be the guardian of his own interests."[3]

Appo told Syle he was born in 1825 in Zhusan, an island off the mouth of the Yangtze River on the midcoast of China, and had lived through the British bombing of Shanghai during the Opium Wars. How much of his biography can be taken at face value is difficult to say, Appo, however, does appear to have been one of the Chinese who took to the trade routes to the West. He claimed to have traveled with Prussian missionary Karl Gutzlaff into forbidden interior sections of China. Gutzlaff mistakenly believed that the Chinese needed only to be exposed to Christianity to convert en masse. (He had proposed that Americans emulate the Prussian practice of sending missionaries on opium trading vessels.) Living on an island under constant battles for control by the West, Appo was in all likelihood among those Chinese nationals who gained access to Western ships after the 1842 Treaty of Nanjing. Zhusan was a strategic island for British and American opium traders. Appo said he then sailed to Yerba Buena in 1847, before the United States claimed the territory. After the discovery of gold at Sutter's Mill, he went to the gold fields and was reportedly involved in killing two Mexicans in self-defense. They had killed one of his partners while attempting to steal their gold. Some time afterward he sailed to Boston as a cook and steward on the *Vandalia*. Later in New Haven, he married an Irish American named Catherine Fitzpatrick. They eventually moved to New York, where he found work at a tea store. They had a daughter and a son. Their son was born on the Fourth of July and they named him George Washington Appo.[4]

Appo functioned well in English and was a shrewd storekeeper. While in the store, Syle was impressed by an incident Appo recounted. A customer wanted to change a dollar note for a small quantity of coffee. Appo told the customer: "You want to change this note, [you] must buy half a pound, then can do." The surprised customer then did as the savvy Appo required.[5]

Appo, it seems, was not totally self-serving. An 1856 *New York Times* reporter called upon "Crimpo" Appo to gain access to cigar peddlers. Appo was willing to talk to the reporter about his countrymen for he hoped "public attention could be directed to the condition of some of them—particularly those who sold cigars in the street—for the cold of Winter would soon debar them from this mode of obtaining a sustenance." Appo took the opportunity to advertise the desperate plight of vendors through the *Times* article. "Being totally unacquainted with the language and customs of this country, they are unfitted for almost any City work, but they are anxious to be employed, and would like situations on farms."[6]

According to journalist Louis Beck's often-cited 1898 book *New York's Chinatown, An Historical Presentation of Its People and Places*, Appo was the first Chinese resident of New York. He was credited as "a man of great intelligence, gifted with a mind whose keenness startled all white men who came in contact with him." "Those associated with him," wrote Beck, "were charmed with his winning manner, and there was no greater pleasure in those days, when Chinamen were still but rarely seen on our streets, than to meet Quimbo Appo in a genial mode and listen to the endless stories he had to relate."[7]

Appo lived and worked at a tea store located at 50 Spring Street, well above the poverty of the Fourth and Sixth Wards. He did not own the store, but apparently earned a decent wage. Tea was a major import item for the port of New York. By 1860 tea merchants in New York handled $8.3 million of a national total of $8.9 million of imported tea.[8] Retailing tea promised opportunities for Chinese in the city.[9] Four fellow tea dealers were visiting Appo when the *Times* reporter arrived to meet him. "One young fellow, quite dandyish in his appearance, wearing a shawl, and all that, announced his intention of learning to read and write the language, to become an American citizen, and to marry an American girl." For this aspiring tea dealer, Appo must have been a successful role model. He could speak English and had married an American woman. Not having much of a Chinese constituency from which to draw customers, operating in a Chinese dialect was not a viable option for these merchants. Being able to effectively communicate with English-speaking New Yorkers, then, was a key prerequisite for these budding merchants to do well. The younger man's attitude clearly indicated a willingness to intermix with his non-Chinese neighbors.[10]

Indeed, this anecdotal journalistic information is supported by what can be found in the New York City census. From the 1820s to the 1870s, a modest but telling number of Chinese settled in the port of New York. It can be called the pre-Chinatown settlement because Chinatown did not really develop until the late 1870s. During this time, one of four Chinese men found in the city were married to Irish women and many had families. These Chinese men took on Anglo first names, and some took Anglo first and last names. They became citizens and appeared to have every intention of staying. William Brown, for example, was a Chinese man who worked as a ship steward. He had lived in New York since 1825 and was married to Rebecca Brown, an Irish woman who had come to New York at the age of 7 and lived in the city for 20 years. Their 6-year-old son William was a native New Yorker. John Huston was born in China and he was 28 years old in 1855. He arrived in New York in 1829 and was married to Margaret Huston, a 26-year-old Irish woman. They had two young daughters, Kate and Mary. He was a seaman and a naturalized U.S. citizen. In 1870, William Assing lived at 66 Cherry St. with his Irish wife Bridget Assing, 33. They had four boys. The oldest was 14 and the youngest 2 months, indicating some stability and longevity in their relationship. He reported a personal wealth of $700, the equivalent of 23 months of pay for a sailor.[11]

It should be emphasized that the documented settlement was small. In 1855, 1865, and 1870 only some 65 Chinese were officially reported to be living on Manhattan Island. Nevertheless, Chinese Irish marriages were sufficiently noticeable in New York City to merit regular comment in the city's newspapers, even warranting caricatures and drawings, which dominated the media's representation of Chinese in New York. *Harper's Weekly* reported in 1857 that 28 Irish women selling apples have "gone the way of matrimony with their elephant-eyed, olive skinned contemporaries." And in 1858 *Yankee Notions* featured an Irish woman, her Chinese husband, and their two Irish-Chinese sons on the cover.[12] In 1869, the completion of the transcontinental railroad inspired a *Harper's Weekly* graphic of two couples, both pairing a Chinese man and an Irish woman, walking arm-in-arm in front of the "Church of St. Confucius."[13] And decades later, in 1890, *Harper's Weekly* devoted a double-page centerfold spread showing a Chinese-Irish couple and their children.[14]

Those familiar with New York immigration and settlement patterns would not be totally surprised by this Chinese–Irish phenomenon. Chinese immigrés could be found in the Fourth and Sixth Wards of Lower Manhattan. The Fourth was located below and eastward of Chatham Square, with the East River as its southeastern border. It was a maritime-oriented ward, the center of the shipbuilding trade and the place where the industry's skilled workers lived. Sailors lodged in the area's many boardinghouses. Just above and to the west of Chatham Square was the Sixth Ward, which encompassed the present-day commercial core of Chinatown. Many Irish lived in these two wards up until the time of the Italian and Jewish immigration in the 1880s. Yet physical proximity alone would not necessarily account for these interethnic relationships. What might have brought Chinese men and Irish women together other than physical proximity?

Carol Groneman's and Hasia Diner's research on Irish women in New York sheds light on some of the shared experiences that laid the basis for these cross-cultural bonds. Groneman found that for Irish women between the ages of 15 and 29, there were 100 women for 80 Irish men. Over the decades a significant number of these women married partners of other ethnic groups. In the 1855 census, some 6.7 percent of these Irish women married non-Irish. Of the 1,430 Irish marriages recorded between 1853 and 1860 at the Sixth Ward's major Roman Catholic parish, the Church of the Transfiguration, 4.7 percent of the Irish women chose non-Irish partners. Though fairly modest statistically, given the large numbers of Irish immigrants in New York, this constituted a significant phenomenon. According to the 1855 census figures, somewhere between 2,707 and 3,762 Irish women in New York married non-Irish. During this same period, no Chinese women were recorded by the census-takers. Indeed, the first recorded birth of a "pure, unadulterated" New York child with both parents of Chinese birth was reported by the *New York Tribune* in 1885.[15]

The nature of port districts combined with Irish and Chinese demographics provided the conditions in which Irish women and Chinese men might come in contact. Because they were immigrants, their comparably modest socioe-conomic standing may have been a further basis of shared experience. Poorer Irish women frequently sold fruits and vegetables on the fringes of established marketplaces. Irish "apple women" were often spotted near City Hall Park, Printing House Square, and the Bowery. From the mentions in newspapers, it appears that a number of them joined together with Chinese men, who also peddled such goods as cigars and Chinese candies in that area.[16]

Besides marrying Chinese men, as Graham Hodges notes in chapter 4 some Irish women entered into relationships with African Americans, despite the concern among antiabolitionists that blacks commingling with whites were about to "mulattoize" whole neighborhoods. For this added reason, the already sensationalized Five Points became identified as a place in which the races mixed indiscriminately. In 1858 the xenophobic, Democratic Party paper, the *New York Evening Day Book* described the Sixth Ward as "the only spot, thank God, in these United States where the Abolition ideas is [*sic*] reduced to practice, [and] whites, negroes, and mongrels readily 'intermarry.'"[17]

Although the phenomenon of marriage across racial-ethnic lines was prob-ably greatly exaggerated by the antiabolitionists, the area was indeed an inter-national district in which cultures from around the world intermixed, forming a hybrid, creolised New York culture. The particular mix of people in New York was unusually diverse, however. The port of New York's rise to national and international importance brought ships and people from all around the world. The early Chinese settlement embodied this multiplicity. In 1835, for example, Lesing Newman was a 23 year old Chinese-born, naturalized citizen of the United States who was signed on to the ship *John Taylor* of New York, bound for Liverpool. That same year Ben Sanchez of China was on the New York ship *Adelaide* heading for Havana. The 1855 census noted a 17-year-old Singmer Dosai residing in the Fourth Ward. He was listed as a "mulatto" sailor (possibly Portuguese?) born in China. A 1856 *New York Times* article noted "a great many" Chinese walking the streets of New York having escaped "brutal task-masters" of the Peruvian Chincha Islands, where indentured "coolie" labor dug guano for fertilizing American farms. Chinese New Yorkers were therefore already embodying a cross-cultural mix of local, Peruvian, Cuban, Irish, and other cultures.[18]

The early small businesses of the area reflected this polyglot international culture. Ah Sue, for example, has been credited with being one of the first Chinese to open a small business. Tired of maritime travel, Sue landed at 62 Cherry Street in 1847, married an Irish woman named Murphy, and opened a small tobacco and candy store serving non-Chinese customers. In order to find a niche within the neighborhood economy, the Chinese had to quickly learn what their non-Chinese neighbors liked to buy. In the best of Lower East Side traditions in the making, the mixing of immigrants and native New Yorkers brought about a mixing of cultural goods as well. This interethnic fertilization also created at least one new form of cultural expression. Tap dancing has been documented as emerging from the Five Points mix of African and Irish dance traditions.[19]

In 1871 the Anglo-Protestant *Harper's Weekly* ran a graphic and article that underscored the creolised nature of these lower Manhattan wards. Entitled "Along the New York Docks," the article pictured an "unaristocratic international restaurant" run by a "good-natured, broad-breasted, jolly-faced" Irish woman catering to "Irishmen [who] jostled against 'niggers'; Chinaman, Frenchmen, Germans, [mingling] in perfect harmony." The quip about harmony was powerfully contradicted by a Chinese man being violently brought to his knees while others blithely carried on.[20] This article articulated a double message characteristic of Protestant Victorian New Yorkers. On the one hand, there was a definite fascination with this creolised downtown culture; on the other hand, there was great disgust and abhorrence of it.

In this worldview, both the Chinese and Irish were considered racial "others." The prodigious diarist, one-time mayor, and upper-class Whig George Templeton Strong clearly articulated how distant they were from Anglo-Protestant normalcy in his view. Strong wrote that the Irish were "almost as remote from us in temperament and constitution as the Chinese."[21] *Yankee Notions'* 1858 cover graphic mentioned earlier bears further examination in this regard. The mock dialogue of "The Result of the Immigration from China" between the Irish Mrs. Chang-Fee-Chow-Chy and the Chinese Mr. Chang-Honey expressed Strong's sentiments but in comic form.

> Mrs. Chang-Fee-Chow-Chy (the better half of the Celestial over the way).—Now, then, Chang-Mike, run home and take Pat-Chow and Rooney-Sing wid ye, and bring the last of the puppy pie for yer daddy. And, do ye mind? bring some praties for yer mother, ye spalpeens.
>
> (To her husband)—How be's ye, Chang Honey?
>
> Chang-Honey—Sky we po kee bang too, mucho puck ti, rum foo, toodie skee sicke.[22]

From this vantage, both the Chinese and the Irish are beyond the pale of civilized behavior.

In his 1870 piece "John Chinaman in New York," Samuel Clemens expressed one aspect of the dominant culture's fascination with the ethnic "mix-up." Clemens described a walk in Manhattan: "As I passed along by one of those monster American tea stores in New York, I found a Chinaman sitting before it acting in the capacity of a sign. Everybody that passed by gave him a steady stare as long as their heads would twist over their shoulders without dislocating their necks, and a group had stopped to stare deliberately." After a long meditation on how shameful Americans should feel that they "degrade a fellow-being" in this manner, "I pitied the friendless Mongol." While liberally protesting the treatment of this man, he titillated his readers with a detailed description of this stranger's odd dress:

Men calling themselves the superior race, the race of culture and of gentle blood, scanned his quaint Chinese hat, with peaked roof and ball on top, and his long queue dangling down his back; his short silken blouse, curiously frogged and figured (and, like the rest of his raiment, rusty, dilapidated, and awkwardly put on); his blue cotton, tight-legged pants, tied close around the ankles; and his clumsy blunt-toed shoes with thick cork soles; and having so scanned him from head to foot, cracked some unseemly joke about his outlandish attire or his melancholy face, and passed on.

Upon touching the man's shoulder in sympathy, Clemens stated: "Cheer up—don't be downhearted. America and Americans are always ready to help the unfortunate. . . . What wages do they pay you here?" The man replied in an Irish accent: "Divil a cint but four dollars a week and find meself; but it's aisy, barrin' the troublesome furrin clothes that's so expinsive."[23]

Such a Chinese–Irish mix-up was funny within the dominant culture because both groups were represented as comic figures. In this case, radical Republican sensibilities expressed their anti-Irish feelings by using their sympathetic Chinese caricatures as foils. A disgruntled Bricklayer's Union representative, for example, complained that the lack of proper building regulations to prevent the frequent collapse of buildings upon workers was due to anti-Irish prejudice. "Our philanthropists say that they are less than the 'nigger'" hence Irish injuries did not matter.[24] Whig and Republican politicians often advocated African American suffrage while denouncing Irish immigrant voters. As early as 1834 the New York *Journal of Commerce* stated: "We have among us a large number of native born COLORED PERSONS, whom the laws prohibit from voting, but who . . . are intelligent, and in many respects FAR BETTER QUALIFIED to participate in our elections than the [Irish] of whom we have been speaking."[25] In a parallel manner, many Whigs and Republicans believed that, like their "colored persons," Chinese were often more fit than the Irish Catholics to be citizens. New York Protestant pluralists rhetorically seemed to prefer blacks and Chinese over "their" despised and far more numerous Irish. Although such pluralism had clear limits, it formulated a widespread consensus among the Protestant elite of Gotham.

Others of the mainstream elite chided all three groups, making them the brunt of crass, but totally acceptable and commonplace public humor that pitted stereotypes of one racialized group against another in jest. Irish–Chinese mix-ups, for example, pervaded nineteenth century political culture, from *Yankee Notions'* 1854 "Hibernian Celestial" and *Harper*'s 1879 "How the Chinaman Might Gain Favor" (figure 5.1) to Allen's Jewel Five Cent Plug trade card and John Denison's 1895 vaudeville farce and mix-up "Patsy O'Wang." It was an enduring cross-cultural theme demonstrating the longlasting tensions felt by the Anglo elite toward their perceived Irish and Chinese inferiors.[26]

This European Protestant obsessive fascination formed the basis of another common Irish and Chinese New Yorker experience. As is well known, the Irish were a particularly favorite target of the Anglo-American elite. Thomas Nast, himself a German émigré, studied the political drawings of *Punch*'s Sir John Tenniel and adapted them to the American context. Acknowledged as the pioneer American political cartoonist, he fully accepted the physiognamatic assumptions informing British caricature of the Irish. As others have demonstrated, Irish men were predominantly represented as an ape-like, prognathous race of thugs.[27] Nast's Irish in *Harper's Weekly*, especially his riot scenes, were quite similar.[28] Such images were also typical of Johannes Keppler's drawings of the Irish. Keppler, the cofounder of the highly successful *Puck*, was the successor to Nast.[29] They differed mainly in the positions they took on the so-called Chinese question. Nast, in a limited sense, supported the Chinese in part because of his radical Republican convictions, but especially because this was a means of demonstrating his antipathy for the Irish. Yet, both Nast and Keppler's representations of Chinese were also informed by the mid–nineteenth century scientific theory and practice of physiognomy.[30]

Not surprisingly, individuals such as William and Bridget Assam also had to endure the condescension of patrician society. Both Chinese and Irish were seen

HOW THE CHINAMAN MIGHT GAIN FAVOR.

This *Harper's Weekly* political cartoon (Apr. 12, 1879) is a typical example of an Irish-Chinese "mix-up." (From the collection of John Kuo Wei Tchen.)

as comic and inferior by the upper classes. Such hierarchic relations were encoded into the established areas of Manhattan Island itself. Indeed, race, ethnicity, and class were indelibly encoded into the spatial arrangements of the early city. As the gentry moved uptown, immigrants, blacks and the working poor remained behind. Blacks could only afford housing in the still sunken and swampy Fifth and Sixth Wards. Before the Draft Riots of 1863, a poor, immigrant, and racially diverse downtown residential district was created in contradistinction to suburbanizing Anglo- and German-Protestant elites moving uptown.[31]

Whether they chose to or not, these Chinese men and Irish women found themselves entering the city in the same Lower East Side neighborhoods. Given the cultural geography of the urban landscape, their shared spatial relations in the city implied a shared economic, immigrant, and situational experience. Differences of appearance, language, and cultural practices were in these cases of intermarriage seemingly overcome by their common concerns and experiences. The Lower East Side not only provided the basis for the intermixing of cultures but also fostered a countervailing phenomenon. The catastrophic violence that befell the Appo household embodied the growing tensions between Chinese and Irish in Lower Manhattan.

The Trial and Contested Stories

Apparently all was not marital bliss between Quimbo Appo and Catherine Fitzpatrick. One of their domestic quarrels erupted in violence and hit front-page headlines in the New York papers. With subsequent cycles of fights and imprisonment, violence turned into a way of life for Appo. Over the course of the next two decades, the upstanding merchant citizen fell from grace. Yet the details of what went wrong remained rather cloudy.

According to Louis Beck, the 1898 chronicler of New York Chinatown, Appo drank liquor. And when he was inebriated he was "a veritable Caliban" who was "dead to all human emotions." "At such times he was transformed into a fiend, with an insatiable craving for blood." He apparently married "a woman of the slums" but "in a fit of rage" cut his wife's throat. He was sentenced to be hanged but on the intervention of his Christian friends gained a new trial and was sentenced for second-degree murder and 10 years' imprisonment. In 1863 he was pardoned. Within a year of his release he quarreled with "a Pole" and killed him. He served five years for this act. Once he was out again, he married "Cork Mag" an Irish woman whom he supposedly knifed. She lived, and he went back to prison for a year. He was then transferred to the State Hospital for the Criminal Insane at Matteawan, where he lived out the rest of his years.[32]

Appo was still living while Beck published his vicarious and touristic book on Chinatown, and Beck described Appo in prison. "To all appearances he is perfectly rational, and for hours he will entertain you with stories of the old days in China and California. . . . But—bad as he is—and this is pitiful—when the Albany night boat passes Matteawan Appo points to the big search light that flashes in her bow and says proudly: 'That is my diamond. They bring it to me every night.'" Appo apparently believed he was a thousand years old. For Beck, "There were two Quimbo Appos—or rather a Jekyll and Hyde Appo—one shrewd, entertaining merchant, full of interesting reminiscences, bright eyed and smiling; the other an inhuman monster, delighting in the worst of crimes."[33] Beck used Quimbo Appo as a metaphor for New York's Chinatown and its residents—a community of unpredictable opposites in which evil lurked behind good at every turn.

The transcript of Quimbo Appo's 1859 murder trial, examined against newspaper coverage of his various crimes and trials, offers some insights into his world as he saw it. The character that emerges is quite different from Louis Beck's Caliban. Contrary to Beck's assertions that Appo "drank," creating in him an "insatiable craving for blood," which led him to cut his wife's throat, Appo was tried for the death of Mary F. Fletcher, his landlady. The location was 47 Oliver Street in the Fourth Ward. Quimbo Appo was returning home. It seems that during a fight between Appo and his wife, Mrs. Fletcher went to quiet them down. A scuffle broke out and she was stabbed and stumbled down the tenement stairs. Neighborhood Irish gathered and called for revenge. Emotions continued to run high the week after the arrests as people tried to steal Appo away to lynch him. During the trial no mention was made of his ever being drunk; testimony in fact indicated quite the opposite.[34] The jury convicted Appo of murder, but they "unanimously recommend[ed] him to mercy." The judge, however, for reasons not stated, sentenced him to be hanged.[35]

The governor of New York State stayed his execution and ordered a retrial. In the retrial, the reasons for his temporary reprieve became obvious. Despite being conversant in English, highly esteemed in the Chinese and larger communities, and a man of some means, Appo was not able to obtain adequate counsel. He retained a former judge as his attorney, but the man failed him miserably, showing up for the trial a half-hour late, unprepared even to make an opening statement. Unfamiliar with the laws of the state, and the "niceties of the English language," Appo was unable to evaluate the magnitude of these and other problems of his defense.[36]

In his retrial, Appo took the stand for the first time. He stated that he had come home to find his wife drunk after celebrating Mrs. Fletcher's birthday. Angered, he began to beat his wife and Mrs. Fletcher, and then other women in the building, came to her rescue. They hit him with their fists and one called him a "China nigger." Another hit him with a flatiron. He admitted stabbing his landlady, but only in self-defense "while endeavoring to escape from her and other women." Other witnesses testifying on his behalf said he was a man of good "peaceable" character, confirmed that Fletcher was not dead after being stabbed, and that all the Irish women "had been drinking intoxicating liquors to great excess."[37] Testimony appealing to stereotypes of Irish intemperance and misogyny were used to cast Appo as a victim and the Irish women as his victimizers. A sympathetic reporter described Catherine Fitzpatrick as a "low Irishwoman habitually drunk who would not cook his meals and neglected him in every particular" and charged that she had just been convicted of larceny and was in jail herself. With the appeal, it was decided that Appo should not be hanged but given a prison sentence of 10 years for the reduced charge of manslaughter.[38]

The trial testimonies suggest tensions over deployed stereotypes of race, to be certain, but also over gender and class. Appo's view of what happened differed significantly from the case of *The People*. In addition, the witnesses called to testify for and against Appo represented opposing perspectives of Irish and Chinese relations.

The prosecution constructed a case in which a violent, irrational, and misogynist Quimbo Appo struck out at his wife. The Irish women in the building came to Catherine Fitzpatrick's defense, and then several of them were stabbed by the crazed Appo, who escaped like a fugitive. Eight women testified for the prosecution. Two were the murdered landlady's daughters, one her sister (who also lived in the building), the sister's friend, and four neighbors. The proceedings depended little on the five men who testified. Patrick Fletcher, Mary's husband, two police officers, and a coroner gave brief statements, and one gave testimony that was withdrawn. The defence of Appo was clearly inept. Only James Barnes, a wheelwright, testified that the women at the Appos' apartment door "thought he would kill someone." Appo was then found guilty by the jury and sentenced to be executed.[39]

At the subsequent appeal, Appo was able to present his side of the story. In sharp contrast to the Irish women friends and relatives of Mary Fletcher who testified for the prosecution, fifteen white male witnesses, all in positions of authority, testified on his behalf.

A Doctor Elwood Irish testified that Appo was "an active and enterprising person—sober and honest, and sociable, quiet, and peaceable in his intercourse with his fellows and neighbors." Then six local men (with such names as Burnham, Whyte, Neubauer, and Briggs) signed a sworn affidavit supporting Irish's statement. Next, six police officers (including three sergeants) stated that Mrs. Fletcher and other women who had testified were known to be drunks. C. F. Williams, for example, stated that Appo had expressed "great anxiety and affection" for his wife and often complained of her "constant and excessive use of intoxicating liquors." In addition, on the day of the incident Mrs. Fletcher and two of the other witnesses were seen "drinking intoxicating liquors to great excess, and . . . they had been in the almost daily habit of so doing for a long time previously." Not only were these women represented as being habitually drunk, but they were also portrayed as unreasonably clannish to the point of not caring about justice. When the officer asked the women about what happened, they refused to help him, stating "they were of the same country as the deceased, and believed that it would disgrace them if they were to assist in preserving the life of a Chinese, or even to testify in his behalf."[40]

Officer James Youngs, who also testified at the first trial for the prosecution, stated he had known Appo for six years and "always considered him to be a very industrious, quiet, inoffensive man" who had never been known to commit a "bad act" or been found intoxicated. Indeed, he "was constantly in the habit" of visiting the station-house to get advice and "inform the police" of "any bad acts of his countrymen" and often helped preserve "order among the Chinese living in the ward." In stark contrast, Mrs. Appo was identified as "an Irish woman" who was regularly drunk and making "his" room "a place of resort for her friends to drink and carouse in," "much to the discomfort and annoyance of [the] defendant." In addition, Mrs. Fletcher was described by Patrolman Youngs as being an "intemperate woman" whom he had found drunk in the streets one day at eleven o'clock in the morning. Finally, two jurors, Mr. Miller and Mr. Grant, testified that they did not believe Appo's actions were premeditated in any way and therefore believed he was not "guilty of murder" and made a "recommendation to mercy."[41]

In all, 15 men of fairly significant local authority testified against 8 neighborhood Irish women. The story the women told was of neighborly concern and caring for an abused wife who was married to a violent, irrational, and dangerous man. Countering such a story was the portrayal of Appo as a law-abiding, industrious, peaceable man who was driven crazy by a drunken wife and her drunken friends. During the appeals process, white male authority held sway and Appo's murder indictment was reduced to manslaughter. His image as a good, hard-working, peaceable member of the Lower Manhattan community prevailed, at least for 1859.

Although there were only two sides to the trial, three viewpoints were articulated. The prosecution represented the views of some neighborhood Irish women who sought to protect Mrs. Appo. The defense represented not only Quimbo Appo's views as a respected member of the Chinese community, but also the class, gendered, and ethnic perspective of Protestant male authority. Officer Youngs and all the police who testified were, after all, the designated guardians of law and order in this Victorian city. Even though individual police officers may have been Irish, they were in this instance deracinated and protectors of the dominant moral order. At this moment in time, the alignment of such authority figures with Appo made all the difference in the outcome of the trial. Without such support during the original trial, he was unable to plead his position. And with such support in the appeals process, the women's case was easily supplanted.

A clear hierarchy can be teased out from this legal proceeding. In 1859 Irish women had more authority than a lone Chinese man, however much less authority than a Chinese man supported by the powers that be. Indeed, from a sheer class mobility perspective, it was better for someone like Catherine Fitzpatrick to marry a Chinese merchant than stay a single woman. As long as Victorian society still valued the Protestant-like Chinaman, she stood to gain social standing. In this particular case, being a working-class Irish woman was about the lowest position one could hold. Being male and behaving with "respectable" values was far more powerful and important. For Appo, and probably other Chinese men, Irish women offered the chance of having a family away from their homeland, yet they remained extremely vulnerable. They had to behave in certain ways that the real and symbolic authorities understood, or else they could easily be victimized and marginalized. Appo's regularly checking with the police, his English-language ability, and his respectable tea merchant status enabled him to be included within a Protestant pluralist moral economy. Even so, he could not stand alone in the eyes of New York law. With an incompetent protector, the tardy and ill-prepared former judge, he could not even defend himself against "low-class," neighborhood Irish women. Clearly, both Chinese men and Irish women were caught in precarious positions of social status and rights, but what about the dominant culture?

At first it would appear that male Victorian authority was in firm control. Yet, why the need to mobilize so many white men on Appo's behalf? Shouldn't a few have been more than enough? And why so much journalistic attention to his trial? If elite authority was so clear-cut, why wasn't the adjudication of the case much more straightforward?

Irish Uplift and Chinese Criminalization

The order of New York genteel society was itself in disarray at this time. The exploding population, the peoples from so many different cultures, the growing dehumanization of the city, the yawning divide between rich and penniless—all gave rise to great civic and private insecurity. The elite had a double problem: they had to reformulate British Victorian culture into American terms that would establish norms of behavior for their own guidance, and they had to acculturate and then assimilate others into their Protestant pluralist hierarchic order. In this time of great urban flux, proper codes of behavior and conduct had to be reestablished for their own children and for the non-Protestant and non-Western European entering Castle Garden.[42]

Within this context, Quimbo Appo's private affairs became a matter of public fascination. In the decade before the Civil War, he was represented by the media as a model citizen of his "race." Yet when he emerged again at war's end, Appo was presented as the embodiment of evil. Indeed, the local Chinese settlement itself became increasingly associated with opium dens, rats, and "criminal" activity. By 1882 Chinese workers were excluded from entering the United States altogether.[43] Although the position of the Irish in the anti-Chinese movement in California has been well documented, the role of New York's Irish in this criminalization and exclusion process has never been explored.[44] During the antebellum decades, the Irish achieved great individual and group accomplishments in Gotham. Yet many improved their status at the expense of others, that is, by demonizing racial "others."

Much immigrant and ethnic history in the United States has been written within the framework of Horatio Alger's *Ragged Dick* narrative: poverty, hard work, individual uplift, and modest success. Mobility is often ascribed to the ability of an ethnic group to take advantage of opportunities or, in the laissez faire ideal, to create their own opportunities for advancement. Such a unilateral approach often acknowledges the complicating factor of the stereotypes imposed on the group or their relations to the dominant structures of politics, economics, or morality. Hence what can be called a bilateral history discusses both fighting discrimination and making contributions through honest hard work.[45] Yet this effort to unravel Chinese and Irish relations within the dominant Anglo-American culture suggests an even more complex dynamic. A trilateral analysis of Irish and Anglo-Americans and Chinese, complicated by race, class mobility, and gender issues, is needed here.

It is well known that during the Draft Riots of 1863 Irish and other denizens of Lower Manhattan attacked fellow African American residents, leaving scores lynched and permanently driving them out of the Five Points area. Indeed, the great majority of Irish immigrants and their families became Democrats, the party that fiercely fought against Republicans and their abolitionist sermonizing about freeing blacks. The rebellion also spread to attacks on brothels and Chinese peddlers in the Fourth Ward, who were "suspected of liaisons with white women." The agitation had now become what seemed an "indiscriminate race riot."[46] Yet, the shift of anger from African to Chinese Americans was not as "indiscriminate" as might appear on the surface. Within the worldview of the Irish immigrant worker, the two were intimately interconnected.

Economic competition has been the most commonly cited reason for Irish antipathy to both blacks and Asians. Certainly, all three groups worked in vulnerable working-class occupations: "Both Irish and black men and women competed for positions as manual laborers, hodcarriers, white-washers, bootblacks, waiters, coachmen, cooks, and servants."[47] The recruitment of Chinese in the Pacific West and of the Irish for labor on the railroads is well known. As anti-Chinese agitation increased in the West, Chinese who migrated eastward took on the lower-status occupation of laundry work, which did not compete with the work of European American men. The elite Republican families of New York usually preferred to hire African American and later Chinese servants and cooks over the "intemperate" Irish. The first and nationally publicized efforts to recruit Chinese laborers in the East were undertaken to break Irish-led strikes in North Adams, Massachusetts, by replacing a Knights of St. Crispin union of male shoe and boot makers and in Belleville, New Jersey, by replacing a group of organized Irish women. Black workers were also used to break Irish strikes. An 1862 Brooklyn race riot was, in part, caused by tobacco workers' demands to fire black employees and rehire Irish, and the subsequent Draft Riots were led by displaced Irish longshoremen.[48] During the 1870s, New York Chinese men were commonly represented as displacing Irish and black women. Or, in the nineteenth-century language of urban stereotypes, "John Chinaman" was soon competing with "Bridget" and "Dinah" in washing dirty clothes, cleaning houses, and cooking for Victorian urbanites. And the New York media clearly delighted in this competition as a way to solve the annoying "servant problem."[49]

Irish competition with blacks and Chinese undoubtedly existed, and the strategy of replacing organized workers with unsuspecting workers of another culture was quite common, yet it is not a sufficient explanation for Irish antiblack and anti-Chinese feelings and actions. Few blacks actually took over Irish work; in fact, quite the opposite was the case. The same can be said for Chinese workers in California. Irish aggressively displaced occupational niches for both groups.[50] Irish fears need more than a socioeconomic explanation.

In finding a place for themselves in New York, the Irish among others sought to affirm their personal identities and to improve their lot. The creolised, international culture of Lower Manhattan at once dissolved national boundaries and reinforced them. Recent arrivals from Ireland found themselves rather unexpectedly to be hyphenated Irish-American ethnics by "descent" and denizens of a very mixed port neighborhood. Irish men and women could intermingle both culturally and physically with individuals of other cultures, while discovering how "Irish" they truly were. Hence, distinctively New York relationships were formed by the coupling of Irish women and African American men or Irish women and Chinese men, an intercultural relationship practice also common in other port cities such as the Limehouse District of East London, and especially in the more fluid plural cultures of the Caribbean and Latin American. Within the Anglo-American context, however, such practices were abhorred. On this count, the *New York Evening Day Book*, which catered specifically to Democratic and working-class sentiments, identified an Irish Five Pointer's existential dilemma. In 1858 the xenophobic newspaper wrote: "Sin, debauchery, and crime have destroyed all natural and truthful perceptions of their specific relations, and the white woman, corrupted and lost, of course sinks to the level of the negro."[51] The practice of Irish women marrying non-Irish men became a public and political matter. Here a survival strategy for women clashed with that of politically oriented men.

Good Irish male Democrats, who since 1827 were qualified to vote, were caught in a highly vulnerable and contradictory position. Reigning "scientific" notions of "natural" and "truthful" "specific relations" dictated that the mixing of races resulted in harmful and tragic consequences, debasing what were considered higher pedigrees to lower bastardized ones. The very coining of that ugly and still-used term "miscegenation" illustrates the position that Irish men would increasingly play in repressing Irish women's sexual and conjugal relationships with non-Irish and particular non-European Americans.

On Christmas day in 1863, complimentary copies of an anonymously penned pamphlet were sent out to a number of prominent antislavery leaders in the country. The seventy-two page pamphlet, *Miscegenation: The Theory of the Blending of the Races, Applied to the American White Man and Negro*, was being sold at New York newsstands for a quarter. The author asserted that the commonly used term "amalgamation" was an inadequate word. It referred to the "union of metals with quicksilver, and was in fact only borrowed for an emergency, and should now be returned to its proper significations." Instead, building on the popular racial sciences of physiognamy and phrenology, the pamphleteer offered a combination of the Latin *miscere* (to mix) with *genus* (race). The writer also argued that a more precise term could be found for black and white unions, that of *melaleukation,* from the Greek *melas* (black) and *leukos* (white). Written with the flourish of a seemingly committed abolitionist, the pamphleteer stood on the side of monogeneticists, arguing that "all the tribes which inhabit the earth were originally derived from one type" and that if "any fact is well established in history, it is that the miscegenetic or mixed races are much superior, mentally, physically, and morally, to those pure or unmixed." Hence, "all that is needed to make us the finest race on earth is to engraft upon our stock the negro element; the blood of the negro is the most precious because it is the most unlike any other that enters into the composition of our national life." The writer further asserted, far more radically than any abolitionist of the time, that "our Presidents" thought it "desirable the white man should marry the black woman and the white woman the black man—that the race should become melaleuketic before it becomes miscegentic." And the next steps would be to open California to an Asian racial intermixture that would create "a composite race which will hereafter rule this continent." The "leaders of Progress," to use the language of radical Republicans, "urge miscegenetic reform."[52] What was ascribed by the *Day Book* to be developing in Lower Manhattan, was now confirmed to be the abolitionist ideal—whites freely commingling with blacks and Chinese to create the new America.

The pamphlet, it turns out, was a Democratic hoax, written by two reporters for the *New York World*, David Goodman Croly and George Wakeman. Of the latter, little is known. He was 22 years old, a "clever young journalist" who the elder Croly had drawn into the collaboration. More important, in any case, was Croly. He was an Irish immigrant who was a proud, independent, and successful Democrat. He began in New York as a young apprentice silversmith, married a pioneer female journalist, bought a midwestern newspaper owned by his wife's relative, and made it into an "independent" Democratic newspaper. He returned to New York to become the city editor of the *World* just before the Civil War. Croly and Wakeman never revealed their hand in the pamphlet and their authorship was not made public until Wakeman's *World* obituary tipped his role in 1870. Their "clever" work sparked a firestorm of controversy reprinted in newspapers all across the nation and in Europe and ultimately echoed in the halls of Congress. During this Civil War period, miscegenation became the central issue in the national debates for the 1864 presidential campaign, eventually forcing radical Republicans like Thomas Nast to retreat.[53]

As an Irish New Yorker, Croly was well-attuned to both the mainstream image of Five Points Irish and the actual experience of the international district. With the Draft Riots still fresh in the minds of the reader, the *Miscegenation* pamphlet picked at a raw scab. "Notwithstanding the apparent antagonism which exists between the Irish and negroes on this continent," the masquerading Republican writers focused on Irish-African sexual unions, "wherever there is a poor community of Irish in the North they naturally herd with the poor negroes . . . connubial relations are formed between the black men and white Irish women . . . pleasant to both parties, and were it not for the unhappy prejudice which exists, such unions would be very much more frequent." Then, in spirited exaggeration, Croly and Wakeman deliberately transgressed the usual bounds of radical Republican arguments.

> The white Irishwoman loves the black man, and in the old country . . . the negro is sure of the handsomest among the poor white females. . . . The fusion, whenever it takes place, will be of infinite service to the Irish. They are a more brutal race and lower in civilization than the negro . . . coarse-grained, revengeful, unintellectual . . . below the level of the most degraded negro. Take an equal number of negroes and irish [*sic*] from among the lowest communities of the City of New York, and the former will be found far superior to the latter in cleanliness, education, moral feelings, beauty of form and feature, and natural sense.

The very same racial scientific language that was being used against the Irish and blacks was used here to assert that the Irish were lower than blacks. Irish were biologically inferior. The "prognathous skull, the projecting mouth, the flat and open nostril" were stated in positivist fashion to be characteristics of the "inhabitants of Sligo and Mayo." Only genetic intermixing could improve such lowly human stock.[54] Republican views were taken to such an extreme that they had to inflame even the most Protestant-oriented of lace curtain Irish. Croly understood what would raise the "ire" of his fellow countrymen and used this insight to advance the cause of the Democratic Party and those who rebelled against conscription. It was not until November 1, just before the actual election, that the pamphlet was revealed as a "hoax" and that "two young [and unnamed] Democrats humbugged the political world."[55]

David Croly was but one of a number of Irish male New Yorkers who played a key role in further racializing the political culture of the era. In various efforts to improve their lot, aspiring Irish writers and performers took advantage of opportunities available to them in the expanding commercial culture. The publishing industry was already well established by Protestant elites; however, new forms of commercial culture were open for Irish involvement. The Bowery, with its accessible, popular forms of entertainments, as opposed to the far more proper Broadway venues, was a dynamic commercial marketplace for mechanics, self-styled "Bowery Boys," and newly arriving immigrants.[56] And such creative individuals as Ned Harrigan and Chuck Connors who made their careers on the Bowery stage showed how generations of Irish performers were able to build their success on stereotyped representations of themselves and others in this dynamic, complex popular culture.

Edward Harrigan has been often called the "American Dickens" and with his partner Tony Hart, the "American Gilbert and Sullivan." After leaving minstrelsy for variety theater in 1873, Harrigan wrote a series of plays that portrayed everyday ethnic life in the Lower East Side for the basically male, Bowery theater-going audience. In contrast to the gross Irish caricatures of minstrelsy, Harrigan developed Irish portraits of much greater depth and range. He still borrowed on the long-established stereotypes of Hibernian laziness, brawling, and drinking, but the main character, Dan Mulligan, was more of a positive and realistic figure that Irish audiences could identity with. Mulligan immigrated in 1848, fought in the Civil War, bought a grocery store, cared about his community, and became a successful local politician. As Robert Toll has pointed out, Harrigan's audiences laughed both at and with his Irish.[57] He wrote for a popular multiethnic, Euro-American, male audience that wanted a fast pace and clear-cut contrasts. In effect, Harrigan broke through the Anglo-Protestant representational hierarchy of ethnic and racial groups by injecting a positive Irish image onto the commercial stage. Irish were in effect made somewhat normative.[58]

Chinese and African Americans were also among his stock characters. Although his Irish representations had broken past the anorexic bounds of minstrelsy, his depictions of these two groups had not. Blackface minstrelsy provided Irish Democrats with an empowering sense of their place in American culture and politics.[59] The significance of Chinese stage caricatures with regard to policies of Chinese exclusion and segregation in the United States has yet to be fully explored. While Denis Kearny was leading the Workingmen's Party movement against Chinese immigration on the Pacific Coast, Harrigan was representing Chinese on the New York stage. Drawing on decades of Chinese caricatures in melodrama and minstrelsy from the 1870s into the 1880s he regularly referred to Chinese as part of the Five Points scene. A lustful, laundry man named Hog-Eye who spoke pidgin-English and had a penchant for stealing clothing was Harrigan's main comic antagonist of Dan Mulligan. In this district, which Anglo-and German-Protestants considered to be filled with "heathens" of all types, Hog-Eye was the heathen's heathen, the Irish other's other. His exaggerated "yellowface" appearance, his bumbling yet constant desire to lure Irish women into smoking opium, his inability to honestly compete with Irish washerwomen, and his childlike speech were all performed with great comic effect on the white male audiences.[60] Harrigan drew on the well-known presence of Chinese–Irish couples and families in the Lower East Side and played out scenes pitting his oddball Chinese against his dignified, if sometimes flawed, Irish heroes and heroines.

In contrast to African New Yorkers, Chinese did not have any individuals successfully writing or performing as minstrels or in variety venues. Their small numbers and language difficulties combined with societal marginalization did not make for a hospitable environment for such involvement in commercial theater. They had no Harrigan, no Bert Williams, and no audience base to break the bounds of one-dimensional portrayals fostered by the commercial culture. Given this vacuum, Irish writers and performers played a particularly strategic role in presuming to represent "Chinese" on the New York stage, in the work of Harrigan and then, in more pronounced fashion, through that of the professional Bowery B'hoy persona of "Chuck" Connors.

George Washington O'Connor was one of New York's best-known local celebrities at the turn of the century. Having been a prizefighter of some minor success, he promoted himself as a street-wise philosopher to a metropolitan media eager to feature stories of local "color." He cultivated his persona by evoking a fading era of Irish immigrant bravado and community on the Lower East Side that was now displaced by Italian and Jewish immigration, of the type celebrated by the elder Harrigan. He spoke in a heavy "dese-dem-dose" argot and was a masterful performance artist and storyteller. He took advantage of the growing, late-1890s interest in New York's Chinese settlement by giving tours to uptown "rubberneckers" of Mott Street stores, Chinese restaurants on Pell Street, "exotic" gift shops, and staged opium dens with scandalous white women. Richard Fox, one among many of Connors' notable friends, publisher of the *Police Gazette*, claimed Connors knew Chinatown better than anyone else. Given this self-cultivated image, Connors was regularly referred to by the media as the "mayor of Chinatown." Besides his regular mention in New York papers, he had enough of a popular following to appear on stage, was featured in pamphlet versions of his tours, and had a book entitled *Bowery Life* featuring his routines.[61] By becoming the tour guide for uptown Americans and emphasizing the "otherness" of Chinatown, Connors was able to endear himself to the media and the media-consuming public. In a sense, by playing the role of an interpreter on behalf of the voiceless Chinese, he was able to gain authority and win a role within mainstream society.[62]

Edward Harrigan and Chuck Connors, by virtue of the Irish proximity to New York's Chinese settlement and the upward mobility into commercial theater, helped craft stereotypic representations of the Chinese. Because the Chinese lacked the power to speak for themselves, these two Irish cultural producers, among others, were able to fabricate how Chinese were to be represented in the popular culture. By mimicking this community with certain elements of Lower

East Side verisimilitude, Chinese were made into Irish "others." This phenomenon occurred with many Irish, among other European American actors and artists, representing blacks in blackface. However, to the limited degree that African American performers were able to enter into the commercial culture, they were able to somewhat mitigate anti-black stereotypes. (And one may well speculate: if the predominantly Irish Draft Riots had not pushed out the local black community in 1863, would someone like Connors have assumed the role of the "mayor" of "Little Africa"?) What becomes quite clear, however, is that the Irish discourse on the Chinese was fully embedded within the preestablished power relations of New York City. Harrigan's and Connors' representations of this group were essentially identical to those of Nast and Keppler. Those graphic artists' assumption of the racially informed principles of British physiognamy-informed drawing were made three dimensional by Harrigan's stage caricatures and Connors' tours. In effect, these two performers were able to break out of their Lower Manhattan ghetto by using the Bowery stage as their vehicle for success and recognition.

How can this phenomenon of New York Irish prejudice be explained? Sociologist Emile Durkheim insisted that "frameworks of knowledge . . . built at the inception of a society" were important in structuring the relations of power between dominant and marginalized social groups. Race became a fundamental marker determining U.S. social relations in the country's European colonial past, when, as part of the so-called New World, it was "discovered" as part of the expanding world system of capitalism. For the purposes of this discussion, it is important to note that the port of New York was founded during the search for an alternative passage to the "Indies." And the subsequent development of the trade with India and China involved those two empires in the periphery of the globalizing system. Africa was also drawn in to the Western orbit—deemed useful to the West mainly for the slave labor its tribal elite were willing to offer to traders. A racially constructed hierarchy, then, was structurally embedded with the codification of Africans with slavery in the Virginia slave laws of the later seventeenth century *and* with the inherited "orientalism," in the sense that Edward Said has used the term, from Europe.[63]

Given the fundamental domestic social dichotomy of white and free versus black and unfree, American social identities have been inextricably tied into a basic hierarchy of race—a hierarchy quickly complicated by other migrants and immigrants variously defined as "ethnic" or "racial" groups. Within the discourse of Irish–British relations, colonized Irish Catholics were de facto cast as an inferior race. Yet when Irish entered the black/white discourse of the United States, they could occupy a more ambiguous position in the social hierarchy. Irish Catholics were both despised by Protestant patricians and privileged over African slaves and freed men. Yet, many Irish were able to gain certain power and improve their lot via westward migration, involvement with urban politics (taking advantage of the 1827 amendment of universal white male suffrage), and entry into the burgeoning commercial culture of the American stage.[64] In the face of mainstream antipathy, positive Irish American identity was being forged within the preexisting discourse of pro-Protestant white and anti-black Americanism. The classic means for Irish Catholics to defuse longstanding Anglo-American and European-Protestant hatred toward them was to symbolically displace such low valuation placed on them onto an even lower group.

Chinese entering the port of New York after the 1842 Opium Wars and after New York had already benefited from the China trade were treated by the Anglo-Protestant elite in an ambivalent manner. Still somewhat influenced by romantic Enlightenment interest in Confucius, the Great Wall, the Grand Canal, the civil service system, and most of all the highly desired luxuries China produced for export, "gentlemanly" Chinese, such as Quimbo Appo, were still admired. At the same time, Protestant missionaries and traders eager to increase their profits from opium and other goods resented all resistance Chinese people offered to their notions of progress and modernization. Once admired for its splendors and wisdom, China became increasingly measured by how friendly it was to Western economic and cultural expansion. Chinese workers entering the port of New York at this time not only walked into a preestablished spatial hierarchy but were also deemed targets of racial backwardness and ridicule, the perfect foil for progressive, Anglo-Saxon, and Protestant patrician society becoming more and more assured of its self-declared special destiny.

Within this Anglo-Saxon discourse, Irish New Yorkers played a key role in broadening the Anglo-American identity to include Celtics, another constructed "race" as part of a pan-European race of "whites." By emphasizing Irish humanity and exaggerating African and Chinese differences within the given parameters of New York commercial culture, the Irish performers were able to re-create themselves in the eyes of the larger society. Their "otherness" could be reified in the United States into a pan-Euro-American "whiteness" precisely because of the existence of African Americans and Chinese immigrants who could be constituted as Irish "others." Irish women calling Quimbo Appo a "China nigger" was a means to further distance Irish from those that they were often associated with in New York. Indeed, native New Yorkers frequently referred to their Roman Catholic brethren as "white niggers" or "Irish niggers." Irish patriarchs, in particular, but Irish families in general, played out a real life drama of tragic proportions. "By castrating Negro men, by rending asunder an Irish woman guilty of intermarriage, and by torturing and killing Negro prostitutes, the Irish were exorcising their guilt feelings, denying their fantasies, and re-affirming their allegiance to their families, their community, and their dreams." Their "others" must be created and defeated, so that Irish American identities could flourish more freely.[65]

The competing configurations of a shared low (to upper-low) position of Chinese men and Irish women and Nast's Anglo/high, Chinese/upper low, and

Irish/low formulation ultimately gave way to the Anglo/high, Irish/upper low, and Chinese–black/low hierarchy of moral and social value.[66] The alliance between local Protestant, male authority, and Appo over Irish women, as demonstrated in his second trial, had been displaced by an alliance of pan-white racial purists over non-European Americans and mixed "mongrel" New Yorkers.

The intercultural dynamic indicated by my historical research is one in which New York's Irish had a special, if ambiguous, relationship to the local Chinese community. Although earlier in the century the two groups had shared enough to produce Irish–Chinese families, by the end of the century several generations of "professional" Irish aggressively moving uptown, both figuratively and in reality, took advantage of their unique experiential resources for elaborating ethnic and racial stereotypes gained from living in Lower Manhattan.[67] And because they had prerequisite talents and skills for entering into New York commercial stage culture just at the point of its expansion, the Irish were in a unique position to build up their own image in mainstream society while creating new "heathens" to displace their longstanding negative image. In much the way that Jean Baker analyzed the cultural milieu of Irish Democrats in New York—a milieu that effectively marshaled political support in opposition to the freeing of blacks and radical reconstruction—I have attempted to provide the cultural background that made possible the passage of the 1882 Chinese Exclusion Law and segregation of the Chinese into isolated ghetto communities.

The Irish did not magically become white. They helped to make it so, after the Civil War. They became active players in city politics but still experienced discrimination based on their ascribed racialist "character" and their non-Protestant religion and values. Yet New York pluralism became more complex and segmented; and in addition to class and Protestant values, "whiteness" became a new unifying category, making it possible for the Irish and other non-Protestants to become more integrated into the ever-reformulating hierarchy, while at the same time satisfying the Victorian need to discipline the self and obsess on targeted others. In this regard, Irish women became the target for what nowadays would be termed "ethnic cleansing." Irish men were able to become Americanized by actively participating in racial masquerades of the established political culture. And by so doing they became increasingly viewed as "white." Upward mobility within this highly constrained and segmented hierarchy privileged ethnic politics over multiethnic racial combinations. Being an Irish American, even within the highly negative view created by elite, radical Republicans, constituted the primary means for a positive identity formation and a chance of making life better. Irish Catholics could join mainstream Protestant audiences and voters in laughing at the wretched, comic antics of whites masquerading in blackface and yellowface. Just as *Yankee Notions* depicted Irish Chinese mix-ups decades earlier, in post-Reconstruction America many Irish joined in laughing at their own mix-ups. Now, however, they also had the power to dehumanize others and humanize themselves. During an era in which Irish and Anglos railed against crossing the racial borders they created, the skits and short stories about Chinese men and Irish women took on a highly moral tone. Their amorous relations were now taboo and not simply descriptive and odd. To transgress such borders meant degradation of a whole people. Therefore, to laugh at a postcard of a vaudeville sketch showing an aggressive lowly Irish wench trying to attract a Chinese laundry operator was a way to reassure oneself that oneself was not that silly. To thrill in the reading of Edward Townsend's lurid short stories of Chinese men intermingling with Irish women in Chinatown was a way to be both titillated and repulsed.[68] The comedy and drama did not lay with the African and Chinese caricatures; it was thought those folks could not help but be the way they were portrayed. The action was with the Irish women who had some choice. They were "white" and did not need to lower themselves.

Irish advancement in New York, therefore, was in part premised on their learning the unwritten rules of racial pluralist politics in the metropolis. In sheer political terms, power could be gained by appealing to and reformulating the prejudices and emotions of a pan-European-American, male, working-class audience composed of both immigrants and natives to unite in fighting against and laughing at lowly non-whites and miscegenators. By late century, Irish women, from Catherine Fitzpatrick to the staged "Bridgets," were essentially told to make a choice, or else.

Appo Revisited

In 1863, Appo was pardoned from prison and moved back to Lower Manhattan. After the 1859 trial, Catherine Fitzpatrick moved with their daughter to California where her brother lived, but the ship crashed off the Pacific coast and everyone was killed. Their son, George Washington Appo, was left behind to be raised on Donovan's Lane.[69] Quimbo Appo did return to his old Lower Manhattan haunts. If he was not a man who used physical force before he went to prison, he appears to have become prone to fights after release. He was accused and convicted of "justifiable homicide" in the killing of a Lizzie Williams, for which he served one year. Now identified by newspapers as "the notorious Chinese ruffian," he later was found guilty of assault in a fight and sentenced to five years in prison. He was pardoned in 1875, at which time he was again convicted for brutally kicking a German woman. Six months later he set up a cigar stand but was arrested for not bearing the required tax stamp license.[70]

In 1876 Appo committed another murder, an incident that characterized his acts of violence and was perversely reminiscent of Bret Harte's fictional Chinese character Ah Sin in his wildly successful 1870 "Truthful James" poem.[71] While lodged at a boardinghouse on Chatham Street, he played checkers with a man named Kelly. Proud of his skills at checkers, he beat the man several times, winning small wagers each game. Appo went to bed while the much larger Kelly went off angrily and had a few drinks. Later Kelly returned to the lodging house, dragged Appo out of bed, blackened his eye, and kicked him down the stairs. Appo drew his penknife and stabbed the approaching Kelly three times. Kelly died and Appo was once again sentenced to manslaughter, this time for seven years.[72]

The coincidence of fiction preceding event is not entirely without relation—experience as lived was undoubtedly influenced by developing stereotypes, popular representations in the commercial culture, and the dominant political culture of the city. The scapegoating of Irish "others" during the Draft Riots and Appo's return to the neighborhood should be understood together as formulating a calculus of violence between ethnic racial groups. Any sympathy for Appo expressed earlier by reporters had now turned into intolerance. In part, no doubt, this shift reflects Appo's later pattern of involvement with violence, but it was also indicative of a larger change in the representation of Chinese between the 1850s and 1880s. The *New York Times* called him "one of the most desperate criminals in the city." The *New York Herald* described him as "a fiend in human shape." And the *New York Tribune* revealed more about the cultural issues by writing about him within a specifically racial discourse. Appo's actions, according to Horace Greeley, was "an instance of the uncurbed barbarian temper of the East brought into collision with the colder habits of our Saxon civilization." Not only was it thought that more stringent laws should be passed to keep recidivist criminals in jail, Appo's criminality was used as evidence that all Chinese immigration should be curbed. This image was so deeply associated with Appo that even upon his death in 1912 he was still referred to as the "famous Chinese devil man."[73]

It is clear that Quimbo Appo had become a violent man. The doctor explained Appo's violence as follows:

> Patient says that ever since the close of the late Civil War he has received revelation from the spirits and "ciples" (disciples) and that he has had assurances from these sources that whatever he should consider it right to do would be considered a good act by God Almighty, no matter what it might be in the light of the human law. He further says that he has been the special subject of the "temptations" by evil spirits for many years and that these "tengatations," as he calls them, have been the source of all his crimes. He says that whenever one of these temptations has been about to beset him, he has been forewarned by spirits and assured that he would come out all "light" (right) in the end, no matter what he did; and, on studying the homicides he has committed, it will be found that in nearly all, some aggravating act of the victim led to the commission of the crime and to a mitigation of the punishment. From his frequent escapes from capital punishment, patient has acquired the delusions that no one can kill him or seriously injure him; and from his many years' imprisonment (18) he regards himself as a protegee of the State. . . . Patient is a devout Roman Catholic; expresses himself as ready to die at any time and says he is "going to Heaven, sure."

While it would be easy to diagnose Appo in contemporary terms as having delusions of grandeur and a persecution complex, such an analysis would tend to underestimate two powerful social influences of his time.

First, his patient records were full of late-nineteenth-century scientific language premised on racially charged notions of biological determinism. In striking contrast to the judgment of the *New-York Times* reporter who observed Appo as a shrewd and most intelligent businessman, this examining doctor authoritatively stated Appo "has many of the characteristics of the Mongolian type" and "he is possessed of little or no education and is of an inferior order of intelligent development, resembling in many respects a child." Like Harte's Ah Sin and all the pidgin-English-speaking and childlike "Chinamen" in popular culture, Appo was described within a scientifically "proven" racial hierarchy. As evidenced by their once great culture, the Chinese were clearly superior to lowly Africans and African Americans who were thought to be suspended in the "foetal" stage of human development, but far inferior to European and European-originated whites, who were considered full adults. As if to prove these qualitative racial determinations, the doctor described Appo as having a "small and well shaped" head. And in the empiricist tradition of Drs. Morton, Gliddon, and Nott, he attached a full page of 24 "cephalometrical" measurements of his head, including that of circumference, volume, "great transverse diameter," facial angle, and "angle of prognathism," all in centimeters. In addition, when filling out "Is the patient addicted to self abuse?" he rendered the less-than-exact answer: "probably." In Victorian science masturbation was commonly thought to be a cause of insanity, especially among women.[74] As further evidence of Appo's childlike nature, the doctor recorded examples of Appo's delusions. The loss of a game of checkers was said to be due to a political or professional party of one type or another, "Abe Lincoln's party," the "Doctor's party," the "Superintendent's party" or the "Fenian's party." The doctor also reported that fellow inmates purposely teased him because they enjoyed "listening to his 'pidgin' English." In a sense, Appo's irritable nature made it easy for others to provoke him into putting on what could be described as a mock-yellowface show, replete with the comic and childish expressions of an Ah Sin.

What was the process of Appo's criminalization? What was the danger he came to represent to society? Contrary to the representation of Appo as somehow being imprisoned by his biological racialness, he clearly exemplified strong intercultural influences. His doctor's notations indicate that he had Western tattoos on both arms, a possible practice of Chinese who had visited international port cities. According to one prison admission record, the left forearm featured "the Goddess of Liberty & the Crucifixion" and the right forearm displayed a "Spanish dancing Girl & Girl with a flag & emblem skull & cross bones."[75] He did not shave his head, nor did he wear a queue as all Chinese men, even those overseas, were subject to wear. Indeed, he adopted the distinctly European and American predilection of some bald men by wearing a wig. He had become so imbued with Roman Catholicism that even his delusional fantasies were punctuated with Catholic imagery, such as his vision of the Virgin Mary. In this regard, Appo's experience was remarkably similar to the conversion of John Hu, the Jesuit committed to an asylum in France in 1723. In both cases, these Chinese Christians experienced their faith too vividly and too excessively to seem "normal." Appo in fact occasionally claimed he was the "All Powerful" and the "Second God." At other times, he either feared or identified with the Irish. In 1885 he so identified with the Irish that he believed he was "suffering for the cause of Ireland and that he must suffer until she is free."[76]

What drove Appo to insanity? It is probably impossible to arrive at a definitive answer. For whatever reasons, he clearly suffered from delusions of grandeur and suspected myriad conspiracies. If his response to life was skewed, the social pressures he felt were quite real. Many political parties, "Fenians," and professional authorities were hostile to the Chinese. In contrast to the self-protective isolation of the Chinese within the occupational protection of the hand laundry, his lashing back had repeatedly landed him behind prison bars. In a society that mounted increased racial hostility toward being Chinese and being a mixture of Chinese and Irish, Appo had little room to breathe. As a once highly respected Chinese New York man who repeatedly rebelled against those who he sensed did him an injustice, he became a criminal and was declared insane. If Appo was not insane when he entered Matteawan, he surely lost touch with any semblance of reality the longer he was jailed.

In 1882, the year in which the Chinese Exclusion Laws were passed by the U.S. Congress, Appo complained to prison officials that he should have been released but "the Democratic party" was in conspiracy against him and had prevailed upon the governor to withhold his commutation of sentence for political reasons.[77] His seven-year term was in fact completed by that date, but little did he realize that he would never be released. In an oddly insightful way, Appo had diagnosed the source of his woes. Shifting political winds had conspired against him, though of course not in the personal and paranoid way that he felt.

Quimbo Appo, like Irish women who had relations with non-white men, transgressed the reformulating racial boundaries of Lower Manhattan. If Appo had committed his crimes of passion and violence within the confines of the Chinese settlement, it is questionable if they would have been given any public notice. Appo's crimes, however, were directed at the non-Chinese that he lived with and came into contact with. In effect, Appo was what Croly would have defined as a "miscegenator," a person who mixed with non-Chinese New Yorkers. As a free-spirited and intelligent individual acting on his own behalf, he was viewed as dangerous and had to be controlled. And as a cultural symbol of racial impurity, he had to be made marginal and criminalized. In this sense,

Appo's paranoia about Fenians, Democrats, and politicians trying to get him were not simply delusional. These fears were grounded in actual power dynamics occurring in lower Manhattan. His fall from grace as a respected merchant and spokesman to a loathed Chinese "devil-man" was not entirely of his own doing.

While living in New York and living in prison, Appo's hybrid, multifaceted life became increasingly limited. Both scientific and popular yellowface stereotypes were used to measure his "normality." Even in the asylum, fellow inmates provoked him so that he would perform in pidgin English for their amusement. In effect, his efforts to cross cultural borders became a source of amusement and terrible fascination, which ultimately had to be punished. The signals to the Chinese community were clear, within Anglo-American orientalism these people would be forever viewed as foreigners. Settling and intermingling was discouraged. What sociologist Paul Siu has called a "sojourner" mentality developed. Hence, post-1870 Chinese increasingly gravitated toward opening small hand laundry operations that were highly mobile and insulated from the larger society.[78] Laundries, then, became the dominant occupation of New York Chinese right up to the recent Civil Rights era of the 1960s. Chinese did not and could not represent themselves. That terrain had been claimed by Irish New Yorkers, among others. The sympathy and respect that Appo held with the press in the 1850s gave way to Chuck Connors acting as the "mayor" of Chinatown for uptown rubberneckers.

Quimbo Appo and, by extension, other New York Chinese came to be represented as either Dr. Jekyls or Mr. Hydes. Yet it was the historical terrain *between* such Victorian polarities of light and shadow, good and evil that the true experience of the Chinese in New York was actually lived. The particular, local experiences of a group such as the Chinese New Yorkers, necessarily leads to larger questions of interracial relations, which in this case were played out as Chinese–Irish relations. That configuration leads to an understanding of the broader relations of historical power as expressed in New York City and provides a penetrating and realistic historical analysis of the shared, interrelated, and still usable past.

CHAPTER 6

Illness and Medical Care among Irish Immigrants in Antebellum New York

O N JANUARY 1, 1892, Annie Moore, a 15-year-old whom the *New York Times* described as a "rosy-cheeked Irish girl" from County Cork became the first immigrant to enter the United States via Ellis Island, the federal government's new immigration depot in New York harbor. Ferried from her ship, the *Nevada*, to Ellis Island with her two brothers and other immigrants for medical inspection and processing, young Ms. Moore was preselected to be first off the boat and into the depot. She was met by a beaming John B. Weber, immigration commissioner for the port of New York. Weber came forward after Moore's name was written in the registry book and presented the girl with a $10 gold piece to commemorate the occasion.[1]

After quickly passing before the watchful gaze of the inspecting physicians of the U.S. Marine and Hospital Service and answering the questions of Immigration Bureau Officials, the three youngsters were admitted. Annie Moore's "rosy-cheeks" had not deceived. According to the Ellis Island physicians, she was physically and morally fit for America.

The opening of Ellis Island was news, but the arrival of yet another Irish immigrant girl and two boys in New York was hardly a notable event in the nineteenth century. Almost four million Irish, most of them Catholics from Ireland's southern provinces, had arrived in the United States in flight from hunger, poverty, Protestant abuse, and English domination. Nor was it surprising that the newcomers, including Annie Moore, were required to stand the scrutiny of the uniformed physicians of the United States Marine and Hospital Service (later renamed the U.S. Public Health Service). Apprehensions about the health and vitality of immigrants arriving in the United States long predated both Ellis Island and even the germ theory of disease derived in the 1880s from the research of Germany's Robert Koch, France's Louis Pasteur, and England's Joseph Lister.

The menace of diseases from afar, borne by the bodies of immigrants and refugees, and the American public's response to that possibility have been intertwined with nativism and ethnic prejudice throughout American history. Often, the native-born grudgingly welcomed immigrants contingent on their physical health and intellectual vitality, striving to admit only those most fit and able to compete for the material rewards of life in the United States. Just as often, the native-born have suggested that regardless of who was admitted, the country's unique blend of individual liberty, capitalism, and political democracy could transform downtrodden and oppressed humanity from every corner of the globe into new and improved beings, denizens of a country singled out by Providence for special blessing. Always, Americans have believed that immigrants posed a threat. They have feared that poor health and frail physiques might make of immigrants burdens rather than assets; might spread infectious diseases among the native-born, undermining the advantages of the very society that offered freedom and opportunity to those who could find it nowhere else.

Historians of immigration and historians of medicine have only begun to explore the linkages between nativism and the social construction of health and disease in different eras of American history.[2] One such study treating the mid–nineteenth century is Charles Rosenberg's now classic volume, *The Cholera Years*.[3] Rosenberg demonstrates how nativists in New York City stigmatized Irish immigrants with responsibility for this dreaded infectious disease, a disease that was actually triggered by living conditions in the host nation. In Rosenberg's study the voice of nativist prejudice is unmistakable. Similarly, historian of medicine Gerald Grob has described how mental illness of institutionalized Irish immigrants was attributed to an inherent instability characteristic of the new arrivals. In both instances, disease was socially constructed by nativists to stigmatize Irish immigrants.

The next logical step for historical inquiry is to place the association of the Irish and disease within the larger context of immigration to America. Medicalized bigotry caused a worried public to demand protection from state governments, thereby ushering in a new era in immigration inspection and processing. Likewise, nativist antagonism prompted a response from the Irish community. Irish immigrants were not passive pawns, nor were those individuals and institutions who assumed responsibility for their welfare content to look on passively, as newcomers suffered physical pain and spiritual deprivation, bartering ethnic pride and religious customs in return for badly needed medical care.

The experience of Irish immigrants in New York during the nation's first great wave of immigration, which occurred before the Civil War, offers an opportunity to analyze the foreign-born's response to medical stigmatization. It also provides an opportunity to comprehend the means and motives of those individuals and institutions that sought to deflect the nativist assault while providing for the health care of Irish arrivals.

The earliest precaution taken against the threat of disease from abroad by Americans concerned only infectious disease. It was the quarantine of arriving ships, a procedure known and practiced throughout Europe. In the late eighteenth and early nineteenth centuries, transatlantic voyages were perilous and public health in ports such as New York City were protected only by quarantine procedures. Bedlow's Island (later spelled Bedloe's) was the quarantine station with a port physician appointed. He was charged with inspecting all incoming vessels that he suspected of carrying infection and reporting conditions aboard to the governor or, at times, to the mayor, who would then decide whether a ship should be quarantined and for how long. Immigrants quarantined for any length of time in the port of New York were generally sent to the Marine Hospital at Red Hook.[4]

Because shipmasters sought to maximize profits by cramming into their holds as many immigrants as possible, shipboard illness and even mortality was quite common. Typhus and diarrhea often ravaged tightly packed passengers to the New World. Friedrich Kapp, one of New York's Commissioners of Emigration, wrote in 1870 that "the lower deck of an emigrant vessel as late as 1819, was no better than that of a slaver or a coolie ship; the passengers were just as crowded, and just as little thought of, as those unfortunate beings from Africa or China." According to Kapp, "Ten deaths among one hundred passengers was nothing extraordinary; twenty per cent was not unheard of; and there were cases of 400 out of 1,200 passengers being buried before the ships left port."[5] In New York, the Marine Hospital filled to capacity when several ships docked at the same time.

But the Asiatic cholera epidemic of 1832 proved that quarantines were insufficient. A silent traveler from abroad, cholera rode into New York and other east coast ports even as an increasingly large number of foreign-born were arriving. An acute infection with symptoms of diarrhea, vomiting, muscular cramps, dehydration, and collapse, cholera in the nineteenth century was a deadly disease. It is now known that cholera is caused by the ingestion of water or foods contaminated by the excrement of infected persons. In 1832, many Americans believed that cholera was caused by the Irish.

Why the Irish? Between 1820 and 1830, America's busiest port, New York, received 92,884 newcomers, 81,827 of them from England and Ireland and another 7,729 from Germany.[6] Later, between 1840 and 1860, hard times would send an additional 1.8 million Irish hurtling toward North America. A great majority of the Irish who arrived in New York City migrated elsewhere within three to four years, only to be replaced by others. Still, by 1860 there were 203,740 foreign-born Irish living in New York City; one of every four New Yorkers was Irish.[7] There they were reviled by the native-born, largely of Protestant English ancestry, sometimes for their Irishness and at others for their Catholicism.[8] Living in run-down shanties and tenements, Irish immigrants felled during the 1832 cholera epidemic were believed by many of the native-born to have died of individual vices typical of their group, a punishment divinely determined that might be spread to those undeserving of such retribution. And what were these vices? Intemperance and a lack of cleanliness were the character flaws most responsible for the sickness suffered by the "low Irish" who were crammed into city slums, according to a New York Board of Health report.[9] Irish-haters such as journalist Hezekiah Niles, editor of *Niles Weekly Register*, blamed the Irish for taking the jobs of native-born workers, adding to the public's burdens by cramming the urban almshouses with their destitute, opening saloons to lure thirsty and gullible workers, and perverting local politics with their smooth-talking ward heelers.[10] Was cholera bred in bars and political clubhouses? Anti-Irish nativists were only too anxious to answer with a grimace and a nod.

That so many of those Irish stricken in New York were Roman Catholic did not escape public notice. However, not all Protestant clergymen agreed on the details of cholera's social construction as the Irish Catholic disease. Some clergymen saw the disease as a literal result of man's sinfulness. In a sermon preached on a day of "public fasting, humiliation, and prayer," one minister declared that cholera was "not *caused* by intemperance and filth, in themselves, but it is a *scourge*, a rod in the hand of God."[11] Others, of a more liberal bent, suggested that cholera was not a scourge sent by God with the intention of punishing man, but rather a disease that existed in nature and was the result of man's violations of natural law. Thus, drinking or eating to excess, or failing to keep oneself clean were failures to conform in body and soul to the divine plan.[12]

Still, most native-born Americans did not suggest that the Irish were inherently flawed. Rather, the success of Roman Catholicism among the Irish and the influence of priests in the Irish community was attributed by many American Protestants to environmental factors such as poverty, oppression, and misgovernment. Catholicism thrived, Protestants thought, because Irish minds were limited in their imagination by a lack of education and economic independence. The church merely benefited from Irish ignorance and desperation. Similarly, the inclination of the Irish toward drink was seen as a moral failing derived from the need to escape the misery of their condition. In short, Irish immigrants were often regarded not as moral profligates, the wages of whose sins were disease, but as victims of bad circumstances, whose shortcomings could be cured.[13] Yale president, the Reverend Timothy Dwight, denied that the Irish in New England had a "native character" that inclined them to immoral ways. His prescription was: "Give them the same advantages which are enjoyed by others, and they will stand upon a level with any of their neighbors."[14] A level field of competition could be achieved by changing the immigrants' living conditions; the individuals themselves need not be excluded from society. However, others were less sanguine. In one of his nativist tracts, the sire of the telegraph, Samuel F. B. Morse, despaired because so many of the newcomers were Catholics, who "obey their priests as demigods, from the habit of their whole lives," and were unlikely to be disabused of their illusions simply because of their arrival in the United States.[15]

The famine of the mid-1840s loosed yet more Irish Catholics across the Atlantic. Those leaving from the English port of Liverpool were required to stand a medical inspection conducted by British government physicians. A doctor who made the crossing many times on American ships wrote a letter to the *New York Times* in 1851 describing a perfunctory exam at best, but one that bordered upon charade. Each passenger "inspected" by the doctors was required to stick out his or her tongue while overburdened physicians barely glanced up from their papers. Passengers infested with vermin or in the early stages of smallpox were often overlooked. On busy days when several ships were departing, as many as a thousand travelers might pass before a team of two doctors who, standing behind a small window, asked each emigrant whether they were well, glanced at tongues, and stamped tickets speedily.[16] Complaints did reach the ears of British emigration commissioners urging more thorough inspections to prevent shipboard disease. However, the commissioners dismissed these complaints, arguing that most shipboard disease was the result of changes of diet, seasickness, fear, and other such conditions that compromised the body, making it vulnerable to disease.[17]

Examining physicians freely admitted that emigrants were not stripped and that, beyond taking pulses and examining tongues, they closely scrutinized only hands in the search for symptoms of serious ailments. Rejections were for typhus fever, childhood diseases, or infectious eye diseases such as ophthalmia. The physicians defended their exams, noting that they differed little from those given army inductees and convicts, where prisoners were lined up in the jailyard as a doctor walked before them in search of those who might be ill. When asked if immigrants suffering from consumption were rejected, a physician said no, because it was not an infectious disease.[18]

Medical inspection of emigrants certainly cannot be characterized as thorough, but it would be a mistake to dismiss them as egregiously superficial. By the 1840s and 1850s the state of medical knowledge, especially that relating to infectious disease, remained thin. Diagnostic techniques were few in number and highly impressionistic in nature. Acute observation and the physician's judgment were still the most reliable instruments at hand.[19] Equally significant may be the method of physician payment, a pound for every hundred persons inspected. By 1854, Liverpool had three full-time positions and had switched from piecework to a fixed annual salary of £400.[20]

A second cholera epidemic struck in 1849. It appeared to spread north from Philadelphia to New York and Boston. Although the figures were skewed by wealthier, native-born Americans who tended to avoid hospitals when ill, a tabulation of hospital statistics for six cities (Cincinnati, New York, Buffalo, Brooklyn, Boston, and New Orleans) compiled by Charles Rosenberg reveals that 4,309 of 5,301 patients during the height of the 1849 cholera epidemic were listed as foreign-born. More than 40 percent of those dying of cholera in New York were of Irish birth.[21] As in 1832, the connection seemed obvious to many. Were not the Irish homes the poorest in drainage, least well ventilated, and most crowded? And was not poverty a product of moral shortcomings?

Fewer native-born Americans in 1849 than in 1832 viewed cholera as a direct act of retribution upon the sinful and spiritually unworthy Irish Catholics. Although many continued to see a social dimension to the disease, the public response was more directed at blocking the entry of those already diseased than in deciphering God's judgments.

In May 1855 an old fort at the tip of Manhattan, Castle Garden, was leased, renovated, and on August 1 reopened as a state immigration reception center: New York's Emigrant Landing Depot. The quarantine procedures would now be supplemented by the individual examination of immigrants. Every vessel bringing immigrants had to anchor at the Quarantine Station, 6 miles below New York City. There, a New York State emigration officer boarded to ascertain a count of passengers, deaths during the voyage, the degree and kind of illnesses suffered during the trip, and the overall cleanliness of the vessel. A report was sent to the general agent and superintendent at Castle Garden and the boarding officer remained on the ship as it steamed up the bay to ensure that no one from the ship contacted anyone on shore before the authorized disembarkation of emigrants. This prohibition was destined to inhibit the activity of runners and swindlers who accosted arriving immigrants with schemes and scams.

Once the ship was anchored near the depot, a New York City policeman detailed to Castle Garden assumed authority. Passengers were transferred to the jurisdiction of the Landing Department. After a customs inspection of luggage, the immigrants and their belongings boarded barges and tugs that took them to the Castle Garden pier. There, passengers were examined by a state medical officer to discover "if any sick have passed the Health authorities at Quarantine (who are thereupon transferred by steamer to the hospitals on Ward's or Blackwell's Island), and likewise to select all subject to special bonds under the law—as blind persons, cripples, lunatics, or any others who are likely to become a future charge." After examination, the migrants were directed into a rotunda in the center of the depot, where they registered their names, nationalities, former places of residence, and intended destination.[22]

Thus by the mid-1850s each immigrant was subjected to two medical examinations before landing in the United States, followed by a more general health inquiry by the quarantine officer. Fear of infectious disease from abroad had triggered entirely new processes and procedures in public health policy. Still, many Americans continued to hold the foreign-born responsible for disease in general, not just cholera. A nativist physician, Dr. Samuel Busey, wrote in 1856, "In the cities, those direful and pestilential diseases, ship fever, yellow fever, and small pox, are almost exclusively confined to the filthy alleys, lanes, and streets, and low, damp, filthy and ill-ventilated haunts, which are exclusively tenanted by foreigners."[23]

Whether or not the Irish were suffering more or less than other impoverished new arrivals, it is certainly true that their plight often led to institutionalization where they could be counted. Natives of Ireland accounted for 53.9 percent of New York City's foreign-born population in 1855, but at the city's Bellevue Hospital, 85.0 percent of all patients of foreign birth had been born in Ireland.[24] Statistical data allowed New York officials to appreciate the dimension of the problems facing the newcomers and their hosts. At times, however, distortions in the data shed false light on the extent of the plight of the Irish, as in the case of mental illness.

Mental illness, if not an epidemic disease such as cholera, nevertheless seemed to native-born Americans every bit as pervasive among the Irish. In the mid–nineteenth century, insanity was defined by aberrant behavior. Discussions of etiology were protean and quite general in character, reflecting broad social perceptions and prevailing religious, moral, and cultural values. Most physicians believed that insanity grew out of a violation of physical, mental, and moral laws that, when properly understood and obeyed, resulted in the highest development of the white Anglo-Saxon Protestant race, indeed of all civilization. Abnormality in the population might be traced to the increasing rigors of civilization, the immigration of those already on the road to degeneracy, an inherited predisposition to mental illness, or external elements—an endless list that included alcohol, sexual excesses, improper nutrition, grief, or anxiety.[25]

Irish immigrants appeared to have the highest rates of illness in general, and the highest rates of insanity, according to published data of the era. In New York, three-fourths of the admissions to the city lunatic asylum on Blackwell's Island from 1849 to 1859 were immigrants; two-thirds of these were Irish. Trying to account for these skewed figures, the asylum's resident physician speculated that "either the ratio of insane is very much less among the natives, or they are kept at their homes. Probably the first supposition is true, and this may arise in part from the shipment of the insane from Europe during a lucid interval." Clearly, the native-born preferred taking care of sick relatives at home, which left a preponderance of foreign-born in existing institutions. In 1854 physician Edward Jarvis calculated that, while only 43 percent of the poor insane ended up in a state institution, almost every one from among the foreigners did. One reason was the stigma attached to those native-born who allowed kin to be hospitalized in an era when the curable were expected to get better at home, and hospitals were places for the impoverished to die. Another reason was the desire on the part of the more affluent to avoid exposing loved ones to the poor conditions in mental hospitals where they might associate with society's bottom rung, especially the foreign-born.[26]

Although there is little doubt that Irish immigrants in New York City and elsewhere were institutionalized while the native-born deranged were treated at home, rates of institutionalization were not disproportionate to the size of the Irish immigrant population. More sophisticated techniques of statistical analysis developed after 1900 suggested that mid-nineteenth-century data on the admissions of immigrants to mental hospitals were greatly distorted: "When the institutionalized population was analyzed in terms of the age distribution of the entire native and foreign-born population, for example, the relative proportion of immigrants in hospitals declined precipitously." Additional corrections for sex distribution and urban rural residence still further explained the discrepancy between newcomer and native-born rates of mental disease.[27]

Data inaccuracies aside, the popular perception at midcentury was that the Irish immigrant had a greater propensity to mental illness than his or her host. Patterns of aberrant behavior diagnosed as insanity in the 1840s seemed quite common among newly arrived immigrants. The governors of the New York Almshouse attributed the condition to "privations on shipboard," or "the changes incident to arriving in a strange land," and "to want of sufficient nourishment." At least some of these conditions were judged to be temporary. In 1854 of the 100 patients admitted to New York's Lunatic Asylum and chargeable to the state's commissioners of emigration, 35 had been in New York City less than one year. Many of these were diagnosed as temporarily deranged and were later pronounced recovered and released.[28]

Both Irish men and women were reported as being particularly susceptible to schizophrenia and alcohol-related syndromes after immigration. One physician, perhaps looking through the gender kaleidoscope of his era, claimed that young women arrivals seemed especially prone to mental illness. He attributed it to "the combined moral and physical influences of their leaving the homes of their childhood, their coming almost destitute to a strange land, and often after great suffering."[29] Irish women appeared to be more vulnerable to mental disease than women of other groups if judged by the large number found in hospitals and asylums. However, the high rate of institutionalization may be accounted for by the fact that many Irish women emigrated alone and had no one to care for them in time of illness. A New York physician treating patients on Blackwell's Island commented on the large number of Irish women there, but he attributed their illnesses to environmental strains rather than to a predisposition to mental instability. Other sources observed that Irish women, who often married late and came to America alone in search of work as domestics or teachers, seemed more homesick for the parents and siblings they left behind than did Irish males, although more recent scholarship suggests that the males may have been even more vulnerable than the females.[30] Still, well into the twentieth century more than two-thirds of institutionalized Irish insane were women and the Irish continued to be the largest immigrant group in American insane asylums.[31]

Once institutionalized, the Irish suffered from anti-Catholicism on the part of many Protestants in charge of mental institutions. The trusting relationship between physician and patient necessary for therapy was disrupted by unbridgeable ethnic differences and prejudice. Common religion, values, and culture were absent and even sympathetic physicians found themselves at a loss. One physician confessed his inability to approach his foreign-born patients "in the proper way." He puzzled, "Modes of address like those used in our intercourse with our own people, generally fall upon their ears like an unknown tongue, or are comprehended just enough to render the whole misunderstood, and thereby excite feelings very different from such as we intended." Another superintendent regretted that his personnel could not easily gain the trust of immigrant patients, "for they seem jealous of our motives" and embarrassed by language difficulties, together significant obstacles to successful therapy and recovery.[32] The very foreignness of the immigrant mental patient seems to have contributed in part to undermining "the original postulates of the asylum movement" that sought to "re-create both in and out of the asylum, a well ordered, balanced, harmonious, and ultimately homogeneous community." Homogeneity was impossible in an ethnically pluralist nation. However, dangers posed by the mentally ill, perhaps even criminally insane, from abroad lent support for "straight-forward incarceration" as legitimate use for the asylum in protecting society from these less than desirable newcomers.[33]

Some professionals believed that the inner strength of those who undertook a journey to a foreign land predisposed the mentally ill among them to benefit from treatment. But again, cultural imperative influenced medical assessment. Germans were praised for possessing "a healthy and elastic mental constitution." They seemed "docile and affectionate" to their doctors and quick to express gratitude. The reverse was said of the Irish, who were described as less intelligent, resourceful, refined, or self-possessed than the native born or patients of other groups. Ralph L. Parsons, superintendent of the New York City Lunatic Asylum on Blackwell's Island described many of the Irish he saw as "persons of exceptionally bad habits." He believed the Irish patients to be of a "low order of intelligence, and very many of them have imperfectly developed brains. When such persons become insane, I am inclined to think that the prognosis is peculiarly unfavorable." In some cases superintendents sought to segregate the foreign-born mentally ill from the native-born on the grounds that the two groups of patients differed so in temperament.[34]

The prevalence of insanity among the Irish contributed to an evolving racial nativism. As historian John Higham and others have noted, concepts of race remained vague before the Civil War and the obvious physical similarities between the Irish immigrants and native-born Anglo-Americans hardly encouraged serious scientific argument for the two as distinctive races.[35] However, opponents of continued Irish immigration argued that it was more than the economic circumstances engendered by the famine that made the Irish undesirable additions to the republic; hereditary characteristics defined the Irish as beings of an inferior order.[36]

Although few actually read the studies of European ethnologists, many Americans were interested in the study of humankind. The popular press was filled with speculation on the value of various techniques to measure and define national characteristics with scientific precision, often referring to nationality as "race." Not surprisingly, Irish immigrants were a topic of much interest and their features were subjected to frequent phrenological and physiognomical analysis. An 1851 *Harper's* Magazine article discussing two Irish newcomers described the "Celtic physiognomy" as "distinctly marked—the small and somewhat upturned nose, the black tint of the skin; the eyes now looking gray, now black; the freckled cheek, and sandy hair. Beard and whiskers covered half the face, and short, square-shouldered bodies were bent forward with eager impatience."[37] Similar descriptions appeared frequently. Faces were often portrayed as simian-like with extended cheekbones, upturned nose and protruding teeth. Newspaper and magazine caricatures reflected these stereotypes or traced out derogatory phrenological charts of the head. Late in the nineteenth century, renowned cartoonist Thomas Nast continued to depict the Irishman and ape as closely related.

Irishmen were also portrayed as short and stocky, the very physique that pseudoscientists associated with people who were not very active, but somewhat "slothful" or "lazy." Many Irishmen were depicted as having coarse red hair, precisely the kind thought to indicate an "excitable," "sociable," or "gushing" personal manner. If Irish were ruddy-complexioned, this was seen as a sign that they were given to raw, unrestrained passions and self-indulgence. Those with dark eyes could be expected to be arduous or excessively sensuous. According to phrenologists in the 1850s, such individuals would not be contented with indoor or sedentary labor but would gravitate toward outdoor occupations because they required "a great amount of air and exercise."[38] That many of the Irish who arrived in midcentury worked on the docks or the railroads seemed to confirm their "scientific" profile. It did not occur to readers of Orson and Lorenzo Fowlers's *New Illustrated Self-Instructor in Phrenology and Physiology* (1859) or James Redfield's *Outline of a New System of Physiognomy* (1850) that the authors might have ascribed a certain personality profile to those physical characteristics already part of the Irish stereotype.

The Irish response to nativist charges that they were health menaces were not collective or systematic. But many seemed sensitive to charges of cultural or social inferiority; they seemed determined to demonstrate that the Irish were already fully capable of holding their own on the level American playing field. A compendium of commentary on the physical attributes of the Irish published in 1899 contained ample testimony from earlier in the century attesting to the robust good health of the Irish population, that "the Irish are dowered with nature's gifts in as high a degree as any people on earth." Objecting to the demeaning characterization of the Irish in the English journal, *Punch*, where the Irishman was parodied as a "low and savage type" adorned with "a tattered coat kneebreeches, a battered hat, a clay pipe, a sillelah," the author was equally vehement in his denunciation of antebellum American nativist literature, which "surpassed in savagery even the odious caricatures" of *Punch*. As for those who claimed Irish inferiority a product of the potato diet, an eighteenth-century Englishman, Arthur Young, was quoted observing that "the food of the common Irish is potatoes and milk; it is said not to be sufficiently nourishing for the support of hard labour; but this opinion is very amazing in a country, many of whose poor people are as athletic in their form, as robust, and as capable of enduring labour as any upon earth."[39] Of course that was true before the physical trials of emigration and settling in a new country.

After the exodus to America, well-off Irishmen who had achieved or been born to some measure of wealth and social standing sought to impose their social values on the Irish-immigrant masses as a means of ensuring their own influence and prestige in the new land. They often forged alliances with the Catholic Church in America. Both hoped to impose social control upon impoverished Irish Catholic immigrants by encouraging "industry, thrift, sobriety, self-control, and domestic purity," habits that would cement newcomers to the Church in America and shape citizens willing to be led by those who already considered themselves to be their group's stewards.[40] These patterns also held true for matters of health and health care.

Educated Irish shared the prevailing belief that the origins of disease were in miasmas, gaseous vapors arising from decaying organic matter. The idea that filth caused disease was beginning to take hold in Ireland in the early decades of the nineteenth century much as it was elsewhere in the Atlantic community. With qualified physicians "rare and expensive," however, their services had been largely limited to the rich in Ireland, while the majority of the Irish used local healers armed with folk remedies to treat the symptoms of particular ailments.[41] After emigration, Irish-born physicians living in the United States extended medical treatment to the needy newcomers in a spirit of altruism and to prevent the ill health of impoverished newcomers and their folk remedies from becoming an embarrassment to all Irishmen. Prominent Irish physicians in New York, committed to encouraging American middle-class behaviors among the newcomers, took special care of their own, perhaps because they had the most to lose if Americans attributed their negative perception of the Irish masses to all Irish. One of these was Dr. William James MacNeven, who arrived in the United States on July 4, 1805.

William MacNeven's background was atypical of Irish newcomers in almost every respect.[42] He was born to wealth in 1763, the son of landed Irish Catholic aristocracy. He was raised in Prague by an uncle who was titled nobility and a physician. William, too, became a physician, completing his studies in Vienna and returning to Ireland, where he sought a cure for his countrymen's ills in politics. He was a delegate to Ireland's Catholic Convention of 1793, commonly called the Back-Lane Parliament, serving until 1798, when he was arrested for his role in the Irish rebellion. After his release in 1802, he emigrated with two other Irish radicals, Thomas Addis Emmet and William Sampson.

MacNeven settled in New York City, where he taught medical sciences and established himself as a respected member of New York's literary society. He continued to work for Irish nationalism, but unlike many Irish exiles who were too busy with the issues to touch the lives of individual sufferers, MacNeven used his medical skills to help his fellow immigrants, whom he well knew were not inherently diseased, but suffering the side effects of emigration, poverty, and deprivation. He was known to treat the poor for no fee.[43] He often attended sick or dying immigrants who were stricken during their journey to America and were in desperate need of care when they reached New York. He offered individuals instruction in how to live a healthy life in America and created an emigrant aid society that sought to relieve unhealthy urban congestion by colonizing newcomers in the West.

William MacNeven's efforts in behalf of the health of the Irish poor and his advocacy of standards of health and hygiene drew the approval of those of his own class—both Irish and non-Irish alike, and may in part account for his immense popularity. When he died in 1841, he was regarded by many as the "recognized leader of the Catholic Irish community in New York."[44] MacNeven looked upon the cholera epidemic's victims with compassion, but also as newcomers whose habits of life must be changed if they were to be healthy wage-earners and acceptable to their non-Irish countrymen.

The clamor for Irish immigrants to assimilate, to become more "American," was heard and answered at the altar where most of them worshipped. The Roman Catholic Church set out not only to assist stricken immigrants but to do so in a manner consistent with the faith, as it had done historically in other countries.[45] Individual religious responded promptly to the 1832 epidemic. The Sisters of Charity nursed cholera victims in New York and other cities. Father Felix Varela, a native of Cuba who became much beloved among New York's Irish Catholics, "lived in the hospitals" during the epidemic.[46] Even so, attacks on the Catholic clergy by Protestant newspapermen were not uncommon. During the 1849 cholera epidemic, the distinguished editor of the *New York Herald*, James Gordon Bennett, chided New York's equally well-known Catholic bishop, John Hughes, for vacationing at Saratoga Springs while his clergy labored to comfort those dying of cholera.[47] Neither the church nor Hughes was indifferent to the suffering among newcomers or to the ways in which opponents of the Catholic Church sought to capitalize on it. Their response was institutional, the building of a Catholic hospital in New York City.

In 1830 New York's Bishop John Dubois wrote to the secretary of the Association for the Propagation of the Faith in Lyons, describing his diocese and its needs. One of the most urgent was "a hospital in New York, where a number of the emigrants who daily arrive and suffer for want of attention might regain both corporal and spiritual health." He regretted that newcomers in need of medical care were being treated in a hospital three miles outside the city, one "administered by Protestants." Nor could he even adequately care for the spiritual wants of "the seven hundred Catholic sick who are in that institution [probably Bellevue]."[48] Four years later, after the onset of the cholera epidemic had created even more pressing needs, Bishop Dubois called for the creation of a Catholic hospital that would "afford our poor emigrants, particularly from Ireland, the necessary relief, attendance in sickness and spiritual comfort, amidst the disease of a climate new to them."[49] Dubois was one of many Catholic priests troubled by the Protestant ethos of American public institutions, including schools and orphanages, as well as hospitals. In private and public institutions operated by Protestants, priests were frequently denied access to Catholic patients. Protestant clergy converted the elderly on their deathbeds and often conducted Protestant services in juvenile wards to capture young minds and hearts.[50] The New York bishop well understood that maintaining a hospital, especially one that would serve the immigrant poor would be a way to battle Protestants for newcomers' souls, to provide an institutional identification for Catholic migrants, much in the way that churches and fraternal organizations did.[51]

In 1847, a year after a second cholera epidemic in 1846, Bishop John Hughes published a pastoral letter attacking the intrusion of Protestant clergy upon Catholic public hospital patients and called for the establishment of a Catholic hospital in New York to care for immigrants.[52] Examples of the warfare for souls was plentiful. In early 1848 a young illiterate Irish Catholic girl, Ellen Duffy, published an affidavit in which she claimed that, while living in the House of Industry, a private nonsectarian benevolent institution to help the poor find employment, she took sick and was denied the ministrations of a Catholic priest after specifically requesting them. She claimed that one of the assistant managers of the institution, a Miss Balch, had told her, "Ellen, you do not want any Catholic clergyman, you want my minister." Father George McCloskey, who had been summoned by one of Ellen's friends and was denied access to her until she was moved to Bellevue Hospital, confirmed that he had been summoned by one of Ellen's friends and denied access to her until she was moved to Bellevue Hospital. Even his efforts to secure the intervention of a New York alderman had come to nought.[53] As in the case of the parochial school, the Catholic hospital seemed to church leaders an essential fortress against the assaults of proselytizing Protestants.[54]

In 1849 St. Vincent's Hospital opened its doors in Lower Manhattan, on East 13th Street. The first published report on the institution left little doubt about why it was founded. "Although a Catholic institution, its doors are ever opened to the afflicted of all denominations who seek admission, and who may be attended during their illness by their own ministers, if desirable."[55] St. Vincent's was not only a response to the specific disease accusations of the cholera years, it was a response to persistent Protestant conversion efforts. The hospital was staffed by the Sisters of Charity under the leadership of Hughes's sister, Sister Mary Angela Hughes. The Sisters' founder, Mother Elizabeth Ann Seton (later the first canonized saint of American birth), was the daughter of Dr. Richard Bayley, a physician and health inspector of immigrants in the port of New York. He died of yellow fever contracted from his patients at the Quarantine Hospital on Staten Island. Elizabeth Seton married, but by 1803 was a penniless widow. She converted to Catholicism the following year and five years later founded the Sisters of Charity.[56]

The Sisters were well experienced with hospitals and understood the enormous potential for linking cures for the body to those that their faith offered the soul. Indeed, some argue that the Sisters' spiritual concerns both for themselves and their patients fueled the fires of their zealous efforts to offer medical care and comfort to beleaguered newcomers.[57] In 1828 five of them had started the first Catholic Hospital in the United States in St. Louis.[58] Later, in 1834, they were asked by the governors of the public hospital in New Orleans to take charge of the Charity Hospital, which was sinking under the burden of victims of a hurricane and fire, as well as numerous leprosy cases. In New York, the Sisters were already well known for their work with cholera patients during the 1832 epidemic.

In 1849 St. Vincent's Hospital had a 30-bed capacity; by 1861, the hospital had moved to West 11th Street and its facilities had been expanded to accommodate 150 patients. At the turn of the century, it was treating in excess of 3,500 patients annually.[59] Although the hospital was open to all the city's Catholics, the inability of the Sisters of Charity to speak German contributed to its becoming a largely Irish Catholic institution, especially after the German Sisters of the Poor St. Francis founded St. Francis Hospital on New York's Lower East Side in 1865. By the turn of the century, even as immigrants from southern and eastern Europe were pouring into Lower Manhattan, more than a quarter of the hospital's patients remained Irish.[60]

St. Vincent's Hospital made a favorable impression on the distinguished surgeon, Dr. William Van Buren, who toured the facility early in 1850. In a published article he remarked, "We found the hospital rooms large and airy and we need not say, remarkable for cleanliness and order. There are ample accommodations for a large number of patients and everything betokens the careful, kind and conscientious attention to the needs of the sick which so powerfully assists recovery from disease." Even more important, St. Vincent's quickly captured the hearts of those it was founded to serve. Typical was the patient whom surgeon Van Buren described as "a true Irishman." Responding to an inquiry about the discomfort he was feeling after the removal of a cancer from his lip and cheek, this patient answered, "Sure I suffered, but did not our Blessed Savior suffer more for me on the cross? I thank God Almighty that He has been pleased to send me here, where I have so well got rid of it!"[61]

St. Vincent's Hospital not only allowed patients to draw upon the comforts of their faith in their suffering, it enhanced patients' dignity by charging modest fees rather than setting up as an almshouse. In 1858, a physician in Manhattan's New York Hospital observed that working-class Irish preferred St. Vincent's to his own institution and seemed not to mind paying their way. The Sisters of Charity well understood the charitable needs of the community they served. As St. Vincent's annual report noted in 1858, "Although the terms for board and medical attendance are three dollars per week, nevertheless many patients are received free."[62]

Still, there were never enough resources. The report lamented, "Daily are they [the Sisters of Charity] obliged, with pain and sorrow to turn away some poor afflicted one whose means will not allow him to pay even a part of the small sum asked for admission. It is impossible for the Sisters to accommodate all the poor patients who apply for aid and medical treatment. Often are they obliged even to furnish some of them with articles of clothing, besides receiving them as free patients." As always, the church appealed to the philanthropy of its flock, encouraging Catholic New Yorkers to purchase "yearly subscriptions which would secure free beds, and thus afford relief to many of the poor suffering creatures."[63] By the turn of the century, the needs were still great. Of the 3,681 patients treated at the hospital, 1,161 were total charity cases, 1,255 were receiving partial assistance, and 1,265 (a third), were paying for their care.[64] Clearly, the needs of the New York community were not atypical. In 1885 there were 154 hospitals run by Catholic orders in the United States, more than the total number of hospitals of all kinds that had existed when the Civil War ended in 1865.[65] To paraphrase the title of Charles Rosenberg's volume on hospitals, Irish Catholics truly did transform the "care of strangers" into the care of their own.

The arrival of millions of Irish also did truly transform the face of American immigration. Vague fears of strangers coalesced into specific stigmatization of a particular group. Preexisting anti-Catholic sentiments and the sheer size of the migration sent shock waves of apprehension through native-born Americans, especially in port cities such as New York where the presence of the Irish was most visible and where sick or disabled newcomers most strained existing facilities for care of the sick and impoverished. Half a century later, nativists would again justify their restrictive policies by claiming that the Chinese brought plague, the Italians polio, and the Jews tuberculosis.

This medicalization of prejudice against the Irish inspired the passage of state legislation and the establishment of administrative procedures to effect the inspection and regulation of immigrants. No longer did perfunctory preboarding medical examinations and routine quarantine procedures seem adequate to protect the public health from foreign health menaces. Indeed, during the next great wave of immigration responsibilities for the inspection and processing of immigration would be further formalized and transferred from state to federal jurisdiction.

Even as nativists marshaled their legal and administrative resources to repel the Irish, immigrants learned that they, too, must coordinate a response to the enemies who would stigmatize them as unfit for America and bar the country's door against them. Newcomers with needed skills and resources defended their group's welfare through the direct delivery of services, including medical care. Others channeled their philanthropy through their church or other organizations to build institutions that would parallel those of the native-born. Precedents of self-help set by the Irish and the Catholic Church in antebellum New York would become routine among immigrants arriving half a century later.

The association of the Irish and disease in the mid–nineteenth century marks an early appearance of the medicalization of prejudice, an important theme of American nativism, and a historical perennial that must be placed in the dual context of both the history of migration and the history of American medicine. Like all perennials, this one continues to flower periodically.[66] In the 1980s and 1990s, the United States again has been in the midst of a wave of immigration that nativists abhor and again, a disease has been socially constructed to the disadvantage of a particular group. The sad experiences of the Haitian immigrants, stigmatized a decade ago with accusations about their alleged susceptibility to AIDS, stands as a contemporary reminder that illnesses and values, lifestyles, foreignness and danger continue to be metaphors for each other and to nourish preexisting prejudices.[67] However, patterns of assistance and altruism, too, often reappear and, at times, the same institutions that served the foreign-born in the past continue their mission in the present. Haitian immigrants and other Catholic newcomers from the Caribbean and Southeast Asia receive free or low-cost health care and attention to their spiritual needs at St. Vincent's Hospital, much as Irish immigrants of earlier generations did in antebellum New York.

William E. Devlin

CHAPTER 7

Shrewd Irishmen

IRISH ENTREPRENEURS AND ARTISANS IN

NEW YORK'S CLOTHING INDUSTRY,

1830–1880

I N 1852 a reporter for a grandiloquent New York City paper called the *Atlas* penned a description of a prospering men's clothing store, Union Hall. The six floors of this "splendid freestone edifice" at Nassau and Fulton Streets, in the heart of what was then the city's garment district, were apparently a hive of activity. Each floor housed a branch of the men's clothing trade as it was then practiced: custom tailoring took place on one floor, the manufacture of "ready-made" clothing for men and boys took place on another, and a retail salesroom and wholesale warehouse space occupied the remaining floors. As a men's clothing store, Union Hall could be "surpassed by few in the city," the writer declared. He was "surprised and amazed . . . by the amount of commerce and thrift [he] witnessed. On every side were large cases and other packages, addressed to merchants in almost every state and city of the Union, waiting only to be transmitted to their respective places of destination, a la railway and steamer."

Success stories in the garment business are a New York staple, familiarly with a Jewish protagonist. But at the helm of Union Hall was a County Tyrone native, Patrick Rogers. "He has by industry, intelligence, and prudent and careful watch on his credit, succeeded in building up a large business," a hard-nosed credit agent wrote of Rogers in 1852. He had landed in New York only half-trained as a tailor a scant 16 years before. By 1852 he owned, besides his business, a comfortable home in Williamsburg.[1]

This chapter examines New York's clothing industry as an avenue for the economic survival, assimilation, and advancement of Irish immigrants during the middle years of the nineteenth century, particularly for artisans and entrepreneurs who, like Patrick Rogers, had aspirations beyond mere survival. The discussion focuses on two occupational groups, tailors and hatters, distinct but related trades in which some Irish immigrants enjoyed visible success.

During the period of the Great Migration not only did individuals like Rogers make their mark in the city's clothing business but the industry was a major point of entry into the economic life of the city for thousands of Irish immigrants. In 1855 the New York State census identified more than 11,000 Irish-born New Yorkers working in what had become the city's largest industry, making men's suits, shirts and shoes, hats and caps, and women's dresses, hoop skirts, and millinery. They accounted for one of every eight Irish immigrants employed in the city and for approximately 36 percent of the local industry's work force.[2]

The workers of concern in this discussion consist of the presumably skilled and sometimes entrepreneurial population probably numbering about 2,000 by 1860, that included artisans and merchants who sold "ready-made" or used clothing but did not necessarily produce it themselves. From their ranks emerged leaders—in business, in the union movement, even in the creative side of designing clothing. Yet these trades, especially tailoring, were largely abandoned by the Irish by 1890. The central questions to be considered here are why the clothing industry became so important to the New York Irish during this period, how it might have led to individual economic independence and security, what consequences this might have had for the Irish immigrant community, and why the Irish were supplanted in the industry by newer groups, in a process of ethnic succession that continues to this day.

This is largely unexplored territory. Studies of New York's clothing industry unfailingly note an Irish presence during this period but supply few details. And the army of domestic servants and day laborers who streamed into New York from the famine-stricken Irish countryside during this period has tended to command the attention of scholars and popular historians alike, monopolizing the usual image of this immigrant population. Therefore, although the plight of the nineteenth-century seamstress, often an immigrant, has been studied in some depth, left unanswered is the question of whether there were identifiable groups of skilled Irish workers in the city and how they fared during this period. A number of questions immediately arise in the case of tailors and hatters: Were they simply victims of a ruthlessly exploitive industry undergoing a transition to mass production? Was their presence an indication of a decline of artisanal skills and traditions? How were they accepted by native workers and employers? What skills did they bring? How were they able to adapt to conditions in the industry, start businesses, compete with native Americans, as Patrick Rogers did?[3]

The answers to these questions begin to emerge in an examination of prefamine Ireland. There, tailoring was a significant urban trade, one of the island's five largest trade groups in 1831, claiming between 15,000 and 30,000 practitioners. Both tailors and hatters tended naturally to live in Ireland's cities and larger towns. They also tended to be concentrated in its better-developed areas, where they serviced the gentry, prosperous farmers, and fellow town dwellers. Cottiers and other rural and urban poor whose clothing was not homemade relied on a huge trade in secondhand garments, originating at huge fairs outside London. Travelers in prefamine Ireland seldom failed to note the multitudes of people they observed wearing rags or clothing long out of fashion.[4]

In Ireland both tailoring and hatting were organized trades in the early nineteenth century. Tailors in particular were considered "a strong combination," with rights under the Irish statutes to petition for increases in wages or to regulate work hours. Irish hatters reportedly had ties to English journeymen's societies in their trade.[5]

But most Irish clothing artisans faced a bleak future of insecurity and poverty if they remained at home. Their living standards and social status were not high to begin with: "most townspeople—artisans and laborers—lived barely above subsistence level in filthy, congested and disease-ridden slums and 'cabin suburbs.'" Their education was rudimentary and short, invariably terminating with an apprenticeship at the age of 12 or 14, if not younger. And British society accorded low status to most tradesmen. The masculinity of tailors was derided in the popular expression "it takes nine snippies to make a man," while hatters had to contend with "drunk as a hatter" or "mad as a hatter," the latter expression a reference to the uncontrollable palsy some older hatters developed as a result of long exposure to the mercury used on fur to help make it into felt, from which most hats were made.[6]

Most of Ireland's nascent industries collapsed under the Union, and as the early decades of the nineteenth century progressed the agricultural economy deteriorated. Many of the big provincial towns began to lose population. Those who drifted into the towns and cities tended to be landless paupers evicted from nearby estates, hardly a promising clientele for the makers of clothes. While the hopeless country folk swarmed into the city slums, the skilled artisans of the towns joined with shopkeepers and professional men in "the vanguard of the exodus to America, where . . . [they] were likely to succeed."[7]

Some emigrated first to England, like Dublin-born tailor Robert Crowe, who left a brief memoir of his eventful life. Crowe learned his trade in a brief apprenticeship "in the sweating dens of London." Like Crowe, many Irish tailors in England often moved on again to America, attracted especially to New York. There, wages for tailors during the 1830s were reputed to be one-third higher than in London. Moreover, New York's already notorious high prices and living costs may not have been a significant deterrent to craftsmen accustomed to those of Dublin, considered the most expensive city in the British Empire.[8]

The vanguard of emigration of Irish clothing artisans began to arrive early in New York; city directories of the 1780s and 1790s list several Irish-surnamed tailors and hatters. Newcomers generally found their first homes in the city in the old houses and new tenements within walking distance of the Second Ward, where the city's clothing businesses were concentrated, among the huge, fluid, and largely Irish population of sailors, laborers, and smiths of the downtown wards. Even in these generally poor locations, newly arrived artisans of the 1830s, 1840s, and 1850s could find visibly successful predecessors. During the 1820s a New York-born Irish American, James Leary, had revolutionized the city's hat trade by introducing a low-priced hat napped with nutria fur for half the price of the more stylish beaver. By the late 1840s Leary, who frequently traveled to Europe to pick up on the latest French hat styles, was being touted as "the arbiter of fashion" for the city's retail hat trade, his shop a training ground for many of the city's hat retailers, some of whom were Irish immigrants. But there were also precedents for success by recent Irish immigrants. A handful of tailors identified in the 1855 New York State census of seven downtown wards owned real property, and 24, about 3 percent of the total, had their own household servants.[9]

The numbers of Irish tailors and Irish-owned clothing businesses in the city surged during the 1830s, and during each year of the famine period of 1847–55, about a hundred Irish tailors settled in the city. U.S. Census Bureau figures from the years between 1875 and 1914, when immigrant tailors began to be identified by nationality, record between 40 and 177 of them entering the United States directly from Ireland each year. Some of these settled in New York, and Irish tailors no doubt accounted for a substantial proportion of the nearly 8,000 recorded as arriving from England during that period.[10]

The New York State census of 1855 and much anecdotal evidence suggests that most Irish immigrant tailors and hatters were artisans with some level of training who emigrated in their 20s or early 30s with the expectation of supporting a family. Sixty percent of almost a thousand tailors sampled from seven wards in the state census were married and 46 percent had between one and four children. Moreover, they were likely to be the sole, or at least the primary support of their families. Only a small percentage (6%) lived with parents or other kin. Only 10 percent had working spouses or working children, and almost a third of these lived in one ward, the Sixth. Only 16 percent kept boarders. The range of age levels found also suggests that both tailors and hatters tended to remain in their craft through their lifetimes. The rate of literacy was high, suggesting at least some schooling, although those in the postfamine group were three times as likely to be illiterate or semiliterate (10%) than those who had arrived earlier (3%). The 82 Irish hatters sampled were working in a conservative trade in which traditional craft practices were only slowly giving way to mechanization. They were quicker than tailors to become naturalized (43% as opposed to 27%), and more likely to have father and son in the same

173

*Irish Entrepreneurs
and Artisans in
New York's
Clothing Industry,
1830–1880*

profession (12 examples), reflecting a still-breathing tradition of passing on traditional skills. Less than half of the hatters were married, none of those who were had working spouses, and only one-fifth had children. These living arrangements allowed them freedom to travel and fend about for work when and where it was available, as true journeymen. Whether they emigrated as trained artisans or learned their trade here, the Irish in the hatting trade appear to have adapted readily to an artisan culture with roots in the Middle Ages.[11]

This was clearly a population possessing at least some skills, and, usually, some education. They had as well some experience of urban living and conditions, if not on quite the scale they found in New York, a city that worked at "a railroad pace." Finally, that same urban background would suggest that most, if not all, were English-speaking, a factor that would have allowed them to move directly into the mainstream of the growing clothing industry.

That growth since the beginning of the nineteenth century had been nothing short of spectacular. The beginnings of mass production of presized, or ready-made clothing (today it would be called "off the rack") created a revolution in American dress. The city's first clothing stores coalesced around the docks of South and Pearl Streets, where ready-made clothing originated as a convenience to sailors who could not wait for fitted, tailor-made garments. During the early decades of the nineteenth-century dealers in presized, manufactured clothing, or clothiers, began to sell to the general male populace. The more egalitarian modes of male dress ushered in by the French Revolution (especially frock coats and trousers) made men's clothing easier to mass produce, and its convenience made it popular. Soon ready-made coats, felt hats, and suits were being exported to the South via the "cotton triangle" between New York's port, southern ports, and Europe, and to the West via the Hudson River and the Erie Canal. The industry entered a prolonged period of takeoff, protected by a tariff of up to 50 percent and fueled by the demand of a growing urban middle class and professional population. By 1860 New York City's 30,000 clothing workers were annually producing about 40 percent of the country's total output of clothing. Later, strengthened by the beginnings in earnest of a garment industry for women, production tripled between the end of the Civil War and 1880. Analogous developments occurred in hatting. Manhattan became the nation's capital for the production of the tall, expensive silk hats favored by the elite, but its chief role was as the entrepôt for millions of hats produced in its hinterlands, particularly in centers in Connecticut and New Jersey, and later Brooklyn and Yonkers.[12]

A clothing district developed in the city, centered on the Second Ward and emerging first downtown in the Nassau and Fulton Street area, but by the 1840s moving to lower Broadway, where the multitude of retail stores and fine hotels appealed to country merchants on semiannual buying trips to the city, and moving northward over time up that avenue following the movement of the dry goods trade. A cheaper mirror image of Broadway competed a few blocks east on the Bowery, while Chatham Square became a favorite slumming destination for middle-class New Yorkers who enjoyed the bazaar-like atmosphere of its mostly Jewish-owned secondhand clothing stores. Finally, sailors' clothing stores clung to the seedy docks around West Street, many of them with a grog shop on the side. The Irish would work and start businesses in all these locations.

Throughout this period of growth, immigrant clothing artisans of all nationalities were welcomed. "It is always difficult to get skilled labor . . . , a clothing manufacturer complained to *Clothier & Furnisher* Magazine in 1883, "there is always a demand for good workmen, and we all steal from each other without compunction." Some immigrants even followed traditional craft practices in securing employment. The tailor Robert Crowe brought with him a letter of recommendation from his previous employer when he emigrated to New York in 1856, which "procured [him] immediate work." Irish workmen in these trades seem to have borne no particular stigma; the British hatter James Dawson Burn, who worked beside immigrants of many nationalities in the back shops of the New York metropolitan area in the 1860s, found Irish workmen to be "among the most useful of the industrial members of the community in this country . . . not less industrious than the Germans," but more sensitive to perceived insults and more "impulsive."[13]

But the clothing industry also fed unashamedly on immigrant labor, both skilled and unskilled. No other American industry was so dominated by the foreign-born: 53 percent of all tailors and tailoresses in the country were foreign-born in 1880, according to federal census figures, while 95 percent of New York's tailors and two-thirds of its hatters were in this category in 1855.

The demands of mass production and the availability of sources of potentially cheap labor fundamentally changed the clothing trades, especially tailoring. Instead of mechanizing hand processes, as occurred over a long period of time in hatting, garments came to be designed and precut in huge quantities by highly skilled tailors called cutters, then contracted out for assembly (sewing) to journeymen tailors, seamstresses, or virtually any responsible party willing to contract or subcontract for the work. Many Irish tailors listed in the 1855 state census, particularly the newly arrived, had been sucked into living in boardinghouses owned by grocers, liquor dealers, or other tailors who contracted for work from clothing manufacturers. Forty of these proto-sweatshops for tailors and shoemakers existed in the Sixth Ward alone in 1855. Virtually all workers were paid at piece rates, which could fluctuate rapidly.[14]

The practices of contracting and outwork continually drove wages down with the result that the ready-made clothing industry became the lowest paid in the city. Union leader Edward Mallon told a rally of striking tailors in 1850 that those employed by southern trade manufacturers could expect "75 cents a day . . . and I would assert that far the greater number make less . . . (and) the majority of them have families to support. The average number of members in each

175

*Irish Entrepreneurs
and Artisans in
New York's
Clothing Industry,
1830–1880*

family may be taken at four. A man cannot rent a room, and bedroom to shelter them on the third story of an ill-ventilated house, for less than $6 a month. Then he has $12 per month to provide fuel, food and raiment for them. Thus they are entirely debarred from all the enjoyments of life, and scarcely able to subsist in the most wretched and miserable manner." Wages were better for hatters, who retained a rough parity with other skilled trades, but even the $10 weekly foreman's pay offered Charles Knox by his employer in 1844 would translate into a $500 annual wage, a figure rated by contemporary city newspaper editors as "a bare minimum" to support a family in the city "without want."[15]

The subdivision of labor in these two crafts had other impacts on the Irish. In both tailoring and hatting the average craftsman trained in traditional ways of making a product from start to finish was gradually reduced to doing essentially semiskilled assembly work or machine operation. The remaining jobs in the two trades that required special skills became more valuable, and the resulting job hierarchy favored the well-connected. Cutters in the large clothing houses, for example, earned on average a third more than tailors and were seldom laid off, even during financial panics when they had no work to do. The new semimechanized hatting practiced during this period nonetheless required deftness of touch and experienced judgment, especially on the part of the finishers who used sandpaper, blocks, irons, and other tools to shape rough cones of felt into finished hats. The Irish were at first barely represented in these upper levels of the job hierarchy. Only seven Irish-born cutters could be found in seven wards in the 1855 state census, and almost all of those hatters who identified themselves as finishers were American-born or Germans. And with the glut of readily available immigrant workers, the long-troubled institution of apprenticeship withered away in the city's tailoring trade. In 1861 the *Times* reported that "it would be hard to find six American boys in the city who are being brought up to the tailoring business." Newly arrived Irish tailors would have worked primarily on coats, the heaviest and most complex of male garments, and would have had to compete with the city's many low-paid sewing women for work on pants or vests. Most New York hatters worked in small finishing shops or in silk hat manufactories of up to 60 workers.[16]

The clothing trades were a harrowing way of making a living for other reasons as well. The industry's traditional production schedule, centered around spring and fall buying seasons, made employment unsteady and necessitated a constant shifting about for work. Clothing workers and their families regulated their lives by the production seasons. For example, four children of one clothing worker were all born between May 1 and June 23, indicating a conception date in late August or early September, a "dull season" in the trade. Because they produced consumer products sensitive to demand, the two trades under study here were hard hit by the financial panics of 1854, 1857, and 1873, which abruptly disrupted employment for the majority of the city's clothing workers.

And each trade had its own unique health hazards. Tailors suffered from indigestion, poor posture and stooping, poor eyesight, exhaustion, liver diseases, and consumption; hatters from the effects of wood alcohol and mercury. Job security was nonexistent except among cutters and other top hands, and no provision for old age existed in either trade. The pathetic fate of one Irish tailor, Cornelius Doris of Hudson Street, is recounted matter-of-factly in the field agent reports of the R. G. Dun & Co. Doris arrived in the city in 1841 and worked actively into the 1850s, but by the end of the decade he was described as "drying out" and later, "in ill health . . . about used up." The Irish American Daniel Edward Ryan wrote that even the aristocratic clothing cutters and foremen had reason to dread advancing age. Their reward, he wrote, "after a slaves life of years upon years . . . [was] premature old age, and a bench in a corner of the cutting room, as a 'Buzzard cutter' on a legacy of a boy's wages."[17]

That the record of the Irish under these conditions was anything besides victimhood is surprising. But it also reveals, on the part of some, adaptability, opportunism, and assertiveness of their rights as workers. One reason for this adaptability was the incredible diversity and complexity of New York's clothing industry during this period. The industry was subdivided into numerous distinct trades, market segments, and work practices. The existing evidence suggests that Irish tailors gravitated toward the areas they were most familiar with in Ireland: custom tailoring, unions, even the secondhand clothing trade. The U.S. Industrial Commission reported in 1901, after the Irish had largely disappeared from tailoring in the city, that "it [had been] customary for the Irish tailor to work in the back shop of the merchant tailor." In his 1905 study of the city's clothing industry, Professor Jesse Pope asserted that the custom trade had been the Irishman's ticket to upward mobility, that as a group the Irish had been pushed upward in the industry by newcomers. "From the custom trade," he wrote, "they became the manufacturers, the cutters, the foremen who directed the industry," controlling the cutting trade into the 1880s.[18]

Contemporary sources corroborate at least an Irish attraction to custom tailoring. The market for custom-tailored clothes remained large in the city, despite the popularity of ready-made clothing. One reason for this demand was timeworn tradition; another was quality. It was not until the late 1870s that manufacturers felt confident enough to proclaim that ready-made clothes equaled the product of the custom tailor. The average journeyman's skill thus remained essential, and merchant tailors (those who owned their own shops and employed journeymen) as well as the custom departments of the large men's clothing houses paid more than the ready-made manufacturers for their higher-quality garments. But the selling season was short in the custom trade, sometimes only 24 weeks or less. Off-season, depending on the demand, journeymen could produce cheaper clothing for their employer, shift to taking out ready-made work for themselves from the big men's clothing houses, or become contractors and subcontractors, employing other journeymen or seamstresses.

177

*Irish Entrepreneurs
and Artisans in
New York's
Clothing Industry,
1830–1880*

Some contracting journeymen were capable of producing up to a thousand coats in a week, and "by the fifties, many journeymen in shoemaking and tailoring—either as heads of households or as garret masters—also exercised some of the prerogatives of the small employer," albeit at the cost of exploiting their own countrymen. But it was thus possible for skilled tailors, as most of the Irish seem to have been, to manipulate the seasonal production schedule to their advantage, if times were good. A kind of independence could result, bemoaned by a manufacturer in an article in *Clothier and Furnisher* in 1883: "In the Fall (the best hands) return to their custom work at about such prices as they choose to ask. You can't talk any 'poor tailor' to me," he complained, "no labor is more independent than the men who make clothes." Independence was taken for granted in hatting, where skilled journeymen customarily shifted from shop to shop or even from city to city for work between seasons or for better wages.[19]

The record also shows some Irish families adapting to conditions by working as a unit. As already mentioned, the sons of several Irish hatters in the city in 1855 were learning the trade as apprentices, presumably with their fathers. The state census of 1855 also reveals that a number of tailors' wives in the Sixth Ward were sewing at home alongside their husbands as "tailoresses." Some Irish tailors also apparently practiced what was called "the family system," usually associated with Germans, by putting all the family members to work. An R. G. Dun & Co. field agent reported of merchant tailor James Murray of 18 Clarkson Street during the 1850s that "he works hard at his business and makes all his family work hard . . . he and his family do nearly all the work."[20]

There is also evidence that Irish clothing artisans placed great value in saving some of what they were able to earn. An 1857 survey of six New York savings banks, including the Emigrant Industrial Savings Bank whose depositors were 80 percent Irish, found clothing workers as a group to be the third largest group of depositors by occupation, after domestics and boardinghouse keepers. Most of the deposits were small amounts, between $10 and $20. Although a majority of depositors surveyed were women, some 1,200 were male tailors. Savings provided the capital for numerous Irish clothing businesses, and the adjectives "frugal" and "saving" appear frequently in the credit reports of R. G. Dun & Co. field agents on Irish tailors, hatters, clothiers, and hat dealers.[21]

Irish tailors and hatters were also quick to join labor organizations and eventually to organize them where they did not exist. New York's existing journeymen's societies at first resisted admitting immigrant artisans, but by 1850 the Irish were so numerous in them that an English-speaking union of tailors that participated in a citywide strike against southern trade employers was called the "Irish" union, even though it contained men of several nationalities. Its leadership was Irish; men like Joseph Donnelly, George Clancy, and William Leonard forged a coalition with German-speaking unionists and acted as spokesmen for both groups to employers and to the press.[22]

Trade organizations were often short-lived in the clothing industry, with its plethora of employers and contractors, reliance on piecework, and competing forms of cheap labor. But among custom tailors, where the Irish were concentrated, a permanent union emerged in 1862. One of the founders of the Custom Tailors Benevolent and Protective Union that year was Robert Crowe, who left an account of its founding. In his autobiography, Crowe described how wartime conditions had inflated prices in the city while wages had remained stagnant, while, he recalled, "no form of combination then existed to protect the interest of the worker." In six months, he reported, 2,000 journeymen tailors had been enticed to join the new union, and the organization's efforts "had doubled the prices of garments throughout the city." Over the next 15 years Crowe's union exerted a stabilizing influence on piecework prices and on employment in the custom tailoring trade, despite the complex task of negotiating piece rates with literally hundreds of employers. A survey of wages and unemployment in the city's trades in the *New York Times* in 1876, when they were still suffering from the panic of 1873, rated both the tailors' and hatters' as "strong societies." The survey found that most "society men" continued to be employed during the depressed times at prepanic wages. Robert Crowe served as the organization's secretary, participated in an abortive effort to found a national organization after the Civil War, and chaired the 1883 convention in Philadelphia that created the first permanent national tailors' union, the Journeyman Tailors' Union of America.[23]

Irish leadership is more difficult to find among the hatters in the city until the 1870s, when several Irish officers appear in hatting organizations. But the Irish were strongly represented in the leadership of national hatting unions, including James P. Maher, who grew up in Brooklyn during the latter part of the period under study here and who later became treasurer of the United Hatters and a U.S. representative from New Jersey.[24]

The most prominent Irish clothing worker in the city's labor movement was a radical tailor named Robert Blissert. A skilled and inflammatory speaker, the Irish-born Blissert emigrated to New York from London after the Civil War and began working for fashionable Park Avenue tailors. Already a socialist, he was appalled by conditions in New York, particularly by the tenements, which he called "little better than cages." He quickly became active in the Journeyman Tailors' Union, and in 1870 he emerged as one of a group attempting to organize a workingmen's party in the city. A year later he was an officer of a national parent organization for workingmen's cooperatives. Blissert's voice of disillusion and revolution soon began to appear in the city's press, which in 1872 quoted his speeches to strikers for an eight-hour day. His career as a labor leader reached an apex in 1882, when he was chosen as the first acting president of New York City's Central Labor Union. As that body's president, Blissert, whose radicalism was tinged with Irish nationalism, organized a mass rally in Union Square to welcome Land Leaguer Michael Davitt to the city. Soon after that,

Blissert dropped out of the public eye to run his own tailoring business for the next 12 years. According to an R. G. Dun & Co. field agent's report, his credit was guaranteed by "a wealthy merchant," whose patronage allowed Blissert to continue his radical activities to some extent.[25]

Pope's scenario of Irish upward mobility into "the cutting trade" and manufacturing was another form of adaptation that has some basis in fact. The cutter's trade could be a step toward a foreman's position and even higher management; during the 1850s Irish-born cutters William P. O'Hara and John Devlin became partners in major city clothing firms despite having no capital to contribute. Between 1855 and 1880 Irish cutters increased from a bare handful—only seven Irish-born cutters could be found in seven downtown wards in the state census of 1855—to a substantial number. Cutters with Irish surnames listed in *Trow's City Directory of 1880* number 169. But even that number accounts for at best 15 percent of the city's total. Pope's perception of Irish "control" of the cutting trade may have been colored by the fact that in the 1870s and 1880s Irish cutters and foremen were being employed by some of the leading clothing houses, including Brooks Brothers, and by the influence of Daniel Edward Ryan.[26]

Son of an Irish tailor who had settled in Kentucky, Ryan began designing clothes as a youth and was recruited by New York clothiers impressed by his exhibit at the Cincinnati Exposition of 1873. Ryan dreamed of being an independent designer, but instead wound up working at good salaries ($5,000 in 1880) for a succession of big clothing houses, including Browning, King, and Sweet, Orr & Co. He may have been the earliest recognized American clothing designer. He was noted in the trade for the fine fit of his design and his attention to detail, particularly in boys' suits. He did public relations for the American clothing industry abroad; with his neat Vandyke beard, flowing moustache, and ramrod-straight posture, he was dubbed "the very embodiment of what a well-dressed gentleman ought to be" by the *Tailor and Cutter* magazine of London after a trip there in 1885.[27]

For several years Ryan led a campaign, at least partly successful, to improve the professional standards and pay of clothing cutters and foremen. He oversaw the organization of the New York Cutters' and Tailors' Association in February 1881 and edited the organization's journal for a year. In his writings Ryan urged clothing manufacturers to abandon their concept of a foreman or head cutter as a glorified shop manager and think of him instead as a creative designer, "your Rubens, your Raphael, your Vandyke." The obvious embodiment of this image, of course, was Ryan himself. His influence seems to have waned after the 1880s, although he continued to work in the industry until his death in 1912.[28]

Finally, starting a clothing business of their own became an attainable goal for Irish immigrants during this period. Indeed, the clothing industry "provided the best opportunities for immigrant workers to advance to ownership status." Capital requirements for a custom tailoring, hat contracting, or small retail clothing business or hat dealership were relatively light during this period, generally less than $1,000, as the prevalence of hand production obviated the need for any extensive investment in machinery or plant. Manhattan rents were high, but most Irish immigrants began their businesses, naturally enough, in modest low-rent locations, then moved to progressively better situations as they became more successful. The R. G. Dun & Co. field agent reports provide a portrait of the startup of one clothing business involving an Irish American. William Braisted and William Dougherty, both newly married and each with living expenses of "but $250 a year," began a custom tailoring business in 1854. With joint capital of $1,000, which they had saved while working for Dougherty's father for the previous nine years, they rented "the rear of Bodine's hat store" at 299 Broadway and purchased a supply of cloth. By 1858 they were reported to be "doing a large and fashionable custom business," and by 1864 they had two locations on Broadway and were worth $10,000–12,000. Hatter Charles Knox recorded a similar beginning, starting a small contracting business in a basement with a $250 bonus from his former master, then moving to a 6-by-10-foot space on the corner of Fulton and Dutch Streets known as "the Little Hole in the Wall," where he could reach any hat on the shelves while standing in the center of the room. But once established in a good location like Broadway, success could come swiftly. R. G. Dun & Co. field agents recorded that 31-year-old tailor Daniel Kennedy set up a shop on the ground floor of the fashionable Astor House hotel in 1855, using $2,000 in savings. In a year's time he doubled this investment on the strength of $20,000 in sales.[29]

Another advantage to the new immigrant was the absence of sophisticated business practices in the city's clothing industry during this period. Retail clothing businesses projected an air of gentility and sophistication, but their actual operations were quite casual. "Advertising was not thought necessary," recalled one veteran of the retail trade on Fulton Street in the 1870s, "just a sign bearing the firm name over the door and a stock of goods inside the store. . . . There was no dating of bills or trouble about terms . . . everything was understood by the seller and buyer." One R. G. Dun & Co. field agent recorded that clothing dealer James Casey was "a shrewd Irishman," but did "a peculiar business . . . keeps no bank account, gives no notes." Into this milieu the Irish, with their knowledge of English and previous urban experience, could move readily.[30]

The prevailing practice of intracommunal patronage further aided the immigrant entrepreneur. To the clothier or hatter, New York City was filled with potential customers. Between 1840 and 1860 its population increased from 312,000 to 813,000, while it regularly attracted some 20,000 travelers a year, most of them on business, as well as a floating mass of hundreds of thousands of others who passed through the port or remained briefly in the city on their way to other destinations. Permanent newcomers during these years were for the most part immigrants, mostly Irish and German, who swelled the ranks of

181

*Irish Entrepreneurs
and Artisans in
New York's
Clothing Industry,
1830–1880*

the city's working class and usually showed a marked interest in bettering themselves. For the recently arrived, dressing like an American was an indispensable part of becoming one. The British hatter James Dawson Burn, writing in the 1860s, observed of the young Irish in New York that "after arriving in this country . . . the young Hibernian speedily has himself tailored into external respectability. He begins to walk with his head erect, and soon that slouching servility and fawning sycophancy to people above his own grade, which made him a slave in all but the fetters [in Ireland], is cast aside, as he dons the character of a free citizen of the United States." These newly arrived Irish tended to patronize clothing businesses run by their fellow countrymen, some of whom advertised in The *Irish-American* and other Irish newspapers. Thus an R. G. Dun & Co. field agent could report in the 1850s of Irish-born tailor James Lapin, who had started his own "fashionable tailoring" business at 23 Chambers Street after working as a cutter for another Irish clothier and saving about $400, that he "has done very well . . . & has a good run of custom, from his Countrymen particularly, who pay cash." Bowery hatter John Callahan advertised heavily in the city's Irish newspapers before St. Patrick's Day, touting himself as "the outfitter" for the parade, and keeping his store open late for several weeks beforehand. The immigrants who patronized such businesses tended to pay for their purchases in cash, an advantage to the small or large clothing merchant or artisan trying to save or deal with complex credit arrangements. The other side of this coin was the practice of intracommunal hiring. Those Irish who founded successful businesses often hired their fellow countrymen. There is evidence that large employers like Devlin & Co., James Leary, and Edward Fox employed Irish immigrants; hatter Charles Knox hired so many from his native County Donegal that a county society sprouted in the vicinity of his Brooklyn factory.[31]

Finally, the diversity of New York's clothing trade, with its multiplicity of what economists call "niche markets," was a stimulus to immigrant entrepreneurs. By the 1850s Irish-owned clothing businesses in New York City numbered in the hundreds, exploiting a broad range of such niches. The 1855 New York State census identified as Irish 81 of New York City's 403 clothiers, about 20 percent of the total. The business listings in *Trow's City Directory of 1854* also show 86 Irish-surnamed merchant tailors, 16 secondhand clothing dealers, and 26 retail dealers in hats. Irish immigrants continued to start new clothing businesses in the city through the immediate post–Civil War era, when the 1870 U.S. Census of Industry recorded 30 new Irish-owned garment enterprises in the Fourteenth Ward alone. Some Irish immigrants who could combine superior artisanal skills with personal charm succeeded in the city's elite custom order trade in men's clothing or hats, the carriage trade as it were. At this time, New York City "boasted the wealthiest elite market in the country." Of several successful examples, the best-known was hatter Charles Knox, who could, it was said, "step up to the bench and perform any operation of manufacture as well as the best" of his workmen. Knox cultivated the friendship as well as the custom of the city's newspaper editors, political and business leaders, and visiting celebrities, measuring them personally for their new silk hat while chatting with them in Windsor chairs set up in the front room of his Broadway store, and keeping their head measurements systematically on file.[32]

At the other end of the scale, the city's secondhand clothing trade consistently attracted Irish dealers from the 1850s on, who numbered between one and two dozen in any given year until the 1880s. They included both men and women; half a dozen of the Irish secondhand clothing dealers on Baxter Street in the early 1870s were women. This is not surprising; Irish women had been an integral part of this trade as "mokers" who wheeled carts through the slums of East London exchanging crockery for "the workmen's castoff Sunday clothes." The secondhand trade in the city was dominated from the beginning by Jews, and among the Irish secondhand dealers was one, Henry Regan, identified in credit reports as Jewish as well as Irish. For some the secondhand trade was profitable. It included "renovating" clothes and had a national as well as local market, serviced by men like John K. Murray who sold both new and used clothing in the city and western markets. He was reported in 1850 to be "well off . . . easy in his circumstances."[33]

Irish women also seem to have sometimes found other opportunities for clothing businesses besides the secondhand clothing shops of Baxter Street. There were artisans like Rosanna Donnelly, who was listed in the 1870 U.S. census of industry as owner of a "shirt manufactory" in the Fourteenth Ward with $1,200 capital invested. She was producing $2,000 worth of shirts a year on a single sewing machine. In general, however, women could be found in business in poor neighborhoods, working with husbands or fathers or inheriting businesses as widows or heirs, in line with the customs and property laws of the time. Despite these limitations, some were recognized for their business abilities. Catherine Hanley took over her husband's business in sailor's clothing at 213 West Street when he died in 1849 and ran it with the help of her daughter for 22 years. "She continues the business and is well able to do it," a credit agent commented in 1850. A daughter of "shrewd Irishman" James Casey singlehandedly ran one of her father's businesses, another sailor's clothing store at 199 Roosevelt Street. Casey left his substantial estate (worth about $20,000) to his two daughters when he died in 1866.[34]

If starting a small business was not uncommon, it was very difficult for an immigrant to move into the ranks of the city's big clothing manufacturers and retailers. Yankee merchant-capitalists like the Brooks Brothers, "all of whom displayed a strong talent for organizing large enterprises efficiently," and whose partnerships consisted primarily of men related by blood or marriage, dominated the ready-made clothing industry. Most catered to the city's retail trade as well as supplying ready-made coats, pants, and vests to distant domestic and sometimes foreign markets. They raised "imposing downtown structures of four to seven stories situated in the heart of the business district." The most successful of the city's hat dealers had started out as artisans but occupied similar buildings, where customers browsed or were fitted for hats on the ground floor while journeymen labored on the upper floors.[35]

Irish immigrants faced a number of special problems in breaking into this exclusive world. Capital requirements were substantial, particularly for cash on hand to meet obligations through "dull seasons," and while awaiting the payments of faraway customers in the West or South on six-month (or longer) terms of credit. As a consequence good credit, the trust of suppliers, and usually wealthy backers were vital for even the largest firms. Management skills and a "system" were considered indispensable. Moreover, an immigrant wishing to compete in the national marketplace had little or no knowledge of American regional tastes in clothes.

The business carried substantial risks, of which the ill-starred business career of clothier Rogers provides a running catalog. In the years following the *Atlas's* glowing portrait of him, he experienced virtually every disaster inherent in the clothing business, forcing him repeatedly to "take in sail," as he called it: overextension, which forced the closing of two of his three stores, one in New York and one in Charleston, South Carolina, in 1852; the depressions of 1854 and 1857, which he withstood "to the surprise of many" in the trade; the burning of his remaining store in 1855 (he was insured); and in 1856 a suit brought against him by a former partner (he won). By 1860 he had been forced to bring in new partners and seemed secure, but only a few years later he died in a carriage accident at the age of 46. His sons took over the business but gave up after they, too, were burned out the following year.[36]

Patrick Rogers was not the only Irish immigrant to reach the top in New York City's clothing industry. Clothiers Edward Fox of Broadway and the McEvoy family of Grand Street, the hatter James Leary, mentioned earlier, and hatting middleman (jobber) Patrick Corbitt, son of a widowed Irish woman raised in Connecticut and sponsored by some of that state's biggest hat manufacturers, all accumulated fortunes or a net worth in the range of $100,000 at different times. But most of these were short-lived, brought down by poor real estate investments in Fox's case and premature death in Corbitt's.[37]

Two Irish immigrants deserve attention here, as they not only founded successful and lasting businesses, but in different ways influenced the industry itself. Even their buildings were landmarks in their day. During the 1860s and 1870s a New Yorker strolling up Broadway could not fail to notice the six-story Knox Building at 212 Broadway, every available space emblazoned with the name of its owner, where most of New York's bankers, politicians, and celebrities bought their hats. Just a few blocks north was the white marble Renaissance-style building of Daniel Devlin & Co., surrounded by a ground-floor colonnade of Corinthian columns and boasting the biggest display window in the city. Devlin & Co. had pioneered quality discount clothing and was the biggest men's clothier in the city outside of Brooks Brothers. The owners of these two leading garment businesses, located just blocks apart in downtown New York, had grown up on opposite sides of Lough Swilly, in County Donegal. Both had changed the way their respective trades were practiced and were among the best-known businessmen in their fields in the nation as well as the city.

Daniel Devlin had emigrated to the United States in his teens as a "merchant tailor" with a sense of adventure and a desire to work for himself. Landing in 1834, he immediately went west, where he clerked on a Mississippi River steamboat and for a maker of "Kentucky jeans" before establishing a successful clothing business in Louisville, Kentucky. In 1844 he came to New York to marry the daughter of a wealthy Irish immigrant fruit importer, Luke Corrigan. His father-in-law then backed him financially as he set up a Western trade business in ready-made clothing, capitalizing on his Louisville connections. He soon added a profitable custom tailoring business that captured the patronage of "the city's leading Catholics," providing him with a cash base with which to expand. By 1849 he had brought his brother Jeremiah over from Ireland as a partner and had built up a business of close to $160,000 a year. A decade later, following a move to Broadway, he was doing nearly 10 times that. By then Devlin & Co. claimed a work force of 150 cutters and clerks and 2,000 outwork hands and shipped its products to all parts of the United States, as well as to Cuba, South America, and Hawaii. It would last for 53 years, and at its apex after the Civil War the company had three big stores on Broadway; had branches in Washington, D.C., Richmond, Virginia, Annapolis, Maryland, and Lexington,

Daniel Devlin, from County Donegal, was one of the pioneers of the men's ready-to-wear market. This detail from a Devlin & Co. billhead dated October 7, 1863, shows the company building at the corner of Broadway and Grand Street. (Collection of The New-York Historical Society.)

Kentucky (and possibly one in Londonderry, Ireland); and supplied fashionable men's clothing and military uniforms to a nationwide clientele that ranged from small-town bands in New England to the U.S. Naval Academy.[38]

Early on Daniel Devlin established an efficient system of production, organization, and sales that was still "running like clockwork" in 1877, the *Clothier and Hatter* reported, 10 years after his death. His idea of departmentalizing the different branches of the operation was imitated by others like Patrick Rogers. Cutters were transformed into specialists in one article of clothing. Partners participated in managing departments, and his extended family played an important role in the operation; brothers seem to have handled company affairs in Charleston and New Orleans before the Civil War, and cousins managed the clerical clothing department and the branch store in Richmond in the 1870s. Devlin was quick to adapt other innovations as well; he was one of the only city manufacturers to be using sewing machines in 1855. Service was a keynote of the stores; they swarmed with clerks, and in the 1870s the company even recalled a lot of suits made from a material that was found to fade in sunlight. The company advertised liberally all over its selling area (even in small town papers), exhibited at the Philadelphia Centennial Exposition, and during the 1870s published a series of catalogs and guidebooks to popular places like Central Park.[39]

Daniel Devlin also broke the prevailing practice of negotiable pricing, usually bargained to the advantage of the seller. He introduced a form of discount pricing that, the firm claimed, "caused a revolution" in the city's clothing trade. Devlin & Co.'s advertising motto was "low profits, promptness, and cash"; it claimed that "gentlemen and lads can walk in . . . and in five minutes walk out again, arrayed in all the glories of the well-dressed man of the period." The lower pricing for good-quality clothes made the store popular with upwardly mobile immigrants, a factor that became a keystone of the business's success. The field agent reports of R. G. Dun & Co. state repeatedly that the firm had not only "a large custom from the Catholics," that is to say, the Irish, of New York, but "a large Roman Catholic trade throughout the country . . . having the patronage of the most influential Catholics in this city, they exert a great influence in other parts of the country as well . . . [giving him] a large wholesale patronage at the South and West." And whether from a sense of justice and charity or the "shrewd" business sense he was credited with by his contemporaries, Daniel Devlin also encouraged intracommunal patronage by identifying himself strongly with the interests of the city's immigrant working class. He paid his employees adequately by the standards of the day (as did several other successful Irish employers—Charles Knox, Patrick Rogers, and Edward Fox—according to available statistics). He extended production seasons to keep his workers employed, and was so well-liked by the unions that a speaker at a tailors' strike rally in 1850 singled him out as "a friend of the workingman." He was deeply involved in a multitude of the city's Catholic and Irish institutions, particularly the

Institute for the Protection of Catholic Children, the Emigrant Industrial Savings Bank, for which he served as treasurer for seven years, and the Friendly Sons of St. Patrick. During the Civil War, Devlin & Co. furnished uniforms gratis to the Irish Brigade, while Daniel served as chairman of its Executive Committee.[40]

Daniel Devlin's "shrewd" business sense, his ability to "make money fast" by anticipating trends in a volatile business environment, even his occasional ruthlessness were much commented on by his contemporaries. He was the only immigrant clothier to be active in public service during this era of Mayor George Opdyke and President Andrew Johnson (both former tailors); he served as city chamberlain (treasurer) from 1860 until he died in 1867. Devlin & Co. survived his death but floundered badly during the 1870s. A stock fraud case involving oil land in Ohio was settled against his estate after his death. The long period of depression and stagnation between 1873 and 1877 was complicated by mismanagement and corruption within the firm, particularly a skimming operation on its books that drained all its profits for several years. In 1880 the company shut down all its branches and consolidated into the Warren Street store, limping on until it was assigned in 1897.[41]

Charles Knox parlayed a genius for self-promotion and a reputation as hatter to the rich and famous into a national line of fine hats that proved to be the most enduring of the Irish-owned clothing businesses of the period. Knox built his reputation on the quality of his hats. The trade magazine *Clothier and Hatter* credited Knox with having "led the way in asserting (American) independence of English styles by proving his ability to originate more graceful shapes than could be imported." Even more significant was his innovative use of advertising, on which he lavished huge sums for the day. Knox bypassed the ad columns for the news pages. Newspapers eager for filler material were happy to print seemingly informative articles Knox sent them on current topics, but which after a few paragraphs turned into paeans to Knox hats. He garnered much free publicity by leading the two-year public fight against the Loew footbridge across Broadway at Fulton Street (the structure blocked light and access to his store) in the mid-1860s.

Knox expanded steadily through the 1870s and 1880s, establishing a store uptown under the Fifth Avenue Hotel, called by *Clothier and Hatter* "the most elegant establishment of this kind in the country." Despite the elder Knox's solid reputation, he nearly met ruin twice, in 1863 and 1878, but wealthy friends bailed him out. He gradually built up a wholesale operation, which by 1885 had grown too large for his downtown building, and he moved his manufacturing facilities to a huge new factory in Brooklyn. By that time his product line had expanded from silk hats to include items like police helmets which became standard issue for many of the country's big-city departments. Like Daniel Devlin, Knox had also been an active supporter of the Irish Brigade, recruiting a company of troops when the war broke out. His son Edward was a colonel in the unit and was awarded the Congressional Medal of Honor. Edward Knox took over the company after his father's death in 1895, but when his own health began to fail in 1913 the company was sold to outsiders. Knox Hats were eventually absorbed into the giant Connecticut-based Hat Corporation of America, which continued to make and market the line into the 1950s.[42]

Successful Irish entrepreneurs in the clothing trades behaved much the same as did their contemporaries who had succeeded. They tended to move out of the city, particularly during the early 1850s, to the then-suburbs: Rogers to Williamsburg, Leary to an estate on Staten Island, Daniel Devlin to an Italianate villa overlooking the Hudson in Manhattanville. James Leary sent his children to be educated in the city's best private and public schools alongside the likes of William B. Astor; Daniel Devlin entertained fellow members of the city's Catholic elite on board his yacht. Daniel Devlin and Charles Knox owned acreage, houses, and hotels; Knox was said to be "one of the largest property owners in the city, owning 28 private houses, three hotels and a farm of 33 acres in the Bronx." Clothier Edward Fox, one of the pioneer clothiers of Broadway,

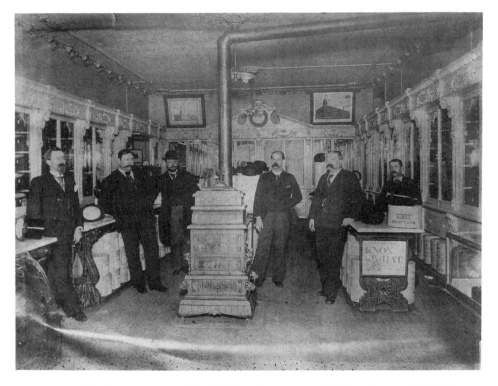

The interior of the Knox Hat store at No. 212 Broadway, corner of Fulton Street, c. 1870s. County Donegal native Charles Knox, one of New York's most important hatters, was a genius at self-promotion and advertising. The exterior of this five-story building was emblazoned on every available space with the name "Knox," and Knox hats were nationally known down to the 1950s. (Collection of The New-York Historical Society.)

owed much of his six-figure wealth to real estate speculation; "he makes good hits," the New York Trade Agency reported. But even individuals of more modest means put some of their resources into buildings and undeveloped lots in Manhattan, Brooklyn, and Westchester. Patrick Colligan, owner of a small sailors' clothing business at 323 West Street, not only "had money at interest" but owned five dilapidated old frame buildings with three storefronts "worth $10,000 mortgaged." Even the radical labor activist and tailor Robert Blissert caught this speculative fever in the 1880s, buying acreage and lots at Whitestone at auction for $200; by 1886 it was reported to be worth $1,500. In fact, of more than 60 entries on Irish clothing business owners, both large and small, found in the R. G. Dun & Co. field agent reports, about a third owned real estate, often undeveloped or rented.[43]

The strong Irish presence in the clothing trades came to an almost abrupt end in the 1870s. By the end of that decade, the Irish in New York's clothing industry were in a swift decline in numbers and influence, as evidenced by the listings in the city's business directories. In *Wilson's Business Directory for 1880* only 7 Irish-surnamed clothiers are listed, as opposed to 56 (81 in the state census) in 1855, and the number of Irish-surnamed secondhand clothing dealers had dropped to 7 from 15 only five years before. Only the number of retail hat dealers held steady at 25, and a number of new Irish-surnamed dealers in the new specialty of gentleman's furnishing stores had appeared. But in *Trow's Business Directory for 1892* the Irish presence is a mere trace: 5 retail and wholesale clothiers and 5 secondhand clothing dealers. The Irish abandoned this industry that had been such an important economic gateway for several reasons. Clearly, they no longer saw the clothing industry as a source of real opportunities. The long depression that followed the panic of 1873 not only shook giants like Devlin & Co. and Knox but it winnowed out many smaller Irish-owned clothing firms. Moreover, even if tailoring and hatting in the city started a road to riches for a few and brought others to the brink of entry into the city's middle class, for most these trades meant a lifetime of struggle to keep working, of near-poverty and tedious work, "a fight against mishaps, disappointments and adversity," as an Irish immigrant shoemaker described his lot. Unions could help guarantee good wages and continuous work, but none of the trades could offer security in old age. As immigrants who had arrived in the 1840s and 1850s aged, those who could find a way to get out did so. By the 1870s, Unionists George Clancy and Robert Crowe had jobs as city inspectors, and many others had left their trade or the city. Most of the second generation of Irish in the city looked for opportunites outside the largely sweated clothing trades. As the *Brooklyn Eagle* noted in 1884, "American boys," who by this time included second-generation Irish Americans, "avoid tailoring, preferring to enter stores as clerks to sitting cross-legged on a table or trying to learn the genius-requiring art of cutting," despite the fact that "a cutter makes a salary nearly four times as great as that given an adult clerk." Moreover, Irish-founded clothing businesses, with the notable exception of Knox Hats, were not carried on for long beyond the lifetimes of the original founders. The great majority of their businesses were small, and turnover in the style-sensitive industry was high. Irish-owned businesses identified in the R. G. Dun & Co. field agent reports failed for a variety of reasons: financial panics, the most common; the outbreak of "the Rebellion"; business misjudgments; a corrupt partner; alcohol abuse in a few cases and overextended or shaky credit in others. In my sample from the R. G. Dun & Co. field agent reports of 44 Irish-owned businesses active during the 1850s, 7 moved out of the city, 3 proprietors died, and 15 failed or otherwise went out of business before the end of the decade, a turnover rate of more than 50 percent. Moreover, the movement of the Irish masses out of their first downtown neighborhoods depleted the ethnic population base for intracommunal patronage that had helped to establish and sustain their countrymen in the custom and retail trades.[44]

The Irish were replaced on the ground floor of the clothing industry by newer immigrant groups. Germans had begun to outnumber them as early as 1855. The late 1870s and 1880s saw the beginnings of a huge new wave of hundreds of thousands of Jewish tailors, emigrating from Germany and Austria-Hungary at first and later from Russia. Only 3.5 percent of the tailors who entered the United States between 1875 and 1898 were Irish, along with a portion of the 7.3 percent counted as English. Over the next 16 years, as the immigration of Jewish tailors swelled to a total of nearly a quarter million, that percentage declined to an imperceptible 0.5 percent.[45]

Technological changes in clothing manufacturing favored these newer immigrants. Most significantly, with the increasing use of sewing machines (first introduced two decades earlier but slow to be adopted) and the cutting knife, the first clothing factories began to appear in New York in the 1870s. Hundreds of operatives in these factories assembled garments at huge banks of machines. The growing number of German employers hired Jewish male tailors to operate sewing machines to replace sewing women because of their physical strength. Finally, during the 1880s Russian Jewish tailors introduced the task system, wherein teams of tailors working on specialized tasks lowered the labor cost of making men's coats, the mainstay of Irish American tailors, by 25 percent between 1876 and 1883.

Hatting in the city changed as well. As the silk hat declined somewhat in popularity after the Civil War, losing ground as a dress hat to the newly introduced derby, production shifted from the city's small manufactories to Brooklyn, which developed one of the nation's largest concentrations of hat factories (Knox's among them). Manhattan, however, retained its role as sales and distribution center, and continued to provide fertile ground for retail hat businesses. In this line, the numbers of Irish remained steady as they declined elsewhere in the clothing trades. There were as many Irish-surnamed hat retailers in the city directories of the 1880s and 1890s, about two dozen, as there had been in the 1850s, the only area where this was true.[46]

Moreover, the Irish had almost nothing to do with the period of takeoff experienced by the clothing industry after the Civil War, when pent-up postwar demand, population growth, and immigration sent production soaring. Some Irish entrepreneurs had proved astute in finding ways to expand the markets for their products through pricing and advertising, but they operated within spheres of the industry that can be seen as readily transferable from Ireland, as witnessed by their gravitation to custom tailoring and to the trade in secondhand clothing. It would be entrepreneurs from other groups, particularly German and later Russian Jews (along with the few surviving Yankee firms like Brooks Brothers and Browning, King), who would bring the industry into the mass consumer markets of the twentieth century through product innovation. A case in point is women's clothing. A few of the city's first cloak dealers were Irish, and the biggest hoop skirt manufacturer in the city in 1860 was an immigrant from England with the intriguingly Gaelic name of Austin Kelly. But on the whole the Irish had almost nothing to do with the rise of the women's garment industry, the fastest-growing segment of the industry after the Civil War, which in only 50 years achieved parity in production with men's clothing. It was pioneered by Jews, as were most other new product lines in men's clothing. In the 1850s Jewish enterprise had been largely confined to the secondhand clothing trade of Chatham Street and to a few shirt manufacturers. By 1887, after earlier German Jewish entrepreneurs had become established and the influx from Russia had begun, the trade magazine *Clothier and Furnisher* credited Jews with "control of seven-eighths" of the clothing trade, with "a monopoly" of the shirt manufacturing industry, and with pioneering the mass production of cloaks and undergarments for both men and women. Jewish entrepreneurs had little competition from existing businesses in these new lines, and opened up the potential for literally thousands of Jewish contractors to supply them.[47]

This process of ethnic succession in the garment industry continues to this day and has been documented in recent years. In the contemporary women's garment industry in New York, Chinese and Dominican workers and entrepreneurs are replacing the Jews and Italians who were formerly dominant. Several factors at work here are "opportunity structures"—economic factors within specific industries—which encourage entrepreneurship on the part of new immigrants and are as essential to the success of their enterprises as "cultural" factors such as a historic predisposition to business or the willingness to work hard. These internal factors include immigrant access to ownership positions because of expansion within an industry or abandonment by the native-born; low entry barriers, including low capital requirements; "blocked mobility" or a lack of opportunities in other fields, and "ethnic resources," including access to capital and ethnic networking, which for some immigrant entrepreneurs enabled them to hire reliable and motivated workers. It is not difficult to see how a convergence of these same factors in New York City's clothing industry of the 1830s and 1840s created a window of opportunity for the Irish: a rapidly

191

*Irish Entrepreneurs
and Artisans in
New York's
Clothing Industry,
1830–1880*

expanding industry that encouraged newcomers and accommodated a plethora of market niches; low capital requirements for starting a small business; and a tendency within New York's huge and rapidly expanding immigrant communities to buy from and employ people from their old homelands.[48]

The Irish never dominated the clothing industry in the way that the Jews came to. But the fact that they took advantage of such opportunities as they saw suggests in part an entrepreneurial spirit not usually associated with them, but it seems to have existed among them in other fields in New York as well. The experience of the Irish in the clothing trades in New York clearly differs from that of the Boston Irish. There, the "Boston system" of ready-made clothing manufacturing, a form of factory production combining limited mechanization with an "infinite subdivision of labor" to virtually eliminate the skilled artisan entirely, was built on unskilled and cheap Irish labor.[49] In New York, with little space available on Manhattan for heavy industry, the city's manufacturing economy mushroomed in the early nineteenth century through an expansion of what has been referred to as the skill-intensive "consumer finishing trades."[50] These included trades that in their preindustrial form were skill-intensive and attracted individuals trained in them in their home countries. Some recent historians have seen the entrance of Irish and German immigrants into contracting-dominated trades like tailoring as evidence of those trades becoming "de-skilled." On the contrary, the bulk of the Irish in tailoring and hatting in New York, with their gravitation to the custom trade and their multitude of small and large businesses, suggests a population of skilled artisans. Their early tendency to organize also suggests they were workers who were aware of the value of their skills. Some of the Irish tailors and hatters who settled in New York seem to have attained a kind of stability and independence, and a few made it into the middle class as cutters, custom tailors, or small business owners. R. G. Dun & Co. field agents frequently refer to Irish subjects as "frugal," "saving," "hardworking," or "shrewd," hardly the stereotype of the famine-era immigrant. Most of these artisans appear to have made an effort to put money away in banks; the more entrepreneurial moved to protect their gains by acquiring real estate.

Moreover, the tremendous diversity and expansion of New York's clothing industry attracted the creative, like Daniel Edward Ryan, and those with clearly entrepreneurial goals, like Daniel Devlin or Patrick Rogers, along with those focused simply on surviving and supporting a family. The earliest-comers among them were clearly favored as the industry's expansion accelerated, but the Irish continued to perceive the clothing business as a source of opportunity after the Civil War. The most successful of these Irish clothiers, tailors, and hatters eagerly embraced a role as gatekeepers to respectability for the city's immigrants, the source for a $5 hat that looked just like an expensive beaver or for a discounted suit from one of Broadway's most elegant clothing palaces. Neither initiators nor the sole proponents of the movement toward the "democratization" of dress in America that began during the nineteenth century and that virtually erased the visual distinctions in status signaled by different kinds and grades of clothing, they nonetheless seem to have been among its most enthusiastic proponents. The presence of some Scotch-Irish among them cannot account for the proclivity for business some of them showed. Of the three major figures studied here whose religious background is known, two, Rogers and Devlin, were Catholics, as were James Leary and hat jobber Patrick Corbitt. That the former two and Charles Knox were natives of Ulster indicates mainly that because it was Ireland's most prosperous and urbanized province they were better able to envision and plan for success than were those from poorer parts of the island.[51]

If political prowess, rather than business enterprise, has traditionally been credited for the eventual Irish success in America, then perhaps New York's case deserves a closer look, particularly in terms of elite formation. The numbers and percentage of Irish in the city's construction and maritime trades in the 1855 state census closely resemble those in clothing. Although some recent historians have seen this influx as evidence of a decline in artisan traditions in these trades, to the ethnic historian they can begin to tell another story, of an opportunity perceived by artisans trained elsewhere. New York, as the nation's largest population center, busiest port, and financial hub, was likewise an incubator for small and large businesses. It is significant that the Irish were abundantly represented here, too, the 1855 state census revealing them to be the single largest ethnic group of "shopkeepers" in the city. Irish immigrant businesses founded or active during this period ranged from neighborhood grocers and junk dealers to the city's largest, the department stores of Alexander T. Stewart and Hugh O'Neill, the construction company of John Crimmins, and the shipyard of John Roach. The success of these businesses had a direct impact on the Irish immigrant. Most of them provided employment, of course, but perhaps the most significant effects were connected to the strength of institutions that sustained or helped the immigrant advance in his or her new country. For clothier Daniel Devlin had counterparts in other fields in the city: successful Irish-born businessmen like James Kerrigan, Andrew Carrigan, Henry Hoguet, Hugh Kelly, Terence Donnelly, and numerous others who formed a Catholic elite that helped finance and provide lay leadership for the growth of the Catholic Church in the metropolis, and that founded and directed other institutions that assisted the immigrant, from the Catholic Protectory to the Emigrant Industrial Savings Bank.[52]

Edward K. Spann

CHAPTER 8

Union Green

THE IRISH COMMUNITY AND

THE CIVIL WAR

THE CIVIL WAR offered Irish Americans in New York and elsewhere a unique opportunity to establish themselves as American citizens and patriots. After decades of nativist agitation against them, many Irish volunteered to defend the nation against the rebellious South. The Irish soldier in the Union cause, said Charles Halpine, himself a volunteer as well as a journalist, was motivated by "the thought that he was earning a title, which no foul tongue or niggardly heart would dare to dispute, to the full equality and fraternity of an American citizen." In all, more than 140,000 men of Irish birth fought for the Union, roughly a third from New York City and vicinity. In four years of bloody conflict they strengthened their claim on America, although this achievement became tinged with disappointment and was obscured by increasing opposition to the direction of the war.[1]

Throughout, this "Union Green" was motivated by special Irish concerns as well as American patriotism and did not claim to stand for a true blue devotion to every aspect of the war effort. From the start, the Irish had no confidence in the Union government of Abraham Lincoln and his Republican party. Before the war, they had supported the Democratic party, identifying the Republicans with a nativistic "puritanism" that threatened their religion and their general interests. They especially condemned Republican leanings toward abolitionism as favoring black people over white people like themselves.[2] Although not necessarily sympathetic to slavery, many sympathized with the slaveholding south as a defender of the established order against abolitionism and intrusive power. In February 1861, for instance, the *New York Irish-American* urged its readers not to fight against southern secessionism: "We deprecate the idea of Irish-Americans—who have themselves suffered so much for opinions sake not only at home but *here even*—volunteering to coerce those with whom they have no direct connection." It was with such thoughts that the Irish patriot John Mitchel, the grandfather of a future mayor of New York, joined the Confederacy, eventually sacrificing two of his sons to that cause.[3]

When the Confederacy attacked Fort Sumter on April 12, 1861, however, most of the New York Irish were ready to defend the Union. Earlier, many of the men had participated in various militia units like the "Erin Guard" and the "Irish National Grenadiers." Generally, these amateur soldiers did little beyond marching in the annual St. Patrick's Day parade, but they did acquire at least a little experience with arms and tactics. Many believed that they were training themselves not only for the defense of America but also for the armed liberation of Ireland from English rule. In 1853, when the Crimean War promised to weaken British power, they formed three regiments for that purpose, and in 1859, with the prospect of war between England and France, the *Irish-American* declared it "the sacred duty of every Irishman at home and abroad to prepare himself to fight the battle of his country [Ireland] and kindred when and how he may."[4]

In 1860 this militancy made the strongest Irish militia unit, the Sixty-ninth Regiment, a focus of controversy. By then, the regiment had elected as its commander a future military hero, Michael Corcoran. Born in Donegal in 1827, Corcoran had in 1849 migrated to New York, where he became a leading figure in the Fenian movement for Irish freedom.[5] In 1860 he won much attention when he refused to parade the Sixty-ninth for the visiting Prince of Wales, a disobedience that involved him in a lengthy court-martial proceeding in early 1861. When the Confederates attacked Fort Sumter, however, Corcoran called on all men to defend the Union and his trial was quashed, encouraging a rush of Irish volunteers into the military, especially into the Sixty-ninth Regiment.[6]

Not all Irish opinion favored the war effort. The *Freeman's Journal*, the leading Catholic newspaper in the city, was so hostile to the Union government that it was banned from the federal mails (it was, in effect, suppressed) until its editor, James McMaster, pledged that it would "not be devoted to the overthrow of the Constitution and the Union." Even the *Journal*, however, expressed pride in the willingness of Irishmen to volunteer for service. In any case, its influence was outweighed by the *Irish-American*, the leading journal of secular opinion, which ardently supported the Union military effort throughout the war despite its dislike of Lincoln and abolitionism. This newspaper—which devoted most of its front page to "home" news from Ireland—claimed a circulation of more than 33,000 in 1861.[7]

Additional support came from the Irish-Catholic hierarchy, most notably from Archbishop John Hughes. Soon after Fort Sumter, Hughes wrote confidentially to the Lincoln administration that since the Sixty-ninth regiment consisted almost entirely of Irish Catholics he took "a deep interest on the honor & bravery with which they shall conduct themselves during the campaign."[8] The archbishop's interests extended beyond his favorite regiment. Responding to a southerner's argument that Irish Catholics had no obligation to a society that had often despised them, he declared that all naturalized citizens ought to defend the nation that had granted them citizenship. In confirmation of this position, churches in New York flew the national flag, provoking one southern Catholic to warn that their practice might "bring down the curse of God" on them.[9]

Such support was important for the Union cause. In 1860, there were upward of 200,000 Irish-born people in New York, a full one-quarter of the city's population, a formidable human mass at the economic center of the nation and a major source of manpower. Irishmen volunteered for service in many other regiments besides the Sixty-ninth. Another was the Seventy-fifth Regiment, the "Irish Rifles," originally formed in the 1850s with the hope of freeing Ireland; in 1861, the Seventy-fifth was recruited to near full strength in a week. By one count, at least 10 other regiments formed in the city had numerous Irish recruits. The Union flag, said the *Irish-American*, "shall never be trailed in the dust if Irish-American hearts and heads can keep it gloriously aloft."[10]

Undoubtedly, one cause of this rush to service was the high rate of unemployment among Irishmen, which was bad enough during normal times but was made all the worse by the economic uncertainties arising from secession. In April, the *Irish-American* said that many of the volunteers were workers whose situation had become "almost disastrous."[11] Beyond the need for money, though, a dual patriotism—one often enhanced by the glamour of military life—inspired men to volunteer both to prove their devotion to the Union and to advance their hopes for a free Ireland. In 1862, Archbishop Hughes said that many had enlisted with the thought of preparing themselves, by "becoming thoroughly acquainted with the implements of war," for the liberation of their homeland. In this American and Irish patriotism there seemed no contradiction.[12]

Although there were enlistments in many military units, it was the Sixty-ninth that symbolized Irish involvement in the war, and when on April 23 it left New York it was given an enthusiastic send-off, the various Irish civic societies joining it in a procession through the streets under "waving banners—the harp of Erin kissing the stars and stripes." When the regiment reached Washington, it marched through a cheering crowd of onlookers to its temporary home at Georgetown College. After receiving some training in military tactics, the Sixty-ninth was moved to the Virginia side of the Potomac for the defense of Washington.[13]

In May, the *Freeman's Journal* expressed the hope that the Confederates would not attack a regiment of "men who have been in politics the steadfast friends of the South." This hope was shattered in July by the first battle of Bull Run. In what was otherwise an ignominious defeat for the Union, the Sixty-ninth won praise by bravely sustaining the fight until, under orders, it withdrew without panic, but it suffered heavy losses, including 39 killed. Many of its men were captured; one of them was Colonel Corcoran, who was to spend the next year in a Confederate prison.[14]

These losses deeply affected the Irish American community in New York, impelling it to initiate cooperative efforts that were to strengthen it during the war years. From the beginning, the community had provided support for its fighting men. In April, for instance, the Friendly Sons of St. Patrick contributed some $1,500 to help equip and sustain the Sixty-ninth, and Judge Charles P. Daly headed a committee to provide similar support for the Seventy-fifth.

Departure of the Sixty-ninth Regiment on April 23, 1861, as it passed Old St. Patrick's Cathedral and Hibernian Hall at Mott and Prince Streets. The Sixty-ninth was an all-Irish unit of the New York State Militia, which became part of the Irish Brigade that was formed by Thomas Francis Meagher later that year. Recruiting for the Union army among the New York Irish emphasized support for the Constitution and duty to one's country that was easily reconciled with the sentiments of Irish nationalism. The green flag of Ireland flew at all recruiting rallies and Irish patriotism (that is, good citizenship) was reflected in headlines like "The Emerald Isle Will Aid the Gem of the Ocean." (Lithograph by Sarony, Major & Knapp. Collection of The New-York Historical Society.)

Recognizing that the families of volunteers often had little money, the community formed a relief committee to provide for their support. By May several thousand dollars had been raised, with contributors vowing to continue their support as long as the men were in the field.[15]

The Battle of Bull Run abruptly forced an expansion of this effort by creating a class of widows and orphans, and in August the community raised money for their relief by holding a "festival" at Jones' Wood, charging 25 cents admission. It was estimated that some 60,000 people attended the event, one of the largest crowds ever to assemble in the city. Until the end of winter, the thousands of dollars raised at Jones' Wood and elsewhere were distributed to the dependents of volunteers who had been killed, wounded, or captured.[16] Although assistance became available from other sources, including the city government, community support for families met a critical need. In December 1861, when public relief temporarily ran out, some 200 desperate wives of soldiers gathered in Tompkins Square to protest, as one of them put it, that "you have got me men into the souldiers, and now you have to kepe us from starving."[17]

This organized relief effort helped to prepare the way for the greatest Irish military adventure of the war. In late July the Sixty-ninth returned home, having lost nearly 20 percent of its 1,276 men. It received an enthusiastic welcome on its march through the city. When its battle flags came into view, said a reporter, "their rapped and discolored appearance excited the most vehement applause."[18] Technically, it was to be disbanded, having completed the three months for which it had been enlisted, but many of its men were eager to return to combat. Moreover, the regiment was becoming the nucleus for an ambitious military plan, the creation of a whole Irish brigade consisting of several regiments from New York City. The idea had the sanction of tradition, there having been Irish brigades in service for various governments as early as the eighteenth century. In the late 1850s an Irish brigade had fought for the Papal states, winning the gratitude of the Pope for its faithful service.[19]

More than a month before the Sixty-ninth returned, the *Irish-American* had urged the organization of Irish soldiers from the city into one powerful force: "Would it not revive the inspiring memories of the Irish Brigade in other lands, and stimulate our armed countrymen in the ranks of the Union host to rival the deeds which history has immortalized." There were some doubts about the plan. Although Archbishop Hughes liked it as a way to protect the Catholic faithful in a largely Protestant army, he was concerned about ethnic labeling, warning that if military units were specifically linked to Irish, German, and other ethnic groups "there will be trouble among the troops even before the enemy comes into sight."[20] By September, however, the Irish community was ready to create its own brigade, and had found the man to lead it.

With Corcoran in a Confederate prison, attention focused on Thomas Francis Meagher. In 1849, the rebellious Meagher had been exiled by British authorities from Ireland to Tasmania, from which he eventually escaped to New York City.

Within a few years after his escape, he had become an American citizen, married the daughter of a rich New Yorker, and founded the weekly *Irish News*.[21] He brought this same energy to the military. When war broke out, he raised his own company, the Irish Zouaves, and succeeded in attaching it to Corcoran's Sixty-ninth Regiment. At Bull Run, he won the notice of one observer: "He rode a splendid white horse. He lost his cap, and was remarkable in his bare head, urging his men forward." Not all reports were so favorable: Some officers of the Sixty-ninth later told Maria Daly, the wife of community leader Judge Charles P. Daly, that in the battle Meagher "had just enough sense and elation to rush forward and afterward fell from his horse drunk, and was picked up by the troopers."[22]

Whatever the truth, Meagher succeeded in winning community support for himself and for the brigade, in part by carrying his message to such places as Niblo's Theater, where he spoke to a packed audience gathered to see the Irish comedy, "Colleen Bawn." Recruitment began with the Sixty-ninth, each of the eight companies of the regiment recruiting through its own office in a distinct location, increasing the chance that the men in a company would be drawn from the same neighborhood. Father William Corby, a chaplain, said later that the members of the brigade were "healthy, intelligent men far above average," many having a good education including "seven first-class lawyers." Before the end of 1861, more than two thousand volunteers had been organized into three regiments from New York City, the 63rd, 69th, and the 88th.[23]

The months of preparation in late 1861 energized the community. Determined to "sustain the Brigade at every cost," businessmen and other leaders formed the Irish Brigade Committee to provide long-term support for the men and their families. Soon its various subcommittees were "earnestly at work" collecting money, encouraging recruitment, and equipping the men for battlefield life. Of great symbolic importance was the effort to furnish identifying flags and banners for the regiments, a task that fell especially to women; such flags were intended to represent the community in battle and became a strong inducement for heroic action. After one member of the Sixty-ninth had disgraced himself at Bull Run by abandoning the regimental flag, Maria Daly noted with some relish that he did not dare show his face in New York, some of the men having "declared he shall be shot if he does."[24] This disgrace was not repeated.

In the middle of November, a crowd gathered at the camp of the Sixty-third regiment (the third regiment of the brigade) to witness the presentation of the regimental colors. With the troops drawn up in formation—"they looked magnificent," wrote a reporter, the young women responsible for making the flags formally presented their work, including a special green flag inscribed with the motto, "wounded but not conquered." Similar ceremonies were held for the other units. Mrs. Meagher presented the colors to the Eighty-eighth Regiment, making it as it was sometimes called "Mrs. Meagher's Own." To the Sixty-ninth went the special flag made by Tiffany and Company under arrangements with a committee of women headed by Maria Daly—a green flag with an Irish harp at its center.[25]

Threaded through these ceremonies was the hope that service and sacrifice in war would, in the words of one speaker, end "forever the charges against the naturalized citizen and the Catholic, as being unworthy of citizenship." Often mixed with this American patriotism were avowals of continued devotion to the Irish homeland, such as the declaration of a brigade chaplain, J. M. Dillon, that he "did not love America less but he loved Ireland more." Another speaker said of one green regimental flag that "it reminds us we are exiles from our native land . . . the symbol of the hopes, the memories, the past glories and future destinies of a chivalrous people."[26]

The Irish Brigade also was infused with the Catholic religion. Although Archbishop Hughes had warned against ethnic labels, he favored military units in which Irish Catholics could practice their faith under the guidance of Catholic chaplains. Chaplains had served from the beginning with the old Sixty-ninth. Reverend R. J. Mooney, pastor of St. Bridget's Church in Tompkins Square, accompanied the regiment south, endeavoring with some success to make the men "good christians and brave soldiers—a body of patriots." Mooney returned home before the Battle of Bull Run, but his successor, Father O'Reilly, narrowly escaped death in the battle, "his clothes being perforated with bullets, while attending the wounded in the field."[27] Such men helped to set the standards for the chaplains of the Irish brigade.

In a predominantly Protestant military, the priests played a special role as protectors of the Catholic faith and morality, holding services, hearing confessions, and giving last rites. They also were important links between the men and their families at home, helping to maintain a correspondence between them and also trying to ensure that the men used their pay—eventually millions of dollars—to support their dependents. In August 1862, for instance, the wife of one soldier wrote to Father William Corby (chaplain of the Eighty-eighth Regiment and a future president of Notre Dame University) complaining that she had not heard from her husband for more than five months, "and me and the children are in complete want. He toled [*sic*] me in his last letter that he gave you . . . 24 dollars and if he did please send it on." Corby and the others acted as bankers for the men, arranging the transfer of their pay to their homes and also taking charge of their savings.[28]

And so priestly black mixed with Irish green and Union blue to make a special unit. Later, Father Corby would describe the Irish Brigade as a "body of about 4,000 Catholics marching—most of them—to death but also to the glory of their Church and country." The full extent of this destiny was not immediately realized. In late 1861 the brigade left New York, evoking cheers and tearful goodbyes. Throughout most of its first six months in Virginia as part of the Army of the Potomac, it was generally sheltered from both glory and death by the cautious strategy of General George B. McClellan. In the spring of 1862, however, McClellan initiated the Peninsula Campaign, and in June the brigade received its baptism of blood at the Battle of Fair Oaks, suffering heavy losses, with more to follow.[29]

In July 1862 Meagher returned to New York hoping to recruit 2,000 men to bring the brigade to full strength. On July 25 people crowded into the Seventh Regiment Armory to hear him recount his losses and appeal to their Irish as well as American patriotism.[30] Indirectly, his effort received the support of Archbishop Hughes, who had spent the previous months in Europe speaking for the Union cause. Returning in July, Hughes gave what the *New York Times* termed a "War Sermon," in which he urged a maximum military effort to bring the war to an early end. Later, he justified his call as being in the interest of humanity and peace, adding that "the country, as I knew it was one, and I hope it shall never be called upon to recognize it as two."[31]

Both Meagher and the Archbishop were soon overshadowed by Michael Corcoran, who in August was finally freed in a prisoner exchange from a Confederate prison. Having been appointed a Brigadier-General, he reached New York City on August 22, where he received what the *Irish-American* called the greatest "ovation extended by the Empire City to any public man of modern times," including a grand procession of the Irish civic societies. Such was the enthusiasm, said the *Irish-American*, that Corcoran could have raised a whole division of 10,000 men, exciting hopes that "all the Irish valor, endurance, and energy that this war had called forth might be concentrated in one grand army." It soon became apparent, however, that Corcoran had no interest in sharing a command with Meagher. By the end of September he had begun to organize his own brigade, the "Corcoran Legion," having persuaded the city government to give a special bonus to early enlistees in it.[32]

In a month, more than 4,000 recruits, many of them from outside the city, were hastily assembled into four regiments, and in late October Archbishop Hughes, assisted by 10 priests, gave them a mass blessing. One of the recruits was the archbishop's nephew, Tracy P. Hughes, a member of General Corcoran's staff. It was, said a reporter, "a most impressive sight to see over four thousand men kneeling, in reverence, under the bright sky." In November the regiments boarded transports, and by the end of the month they were in Virginia. After its whirlwind organization, however, the Corcoran Legion was to see little action for nearly a year.[33]

In contrast, the last months of 1862 brought bloody disaster to the Irish Brigade. On September 17 Meagher's partly reinforced regiments were thrown into battle at Antietam, where they fought with reckless courage. In one phase of the battle the men advanced up a hill under their green banners in the face of deadly fire from entrenched Confederate units, cheering as they went until they had forced the enemy to retreat. The colors of the Sixty-third Regiment, wrote a reporter, "were shot down sixteen times, and on each occasion a man was ready to spring forward and place the colors in front." During this one battle, 506 of the brigade's 3,000 men were either killed or wounded.[34]

Five years later, John F. Maguire, in *The Irish in America*, said that Irish American military organizations like the brigade imposed on their members far more than the ordinary dangers of military life: because of his dual loyalty, the Irish-American soldier was doubly driven by concern for reputation, "for if he fought as an American citizen, he also fought as an Irish exile."[35] Beyond that, members of the brigade also felt a special obligation to the Irish community in New York, of which they were reminded by their battle flags, the gift of the community. It was a heady but also dangerous mixture of loyalties, a recipe for reckless heroism.

Less than two months after Antietam, this pattern repeated itself at Fredericksburg. On the morning of the battle, Meagher instructed his men to wear sprigs of green boxwood in their caps as signs of their Irish identity. On that day, December 13, they were ordered to charge the Confederates entrenched on Marye's Heights. They had advanced to within a hundred yards of the top when they were hit by a barrage of fire that mowed them down, said one observer, like "corn before the sickle."[36] Perhaps as many as half of the men involved in the charge were either killed or wounded. "It will be," predicted one of the survivors, "a sad, sad Christmas by many an Irish hearthstone." After Fredericksburg, said one observer, "the Brigade, in fact, no longer exists!" In three main battles between June and December 1862, it had suffered at least 1,200 casualties.[37]

One glimmer of light in this gloom was the improved medical care given to the wounded, thanks in no small part to the efforts of women. Maria Daly, for instance, visited the sick and wounded in a local military infirmary, bringing old sheets, towels, clothes, and anything else that might serve as bandages. More professional care came from a dedicated group of nursing nuns. In the first month of the war, the Sisters of Charity in the New York diocese volunteered to serve as military nurses. Initially, Archbishop Hughes balked at losing women needed for the care of the sick at home, but he soon relented, and by June 1861 the *Freeman's Journal* could announce that nuns from several orders were "hurrying to scores of the Hospitals" set up for the Union Army. And more were to follow: in 1862, for instance, nine Sisters of Mercy left their convent on Houston Street to take charge of a military hospital at Beaufort, North Carolina.[38]

Much of the nursing was done in New York City. At Saint Vincent's Hospital, the Sisters of Charity took care of some of the wounded soldiers returned to the city. Lieutenant Bernard S. O'Neil, seriously wounded in the left arm at Fredericksburg, resorted to Saint Vincent's in early 1863 when military surgeons were unable to repair all the damage; at the hospital, he was able to recover—only to rejoin the war and to die in 1864. After Antietam, the sheer volume of casualties demanded a rapid enlargement of care, and in October 1862 the former St. Joseph Academy in Central Park was converted into a military hospital, with the Sisters of Charity in charge of nursing. It was a demanding mission, involving 20 wards, some large and many filled to overflowing—and it could be dangerous: Sister M. Prudentia Bradley died in 1864 of a disease contracted during her work, but these devoted women succeeded in confirming their reputations as, in the words of one admirer, "the most faithful nurses in the world."[39]

At the same time, the Irish community was attempting to take care of children orphaned by the war, a problem compounded in the fall of 1862 when the Catholic Orphanage in Brooklyn was destroyed by fire. Following the bloodbaths at Antietam and Fredericksburg, one community leader, Richard O'Gorman, estimated that nationally there were "tens of thousands of orphans whose fathers had given their blood to this country." Especially disturbing was the increasing number of homeless children. Some of them came under the care of the Children's Aid Society, but this was of little comfort to Irish leaders, who had long viewed the Society as a Protestant agency eager to kidnap Catholic children away from their faith. In December 1862 laymen like O'Gorman met with Archbishop Hughes to organize the Catholic Protectory for homeless and wayward children, and in May 1863 the new institution opened its doors. By the end of the year, the Protectory was providing a home for over a thousand children.[40]

The war years also saw other organized efforts to aid the unfortunate. In the spring of 1863 the community was active in raising money for the relief of the suffering poor of Ireland, the homeland being threatened by a famine as severe as that of the 1840s. More attention went to meeting needs at home, especially the needs of women. In February 1863 Maria Daly tried to interest the church in a project to resettle widows and orphans in a Catholic farm colony, each widow's family to be attached to a family with a male head. Nothing came of this, but the often desperate needs of poor working women, many of whom were Irish, did bring the formation in late 1863 of the Working Women's Protective Union, headed by Maria's husband, Judge C. P. Daly. This organization provided support for seamstresses and other workers throughout the war, in 1865 helping to form the first known Catholic day nursery for working mothers.[41]

The community had some opportunity to celebrate its wartime contributions. In January 1863 it attended a "Grand Requiem Mass" held at Saint Patrick's Cathedral for all those who had died in Irish units since the fighting began. In his panegyric, Father O'Reilly (the chaplain of the old Sixty-ninth at Bull Run) declared that the men under their green flags and star-spangled banners had marched gladly into conflict, "rushing joyously to the battlefield like bridegrooms to their nuptials." They had done so, said O'Reilly, out of deep reverence to the nation, the Constitution, and to God, guided by a profoundly conservative respect for all legitimate authority. In March the celebration was more joyful when on Saint Patrick's Day a large new gunboat was christened the *Shamrock* to honor Irish patriotism. "No ship launched at Brooklyn," said a reporter, "was ever greeted with applause so boisterous."[42]

The year 1863, however, brought a severe crisis in the community regarding both the war and authority. Early in the year, Meagher attempted to replenish the depleted ranks of the Irish Brigade without much success. In part, this resulted from his own much diminished image: within the community, critics condemned him for the horrendous losses suffered by the brigade, and there were new rumors of his drunkenness. On the other hand, Meagher and his supporters blamed the failure on the refusal of the Lincoln administration to permit the brigade to return home for purposes of rest and recruitment. The situation grew even more desperate in May when fighting at Chancellorsville reduced the brigade to a few hundred men, evoking charges that the administration was willing to sacrifice "the heroes of the Green" to the last man. When he was again refused permission to bring his men home, Meagher resigned his command. The brigade survived without him, but in a much diminished form, fighting at Gettysburg as a battalion of six companies under the command of Colonel Patrick Kelly.[43]

Resentment was intensified by the Emancipation Proclamation, which, in Irish eyes, changed the character of the war for the worse. Where the early war had invited patriotic efforts to defend the traditional Union, it now seemed to demand acceptance of a hated abolitionism, leading the *Irish-American* to condemn the "Negrophilism" of the administration and "the irredeemable malignity of the Abolition hatred of our race." Emancipation threatened to intensify the competition of blacks for Irish jobs and to extend that competition to the battlefield by opening the ranks of the Union Army to black soldiers, diminishing the sacrifices made by the heroes of the green and weakening their bid for acceptance as citizens When it was argued that black military service would diminish the number of white casualties, the bitterly antiwar *Weekly Day-Book* warned that "equality as a soldier means equality at the ballot-box, equality everywhere," an equality that meant that Irish workers would be "degraded to a level with negroes."[44]

Tensions were further deepened by economic conditions. In some respects, the war brought significant benefits to the Irish population, providing employment for thousands of men and women in war-related industries and generating millions of dollars in military pay and support money. By 1865 the city's leading welfare agency could conclude that "there was less suffering from indigence in the city than in any proceeding four years in our history." At the same time, the war brought a vicious inflation that bore heavily on workers, especially on unskilled laborers, many of whom were Irish. In March 1863 some 6,000 angry workers met to protest this situation and to hear their chairman, Charles McCarthy, call for the creation of one big union of all-*white* workers in support of higher wages. Tensions were further increased by the use of blacks as strike-breakers. In June 1863, for instance, some 3,000 striking longshoremen, most of whom were Irish, were forced to watch as black men, under police protection, took their jobs on the docks.[45]

Resentment found a focus in the Conscription Act passed by Congress in March 1863. Earlier, Archbishop Hughes and other leaders had favored a draft as a way to ensure that it would not be only the Irish poor who bore the brunt of battle, but the Conscription Act seemed like more discrimination, since it exempted those men who either paid $300 commutation money or provided a suitable substitute. Contrary to Hughes's hopes, this draft threatened to make the war even more a poor man's fight. The result was widespread condemnation of the act even though its enforcement in the city was assigned to Colonel Robert Nugent, one of the heroes of the old Sixty-ninth Regiment. As if to light the fuse, the *Freeman's Journal* declared that not to resist the "outrage" of conscription would be "an apathy that denotes an enervated, emasculated and slavish people."[46] There was no apathy.

When on July 11 an attempt was made to begin the draft, a series of savage riots broke out in the Irish sections of the city.[47] Much of the accumulated anger was vented against blacks, some of them being thrown into the river by outraged longshoreman and others lynched. But the rioters attacked whites as well. They attempted to burn Colonel Nugent's house, entering one room that contained portraits of Nugent, Meagher, and Corcoran; they slashed the pictures of Nugent and Meagher but left that of Corcoran untouched. Within hours after leading a small military force to beat back one mob, Colonel Henry O'Brien fell into the mob's hands and was cruelly beaten and shot, his broken body finally being hung on a lamppost.[48]

It was four days before what the *Irish-American* called "a saturnalia of pillage and violence" was suppressed by the police and by military units called into the city. The extent of the violence and the fact that it required intervention by the Union army has led some historians to call the riots an "insurrection." On the whole, however, this violence lacked the organization and direction of a true revolt against authority. Basically, it was an eruption of the frustrations that had accumulated throughout the first half of 1862, serving both as a catharsis for past feelings and more tangibly as a modifier of draft policy. Subsequently, the threat of conscription and, therefore, of further rioting was substantially reduced by local policies encouraging voluntary enlistments and providing exemption money for, among others, the city's volunteer fire companies, a leading source of disorder.[49]

The affair was a severe blow to the reputation of the Irish community. Many of the rioters were not Irish, and many of those who opposed the riot were Irish; indeed, one of the few undoubted heroes was young Paddy McCafferty who organized a rescue of the children in the Colored Orphan's Asylum from a threatening mob. But many of the most identifiable rioters were Irish, women as well as men. "Stalwart young vixens and withered old hags," wrote George Templeton Strong of Irish women, "were swarming everywhere, all cursing the 'bloody draft' and egging on their men to mishcief." In August the *Irish-American* indignantly denied a rumor that Irish servant girls were planning to burn down the homes of their employers. Undoubtedly, many influential people agreed with Strong that "the atrocities these Celtic devils perpetrated can hardly be paralleled in the history of human cruelty." In contrast, social leaders applauded the victims of Irish rage, black Americans, who were reported by the city's leading charitable society to have been "honored by the elite of the city with public ovations. They have been marshalled 'in all pomp and circumstances of glorious war' on our public squares, and escorted in military array, with banners and martial music, through our busiest streets and most beautiful avenues."[50]

This contrasting treatment and the growing military involvement of African Americans in the war only added to the gloom of a depressing year. In December 1863 Irish military zeal was further diminished when the community lost its greatest hero, Michael Corcoran, who died not in combat but from a riding accident. Many mourned his death, some because it left Meagher, who they had come to detest, as the foremost Irish military leader, and others because they saw in Corcoran not only a war hero but a future redeemer of Ireland from British rule.[51]

Amid the gloom of 1863, one joyful ray was shed by "Private Miles O'Reilly of the Forty-seventh New York Volunteers," the fictional hero created by Charles Graham Halpine. Halpine, a native of Ireland, had left a career as a writer and journalist in New York to join the war, first as an officer in the old Sixty-ninth Regiment and then as a member of the staff of General David Hunter. After the Draft Riots, he was reassigned to New York City. By the end of 1863 he had published enough pieces featuring Miles O'Reilly for the *Irish-American* to say that only the president was better known than O'Reilly and for Horace Greeley's *Tribune* to declare that he projected "a halo of gayety over the harsh and rugged features of these anxious days." Halpine soon collected his pieces in *The Life and Adventures, Songs, Services and Speeches of Private Miles O'Reilly*, where he described Miles as having "the usual strong type of Irish forehead—the perceptive bumps, immediately above the eyes being extremely prominent."[52]

As the nation's leading "military minstrel," Miles composes verses in support of the war, including defense of the use of black soldiers, "Sambo's Right to Be Kilt," where he says he would not object if "Sambo's body" stopped a bullet directed at him. More idealistically, he writes in his "Song of the Soldiers":

> By the baptism of the banner,
> Brothers of one church are we!
> Creed nor faction can divide us,
> Still whatever fate betide us,
> Children of the flag are we!

In such lines, Halpine worked against Irish alienation from the war and at the same time called national attention to what the *Irish-American* termed "the military glory of the citizen soldiers of America," especially the New York Irish, thereby undoing at least some of the damage resulting from the Draft Riots.[53]

The opening of 1864 brought another break in the gloom when the remnants of the Irish Brigade were finally allowed to return home to New York on furlough, and on January 16 Meagher and other officers held a great banquet dedicated to all the veterans of the brigade. In the banquet hall, whose galleries were filled with onlookers, including many war widows dressed in black, the officers saluted the enlisted men, a characteristic Irish gesture, said the *Irish-American*, "of the blood and brotherhood that united the chieftains of old to his clansman."[54]

The banquet initiated a generally successful effort to replenish the three New York regiments of the brigade. By April, it was back in Virginia preparing for a new phase of the war. Combined with the Irish Legion, which had yet to experience numerous losses in battle, it represented a renewed Irish military presence in the war. This new force, however, was soon to experience the same old bloodshed. In his poem "April 20, 1864," celebrating the third anniversary of the Sixty-ninth Regiment, Charles Halpine remembered when the regiment had first entered into what was then thought to be a short conflict, when "beneath a cloudless heaven twinkled a thousand bayonets." But the war had not been short:

> Of the thousand stalwart bayonets
> Two hundred march today
> Hundreds lie in Virginia swamps
> And hundreds in Maryland clay
> And other hundreds less happily drag
> Their shattered limbs around.[55]

And so it was to be again in the months that followed the brigade's return to war. Soon, both the brigade and the legion became involved in Grant's bloody campaign to take Richmond, each suffering terrible losses. In an assault on Petersburg, the brigade lost its commanding officer, Colonel Patrick Kelly. Kelly, who had fought in every campaign of the brigade, was brought home for burial in an impressive ceremony at Calvary Cemetery. By this time, funerals had replaced flag presentations as the most common military ceremony. The brigade's casualties in less than two months totaled nearly a thousand men, and more were to follow, leading military authorities to order the consolidation of the remains of the three New York regiments into a single unit.[56]

Again, the Irish had reason to be dissatisfied with military policy, and this time during a presidential election year. Whatever their view of the war, the great majority had remained loyal to the Democratic party, leading an exasperated Meagher, one of the few exceptions, to complain in a public—and much condemned—letter that most of his countrymen had allowed themselves "to be bamboozled into being obstinate herds in the political field."[57] Actually, there was reason for this loyalty since the Democrat-controlled city and county government provided millions of dollars of aid for the Irish poor. During the war years, for instance, the city council appropriated more than $6 million to assist the indigent families of volunteers. And the New York County Board of Supervisors provided more than $10 million in bonus money for military volunteers—a program that not only gave as much as $700 to volunteers but also, by encouraging voluntary enlistments, reduced the threat of a local draft. This bonus money was distributed by the five-man County Committee on Recruiting, whose most conspicuous member was Willam M. Tweed; with the help of such programs, Tweed would soon make himself the "Boss of New York."[58]

Beyond self-interest, the Democratic party also appealed to the average Irishman's vision of the American Republic. Of all major ethnic groups, the Irish generally were the most conservative, their Catholic faith reenforcing a reverence for traditions. Their deeply traditionalist view of warfare, with its emphasis on personal honor and reckless courage, undoubtedly contributed to the high casualty rates of the Irish Brigade, fighting under the conditions of perhaps the world's first modern war. This same traditionalism was evident in Irish political and social thought, which strongly favored individual rights, local control, and the preservation of the existing social order, especially in race relations; Irish Democrats had been the most hostile to eliminating discrimination against black voting in New York. Archbishop Hughes summed up the general attitude when in October 1861 he warned that while his flock was willing to fight to the death to preserve the old Union, it would "turn away in disgust" from a war against slavery.[59]

Whereas the principles and practices of the democracy appealed to Irish conservatism, the Republican party stood for threatening change, for a meddlesome and intrusive government, for efforts to change the social order, and for the competition of black people. Few disagreed with the *Irish-American* when it denounced the "narrow bigotry and persistent intolerance" of Lincoln and his party. Although the Irish community was antiadministration, this did not mean that it was necessarily antiwar. Charles P. Daly, an important community leader, was bitterly anti-Lincoln but was also a strong supporter of the war effort, as was the important Democratic politician, James T. Brady; in one speech, Brady alluded to his Irish heritage in virtually the same breath in which he proclaimed himself a "Yankee," defining that term to include anyone who supported the war against the Confederate South. In 1864 Brady, Charles Halpine, and other Irish Democrats favored committing their party to a vigorous prosecution of the war as the best way to achieve a favorable peace and the restoration of the old union.[60]

At the same time, the disillusionments of 1863 had strengthened antiwar tendencies within the community, providing encouragement for Copperhead opposition to the war effort. Irish leaders like Richard O'Gorman (an organizer of wartime relief efforts) and Daniel Devlin were prominent in the movement to achieve peace at virtually any price. Among Irish newspapers, the *Freeman's Journal* supported the movement, as did the *Metropolitan Record*, whose editor, John Mullaly, was arrested in 1864 for publishing allegedly "incendiary, disloyal, and traitorous" articles; Mullaly had condemned the draft and war policy in general, with the warning that they could bring "five hundred thousand more victims to Abolitionism." The chief political agency for the peace movement was a faction within the local Democratic party headed by John McKeon. In 1863, the McKeon faction, running against other Democrats as well as Republicans, had been able to elect an antiwar extremist, G. Godfrey Gunther, as mayor of the city, much of Gunther's support coming from Irishmen.[61]

On the question of continuing the war, the Irish community was deeply divided, the strong pro-war *Irish-American* more than balancing Mullaly's *Metropolitan Record*, but this disunity was countered by a general aversion to Lincoln and his party. In the presidential election of 1864, Republicans made some effort to win Irish votes, recognizing their importance in winning the city and the state. Shortly before the election, Daniel Daughtery warned that Lincoln's defeat would simply allow the Confederacy the opportunity to find "Hessians" to fight its battles and continue the war. "Was any Irishmen in favor of that?" The community, however, heavily favored the Democratic candidate, General George B. McClellan, whose cautious polices as commander of the Army of the Potomac earlier had at least saved lives and who plainly was no abolitionist. More than 90 percent of the vote in the heavily Irish Sixth Ward went for him, and he carried the entire city by a more than two-to-one majority. Lincoln may have lost the city, but he won the presidency, underlining the isolation of the New York Irish from national trends.[62]

Grumble though they might, critics had no choice but to accept Lincoln's reelection, especially since it was linked to what was plainly becoming an inevitable Union victory. Although most Irishmen continued to despise the Great Emancipator, some were saddened by his assassination in April 1865, concluding with the *Freeman's Journal* that the president had started to move toward more moderate policies and away from "the fanatical portion of the Puritans" who favored the abolition of slavery and interracial justice.[63]

The war dragged on into 1865, producing more casualties, one of the last being Colonel Matthew Murphy, the commander of the Irish Legion. Two hundred seventy died in April from wounds received two months earlier, but by that time Lee had surrendered at Appomattox. And in the early summer, the Irish units of a rapidly demobilizing Union army returned home. In mid-June came some 700 members of the Irish Brigade, marching one last time through the streets of the city: "The men looked strong and hardy; their faces, bronzed by the exposure of years, were wreathed with smiles and bestowed with tears as cheer upon cheer rent the air." Soon after, the remnants of the Irish Legion reached the city, to be given a similar reception as they marched to the Centre Street Market Armory, where they stacked their arms and were treated to "a beautiful collation" before dispersing into civilian life.[64]

Notably absent from these affairs was Thomas Francis Meagher. In the presidential election, Meagher had openly supported Lincoln, and he expected to be rewarded for his services with an appointment as a territorial governor. In May 1865 he resigned from the military, eventually to be appointed territorial secretary and acting governor of Montana Territory. It was a new but short adventure for the 42-year-old Meagher, for on July 1, 1867, after a drinking bout, he toppled off the steamboat on which he was riding and drowned in the Missouri River.[65]

And so, in such varied ways, ended the war—at least for most. For some, there remained the old hope for a military liberation of Ireland. This idea animated the Fenian Brotherhood, which had organized numerous "circles" within the Union army. In January 1865, with the prospect of peace, the strongly Fenian *Irish-American* dreamed of uniting Irishmen who had fought in the Confederate as well as Union armies—battle-hardened veterans all—to overthrow British rule. But many of the Fenians, like Corcoran, had died in the war, and the dreams of grand conquests fizzled in an unsuccessful invasion of Canada in May 1866. The Fenians attempted another invasion in 1870 with the same result.[66]

By then, probably most Irish Americans of the Civil War generation had come to identify themselves with the United States, whose soil had both absorbed their blood and provided a ground for their aspirations, while their loyalty to the old country was fading into sentiments for St. Patrick's Day. Although the war had brought profound disappointments, it had also forced an unprecedented involvement in important affairs. Four years of cooperation in support of the regiments in the fields and of the needy at home had strengthened the community in New York, rooting it firmly in American conditions. And four years of outrage over Republican policy had deepened involvement in the Democratic party, bringing one step closer the time when the Irish would dominate the local party and make themselves a power in American politics. Eventually, they would forge a coalition with the Democratic South, which would revive much of the old racial order.

The war by no means eliminated nativist hostility to the Irish, but it did make it far more difficult to deny them a place in America. As memories of the Draft Riots and of Copperhead politics faded away, there remained in battlefield accounts and on the markers over thousands of graves concrete evidence that the Irishman was, in the words of one Union general, "a gallant soldier and loyal citizen." Although in important respects Irish Americans had been on the "wrong" side regarding war policy, in the light of their service and sacrifice there was much less reason than before to doubt that they were citizens and patriots in their adopted land.[67]

THE TIGER'S SHARE.

TAMMANY—"I'm monarch of all I survey;
    My rule there is none to dispute.
From Harlem right down to the bay
    I'm lord of the man and the brute.

1877 to 1914

PART III

THE TURN OF THE CENTURY

The "Tammany Tiger," with a shamrock in his hat, sits astride
Manhattan in this c. 1890 lithograph. The Society of St.
Tammany was closely associated with Democratic politics in
New York County from the middle of the nineteenth century.
Irish immigrants, spurned by Republican nativism, voted
Democrat. Their party loyalty on election day was in exchange
for social benefits like jobs, food, shelter, loans, recreation, and
solidarity. In 1872, John Kelly became the first Irish Catholic
leader of Tammany Hall; until 1948, a succession of Irish bosses
honed an urban political machine that provided public works
and civil service employment for thousands of immigrants.
Tammany was behind the election of the City's first Irish
Catholic mayor, the businessman William R. Grace in 1880,
and groomed men such as Al Smith, James Farley, and Robert
Wagner Sr. for state and national politics. (Museum of the City
of New York. Gift of Mrs. Bella C. Landauer.)

Lawrence J. McCaffrey

OVERVIEW
Forging Forward and Looking Back

I N THE summer of 1912 my father, John Thomas McCaffrey, left Sligo on a White Star Line passenger ship bound for New York. Unlike most of the young men and women leaving Ireland for the United States, he had a farm, 40 acres of mostly bog and rocks in the townland of Dowra, County Cavan, at the foot of Cuilcagh Mountain, a few hundred yards from the Shannon Pot, the source of Ireland's magnificent river. Economic realities drove most Irish emigrants from the land of their birth. Only one son could inherit the farm; only one daughter could have a dowry to marry. Outside the Belfast area there were few employment prospects in industry, and small Irish farms needed little agricultural labor. Some lads joined the Royal Irish Constabulary, enlisted in the British armed forces, or found jobs in towns. Some lassies worked in shops or as domestic servants in the big houses of a fading gentry class, in cottages of prosperous farmers, or in middle-class homes in Irish cities and towns. And there was always the church. A considerable number of young Catholics became priests, nuns, or brothers. But the vast majority had to leave home to make a decent living, and after 1840 most of them preferred the United States to Britain or other parts of its Empire. Many Irish religious also departed Ireland to serve the spiritual needs of the diaspora or to do missionary work in the British colonies.

From 1877 to 1914 young Irish Catholics continued to flock to America as they had in earlier times. This group of emigrants, my father among them, left

Ireland first because of the agricultural depression in the late 1870s, which hit the western part of the country particularly hard, and subsequently because of a desire to escape a lifetime of boredom in a stagnant economy and a peasant Catholic puritanism that encouraged gender segregation and hard drinking as a relief for sexual frustration. Staying in Ireland meant not only depressing monotony but also arranged and usually loveless marriages or permanent celibacy. Options were particularly limited for young women, and they, even more than their brothers, decided that the United States, with all of its hardships, was a promising alternative to rural Ireland.[1]

The Irish Catholic immigrants who entered the United States during the nineteenth century were for the most part socially and economically handicapped. Many were illiterate, few were skilled in either agriculture or industry, and some were more fluent in Irish than English. These liabilities froze them into the lowest levels of the unskilled labor and domestic servant classes. Famine refugees, especially those who left after 1847, represented the nadir of the Irish exodus.

Life in a rural, Catholic, sometimes Irish-speaking culture did not prepare Irish immigrants for urban, industrial, Protestant America. Traumatized by the transition from the familiar Old World to the strange New World, they experienced a slow and painful adaptation. They became urban America's first group social problem. Their crime, filth, alcoholism, mental disorders, violence, and family collapses irritated Anglo-Protestants, but not as much as their religion. Anglo-America inherited its no-popery bigotry from Anglo-Saxon England as the core of a nativism insisting that Catholicism represented an alien, subversive religion that threatened American culture and institutions.[2]

My father's generation participated in the final stages of a mass emigration whose members had experienced a steady improvement in education and economic fortunes since 1850. Because the Famine had eliminated at least 2½ million people from the landscape, forced survivors to take a more prudent look at marriage, and institutionalized emigration, it cleared the way for a more prosperous Ireland. Tenant farmers replaced agricultural laborers as the most numerous class, and the size of their holdings gradually increased from 1840 to 1900, as Ireland went from Europe's most to least densely populated country.

Political activity also contributed to positive change. In response to Catholic, agrarian, and nationalist agitations, British Liberal governments between 1860 and 1890 disestablished the Protestant church, legalized secure tenures at fair rents, loaned money to farmers to purchase their holdings, democratized the Irish franchise, and concluded an alliance with Irish constitutional nationalism, encouraging hopes for self-government. In the 1880s and 1890s, British Conservative governments, hoping to discourage nationalist enthusiasms, converted tenant farmers into peasant proprietors; created a congested districts board that opened agricultural and technical schools, equipped and instructed fishermen, and organized a cottage textile industry; and financed public works projects such as railway and road construction and land-improving drainage projects.

By 1914 Ireland was considerably more prosperous than in 1870, though still a poor, underdeveloped country. With the help of the population decrease, the reform efforts, and dollar gifts from children in the United States, living standards rose appreciably. Rural cottages were larger and more comfortable. Potatoes remained a key element in the diet, but farmer's wives supplemented them with bread, butter, milk, eggs, cereals, vegetables, and occasionally meat.[3]

Education also improved. In 1831 the British government established a system of national education to Anglicize recently emancipated Irish Catholics. National schools probably hastened the decline of Irish and the spread of English as the vernacular, but increased literacy multiplied the reading audience for nationalist books, newspapers, and periodicals. In general, the schools provided a sound basic education. By 1900 about 95 percent of Irish emigrants were literate.[4]

My father was a tribute to the national schools. He was forced to leave school and work on the farm after the sixth grade (his father and seven of his brothers and sisters had died of tuberculosis), but the instruction of Master McHugh inspired him to read nationalist versions of Irish history, pre-Revival Irish literature (especially the novels of Charles Kickham), and Shakespeare's plays.

Better living conditions, literacy, and nationalist aspirations reduced Catholic and Gaelic fatalism and pessimism. Furthermore, a reformed and revitalized church helped to refine and discipline the Irish character. On his visit to Ireland in 1835, Alexis de Tocqueville observed that Irish Catholics were more devout than those on the Continent, but ignorance, superstition, and religious indifference pervaded the poor, largely Gaelic, underdeveloped, and densely populated parts of the country.[5] The people in these areas lacked adequate numbers of clergy and chapels. Priests were not well educated, and bishops scandalized their flocks by publicly quarreling over the relationship between Catholicism and nationalism and the British government's Irish policy.

The Famine had a brutal effect on Irish Catholic society, particularly its poorest members, and therefore the most ignorant and superstitious portion of the population. With their disappearance, the church was better able to instruct and minister to the more affluent, better-educated survivors.[6]

In the last year of the Famine, Pius IX appointed Paul Cullen, rector of the Irish college in Rome, archbishop of Armagh. In 1852 he moved to Dublin, where, until his death in 1878, he dominated Irish Catholicism. Cardinal Cullen reformed and romanized the religion in Ireland, building chapels and schools, improving clerical education, enforcing a public appearance of harmony among the bishops, and persuading the laity to attend mass and devotions diligently, receive the sacraments, and contribute pennies, shillings, and pounds to the church in Ireland, Rome, and foreign missions.[7]

Cullen distrusted nationalism because it presented both secular and Gallican competition to his ultramontane Catholicism, but it did contribute to his "devotional revolution." Since the 1820s, when Daniel O'Connell had transformed the people's religious identity into a sense of nationality, Catholicism and Irishness had become inseparable. Young Ireland's cultural nationalism, increased literacy, and agitations for tenant rights and home rule had spread and intensified nationalism. And as the Irish became more nationalist, they also became more devoutly Catholic. This religion's affiliation in turn became a visible sign of ethnicity.[8]

Although the devotional revolution played an important role in civilizing and disciplining the Irish character, it also had a negative effect. Reinforcing the economic need for more prudent marriage patterns, the church's emphasis on chastity and its obsession with sins of the flesh contributed to the dullness of Irish rural life and the social segregation of men and women that persuaded so many to leave the country.

Not only were Irish immigrants in the late nineteenth and early twentieth centuries culturally, socially, and religiously more scrubbed and polished than preceding generations, they also had a more pleasant journey to and reception in New York. Since the 1850s steamships had reduced the time of the journey from five to two weeks or less and were more comfortable and sanitary than sailing vessels. Arriving in New York, new Americans no longer had to suffer a barrage of runners, mostly Irish, meeting them on the dock, grabbing their scruffy baggage, and hustling them off to filthy boardinghouses/grog shops whose landlords, again usually Irish, cheated them out of their meager poke.

In 1855 Castle Garden, at the lower tip of Manhattan, opened to help immigrants make the transition from Europe to the United States. Once Fort Clinton and then an opera house, it had facilities for bathing, cooking, changing currency, collecting and mailing letters, depositing valuables, purchasing railroad and riverboat tickets, and obtaining advice from representatives of religious and benevolent societies. When they left the main building, immigrants could consult employment agencies staffed with translators. Castle Garden officials provided luggage carriers and directed them to respectable boardinghouses. In 1892 Ellis Island replaced Castle Garden and improved on its services.[9]

When my father arrived in New York, it was a city with a strong Irish flavor. In 1870 more than 200,000 Irish immigrants (21.4% of the city's population) lived in Manhattan, and 73,985 (18.7%) resided in Brooklyn.[10] By 1884 some 40 percent of New Yorkers were of Irish extraction, 5 percent more than Germans, the second largest group.[11] In 1890, 196,372, or 24 percent of all Brooklyn Caucasians, had Irish immigrant mothers, the largest foreign-born maternity figure for the city. For New York the numbers were 399,348, or 26.8 percent, second to the German 27 percent.[12] In 1898 the Greater New York Charter merged Manhattan and Brooklyn, the number one and number three Irish metropolitan centers in the United States.[13] Although Russian Jewish and Italian immigrations reduced New York's Irish and German ambiences in the late nineteenth century, in 1900 people of Irish stock still accounted for 22 percent of New York's almost three million residents.[14]

Despite their improved quality, post-1870 Irish immigrants still arrived with fewer skills than Anglo-Americans or immigrants from other parts of northern Europe, particularly Germany. Consequently, they had to settle for casual, unskilled, dangerous, dirty, unhealthy, and menial jobs. Men worked in stables or drove horses as dairymen or cabbies, loaded and unloaded ships on the docks, swept out factories and saloons, dug foundations and carried hods on construction sites, and served people in restaurants and bars.[15]

Some women found employment in factories, garment district sweatshops, and restaurants, and others became domestics, an occupation that Anglo-Protestants tended to dismiss as degrading. Many parents of non-Irish ethnics also worried about having their daughters work in the homes of strangers. But to single Irish women, domestic service meant comfortable living quarters, nourishing food, clean clothing, a taste of civilized living, and, in view of the room and board, offered better pay than work in a factory, mill, or the garment industry. In general, Irish women were more sober and responsible than Irish men. They saved their money, sending it home in the form of ship passages for siblings or in cash or bank drafts to help their parents. And they contributed a significant amount of their income to the Catholic church.

If husbands did not desert them or perish early from diseases associated with hard and hazardous labor, married Irish women were unlikely to work outside the home. Matriarchs concentrated their energies on their families, pushing spouses and children toward middle-class respectability. Abandoned wives or widows often returned to work outside the home, but many supported themselves and their children by taking in borders and by sewing. Occasionally married women with working husbands also became landladies or seamstresses to supplement family incomes.[16]

Around the turn of the century, the health and social ills associated with poverty continued to plague Irish neighborhoods. There was little space for cleanliness or privacy in overcrowded tenements. The contents of outdoor toilets spilled into streets and courtyards. Odors and bacteria from human excrement and urine, slaughter and gas houses, and animal offal, particularly from cart horses, fouled the air and contributed to disease and high mortality. Irish neighborhoods on the Lower East Side (Five Points and the Fourth Ward), the middle East Side (the Gas House district), and the middle West Side (Chelsea and Hell's Kitchen) were afflicted with alcoholism, brutality, crime, despair, and family conflict. Physical and mental disease also took a heavy toll. Tuberculosis, depression, and schizophrenia ravaged Irish America as they did

Ireland. Husbands sodden with drink beat wives who often retaliated with fists, skillets, or other kitchen implements. Men frequently deserted families. Youngsters ran wild in the streets. A few young women became prostitutes and petty thieves, but young men were more likely to turn to a criminal life. Street gangs proliferated in Irish neighborhoods. Some were connected with volunteer fire companies and Tammany politics. Gang members protected the ballot boxes of their patrons and destroyed those of their enemies. They also intimidated opposition voters. Hell's Kitchen probably was the most violent Irish section of New York. Police found it impossible to control the gangs there, leaving the turf to the Gophers, Gorillas, the Parlor Mob, and the Rhodes Gang.[17]

Male recreation reflected the cruelty and crudity of tenement life. Boys swam in the garbage- and sewage-infested East and Hudson rivers. Their older brothers and fathers enjoyed bare-knuckle fighting or placing bets at the dog and rat pits, where assorted mixed and pure-bred terriers competed in killing rodents and each other. Cock fighting was another wagering "sport" relished by men.

Upper- and middle-class New Yorkers still remembered the Irish violence of the Draft Riots of 1863 and the Orange Riots of 1870 and 1871.[18] Those incidents and the heavy Irish involvement in crime and social disorder confirmed nativist opinion that Irish Catholics were a cancer eating away at the vitals of their city. Inheriting Anglo-Saxon or Scots-Irish ancestral prejudices, they were convinced that Protestantism represented liberty, reason, industry, and order, whereas Catholic authoritarianism nurtured ignorance, irrationality, and superstition. As leaders of the Catholic Church in the United States and as influential citizens in urban politics, the Irish took the brunt of anti-Catholic prejudice.

American novels and plays featured negative Irish stereotypes. Ignorant and foolish Biddys and Paddys wandered through fiction and across theater stages. *Harper's Weekly* cartoonist Thomas Nast, in his attacks on Tammany Hall during the late 1800s, depicted its army of Irish voters as menacing, simian-featured monsters, a caricature projected in other newspapers and periodicals. In cartoons, novels, and plays the Irish were either alcoholic, shillelagh-wielding thugs or loquacious but ignorant fools, blundering through life, obviously in need of Anglo-Protestant guidance. Anti-Irish Catholic prejudice had racist overtones, suggesting that only inferior people would choose such a debased religion.[19]

Although their faith targeted the Irish for nativist animosity, Catholicism as well as nationalism and politics instilled pride, dignity, and hope. Catholicism played a particularly important role: its liturgy and sacraments bridged the chasm between rural Ireland and urban America, providing psychological and spiritual comfort in a strange and hostile environment. Catholic parishes in American cities functioned as rural villages preserving a sense of community.[20]

Cullen's devotional revolution spread to the American branch of the Irish spiritual empire. Post-1877 immigrants knew their religion and practiced it more diligently and regularly than those who had come before.[21] Compared with other ethnics of their gender, Irish men were well represented at church services. But as Colleen McDannell explains in chapter 9, Irish women were the pillars of the church just as they were of the Irish family. They were more regular in their attendance at mass and devotions and the reception of the sacraments, and they gave their enthusiasm, as well as their time and money, to the support of the parish.

Irish American bishops, like their Irish counterparts, were strong champions of ultramontanism and displayed an aggressive Catholicism in promoting the building of churches and schools. In 1864 John McCloskey, America's first cardinal, became archbishop of New York. Fifteen years later he completed the construction of St. Patrick's Cathedral on Fifth Avenue, started by his predecessor, Archbishop John Hughes. St. Patrick's was a monument to the spirit and zeal of Irish American Catholicism. McCloskey was an organizer as well as a builder. He divided parishes into smaller units, strengthening them as communities, enabling priests to establish closer contacts with the laity.

New York's archbishops would have liked to shelter all Catholic children from Protestant and secular influences through parochial education, but in 1870 only 68 percent of New York parishes had schools, which enrolled about 19 percent of the city's Catholic youngsters. They had difficulty achieving the ideal because the church was dependent on the generosity of devout but economically strapped parishioners. In addition, Catholic leaders had few reasons to complain of public education. Irish political power kept nativist propaganda out of neighborhood schools, and many of their teachers and administrators, usually women, were Irish Catholics.[22]

Because Catholicism insists that the sacraments are essential to salvation, its priests have enjoyed more respect and power than the clergy of other faiths. And in Ireland the laity have been especially partial to their priests because they symbolize a religion that is also part and parcel of Irish culture and nationality. Unlike Continental Catholicism, the Irish variety has been associated with the peasantry not the aristocracy. Priests praised popular sovereignty and participated in agitations for economic and social justice and national independence. Priests, nuns, and brothers were the only educated Catholics in rural Ireland, with the exception of teachers. Parish priests shared influence and competed with Anglo-Protestant landlords for peasant deference. Irish Catholics sent their best and brightest sons and daughters into the church. A priest in the family brought distinction to all of its members. Because of the clergy's secular as well as religious importance, parishioners asked clerical advice on worldly and spiritual matters.

In the United States, Catholicism continued to be a significant presence in Irish life. Not only did priests say mass, hear confessions, visit the sick and the old, marry the young, and bury the dead, but they also verbally chastised alcoholic and abusive husbands, wayward wives, and delinquent children and adolescents. Clerical guidance and moral discipline instilled by nuns and brothers in Catholic schools speeded Irish economic mobility and respectability.

The Catholic Church functioned as a social service as well as a religious and educational institution. At a time when city governments did little to lessen the effects of poverty, Catholic hospitals, orphanages, and shelters for the hungry and homeless did much to alleviate human suffering. The clergy also attempted to address one of the main causes of much Irish misery: alcoholism. From the time Father Theobald Mathew, the Cork Capuchin temperance leader, visited the United States in 1851, American Catholicism had challenged alcohol addiction. The St. Vincent De Paul Society, church councils, parish temperance societies, and the Catholic Total Abstinence Union of America (1872) all denounced excessive drinking as a cause of immorality, family disharmony, and poverty.

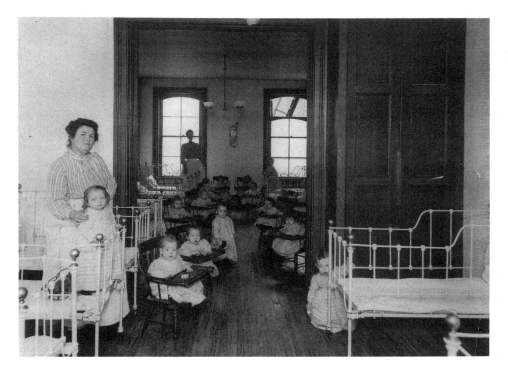

The Sisters of Mercy cared for and educated hundreds of the neglected or orphaned children of the immigrant poor at St. Vincent's Nursery on Graham Street (Taaffe Place) in Brooklyn, pictured here in 1902. After 1875, when the Children's Law made public funds available to religious institutions, Catholic child care expanded rapidly, offering alternatives to Protestant efforts like the Children's Aid Society, which had been looked upon with suspicion. By 1890, religious orders of Irish and Irish American women were caring for more than 13,000 children in orphan asylums and industrial homes throughout the city, including the Catholic Protectory in the Bronx and the Mission of the Immaculate Virgin at Mount Loretto on Staten Island. (Courtesy of the Sisters of Mercy, Brooklyn Regional Community.)

Many young Catholics took total abstinence pledges at confirmation, as did older members of congregations at parish missions. Temperance in the nineteenth century was "what birth control was to mid-twentieth-century Catholicism; the *cause célèbre* of moral reform."[23] Catholic pressures did curb the beer and whiskey thirsts of many Irish Catholics, but drinking remained an important part of their culture (the neighborhood saloon was a social and political club), and often it was an escape from the anguish of wretched lives.

Although Catholic social services did much to ameliorate the consequences of poverty, the New York hierarchy and clergy failed to attend to its causes. As John Cardinal McCloskey's coadjutor from 1880 to 1885 and then as his successor from 1885 to 1902, Michael Augustine Corrigan established New York as the citadel of American conservative and authoritarian Catholicism, a reputation it still retains. Corrigan was a pious and dedicated priest and gave much of himself to the administration of his archdiocese, but he had little concern for the material needs of his people. Like many Catholic bishops and priests, more often in the East than in other parts of the country, Corrigan believed that working-class reform movements were tainted by secular materialism or the Protestant social gospel. The archbishop viewed poverty as part of the natural order, a product of original sin. He promised his flock that those who suffered the misfortunes of this world with Christian resignation would be rewarded with eternal bliss in the next.

Corrigan warned reformers that they should not try to eliminate poverty by interfering with private property.[24] Convinced that socialists had infiltrated the labor movement, he led other bishops in opposing unions. Corrigan advised Leo XIII to proscribe the Knights of Labor, who had made the first significant attempt to organize American workers on a national scale. When the pope issued the encyclical *Rerum Novarum* in 1891, New York's archbishop interpreted it as a defense of private property and an attack on socialism more than an appeal for social justice.[25]

Corrigan distrusted American culture, which he saw as a threat to the faith of the laity. He and his mentor, Bishop Bernard McQuaid of Rochester, allied with German American prelates in the Midwest, promoted ethnicity as a form of Catholic cultural isolation. Corrigan and McQuaid battled Archbishop John Ireland (St. Paul), James Cardinal Gibbons (Baltimore), and other members of the hierarchy who insisted that not only were Americanism and Catholicism compatible, but liberal democracy gave the church an opportunity to flourish. Americanist bishops encouraged Catholics to fraternize with members of other faiths, praised and tried to cooperate with public schools, and believed that if their church refused to identify with the economic and social problems of the laity, it, like the European church, would lose the urban working class. Gibbons' visit to Rome prevented a condemnation of the Knights of Labor, but in 1899 Leo XIII, at the urging of Corrigan, McQuaid, and members of the French hierarchy, labeled distorted views of Ireland and his friends as an Americanist heresy. The archbishop of New York won a major victory over his St. Paul enemy, but the controversy cost them both red hats.[26]

If Catholicism was religion, culture, and nationality for the New York Irish, politics gave them access to power and economic opportunity. It was the only skill they brought with them from Ireland. In agitations for Catholic emancipation and repeal of the union with Britain, Daniel O'Connell organized the Irish masses for political action and instructed them in the effectiveness of organized public opinion.[27] In the 1880s, under the leadership of Charles Stewart Parnell, members of Parliament who promoted home rule were the most disciplined at Westminster.

Since nationalist politics in Ireland opposed Anglo-Protestant landlordism, it was only natural that the Irish in America would feel comfortable in the antiaristocratic party of Jefferson and Jackson. Actually, pragmatic more than ideological considerations determined their choice. Democratic politicians were less nativist than Federalists, Whigs, or Republicans; hastened Irish naturalization; and found the immigrants jobs.

The idea that politics enabled the Irish to achieve economic and social mobility has been rejected in some quarters for the view that political jobs actually kept them in low-level blue-collar or white-collar employment.[28] Although it is true that the Irish were so fascinated with politics that they neglected other American opportunities, until well into the twentieth century Protestant control of business and the professions in New York and other cities excluded or put quotas on Catholic and Jewish as well as African American participation. Therefore the Irish applied their talents to the achievement of power and influence in the Catholic Church, politics, and the labor movement. For people who suffered poverty in rural Ireland and urban America, security was a primary objective. Employment connected with politics was relatively stable and often supplemented by pensions, thus providing a base of confidence that eventually launched Irish America into the middle class.

After the fall of the Tweed Ring in 1871, intelligent, self-educated, devoutly Catholic, American-born John Kelly became Tammany leader, initiating an Irish ascendancy at the hall that lasted until after World War II. Distinguishing between "honest" graft, which was a fee for services rendered, and "dishonest" graft, which he defined as outright stealing from the public purse, Kelly purged Tammany of the flagrant corruption of the Tweed years. He also restructured Tammany on the hierarchical model of the Catholic Church.[29] In 1886 Richard Croker, Kelly's protégé, replaced him as Tammany boss. A Famine refugee at the age of three, Croker began his political career as a Tammany street thug. He was shrewd, if ignorant, and skilled at manipulating political power. His reign was a record of ruthless power and massive corruption. Scandal finally forced Croker's resignation. In 1903 he retired to Ireland as a multimillionaire horse breeder and a verbal supporter of, and financial contributor to, home rule nationalism.[30]

Under Kelly and for most of Croker's tenure, Tammany was limited in what it could do for its working class constituency because of its alliance with Democratic Party factions Irving Hall and County Democrats, or Swallow Tail bankers, businessmen, industrialists, and lawyers with a conservative agenda. Popular maverick politicians, such as Sheriff Jimmy "The Famous" O'Brien and former heavyweight boxing champion John Morrissey, who became a reform member of Congress and a state senator, challenged Tammany leadership in Irish circles. Unlike more recent political machines, Tammany could not really select candidates or control them once they were in office.[31]

Despite the complaints of nativist writer Paul Bocock and Theodore Roosevelt that the Irish were corrupting New York politics, their influence actually declined as their numbers increased.[32] From 1844 to 1884 the Irish percentage of the population rose from about 20 to 40 percent, but they held only 14 percent of Tammany leadership positions compared with the Swallow Tail's 64 percent.[33]

Although Tammany was negligent in responding to working-class complaints, individual politicians such as Big Tim Sullivan in the Bowery and George Washington Plunkitt in Hell's Kitchen did cater to voter needs. Sullivan, the most powerful politician in lower Manhattan, a nonsmoking, nongambling teetotaler, bought food and clothing and paid rent for the poor from vice protection graft (he was accused of but denied prostitution connections). The "King of the Bowery" also championed organized labor and social and political feminism.[34] Plunkitt's "diary" records conscientious attendance at Irish, German, Italian, and Jewish wakes and weddings, gifts for the bride, flowers for the deceased, licenses for push cart operators, shelters for fire victims, and bail for prisoners.[35] The concerns and services of individual Tammany politicians blunted working-class anger, curbing violent protest, but like Catholic social services, they did not attack the sources of poverty or institute a comprehensive program of change.

Irish American nationalism provided an idealism missing in politics and, to a certain extent, a social justice agenda missing in New York Catholicism. In 1858 Michael Doheny and John O'Mahony, two veterans of the 1848 Young Ireland Rebellion, founded the Fenian Brotherhood, the American wing of the Irish Republican Brotherhood.[36] Fenianism expressed the alienation of bitter people living in ghettos of mind and place and blaming British rule in Ireland for banishing them to a land where they continued to experience Anglo-Protestant nativism.

Because of the movement's failed 1867 uprising in Ireland and unsuccessful invasions of Canada, the hostility of the Grant administration in Washington, and internal factionalism, by 1870 American Fenianism had almost died out. The Clan na Gael took its place as the most effective voice of Irish American nationalism. Jerome J. Collins, science editor of the *New York Herald*, founded the Clan in 1887, but it was Irish Republican Brotherhood exile John Devoy, a British prison parolee who settled in New York in the 1870s as editor of the *Gaelic American*, who became the Clan's dominant personality.

At its peak, the Clan had about 40,000 members and the emotional and financial backing of many other Irish Americans. Its aspirations and sentiments lay more with the upper-working and middle classes than did Fenianism. Clansmen were hungry for respectability. Many were convinced that Irish Americans had failed to be accepted socially because of Ireland's state of bondage. They believed that if they could liberate Ireland from British colonialism, they would be able to elevate their own status.[37] But the ties between Irish nationalism and Irish Catholicism, and the fanatic Anglophobia of the former, antagonized American elites who viewed Britain as their cultural homeland. Irish nationalism's provocation of American nativism was evident when Irish and German Americans agitated for neutrality in the early stages of World War I. Most Anglo-Americans shared the British view that the 1916 Easter Week rebellion in Dublin was a despicable stab in the back, and few of them sympathized with Ireland's struggle for freedom during the 1919–21 Anglo-Irish War.[38]

Irish American nationalism had important economic and social implications as well. In 1870 Galway native Patrick Ford, infuriated by his experience with anti-Irish nativism in Boston, began publishing the Brooklyn-based *Irish World*, the most widely read and influential Irish American newspaper in the country. Its columns and editorials linked landlordism in Ireland and industrial capitalism in the United States as twin scourges and urged populist revolts against both. Ford complained that the Clan na Gael was too focused on revolutionary republicanism, and that it needed an economic dimension to capture the enthusiasm of Irish peasants and Irish American workers.[39]

Ireland's agricultural depression of the late 1870s gave weight to Ford's position. As a result, the Clan in 1878 formulated its New Departure strategy, which consisted of a campaign against Irish landlordism designed to enlist the support of the rural masses for its ultimate revolutionary objective. Devoy sent Michael Davitt, a Fenian paroled from a British prison who was visiting in the United States, back to Ireland to mobilize and organize farmers for the land war. Davitt founded the National Land League in 1879. Charles Stewart Parnell, a Protestant landlord member of the Irish Parliamentary Party, but a dissenter from the conciliatory policies of its chair, Isaac Butt, decided to offer his services to the league. On Davitt's invitation, Parnell became its president.[40]

The American Land League launched in New York, its many branches, and other Irish American organizations financed the campaign against landlordism. American money, Irish peasant determination and solidarity, and aggressive tactics, mainly economic and social isolation (boycotting) of those who cooperated with landlordism, eventually won out. In 1882 William E. Gladstone's Liberal government conceded fixed tenures, at fair rents, with the free sale of interests in holdings to Irish farmers. This legislation was a major step toward the final solution of the Irish land question, peasant proprietorship.[41]

Parnell used agrarian agitation to capture the leadership of the Irish Parliamentary Party. Much to the consternation of Irish American revolutionary republicans, he used surplus Land League funds and other Irish American financial contributions to support local self-government rather than complete separation from Britain. Most Irish American nationalists affiliated with organizations in favor of home rule, such as the Irish National League of America and its successor the United Irish League of America, which funded the Irish party at Westminster. The Clan na Gael, however, in conjunction with the Irish Republican Brotherhood, upheld the objectives of revolutionary republicanism. John Devoy and others participated in planning the Easter Week rebellion. All of Irish American nationalism rallied to the Sinn Fein cause during the 1919–21 Anglo-Irish War.

In chapter 13 David Brundage argues that the Clan na Gael was radical in its tactics and goals, but conservative in regard to economic and social issues. The New Departure pleaded the case for Irish tenant farmers as a short-range strategy to enlist them for revolutionary republicanism. It was not a long-range program of social justice. Clan leaders were too focused on Ireland to worry about the problems of the American working class. And after the 1880s Catholic pressures stilled the once radical voice of Patrick Ford. At the same time, Irish American home rule nationalists, while fearing socialism, sympathized with trade unionism and the women's suffrage movement.

In Ireland, following the 1890 divorce scandal, the subsequent fall of Parnell, and the nine-year split in the Irish Home Rule Party, a cultural revival captured the emotional and intellectual loyalty of many nationalists. As John T. Ridge explains in chapter 11, the spirit of revival spread to America in the 1890s in the form of county social clubs. Inspired by the Gaelic Athletic Association in Ireland, county teams competed with each other in New York. Chapter 10, by Kenneth Nilsen, reveals a "Hidden Ireland" of close to 80,000 Irish speakers in New York at this time. He discusses Irish language sections of such newspapers as the *Irish American* and the *United Irishman*, as well as Gaelic organizations and Irish language groups all over metropolitan New York. According to Nilsen, Irish-language enthusiasts in the United States anticipated Gaelic League efforts in Ireland.

Concerned with the problem of preserving Irish culture in the United States, Michael J. Logan, an immigrant from Galway and principal of Our Lady of Victory school in Brooklyn, began publishing the *Gael (An Gaodhal)* in 1881. It survived until 1904, four years after Logan's death. The *Gael* informed Irish Americans of the richness of Irish art and music and encouraged them to read and study Irish literature and history. From its Brooklyn base the *Gael* reported on Gaelic nationalism activities in Ireland and all over the United States and advertised the existence and times of meetings of organizations involved with the Irish language and culture. In 1890 there were two such organizations in Brooklyn, three in Manhattan, and one in Yonkers.[42]

Irish and Irish American cultural nationalism of the late nineteenth century responded to Anglo-Saxon racism that was popular in academic, political, and journalist circles and among the British and American upper and middle classes. This new version of nativism described Catholic Celts as unstable, emotional, and slavish, badly in need of Anglo-Saxon masters. In its most malicious forms, it insinuated that mentally and physically the Irish had not advanced much beyond apes.[43]

Cultural nationalism did much to instill self-esteem in a people who needed an ego lift. But it also permitted many Irish Americans to escape into a largely romanticized Irish past while ignoring the realities of the American present, thereby increasing rather than diminishing their alienation. Cultural nationalism had a negative effect on the development of Irish American literature in that it postponed honest investigations into and descriptions of Irish American urban misery. It also fostered a narrow-minded provincial approach to art and literature.[44] In 1911 the Abbey Theatre's presentation of John Millington Synge's *The Playboy of the Western World* received the same kind of negative reception in New York that it had experienced four years earlier in Dublin. Defensive thin-skinned audiences in both cities could not tolerate the playwright's depiction of the Irish peasantry as less than the idealized spiritual, antimaterialist Gael.

Most of the New York Irish did not flounder in the mists of a Celtic twilight. They directed their energies to more immediate and pressing concerns. Impatient with Tammany's conservative Swallow Tail alliance and its reluctance to respond to working-class issues, Patrick Ford and Father Edward McGlynn, pastor of St. Stephen's parish, supported the 1886 mayoral candidacy of Henry George, the single-tax proponent. George's advocacy of the Land League and close ties to Michael Davitt and Ford gave him many friends in the Irish community. Archbishop Corrigan, however, feared that Catholic workers were under the spell of a pied piper of socialism and ordered McGlynn to withdraw from George's campaign. When the priest refused to obey, Corrigan suspended him, a decision that Rome later reversed.[45] Combined with Tammany voter manipulation, the archbishop's opposition no doubt helped Swallow Tail Abram S. Hewitt win the election. But the 67,000 votes that went to George indicated strong Irish (especially second-generation) and German working-class support. He received 34 percent of the votes in Irish lower and midtown districts.[46]

Clan na Gaelers also challenged Tammany. Devoy and others despised the compromise and the pragmatism of Irish American politics. They also resented the way that Democrats took the Irish vote for granted and advised Irish Americans to cast ballots for pro-Irish nationalism office seekers of any party. In 1884 and 1888 Devoy and his associates endorsed Republican presidential candidates, but by engaging in American politics they shattered many idealistic illusions that surrounded revolutionary republicanism, and they could not compete with politicians closer to and more familiar with the needs of the people. Irish voters did not have difficulty voting for Henry George, a friend of Ireland, but did so for a party crusading against "rum, Romanism, and rebellion."[47]

Increasingly, Irish Americans turned from politics to the labor movement to redress their economic and social grievances. But their skills in the former meant that they were overrepresented in the upper echelons of the latter. In Chapter 12 John R. McKivigan and Thomas J. Robertson discuss Irish leadership of New York unions, the Knights of Labor, and radical political movements such as the Independent Labor Party, the Socialist Labor Party, and the United Labor Party. The Irish were also prominent in a more conservative expression of working-class consciousness. In 1900 Irish Americans held almost half of American Federation of Labor union presidencies.[48]

More than Tammany political or Catholic values, Irish nationalism inspired Irish American labor radicalism. Boycotting was a contribution of the 1880s Irish land war to the American labor movement. In Ireland the strategy socially ostracized agents of landlordism. In America it was applied through economic sanctions against unfair employers.[49] "Cautious and conservative in local politics, the Irish-controlled building trades set a record for industrial conflict, generating nearly three times as many strikes, boycotts, and sympathy strikes as other industries such as mining."[50]

There was a negative as well as a positive side to the Irish impact on the labor movement. As McKivigan and Robertson point out, early in the nineteenth century Irish stevedores banded together to exclude African American and other ethnics from the docks. They also show how Irish-led unions of the late nineteenth and twentieth century manifested prejudices against non-whites and new immigrants in accepting and rejecting members.

After Tammany survived confrontations with Irish labor and Irish national-ism, its leaders came to realize that they could no longer appease working-class voters with coal, food baskets, and political blarney. Following the lead of Tim Sullivan in the Bowery and Henry Purroy, a city fire commissioner, in the Twenty-Fourth Ward, Tammany established political clubs throughout the city. These groups provided social entertainment, including boat trips and clam-bakes, for the entire family, and took a close personal interest in neighborhood people. Factionalism in Swallow Tail ranks and social networking enabled Tammany to fight off threats from mavericks, select and mobilize votes for candidates, control them in office, and formulate policies attractive to an essentially proletarian constituency.[51] McKivigan and Robertson emphasize that the conservative urgings of the Catholic Church combined with Tammany patronage of and alliance with organized labor plus its employment of Irish civil servants, policemen, and firemen, as well as some Irish occupational mobility, took the strength out of lingering Irish radicalism.

In 1902 American-born, working-class Charles Francis Murphy took charge of Tammany. Although a conscientious, puritanical Catholic who never cursed or smoked and seldom drank, Murphy owned four saloons, which functioned as Irish political and social clubs. Although verbally inarticulate, he was a political genius, a master organizer, and a shrewd judge of situations and talent. Alfred E. Smith, a multiterm governor in Albany and pioneer of the New Deal, and Robert F. Wagner, New York's effective and distinguished senator in Washington, were Murphy protégés.

Murphy believed that the government had an obligation to serve the common good and thus to solve economic and social problems. He had more influence in Albany than Kelly or Croker. Friendly governors provided patronage funds for Tammany and vetoed the antimachine bills of hostile legislatures. When many middle-class Protestant opponents of increased assessments moved to the suburbs, Murphy taxed absentee landlords and businesses and applied the income and patronage funds to public works and social welfare programs.[52]

Many journalists and novelists have exaggerated and romanticized the positive side of Irish politics and its power broker significance. Although the political machines may have helped incorporate other ethnics into the system, Tammany clearly reserved the largest share of patronage plums for the Irish, satisfying others with such trinkets as coal, food baskets, and push cart licenses.[53] Under Tammany rule, New York fell far short of paradise and Irish politicians were mostly concerned with their own kind. At the same time, they had a more benevolent attitude toward other Catholics and Jews than did Anglo-Protestants, who conceived of reform in moral rather than in economic or social terms.[54]

The same year that Murphy became Tammany boss, Irish-born John M. Farley succeeded Corrigan as archbishop and later became New York's second cardinal. While far from liberal, he was warmer and more flexible than his predecessor. Farley encouraged the endeavors of priests at St. Joseph's Seminary, at Dunwoodie in Yonkers, one of the few Catholic intellectual centers in the United States. In 1905 Fathers Francis P. Duffy and John F. Brady of the philosophy department started the *New York Review* with the seminary president, Reverend James A. Driscoll, a highly respected theologian, as editor. Its reading audience was small, but the journal represented an important European and American Catholic voice in opposition to a rigid Thomistic philosophy and theology that insisted on a static church impervious to the contemporary world. Like John Henry Cardinal Newman, the *Review*'s editor and writers believed that knowledge of God and his purpose evolved through time. They wanted the church to accept historical development and to come to terms with discoveries and ideas in the sciences, social sciences, and humanities. In 1907 Pius X's encyclical, *Pascendi Dominici Gregis*, condemned as heretical the criticism of neoscholasticism and the effort to bring the church up to date. Farley and other members of the American hierarchy submitted to Rome. Pius X's "reign of terror" against Modernism and intellectualism shut down the *New York Review* in 1908 and forced Driscoll and Duffy out of the seminary into parish work.[55]

Duffy became pastor of Holy Cross in Hell's Kitchen and then the famous chaplain of the Fighting 69th in World War I.

At the turn of the century the New York Irish were still stumbling along the road to American success. They had the highest percentage, 39.3, of unskilled workers in the city, and 25.4 percent were semiskilled. Both groups supplied their brawn to the construction of the East and West Side elevated railways in the 1870s, the building of the Brooklyn Bridge between 1869 and 1883, and the digging of the subway system after 1900. Many Irish men and women remained part of the service economy as waiters, waitresses, hotel employees, bartenders, and domestic servants.[56] The slow pace of occupational mobility perpetuated the social problems of alcoholism, crime, and brutality that victimized Irish individuals and neighborhoods.[57]

Irish bigotry toward other minorities expressed American disappointments, failures, and insecurities. Physically, the Irish resided in the most cosmopolitan of American cities; psychologically, they lived in peasant villages, fearing the unfamiliar. Much of their resentment of Eastern European Jews derived from traditional Christian anti-Semitism, some from jealousy of a people who arrived later and rose faster. Even Patrick Ford's *Irish World* echoed the attacks of American populism on usurious Shylocks.[58] Irish prejudice was not restricted to African Americans and Jews; it was also directed at Italians, who were considered inferior non-English speaking Catholics.[59]

Despite the poverty and social disorder, the sluggish rate of occupational mobility, the moral discipline of Catholicism, and the idealism of nationalism, the situation was getting better for the New York Irish. By 1900 about 23 percent of Irish workers were skilled, second to the German 29.9 percent.[60] On the waterfront, in packing houses, in factories, and on construction sites, they were foremen as well as laborers. On railroads there were fewer Irish navvies and more engineers, firemen, switchmen, levermen, clerks, and telegraphers. Streetcar, elevated railway, and subway riders noticed that quite a few conductors and motormen spoke with a brogue. On building sites, Irish bricklayers, carpenters, plasterers, painters, plumbers, steamfitters, and electricians began to match and then exceed the numbers of diggers and hod carriers. Political power meant that city public works projects went to Irish contractors who employed coethnics in the skilled building trades. They in turn hired unskilled Irish laborers.[61] The distinction between unskilled and skilled became generational, the difference between immigrant greenhorn fathers and narrowback sons.

The security of the civil service greatly attracted people who could still remember poverty, eviction, and famine in Ireland and difficult American adjustments. The Irish staffed the police and fire departments, the post office, and the government bureaucracy. Curiosity, writing skills, the search for adventure, and a hearty drinking tradition drew Irish talent to journalism. From

1890 to 1900 the number of New York Irish in high white-collar occupations grew from 4.3 to 10.3 percent, which was below the German 18.8 percent but above that of New Yorkers with British and Canadian backgrounds.[62]

Irish families provided the Catholic Church with most of its priests, nuns, and brothers. As politics became more connected with law than with saloons—not necessarily a moral improvement—many young men became attorneys. And Irish medical school graduates served the health needs of their people. Between 1870 and 1910 Irish small businesses also increased in number; there were many Irish saloon keepers, Irish-owned grocery, clothing, hardware, and other small shops that catered to neighborhood clienteles.

Nuns, many from Ireland, taught in parochial schools, nursed in Catholic hospitals, and operated orphanages and sanitariums. They were role models for young Irish lay women who were in the vanguard of an advancing New York Irish community. Daughters of mothers who had been domestic servants or who had worked in factories, mills, or the garment industry sweatshops became teachers and nurses. In 1900 American women with Irish-born parents exceeded the "combined total of all female teachers with English or German parents."[63] Eight years later, fathers of 20.7 percent of New York's

The opening of a new police station at 153 East 67th Street was the occasion for a formal portrait in November 1887. The 25th Precinct covered the blocks from Fifth Avenue to the East River between 57th and 79th Streets, a ward that in 1890 was 26 percent Irish by birth or descent. The neighborhood cop was one of the most visible "Irish" occupations in late-nineteenth-century New York City, partly because of Tammany influence and partly because of the 95 percent literacy rate among Irish immigrants. (From the collection of Anne T. Murphy.)

public school teachers had been born in Ireland.[64] Nuns and the women they taught and inspired achieved leadership positions as school principals, college presidents, and hospital directors. They were America's first group of professional women.[65]

With rising incomes and expectations, many Irish families in the upper-working and lower middle class deserted their old neighborhoods for new ones in Manhattan's Upper East and West Side and the Bronx. In Brooklyn they left the vicinity of the Navy Yard for Flatbush and other residential areas. Ambitious families sent their sons to St. John's College (renamed Fordham in 1907) in the Bronx to be educated by the Jesuits, to the Christian Brothers at Manhattan College, to the Vincentians at St. John's College in Brooklyn, or to the Franciscans at St. Francis College, also in Brooklyn. They enrolled their daughters in the Sisters of Charity's College of Mount Saint Vincent in Riverdale. Young women from affluent families attended Manhattanville College of the Sacred Heart. But most Irish women trained for professions in teacher's colleges or in hospital nursing programs.

Show business and sports featured Irish performers and athletes. They entertained and released the frustrations of the general public. They also served as ethnic heroes. Urban poverty and adversity bred strong, hard, and bitter young naturals for the boxing ring. Until Joe Louis in the 1930s, the Irish dominated that violent sport. At the turn of the century they also were closely associated with baseball, the national pastime. With Bill McGunnigle as manager and players named Collins, Burns, O'Brien, Corkhill, Daly, and Terry, the Brooklyn Dodgers won the National League pennant in 1890. In 1899 and 1900 they again were champions when McGann, Daly, Casey, Keeler (Wee Willie), Kelley, Farrel, Jennings, McGuire, Dunn, Hughes, Kennedy, McJames, and McGinnity played for manager Ned Hanlon. In 1904 John J. McGraw managed the National League champion New York Giants. A year later they won the World Series, defeating Connie Mack's Philadelphia Athletics. McGraw had McGann, Devlin, Donlin, Shannon, Browne, Bresnahan, McCormick, Donlin, and McGinnity in the starting line up. The McGraw-led Giants won National League pennants in 1911, 1912, and 1913, with the assistance of players Doyle, Devlin, Murray, and Burns. The Giants owned but shared the Polo Grounds with the New York Yankees, a team that also featured a number of Irish Americans.[66] Because baseball was the country's most popular sport, closely linked to the mythical image of a rural Protestant nation, Irish players came to represent American adaptability and their skills in this arena gave them a more acceptable persona than boxing prowess. But athleticism also reinforced nativist opinion that the Irish were strong of back but weak of mind.

Irish American actors, dancers, singers, acrobats, and comedians appeared on vaudeville stages and in theaters. In plays and comedy sketches the Irish were evolving into more acceptable representatives of their people than the Paddys and Biddys of former days. People were laughing with, rather than at, them.

Dublin-born playwright and actor Dion Boucicault (1820–90) settled in New York and had an important impact on the development of American theater. His work influenced George M. Cohan, the Irish American king of Broadway.[67] Boucicault's Irish plays *The Colleen Bawn* (1860), *Arrah-na-Pogue* (1864), *The O'Dowd* (1873), and *The Shaughraun* (1874) remained popular with New York audiences into the twentieth century. His peasants were witty not foolish, courageous without being violent, and intelligent instead of ignorant or stupid. In clever ways, they outsmarted landlords, constables, and British officials. Boucicault's plays were pro-nationalist, but inoffensive to Anglo-Protestants in the audience.

The sketches that Edward Harrigan and Tony Hart (Anthony Cannon) wrote and performed from the 1870s through the 1890s, included songs composed by Harrigan and his father-in-law, David Braham. They depicted New York's Irish in humorous yet sympathetic interactions among themselves and with other ethnics. Despite their foibles, Harrigan's and Hart's characters were likable, hard-working, and decent people.[68]

In addition to the comic songs of Harrigan and Braham, other forms of music celebrated Irish America. In 1906 the great Irish tenor John McCormack began to make records. They and his concerts popularized Irish music in theaters and drawing rooms as well as in music halls. McCormack's renditions of Thomas Moore's *Melodies* advanced the Irish quest for respectability. Chauncey Olcott (1860–1932), an actor-singer, wrote plays filled with songs, many of his own, about Irish subjects. He tried them out in Irish Brooklyn and Bronx neighborhoods before taking them to Broadway. The lyrics Olcott pleasantly sang were sentimental and romantic, and about the Irish icons of home and mother, but they appealed to the Irish upper working and middle classes, as well as to other Americans. He popularized "When Irish Eyes are Smiling" and "Mother Machree." They still thrill some Irish hearts.

Songwriters of the late nineteenth and early twentieth centuries found the Irish good subject material and treated them favorably.[69] An interesting question is why the "hard-working, disciplined, sober, competitive, Protestant America of the early twentieth century [bought] into the image of the light-hearted, home-loving, quick tempered but genial, sentimental, loyal, extravagant, hard-drinking, Irish, who dared to love Ireland as much as America." The answer perhaps lies in the timing: "In the early decades of the twentieth century, as the culture of the factory and office reshaped the American character, the popular image of the Irish represented an alternative to the white-collar, organization man of the new urban business culture. The Irish of the popular songs had come to embody simple, old fashioned virtues: simple, romantic love, as opposed to sex: mother love and filial piety; geniality and neighborliness; hard work and hard play; loyalty and patriotism. The more America changed, the more Ireland and Irishness became repositories for the qualities that might be lost."[70]

George M. Cohan was a personification of Irishness that other Americans appreciated. The son of vaudevillians, Cohan became the most famous and successful combination of actor, singer, dancer, songwriter, and playwright in the United States. His work was filled with Irish wit, humor, and exuberance and unabashed American patriotism. During World Wars I and II, Cohan's songs lifted the morale of American servicemen and civilians and increased their love of country. Other Irish Americans shared his view that no matter what some others might think, they were red, white, and blue Yankee Doodle Dandys.[71]

After passing through Ellis Island, my father went to work in one of the Butler grocery stores, found a place to live in an Irish widow's crowded Hell's Kitchen rooming house, sharing space with old Cavan friends and new ones from other Irish counties. He quickly became a staunch Democrat, a dedicated union member, and a baseball fan. He improved his economic situation by taking a job as a streetcar conductor, but in 1916 lost it to scab labor in a transit workers' strike. In search of a new one, he dug ditches in Lynn, Massachusetts, and eventually found his way to Chicago, where he worked in packing houses, steel mills, the Pullman company plant, and finally ended up as a lever man on the railroad.

My father considered his New York introduction to urban America the most exciting period of his life. During World War II, when I would return home on leave from Coast Guard duties in New York, he would grill me for hours about the places he formerly frequented. In the late 1950s he revisited them personally.

From my father and other Irish immigrants of his time, I learned that their experience in a Protestant nativist country, propelled by competitive industrial capitalism, was difficult. Frequently they nostalgically recalled the relaxed pace of Catholic, agrarian Ireland, but not for long. Unlike the culturally dysfunctional exiles that inhabit the pages of Kerby Miller's *Emigrants and Exiles,* the overwhelming majority of Irish immigrants in New York and other American cities knew that the United States liberated them from the dreary, static life of rural Ireland.[72] Urban America was a formidable challenge, but one full of adventure and promise. In it Irish Americans found a permanent niche as labor leaders, professionals, athletes, and entertainers, and as decent, hard-working family men and women. Many had the opportunity to see their daughters and sons rise to heights unthinkable in the Ireland they left.

My father insisted that his children be Irish; his lessons in Irish history were continual. But he frequently said to me: "You know I love Ireland, but never forget that America is the greatest country in the world." In the transitional period, 1877–1914, most of the New York Irish were beginning to have the same opinion.

Colleen McDannell

CHAPTER 9

Going to the Ladies' Fair

IRISH CATHOLICS IN NEW YORK CITY,

1870–1900

ACCORDING TO American religious historians, Catholicism in the United States has been dominated by the Irish and their children. They cite statistical surveys of the ethnic heritage of bishops, clergy, and nuns to prove that Irish Americans embraced the religious life with unsurpassed enthusiasm. Sociologists and novelists detect a distinctly Irish combination of spirituality and culture. Even a musicologist has recently argued that the influence of Irish American sentimental music explains why Catholics do not sing in their churches.[1] In standard American Catholic history, the Irish are presented—in some ways—like the Puritans. "The" Irish experience has shaped Catholicism just as "the" Puritan experience shaped American Protestantism. Puritanism provided the foundation both for American virtues (hard work, piety, the sense of mission) and for American vices (prudery, arrogance, religious intolerance). In the same way, the Irish have been portrayed simultaneously as the reason behind the success of the American Catholic Church (financial support, concern for vocations, devotionalism) and the source of its problems (narrow religious legalism, hierarchical power monopolies, sentimentality). The critical difference, however, lies in the extent to which scholars have attempted to understand these two influential religious forces in American culture. The Puritans have received longstanding and sophisticated scholarly appraisal. From the insightful concern of Perry Miller to the revisionist impulses of Amanda Porterfield, scholarly studies have explained a great deal about the complexities of Puritanism(s).[2] Irish American Catholicism, by contrast, has received almost no attention from historians.

With a few notable exceptions, Catholic belief and behavior have not been considered a significant category for historical investigation.[3] Even fewer historians have attempted to describe the characteristics of Irish American Catholicism. Although they have rushed to document labor patterns, working-class entertainments, and the social construction of gender, historians have shown little interest in understanding the religious mentality of ethnic groups. Scholars have relied on overgeneralized, underresearched, and historically unsubstantiated descriptions of "Irish American Catholicism" such as this one: "the Irish immigrants preferred the Gothic-style church they had known in Ireland; emphasized the glories of Saints Patrick, Bridget, Brendan, and Columban; wanted a simple ascetic piety consistent with Irish Catholic culture; expected to hear sermons on temperance and sexual morality; joined the Ancient Order of the Hibernians with as much enthusiasm as they did the Archconfraternity of the Holy Rosary; continued practicing the devotions they had learned in Ireland; and demanded Irish or Irish-American priests."[4] Scholars and writers assume that something called Irish American Catholicism exists and that it has not changed over the centuries.

If the Irish are to American Catholicism what the Puritans are to American Protestantism, why the paucity of historical studies? Why is there no tradition of studies on Irish American Catholicism that can be challenged and revised by new scholarship? One of the reasons is that, unlike the Puritans, the Irish did not feel compelled to write down their spiritual trials and triumphs. While the Irish went to mass, sodality meetings, and parish schools, they did not put pen to paper and detail their feelings about Catholic life. Little is known about how they felt going to confession or challenging the authority of the parish priest. If such reflections were written down, they have not been preserved in libraries and archives. Although it is possible to construct the religious worldview of early-twentieth-century Catholics through oral history, one must not assume that those Irish attitudes and activities merely continue the beliefs of earlier generations. And although there are Catholic novels, devotional tracts, and schoolbooks, the nagging thought persists: Were the Irish really like this? To answer this question and some related ones—Is there an Irish American Catholicism? What might it look like? How has it changed?—one must consider sources that might not at first glance seem particularly spiritual. Since the Irish left little written evidence about their religious feelings, their religious behavior must be the guide.

In this chapter I do not attempt to speak about "the" Irish American Catholicism. Rather, I concentrate on one group of Irish, those who belonged to Manhattan parishes during the last third of the nineteenth century. To determine what the Irish were doing if they were not behaving like good Puritans and keeping spiritual diaries, I searched the New York archdiocesan archives, located the dusty records kept by parish priests, and scanned the city's newspapers.[5] What I found was that Irish New Yorkers wrote about their parish fairs. These fund-raising fairs involved the whole parish, with lay people providing the organization, design, and labor, as well as attending the event. Unlike church activities directed by Rome and organized by the clergy, parish fairs provide an indication of the religious behavior of the average Irish woman, man, and child. Thus it is useful to consider what went on at the fair, what kind of goods were raffled, and who helped organize the events. Fairs were essential to parish life because Irish Catholics expected fancy churches, useful social services, and free parochial schools. They were willing to pay for this elaborate institutional Catholicism not only by attending fairs but also by paying attention to every aspect of their religious lives. Irish Catholics were not otherworldly, ascetic, anti-Protestant believers devoted to St. Patrick. They represented a diversity of religious experience, as can be seen by comparing the parish fairs to the more well-known St. Patrick's Day parade. With the decline of the fairs in the early twentieth century, Irish American Catholicism entered a new phase.

The charity bazaar or fund-raising fair is so much a part of American cultural life that it is almost invisible. The typical nineteenth-century fair took place on a holiday or in the period before Christmas, in public rented space, and women were involved in the organization and execution.[6] In the antebellum period, handiwork produced by women dominated the fairs. By midcentury the handiwork had to be functional as well as decorative. The environment of the fair was constructed to encourage people to visit and to buy. Donated goods and foodstuffs were sold, and the profits went to the community, church, or social organization. Most fairs were modest in scope and accomplishments. The antislavery fairs of the 1830s, however, set the stage for the monumental Civil War fairs of the 1860s. The first Sanitary Commission fair for the support of the Northern cause was held in 1863 in Chicago and netted between $68,000 and $100,000. A later Boston fair raised $146,000, and the Philadelphia fair more than $1 million.[7] The publicity surrounding these fairs heightened the interest in fairs everywhere. Whether the fair was a small event to help raise money for a local church or a large one expecting to gross thousands of dollars, the basics were the same: women raised money for communal needs through the exchange of goods for cash.

During the nineteenth century, "ladies' fairs" were a successful means of raising funds for New York Catholic parishes as well as for other groups. The earliest mention of a Catholic fair that I have located was an 1834 benefit for orphans held at "Niblo's Saloon." Advertisements for the fair described the sale of "fancy articles from France" but gave no information on what happened at the fair.[8] Mention of fairs in Catholic newspapers became more frequent in the late 1850s. A Catholic newspaper article compared Catholic fairs to the exhibitions held in the Crystal Palace (1853) before its 1858 fiery demise.[9] A flurry of parish fairs took place in the 1870s and 1880s, perhaps following in the footsteps of the 1864 New York Metropolitan Fair and the 1876 Centennial Exhibition held in Philadelphia. The Metropolitan Fair, for instance, raised $2 million for the Northern cause in the Civil War.[10] New York Catholics in 1878 could view the latest inventions at the American Institute Exhibition and a 1,500-pound cheese at the Dairy Fair.[11] Or they could read about the "Methodist Church Fair" in the *New York Times* or learn "Some Hints for Charity Fairs" from *Harper's Bazaar*.[12] For New Yorkers, exhibitions and fairs provided popular entertainment in the days before Coney Island and nickel movies. They were the primary way to display manufactured goods before the advent of the department store. Fairs were so popular and so successful that Catholics quickly jumped on the "fair wagon."

For the Irish Catholics of the city who dominated parish fairs on every level, fund-raising fairs not only fit into an American social pattern, they also recalled church life in the Old World. Charity fairs were popular in Europe as well as in America. Between 1840 and 1870, bazaars in Ireland helped pay for church building.[13] The fund-raising enterprises of the European Irish "would make the most hard-headed exponent of the Protestant ethic gasp."[14] Bazaars were also popular in England; in 1904 a society periodical reported on more than 50 bazaars in a six-month period.[15] Consequently, the Irish on both sides of the Atlantic understood what fairs were and their significance to the community. Fairs were not a strange American custom but an activity the Irish understood. Likewise, fairs were not something exclusively Irish. They were both European and American.

Like other groups, Catholics held fairs either in public buildings or at the church. In 1868 St. Vincent Ferrer parish held its fair in the newly built Tammany Hall and 11 years later it provided space for St. Ann's fair. In 1879 the Paulist Fathers had their fair at Lyric Hall.[16] The grandest fair of the period was held in the nave of St. Patrick's Cathedral, before its dedication. More frequently, fairs were held in the basement of the church (St. Anthony, 1869; St. Teresa, St. Peter, and St. Agnes all in 1879) or in a school hall (St. Lawrence, 1879; St. Francis Xavier, 1880). As parishes built churches and schools, fairs were moved from civic buildings, but Catholics continued to emphasize their public nature. Fair organizers wanted to appeal to all of New York City's citizens to attract both donated goods and dollars.

After an initial call from the pastor, women took over the organization and running of the fairs. They collected donated items, created the festive environment in the hall, staffed the tables, cooked and provided the foods, and supervised the whole affair. While men might build booths, act as bouncers, or take tickets, women typically directed male activities. Women made up the general plans, told men how to execute them, and supervised the collection of money. In the fair environment, male and female roles were reversed. There

Irish Catholics in New York City, 1870–1900

were a few exceptions to this pattern. Because of its size and prestige, the cathedral fair of 1878 did have a male "committee of managers," and St. Anthony's parish (1869) had male officers and a male executive committee. Even at the cathedral fair, however, those who staffed the fair and collected the donated goods were primarily women. Catholic fairs were no different from other fund-raising fairs where women supplemented their domestic roles with socially approved fair activities. Through such events, women developed and demonstrated their creativity, energy, ambitions, and social concerns in the public sphere.

Since most Catholic fairs stayed open late into the night every day for one month, parish women took on tremendous responsibilities. In 1886 when the pastor of St. James asked for "lady" volunteers for the church's biennial fair, 250 women showed up. According to parish reports, "Immediately not only our parish, but the city was invaded by this small army, equipped with book and pencil, persuasive tongue and beseeching eyes."[17] Newspaper articles and fair souvenir booklets describe these women as a combination of soldier and seducer. The women possessed both the powers of "persuasion and argument" and were "as regular and well ordered as a regiment of soldiers."[18] There is no indication that women might be viewed as unsuitable for such public duties; rather, they were perceived as naturally inclined for such work. Catholic fair women, in the same manner as all fair women, influenced the growth and security of their parishes by their fund-raising activities.

It is impossible to identify precisely the women who worked at parish fairs. Although the cathedral fair of 1878 published lists of women who staffed the various parish booths, the similarity of Irish names makes it difficult to find these individuals in census materials. Women also tended not to list their occupations in city directories.[19] The few women located suggest that fair workers reflected the class and occupation of Irish women in general. Miss Nora Cunningham, who staffed Transfiguration table at the cathedral fair, worked in gentleman's furnishings. Miss Mary Reilly was a teacher. Miss Annie Campbell, from St. James's parish, was a nurse and Sarah Kane a dressmaker. Miss Maggie Dunn (St. Bernard) and Miss Mary Dowd (Holy Name of Jesus) were also in the needle trades. Married women were frequently listed with only their husband's name. Mrs. Jeremiah Devlin's husband (St. Francis Xavier) was in clothing, Mrs. William Clary's husband (St. Anthony) was a laborer, and Mrs. Owen Moran's husband (St. Vincent Ferrer) a mason builder. Widows also helped with the fair. Since these occupations were typical of the Irish in nineteenth-century New York, the fair workers probably reflected the female Irish population in general. Although the notable absence of servants might indicate the middle-class nature of the cathedral fair, it more likely that Irish domestics did not list their occupations in city directories. The women who helped with parish fairs were widows and single and married women of all classes.

The fair women created a "fairy land" environment.[20] In 1878 gas donated from New York Mutual lit the interior of the cathedral. In 1886 donated electricity made St. James's basement glow. Banners, mottos, pictures, and flags decorated the walls. Cut flowers were creatively woven into floral "pavilions" (St. Patrick's Cathedral, 1878) or "bowers" (St. Agnes, 1879). St. Lawrence's grand ladies' fair (1879) not only had potted plants and flowers but canaries in cages and an aquarium. St. Agnes's fair exhibited "a statue of 'liberty lighting the world,'" executed in nougat. In all of the fairs, orchestras and bands serenaded the fairgoers with music. Refreshments at the cathedral fair included oysters (stewed, pickled, raw), salmon, sardines, turkey, chicken, chicken and lobster salad, cold cuts, and various desserts. Fairgoers washed down their dinners with wine, sherry, port, claret punch, ale, beer, and lager. At St. Ann's fair (1879), however, they were limited to coffee, tea, and lemonade. Men amused themselves in the shooting galleries, at billiards, and in smoking rooms or watched demonstrations of the newly invented telephone and phonograph. Punch and Judy puppets, miniature horse races, minstrel performances, and magic lantern shows delighted the children.[21]

Even more impressive was the vast wealth of goods displayed on draped tables. While most parishes maintained between 10 and 15 tables, the fair at the Cathedral boasted 45. The dazzling array of booty was all within the grasp of the fairgoers. Rather than sell the goods, as most fairs did, Catholic fairs asked people to buy raffle tickets for the donated items the women had collected. They could buy several chances to win a particular item they liked. Toward the end of the fair, everything was raffled. The raffling of goods was most likely due to the lack of Catholic purchasing power. Whereas the Protestant population comprised rich as well as poor individuals, New York Catholics were disproportionately from the working class. If parishes had depended on their wealthy members to buy expensive items, they would have found that Catholics came to look but not to buy. By raffling the goods, parish fairs drew in many people from diverse social backgrounds. Rich and poor could all buy chances for goods. Luck, rather than wealth and status, played an important part at the fair. Catholics were not merely consumers purchasing donated goods as they would at any department store. Raffling emphasized that wealth could be accumulated through luck or the grace of God, in addition to hard work and sharp trading. Prizes challenged the rational market system, in which prices were fixed. Raffling goods introduced unpredictable elements into consumerism. Because the more affluent could afford to buy several tickets and thus increase their chances of winning an item, however, purchasing power was not entirely irrelevant. Nevertheless, the organizers promoted the illusion that the fair was fair.

The types of the goods did not differ from parish fair to parish fair; wealthier parishes merely displayed more articles. Donations included basics such as coal and flour as well as household goods, art, and religious articles. Lord & Taylor's, Tiffany's, and other department stores contributed furniture, pianos and parlor organs, sewing machines, "a new patented type-writer" (St. Francis Xavier,

1880), and baby carriages. Parlor and dining room accouterments included china tea sets, silver pitchers, fire screens, a Swiss clock, and even a case of stuffed birds. His Eminence Cardinal McCloskey won a bird cage at the cathedral fair. Men could come home with gold pens, walking canes, fishing equipment, and gentlemen's toilet sets. Children marveled at dolls and their carriages, toy kitchens, model ships, and even a live goat "with a silver-mounted harness and a cunning wagon" (St. Lawrence, 1879). Perhaps the most unusual fair prize was won by Mrs. K. Emerson at St. Patrick's Cathedral. She acquired a "bleating lamb" bedecked in pink ribbons, christened "Mary's Little Lamb," and present throughout the fair in a cage.[22]

Not surprisingly, most fairs did not include live animals. More typical were explicitly Catholic chromolithographs, paintings, and embroidered pictures. Illustrations of the pope, American bishops, and local priests were numerous. Chromos and oil paintings included those of Christ (Ecco Homo, Sacred Heart, Easter Morn), Mary (Mater Dolorosa, Our Lady with Lilies, the Grotto of Lourdes), and the saints (St. Joseph, St. Aloysius, St. Cecilia, St. Patrick). Tables at the cathedral included a "picture of the Infant Jesus worked in floss silk" and an original oil of the Virgin and Child by Father Richard L. Burtsell, supporter of the controversial Father Edward McGlynn.[23] The arts were an integral part of the delights of the fair.

Religious goods crowded the tables, often acting as centerpieces. Lucky ticketholders won finely wrought crucifixes in gold and ebony, as well as imported holy water fonts. Religious books, including family Bibles, were quite popular. As would be expected at a Catholic fair, the women raffled statues of the Blessed Virgin Mary, the Sacred Heart, and the various saints (St. Stanislaus, St. Louis, St. Teresa, Infant Jesus). Elaborate shrines were also donated and eventually found their ways into Catholic homes via the fairs. At the "Children of Mary" table (St. Lawrence, 1879), a statue of Mary was "enshrined in a beautiful niche of pale blue and white muslin" complete with lambrequins of silk chenille fringe. St. James's parishioners (1886) were especially proud of an 8-foot-high altar displaying a statue of Our Lady of Lourdes. The fairs of the cathedral (1878), St. Francis Xavier (1879), St. Gabriel (1879), and St. Teresa (1879) all offered large shrines of the Lourdes grotto. At least five parish fairs raffled wax crosses, while others offered marble and Easter crosses, a doll dressed as a Sister of Notre Dame, and even prie-dieus.[24]

The assembled wealth included goods that reflected the Irish heritage of the fair organizers and participants. While the New York archdiocese had German, French, Italian, Polish, and Canadian national parishes, apparently none of these churches held major fairs between 1870 and 1900.[25] Other Catholics preferred the "bazaar," which was of shorter duration and sold goods instead of raffling them, often just before Christmas. Irish Catholics asserted their national heritage by taking chances to win portraits of political figures, bog oak canes, paintings of scenes from the "Emerald Isle," or a "Tipperary Flag of the 69th."

The pastor of St. Teresa's donated several gifts he received during a recent trip to Ireland, including a banner from nuns in Kildare. St. Lawrence's fair had a table staffed by salesmen from Lord & Taylor's that boasted "a 'maid of Erin, dressed in green satin and leaning against a harp entwined with ivy," the Ten Commandments written in Irish, a portrait of Daniel O'Connell from a convent in Dublin, an autograph of O'Connell "embellished by *real* shamrocks," a "bog deal cross," a "blackthorn walking stick," an oil painting of St. Patrick, a shield of white satin embroidered with shamrocks, and a Belleek whisky flask.[26] Although Swiss clocks and Japanese vases had their places at the tables, only Irish goods made statements of ethnic sentiment.

Fairs not only displayed elaborate goods and foods, they also provided an opportunity for friendly competition among individuals and organizations. Fair personality contests included parish men, women, and Catholic clergy, as well as public, non-Catholic figures and groups. In order to raise money, organizers developed popularity contests in which fairgoers could purchase a vote for a favorite parish city militia regiment (St. Francis Xavier), police captain (St. Lawrence), boat club (St. Francis Xavier), military general (Cathedral), or fireman (St. Agnes). In 1880 at St. Bernard's fair, a contest was held between beer brewers and "maltsters" of the city. The company that garnered the most votes won a silver-mounted ale keg described as a "very handy work of art." At St. Agnes's fair, the most popular lady would be presented a pair of earrings, the best-beloved clergyman a liturgical stole, and the gentleman with the most votes would receive a gold-headed cane so he could "walk through life with 'gold in his hand,' if not in his pocket."[27] Catholics constructed contests based on personality rather than success. It was the most popular fireman, not necessarily the most successful one who would win votes. As in the case of taking chances on donated goods rather than buying them, Catholics subverted the Victorian notion that hard work led to success, which in turn led to wealth. At the fairs luck and popularity could make one a winner. Men and women won prizes not because they were accomplished in their occupations but because they had appealing personalities. The person, not the job, was rewarded.

Those who visited the fairs that flourished in New York between 1870 and 1890 must have found the cause, environment, and goods appealing because they joined in the festivities and spent their money. More than 20,000 people, including the mayor and various New York dignitaries, attended opening night celebrations at St. Patrick's Cathedral fair in 1878. In spite of the economic depression of the late 1870s, New Yorkers paid the quarter admission fee and most bought raffle chances for one dollar. Not everyone who came to the cathedral fair was willing to gamble on raffle tickets. The *New York Times* reported that two men were arrested for "attempting to steal a gold watch and chain from St. Cecilia's table."[28] Such pilfering had no financial impact. The *Catholic Herald* estimated that fair receipts averaged $6,000 a day and would realize half a million dollars at the end of its 42-day run.[29] The success of the cathedral fair, in which most of New York's parishes participated, probably encouraged other parishes. In 1879 St. Rose and St. Bridget's churches each earned upward of $5,000 while spending only a bit more than a hundred dollars on expenses. In 1880 St. Alphonsus raised $11,000, and two years later it grossed almost the same amount ($10,800).[30]

Comparing fair income to the other means of parish support demonstrates how significant this activity was to the life of the parish. St. Bernard's church reported in 1879 that its three-week long fair grossed $8,764. This was only $550 less than its total yearly pew and seat rental income. That same year, the wealthier Holy Cross church, received $19,693 from yearly seat, pew, and plate

Detail of the crowd of twenty thousand who attended the opening celebrations of the Grand Fair of the Roman Catholic Churches of New York City on October 22, 1878. The fair was held in the unconsecrated nave of the new St. Patrick's Cathedral for forty-two days and netted $172,625 toward the completion of its construction. Each of the city's forty-five parishes were represented by a booth, laden with goods available for raffle, and staffed by women. Such "mixing of religion and consumerism" was common in the nineteenth century. (*Frank Leslie's Illustrated.* Museum of the City of New York. J. Clarence Davies Collection.)

collections while its fair grossed $5,013. Their ladies' fair and a one-day "Festival in Elm Park" earned almost five times as much as a revival mission held by Dominican Fathers ($6,684 versus $1,431).[31] Not surprisingly, when bad weather slowed down attendance at a 1875 fair, Father Richard L. Burtsell would write in his diary that he "spoke plainly at all the Masses complaining of the wretched attendance at the Fair."[32] Successful fairs were crucial for the financial well-being of New York's parishes, and the clergy expected their parishioners to contribute.

The fairs that flourished in New York parishes from 1870 to 1890 provide a degree of insight into Irish Catholicism as experienced by urban immigrants. Fairs occurred frequently in the late nineteenth century because the New York Irish were willing to support an expensive, and expansive, parish system. In 1850 Manhattan had 21 Catholic parishes. Twenty years later the number had doubled, to 42. Between 1870 and 1890, the archdiocese added 30 more parishes, bringing the Manhattan total to 72. This growth was duplicated again between 1890 and 1910, when 31 more parishes were established. By 1920 there were 114 parishes in Manhattan, with only Christ Church having closed in 1837. After the First World War, population changes in New York City radically altered the number of Catholics in Manhattan, and churches experienced a sharp decline in their congregations. Some eventually had to close.[33]

It cost more to create a Catholic parish in New York City than a Protestant one. The churches the Irish attended were decorated with imported art and statuary, ornate altars, fine wooden pews, and grand organs. They included the latest innovations in heating and lighting. Priests required sets of embroidered vestments and sacred vessels. At first, a congregation might hold services in a simple sanctuary, perhaps in the basement, while saving to build a more elaborate sacred environment. Holy Name (founded in 1868) and Our Lady of Lourdes (founded in 1901) illustrate this trend. Both originally had simple altars with limited amounts of statuary. Over the years, each became increasingly laden with French gothic decorations. In 1898 the newly rebuilt Church of St. Agnes had five altars instead of the former three, marble floors instead of wood, a new organ, and 50 stained-glass windows. Frequently, fires destroyed churches, and this provoked renewed building spurts. St. Augustine's church in the Bronx was founded in 1849, renovated in 1881, received new stained glass in 1884, a new vestry in 1885, a new rectory in 1886, a new parish school in 1887–89, a new grand organ in 1890, and then the whole complex burned to the ground in 1894. When new forms of technology arrived, churches did not hesitate to utilize them. In 1899 St. Teresa's church erected a huge electric cross that could be seen "from any point of greater New York."[34] The Irish gave their time, money, and energy to build palaces where the "Real Presence" of God would dwell. The dazzling delights of the church were to lift the soul into the realm of the divine.[35]

The Irish ran fairs not only to build churches but to support other ancillary religious institutions. After the 1860s, bishops had assumed that parishes would maintain a parochial school. Bishop John Hughes (d. 1864) wanted "to build the school-house first and the church afterwards."[36] My calculations based on Catholic directories and parish histories indicate that by 1870 at least 50 percent of Manhattan parishes sponsored either parochial or private schools. By 1880 close to 60 percent of all parishes and 62 percent of all predominantly Irish parishes had schools. If the churches founded before 1900 are counted, 80 percent had parochial schools by the turn of the century. The 1884 Baltimore Council declaration that every parish should have a school and that all Catholic parents should send their children to it had a major impact on New York City parishes. The Irish sent their children to these schools to the extent they could afford it, since a child at school was a child who was not working. School funding would prove to be a continual financial concern to Manhattan parishes.

In addition to school expenses, the parish would need to buy, furnish, and maintain a suitable home for five or six priests and their servants. The sisters would also need a convent. Most of the women who taught New York's Catholic girls were not cloistered nuns, but in 1907 the 30 cloistered sisters who staffed St. Michael's parish school were provided a paved, roof-top recreational area for their private use. The sisters also merited an "electric elevator" in their convent.[37] New York Catholic parishes also supplied housing for the brothers who taught the boys.[38] In addition to schools, some parishes supported their own orphanages. In 1888 St. James's parish orphanage sheltered 200 children; it operated until 1929.[39] Parishes like St. Paul the Apostle and St. Ann organized day nurseries. During 1892, St. Paul's nursery fed more than 14,000 children and the church's *Monthly Calendar* boasted that because of its activities "the mothers of the children have earned $10,000 during the year."[40] St. Paul's also ran an employment service for women.

By the end of the century, parishes would also be expected to contribute to building the diocesan seminary in Yonkers, constructing the Catholic University in Washington, D.C., and supporting a variety of national charities determined by the bishop. In 1890 these charities included the African Mission, Colored Home, and the St. Vincent de Paul Society. Sometimes pastors questioned the continual collecting for national Catholic concerns. Father J. H. McMahon in a letter to Cardinal John M. Farley in 1904 asked for permission *not* to take up a collection for the Catholic University, noting that it was "merely a university" and therefore did not merit special attention.[41]

In 1878 New York Catholic churches had a combined debt of $3.04 million, which was three times the debt of New York Episcopalians, who were the second most indebted group, and six times that of Presbyterians.[42] Although similar statistics are not available for the latter part of the century, when Catholics became even more numerous in New York, the list of parish activities only increased over the years. Paying for fancy churches, schools, social welfare organizations, and diocesan and national charities placed a heavy burden on parishioners. Perhaps the only unarguable statement that can be made about New York Irish Catholicism is that it was expensive.

Parish fairs were only one way—albeit a very lucrative way—of supporting Catholic activities. Catholics were charged for every aspect of their religious life. Parishes charged quarterly pew rents. Those who could not afford pews were charged a seat fee. In 1894 the Paulists, noted for their American outlook, still charged a dime for a seat at the 8:00, 9:00, and 10:30 Sunday masses and a nickel for 6:00 and 7:00 a.m. services. The 5:30 Sunday morning mass, however, was free.[43] In addition to seat rentals, plate collections were taken up during the Offertory of the Mass. In 1889 St. Bridget's church collected $1,824.90 in quarterly pew rent, $6,703.61 in seat rent, and $4,723.70 from the plate.[44] All sodalities and societies charged a monthly membership fee.

Although it was not obligatory, Catholics were strongly encouraged to have funeral masses said for the dead. The family had to pay for such masses because they required the services of priests, altar boys, and sextons, and perhaps even the choir. Part of the payment went to the priest who said the mass with the rest divided among the others. St. Bridget's church required the expenses for funeral masses to be paid in advance, "and the corpse [to] be brought to the Church before 10 A.M. The Mass will commence at that hour even if the funeral [group] is not present. . . . without its observance the Clergy are kept uselessly waiting for an entire afternoon and prevented from attending to other duties." The cost of a solemn high mass with celebrant, deacon, subdeacon, and choir was $40. If only the priest and choir were present, it dropped to $25. A low requiem mass with no singing was only $10.[45] Parishioners were enjoined not to waste their money on wakes and elaborate funeral sculpture but, instead to pay for a solemn high funeral mass and a series of masses said for the deceased person's soul. All parish activities involved money.

From the accounts of the fairs and the descriptions of late nineteenth- and early-twentieth-century parishes, it is clear that the New World Irish expected elaborate churches and were willing to pay for them. The parish was not inflicted on the Irish by bishops and priests looking merely for self-aggrandizement and social status. Parishes fulfilled the social, emotional, and spiritual needs of the Irish. The enthusiasm with which the Irish participated in the fairs suggests that the fantasy environment that they created reflected the lush atmosphere of the churches. Paid choirs, orchestras, processions both inside and outside the church, and the ever-increasing number of statues and stained-glass windows made the church, like the fair, a journey into another world. In 1890, for instance, St. James church paid more for its choir ($1,991) than it did for its orphanage ($1,375).[46] Between 1865 and 1910 Irish Catholic churches in New York City became increasingly baroque in decoration and theatrical in liturgy. The notion that the Irish were satisfied with austere physical surroundings while the French and Germans indulged in religious sensuality is wrong. The New York Irish, like other Catholics, built ornate churches. The average Catholic who did not want to have the elaborate parish with its dazzling church, school, and social services could have resisted paying for it.

Through the fairs, the New York Irish created an environment for unabashed consumer voyeurism. These Catholics did not distinguish between piety, artistic sentiment, domesticity, and enjoyment. Placing a shrine of Our Lady of Lourdes on the same table with tea sets, gold watches, a painting of Mt. Etna, and a sewing machine caused no consternation. Religion was not trivialized by setting statues of the Blessed Virgin next to household goods. In keeping with general Victorian sentiments, the Irish did not see material wealth as a barrier to the Christian spirit.[47] The sacramental character of Catholicism, which asserts that the divine can be present in the physical world, permitted an additional theological justification for the association of material goods and spiritual values. Contrary to the view that Irish Catholicism contains an ascetic streak, the New York fairs reveal a people fascinated with American economic abundance.

Likewise, the image of Irish Catholicism as dreary, pessimistic, guilt-ridden, and not sensual is challenged by the vibrant fantasy and good humor of the fairs. At the fair, entertainment and piety went hand in hand. The fairs provided a means of enjoying, even if only for an evening, the lush materialism of urban existence. Like the department store, fairs displayed the consumer goods of a flourishing industrial society. Parish fairs served as legitimate avenues for socializing, witnessing the wealth of the city, and having fun while doing one's religious duty. In an article entitled "The Theology of the Fair," the pastor of the Church of St. Agnes called Protestant critics who disapprove of fairs "walking vinegar-casks of New England theology." Father Brann relates the tale of an angry Scot who, on seeing a jolly Irishman going to mass asked rhetorically, "Dinna ye know that it is na allowed to whastle on Sunday?" Parish fairs were extremely successful at luring people to spend their money because they created an environment of materialism and fantasy blessed by religious associations.[48]

The fairs of the 1870s and 1880s depended on the willingness of large numbers of Catholics to each contribute a small amount for the general good. The large donations that supported New York's Protestant and cultural establishments, were unavailable even for the cathedral. Parishes took seriously the diverse social standing of New York's Catholics. To encourage support of their fair, St. Paul's bulletin explained that "Vanderbilt might put up our splendid school and hall; but then that Vanderbilt would have all the glory and honor and merit, and thousands of people in our parish would be cast aside and deprived of their share of the glory and honor and merit. Thank God! we have no millionaires to deprive our people of the opportunity of showing that they have in them a virtue which rich men seldom possess—the virtue of generosity that demands self-denial!"[49] Fairs were essential for the growth of the church, so the parishioners, involvement and interests had to be taken seriously. While priests certainly were leaders in their parishes, it was the ability of the Irish to work together on communal projects such as fairs that enabled the parish to prosper. Since items were raffled rather than sold, even the poor had a chance to bring home a wanted prize. "In a word," summarized St. James's fair organizers, "everything is fair."[50]

The fairs suggest that Protestant–Catholic relationships in New York could be amiable and supportive. In 1886 St. James parish reported that among the "vanquished victims" of their donation solicitors were "The American, the Celt, the descendant of Abraham, the sojourner from the Celestial Empire [Chinese], Protestant and Catholic, politician and lawyer, statesman and mechanic."[51] The non-Catholics who owned department stores, the gas and electric companies, art galleries, and jewelry shops willingly donated goods to support Catholic parishes. The Irish could not have been able to put on such elaborate fairs without the help of wealthier non-Catholics. Although the majority of fairgoers most likely were Catholics, the cathedral fair attracted many non-Catholic dignitaries, and most likely part of the half million dollars raised came out of non-Catholic pockets.

Irish Catholics also seemed willing to raffle and use what might be considered Protestant religious goods. Family Bibles and wax crosses found their way onto many fair tables. While the family Bibles probably had approved Catholic translations, wax crosses have no connection to Catholic iconography and were popular Protestant parlor decorations.[52] Catholic New Yorkers apparently had little difficulty accepting certain nonsectarian Christian artifacts. They also adapted Victorian fancywork, such as embroidery with silk floss, to Catholic themes. While the poor and working class could gain spiritual merit from contributing to the fair, the displayed objects reflected a middle-class Victorian taste shared by Protestants and Catholics. Through the fairs, an informal education was offered in what should be consumed and how one should behave in elegant surroundings. The table displays helped the upwardly mobile (or upwardly aspirant) learn what was considered beautiful, tasteful, and pious. Fairs showed New York Catholics what they should desire and demonstrated that those desired goods were not in conflict with religious sentiments or political ideology. Catholics did not need to give up either their religion or their ethnicity to become a part of America's consumer culture.

The Catholic items raffled at the fairs not only schooled the Irish in Victorian consumer culture, they also defined Irish private piety. During this period, only certain religious figures entered Irish devotional life. Statues and pictures of St. Joseph and the Blessed Virgin were quite common, but the saints who would become icons of Catholicism in the twentieth century are entirely absent. Devotion to St. Jude and St. Therese, the Little Flower, did not exist in the nineteenth century.[53] The Sacred Heart of Jesus also appeared both in statuary and art, but again, not with the same strength as it would later. By far the most popular sacred character was Our Lady of Lourdes. Although the appearance of Mary to the French peasant Bernadette had occurred in 1858, her cult was not introduced in the United States until 1870. Rather than promoting Irish saints like Patrick or Bridget, the New York Irish preferred to focus on this contemporary apparition.

Nineteenth-century church fairs, of whatever denominational or ethnic flavor, were run by women. New York parish fairs were no different. Irish women, however, managed successful fairs because fairs utilized their social skills: an understanding of Victorian middle-class culture and confidence in women's economic prowess. Fairs provide another example of how Irish women introduced the "manners and accouterments of the middle class" and "spearheaded the push upward" on the social ladder.[54] Irish women not only understood what was needed to put on a tastefully proper fair, they also knew how to manage money so the fair would reach its financial goals. Women's contributions were not overwhelmed by the philanthropy of a few wealthy men. If it is true that women claimed the economic arena while the men appropriated the political, then the fairs would fall under women's purview. Irish women organized parish fairs not necessarily because they felt they were more pious but because they and the men understood each other's sphere of competency.

Irish women, as well as their parishes, benefited from fair activities. A first glance at New York churches reveals that women fully used the parish for their own social, economic, and spiritual growth. Although the exact number of women and men who attended Sunday mass is not known, a survey of missions by the Paulist fathers in Manhattan parishes indicates that more women attended their revival missions than men. At a typical mission, roughly 60 percent of the communicants were women and 40 percent were men.[55] Irish women prayed in the churches they funded. Because of the larger number of Irish women domestics, some parishes had extremely high numbers of women. In 1888 a Paulist priest commented that Holy Innocents, parish was "decidedly a 'woman's parish: that is, it is situated in a 'hotel and brownstone, district, and, having in it but few tenement houses, the church going population is chiefly composed of domestics."[56] In every parish school, the number of girls in attendance outnumbered the number of boys, the difference ranging from slightly more than 50 percent girls to as high as 60 percent. Boys were put to work while girls could more easily be permitted to stay in school. Women took advantage of church nurseries and employment bureaus. At St. Teresa's church, the notes of the St. Vincent de Paul society indicate that women came to collect shoes and rent money for their families. While women's names were noted in the society's minutes, their husband's names were not.[57] Women helped with fairs not only because it was a womanly thing to do but because the parish helped them survive in a harsh urban environment while furnishing them a place to cultivate their spiritual selves.

For women with middle-class aspirations, organizing parish fairs taught them valuable skills for supporting future political or social causes. Since Irish American women did not have the leisure time available to their more affluent Protestant neighbors, parish fairs could not rely on selling ladies' fancywork. The New York Irish probably would not have spent their hard-earned money on pincushions, dolls, and penwipers in any case. For Catholic parish fairs, women had to find merchants willing to donate bedroom sets, coal, flour, and hunting equipment. Free gas and electricity also had to be found. Women had to know who would donate what and how to exert the right amount of pressure. Design and artistic skills were exercised cleverly to transform a school base-ment hall into a fantasy land conducive to risking 50¢ on a chance to win a statue of Our Lady of Lourdes. Women practiced cajoling men to help with the heavy work while keeping them from taking over the fair itself. Irish women benefited both from parish activities funded by the fair and by the skills they learned in organizing the event.

The parish fairs of New York may be contrasted with the more famous and enduring St. Patrick's Day parade and celebrations.[58] Irish lay men controlled the parades while Irish women ran the fairs. The parades took place in public space where men felt most comfortable. The fairs were held indoors, in space that could be transformed into a semidomestic environment by filling it with food and household goods. Men were marginal actors at the fair; they helped but did not control. Women were the onlookers at the St. Patrick's Day parades. Only in the last part of the twentieth century were they permitted to attend some of the St. Patrick's Day festivities before the parade as members of women's auxiliaries to the male fraternal associations.

Whereas the parade could be seen as a male display on the street, the fairs reinforced the relationship between economic abundance and the social and religious order. Women raised money for their parishes rather than spending it on lavish St. Patrick's Day dinners, parade regalia, and drink. Fairs showed the Irish what decorations to put in their homes, which religious devotions were in vogue, and how to properly socialize with each other. The intermingling of Victorian sensibilities and Catholic piety was distinctly pedagological. In spite of the best intentions of their organizers, St. Patrick's Day parades frequently led to too much drinking, brawls, and disorder. When disturbances got out of hand, some Catholic newspapers urged men to forgo the parade and instead donate money to charity or to Irish causes. But the parades continued because they were not designed to provide an exercise in Victorian sensibilities. St. Pat-rick's Day parades demonstrated the stamina and the pride of Irish men. Drinking, dining, and symbolic expressions of Irish presence were as much a part of the parade as St. Patrick was.

The St. Patrick's Day parade promoted Irish political and ethnic spirit, while the fairs supported the individual Catholic parish. Although New York parishes were predominately Irish, the goal of the fair was to support a religious cause that in turn would help the Catholic community. The ethnic goods displayed emphasized Irish cultural memories and not a nationalism that could rival Catholicism. The goods both reflected Irish history and served to create a distinct American Irish consciousness. The fairs had a decidedly Irish flavor, but unlike the St. Patrick's Day parade, they kept ethnicity under religious control. Nationalism, either American or Irish, took a back seat to the immediate needs of the parish. Although the St. Patrick's Day parade separated the Irish from other Catholics in America, fairs served to inculcate parish (rather than ethnic) loyalty.

It is difficult to say what caused the elaborate parish fair to die out. By the end of the century, Catholic newspapers no longer published articles about month-long parish fairs. Instead, euchre (a card game somewhat like bridge) and short-term bazaars raised money. Churches were still being built and renovated, but fairs no longer served their former purpose.

By the twentieth century New Yorkers had the choice of many different forms of entertainment. Large dance halls were being built, more department stores displayed richer and less expensive goods, Coney Island was in full swing, and amusement parks produced exciting fantasy environments. Ladies' fairs could not compete with commercial amusements that offered acceptable enjoyments to the middle class. Euchre, which demanded more concentration and supplied a more intellectual form of relaxation, appealed to a more selective group of Catholics and thus could not raise as much money as the fairs. Consequently, other avenues of fund-raising needed to be explored. By 1895 the Knights of Columbus had been established in New York City, and these men assumed the role of parish fund-raisers.

Changes in the ethnic makeup of New York also affected fund-raising activities. By the late nineteenth century some parishes that were once all Irish now housed Italians or Syrians in their basements. Italians worshipped in the basement of St. Bridget's church for fifteen years before their own church was built.[59] Assimilation of new Catholic immigrants into Irish parishes was troublesome because of language barriers and differing cultural styles. As a result, large-scale fund-raising by parishes with heterogeneous populations became difficult.

Finally, changes in the ways the Irish understood their Catholicism might have made the fairs anachronistic. Irish Catholicism is not a fixed set of traditions passed from the Old World to the New. As social, cultural, and religious changes occur, the texture of Irish Catholicism also must change. As the Irish became more Americanized, it is possible that religious expression became more individual and private, less communal and public. Perhaps the mixing of religion and consumerism, the acceptance of Protestant religious goods and arts, the delight in the senses, and the demonstration of women's economic competence no longer described the Irish Catholicism of the early twentieth century. Although one might like to think that religion is eternal and unchanging, how religion is experienced and expressed is constantly in flux. The ladies' fair may be emblematic of Irish Catholicism in New York City at a particular time, but other religious organizations or causes might be a more appropriate lens for other places and periods. Those entrées into the world of Irish Catholics also need to be examined in order to arrive at a deeper understanding of Irish American Catholicism.

Kenneth E. Nilsen

CHAPTER 10

The Irish Language in New York,
1850–1900

Óró, mhíle grá, nach fada siar tá céibh New York
is tá mo tharraint ann.
(Oh, my love, New York quay is far to the West and that is
where I'm heading.)

—*traditional rhyme, Connemara*

THE NINETEENTH-CENTURY New York diarist, George Templeton Strong, describes the following scene in his entry for July 7, 1857:

> Yesterday morning I was spectator of a strange, weird, painful scene. Certain houses of John Watts DePeyster are to be erected on the northwest corner of this street and Fourth Avenue, and the deep excavations therefor are in progress. Seeing a crowd on the corner, I stopped and made my way to a front place. The earth had caved in a few minutes before and crushed the breath out of a pair of ill-starred Celtic laborers. They had just been dragged, or dug, out and lay white and stark on the ground where they had been working, ten or twelve feet below the level of the street. Around them were a few men who had got them out, I suppose, and fifteen or twenty Irish women, wives, kinfolk or friends, who had got down there in some inexplicable way. The men were listless and inert enough, but not so the women. I suppose they were "keening"; all together were raising a wild, unearthly cry, half shriek and half song, wailing as a score of daylight Banshees, clapping their hands and gesticulating passionately. Now and then one of them would throw herself down on one of the corpses, or wipe some trace of defilement from the face of the dead man with her apron, slowly and carefully, and then resume her lament. It was an uncanny sound to hear, quite new to me. Beethoven would have interpreted it into music worse than the allegretto of the *Seventh Symphony*. Our Celtic fellow citizens are almost as remote from us in temperament and constitution as the Chinese.[1]

Strong's oft-quoted diary has many references to the Irish, most of them uncomplimentary. The New York of Strong's time was quickly changing to a city where the Irish would be one of the most numerous groups. Though not explicitly stated by Strong, it seems reasonable to assume that the women he mentions were keening in the Irish language, and perhaps this added to Strong's feeling of remoteness.

The Irish were by no means the only foreigners G. T. Strong would have come across in his perambulations in mid-nineteenth-century New York, for at that time the city was teeming with immigrants who spoke a wide variety of languages. German-speaking immigrants, for instance, were especially numerous and had several newspapers in their own language, such as *New Yorker* Staats-Zeitung and *Deutsche Schnellpost,* and also a number of German churches, both Catholic and Protestant. The French, too, had a newspaper, *Le Courrier des États-Unis,* and several French-language churches, including one Protestant church. An Italian newspaper, *Eco d'Italia,* was being published in the city as early as 1851. More significant, however, the Welsh, who numbered only several thousand and who like the Irish came from the United Kingdom, published a Welsh-language newspaper in New York City in the 1850s and had two Welsh-language churches as early as the 1830s.

It is interesting to note that in 1848 the state of New York enacted a law requiring boardinghouses for immigrants to post signs listing their prices in the "English, German, Dutch, French and Welsh language." No mention is made of the Irish language in spite of the fact that Irish immigration was soaring because of the Great Famine. This disparity between the recognition of Welsh and Irish is due to several factors. First, a higher percentage of Welsh immigrants were Welsh-speaking, probably more than 75 percent (even today 18% of the Welsh are native Welsh speakers compared with 1–2% of the entire Irish population who are *native* Irish speakers). Second, Welsh publishing was in a relatively healthy condition in Wales, and a far higher percentage of its speakers could read the language. And third, the Welsh clergy, unlike most of the Irish clergy, did not abandon their native language. In Ireland, the Irish language was proscribed from the legal and educational systems, denied access to the printing press, and virtually abandoned by the Catholic middle and upper classes and the clergy. Daniel O'Connell's lack of support of the Irish language, for instance, is well known. Given these circumstances and the fact that the majority of Irish-speaking immigrants were illiterate, it is hardly surprising that the language received scant acknowledgment in its new home. Indeed, even Irish American historians perpetuated the simplistic view that all Irish immigrants were English speakers. In fact, Irish immigrants fell into three linguistic categories: monolingual English speakers, bilingual Irish/English speakers, and monolingual Irish speakers.

In recent years investigators have begun to deal with the long-neglected question of Irish-speaking immigrants in this country. One of the difficulties in handling this topic is the question of what percentage of incoming Irish were Irish speakers. Some scholars believe that the percentage of Irish-speaking immigrants rose as a result of the Famine. They point to the rise in emigration from counties with considerable Irish-speaking districts. Others maintain that approximately 28 percent of the Irish arriving in the United States in the 1850s were Irish speakers.[2] This percentage suggests that of the 259,000 Irish-born immigrants living in New York City and Brooklyn in 1860, approximately 73,000 were Irish speakers. Estimates based on material from the *Irish World* (1898–99) indicate that there were 400,000 Irish speakers in this country in the 1890s, with 70,000 in New York, 40,000 in Philadelphia, 30,000 each in Boston and Chicago, and 2,000 in Yonkers.[3]

Although the influx of Irish speakers may have been particularly high in the period after the Famine, a number of factors suggest that Irish speakers represented a substantial portion of Irish immigrants in prefamine times. First, the percentage of Irish speakers in Ireland increases the further one goes back in time. In 1800 about half of the Irish were Irish-speaking. In fact, the number of Irish speakers in the decades before the Famine was greater than has previously been recognized.[4]

It can also be shown that Irish speakers were in the United States—in Virginia, New England, and Pennsylvania—long before the famine years.[5] A number of the United Irishmen who came to the United States after the 1798 rebellion were Irish speakers. Perhaps the most prominent of these was Dr. William James MacNeven, who was born in Ballynahowna, County Galway, in 1764. MacNeven, along with other United Irishmen, was taken prisoner on March 12, 1798, and lodged in Kilmainham. "Later he was sent to Scotland, where in prison he translated many of the Ossianic tales, being a fluent speaker of Irish."[6] MacNeven arrived in New York City in 1805 and became one of the city's most respected physicians. He was also involved in several organizations that aided newly arrived immigrants. He is credited with the idea of erecting a monument to Thomas Addis Emmet in St. Paul's churchyard. The Irish inscription on the Emmet monument, which was erected in 1830, was the first public use of the Irish language in New York.[7] A monument to MacNeven, also in the churchyard of St. Paul's, which was raised in 1867, bears inscriptions in Irish, English, and Latin and was fashioned by the Irish-speaking Draddy brothers.[8]

For many who came, Irish was their only language. The parents of Reverend Edward McGlynn (b. 1837), for example, arrived in New York from Donegal in 1824 "gan d'urlabhra acu ach Gaeilge" (without any language but Irish).[9]

Probably the most notable Irish monoglot speaker to arrive in this country in the prefamine years was Pádraig Phiarais Cúndún (Patrick Condon), who settled with his family in 1826 in Deerfield, New York, just outside of Utica. His letters and poems, written in upstate New York to his neighbors in Ballymacoda, County Cork, represent the most important body of prefamine writing in Irish from the United States.[10] In his letters Condon mentions many of his Cork neighbors, all presumably Irish speakers, who came out to America. He ends most of his letters with the words: "Scríobh chugam go luath insan teangain Ghaeilge" (write to me soon in the Irish language).

Other Cork Irish speakers made their way to New York City in the prefamine decades. One such immigrant was Thomas Crimmins, who related to O'Donovan Rossa that he had crossed the Atlantic in 1835 on a sailing ship with 86 gold sovereigns in his pocket. His purpose in coming to America was to make inquiries about property that had belonged to David Reidy, a distant relative and 1798 exile, who died in New York City a few years after the War of 1812. O'Donovan Rossa met Crimmins in New York in the 1890s and received from him much valuable information concerning the 1798 exiles in New York. Rossa, a native speaker of Irish, states: "I went to Thomas Crimmins' house for the special purpose of taking from him, an elegy in the Irish language, that he had by heart, on the death of an uncle of his, Daniel Barry."[11]

Another Cork Irish speaker who arrived in New York before the Famine was Daniel Draddy from a family of stonecutters and scribes. Daniel was apparently the son or nephew of John Draddy (Seán Ó Dreada), a prolific Cork scribe who often listed his profession as "snoigheadóir cloiche" (stone carver). In fact, one of the few early-nineteenth-century Irish language tomb inscriptions in County Cork is an epitaph carved by Seán Ó Dreada in 1831 on the stone of the Cork antiquarian, Denis O'Flyn, in Dunbulloge churchyard.[12] Daniel, presumably John's son, is listed as a stonecutter in the New York City directories as early as 1843.[13] Daniel is also mentioned by Jeremiah O'Donovan, the grandiloquent Corkonian and Irish speaker, in his book *A Brief Account of the Author's Interview with His Countrymen*, which seems to include a reference to every Irishman living in this country at the time: "Mr. Daniel Draddy; this gentleman is from the City of Cork, and keeps an extensive marble establishment in 23rd Street near the East River. . . . Mr. Draddy . . . is a mechanic of the highest grade, has a well-cultivated mind, he is a great historian, and writes the Irish language druidically, in a word, he is an honer [sic] to his country."[14] Nearly 20 years later, the Irish-speaking Cork priest Reverend Michael B. Buckley mentions having met the Draddy family on his trip to New York in 1870–71: "Miss Flynn, is also here, so are a whole family of Draddys, of Quaker Road, out here for the last thirty years—a mother and three sons. At home they were stonecutters; here they are "sculptors"—a most respectable family indeed. We had a very pleasant evening; some capital singing, and agreeable dancing. The old lady Mrs. Draddy danced as gaily as if she were only fifteen.[15]

These descriptions provide just a glimpse into the lives of a mere handful of Irish speakers in the United States in the period before the Famine. For the majority of Irish-speaking immigrants there is no information. Since most of them, unlike the Draddys and Patrick Condon, were illiterate in Irish, they left behind no record of their language. The use of Irish and its prestige declined rapidly in Ireland during the first half of the nineteenth century, a trend that was accelerated when the Famine struck. Hardest hit were the poor regions of Ireland, which were also the areas with the highest concentrations of Irish speakers. From 1847 to 1853 more than a million Irish immigrants entered the United States. The arrival of these Famine Irish speakers "gave Irish-America at mid-century a decidedly Gaelic cast": during the late 1840s port officials occasionally remarked on the inability of entire shiploads of emigrants to speak English, while shipping agents touted some shipmasters' fluency in Irish as 'a great advantage to Passengers.'"[16] As the ships arrived at the pier, they were boarded by "runners" many of whom were disreputable and would try to swindle the immigrants of their savings. In an address to emigrants, delivered on March 27, 1847, Gregory Dillon of the Irish Emigrant Society of New York warned prospective travelers of the dangers that faced them when their ships came into port:

> Upon the coming of the ship into the harbour of New York, she will be boarded by an agent of this society, by whose directions it will be advantageous for you to be guided. She will also be boarded by a large number of persons known as "runners," many of whom are Irishmen speaking the Irish language who . . . apply to emigrants to take board and lodging at the different board-houses for which they may be employed. . . . They will agree to furnish you . . . board at a trifling price, and after having got you and your baggage at their houses will . . . demand 2, 3 and 4 times what they agreed. . . . and will refuse to permit your baggage . . . to leave their premises until their extortionate charge be paid, and will perhaps maltreat you besides.[17]

The state of New York realized the need for laws to help protect the arriving immigrants. In 1848, a year in which 151,003 Irish entered the United States, the legislature passed "an act for the protection of Immigrants arriving in the State of New York."[18] As mentioned above, the act makes several references to the need for signs in certain native languages of the newcomers. Section three, for instance, states:

> All persons keeping houses in any of the cities of this state for the purpose of boarding immigrant passengers shall be required to have a license for said purpose from the mayor of the city. . . . Every keeper of such boarding house shall under a penalty of fifty dollars cause to be kept conspicuously posted in the public rooms of such house in the English, German, Dutch, French and Welsh language a list of the rates of prices which will be charged immigrants per day and week for boarding and lodging and also the rates for separate meals.[19]

Despite the fact that Irish immigration was reaching peak levels, the law made no reference to the Irish language. But this does not mean that Irish speakers were not arriving in large numbers.

There were those who were fully cognizant of the incoming waves of Irish speakers. Charlotte Grace O'Brien, who worked with Irish emigrants on both sides of the Atlantic, spoke of the particularly difficult plight of the monolingual Irish-speaking immigrants in her lines:

Speechless! ay, speechless, for their Gaelic tongue
Is dead; as wanderers from some far-off age
They strike against the shore so human life, to wage
A too unequal fight with toil and wrong.[20]

There is some evidence to suggest that the Democratic Party in New York kept its grip on the Irish vote by using Irish-speaking ward captains.[21] Irish-born David Nagle of New York, for instance, "urged his party's leaders to approach Irish voters only through 'men who understand the Irish language and speak it fluently, as it is the language best understood and most applicable to touch the feelings of the Irish heart.'"[22] Further evidence suggests that the number of Irish speakers was so high in New York at this time that the clergy made some effort to use Irish with their flocks. Even in 1846 Father Joseph Burke from Donegal, pastor of St. Columba's Church on West 25 Street, reportedly addressed his flock in the Irish language, and documents of the American Protestant Society dating from the late 1840s claim that five-eighths of the Irish in New York were Irish-speaking at this time.[23] This group actively used the Irish language in New York, Pennsylvania, and Ohio in its effort to convert Irish-speaking Catholics to Protestantism. This method of proselytism had been in use for decades in Ireland and also in New Brunswick, Canada, in the 1830s.[24]

Even more compelling are the records of the American and Foreign Christian Union, established in New York in 1849, which expanded on the work of the American Protestant Society. The publications of this organization contain reports of the Irish-speaking colporteurs, themselves converts from Catholicism, who attempted to convert their compatriots by bringing the Gospel to them in their own language. Patrick J. Leo, for one, preached widely in Irish to his countrymen in various Protestant churches in New York and New Jersey. Leo states in one of his reports: "I lecture in the several Evangelical Churches, and invite my countrymen . . . Sometimes I lecture to them in Irish so that they may more clearly understand me. . . . It is an inducement for them to come, to hear their own language."[25] The American and Foreign Christian Union and allied groups such as the American Bible Society provided ready employment for newly arrived Irish-speaking converts like the Maynooth-educated Mayoman George McNamara, who forsook the priesthood in Ireland in the late 1840s and who, within weeks of his arrival in New York City in 1852, applied for and was granted a position as colporteur. The one surviving set of original handwritten reports by a colporteur, named Michael McNulty, shows on every page the writer's dedication to his language and religion as he trod the streets of Lower Manhattan attempting to convert his compatriots. The final page of the 12 manuscript pages even includes three quatrains of a religious hymn in Irish written in the Irish script.[26] There is little reason to believe that these proselytizers were successful in their conversion efforts, but their reports provide some of the strongest evidence for the widespread use of Irish among Irish immigrants in New York City in the mid–nineteenth century.

At this time, according to the *Irish-American* (June 27, 1857), "the Irish-speaking population of New York, it is well known, may be numbered by thousands." Not long after the *Irish World* (Sept. 28, 1872, 4) reported that one of the New York City wards made an unsuccessful attempt to introduce Irish into the school curriculum.[27] Indeed, Irish was spoken in many New York households, and naturally enough it was the first language learned by children in these families. Such was the case of MAC GARAVA, the writer of a letter from "Jamesville, Pa." to the *Irish World* (Mar. 15, 1873) in response to an earlier letter by SIGMA, stating that he had never met an Irish-American who could speak Irish:

> As an Irish-American, born in this country, I feel called upon to refute the assertion. "Sigma" may have meant well enough, but his mistake must not pass by uncorrected. Mr. Editor, I was born in Brooklyn, L.I., where I spent some years. I am the second of a family of six children—the oldest a girl of twenty-six, the youngest a boy of six—*all of whom can, and do, speak Irish in public and private,* and are not ashamed of it. . . . The statement that Irish-Americans feel it a disgrace to speak the Celtic language is something new to us, though we are Americans by birth. Not only are we willing to talk the mother tongue, but we are also willing to fight for Erin's freedom, that she may teach and talk it at will. Perhaps I might be laughed at for saying that I know a child, born in America, and nearly eight years old, that can speak nothing but Irish!

Another native New Yorker who also apparently learned Irish in his infancy was P. J. Kenedy, the Catholic bookseller and publisher, born in Manhattan in 1843. In an interesting editorial in the *United Irishman* (Oct. 31, 1885) entitled "Priseach-Bhuidhe Patriotism," O'Donovan Rossa incidentally mentions Kenedy and his knowledge of Irish:

> The men of the Ancient Order of Hibernians had a picnic in Jones' Woods the 15th of August last. I went up to see the gathering of the Hibernians, and met in the woods P. J. Kenedy, the bookseller, of No. 5 Barclay street. He and I talked, and walked about the Woods all day, and after nightfall came, came home together. Mr. Kenedy speaks the Irish language, and now and again we talked Irish. On our way toward the Brooklyn Bridge we passed Mott street and Baxter street and the Five Points. Passing them by at Chatham square Mr. Kenedy said, as he pointed up Mott street, "I could kiss every stone in that street." The expression staggered me somewhat, as the locality is principally inhabited by poor people—American, Israelites, Irish, Chinese and Italians—and I looked inquiringly at Mr. Kenedy, as much as to say, "What do you mean?" After a while I did ask him what did he mean by the expression, and he told me it was there in Mott street he was born, and there he grew up a boy, and lived till manhood; there his dreams took him at night and brought him to the fireside of his father and mother and to the associations of youth and early home. I feel some way that that expression of Mr. Kennedy's [*sic*] has expanded my mind—that expression of his that he could kiss every stone around Mott street, Baxter street and the Five Points.

An article on Michael J. O'Lenihan in the *Gael* (Oct. 1900, 283) also mentions Irish being spoken by native New Yorkers. At the age of five, O'Lenihan came to New York with his parents from their native Mallow, County Cork. The family apparently continued to speak Irish in New York: "So thoroughly Irish was the atmosphere in which he was reared, that he recalls with pride his youthful companions, many of them born in New York City, who generally settled all their boyish arguments in the Gaelic."[28]

The great majority of immigrant Irish speakers would have belonged to the working classes. Although they were mostly illiterate in Irish, among them there would have been one or two who could read Irish and some who even had Irish manuscripts. To this latter category belonged a remarkable group of Irishmen who arrived along with the famine immigrants. These were the Young Irelanders. After their failed attempt at revolt in 1848, many of the prominent figures of this group found their way to America. A number of them, such as John O'Mahony, Michael Doheny, Michael Cavanagh, and John T. Rowland of Drogheda, were native Irish speakers and, indeed, excellent Irish scholars. Many of them continued to be involved in political organizations dedicated to attaining Irish freedom, but in spite of all their political involvements they still had time to cultivate their native language in New York City.

One of the most important sources of information on the Irish in New York in the last century, and one that has been largely overlooked by those who have written on this subject, is the weekly New York paper the *Irish-American*, which started publication in 1849. Like so many Irish and Irish American weeklies of that era, its Irish language content was at first limited to the occasional word or phrase in a song or a poem, spelled in that peculiar orthography that is neither proper English nor Irish. One occasional contributor to the "Poet's Corner" was WBR, a resident of New York, whose poems were patriotic in tone. One of his compositions in praise of the Irish language is entitled "Stanzas for Kossuth" (Louis Kossuth, the Hungarian patriot) and concludes with the words: "Sios lesh a Ghoul a nis, suas lesh a Ghael go doe" (Down with the foreigner now and up with the Gael forever, *Irish-American*, Jan. 31, 1852).

In a similar vein, a piece was contributed on May 10, 1851, with the title of the popular Irish song "Is go de sin din te sin na bannan sin do?" (What is that to him whom it does not concern). This patriotic poem, contributed by "Eiranach" (an early pen name of Michael Doheny), is completely in English except for the last line of each stanza, which is identical to the title.[29]

The first full piece of Irish to appear in the paper is a three-stanza ditty placed inconspicuously between two English poems in the "Poet's Corner" on June 21, 1851. It is addressed "To the Editor of the Irish-American," is written in a fairly standard orthography—printed, of course, in roman characters—and, perhaps not surprisingly, is full of typographical errors, which makes it difficult to decipher in places. But since this tribute to a pub on Duane Street is probably the first Irish poem composed in the United States to be published, it seems appropriate to print it here in a partly corrected text:

TO THE EDITOR OF THE IRISH-AMERICAN June 7th, 1851

Gach Oigfhear calma lan mheanamnach fioraonda
'Na mein leis sealad a chathamh le pleisiur;
Go Duane street tagach go tapa 'sa steach don Daisy,
Mar a bhfuil ceol da spreaga mar chantain na bhfioreanla.

Ata an sud gan bhladareacht measareacht fioraondachd,
Ata aun brandy go farsin agus fion da thaosga;
Gin gan easba mar mheasaim agus beoir le heiliomh,
Aig an Leomhan mear calma, do mhathaimh agus do chru na Gaoidhilimh.

A se Seamus an farare geanamnach lan eagneach,
D'fhior fhuil chathaseach chlar banaba ba mhor eiliomh;
O'Daoir nar mheata a n-am catha chum namhaid do fhleasga,
Le hard ghniomh aigionta da dtreasgairt da mbrugh 'sda leirsgrios.

(Let every stout, spirited, well-met young fellow
who wants to spend some time in pleasure
come quickly to Duane Street and into the Daisy
where music is playing like the song of the birds.

There he'll find moderation and decency without boasting
Brandy in plenty and wine being poured
No lack of gin, I believe, and beer for the asking
from that brave Lion of the noble lineage of the Gaels.

James is the cheerful, mindful guardian
of the true blood of the Plain of Banba of great fame
O'Dwyer never cowardly at the break of battle in blasting the enemy
with a high noble deed, defeating them, crushing them and destroying them.)

The Séamas Ó Daoir mentioned in the poem would seem to have been James O'Dwyer who, according to *Wilson's Business Directory of New-York City* for 1851 and 1852, was the proprietor of a "porter house" at 21 Duane Street. The poem provides a window into the Irish-speaking side of New York City of 1851, which is known to have existed but disappeared leaving few traces.

This stray piece of Irish is the sole example in the early years of the paper. In 1854 a series of translations from the Irish began to appear that were the work of Michael Doheny, a Tipperary native who had left Ireland after the failed revolt of 1848. In his book *The Felon's Track*, published in New York in 1849, he mentions his own knowledge of Irish several times as he describes how he and his companion, James Stephens, eluded the authorities. Doheny's early translations include "A phlur na m-ban doun og," "Slan le Maig," and "Si gra mo croidhe, Eibhlin na g-cine ban."

A close friend of Doheny was John O'Mahony. O'Mahony, too, had been a member of the Young Ireland movement, which, like similar movements throughout Europe at the time, espoused freedom and equality for oppressed nations along with an increased cultural awareness through the cultivation of minority languages. O'Mahony, a native Irish speaker like Doheny, was one of several Young Irelanders who recognized the need to maintain the Irish language as part of Irish nationality. After the failed Irish uprising in 1848, he fled to Paris where he spent several years before coming to New York in 1853. One of the finest Irish language scholars of the time, he spent his first few years in Brooklyn working on his translation into English of Geoffrey Keating's *Foras Feasa ar Éirinn* (History of Ireland).[30] An excerpt of the translation appeared in the *Irish-American* on October 11, 1856. The completed work was published in New York in 1857 by P. M. Haverty with an introduction by Michael Doheny.[31] A letter by William Smith O'Brien pointing out the desirability of printing the original Irish alongside the translation sparked the following reaction from the *Irish-American*:[32]

> Mr. O'Mahony, we are quite sure, would have met Mr. O'Brien's patriotic desire had he had an opportunity of procuring Irish type. It is a strange fact that it is only in the city of London *Irish types* are cast. In Dublin, we have been informed, casting and selling Irish types is not pursued as a trade. Rather than procure such a font from London (the stronghold of the Irish enemy),[33] we have given an order for a font of *Irish type* in the original character, to be cast in the city of New York. Major James Conner (whose name has a fine Irish sound and who feels proud of his Irish descent) will shortly produce from his celebrated foundry a complete and beautiful "font of type" in the original Irish character, for the *Irish-American*. Mr. Haverty, the enterprising publisher of Irish works, 110 Fulton street, has made every effort to obtain, both in Dublin and here, Irish types wherewith to print in the Irish character the words required for his purpose in his projected publication of Irish music.
>
> To Mr. Haverty we are indebted for the facilities which have enabled us to accomplish in America that which even Ireland fails to furnish—namely, the resuscitation in print of the Irish language.
>
> Shortly, we trust, our readers will have an opportunity to peruse in the original Irish character the entire of Archbishop MacHale's beautiful series of Moore's Melodies rendered into Irish. We expect to be able to follow these by the publication of other Irish works of equal merit in the same type. We will have to leave to our readers whether this enterprise be not worthy of commendation.

In the July 18, 1857, issue the paper's editorial includes a note, "Our Irish Type," which says the type has arrived and that the paper will begin publishing Irish poetry and prose with translations the following week. An example of the type is included in an advertisement for O'Mahony's translation. This was the first set of Irish type ever produced in the New World.[34]

The following week, on July 25, 1857, the paper introduced its Irish-language column, "Our Gaelic Department." This was to be a regular feature of the paper, albeit with significant lapses, until it ceased publication in 1915, by which time it had printed nearly 1,500 Gaelic columns.

The first anonymous Irish-language editor was apparently Michael Doheny, who received generous assistance from John O'Mahony.[35] The material consisted largely of traditional poetry and songs, much of which had not been previously published. Very little was published that might be called "current events." There was no such tradition in Irish, and when the *Irish-American* initiated its Gaelic Department, it was the only weekly publication in the world with such a feature. Doheny and O'Mahony both had Irish manuscripts, and a fair number of manuscripts were owned by other Irish immigrants.[36] One example is the manuscript of Pádraig Phiarais Cúndún, which was loaned to the *Irish-American*. In a note to Cúndún's *Om chroidhe mo sgread* published on January 9, 1858, the editor says:

> A MS. volume, containing many of the compositions of this bard of our own times, has been placed at our disposal by his son, Mr. Pierce Condon, of South Brooklyn—Several of them are of considerable merit. . . . The most recent composition of our bard that we have seen was written upon the miseries of his country in 1849. . . . In it we find that after an exile of nearly thirty years his heart burned with as ardent a love of his native soil and ancient faith and with as thorough a hatred of its foreign tyrants as did any of his predecessors of the days of Clarach, O'Toomy and their contemporaries. The race of Irish bards we deemed extinct, but the fact that the subject of this note sang of his Fatherland, in his native tongue, to the American wilds up to the last year, causes us to hope that the Gaelic Muse will flourish again, and that even now she may have worshippers in many an obscure retreat, whose poems may not prove unworthy of the olden Fileadha.

Most of the early columns were accompanied by extensive introductory notes and footnotes in minute print. For instance, in discussing Micheal Mac Pheadair Ui Longáin's poem on the Rosary, *Is tuirseach fá dhaor-smacht péine a bh-fad sínn* (*Irish-American* Dec. 11, 1858), the Gaelic editor points out that "the above song was composed to the air to which a metrical version of the paidrín páirteach was wont to be chanted."

Occasionally, appeals were made to the public to supply material. One such call, printed on October 2, 1858, listed the names of a number of Irish poems and then requested: "Persons who may have these or any other of our good old popular songs by heart, but who cannot write Irish themselves, may have them transcribed, and eventually translated and published, by calling at our office." Other material was taken from published works such as Charlotte Brooke's *Reliques*, Hardiman's *Irish Minstrelsy*, O'Daly's *Poets and Poetry of Munster*, the *Transactions of the Ossianic Society*, and, of course, Archbishop MacHale's Gaelic translations of Moore's "Melodies." The Gaelic editors also had access to some lesser-known works, such as the one mentioned in a note after "Seilg Ghleanna An Smóil" (*Irish-American*, Nov. 16, 1861):

> In an unfinished work, entitled, *The Introduction to an Universal Irish Grammar, &c*, printed (although without place or date) at Carrick on Suir, by one Stacy about the year 1800, and now excessively rare, an imperfect copy of this poem is given in the Roman character; and it also contains a portion of another poem, written dialogue wise, by William Meagher, of Nine mile House, county Tipperary, an excellent Irish Scholar, on a sow that destroyed his collection of Irish MSS.

The public greeted the Gaelic department enthusiastically. One reader who signs himself "Street Peddler" says, after expressing his joy at seeing the Irish column, that he hopes it will encourage Irishmen in America to cultivate their language. He mentions a problem all immigrants faced, namely, acculturation, and he advises them not to give up their native culture:

> Some say that attachment to native language and native land is dangerous to good citizenship, just as if strangers can expect love or respect from those who cannot afford the same to their near kindred, but rather on the contrary hate and vilify their own flesh and blood. Let not the people be shamed out of their anxiety for this acquirement by any such silly and ignorant objections equally applicable to other tongues, but let such tend rather to increase the obligation of its study. I hope, therefore, that my countrymen will yield to no such nonsense, but at once unite in one solid phalanx to encourage this noble and patriotic struggle, so that if ever we will have a nation we shall also have a prospect of our native tongue.

The poetry in the Irish language column stirred the *Daily News* to call for the establishment of Irish classes:

> In such a city as New York, where half the population is Irish or of Irish descent, there should be facilities for instruction in a language which boasts such noble gems of poetry as the Erse. For this reason, as well as others, we call upon our authorities to establish, upon a broad basis the recommendation of our energetic and far-sighted Mayor in reference to a University, in which we might find chairs, perhaps, for the heroic Irish, with her songs and epic rhapsodies, as well as one of the Anglo-Saxon, with its meagre and stunted shoots, which have, however, at last expanded into the magnificent strains of Shakespeare and Milton.[37]

On October 17, 1857, the paper published what is certainly the first Gaelic letter to the editor to be printed in America. The high quality of the paper's Gaelic columns reflects the erudition of its anonymous Gaelic editors. In a letter to the paper, John O'Daly of Dublin, the noted Irish-language editor and publisher, wrote that one "of the ablest Celtic scholars living" was John O'Mahony of New York. The editors of the *Irish-American* were well aware of the leadership their paper was showing in respect to the Irish language. On April 17, 1858, it announced on page 1 that "The Celtic Tongue" would be a regular feature of the Dublin *Nation* as of March 20: "It is a source of no little gratification to us to find that our example has already begun to produce good effects, and that we may now calculate with certainty on a combined, vigorous effort, on both sides of the Atlantic, to rescue from oblivion the venerable tongue of our beloved Fatherland."

The Gaelic column continued each week through 1861, but in 1862 only 32 issues had a Gaelic column, and in 1863 there were only 23, most of which were Irish lessons. There were a number of reasons for the decline. One was undoubtedly the onset of the Civil War in 1861. O'Mahony and others enlisted in the Union army. In April 1862 Michael Doheny died, and the *Irish-American*'s editorial notice of his death made no mention of his contributions to the paper. The Gaelic column by this time had been given over largely to "Easy Lessons In Irish," and the column seems to have come to a temporary end by the close of 1863.

Another reason for the decline of the column was the fact that in 1859 O'Mahony, along with Michael Doheny, Michael Cavanagh, and several other members of the New York Branch of the Ossianic Society, started their own paper, the *Phoenix*. One important member of the New York Ossianic Society and *Phoenix* contributor was David O'Keeffe who, in the years 1858–61, was transcribing a copy of *Cúirt a' Mheadhon Oidhche* (*The Midnight Court*) and other Munster poetry that is now Ferriter Manuscript 33 in the collection of University College, Dublin. Both O'Keeffe and Thomas Norris, another member of the Ossianic Society, were to become important figures in the Irish-language revival movement in the late 1870s and 1890s.

Although the *Phoenix* included fragments of Irish, especially about the origins of Irish surnames and place names, from the beginning (June 4, 1859), it never seems to have had an all-Gaelic column. Irish language and literature were a concern of the editors, however, and in the case of O'Mahony the ancient *Fianna* of literature clearly served as a model for the nascent Fenian organization. In the first issue, O'Mahony discoursed on the *Fianna*: "The principal duties of the Fenian Order in Ireland, called *Fiann na h-Eirenn* in our vernacular, were, to defend the country." Later issues of the paper carried reports of the meetings of the New York Ossianic Society and also first-page advertisements by that society announcing the sale of copies of John O'Daly's *Munster Poets* and *Self-Instruction in Irish* (*Phoenix*, Apr. 14, 1860). The same issue also has an interesting article on faction fights entitled "The O'Lucies and the Shillelagh," which ends with a stanza in Irish and is signed "Daithbhidh O'Caeimh."

The *Phoenix* for January 26, 1861, announced the formation of an Irish class in New York, possibly the first such venture in North America. A letter by David O'Keeffe printed in the *Irish-American* (Nov. 26, 1878) many years later gives some important details about this society and summarizes the reasons for its demise:

> In 1859 appeared the *Phoenix*, and had a very able staff of writers. Col. Michael Doheny, James Roche, and Patrick O'Dea,—Mr. O'Mahony taking charge of the Irish column. I then wrote several articles for this paper, mostly about Irish · matters. Mr. O'Mahony called on me that we might establish a branch of the "Ossianic Society" in New York. We did so. We called a meeting and we were very successful. There flocked around us men of talent and learning. . . . Nearly all of the members of that splendid Society are now no more. . . . The New York branch held its meetings in No. 6 Centre street. At a meeting could be seen T. F. Meagher, Dr. Nicholas Drew, Dr. O'Hanlon, Dr. Shanahan, Col. Michael Doheny, James Roche, John O'Mahony, Captain Norris, Col. Michael Corcoran, of the 69th; Frederick Duggan, John Egan, Michael Coughlan, John D. Sullivan, and many more that I need not mention. In the year 1860 we were very

prosperous, fully recognized by the parent society, which sent us several cases of books. . . . I fear it will never be my lot to mingle with so many fine spirits,—men of vast learning and research, yet mild as children. There was the eloquent Thomas F. Meagher, the witty O'Dea, who in answer to me when I said that the Irish was a splendid language for prayer, caused a hearty laugh, when he dryly said, "Do they understand Irish *up-stairs*?"—the high-minded Dr. Shanahan and the genial Dr. O'Hanlon, with a sweet smile on his face, and sometimes shy as a young girl, when O'Dea used to repeat some strong passage of *Cúirt a Mheodhanoidhche.* In the Fall of 1860, Abraham Lincoln was elected, the South seceded; Mr. O'Mahony went to Ireland. His last words were to Mr. Michael Cavanagh, "If any thing should happen to me, give my Irish books to Mr. O'Keeffe." Nearly all our members went to the war, and many never came back. As a matter of course, our society got broken up. . . . What position I then occupied in our society can be easily seen by referring to the *Phoenix* of 1860. I am now the only active member of the "Ossianic Society" connected with the Irish language.

Irish-language activity in general seems to have been abandoned in New York during the rest of the Civil War and the period of Fenian activity that followed. It should be noted, however, that many of the Irish who fought in the war, especially in the Sixty-ninth and Eighty-eighth regiments, were Irish speakers. Indeed, the flag of the Irish Brigade carried the Gaelic words of Oisín "Riamh nár dhruid ó sbairn lann" (who never retreated from the clash of spears).[38] Referring to soldiers of his Eighty-eighth Regiment, Captain W. L. D. O'Grady wrote, "A few spoke nothing but Gaelic when they enlisted from the very gates of Castle Garden."[39] In the postwar years, one event with an Irish-language connection worth noting was the erection of the monument in June 1867 to Dr. William James MacNeven, referred to earlier.

In January 1869 the *Irish-American* Gaelic column reappeared. Perhaps this was prompted at least in part by the fact that John O'Mahony's rival *Irish People* was about to start its own Gaelic column. O'Mahony's commitment to the language was unwavering, and according to Devoy, "he looked forward to the restoration of Gaelic as one of the certain results of the achievement of national independence."[40] O'Mahony announced his intention to begin a Gaelic column in the issue of February 2, 1869:

Our Gaelic-speaking readers, and, indeed, all who truly love our fatherland and revere the traditions of our old race, will rejoice to learn that we shall inaugurate the commencement of our seventh volume by opening a CELTIC DEPARTMENT in this paper. It will consist, in the first place, of careful selections, in the original Gaelic, from the works of the best and most popular native bards, with rhythmical translations and explanatory annotations in English; and, in the next place, of prose translations of ancient historical traits and romances, which shall be carefully annotated also. For this, we have ordered a special font of type, in order to avoid the inconvenience and unsightliness resulting from the employment of the ordinary characters in printing our native language. Our facilities for making this department both instructive and entertaining can scarcely be equalled by any Irish journal now published on the American continent; and we feel confident in succeeding in our attempt, provided we receive any reasonable support from our compatriots. The Gaelic Department will be opened in our next issue (for the week ending Feb. 13, 1869).

The type the *Irish People* employed was a somewhat strange style of printing Irish in which the acute accent was replaced by a macron and the dot of aspiration by an apostrophe.[41] The content was much the same as that of the Gaelic columns of the *Irish-American:* mainly traditional poetry with notes by Melgola (a pen name of O'Mahony) and translations into English by M. Doheny, M. J. Heffernan of Brooklyn, Michael Cavanagh (under the pen name *Cloch an Chúinne*), and others. Fittingly, the first piece selected by O'Mahony for the "Celtic Department" was a sixteenth-century war ode by Angus O'Daly, chief bard of the renowned Feagh McHugh O'Byrne, inciting the Gaels to battle (*Irish People*, Mar. 3, 1869). The printing of an Irish-language letter (*Irish People*, July 27, 1869) from Splancach Ua Braonāin of Sligo inspired a lively response from readers, to judge from the "Answers to Correspondents" column. One correspondent, Brian Rābach Ua Cuiridh, was told:

> We are glad to learn that the Irish letter of your friend, *Splancach Ua Braonain*, gave you so pleasant a surprise. He knows his native tongue well. . . . The only liberty we took with his original text, was to restore the classic orthography of his words wherever he had deviated therefrom. . . . With respect to communicating with and from Ireland in Gaelic on important revolutionary matters, we do not advise it. For the British enemy have renegade spies in pay who know Gaelic as well as any of us. But we would gladly encourage our countrymen in this country and at home to avail themselves of our columns in publishing such spirited and *discreet* communications in our vernacular, as those of *Ua Braonain*. . . .We have made a move which we hope to see followed ere long by every Irish national journal in America. Indeed, some of them already find their market in imitating the example we have set them, and rejoice at it.

An answer to John Jones of Keokuk, Iowa (*Irish People*, Aug. 17, 1869), stated that the paper did not "at present know of any place where you could find *profitable* employment as a teacher of Gaelic or Irish. The taste for that kind of study is but just awakening among our fellow-countrymen at this side of the Atlantic . . . We would feel gratified by your sending us . . . a list of the contents of your Gaelic 'Manuscripts.' We have a knowledge of nearly all the works that have been printed. Want of space alone prevents our giving insertion to your excellent translation." In the same issue *Scail-leastrach Ua Cuilcin* was told:

> We are forced to postpone the insertion of your Gaelic communication to next week. The appearance of your friend, *Splancach*, has caused a great excitement among our Gaelic-speaking readers. If it continues we will have to devote part of our space each week to contributions in our native tongue. The time may come when it may be advisable to publish a paper exclusively in that language. The fact of not knowing the received spelling of words should not deter any one from Gaelic composition. Phonetic spelling is equally intelligible to us when the language itself is pure, and the meaning clearly and well put. We cannot

become all at once adepts in spelling Gaelic, however well we speak it orally. Any lapses of our correspondents in orthography shall be set right before sending their copy to the printer.

The following week (Aug. 24, 1869), "Athenry" of Brooklyn received the answer, "Any of your Irish-speaking neighbors could have answered your question, and Brooklyn contains as many persons who speak our vernacular Gaelic as Cork City."

O'Mahony occasionally provided some interesting details in the introductions to the Gaelic pieces. Thus while discussing "The Maiden Widow" (*Irish People*, Mar. 30, 1869), he notes that "it was taken down some thirty years since from oral repetition by a student of the Irish tongue, who heard it sung at a harvest gathering at Kilbeheny, by a peasant girl of the Gaultie side."

The Gaelic column continued in the *Irish People* through mid-1871 but apparently disappeared after that. In 1870 many of the paper's Gaelic columns were recycled in the weekly literary periodical the *Emerald*, and in 1871 the articles were republished the following week in the *Sunburst*, a periodical that took its title from the name of one of the flags of the *Fianna*.

As mentioned above, the new column of the *Irish-American* started in January, 1869. At first it contained pieces taken mainly from earlier *Irish-American* columns. But after printing a Doheny translation without acknowledgment in the issue of April 17, 1869, the editor of the *Irish-American*, P. J. Meehan, was severely attacked by O'Mahony in the *Irish People*. After a hiatus of two months, the column started again on June 26, 1869, with a Gaelic editor using the pen name "Boru." Boru presents a number of poems, some of which are Irish translations of English-language material. It is hardly surprising that someone with the *nom de plume* Boru should show a preference for Clare poets. He includes pieces from Seán Llúid, Eamon Mac Giolla Iasachta, Aindrias Mac Cruitín, and Brian Merriman and four poems by Tomás Ó Miodhacháin. In his notes on "Aithrighe Sheaghain Do Horadh," the Gaelic editor mentions his source: "We have recovered the present Gaelic copy from an old and almost illegible manuscript, written in English character" (*Irish-American*, Jan. 15, 1870). He signs the piece "WILLIAM RUSSELL" (BORU). From this article on, he signs himself either W. R. or William Russell. The last article in this series appeared on September 16, 1871.[42] By this time the *Irish-American* had published more than 300 Gaelic columns. For the years 1872–76 they published only three Gaelic items (two items in Aug. 1874 and one in 1876).

It is interesting to note that shortly after the Gaelic columns had been dropped by the *Irish-American* and the *Irish People*, the language cause found support in the columns of Patrick Ford's *Irish World*. This support did not seem likely to materialize at first. As an early editorial explained: "We do not ask that any one should, at this day, set about learning Irish; nor do we intend to open a Gaelic department in the *Irish World*. The one would be as unfeasible as the other idle. For all practical purposes in life the English language—hateful though the admission be—is, and must continue to be, our means of communication. But if the Irish language cannot be studied, it should, at least be held in reverence. . . . It is a grand relic of the olden world literature, and on this account alone, if for no other consideration, it should command respect" (*Irish World*, Jan. 27, 1872).

Ford's paper soon started to receive a spate of letters on the subject. Most were in favor of the language. Some writers, such as Jas. E. Murray of Willimantic, Connecticut, urged Ford to institute an Irish column in the paper: "Why could not you, Mr. Editor, give us in your welcome weekly *Irish World*, some few such proverbs and witticisms in the Irish language, in ordinary type, with the translations in English" (*Irish World*, Feb. 10, 1872). But Ford had no intention of instituting an Irish department, and such a column was not to become part of the *Irish World* until March 1899.[43]

In the May 25, 1872, issue, Ford published the now famous letter by THE GAEL (Michael Logan of Brooklyn) calling for the cultivation of the Irish language through the establishment of Irish classes "in every Irish society in the Union" and the publication of Irish lessons in the *Irish World*. "I will gratuitously give lessons in the original Irish," Logan continued, "to any society of Irishmen in Brooklyn."

Logan was true to his word and soon organized an Irish class in Our Lady of Victory School in Brooklyn.[44] The columns of the *Irish World* continued to reverberate with calls from all over the nation for the revival of Irish via the establishment of classes, associations, and an Irish-language journal. On March 22, 1873, under the heading "The Irish Language," the paper noted that "the restoration of the Celtic language having now been agitated at great length in the *Irish World*, all future communications on the subject must be as brief as possible. Otherwise, we cannot publish them."

But the letters kept coming in. P. J. Daly of Boston reported on the first meeting in that city to organize an Irish-language society (*Irish World*, May 10, 1873). In Manhattan, Patrick Logan of the Total Abstinence Society of St. Columba's Parish, announced the society intended to begin an Irish class (*Irish World*, May 24, 1873). In January 1875 Michael Logan established the Brooklyn Philo-Celtic Society.

Logan was to spend the rest of his life working for the Irish language. Born in Curraghderry near Miltown in County Galway in 1836, he received his education at St. Jarlath's under Reverend Ulick Bourke.[45] He came to America in 1871. He was to become most noted for his largely Irish-language periodical *An Gaodhal*, which he published in Brooklyn from 1881 until his death in 1899.

The work of the Brooklyn and Boston Philo-Celtic societies seems to have spurred the Irish in Ireland to found the Society for the Preservation of the Irish Language in Dublin in December 1876. The activity of this society in turn seems to have rebounded across the Atlantic and given rise to a revitalized interest in Irish. In 1877 the *Irish-American* revived its Gaelic column. In 1878 Irish language societies sprang up not only in the New York and New Jersey region but all over the Northeast. The emergence of these groups is chronicled in the pages of the *Irish-American* and attests to a strong interest in the language among many in this country. The New York Philo-Celtic Society was founded in May 1878 with David O'Keeffe, "the Patriarch," as teacher. A Jersey City

Aloysius O'Kelly's elaborately decorated cover for *The Gael* is a good example of the iconography surrounding the Gaelic Revival movement at the turn of the century. A "bi-lingual magazine devoted to the promotion of the Irish language, literature, music, and art of Ireland," *The Gael* was published monthly in New York between 1881 and 1904. It was founded by County Galway native Michael Logan and later edited by an Irish American, Miss Geraldine M. Haverty. (Courtesy of Angela M. Carter.)

branch was established in June 1878. In July came the notice of another group in Manhattan, the Society for the Preservation of the Irish Language, which had close links to Michael Logan's Brooklyn group. Later in July came word that a Philo-Celtic Society had been started in Elmira, New York. In August two more "schools" were opened, one at St. Columba's Church and the other known as "the Uptown Irish class," which met at 193 First Avenue. In the following months other branches were established at 1110 Second Avenue, in the Fort Washington area, and at 561 Eleventh Avenue (which soon moved to 358 West 43rd Street). In November, one correspondent wrote that there were 1,100 members of these various groups in New York, Brooklyn, and New Jersey.[46]

A certain sense of rivalry grew up among many of these groups, and sometimes bitter accusations were made. David O'Keeffe and his supporters, for instance, were never willing to acknowledge Michael Logan as the father of the Irish-language revival in America since O'Keeffe had been involved in promoting Irish long before Logan came to this country. Furthermore, O'Keeffe's group raised serious questions about Logan's command of Irish.[47]

Nevertheless, the groups continued to expand. At first, some classes used lessons printed in the Gaelic column of the *Irish-American* as their reading material, but the *Irish-American* soon published the lessons in book format. The paper also included a small section of Irish in its yearly *Irish-American Almanac*, and in 1879 it published P. W. Joyce's *Grammar of the Irish Language* and in 1880 a booklet of Moore's 'Melodies' accompanied by the translations into Irish of Archbishop MacHale.

Many of the teachers of these classes were excellent Irish speakers, and some seem to have been accomplished Irish scholars. Foremost of all, perhaps, was David O'Keeffe who, as already mentioned, was transcribing Irish manuscripts in the late 1850s. O'Keeffe continued teaching for a number of years and contributed numerous pieces to the columns of the *Irish-American* in the 1880s. Possibly even more impressive was Daniel Magner, who taught at the Fort Washington classes and transcribed an imposing amount of Irish literature from manuscripts that he then published in the *Irish-American* in the 1880s and 1890s.[48]

The students came from a variety of backgrounds. They included Irish speakers, Irish Americans, and a few with no Irish connections at all. One member of the Dublin Irish-language group, Thomas O'Neill Russell, came to the United States in 1878 and immediately involved himself with the movement in this country. A Protestant native of the Athlone district, he was sometimes accused of being a British spy! This was partly due to his predilection for entering into heated arguments over arcane points of Irish grammar, despite the fact that his own command of Irish was quite poor.

One student who attended the early classes with his father was William H. McLees. Born in New York City, McLees lived most of his life in nearby New Jersey and worked for the Sterling Engraving Company, New York. In his spare time, he worked on compiling an English-Irish dictionary that had reached more than 9,000 handwritten pages by the time of McLees's death in 1953.[49]

Patrick O'Beirn, a native Irish speaker from Donegal, learned to write Irish at the classes. He put his talents to work writing poetry and soon became by far the most significant Irish language poet of the revival in the United States. An elegy he wrote in Irish for Ulysses S. Grant was printed in the New York *Herald* on August 10, 1885. His works covered the language revival movement, politics, nature, history, love, and humor. His poetry, along with that of Douglas Hyde, heralded the tentative beginning of a new era in Irish poetry.[50] His finest poem, "Adhbhar ár m-Bróin" (The cause of our Sorrow) (*Irish-American*, Feb. 12, 1887, 3), was written shortly after Father Edward McGlynn had been suspended from his duties at St. Stephen's Parish by the Archbishop of New York, M. A. Corrigan. McGlynn had been dismissed for his outspoken political views, which included support of Henry George. Pádraic's poem expresses powerfully the love and reverence the people had for Dr. McGlynn and their feeling of helplessness in the conflict. McGlynn is not mentioned by name in the poem and it is certain, given the editorial stance of the paper, that the piece would not have been printed had it been written in English.

A number of the Catholic clergy, some of whom were native Irish speakers, took an interest in these classes, which were often held in church halls and schools, sometimes with a clergyman in attendance. Father McAleer supported the classes at St. Columba's parish on West 25th Street where he "took his first lesson in Gaelic" (*Irish-American*, Sept. 21, 1878). A class was established in Jersey City in September 1878 at the Academy of St. Paul of the Cross, and the pastor of the parish, Reverend J. P. Smyth, is described as "a Celtic scholar of no mean ability" (*Irish-American*, Sept. 28, 1878). Father Patrick Hennessy of St. Patrick's Church, Jersey City, apparently studied Irish to be able to communicate more easily with his flock. He established an Irish class in his parish, as reported in the *Irish-American* on December 21, 1878:

> The highly esteemed and much beloved Father Hennessy, of St. Patrick's Church, Jersey City, . . . has recently engaged the services of an accomplished Irish Professor, Mr. Tenpenny . . . He felt proud to say he was, like a great many then listening to him, once ignorant of the Irish language; but he could not feel happy until by study and perseverance, he acquired a grammatical knowledge of it. . . . It is a great blessing and comfort to those of St. Patrick's congregation, and others, who cannot speak the English language, to know that not only Father Hennessy, but his active, pious and exemplary assistant, the Rev. Father Downes, can speak the Irish language fluently and thereby give them spiritual advice and hear their confessions in their own native tongue.

Father Thomas Fitzgerald, a fluent Irish speaker, was closely connected with the language movement in Brooklyn throughout the 1880s and composed an interesting poem in Irish to Father Patrick Hennessy on the latter's twenty-fifth anniversary in the priesthood.

One feature of the Irish-language movement that must be treated is the question of political involvement. Although by and large these groups supported efforts for Irish freedom, it would be wrong to overemphasize the degree to which they were politically motivated. This is not to say that people with a political agenda did not participate in the language movement. One of the most famous students of the classes was Jeremiah O'Donovan Rossa. Rossa had spent his early years living with his grandparents in West Cork, speaking principally Irish. In later years as a shopkeeper in Skibbereen, Rossa had his name painted in Irish above the door. When he was arrested by the British in 1865, he had in his possession a number of Irish manuscripts that have never been recovered. He started his own highly political paper, the *United Irishman,* in New York in 1881 and included a certain amount of Irish in the paper, printed in roman type with no accent marks. Although the Irish content consisted mainly of traditional poems and proverbs, Rossa, who wrote nearly the entire paper, frequently capped off an editorial, article, or a letter to the editor with an asseveration in Irish. For instance, after a one-line notice from the *Boston Pilot* stating, "Michael Davitt is in Egypt," Rossa quipped "Mola 's buidhechas le Dia! iss fad' o bhaile air seachran ruithean moran daoine" (Praise and thanks to God. It's far from home many people run astray) (*United Irishman,* June 13, 1885, 4). But barbs of this sort were generally aimed at the English, such as one that appeared after a piece on Earl Carnarvon, Lord Lieutenant of Ireland: "Go m-beirean dia'al leis iad-go h-aon dia'al aco" (May the devil take them—every single devil of them) (*United Irishman,* Sept. 12, 1885, 2). Rossa occasionally inserted a notice in Irish like the one that appeared on September 10, 1887: "Ni bheig aon papeir aguinn an t-seacht'uin seo chughain" (There will be no paper next week). It is interesting to note also that a number of the paper's subscribers wrote their names in Irish.

There had been a number of calls for an Irish-language journal, and with so many students enrolled in classes the time seemed right. In 1881 Michael Logan started to publish *An Gaodhal* in Brooklyn. This largely Irish-language journal marked an important advance in the Irish movement in America. Like the *Irish-American,* it provided a forum for language enthusiasts, fledgling authors, and collectors of Irish folklore. It also seems to have been a catalyst in moving the newly founded Gaelic Union of Dublin to begin publishing its own periodical, the *Gaelic Journal,* in 1882. Logan died in 1899, but *An Gaodhal* continued to be published until 1904.

By the 1880s and 1890s the Irish language had established a definite presence in New York. Every week one could buy the *Irish-American* and the *United Irishman* with their columns of Gaelic. The monthly *An Gaodhal* was almost entirely devoted to Irish-language matters. Other periodicals such as the *Celtic Monthly* and later the *Celtic Magazine,* both edited by James Haltigan, had Gaelic departments. On Thanksgiving night 1884, a Gaelic operetta was performed in Steinway Hall and reviewed by the leading New York newspapers. In 1885 Kerry native and Brooklyn resident Captain Thomas Norris delivered an address in Irish at the inauguration of President Grover Cleveland in Washington. Irish classes were given nearly every night of the week at one or another of a variety of locations by a large number of Philo-Celtic societies. Some of these societies, such as the New York Gaelic Society, continued in existence for many years and served to acquaint generation after generation of New Yorkers with a part of their linguistic heritage unavailable to them in the schools and universities of their city. Since the days of the Ossianic Society and the initiation of the Gaelic column in the *Irish-American*, Irish-language activity in New York had supported and stimulated the language movement in Ireland. This support was to continue for several decades, and, in fact, Douglas Hyde's brief acquaintance with the Gaelic societies during his trip to New York in 1891 seems to have been a factor in guiding him to establish the Gaelic League in Dublin in 1893.[51]

Although the Irish-language activity during this period was truly impressive, what remains of it is merely the tip of the iceberg, records left to posterity by those involved in the language movement. The vast majority of undocumented Irish speakers, some of whom never learned English and most of whom never belonged to a language movement, remain unknown to historians. Only diligent probing will yield occasional traces of their existence such as this notice from the "Brooklyn Echoes" column of the *Irish-American* (June 18, 1887, 5):

"Catharine Hanaford, a poor Irishwoman, aged 80 years, hailing from Galway and speaking Gaelic only, being utterly ignorant of the English language, was found wandering in the Sixth Precinct last Friday evening. Justice Nachor sent her to the Almshouse. It is said that she has two daughters living in Greenpoint."

Another example of the existence in this country of a Gaelic underground culture is provided by Captain Thomas Norris in the *United Irishman* (July 4, 1885, 4):

> "Irish Caoiners in America" Captain Thomas Norris—Yes, there are Irish caoiners in this country that have reason to caoin far away from home. Over near Coill-an-Uimire, in Brooklyn, where we live, we were at an Irish wake the other night. It was the wake of a young Irish girl who had been married a year before this. The caoiner was an old country neighbor. She had not been asked to the wedding, and now at the wake she could not repress her satire. A verse of her caoin was:
>
> Mo chara 's mo stor thu
> Do h-iarradh me air do thoraibh
> Nior h-iarradh me air do phosa.
> Ni iosfain punt feola
> A's do dheunach gluine no dho me.
>
> (My friend and my love,
> I am invited to your wake

But was not invited to your wedding.
I would not have eaten a pound of meat
And a glass or two would have sufficed me.)

From George Templeton Strong to Captain Thomas Norris, many nineteenth-century New Yorkers were familiar with Irish immigrants who sounded distinctly different from their American neighbors. Yet despite the fact that Irish speakers numbered between 70,000 and 80,000 in the New York City area in the second half of the nineteenth century, their impact on the historical record has been almost nil, especially when compared with that of numerically less significant immigrant groups. I have attempted to correct this imbalance and to illustrate that the question of the Irish language in nineteenth-century New York cannot be dismissed by mere reference to a "language movement." In fact, the language was used by thousands in New York who came from a variety of backgrounds. Some—like John O'Mahony, Michael Doheny, and O'Donovan Rossa—were political refugees. Others like the Irish-speaking colporteurs who stressed the use of Irish in their work, did not show the slightest interest in Irish political freedom. For the majority of Irish speakers, Irish was the language that was most natural for them to use with family, friends, and neighbors. It is an encouraging sign that modern researchers are starting to hear the voices of the many Irish immigrants who arrived in this city with their language and culture intact.

CHAPTER 11

Irish County Societies in New York,

1880–1914

SOCIETIES ENROLLING only immigrants from the same villages or provinces in the old country have been common among most ethnic groups coming to America. Most such organizations faded out in subsequent generations as provincial loyalties gave way to broader national or religious associations. One exception was the Irish county societies, which evolved differently. Irish county associations were weak during the heaviest flow of Irish immigration in the famine years of the 1840s and 1850s. It was only in the late nineteenth and early twentieth centuries, with a renewed flow of immigrants and the revival of Irish political and cultural nationalism, that Irish county societies finally took root and flourished in New York.

The First County Societies

Since the founding of the Friendly Sons of St. Patrick in 1784, there has been a long succession of Irish societies of all types and purposes. The majority were purely social groups, some were of a fraternal nature, and others had a religious, benevolent, and political orientation, political primarily in regard to Ireland's nationhood, but occasionally in the domestic sense as well. The majority of the organizations enjoyed but a short life, unable to maintain the initial enthusiasm that had set them to organizing. The typical life span of an Irish society in the mid-nineteenth century was no more than 25 or 30 years.[1]

The new generation of immigrants arriving in New York in the late 1840s and 1850s had fled Ireland and its declining agricultural prospects in desperation. Unlike many of the Irish who had arrived a decade earlier, they were ill-prepared for the New World. In order to make the transition to American life as easy as possible, the newcomers founded a large number of groups, ranging from labor unions to temperance societies. The social world created by these organizations emphasized the common bonds of Irishness regardless of their members' county of origin in Ireland.[2]

The size of the Irish immigrant wave arriving in Manhattan caused whole neighborhoods to develop an Irish character. While the availability of cheap housing and ready employment might have been the initial reason for attracting immigrants to a particular neighborhood, the comfort of living with people of the same cultural background soon became a prime factor in determining where an immigrant would settle.[3] But New York's Irish as well as German neighborhoods were still only temporary areas of settlement for most immigrants. A high rate of mobility out of the city (55% for the Irish and 58% for the Germans) between 1850 and 1869 indicates that the ethnic neighborhoods were in a constant state of flux and consequently dependent on new arrivals for their distinctive character.[4]

Despite the high degree of mobility, New York's early Irish neighborhoods remained more or less intact until the close of the nineteenth century. Several principally Irish sections of the city were distinguished not only by their Irishness but by a particular stamp of Irishness, since in some places immigrants from specific counties predominated, or at least were present in significant numbers. Those counties that supplied the largest numbers of emigrants in the 1850s were more likely to form a recognizable enclave. Consequently the old Fourth Ward for Kerry people and Seventh Ward for Cork people were well known as "Kerry" and "Cork" wards to the New York Irish.[5] But it was not just the big county groups that tended to gather together in the city; smaller pockets from other counties in Ireland were to be found elsewhere in Manhattan.[6]

A county enclave like the Kerry neighborhood in the Fourth Ward, however, contained only a portion of the immigrants from that county in the city. People from Kerry, as was the case with the other 31 Irish counties, were to be found all over the city, but many of them had once been residents in one of the old downtown county enclaves. In several instances, a county enclave served later not only as a base for the organization of a county society itself, but as a rallying point for exiles from around the city and beyond. The Fourth Ward and vicinity gave birth to the first Kerry Association in the 1850s, and for many years afterward the ward remained a factor in its membership and activities.

The immigrant's first neighborhood in America often evoked a nostalgia similar to the pinings felt for the old country itself. Manhattan, as the first place of settlement and geographic focus for so many immigrants, became a drawing card for the county organizations as older immigrants returned to their original neighborhoods for their social gatherings. It was no accident that practically all these gatherings came to be described as "reunions."[7]

Oddly enough, the first county organization, the Sligo Young Men's Association formed in September 1849, was composed not of struggling recent immigrants, but of relatively comfortable middle-class members.[8] Its birth also marked a shift in the pattern of Irish emigration away from the north and the east of Ireland to the western seaboard.[9] The *Irish-American* (Feb. 3, 1850) welcomed the new group:

> We are gratified, truly, to see the organization of these associations. They give a becoming reply to the calumnious statement that our position in America was one of "poverty and shame." They show that it is (Thank God) far otherwise with those of our people who are industrious, thrifty and well conducted. We are willing to admit that the idle and conceited Irish half sir, and the muddling intemperate, have nothing to expect but poverty and shame; and if our name be a reproach in this region of dignified labor and active enterprise, we have such as they alone to blame for it.

The Sligo Young Men was an organization composed of businessmen, tradesmen, and the "respectable" classes.[10] Indeed, it is unlikely that unskilled laborers would have been able to afford the one dollar charged at their second annual dinner and ball in 1851. Sligo's social evenings resembled the intimate upper-class suppers of the Friendly Sons of St. Patrick, with its rigid structure of formal toasts and mutual self-congratulations. D. F. Ferguson, one of the founders of the Sligo Young Men, wrote that the organization's purpose was to disseminate "the great principles of Friendship, Love and Charity, and to form a powerful union of Irishmen to amend the social condition of the poorer classes of their brothers, here and in Ireland, as far as in them lies."[11]

Despite the sympathetic coverage that the new county society received from the *Irish-American,* the newspaper was plainly concerned about the threat of sectionalism posed by the Sligo Young Men's organization. Factional squabbles between competing gangs of Irish laborers had degenerated into fights between different county groups in 1850 and 1851, and it was gently suggested that the new organization change its name or form a military company instead. As the paper reported on August 10, 1850, the Sligo Men did both, forming an independent military company named after their native county and altering the name of the society to conceal its sectionality by adopting the somewhat grand name of "Order of United Irishmen—Sligo Grand Lodge No. 1."

The name change seemed to do the trick. The Sligo Association prospered in a modest way and was much more successful than several other county societies formed shortly afterward in the 1850s, such as Cavan, Kerry, Galway, Monaghan, and Tyrone. It was also the only one of this group to survive down to the era of the big wave of county society organization and reorganization in the early 1880s.

The organizations of sectional affinity covered in the Irish American weeklies of the 1850s varied somewhat in character and can be divided into four or five categories. First, there were the purely social organizations such as the Sligo Young Men and the Kerry Men's Association.[12] Second, there were military societies like the Fermanagh Republican Guards and the Limerick Guards, who spent most of their time practicing the military arts but had a social aspect too, to judge by their frequent entertainments and dances. Third, there were athletic clubs like the Meath Football Club. Fourth, a number of special-purpose organizations like the Donegal Relief Fund arose in direct response to the threat of famine in parts of Donegal. Perhaps a fifth category would be the town societies, which carried the local appeal of the county societies a step further. These societies represented towns from all the provinces and included such diverse locations as Mallow, Cootehill, Athlone, and Dungannon.

Although certain of these societies, such as Sligo and Athlone, were clearly middle-class in character, it is difficult to place most of the others. The members of the military societies probably approached middle-class status; since they were independent companies, however, their members received no pay and were therefore obliged to equip themselves with uniform, weaponry, and supplies at their own expense. Several contemporary accounts of the social events of the military companies indicate a preference for rather elaborate social affairs accompanied by relatively expensive formal sit-down dinners. Since detailed coverage of the social events of the county societies was usually lavished only on the grander functions in the Irish American press, however, most of the county and local societies in the 1850s were only briefly mentioned in press accounts.[13]

The county societies formed an obscure and small part of Irish New York for almost 30 years. In contrast, the Ancient Order of Hibernians (AOH)—which was organized by parish, neighborhood, or sometimes occupation, but never by county origin—enjoyed the most spectacular growth of any of the Irish societies in the 1850s through the 1870s. New York Irish American weekly newspapers like the *Irish News* gave their blessing and encouragement to the AOH in the early 1850s because its Irish nationalist approach erased divisive sectionalism among the Irish in labor competition.[14]

The AOH, unlike the county organizations, was a Catholic fraternal society that strongly linked ethnicity and Catholicism. It was a mass organization of decidedly working-class background that had a social, political, and religious agenda. Because of its broad appeal to Catholics, Irish nationalists, and laborers, membership in the Hibernians represented much more than just ethnic identity and old country nostalgia. The AOH made a point of being highly visible.

Up to the 1880s the county societies tended to be more middle-class, apolitical, and certainly less sectarian than the AOH and remained isolated from other Irish societies in the city. The social aspect of the county organizations was an end in itself, and they managed to ignore most of the political and social turmoil in Ireland and New York.[15]

By the 1870s there were at least 18 county organizations out of a possible 32 Irish counties operating in the city: Kerry, Cork, Tipperary, Limerick, Waterford, Mayo, Galway, Roscommon, Sligo, Leitrim, Carlow, Dublin, Meath, Monaghan, Armagh, Cavan, Fermanagh, and Tyrone. Despite their growing number, these organizations had not entirely shed the stigma of sectionality. A Corkmen's Association, for example, was formed in May 1874, but by 1877 it had changed its name to the Shandon Club in response to criticism of the alleged sectional narrowness of the organization. Even so, it remained an organization of Corkmen under the cloak of the romantic image of Shandon. Other county societies similarly disguised their sectionality. The Meath Association was known as the Knights of Tara after the seat of the ancient high kingship of Ireland, and the Wexford Men usually went by the name of the '98 Club, in memory of the insurrection in that county in 1798.

By the mid-1870s many county organizations had either died out or fallen into decline. This was the result of a combination of factors. Industrial expansion in the early 1870s was followed by a sharp downturn in the middle years of the decade that caused considerable unemployment. For the first time since the 1840s, there was a dramatic drop in Irish immigration in the late 1870s, cutting the county societies off from their principal source of recruitment: the newcomers who usually harbored the strongest feelings for home. Competition from other Irish and Catholic societies was great since they were larger and could better withstand periods of peak demand on sick and death benefits than the relatively tiny county societies. Probably most significantly, the county societies were unable to focus on substantive Irish issues, although they did tackle with great success the question of the Irish Land League in the early 1880s.[16]

The Irish Land War

Conditions in 1880 were ripe for the development of Irish county societies in the city since their traditional rivals, the Irish fraternal orders, had suffered major reverses. The St. Patrick's Mutual Alliance, a powerful Irish political and fraternal society, had collapsed in 1876–77, along with its patron, Richard Connolly of the Tweed Ring. The Ancient Order of Hibernians, the largest of the Irish societies, became mired in a spell of bad publicity when the Molly Maguire episode received national attention in 1876. Soon afterward the AOH split into two bitterly opposed factions over an unrelated leadership squabble. The last of the major societies, the Father Mathew Total Abstinence and Benevolent Society, went into its own decline in the late 1870s and in less than a decade would be almost defunct. By 1880 Irish organizational life had reached its lowest point in more than 35 years.[17]

The agricultural distress in Ireland then propelled a new large wave of immigration into the city, much of it from the counties, where a "land war" was raging. After several years of low immigration, the influx from Ireland exploded. Immigrants numbering 71,000 in 1880, 72,000 in 1881, and 105,000 in 1882 arrived in the city, many of them with bitter personal reminiscences of the struggle between landlord and tenant. These new immigrants were destined to play an important part in the development of the county societies.[18]

The new wave of immigration coincided with an economic recovery. It was easier for these newcomers to fit into New York life than the completely destitute wave of immigrants that had followed the famine in the late 1840s. Better off economically and often comforted by established relatives and friends, they were also able to help out materially in fund-raising efforts in New York for the Irish Land League, the reform organization in Ireland.

In the late 1870s Kerry, where frequent evictions were taking place, was one of the most troubled counties in Ireland. A group of Kerrymen had first come together in early 1881 in New York to bury an indigent fellow immigrant, but by the time they were ready to form a permanent society in March of 1881 it was only the Irish land struggle that mattered. On April 9, 1881, the *Irish-American* reported that hundreds had been "compelled" to abandon their homes and friends in Kerry, "in consequence of the tyranny of the Dennys, the Herberts, the Husseys, the Browns, the Crosbies, the Trenches and others, who sucked the life-blood out of the tenantry." The paper urged those who had come to New York by a united action here prove to those rapacious tyrants that although three thousand miles away from the homes of your childhood, you are still, in spirit, with your kindred at home, and that you are willing and ready to assist them to the best of your ability, both financially and physically, in their efforts against landlordism or any other ism."

At the initial meeting of the Kerrymen's Patriotic and Benevolent Society, more than 100 men signed up, all of them natives of Kerry. The object of the association, as stated in the *Irish-American* (July 30, 1881), was "to render as far as practicable financial and moral aid to the people of Kerry in any effort to improve their condition, and to afford assistance in deserving cases to such Kerrymen and their families in New York as may need assistance." The paper also noted that the new Kerry Association would soon be sponsoring an address at the Cooper Union by the Reverend Michael O'Connor, the parish priest of Ballybunion, County Kerry, who had come to New York expressly to raise money for the embattled tenants of the Harence estate.

The Kerrymen's Society served as a model for a new breed of county society that not only incorporated the traditional social activities of its predecessors but committed itself to Irish political and cultural issues, along with a much stronger benefits program for its members. For the remainder of 1881 and for the following two years, the Kerrymen and a few close allies among the other county organizations conducted a missionary effort to start new county societies and to mold existing county societies in their activist image.

Kerry's nationalist fervor was shared by most of the new county organizations. The members of county societies were able to enjoy the sensation of being 3,000 miles away from Ireland while remaining involved in activities that would determine the future of their place of birth. They were no longer faceless emigrants who were lost to the old country forever, but faithful sons of their county, anxious to improve the lot of their kin at home. When the Wexford (the '98 Club) and Galway societies hosted the members of Parliament for their old counties at the Cooper Union, they did so not just as ordinary exiles but as "the sons and brothers of your constituents" (*Irish-American*, Feb. 18, 1882).

The Irish Confederation

The independence and separateness of the 21 county societies formed by 1883 were seen as an inherent weakness, and leaders of some of the better-organized county associations began to lay plans for a central organization of all the counties. Its aim was to turn the county societies into a movement similar to the AOH or Clan na Gael and at the same time help dispel the aura of sectionalism. The movement was led by the Kerry, Wexford, and Tipperary societies, and its advocates proposed a central body in which each county would have one equal vote in order to dispel "that spirit of petty jealousy which has long existed" (*Irish-American*, Mar. 4, 1882).

Delegates from many county societies conferred in late 1882 at Military Hall on the Bowery with all the self-importance of the Founding Fathers at Philadelphia. Indeed, they obviously felt that they were hardening in the same mold of history that had united the 13 colonies. For many a frustrated Irish nationalist the all-Ireland delegate society offered a substitute for a real 32-county Irish Republic. According to the *Irish-American* (Jan. 20, 1883), the delegates acted as if they were forming a surrogate Ireland right in the city of New York, and it took several weeks of wrangling before a central organization was formed. Shortly thereafter, the new organization, the Irish Confederation of America, issued its first public statement, rather grandly styled as the "Address of the Irish Confederation of America: To Those Who Love Liberty and Hate Oppression," an appeal patterned after the "Address of the American Congress to the People of Ireland" of 1775. Somewhat ironically, in view of its dependence on new arrivals from Ireland, the confederation endorsed the Irish Land League in order to "prevent the bravest and best men of Ireland being forced to emigrate" (*Irish-American*, Feb. 10, 1883).

The confederation was intended to be the mirror image of Ireland in America and based itself directly on the American Constitution. Irishmen of every creed would be united in New York. If Ireland could be created in miniature in America, why could the same not be done in Ireland? Unfortunately, it proved to be a difficult task to unify the Irish counties for joint fund-raising efforts or to get them to come to one another's assistance. The Donegal Association witnessed firsthand the lack of response from the other counties when it hosted journalist James Redpath at the Cooper Union. According to the *Catholic Review* of New York (Jan. 13, 1883) the association was forced to fall back on its own members and supporters in order to fill the hall for Redpath's firsthand account of the distress of Donegal.

Unlike the AOH and Clan na Gael, whose central ruling body had the power to direct and often obligate its branches for various projects, the confederation enjoyed no such power. Moreover, many other societies and individuals, a good number represented by visiting priests from Ireland, made direct appeals to the county organizations. This severely taxed their ability to respond to the appeals of their brother county societies. Although 30 counties had indicated they were interested in joining the Irish Confederation, by the time of its first great fund-raiser, a massive demonstration in the great hall of the Cooper Union, the meeting got off to a shaky start. The *Irish-American* (Feb. 10, 1883) reported: "Accounts received during the past week reveal the pitiable condition of the people in the counties of Donegal, Sligo, Mayo, Galway, Clare and Kerry; and it is singular that, with the exception of Kerry and Donegal, the counties where misery is most prevailing in Ireland and which have organizations in this city have not yet sent their representatives to act in concert with the members of the County Associations constituting the Irish Confederation."

The confederation's mass meeting scheduled for February 23, 1883, however, initially won the backing of civic and political leaders and the promise of Mayor Franklin Edson to serve as chairman. Even the extraordinary seemed possible. J. Neil Darrah, a prominent member of the Derry Association, which had repeatedly stressed that it was "irrespective of class or creed," announced that "the Grand Master of the Orange Lodges, Francis Vaik, had promised to come, with many officers of Orange lodges and would lend the Orange flag to be entwined with the green flag on that evening" (*Irish-American*, Mar. 3, 1883).

The appearance of the Orange and Green on any platform in New York would have been a uniquely remarkable historic occasion and would have accomplished something virtually unthinkable at home in Ireland. Mayor Edson issued a letter at the last minute, however, stating that the meeting was "a matter of Irish politics" and therefore he would not be coming. The mayor simply took offense to the slogan "Ireland for the Irish" on the ticket of admission, which he claimed was nothing but a blatant political statement. The mayor's action caused others to balk at an appearance that included Orangemen.

Left largely to itself, the Irish community's gathering at Cooper Union was hardly distinguishable from any other Irish nationalist rally and like them included participants from the Roman Catholic clergy. At least 10 Roman Catholic priests occupied seats on the platform. The controversial Father Edward McGlynn delivered one of the principal addresses. The *Irish-American*

(March 17, 1883) observed that an Irish Protestant nationalist, the Reverend Doctor H. M. Gallaher of the Hanson Place Baptist Church in Brooklyn, did make a valiant effort to compensate for the apparent lack of diversity.

In the end, only 14 associations, those that had already joined the Irish Confederation, had answered the call: Cork, Kerry, Tipperary, Limerick, Wexford, King's, Kilkenny, Galway, Roscommon, Derry, Donegal, Antrim, Tyrone, and Cavan. Although $1,600 was raised and sent to Ireland for distribution by the bishop of Meath, the figure was just a little more than double what one county, Donegal, had managed to raise by itself earlier in the year.

The Irish Confederation survived only to the late 1880s. The temporarily improved conditions in Ireland robbed the confederation of the urgency of its mission. County societies were drawn into other alliances for the first time, as could be seen from their increasing participation in the annual St. Patrick's Day parade. It seemed that just as many links drew the county societies to other Irish organizations in the city as drew them to each other.

The Counties Reorganize

When Ireland once again experienced agricultural distress in the late 1880s, the Irish county movement became revitalized as eyes focused on an Ireland in need. A new wave of reorganization and expansion took place, and several new county organizations appeared.[19]

By September 1890 Brooklyn had 5 separate county societies, and the following January, 21 Irish county societies there came together to form the Federation of Irish County Societies of Brooklyn. The Brooklyn federation, rather than the individual county organizations, was to take care of the benefits plan from a central fund and thus permit even the smallest counties to provide benefits. A family would receive the substantial sum of $250 on the death of a federation member and $100 on the death of someone from the member's family. County activity in Brooklyn diminished after consolidation with New York in 1898, but in its brief period of glory the Brooklyn societies were comparable to the county societies across the river. Indeed, the Donegal Association had for a time in the late 1880s abandoned meetings in Manhattan for an area just to the south of the old Brooklyn Navy Yard where Donegal immigrants had concentrated.[20]

With famine again threatening Ireland, the county societies of both New York and Brooklyn returned to Cooper Union to raise money for relief efforts. The meeting featured appearances by visitors John Dillon and William O'Brien, members of Parliament, and raised $1,600, which was sent, through Irish-born financier Eugene Kelly's banking-house to Ireland.[21]

There were now more county organizations in Manhattan than ever before and the idea of formally uniting them gathered momentum. A meeting of "60 county organizations," a figure that probably included Irish local, regional, and town societies, considered new plans "to bring all parts of Ireland into social contact." But once again not all the county societies remained interested by the time the new central body, the United Irish County Association, got under way in April 1891. Although 16 of the 22 existing county societies participated at the concluding negotiations, only 9 agreed to the final terms and formed the United Irish Counties (UIC). The new central organization borrowed from the Brooklyn counties amalgam and provided for a fund of centrally disbursed death benefits. The UIC managed to pick up a few additional county affiliates and was socially visible in the Irish community over the next couple of years, holding a Grand Union Ball annually up to at least 1896, but it seems to have faded into oblivion about 1897.[22]

The second failure to unite the counties in a central body did not mean that individual counties could not work together when quick action was needed. When a letter to the *New York Times* in the spring of 1893 called attention to the fact that the Central Park Zoo had the unofficial policy of naming monkeys and chimpanzees with nicknames like Mike, Paddy, Biddy, and Crowley, the Mayo, Kerry, Clare, and Longford organizations called a hasty meeting at Ledwith Hall to launch a formal protest with the park commissioners. According to the *Irish World* (Apr. 22, 1893), "It was held by the projectors of the meeting that they liked fun, but humor with a hot end to it was dangerous and unpleasant. It was all very well to call a monkey Mr. Crowley, but none of the other apes had as yet been christened Uncle Sam, Isaac, Hubert Edward, Napoleon or Bismarck, and it was discrimination." The park commissioners met a week later and issued a resolution forbidding the "practice of applying to the animals of the zoological collection names that are likely to be offensive to persons of any race or nationality, and such practice is hereby prohibited" (*Irish World*, May 6, 1893).

The Irish counties could and did work well with the other Irish fraternal and social organizations as well. The Irish had long been embarrassed by the fact that not a single building in Manhattan was actually owned by any of the numerous Irish societies, in contrast to other ethnic groups, most noticeably the Germans, who owned several well-appointed and centrally located buildings. The Irish Palace Building Association, founded in 1896 in an attempt to correct that omission, proved to be one of the most successful financial efforts ever made to acquire a central meeting place for the Irish societies of New York. It was the brainchild of several prominent members of the Irish Volunteers, an organization of independent Irish military companies outside the government, and Clan na Gael, the militant nationalist society pledged to liberate Ireland by physical force.

In order to raise funds for the proposed Irish Palace Building, a grandiose edifice that was to include not only a library but a shooting range and riding school, an Irish Fair was held for the entire month of May in 1897 at the Grand Central Palace, Lexington Avenue and 43rd Street. Although the project was run by and for the Irish Volunteers, the county societies provided most of the workers. The enthusiasm ran so high that for the first time there were both men's and women's organizations for all of Ireland's 32 counties, even if some lasted no longer than the fair itself. The groups staffed booths for each county in Ireland. The booths were filled with paintings, crafts, and curiosities, and they vied with one another to produce the best exhibit. Many novel features kept the crowds, both Irish and non-Irish, coming, and the fair was a tremendous financial and social success. The favorite exhibit with the Irish was the giant topographical map of Ireland, which offered poignant reminders of the immigrants' attachment to their place of birth:

> In a long, rectangular space, fenced off within a space that forms a promenade around the four sides, and entered by five columned archways, surmounted by a huge green shamrock, is, upon the floor, a topographical map of Ireland, marked off into 32 county spaces, cast in the exact form of the Irish county it represents. These spaces are filled with the veritable Irish soil of the county, gathered by McVeigh, and duly attested as truly genuine. For the low price of ten cents one can tramp all over Ireland. It was a clever conception, that has given great delight to thousands who never thought to stand again on Irish soil, and many a pathetic scene is witnessed daily. One poor woman—Kate Murphy by name, and 80 years old—knelt down and kissed the soil of Fermanagh; then, crossing herself, proceeded to say her prayers, unmindful of the crowd around her. While thus kneeling a photographer took a flashlight picture of her. The flash was a revelation to the simple hearted creature, who seemed to think it a light from heaven, and was awed into reverential silence. When she finally stepped off the Irish soil she sighed sadly and clung to the fence, still gazing at "Old Ireland." She kept looking backward as she walked away, as if bidding a long farewell. (*Irish World*, May 22, 1897)

Shortly afterward the county societies were unpleasantly surprised to learn that they would have no share in the proceeds or in the future direction of the Irish Palace. The counties represented by Mayo, Kildare, Cork, Galway, Limerick, and Sligo sued, but the decision was made against them, even though their work had made the fair a success.[23]

Occasionally, the county organizations became involved in American politics. When American Anglophiles introduced a bill in the U.S. Senate in 1896 proposing an arbitration treaty that would set up a process to peacefully mediate disputes between the United States and Britain, the counties were able to join with other organizations to oppose it. A new organization, the United Irish Societies, was formed, with Jeremiah Healy of the Corkmen's Patriotic and Benevolent Society as its first chairman, and the Irish county societies were destined to play a large part in it.[24]

The combination of pressure from organized Irish and German groups across the country coupled with strong isolationist sentiment in America caused the treaty to be defeated. The Irish counties could share in a small way in the victory.

The dream of many of the leaders of the Irish county movement in the 1880s and the 1890s had been to establish a working model of an independent Irish republican government in the form of a united Irish counties organization in the city, but New York's Irish population and the population of Ireland were in reality quite different. In 1880 the Irish-born population of Manhattan totaled 198,595 and that of Brooklyn 78,814, and certainly every county in Ireland was to be found in those two, at that time, independent cities.[25] Despite their large size, these two Irish communities were in no way a mirror image of the old country. They were the product of peculiar geographic, economic, and social forces in both Ireland and America, forces that propelled high emigration from the more distressed areas in Ireland, in general the western seaboard, and that in America channeled the flow to and away from New York according to family connections and labor opportunities. New York's Irish community therefore drew strongly from some areas in Ireland and weakly from others.

A sampling of just under 13,000 immigrants arriving in New York in the spring and early summer of 1882 shows clearly that the composition of New York's Irish population differed from that of Ireland as reported in the census of 1881 (table 11.1).

The proportion of immigrants from the provinces of Connaught and Munster arriving in New York in the 1882 sampling was much greater than the share each of those provinces held in the actual population of Ireland in 1881. In contrast, Ulster and Leinster were far less well represented in immigrant arrivals in comparison with the 1881 census. New York's Irish population reflected an immigration that was coming from the distressed rural districts where the land war was in full swing. Emigration from the more prosperous Northeast and Leinster was not at the same level.

When viewed on a provincial basis, New York's share of the immigrants closely resembled the share to all American destinations as a whole. Only Leinster showed a slightly greater preference for a New York destination.

TABLE 11.1. Population of Ireland by Province, 1881, and Irish Immigrant Arrivals to All Destinations and New York City, May 6 to July 29, 1882

			Immigration (3 months), 1882			
Province	Population, 1881	Percent	All destinations	Percent	New York City	Percent
Ulster	1,743,075	34	3,111	24	1,160	22
Connacht	821,657	16	3,304	25.5	1,235	24
Munster	1,331,115	26	4,461	34.5	1,781	34
Leinster	1,278,989	25	2,073	16	1,029	20
Ireland	5,174,836	100	12,949	100	5,205	100

Source: "Arrivals from Ireland," *Irish Nation,* May 6, 1882, to July 29, 1882.

Substantial differences in the pattern of immigration from various counties of Ireland only become apparent when the immigrant arrivals are broken down by county of origin. Here it is evident that individual counties differed widely from one another in their preference for settlement in New York City.

In absolute numbers, the counties with the largest populations in the 1881 census of Ireland commonly appear near the top of New York's destination numerical totals. In several instances, however, some of the immigrant stream to the city from smaller counties contributed a number of immigrants out of proportion to their position in the 1881 census.

An average of 40 percent of the total Irish immigrant arrivals in the 1882 sampling indicated settlement in New York City (New York and Brooklyn), and the greater or lesser preference of individual counties for New York City can be measured against this figure. It is apparent from table 11.2 that some large immigration counties were underrepresented among the New York immigrants. Donegal and Mayo, for example (each with only 28% of their immigrants settling in New York) contributed small numbers of their total immigrants in the 1882 sampling. Antrim had even a smaller percentage (27%) of its immigrants locating in the city.[26]

Regionally, it can be said that all of northern Ulster (Donegal, Derry, Tyrone, Antrim, and Down) was noticeably less likely to send a major share of its immigrants to New York. The same pattern can be seen for Roscommon, Mayo, and Kerry. The northern half of Leinster and the southern Ulster counties of Monaghan and Cavan formed a region of above-average immigration to New York City and constituted a contiguous region that covered a large slice of north-central Ireland.

Just as patterns of immigration varied from one part of the United States to another, there is some evidence to suggest the same variables were acting within the confines of today's New York City limits (table 11.3). Only about 4 percent of the total 1882 sampling listed Brooklyn as their destination and only 10 percent of the combined Brooklyn and Manhattan total (that is, New York City).[27] The counties with the largest number of immigrants to Brooklyn were very different from those high on the Manhattan totals. Counties that are not significant in Manhattan's influx (Donegal, Longford, and Westmeath) contributed substantially to Brooklyn's Irish population. Regional and county patterns were significant in immigration to New York City. They made the city not only different from Ireland as a whole but different from other Irish communities across the United States.

The Counties and Athletics

It was unexpectedly through competitive sports, the ancient games of Gaelic hurling and football, that a firm link was finally established between the county societies. Although Irish sport had a long tradition in New York before the turn

TABLE 11.2. Irish Immigrants to New York City, including Brooklyn, and Percentage of Immigrants Indicating This Destination, May 6 to July 29, 1882

Origin	Total immigration	New York City arrivals	Percent	Rank of New York City	Rank of all destinations
Ireland	12,949	5,205	40		
Province					
Munster	4,461	1,781	40	1	1
Connaught	3,304	1,235	37	2	2
Ulster	3,111	1,160	37	3	3
Leinster	2,073	1,029	50	4	4
County					
Cork	1,302	507	39	1	1
Kerry	1,090	361	33	2	2
Galway	779	331	43	3	4
Limerick	679	297	44	4	5
Tipperary	582	289	50	5	8
Mayo	1,011	285	28	6	3
Cavan	486	271	56	7	10
Leitrim	449	219	49	8	11
Clare	509	217	43	9	9
Roscommon	621	200	32	10	7
Sligo	444	200	45	11	12
Donegal	644	177	28	12	6
Longford	237	151	64	13	19
Monaghan	289	149	52	14	17
Tyrone	387	131	34	15	14
Westmeath	214	120	56	16	24
Meath	220	116	53	17	21
Dublin	188	112	60	18	25
Kilkenny	215	111	52	19	23
Antrim	497	110	27	20	13
Waterford	299	110	39	21	16
Derry	312	98	31	22	15
Armagh	226	91	40	23	20
Wexford	244	84	34	24	18
Queens (Laois)	186	77	40	25	26
Kings (Offaly)	133	71	54	26	29
Down	216	68	32	27	22
Fermanagh	144	65	45	28	27
Louth	117	64	55	29	31
Kildare	137	50	37	30	28
Carlow	121	46	38	31	30
Wicklow	61	27	44	32	32

Source: "Arrivals from Ireland," *Irish Nation*, May 6 to July 29, 1882.

TABLE 11.3 Immigrants to Manhattan and Brooklyn, May 6 to July 29, 1882

Origin	Brooklyn		Ratio of Brooklyn to Manhattan (percent)	Rank of Brooklyn	Rank of Manhattan
	Number	Percent			
Total Ireland	511	4	10		
Provinces					
Connaught	146	4	12	1	2
Ulster	141	5	12	2	3
Leinster	115	6	11	3	4
Munster	108	2	6	4	1
Counties					
Donegal	44	7	25	1	13
Mayo	39	4	14	2	6
Leitrim	38	9	17	3	9
Longford	36	15	24	4	15
Cavan	29	6	11	5	7
Westmeath	26	12	22	6	21
Sligo	25	6	13	7	11
Limerick	25	4	8	8	5
Tipperary	25	4	9	9	4
Kerry	25	2	7	10	2
Roscommon	23	4	12	11	10
Galway	21	3	6	12	3
Cork	15	1	3	13	1
Down	14	4	21	14	29
Clare	14	3	6	15	8
Derry	12	4	12	16	22
Queens (Laois)	12	7	16	17	25
Antrim	11	1	10	18	20
Monaghan	11	4	7	19	12
Armagh	9	4	10	20	24
Kings (Offaly)	9	7	13	21	27
Meath	9	4	8	22	16
Kildare	7	5	14	23	31
Fermanagh	6	4	9	24	28
Kilkenny	6	3	5	25	19
Dublin	6	3	5	26	17
Tyrone	5	3	4	27	14
Waterford	5	2	5	28	18
Wicklow	3	5	11	29	32
Carlow	1	0	2	30	30
Wexford	0	0	0	31	31
Louth	0	0	0	31	31

Source: "Arrivals from Ireland," *Irish Nation*, May 6 to July 29, 1882.

of the century, it been left to the independent Gaelic football and hurling clubs. This circumstance changed abruptly when the county societies organized their own teams. It soon became necessary for the counties to come together to regulate and promote the games.

The city's Irish had about a dozen particularly well-known teams in the 1890s, such as the Irish Americans, the Barrys, the Wolfe Tones, the Stars of Erin, the Mitchels, the Thomas Francis Meaghers, the Emmets, and the Kickhams. None of the teams bore specific county names, although at least one, the Kickhams, was composed almost entirely of Tipperary men. The first team with a county name was the Kilkenny Football Team in 1898. After 1900 each county organization began forming its own football or hurling team, and in a few years the use of nationalist titles or the names of patriots from Irish history for team names was abandoned. When the time came in 1904, the Kickhams merely changed their name to the Tipperary Football Team.[28]

Land for the first athletic park specifically for Irish games, Celtic Park, was purchased in late 1897 in the Laurel Hill section of Queens. It was only a ten-minute ride from the Long Island City terminus of the 34th Street ferry, so it was convenient for all of Manhattan, as well as adjacent parts of Brooklyn. It was also close to Calvary Cemetery, the "City of the Celtic Dead," which was a sad place of Sunday pilgrimage for all too many Irish families grieving the early loss of a loved one. The cemetery traffic and clever promotion by the private owners of Celtic Park, several of whom were known members of the Irish county associations, made the sportsground an instant success. Every Sunday the Irish filled the grounds to see not only Gaelic games but foot races, weight throwing, jumping contests, and even bicycle races. Sport was an important part of self-esteem for the Irish immigrant, and even the U.S. Olympic team received financial support from county organizations in the era when the U.S. team featured several well-known Irish-born athletes who often competed at Celtic Park. As reported in the *Irish-American* (May 18, 1912), "The Galway men feel that in aiding clean sport in this way they are promoting the interests of our race in this city and throughout the nation, it being well known fact that America in large measure owes her devotion to track athletes to the Irish and Irish-American race within her borders. This is a matter for self-gratulation to every Irishman, who sees this sustained all the claims of his race in manly sport, and thereby refuted many of the ignorant calumnies cast upon us by our enemies, who have tried to depict us as a debauched and inferior race."

In their early years the Irish counties participated in such varied competitions as shuffleboard and cricket, but interest in non-Gaelic sports was fading rapidly. The Queens (Laois) County Cricket Team was one of the best in New York soon after its foundation in 1900 and practiced playing the teams from British steamships visiting the city. The Queens County team was not, however, composed of the scions of the Anglo-Irish manor houses; the members, said the *Gaelic American* (Apr. 2, 1906), were "hard working men" with names like

Delaney, Flynn, Gleason, and McGrath. Because of the growing enthusiasm for Gaelic sports, cricket was quickly replaced by a Gaelic football team. The popularity of Irish sport on occasion brought the matches right into Manhattan's Madison Square Garden where, to the surprise of many, "interest in the game was intense among native American spectators," many of whom saw a Gaelic match for the first time (*Gaelic American*, Feb. 11, 1905).

The playing field gave each county a chance to prove its worth and brought to some of them fame and financial prosperity. The Irish Counties Athletic Union (ICAU) was formed by several county organizations in 1904 to coordinate the matches of the county teams, and this organization later became known as the United Irish Counties. According to the *Irish Advocate* (July 4, 1913), the Gaelic athletic movement emphasized the fellowship of sport among all the Irish counties. On most occasions the contestants lived up to the ideal, but sport was raw competition and success was measured in goals and points. Consequently, local pride and local passion sometimes took precedence.[29]

Celtic Park rested in the hands of private individuals whose motivations mixed patriotism and profit in varying degrees. The Irish American Athletic Club, an association created by the Celtic Park principals to foster both Gaelic and non-Gaelic sporting events, was, moreover, the athletic power at Celtic Park and was an obvious rival to the Irish Counties Athletic Union. Many of the teams of the Irish counties, particularly the smaller ones that formed the heart of the ICAU, asked for better terms from the proprietors, but they were not forthcoming.[30]

Four teams known as the "Big Four"—Cork, Kerry, Kildare, and Kilkenny—were the biggest drawing cards at Celtic Park and consequently split big receipts whenever they played there. The Big Four were quite content with conditions as they existed. The "equal voice" concept of the Irish Counties Athletic Union held little sway for the counties that had fashioned superior teams and had worked hard to achieve success.[31]

In 1907 the ICAU purchased grounds in the Wakefield section of Yonkers for a new rival park. For the most part, the move was not supported by "the Big Four," which could see no advantage in such a financially risky and relatively remote location. The ICAU mobilized all its members (24 affiliated counties in June 1909) into a united front and tried to prevent any county from sending teams to Celtic Park. According to the *Irish Advocate* (June 26, 1909), some counties balked at this:

> Kerrymen never stood aside when called upon to do a charitable, manly, or national act; and it does not matter what movement is started for the welfare of our oppressed and downtrodden country, the sons and daughters of the "Kingdom" are there doing the work. It would be a sorry day for Kerrymen to come to 341 W. 47th street (I.C.A.U. headquarters) to learn the rudiments of nationality and the duty to the land of their birth. The society will march on as it has done in the past and will not be bulldozed by any threats that may

emanate from a few irresponsible men who claim all the virtues and find fault with men who differ from them, whether it be in the journalistic or football field.

The 9½ acre Irish Park at Wakefield was to prove an even bigger failure than the Irish Palace Building Association for the counties. The purchase price of $70,000 was far more than the $30,000 the county associations were able to come up with, and a mortgage of $48,000 and a second mortgage for improvements of $9,000 soon hung over their heads. The city of Yonkers then invoked its blue laws against the charging of admission for sport on Sundays, and the fate of Wakefield Park was sealed. Although several county-sponsored events were held at the park before foreclosure finally came in 1910, the participating county organizations lost all their investment in the final collapse. The loss of Wakefield Park was not fatal to the ICAU, but several county societies, including Cork and Meath, split in two over its ramifications. [32]

The ICAU became the United Irish Counties and prospered under that name despite Wakefield Park. Control of Gaelic games passed over to the Gaelic Athletic Association in 1914 and with it most of the controversies that arose over the playing field. All 32 Irish counties did not affiliate with the UIC until the 1930s.[33]

Establishing a Place in the Irish Community

All the county societies based their membership appeals primarily on natives of their respective counties. It may not always have been a formal part of the by-laws, but it was clearly their expectation that few but actual immigrants would be interested in joining such an old country society. The rhetoric of the county societies in the Irish American weeklies in the 1880s and right up to World War I was therefore plainly addressed to "Meath Men," "Leitrim Men," "Tipperarymen," or the like. Some county organizations admitted American-born Irish, but others chose not to be so broad in their admission qualifications. In any case, in those organizations where they were admitted, they do not seem to have been very numerous.[34]

Restrictive membership qualifications in some of the county organizations were relaxed early in their development. In March of 1883 the Limerick association announced that "any gentlemen who is a native of Co. Limerick is eligible to membership," but by August it had broadened qualifications to include as "persons entitled to membership Irishmen, sons of Irishmen, of good moral character."[35] Wexford had amended its native-born restriction early in the following year to "all Wexfordmen and their descendants," and Cork had changed its qualifications to "all Corkmen and sons of Corkmen" by 1890. The restriction to native-born Irish did not entirely vanish, however; on their organization in 1887, the Dublinmen qualified membership to "natives of

Dublin, city and county." The newly organized County Down Men, noted the *Irish Advocate* (Mar. 12, 1904), appealed only to men "who hailed from County Down" in 1904. The trend was certainly toward a more liberal interpretation of qualifications for membership, but the rhetoric used by the county societies in their appeals for membership was always directed at the Irish-born. Providing the means for actual "exiles" to socialize with one another was the cornerstone of the county societies, and it is probable that the Irish-born in the organizations exceeded 95 percent up to the World War I period.[36]

One of the early county societies, County Derry, altered its qualifications most radically of all. At its formation in late 1882 Derry had appealed to all men of that county to join, but after a couple of months passed without much success, Derry welcomed "all persons of both sexes, born in Co. Derry, or their descendants" (*Irish-American*, Jan. 20, 1883). Although women were welcomed into the association, the franchise apparently did not extend to holding office, since all the offices remained exclusively for men.[37]

With few exceptions, notably the Gaelic League and Philo-Celtic Society, most Irish organizations remained either exclusively male or female.[38] The first mass movement with the participation of Irish American women came in the 1880s, when American branches of the Ladies Land League were organized by such notables as the Parnell sisters and Ellen Ford of the *Irish World*. The New

Couples meet halfway during the fourth figure of the Irish quadrille at a dance class sponsored by the County Monaghan Men's Society of New York in 1905. Such associations, usually called "patriotic and benevolent societies," were based on place of origin in Ireland. They underwent a tremendous boost in popularity as a result of heavy immigration after 1880, which coincided with the revival of interest in cultural pursuits such as traditional Irish music and dance. (Library of Congress.)

York branches of this organization certainly served as models for the ladies' county organizations that came into being, although for only a short time at this time.[39]

The membership of the men's county organizations grew as time passed, but the ladies' organizations were for the most part only temporary. The members were usually single young immigrants who soon found their way into marriage and out of Irish organizational life.[40]

Not surprisingly, almost all of county ladies organizations met on Thursday evenings, the so-called "maid's night out," because many of their single young members worked as domestics. Living at the house of their employers, they could not receive their prospective suitors as they had in their homes in Ireland. Consequently, the ladies' county societies organized dances and socials, held at various halls around the city, as a substitute for the fireside at home. The entertainments the ladies' societies ran were designed to give young women a social opportunity to meet men of the same ethnic and social background as themselves. Some of the few older ladies of the society usually headed the reception committee at the door and acted as intermediaries in the matching of boy with girl. The men's county organizations used their socials in a similar manner, but because the men were not tied to the home after marriage as much as the ladies, it was only the ladies' societies that inevitably suffered a decline.[41] A typical symbiotic relationship existed between the Kings (Offaly) County societies:

> The inducement we offer to the fellows to come to patronize our ball are probably the greatest on earth, namely the Kings Co. beauties. You may ask are they more beautiful than any other county girls. Well, they certainly must be, for it was only last year they could muster up single ones enough to form a young ladies association. They are grabbed up the minute they land, so that it was only allowing those who were just after being married to join the association that they ever managed to form it. With such an attraction I'm sure we will be able to find standing room for the men.
>
> Now for the young ladies. Will they not find attraction enough in the famous Kings County Hurling team? Have they not proven time and again that they have few if any equals. I'm sure in years to come, when some young lady that will attend our ball and falls in love and gets married to one of the team, it will make her neighbor turn green with envy when she tells her her husband is one of that intrepid band of hurlers. This is your opportunity, ladies. (*Irish-American*, Nov. 26, 1910)

Most members of the ladies' societies remained with them until they were married. In 1910 there were 26 ladies' county organizations. The total number of officers was 271, of whom 238 (or 88%) were single women. Of the 33 married women, 20 served as senior officers, either as presidents, vice presidents, or trustees.[42]

The longevity of the men's county organizations contrasted sharply with the ladies because men simply stayed members longer, if not for life. Practically all the county associations that came into existence in the 1880s tacked the appellation "benevolent" to its name, and this seemed to offer an immediate advantage over the purely social county organization. In the long run, it obligated members to continue membership or forfeit the advantages their dues had already paid for. The Meath association, which was known as the Knights of Tara, was a popular association in the 1870s but became moribund by the close of the decade. When it was reorganized in April of 1882, said the *Irish-American* (Apr. 8, 1883), it "rolled up" members "far beyond expectations due to the introduction of the benevolent clause in its constitution."

The paper also reported (Aug. 4, 1883) that the Limerick Men's Patriotic and Benevolent Association paid a member, after one year in good standing, $5 a week in sick benefits, and upon the death of a member the sum of $50 was presented to the family of the deceased. It is remarkable how little the level of benefits changed over the years. The Cork, Sligo, Roscommon, and Donegal associations were still dispensing sick benefits at the same rate of $5 a week between 1910 and 1912. Death benefits ranged from $75 to $100 for the death of a member and about half that amount for the death of a spouse.[43]

Many of the county societies also purchased burial plots in Catholic cemeteries for emergency use. This was indeed the reason that had brought several of the county organizations together in the first place, since burial in a pauper's plot was considered a terrible disgrace among the immigrants. For societies like the Claremen, a proper burial was more than just charity: "In conclusion let me say that the mission of the Clare Men's Society is a holy one. It has brought cherished hope to the sickman's door, it has brought happiness to the widow and orphan and its outstretched hands have succored the poor and oftentimes the homeless. The good ship carries her human freight o'er turbulent waters, so does the Clare Men's Society safely guard the precious souls who are committed to her care, never withholding the glad hand or affable works of consolation which are so dear to the distressed." (*Irish Advocate*, July 30, 1904)

In the late nineteenth and early twentieth centuries the county organizations assumed a dominant role in the social life of the Irish of Manhattan, but none of the county societies were ever satisfied with the number of members they managed to bring into their ranks. Societies representing counties with the lowest number of immigrants in the city had difficulty surviving, of course. The chairman of the Carlow Men's Society pointed out in the *Irish Advocate* (Apr. 9, 1910): "While there are some thousands of County Carlow men in this city, only a comparatively small number could be found to come together."

Even at the best of times the county societies in New York had in their ranks only a small fraction of the total number of immigrants. As far as can be determined, the membership of the county associations in the early 1880s ranged from about 100 for the smaller societies to 250 or more for the more successful ones. Twenty years later only a few societies had progressed much beyond that. For example, Kilkenny had 258 members in 1909 and Galway about 400, Cork 410, and Kerry just over 700 members in 1910.[44] The total membership of the Irish county organizations probably amounted to 4,000 to 5,000 at this time.

One of the more successful county societies summed up the difficulty in recruiting their county men in these terms: "All of the Corkmen of New York and vicinity are not members for various reasons—some are not energetic enough to take a hand in the great work; some are not healthy enough for acceptance; some are members of various other organizations and some are too well blessed with the things of the world to think of laboring among their countrymen with whom fate has played falsely and opportunity has severely ignored" (*Irish Advocate,* Apr. 16, 1910).

Up to World War I the county societies drew their membership mainly from Manhattan. Very few joined from Brooklyn and the outer boroughs. On its dissolution in 1917, the Corkmen's Mutual Aid Society, for example, had 120 members, of whom 86 percent were residents of Manhattan.[45]

The consolidated city of New York was a huge place, and the distances from one borough to the next were often equal to the distances between one Irish county and another. The county societies demanded the active participation of their members at frequent meetings and often levied fines for failing to participate at meetings and events. This discouraged those who could not conveniently reach Manhattan from becoming members.[46]

Far greater numbers coming from much further afield could be counted on to support the frequent social events of the counties. It was common for many of the counties to have 3,000 guests or more at their major dances, and as many as 6,000 attended the sailing excursions in the summertime. It was at these mammoth gatherings that the county organizations came closest to fulfilling, at least numerically, their ideal of uniting all their exiled countrymen in New York.

The concentration of county organization members in Manhattan had, however, no lasting effect on the borough, even in neighborhoods where individual counties had established an enclave. No neighborhood at the turn of the century was as closely identified with a specific county as was County Clare with the western section of Greenwich Village. The Claremen were so firmly entrenched there by 1900 and for at least the next two decades that the area's Irish gave "one of the principal thoroughfares the nickname of County Clare Street."[47] When the Irish-born declined in this neighborhood after World War I, the County Clare organization moved out of the neighborhood because their still numerous descendants were not interested in perpetuating old country traditions. A vigorous Irish American social life remained in the West Village, but in the 1930s it was to be found mainly in the church, athletic, and political clubs.

> In contrast to the Italian group whose social organization was based on Old World associations, the social structure of the Irish community, acclimatized through more than a generation of American residence, rested upon a distinctive

adaption to life in America—a structure which remained unchanged except in so far as the disintegration of the community broke it. This social structure rested primarily on three foundations, the Church, the political club, and the neighborhood which the Irish had made theirs in a way that the Italians never did. Irish county clubs, the partial equivalent of Italian mutual benefit societies (though never so generally inclusive because they lacked the mutual benefit features of the Italian societies), played no considerable part in the lives of the local Irish within memory of any except the oldest inhabitants. Rather, associations based upon the length of time and the place of their American residence, their American interests and successes, gave to the Irish community in the twentieth century its social form.[48]

Rather than adapt itself to the new world, the county societies remained fundamentally dedicated to the preservation of the ties between old country exiles. Essential to this was the "old boy's network" of older established immigrants who stood willing to help the newer ones. The Sligo organization's physician, Dr. J. C. Hanan, pointed out the material advantages of membership at a banquet address in 1904:

> You not only meet friends of your childhood days but you will become associated with men who are higher up in the world than you are and in that way you will have a chance at elevating yourself to some noble point in the history of mankind. Dr. Hanan said "When I came to this country, which is not a few years ago, Irishmen at that time had but little education, some none and they were formed for hard work, yes, slaving work, but today you see Irishmen in a different state, they are businessmen, clerks, bookkeepers and in almost every Irish County organization whereby you will be enlightened in everything that is going on. (*Irish Advocate*, July 30, 1904)

Although the bulk of the membership appears to have remained working class, the associations attracted a good number of professionals and prominent merchants to leadership positions. Every society seemed to have its doctors, lawyers, and successful contractors serving as officers, many of whom had a network of contacts in a variety of industries such as stevedoring, carpentry and construction work, and government employment. County societies were therefore excellent places to land a job.[49] Sometimes a prominent leader was also the head of a union, as was Longford's James Lennon in 1908. Lennon brought many members into the sheet metal trade, and leaders in the Donegal Association found employment for immigrants in construction and tunnel work (sand hogs). From early in the century, Kerrymen dominated the Paper Handlers Union, whose members initially came from the Kerry neighborhood close to the old downtown printing-house district. Kerry also had good connections within the police department. Limerick had a powerful leader in Tim Healy, who was for many years the head of the Stationary Engineers Union—a source of many jobs in building maintenance. Clare immigrants were heavily employed as longshoremen on the Lower West Side, near 14th Street, and this factor certainly kept them together as a group in this neighborhood after all the other county enclaves had practically vanished.[50]

Because of just a few influential people, large numbers of newcomers were brought into trades and occupations by the county organizations. Longford went on to establish a formal labor bureau to get jobs for members in 1908, but the idea was adopted by the entire Irish Counties Athletic Union for all the members of its affiliated county organizations in the years before World War I.[51]

Every society seemed to have its resident politicians who were instrumental in connecting members to jobs in the public and private sector. The county societies were glad to return the favors at election time. This also worked for politicians who were not members, like William R. Hearst, whose race for governor in 1906 was backed by the Irish Counties Athletic Union, and John Purroy Mitchel, whose mayoral race in 1913 was boosted by a formal Irish Counties Campaign Committee.[52]

Some of the most active politicians in the county organizations, like Denis Buckley, a West Side undertaker known as the "Mayor of Tenth Avenue," were content with just having their own namesake organization to wield power and influence in their own neighborhood. Buckley, for several terms president of the Kerrymen and known to them as "The Big Chief," became "an important factor in the political arena in his district."[53] Namesake organizations like Buckley's abounded among individuals active in the county organizations. Two of the best-known associations in the period before World War I were the William J. Crowley Association, named after the several times president of the Clare Association, and the James J. Hagan Association, named for the prominent Longford orator, both of whom received the endorsement of the Irish Counties Athletic Union in their runs for office.[54]

Irish politics was a never-ending source of interest for the county organizations. From the 1880s until the Easter Week Rising in 1916, and to some extent even beyond this, the Irish county societies were in the corner of the constitutional nationalist movement in Ireland. The Irish Parliamentary Party leaders visiting New York could always count on the counties' moral and financial support, since many of the leaders of the county organizations were members of the United Irish League, the American support group.

The counties were in the habit of issuing resolutions on most matters of Irish political development which were almost invariably sent to the sitting member of Parliament for their respective old country constituencies. Consequently, connections with the Irish members at Westminster were constantly being reinforced. When these members of Parliament visited the United States, which most of them did regularly to raise funds, they were often treated to formal dinners in their honor. This suited many of the more prosperous leaders of the county organizations, who also tended to be the chief supporters of the Parliamentary Party. Leading professionals and businessmen in the New York Irish community such as the physician Dr. Joseph P. Brennan of the Westmeath Men, the dry goods merchant Edward O'Flaherty of the Wexford Men, his partner Stephen McFarland of the Leitrim Men, and many others took the county societies out of the realm of the 25¢ annual dance at Tammany Hall to the more refined air of the hotel ballroom.

There were also many physical force men of Clan na Gael in the county organizations, but as a secret oath-bound society their numbers were comparatively small. The militants remained in the background and managed to exercise their influence in more subtle ways. Rather than make overt statements in favor of the physical force movement, the militantly nationalist societies often chose instead to publicly support individuals who had been imprisoned in Ireland because of their revolutionary activities. In this manner they could unofficially identify with militant nationalism while continuing to back the Parliamentary moderates.

On the surface, the County Mayo Men's support for P. W. Nally, the imprisoned Irish Revolutionary Brotherhood Centre for Connaught, in the 1880s and early 1890s was a charitable action. But the long agitation for his release and the perpetuation of his memory after his death with annual observances satisfied a militant faction within the organization and kept the physical force option alive.[55] Similarly, Galway chose in 1905 to offer a testimonial to released prisoner Patrick Finnegan, an unrepentant militant, who had been released after a 20-year term.[56] Nevertheless, through the Irish Counties Athletic Union both societies unanimously endorsed Redmond and his party.[57]

County Tyrone Men in the late 1890s were said to have "a general lack of interest in the politics attending the Home Rule for Ireland program of the Irish Parliamentary Party." This feeling was certainly fortified in 1900 when Thomas Clarke, later to be one of the martyred leaders of the 1916 uprising, joined the association and served for a few years as an officer.[58] The County Roscommon Society had as a leading member and officer for more than 30 years, Thomas Rock, an associate of the old Fenian John Devoy. Rock was a founder and president of the Sinn Fein Society of New York and used his influence to gain small victories. Consequently, Roscommon donated money in 1904 to the Irish Republican Brotherhood monument in Calvary Cemetery without much opposition, even though it was clearly a project of the physical force movement.[59]

The Irish county societies could best identify with the more practical aspects of nationalism. It was for this reason that the land war was still occupying their attention in 1911 and 1912, when more than 10,000 families who had been evicted before the turn of the century had still not been reinstated on their farms. The Clare Association at one point refused all requests for charitable aid from the bishop of Killaloe because one of his priests held the land of an evicted tenant. In several instances the county association's direct intercession with Irish members of Parliament resulted in the restoration of longstanding claims of evicted tenants.[60]

The activities of the Irish county societies were clearly aimed at the Irish-born and toward the Old World. The future of their organizations, as most of the members saw it, was simply to be cast adrift with the ups and downs of immigration. There could be little hope for survival beyond the day when immigration stopped. Despite the forays into American and Irish politics, their organizations played a primarily social role and were designed to fill the void in the lives of those immigrants who felt the particular need to remain close to old country ways and old country people.

Epilogue

World War I had a dramatic effect on the Irish county organizations. Many of its members found their way into the American army as officers and enlisted men, particularly in the old Irish 69th Regiment, a unit that had traditionally recruited from its ranks. The Irish American weeklies in late 1917 and 1918 detailed the pathetic stories of the many who succumbed to war and disease.[61]

The cause of independence for Ireland and the establishment of an Irish Republic was quickly taken up by all the county organizations following the 1916 uprising in Ireland. Just as they had responded to local agricultural agitation in Ireland in the nineteenth century, the counties targeted relief efforts toward fund-raising for the Republican cause and for the families whose homes had been burned or destroyed during the guerrilla war. Leaders like Eamon de Valera came to them personally for help and quickly won their support. The Irish Civil War divided and destroyed some of the counties, and it was not until the 1930s that societies representing all 32 Irish counties would exist in New York.[62]

The cutoff of immigration during World War I, the depression years, and World War II forced the counties to rethink their membership appeals. Increasing numbers of American-born Irish found their way into the societies to the point where 40 percent of the membership were born outside of Ireland. Virtually all the county societies shelved the separate men's and women's organizations in favor of unified societies.[63]

Geographically, the old dependence on a Manhattan-based membership eroded as the Irish population spread in all directions. So great has been the change since then that some societies no longer hold their meetings inside the city limits. Membership has declined dramatically for most of the counties, although social events still have the same character of "reunions" and draw many more than just the members. Unless immigration from Ireland is cut off completely, the majority of county societies will probably continue in relative prosperity for many years to come.

John R. McKivigan and Thomas J. Robertson

CHAPTER 12

The Irish American Worker in Transition, 1877–1914

NEW YORK CITY AS A TEST CASE

FROM THE time of the Civil War to the early twentieth century, Irish Americans in the New York City labor movement evolved from unskilled and unorganized laborers into militant and radical opponents of the emerging industrial capitalist order and subsequently into the leaders of a conservative labor union bureaucracy. That metamorphosis is the subject of this chapter. The aspects of particular interest here are the role of Irish Americans in the unprecedented explosion of working-class political radicalism and trade union militancy in New York City in the 1870s and 1880s; the demographic, economic, cultural, and political trends that led to the decline of this radical activism during the quarter century after 1890; and the influence of these factors, along with internal developments in the labor movement, on the Irish workers' decision to adopt a more "business-oriented" approach to solving their problems.

As a consequence of the Great Famine and an overpopulated agrarian economy, a heavy stream of Irish refugees arrived in New York City during the 1840s and 1850s. Lacking the financial resources to establish themselves as farmers in this country, large numbers of Irish immigrants remained in New York to supply the human material for the city's rapid development as a manufacturing and transportation center in the early nineteenth century. Before the Civil War, Irish immigrants became the largest element in the city's unskilled labor pool, particularly in service and domestic jobs. The city's transportation industry, especially its docks, also depended heavily on the brawn of the Irish. Irish gains came despite resistance from American workers, particularly among the cartmen, who unsuccessfully attempted to maintain their control over jobs in their field by trying to fan nativist sentiment. At the same time, intense competition between the Irish and African Americans for employment in many unskilled trades produced considerable violence, culminating in five days of race rioting during the Civil War.[1]

By 1890, more than one-third of New York City's population were either Irish immigrants or their descendants. According to that year's U.S. Census, the population of New York City was approximately 1.5 million and included nearly 200,000 Irish-born and another 400,000 second-generation Irish. In addition, third- and even fourth-generation Irish Americans further swelled that total, creating what one Irish immigrant described as "a little Dublin."[2] By the end of

Laying street railway tracks at Broadway and 14th Street, c. 1891. What William Sampson observed in 1825 ("Is not this city prospering and growing by the labor of the poor Irish, who swell the capital of our rich proprietors by their hard and daily work?") was equally relevant more than half a century later as immigration from Ireland continued to keep pace with New York's physical expansion. Irish men benefited the most from municipal improvements projects, such as laying water and gas pipes, opening and lighting streets, excavating and filling land, and building bridges, tunnels, and transit facilities. Although the New York Irish were occupationally diverse by the turn of the century, "pick-and-shovel" work was often a new immigrant's first job in the city. (Drawing by Hughson Hawley. Museum of the City of New York. Gift of Colonel Thomas Crimmins.)

the nineteenth century, a small "lace curtain" middle class had emerged among the city's Irish. These professionals and small-scale entrepreneurs and construction contractors, together with Tammany Hall politicians and the bulk of the Roman Catholic clergy, eventually created a significant conservative force among New York City's Irish population.[3]

Despite the gains of some individuals, the large majority of the city's Irish remained in the working class well into the next century. In time, many Irish immigrants and their children acquired skills and began entering New York City's woodworking, metal, construction, and clothing trades, and the proportion of unskilled workers among the Irish declined after the Civil War. The arrival of additional immigrants throughout the late 1800s, however, resulted in a continuing Irish presence in unskilled fields into the twentieth century.[4]

These Irish workers ultimately played a key role in determining the outcome of competition between two rival, but far from distinct, forms of pro-labor activity within the late-nineteenth-century New York City labor movement. One sought to maintain the independence of workers in the face of industrialization through a re-creation of antebellum workingmen's organizations, which espoused worker cooperatives, eschewed strikes, and embraced third-party politics. This movement could trace its roots back to the Jacksonian era Workingmen's party and trades unions, if not all the way back to the Revolutionary era "Jack-and Tar" mobs.[5] The alternative to this reform ideology centered in the struggling trade union movement. Rather than attempting social reform, the trade unions bowed to the inevitability of the wage system and sought "immediate material improvements within the frame-work of existing institutions." The trade unions focused more on bread-and-butter issues of wages, hours, and working conditions.[6] For most workers, distinctions between these wings of the labor movement in terms of tactics and goals were far from clear in the 1870s and 1880s. The strong impress of Irish traditions and practices on all parts of the city's working class only added to the ambiguity and confusion within the labor movement.[7]

After the Civil War, the famine-era Irish, joined by their children and subsequent immigrants, began to play an important role in New York City's nascent labor movement. John McHugh headed the city's dockworkers' union. Joseph Wilkinson led an organization of journeymen tailors. Peter J. McGuire was the president of the powerful Brotherhood of Carpenters and Joiners. Some of these individuals had first spent time working in Britain's burgeoning industrial cities such as Manchester and Liverpool before migrating to the United States. There they had observed and sometimes participated in the birth of British trade union movement. Until well into the next century, Irish Americans dominated the leadership of most of the city's principal unions, outside those in the needle trades.[8]

In the 1860s and 1870s, Irish American labor leaders played a prominent role in the eight-hour day movement in the city. The fledgling unions tried to coordinate their campaign through early citywide trade assemblies, first the Workingmen's Union and later the Amalgamated Trades and Labor Union (ATLU). Among the leaders of these early labor councils were Thomas Masterson of the Shoemakers and Joseph Wilkinson and Robert Blissert, both tailors.[9] After the painters, plasters, and bricklayers had won the eight-hour day through strikes, an uncoordinated series of work stoppages by a wide range of unions occurred in spring 1872 to replicate that goal. Collective action by employers, however, thwarted the effort in most industries. Unsuccessful attempts to launch a labor party occurred periodically in the early 1870s. Locally run independent "workingmen's" candidates likewise fared poorly at the polls.[10]

The best known of the city's Irish American union leaders of the era was Peter J. McGuire. Son of an immigrant Irish department store porter on the Lower East Side of New York City, McGuire was apprenticed as a woodjoiner. He joined the International Workingmen's Association and helped launch the Social Democratic Party (later the Socialist Labor Party). A founder of the United Brotherhood of Carpenters and Joiners, McGuire became its first secretary in 1881. As the new union's principal executive officer, McGuire moved its headquarters to New York City, where he became active in the eight-hour-day movement. McGuire was one of the sponsors of the first Labor Day celebration in which marching unionists carried banners displaying Irish nationalist slogans. While espousing what he called a "Socialism of a Trades Union Kind," McGuire was active in creating the American Federation of Labor (AFL) in 1886 and remained one of its vice presidents until 1900.[11]

Competing with the trade unions to represent the city's workers was the Knights of Labor. The Knights denounced the wage labor system and advocated programs of education, land redistribution, legislative lobbying, and cooperative enterprise to replace it. In 1881 Terence V. Powderly of Scranton, Pennsylvania, rose to the Knights' top rank of grand master workman. Powderly strongly endorsed the Knights' cooperative and legislative programs but privately disapproved of confrontational tactics such as strikes. His Irish ancestry and active support for Irish causes helped make the Knights of Labor organization popular among the city's Irish American workers.[12]

Knights in New York City affiliated either in trade or mixed assemblies. Trade assemblies—such as the Progressive Painters, the Cooperative Shirtmakers, the Ale and Porter Brewers Association, the Salamander Association of Boiler and Pipe Covers, and the Amalgamated Carpenters—functioned in similar ways to trade unions. Most of the city's trade assemblies were headed by Irish American officers.[13] The city's mixed assemblies contained members from diverse occupations, including many middle-class reformers. The largest of these was District Assembly 49, which contained 400 local assemblies. This politically radical mixed assembly was headed by District Master Workman Thomas B. McGuire and supported by such Irish American officers as James Quinn, George E. Murray, William McNaire, and John Costello.[14] McGuire once bragged about the erudition displayed at his group's meetings. "If you could hear our members quoting Spencer, Mill, Ricardo, Walter, Marx, Laselles, Pruddon [sic] and other political economists, you would think you had struck a convention of teachers of the science which has enslaved us."[15]

By the 1880s the city had a number of pro-labor periodicals that gave sympathetic coverage to the activities of the Irish American working-class leaders. The most widely read of these papers was the New York *Irish World*, which carried the revealing subtitle *Industrial Liberator*. Edited by Irish American Patrick Ford, the *Irish World* endorsed such programs as temperance, western migration, and vocational education. Ford's editorials urged the fledgling labor movement to help the economically impoverished Irish immigrants improve themselves.[16]

Irish Americans of all classes were heavily influenced by the ebbs and peaks of the nationalist movement in their old homeland. The republican strivings of both the Fenians of the 1860s and the Clan na Gael of the 1870s received strong support from the city's burgeoning Irish community. A revival of nationalist protests in Ireland in the 1880s, centered on the land tenure issue and led by parliamentarian Charles Stewart Parnell, spurred the New York Irish to renewed activism.[17] During the spring and summer of 1880, in connection with Parnell's successful tour of the United States, branches of the Land League grew around the country. The Land League flourished in New York City, drawing on the city's large Irish American population and profiting from the support and influence of Tammany Hall, as well as several pro–Land League newspapers. Irish American workers in New York City created "Spread the Light Clubs" and Tenant Leagues, all in support of Land League issues.[18]

The Land League had a profound effect on Irish American labor in New York City. Influenced by the Land League's use of the boycott against Irish landlords, the city's Irish-dominated labor groups, for example, launched an extensive program of "labor boycotts" during the 1880s. Originally a tool of social control and ostracism in rural Ireland, the transplanted boycott in the United States attempted to serve the same purpose, but it was transformed from a social to an economic tactic as a result of the changing nature of work and the diversity of populations in industrializing America. Through boycotts aimed at economic disruption many Irish labor groups sought to obtain higher wages and better working conditions in a wide range of industries.[19]

The traditional roots of the boycott tactic were apparent in the Freighthandlers strike of 1882. Led by union president Jeremiah Murphy, a recent immigrant from Cork, the freighthandlers used the boycott to rein in union members who were breaking ranks and returning to work. Blacklists were created and circulars were printed and distributed giving the names of those not adhering to the strike. Strike leader Murphy declared that "every man upon it should be shunned like a leper."[20] By the end of the decade, however, the boycott could be applied in two different ways: "let alone" and "let severely alone."

According to Knights of Labor Secretary Patrick Doody, "let alone" was the economic tactic of not buying goods, while "let severely alone" is the traditional Irish definition of "almost driving and starving a man to death, driving him out of the world, extermination."[21]

While the use of the boycott expanded steadily in the mid-1880s, some Irish American labor groups also sought to enter the political arena. On January 30, 1882, a collection of trades unions and semiskilled and unskilled workingmen's associations held a mass meeting of more than 12,000 at Cooper's Institute to demonstrate support for Irish tenants and workingmen battling English landlordism. The success of the meeting caused the leadership of several participating unions to consider creating a worker's organization that would allow for a "concentrating [of] the working classes for their own natural protection, education, and development."[22] This idea for a workers organization became the Central Labor Union (CLU).

From this start, the CLU grew rapidly into a confederation of more than 200 trade unions and political reform groups. Most of the city's traditional craft unions, once united in the now defunct ATLU, immediately joined. Many Knights assemblies, sometimes under different names, were also represented in the CLU. According to one contemporary observer, nearly half of the CLU delegates were Knights of Labor and their sympathizers. Middle-class reformers and socialists also affiliated. Prominent in the creation and leadership of the CLU were Irish Americans such as James McMackin and John Devitt, members of the Painter's Union, Frank Ferrell of "the Eccentric Engineers," Thomas Ford of the Brass Workers, and Patrick Doody, secretary of the Knights' District Assembly 49.[23]

The most influential of the CLU's Irish American leaders was Robert Blissert, a journeyman tailor. Born to Irish parents in Lancashire in 1843, Blissert migrated to the United States in 1867 after being blacklisted as a striker in Britain. He worked for James W. Bell's tailoring firm and became active in the International Workingmen's Association and the Amalgamated Trades and Labor Union in the 1870s. Already a strong believer in a politicized union movement, Blissert strove to combine the supporters of Irish nationalism and American labor. In particular, he championed the boycott tactic, telling one mass meeting, "I bless Ireland for St. Boycott, and we want those who try to crush it to know that it is but a baby as yet, but if they understood what a stalwart mother and father it has, they would respect it."[24]

The unprecedented political militancy of Irish American labor threatened traditional voting alignments in the city. Long a bastion of "machine politics," New York City's "bosses" had facilitated the rapid and often illegal naturalization of tens of thousands of Irish immigrant voters in the 1850s and 1860s.[25] In return for their rapid incorporation into the city's political community, Irish American voters traditionally supported the Democratic party. Irish-dominated wards in Lower and Midtown Manhattan gave the Democrats an average of two-thirds of their votes in the 1870s and 1880s. With their rapidly expanding numbers, the Irish began to play increasingly influential roles inside the party's Tammany Hall political machine after the Civil War, culminating in the selection of "Honest John" Kelly as Tammany leader in 1872. In 1880 Tammany elected the city's first Irish-born Roman Catholic mayor, William R. Grace.[26]

Irish American political leaders were in general more conservative than their working-class counterparts on labor, fiscal, and social issues. In large part, this was due to the needs of the political "machine" to build a broadly based electoral coalition and placate the city's business community. Ironically, Tammany Hall had managed its recovery of political dominance after the scandals of the Tweed Ring era in the early 1870s by demonstrating to the city's bankers, lawyers, and businessmen that it could run local government on a tight budget.[27]

The CLU soon discovered how hard it was to challenge Tammany Hall for the loyalty of the Irish American electorate. Many Irish Americans backed the mayoral candidacy of John W. Franklin, president of the Bricklayers' Union, sponsored by the Central Labor Union in 1882, but Franklin and the other CLU-backed candidates were crushed at the polls. The soundness of the defeat caused the CLU, and most member unions, to forsake politics and concentrate on other avenues of assisting the workers of New York City.[28]

While frustrated in the political arena, labor groups experienced increasing success in economic disputes through boycotts in such trades as hatmaking, shoemaking, typesetting, brewing, and baking industries. Many non-Irish American labor groups in New York City were also now using the boycott. There were approximately 165 boycotts in New York City in 1886. The widespread, and often effective, use of the boycott was a concern of businessmen and government officials alike. The Bureau of Labor Statistics for New York offered an explanation for the proliferating use of the boycott: "the strike is negotiation, the boycott is action."[29]

The use of the boycott continued in force in New York City until labor encountered a series of arrests and hostile court decisions in 1886. Through questionable interpretation of the New York Penal Code, boycotters and labor leaders were often arrested for a variety of crimes, most commonly conspiracy, coercion, and extortion. Often opposed to organized labor, the judge usually found in favor of the prosecution.[30] The legal setbacks that boycotting Irish American workers encountered in New York City in 1886 helped set the stage for an unprecedented political rebellion. That year, Irish American voters were conspicuous in Henry George's mayoral campaign.

Henry George's support of the Irish Land League and other Irish causes provided strong backing for his candidacy in many of the Irish communities of New York City. While George's theories received varying degrees of acceptance in this country, his work on land reform was eagerly embraced by many in Ireland, most notably Irish agrarian reformer Michael Davitt. George's efforts on behalf of the Irish peasantry and the compatibility of his "single-tax" platform with the "producer's ideology" of the Irish Americans helped break down dogged Irish loyalty to the Democrats.[31]

In early 1886 George had just returned from a very successful lecture tour of Great Britain, which was widely chronicled in the Irish American press in and around New York. George's *Progress and Poverty* was not only selling well in the United States but was extremely popular in Great Britain and Europe. Selected by the CLU-organized "Independent Labor Party of New York and vicinity," George became the candidate of a loose coalition of more than 150 labor and social organizations.[32]

The Independent Labor party (ILP) was a collection of strange bedfellows. The Socialist Labor party was well represented in the ILP, as were members of the Knights of Labor and the fledgling American Federation of Labor. The SLP, while not holding prominent positions in the leadership of the CLU, was extremely influential in urging the creation of the ILP and pursuing political action.[33]

The developing breadth of the George coalition in the 1886 election disturbed the power brokers of Tammany, while the radical platform of the CLU irritated the leadership of the New York Catholic archdiocese. On October 25, just one week before the election, Tammany representative Joseph J. O'Donohue wrote to Monsignor Thomas S. Preston, vicar-general of the New York diocese and Tammany supporter, about a "rumor" that the church was backing Henry George. Preston replied, "I can state with confidence that the majority of the Catholic clergy in this city are opposed to the candidacy of Mr. George. . . . His principles, logically carried out, would prove the ruin of the working-men he professes to befriend."[34]

This exchange of letters between O'Donohue and Preston was a carefully orchestrated campaign ploy. Tammany knew the Irish-controlled hierarchy of the New York diocese was not supporting George, but a public exchange of the letters published in the newspapers and printed on fliers distributed in the Irish neighborhoods was undertaken to alert the Irish community that a vote for George would be against the wishes of the church. The traditionally pro-Democratic *Irish-American* echoed the religious tone of the attack on George and condemned his "imaginative visions of Socialistic equality that have been used by such charlatans to dazzle the understanding of mankind ever since the day . . . [of] the Serpent in the Garden of Eden."[35]

The church's attacks on George had mixed results in the Irish American community. When the Catholic Church and Tammany initiated rumors that Terrance Powderly, a strong, behind-the-scenes backer of the George candidacy, actually opposed George, the grand master workman increased his public efforts to rally the Knights behind the campaign.[36] In contrast, Ford's *Irish World* buckled to the combined conservative pressure and gave George only half-hearted support and thereafter never ventured beyond mild liberal positions on economic questions.[37]

No doubt George was hurt by the combined opposition of the church and
Tammany, but he nonetheless polled some impressive vote totals in Irish
districts. Official totals showed George with 68,000 votes, finishing second to
Tammany-backed Abram Hewitt, who claimed 90,000 ballots, yet ahead of
Republican candidate Theodore Roosevelt at 60,000 votes.[38] Careful analysis of
the Irish American voting in this election, however, reveals that the ILP had cut
strongly into Tammany's support in working-class Irish neighborhoods, especially among those skilled workers who were heavily involved in the labor
unrest earlier in the decade.[39]

Immediately following the election, the campaign's leadership organized a
central committee to continue the issues of the campaign and take full advantage of the success of the George candidacy. This committee consisted of John
McMackin, a member of the Knights of Labor and George's campaign manager;
Father Edward McGlynn, a self-proclaimed radical Roman Catholic priest; and
James Redpath, a journalist whose reports on the boycott tactics of the Irish had
been widely reprinted in the city. These three men directed the development of
a new political party: the United Labor party (ULP).[40]

Created without the consultation of the CLU or other groups involved in the
George campaign, the ULP suffered immediately from internal division. As the
controlling George faction entrenched deeper into a myopic and self-indulgent
vision of single-tax and land reform, the cohesion of the ILP evident during the
campaign gave way. Bickering and factionalism replaced idealism. As the
coalition slowly collapsed, the ULP became vulnerable to outside attacks.[41]

The conservative archbishop of the city, Michael A. Corrigan, proved an implacable foe of the ULP. Corrigan began a letter-writing campaign in the local
newspapers that warned Catholics that George's stand on property rights contra-
vened Catholic doctrine. He characterized George's position as a radical plan to
seize all land and establish communal ownership. On November 21, 1886, Corrigan
issued a letter that "defended private property in the land as being in accordance
with God's laws and economic necessities." While not mentioning Henry George
by name, Corrigan warned readers "to be zealously on your guard against certain
unsound principles and theories which assail the rights of property."[42]

George responded vigorously and accused the Catholic Church of being a
Tammany tool. This quarrel certainly damaged the ULP among some Irish
Catholics, but before its impact was apparent the group unraveled in quarrels
first between George's middle-class followers and the socialists and then the
George faction and the trade unions. George and his single-tax proponents
moved to create the platform of the ULP with his own economic planks. George
alienated the SLP by stating that "state socialism, with its childish notions of
making all capital the common property of the state . . . is an exotic, born of
European conditions that cannot flourish on American soil."[43] Seeking total
control over the ULP, the George faction ousted the socialists from the party by
disallowing dual membership in political organizations.

By the fall of 1887, with the expulsion of the SLP and the growing ambivalence of many labor groups to the direction of the new party, the ULP was a shell of what it had been the year before. The decline in support for the ULP was evident during the New York State elections of 1887 in which George, under the ULP banner, ran for secretary of state but received just 72,000 votes. In 1888, dismayed by the poor election results and frustrated with the inability to promote his economic plans through working-class organizations, George bolted the ULP for the more middle-class Democratic Party and became an ardent backer of Grover Cleveland's presidential reelection bid.[44]

When George left the ULP, what remained of it fell into the hands of Father Edward McGlynn, the son of Irish-immigrant parents and pastor of St. Stephen's, the largest Catholic parish in the city. McGlynn launched the Anti-Poverty Society, which attracted hearty support from both his working-class Irish parishioners and Protestant middle-class reformers. Appalled by what he perceived as McGlynn's radical views and at the urging of Tammany leaders, Corrigan first removed McGlynn from his parish and then excommunicated him for his unswerving support for labor causes. Undaunted, McGlynn and his Anti-Poverty Society continued to battle for causes such as child labor and antimonopoly laws. Many local Irish labor leaders rallied to McGlynn's side and denounced his excommunication. To quash support for McGlynn among the Catholic clergy and laity, Corrigan declared attendance at Anti-Poverty Society meetings sinful.[45] The strong condemnation of McGlynn from New York City's Catholic hierarchy eventually caused some labor leaders such as Powderly of the Knights to drop their support for the defrocked priest rather than risk the Knights' newly established rapprochement with the Roman Catholic Church. In retaliation, McGlynn publicly denounced Powderly's active courting of Roman Catholic prelates, including Pope Leo XIII. Pro-Knights newspaper editor John Swinton detested McGlynn, whom he declared "has done more mischief to the cause of labor by hurling the religious firebrand into Labor's camp than has been done by all of the attacks of its capitalist enemies."[46] As a result of the combined attacks of the church and the Knights, attendance rapidly declined at Anti-Poverty Society meetings. Although the pope rescinded McGlynn's excommunication in late 1892, Corrigan supplied the *coup de grace* to the still contentious priest's influence upon the Irish American working class by transferring him to a parish in upstate New York in 1894.[47]

At the same time the ULP disintegrated, the Knights of Labor in New York City began a slow but steady decline. The highly publicized defeat of strikes by western Knights' locals in 1886 and antiradical hysteria produced by the Chicago Haymarket Square bombing the same year hurt the Knights nationwide. Locally, the defeat of strikes by the city's longshoremen in 1887 and by Brooklyn trolley operators in 1895 cost the Knights several thousand predominantly Irish members. There was also growing competition and antagonism between the Knights' trade assemblies and trade unions affiliated with the new

AFL. Locals of P. J. McGuire's carpenters and Samuel Gomper's cigarmakers, in particular, angrily charged that Knights scabbed against their strikes and therefore retaliated in kind. Likewise, both groups generally ignored boycotts called by the other. Defections of individual Knights and entire trades assemblies ran at a high rate in the late 1880s. For example, Harry J. Skeffington led his shoemaker assemblies from the Knights into the Boot and Shoe Workers' International Union (AFL) in 1889. A mass rally of New York City area Knights at Cooper Union in July 1890, addressed by Powderly and T. B. McGuire, failed to halt the steady flow.[48] Although appeals to Irish American sympathies remained a staple of Knights' propaganda, the group's membership in the city, as across the nation, dwindled in the 1890s. The CLU, changing its name to the Central Federated Union of New York City in 1899, even became an AFL regional affiliate. Embarrassing squabbles between Knights' District Assembly 49 and national leaders in 1895 over entering into political alliances with the socialists ended what remained of the Knights' effectiveness in the city.[49]

In the 1890s support among Irish American workers for radical political projects slowly ebbed. The fracturing of the ULP and the decline of the Knights of Labor created a vacuum in radical Irish American political participation. At the same time, a number of significant demographic, economic, social, and political trends helped move Irish American workers in a more conservative direction.

Starting in the 1880s, heavy waves of immigration from southern and eastern Europe flooded New York, transforming forever the face of the city's working class. By 1900 more than two-thirds of New York's newcomers were from Italy, Greece, Russia, Poland, and the Balkans.[50]

Frequently overlooked in this mammoth wave of arrivals from predominantly southern and eastern Europe were significant members of Irish women and men. After 1880 most Irish immigrants were from the island's westernmost counties. Overpopulation and a renewal of famine forced tens of thousands from these heavily agricultural counties. Without any urban experience or skills, this later generation of Irish immigrants were forced into competition with the "New Immigrants" for the declining number of unskilled laborers' jobs.[51]

The New Immigrants immediately entered into economic competition with the Irish by displacing the Irish from many unskilled occupations. One exception was the area of domestic jobs, where many of the newly arrived Irish American women worked but members of most other ethnic groups avoided. The total number of domestic jobs in the city, however, went into decline after the turn of the century.[52]

In the skilled trades, the Irish were more successful in defending themselves from competition from the newer immigrants. In the city's building trades, such as the plumbers and the masons, Irish-dominated unions adopted nepotistic membership requirements that kept out the new arrivals. Irishmen in these unions believed the resultant high group solidarity among workers in these trade unions was essential in order to prevent scabbing. Similarly, the Irish used their political connections to entrench themselves in both skilled and unskilled city government jobs for policemen, firefighters, rapid transit workers, and school teachers, even before those workers had their unions recognized.[53]

By 1900 significant numbers of the city's Irish had moved up into the ranks of professionals and entrepreneurs, especially contractors in the building trades. This economic mobility even included former working-class leaders such as Robert Blissert, who opened his own tailor shop in the mid-1880s and soon after disappeared from labor rallies. The expansion of certain industries in the city, especially textiles and light manufacturing, allowed thousands of male Irish Americans to move into the lower rungs of management and middle-class respectability. Their knowledge of the English language and their political connections assisted their rise into foremen and superintendent positions as well as into white-collar clerical jobs. Likewise, thousands of second and subsequent generations of Irish American women found employment in such professions as teaching, nursing, and clerical work. Some observers claim that New York's Irish had reached "class-structure parity" with the Anglo-Saxons by the early twentieth century.[54]

As a consequence of this economic mobility, a large majority of Irish Americans moved northward in the city or to Long Island, leaving their original neighborhoods in Lower Manhattan to the more recently arrived immigrant groups. The remaining Irish American working-class enclaves, such as Hell's Kitchen, however, were regarded as among the city's poorest and roughest in the early twentieth century. Contemporary studies found health conditions among the Irish in these latter neighborhoods as bad as any of the New Immigrant groups, with crime and alcoholism rates often considerably worse. Because this new wave of Irish immigrants lagged behind their earlier-arriving countrymen, the Irish were among the most economically and occupationally diverse ethnic group in New York City in the early twentieth century.[55] In addition to these demographic and economic trends, local political forces guided Irish American workers back from earlier flirtations with radicalism and toward the Democratic Party.[56] After the defeat of Henry George, a few "liberal" Irish leaders such as Patrick Ford tried vainly to attract Irish Catholics into the Republican camp. The volatile issue of enforcing the Sunday closing of saloons demanded by the rural-dominated state Republican Party, however, severely handicapped that party's candidates in the city from the 1880s on. Likewise, the prominent role of nativist organizations such as the American Protective Association in backing the Republicans disinclined most Irish Americans from the party of Lincoln.[57]

In 1899 the city's principal trade unions briefly revived the Independent Labor Party as a vehicle to protest against Tammany Hall's lax enforcement of wage and hour laws on public works projects. The ILP's platform favored such programs as municipal ownership of public utilities, improved public education, enforcement of eight-hour-day laws, and a ban on child labor and tenement sweatshops. Acknowledging Tammany's strength, the ILP conducted negotiations with the Republican party that ultimately produced a "Fusion" ticket. While Republicans monopolized most places on the ticket, William O'Brien of the city building trades council received the Fusion nomination for sheriff. Dissension broke out in labor's ranks, however, because the Fusion ticket nominated conservative Republicans to run against two Tammany-backed state assembly incumbents who were active trade unionists. Although O'Brien led the Fusion ticket with almost 40 percent of the votes, Tammany triumphed in all the races because working-class districts continued to vote Democratic.[58]

The most serious challenge to the Irish American–Tammany Hall alliance came in 1905 when William Randolph Hearst campaigned on a platform championing public ownership of the city's utilities as the way to break the corrupt influence of the franchise holders in politics. Branding his Tammany opponent George B. McClellan an Anglophile, Hearst ran even with Tammany in Irish wards and lost by the narrowest of margins.[59]

Tammany leaders heeded these warnings. By 1910 the Irish proportion of New York's population had fallen to only 15 percent, but they controlled all but a handful of the city's Democratic Party district chairmanships and nearly half of the party's ballot positions for local offices. The latter generation of Irish bosses, especially Richard Croker and Charles Francis Murphy, discarded the fiscal restraint of the Kelly era and rapidly expanded the city's public payroll. As a consequence, the public sector employed a full one-third of first-, second-, and third-generation Irish Americans in 1930 compared with just 6 percent in 1900. This patronage helped produce a heavy concentration of Irish in jobs on the fire and police departments and in municipally owned subways, streetcars, waterworks, and port facilities. Many of the city's Irish middle class worked on the public payroll, especially in the public schools, and thousands of others labored in construction jobs tied to city expenditures. For second-generation Irish American women, jobs as schoolteachers were the most sought-after career. Such patronage policies would help to bind the Irish working class and much of the middle class to Tammany Hall for another generation.[60]

At the turn of the century, Tammany even managed to bring entire labor unions inside its organization. In 1901, pro-Democratic labor leaders affiliated their organizations with the Workingmen's Political League of New York City, which opponents condemned as a tool of Tammany. Likewise, individual Irish American labor leaders, such as Thomas M. Farley, the walking delegate of the cement-layers' union, became influential Democratic politicians. The son of immigrant parents, Farley was a lifelong resident of the Yorkville neighborhood who rose through political ranks to the Office of Sheriff before being brought down for corruption.[61] So both individually and organizationally, Irish American labor in New York City had largely become an arm of the Democratic Party by the twentieth century.

This alliance paid further dividends in the next few decades. The Democrats at both the city and state level began to initiate a wide range of "progressive" legislation beneficial to labor. Although intraparty fighting between Tammany and upstate Democrats delayed passage of some measures, the state legislature enacted workers' compensation, health insurance, child labor controls, and other legislation long desired by the city's unions. As a modern urban "liberal" character took shape, links between the Democrats and labor further solidified.[62]

Meanwhile, the Roman Catholic Church, dominated by Irish American prelates, became more uniformly arraigned against the more radical forms of labor protest after the 1880s. While in other parts of the nation some Catholic prelates such as James Cardinal Gibbons supported workingmen's movements, most notably the Knights of Labor, Archbishop Corrigan and his successor, John Farley, remained among the American church's leading conservatives on economic issues in the American Catholic hierarchy. The archdiocese's newspaper, the *New York Catholic Review*, advocated compulsory arbitration of labor disputes as a means of avoiding violent and potentially revolutionary strikes. The pro-Tammany *Irish-American* declared strikes "the illegitimate fruit of greed and inhumanity" on the part of both labor and management.[63] Even relatively liberal Catholic voices, such as Patrick Ford, abandoned public support for trade union tactics, including strikes, and championed progressive reformism as the best bulwark against socialism.[64]

After the issuance of Pope Leo XIII's encyclical *Rerum Novarum* in 1891, which endorsed moderate social reform programs, the Catholic hierarchy's relations warmed with the heavily Irish leadership of the city's AFL-affiliated trade unions. Church leaders observed that most of these union leaders shared their strong antisocialist beliefs and sought ways to assist them in the labor movement. The New York archdiocese sponsored antisocialist lecture series and other propaganda aimed at workingmen. Likewise, the heavily Irish American Catholic lay fraternity Knights of Columbus adopted an antisocialist and superpatriotic propaganda stance. New York City Irish American labor leaders also were represented among the activists in the Militia of Christ for Social Service (later renamed the Social Service Commission), an antisocialist labor group organized by Father Peter Deitz.[65] The hold of the Catholic Church on the heavily Irish trade union leadership led the *International Socialist Review* to charge that the church was virtually "controlling the AFL."[66]

In contrast to past practice, Irish nationalism offered no radical counterbalance to the church's conservatism within the Irish American community. The Irish nationalist cause was badly disrupted in the late 1880s and the 1890s by disputes over adopting home rule rather than independence as its principal objective. Charles Parnell's control of the movement had been shaken by a sex scandal and then ended by his premature death in 1891. A badly factionalized movement dissipated much of its previous energy.[67] A revival of interest in the

Irish nationalist cause following the Boer War of 1899 proved far more conservative in its influence on the city's working class than the Land League movement of the 1880s. The movement was promoted strongly by editors such as Patrick Ford of the *Irish World* and John Devoy of his new *Gaelic American*, and New York City became the headquarters for its principal organizations, the United Irish League of America and a revived Clan na Gael. The movement's intention to unite all Irish Americans on behalf of their homeland, however, made it avoid any hint of radicalism that could alienate the influential clergy or middle class. Such preoccupation with political events in the Old Country proved a constant drain of attention and energy away from problems facing Irish American workers.[68]

By the turn of the century such conservative trends had begun moving Irish American workers noticeably away from their earlier radicalism. Tension among old and "New" immigrant groups, modest economic advancement by some workers, ties to Tammany Hall, the influence of the Roman Catholic Church, and intense rivalry among labor organizations combined to make the Irish Americans distance themselves from labor radicalism. Studies of voting patterns in the city's working-class districts reveal that the Irish supplied little support for socialist candidates. In fact, one scholar has labeled the Irish as the "missing factor" in the socialist movement in New York City at this time. Despite these conservative influences, the radical strain did not disappear completely among Irish American laborers in the city. A significant minority of Irish American working-class leaders would strive to keep alive militant labor traditions into the twentieth century.[69]

During the 1890s, the Socialist Labor party, now under the leadership of former Columbia professor and ex-George-backer, Daniel DeLeon, moved slowly away from direct political action and sought change through trade unionism.[70] In New York City, the SLP's plan was to "bore from within" after taking control of Knights' District Assembly 49. Although at this time the SLP consisted predominantly of Germans and east European Jews, the party was successful in gaining control of District Assembly 49 through the work of "a jovial, ruddy-cheeked Irishman" named Patrick Murphy. Murphy was the secretary of District Assembly 49, as well as a member of the SLP and an ardent supporter of DeLeon. The SLP's success with District Assembly 49, however, was short lived. A concerted effort on the part of the National Executive Board of the Knights of Labor ousted Murphy, DeLeon, and the socialists in District Assembly 49 in 1895, after a two-year struggle.[71] Over the next several years, the SLP engaged in countless conflicts with rival socialist and labor organizations and slowly disintegrated from what one historian described as "endemic intrigue and fratricide."[72]

The Socialist Party of America, founded in 1901 and led by Eugene V. Debs, attempted to court the New York City Irish in the first two decades on the twentieth century. Irish American candidates, such as typographical union leader Edward Cassiday, frequently appeared on local Socialist tickets.[73] A recently arrived immigrant, James Connolly organized the Irish Socialist Federation (ISF) and edited its newspaper, the *Harp*, in New York City.[74] Editorials in the *Harp* denounced the craft unionism of the American Federation of Labor and warmly praised the protoindustrial unionism of the Industrial Workers of the World.[75] The *Harp* also defended radical political activists from the accusations of atheism by the Catholic clergy, declaring that "it is not Socialism but Capitalism that is opposed to religion; Capitalism is social cannibalism, the devouring of man by man."[76] The sharp rhetoric notwithstanding, the *Harp* failed to secure a significant circulation, and membership in the ISF remained small.[77]

Another exception to the growing conservative trend was Leonora O'Reilly. Originally a Knight, O'Reilly became an active member of the United Garment Workers and later an organizer for the New York Women's Trade Union League. In the first decade of the twentieth century, O'Reilly helped lead successful strikes and negotiate contracts for female laundry workers, hat trimmers, and garment workers. Having quit the Catholic Church at an early age, O'Reilly proved immune to its blandishments against reformist-brand socialism. She campaigned actively for socialist candidates as well as for women's suffrage.[78]

Despite the efforts of key individuals, the Socialist Party and other alternative organizations in New York City failed to break the hold of Tammany Hall on the Irish American vote. As already noted, such factors as political patronage and Catholic propaganda helped turn the Irish against the socialists. Factors inside the labor movement also contributed to this outcome. Unlike most European socialist parties of the period, Debs's Socialist Party of America lacked a strong base in the trade unions. However, the party in New York City did develop a following among union members. Most of these pro-socialist unions, however, lay outside the AFL, such as the Amalgamated Clothing Workers. Their membership also came largely from among Jewish immigrant workers. In several cases, these unions competed with AFL unions in the same trade. These jurisdictional disputes pushed Irish American workers even farther from the socialists.[79]

The Industrial Workers of the World (IWW) likewise won little support from the city's Irish.[80] The Wobblies did organize and assist in several strikes of the New York hotel and restaurant workers between 1905 and 1913. The workers' desire for bread-and-butter gains, however, and lack of trade union background overshadowed the Wobblies' desire for protracted class struggle. After a flurry of activity and the creation of the short-lived Hotel Workers Industrial Union in 1912, each of the three strikes crumbled without creating any permanent radical organization. There were also IWW-supported strikes in the shoe industry in Brooklyn in 1910–11, but these strikes were also ultimately beaten when President John F. Tobin of the AFL's Boot and Shoe Workers' Union ordered affiliated unions to cease all forms of support to the strikers.[81] It seems that by the first decades of the twentieth century the militancy and radicalism engendered by the IWW found little quarter among the increasingly conservative Irish American workers of New York City.[82]

Despite some significant exceptions, the majority of Irish American workers and their leaders in New York City were moving in a more conservative direction. Irish Americans played a leading role in guiding the New York City labor movement by the beginning of this century into forms immediately recognizable today: frequently authoritarian, occasionally corrupt, customarily nepotistic, and almost invariably wedded to the Democratic Party.

Nationwide, by the early twentieth century the Irish had risen to the top of many of the international unions and the executive board of the American Federation of Labor. Irish Americans from New York City, first Peter J. McGuire and then Frank Duffy of the Carpenters and Joseph A. Mullaney of the Asbestos Workers, headed their internationals in the early twentieth century. In New York City, the Irish dominated the Central Federated Union of New York City (CFU) and most of its member unions. In the first two decades of the twentieth century John Kennedy headed the city's Brotherhood of Butcher Workmen; William D. Mahon headed the Amalgamated Association of Street Railway Employees, and Timothy Healy presided over the International Brotherhood of Stationery Firemen. What makes this trend even more significant was that the Irish dominance of union leadership came at a time when the Irish formed a declining minority of the working class, both nationally and in the city.[83]

The decline of the ethnic bond between the leadership and rank-and-file in many unions would have several important ramifications for the development of the city's labor movement. While well-practiced political skills and, in many cases, the ability to deliver tangible gains to their membership helped the Irish union leaders retain their posts, sometimes for decades, less creditable factors also played a role. Challenges for union leadership from both socialists and the New Immigrant rank-and-file members led the Irish officers of such unions as the Asbestos Workers to adopt election rules that made them practically invincible.[84]

Entrenchment in office offered potentially great rewards to city labor leaders. In the building trades, Irish union leaders such as Frank Duffy of the Carpenters and Thomas A. Murray of the Bricklayers helped erect jurisdictional rules that bred corruption in the construction industry. For example, the policy of giving the business agents the power to call strikes enabled union leaders in the building trades to extort graft from contractors eager to finish projects. At the same time, union officials often pushed through increases that doubled or tripled their salaries.[85]

One of the few changes in union leadership symbolized the new attitudes in the city's labor movement. In 1901 Frank Duffy ousted McGuire as secretary-general of the United Brotherhood of Carpenters and Joiners of America. Duffy quickly moved that union in a more conventional direction away from

McGuire's moderate brand of "trades union socialism."[86] Duffy broke an earlier agreement by McGuire with the Amalgamated Woodworkers International Union not to contest their organization and representation of "Joiners," (that is, cabinetmakers). This was typical of Duffy's aggressiveness in organizing and resulted in hundreds of jurisdictional strikes and authorized "scabbing" that weakened all of the city's building trades in the early decades of the century. With some justification, critics charged that Carpenters' officials often called these strikes to extort money from contractors.[87]

Another consequence of demographic factors in shaping the city's unions was the defensive posture that most Irish-led unions adopted toward the New Immigrants and racial minorities in their membership policies. The CFU and many local Irish American labor leaders supported the AFL's lobbying for more restrictive immigration policies toward the southern and eastern Europeans.[88] Some Irish-led union locals, such as those of the shoe workers, painters and paperhangers, plumbers and gas fitters, and hotel and restaurant employees either adopted nativist tests into their membership rules or raised initiation fees to high levels to keep out most New Immigrants and blacks.[89]

The most significant local example of this trend was the troubled relations between the city's Irish-led trades unions and those affiliated with the United Hebrew Trades (UHT) at the start of the century. Although founded in 1887, the UHT only became a significant labor force after successful strikes in the garment industry in 1910.[90] The Irish presence in the clothing trades had been in decline since the 1870s, when they had composed a significant minority of the members of the Knights' Gotham City Cutters locals. By the end of the century, the remaining Irish American tailors and cutters were found in locals of the AFL's United Garment Workers of America (UGWA), especially among its officers. The older craft unions of skilled garment workers were overwhelmed by the simultaneous arrival of the heavy wave of eastern European tailors and new machinery and labor practices that undercut the wages and status of workers in the industry. As the UGWA faltered, the UHT unions succeeded by enthusiastically organizing the New Immigrant workers across traditional craft lines throughout the garment industry.[91]

It was a combination of ethnic tensions and disputes between craft versus industrial unionism, therefore, that moved the Irish leaders of the CFU and even Gompers of the AFL to reject the predominantly Jewish Amalgamated Clothing Workers as a "dual union" to the AFL-affiliated UGWA. Despite the UHT's efforts to claim neutrality in the disputes between rival unions in the men's garment industry, the AFL ordered its affiliates to quit the group. The UHT shrank to insignificance, but the ACWU survived, permitting counterproductive dual unionism to persist in the men's garment industry. Although the AFL and CFU admitted the heavily Jewish and eastern European International Ladies Garment Workers Union, resentment in the CFU and the AFL was frequently voiced over its members' leftist political sympathies. The struggles with the

UHT unions reinforced the city's Irish trade union leaders' hostility toward the New Immigrants and industrial unionism.[92]

A final sign of the Irish impact on the city's trade unionism was labor's close alliance with Tammany Hall and through it with the national Democratic party. Through patronage policies, Tammany's Irish leaders granted their working-class countrymen and the labor movement a preferential place in what one historian has dubbed the city's "welfare democracy." Pro-union policies enacted during World War I by Woodrow Wilson's Democratic administration persuaded the cautious leaders of the AFL, as well as of the CFU, to endorse the Democrats in 1920. The post–World War I wave of antiradicalism also initiated by the Wilson administration received the endorsement of the city's Irish trade union leaders, who voiced pleasure at the harassment and even deportation of rivals for working-class leadership, especially those in the IWW and the UHT. Although the war temporarily increased support for Debs's party among some ethnic groups, the city's Irish continued to boycott the socialists and vote Democratic. As a result, the socialist movement declined after 1920, and the city's predominantly Irish labor leaders made their unions the dependable junior partners of Tammany and the Democratic Party.[93]

The gradual evolution in the character of the working-class Irish in the late nineteenth and early twentieth centuries roughly paralleled similar developments among their compatriots in other parts of the United States. Even in regions such as the West Coast, where Irish Americans experienced greater economic mobility, the general trend of the group's disproportionately heavy representation in leadership of the labor movement prevailed. While imported tactics such as the boycott were less common than in New York City, Irish American workers in other parts of the United States also displayed significant community solidarity in support of labor efforts to redress the abuses of late-nineteenth-century industrial capitalism. Evidence of the strong connection between revived enthusiasm for Irish nationalism and working-class activism in the 1870s and 1880s similar to that in New York City occurred in several other communities. In time, however, the trend toward growing conservatism that was so noticeable in New York became visible elsewhere among the Irish immigrants and their descendants. Although the New England Irish trailed other regions in upward mobility, even there the growth of a middle class tempered radicalism within their group. Likewise, while in some cities Catholic prelates were more supportive of the trade union movement than those of New York City, nationwide almost all members of the church hierarchy opposed socialism and conducted an apparently effective antisocialist crusade among the Irish and other Catholic groups. Finally, although Irishmen in some cities never achieved Tammany's near total control of local politics, Irish workers in most American cities eschewed independent parties or socialism and aligned themselves with the Democratic Party, just as they did in New York. Despite allowance for numerous local variations, the growing conservatism of Irish

American workers in New York City at the turn of the century appears part of a national trend.[94]

Although the above trends helped to elevate large numbers of working-class Irish Americans, they often had a long-term detrimental impact on the development of the city's labor movement. The undemocratic structure and corrupt practices that characterized some of their unions proved a ready weapon for organized labor's enemies to attack it. In order to reduce competition from new workers, the Irish American labor leaders instituted restrictive membership policies. This strategy left unions vulnerable to later advances in technology that undercut the bargaining position of organized skilled workers in many industries. At the same time, these exclusionary policies significantly contributed to the stratification of the city's labor market, which left the unorganized majority of workers more exposed to exploitation. The firm alliance of city unions and Tammany Hall helped isolate radical political movements from the working class, while permitting Democratic politicians to treat labor as a captive special interest. Although the visible influence of Irish Americans in most New York City labor unions has long disappeared, the impress of the experiences of their ancestors of a century ago can still be discerned.

David Brundage

CHAPTER 13

"In Time of Peace, Prepare for War"

KEY THEMES IN THE SOCIAL THOUGHT OF

NEW YORK'S IRISH NATIONALISTS, 1890–1916

From THE Young Ireland movement of the 1840s to the founding of the Irish Free State in the 1920s, Irish immigrants in the United States provided vital assistance to the cause of Irish nationalism. At two points in its history, Irish nationalism became a genuine mass movement in this country. In the early 1880s branches of the American Land League sprang up in towns and cities across America to provide support for the agrarian reform and home rule movements in Ireland. By 1881 the Land League had organized more than 1,500 branches around the country and had raised more than half a million dollars, drawing especially heavy support from the Irish American working class. Between 1916 and 1921 Irish nationalism again became a mass movement. The mobilization of the immigrant community hit its peak in the aftermath of World War I, when the American Association for the Recognition of the Irish Republic claimed 700,000 members and when Irish Americans raised more than $10 million for the independence movement in their homeland. Here were classic examples of what Ernest Gellner calls "diaspora nationalism," the phenomenon of nationalist enthusiasm among a people living outside the borders of their relevant nation state.[1]

Between these two eras of nationalist upheaval, however, the situation was entirely different. In the years from 1890 to 1916, Irish American nationalists were few in number, a small cadre of activists and propagandists who struggled to follow their movement's dictum, "in time of peace, prepare for war." Yet a study of the movement in these years, especially one focused on the social thought of its leaders, is important for two reasons. First, it can help us to assess the ideological legacy left by the Land League, to measure the extent to which the social and political radicalism characteristic of many Irish American nationalists in the 1880s persisted into later years. Second, it can provide a basis for understanding the ideological character of the mass movement that emerged after 1916, for many nationalist leaders in the years 1890–1916 went on to become leaders of this larger movement. The patterns of social thought that they developed in this period would do much to shape the more broadly based movement of later years.

In this chapter, I explore some key themes in the social thought of New York City's Irish nationalists. Other cities, such as Boston, Philadelphia, San Francisco, and Chicago, also witnessed significant nationalist activity in these years, but New York remained the epicenter of the movement, the main locus of activities for constitutional home rulers and separatist revolutionaries alike. I discuss the ideas of both of these wings of the movement here, with particular attention to three issues: social class and socialism; religion and the Catholic Church; and gender and women's rights. Taken together, these three issues provide a set of coordinates useful in analyzing the social thought of New York's Irish nationalists.

In the 1880s a close connection existed between ideas on these three issues. Irish American nationalists of this era who could be called "radicals"—that is, men and women who lamented the existence of class inequality and monopoly and who proposed sweeping solutions to remedy these problems—also frequently criticized the power of the church hierarchy and adopted an egalitarian attitude toward women's rights and the participation of women in the nationalist movement. On the other hand, those who could be called "conservatives" when it came to issues of social class and the economic system generally voiced uncritical support for the church hierarchy and opposed women's rights and women's activism. But this ideological consistency broke down after 1890. The views of an individual nationalist on, say, social class, no longer served as a guide to his or her views on other issues. Corporate lawyer John Quinn, for example, was a vehement opponent of socialism, but also a sharp critic of the Catholic hierarchy. Labor activist James Connolly was a socialist, but also a Catholic and not especially anticlerical. As Tom Garvin has recently argued, a degree of ideological incoherence marked the thought of early-twentieth-century Irish nationalists both in America and in Ireland.[2]

The Irish nationalist movement's great achievement in the 1880s was to bring together three traditional currents of nineteenth-century Irish protest: the revolutionary republicanism of the Fenians, the efforts of parliamentary leaders like Charles Stewart Parnell to achieve home rule, and the social and economic struggles of the agrarian poor. The merging of these currents was the essence of the so-called New Departure, which had a tremendous impact in New York. Here the Fenian exile John Devoy (an architect of the New Departure as a whole) joined forces with middle-class Irish American home rulers and with the Irish American radical Patrick Ford, whose widely circulated weekly newspaper, the *Irish World and American Industrial Liberator*, served as the voice of the most politically active sector of the Irish American working class.[3]

The *Irish World* had supported trade unions, strikes, and labor reform movements like the Greenback-Labor Party as early as the 1870s. In the early 1880s the paper began drawing parallels between the land struggle in Ireland and the labor struggle in the United States, arguing that monopoly was the central social problem in both countries. "The cause of the poor in Donegal is the cause of the factory slave in Fall River," Ford proclaimed. In some areas of the country, particularly the industrial belt of New England and the mining regions of Pennsylvania and the Far West, working-class branches of the American Land League emerged, sometimes virtually merging with local Knights of Labor assemblies. In these areas, a "symbiotic relationship between class-conscious unionism and Irish national consciousness" was clearly visible.[4]

In New York City, the Land League's leadership was dominated by anti-Ford conservatives, men from the growing Irish American middle class. The city's leading Irish newspaper, the *Irish-American*, reflected their outlook, following a conservative course both in American politics and in the politics of Irish nationalism. But even in New York a strong connection existed between the labor movement and the struggle against the Irish land system. In January 1882, some 12,000 trade unionists met at Cooper Union to back the No-Rent Manifesto then being promulgated by the Land League in Ireland. Under a banner declaring that "the No Rent battle of Ireland is the battle of workingmen the world over," prominent labor reformers like Robert Blissert, George McNeill, and Peter J. McGuire drew attention to what McGuire, leader of New York's carpenters, called "the simultude [sic] of the slave system at home and abroad." In the wake of this meeting, New York labor activists formed the city's Central Labor Union (CLU). The first plank of its declaration of principles stated that land should be "the common property of the people."[5]

It was also in New York that some of the most radical dimensions of Irish American nationalism came to the surface. In 1882 Dr. Edward McGlynn, pastor of the sprawling working-class parish of St. Stephen's in Lower Manhattan, began to champion both Michael Davitt's sweeping land nationalization plan for Ireland and Henry George's single-tax reform for America. In the Anti-Poverty Society that he founded and in his many powerful speeches, he developed a distinctively Irish and Catholic version of the social gospel. "Christ himself was but an evicted peasant," McGlynn told a rally for Davitt organized by the Central Labor Union in June 1882. "He came to preach a gospel of liberty to the slave, of justice to the poor, of paying the full hire to the workman."[6]

Even more significant was Henry George's 1886 campaign for mayor of New York. George, whose widely read single-tax tract, *Progress and Poverty,* had been extremely influential in the American labor movement, had also been a key supporter of the Ford wing of the Land League, writing pamphlets on the Irish land question and serving as the *Irish World's* correspondent in Ireland in 1881. In turn, Davitt and Ford had done much to publicize *Progress and Poverty,* and Irish American supporters of the Land League had constituted George's first major constituency. Not surprisingly, large numbers of New York City's Irish Americans rallied behind George's challenge to Tammany Hall. Although he lost the election, George polled a remarkable 68,000 votes. Both Ford and McGlynn worked in the reformer's campaign, which was also backed by the CLU and the Knights of Labor. McGlynn's participation in the campaign and his subsequent refusal to explain his position led to his excommunication in 1887, but a massive outpouring of support from his Irish American parishioners revealed the appeal of this distinctive brand of radicalism.[7]

Significantly, New York City's Irish radicals also endorsed a new departure in the relationship of women to nationalist and social reform movements in these years. The *Irish World,* for example, backed women's rights along with labor and land reform. In addition, it was in New York that Fanny Parnell (Charles's sister) and Jane Byrne organized the Ladies Land League in October 1880. Over the next two years, militant Ladies Land League branches, often independent of male control, appeared in several American cities. In Ireland itself, the emergence of the Ladies Land League marked a change of gigantic proportions: it was the first formally organized expression of female protest in Irish history and Anna Parnell, another Parnell sister, became the first woman to occupy a prominent position in Irish public life. "In the Irish Land League cause, the best men were the women," Henry George told a group of striking New York telegraph operators in 1883, obviously thinking this the greatest praise he could give. McGlynn, meanwhile, became a vigorous champion of women's rights. In 1882 he defied the conservative bishop of Cleveland, Richard Gilmour, by speaking to a Land League branch in that city whose female members Gilmour had excommunicated for their activism. In turn, activist Irish American women rallied behind McGlynn: his Anti-Poverty Society attracted a disproportionately large number of women supporters in the 1880s and 1890s, and women were prominent in the rallies organized to defend the priest after his excommunication.[8]

McGlynn's defiance of the Catholic hierarchy illustrates another dimension of radical Irish nationalism in New York: it encouraged secularism and anti-clericalism among the city's Irish American population. Without ever repudiating the church, the *Irish World's* Patrick Ford was highly critical of the Catholic hierarchy in the early and mid-1880s. If the Pope opposed the struggle for the Irish nation, Ford argued in 1884, then Irish Americans should simply ignore the pope. Philip Bagenal, an English observer of American society in these years, believed that the *Irish World's* popularity indicated that the church was losing its influence among the American Irish. The excommunication of McGlynn probably accentuated the trend toward secularism among Irish New Yorkers. For example, Thomas Flynn, father of the famous twentieth-century labor radical Elizabeth Gurley Flynn and a supporter of both George and McGlynn, left the church following the McGlynn affair. He was surely not the only Irish American New Yorker to do so.[9]

The unity of Irish American nationalism in the early 1880s proved to be short lived. In 1882 the Land League in Ireland was torn apart by conflict over Davitt's land nationalization proposal, and in the following year it was replaced by the Irish National League, a much more moderate organization dominated thoroughly by Parnell. Parallel developments occurred in America, where an Irish National League of America was established under more consistently conservative leadership. Disunity within the movement was furthered by the fall of Parnell himself in 1890 and the subsequent collapse of the Irish National League. Meanwhile, Irish American working-class radicals seemed to lose interest in Ireland altogether, throwing themselves into the building of trade unions or into political reform movements. Yet some, though not all, of the themes that had characterized the New Departure continued to shape the social thought of New York's Irish nationalists after 1890. The remainder of this chapter is concerned with this influence, both in the constitutional home rule wing of New York's Irish American nationalist movement and its separatist revolutionary wing.[10]

Shortly after the fall of Parnell, the American wing of the Irish Parliamentary Party (IPP), centered in New York, began to rebuild itself. In May 1891 anti-Parnellites among America's Irish nationalists gathered at New York's Hoffman House and established the Irish National Federation of America (INFA). They elected Thomas Addis Emmet, a prominent New York City physician, vigorous Parnell opponent, and grandnephew of the famous Irish revolutionary Robert Emmet, as their president. The INFA's goal was to line up American opinion behind Irish home rule and to raise funds for the Irish Parliamentary Party. The organization grew quickly and by 1893 had established 150 branches. A number of public rallies were held, including a hugely successful mass meeting at the Academy of Music in New York City in March 1893, where New York's well-known member of Congress, Bourke Cockran, served as the featured speaker. Nevertheless, the defeat of a Home Rule Bill in Parliament and continuing conflict in the Irish Parliamentary Party effectively killed the INFA, though it continued to maintain a formal existence through the decade.[11]

Only after the turn of the century, when the main factions of the Irish Parliamentary Party reunited under the leadership of John Redmond, did the situation begin to improve. The United Irish League of America (UILA), named after William O'Brien's recently formed United Irish League, was founded in

1901 to replace the now moribund INFA. Heartily endorsed by Patrick Ford's *Irish World*, the UILA quickly formed branches in the New York area and, soon thereafter, throughout the country. Redmond toured the United States in late 1901, focusing attention on the new organization and on the renewed dynamism in the Irish home rule movement. By the end of 1902 the UILA claimed more than 200 branches throughout the United States and had raised at least £10,000 for the IPP.[12]

Over the next decade, the UILA played a critical role in financing the IPP. The American organization provided approximately £50,000 to the party during these years, leading Redmond's English opponents to caricature him as the "Dollar Dictator." In the 1910–14 period, the IPP's strategy, backed by Irish American financial support, began to show results. The election of 1910 made it clear that the Liberal Party now depended on Redmond and the IPP to remain in power. Responding to this new political situation, Liberals reformed the House of Lords in 1911 so that it could only delay, no longer defeat, legislation. In the following year a new Irish Home Rule bill was introduced in Parliament. Irish Americans across the nation, finally seeing home rule on the horizon, now rallied behind the UILA. Membership soared, and American politicians from William Howard Taft to Theodore Roosevelt to Woodrow Wilson went on record with pro–home rule statements. The parliamentary wing of the nationalist movement was at high tide, in New York and throughout the United States, as well as in Ireland.

But what did New York's home rulers stand for, beyond home rule? What was their vision of a post–home rule Ireland? One aspect of that vision concerned religion and the role of the Catholic Church, a central institution within both Irish and Irish American society. But, astonishingly, John Redmond and the IPP as a whole had devoted very little thought to the role of the Catholic Church within a post–home rule social order, leaving no orthodox home rule position on this crucial matter. There was a wide range of opinion within the New York home rule movement on this question. At one extreme was Patrick Ford. Although the editor had once been a vocal critic of the church hierarchy, he changed course dramatically after 1886. As he repudiated his earlier radicalism and moved toward the political center, Ford also drew closer to the church. As early as 1887 Ford was attacking his erstwhile allies, George and McGlynn, for their criticisms of the hierarchy. From then until his death in 1913 Ford consistently lined up behind the church, viewing that institution as a guardian of public morality and as a bulwark against social radicalism.[13]

At the other end of the spectrum was John Quinn. A successful New York lawyer and active Irish constitutional nationalist in the early twentieth century, Quinn was perhaps best known as a patron of the arts. His vigorous support for artistic freedom led him toward an extremely critical view of the Catholic Church's interference with the arts and what he perceived as its domination of Irish and Irish American intellectual life. "You will never be able really to make a successful art movement in Ireland until you have accomplished two things—broken the power of the church and secured an educated audience," he wrote W. B. Yeats in 1906. "Perhaps I should have said only one thing, namely broken the power of the church, because when the power of the church is broken education will come."[14]

The center of gravity in the UILA lay somewhere between these poles. It is interesting to note that just one of the eight New York City members of the UILA's National Executive Committee in 1904 was a priest. This suggests that while Catholic clergymen were not excluded from the organization, neither did they exercise much formal power within in it. The UILA was very much a secular organization. Its New York supporters resembled Ireland's home rulers who, while overwhelmingly Catholic in religion, were nationalists of the "assimilationist" variety. The middle-class home rule leaders of early-twentieth-century Ireland had long been immersed in British political and cultural life, admired its liberal ideals, and were secularist in their basic outlook. They were disturbed, to be sure, by the anti-Irish Catholic bias they perceived in English culture, but they believed that this bias could be eliminated by the reestablishment of an autonomous Irish legislature. They had no sense of Ireland as a distinctive civilization but rather hoped that its post–home rule institutions could be modeled along English liberal lines, so that Ireland could be given its deserved standing as a full partner in the British imperial enterprise. Such views were widely held among New York's home rulers, and not only by Quinn, who eventually found himself isolated by his extreme identification with English civilization and by his unwavering pro-war stance. Cultural attitudes like these account for the support many Irish American New Yorkers gave to England in the first months of World War I. "The English people are fighting the battle of civilization," Bourke Cockran proclaimed in 1915. At a Carnegie Hall commemoration for the men executed by the British following the 1916 Easter Rising, when Cockran was interrupted by shouts of "Down with England," he shouted back, "I say not down with England but up with Ireland."[15]

But there were other sides to this cultural stance. If it could lead to support for war and imperialism and a disregard for Irish culture, it could also help shape a powerful vision of Catholic–Protestant unity, which accounted for the unwillingness of most of New York's home rulers to consider the temporary partition of Ireland proposed by the Liberals in 1914. "While the Orangeman differs widely from the Irish Catholic, each of them resembles the other more than anybody else in the world," Cockran wrote to Moreton Frewen in 1914, going on to argue that the Catholic hierarchy in Ireland needed to take the lead in reassuring northern Protestants that it did not seek to create a Catholic state.[16]

The home rulers' views on social class and on socialism were as significant as their ideas about religion. These views were rooted in the social background of New York's home rule leaders, who were, on the whole, individuals of wealth and high social standing. The INFA, for example, was not only headed by the prominent and well-to-do Emmet, but its first treasurer was Eugene Kelley, the millionaire president of the Emigrant Savings Bank. Following Kelley's death in late 1894, the INFA's Board of Trustees elected John D. Crimmins to succeed him. Crimmins was one of New York's wealthiest builders and contractors, whose firm had constructed much of the city's elevated transit system in the late 1870s, at times employing as many as 12,000 workers. At the turn of the century, Crimmins played a key role in organizing a so-called millionaire committee, a group made up of what John Redmond called "the better class of Irish men of New York," to coordinate financial contributions to the IPP. The group disbanded after the UILA got on its feet, but the UILA itself continued to attract support from upper- and middle-class Irish Americans in the city. John Quinn, for example, was a wealthy corporate lawyer, and both Cockran and New York Judge Martin J. Keogh, another leader, were men of considerable means.[17]

It should also be noted that New York City was witnessing a sharp growth of class conflict and labor radicalism in these years. New York's Socialist Party grew steadily after its 1901 founding, particularly after 1908, when it began establishing deep roots in several immigrant working-class neighborhoods. A lively left-wing bohemian culture also began to take shape in the city, with its center in Greenwich Village. Perhaps most important, the city was torn apart by large strikes, especially those of Jewish and Italian garment workers in the years 1909–1913.[18]

The Irish American community was not totally isolated from these developments. In the 1890s, Irish American shoeworkers in Massachusetts had been crucial in providing the American socialist movement with some of its first electoral victories. The Western Federation of Miners, dominated by Irish immigrants and Irish Americans, adopted socialism as its official policy in 1903. Meanwhile, in New York City the left-wing sojourner James Connolly established the Irish Socialist Federation (ISF) specifically to appeal to Irish American workers in the city. Many historians have dismissed the influence of Connolly and the ISF, pointing to its small membership and the low Socialist Party vote in Irish neighborhoods. Yet the threat of socialist influence among the city's Irish working class was always present. On Connolly's first speaking visit to New York in 1902, for example, every seat in the Cooper Union was taken. Bitterly fought strikes involving New York's Irish American teamsters and public transport workers in the early twentieth century also brought some of them into contact with friendly socialists. And there was certainly a kind of heroic mystique attached to Connolly, Elizabeth Gurley Flynn, James Larkin, and other Irish labor radicals, especially those associated with the Industrial Workers of the World. In the early 1910s William O'Dwyer, later mayor of New York but at that time a member of the city's hod carriers union, followed very closely the activities of "the IWWs, the Socialists, here and in the West." As O'Dwyer recalled many years later, "their programs, the articles that were written on them, the daily news that was carried on them and the magazine articles—those things happened to bring us to a realization of the things that were wrong in our civilization."[19]

The prospect of socialism's rise among New York's Irish workers haunted the middle- and upper-class leaders of the UILA. Though they may have been divided on the question of the role of the church, Patrick Ford and John Quinn were united in their condemnation of militant labor activity and socialism. By the early twentieth century, Ford opposed trade unionism, strikes, and all other forms of assertive labor activism. His *Irish World* now held up "self-made" men of wealth like Thomas Addis Emmet and John D. Crimmins as individuals for workers to emulate and denounced socialism as immoral and atheistic. In a similar vein were Quinn's comments on the radical culture of Greenwich Village, expressed in a 1917 letter to Ezra Pound: "I don't know whether you know the pseudo-Bohemianism of Washington Square. It is nauseating to a decent man who doesn't need artificial sexual stimulation. It is a vulgar, disgusting conglomerate of second and third-rate artists and would-be artists, of I.W.W. agitators, of sluts kept or casual, clean and unclean, of Socialists and near Socialists, or poetasters and pimps. . . . But hell, words fail me to express my contempt for the whole damned bunch." In light of such attitudes, it is not surprising to find the New York Municipal Council of the UILA denouncing James Larkin and his comrade Cornelius Lehane for their socialist speeches in 1914.[20]

Hostility to labor radicalism did not necessarily mean opposition to moderate forms of trade unionism or to progressive labor reform measures. Mayor John Purroy Mitchel, for example, played a conciliatory role in the 1910 New York garment strike, criticizing the antiunion bias of the courts and condemning the "violent and disorderly" activities of "both sides" in the dispute. And Tammany Hall leader Charles F. Murphy was in many ways a genuine progressive, a supporter of woman's suffrage and progressive labor legislation. Both of these politicians were closely identified with New York's Irish home rule movement. But both also regarded anything more radical than progressive labor legislation and "pure-and-simple" trade unionism as beyond the pale.[21]

Murphy's support for woman's suffrage raises the question of the relationship of women to constitutional Irish nationalism in New York. Although Irish American women were not active in the INFA in the 1890s, they took on active roles in the UILA from its very beginnings. Of the 149 New York City delegates to the second national convention of the UILA in 1904, 11 were women. One of them was Mary O'Flaherty, who was elected to the National Executive Committee of the organization. To thunderous applause, Chicago's John F. Finerty, accepting reelection as president of the UILA, devoted much of his speech to calling on Irish American women to enter the movement:

> We must never forget that the women of the Irish race have been the priestesses of the Irish race, we must not forget the breach of Limerick, where they hurled back the grenadiers (applause), we must not forget the slopes of Vinegar Hill,

where, green flag flying, and with the shells of General Lake bursting, they bled and died side by side with the men of their race (applause). . . . I say to the women of our race who are assembled here and who may assemble elsewhere, that they can do much for our cause.[22]

Such language did not necessarily mean that the UILA was committed to women's rights. Both IPP leader John Redmond and his deputy, John Dillon, were strong opponents of woman's suffrage and the IPP actually played a crucial role in preventing parliamentary action on votes for women in Britain. Yet on this point the Irish leaders faced considerable opposition, not only from suffragists in Ireland but also from Irish American women in the home rule movement. When Redmond traveled to the United States in September 1910, for example, UILA women told him that they would not provide him with funds unless he changed his position on the vote. Though they did not prevail on this occasion (Redmond left America with $100,000 in election funds), women were making their presence felt within the UILA. UILA women undoubtedly figured among those at the huge May 1912 suffrage demonstration in New York, for one of that demonstration's demands was the extension of the vote to Irish women in the Home Rule Bill introduced that year.[23]

New York's Irish American female nationalists came to the fore with the tumultuous events of 1914. In March of that year, a large meeting was held at Carnegie Hall to protest "the dismemberment of the Island," a reference to Asquith's plan for a partition of Ireland. The meeting had been called, according to Bourke Cockran, "exclusively by women," UILA activists. Later in the year, Dr. Gertrude B. Kelly, a well-known New York physician and woman's suffrage advocate with political roots in Henry George's single tax crusade, emerged as a leader of the opposition to Redmond's endorsement of the war and his pledge of Irish support. She couched her antiwar and anti-imperialist arguments against Redmond in highly charged and highly gendered language:

> May I, as a woman, an Irishwoman and a physician, spokeswoman of hundreds, thousands of my sisters at home and abroad, ask our leaders what it is they propose to Ireland to do—commit suicide? Admitting for the moment that this is a "most righteous war"—not "a war of iron and coal"—a war between titans for commercial supremacy—why should little Ireland have to do what the United States, Switzerland, etc. do not? Is Home Rule to be secured for the cattle and the sheep when the young men of Ireland are slaughtered, the old men and the old women left sonless, the young women obliged to emigrate to bring up sons for men of other climes?[24]

In their unified and vigorous condemnation of labor radicalism and militant working-class activity, then, New York's home rulers broke sharply with some of the most important ideas of the New Departure. But in their generally secular orientation, their openness to women's participation, and their support for woman's suffrage, they illustrated the continuing vitality of at least part of the Land League's legacy.

If parliamentary nationalism occupied center stage in the opening years of the twentieth century, it did not do so unopposed. Moderate home rulers were dogged by constant criticism from revolutionary separatists in the Clan na Gael, the most important and long-lived Irish revolutionary organization in American history. Established in 1867 as the main heir of the Fenians (John Devoy saw the organization as an expression of "reorganized Fenianism"), the Clan nonetheless was discredited after a British dynamite campaign in 1883 and experienced bitter and debilitating factionalism over the next 16 years. But in July 1900 the organization reunited under the leadership of Devoy, New York's Daniel Cohalan, and Philadelphia's Joseph McGarrity. Using Devoy's weekly newspaper the *Gaelic American* to attack the IPP, the UILA, and the very objective of home rule, the Clan called for physical force to establish a fully independent Irish republic. Though overshadowed by the larger and more respectable UILA, the Clan built a national membership of about 40,000 by 1910. Moreover, it had a huge influence beyond its numbers. The Clan provided critical support for nationalist cultural and political movements in Ireland, such as the Gaelic League, the Gaelic Athletic Association, Sinn Fein, the Irish Volunteers, and the Irish Republican Brotherhood, which planned and carried out the 1916 Easter Uprising. As with the constitutional movement, New York was the main center for Irish revolutionary activity in the United States.[25]

Yet, like their counterparts in Ireland, New York's revolutionary nationalists were "radical in style and means, but not in ends." Their ideas about proper women's roles provide a case in point. The Clan na Gael permitted female nationalist supporters to join its women's auxiliaries but, in marked contrast to the broad participation of women in the UILA, these organizations were subsidiary ones, dominated entirely by men. Mary J. O'Donovan Rossa, widow of the old Fenian Jeremiah O'Donovan Rossa and a member of the Clan's women's auxiliary in New York, expressed the dominant view within the Clan when she wrote to Devoy in 1915 that women's auxiliaries "must be absolutely under obedience to the authorised men and take willing guidance from them." Rossa *did* support woman's suffrage, conceding that "every woman does these days." But she nonetheless proclaimed herself "old-fashioned enough still to cling to the notion that men are the lords of creation and women at their best when kindly cooperating in all that reason and conscience approve, and under guidance, with modesty, not self-asserting." When it came to women in the movement, Rossa "would give the men a *despotism* over them and ban whoever murmured."[26]

It is difficult to know how many New York women actually joined the Clan's auxiliary. Certainly some were so committed to the Irish struggle that they were willing to put up with this kind of systematic subordination and others may have simply accepted the subordination as appropriate. But many women who sympathized with the ultimate goals of the movement may have had qualms, not only about the role of women within it, but also about the violent methods advocated by revolutionary republicans, methods that conflicted sharply with the conception of "womanhood" that many Irish American women maintained. As Dr. Gertrude Kelly explained, "we women have hesitated to give our adherence to the physical force party, not that we did not sympathise to the utmost with its aims, but that in our capacity as conservators of the race we hoped to call a halt to the immolation of Irish youth." In addition, the style of the Clan prior to 1916 revolved around a kind of cult of male revolutionary "brotherhood," an aggressive assertion of masculinity that left little space for women. It is not surprising that many Irish American women kept their distance from this wing of the movement.[27]

Although the Clan did attract Irish American working-class men, it was almost totally indifferent to the question of class inequality. Devoy, it is true, got along well with James Connolly during the latter's stay in New York, mainly because both men shared a hostility to what they regarded as the timidity of the home rule movement in Ireland and America. Like Connolly, Devoy often asserted that upper-class Irish Americans were unlikely to be staunch nationalists, simply because they were too contented. But Devoy was no more sympathetic to Connolly's socialist views than he had been to Davitt's and Ford's social radicalism in the 1880s. Indeed, with the exception of his support for the New Departure, the Fenian pioneer demonstrated a striking consistency over his entire career: he resisted all efforts to dilute pure nationalism with any kind of social program.[28]

There were others in the Devoy wing of the movement who took an even more conservative position. In the 1910 garment strike, New York Supreme Court Justice John W. Goff, a prominent Irish separatist, handed down a sweeping injunction against the clothing workers that, for the first time in New York state history, permanently restrained strikers from peaceful picketing and prohibited them from interfering in any way with those seeking to work. American Federation of Labor president Samuel Gompers called Goff's ruling an example of the "tyranny of autocratic methods of concentrated capital and greed."[29]

A similar conservatism could be seen in the Clan's views on Catholicism. The original Fenians had been thoroughly secular, many of them adopting strong anticlerical positions. Yet the church's growing importance in both Irish and Irish American life after the so-called devotional revolution of the mid–nineteenth century caused later generations of separatist revolutionaries to back off from this stance. Nowhere in the ranks of the Clan na Gael could be found the kind of anticlericalism exhibited by John Quinn or, before him, the supporters of Henry George and Edward McGlynn. Even the socialist James Connolly gave support to the church, striving in his writings and speeches to prove that Catholicism and socialism were compatible. Roger Casement, the most famous Protestant connected to the 1916 Easter Rising and a figure with close ties to the Clan na Gael in America, symbolized the near total identification of Catholicism and revolutionary separatism: shortly before his execution, he was received into the church.[30]

The more radical ideas and programs of the Land League era, then, played almost no role at all in the social thought of New York's revolutionary separatists between 1890 and 1916. Class inequality and socialism were simply not matters of concern for most of them. In their ideas on gender and religion, they actually appeared more conservative than their counterparts in the city's home rule movement.

World War I and John Redmond's decision to support the British war effort and accept a postponement of home rule transformed the Irish nationalist movement in New York and elsewhere, undermining support for the UILA and leading to a sharp rise in the fortunes of the revolutionary wing of the movement. "The general impression here is that Redmond is either a bungler or a

333
*Key Themes in the
Social Thought of
New York's
Irish Nationalists,
1890–1916*

Members of the St. Columcille Branch of the Friends of Irish Freedom marched on St. Patrick's Day in 1919, one year after women made their official appearance in New York's annual parade. The FOIF was an American organization with national headquarters in New York. The FOIF supported Ireland's new republican party, Sinn Fein, in its effort to gain independence from Great Britain. There were scores of local branches in the city, like this one from St. Columba's parish in Chelsea. (Museum of the City of New York.)

traitor," wrote a New York home ruler in early 1915. "The UIL in New York city has been reduced to a skeleton." The Clan na Gael now sprang to life, calling for a convention of the Irish race that would lead in 1916 to the creation of the Friends of Irish Freedom, a mass membership American organization favoring an independent Irish republic.[31]

The Easter Rising and the British executions of its leaders finished off the UILA and the IPP alike, further strengthening nationalism's revolutionary wing in both Ireland and the United States. The new phase of the movement in New York was opened by a huge Carnegie Hall meeting in May 1916, where John Devoy shared the platform with Bourke Cockran, who now repudiated many of his earlier positions. Revolutionary Irish nationalism would soon become a mass movement in New York and other American cities: the Friends of Irish Freedom claimed more than 275,000 members by 1919, for example. Yet, in ways that require further investigation, the character of this mass movement continued to be shaped by the social thought of the men and women who dominated Irish American nationalism in the years between 1890 and 1916.

1914 to 1945

PART IV

THE EARLY TWENTIETH CENTURY

The first grade class at St. Patrick's School on Kent Avenue, just south of the Navy Yard in Brooklyn, in 1917. At a time when the antihyphenate climate was calling the loyalties of Irish Americans into question, Catholicism emphasized patriotism. St. Patrick's was a free parochial school staffed by the Sisters of Mercy, an Irish order of nuns who had come to Brooklyn in 1855. An education in New York City had an distinct Irish flavor from the second half of the nineteenth century. In addition to several Irish religious orders working in Catholic schools, large numbers of second-generation Irish American women began teaching in the public school system. (Courtesy of the Sisters of Mercy, Brooklyn Regional Community.)

Chris McNickle

OVERVIEW
When New York Was Irish,
and After

By 1914, a second and third generation of American-born Irish had not only figured out how the nation's premier metropolis worked but had given it an indelible imprint of their own and had begun to enjoy the success that comes with commanding a city's affairs. By 1945, when the United States finally left behind the economic catastrophe of the Great Depression and assumed its position as the world's most powerful nation, the Irish were merely first among equals in New York and fading as a group. Their moment was ending, while the rapid economic and educational advances of Jewish New Yorkers, apparent as early as the first decades of the twentieth century, were carrying that group to the center of New York's ethnic kaleidoscope.

The Irish ruled New York from the end of the nineteenth century through the 1920s. They controlled its government and politics, dominated construction and building, moved into the professions and managerial classes, and benefited, perhaps disproportionately, from the general prosperity of the times. By the third decade of the twentieth century the group was economically and socially diverse, and its sense of identity was weakening. Then came the depression. The economic collapse hit the Irish very hard and appears to have halted their upward momentum in its tracks. The financial decline coincided with a political lapse for the Irish, so the group faced tough times without control over City Hall and without the help, just when they needed it most, of an institution they had come to think of as their own. The difficult struggle of the 1930s resolidified the sense of cohesion that Irish New Yorkers felt toward each other. The group renewed its upward ascent after the end of the Second World War, but by then Irish domination of the metropolis was over.

The way New York's Irish thought of themselves was in flux during this period. Their rise in stature made it hard for them to maintain a self-image as a downtrodden yet defiant group, set upon by wealthy, mean-spirited Protestant Americans. It was tougher to feel like the underdog when they were on top, to cry discrimination when the men wielding power were of their own stock, to bemoan the lack of respect for their customs when American traditions and their own flowed increasingly together into a single pool. The arrival of millions of new immigrants more different from old-stock Americans than the Irish intensified the confusion. By comparison, the Irish were respectable. This new reality fit them uncomfortably for a time as they searched for a way to be wealthy and powerful, yet remain simple and humble as they liked to think of themselves. This theme recurs in a variety of ways in the next three chapters.

The Irish impact on the politics of New York was especially pronounced. For 27 years, beginning with "Honest John" Kelly in 1871, Irish Catholic politicians led Tammany Hall, the Democratic organization that dominated the city's political affairs. Between 1902 and 1932 the organization was at the peak of its power. The basic premise of the Tammany machine was simple and effective. The vast majority of a city's people, especially its immigrant slum dwellers, struggled to overcome life's daily challenges. By offering tangible help the Democratic organization earned the gratitude of citizens in the form of a vote on election day. The politicians then used the power that came with victory to enrich themselves and to offer more help to the people in their districts, thus perpetuating their rule.[1]

The Irish proved masters at providing political patronage positions to satisfy the immigrant's desperate need for a job and to create a loyal voter at the same time. By the turn of the century Tammany controlled about 60,000 government posts with salaries totaling $90 million a year. But always more voters existed than jobs, so professional politicians relied on additional tools to expand their support. They exercised influence over judges and police on behalf of potential voters, they offered families help in the event of eviction or a fire, they sponsored summer picnics and social clubs, and on and on. And when these many tactics proved insufficient to keep their candidates in office, Tammany politicians resorted to fraud.[2]

New York's Irish were well suited for the tasks of politics. At the end of the nineteenth century their numbers were great, and geographically concentrated. This made organizing easy. The hierarchical nature of the Catholic Church and its demand for discipline offered an effective model for a political party to follow. And when they arrived in the United States, the Irish already had a long, if perverse acquaintance with an Anglo-Saxon political system. They had learned from the English about electoral fraud, judicial chicanery, and manipulation of the rules for partisan advantage. They understood politics as the means one group used to secure power for itself, to hold onto it and to exploit it. Morality had nothing to do with it, nor did any grand ideology. For the Irish, politics differed from other professions only in detail. It was a way to earn a living.[3]

The system was well established when Charles Francis Murphy inherited control of the machine in 1902, but it was under siege. Twice within a decade, in 1894 and again in 1901, reformers had turned Tammany from office by persuading large numbers of non-Irish immigrants, principally Jews, to vote against the Democrats. Under Murphy, the machine solidified the allegiance of Jewish voters and added them to the traditional electoral strength of the Democratic Party's Irish base. This coalition was powerful enough to win his candidates an impressive string of victories. Between 1903 and 1921 the Democrats conquered the mayoralty five times in six contests and controlled the Board of Estimate and Board of Aldermen. Murphy's machine dominated the state legislature for much of the period, and it elected Al Smith governor of New York State for the first time in 1918. Smith went on to run for president in 1928.[4]

Murphy's genius lay in his recognition that building a winning coalition required Tammany to respond to the rapidly changing composition of the city; the arrival of enormous numbers of Italians and Jews was diluting the influence of Irish voters. In 1880 more than one-third of New Yorkers were of identifiably Irish stock, a higher proportion than any other group. By 1910 the proportion had dropped to less than 1 in 5. By 1945 it was fewer than 1 in 10. In contrast, Jews contributed just 5 percent of the city's total population in 1880, but more than 17 percent by the turn of the century. In 1920 nearly 30 percent of New Yorkers were Jewish, and by 1945 some two million Jews still constituted more than a quarter of the total population. An insignificant number of Italians in 1880 exploded to half a million by 1910, more than 10 percent of the city's population at the time. Two decades later more than a million Italians made up 20 percent of the city, with their numbers increasing modestly thereafter.[5]

New York's large Italian population consisted principally of immigrant peasants with no formal experience with democracy and little understanding of the electoral process. They tended to be unconcerned with citizenship and indifferent about the right to vote. According to one estimate, as late as 1911 only 15,000 Italians were registered to vote in New York City. Consequently, it was not the Italians who Murphy needed to bolt to the machine. It was Jewish New Yorkers—who voted in greater proportions than any group save the Irish—who became crucial to the Democratic coalition. Bringing them in required three things. First, Tammany had to remove the moral taint that colored the Democrats when the quest for riches led them to protect criminals to a greater extent than voters could bear. Jewish voters were more sensitive to this issue than other immigrants, and reformers periodically used Tammany complicity with organized vice as a lever to pull them away from the Democrats. Second, the machine had to use its political power to defend Jews against anti-Semitism. Third, it had to defuse the philosophical appeal to Jewish voters of the Socialist Party, and of the Republican Party, which possessed a strong progressive wing in New York early in the century.[6]

Removing the moral taint on Tammany came easily to Murphy. Although he was a street-toughened barkeeper by profession, he was also a "thorough-going puritan" according to his biographer. He barely drank and prostitution deeply offended his religious convictions. After rising to power he rapidly rid the party of the members most infected with vice. Protecting Jews against anti-Semitism required symbolic gestures more than anything else. As a group that had known its share of discrimination, many Irish found the task appealing, and it did not require much sharing of the jobs and contracts that the Irish coveted for themselves.[7]

The most enduring characteristic of the machine under Murphy, and a crucial part of the effort to attract Jewish voters to it, was the party's commitment to far-reaching social legislation. The huge influx of eastern European Jews familiar and comfortable with socialist thought provided a strong electoral base for New York City's Socialist Party beginning in the last decade of the nineteenth century. For a time, in an effort to maintain a broadly based and ideologically pure appeal, Socialist organizers denied the increasing Jewishness of their party. (The denials were typically made in Yiddish.) But the party's tacticians learned that fusing socialist thought to Yiddish culture strengthened it with its Jewish core. By the first decade of the twentieth century the Socialists threatened to become the political voice of Jewish immigrant workers. The risks for Tammany Hall were great.[8]

Encouraged to respond by his most talented young candidates—Al Smith, Robert F. Wagner, Jimmy Walker, and others—Murphy elected to "give the people what they want." He allowed his men to pass social welfare legislation that helped workers and the poor provided it did not weaken the political prerogatives of the machine. This important decision in great measure neutralized the attractiveness of the Socialists. It also robbed the Republicans of their appeal to many of New York's influential German Jews. The first decade of the twentieth century was the era of Theodore Roosevelt, Charles Evans Hughes, and Oscar Straus for the New York State GOP. These party leaders were bona fide progressives who appealed to the cautious liberalism of the city's German Jewish elite. The combination of Democratic commitment to progressive reform and a resurgence of Republican conservatism after the failed Bull Moose campaign of 1912 pushed the group toward the Democrats.[9]

The Irish built political machines in cities throughout the United States in the late nineteenth and early twentieth centuries, but the New York machine was distinctive in its reliance on an alliance with another group the size of the city's enormous Jewish population. The number of Jews is New York had surpassed the Irish by 1914, yet the Irish continued to dominate the machine for decades because of their ability to coopt Jewish political priorities. New York, since its earliest days, has been more intensely cosmopolitan than other American cities, and cooperation among diverse groups has been particularly important. It may be that Murphy's genius resulted from having grown up in a political environment that demanded an unusual degree of accommodation to succeed.[10]

Compare the experience in New York in the first half of the twentieth century with that in Boston, for instance. At peak times, the Irish constituted an absolute majority in Boston, but only a third of the population in New York. Yet, the machine never ran as efficiently on the Charles River as it did on the Hudson. Boston's Irish clansmen spent nearly as much time battling among themselves as they did combating the city's Yankee elite. James Michael Curley is well remembered, but it is for his personal outrageousness. He was a spectacular one-man show, irrepressible, but not responsible for the creation of an enduring institution. Boston's Democratic Party bears no name like Tammany to give it an identity and to reflect a special standing. In Chicago, the senior Richard Daley ultimately lent his name to the city's machine, and it functioned as well as any. But it had required a Czech named Anton Cermak to reduce the conflicts of Chicago's Irish politicians to a smoothly functioning machine in the 1930s. A coincidence, perhaps, but it may be that establishing cooperation among Chicago's Irish required an outsider, a leader neutral in the fratricidal battles of that city's Celtic chieftains. New York's tradition is different. It was an Irish Catholic leader, Murphy, who proved the greatest of the city's coalition builders. And when he ruled, Tammany reached greater heights than any political machine of its time. It is worth emphasizing that pragmatism inspired Murphy's penchant for accommodation. The force of Jewish electoral strength motivated him; Italians received short shrift from Tammany until the 1930s and 1940s, when they began voting in numbers large enough to affect election outcomes.[11]

Implicit in Murphy's rule was the recognition that respectability mattered. Winning the confidence of the city's population required adherence to certain moral standards and a commitment to using the tools of government to help people, not just to plunder public coffers. In 1913 a police scandal and the fallout from a political battle between Murphy and New York State governor William Sulzer prevented Tammany from portraying itself as respectable. These events allowed a non-Tammany Irish Catholic Democrat, John Purroy Mitchel, to win the mayoralty for a single term. In chapter 15 John F. McClymer compares Mitchel's career with Al Smith's to show how much some Irish aspired to respectability, as well as how difficult it was to achieve and still retain the common touch the Irish considered part of their heritage.[12]

The tension between respectability and Irish authenticity emerges persistently during this period because the Irish were becoming respectable so rapidly, especially in comparison with the large numbers of Jewish and Italian immigrants arriving in New York. These newcomers were more different from older-stock Americans than the Irish were. They had just landed and did not know their new nation's customs. They spoke different languages, dressed differently, and behaved differently. The Jewish religion, as practiced by the eastern Europeans crowding into the Lower East Side, was foreign to Americans. In the early years of the century many New Yorkers thought that the city's large Jewish population was the source of its most pressing problems. In 1908 the commissioner of police declared (without evidence) that Jews committed half the crimes in the city. Italian Catholicism had an unfamiliar Mediterranean flavor to it, and the influx of hundreds of thousands of men and women from the land of the pope intensified the fears of Anglo-Saxon nativists who suspected a dual loyalty to the United States and Rome. By the end of prohibition the public had come to associate organized crime with New York's Italians. The Irish were highly respectable by comparison, more like the older generations of Americans who still laid claim, even if with decreasing confidence, to the right to determine what it meant to be American and to hold American values.[13]

Yet, the greater respectability of the Irish came not just by comparison with others, but from their own accomplishments as well. Some time before 1910 the Irish began attending college in greater proportion than the national average for non-Hispanic whites: about one out of four Irish Catholics of college age compared with about one out of five of the general population. By the 1930s the Irish had achieved rough parity in educational level with the population at large across all age groups. In the early years of the century the Irish still held many of the city's lower-middle-class jobs—clerk, policeman, city government employee, transit worker, and the like. But by the 1920s they were already more likely to hold a managerial or professional job than was the typical American. The trend continued until it became twice as likely for the Irish to have attained that level than others. Some evidence suggests that Irish educational advancement was greater in midwestern and nonurban settings than in New York (and Boston), but there is little doubt that the Irish were moving up in Gotham during the first decades of the twentieth century, even if at a modestly slower pace than elsewhere.[14]

Academics have given scant attention to Irish success in business. Scholars acknowledge that the group ran its share of neighborhood franchises—such as saloons, restaurants, groceries, and hardware stores. The research also admits to advances by late in the last century in the fields of building and contracting, businesses that benefited from Irish ties to local politicians. These tended to be small, family-run affairs that yielded handsome livings when things went well but risked bankruptcy when they did not. Even those that survived lean times rarely grew beyond local stature. Like other immigrant groups, the Irish financed home construction in their neighborhoods through the creation of savings banks. The Irish-dominated Emigrant Industrial Savings Bank was one of New York's largest, and its officers were wealthy men, although few savings banks swelled to comparable size.[15]

Chapter 16, by Marion Casey, brings to light several points about Irish residential patterns in New York. By early in the century New York's Irish included a fair number of wealthy real estate developers and land speculators. These men (and it appears they were only men) constructed middle-class housing and benefited from the growing ranks of Irish New Yorkers who sought, and could afford, better living conditions. The evidence suggests that the period between 1910 and 1930 was one of rapid advancement for the Irish in a broad range of occupations, including business and the professions. As the chapter also makes clear, for many Irish the quest for more pleasant surroundings was not linked to a desire for greater stature or a better address. Even as their lot in life improved, many Irish found themselves ambivalent about the outward trappings of success. It conflicted with their sense of themselves.

The 1919 freshman Latin class at St. Francis College, in the Cobble Hill section of Brooklyn, shown with their Classics teacher, Brother Columba Reilly, O.S.F. Reilly, a native of County Meath, became president of the College in 1925. The Franciscan Brothers came to Brooklyn from County Galway in 1858 at the invitation of Bishop Loughlin. By the end of the nineteenth century, Brothers from Ireland were teaching the sons of Irish immigrants in a dozen elementary schools, two high schools, and a liberal arts college in the Diocese of Brooklyn. Other Catholic colleges training young men for the professions included St. John's in Fordham (est. 1841), St. Francis Xavier (est. 1847) on West 16th Street, and Manhattan College (est. 1849). (From the Archives of the Franciscan Brothers of Brooklyn.)

Traditional interpretation of Irish participation in the world of finance—where the serious money was (and is) in New York, and where achievement translates into real power and influence on a national scale—is that it was off limits in the first half of the century. The exceptions are used to prove the rule. Joseph Kennedy came from Boston to pursue his ambitions, but Wall Street kept him at its edges. He prospered from his own shrewd judgments but was never invited into the closed club of old-stock Protestant investment bankers who thought little of the Irish.

There is much that is true in the picture, but it does not seem entirely correct. Kennedy left Boston for New York because he perceived it as being more wide open, offering more room for someone like him to maneuver. New York's financial elite was simply no match for Boston's Brahmins when it came to directing hostility toward the Irish, and New York's financial industry was too big in national and international scope to control tightly. It seems hard to contend that Kennedy's career suffered because of discrimination against him, even if many disliked him and he resented the unwillingness of Wall Street's elite to accept him.[16]

Anecdotal evidence of Irish success in New York's financial industry during the first three decades of the century abounds, particularly during the 1920s when markets soared to dizzying heights and the local and national economies knew extraordinary prosperity. For example, Tommy Corcoran, one of Franklin Roosevelt's chief aides, arrived at the New Deal via a Wall Street law firm that specialized in securities law. William Shannon pointed out that by the 1960s one began to find obituaries in the *New York Times* that read like this: "Peter McDermott, who entered Wall Street as a runner and office boy in 1902 and rose to become a wealthy broker, died Tuesday." It goes on to note that the man established his own brokerage firm in 1925 and that he served for several years as a director of the Hibernia Trust Company, a bank unlikely to have been owned by WASPS. In 1961, when consolidation of two of New York's largest banks created the fourth largest banking corporation in the country, Manufacturers Hanover Trust, Horace C. Flanigan became the chairman of the new entity's executive committee with compensation in excess of $2 million, a suite at the Waldorf Astoria Hotel, a corporate jet, and a limousine. Flanigan was an Irish Catholic who had graduated college with a degree in engineering in 1912, and who had become a vice president and director of the Hanover Bank by 1931. The contrast between these profiles and the position of the Irish a century earlier, as Leo Hershkowitz and Hasia Diner describe it in their overviews, is vivid.[17]

If one adds the economic boom times of the 1920s to the simple but impressive fact that the Irish were more college bound than others by then, and on average about as well educated, it is hard to imagine that their role in New York's major industries, including the financial industry, did not progress strongly during this time. They did not yet run the city's national financial institutions; that was still the province of Morgan, Rockefeller, Harriman, and their crowd, and of German Jews who had followed their need to finance trade into investment banking. But the Irish by the 1920s worked in financial firms, benefited significantly, and set the stage in the first half of the century for a more prominent role in New York's financial industry in the second half. More research on the topic is in order.

More widely recognized is Irish success in literature and the theater. In the nineteenth century Irish American writing went through three phases. The first, in the years before 1840, consisted of a confident prefamine generation that wrote self-deprecating stories for a highly literate general audience. The second generation emerged from the famine Irish in the years between 1850 and 1875. These novels were conservative and practical, offering guidance to recent immigrants from Ireland to help them make it in the new world. Characters were stereotypes, the rhetoric was sentimental, conflicts were simple and the moralizing clear. The third generation appeared in the last quarter of the nineteenth century. The audience had become more middle-class, but was still largely Irish. The stories had more texture than those of the earlier generation, and with greater human insight began to "count the costs and assess the damages of the previous generation's experience," according to Charles Fanning, a critic of Irish American literature.[18]

For a generation after the turn of the century Irish American writers produced little of note. The rise of nativism in the country discouraged people of all backgrounds from celebrating their ethnic heritage. The pressure to define oneself as 100 percent American during World War I was great, and the two years of "troubles" that reduced Ireland to civil war following the partition of 1921 left Irish Americans less eager than they had been to insist on their cultural roots.[19]

Not until James Farrell created Studs Lonigan in 1932 did a new generation of thoroughly authentic Irish American writing begin. But in 1925, with publication of *The Great Gatsby*, F. Scott Fitzgerald became America's first major Irish Catholic novelist accepted by a broad public audience. *Gatsby* has become *the* work of fiction that captures the spirit of urban American life in the 1920s. Fitzgerald was born in St. Paul, Minnesota, but he wrote *Gatsby* in and around New York, and it is in and around the city where the plot unfolds. To hold the literary position the book has achieved it had to take place there. New York City is America's national metropolis. Nowhere else could provide as full a context for a vignette of the jazz age, the superficial society it spawned, the spectacle of great wealth, and the tragedy that can follow when people accumulate money rapidly and without regard to morals.[20]

The significance of Fitzgerald's Irishness to his writing is a matter of some debate. He himself made little of it, but when Malcolm Cowley assessed Fitzgerald's work, he concluded that his "Irishness was a little disguised, but it remained an undertone in all his stories; it gave him a sense of standing apart that sharpened his observation of social differences." Another critic, Robert E.

Rhodes, detects in Fitzgerald's works an evolution of his attitude toward the Irish that counterbalances his view of the rich. "From something close to unquestioning adulation of wealth in *This Side of Paradise* to vaguely ambivalent feelings in *The Beautiful and the Damned* to fairly strong condemnation in *The Great Gatsby*, Fitzgerald moved to severe criticism in *Tender Is the Night*. This movement is paralleled by that from Fitzgerald's rejection of the Irish, to their moderate acceptability, to Irish Dick Diver's victimization by power and wealth [in *Tender Is the Night*]."[21]

To judge from his novels, Fitzgerald became increasingly comfortable with his Irishness as his life progressed. As a young man he moved away from his Irish Catholic roots as a matter of philosophical disposition, but also to distance himself from the stereotype of the unskilled and uneducated worker. Recognition of Fitzgerald as a major novelist shows how far Irish Americans had risen by the 1920s, and the recognition mattered quite a lot to the man. Fitzgerald's Princeton education and his acceptance by the nation's substantially Protestant literary elite meant that he had achieved respectability. Yet, his wild behavior seemed almost a personal statement that he would not allow the quest for acceptance to force him to conform. He once described himself as possessing a "two-cylinder inferiority complex," the result of a youth spent "alternately crawling in front of the kitchen maids and insulting the great." It suggests the ongoing tension many Irish of the period experienced between a desire for respectability and an unwillingness to submit entirely to the ways of the respectable classes.[22]

This same tension is apparent in the career of John O'Hara, an Irish Catholic writer who traveled to New York from rural Pennsylvania in the mid-1920s. He first achieved fame in 1934 with his novel, *Appointment in Samarra*, followed rapidly by publication in 1935 of *Butterfield 8*. In the latter, James Malloy, a young Irish newspaperman, begins a heart-to-heart talk with his girl friend this way: "I want to tell you something about myself that will help to explain a lot of things about me. . . . First of all, I am a Mick." He goes on to tell her not be fooled by the fact that he wears Brooks Brothers suits and does not eat salad with a spoon. He is still a Mick, and the Irish, he declares, are, "non-assimilable."[23]

The segment is more than a little autobiographical. For O'Hara, the desire for acceptance by the non-Catholic world was intensely obvious. One friend recounted how he used to sit in the window of his East Side apartment and watch the yachts go by. Armed with binoculars and a copy of the Social Register, he used to check the flags of the boats to see whose was whose. While his success brought him close to the affluent and socially prominent, "he was as much observer as participant," according to one writer who knew him. Another friend recalled that "he yearned to belong to a socially elite club." It all had to do with his complex that an Irish Catholic from Pottsville, Pennsylvania, could never achieve real respectability in the United States. In the words of one critic, to

O'Hara, being Irish was an "underlying dominant problem . . . and every 'Mick' who had the misfortune to find his or her way into his stories had a share in the deprivation with which he believed life handicapped him." For many Irish such doubts and ambivalences about their ethnic identity persisted throughout the 1930s and 1940s. Not until the country elected John Kennedy president in 1960 would the insecurities finally recede.[24]

Fitzgerald and O'Hara made their marks in New York, the country's literary capital. Both were Irish Catholic writers, but neither one wrote novels that were representative of Irish Americans as a group. A third great Irish novelist of the period, James T. Farrell, did. He created the character of Studs Lonigan on the South Side of Chicago. Farrell tells the story of a young Irish American boy coming of age and growing into manhood in a working-class Irish neighborhood during the depression. The story fits better in Chicago than New York. The stark authenticity of the tale, what Farrell called the spiritual impoverishment of the Irish American working class that endured even after the group had achieved a measure of economic stability, makes it harder to set in New York. On the one hand most of the conditions and attitudes Farrell writes about existed in New York's Irish neighborhoods. Indeed, a literary school of regional realists grew up in Farrell's wake, including a New York contingent. Harry Sylvester wrote *Moon Gaffney* (1940) about the Brooklyn Irish, Howard Breslin wrote of the Irish living in the South Bronx in *Let Go of Yesterday* (1950), and there were others. Yet, New York City possesses a glamour, an excitement, and a national stature that interferes with the insularity of its communities, the working-class Irish ones included. In Chicago, Bridgeport spawned Richard J. Daley; in Manhattan, Hell's Kitchen spawned Daniel Patrick Moynihan. The similarities are evident, but so are the differences.[25]

Broadway is part of New York's glamour, and it was there during the 1920s, 1930s, and 1940s that Eugene O'Neill made his mark with *The Iceman Cometh, A Long Day's Journey into Night,* and other plays. This is another example of an Irish American achieving new heights during the first decades of the twentieth century. Because New York was the nation's drama capital, O'Neill's career could not have reached the same degree of success elsewhere. His plays exhibited a romance and fatalism, an ambivalence toward alcohol and sex, and a fondness for the dark side of life that was evident in much of the drama emerging from Ireland in the first quarter of the twentieth century. These works also accurately reflected the attitudes and emotions of the American Irish of his day. It is through the prism of their Irishness that the characters in *A Long Day's Journey into Night,* the Tyrone family, display universal emotions. The broad appeal of O'Neill's work is achieved with a distinctly Irish style, and there is much about it that is New York as well. *The Iceman Cometh* takes place in a local bar in Greenwich Village, for example.[26]

The Irish were fending for themselves quite well in New York by the 1920s. If they were not yet rich as a group, increasingly they lived in middle-class comfort. Many of their own had achieved notable national success. They still felt discriminated against, but momentum was on their side. One of the glues that holds ethnic consciousness in place is the threat from others, and its grip on New York's Irish was starting to weaken as the power the Irish wielded became ever more apparent. Between 1915 and 1917, for example, Mayor John Purroy Mitchel instituted educational reforms known as the Gary Plan. To many Irish New Yorkers the program appeared to sacrifice the quality of education delivered to the children of the city's working class, including large numbers of Irish Catholic students, to keep the taxes paid by the wealthy low. In response, Irish Catholic lay and religious leaders teamed up with Jewish leaders to have the plan repealed. In 1917 this same coalition helped topple Mitchel's administration. In the short term, the effort by a public official to impose an unwanted policy on the Irish no doubt increased the group's sense of vulnerability. But the completeness of their victory made it clear that New York's Irish held the power to protect themselves against perceived cultural onslaughts.[27]

Contrast this episode with the group's experience in the 1840s. As the incipient national movement for public education gathered momentum in New York, the city's Irish Catholics wanted schooling for their children, but faced a conflict. "How can we think of sending our children to those schools in which every artifice is resorted to in order to reduce them from their religion?" John Power, the vicar general of the archdiocese of New York asked after assessing the philosophical orientation of public school classes. The curriculum was indisputably Protestant. In response, John Hughes, the city's fierce Irish Catholic archbishop, created a vast parochial school system financed by the city's many Catholic parishioners. It was the only way to ensure that his worshipers could educate their children in their own faith. In short, unable to control the formal powers of government held by Protestants, Hughes did what the Irish had done for centuries to circumvent British laws in Ireland. He instituted an Irish-dominated shadow system.[28]

By 1917 things were different. New York's Irish exerted enough control over the formal government to insist that their views be respected. For more than three decades following the Gary Plan controversy, New York experienced no educational issue of comparable emotional intensity to Catholics. No prudent leader dared raise one. It is no coincidence that the next struggle over New York's school system to strike a raw Irish Catholic nerve did not occur until 1949. That year Representative Graham Barden proposed to forbid the use of federal funds for parochial schools, and many New Yorkers supported the bill, even though the Irish opposed it. By 1949 the Irish were first in the ethnic pecking order of the metropolis by only a slim margin, and once again others were prepared to test them.[29]

The role of the Catholic Church in New York City in the first decades of the twentieth century is instructive. Late in the nineteenth century a significant minority of radical Catholics, of whom Father Edward McGlynn was the most noted leader, militated for social change. As the Irish continued to rise in wealth and stature, this wing faded until traditionalists completely dominated the leadership of New York's archdiocese. The church tended to its flock and ministered diligently to the needs of the poor during the depression but did not maintain as high a profile during the 1920s as at other times in the city's history. In significant measure, it did not have to. Catholic New Yorkers—and the Irish dominated the Catholic Church in New York—were well protected and served by other institutions. They could afford a weaker church. One result was that when Francis Spellman was named archbishop of New York in 1939 he inherited an impressive organization with more than 2,500 priests, 10,000 nuns, and 2 million members, but it was $26 million in debt. He rapidly set about reversing the church's fortunes lest it lose its place. New York's Irish, by then, were beginning to fear as much.[30]

If hostility from others is one glue that binds the members of an ethnic group together in the United States, a common sense of purpose regarding their ancestral homeland is another. In New York, throughout the late nineteenth and early twentieth centuries, a small, committed band of nationalists called on their fellow Irish Americans to support a movement to chase the English from Ireland by force of arms. Daniel Florence Cohalan, an influential local politician, eventually promoted by Tammany to a New York State judgeship, was prominent among New York's more radical Irish leaders. In the first decade of the twentieth century he became a moving force behind the Clan na Gael, a brotherhood bound together by secret oath, first established in 1867 to help organize support for Irish radicals fighting the English. His ally, John Devoy, created *The Gaelic American* in 1903. This weekly adopted an editorial policy opposed to the efforts of Irish leader John Redmond to achieve home rule through compromise and accommodation with the English. The newspaper ultimately achieved a circulation of 30,000. It rivaled in size the more established *Irish-American*, which hewed a pro–home rule line until 1913, when family succession led to a new editor and a new policy in support of full independence. Together, these two publications provided a consistent forum for promotion of the Irish republican cause.[31]

The men and women living in Ireland had to contend with the practical considerations of dealing with English rule in their daily lives and benefited from incremental improvements on specific issues. These realities tended to temper their political opinions toward the English. Irish Americans, on the other hand, had the luxury of indulging fully their emotions about centuries of cruel injustice. They also experienced a need to assert their identity in a land filled with people different from them. As a result, Irish American rhetoric on the subject of Irish independence was more uniformly radical than the opinions of the Irish still living in the country at the turn of the century. The shared emotion gave Irish Americans a unifying sense of purpose with respect to their homeland. Yet, despite the harsh words, before the First World War most Irish Americans were content with proposals for home rule, and few spent much time actively working toward the cause of Irish freedom. They were too busy tending to their own parochial needs.[32]

During the first two decades of the twentieth century, a period of radicalization took place in Ireland with respect to English rule. When the British fought the Boer War for control of South Africa, Ireland developed a strong, militant, anticolonial movement in opposition. This movement erupted with renewed force at the outbreak of World War I, and many Irish refused to serve in the British army. When the Liberal government in England submitted a Home Rule Bill in 1912, it galvanized Ulster Protestants in the north and Catholic nationalists in the south. Secret military organizing accelerated among both groups laying the foundation for civil war later. In 1916 the failed Easter Rebellion originally elicited only modest reaction. Many dismissed the rebels as dreamers or fools to have thought that seizing the downtown Dublin post office by force of arms would ignite a general rebellion. But when the English imposed the death penalty on the principal organizers, they created martyrs, and Irish demands for greater control over their destiny took on renewed force.[33]

Irish American radicals intensified their efforts in response to the accelerating pace of activity overseas. In New York, the *Gaelic American* adopted a pro-German position at the outbreak of war in Europe linking the cause of Irish independence to the defeat of the British. Most Irish Americans opposed U.S. intervention on either side. There was certainly no desire to come to the aid of the English, but there was little belief that support for Germany was worthwhile either. Simply put, except for the radicals, the cost of war was too great a price to pay for the goal of Irish freedom.[34]

The attitude of the majority of Irish Americans began to change after the Easter Rebellion executions. The harshness of the English response to the uprising shocked them and created a ground swell of emotional support for independence. Yet, when America entered the war on the side of the British, only the most radical Irish leaders refused to salute smartly and rally 'round the flag. Irish Americans volunteered for the armed forces by the thousands. In New York, Catholic Church leaders sought to remove the issue of Irish independence from public debate until the war ended for fear that criticism of America's British ally would be perceived as unpatriotic. But other New Yorkers, including Daniel Cohalan, insisted that Irish independence be among America's war aims. And as the war drew to a close, Irish Americans sensed a match between their desire for Irish independence and President Woodrow Wilson's commitment to a new set of rules for international behavior, particularly his call for national self-determination for ethnic minorities.[35]

"From January 1918 to June 1919, the Irish in America worked with ferocious vigor to force the administration to include Ireland under the umbrella of American war aims," historian Joseph O'Grady has written. The major Irish American organizations in New York—the Friendly Sons of St. Patrick, the Ancient Order of Hibernians, the New York Chapter of the Knights of Columbus—sent petitions signed by thousands to the president. On December 10, 1918, the Friends of Irish Freedom sponsored a rally at Madison Square Garden attended by 15,000 people, according to newspaper reports. Frank Walsh, a prominent Irish New Yorker, led the American Commission on Irish Independence that traveled to France to insist that the president respect the demands of the Irish. When Wilson returned to the United States without a treaty granting Ireland's freedom, he was perceived as a traitor to the Irish cause, and bitterly denounced.[36]

In the immediately following years, the New York Irish adopted wholesale the stand that radical Irish leaders had taken for decades. Strong support emerged for Irish volunteers who fought against the British in the Anglo-Irish War of 1919–21, and when Eamon de Valera traveled to New York in 1920 seeking support for Sinn Fein and an independent Irish Republic, New York's Irish population raised $10 million for his cause. Joe Doyle captures the emotional commitment New York's Irish felt toward the demand for independence at this time in his discussion of the 1920 dock strike in chapter 14. Although the dockers he writes about were themselves members of the working class, the leadership of the American Women Pickets for the Enforcement of American War Aims who supported the strikers was decidedly from the middle and upper middle class. Dedication to bringing independence to Ireland cut across social barriers. It provided New York's Irish, by 1920 a diverse group of people with a broad range of educational, social, and professional backgrounds, a common sense of identity.[37]

Events, however, left Irish Americans confused about their ancestral home as the 1920s began. On December 23, 1920, the British Parliament created two governments in Ireland—one in Belfast for the 6 predominantly Protestant counties in the north, and another in Dublin for the 26 overwhelmingly Catholic counties in the south. When the Irish and English signed a treaty ending formal combat in 1921, the nation was split. Some Irish thought the arrangement was an enormous step forward and that in time the northern counties would reunite with the south. Others thought that if they did not insist on one united republic then and there, they would miss the chance for generations to come, if not forever. The dispute erupted into a civil war that hardened political factions within Ireland for decades. Choosing between brothers was a very different proposition for Irish Americans than siding with their relatives against the English. Irish American interest in Irish affairs persisted, of course, but with diminished intensity. And the complexity of the new situation and the disagreement among the Irish themselves over how best to respond robbed the group of a unifying cause. Perversely, the success of the Irish nationalist movement in securing independence for 26 counties weakened a bond that had helped Irish New Yorkers maintain their identity.[38]

Perhaps the economic boom and good times of the 1920s eased the pain that the conflict in Ireland caused New York's Irish. All the city's people benefited from the strong economy that fueled development and growth, but because they had been in New York longer than other immigrant groups, and because of their unique political connections during a time of extensive building and construction, the Irish probably prospered more than most others during the 1920s. The decade also saw the imposition of prohibition, which New Yorkers ignored with a vengeance. Illegal liquor made mobsters rich, and while the gangsters of the time were not notably Irish, prohibition enriched an Irish-dominated police force that participated eagerly in the effort to frustrate federal agents trying to enforce what many Americans thought was a silly law.[39]

In 1925 New Yorkers elected Jimmy Walker mayor. A handsome man, a one-time song writer and singer, Walker possessed a wit that charmed the public. In his dress and style he epitomized the city's sophistication, and the ever rising aspirations of its Irish. Al Smith's bid for the presidency showed those aspirations to be higher still in 1928. But the nation's rejection of Smith, by an embarrassingly large margin, was quite a blow. The challenger's loss was due in great measure to the prevailing prosperity, and to Smith's lack of understanding of America beyond 14th Street. The Tammany man simply did not realize how much so many American men and women distrusted the country's great urban centers. But there was a strong measure of anti-Catholic bigotry behind the defeat, and it was on this that the Irish focused, because it stung them. America roundly rejected their quest to be respectable *and* Irish.[40]

An undertone of harsh nativism had accompanied the prosperity of the 1920s, but in New York the Irish had dominated local affairs sufficiently to insulate themselves and other immigrants from the hatred festering in the land. Smith's battering reminded them that they still had not won complete acceptance. The stock market crash of 1929 and the Great Depression that followed reminded them no less than others of the fragility of their economic security. Most New Yorkers suffered horribly from the depression, but perversely the Irish, better off than many other groups, may have felt the greatest relative decline. They were upwardly mobile at the time, poised to benefit more than most from good times, and more vulnerable when the prosperity faded. Wealthy Protestants who had a lot lost a lot, but still had a lot left. Newer immigrant groups, notably the Italians, were still struggling in poverty and typically had relatively little to lose.

There were some Irish in the camp of the wealthy, and many in the camp of the poor, but it seems there were a disproportionate number in between, a rising middle class on the verge of making it, who felt cut off at the knees by the economic decline.

The Irish lost their informal support system as well. In tough times they should have been able to use their political control of government to reduce the impact of the depression. They could not. When Smith ran for president in 1928, he was replaced by Franklin Roosevelt as governor. Roosevelt became president in 1932 and was succeeded in the governor's mansion by Herbert Lehman. The first man was Protestant, the second Jewish. Roosevelt was at odds with the New York machine, and Lehman, although he owed his career to Tammany, was never really one of them. Jimmy Walker, when not too busy entertaining himself with a high-profile extramarital affair in illegal speakeasies around the city, took enough graft to get caught by a special investigating committee and resigned the mayoralty in disgrace in 1932. The scandal helped Fiorello LaGuardia win Jewish voters away from Tammany in 1933, which, coupled with strong support from his fellow Italians, put the Little Flower in City Hall. The irrepressible reformer stayed there for a dozen years. The result was that New York's Irish received fewer patronage positions from the city, state, and federal government than they had in a long while, at a time when they particularly needed it. A disproportionate share began to go to Jewish New Yorkers. (Ed Flynn in the Bronx maintained excellent relations with President Roosevelt and Governor Lehman and endured much better than other Irish Democratic political leaders.)[41]

Tough economic times often bring out the worst in a people. Displacement by others tends to do the same. The Irish faced financial hardship *and* a loss of place as the 1930s evolved. Many bore their burden with Irish stoicism, but others responded differently. Father Charles E. Coughlin's radio messages inspired a broad following among New York's Irish. His appeals began temperately enough. At first, they seemed to offer spiritual nourishment and economic programs for a more humane and just society. In time, they shifted in tone and became hostile. They cast blame for hard times on an amorphous group of domestic and international conspirators, including Jews. In and of themselves the anti-Semitic tracts caused fear and anger among New York's large Jewish population. When groups of Irish Catholics responded physically to Coughlin's cranky calls to put down Jews, the anxieties moved from the abstract to the real.[42]

Part of Coughlin's appeal to the Irish came from his fierce anticommunist rhetoric. By 1930 Pope Pius XI had urged Americans to be wary of communism and its avowed atheism, lest people facing economic hardship be seduced by its allure. In 1937 he declared communism the world's greatest threat and called on Catholics to crusade against it. In New York, during the depression, the Communist Party was indeed gaining momentum, and the party was associated with the city's Jews. While Jewish involvement in Communist organizing has been exaggerated, the political traditions eastern European Jews brought to the United States included a much higher tolerance for communism than was typical of the Irish. And by the 1930s Jews had advanced on the Irish economically, educationally, and in terms of social status. The combination turned out to be potent.[43]

In 1938 a group of disaffected Irish in Brooklyn created the Christian Front for the specific purpose of taking up Father Coughlin's call to repress "Jews and Communists" (the two terms were used almost interchangeably). The front included some Germans and Italians, but its membership was overwhelmingly Irish. It boycotted Jewish stores and plotted violent acts against Jewish organizations and in Jewish neighborhoods. An even more extreme offshoot, the Christian Mobilizers, developed in the Bronx and Manhattan.

Martin Kelly and Michael Carroll, both from Ahascragh, County Galway, model their new IRT motorman uniforms in the Bronx, c. 1929. Train drivers were an elite group in transit and were thus one of the last holdouts to the labor organizing efforts of New York City's Transport Workers Union. During the 1930s, about 50 percent of the TWU's membership were natives of Ireland, including its president, Michael J. Quill. Many were recruited through the Clan na Gael, an American branch of the Irish republican movement. (From the collection of Martin J. Kelly.)

Many Irish Catholic leaders supported the group, while others at least tolerated it to avoid offending their fellow Irish. Only occasionally did Irish leaders speak out against it. During the Second World War the imperative for unity against a foreign foe overpowered the appeal of the front, and efforts to revive it after the war met with little success. In the wake of Nazi death camps and extermination furnaces, anti-Semitism found few champions in New York City.[44]

Irish right-wing fanaticism was one reaction to the 1930s, left-wing militancy was another. Irish union organizing in the United States had periodically included radical movements like the Molly Maguires of the Pennsylvania coal fields. In the late nineteenth century New York City had been home to potent worker groups and the Irish had been active participants. During the depression the Irish played an active role in New York's reenergized labor movement. Mike Quill, for instance, helped seize a power plant to make the point by force of arms that workers had the right to organize. He ended up heading the heavily Irish Transport Workers Union and remained one of the most colorful and powerful union leaders in the city for decades, unsurpassed in his ability to launch rhetorical rebellions, even if his behavior was more tame than his words and gestures. The city's powerful trade unions, heavily Irish in composition, developed during this time as well.[45]

Most of the Irish, of course, were neither left-wing nor right-wing extremists. They endured the depression as best they could without dramatic actions. As World War II approached, most Irish supported a policy of neutrality. The group displayed scant enthusiasm for a U.S. alignment with either England or with the Soviet Union. Once war broke out, most Irish joined the effort to defend the United States with full patriotic fervor, although isolationist elements persisted. Irish soldiers came home from the war, like others, matured by the experience and ready to return to civilian life and a better future.[46]

In 1945 things appeared to return to normal for the Irish when New York elected William O'Dwyer mayor. The return of an Irish Catholic Democrat to City Hall was welcome, but to win, O'Dwyer had campaigned with a balanced ticket that included an Italian City Council president and a Jewish comptroller. In days gone by the Irish typically had claimed all of the citywide posts. There was no escaping the conclusion that New York's future would be colored less emerald than its past.[47]

In the decades that followed the Irish returned to a path of upward mobility. The group knew more success in business, the professions, literary endeavors, and belatedly academia. But their numbers in the city dwindled, and their presence diminished. They ceased to dominate the metropolis, even if the city owed much of its style to them. By the 1960s

Jewish influence was predominant in New York, and the Irish assumed their place alongside the city's other ethnic groups. They remained one of the most important elements of New York's constantly changing human mosaic, and one of the few that could claim they once ruled the city, as the next three chapters make clear.

Joe Doyle

CHAPTER 14

Striking for Ireland on the New York Docks

ON AUGUST 27, 1920, a spectacular strike broke out on Manhattan's West Side piers. Thirty women, protesting the arrests of two Irishmen, Archbishop Daniel Mannix, and Cork mayor Terence Mac-Swiney, incited the coal stokers aboard a British passenger liner to strike their ship. The Irish longshoremen working the West Side docks immediately joined them on strike. The women protesters convinced the African American longshoremen and Italian coal passers at work that day on British ships to strike as well. By midafternoon thousands of longshoremen were marching up the West Side waterfront crying, "All Off," and shutting down loading operations on every British ship in port.

The strike lasted three and a half weeks. It idled thousands of longshoremen and caused more than 100 "British seamen" (including a number of Irish cooks and chambermaids working the transatlantic liners) to be fired and blacklisted.[1] It spread to Brooklyn and Boston and was called by the *New York Sun*: "the first purely political strike of workingmen in the history of the United States" (Aug. 28, 1920). This little-known strike, the women who led it, and their ad hoc organization, the American Women Pickets for the Enforcement of America's War Aims, illuminate a crucial period in the history of the Irish independence movement in America, from the 1916 Easter Rising until the 1921 treaty that established the Irish Free State.

During these crucial years women provided some of the most dynamic leadership in the nationalist movement.

The American Women Pickets' campaign in 1920 for Ireland's freedom had a powerful precedent. The Ladies Land League, from its founding in October 1880 to its demise in August 1882, electrified the nationalist community both in the United States and in Ireland. That movement, led by Charles Parnell's sisters Anna and Fanny (assisted by scores of American Irish, including Marguerite Moore, who 38 years later played a role in the events leading up to the 1920 strike), built enormous support for the Land League while Charles Parnell was a prisoner in Kilmainham Jail.

Charles Parnell's mother, Mrs. Delia Parnell, and Ellen A. Ford (sister of Patrick Ford, editor of the *Irish World and American Industrial Liberator*) spoke three and four nights a week in towns throughout the United States, collecting thousands of dollars to aid Land League organizing efforts in Ireland.[2] Within months of its founding the Ladies Land League had organized dozens of branches nationwide, boasting 50 to 200 women apiece.[3] New York had so many branches that they were organized ward by ward in Irish neighborhoods.[4] In Ireland, Anna Parnell was even more successful, organizing 420 chapters of the Ladies Land League.[5] Soon after Charles Parnell was released from Kilmainham, however, he pressured the Ladies Land League to go out of existence. (And no women were permitted to join the reorganized Irish National League.) In their two years of operation, the Ladies Land Leaguers had proved themselves able administrators, tacticians, orators, fundraisers, and propagandists.[6] Why is it then, that "for the next 20 years no group of women activists emerged"?[7]

Historian Hasia Diner contends that most nineteenth-century American Irish women apparently believed that women and men should have "separate spheres," with the women's sphere (after marriage) principally in the home.[8] Professor Diner documents a proliferation of single Irish women in the American work force and chronicles a dozen nineteenth-century Irish American women who achieved prominence organizing women workers. But apart from those who were active in the Ladies Land League, she found no women who figured prominently in Democratic Party politics or in the nineteenth-century nationalist struggle.[9]

It is possible that activities of Irish American women in the nineteenth-century nationalist movement simply went undocumented. Patrick Ford, whose *Irish World* had a weekly circulation of 125,000 by the turn of the century and was "the paper of record" in the American Irish community, disapproved of women activists.[10] After 1882, when the Ladies Land League folded, until the twentieth century women in the Irish independence movement virtually disappear from the pages of the *Irish World.*

The only women Ford chronicled during that period were saints, nuns, and, on rare occasions, women involved in labor disputes.[11] The closest he came to showing women involved in the nationalist struggle was to print iconographic engravings of women symbolizing distressed Ireland. Ford did begin a woman's page in 1894 (perhaps in response to the sanctioning that year of Ancient Order of Hibernians women's auxiliaries). But he restricted the women's page to recipes, fashion news, and child-rearing tips.[12]

In the twentieth century, on the other hand, the *Irish World* reads like a different newspaper. Even before Patrick Ford died in 1913 and his brother Robert took over as editor, issue after issue featured articles about women poets, women patriots in Irish history, and contemporary women active in the independence movement: Constance Markievicz, Helena Maloney (who reportedly threw a hatchet at Prime Minister Herbert Asquith when he visited Ireland in 1912), and others.[13] After the Easter Rising, interviews appeared regularly with the widows of the executed 1916 leaders.

What happened to make women so visible in the twentieth-century Irish movement in the United States? Clearly, the surge of activity in Ireland by Lady Gregory, Maud Gonne, and women active in the Gaelic League and nationalist cultural revival inspired women in the United States. The burgeoning women's suffrage movement encouraged American women to play an active role in a movement that had been hitherto dominated by men.

The new ladies auxiliaries to Irish American fraternals also helped women gain power and authority in the nationalist movement. In June 1918 Mary McWhorter, president of the Ladies Auxiliary to the Ancient Order of Hibernians (AOH), led a delegation to the White House of mothers with sons fighting overseas. They delivered a petition bearing 600,000 signatures demanding that President Woodrow Wilson pressure England to free Ireland after the war. McWhorter's Ladies Auxiliary to the AOH numbered 75,000 members in 1920!

Perhaps most important, women in the nationalist movement in the years following the Easter Rising, like their Ladies Land League forebears, were able to fill a vacuum of power. Once the United States entered World War I, in April 1917, Irish American men who continued to speak out against the war were denounced as traitors. The British-bashing satirical journal *Bull*, which Jeremiah O'Leary published, was suppressed by the government and O'Leary tried for sedition. American Irish women, however, could and did criticize the war without governmental reprisal.

Women reached a watershed in their rise to prominence in the Irish nationalist movement in the United States in October 1914. Dr. Gertrude B. Kelly, a revered name in the American Irish community, issued a call, "to the women of Irish blood," to join the first American chapter of the Cumann na mBan, the Irish Women's Council.[14] Hundreds of women responded, gathering the following month at a public meeting at the Hotel McAlpin. Their first task, as outlined by Dr. Kelly and Mary Colum, wife of poet Padraic Colum and a Dublin member of the recently formed Cumann na mBan, was to follow the lead of the Cumann na mBan in Ireland and raise funds and public sympathy for Eoin MacNeill's nationalist militia, the Irish Volunteers.

To that end, Dr. Kelly's chapter of the Irish Women's Council invited many leading figures in the Irish independence movement, especially those touring America, to address their meetings. Her efforts were reproduced throughout the United States by similar groups of Irish and American Irish women committed to the nationalist struggle. Between 1916 and 1921 Hannah Sheehy-Skeffington, Eamon de Valera, Nora Connolly, and Mary and Muriel MacSwiney spoke to meetings of women nationalists all across America.

When America entered the war, women of the Irish Progressive League (IPL), a robust grouping of militants and socialists, wrote pamphlets, spoke on street corners, and staged protest demonstrations denouncing British rule in Ireland, while the AOH, the Friends of Irish Freedom, and the most prominent men in the nationalist movement demurred from criticizing America's wartime ally. Hannah Sheehy-Skeffington and Mary McWhorter secured White House meetings with President Wilson to present their appeals for Irish freedom. Leonora O'Reilly corralled support from leaders of the American labor movement.[15] Eileen Curran and Deborah Bierne organized Irish theater companies.

After the close of the war the Irish nationalist movement in the United States swelled to immense proportions. A single organization, the American Association for the Recognition of the Irish Republic, had 700,000 members by 1921. And its rival, the Friends of Irish Freedom, had 95,000 followers as well.

It is no exaggeration to say that a fever for independence gripped the Irish community in New York City in 1920. Parochial school children marched in Fianna battle sashes on St. Patrick's Day. Independence rallies regularly filled 15,000-seat Madison Square Garden (twice in the month of August alone). Street orators for Irish freedom spoke "every night of the week" in Irish neighborhoods: at Tremont and Washington avenues in the Bronx, on Monday evenings; at Seventh Avenue and 125th Street, on Tuesdays; at Broadway and 37th Street, Wednesdays; at Willis Avenue and 148th Street, Thursdays; at Fourth and Atlantic Avenues, Saturday nights; and at 14th Street, at Times Square, and at elevated subway platforms. They took time off only on Friday nights to attend Jeremiah O'Leary's fiery training sessions.[16] At every turn in the feverish months of 1920, American Irish women played principal roles in the independence movement: sharing the work, the headlines, and the decision making.

The Women Pickets for the Enforcement of America's War Aims was conceived originally as a lobbying group of newly enfranchised women voters with an Irish agenda. In March 1920 some 60 Irish American women were recruited for a congressional lobbying campaign by Dr. William J. Maloney, a key figure in the American Irish independence movement.[17] The lobbyists were to poll members of Congress on their attitudes toward Illinois Representative William Mason's bill to open up consular offices in Dublin (as a first step toward formally recognizing the Irish republic).

On March 20, however, Cork mayor Tomas MacCurtain was shot dead in his home by Royal Irish Constabulary troops. Three days later, British troops killed two more Irishmen and began a massive deployment of British gunships and troops. Hannah Sheehy-Skeffington telegrammed from Dublin that a massacre was imminent, to frighten Irish rebels into submission.[18] Sheehy-Skeffington implored her American colleagues to protest immediately.

Dr. Maloney asked Gertrude Corless, an editorial writer and wife of a prominent Irish American, to convene an emergency meeting in her New York apartment.[19] The women who were to have conducted the lobbying campaign for the Mason bill were requested instead to take part in a protest at the British embassy in Washington. Maloney and Corless hoped that a spirited protest would generate enough publicity internationally to focus press attention on the actions of Britain's army in Ireland and prevent a bloodbath.

Overnight, The American Women Pickets for the Enforcement of America's War Aims took form. Gertrude Corless contacted women sympathizers from Philadelphia, Boston, St. Louis, and Pittsburgh. Gertrude Kelly's American arm of the Cumann na mBan was enlisted, as was the Irish Progressive League.[20] The group's first contingent marched on Congress the following day, April 1, 1920. The organization took its name from Woodrow Wilson's "war aims" of self-determination for small nations and "a war to end wars."[21] The Women Pickets asserted that the self-determination of the Irish people had been manifested in the 70 percent majority (73 of the 105 Irish seats in Parliament) won by the nationalist Sinn Fein Party in the December 1918 parliamentary elections.[22] The Women Pickets wanted President Wilson to recognize the Irish "republic" mandated by the those elections, and to enforce an end to England's war on Ireland.

The protest at the British embassy took off like a rocket April 2. It was the lead story the next day in the *New York Times*, the *Washington Star*, and many other papers. With their strident placards: "England, American Women Condemn Your Reign of Terror in the Irish Republic," "America Cannot Continue Relations with an England Ruled by Assassins," and Corless's inflammatory rhetoric: "We picketed the embassy on Good Friday to remind Great Britain and the State Department of the crucifixion of Christ and to call attention that Ireland was being crucified,"[23] the Women Pickets made great newspaper "copy." Made up of suffragists, socialites, professional women, mothers of World War I soldiers, and actresses, the Women Pickets were articulate and colorful.[24]

The Women Pickets set up headquarters in the Hotel Lafayette, the Washington base for many of the women's suffrage leaders. Corless and her chief aide, Kathleen O'Brennan (a recent Irish immigrant and sister-in-law of executed 1916 leader Eamonn Ceannt), posted pickets outside the British embassy, drew up shifts of duty, sent out fresh pickets every two hours—by motorcar—and announced a campaign for operational funds, with the *Irish World* newspaper to act as fiscal agent.[25]

The Women Pickets seem to have modeled their campaign on suffragist Alice Paul's strategy of deliberate provocation. Among their leading members,

Dr. Gertrude Kelly and Leonora O'Reilly were prominent suffragists, as were Marguerite Moore and Hannah Sheehy-Skeffington (whom many of the Women Pickets knew from her agitational work in the United States in 1916 and 1917). Mrs. Sheehy-Skeffington wrote an article in 1918, "How the Pickets Won the Vote," applauding Alice Paul's confrontational tactics.[26] In keeping with these aggressive tactics, they carried placards with slogans like: "Down with British Militarism," and "England, Hands off the Women of the Irish Republic."[27] They even chained themselves to the embassy gates to guarantee they would be arrested. Once arrested, a number of the Women Pickets—like Alice Paul's suffragists before them—refused bail.[28]

They adroitly manipulated their press coverage. Newspapers ran photographs of elegantly dressed Women Pickets behind bars and quoted their truculent statements about English rule in Ireland. Reporters and newsreel crews delighted in their quirky militancy.[29] A week into the campaign the Women Pickets "bombed" the British embassy with leaflets denouncing Britain's military campaign in Ireland. "The Irish aviatrix" doing the bombing was a Manhattan actress of Irish parentage, Mollie Carroll, who looked so dashing in aviator's garb that her photo made newspapers across the country the next day.[30]

Newspapers ran editorials excoriating the pickets as "petticoated friends of Irish independence," while printing enthusiastic front-page stories about each new stunt the women pulled.[31] Picket captain Mrs. James Walsh assured reporters: "Our numbers are augmented hourly."

The Women Pickets set out to prevent a massacre in Ireland by creating a publicity blitz, and for the two weeks that the women picketed the British embassy no casualties at all were inflicted on the Irish people. Dr. Maloney expressed his thanks to the women for their marvelous work, expecting they would disband. To Maloney's consternation, they did not.

In subsequent months the Women Pickets lobbied individual members of Congress, arranged protests in a dozen states, interrupted "Empire Day" at the Philadelphia Opera House, picketed British diplomats visiting the United States, and burned British flags (on the steps of the Treasury Department, in one instance, before an audience of 500 bystanders and federal employees). On June 1, 1920, they invaded Congress, disrupting the House and Senate simultaneously with speeches from the galleries on the order of "Why Don't You Take the Savage Hun Out of Ireland?"[32]

Dr. Maloney began to consider the Women Pickets cranks, an embarrassment to Ireland's diplomatic efforts in the United States. To judge from the financial contributions streaming into their Picket Fund, the nationalist community disagreed.[33] Buoyed by the community's response, the leading players in the Women Pickets' "Washington skirmish" (as they called it) took on key roles in the waterfront strike later that summer, adding further to their numerous activities on behalf of the Irish cause.

One of these key players was Dr. Gertrude B. Kelly, an eminent New York surgeon born in Waterford and raised in the United States. In addition to founding the American chapter of the Cumann na mBan in 1914, she co-founded the Irish Progressive League in 1917 and belonged, by her own admission, to "every Irish society on record." Kelly had been very active in the Redmondite United Irish League and involved in political affairs as far back as Henry George's 1880s single-tax movement.[34] Like Gertrude Corless, she had championed Jeremiah O'Leary during his imprisonment and trial for sedition during World War I.[35]

Washington pickets Helen Golden, Margaret Hickey, and Leonora O'Reilly were, along with Dr. Kelly and Hannah Sheehy Skeffington, Peter Golden, Padraic and Mary Colum, guiding forces behind the Irish Progressive League.[36] In her memoirs, Colum calls the IPL "the young people's organization." IPL members were for socialism, suffragism, and a Gaelic-speaking Ireland. They distrusted John Devoy's chief adviser Daniel Cohalan, a New York Supreme Court judge and Tammany kingpin, and old-line politicians who claimed to speak for the Irish in America. For political direction they looked instead to the military and political leaders who emerged from the 1916 Easter Rising.[37]

During the summer of 1920 the American Irish community split on the question of who, indeed, should provide political direction. Eamon de Valera, who was in the United States seeking money and diplomatic recognition for the Irish republic, claimed the right, as elected head of Dáil Éireann, the revolutionaries' unofficial parliament, to lead nationalist supporters in the United States as well as in Ireland. Judge Cohalan and the old Fenian John Devoy, leader of the Clan na Gael and editor of its newspaper the *Gaelic American*, disputed de Valera's right to make policy for the American Irish.[38] The Friends of Irish Freedom (FOIF), which numbered 275,000 members in 1920, split wide open over the dispute. Devoy and Cohalan received the official backing of the FOIF's executive committee (most of whose members they had handpicked). Most of the rank and file sided with de Valera. The FOIF quickly lost more than 180,000 members.[39]

With the American arm of the independence movement temporarily in shambles and its male leadership almost wholly absorbed during the summer of 1920 with political infighting, it was again the Women Pickets who seized the initiative in the nationalist movement. Dr. Gertrude Kelly and IPL members Margaret Warner and Kathleen Sheehan worked with Father Flanagan from the Carmelite Priory on East 29th Street—a hotbed of nationalist activity—to organize a dramatic rally on July 31 at the White Star Lines docks on Manhattan's West Side.[40]

The occasion was a send-off for Daniel Mannix, the Irish-born archbishop of Melbourne, Australia. Mannix was an outspoken critic of English rule in Ireland and the leader of two successful wartime anticonscription campaigns in Australia. In 1920 Mannix journeyed from Australia to San Francisco and then by train to New York to catch a ship to Ireland. During the months of June and July hundreds of thousands of Americans turned out to hear Mannix speak at massive rallies staged along his route east.[41]

In New York, Mannix was the featured speaker at a gathering at Madison Square Garden. Mayor John F. Hylan granted him the freedom of the city, and a testimonial dinner was held in Mannix's honor at the Waldorf-Astoria Hotel. Lloyd George had publicly stated he would not allow Mannix passage to Ireland. A reported 15,000 New Yorkers turned out at Pier 60 at the foot of West 20th Street on July 31 to see that he did.[42]

Mannix's "bon voyage" party, as events transpired, directly set the stage for the great ship strike a month later. "Not since the arrival of the *Carpathia* [bearing the survivors from the *Titanic*] has there been such a tense and hairtrigger crowd assembled about the Chelsea piers," a *New York Times* reporter said of the crowd awaiting Mannix's arrival outside Pier 60.[43] The stewards' department of Mannix's ship, the *Baltic*, refused to sail if Mannix boarded. The *Baltic's* engine room gang were equally adamant: *unless* Mannix boarded, the ship would not sail. Between 40 and 100 Women Pickets (the newspaper accounts vary) decided to go on the offensive.

They were dressed in white, with green capes, and they carried the neatly lettered signs with grandiloquent slogans that were their trademark: "There Can Be No Peace While British Militarism Rules the World," "Armenians Massacred: Intervention—Irishmen Massacred: Silence," "Mannix: The World Looks to You to Save Democracy," "Freedom—America 1776, Ireland 1916." One placard showed a map of Ireland in green surrounded by an expanse of blue sea, with the legend: "God Has Defined the Boundaries of Ireland."[44]

A phalanx of Women Pickets led the crowd up to a solid row of policemen barring the entrance to Pier 60. Feinting first at an end run, the women wheeled and rushed the police lines. The huge crowd followed the pickets past the police and onto the dock.

According to the New York daily newspapers, the events that followed on the dock assumed mythic proportions: Mannix was serenaded by the Fighting 69th regimental band, which the White Star Line had banned from the docks. Longshoremen repeatedly halted Archbishop Mannix's progress toward the gangway by insisting on kissing his ring. An English coal merchant sailing aboard the *Baltic* reportedly booed Mannix (he told interviewers afterward he was booing the Irish protesters, not Mannix) and was mauled by longshoremen in a fracas that sent one police detective to the hospital and whipped the mob of Irish enthusiasts on the docks into a near frenzy.

Eamon de Valera, whom English authorities considered an escaped prisoner (he had broken out of a British jail), materialized on the upper deck of the *Baltic* beside Mannix and made a brief, characteristically arch speech. Mannix, also characteristically, made a speech of haunting eloquence. A half dozen longshoremen carried de Valera triumphantly back to the dock and Mannix's ship sailed.

En route to Ireland, however, two British destroyers stopped the *Baltic* at sea and arrested Archbishop Mannix. He was released in Penzance, Cornwall, and handed orders refusing him permission to travel to Ireland, Liverpool, Manchester, or Glasgow.[45]

Mannix's arrest at sea backfired spectacularly. The naval action drew international criticism. In New York a Madison Square Garden rally scheduled for August 15 was reorganized to make Mannix's abduction the central issue. Several of New York's Women Pickets paraded placards: "Up Mannix—Down with the Pirates of Penzance" and "Yo Ho Ho for a Pirate's Life." Major Michael Kelly of the Fighting 69th quipped: "The great British Navy that was bottled up during the war dared to venture out into the high seas."[46]

A quiet announcement at the meeting went almost unnoticed: Terence MacSwiney, lord mayor of Cork City and a republican military commander, had been arrested August 12 by British troops. He vowed to stay on a hunger strike until he was released.

To protest MacSwiney's imprisonment, the Women Pickets decided to form another picket line. On Monday, August 23, seven of their number marched outside the British consulate on Whitehall Street at the tip of Manhattan. With their usual gift for sloganeering, they made the front page of New York's major daily newspapers the next day.

There were few enough pickets at the Whitehall protest that reporters had a chance to interview them individually. Dr. Gertrude Kelly and Helen Golden were among the pickets interviewed. Golden was acting secretary of the Irish Progressive League. Three of the pickets were members of an Irish repertory company, the Celtic Players, which had ties to the IPL and was committed to popularizing in America the works of Ireland's Gaelic Renaissance: John Millington Synge, Lady Gregory, William Butler Yeats, Padraic Pearse, and others.[47] Eileen Curran, much quoted during the Whitehall Street protests, headed the company. She was about to play the greatest role of her life.

The second day of their picketing, an employee of the U.S. Navy office located directly above the British Consulate dumped a bucket of water on the women picketing below. Reporters treated the incident as symbolic of the hopelessness of the women's effort to free Terence MacSwiney with a New York picket line.

On August 27, however, approximately 30 Women Pickets moved from Whitehall Street to the West Side pier where Mannix's late ship, the *Baltic*, was returning to port that morning. They carried a new banner, with the watchwords: "British Body Snatchers." The women talked to longshoremen during their noontime lunch break and passed out three-by-five-inch handbills calling for a boycott against British shipping. A group of longshoremen accompanied the women to Pier 59, where the *Baltic* lay anchored.

Looming above them, on the deck of the Baltic, members of the engine room crew were milling around on their lunch break. The *New York Times* (Aug. 28, 1920) reported that one of the Women Pickets climbed on top of a parked truck and shouted up to them "a violent speech." The British seamen appeared to listen to the picket's harangue and then disappeared from the deck of *Baltic*. After a number of minutes passed, a reported 50 to 150 stokers from the crew of the *Baltic* agreed to quit work in sympathy with MacSwiney and Mannix.

These were the same engine room hands who had threatened to strike the *Baltic* on July 31 if White Star Line management refused passage to Archbishop Mannix. Outraged by Mannix's arrest at sea, they threatened to shut down the engines the morning of August 27 when their skipper, fearing a disturbance in port, attempted at the last minute to divert the *Baltic* away from New York harbor.[48] (In preceding weeks there had been pledges by the British labor movement to boycott arms shipments to the British army in Ireland.)

With the *Baltic*'s striking coal stokers and longshoremen in tow, the Women Pickets marched to Pier 60 where the *Olympic* was berthed. The *Olympic*'s longshoremen were implored to strike to free MacSwiney and compel Archbishop Mannix's passage to Ireland. Although many of the Chelsea longshoremen were first-and second-generation Irishmen, it was a large request to ask them to strike. Missing a day's pay was a difficult sacrifice, given the hit-or-miss nature of their employment—the men shaped up daily for work. The Chelsea longshoremen had already borne the brunt of their union officials' wrath the year before when they had led a month-long wildcat strike for better wages.[49]

Throwing caution to the winds, the longshoremen working the *Olympic* hung up their cargo hooks and joined the strike. Why they did so is cause for speculation: 92-year-old Teddy Gleason, who went to work on the West Side docks in 1917 (and served as president of the International Longshoremen's Association from 1963 to 1987) recalled the West Side longshoremen were attuned to the struggles of Ireland, and endless collections were taken up on the waterfront for successive Irish relief funds. In addition, longshore work gangs tended to be made up exclusively of men from the same county, reinforcing their nationalist sentiments.[50]

Long-time president of Chelsea Longshore Local 791 Joe Ryan refused to support the walkout. Although Ryan had been named to a council of New York labor leaders seeking united labor action on Ireland's behalf, he declared the walkout would impede pending contract negotiations. "All the men will be back to work this morning, a good night's sleep will cause them to forget all about Ireland," an unnamed officer of the ILA told reporters.[51]

Without authorization from their union, the longshoremen working the *Acquitania*, *Pannonia*, and *Celtic* on August 27 quit work at the Women Pickets' call. The growing army of strikers paraded from pier to pier, calling on the longshoremen at each dock to down their tools and join the strike.

Newspaper accounts report that the strike seemed to hang in the balance when the mob of strikers reached the Red Star Line's *Finland*, which was being worked by gangs of African American longshoremen. Irish and African American longshoremen in New York City had been at each other's throats since at least the 1850s.[52] Among the first African Americans lynched in the 1863 Draft Riots were longshoremen who had been competing for jobs with the Irish on the West Side docks.

Irish longshoremen had been excluding African Americans from employment on the docks ever since. African American longshoremen fought back when they could. A milestone strike in New York harbor in 1887 involving 50,000 waterfront workers affiliated with the Knights of Labor was broken, in part, by the importation of African American longshoremen. The National Steamship Line and Atlantic Transport Company used the same tactics to break subsequent strikes, as did the Ward Line in 1895, which hired African American longshoremen exclusively from that time forward. Although the successive longshore unions that succeeded the Knights—the American Longshoremen's Union, the reconstituted Longshoremen's Union Protective Association, and the International Longshoremen's Association—all formally banned racial discrimination, segregated locals emerged.[53] In short, a great deal of history soured the deliberations of 300 African American and Italian longshoremen over whether to join the August 27 strike for Irish freedom.

The *Finland*'s work crew of African American longshoremen broke out of their caucus and joined their fellow workers on strike. They swung into the rear of the line of march, reportedly to the cheers of the longshoremen awaiting them. The Women Pickets next led the African American longshore gangs working the *Norman Monarch* out on strike.[54]

The decision of African American longshoremen to join the strike appears to have been influenced by Marcus Garvey, an outspoken champion of Irish freedom. In two separate addresses during the International Convention of the Negro Peoples of the World (which was taking place at the same time as the shipping strike, and which self-consciously was organized in imitation of the Irish Race Conventions of 1916, 1918, and 1919), Garvey declared his solidarity with the Irish independence struggle.[55]

When a strike call was inadvertently made at the French Lines dock, out came longshoremen and a number of French seamen. By 4:30 p.m. every British ship on the West Side was tied up. James Lynch, organizer for the Marine, Firemen, Oilers and Watertenders Union, called for a boycott against British shipping "from Galveston, Texas to Portland, Maine."[56]

"Well, we did it," strike leader Eileen Curran told reporters: "We're trying to show the English that American women of Irish birth can keep them busier than they've ever been in their lives. Let them release MacSwiney and then we'll begin a new effort to compel them to let Archbishop Mannix into Ireland. The men are with us. I knew they would be."[57] The Women Pickets sent a telegram that afternoon to Lloyd George: "The sound of death in the throat of Terence MacSwiney is the death knell of your adventure in Ireland. We hear the bells tolling. The people are gathering. Oil your tanks. Polish up your guns."

The success of the Women Pickets in closing down the West Side docks was capped that evening with a master stroke of public relations. The Lexington Opera House was rented for a victory rally. Through the combined organizational abilities of Eileen Curran's Celtic Players, Frank P. Walsh's American Commission on Irish Independence, Helen Golden and Margaret Hickey's Irish Progressive League, and Dr. Gertrude Kelly's Cumann na mBan, the audience attracted to the Lexington Opera House that evening was twice its seating capacity.

At 8:30 p.m., August 27, as the New York *American* prepared a banner headline for the next day's paper: "Great Ship Strike Here as M'Swiney Slumps," Frank P. Walsh gaveled to order some 3,500 people inside the Lexington Opera House.[58] Simultaneously, Reverend John Dooley of Corpus Christi Church called to order an equal number of people outside the hall, on the steps of the auditorium. (Speakers repeated their talks, for the benefit of the spillover meeting.) Meanwhile, a third meeting, of striking longshoremen and nationalist sympathizers, sponsored by the Friends of Irish Freedom, was taking place at the Twenty-third Street Opera House (formerly the Pike Opera House). As all three meetings got under way, the heroes of the hour, the coal stokers from the *Baltic*, were transported up to the 51st Street Lexington Opera House in chartered Fifth Avenue buses.

Newspaper accounts of the Lexington Opera House meeting describe an audience carried away with emotion. When 50 British coal stokers from the *Baltic* marched into hall, the standing-room-only crowd "howled" with joy. Walsh saluted the British seamen: "Perhaps we are standing at the dawn of a new era. These men who have marched onto the stage today symbolize the resistless force of labor in the world today." For many in the hall that night it seemed a fact that Britain's mastery of the ocean, the linchpin of its empire, had been challenged that day in New York harbor.[59]

For three and half hours the crowd cheered speeches by Major Kelly of the Fighting 69th Infantry, Judge Goff, Patrick McCartan, Harry Boland, and Liam Mellows—the leading lights of the Irish independence movement (or more precisely, that part of the movement that had sided with Eamon de Valera against Devoy and Cohalan). Each speaker expressed in passionate, often eloquent, rhetoric the same sentiment: the old Fenian dream of striking the blow from America that would free Ireland had been realized that day on the Chelsea docks.

De Valera gave a speech the *Irish World* (Sept. 4, 1920, 1) called "the most impassioned address he ever delivered." MacSwiney was a personal friend, and de Valera saw in the sympathy strike a fleeting chance to save his friend's life. He invoked the image of MacSwiney's young wife, with her babe in arms, and blasted the *New York Times*, which that day in an editorial had called Mac-Swiney "a suicide." (Immediately there were cries from a woman's voice in the audience of "Let us picket the *New York Times*!" and "Picket the *Times* When the Meeting is Over!")[60] de Valera invoked, too, the image of the key to the Bastille, which he had viewed at Mount Vernon. Lafayette had entrusted it to Tom Paine to give to George Washington after the fall of the Bastille. "Another Bastille has to fall!" de Valera declaimed, and the audience roared its approval.

Dudley Field Malone, a candidate for governor of New York on the Farmer–Labor Party ticket, made the practical suggestion that a fund be established to help the longshoremen meet expenses while they stayed out on strike. He contributed $50 to start it out. The crowd responded by heaping the various collection baskets with silver coins and larger bills to support the longshoremen.

Walsh closed the meeting by bringing on stage the women who had led the waterfront strike: "When a handful of brave young women today brought their banners to the ships, they singlehandedly set in motion events which shall cause the downfall of that empire which has built up its great power upon crimes committed against weaker nations all over the world."[61] Who were these "brave young women," and what drew them into the fight? Only seven of the 30 women who picketed the ships on August 27 can be traced in the New York City Directory and other sources. Dr. Kelly, Eileen Curran, and Helen Golden have already been mentioned. Joining them were Helen Crowe, a New York librarian; Mary L. Sullivan, a switchboard operator for the New York City Department of Parks; Helen G. Kelly, a Cumann na mBan member; Kathleen Sheehan, a school teacher; and Margaret Warner, an IPL member who with Sheehan had helped plan the bon voyage rally for Archbishop Mannix.[62]

Helen Golden (and a working committee apparently composed of labor leaders and ranking Irish republicans) appears to have orchestrated the strike.[63] Golden was an actress and suffragist from a Protestant Anglo-Saxon family with ties to the Daughters of the American Revolution. She had been drawn into the nationalist movement in 1916 when she met her husband Peter Golden, also an actor. In a dramatic letter to Dr. Kelly written August 23, the first day of picketing at the Whitehall Street British Consulate, Helen Golden apologized for physically confronting Dr. Kelly when the latter suggested the Women Pickets move their picket line that day to the docks. Golden instructed Dr. Kelly that a major action was being planned on the docks for Friday, August 27: "but that must be 'shrouded in darkness' meantime I am trying to get every picket I can to line up for Fri. without letting them know what it's about. 100 pickets if possible. Between now and then mean to Pickett (*sic*) the Consulate for 2 or 3 hrs. every day—just a few girls at a time."[64]

When the Women Pickets reported for duty at 6:30 a.m. on August 28, day two of the strike, they found their previous day's efforts had been severely undermined. New York City police kept the women on the far side of West Street away from the docks. The Cunard and White Star Lines put their ticket sales and administrative corps to work alongside their ships' stewards departments, carrying passengers' luggage onto the ships scheduled to sail that day, in a frantic effort to break the strike. An unknown party hung a sign on the gate to the Cunard Line docks calling the women "House Wreckers." Two of the Women Pickets darted through police lines to remove it.[65]

Approximately 2,000 longshoremen who usually worked the Chelsea docks stayed away from their jobs.[66] Cargo was not loaded. Many ships missed the tide. The *Celtic* sailed without 600 trunks belonging to its steerage passengers. The *Mauretania* had to detour up to Halifax to take on enough coal to get it across the Atlantic. The *Call* reported the *Olympic* left port without 20 of its firemen, "and other ships were similarly shorthanded." The *Pannonia* missed its sailing day completely because its Italian American coal passers refused to work. The rest of the transatlantic liners sailed, however, and it was a grave setback for hopes that the strike could save MacSwiney's life.

Although the British seamen and Irish longshoremen had struck principally in response to the outrageous behavior accorded Archbishop Mannix, the hunger strike of Terence MacSwiney quickly became the central issue in the strike. Just two weeks into MacSwiney's hunger strike, newspaper headlines were blaring: "MacSweney [*sic*] Dying in English Prison."[67] reporters kept a death watch outside London's Brixton Prison, never imagining the mayor of Cork's death agony might stretch out to 74 days. Not only the *New York American*, which courted Irish readers, but the *Times, Sun, Tribune, World,* and other papers ran a front-page column every day, expecting it to be MacSwiney's last.[68]

When African American longshoremen initially returned to work on August 28, a woman picket persuaded them to come back out again. The *World* (Aug. 29, 1920) reported they walked off their jobs, chanting: "Free Africa" and suggested some of their number were Marcus Garvey supporters. The *Times* claimed the men returned to work after the noon hour, but a subsequent message from Garvey and a deputation by Garvey's lieutenant, Reverend J. F. Selkridge, apparently did keep the men from working British ships.[69] Negotiations between the Irish strikers and Garvey's United Negro Improvement Association were conducted by Dudley Field Malone. Malone took 14 Irish longshoremen and sympathizers up to Garvey's Liberty Hall in Harlem, both to explain the strike and to hammer out a resolution of mutual assistance for the future.

On September 10, some 250 African American longshoremen were brought in from other districts to work the White Star Line docks. They were fed and housed on Pier 60 for the duration of the walkout so they would not have to walk through the picket lines.[70] Strikers asked the International Longshoremen's Association to bar the men as strikebreakers. But association officials refused to intervene, on the grounds that the strikebreaking longshoremen were all dues-paying members and the union had not authorized a strike. On September 11 the Women Pickets enlisted a number of African American women to stand at the head of the pier to try to dissuade the men from working.[71]

Since the foreman of the 250 "strikebreakers" working Pier 60 was an African American, and the Garvey movement was strong among longshoremen, Helen Golden invited the man to come to strike headquarters on 23rd Street to meet with her and a representative from the United Negro Improvement Association. Past incidences of "apathetical treatment" by Irish longshoremen, however, doomed their September 13 negotiations. The UNIA representative called for African American longshoremen to boycott British ships on every pier except Pier 60, at the same time expressing the hope that closer cooperation between Irish and African American would be possible in the future.[72]

The strike on the West Side docks achieved significant success in obstructing the loading of cargo on British ships, but it failed to prevent the passenger liners from sailing.[73] The Women Pickets fanned out in early September in a desperate effort to extend the strike. They persuaded 3,000 Brooklyn longshoremen to strike on September 2 and pledge not to work any English vessels "until England recognizes the Irish Republic."[74] Women Pickets led protests in Charlestown and East Boston, and their Boston longshore boycott was a notable success, spreading also to freight handlers and employees of grain elevators. Longshoremen in Philadelphia, New Orleans, Newport News, Galveston, and other cities sent telegrams pledging they, too, would refuse to unload British ships.

Gertrude Corless and Kathleen O'Brennan went to Washington to join suffrage leaders Emma Wold and Eleanor Taylor Marsh, as well as Irish women representatives, in making a personal appeal to Secretary of State Colby for relief for Ireland from British occupation.[75] Jersey City struck. Hoboken started boycotting British ships after speeches there by Leonora O'Reilly and Gertrude Corless. O'Reilly, Dr. Gertrude Kelly, and Kathleen O'Brennan addressed a mass meeting in Bayonne, as well.

A sampling of Leonora O'Reilly's diary entries for August and September 1920 describes how totally the Women Pickets allied with the Irish Progressive League were committed to the waterfront strike: 8/31: "Picket in NY"; 9/1: "Speak to longshoremen at St. V[eronica's] Hall . . . Slept . . . 3 a.m." 9/8: "Home midnight dead tired," September 10: "Plainfield, N.J . . . about 100 people . . . Mrs. C[orless] gets dizzy spells." To make things harder, a New York subway strike forced her to walk to her Manhattan picketing and speaking engagements: "Twice back and forth on shanks' mare to Brooklyn" is O'Reilly's diary entry for September 3.[76]

While this barrage of organizing activity was going on, a number of the Women Pickets were doing double duty, taking part in the street-corner meetings of the Irish Progressive League, as well. The IPL sponsored both a speakers' bureau and a class for neophyte soapboxers, taught by esteemed orators like Leonora O'Reilly and Jeremiah O'Leary. On September 4, Margaret Gilmore, a graduate of Jeremiah O'Leary's soapboxing school, persuaded 1,000 Manhattan warehousemen to stop handling cargo for British ships until MacSwiney was released and British troops left Ireland.[77]

The Women Pickets kept the strike alive for three and a half weeks from their 23rd Street and 10th Avenue headquarters in the Adelphi Hotel. Their "Chelsea Pier Picket" campaign administered a strike fund, with Dr. Gertrude Kelly acting as treasurer, which gave stipends to longshoremen willing to stay out on strike. Funds were solicited through public meetings, street-corner rallies, and an open notice in the *Irish World*. The Cumann na mBan sponsored a successful meeting the first week of September in the Lexington Opera House to raise money for the striking longshoremen. A letter to the editor of the *Gaelic American* estimated that more than $10,000 was distributed to longshoremen through a separate fund administered by the Friends of Irish Freedom.

The Women Pickets received a powerful tribute on September 7 from Muriel MacSwiney. Speaking for her husband, Mrs. MacSwiney thanked the Americans who took part in the shipping strike. She considered that action, and their simultaneous boycott against British manufactures, genuine efforts to save her husband's life, as opposed to the lip service and empty resolutions she had received from organizations in England and America.

On September 21 the longshore strike was called off. The Women Pickets did not save the life Terence MacSwiney. He died October 25 on the seventy-fourth day of his hunger strike. In a sense, the waterfront strike for Terence MacSwiney mirrored the entire American campaign for Ireland's freedom: by herculean labors it managed to achieve a great deal in America, yet made little impact on events in Ireland.

The Women Pickets in widows' weeds were a dramatic presence at the memorial held for Terence MacSwiney on October 31, at the Polo Grounds. De Valera and New York governor Al Smith were featured speakers at the mammoth rally. Newspapers reported upward of 35,000 people attended, with tens of thousands kept outside for lack of seats.[78] The Women Pickets formed an honor guard. One held a placard much photographed the day of the funeral: "One Man Can Save a Nation, As One Man Has Redeemed the World."

The dramatic testimony of Muriel MacSwiney, Terence's widow, at December 1920 hearings of the American Commission on Conditions in Ireland, and her subsequent American speaking tour, may have marked the apogee of women's influence on the nationalist movement in America. The woman's suffrage wave that the Women Pickets seem to have been riding (accounting for the volume of reporting on their activities) crested with the passage of the Nineteenth Amendment. The Irish Progressive League, which in many ways was the engine vitalizing the Women Pickets, submerged its organizational work into de Valera's American Association for the Recognition of the Irish Republic (organized in November of that year). Factionalism on the part of Gertrude Corless may have cost the Women Pickets their place in the histories of the nationalist movement. Corless, like Mary MacSwiney and many of the women in the Dáil Éireann, adamantly refused to accept partition and the treaty. For the next few years Corless occasionally mobilized the remaining members of the Women Pickets. In January 1923 they are reported breaking up a New York City meeting in support of the Irish Free State. In 1925 Corless ran into legal difficulties and dropped out of sight.[79]

Why were the women of the American Irish independence movement able to wield so much influence in the years between the 1916 Easter Rising and the signing of the Treaty in 1921? First, they filled a power vacuum during World War I, just as the Ladies Land League had in 1881. Second, the achievements of Maud Gonne, Constance Markievicz, Mary Colum—and Alice Paul's triumphant generation of suffragists—provided strong role models for activist women. Third, by 1916 the American Irish women in the nationalist movement represented two and a half decades of continuous organizing, of women by women. They were no longer content to be "auxiliaries."

When Gertrude Kelly made her 1914 appeal to "societies of Irish women" to join the Cumann na mBan, she revealed the degree of organization American Irish women had achieved since the mid-1890s: "A.O.H. Auxiliaries, Ladies' County Societies, Gaelic Societies, Industrial Organizations, Benefit Societies, Literary and Dramatic Societies, women of any and no affiliation, without regard to class or creed . . . co-operate with us in securing Ireland's place in the sun."

Through "separate spheres" and years of patient organizing, Gertrude Kelly, Gertrude Corless, Mary McWhorter, Helen Golden, and all the other American Irish women who achieved such marvels between 1916 and 1921 were able to draw from large, resourceful women's nationalist organizations an activist core eager to fight with new tactics for Ireland's independence. The Women Pickets and the Irish Progressive League represented the new generation of Irishmen *and Irishwomen* hailed in Padraic Pearse's proclamation of the Irish Republic, "asserting their right to national freedom" as equals.

CHAPTER 15

Of "Mornin' Glories" and "Fine Old Oaks"

JOHN PURROY MITCHEL, AL SMITH, AND

REFORM AS AN EXPRESSION OF

IRISH-AMERICAN ASPIRATION

O N JULY 6, 1918, Major John Purroy Mitchel, the former "boy mayor" of New York, died during a solo flight at Gerstner Field in Lake Charles, Louisiana. Mitchel, who was not quite 39 years old, had almost completed his training before leading his squadron into combat in France. During the fatal flight he attempted a roll. His altitude was about 500 feet when the plane turned upside down, and he fell out. He had not fastened his safety belt.[1]

"A most engaging and promising personality disappeared from public life," commented Oswald Garrison Villard in an obituary notice in the *Nation*. "Two years ago there was no young man in the United States with such bright prospects before him." The beau ideal of municipal reformers, Mitchel "had all the charm of youth" plus "good looks, dignified and straightforward bearing, and in speaking an admirable address." Even the White House had seemed within his reach, at least to admirers like Villard. Another, Julian Street writing in *Collier's Weekly*, quoted "one of the shrewdest political prognosticators in this country" that "so far as the Democratic party is concerned, Mayor Mitchel is about their best 'white hope' for the presidency." The mayor reminded this unnamed observer of Theodore Roosevelt. "He may make mistakes, but they are the kind of mistakes Roosevelt used to make—likable mistakes; and the mistakes of a strong fighter—and he gets away with them, as Roosevelt always could, through sheer honesty of purpose, energy, and personality."[2]

Nor were these the only public suggestions that the youthful mayor, the son and grandson of Irish immigrants, and a Catholic, would make a credible presidential candidate.[3] Yet, as Villard lamented, "the whirligig of fate spins unceasingly," and Mitchel's political prospects, so brilliant in the early fall of 1917, turned to ashes that November when the Democrat candidate, Judge John Francis ("Red Mike") Hylan, crushed his bid for reelection by 313,956 (48.9%) to 155,497 votes (24.2%).[4] Hylan's two-to-one margin of victory was the largest in New York City history as was his 150,000 plus vote plurality. Mitchel, in fact, barely nosed out Socialist candidate Morris Hillquit, who polled 145,332 votes (22.6%). Rounding out the field was Republican William Bennett, who captured only 55,438 votes (8.6%) in the November election, but who had bested Mitchel by 224 votes in the Republican primary the previous September. On the ticket with Hylan, running for president of the Board of Aldermen, was another ambitious Irish Catholic, Al Smith. No one was suggesting in 1917 or 1918 that he would someday make a plausible presidential candidate. Tammany boss Charles F. Murphy, on the other hand, was thinking about Smith as a likely governor.[5]

Mitchel's story, friend and foe agreed, had a simple moral. He had intelligence, dedication, and many other fine qualities, but he just was not a politician. He was a reformer, and "reformers," as Tammany ward leader George Washington Plunkitt once scornfully remarked to reporter William L. Riordon, "were mornin' glories—looked lovely in the mornin' and withered up in a short time, while the regular machines went on flourishin' forever, like fine old oaks." The reformer, Plunkitt continued, "can make a show for a while, but he always comes down like a rocket."[6]

Despite his flair for metaphor, Plunkitt's point about the urban reformers of the late nineteenth and early twentieth centuries was explicitly prosaic. "Politics is as much a regular business as the grocery or the dry goods or the drug business. You've got to be trained up to it or you're sure to fail." The typical "goo goo," as Plunkitt and his fellow Sachems dismissively referred to good government crusaders like Mitchel, "hasn't been brought up in the difficult business of politics and he makes a mess of it every time." This was why no reform administration had ever succeeded itself.[7]

The temptation to explain Mitchel's triumphs and defeats in terms of Plunkitt's witty, but hard-nosed dicta has proved irresistible, perhaps because no political career in New York history so literally resembled a rocket in flight as did John Purroy Mitchel's. Elected on a Fusion ticket in 1913, with the largest plurality any mayor had received since 1897, he lost four years later by an even wider margin.[8] His victory had led many to predict that Tammany's power in New York was finally about to be overcome.[9] His defeat marked not only the rejuvenation of the Hall, which went on to sweep four consecutive mayoralty races, but also the abrupt end of the "era of genteel reform" in New York.[10]

Mitchel had been "admittedly the ablest and best Mayor New York ever had," according to Oswald Garrison Villard, editor of the *Nation*, a judgment advanced time and again by advocates of "scientific" and "progressive" reform. Theodore Roosevelt, in endorsing Mitchel's bid for reelection in 1917, claimed he had "given us as nearly an ideal administration of the New York City government as I have seen in my lifetime, or as I have heard of since New York became a big city." William Hard, in a two-part article in the *New Republic*, which "sized up" Mitchel's challengers in 1917 and found them wanting, noted that the Mitchel administration "is regarded by most municipal reformers as being among the very last words in municipal administrative technique." He had "against political influence, against commercial influence, against every influence . . . kept his departments sound and honest and . . . confirmed them in instincts and habits of scientific service." He had laid "sure and deep . . . those foundations of efficiency, those traditions of uninfluenced devotion to the public welfare" so necessary for good government.[11]

Yet the same qualities that made Mitchel so superb a mayor, his admirers believed, made him a hopelessly bad politician. Howard Lee McBain, writing in the *National Municipal Review*, the bible of "scientific" urban reform, explained Mitchel's defeat as due to the fact that "he bothered more about being mayor, more about doing a thoroughgoing and clean job in that difficult office, than about making himself solid with party organizations, or building a political machine of his own, or doing the thing that would catch the popular fancy." Further, "in doing this job as it should have been done and as no one else had ever done it, he trod upon the toes of group after group whose class or factional interests stood in the way of the interests of the general public."[12]

Al Smith, whose election as president of the Board of Aldermen in 1917 provided a springboard for his successful gubernatorial campaign in 1918, offered a similar analysis. "Mitchel had a large and powerful independent following. He was a man of unquestioned ability. He brought about many desirable reforms in the administration of city business, but the loose cog in the wheel happened to be the fact that he held a political position and was a thousand miles away from being a politician."[13]

Not every exponent of what can be called the Plunkitt thesis was so generous. Robert Moses, who began his public career as a Mitchel loyalist, and later became one of Smith's closest advisers, dismissed the Fusion administration as an "honest outfit committed to saving rubber bands, using both ends of the pencil and similar efficiency devices, and to the impossible promise of making vast physical improvements without spending any money." Critics like Moses and Mitchel's staunchest defenders alike agreed on his lack of political savvy. He was unable "to make the plain people of the city feel that he is their friend, their supporter, their servant, their leader, their Mayor," as Oswald Garrison Villard put it a week before the election in 1917.[14]

Historians have by and large hewed to the same line, when they have paid attention to Mitchel at all.[15] In reducing his career to an illustration of Plunkitt's witty aphorisms on "very practical politics," however, one runs the risk of falling into the trap, so cogently described by Alexis de Tocqueville, of seeking to make sense of history as though it were simply politics. It is understandable that politicians, "living in the midst of disconnected daily facts, are prone to imagine that everything is attributable to particular incidents, and that the wires which they pull are the same that move the world." Historians should know better.[16] And, in fact, there was much more to Mitchel than Plunkitt's "mornin' glory" metaphor suggests.

His career has much to teach about the end of Progressivism, about the concomitant rise of a new sort of "urban liberalism" that prefigured the New Deal and made Al Smith a national figure, about the origins of the Red Scare in New York and of Tammany's surprising role as defender of civil liberties. Most important, Mitchel's career has much to teach about the ways Irish Americans sought city and national power in the opening decades of the twentieth century. In all of these respects, and especially with regard to the last, Mitchel can serve as a counterpoint to Al Smith.

It is, therefore, time to take a fresh look at Mitchel. He followed a radically different path toward political power than did Smith, but he courted, and for a time very successfully, some of the same reform elements, as well as the same independent voters that Smith would later seek to win over. Between them Mitchel and Smith explored much of the range of Irish American political aspiration between the incorporation of Greater New York in 1897 and the "Brown Derby" campaign of 1928. As a consequence, the career of each makes more sense when seen in the context of the other's.

Mitchel's aim was to prove that an Irish Catholic could have a central role in American life because he could be a more perfect WASP than the members of the Union League Club. This ambition permeated his career as it did his life. It informed his understanding of politics and of reform. It defined his patriotism. It shaped his Catholicism. His message to the Yankee establishment was that in every way that counted he was one of them.

Smith's career exemplified an altogether different vision of how the Irish should fit into American public life. His message was that they, and all the other ethnic groups, were indeed different and that the resulting diversity was healthy. American culture ought to make room for all. Smith, as a result, never sought to distance himself from his ethnic roots, never took off his derby hat, never put away his stogie. Instead he tried to prove to native-born Protestants that he and his were better than they thought, were truer to the basic ideals of America than their critics were themselves.

In this, as in much else, the first two Irish American Catholics to inspire serious speculation about their fitness to run for president were polar opposites.

Mitchel, the son and grandson of Irish immigrants, grew up in a comfortably affluent home in the Bronx. He studied with private tutors, then attended St. John's (later Fordham) College Preparatory School, Columbia College, and New York Law School. His family employed servants and took vacations in New England and on the continent. Both the Mitchels and the Purroys (whose ancestry was Spanish) were active in New York City politics at the highest levels. Mitchel's maternal uncle, Henry Purroy, was the first Bronx member of the Board of Aldermen, in 1874, and became board president in 1876. A sometime ally of Tammany, he went on to become fire commissioner, a position from which he could advance the careers of both his brother, who was a battalion chief in the department, and his brother-in-law, John's father James, who was fire marshall for the city. John Purroy Mitchel's own start in city politics came from family friend William B. Ellison, the city's corporation counsel, who appointed him to investigate charges of inefficiency in the office of Manhattan borough president John F. Ahearn in 1906.[17]

Even more valuable than his Purroy connections in the New York politics of the early twentieth century was the Mitchel name. The first John Mitchel, John Purroy's grandfather, was a celebrated Irish nationalist whose activism in the Young Ireland movement of the 1840s led to his trial and conviction for treason against Great Britain in 1848. Sentenced to 14 years' transportation to Van Diemen's Land, Mitchel escaped to the United States in 1853. He no sooner arrived in New York, to a hero's welcome from the city's Irish immigrants, than he founded the *Citizen,* a newspaper dedicated to the cause of Irish independence. He also developed a loyalty to the Democratic Party and quickly became a noted apologist for slavery. In 1856 he moved his family to Knoxville and started the *Southern Citizen.* In 1860 he moved again, this time to Paris, to better agitate for a free Ireland. In 1862 the Mitchels returned to the South and John Mitchel became editor of the *Richmond Enquirer.* His three sons enlisted in the Confederate army. Of the three, only John Purroy's father survived the fighting, and he lost an arm. In 1865 John Mitchel went back to New York, took over as editor of the *Daily News,* and immediately got into trouble for his pro-Southern editorials. After four months of confinement in Fort Monroe, he went to Paris to work in the Fenian cause, came back to New York to edit the *Irish Citizen,* and in 1875 returned to Ireland to stand for Parliament. The Tories refused to permit him to take his seat, but his Irish constituents insisted upon returning him in the by-election. Before anything further could transpire, Mitchel died on March 20, 1875.[18]

Smith, in contrast, grew up in poverty on Manhattan's Lower East Side. He quit school at age 12 to help support his recently widowed mother, held a variety of jobs during his teens, including several years of working 12- and 13-hour days at the Fulton Fish Market, and found recreation in amateur theatricals and a future in politics. Totally lacking in family connections, he set about becoming "a statesman" in exactly the fashion George Washington Plunkitt recommended. He made himself useful to the local Tammany leader. As he proved himself, he gradually earned more important responsibilities, moving up from subpoena server in the Office of the Commissioner of Jurors in 1895, his first political job, to member of the state assembly in 1903. All of his education, in both politics and the art of governing, came as on-the-job training.[19]

Despite inheriting a name synonymous with Irish nationalism, Mitchel's ambition to be as "American" as New York's Yankee elite led him to cultivate an aristocratic bearing. A 1917 portrait shows him in a characteristic pose—head held high, shoulders back. He made a practice of attending the balls and dinners of "the Four Hundred." He also made a point of refusing, as a hero-worshipping Emanie N. Sachs reported, "to attend passover balls and Labor day rallies. He said: 'I'll be damned if I will. I work hard, don't I? I'm human. I've got to have some recreation. I want to dance with my friends.'" Sachs also described Mitchel striding through his outer office, which was "filled with old friends and new ones, mostly job-hunters." He was "a triumphant, patrician young figure. . . .The blue eyes looked neither to right nor to left. The thin lips, lightly sardonic, pointed in at the corners. The face was aloof." His secretary had urged the mayor not to leave through the outer office. It was "'full of people waiting to see you. They won't like it if you go right through without talking to them.'" Mitchel had replied: "'I haven't time to talk to a lot of empty-headed yaps.'"[20]

To his admirers Mitchel's patrician manner sprang from his genuine disdain for political "show." Julian Street quoted the mayor's secretary about an appearance where Mitchel found himself expected to kiss the "prize baby at a baby show." "'He looked terrified at the idea. . . . I couldn't make him do it.'"[21] Plunkitt could readily have warned Mitchel of the political costs of such fastidiousness. "Puttin' on style don't pay in politics. The people won't stand for it." They did not want politicians who gave themselves airs and acted as though they were better than their constituents. As Plunkitt put it with his usual zest, even he had to be careful. The day before one election, his "enemies circulated a report that I had ordered a $10,000 automobile and a $125 dress suit." He "sent out contradictions as fast as I could," but still lost votes. "The people wouldn't have minded much if I had been accused of robbin' the city treasury, for they're used to slanders of that kind in campaigns, but the automobile and the dress suit were too much for them."[22]

Mitchel's fondness for fancy dress balls can thus seem proof of Al Smith's judgment that the "boy mayor" was "a thousand miles away from being a politician." Certainly Smith never sought to high-hat his supporters. Instead, as Norman Hapgood and Henry Moskowitz wrote in their admiring biography, there was "nothing to put Smith apart from the men in the street, except his brains and his industry." In his dress, forms of recreation, constant willingness to listen to ordinary people, Smith demonstrated that he thought of himself as "one of the majority."[23]

Yet there was more to Mitchel's refusal to dance the two-step on the Lower East Side or attend picnics in Brooklyn than political naiveté mixed with stubbornness. There was a determination to insist upon one social identity and to deny another. This was the charge of his detractors, especially William Randolph Hearst, whose morning *American* and *Evening Journal* portrayed the mayor as a social climber. Of his passion for dancing with the Four Hundred, the *American* wrote:

> Svelte as a fawn in a natural history,
> Limber and swift as a young kangaroo,
> With all of the Russians' interpretive mystery,
> He shakes his emotional shoe.
>
> Opinions may differ about his ability,
> The fussy may look at his record askance,
> But there can't be a doubt of his grace and agility;
> John Purroy Mitchel knows how to dance![24]

Warming to the same theme, the *Evening Journal* wrote in 1917 that "only five years ago, Mr. John Purroy Mitchel was a sharp-faced little ambitious politician, vowing that some day he would get somewhere, and, if possible, as far as Newport." Success, the article continued, had finally crowned his efforts and one "great night" a mayor "breathless" with excitement and "with a bright pink spot on each cheek . . . burst through his front door and cried" out to his wife "'My dear, Mr. Vanderbilt called me Jack.'" Ordinary folk, "satisfied with [their] old friends" and "not tormented by a desire for 'social success,'" could "hardly imagine how the heart beats and the pulse throbs when a man like John Purroy Mitchel with his own ears hears one of the Vanderbilt family say, 'Hello, Jack.'"[25]

Mitchel, the *Evening Journal* charged, was in full flight from his Irish immigrant background. "His name is John Purroy; and in his youth he often heard old, plain friends of the family call him 'Jawn.'" But the mayor had put those days behind him for "when you have struggled up, have got away from what you despise, away from the old associations and have forgotten the old people, the old friendships, the old ties, and have actually heard 'Hello, Jack' from the socially sanctified lips, some happiness will always remain with you," even if the voters should choose to punish you for playing "the Little Brother to the Rich."[26] However vicious the Hearst attacks, they went to the heart of Mitchel's attempt to present himself as a perfect WASP at ease only among the smart set. What made them so effective, and Osward Garrison Villard estimated that they had "poisoned the minds of a good many people" against the mayor, was that they pointed to the fact that, in making his way into high society, John Purroy Mitchel had effectually repudiated his own background.[27]

This was true politically as well as socially, for in Mitchel's hands municipal reform became explicitly anti-Catholic and anti-Irish. This began with Mitchel's determination to surmount his ethnic background by having nothing whatever to do with Tammany. The mayor had a horror of anything that smacked of the sort of politics George Washington Plunkitt and Al Smith practiced and preached. Julian Street asked him in 1917: "'No matter how straight and clean a man may wish to be, doesn't he have to compromise a little bit now and then if he's in politics? Doesn't he have to balance one man, or one crowd, against another? Doesn't he have to trim and be artful, sometimes?'" Mitchel's reply was a prompt "No." "'A man in public office has to associate sometimes with men he doesn't like to associate with, but the idea of being "slick," of "playing the game," is the old idea—the Tammany idea. I don't believe a man has to stoop to such devices. To my mind there is only one course to pursue: *Be right and speak out.*'"[28]

His was an administration of experts, not of political "yaps."[29] One of the most visible was John A. Kingsbury, the Fusion commissioner of public charities. Kingsbury had previously been the assistant secretary of the State Charities Aid Association and then general secretary of the Association for the Improvement of the Condition of the Poor. He was a noted critic of publicly supported charities, particularly of New York's Tammany-inspired system of funneling public money to sectarian orphanages.[30] Most of these were run by the Catholic archdiocese. So when Kingsbury undertook a special investigation of private institutions receiving city funds, the stage was set for a potential confrontation not only between Fusion and Tammany but between the mayor and the cardinal.

Kingsbury appointed a deputy, William J. Doherty, to conduct the investigation and also named individuals associated with Catholic, Jewish, and Protestant institutions to the panel.[31] Almost immediately the Catholic representative resigned. The investigation proceeded without him being replaced. Nor would Mitchel accede to requests from unnamed "Church officials" who "tried to influence the Mayor to end the investigation." He would do no such thing. He would "be right and speak out." "These people are trying to give me orders," he reportedly said to a friend. "I'm the mayor of New York. I don't take orders from anyone, even from them."[32]

Doherty's inquiry turned up irregularities in some 12 Catholic and 14 non-Catholic orphanages. All had cooperated with the Doherty panel, all accepted its recommendations for changes in order to continue receiving city funds, and all actually instituted the required changes. So, had the Fusion administration simply wished to make sure the city's orphans were receiving the best care available, the matter might have ended with Doherty's filing of his report.[33]

In fact, the charities case was just beginning. The reason was that Kingsbury and Mitchel had challenged the competence of the State Board of Charities in initiating the inquiry in the first place, since it was the body that certified the fitness of private institutions to receive city money. And the state board had inspected and approved all 26 of the orphanages Doherty subsequently found deficient. So Mitchel, at Kingsbury's recommendation, urged Governor Charles Seymour Whitman to launch an investigation of the state board. Whitman agreed and put attorney Charles H. Strong, a former president of the City Club, in charge. Strong, the governor promised, "will have an absolutely free hand." For his part, Strong made it clear from the outset that he saw his role as furthering the Fusion administration's agenda. His inquiry would look toward "some simplified system of control of State charitable institutions" and into "the question which Commissioner John A. Kingsbury of New York has raised as to the quality of inspection by the State Board of Charities."[34]

Fusion could only make its case against the state board in the Strong hearings by detailing all of the deficiencies that Doherty had found more than a year before and that even Kingsbury conceded had already been corrected. Catholic officials were irate. Kingsbury's response was a model of incomprehension. Certain people were trying "to create an impression that the Department of Charities is seeking to hamper and harass the institutions of a certain religious denomination," a charge he dismissed as "absurd." The Doherty investigation had looked into "institutions of all denominations."[35]

In fact, Kingsbury financed the printing and the distribution of 7,000 copies of a pamphlet that highlighted the most sensational findings of the Doherty inquiry, including the entirely baseless charge that in one Catholic orphanage "orphans and pigs were fed out of the same utensils." According to William H. Allen, a former Mitchel supporter who had resigned from the Bureau of Municipal Research when it decided to abandon public criticism of the Fusion administration, Kingsbury knew this charge was without foundation but permitted its circulation anyway.[36] Whether the commissioner knowingly engaged in calumny or not, he found himself in a pamphlet war. The Catholic champion was a Brooklyn priest, Father William B. Farrell, and Catholic laity could soon pick up copies of his *A Public Scandal, Charity for Revenue,* and *Priest Baiting in 1916* on their way home from Sunday mass since the archdiocese permitted them to be distributed in all the Catholic churches in the city. William H. Allen estimated that 700,000 of the pamphlets were circulated, each bearing the message "After reading, pass on to your fair-minded neighbor" on its cover.[37]

Father Farrell gave as good as he got. Summoned to testify at the Strong hearings, he accused Strong of doing Kingsbury's and Mitchel's dirty work for them. Strong was engaged in character assassination, he charged. Mayor Mitchel, convinced that Farrell's pamphlets were libelous and that the chancellor of the archdiocese, Monsignor John J. Dunn, in permitting their distribution in the city's Catholic churches, had engaged in a criminal conspiracy with Father Farrell to commit libel, authorized the tapping of the two priests' telephone conversations, as well as those of several other critics of the Doherty report. In May of 1916 the mayor submitted the wiretap evidence to a grand jury; Father Farrell and several of the other objects of the taps immediately demanded that the grand jury consider charges of illegal wiretapping against the mayor. The fat was truly in the fire, especially when state senator George P. Thompson declared that he would hold an investigation of the whole question of the use of wiretaps.[38]

Mitchel decided to testify before the Thompson committee himself, and what he had to say infuriated Catholics everywhere. Some of his "co-religionists" had from the first days of his administration engaged in a "well-organized and purposeful conspiracy" to "obstruct" the legitimate activities of his administration and to "interfere" with "the proper and orderly conduct or control of the private charitable institutions of the city." It amounted to nothing less than "the attempted seizure by the Church of the city government."[39] Catholics had heard such charges before, of course, but not from a fellow Catholic. Mitchel, many decided, was using the charities case to curry favor with the WASP establishment. As state supreme court justice Eugene A. Philbin put it, the mayor was attacking the church out of "a desire to obtain a reputation for being fearless."[40]

If that were his goal, he certainly succeeded. Most of the New York, and the national, press hailed the mayor's "courage" and "independence" in taking on the archdiocese. The *Nation* editorially warned that "if the Catholic authorities in this city are put in the attitude of hounding Mayor Mitchel, a loyal son of their Church, for daring to be independent and humane-minded in the administration of the public charities, they will be doing themselves and their cause deadly hurt." And a year later, during the mayoralty campaign, editor Oswald Garrison Villard rhapsodized that "in going counter to many of his co-religionists and the powerful Catholic Church" Mitchel "gave the greatest exhibition of moral courage ever seen in this city." Julian Street, writing in *Collier's Weekly*, likewise saw "the Charities battle" as a "clear demonstration that Mitchel is a man who cannot be frightened or otherwise dominated by any political or religious influence." More than anything else he had done, "his action in this matter . . . has caught the popular fancy, and has caused him to be spoken of as the 'Fighting Mayor.'"[41]

Street did concede "the regrettable fact that bigoted Protestants seized the opportunity to represent Mitchel as a sort of anti-Catholic champion." What he and Mitchel's other WASP admirers could not see was that their own progressive understanding of the issue struck many Catholics as equally bigoted. The New York *Evening Post*, for example, ran an editorial cartoon showing frightened orphans looking out a window of a building labeled "Dept. of Charities" at a stalking Tammany tiger. The caption read: "The Tiger's Prey" "They Used to Be His Regular Diet—Shall He Have Them Again?" The *Survey* magazine reprinted the cartoon on the cover of its January 14, 1918, issue while inside it ran an article warning of the dangers the orphans faced now that Mitchel was out of office.[42]

Catholics, of course, did not see the Tammany tiger preying upon innocent waifs when they looked at the charities controversy. They saw Sisters of Charity and other women religious, who selflessly devoted their lives to others, under attack. They saw one of their own accusing church officials, including by implication the cardinal, of conspiracy; they saw him placing taps on the phones of a priest and a monsignor, charging those clerics with criminal conspiracy, and insisting on reading the transcripts of their private conversations into the record of the Thompson committee hearings even as Senator Thompson tried to gavel him into silence. They did not see independence and courage; they saw apostasy and opportunism.[43]

Mitchel irked fellow Catholics in little things as well as grand. Not only did he battle the hierarchy in terms that provided ammunition to Protestants they imagined as all too eager to believe that "papists" lacked the independence of conscience to be good Americans, he also developed a grand manner of practicing his religion that seemed to belittle their own parochial loyalties. According to Emanie N. Sachs, Mitchel had a private confessor, a Jesuit who taught at Brooklyn Preparatory School, "who had the right of way to the mayor's office past any one." Having what amounted to a private chaplain, Mitchel never went near the parish church in his own neighborhood, a fact that became notorious when, at a Catholic gathering, a priest came up to the mayor and said, "You don't know me, Mr. Mayor." That was so, Mitchel agreed: "You have the advantage of me." "I am the pastor of your parish," the priest rejoined. Mitchel, according to Sachs, "threw back his head and laughed."[44]

Again, the contrast with Smith is palpable. He devoted pages of his autobiography to extolling St. James's Catholic Church, his neighborhood parish, and its pastor, Monsignor John Kean. His unquestioning loyalty to the pastor is recounted at length in Hapgood's and Moskowitz's campaign biography, *Up from the City Streets.* One revealing anecdote concerned the time when Smith was about 18 and Father Kean sought to prevent the young people of the parish from patronizing the local saloons by getting the St. James's Union, the major young men's club, to give him the power to expel any member he wished for whatever reason he wished. Lots of the young men were ready to object, but not Smith. He told his fellows, "St. James's Union is part of the church. It belongs to the church. We cooperate with the church and it cooperates with us. If the Father wishes to have something to say about it, I think he has a right to control the membership."[45]

It was also at St. James's that Smith discovered his taste for amateur theatricals, and he soon became a regular, indeed a leading, player in the St. James's Dramatic Society. Smith loved to perform, but he wanted to play the hero since the very demonstrative local audiences hissed his villains with a bit too much fervor for his taste. He would play no more villains, he once proclaimed. But Father Kean had other ideas. He called Smith to the rectory, put his hand on his shoulder, and said, "'Alfred, we have over two hundred little orphan girls next door. It is getting harder every year to feed and clothe and care for these girls." The Dramatic Society put on two plays a year to help support the orphanage. What would Smith do? "Al replied in four words: 'Give me the part.'"[46]

If Mitchel transformed social welfare reform into a battle with the church and therefore, given the ethnic makeup of the hierarchy, into a battle with his fellow Irish Americans, he turned several other anti-Tammany measures, most importantly progressive education, into virtual wars with not just the Irish but also with all the nationality groups in the city. Schools were bound to be a major issue once his administration adopted a "pay-as-you-go" policy on all capital expenditures that were not themselves revenue producing.[47] This meant that Fusion would build only those school facilities it could finance out of current revenue. In practice it proved willing to spend even less than that. According to the New York *Evening Post*, a faithful support of the Mitchel administration, the Board of Estimate appropriated $17.05 million for new buildings, alterations, additions, and new sites between 1914 and 1918, but Fusion spent less than $5.0 million.[48]

Given existing overcrowding in the schools, and the fact that previous administrations had been unable to keep up with the city's rapidly growing school-age population despite heavy borrowing to finance new buildings, a pay-as-you-go policy promised to make a bad situation rapidly worse. Mitchel's solution was to bring the Gary Plan to New York. Under it students would spend part of the school day outside their regular classroom learning about art in museums or tools in machine shops or drama in theaters. They would, that is, learn by doing, just as progressive educators advocated. Furthermore, learning, working, and playing would all be integrated into the school day. And, because students did not need to be in the traditional classroom the entire day, several students could use the same seat. This would obviate the need to build extra schools while simultaneously improving the quality of education in the city schools.[49] The Gary Plan, in short, promised "vast improvements," as Robert Moses derisively remarked, without the city needing to spend any extra money.

If the plan were to work, the wholehearted cooperation of the city's teachers would be required—not least of all because it required a lengthening of their work day by 20 percent. But, as John Dewey remarked, "to the teachers" the "administration presented its most brutal face." In 1915, when the Board of Education requested $67,000 for summer school teachers' salaries, Fusion comptroller William A. Prendergast retorted that teachers were already over-paid. None of the teachers' organizations ever "made an effort to produce a larger amount of labor" to justify their salaries. They were only interested in "getting increases of salary for themselves without increase of service." The teachers should volunteer to teach the summer classes for free. Earlier that Spring both Mitchel and Prendergast had testified in Albany on behalf of a bill that would have allowed them to lower teachers' salaries.[50]

Given their conviction that teachers already received too much compensation, it is not surprising that Mitchel and Prendergast believed that salaries should not be increased for teachers in so-called Gary schools despite the increased workload. In detail, the plan, as Fusion proposed it in 1915, called for a longer school day (from five to six hours), a longer school year (from 40 to 44 weeks), a reduction in the number of grammar school years (from eight to seven), no salary increases, prohibition of regular teachers earning extra pay in night or summer schools, a freeze on new school construction, and a 10 percent cut in the number of teachers.[51]

The president of the Board of Education in 1915 was Thomas W. Churchill, a lawyer, former teacher, and long-term Tammany loyalist. He was only too willing to rally the teachers and lead the opposition to the mayor's version of the Gary Plan. For his part, Mitchel, who could appoint only a fifth of the members of the board each year, and thus had to wait until 1916 to command a working majority, was determined to oust Churchill at the earliest opportunity. The mayor charged Churchill with doing Tammany's bidding. Churchill retorted that Mitchel intended to hand the city's schools over to the Rockefeller interests. It was the "tendency of mayors" to "respect the aristocratic voice of the community and to forget the democratic."[52]

Churchill's charge about "Rockefeller interests" running the schools became a major issue, in part because Mitchel appointed Abraham Flexner, an assistant secretary of the Rockefeller-endowed General Education Board, and Raymond B. Fosdick, an employee of the Rockefeller Foundation, to the Board of Education. Also contributing to its plausibility was the fact that Fusion's version of the Gary Plan reduced the number of hours children in the affected schools devoted to traditional academic work. Since these schools were in immigrant neighborhoods where the overcrowding problem was most severe, Churchill and other Mitchel opponents could portray the mayor as consigning the children of the poor to a blue-collar future. Mitchel and Prendergast also played into Tammany's hands by failing to make any effort to explain their plan to the parents and pupils involved while the Hall held countless neighborhood meetings to drum up opposition. As Theodore Roosevelt commented just before the 1917 election, the "so-called Gary school system has become a liability." Parents had a "right to be consulted." "Instead, having agreed that the doctors had fixed up the medicine that would be good for the school patient," Fusion "decided to let the doctor jam it down the patient's throat, whether the patient liked it or not."[53]

At the heart of the Tammany campaign against the Gary Plan was the claim that the reduction in the hours devoted to traditional academic subjects was an effort, in Theodore Roosevelt's paraphrase, "to keep" the children of the poor "in the place of hewers of wood and carriers of water." In early 1916, just as Mitchel wrenched control of the Board of Education from Churchill and Tammany, school superintendent William Henry Maxwell lent credibility to the charge when he released a report from the school system's chief statistician that purported to show that students in Gary Plan schools lagged behind children in comparable schools where the traditional curriculum was still followed.[54]

Advocates of the new plan were outraged. It was not fair to assess progress when the new system was still just being instituted, they argued; furthermore, the schools chosen were not really comparable; and pupils in the Gary Plan schools really did better than chief statistician Burdette R. Buckingham admitted. For their part, Mitchel appointees to the Board of Education were equally willing to play politics with assessments of the plan. The Rockefeller-endowed General Education Board completed in 1916 an evaluation of the public schools of Gary, Indiana, to see how well they compared with schools in other cities. One of its coauthors, Abraham Flexner, was, as noted above, a Mitchel appointee to the Board of Education. The report was extremely critical of the Gary schools and its timely release would have damaged the mayor's position quite substantially. But the General Education Board did not release it until 1918.[55]

Even without the corroborating evidence garnered by Flexner, the Buckingham Report did enormous damage to the Fusion Plan, especially when Superintendent Maxwell weighed in. Buckingham's data, he said, showed that pupils in the Gary schools "are inferior in attainments to the pupils in the schools having the regular course." He did not claim "this test is conclusive" and gave lip service to the idea that the city should continue to experiment with the Gary Plan on a strictly limited basis. On the other hand, he denied the plan would substantially reduce the need for new school building, claimed that pupils in Gary schools were more likely to drop out and just as likely to be truant, calculated that teaching costs went up fastest in plan schools, and concluded that "poorer results, with a cost that is practically prohibitive, will not justify revolutionizing the administration of another school."[56]

"Red Mike" Hylan picked up on the theme. His message to Mitchel, "the Rockefeller Foundation, and to any other private interests" was "hands off our schools." He promised a Hylan administration would give "our boys and girls" the "opportunity to become doctors, lawyers, clergymen," or whatever else they wanted to be "notwithstanding the views of the Rockefeller Board of Education." Socialist candidate Morris Hillquit was equally outspoken, and by October 1917 the city's schools were the scenes of daily rioting, by students and parents alike, over Mitchel's attempt to impose the Gary Plan. At one school more than a thousand pupils went out on strike, smashed windows, attacked other children who sought to enter the building, and hurled rocks at the police who tried to break their picket line. Another 500 students at a second school staged a march in which they carried banners reading "Down with the Gary System" and "Can the Gary System and Mitchel."[57]

The story of the Gary Plan can serve as a paradigm for how Mitchel destroyed progressivism in New York. He turned "scientific" approaches to urban problems into class warfare; he personified the arrogance of expertise; and he brought the latent nativism and antidemocratic ethos of much progressive reform to the fore. A dismayed John Dewey wrote, shortly after Hylan's landslide victory, that "all of the better informed friends of the now defunct Gary system in New York have been aware for some time that its success was fundamentally compromised if not doomed by the autocratic way in which it was formulated and imposed from above." Fusion ought to have followed Thomas Churchill's lead in cultivating better relations with the teachers instead of ousting him as president of the Board of Education. Once Mitchel "broke with him, the situation became largely that described by Carlyle as anarchy plus the constable's club."[58]

There would be reform after 1917, but it would be a new "urban liberalism" built upon a political alliance between machine regulars like Al Smith and Robert Wagner and social and settlement workers like Henry and Belle Moskowitz, along with professionally trained urban planners like Robert Moses. This new coalition would presage the New Deal. It would make Al Smith, Catholic, ethnic, product of the streets of New York, a national figure and, by 1924, a serious candidate for the Democratic nomination for president.[59] The import of John Purroy Mitchel's career for this new urban liberalism, for the alliance of expert reformers and machine politicians, and for the presidential aspirations of Al Smith has proven easy to overlook. Yet it is clear that Smith's later triumphs would not have been possible had Mitchel not failed on so grand a scale. Prior to 1917 and Mitchel's overwhelming defeat, that is, a Smith–reformer alliance was unthinkable since municipal progressives had defined themselves in terms of their opposition to Tammany.

As the *Literary Digest* summarized the situation in the fall of 1917, almost "every important newspaper in the country" endorsed Mitchel and called for "the retention of what they considered the best administration in the city's history." "The nation's eyes" were "on New York," as the *Nation* editorialized, for "in Mitchel for the moment are embodied the hopes of all who would redeem American cities permanently from the shame that has been theirs." Howard Lee McBain, in the *National Municipal Review*, went even further. Democracy itself was on trial in New York in 1917.[60]

Not only was progressive opinion solidly behind the mayor, large numbers of reformers such as the Moskowitzs, and Moses, and virtually the entire staff of the Bureau of Municipal Research, held office in the Mitchel administration. Had Mitchel gained reelection, had he even managed to lose less disastrously, reformers would likely have continued to rally around the Fusion banner.[61] But Mitchel did lose disastrously, and not just in terms of vote totals. He so antagonized the electorate that the Democrats ran on an openly anti-reform platform. "Red Mike" Hylan stumped the city with the promise that, once elected, he would "fill the outgoing trains with 'experts.'" He denounced government by Bureau of Municipal Research personnel as an attack upon the ideal of democracy. "The ancient Greeks called it aristokratia, from which our modern word aristocracy is derived. The present term for it in New York is 'Government by Experts.'" In their place Hylan promised to appoint real New Yorkers, aka regular Democrats, who understood firsthand the problems the voters faced. In such a way, Hylan would restore the city to "the conception of government held by Abraham Lincoln."[62]

In victory Hylan proved as good as his word. "We have had all the reform that we want in this city for some time to come," he announced shortly after taking office. He made short work of the Bureau of Municipal Research staffers Mitchel had appointed, and in their places he named party loyalists whom the *Survey*, an organ of social and settlement workers and a strong backer of the Mitchel administration, described as "unknown or none too favorably known for their acquaintance with progressive thought."[63]

Fusion was dead, and so was the style of reform it had embodied. Progressives like Howard Lee McBain could blame the voters, could conclude that New Yorkers had proven their unfitness for democracy. Other reformers, like William H. Allen, could try to breathe new life into the old Fusion coalition by arguing that the voters turned against Mitchel only after he turned against "genuine" reform.[64] But the hard fact was that Tammany won in 1917 on an explicitly antireform platform, and there was no sign the city's electorate was longing for a new Fusion movement to come along in 1921.[65] So if reformers were to have a future, they would need to develop a new political strategy. In New York that meant working for—and with—some of Tammany's own, Al Smith and Robert Wagner, who, as Oscar Handlin pointed out, "had not been committed to the old progressivism and therefore did not bear the burden of its defeats or—what was even worse—of victories that led only to disappointment."[66]

John Purroy Mitchel's defeat did more than permit the return of Tammany to power, more even than mark the end of "genteel reform" in New York City, thus clearing the way for Smith's new urban liberalism. His decision to run in 1917 as the only true American in the field rather than as a municipal reformer subordinated the usual progressive themes of efficient and "scientific" management to demagogic attacks on "Turk, Teuton, and Tammany" and on "Hearst, Hylan, and the Hohenzollerns." Mitchel directly challenged the patriotism of several of the city's major ethnic groups, particularly the Irish and the Jews, as well as German Americans, and transformed a municipal election into a contest over the meaning of "Americanism." In so doing he echoed Theodore Roosevelt's 1916 campaign for the Republican presidential nomination and foreshadowed the tactics of Attorney General A. Mitchel Palmer, who tried to parley his sensational roundup of alien radicals into the 1920 Democratic presidential nomination, and those of New York state senator Clayton Riley Lusk, who used his chairmanship of a legislative investigating committee to stage his own "Palmer Raids" across the state.[67] The 1917 mayoralty election, therefore, helped inaugurate an era in which issues of loyalty, patriotism, and free speech dominated New York (and national) politics. And it began Smith's, and Tammany's, careers as champions of civil liberties.

Mitchel declared the maintenance of "an aggressive pro-American government in the city of New York" the central issue of the campaign. City Hall, the Fusion platform asserted, "must not be controlled or influenced by enemy sympathizers, or by discontented elements nor must [it] be administered by . . . those whose hesitation and evasion leave doubt of complete devotion" to the war effort. The mayor must be ready and able to "maintain order within, to co-operate with the Federal Government against the menace from without, to detect intrigue, to suppress violence." The government of New York must be "above all intensely loyal and intensely American." Fusion's record in this regard, the platform declared, "is without parallel in the contemporaneous municipal history of the country."[68]

Not content with praising his own Americanism, Mitchel spent much of the campaign traducing that of his opponents. A Fusion "Political Primer," written by Porter Emerson Browne and illustrated by Rea Irwin, for example, portrayed a "Soap Box Ag-i-tat-or" standing next to a street lamp haranguing a small dog. "Does He Want To See the May-or De-feated? Why? Be-cause The May-or Pre-vent-ed Him From Talk-ing Se-di-tion and Stir-ring Up The En-e-mies At Home to Aid and Com-fort the En-e-mies That Our Sol-diers Are Fight-ing A-broad." As Mitchel sympathizer Karl de Schweinitz commented in the *Survey* for November 17, 1917, "most of the 'soap-box agitators' were intensely patriotic Irishmen. Their criticism of British misrule in Ireland led Fusion speakers to denounce them as 'pro-German,' with the result that the Irish vote went solidly against Mayor Mitchel."[69]

Fusion billboards portrayed Mitchel, in uniform, keeping the Tammany tiger at bay with his bayonet. Others showed a soldier urging voters to support Mitchel. In the background William Randolph Hearst and the Kaiser stood together. The *Fusion Flashlight* quoted Elihu Root as saying that a Mitchel defeat would aid Germany: "Many of the young men whom we are sending across the Atlantic will pay with their lives for that encouragement to our enemy."[70]

Hylan responded by reminding voters that patriotism was often the last refuge of scoundrels. For his part, he said, he "would be ashamed to make political capital of the noble sacrifices of men who are giving up their positions, their homes, and in many cases their lives, to answer the call in their country's hour of need." Hillquit, on the other hand, was eager to make an issue of his opposition to the American entry into the war and of his role in drafting the Socialist Party's St. Louis platform that condemned it. "If you want war to continue indefinitely," he told voters, "if you want new millions of your fellows slaughtered and butchered in the hard struggle, and the war in Europe to continue day after day, and this bestial, brutal state of affairs to be prolonged, then vote for the capitalist parties." Otherwise, "vote for me."[71]

Once the campaign was over, Mitchel's supporters conceded that his use of the patriot issue had cost him votes. The Women's Municipal League bulletin, for example, calculated that "thousands" voted against Mitchel because of "his inexcusable bigotry in claiming during the campaign that his particular brand of patriotism was the only kind and all who opposed him were miscreants and traitors." The *New Republic* came to a similar post-mortem. "Most of the Hylan and Hillquit support consisted of undiluted anti-Mitchel votes, cast by men who resented the attempt made by one whom they took to be a class candidate to set himself up as the only pure and undefiled embodiment of patriotism."[72] This, for the *New Republic,* was indeed hindsight. Before the election it ran William Hard's pro-Mitchel analysis of the race in which he accused William Bennett of appealing to the German vote in the Republican primary and "Red Mike" Hylan of doing the same in the general election by refusing to speak out against Germany. Hylan, Hard charged, could not remember the war "in any effectively loyal manner."[73]

Not all of the criticism came after the fact. Even before the votes were in, some Mitchel backers warned that the Fusion attempt to turn the election into a referendum on the war would backfire. Oswald Garrison Villard, writing in the *Nation,* considered Mitchel's "introduction of the Americanism issue" the "greatest tactical mistake" of the campaign. His use of the word "tactical" is revealing here. Mitchel's attacks upon Hylan and his other opponents were baseless, Villard knew. He also knew that in making them Mitchel "deliberately violated a fundamental theory of the good-government campaigns in this city during the last three decades," namely, that "national issues should not be brought into local campaigns." Still, the real problem was that the patriot issue was not working. Such an "appeal to national patriotism might have been in some degree effective in the last few days of the campaign, but it was sprung too early to last."[74]

This narrow focus on tactics enabled Mitchel's supporters to dodge the question of whether his use of the Americanism issue called into question his fitness for office.[75] It also allowed progressives to avoid public acknowledgment of the damage the Fusion administration had done to the reform cause. Karl de Schweinitz, writing in the *Survey,* typified those who believed that the real "issue should have been Tammany versus good government" and who faulted Fusion for not having embarked from the beginning upon "a systematic visitation of the neighborhoods of the city" in an effort to explain "to the people what they were trying to accomplish." "Even the most casual acquaintance with the men and women who were appointed by Mayor Mitchel would have been an education in reform." And, once "the people" had seen the "difference between the Tammany office-holder and the municipal specialist," they would have been "reconciled" to "the few out-of-town experts who took service with the administration."[76] In fact, of course, the real issue of the campaign was, as far as "Red Mike" Hylan was concerned, Tammany versus good government. It was an issue that favored Tammany, for once, and not simply because Fusion had ignored the neighborhoods. It was also Tammany's issue because the administration had succeeded in making reform a term of opprobrium for hundreds of thousands of ethnic voters in New York.

Tactical critiques of the Mitchel campaign also obscured the fact that the mayor began promoting his own conspicuous patriotism, and attacking that of political opponents, as early as 1915, when he marched off to Plattsburg in the middle of August for a month of military training as part of the Preparedness movement.[77] For him the Americanism issue was no mere political tactic, and the suggestion of de Schweinitz (and Villard) that "Fusion campaign managers" turned to it out of the "feeling that during the last three or four weeks of the canvassing an emotional issue was needed" is simply incorrect.[78]

Leading the crusade for "100% Americanism" was how Mitchel came to terms with his own ethnic background. Specifically, it enabled him to repudiate his grandfather's Irish nationalism while claiming his "fighting spirit." It was thus central to his quest to prove himself as American as any Yankee. This, at least, is one way of making sense of Mitchel's ferocity in harassing Irish critics of British rule of their homeland. Fusion police commissioner Arthur Woods had initially instructed his officers to permit demonstrations, so long as the proper permits had been secured. Mitchel, in Oswald Garrison Villard's words, overruled his own commissioner "and so we have had the spectacle of police cars being driven into crowds," "legitimate public meetings" being broken up, and "orators being arrested for speeches that were not seditious" but merely hostile to English policy in Ireland. The result was "a widespread feeling of outrage, particularly among the Irish."[79]

Hylan did not have to do anything in order to benefit from this outrage, for Mitchel's version of the "patriot game" played directly into Tammany's hands.[80] Avoidance of the issue would not work so well in 1918, however, when the Hall nominated Al Smith for governor. Smith would have to pull in some upstate votes where charges that a failure to take a strong stand on the war, indicating a secret appeal to German American and other ethnic voters, might prove fatal. Tammany also had to consider the enormous Socialist vote in the mayoralty race. A strong Socialist vote in 1918 would weaken Smith's chances, if only because he needed to take as large a majority out of the city as he could if he were to carry the state.

Whether for these or other reasons, Tammany Boss Charles F. Murphy decided to make the patriot issue his own in 1918. "We want only Americans . . . whose patriotism is unquestioned" Murphy decreed, and the Democrats worked with Republican district leaders to find Fusion candidates, such as Fiorello La Guardia, to run against Socialists.[81] This certainly worked in La Guardia's case as he easily won reelection over Scott Nearing. It also worked with Smith, who became the first Tammany leader ever to win the governorship.

Tammany's success with the patriotism issue in 1918 did not carry over even to the next year, however: 1919 was a year of great turmoil nationally as unions and corporations squared off in a series of epochal strikes, as political radicals struggled to come to terms with the success of the Bolshevik revolution, and as militant antiradicals organized in the American Legion and the National Defense League to consolidate their wartime gains.[82] Nowhere did feelings run higher than in New York, where the Republican-controlled state legislature established the Joint Committee to Investigate Seditious Activities, chaired by first-term Senator Clayton Riley Lusk from upstate Cortland.[83]

Within a few weeks of the May Day bomb scare, in which a series of explosive devices were mailed to prominent public officials, the Lusk Committee launched a series of spectacular raids, centered on New York City, on a variety of left-wing targets. These included the Soviet Mission, the Rand School for Social Science, and the headquarters of the Industrial Workers of the World (IWW).[84] The justification for the raids, according to Senator Lusk, was evidence reaching his committee that indicated there was "a Bolshevist plan" to "hold up New York City in some unexplained way for an hour, as a spectacular demonstration to the world that the 'Red' brotherhood had developed fighting strength."[85]

Lusk reveled in such vague but menacing charges, and he quickly turned himself into a major political figure. He commandeered the services of the state police and the New York City police to carry out his raids; he successfully called on Governor Smith to authorize an extra term for the state supreme court to process the cases against those arrested, most of whom were immigrants; he held frequent and spectacular press conferences at which he announced ever more elaborate conspiracies were about to be unmasked; and he introduced a series of draconian measures, the "Lusk Laws," to end the Bolshevik threat to New York by censoring movies and regulating settlement house classes.[86]

At first both Governor Smith and Mayor Hylan went along with Lusk's crusade. Smith, for example, told a commencement audience at Cornell just a few days after the first raid that "nothing would be left undone to prevent a spread of radical ideas." Hylan permitted the committee to hold its hearings in City Hall.[87] This sort of cooperation in a Republican-led Red Scare did not last, and Smith in particular moved aggressively to oppose the "Luskers" and to stake out a strong civil libertarian position.

One reason, as Smith made clear in his annual message for 1920, was that the antiradical campaign had quickly turned nativist. Smith protested any link between "the anarchist, the violent revolutionist, the underminer of our institutions," and "the hundreds of thousands of our brothers of alien stock" who "have made America their home" and "helped to build up our great nation by self-respecting labor and . . . citizenship." Smith did not mention Lusk or his committee directly, but he did denounce "as sinister and as an expression of the old know-nothing spirit the attaching to all citizens of foreign birth the stigma of radicalism." Just the opposite was true. Smith insisted on "the fundamental wholesomeness of citizens of foreign birth."[88]

Immigrants and their children had long been Tammany's loyal constituents, and there is no surprise in Smith's speaking out on their behalf. The governor, however, went much further. He also spoke out strongly against the expulsion of five Socialist members of the state assembly. It was "inconceivable," he said, "that a minority party duly constituted and legally organized should be deprived of its right to expression so long as it has honestly, by lawful methods of education and propaganda, succeeded in securing representation." It may have been true, as he had said in his annual message, that during the war "every sane American" recognized the need to relinquish "some of his freedom." But peace meant "we should return to a normal state of mind, and keep our balance, and an even keel." "Our faith in American democracy," he wrote, "is confirmed not only by its results, but by its methods and organs of free expression."[89]

Smith's stand enabled him to claim to be a better, truer American than the nativists. Thus when he vetoed the "Lusk Laws," he said of the one that required a state board to oversee private educational enterprises that "in fundamental principle the bill is vicious. . . .[I]t strikes at the very foundation of one of the most cardinal institutions of our nation—the fundamental right of the people to enjoy full liberty in the domain of idea and speech." The bill also mocked "the profound sanity of the American people" whose patriotism did not require coercion.[90] It was an issue on which the governor felt deeply. So when Smith narrowly lost the governship in 1920, even though he ran a million votes ahead of the national ticket, and the Lusk measures became law, he made them an issue in his 1922 campaign and, with his victory, moved immediately for their repeal. The measure was introduced, fittingly, by Tammany's own Senator James J. Walker.[91]

John Purroy Mitchel and Al Smith both claimed to be real Americans. For Mitchel this meant denying his ethnic patrimony and engaging in American Protective Association–style attacks on the Catholic hierarchy while insisting upon his own Americanism. Smith, in contrast, openly avowed his origins, embraced his church even as he insisted that his Catholicism was entirely compatible with his devotion to the United States, and promoted an inclusive, tolerant definition of what it meant to be an American. Both were reformers, but Mitchel measured progress in terms of efficiency and Smith in terms of the happiness of his constituents. Both believed in free speech, but Mitchel excluded speech that attacked the government itself and then proved himself unable to distinguish between the government and his own administration. Smith believed even in the speech of political radicals because he also believed in the ability of ordinary Americans to listen intelligently. Both men achieved national prominence, Mitchel as the unlikely embodiment of the WASP ideal and Smith as the archetypical ethnic. Both reached great heights. Both fell. One deserved better.

Marion R. Casey

CHAPTER 16

"From the East Side to the Seaside"

IRISH AMERICANS ON THE

MOVE IN NEW YORK CITY

A RECENT POPULAR song by Terence Winch, *When New York Was Irish,* offers a succinct lesson in twentieth-century New York Irish geography: "You could travel from Kingsbridge to Queens or Midtown, from Highbridge to Bay Ridge, from uptown to down, from the East Side to the seaside, sweet summer scenes, we made New York City our island of dreams." Aside from nostalgic value, these lyrics raise some related questions: When did the Irish begin to move out of Manhattan? Where were they going? What prompted the move and how was it managed? What were the implications for social mobility?

From the turn of the century, the ethnic map of New York City began to reflect a changing geographic dispersion of the Irish population. In 1910, approximately 88 percent of the city's Irish immigrants—more than a quarter million—resided in Manhattan and Brooklyn (see table 16.1). By 1960 more than half of all the Irish (immigrant and foreign stock combined) resided in the Bronx and Queens.[1] In addition to this dramatic shift, the number of Irish-born in the entire city (all five boroughs) declined by more than 100,000 between 1910 and 1960, with a corresponding loss for second generation Irish Americans (see table 16.2).[2] Discounting death and declining emigration from Ireland, this loss indicated the beginning of an Irish trend to move beyond the city's borders into neighboring Nassau, Westchester, Rockland, and Bergen counties. After 1960 this trend was even more pronounced.[3]

TABLE 16.1. Number of Irish-born by New York City Borough, 1910–50

Borough	1910	1920	1930	1940	1950
Manhattan	151,052 (60)	116,749 (58)	96,861 (44)	68,996 (38)	49,073 (34)
Brooklyn	70,653 (28)	53,660 (26)	53,571 (24)	39,689 (22)	29,717 (20)
Bronx	18,269 (7)	18,679 (9)	38,816 (18)	42,709 (23)	38,004 (26)
Queens	8,671 (3)	10,618 (5)	27,139 (12)	26,953 (15)	25,277 (18)
Richmond	4,017 (2)	3,744 (2)	4,244 (2)	3,479 (2)	2,737 (2)
Total	252,662	203,450	220,631	181,826	144,808

Source: U.S. Bureau of the Census.
Note: Figures in parentheses are percentages.

Numbers mask the complexity of this Irish diaspora within the New York metropolitan area. The entire city's population was being redistributed during this period, propelled by the rapid suburbanization that was redefining the relationship of the outer boroughs to Manhattan. Not only did the Irish move into parts of the city that were relatively new both to them *and* to New York, but the movement itself had broader social implications. Certainly their migration cannot be understood solely in terms of the classic conceptualization of "social mobility," with its proportionally direct relationship between occupation, class, and residence (that is, a better job enables one to cross class lines and move into a better neighborhood). An examination of the motivations behind Irish migration within New York City at this time confirms that much of it bore little relation to vertical mobility in either occupation or class. Even new immigrants from Ireland were able to by-pass Manhattan in favor of joining relatives and friends in the apartments and houses of the Bronx, Brooklyn, and Queens.

What geographic movement in early-twentieth-century New York did reflect was the search for a better quality of life. For the first time, physical conditions in the city offered a unique opportunity to attain a standard of living that was

TABLE 16.2. Irish Stock, New York City, 1910–60

Year	Total	Foreign-born	Second generation
1910	676,420	252,662	423,758
1920	616,627	211,789	404,838
1930	613,006	220,631	392,375
1940	518,466	181,826	336,640
1950	456,408	144,808	311,600
1960	342,381	114,008	228,373

Source: Ira Rosenwaike, *Population History of New York City* (Syracuse, N.Y., 1972), 203–6.

both comfortable and respectable, yet not dependent upon occupational advancement or even better wages. Likewise, a new address did not always indicate a rise in social status. But perhaps more significantly, it enabled blue-collar workers to enjoy middle-class amenities in their housing and neighborhoods—a style of living that, in the more traditional definition of mobility, should have taken a generation or two longer.

This reality is somewhat at odds with the general twentieth-century perception of the Irish as monolithically white-collar middle-class suburban dwellers or, in other words, as a thoroughly assimilated ethnic group. The Irish, as one of the oldest groups in the city, are commonly believed to epitomize the delicate balance between social mobility and "ethnic succession," wherein succession implies success: as their economic situation improved, they moved on to better housing, replaced by newer immigrants who filled their old jobs and lived in their old neighborhoods. But in New York City ethnic succession ceased to be relevant for a time during the early part of this century as a building boom put a glut of apartments on the market that were both accessible by public transportation and offered more amenities for the same or less money.

How much did these new middle-class living standards reflect appearances rather than economic or social reality for the Irish? Understanding the logistics behind the Irish migratory experience in New York helps to assess their proverbial "ethnic success" story and its implications for assimilation. The Irish played diverse roles in the urban ecology of New York, as renters, homeowners, superintendents, landlords, agents, salesmen, builders, and developers. In this they differed little from other ethnic groups in New York City. But, whereas Jewish and Italian migration is characterized by the unique ethnic stamp they put on the city's modern landscape, the Irish experience was much more typically the New York one. First, the Irish were less dependent on ethnicity in their reasons for moving, and second, they did not always perceive physical movement in terms of upward mobility. Intraurban migration took place for very practical (subjective) reasons and was made possible by a range of options. Their choices were more often affected by citywide developments in housing and transportation than by the need to live in an "ethnic" neighborhood.[4]

The geography of New York City dictated where and when real estate developers operated and, by extension, the direction of intraurban migrations. The city's center was, and continues to be, an island—Manhattan—and expansion from that center has been to two other islands and a portion of the mainland. Before the turn of the century, technological innovations in transportation, especially the streetcar and elevated railroad, enabled New York to urbanize the northern reaches of Manhattan and parts of the Bronx. Such growth had intense political ramifications. Lucrative connections between private companies and City Hall brought contracts for municipal improvements in these new areas, such as water and gas pipes, street openings and lighting, excavations, land fill, bridge and tunnel work, and, of course, transit facilities. The Irish appear on all levels of the construction and real estate industries in New York during this period. By default, they were in the vanguard of the city's physical expansion. Many of the most successful Irish contractors also served on local chambers of commerce, which were anxious to attract improvements to their areas, and a little insider knowledge went a long way in speculative real estate transactions.[5]

From about 1880, when the Ninth Avenue elevated railroad was extended through Manhattan's Upper West Side, the Irish began to actively purchase real estate in the area as well as finance the construction of houses. The Crimmins Construction Company was responsible for much of the new infrastructure and landfill undertaken in the city at this time.[6] John D. Crimmins (1844–1917) was one of the earliest "sagacious operators" making lot transactions on the Upper West Side.[7] Crimmins had done some speculating with lots on the East Side, but as that area's topography lent itself to quicker development than the rocky heights of the West Side, real estate opportunities there (already as far north as Yorkville and Harlem) were "beyond the reach of the speculative builder" by the 1880s. This probably accounts for the Irish preference for West Side real estate at the turn of the century.[8]

Crimmins was also involved in local improvement companies, such as the Property Owners' Association and the West End Association: "In the Riverside Park district of the city particularly, as well as in the district just north of Central Park, his many important investments for improvement were not only profitable for himself but rendered a great public service in developing these fine sections of the city in proper and adequate ways."[9] After the turn of the century, Crimmins was especially building in the area of 171st Street but he was not the first Irishman to be interested in Washington Heights real estate. The area had begun generating a "pronounced speculative movement" as early as May 1891 when, at the Morgenthau Sale of 411 vacant lots, nearly a quarter of the total sale price came from 22 Irish speculators who spent $346,150 on unimproved lots in the area of 178th to 182nd Streets, along Amsterdam, Audubon, Wadsworth and 11th (St. Nicholas) avenues. Five men were responsible for 69 percent of the total value of Irish purchases in this sale: B. F. Kearns ($86,400), John Reilly ($64,375), B. L. Kennelly ($30,850), Michael J. Mulqueen ($27,350) and Patrick Fox ($26,400).[10]

Irish real estate interests were already beginning to focus on undeveloped parts of the Bronx and Long Island at the turn of the century.[11] John P. Dunn (1860–1922), whose father invested the family fortune in improvements in the Fordham area, was president of the Fordham Property Owners' Association and, after appointment as the first head of the Bureau of Street Openings, actively acquired property in the Bronx for city parks as well as streets.[12] The contractor Michael J. Degnon (1856–1925) built the Williamsburg Bridge in 1903, the

Pennsylvania railroad terminal at Long Island City in 1910, and the BMT East River subway tunnel in 1913. He was a director of the Chamber of Commerce of Queens and, by coincidence, president of the Degnon Realty and Terminal Improvement Company, which owned "about 400 acres in Long Island City and Flushing" that were "improved for city homes."[13] As early as 1910 (the year the rail line between Manhattan and Long Island was electrified), the *Irish Advocate* ran advertisements that offered building lots and homes for sale in Jamaica, Floral Park, and "the most exclusive sections."[14] That same year, John D. Crimmins was developing in Astoria, Queens, and Hunt's Point in the Bronx, as well as touring properties in Elmhurst and Flushing in Queens, and Brownsville and New Lots in Brooklyn.[15] The Kennelly Corporation, which had been buying property in Washington Heights at the turn of the century, by 1926 was advertising lots for auction in Amityville, Garden City, Sands Point, and Great Neck in Nassau County; Jamaica, Elmhurst, and Forest Hills in Queens; and Gravesend and Bay Ridge in Brooklyn.[16]

There is no evidence that such real estate activity by the New York Irish was consciously ethnic in its orientation, even though many of the areas they opened up were identified as "Irish" within 20 years or so.[17] On the other hand, parish building in the boroughs was influenced by wealthy Irish speculators and contractors who often had close relationships with the Catholic Church.[18] "Brick and mortar" Catholicism allowed upper- and lower-class Irish interests to work in tandem, because it involved everything from property acquisition in new areas of the city to regular employment in the construction and maintenance of buildings. The advice of Irish real estate interests in site selection, property transactions, and construction contracts had a particularly strong influence if they were parishioners themselves or had other connections. Catholic construction projects provided employment for hundreds of Irish builders, subcontractors, carpenters, plumbers, and electricians. The direction of Irish movement within New York City after 1900 can be plotted by the creation of Catholic parishes and Knights of Columbus councils, both especially numerous in areas becoming identified with the Irish.[19]

Although there had been Irish in the outer boroughs since colonial days, Manhattan was the Irish stronghold until the twentieth century. The Irish initially lived in the immigrant sections bordering the docks on both the lower east and lower west sides of Manhattan. Their economic situations began to stabilize at about the time ethnic succession became a critical factor for the city's available housing stock.[20] In general, their progression northward on the island (on both the east and west sides) followed the development of transit lines and Manhattan real estate, especially lower-and middle-income housing. As early as 1910, the Irish still living in Greenwich Village, Hell's Kitchen, and Chelsea were considered to be remnants of a much larger, nineteenth-century Irish population that had long since moved on to "better surroundings."[21] Within the decade East Side districts, especially around the Gashouse, Kip's Bay and Yorkville, and the blocks west of Central Park became both primary and secondary areas of Irish settlement. That is, they were the first places called home by new Irish immigrants or newly married Irish American couples, and they were often the second stop in an Irish family's intraurban migration.

Irish had been settling in the Bronx from the 1830s when construction projects like the Croton Water Aqueduct, several railroad systems, and then the "El" linked the mainland with Manhattan. The most significant boost to Irish population growth in the Bronx was the arrival of the subway in 1904 and its subsequent extensions, which spurred the construction of lower-income housing in the borough. By 1914 the South Bronx (Mott Haven, Melrose, Morrisania), Highbridge, Fordham, and Kingsbridge were known as Irish areas. Development in the Bronx spilled over into northern Manhattan via the High Bridge and Harlem Bridge connections.

Movement into Brooklyn and Queens, lying east of Manhattan on Long Island, was initially hampered by the East River, which challenged ferry, bridge, and railway connections. The Williamsburg and Manhattan bridges were not built until 1903 and 1909. The subway, the real key to large-scale working-class mobility, did not reach Brooklyn until 1908 and Queens until 1917; full extension in both boroughs was not completed until the 1950s and 1960s, respectively. In Brooklyn, pre–World War I Irish communities still clustered close to the river near the Navy Yard, in Greenpoint and Williamsburg, further east in the area just north of Prospect Park (St. Teresa of Avila parish) and to the south in Flatbush, with nascent sections in Sunset Park and Bay Ridge. In Queens, the Irish were already settled in Long Island City, Astoria, Woodside, and Sunnyside by 1914, spurred especially by the opening of the Queensboro Bridge in 1909. In addition, Rockaway Beach was beginning to develop as an Irish summer resort community.

After the first world war, several factors converged to make better, more affordable housing available to the average New Yorker, and it is no coincidence that the decade 1920–30 witnessed the greatest shifts in Irish settlement in the city.[22] As the subway made new areas accessible, cheap land and New Law requirements for light and ventilation produced experimentation in tenement, apartment house, and tract design. By 1920 profits could be realized by developers who emphasized quality rather than quantity. A building boom ensued, encouraged by several New York State laws granting real estate tax exemptions on the construction of buildings between 1920 and 1926, and a law allowing insurance companies to invest profits in housing for limited dividends. Such changes not only affected private housing construction for the middle-class but also philanthropic efforts to build low-income housing.[23] In 1927 William J. Moore of the American Bond and Mortgage Company commented: "There is a great force at work which has gained surprising velocity since the war—better standards of living. The greatest accelerator of this is advertising—it makes us want better bathrooms, kitchens, heating plants, furniture, radios, pianos, foods.

. . . In the matter of housing there is definite demand for moderate priced apartments in certain sections."[24]

Of all the boroughs, Manhattan was least able to take advantage of the changes in multiple-dwelling construction save for a few areas in Washington Heights and Inwood. The typical Manhattan apartment of the period was three or four rooms in which "space was necessarily at a premium, and such space-saving furniture as folding cots, . . . and drop-leaf tables were popular."[25] Dissatisfaction with such outmoded accommodation in the older sections of Manhattan created an incentive for mobility, encouraging families with children to explore the greater "spatial amenities" of the outer boroughs. In general, accommodations improved the farther north and east of Manhattan that one lived, as newer housing and falling prices were usually to be found in sections recently opened up. People moved simply because they wanted, and could now get, cheaper rents, larger apartments with modern conveniences, and sometimes their own homes. Marriage and employment opportunities, in conjunction with dissatisfaction, also stimulated people to look in new areas. Municipal developments, particularly a general increase in rents, transit expansion, the nickel subway fare, and the construction boom of the 1920s helped spur the movement out from Manhattan after World War I. Between 1910 and 1930 the number of all New Yorkers living in Manhattan dropped from 49 to 27 percent, while the Bronx and Queens more than doubled their percentages.

Irish Americans were part of that movement.[26] The basic pattern of their migration, using Washington Heights as an example, would show some development by the Irish circa 1890–1910 (including lot sales, apartment house construction, and parish building), followed by large-scale movement of Irish into the area. Between 1920 and 1940 the Irish population in Washington Heights almost quadrupled.[27] In fact, after 1910 the Irish from all parts of Manhattan gravitated toward the West Side districts north of Central Park.[28] These Irish were new immigrants for whom Washington Heights was their primary stop in New York City simply because that was where relatives and friends lived; and both first- and second-generation Irish migrating north from lower down in Manhattan to take advantage of improved housing conditions in the area. Since neither the city nor the Irish community was ever static, the scenario is complicated by Irish who were moving *out* of Washington Heights and into new parts of the Bronx or Queens during these same years, in a repeat of the pattern. The first and second generation overlapped in neighborhoods like Washington Heights even as the next stage of migration to Inwood, Fordham, Kingsbridge, Flatbush, and Woodside was taking place for both Irish and Irish Americans. Eventually such outmigration left a remnant population behind in its wake, explaining why there were still some Irish in tenements on the middle East Side during the 1930s and on the Upper West Side in the 1950s who could be displaced by municipal improvements like the Queens-Midtown Tunnel and

Lincoln Center. In Irish New York, the center—if there ever really was one—was always shifting.

It is important to point out, however, that the percentage of Irish-born living in Manhattan still remained higher than for the city's entire population; thus in 1930 Manhattan was home to 44 percent of Irish immigrants (see table 16.3). But this is almost a false statistic because the major Irish areas in Manhattan at this time were Washington Heights and Inwood, which bear the same latitudinal relationship to the city's geography as the West Bronx. In other words, moving to northern Manhattan involved the same psychological factors for the Irish as moving to one of the outer boroughs.[29]

Like most New Yorkers at this time, the Irish were scattering out from their old Manhattan neighborhoods for reasons that simply reflected the realities of their daily relationship with the city.[30] The parish of St. Gregory the Great on the Upper West Side of Manhattan (West 86th to West 92nd Streets, Central Park West to Riverside Drive) provides a good example. It was created in 1909 from the larger Irish parish of Holy Name to the north, probably in response to an increase in population in the area.[31] St. Gregory's was considered to be a "middle-class" parish, peopled predominantly by Irish and Irish Americans who were employed in a variety of occupations, including "lawyers, doctors, brokers and men prominent in public life," as well as "teachers (in public schools), nurses, stenographers, typists, telephone operators, post office clerks, letter carriers, clerks in stores and offices (male and female), chauffeurs, motormen and conductors on the elevated, subway and surface lines, mason builders, carpenters, machinists, plumbers, laborers, domestics, etc." A 1920 survey of the parish found most people living in flats, either three rooms on Columbus and Amsterdam Avenues or in "better-class houses" on side streets like 88th, 90th, and 91st. Rents in the parish had jumped since the war, with two weeks' wages required to be set aside for the landlord where previously one week sufficed; whereas $18 a month paid the

TABLE 16.3. Comparison of City Population by Borough with Irish-born Population, 1910 and 1930

Borough	Total New York City, 1910		Total New York City, 1930		Irish-born, 1910		Irish-born, 1930	
Manhattan	2,331,542	(49)	1,867,312	(27)	151,052	(60)	96,861	(44)
Brooklyn	1,634,351	(34)	2,560,401	(37)	70,653	(28)	53,571	(24)
Bronx	430,980	(9)	1,265,258	(18)	18,269	(7)	38,816	(18)
Queens	284,041	(6)	1,079,129	(16)	8,671	(3)	27,139	(12)
Richmond	85,959	(2)	158,346	(2)	4,017	(2)	3,479	(2)
Total	4,766,883		6,930,446		252,662		220,631	

Source: U.S. Bureau of the Census.

Note: Figures in parentheses are percentages.

rent for three rooms on Columbus Avenue before the war, by 1920 it had risen to $28. The survey's author commented: "I think it can be safely said that generally in this parish rents have gone up at least 100% and the writer knows of some cases wherein the rents of working people have advanced to 150%, thus putting a tremendous strain upon the family budget. It is not a rare thing to meet a parishioner, a wage earner, who, with nearly tears in his eyes, tells of the advance in rent made during the past week and threatened for the next week."[32] Although the Armistice did increase wages in the parish, the author concluded that "the maintenance of the home, according to our people's accustomed standard of living, eats up nearly all of this increase."[33]

Sometimes the city forced moves for municipal improvement schemes or with incentives like tax abatements. In 1921, for example, Marie Walsh's parents moved to Tremont in the Bronx from a brownstone apartment on Manhattan's East Side. Three years later they purchased a single-family house at 3702 Secor Avenue in Edenwald, on the Bronx-Yonkers border. The family's reason for moving again "was the City's offer of a ten-year real estate tax exemption for the period 1921–1930. That was very welcome, but unfortunately offset by assessments for local improvements such as street grading, sewer installations, etc., largely lacking in the newly developed neighborhood."[34] In the mid-1930s, when the area around their East 36th Street apartment (including St. Gabriel's Church) began to be cleared for the approach road of the Queens-Midtown Tunnel, Charlie Mooney's father (a second-generation Irish American) was forced to move his family further up the East Side to 66th Street.[35]

Employment opportunities also served to spread the Irish widely in New York, particularly through ethnic niches like the transit system (subway, elevated and surface lines), grocery chains, and live-in domestic service. During the 1930s and 1940s, the majority of the workers for the Third Avenue Railway, the Fifth Avenue Coach Company, and the transportation departments of the IRT and BMT subway lines were Irish.[36] Most transit workers opted to live near the end of their day's work, that is, close to car barns, train yards, trolley depots, or bus garages in the inner suburbs and northern Manhattan. In Highbridge there was even a complex of connected houses on University Avenue nicknamed "Interborough Row," which was "all Irish."[37] Likewise, the Astoria Light, Heat and Power Company, the Railway Express Company, Guinness and other industries in Queens brought the Irish to Astoria, Long Island City, Woodside, and Sunnyside.[38]

Many new Irish immigrants got their starts in New York working for either Daniel Reeves' or James Butler's extensive grocery operations, and later on the A&P (Atlantic and Pacific Tea Company).[39] Since grocery stores were neighborhood based, it was often easy to live near one's work. James Butler (1855–1934) was a native of County Kilkenny who was doing $15 million dollars worth of business in 200 stores by 1909; eventually he owned 1,100 stores and a $2 million warehouse in Long Island City.[40] County Clare native James Reeves (1871–1957) got his start working for Butler's, and after 13 years invested $6,000 savings into opening his own grocery store. By 1911 he and his brother Daniel had spread to 35 locations; in 1941, when the company merged with Safeway, the number was 750.[41] With such a network of stores, employment with Butler's and Reeves' helped scatter the Irish throughout the city.

Irish women who were employed as waitresses in restaurant chains like Child's, Schrafft's, and Stouffer's could easily commute by subway or bus to their numerous midtown locations from the East or West sides of Manhattan, and even from the Bronx. While the Upper East Side homes of wealthy New Yorkers were convenient to the Irish community of Yorkville, in general live-in domestic work for Irish women spread them widely over the metropolis. But it was a temporary dispersal. In most cases, marriage immediately changed a

St. Simon Stock was a big Irish parish in the Fordham section of the Bronx when Denis Mullins played outfield for the high school baseball team in 1939. His father was an IRT coach inspector from County Cork who emigrated with his children in 1922. Although St. Simon Stock was rumored to have been English, the parish was founded by the Irish Carmelites of 28th Street (Manhattan) and their Irish nationalism was above reproach: they harbored Eamon de Valera during his American sojourn in 1919. (From the collection of Denis J. Mullins.)

woman's relationship to the city's geography, making her more dependent upon the nature of her husband's employment, the family's total income, or the availability of affordable housing.

A variety of subjective reasons (from cross-ventilation in an apartment to relatives in the neighborhood) enabled Irish women in particular to exercise options regarding where the family lived in New York. They were conscious of their neighborhoods (particularly mothers who stayed at home with the children) and proved to be patient and resourceful in their selection of new apartments. In this they were not unusual. A contemporary report by the Harmon National Real Estate Corporation claimed women appraised real estate differently from men: "Provided the purchase price of the parcel is within her means, she will judge it almost entirely by what might be called subjective rather than objective standards." In order of importance, women wanted (1) a view or outlook, (2) proximity to stores, (3) play space for children, (4) nice neighbors, and (5) nearby school and church facilities.[42]

In 1937 Delia Brennan Hayden, from County Sligo, was living with her family on West 80th Street in a five-room railroad flat. She "wanted to move to a nicer apartment" and found one on the corner of 81st Street and Amsterdam Avenue. It was a five-story building, with a corner apartment that had tall ceilings and windows in nearly every room. Dorothy Hayden recalled, "My mother kept an eye on that house, . . . it was a good house" until word came through her network of friends in Holy Trinity parish that there was a vacancy in the building. The rent ($67.50 a month) was not a factor in her decision to move, even though "other people were paying $30–35" in the neighborhood.[43]

In the South Bronx, Mary Gilrane Flynn and two of her friends regularly made a habit of looking at apartments in St. Luke's parish, as a way to pass the time and satisfy their curiosity.[44] Catherine Kennedy recalled that if you were scouting for an new apartment in the Yorkville area, you "would look at the mailboxes to see what names were there, and if you didn't like the names, you didn't go in." Although she moved with her new husband to Fordham in 1924, Kennedy hated the Bronx because she missed all her friends in Manhattan. Within a short period of time, she made a permanent move back to Yorkville.[45] In 1921 Agnes Campbell Sinclair's parents moved from Crown Street (south of Eastern Parkway) in Brooklyn to be nearer to "my mother's friends [who] were all up [around] Rogers Avenue and St. Teresa's parish." Even after they moved to Greenpoint in 1928 to be closer to Mr. Campbell's work at the Socony oil refinery in Long Island City, Mrs. Campbell used to go back to St. Teresa's every week to visit because "she was just comfortable there."[46] Ties of friendship could be reinforced by language, too. St. Teresa's parish and sections of Flatbush to its south attracted large numbers of Irish speakers from County Donegal during the 1930s through the 1950s: "'Donegal Hill,' a name applied to a height in the northern sector of [Prospect] park, became the focal point for Irish families on weekends for picnics and ball playing. Old friends looked forward to the weekly meetings, and it was a place that always seemed to attract a fresh face or two, some of whom had only recently arrived from the old country."[47]

What conclusion can be drawn about this movement? Moving was common, sometimes within parishes, sometimes between neighborhoods, and sometimes between boroughs. The reasons behind this migration were varied. None of it could have been possible without access to new areas in the city, in the development of which many Irish had been involved. But how much of this activity indicates upward social mobility for the Irish?

The practical logistics behind this movement included a variety of strategies, including step-migration while saving, multiple mortgages, multifamily and summer rentals, and self-built houses. Many families took in lodgers to make ends meet. During the Depression, Maureen Griffin Mooney's parents doubled up when they moved to the Bronx in the early years of their marriage: "At one point my mother and father shared an apartment with another married couple; I mean, they actually could not afford their own place."[48] Her father, a native of County Kerry, worked for the Transit Authority. In the days before it was organized, "there was hardly a transit worker whose family could afford an apartment all for itself. Almost every one of them had one room in which he kept other transit workers as roomers."[49] Eileen O'Rourke Simpson's family also took in Irish boarders in their South Bronx home during the 1930s: "I don't think they paid much since most of them were on home relief because it was during the Depression."[50] Widows, like Nora Higgins, were often forced to advertise "Furnished Rooms, Kitchen Privileges" in order to keep making mortgage payments on their homes; she got $5 a week during the 1930s for "the big, front bedroom . . . with the garage thrown in."[51]

Another option was custodial work. The attitude to being a superintendent (or "janitor," depending on the era and type of building) could vary from disdain to practical acceptance. A rent-free apartment as compensation for an often heavy, dirty job made superintendent's work an important financial consideration for Irish families moving to or within the outer boroughs. It was, however, heavily dependent on the labor of women and children, because the men continued to hold down regular jobs. Agnes Campbell Sinclair's parents were janitors in a six-family, cold-water building on Eckfort Street in Greenpoint: "All through the years my mother was a janitor, and my father, they would take the heavy ashes up [from the cellar to street level]. . . . I used to help my mother on a Saturday, and we had the carpets [hall runners], you'd roll them up and take them out on the sidewalk and sweep them, then roll them up and put them back."[52] In addition, Mr. Campbell earned about $25 a week with Socony in Long Island City and Mrs. Campbell took the trolley to Flatbush every day to work as a domestic for a Jewish family. They had only one child.

Hugh O'Rourke emigrated from County Tyrone in 1911. He had steady work as a stationary engineer for the city through the 1920s and 1930s that enabled him to purchase a three-storey brick row house on Concord Avenue (St. Luke's parish in the South Bronx) in 1934. Ten years later, the family had to take a "downwardly mobile step," as Eileen O'Rourke Simpson recalled:

> My father worked for the City of New York all through the Depression making a steady pay check and while his salary was enough during the Depression, I don't believe it was enough for the war years. Maybe there was some inflation. I was a young teenager then and didn't know. We had to give up the house to the bank or whatever and then moved to a not bad duplex apartment in a two family house at Oak Terrace. . . . After about a year or so, we moved again. I think my father wanted to save money to buy a house, so he took a job as a superintendent of a small apartment house at 183rd Street in the Bronx. . . . After a year at that, we moved to a much larger apartment house [25–50 families], where my father was also the superintendent, although he also kept working at his city job with the Department of Corrections.[53]

Her brother remembered that the onus of the superintendent's work fell on his mother and sister because his father had other employment. By 1945 they had saved up enough to purchase a semidetached brick house in Holy Family parish (East Bronx) for $4,500.[54] By contrast, Maureen Griffin Mooney's mother would not consent to being a super: "She would be ashamed . . . I know it was considered a few times because of the fact that the rent was free, especially when she wanted to send us to Catholic schools and tuitions came along. She talked about it but I always remember her telling her friends 'I wouldn't consider being a super.'"[55]

Another family strategy, summer rentals, eventually made a permanent settlement out of Rockaway's "Irish Riviera." From 1914, Rockaway was the site of real estate speculation, which intensified in response to the opening of Cross Bay Boulevard in 1925. With the accompanying construction of summer bungalows and year-round residences, the peninsula began to attract Irish families from Manhattan.[56]

The popularity of a summer in Rockaway was enhanced by the Long Island Railroad, which permitted Irish workingmen to join their families in the evenings or at the weekends with little inconvenience.[57] It was not uncommon for Irish families in Manhattan to give up their apartments entirely, put their household furnishings in storage, and take a room and kitchenette or a small bungalow for the summer. The living was cheap when most of the time was spent outdoors on the beach or boardwalk, and the surplus of apartments in the city meant that incentives, such as a month's free rent and new paint, made a summer in Rockaway a decided advantage. As one woman recalled: "They gave you the first month free; you were supposed to stay three or four years [in the apartment] but these women didn't. The next year, come June, off they'd go again to the beach because it was the only way they could swing the money. They were frugal."[58]

This strategy was actually reciprocal because many of the rentals were run by Irish women; housewives during the year in Manhattan, they were business women for Rockaway summers. Delia Hayden's Aunt Anne, who was raising eight children on the Upper West Side, did rentals from about 1937 in several Rockaway locations, all under the name "The Sligo House." Around 1945, Delia Hayden borrowed $3,000 from her aunt, added $7,000 from her husband's death benefits, and purchased a "big, old-fashioned rambling house" on 85th Street. The "Rose Cottage" had six rooms for rent, including the "living room, dining room and kitchen. Those were the rooms you rented out. The living room would have two double beds in it. . . . You rented what you could rent and what you could get the money for. . . . About $300 for the summer, big airy rooms" in which the closets were converted into kitchenettes.[59]

The main Irish areas of settlement in Rockaway were Seaside and Hammels. By the 1940s deteriorating summer homes in Seaside (that were increasingly being lived in all year) were condemned by the city, forcing families from "Irishtown" to move into Hammels. To address permanent needs in the area, the city built a public housing project north of Rockaway Beach Boulevard. Hammel Houses, 14 six-storey buildings with 712 apartments, were completed in 1954 and occupied by Irish families of "moderate income."[60]

Part of the appeal of inner suburbs like the Bronx, Queens, and Brooklyn was the chance it offered to live under one's own roof. For many Irish a home of their own was the ultimate goal.[61] In a classic example of upward mobility, William O'Dwyer, later mayor of New York, recounted his decision to change jobs and place of residence:

> As a cop I had lived in a lower-middle-class neighborhood, on the second floor of a three-family house [in Sunset Park]. Nineteen twenty-five and 1926 saw some post-war good times, and right from the beginning the decision to leave the police and pursue a law career seemed justified. Now, with our position of relative affluence, Kitty and I decided to move on to the recently-developed upper-middle-class Irish-American colony in Bay Ridge. In time, we bought a house at 449 79th Street, a semi-detached one-family dwelling which was to remain our home until 1946, when I moved to Gracie Mansion.[62]

O'Dwyer is an exception. An upgrade in employment was *not* a prerequisite for home ownership for the Irish in New York. Between the wars, Irish wages were often sufficient to enable a family to raise their standard of living simply by moving.

For example, Frank Vardy's father (a third-generation Irish American who married a 1920s immigrant from County Cavan) was employed as a truck driver for the American Can Company in Brooklyn. From 1934 to 1941 the Vardys lived in a one-bedroom apartment in Bay Ridge, where the rent was $43 a month. In 1940, on a trip to the World's Fair, they drove along Eliot Avenue in Queens and saw a sign for new houses. Although they liked what they saw, it was not until the following year that they purchased a house on 79th Street in Elmhurst. Frank Vardy was told that the reason the family moved was "so the kids would have a big backyard to play in," but the more immediate factors were a $2 rent increase and, with the imminent arrival of a second child, the family had outgrown a one-bedroom apartment. The Vardys paid $6,590 for a brick row house that had three bedrooms, bath, kitchen, living room, basement, and garage. The mortgage was $57 a month, and Mr. Vardy earned $60 a week. He commuted back to Brooklyn to the same job, yet his wages were sufficient to enable him to raise his family's standard of living by moving.[63]

At the other end of the Irish social spectrum, Frank Murphy accomplished the same form of horizontal mobility when he moved his family into an exclusive WASP development in the Bronx. His father, an immigrant from County Wexford, started Murphy Brothers construction company in 1882 and the firm made its reputation with public buildings in the city. It was always Frank Murphy's dream to build a showplace for entertaining. He purchased a corner lot measuring 130 × 100 × 128 × 68 feet from Fieldston, Inc., a private development company in Riverdale, for $11,875 and spent $31,968 on the construction of a twelve-room (three-and-a-half baths) house between 1926 and 1928. Geraldine Murphy Walsh recalled that the development gave her father some trouble approving his plans for the house because he was not using their designer; she believes this was a subtle form of discrimination because the neighbors were not too happy that Catholics were moving in.[64] The only obstacle to Murphy's mobility was his religion, not his occupation or pocketbook.[65]

Financial strategies were just as vital to successful Irish homeownership in New York's inner suburbs. John Cudahy's parents lived at West 106th Street and Amsterdam Avenue until 1923, when they moved to West 163rd Street near the Polo Grounds. His father was employed by the Fifth Avenue Coach Company, yet in 1926 the Cudahys moved again, this time from Manhattan to the South Bronx, buying a three-family house near Willis Avenue in St. Jerome's parish. They were able to swing this move not only because it instantly brought them two tenants but also because Mrs. Cudahy's nephews were

> veterans of the first world war and they had money . . . and they were buying houses on foreclosure. . . . What they did, one fellow Paddy, the Mack they called him, he had this one and he took the mortgage back from my mother and father, that's how it was done to get in. . . . When my folks bought the house they had three mortgages and all you did was pay the interest on the mortgages. I remember with my sister, we used to go down with my mother to this Mr. Donahue, he was down on 57th Street and Tenth Avenue, it was like $125 every six months was the interest or something on his mortgage, until eventually you got enough saved to pay him off. . . . They weren't bank mortgages, you usually had [them] with some relatives or somebody like that.[66]

George Ward from County Galway, a carpenter by trade, decided to build his own house in the Castle Hill section of the Bronx (Holy Family parish) in time for his marriage in 1928. With a neighbor, Mr. Kelly, who was a plumber, Ward bought architectural plans for about $100 and together they built Nos. 2242 and 2244 Lafayette Avenue, where they had been able to acquire the land cheaply because the subway was 20 blocks away. It took them 20 months to build the houses, which were two-family dwellings each containing two seven-room apartments, plus basement and detached garage. They were able to do all the construction work themselves except for the excavation of the basements. George Ward had a $6,000 mortgage on his house and paid it off in full by 1946; he always rented the upstairs apartment and was getting $48 a month for it between 1945 and 1952.[67]

If, as is sometimes argued, the purchase of a house testified to "a search for maximum *security* rather than for mobility out of" a particular class, in New York City even renters could achieve this same sense of security as long as there was a glut of available and affordable housing.[68] Maureen Mooney, the daughter of a transit worker, recalled her mother saying that, in the Bronx,

> during the Depression, a lot of people had to leave their apartments, or were evicted or whatever. There were a lot of empty apartments around, and on Sunday afternoon, if you didn't have too much to do, you went around and looked at all these empty apartments. If you saw one that you liked better, then you moved. They moved several times and I'm not sure it was really for a cheaper apartment; sometimes it was an upgrade or a better bargain or whatever, to get more room. . . . Very often that was something that they did [look at apartments on Sundays].[69]

A home—which in New York's particular parlance often embraced large, airy apartments as well as single and multifamily houses—was to many Irish families an important symbol.[70] The Irish real estate developers Brady, Cryan and Colleran assured their buyers that "a home of your own is not a luxury but a NECESSITY, for it is a bulwark against adversity and a solace in old age."[71] To Nora Durkin Higgins, the wife of a pub owner, "Buckingham Palace, the Taj Mahal and Shangrila were all wrapped up in that six-room, brick, semi-detached dwelling in the Bronx."[72]

Selling this dream to the Irish also provided an opportunity for personal social mobility. County Tipperary native Daniel Gleeson, for example, was a real estate agent with the Schwencke Land and Improvement Company. Through advertisements in the *Irish Advocate,* Gleeson offered $25 to $50 a week for "clean-cut, wideawake Irishmen to work as salesmen" and particularly sought "men now employed and with a large circle of acquaintances."[73] In a 1916 interview, Gleeson told the *Irish Advocate:* "I have made considerable money through real estate and there is no reason why hundreds of young Irish boys don't take advantage of the present wave of prosperity and join the selling forces of live, rock bottom real estate concerns that give big salaries to ambitious workers. Imagine the number of intelligent Irish boys that have to work long hours on street cars, and we all know that the pay they receive is not enough at the present cost of living."[74]

Daniel Gleeson developed a weekly savings plan for the Schwencke Company by which Irish working people could purchase a quarter acre of land in

Nassau County, six miles east of the New York City line, for $1 a week over three years, at 2–3 percent interest.[75] Such small real estate investment, for personal needs, was typical of the New York Irish. In the late 1940s John Cudahy, a second-generation Irish American, opened an insurance and real estate business in a "small room next to the Irish counties" meeting space in the Henry Hudson Hotel in Manhattan. In 1953 he moved the business to Jackson Heights and his family to Middle Village in Queens:

> What we got at the time then was a lot of our peers, our Irish, coming out of Manhattan. And we knew them and we sold [them]. They are still in some of the houses just like ourselves. One family homes, that's what they wanted. They were in the bar business, or motormen on the subways, maybe the wife was a nurse, and they'd saved up. . . . We started to get people like that who had some cash and then you had the first wave of Irish [immigrants] who came over [after World War II]. They became Korean veterans. . . . Then you could get the G.I. Bill of Rights, and for them to move from Manhattan to here, that was a big move. Like the people who were living here, they were moving further out the island, but these [Irish] were moving to this area.[76]

One of John Cudahy's salesmen, Jimmy Lavin from County Mayo, branched out into contracting, buying handy-man specials in Jackson Heights, Rego Park, Elmhurst, Maspeth, and Middle Village. He brought in carpenters and plumbers to install new kitchens and orchid tile in the bathrooms, and attracted mainly Irish people to move into the renovated houses. According to John Cudahy, Lavin "saw that we had the contacts with the people he was interested in selling to, and they were his own kind of people, Irish, they could converse."[77]

As early as 1914 the *Irish Advocate* had cautioned working women against real estate men and their investment schemes.[78] Using Irish salesmen to sell real estate to Irish people was neither a new nor a very widely used method, but it was one the community had seen abused in the past. The technique was developed to a fine art by the firm of Brady, Cryan and Colleran, owners and developers of Massapequa Park. In 1927 they ran full-page ads in the city newspapers announcing the opening of this new community on the south shore of Long Island. Although it was difficult to reach the area, "this did not dampen or discourage the ambitions and imaginations of three young Irishmen who could foresee a great future for this so-called wilderness." In fact, Michael J. Brady, Frank Cryan, and Peter F. Colleran had a vested interest in the development of Massapequa Park, an incorporated village where, in time, Brady and Cryan served as police justices and Colleran as the first mayor.[79]

With a green paper and green ink brochure, Brady, Cryan and Colleran encouraged people to "Stop Paying Rent to the Landlord" and invest their savings instead in homesites or brick houses (selling in 1928 for between $8,000 and $9,000 dollars) along "Tyrconnell Street," "Glengarriff Street," and "Avoca Avenue." On Sunday afternoons over the next several years, they hired special trains to depart Penn Station, New York and Flatbush Avenue, Brooklyn, to bring out prospective buyers: "Many times two trains a day were needed, and, upon one occasion in May, 1929, 5,621 people visited Massapequa Park on four special trains. . . . So great was the real estate business that the sales organization, which began with forty men in October, 1927, within two years was employing 650 full-time salesmen and over 1,000 part-timers to meet the needs of the steady influx of 'pioneers' to Massapequa Park."[80] The firm even recruited "the popular Irish pilot" Captain James J. Fitzmaurice (1898–1965) as a salesman, built an airfield they christened Fitzmaurice Flying Field, and began to fly buyers to Massapequa Park in 1929.[81] They shamelessly exploited the Irish connection:

> Advertisements offering the lots for sale were printed in Irish newspapers, to attract domestics of Irish extraction who were the chief buyers. . . . Beer parties featured the sales rallies and free transportation to and from Massapequa Park were offered as further inducements. . . . Salesmen for the developers featured a rich Irish brogue in their sales talks and Irish songs and dances featured [in] the rallies that were held frequently on the property. . . . It was customary for Colleran and Brady, if they could learn from what county in Ireland a prospective customer came, to put a salesman from that county to work on him.[82]

Sometimes this kind of sales strategy could backfire, however, as in 1936 when Michael Fitzpatrick, of 510 East 156th Street in the Melrose section of the Bronx, filed suit against Brady, Cryan and Colleran for real estate fraud. Fitzpatrick, who was 70 years old and an IRT employee, had purchased two lots on the installment plan, finished paying $495 for them in 1934, then discovered that the lots were not free from incumbrances. In fact, the first mortgage on the property was under foreclosure, and the Nassau County District Attorney's office brought an indictment based on "thirty-five complaints about similar transactions."[83]

But large-scale real estate investment that both appealed to ethnic ties and went beyond immediate personal needs was the domain of relatively few in the New York Irish community. Most Irish developers were motivated more by opportunities for business or personal gain than for any altruistic reasons such as improving the lot of their own. Noonan Plaza in the Highbridge section of the Bronx is a good example. It was built by the Nelden Corporation, Bernard J. Noonan, president, in 1931 at an estimated cost of $2 million. With almost 300 apartments (some of which had two baths), Noonan Plaza is often cited as New York's supreme example of Art Deco apartment house design. Noonan (1876–1943) was a native of County Longford and although he put his own name on a complex that dominated a corner opposite Sacred Heart Church, in an overwhelmingly Irish neighborhood, Noonan Plaza was built "to provide luxury housing for the upper middle-class" and its first tenants were Jewish.[84] Its 15,000-square-foot garden courtyard was "bedecked with shrubbery, fountains, and mosaic walkways, surrounding a pool in the center that was stocked with swans, goldfish and water lilies. . . . a picturesque waterfall . . . [and] Japanese style bridges."[85] Irish American children from the parish recall that their pleasure of this private Eden was contingent upon the permission of the complex's Irish doorman, and they were never permitted access unless accompanied by an adult. It was not until its Jewish occupants began to move out in the late 1950s that Irish Americans started to live in Noonan Plaza.[86]

By contrast, John Stratton O'Leary's Glengariff Construction Company built a series of four-story apartment houses in the East Bronx, south of White Plains Road, in the early 1930s. Each apartment building housed 127 families. From the beginning "O'Leary's Flats," as they were colloquially known, drew Irish families of County Kerry extraction from the South Bronx.[87] Margaret Sullivan married in 1934 and moved from 124th Street in Harlem (All Saints parish) to Cypress Avenue and 138th Street in the Bronx (St. Luke's parish). The following year, she moved with her husband and infant daughter to 1436 Beach Avenue:

> These apartments were newly built, more modern in layout than the old railroad-type flats in the South Bronx. Residents enjoyed more privacy because rooms were laid out off of foyers rather than having to walk through rooms like in older tenements. . . . [During the Depression] wages were low and rents were low, too. Many of my husband's family moved into the O'Leary's Flats within a short period of time and we all helped each other financially and emotionally. John Stratton O'Leary was a good landlord who did not pressure those who were in financial straits.[88]

O'Leary, a native of Kenmare, County Kerry, and a former policeman, was well known in the Bronx Irish community and word of his new apartments spread quickly among neighbors in the South Bronx. Even 20 years later, O'Leary's Flats were attracting South Bronx Irish, the superintendents were all Irish-born, and the rental agent was the Ardree Company (still owned by the O'Leary family). When Vincent Flynn and his wife moved from St. Luke's Parish to Thieriot Avenue in 1957, seven of their relatives were neighbors in O'Leary buildings on the same street.[89]

Perhaps the only clear example of a successful and organic ethnic interplay between land ownership, development, and residential occupancy by the New York Irish is Celtic Park Apartments in Woodside, Queens.[90] In this instance, a non-Irish corporation built housing in an area, and on specific land, that had had Irish affiliations for years. Because that housing was also both modern and affordable, it proved a natural draw for Irish people already familiar with the neighborhood. In 1897 the Irish-American Athletic Club had raised subscriptions for the purchase of nine acres at the far eastern end of Long Island City, just 10 minutes by trolley from the 34th Street ferry. Celtic Park was ideally situated. Irish Americans were already well acquainted with the travel route necessary to get there since the athletic ground was built adjacent to Calvary Cemetery. Celtic Park drew crowds to some spectacular sporting events up to 1914. After the war, for a number of reasons, the club was dissolved and the property sold to the City and Suburban Homes Company for approximately half a million dollars.[91]

The City and Suburban Homes Company was "one of the oldest limited dividend housing corporations in existence" at the time. It consistently selected projects to be developed in locations that had employment and transportation advantages, but also in areas of dense population where a demand for housing was high.[92] The City and Suburban Homes Company built Celtic Park Apartments in 1931, and despite vacancies and arrears in their Manhattan properties due to the Depression, the first section of Celtic Park was almost fully occupied by 1932.[93]

The apartments rented for $15 a room and were equipped with "refrigerators, radio outlets, incinerators, latest type gas ranges and kitchen accessories, tiled bathrooms and foyer halls. . . . [with] a spacious court[yard], with shrubs and lawn."[94] There were now five transportation lines within three blocks of Celtic Park, and the newly built St. Teresa's Catholic Church (1928) was around the corner on 44th Street. Celtic Park was built in a section of Woodside that since the arrival of the subway in 1917 had attracted mainly Irish and German settlers to live in one and two family houses and apartment buildings. The Irish were said to have migrated there from Manhattan's West Side and by the time Celtic Park Apartments opened, Woodside was estimated to be 80 percent Irish.[95]

The paths of Irish dispersion in New York were established within the first three decades of this century and, on the available evidence, some things are clear for the Irish experience. First, speculative real estate interest by the Irish in the city's early inner suburbs—such as Washington Heights, the Bronx, and Long Island (Brooklyn, Queens, Nassau)—predates the movement of Irish residents into these areas by about 20 years. While lot transactions and municipal improvement contracts permitted Irish involvement in the vanguard of the city's expansion, pure Irish geographic mobility had to await the construction of housing in these areas. The Irish followed the general expansion pattern of the city, arriving in the boroughs in the wake of the first transportation developments, and adapting to available (and more diverse) housing stock rather than imprinting a particular style on an area.[96] In the resulting transformation of inner suburb to urban borough, the Irish were involved at all levels of the real estate hierarchy in New York.

Second, migration opportunities were spread primarily by word of mouth within the community, and often involved step-migration (one to three smaller moves prior to a major change). The biggest factor affecting the degree of Irish migration activity between 1900 and 1960 was the availability of modern housing, because the city's stock fluctuated dramatically during the Depression and the second world war. Direct marketing techniques and other ethnic appeals, although they certainly existed, had a limited impact. Irish connections operated on an informal and almost unacknowledged basis in the process. Celtic Park, O'Leary's Flats, and even Noonan Plaza were the exceptions in the New York experience; most Irish did not rent or buy from other Irish. Yet, for Irish builders, investors, landlords, and agents, real estate as a means of personal social mobility cannot be underestimated. By exploiting the migration potential of inner suburbs through the construction of infrastructure, transit, and housing, they gained, at the very least, civic and social recognition within the city's Irish and Catholic communities.

Third, it appears to have been women who looked for housing and moved their families to new areas. In this they were conscious of both improved domestic amenities and the financial strategies needed to realize the move. For the average Irish family, the result was often a horizontal mobility that raised their standard of living without necessarily requiring an additional drain on the household budget. In the process, the Irish got their first real chance to make the break from tenement living in New York. Although it might not mandate a change in employment for the main breadwinner, a change in residence often did bring additional responsibilities to Irish women, especially when it involved becoming a building custodian or taking in boarders. But by and large life in the Bronx, Queens, and Brooklyn meant new-style (modern) apartments and single or multifamily houses, in areas wearing a new aura of respectability. As Bernard Clare described his Queens sales turf in 1927, "the scene was one of bristling prosperity, of zooming lower-middle-class prosperity . . . small town, country, suburbia, all rolled into one, some of it old, some of it beginning to shine like the pictures of happy, happy life in the 'SEP' [Saturday Evening Post]."[97] This, rather than any direct marketing techniques and other ethnic appeals, drove intraurban migration.

As for the implications of this intraurban migration for Irish social mobility, while job advancement, suburban dispersal, and home-ownership rates are usually cited as indicators of social mobility, in early-twentieth-century New York the city's intense development of the outer boroughs offered a means of horizontal mobility that satisfied aspirations usually associated with occupation or class. Economic and social forces that were conquering urban geography combined to offer the Irish better, more comfortable lifestyles. At the same time a variety of domestic and financial strategies enabled them to take advantage of it. A good address could reflect an important social perception of status for the Irish that was not rooted in economics or power. Thus, a unique set of circumstances in New York enabled the Irish to attain standards of living that, under other conditions, might have required at least another generation or extraordinary economic advancement.[98] The result was "modern suburban comfort" that was just as socially acceptable, if not more so, than the traditionally ascribed route of climbing the "ladder."[99]

1945 to 1992

PART V

THE MODERN ERA

Playing football at Gaelic Park, West 240th Street and
Broadway in the Riverdale section of the Bronx, c. 1980. Gaelic
sports, especially football and hurling, have been played in New
York since the turn of the century. Gaelic Park (once known as
Innisfail Park) has been a popular gathering place since it opened
in 1928. In addition to playing fields, stands, and locker rooms,
Gaelic Park had a dance hall. Long-time proprietor John "Kerry"
O'Donnell once said, "More people went astray here than
anywhere else. You would be surprised at the number of
marriages." (Courtesy of the *Irish Echo*.)

David M. Reimers

OVERVIEW
An End and a Beginning

COMMENTING ABOUT New York's Irish in 1963, Daniel Patrick Moynihan wrote, "New York used to be an Irish city. Or so it seemed. There were sixty or seventy years when the Irish were everywhere."[1] That was the case right up until after World War II. New York's mayor from 1946 to 1950 was Irish-born William O'Dwyer, who had risen from the police department through politics to be elected mayor in 1945. Irish political bosses were shaken during the La Guardia years, but men like the Bronx's Edward Flynn remained politically important in the city. And when Flynn died, he was followed by Charles Buckley, a powerful boss in his borough for many years.

The police and fire department were heavily Irish, and Irishmen invariably headed the top spots in those departments. When replacing Police Commissioner Arthur Wallander, a holdover from La Guardia's administration, O'Dwyer chose William O'Brien, and he was succeeded by Thomas Murphy. Although most new school teachers were Jewish after 1940, many of the older teachers were Irish. And so were many other city workers.[2]

Most religious New Yorkers were Roman Catholic, and the church hierarchy was overwhelmingly Irish, headed by Francis Cardinal Spellman, who was just reaching the peak of his secular and spiritual influence after 1945. When Spellman spoke, people and politicians listened. The St. Patrick's Day parades were New York's largest ethnic display, and the number of marchers and onlookers increased after 1945. The 1947 parade drew more than 80,000 marchers, watched by more than a million spectators. And that March 17 was a chilly day. Nor was Irish American cultural life missing. The United Irish Counties Association's annual festival grew in size after its founding in the 1930s; in 1947 it drew a crowd of 30,000 to watch 3,000 participants show their style in music, poetry, hurling, and dozens of games.[3]

Moynihan continued his observation about New York being an Irish city by concluding that the Irish "felt it was their town. It is no longer, and they know it." By 1963 he could clearly see the waning Irish significance in New York City. Most noticeable was the decline in the Irish population. With it came a loss of political and religious power and influence in running the affairs of the city. The Irish population began to drop before 1945. Immigration fell after the turn of the century, although it picked up again briefly in the 1920s, after Ireland had achieved independence from Great Britain. But during the Great Depression, few Europeans, Irish or otherwise, emigrated to the United States. After World War II, Irish immigration began again, but in lesser numbers than in the heyday of the nineteenth century. Nearly 50,000 arrived during the 1950s and another 32,000 during the 1960s; traditionally, about one-quarter of all Irish immigrants settled in New York City.[4]

In 1965 Congress passed a new immigration law that scrapped the national origins provisions favoring the nations of Northern and Western Europe. Although Ireland actually saw its quota increase from 17,000 to 20,000 (every nation now had this same figure), the rules for getting in changed, with preference given to potential immigrants with close family ties to U.S. citizens and with skills needed in the United States. Equally important was the situation in Ireland during the 1960s and 1970s. Economic expansion and participation in the European Common Market in those years caused the Irish economy to grow at a relatively brisk pace, with the result that few young Irish men and women chose to emigrate.[5] City officials found that fewer than 7,500 Irish settled in New York city between 1965 and 1980, and Irish immigration to the city averaged less than 200 annually between 1982 and 1985.[6]

When the Irish economy turned sour in the 1980s and unemployment soared, the Irish found that they lacked the necessary family connections required for immigration to the United States. They came anyway, usually as tourists, and stayed on when their visas expired, living and working illegally. Perhaps as many as 20,000 of these "visitors" remained in New York City.

In chapter 18 Mary Corcoran takes a detailed look at these new, often undocumented, Irish men and women arriving in the 1980s. Driven largely by economic forces to seek better opportunities in the United States, they found conditions in New York City worth risking living without a green card. The men worked mostly in construction and the women, making much lower wages, in child care. Corcoran notes that many of these latest Irish immigrants were highly educated but found little use for their skills in Ireland. Of course, not all were illegal as special immigration laws passed in 1986 and 1990 enabled Ireland to send more immigrants to America.

One section of the Immigration Reform and Control Act of 1986 enabled several thousand of these "New Irish," as they call themselves, to get green cards. Moreover, the Immigration Act of 1990 guaranteed Ireland 48,000 "Morrison" visas over a three-year period and the potential of thousands more after that.[7] Thus Irish immigration, which officially numbered less than 1,000 a year for most of the 1980s, was on the upswing again, and Corcoran believes that it will continue in the 1990s.

The drop in New York City's Irish first-and second-generation population was substantial after 1945. At one point in the nineteenth century, those generations amounted to one-quarter of the city's residents. In 1900 the first and second generation numbered 692,000 of the city's approximately 3 million residents, and still a significant half million in 1940. But by 1960 they numbered only 312,000. A decade later they amounted to 220,000. In 1980 only 42,000 New Yorkers were Irish born, with the vast majority of Irish Americans being third, fourth, or fifth generation. Some 317,000 identified themselves as being of Irish ancestry. Reflecting trends in assimilation and intermarriage, a slightly larger number labeled themselves as having part Irish ancestry, thus bringing the total claiming some Irish ancestry to some 600,000.[8] These figures are not precise, but they show a clear trend: by the 1980s Irish, and part Irish, accounted for less than 10 percent of the city's approximately 7 million people. Preliminary data from the 1990 census indicate that only 535,00 persons identified themselves as being of Irish or part Irish ancestry.[9]

Dropping immigration alone does not account for the fall in the city's Irish population. Irish New Yorkers, like other whites, left the city in droves after World War II to live in the mushrooming suburbs of New York and New Jersey. Almost 95 percent of the city's 7.4 million residents in 1940 were white, but in 1990 they accounted for less than half of a similar-sized population. Improved transportation facilities connecting the city to the suburbs, the migration of jobs out of the city, enhanced incomes, the housing boom, and the desire to escape blacks and Hispanics and find better schools all account for this mass movement of white New Yorkers.

For the most part, white New Yorkers who moved, and the Irish were no exception, were upwardly mobile with the money to purchase homes in the rapidly growing housing tracts of Long Island, New Jersey, and Westchester. By 1950 more than half of the metropolitan area's Irish Americans lived outside the city, and the proportion continued to grow. These tended to be third or later generations with higher incomes than the first two generations. The preliminary 1990 census indicated that approximately twice as many persons of Irish ancestry lived in New Jersey's Bergen County and New York's Rockland, Westchester, Nassau, and Suffolk counties than in New York City. The largest concentrations of Irish Americans were found in Nassau and Suffolk counties on Long Island.[10]

Changes also occurred for those Irish who chose to stay in the city. The city's Irish had begun to move from Lower Manhattan around the turn of the century, especially as subways and bridges connected that borough to the city's four other counties. Upper Manhattan, the Bronx, Brooklyn, and Queens were the most popular residential districts during the booming 1920s. After 1945 even neighborhoods of second-or third-generation Irish lost their appeal as the more prosperous Irish headed for the suburbs, or Queens. Inwood, in the upper West Side of Manhattan, Fordham and Mott Haven in the Bronx, and the East Side found their Hispanic and black population increasing. What was once Hell's Kitchen, a heavily Irish neighborhood on the West Side of midtown Manhattan, experienced gentrification after 1960. That neighborhood's infamous "Westies" Irish mob was either in jail or dispersed by 1990. A holdover from Hell's Kitchen's old Tammany days, James R. McManus, exercised political muscle in 1992 when he successfully won nomination for Jerrold Nadler to replace the recently deceased Ted Weiss in Congress. But such events were unusual in the early 1990s.[11]

Older Irish landmarks disappeared in these neighborhoods. In February 1991 the Mattie Haskins Shamrock Imports closed its doors after 68 years on East 75th Street in Manhattan. A Mexican restaurant replaced it. One commentator noted of that neighborhood, "It used to be a heavily Irish area. But now there's basically nothing Irish that remains."[12]

Of course, neighborhoods did not transform themselves overnight. Just how Irish New Yorkers responded to their new Latino and black neighbors was a complex issue. In chapter 17 Rob Snyder discusses one neighborhood in detail—the Inwood section of Manhattan. He reveals several trends that were repeated in other sections of the city. Irish residents felt they were in control when dealing with Jewish neighbors during the 1940s. But after 1945 Jews began to move out, and Latinos and blacks moved in. Inwood's Irish feared growing crime and their new, mainly Dominican, neighbors. Middle-class and young Irish left first, leaving largely elderly and working-class Irish behind. The mobile Irish men and women found new homes to the north in Westchester or across the river in New Jersey.

By the 1970s Queens contained the largest number of Irish Americans. The 1980 and the 1990 census revealed that about one-third of those claiming some Irish ancestry lived in Queens. Brooklyn was second.[13] The strongest Irish communities were now in neighborhoods like Queens's Woodside, Brooklyn's Bay Ridge, and the Bronx's Norwood.

The postwar periods of prosperity made it possible for many Irish to continue their education and find better jobs in the city's economy. The elite, composed of families like the Murrays, McDonnells, and the Cuddihys, were among the city's richest families. The Fifth Avenue apartment of James Francis McDonnell was at one point the largest in New York: its "dining room chandelier alone was valued at $100,000."[14] Although for most such a style was beyond their dreams, the Irish in general managed to prosper in these years.

Transit workers are a case in point. As the city's subway and bus lines expanded in the twentieth century, the Irish had played a dominant role, so much so that the Interboro Rapid Transit (IRT) was sometimes called the Irish Rapid Transit. Few were in the top, managerial positions, however. Also heavily Irish (90%) was the Third Avenue Railway, most of whose workers were Irish born. Although their numbers varied from line to line, Irish workers had the advantage of speaking English where contact with the public was concerned. The Transport Workers Union, too, was Irish dominated and led by the colorful Irishman Mike Quill. While working in transport was not especially desirable, it represented steady employment. After World War II, better employment beckoned. The transport business steadily took on black and Hispanic workers who saw these as solid working-class jobs with health and other fringe benefits. By 1990 only a sprinkling of Irish workers remained there.[15]

By then fewer Irish New Yorkers could also be found as policemen, waitresses, domestics, or other traditional working-class jobs they had formerly held. Instead, a growing number of postwar New York Irish found jobs in the professions, management, advertising, insurance, banking, selling, and other middle-class and upper-middle-class occupations. As the *New York Times* put it on August 1, 1986, "And if there are fewer policemen in New York who have Irish names, there are more stockbrokers that do. The police commissioner is no longer Robert J. McGuire, but the chairman of the New York Stock Exchange is John J. Phelan Jr." The paper reported Irish American leader Paul O'Dwyer, brother of William O'Dwyer, as saying, "Twenty years ago, if an Irishman had a daughter who was a stenographer he thought he was doing pretty good. Now, the young Irish-Americans want to get into the yuppie class." The 79-year-old O'Dwyer added, "Some of my own grandchildren even!"

Studies of the social and economic status of Americans do show that Irish Americans on the whole had done well by the 1980s and were more successful than other white Americans except Jews. This also seemed to be the case in New York. The 1970 census indicated that second-generation Irish American families there had higher incomes than comparable whites. Although published 1980 census data did not break down by county or city, they revealed that the Irish in New York State did about as well or slightly better than other whites and that their educational levels were higher.[16] The 1990 census information on this point is not yet available.

Yet not all Irish New Yorkers were in the middle class. A mid-1970s study of three Irish neighborhoods revealed a wide distribution of incomes among residents. Although only a small proportion used Aid to Families with Dependent Children, considerably more had used food stamps and unemployment insurance. Among the elderly, especially, incomes were frequently below the national average and median. Whereas the 1980 census revealed that 10 percent of Irish living in New York State over age 25 were college graduates, a much smaller proportion of residents in these neighborhoods were college graduates.[17]

Rob Snyder also points out that working-class Irish still populated neighborhoods such as Inwood in the late 1980s, and the Irish remained prominent among construction workers in the 1990s. Jimmy Breslin's *Table Money* (1986), a fictional account of the "Sandhogs," those Irish American construction workers who helped build tunnels, bridges, and subways, was based on real people. The Irish, along with West Indians and Poles, still dominated this occupation in the early 1990s. One Irish "Sandhog" said about his occupation, "Maybe its only the Irish and the West Indians thick enough to do it."[18] More research, based on the 1990 census and other data, is needed to give an accurate picture of the city's Irish working-class population in the 1990s.

Next to changing neighborhoods, it was in politics that the decline of Irish presence was most noticeable. Building on neighborhood solidarity and the power of Tammany Hall, Irish politicians dominated much of the city's political life during the first decades of the twentieth century. When Jimmy Walker was mayor in the late 1920s, the important Board of Estimate consisted of six Irish Catholics—the mayor, controller, president of the Board of Aldermen, and the borough presidents of Kings, Queens, and Richmond—and two others. The president of the borough of Manhattan was Jewish while a German headed the Bronx.[19]

Throughout the Great Depression the Democratic Party continued to run Irish men for mayor and other key offices, but the corruption of Tammany Hall and the Walker years soured New Yorkers on the old ways of doing public business. Those years belonged to the colorful Italian American Fiorello La Guardia, who ran on the American Labor Party or Republican lines or as a Fusion candidate. The "Little Flower," as he was sometimes called, rewarded Jewish and Italian voters who supported him with a growing number of top-level appointments. Moreover, during the La Guardia years an expanding number of municipal jobs were placed under the civil service, a trend that also worked to the disadvantage of the New York Irish: "Under La Guardia the civil service lost its brogue."[20]

The Irish staged a resurgence of sorts when La Guardia left office on January 1, 1946, and William O'Dwyer succeeded him. His reputation as Brooklyn's district attorney, his wartime service, and image as a friend of labor and civil rights stood him well, and he ran successfully among Jews and Italians as well as Irish voters. A popular leader, he won again in 1949. In spite of his sometime image as a reformer and foe of Tammany Hall, O'Dwyer's days as mayor were numbered. Dissatisfaction among Jewish and Italian voters, who wanted more power and recognition, grew, as did rumors of his ties to organized crime. Changes in his personal life, scandals in the police department, and Senator Estes Kefauver's Senate Special Investigating Committee on Organized Crime revelations, although it produced nothing new about O'Dwyer, finally convinced him to resign from office to accept President Harry S Truman's offer of the ambassadorship to Mexico.[21]

Vincent Impellitteri replaced O'Dwyer in 1950. His years as mayor added little lustre to his reputation. "By early 1953 the average New Yorker realized what political professionals already knew in 1950: Vincent Impellitteri did not know how to be mayor. More than anything else, he did nothing." Although he decided to run as an independent in the 1953 election, he lost to Democrat Robert F. Wagner, who ran well among Irish, black, Jewish, and even many Italian voters.[22]

The new mayor was half Irish; and if that counts, he was the last Irish American mayor of New York. Wagner had good things to say about Irish-run New York City. Looking back in the 1980s he said, "I think it hurts the city that they haven't the brains of the Irish to meet some of these problems we have here today."[23] Yet this son of a famous U.S. senator was hardly in the mode of past Irish American politicians. Wagner did court Tammany Hall for years, but he had attended Yale University and learned his politics from the top, from his father and his friends, not on the streets of New York City.

A popular mayor who got along with most of New York's polyglot voters, Wagner was a pragmatic man. At first he played ball with political bosses, such as the Bronx's Charles Buckley and Tammany's Carmine De Sapio. He also encouraged labor unions to organize, reached out to black voters, and worked to improve city services. Yet he could shift allegiances too, as he did when the reform movement grew during the 1950s.

During the O'Dwyer years, Jewish and Italian politicians tried to build on the gains of the 1930s and were increasingly nominated for office by the city's political parties. During the 1950s, liberal reformers were dissatisfied with the lackluster Tammany Democratic support of presidential candidate Adlai Stevenson in the 1952 and 1956 elections and the workings of New York's Democratic machine. They took their campaigns to local neighborhoods. The reform clubs, especially in Manhattan, ousted the old guard Irish leaders in a number of elections.[24]

In 1949, within Tammany Hall itself, Carmine De Sapio became the first Italian American to head the organization. Clearly, Irish domination and influence were both in sharp decline after 1950. Wagner sensed the changes. Realizing that Tammany Hall was becoming a bad label in New York politics, he broke with the Hall and threw his lot in with the reformers during his bid for a third term as mayor. Whereas he courted Tammany support in 1953, he repudiated it in 1959 and joined the "dump De Sapio" movement. The man Wagner had "always found . . . to be a good man [who] never attempted to interfere with the running of the city" became a liability. When he attacked the bosses and De Sapio, the latter noted: "We are faced with the spectacle of a candidate who seeks reelection on a platform of cleaning up the mess which he himself has created." To the charge that Wagner was running against himself and his record, the mayor reportedly said, "I could find no better opponent."[25]

Following Wagner's retirement, Irish politicians continued their decline in governing the affairs of New York City. William F. Buckley Jr., wealthy editor of the *National Review*, ran for mayor on the Conservative line in 1965, but he was not a serious threat to the major parties, although he did attract some disgruntled Irish voters who were unhappy over their loss of power within the Democratic Party and opposed to the liberalism of WASP liberal Republican John V. Lindsay.[26] In the 1980s Democratic leader and assemblyman Herman D. Farrell was suggested as a potential candidate for mayor; but Farrell, whose grandfather was Irish, was pushed as a black candidate. By the 1980s only a few Irish men and women held key positions in the city's boroughs, and in that decade only Irish American Carol Bellamy, a Protestant, won a election to a citywide office, as city council president in 1981. By the time David Dinkins was inaugurated as mayor in 1990, only one Irish American served as a commissioner of a city agency and he was replaced by an Hispanic.[27]

At the federal level, Irish Americans still won elections after 1960. Senator Daniel Patrick Moynihan was the most notable, but a number won election to the House, and Robert F. Kennedy (until his assassination) and James Buckley (for one term) both served in the U.S. Senate. Neither of these rich men, however, had worked their way up from the streets of New York. They represented the split nature of many New York Irish Americans; James Buckley championed a rising conservatism, while Bobby Kennedy spoke for the liberal wing of the Democratic Party.[28]

In the House traditional Irish politicians like Brooklyn's John Rooney won many elections, but some of the New York Irish House members, such as Brooklyn's Hugh Carey and Manhattan's William Fitz Ryan, were men of wealthy backgrounds, and Ryan had wide support from reformers in his campaign against "bossism."[29]

Municipal Irish political leaders were being replaced first by Jews and Italians and in the 1980s by rising African Americans. The days of Edward Flynn's and Charlie Buckley's power were over, and Buckley even lost his Bronx congressional seat in 1964, a position he had held for 30 years. The neighborhoods reigned over at one time by Flynn and Buckley were increasingly black and Hispanic. Moreover, many Irish New Yorkers even deserted the Democratic Party, in part because of their rising affluence and in part over particular issues. Some Irish had turned against Woodrow Wilson and the Democratic Party in 1920 because the Treaty of Versailles did not grant Ireland its independence, but they generally returned to the Democratic fold during the 1920s and 1930s, even though many disagreed with Franklin Roosevelt's foreign policies.[30]

Yet the postwar changes saw many Irish American New Yorkers switch to the Republican Party. Some were attracted to Republican Joseph McCarthy during the Red Scare of the 1950s. The senator, both Irish and anticommunist, found a ready audience among many Irish New Yorkers. At a controversial breakfast of the police department's Holy Name Society in April 1953, Cardinal Spellman gave McCarthy his support, much to the delight of thousands of cheering policemen.[31] In the 1950s a few worried about a divorced man, Democrat Adlai Stevenson, running against the popular Dwight David Eisenhower, being elected president, but many rallied to the 1960 presidential candidacy of John F. Kennedy. As noted, many Irish politicians also chafed at the growing Jewish liberalism and their loss of power within the New York Democratic Party of the 1950s and 1960s. Others blamed the Democrats for the student uprisings, urban riots, and the debacle in Vietnam during the 1960s.[32] By the early 1960s many Irish New Yorkers were voting Republican, and in 1964 an estimated 55 percent of the city's Irish voters cast their ballots for Senator Barry Goldwater in the 1964 presidential election.[33] The next year Conservative candidate for mayor, William Buckley, attracted 22 percent of the city's Irish voters, with the rest evenly split between the Republicans and Democrats.[34]

Then the civil rights issue moved to northern communities. When Mayor John Lindsay proposed a Civilian Review Board to examine charges of police brutality, it ran into solid opposition from white Catholic New Yorkers. The predominately Irish Patrolmen's Benevolent Association (PBA) joined with the Conservative Party and a variety of civic groups to force a referendum in 1966.[35] While old-line liberal groups favored the board, it went down to defeat, especially in Italian and Irish neighborhoods where voters overwhelmingly rejected it. Irish Americans voted against it by a 4 to 1 margin. No wonder. At that time Irish Americans were the largest ethnic group in the New York police department, and many persons in white neighborhoods had relatives in the department or close ties to the police. They saw the board proposal as a threat to their safety and an attack on their friends and relatives.[36]

The Civilian Review Board was not the only civil rights issue to alienate white voters from the Democratic Party. Affirmative action programs and "quotas" became increasingly polarizing issues after 1970. As New York expanded its public payroll after World War II, blacks were the major gainers; by the 1980s, after decades of underrepresentation, they were overrepresented as New York City employees. By the end of the 1980s African Americans, who accounted for one in four New Yorkers, held more than 30 percent of municipal jobs. These gains were achieved because of pressure by civil rights groups and affirmative action programs, as well as law suits over alleged discrimination in city hiring practices. The largest gains came in the lower-level entry positions and in the health and human services departments.[37]

The city's Irish still had solid representation in the fire department, which was 90 percent white in the early 1990s. They also were well represented among the police, although a growing number of black officers were being hired in the 1980s. More than 95 percent of lieutenants and captains were still white at that time, but Irish New Yorkers lost the top post of police commissioner when Ed Koch appointed an African American, Benjamin Ward, as commissioner. His successor appointed another black to the top post. The top post returned to the Irish in 1992 when Mayor David Dinkins named Raymond Kelly, a long-time member of the police force, commissioner. Kelly acknowledged, however, that recruitment of more blacks was the force's top priority.[38]

Breakthroughs for blacks sometimes caused resentment and court fights. In 1983 scores of mostly white New York City police sergeants charged that the new Police Department examination for promotion to lieutenant designed to overcome racial and sexual bias was unfair. Sergeant Peter J. Mahon, president of the Sergeants Benevolent Association, insisted that revisions were required.[39] As one journalist, discussing Irish voter alienation from the Democrats, put it in 1984, "Most of the guys I grew up with tell you the Democratic Party no longer represents them. They're tired of the quota systems they run into on their civil service jobs . . . the ones who made it down to Wall Street tell you they don't remember any Federal, affirmative-action programs when their fathers were looking for their first jobs in this country."[40]

Nor were Irish New Yorkers thrilled with the prospect of the election of African American David Dinkins in 1989. Dinkins's problem was how to hold on to a solid black and Hispanic vote without losing too many whites to his opponent, Republican Rudolph Giuliani. Although he easily defeated Mayor Ed Koch in the Democratic primary, Dinkins watched as most whites deserted the Democratic Party in the 1989 election; he barely won election, polling only about one in four among Irish voters. It should be noted that he did about the same among other white voters. In the 1993 election, the verdict was reversed with Giuliani barely defeating Dinkins, in another contest in which racial lines were drawn.[41]

Owing little to Irish American voters, Dinkins shunned Irish politicians for the most part and concentrated on groups loyal to him. The highest Irish American official in the early years of the Dinkins administration was the veteran political leader, Paul O'Dwyer, who supported Dinkins in the 1989 mayoralty race. When O'Dwyer was city council president during the 1970s, he gave Dinkins a boost by helping appoint him city clerk. Now Dinkins returned the favor and selected O'Dwyer as the city's representative to the United Nations. O'Dwyer, lasted only a short time, however; he resigned in December 1991, claiming the United Nations was failing to take a more aggressive role in combating human abuses around the world (including Northern Ireland). He felt that his position did not give him enough leeway to be critical.[42]

The city's demography no doubt made the old Irish political machine demise inevitable. Similar developments, along with shifting Irish political allegiances, occurred elsewhere. Although "demographics finally did the Celtic bosses in," the process varied. In Albany, Pittsburgh, and Chicago the machine hung on longer than it did in New York. After Richard Daley's death in 1976, the machine lost to African American Harold Washington in 1983. But following Washington's death, Chicago voters once again picked an Irish American as mayor, this time Jane Byrne and then the son of Richard Daley.[43]

In another Irish-dominated area of organization life, the Roman Catholic Church, the city's demography and changing social attitudes led to both a decline in the church's role in city affairs and a change in the relationship of Irish New Yorkers to the church. But the shift in power was not as drastic as it was in politics, and shifting Irish Catholic attitudes in the city are hard to document.

Although Irish New Yorkers were not a majority of the city's Catholics in 1945, they dominated the clergy and top leadership within the church as they had done for decades. And a good many of the church's welfare organizations were staffed by Irish women. Archbishop John Hughes was the most famous of the city's many Irish American clergy, at least until Francis Cardinal Spellman, who became head of New York's Roman Catholics in 1939. Spellman was born to Irish parents, not in New York City, but in Whitman, Massachusetts. Although Spellman did not particularly emphasize his Irish origins, he nonetheless continued the long domination of the Irish at the head of New York's Catholics; most of the clergy and staff were also Irish. He cultivated his ties to prominent Catholic public officials, Irish or otherwise, and the city's growing Irish middle and upper class. Under Spellman, the church raised considerable sums of money and expanded its schools, charities, and parishes.[44]

But Spellman was interested in things other than parish affairs and church buildings, and he played a prominent role in public life. His critics charged that he exercised undue influence in city politics, while his supporters saw his activities as proper exercises of concern for the spiritual and moral welfare of church members. This concern touched on the lives of non-Catholics as well, as Spellman sought to censor movies and to gain public funds for parochial schools. As noted, he praised Wisconsin Senator Joseph McCarthy and the anticommunist crusades of the 1940s and 1950s. Not all Catholics agreed with Spellman's political positions, such as his open endorsement of Senator McCarthy, nor were they in agreement when the Cardinal criticized the reforms of Vatican II during the 1960s.[45]

Yet many politicians leaders, such as Mayor John V. Lindsay, who disagreed with the cardinal nonetheless had to deal with his influence. At the cardinal's funeral in 1968, notable political leaders attended, including President Lyndon Johnson. Johnson had high regard for Cardinal Spellman because of his warm support for Johnson's war in Vietnam. At the same time, some observers believed that Spellman's power had peaked before the 1960s. Because of his controversial stands on the Vietnam War, contacts with American intelligence agencies, conservative positions on church matters and public aid to religious schools, he overreached himself and brought a backlash against the church's role in politics, with many complaining that his reign "went on too long by half."[46]

His diocese lost some power in 1957 when the Vatican divided the archdiocese of New York into two dioceses, that of Brooklyn and Long Island and that of New York. When Spellman died he was succeeded by the Right Reverend Terrence J. Cooke, a more modest man. An Irish New Yorker who had served under Spellman, Cooke clearly lacked the dynamism of Spellman, but he apparently had no desire for the power and influence of his predecessor. That same year Pope Paul VI named Frank Mugavero, an Italian, head of the Diocese of Brooklyn and Long Island, the first Italian American to hold such a post in New York State.

When Terrence Cardinal Cooke died in 1984, he was succeeded by Archbishop John O'Connor, who like Spellman was Irish but not a New Yorker. In some other ways O'Connor resembled Spellman. A forceful leader, he took strong positions on public and moral issues. While the issue of public aid for religious institutions was still prominent, gay rights, abortion, feminism, AIDS,

Paul O'Dwyer, the County Mayo–born founder of the Irish Institute, with Senator John F. Kennedy, the guest of honor at an Institute fund-raising dinner in New York in 1957. O'Dwyer recalled that Congressman Charles Buckley, the Bronx County Democratic leader, introduced Kennedy that night as "the next president of the United States [but] none of us believed it except Charlie Buckley, his sponsor." Proceeds from dinners like this gave the Institute its West 48th Street building "free and clear and money to use for our other purposes," which included financial support for cultural projects in Ireland and America. Between 1952 and 1982, the Irish Institute building was the best-known address in the city, used by most Irish organizations as their headquarters. (Courtesy of the Irish Institute of New York, Inc.)

and homelessness dominated the debate. O'Connor even cultivated an unusual relationship with Jewish Mayor Ed Koch, but there is no doubt that the church's role in the politics of the city had declined considerably since the 1960s.[47] Supreme Court decisions had halted prayers in the city's public schools and municipal censorship of movies, and the church fought a losing battle over contracts with the city and the issue of discrimination against homosexuals. Nor could O'Connor halt the New York City Board of Education's 1991 decision to distribute condoms to students in an effort to combat AIDS. After that battle, one church leader acknowledged, "The church's influence has shrunk over the years. In the days of Cardinal Spellman there's no doubt that if an issue arose which the cardinal thought had potential impact on family life, he could pick up the phone and speak to leading political lights, and they would give careful thought to what he said." Another official noted that during the early days of Mayor Dinkins's administration phone calls from the church office were rarely returned.[48]

But what of the relationship of Irish New Yorkers to their church? The membership of the church itself was undergoing change. After 1945 it became less Italian and Irish and more Puerto Rican, with many members not sharing the views of their predominately Irish clergy. In an effort to reach the newcomers, Spellman had many priests learn Spanish. And a new wave of Catholic immigrants from the Caribbean, South America, and even Asia entered after 1965. Hispanic membership was estimated to be more than one-third of the total by 1981 and expected to reach 40 percent by the end of the 1990s.[49] In 1989 the archdiocese formed its first parish for the city's new Korean immigrants, St. John Nam in the Bronx, which was serving 400 families one year later.[50]

Nationally, and also in New York under Cardinal Spellman's leadership, Catholicism came of age just after World War II in terms of vigorous growth and an expanding institutional base, including parochial schools.[51] But the upheavals of the 1960s combined with demographic changes, and financial woes beset American Catholicism. New York City's Roman Catholic Church closed many of its schools in the face of rising costs and the loss of its Irish and other white pupils who had moved to the suburbs. Overall, Catholic school enrollment nationally and in New York City changed and dropped substantially between 1960 and 1990.[52] Cardinal Hayes High School in the Bronx is a case in point. Opened in 1942 as an elite all-white high school, it changed as the Bronx did. By 1992 Cardinal Hayes High School's student body was 99 percent black and Hispanic and "far less Catholic." The recession in the early 1990s forced more cuts. The Archdiocese of Brooklyn reported "difficult economic times" and retrenchment, while the Archdiocese of New York imposed a salary freeze on its lay employees and priests.[53]

With the more affluent Irish and other Catholics finding other social and economic opportunities after World War II, recruitment of young men and women to serve the church as priests and members of religious orders became more difficult. Bishop Mugavero of Brooklyn reported that in 1960 his diocese ordained 32 men to work in the diocese but in 1984 the figure had dropped to 4. "The vocation crisis is hitting us full force," he said.[54]

While new social and economic opportunities no doubt account for service to the church appearing less attractive to Irish Americans, other post-1960 social changes also played a role. Disputes erupted over abortion, divorce and remarriage, birth control, the possible ordination of women as priests, homosexuality, and the reforms of Vatican II, prompting many Catholics to leave the church or modify their religious practices and beliefs. Data gathered by polling experts, none of which singles out Irish New Yorkers, reveal that a growing number of Catholics rejected church teaching on these issues. For example, in 1986 the Gallup survey found that 74 percent of Catholics believed women should be ordained, a figure up from 29 percent in 1974.[55]

Did Irish Catholics in New York follow these national trends? No detailed published study exists of the relationship of the city's Irish to their church, but there is reason to believe that many Irish American New Yorkers were part of the national trends. Before *Humanae Vitae,* the Pope's encyclical against birth control devices, about two-thirds of church members attended church every week, but after the figure dropped to 50 percent.[56] In the mid-1970s about 45 percent of the Catholics in New York's Irish communities attended mass weekly, a figure slight below the national one.[57] And about half of the New Irish immigrants of the 1980s attended church less regularly than they did in Ireland.[58] Data indicate that it is the young and more educated and well-to-do Catholics who have become more disenchanted with church teaching, and the city's Irish were among the better-off Catholics.

Although many Catholics were disagreeing with church teachings, they nonetheless regarded themselves as devout and believed that one could be a good Catholic even if divorced or using oral contraceptives. A *New York Times*–CBS poll even found that a majority believed that a person engaging in homosexual relations can "still be a good Catholic" (Sept. 10, 1987). The Archdiocese of New York found in a mid-1980s survey that of the city's main ethnic groups, the Irish were the "most comfortable" with the church.[59] The figure is not surprising in view of the Irish presence among religious leaders. Clearly a detailed study of Irish Catholics in New York City is needed before the post–World War II changes can be fully understood. The Archdiocese of New York conducted a survey of Hispanics in 1981, but not of the Irish.

In individual cases Irish New Yorkers found themselves in conflict with the church hierarchy. Bronx Assemblyman John Dearie, for example, was barred from speaking at functions sponsored by his parish because he had voted in favor of Medicaid funds to pay for abortions.[60]

But no issue aroused so much public controversy within the Irish community as homosexuality and church teaching. Jesuit priests had been conducting special masses for homosexual members of Dignity, a homosexual Roman

Catholic group at the Church of St. Francis Xavier in Manhattan under the rectorship of the Reverend Michael E. Donahue. In 1987 the Diocese of New York ordered the masses discontinued. A similar ban was ordered in the Diocese of Brooklyn.[61]

Then the gay rights issue directly confronted the city's Irish Americans at the St. Patrick's Day parade in 1991. The parade's committee refused to allow the Irish Lesbian and Gay Organization (ILGO) the right to march in the parade. In an effort to reach a compromise an Irish group, Division 7 of the Manhattan Ancient Order of Hibernians (AOH), invited ILGO to march with them, but under Division 7's banner. Mayor Dinkins then chose to march with Division 7 and the gay group, instead of the mayor's customary position at the head of the parade. During the march the mayor was booed and shelled with beer cans. Although refusing to take a public position, John Cardinal O'Connor's opposition to homosexuality was well known, and he clearly did not agree with the mayor's position.[62] Many believed that the parade was not only a celebration of Irish heritage but also of Catholicism; hence they did not want ILGO to march.[63] Speaking for the 1992 St. Patrick's Day committee, Frank Beirne, chief organizer of the event for years, explained in 1992, "No group that has a position contrary to the teachings of our Catholic faith has a place in our parade."[64] But many Irish Americans within the AOH thought that ILGO should participate.[65] As a result, an internal fight within divisions of AOH erupted.

The issue was not settled by the compromise reached in 1991. As planning proceeded for the 1992 parade, the parade committee once again banned ILGO, as well as Division 7. ILGO appeared to be in a uncompromising mood and demanded, as Irish men and women, the right to march under their own banner. Looming in the background was the protest of the City's Human Rights Commission and the possibility that the parade committee would lose its parade permit. Indeed, in January City Hall took away the permit to organize the St. Patrick's Day parade from the AOH division that had been running it for more than a century. The state division that assumed control, however, also insisted on banning ILGO.[66] As a result, ILGO did not receive permission to joint the 1992 parade. Moreover, a federal court, ruling on an appeal by the Dinkins's administration and ILGO, upheld the denial of the ILGO's right to march. But the court's decision was based on narrow grounds, leaving the issue unresolved. Following the decision to ban ILGO, Mayor Dinkins and a number of prominent officials refused to march, and ILGO staged a demonstration to protest its omission from the parade. In 1994, with the ILGO still banned, the new mayor, Rudolph Giuliani, marched with the parade.[67]

As Irish immigration declined and Irish Americans moved to the suburbs, rose up the economic ladder, and increasingly assimilated into the mainstream of American society, old causes and cultures declined, but by no means disappeared. The renewed troubles in Northern Ireland in 1969 triggered the traditional anti-British sentiment among Irish Americans, and some focused their attention once again on Northern Ireland's troubles. When British soldiers fired on and killed 13 Roman Catholic civil rights demonstrators in Derry on January 1972, Irish Americans expressed their shock and with others labeled the event "Bloody Sunday." The *Irish Echo* called it an "incredible mad dog . . . attack by British troops on unarmed civilians" (Feb. 5, 1972). Some wore black armbands, while others carried banners proclaiming "England Get Out of Ireland" during the 1972 St. Patrick's Day parade.[68] Thereafter an annual testimonial dinner in memory of "Bloody Sunday" was sponsored by the pro-republican Irish Northern Aid Committee (Noraid).[69]

Located in the Bronx, Noraid was accused by the American, Irish, and British governments of supplying armed assistance to the Irish Republican Army (IRA). The *Irish People,* the voice of the Irish republican cause in Northern Ireland, was also published in the New York. Noraid came under governmental attack

Each of New York's Irish county societies have a richly decorated banner, often depicting heroic figures from their locale. County Antrim had a new banner made in 1981 that commemorated the first three of ten Irish republican political prisoners who died on hunger strike in Northern Ireland that year. These deaths galvanized support in New York, and street demonstrations, such as this protest against the visit of the Prince of Wales, were common during the 1980s. When the Prince of Wales visited New York in 1860, 121 years earlier, County Sligo–born Colonel Michael Corcoran refused to call out the Sixty-ninth Regiment to parade for his review. (Photograph by Peter Dolan. From the collection of the New York Irish History Roundtable.)

for gun-running to Northern Ireland, but its New York leaders were never convicted. However, several Irish Americans with ties to Noraid were indicted, tried, and found guilty of illegally smuggling weapons.[70]

While outrage against the British might have peaked in 1972, some Irish groups continued their support for unity for Ireland and those IRA prisoners who died during a hunger strike in 1981. Yet Noraid had few members, and the circulation of the *Irish People* was small—only about 5,000, compared with the *Irish Echo*'s nearly 50,000. Moreover, the IRA was criticized by a number of important Irish Americans who deplored violence. In 1983, when the St. Patrick's Day parade committee selected Michael Flannery—a Noraid founder, civil war veteran, and an outspoken supporter of the IRA—to be grand marshal, Governor Hugh Carey, who had been grand marshal in 1976, said he would not march that year. Senator Moynihan also refused to join the 1983 parade, and Terrence Cardinal Cooke broke tradition by refusing to receive Flannery on the steps of St. Patrick's Cathedral as the marchers streamed by. After Flannery passed, Cooke appeared and waved to the procession. Before mass, he talked to Flannery

435

*An End and
a Beginning*

Michael Flannery, grand marshal of the controversial 1983 St. Patrick's Day parade, meets the press in front of the Fifth Avenue reviewing stand. Flannery emigrated from County Tipperary in the 1920s and was respected for decades of service with various organizations in the New York Irish community. Nevertheless, Irish and Catholic leaders boycotted the parade that year because Flannery had strong republican convictions. He was also one of the founders of Irish Northern Aid (Noraid), which since 1969 had been the most high-profile American organization supporting the republican movement in Northern Ireland. For twenty years Noraid raised money for the families of political prisoners and repeatedly battled charges of gun-running to the Irish Republican Army. (Photograph by Peter Dolan. From the collection of the New York Irish History Roundtable.)

inside the cathedral and expressed his disapproval of violence and terrorism. From Dublin, Prime Minister Garret FitzGerald criticized those Irish Americans who gave money or encouragement to the IRA and regretted the selection of Flannery.[71]

Of course, many Irish Americans did not agree with Carey, Moynihan, and other boycotters. The mainstream *Irish Echo* supported the choice of Flannery as democratic and reported its letters were running 10 to 1 in his favor.[72] It also noted that Flannery was well respected in the Irish American community for his many activities. Speaking of Moynihan, one retired police officer declared, "I personally like Moynihan, but I don't think it's time for him to cast stones. I think he and the others are talking English."[73] Some observers saw the division over the IRA and Northern Ireland as generational, one in which the third, fourth, and fifth generations of Irish Americans who had assimilated into the mainstream of American society demonstrated little interest in the controversy. The more militant supporters of Ireland's cause were found among the first and second generations, while most Irish American politicians maintained a "careful stance" about affairs in Northern Ireland.[74] Although further research is needed to ascertain Irish American attitudes, it is important to note that Noraid was founded by Irish immigrants like Flannery.[75]

One IRA and Northern Ireland cause that seemed to cross generational lines and even win support from many non-Irish was that of IRA member Joe Doherty, who became a folk hero of sorts. Doherty was convicted in 1981 on charges of killing a British army captain in an ambush. He escaped from a British jail and made his way to America, where he claimed political asylum when seized in 1983. In 1985 a federal judge agreed, but the Justice Department then tried to deport him for entering the United States illegally. Doherty's friends fought in the courts, and eventually his case reached the U.S. Supreme Court. All the while Doherty remained in custody, in New York and Pennsylvania jails. In 1992 the court held against him, paving the way for his deportation in February.[76] Irish Americans rallied to Doherty's defense, but so did many others. The U.N. high commissioner for refugees filed a brief before the Supreme Court, as did more than 100 members of the U.S. Congress.[77] In New York David Dinkins and a number of politicians supported his cause during the 1989 mayoralty race. The next year the newly elected mayor, leading the 1990 St. Patrick's Day parade, wore a black shillelagh and a "Free Joe Doherty" button, and before he was deported the mayor visited Doherty to lend his support.[78] So popular was Doherty that in 1991 a storm of protest erupted when the *Irish People* dropped his column because he criticized an IRA decision to plant a bomb near a hospital. The *Irish People* then reversed itself and restored Doherty as a columnist.[79]

Popular causes like Joe Doherty kept Irish traditions alive, but refusal to "talk English" was also reenforced by the great variety of social and cultural Irish organizations in New York City. A glance at the *Irish Echo* over the years reveals a vast number of Irish American organizations and cultural events, including radio shows and live performances. The republican cause is nearly always present at the St. Patrick's Day parade, which draws upward of 100,000 marchers annually. During the controversial 1983 parade, for example the Fire Department Emerald Society carried their usual sign, "England, Get Out of Ireland."[80]

A growing interest in New York Irish history culminated when the New York Irish History Roundtable was organized in 1984 and began publication of the annual journal *New York Irish History* two years later. The publication of this volume is another example of the attempt to recapture the City's Irish history.

The postwar years also witnessed the organization of Emerald Societies along occupational lines, with a Grand Council of United Emerald Societies being established in 1975. The Pipes and Drums Band of the New York City Fire Department Emerald Society celebrated its thirtieth anniversary in 1992. New cultural events have attracted thousands, and the city now has an Irish arts center and an Irish repertory theater. When the Irish Arts Center was created by Brian Heron, an immigrant, he said it was to boost a declining Irish heritage in the United States: "There are few real Irish people in the United States. They know little about authentic Irish culture, and care less. The Irish American is a victim of cultural disintegration, as much as the Mayan Indian. We have to go back to the beginning, to learn again what it means to be Irish."[81]

Chapters 19 and 20 focus on Irish American identity and culture. In chapter 19 Rebecca Miller argues that the Irish New York music scene in the 1950s rested mostly on popular American and Irish American music, with big bands and dances being very popular, particularly at Manhattan's City Center, which packed in Irish immigrants and some Irish Americans on Saturday nights. During the 1960s, she suggests, new immigrants helped stimulate a revival of traditional Irish music with many young Irish American New Yorkers flocking to learn the traditional steps.

In chapter 20 Charles Fanning surveys Irish American writing of recent years in poetry, short stories, and novels. He notes the role of ethnicity in these writings and sees a richness of themes in the various writers, attesting to a live Irish American tradition.

Some Irish Americans, such as a board member of the Irish Arts Center in the Bronx, dismissed the Irish ethnic revival as "faddish." "This new ethnicity is horribly unauthentic, only shades removed from green hats, green bagels and green beer. Not the stuff of nationhood." He concluded, "We've married Italian girls and moved to the suburbs." Yet an Irish troubadour who had performed in the city for 30 years said in 1986 that he was getting more reaction at his bar than he had ever before. "A wonderful number of people speak to me after performances about Gaelic lessons and books to read by writers from Ireland and music."[82] Irish American identity might have changed, as Miller and Fanning note, but it was alive.

Irish American ethnicity was no doubt most alive among the first and second generations. It was they who participated in and supported the city's Irish American cultural institutions, including such public displays as the St. Patrick's Day parade. It was mostly the first generation that rallied to the cause of Northern Ireland.

But most Irish New Yorkers are members of the third or greater generations. Many have married non-Irish, no longer live in predominately Irish American communities, and no longer partake of Irish American culture. With the decline of anti-Catholicism and anti-Irish bigotry after World War II, Irish Americans found new opportunities that their grandfathers never dreamed of. They could identify with their Irishness, however vague, or could choose to ignore it, and many did.

The new wave of Irish immigrants arriving during the 1980s and the potential of still greater numbers in the years ahead suggest the possibility of further reinforcement of Irish and Irish American culture. In chapter 18 Mary Corcoran finds that the New Irish reinforced old Irish American neighborhoods while at the same time maintaining their own style and close connections to Ireland.[83]

In 1988 their growing presence prompted the New York City Police Department to establish a New Immigrants Unit to work with them and the Catholic Church to make a special effort to assist them.[84] As Rebecca Miller notes, they already have made an impact on the New York music scene. In addition, they have contributed to a revival of Gaelic sports in the New York area.[85] The newcomers have also established their own newspaper, the *Irish Voice*, which carries extensive coverage of immigration matters. In its first issue (Dec. 5, 1987), the *Voice* said that most of the latest Irish it surveyed wanted to remain in America and that it would be uncompromising in working to legalize their status.

Their numbers were too small to expect them to lead a revival of New York Irish American politics. But the *Irish Voice* was prophetic about the future of these undocumented aliens. The Irish Immigration Reform Movement, organized by the New Irish, won support, as Corcoran notes, from older Irish New Yorkers and succeeded in opening up a few visas for Ireland by means of a lottery included in the Immigration Reform and Control Act of 1986. More stunning was the inclusion of the Morrison visas in the previously mentioned Immigration Act of 1990 that guaranteed Ireland 48,000 immigrant visas over a three-year period and potentially more after that.[86] While Ireland's economy remained depressed in the early 1990s, conditions in New York City were not conducive to attract new immigrants. Many Morrison visas winners might not choose to emigrate to America.[87] But if they did, the way was paved for new Irish immigration to New York City and a renewed Irish American presence in its social and economic life.[88]

Robert W. Snyder

CHAPTER 17

The Neighborhood Changed

THE IRISH OF WASHINGTON

HEIGHTS AND INWOOD SINCE 1945

IN 1945, the accents heard on the streets of Washington Heights and Inwood spoke more of Dublin than of Santo Domingo. More doorbells were labeled Murphy than Morales. By the 1990s, all that had changed. Most of the Irish were gone, and the northern tip of Manhattan had been transformed into the largest Dominican neighborhood in the United States.

The Irish who left bear an enduring sense of loss for all they left behind. In suburban living rooms, conversations about the old neighborhood swing from nostalgia for childhood to anger at how dangerous the old streets look today. Parents lament that their suburban children will never have the street smarts acquired on New York pavements. Then they thank God that they will never know the violence that engulfs the city today.

The Irish who stayed find their turf seriously diminished. Some speak of the situation in military terms: a handful of old-timers are "dug in" east of Broadway; a tavern remains as a "redoubt" on Dyckman Street. The military metaphors are disturbing but not surprising. After all, social scientists analyze changing neighborhoods in terms of the invasion phase when a new group appears and the conflict phase when newcomers and old-timers clash. And the Irish of northern Manhattan truly feel that their old world was invaded and conquered by Latinos.[1]

But such comparisons cause more problems than they solve. They turn newcomers into enemies, and make it appear that Irish people were pushed out of places like the Heights and Inwood against their will, pure and simple. The truth was more complicated. The Irish were both pulled and pushed from the neighborhood. And they responded to both forces with their own interests uppermost in mind, namely, the desire to provide good housing for their families and the desire to live in a community with a distinctly Irish identity.

The pull was the pull of suburbia, which caught so many city dwellers after World War II. The Irish of Washington Heights and Inwood were lured from the city by suburban amenities: a lawn, a garage, quiet streets, and relaxation at the end of a day's work. Automobiles bought with good wages, highways built with government money, and homes purchased with federally subsidized mortgages all enabled Irish of the financially secure working class and middle class to move to tree-lined streets that their parents had only imagined. The move to the suburbs would place these Irish in settings quite different from the city they left behind—towns an hour or more's drive from the city, where the nuclear family in a single home, and not the neighborhood, would be the focal point of Irish identity. But the departure was consistent with what had led their ancestors to work their way out of lower Manhattan, north to Vinegar Hill around Amsterdam Avenue and the west 130s, and finally to the Heights and Inwood: the drive for good family living conditions.

The push was the push of crime and disorder, whose increase in the 1960s and 1970s made life in so many cities dangerous and insecure. But the Irish response to crime was deeply influenced by something they valued long before crime tore at their neighborhood: the desire to live in an identifiably Irish community. In Washington Heights and Inwood, that meant living on a block or in an apartment building with many Irish families. The adjacent streets or buildings might be populated by strangers—first Jews, later Dominicans—but through concentration of their own numbers, the Irish established environments in which the people they dealt with on a day-to-day basis were mostly just like them. Life in such enclaves seemed safe and secure. In their desire to live in this way, the Irish were no more insular than any other ethnic group.

Ironically, this relative isolation would make them feel less secure when crime and racial and ethnic diversity increased in their neighborhoods: "Where boundaries between social groups are sharp and bridged by few social ties or shared memberships in organizations, even a moderate crime rate will generate fear, which then further exacerbates the boundaries within the neighborhood." Contrary to the belief that close-knit neighborhoods make people feel safe, northern Manhattan's Irish communities, lacking substantial ties to other ethnic communities in the neighborhood, made their residents more fearful because they reduced their residents' contact with blacks and Latinos. The isolated Irish could not distinguish benign neighbors from threatening strangers.[2]

In a pattern repeated between other ethnic groups in other neighborhoods threatened by crime, the lack of communication between Irish and Dominicans—a failure of communication for which each group can be held partly responsible—heightened the fear that the Irish felt in their own neighborhood. In a tragic but familiar pattern, fear of crime made whites fear all people of color. The more productive response, which would have been to unite with the majority of the newcomers in opposition to the violence and disorder that threatened them both, was never realized in a significant way.

The story of this process is more than a piece of Irish history. It is an American story with an Irish inflection, one that has been repeated for many ethnic groups in many neighborhoods and cities since the 1940s. It is about how crime destroyed street life in American cities, and how that transformed the shape and texture of ethnic culture. It is about how the United States went from being an urban nation to a suburban nation. It is about how white people combined fear of crime and fear of people of color. And it is the ironic story of how a deep desire for good housing and identifiably Irish communities helped to destroy a neighborhood way of life that many Irish Americans loved.

The Heights and Inwood, essentially Manhattan north of 155th Street, were a hilly farming area in the seventeenth century and a battleground in the American Revolution. During the nineteenth century, the old farms were bought up by wealthy New Yorkers and consolidated into suburban estates. The area looked and felt far from the bustle of midtown.[3]

Great changes began with the arrival of mass transit. The Broadway subway opened service to 157 Street in 1904, and then on north through Inwood to Kingsbridge in the Bronx in 1906. Contrary to neighborhood boosters' wishes, it did not stimulate the construction of "high class residence property." Instead, modified old-law tenements were built, mostly east of Broadway. It was housing that one Heights resident, Leo Shanley, called "grim, but comfortable." Into it moved large numbers of Irish Americans and a smaller number of Jews. "You kept improving yourself," says Sister Veronica of Good Shepherd parish of the many Inwood Irish who moved up from parishes in Harlem.[4]

Another housing boom in the 1920s and the completion of the IND subway line in 1932 gave the Heights and Inwood much of its present face: simpler housing to the east of Broadway, more elaborate housing to the west. Broadway also became a boundary marker for differences of class and ethnicity. Mostly middle class, Jewish streets lay to the west, more mixed Jewish and Irish working-class streets lay to the east. Dyckman Street cut across Broadway and separated the Heights to the south from Inwood to the north. The George Washington Bridge, completed in 1931, provided a motor route to the rest of the nation across the Hudson River. Great green parks—Highbridge, Fort Tryon, Isham, and Inwood Hill—softened the concrete and made the new neighborhood a desirable place to live.[5]

The Irish of the neighborhood in these years were working-class people of modest means. The area had a reputation for being the home of many transit workers. Geographically there was not one Irish community in the Heights and Inwood, but many communities that collectively formed an Irish archipelago. In 1940, the Irish in the Heights and Inwood numbered 23,900, or about 11.7 percent of the neighborhood's population. (Jews, the largest other group in the neighborhood, numbered approximately 73,100, or 35.8 percent of the population.) Of the Irish-born, many were immigrants from Kerry and Mayo.[6]

The broadest outlines of the Irish community were established through a string of Roman Catholic parishes, from Saint Rose of Lima at the southern end of the Heights to Good Shepherd to the north in Inwood. (To this day, former residents do not say, "I lived in the south-central part of Washington Heights," but "I lived in Incarnation parish.") Within parishes, people typically identified most with an area of a few blocks, defined by the homes of family and friends. "Your whole life was your neighborhood, your home, your parish, your block," recalls Buddy McGee. McGee grew up in Inwood after moving there in the 1940s from Vinegar Hill, which Irish residents fled after the riots in nearby Harlem in 1943. Mrs. Norene Walck, nee Lane, who grew up in the Heights during the 1930s and 1940s, recalled: "Your social life stayed in the neighborhood. It was comforting, you belonged." A change of five blocks, she said, could make you a stranger.[7]

Older Irish Americans in the neighborhood remember the 1930s and 1940s as a benign period. For married adults, social life consisted of church events, family gatherings with "kitchen music" on accordion or fiddle, Saturday night social visits to taverns with neatly dressed children in tow, and the activities of Ancient Order of Hibernians Division 3, founded in northern Manhattan in 1936. Young, single adults went to bars, Irish dances at places like the Innisfail Hall or Leitrim House, and Irish football matches at Gaelic Park just to the north in the Bronx. Children swarmed through the halls of apartment buildings, playing in and out of apartments whose doors were never locked, then surged outside for street games: box ball, curb ball, and stickball. At least once a week, there was the "ritual," as McGee put it, of trips to the movies. The Indian rock shelters of Inwood Hill Park offered plenty of opportunities for adventures, and the Hudson and Harlem rivers beckoned to swimmers.[8]

Order was kept by a combination of beat cops and a network of watchful mothers who amounted to a neighborhood surveillance system. "You knew everybody, everybody knew you," recalled McGee. "You couldn't do nothing wrong, because Mrs. Murphy would see you and say, 'Mrs. McGee, I seen your son smoking a cigarette.' And that was it."[9]

Asked in 1991 about those years, older people who lived in the neighborhood emphasize how everyone got along and no one feared crime. Yet during the Depression and World War II, Washington Heights and Inwood were hardly islands of peace. Irish–Jewish relations in the 1920s were distant. The Irish and Jews who moved into the neighborhood tended to cluster among their own kind in particular buildings or on particular streets. If either group increased in

significant numbers, the other often moved out. The situation deteriorated in
the 1930s for many reasons. Beyond simple anti-Semitism, there was competition for housing as more Jews—including German refugees—moved into the
neighborhood. Working-class Irish resented the relative affluence of those Jews
who lived on the west side of Broadway. Residents were also influenced by Irish
political insecurity over the decline of Tammany, disputes over the Spanish
Civil War in which many Jews supported the Loyalists and many Irish Catholics
supported Franco, and Irish–Jewish differences over Great Britain. To the Jews,
especially the refugee German Jews, Britain was an opponent of Hitler to be
supported. To the Irish, Britain was an oppressor to be shunned.[10]

The pressure of these political and economic developments transformed
Irish–Jewish relations from chilly to actively hostile. From the late 1930s
through World War II, the neighborhood was scarred by violent acts of anti-Semitism. The main perpetrators were Irish youth gangs, particularly the Amsterdams and the Shamrocks, and the Christian Front and Christian Mobilizers,
two ultra-right-wing groups influenced by the ideas of the radio priest Father
Charles E. Coughlin. Coughlin, a right-wing populist from Michigan, laced his
writings and broadcasts with anti-Semitism.

The Front and Mobilizers appeared in the Heights and Inwood in 1939. From
competition for apartments to resentment at Mayor Fiorello LaGuardia's rout
of Irish Tammany, from unemployment to international communism, the Front
and the Mobilizers had a solution: blame the Jews. During the war years, Front
and Mobilizer rallies were succeeded by vandalism of synagogues, insults
blaming Jews for the war, and Irish gang attacks on Jewish youths.[11] It would
be wrong to conclude from such actions that all Irish were bigots. The staunchly
liberal attorney Paul O'Dwyer, for example, was a vigorous opponent of both
right-wingers and anti-Semites. And some Irish residents of Washington Heights,
like the young Mrs. Walck, had Jewish friends. Nevertheless, the antipathy
toward Jews was shared by more than a small minority of the neighborhood's
Irish.[12]

Public pressure brought a solution of sorts in 1944, through a combination
of aggressive policing, organization of Jewish defense units and school escorts,
and a condemnation of prejudice by Catholic, Protestant, and Jewish religious
leaders. The end of World War II further eased tensions, along with postwar
prosperity, civic groups organized to counter bigotry, and the emergence of a
political consensus against anti-Semitism that made any association with it a
liability.[13]

Bitterness remained, however. A report issued in 1954 by the Protestant
Council of the City of New York called Catholic–Jewish relations in the
neighborhood "tenuous" and noted the prevalence of anti-Semitic graffiti at
Eastertime and Halloween.[14] Down into the 1990s, individual Irish and Jews in
the Heights and Inwood could be heard speaking of each other in unpleasant
terms.[15] But by then, the conflict between them had long ceased to be the central

reference point of life and politics in northern Manhattan. Instead, both the Irish and the Jews were defining their place largely by their relationship to blacks and Latinos.

The postwar years brought better economic times for the transit workers, construction workers, firefighters, and police officers who gave the neighborhood's Irish community so much of its flavor. The old sociability of the prewar years resumed—with the addition, thanks to the baby boom, of many new Irish American children.

By 1950 the area's Irish population was up to at least 27,000, concentrated in Incarnation parish in south-central Washington Heights and Good Shepherd in Inwood. Modest numbers of Irish were also scattered through the streets of the eastern Heights and Inwood that connected the two parishes. Even in sections where the Irish were most concentrated, they numbered little more than a fifth of the population. But through their networks of pubs and parishes, and their presence on the streets, they felt that their neighborhoods were very much their own.[16]

Charles Walck, who lived in the Heights between voyages as a merchant seaman in 1948 and 1949, recalls how he and his friends enjoyed the freedom of the streets in their nighttime revels. "We used to start at 165th Street at Broadway—Kent House it used to be named—and work our way up to the Homestead. . . . I mean, we had a regular routine on Saturday night. We'd jump the Anchor Inn up on Broadway because they had a live band . . . toodle up to Dyckman Street, usually end up around the Homestead . . . usually wander down and end up in a place called Bradley's between 165th and 166th on the west side of Amsterdam Avenue, an old Irish bar—white-tiled floors, spittoons, sawdust—sit in the back room and sing all night."[18]

As before the war, the neighborhood was still patrolled by beat cops who "knew everybody," one of whom was notorious for slapping any teenagers he caught smoking. The gravity of the offense and the acceptance of the penalty testify to a low level of lawbreaking and the strength of the policeman's authority. "You didn't argue with the cop on the beat. He didn't brutalize, but he thought nothing of walloping you across the ass with a nightstick if you gave him any lip, or give you a slap in the face. And you didn't go home and tell your parents, 'A cop slapped me!'" For the former Norene Lane, who married Mr. Walck and settled into an apartment on 169 Street between Amsterdam and Audubon in 1955, the neighborhood buzzed with mothers and children in the middle of the baby boom.[18]

Further north, in Inwood, life in the late 1940s and early 1950s continued much as it had before World War II. Out of the crowded little linoleum-floored apartments spilled waves of children. For the boys, there was the neighborhood's well-developed world of sports and street gangs. McGee recalls, "Each block or couple of blocks had a gang like the Alley Cats, the Rams, the Eagles. They were called gangs, but actually they were just teams. I hung out with the guys on

Dyckman Street who had a team down there called the Alley Cats. Each guy had a different helmet. If you had a pair of cleats, your father had a full-time job."[19] Some of the gangs were fighting gangs, like the Eagles from Inwood, full of "hard case" guys who fought for prestige or girls. "But that was with a fist," says McGee. "You very seldom saw anybody use a bat or a chain or anything. . . . If you had a black eye or a cut on your face, you were a big man. 'Hey, I was in the rumble.'"[20]

The gangs had bravado, but stickball, football and basketball games settled more rivalries than rumbles. When rumbles did break out, they were often choreographed for maximum display and minimum damage—"more bark than bite," says Kathleen O'Halloran, who grew up in Inwood and briefly belonged to a gang—much to her father's displeasure. She recalls the typical encounter as a case of "bluff, posture, throw the odd punch."[21] O'Halloran recalls that the girls were expected to provide "support staff" for the boys and then marry "as early as humanly possible." But for her, the overwhelming characteristic of her childhood neighborhoods—204th Street and Tenth Avenue from 1945 to 1955, then Seaman Avenue and 218th Street until 1965—was their Hibernian homogeneity. They seemed isolated from the rest of the city. It was not that the Irish were the only people in her vicinity. Around 204th Street and Tenth Avenue in 1950, the Irish were about a fifth of the population; around 218th Street and Seaman Avenue in 1960, they were about 17 percent of the neighborhood.[22]

The Irishness of O'Halloran's childhood, which was typical, was established by organizing her life so that her closest contacts were with other Irish Americans. At school, in Good Shepherd parish, her day opened with the singing of Ireland's national anthem, "The Soldier's Song." At home, her family tutored her in a decidedly republican version of Irish history. Out on the town as an adolescent, she went to Catholic Youth Organization dances in St. Jude's parish where rock and roll alternated with Irish folk dancing. "At first, when the neighborhood was all Irish, it took me a long time to figure out that there were other people in the world besides Irish people." When she did, she was adventurous enough to find friends among Orthodox Jews, blacks and Latinos. O'Halloran's social life and recreation were satisfied almost entirely in the neighborhood. "I never went downtown until I was a teenager," she recalls. "To go downtown to Times Square when I was 15 (in 1957) was an absolute mindblower—we were as green as grass."[23]

But in southeastern Washington Heights, there were stirrings of change. Black real estate dealers bought up some of the small private homes in the area, and operated them as overcrowded rooming houses catering to black and Puerto Rican tenants. Black and Puerto Rican superintendents began to appear in some of the rooming houses that catered to white tenants. Puerto Rican families from East Harlem and the east twenties in Manhattan began to move into the neighborhood.[24] Like the Irish and the Jews before them, blacks and Puerto Ricans saw the Heights as a desirable neighborhood. A move there was a step up. One Reverend Perez, a Puerto Rican minister in a Presbyterian Church, received many requests for information on Heights apartments. "This is one of the few nice places where relatively poor people can live," he concluded.[25]

By 1950, the population of southern Washington Heights was almost one-third non-white. In the flux of arrivals and departures, some of the old informal mothers' networks that kept order dissolved; the racial rifts between the white old-timers and black and Latino newcomers meant that they would not be rebuilt. In 1954, a city study noted that delinquency rates in the southern and eastern portions of the Heights were exceeded only by those of the city's most dangerous neighborhoods. In June 1955 the city's Youth Board, created in 1948 to fight juvenile delinquency, extended its activities into the Heights all the way to Dyckman Street.[26]

For Irish residents, the arrival of blacks and Puerto Ricans, coupled with a rise in gang activity and crime, made the streets seem threatening. As a child, Mrs. Walck would go out to the candy store at 9:45 p.m. to buy the early edition of the *Daily News*. By 1953, with gangs and robberies increasing, the routine began to feel dangerous. "It had gotten to the point that if I went out, when I came home, I would ring the bell downstairs and may father would walk out and talk to me as I was walking up the stairs, because things had happened on the staircases. . . . Now this was the place you ran up a million times when you were a kid. And all of a sudden you had to have this whole routine."[27]

No one set out a welcome mat for the newcomers. A report on Washington Heights written for the Protestant Council of the City of New York in 1954 noted: "With the population mobility and the inroads of Puerto Ricans and Negroes, human relations problems have mounted. Several incidents were reported, such as the throwing of an incendiary bomb into an apartment house occupied by Puerto Ricans at 182nd Street and Audubon Avenue. Although the offenders were never apprehended, community sentiment attributes this incident as arising from the tensions between the Irish and Puerto Rican groups in the community."[28] In such an atmosphere, both the newcomers and the Irish began to see themselves as aggrieved victims. To blacks and Puerto Ricans, the Irish were an entrenched force that denied them their right to live in a good neighborhood. To the Irish, the blacks and Puerto Ricans were invaders who would transform their neighborhood. Both claims were one-sided, but with the poisonous state of the streets, partisans of any faction could find enough to substantiate their claims.

For many Irish, a July night in 1957 marked a turning point for the neighborhood. Two Heights teenagers, Michael Farmer and Roger McShane, entered Highbridge Park to sneak an after-hours swim in the pool. The park, located on Amsterdam Avenue between 155th Street and Dyckman Street, with a pool at 173rd Street, had been a flashpoint in the days of hostility between Irish and Jewish youths. Lately it had become the focal point of fights between blacks, whites, and Puerto Ricans. Inside the park they met the Egyptian Dragons, a gang of blacks, Latinos, and a smattering of whites whose turf lay south of the Heights. The Dragons attacked.[29]

Farmer was stabbed and beaten on the spot. McShane tried to escape but was chased down and assaulted. He staggered out of the park bleeding from stab wounds. When a taxi driver picked him up, he pleaded, "Find my friend." Police found Farmer mortally wounded, lying in a clump of bushes. He died in Mother Cabrini Memorial Hospital minutes after midnight. McShane, initially in critical condition, survived.[30]

The police traced the incident to a dispute between the Egyptian Dragons and the Jesters, a mostly Irish group with a few black members that was more a ball club than a gang. According to the *New York Post*, the two gangs had played a game of stickball with a bet of 50¢ per player riding on the outcome. The Dragons lost but refused to pay up. When the Jesters attempted to collect, the Dragons retaliated: 40 Dragons jumped 5 Jesters near the Washington Bridge over the Harlem River; one 15-year-old Jester was struck on the head with a chain and a padlock. The wound required 15 stitches. Police also received a report that a Dragon stabbed a Jester in a separate incident. Noting that there were whites in the Dragons and blacks in the Jesters, the police argued that Farmer's murder was not racially motivated. Neighborhood residents and gang members, however, blamed the attack on racial tensions that had been increasing in the neighborhood. An anonymous source from the Youth Board charged that the local police precinct on Wadsworth Avenue was crude and inept in its responses to longstanding racial disturbances.[31]

It would be wrong to describe the killing as either a racial slaying or a gang killing over turf, as if the two were unrelated. The killing was the product of a gang conflict at a time when gang identity was powerfully shaped by the racial and ethnic groups that dominated particular turf. It was no accident that most of the Jesters, drawn from the Heights, were white, and that most of the Dragons, drawn more from the streets bordering Harlem to the south, were black and Latino. As whites moved out of the southern Heights, white youths who remained in the neighborhood joined predominantly black and Latino gangs to ally themselves with the rising ethnic factions in their neighborhood. Black and Latino youths who moved into largely white neighborhoods would seek membership in mostly white gangs for similar reasons. In neighborhoods demarcated by racially defined turf, such minimal integration did not undo the racial and ethnic animosities held by gang members.[32]

White residents observed that the majority of those accused in court were blacks and Latinos. Lacking friendly ties with blacks and Latinos that would have helped them distinguish between dangerous delinquents and ordinary teenagers, many jumped to the conclusion that all black and Latino youths were a threat.

The killing of Farmer and its direct relationship to mounting concern over gangs and delinquency drew attention to the trial. Eleven juveniles were sent to reformatories. Seven other members of the Egyptian Dragons were tried for murder: Luis Alvarez and George Melendez, both born in Puerto Rico, Leonci DeLeon from the Dominican Republic, Charles Horton and Leroy Birch, both African Americans, and Richard Hills and John McCarthy, both white. After a sensational trial, Alvarez and Horton were convicted of second-degree murder, while Birch and DeLeon were convicted of second-degree manslaughter. Their sentences ranged from five years to life. Hills, McCarthy, and Melendez were all found not guilty.[33]

A team of researchers sent into the southeast Heights by the New York City Community Mental Health Board interviewed 125 residents about their reactions to the incident. They found widespread attitudes of "hopelessness, helplessness and fear," with little expectation that the underlying problem of crime and gang violence would change. Many criticized the police for their inability to solve the gang problem. The reactions did not automatically follow racial or ethnic lines: among the children they interviewed were black and Puerto Rican youngsters consumed with fear, and a young Puerto Rican who claimed to have been friendly with Farmer. The researchers noted that many parents were beginning to keep their children indoors under supervision.

> As a result of the tension in the neighborhood there has been an increasing restriction upon the activities of children. This restriction has been growing over the past three years, but was tightened up markedly by parents during the past two weeks. A considerable portion of parents now keep their children at home both during the day and after dark. Others are compelling their children to be in the home before dusk. An added restriction in the choice of friends is occurring. Others are directing their children to run away from groups of boys and not to use the High Bridge pool.
> Some children interviewed stated that they refused to go out of their homes and were afraid to stay home alone. Some children now for the first time are carrying knives for safety. Both children and parents in many instances expressed hostility to parents for being restricted and shut up.

The freedom of the streets that had once been so attractive to a generation that grew up in the Heights was coming to an end, as it eventually would for so many New Yorkers.[34]

For Mr. and Mrs. Walck and their young son, the murder had a decisive impact. "Two weeks later we moved out of the Heights," Mrs. Walck recalls. "It was over. It was the end. . . . I still loved it, but I knew we had Jimmy [her son] and we had to get out of there." The Walcks left for Queens, the first step in a process that would lead them to settle in the suburban town of Dumont, New Jersey. It was not easy for her to depart: "When we were leaving that apartment in Washington Heights, I cried."[35]

As the 1950s ended, there was no mistaking that Washington Heights was a changing neighborhood. In a report on the area written for the Columbia-Washington Heights Community Mental Health Project, Lee A. Lendt observed that the arrival of Latinos—and above all blacks—in the southern part of the Heights was causing many white residents to reevaluate the imaginary boundary line they drew between their own community and black Harlem to the south.

In the 1950s it was common to say that "Washington Heights stops where Harlem begins." But as blacks struggling into the working and middle classes began moving further north into the Heights, the boundary line between Harlem and the Heights grew vague. A black family living at 156th Street and Amsterdam Avenue would feel lucky to have moved into Washington Heights. But as Lendt discovered, a common white reaction would be to revise the southern border of Washington Heights. If blacks lived on 156th Street, whites thought it was no longer in the Heights. And so they preserved the Heights' white identity—at least in their minds.[36]

Lendt also noticed a gulf between the newest arrivals and community leaders in the Heights. It was "most astonishing," he wrote, yet "only a few of the leaders interviewed seemed to display any knowledge of the Negro community. It was generally admitted—with regret—that a large part of the area was inhabited by Negroes. Little, if any, contact had been made with these people by either political or non-political leaders." (93). Evaluating the situation in the Heights, Lendt concluded that the great distance between blacks and whites had to be bridged. "It seems obvious that some understanding and communication must take place between the residents of Washington Heights and their southern neighbors, if the transition to integration of Negroes into what is now a predominantly white community is to take place with a minimum of conflict. There will be some conflict, no doubt, no matter what the preparation, but the present fear-induced isolation expressed by the leadership group in Washington Heights will certainly have to change" (99). Lendt was right about the long-term costs of "fear-induced isolation," but wrong about the certainty that it would be overcome.

The 1960 census, counting as Irish anyone Irish-born or American-born of one or both Irish parents, listed 18,971 Irish in the Heights and Inwood, a decline from 1950. Incarnation and Good Shepherd were still the southern and northern anchors of the community. But the southern end of the Heights was losing Irish inhabitants, as the Irish moved north to escape the changes in their old neighborhood.[37]

Inwood remained relatively untouched by the changes in the Heights. True, in the early 1950s the opening of the Dyckman Houses public housing in northeastern Inwood had prompted muttering among some of the Irish that "they," the blacks, were coming to drive them from Inwood.[38] But as late as the middle 1960s in Inwood, the continuities with earlier decades were strong. Park Terrace was still ritzy and Inwood Hill Park still offered woodland adventures. Jim Carroll—hustler, hipster, basketball player and future writer—moved in at the age of 13 in 1963. In his book, *The Basketball Diaries*, he noted, "hallways in my building and each park bench filled with chattering old Irish ladies either gossiping or saying the rosary, or men long time here or younger ones right off the boat huddling in floppy overcoats in front of drug stores discussing their operations, ball scores or the Commie threat. Guys my age strictly All-American, though most of the various crowds do the beer-drinking scene on weekends."[39]

The 1970 census recorded a drop in the Irish American population of the Heights and Inwood, both native and foreign-born: from 18,971 in 1960 to 12,919 in 1970 as more people moved to the suburbs. In earlier decades, the Irish had established their enclaves within the neighborhood; now, with suburban housing available, they headed west across the Hudson to Bergen County, New Jersey, or north to Rockland County, New York. Although such suburbs lacked the intensely communal environment of the city they left behind, they fulfilled the long-standing desire for good family living conditions. Moreover, they were far removed from the heterogeneity of the city and its increasing crime. Those who remained in Manhattan continued moving north. Incarnation parish now contained a low percentage of the area's Irish, who were relocating in the upper end of the Heights, north of 187 Street—for the most part east of Broadway—and in Inwood.[40]

By the early 1970s, Inwood Irish were more and more disturbed by the increases in crime, disorder, and racial conflict that swept American cities. Inwood until the 1980s remained relatively safe compared with the truly violent areas of New York, for its crime rates well below those for the city as a whole. In 1970, the 34th Precinct had 11 murders per 100,000 people, while the city had 15; the 34th had 616 robberies per 100,000 people, while the city had 938. But it was increasingly perceived as a dangerous place.[41]

It did little good to tell the Irish who remembered the relatively peaceful streets of the 1930s and 1940s that the northern Heights and Inwood were safer than most crime-ravaged city neighborhoods. They knew without being told that they lived in a state of danger greater than they had ever known, and they did not like it.

The old tensions with the Jews, and the gang fights of the 1950s, looked tame by comparison. Those Irish who were involved in the conflict with the Jews were mostly dishing it out. The gang fights of the 1950s with blacks and Latinos were most likely to involve adolescents. In contrast, robberies, muggings, and rapes struck a much wider range of people, especially the elderly. And burglaries made people feel vulnerable even in their own homes.

It was not just the reality of crime that hurt. It was also the perception of crime and the raw fear that seeped into every corner of daily life. News of crime entered every home—in family conversation, in newspapers, and on television. Almost every decision about the world outside involved some calculation of risk, from riding the subway to going out to buy a newspaper late at night. At its best, life on a block in northern Manhattan once made many Irish feel like part of one big happy family. Now they felt more like vulnerable individuals—alone, isolated, and fearful of the sound of footsteps behind them on a dark street.

Fear of crime combined with a rush of changes that signaled the end of life as the Inwood Irish had recently known it: graffiti, loud street noise, the turmoil of the Vietnam War (which took a large number of Inwood men), and the challenge of living with an increasing number of Latino neighbors. Political conflicts raged between old-timers and newcomers.[42]

Old sources of stability like the police seemed inadequate against the threat of crime. Of course, crime was a problem for the entire city and nation. Officers from one precinct could not be expected to bring tranquility to northern Manhattan all by themselves. Nevertheless, as crime increased, some Washington Heights and Inwood residents looked at the police with a mixture of desperation, disappointment, and skepticism. In Inwood and many other places, frustration with police failure to prevent crime contributed to a skepticism toward government institutions that mushroomed into the antigovernment mood of the 1980s and 1990s.

From the Irish perspective, the neighborhood became smaller and less secure. As in so many other city neighborhoods, the gregarious ways of the 1940s were lost in the Great Fear of the 1960s and 1970s. The newcomers who made many Inwood Irish feel threatened were largely Dominicans. Arriving in the neighborhood when crime was already a painful fact of life and living without significant ties to the Irish community, their presence was bound to raise the level of anxiety among the Irish. Unfortunately, this sense of alarm blinded both the Dominicans and the Irish to all that they had in common.

The Dominicans, natives of an impoverished island nation, came to the United States in increasing numbers after the mid-1960s. Like the Irish who defined themselves through their struggle with imperial Britain, the Dominicans were deeply influenced by life under the imperial domination of the United States—expressed as recently as the 1965 "intervention." Both shared the Roman Catholic faith, although significant numbers of Dominicans were also Pentecostals. Like the Irish before them, the Dominicans came to New York to work their way out of oppressive poverty (although often with an eye to returning to the Dominican Republic once they had acquired a stake.) In Washington Heights and Inwood, they found many of the amenities that had lured the Irish decades before: available housing, large parks, and convenient mass transit. Many Dominicans found low-wage work in service industries and manufacturing, the late-twentieth-century's version of the ditch digging and domestic service jobs that had occupied so many Irish 150 years earlier. Monsignor Thomas Leonard, who grew up in an Irish parish in New York and later ministered to the Irish and Dominicans in Incarnation, found the Irish and Dominicans "so alike, it's uncanny."[43]

But few had the knowledge of both Irish and Dominicans that enabled Monsignor Leonard to recognize their shared traits. The Dominicans who moved to the Heights and Inwood were first-generation immigrants making a wrenching adjustment from the Caribbean to the United States—much as the first-generation Irish immigrants in the Five Points had made their own difficult adaptation to American life a century earlier. In a sense, when the Heights-Inwood Irish looked at the Dominicans, they glimpsed the shadow of their own ancestors. If they did not like what they saw, it was partly a testament to the enormous difference between the Irish Americans of the twentieth century and those of the nineteenth.

To complicate matters, the Irish and the Dominicans lacked a common language. A weekly newspaper edited by Barry Dunleavey, *Heights-Inwood*, experimented with bilingual editions. They had little success.[44]

The social and cultural distance between the Irish and the Dominicans was also a measure of the failure of civic institutions to bring the two groups together to nurture a sense of common ground. In the Heights and Inwood the old Democratic political organizations failed to integrate people of color into political life as they had previous generations of white immigrants. The political clubs were not really interested in the task; moreover, they were no longer a significant source of power that provided openings for black and Latino politicians. The urban community action programs of the Great Society and Mayor John V. Lindsay deliberately sought to by-pass the old Democratic machines and create alternative sources of power and social services in city neighborhoods. These new institutions—often rooted in ethnic or activist politics motivated by individual groups or issues—were not well suited to the task of bringing different peoples together to form a common agenda out of disparate concerns.[45]

Religious institutions were not much more effective at bringing together the Irish and the newcomers. Although some black and Latino youths attended the parochial school system, most attended public schools—and were thus beyond acquaintance with young Irish people who were concentrated in the parochial system. Efforts by local churches and political leaders were ultimately inadequate, in part because of Irish and Dominican indifference and in part because many Dominicans, hopeful of moving back to the Dominican Republic, lagged in committing themselves to permanent residence in New York.[46]

In northern Manhattan, as elsewhere in the city, those who suffered most from increases in crime were the black and Latino poor. But by the 1970s, when Inwood Irish walked through Incarnation parish to the south heard Spanish accents on the streets and saw bodegas on the corners, they sensed trouble. Inwood, especially the streets east of Broadway, seemed next in line for great changes.

Tom Mullany, who moved into Inwood after marrying at Good Shepherd in 1963, recalls that by 1970 reports of crimes and store robberies began to be the fearful stuff of everyday conversation. When he looked from Good Shepherd toward parishes to the south and east, the future looked ominous. "In Queen of Martyrs," he recalls, "we were aware of changes there. And in St. Jude's." Again, the miliary metaphor: "There was a sense that the circle was starting to form and encircle the area."[47]

One of the first things to go was the old Inwood bar scene—it no longer seemed safe to stroll from tavern to tavern late at night. "The fear of violence sends people home early," noted the weekly newspaper *Heights-Inwood* in 1974, "and more bartenders are locking out persons they don't know after midnight." One short article listed four holdups and shootings. Two of them took place in the month of July 1974: an off-duty policeman shot in a holdup at Cannon's Pub on Dyckman Street and a bartender and suspect shot in a holdup at the Vinegar Hill Bar at Tenth Avenue and West 215th Street. The article also recalled a shootout that thwarted a holdup at the Park Gate Bar at Broadway and Arden Street in February 1973, and an apparent holdup at the Inn Between Bar and Grill on 207th Street and Sherman Avenue in October 1972. There, gunmen shot and killed bar owner James Rayill and wounded his brother and co-owner Brian.[48]

Bartenders became reluctant to work the night shift, and bar owners installed locks and buzzers on their doors. Social life was transformed as peak business hours shifted from nighttime to 4–6 p.m. "Everybody who's at a bar at night is afraid," said a customer *Heights-Inwood* interviewed at O'Donnell's on West 207th Street. "Whenever the door opens, everyone looks around."[49]

As O'Halloran recalls it, "The changes seemed to come awfully fast—once it started, it was not gradual . . . one day it was all of us, then the next day it was the Dyckman Houses, then after that, all of a sudden—you wouldn't go to Dyckman Street for two weeks, and you'd go down there and there'd be a Spanish sign up there where an Irish deli used to be." Among some of the Irish there is a hint of bitterness towards those who left, as if their departures diminished the Irish community and its security.[50]

The sense of siege in the neighborhood was heightened by the cultural conflict between the old-timers and Latino newcomers. The streets became a battleground. The Irish blamed the Dominicans for making them filthy, much as native New Yorkers had blamed the immigrant Irish for fouling the streets in the nineteenth century. But the loudest complaints were about noise. When Dominicans blasted their music at levels where you could virtually feel the sound waves, older residents were infuriated. Whatever the motive for such sonic display—a territorial assertion, delight in a high-tech music system that symbolized achievement of the good life in America, or alternative concepts of public order—it bred hostility between the Irish and the Dominicans.

It also put the police in the almost impossible situation of being asked to mediate a culture war. "This clash," the police reported to a municipal task force on the Heights and Inwood in 1978, "at the risk of over-simplification, is the gap between the older, established but smaller community that remains, with their intransigently traditional and vocal views, unable to comprehend the norms, traditions and customs of the more recent arrivals. This later and dominant (population) is not compelled to assimilate as others have in the past due to their great numbers. . . . The police are looked to as a buffer in settling the societal differences, often occupying enormous police time and resources, sometimes defying categorization and definition."[51] The police report grasped the difficulty of mediating cultural disputes between different ethnic groups, but as a history lesson it was incomplete. The belief that new immigrants were "not compelled to assimilate as others have in the past" overestimated the assimilation of the older generations in the neighborhood. It also showed no sense of the wrenching conflicts that accompanied earlier immigrants' adjustments to American life, particularly those that involved the Irish: fights over public education, the Draft Riots and Civil War, hostility to Britain in two world wars, and conflicts with the Jews in the 1930s and 1940s.

The Irish of Washington Heights and Inwood—along with their police officers—were living through a classic American dispute between natives and immigrants. Although such episodes have never been pleasant, the participants in the Heights and Inwood might have taken some comfort in the knowledge that they are not unprecedented and eventually resolved. But the shortness of their own memories and a tendency to romanticize earlier days in the city increased Irish residents' sensitivity to the problems and dislocations they saw around them.

Cathy Finnerty, born in 1964 to a Jewish mother and an Irish Catholic father, proud to spend her childhood in the integrated Dyckman houses, felt the pace of change in the neighborhood quicken in the middle 1970s. Finnerty and her sister devised routes to their home that enabled visitors to avoid the noise and dirt of Dyckman Street and Nagle Avenue. When her relatives visited in July 1976, she felt shame. "I remember being so incredibly embarrassed about the neighborhood, feeling so ashamed that this was where we lived. These were my suburban relatives, and there were all these kids out on the street blasting their music, and firecrackers going off. It just seemed like a ghetto, it felt like we lived in the ghetto. And I could tell that my cousins were really uncomfortable, that they thought we were really poor, and just feeling so ashamed."[52]

For many, the pressures of neighborhood that rocked Inwood in the 1970s were too much. They left for the suburbs. "The neighborhood started changing," McGee recalls, "and a lot of guys were finally able—they had jobs as cops, firemen, construction workers, in other words they had fairly decent wages—so they said let's get the hell out of the city and go rear our kids in the country, away from the changing neighborhood. And a lot of them went to Jersey, up to Bergen County, a lot more went to Long Island. Wherever the housing was reasonable."[53]

A year of moonlighting for Fordham Cab brought in enough money for a downpayment. Husbands and wives quarreled over whether to move, and whether to wait until the children finished school before leaving. Visits to friends who had already moved out brought no end to the discussion. "You'd go out visiting," Mullany recalls, "the first question when you were walking through the door—even before you had your coat off—was 'When are you going to get out of there? Why subject the kids?'"[54]

Ethnic diversity alone—in the person of Dominicans—did not drive the Irish from the neighborhood. They had, after all, learned to share it with the Jews in an earlier generation. "And don't kid yourself," recalls Michael Cohn, a German-Jewish refugee who settled in the Heights. "We were just as unpopular as the Dominicans."[55] What many of the Irish found unbearable was the fear that emerged from the combination of crime, ethnic diversity, and the absence of significant ties between themselves and the Dominicans. The gulf between the Irish and the Dominicans, for which both groups are partly to blame, made strangers seem both alien and physically threatening.

Decades earlier, a significant number of the Irish had disliked their Jewish neighbors. But they stereotyped them as economic and political competitors, not as street toughs, and with some reason. The Jews of Washington Heights posed no challenge to the Irish domination of the streets. The new Latino neighbors were different. Young and growing in number, with their share of tough young men, their presence challenged the Irish residents' rule of the neighborhood. For some of the Irish, it was enough to push them to the suburbs. And even for those whose departures were more a case of being pulled from the neighborhood by the lure of lawns and neat little houses, it was enough to make the departure feel like a hasty retreat.

Nevertheless, the Irish departure from the Heights and Inwood was also a tribute to the modest but gratifying prosperity of Irish Americans. Unionized jobs with solid and steady paychecks, combined with the growing ascent of the Irish into professional occupations, gave Irish city-dwellers the option of moving to the suburbs. Fortified by the security of their unions and their professions they could afford to leave the city, with its neighborhood networks of life and labor, without suffering any economic disadvantage. The prosperity they enjoyed in the decades after World War II may have been rooted in the economy of New York City, but that same prosperity enabled the Irish to leave the city and its heterogeneity altogether.

Rockland County in New York, with its relatively inexpensive housing and easy access to the city by highway, became a popular destination, particularly for police officers and firefighters compelled by law to live in-state. Eileen Quinn, who remained in Inwood, has noted the result when visiting friends in Nanuet in Rockland County: "Walking out of mass up there is like being back in the neighborhood."[56]

By 1980, the Irish and Jewish presence that had once defined the Heights and Inwood was fading before the new Latino ascendancy. Even the German Jews of Washington Heights, who clung to their neighborhood, declined by 56 percent, from 24,226 in 1960 to 10,507 in 1980. Those who remained clustered in the northwest section of the Heights along Fort Washington Avenue, much as the Irish clustered in Inwood, leaving the southern part of the neighborhood to Dominicans and other Latinos.[57] The numbers of the Irish as a whole diminished less rapidly, by 38 percent in the same years, from 18,971 in 1960 to 11,718 in 1980. The Irish, concentrated in the working class, were less likely than their Jewish neighbors to have the money to move to the suburbs. Those Irish who stayed in the neighborhood often stayed because they could not afford to leave. Those who remained moved within the Heights and Inwood to areas with the most Irish and the fewest Latinos.[58] Since the early years of the century, the Irish had been the inhabitants of the simple apartments east of Broadway. Now, flight from neighborhood change, coupled with some measure of financial security, led them to the more polished streets north of Dyckman and west of Broadway, like Park Terrace. The Hibernian archipelago of the Heights and Inwood was reduced to one tiny island.[59]

Ironically, the contraction and consolidation of the Heights-Inwood Irish community created neighborhoods more densely Irish than those of earlier years, when the Irish were spread more widely across northern Manhattan. In 1950, the Irish had averaged about 20 percent of the population in the census tracts around Incarnation and Good Shepherd. In 1980, with only a small number of Irish left around Incarnation and most of the remainder squeezed into the census tracts west of Broadway around Good Shepherd, they averaged thirty percent of the population.[60] Yet if Inwood was becoming more densely Irish, it was hardly exclusive. Some 27 percent of the "Irish" inhabitants were American-born individuals, children of one Irish parent plus another nationality. Signs of intermarriage crept into the Good Shepherd school yearbook, where "Hispanic" names appeared under "Irish" faces and "Irish" names appeared under "Hispanic" faces.[61]

In the mid-1980s the Heights and Inwood—often seen as a barometer of working and middle-class New York—reeled under a new threat: the trade in crack cocaine. The Heights became a center for the sale of the drug, partly because the George Washington Bridge gave buyers easy access to the neighborhood. Dominicans were prominent in the trade, usually with other Latinos and African Americans as business partners and suburban whites as customers.[62] Of course, drugs were always present in the Heights and Inwood if you consider alcohol a drug. Alcoholism had long been a problem in Inwood, where some residents bragged that there were 110 bars in 10 square blocks.[63] But the violence that surrounded the crack trade brought neighborhood crime to unprecedented levels.

Armed robberies increased, and even if they remained below citywide rates, they brought the level of fear in the neighborhood to new levels. Worst of all, the area's murder rate began to climb. In the late 1980s and early 1990s, the 34th Precinct became one of the most murderous in the city. In 1990 alone, there were 103 murders in the 34th—a murder rate of 52 per 100,000 inhabitants at a time when the citywide rate hovered around 30. Lurid reports of crack and violence in the Heights became a journalistic staple. Most murders and the worst ravages of crime and the drug trade were concentrated in the southeastern portion of the precinct, around 162d Street, from which the Irish had long departed. Dominicans, living at the epicenter of the drug wars, suffered most from the violence. But reports of gunfights and robberies cast a frightening shadow over the rest of northern Manhattan, including the remaining Irish areas.[64]

The changes that afflicted New York in the decades after World War II struck with cruel force in Washington Heights. To paraphrase a comment about another city, in some ways it seemed that wherever New York was going, Washington Heights and Inwood got there first. True, the neighborhood did not decline into the empty lots of the South Bronx. But the pain of Washington Heights and Inwood seemed to indicate that in the future, the average level of prosperity, security, and justice in the city would be lower than it had been in the past.

Poverty spread through streets that were once the epitome of working-class and middle-class New York. The solid comfort of areas like upper Fort Washington Avenue in the Heights and Park Terrace in Inwood obscured the growing misery in the rest of the neighborhood. In 1989, a study commissioned by the Northern Manhattan Improvement Corporation revealed greater-than-imagined distress in the Heights and Inwood: high levels of poverty among single-parent families and elderly, a high birth rate, a large foreign-born population making the always difficult adjustment to New York City, overcrowded schools, and sweatshops.[65]

The response in the Inwood of the late 1980s, as in the Heights of the late 1950s, was to draw a boundary that excluded the people and the trouble to the south. As Sergeant Robert Parente of the 34th Precinct noted, "If you're from Washington Heights, you probably think of Inwood as just a section of the neighborhood. But if you're from Inwood you're more likely to think of it as separate. That's mainly because people don't want to be associated with Washington Heights' reputation as the crack capital of the world."[66] Former residents looked on with a mixture of sorrow, confusion and anger. From her office in New Jersey, Mrs. Walck can look across the Hudson to the Heights. Even at a distance, she recognizes familiar buildings. On occasion she returns for a visit and is disturbed by what she sees. "I have a problem that the neighborhood changed so much," she says. "I really do. I have a problem when I go in there and see it now. . . . I've always wanted to go back there and say stop this, this was beautiful, it could have been beautiful for you, too."[67]

But the Heights and Inwood could not be the same neighborhood for both the Irish and the Dominicans because the city of the 1990s was not the city of the 1940s. Over the course of those fifty years, New York had changed enormously. The manufacturing base that sustained its working class declined. Its lower middle class felt increasingly insecure. Its middle class fled to the suburbs. Its manufacturing base declined. Its poor increased in number. Its social services and education system were stretched to the breaking point. Its crime rate increased to catastrophic levels. Its increasingly diverse people fought amongst themselves. When New Yorkers looked around in the 1990s, they saw pervasive evidence of social decay, from the homeless people sleeping on the sidewalks to the bars bolted across apartment windows to keep out burglars.[68]

The difference between the city and neighborhood of yesterday and today is apparent when departed Inwood Irish meet with today's remaining residents. O'Halloran recalls a neighborhood reunion in 1984. The talk flew fast, but the conversation was about the past—the present held no common bonds. "You'd say 'What are you doing now?'" recalls O'Halloran, "and that takes up two lines. And then it's 'You remember when?' with nostalgia weighing the whole thing." Similar scenes occurred at a reunion for Good Shepherd parish held in 1987.[69]

As younger people leave for the suburbs, Inwood's Irish community is defined more and more by older people. "The kids in Rockland and New Jersey," says Sister Elizabeth Tierney of Good Shepherd, "spend their time worrying about Mom back here. Then they take her out to the suburbs for the weekend, but she can't wait to get back to her place." For so many, she says, the lure of "the church, the neighbors" and "familiar surroundings" keep them rooted in the neighborhood. As Eileen Quinn, a woman long active in local politics puts it, "Taking me out of Inwood would be like taking the Pope out of the Vatican."[70]

"This is our neighborhood, this is our parish," says McGee. "And most of us that are here, like myself, wouldn't leave. You could give me a house out in Rockland County or a place in Jersey, I wouldn't take it. . . . It's homelike, you know so many people, you grew up in the neighborhood. There are great friendships here, friendships that last years and years. It's like an extended family."[71]

As the 1990s began, people like McGee were a decreasing portion of Inwood's population. The 1990 census counted almost 200,000 people in Washington Heights and Inwood; 67 percent were of Hispanic origin, 11 percent African Americans. The 18.7 percent "white non-Hispanics" in the neighborhood included both the Irish and the Jews. One older Irishwoman, Nora Goodwin, ventured that all the changes in the neighborhood left the Jews and the Irish with more in common. "They're just like us now," she says, "nearly extinct."[72]

As the history of Irish–Jewish relations in the neighborhood shows, ethnic conflicts in New York are not fixed and unchanging. In the 1990s, a Jewish city councilman, Stanley E. Michels, was representing the Irish of Inwood. In stark contrast to the dark days of bigotry in World War II, he was warmly welcomed at meetings of the Ancient Order of Hibernians and Good Shepherd ceilis.

Relations between the Irish and Latinos are a different story. At their worst, they resemble the dynamic of siege within siege that the Irish poet Seamus Heaney observed in northern Ireland. There, a Catholic minority is besieged by a Protestant majority that is besieged by the larger Catholic population of Ireland. Inwood had its own version: a small Irish American community felt besieged by a larger Dominican community that felt itself despised by the rest of the United States. In such situations, where all feel threatened, there is little room for communication and less for empathy.[73]

The full weight of this tragedy fell on one Irish family in October 1991. A mother and father, long-time residents of Inwood who met in Hughie's Bar on 207th Street, went out to celebrate their nineteenth wedding anniversary. They left behind in their apartment on Isham Street two daughters, ages 13 an 17. When the daughters' 14-year-old friend arrived with two little children in tow, two Spanish-speaking men armed with a knife and a gun forced their way into the apartment behind them. They ransacked the apartment and raped the three teenage girls.[74]

In the days that followed, much was revealed. A Dominican neighbor was "shocked and upset" that even though he was at home next door, he heard no noise. The oldest daughter leveled a small part of the blame at her parents, for not moving out earlier. Her mother now vowed to leave. In court, one of the accused men confessed that he had already robbed and raped in as many as 10 households of Dominican immigrants. And the girls' father asked a question that goes to the heart of crime's blight on Washington Heights, Inwood, and all city life. "Do we have to isolate one another?" he asked. "Do we have to continue to run?"[75]

Ironically, the Irish who remain in Inwood probably have a better-developed sense of dealing with ethnic and racial diversity than their cousins in the suburbs, who live in more homogeneous environments. Occasionally, such Irish Inwoodites and the newcomers achieved an inclusive sense of community: Frank Hoare, an Irish American Democratic district leader speaking at a memorial service for Israel Ortiz, a Puerto Rican grocer murdered in his Inwood store; Carlos Estevez and Joseph Atif, an African American, coming to the rescue of Charlotte O'Brian in a mugging; elderly Irish invited to Dominican weddings in Incarnation parish; the congenial integration of Coogan's bar and restaurant at 169th Street and Broadway. Such scenes testified to the best that was possible for the Irish and their neighbors in Washington Heights and Inwood. Tragically, there were not enough episodes like them to reverse currents of fear and separation.[76]

The solution to this impasse, in Inwood and elsewhere, is not to simply decrease levels of crime, although that would help. It is also to create civic institutions, lines of communication and shared political interests between communities like those of the Irish and Dominicans that reduce the uncertainty and hostility that poison meetings between strangers in a time of crime.[77]

In 1992, there are still signs of the Irish in Washington Heights and Inwood that certify their share in the neighborhood's history. They are thickest around the intersection of Broadway and 207th Street: the accents of the elderly people, signs for the Tara Irish Gift Shop and the Piper's Kilt tavern, an advertisement in a butcher's window for Irish sausages.

The Irish who left such scenes for the suburbs will be participants in a new chapter in American history: the challenge of maintaining an ethnic identity in suburban towns far removed from city neighborhoods, whose intensely shared streetlife once did so much to shape the consciousness of so many Irish. The Irish in the suburbs will have two major factors in their favor. One, to be Irish in the late twentieth century, unlike in previous eras, is not to be part of the bitter controversies over education, politics, and American ties to Britain that complicated life for previous generations of Irish Americans. Two, since they are white Americans, their ethnic identity does not readily subject them to bigotry and stereotyping that still afflict people of color. For blacks, Latinos, and Asians, the question of affiliation is decided by appearance. For Irish Americans, ethnic affiliation will become more and more a matter of choice—a choice that carries relatively few negative consequences.[78]

In suburbia, the content and continuity of Irish identity can no longer be assumed. It will have to be constantly re-created if it is to endure. Expressions of Irishness will assume new configurations, with no one of them paramount. Sometimes they will be public—attendance at the Saint Patrick's Day parade, participation in an Irish republican demonstration. More often, they will be private: fondness for Irish music, step-dancing lessons for the kids, a vacation in Ireland. In the towns of Rockland County, Long Island, and northern New Jersey, the Irish will be challenged to develop a new kind of ethnicity, one rooted less in neighborhood relationships and more in emotional attachment to an identity that requires regular and deliberate reinforcement.[79]

The streets of Washington Heights and Inwood represent a kind of place that is disappearing: a big-city Irish neighborhood. But through their sons and daughters who left for the suburbs, there to create new kinds of Irish communities, the echo of their lessons will continue to shape what it means to be Irish in America.

CHAPTER 18

Emigrants, *Eirepreneurs,* and Opportunists

A SOCIAL PROFILE OF RECENT IRISH IMMIGRATION IN NEW YORK CITY

DURING THE 1980s many thousands of Irish people entered the United States seeking work. This exodus was precipitated by a deterioration in Ireland's economic fortunes. The relative prosperity that had characterized the Irish economy in the 1960s and early 1970s was short-lived. Worldwide recession in the wake of the oil crisis of 1973 effectively destroyed the dream of Irish prosperity. Instead, the reality was a prolonged period of economic stagnation, from which Ireland has been the slowest of all the Organisation for Economic Co-operation and Development (OECD) member countries to recover.[1] Despite a modest growth rate and low inflation, the Irish economy has been beset by unemployment (currently upward of 20%) and up until recent years, high net emigration. The fate of these new immigrants in the Irish American community, especially those known as "illegals," is the subject of this chapter.[2]

The Irish, in common with other peripheral nation-states (particularly those located in the developing world) are acutely implicated in the "international nomadism of modern life."[3] Between 1980 and 1990, net outward migration totaled 216,000, which is equivalent to 6 percent or more of the population, with the bulk of emigrants leaving after 1985 (table 18.1). The annual average migratory outflow rose to nearly 34,000 between 1986 and 1990. This coupled with the decline in natural increase resulted in an overall population decrease.[4]

Following the general upward trend in Irish emigration in the 1980s, legal immigration to the United States rose steadily during the decade (table 18.2). Prospective Irish emigrants were the main beneficiaries of a short-term scheme to increase the flow of immigration from countries that had been adversely affected by the provisions of the 1965 Immigration Act. The NP-5 visa program, which was enacted as a provision of the Immigration Reform and Control Act (1986), offered 40,000 special visas over the period 1987–90 to the 36 countries that had been traditional sources of emigration to the United States. The visas, popularly known as Donnelly visas after the member of Congress who initiated the scheme, were offered to applicants who were randomly selected from a mail registration list. Unlike normal visas based on the family reunification or preference system, these special NP-5 visas did not require applicants to have special skills that are in short supply in the United States or to have a job offer from a U.S. employer. In all, 16,329 visas were issued to Irish applicants between 1987 and 1990. The Immigration Act of 1990 established a second lottery system that would distribute 120,000 visas to 34 countries over a period of three years, beginning in October 1991 and ending in October 1993. Under the terms of this act (whose chief congressional architect was Representative Bruce Morrison), Ireland was guaranteed 16,000 visas a year for three years—a total of 48,000 in all. These lotteries greatly augmented the standard allocation of immigrant visas, which averaged 1,000 per year in the early 1980s.

These official statistics fail to reflect, however, the high level of illegal Irish immigration to the United States throughout the 1980s. During those years, tens of thousands of Irish people entered the United States legally on temporary visitors' visas. When the visas expired, they simply failed to return home,

TABLE 18.1. *Net Irish Emigration,*
1980–90

Year, ending April	Net emigration
1980	8,000
1981	(2,000)[a]
1982	1,000
1983	14,000
1984	9,000
1985	20,000
1986	28,000
1987	27,000
1988	32,000
1989	46,000
1990	31,000

Source: Dublin: Central Statistics Office.

[a] Figure in parentheses denotes net immigration.

jeopardizing their legal status by seeking work without the proper documentation. Hence, they became undocumented workers in the American economy, held in check by a metaphorical border that separates the legal citizenry from the twilight world of the illegal alien. Most of these new immigrants have settled in the cities of New York, Boston, Chicago, and San Francisco, where vibrant "new Irish" communities have emerged in recent years.

Typology of Recent Irish Immigrants

The specific character of any particular wave of emigration will vary according to the prevailing circumstances. The anatomy of recent Irish immigration to the United States, therefore, must be examined in terms of the relevant push and pull factors, as well as the structural and social contexts in which these migratory flows take place. Recent Irish immigration to the United States has proceeded in the form of two population flows, one occurring through normal legal channels and the other occurring clandestinely. Five types of immigrant can be identified within these population flows: (1) bread-and-butter immigrants, (2) disaffected adventurers, (3) holiday-takers who make up the illegal population, (4) *eirepreneurs*, and (5) opportunistic emigrants who are legally resident in the United States.

Bread-and-Butter Immigrants

Approximately one-third of the illegal immigrants interviewed for this study saw themselves primarily as economic refugees. They cited underemployment,

TABLE 18.2. Immigrants Admitted to the United States from Ireland, 1980–90

Fiscal year	Irish nationals[a]
1980	1,006
1981	902
1982	949
1983	1,101
1984	1,223
1985	1,397
1986	1,839
1987	2,921 (1,812)
1988	3,458 (2,367)
1989	9,894 (8,846)
1990	4,479 (3,554)

Sources: For 1980–86, 1984 INS Statistical Yearbook and Irish Consulate, New York; for 1987–90, American Embassy, Dublin.

[a]Figures in parentheses indicate number holding NP-5 visas.

seasonal unemployment, and business failure as factors precipitating the decision to leave. Unable to find work in their locale, they were willing to uproot themselves and emigrate. The decision to go to New York City was often made in the context of a familial or personal history of emigration. The opportunity to work and the lure of a regular income in cities like New York generally outweighed concerns about illegal status. Frank, from County Cavan, first left Ireland when he was just 17 years old. A welder by trade, he could see no future in Ireland: "I did try to get work in Ireland but I could only get menial jobs. My last job was working for a small firm. We did welding jobs around the country mainly for co-operatives, but as agriculture declined we got less work, and things got progressively slower. In 1979 I moved to Germany, and then within the year I headed on to New York."[5]

Sean, a native of Mayo, spent summers working in England alongside his brothers, from the age of 15 years. After an abortive year in college, he moved to England to work in construction and then on to the Netherlands:

> In the early 1980s the bottom fell out of the construction industry in Holland. I found myself with my back against the wall. I didn't want to go back to England, I didn't want to go back into construction because I had worked harder than anyone in that line. My idea was to set up my own business in Ireland. I wanted to set up a restaurant and wine business but I got no help from the IDA (Industrial Development Authority). Within months my savings were squandered. I tried England again but I couldn't take the anti-Irish jokes and the way the Irish were looked down upon. For me, it was preferable to be illegal here than to be prejudiced against over there.[6]

Of all recent Irish immigrants, this group has had the least choice in terms of making the decision to emigrate. Hence, they are the most likely to make a permanent commitment to the host country, given the opportunity to do so. The bread-and-butter immigrants therefore most closely approximate the settler immigration pattern that has characterized Irish emigration to the United States in the past.

Disaffected Adventurers

It is not unemployment as such but the absence of an adequate opportunity structure that induces immigrants in this category to leave. The scarcity of jobs with good career prospects in Ireland has produced a generation of workers who feel trapped and frustrated. They see little prospect for promotion, career advancement, or skills development.

Johnny had a good job with a Supermarket chain store in a rural town: "I just got fed up with the job. The money was lousy and I worked like a slave—often working crazy hours. You were paid for a 40-hour week even if you put in an 80-hour week. There was no overtime, no thanks. Promotion might have brought more money, but the tax would kill you."[7]

New York City exerts a pull because it holds out the prospect of starting over in an exciting, fast-paced, urban environment. Immigrants are challenged to survive in a less sheltered but ultimately more rewarding environment, at least in monetary terms. Timmy, a native of the West of Ireland, is typical of this group. He had a job with a state-sponsored company before emigrating to the United States. As he said, "he had it made" because the job was permanent and pensionable:

> But it was a dead-end job. I was a semiskilled laborer and I couldn't really work my way up. The work was boring and I never liked the boss's attitude. Overall I would say that the conditions under which I worked were not favorable. The money was good but the tax took a huge slice out.
>
> I was 25 years old and couldn't see a future for myself in that situation unless I were to get married, get a mortgage and then just wait for a family to arrive, and hang on in there to get the pension. That scenario held no attraction for me.[8]

Timmy's decision to leave was more a question of choice than one of force, but a choice made in the context of very limited options.

Many of the disaffected use their time in New York to work hard and save money. They are future-oriented in the sense that they accumulate capital with a view to making good investments in the years to come.[9] Disaffected by the absence of opportunity in Ireland, they are excluded by their illegal status from pursuing opportunities in New York. Most express the desire to invest their savings in property or in business in Ireland, but in a stagnant or uncertain economic climate those options are limited. In general, the disaffected aspire toward a transnational existence, a lifestyle that would allow them to enjoy the advantages of both the home and host countries. Thus, they speak of developing work or business interests that would allow them to commute on a regular basis between Ireland and New York City. They would therefore not have to make a firm commitment to either place. Such aspirations are idealistic. In the first place, these immigrants would have to regularize their status before such options could be considered. Second, if they begin to marry, settle, and start families, career options that require mobility will become increasingly unrealistic. Such expressions of a desire for a transnational existence, however idealistic, indicate that for this group of illegals their status as immigrants remains unresolved.

Holiday-takers

The third category may be described as extended holiday-takers—people who come from relatively well-off middle-class families, who stand to inherit a farm or a small business when they return home. They see their time in New York as an extended working holiday, before settling down to adulthood and its attendant responsibilities. One such visitor "saw it as an adventure, a way to make money. I had a small business at home which was viable and making money. As a matter of fact, I was probably making more then than I am now! But I was getting a bit fed up with it, especially because it took so much work. So I sold it at the beginning of the Summer and came out here."[10] Another felt the need to explore his potential abroad: "I'm from a prosperous family in the Southeast. Two of my brothers are well set up at home, one is in England and the other is a professional out here. My parents run the family business, a bar, which is actually in my name. Even though I had a great lifestyle, I felt I had more potential than I was using at home. So I came to the States. I have had great times here and managed to save a few dollars too!"[11]

The trip to the United States involves no risk (even if they are unlucky enough to be apprehended) because they have every intention of returning. More important, they generally have a livelihood to which to return. They are neither settlers nor conventional sojourners, but temporary visitors for whom a period as an illegal alien in the United States is little more than an aberration in an otherwise conventional life structure.

The Eirepreneurs

Given the primary position of the United States in the global economy, migratory flows of necessity extend beyond the national boundaries to include foreigners who are either highly skilled or have impressive credentials. The educated middle-class Irish elite increasingly form part of this transnational flow. Dubbed *eirepreneurs* by one Irish print journalist, these emigrants are cashing in on the social capital they accumulated in Ireland, to the benefit of metropolitan economies, and at the expense of our own peripheral one.[12]

There is now considerable evidence that a high level of emigration is occurring among Ireland's technical and professional graduates, which amounts to a brain drain.[13] Thirty-six percent of those who qualified with a primary degree in 1988 emigrated from Ireland. A breakdown of that figure reveals even higher rates of emigration within certain disciplines. For example, 48 percent of engineering graduates, 43 percent of arts and social science graduates, and 42 percent of architecture graduates emigrated in 1988. In terms of pattern and destination, Irish graduates follow the general emigration trend, with the majority going to Britain, the United States, and the European Union, in that order.[14] Not surprisingly, with few opportunities available at home, they are attracted to the core cities of the world economy. These cities offer an elite job market characterized by excellent benefits and remuneration.[15] In New York City, Ireland's educated elite, armed with the necessary visas, have begun to carve out careers for themselves in a range of professions including international finance and banking, insurance, the law, public relations, media, and advertising. According to young professionals working in New York City, the Irish standard of training is well recognized in America as being very high.[16] In addition, hard work is rewarded through salary bonuses and opportunities for advancement.

Since legal immigrants face no restrictions on travel in and out of the country, frequent trips home are possible. In addition, because these immigrants are tied into professional networks rather than immigrant networks, they are much less ethnically bounded in terms of their social interaction. They are therefore much more likely (than the undocumented) to assimilate. Since remuneration, benefits, and opportunity structures are significantly better in New York City, there is little incentive (or desire) among the educated elite to return home at least in the short term. A recent study on Irish accountants in the international labor market bears this out.[17] The *eirepreneurs* in that case made a rational choice about career development when choosing to go abroad. London and New York were the destinations of those who were serious about developing their careers. The Cayman Islands was the destination of those seeking fun.

As is the case in the undocumented sector, immigrant jobs ultimately depend on the vitality of the U.S. economy. Graduate recruitment through legal channels, like clandestine immigration, will ebb and flow in tandem with the trends in the global economic cycles.

Opportunistic Emigrants

Lottery winners (that is, Donnelly and Morrison visa holders, who were *resident in Ireland* at the time of their application) require separate classification. They are unique among the immigrant groups in that their decision to emigrate was a passive rather than an active one. The decision to leave was made *for* them by virtue of their selection for a visa through the lottery system.

These are not emigrants in the traditional sense of the term because they travel to the States not so much by choice but by chance. Had they not won a lottery visa, it is unlikely that they would ever have left Ireland. As such, they are one of the groups least prepared for emigration. Indeed, service providers in New York found that Donnelly visa holders were far more likely to suffer problems of adjustment than illegals, often because they came to the United States without appropriate contacts and networks.[18]

Impressionistic evidence (further research is needed in this area) suggests that many were pushed into going by families who saw a legal passage to the United States as a solution to the family member who "was at a loose end" or "had not yet settled down." Support for such decisions is implicitly underpinned by a culture of emigration that exists in Irish society.[19] Many of the opportunistic immigrants are fundamentally unsuited to emigration, but the visas were held up as glittering prizes that could not be passed up. The failure to take up the gauntlet after "winning" a lottery visa would invite acute social embarrassment. So these young people became emigrants by default rather than by design.

According to American embassy sources in Dublin, about one-third of the Donnelly visas issued went to undocumented immigrants resident in the United States.[20] The remainder (approximately 10,000 over four years) were awarded to Irish residents, the overwhelming majority of whom ostensibly left jobs in Ireland in order to take up the opportunity of legal residence in the United States. Not surprisingly, many of those who took up the initial offer of a visa have since returned to Ireland, or never seriously left Ireland in the first place. The visas constitute an "insurance policy" that might be cashed in at some future point in time. If these visas could be bequeathed to other family members, their holders would no doubt do so.

To maintain the visa, they simply enter the United States at least once a year for a specified period, after which residency is no longer a requirement. Ironically, while these visas are now literally rotting in drawers all over Ireland, undocumented Irish workers continue to face the rigors of illegality in the United States.

There is an element of class stratification implicit in the typology outlined above. The bread-and-butter immigrants, drawn primarily from the lower middle class and working class, are closest to the economic refugee model, in that they feel forced by economic necessity to leave. Like the majority of their predecessors, they are the most likely (of all the immigrant categories) to settle in the United States, if given the chance to do so. The *eirepreneurs* and the holiday-takers, in contrast, are drawn from Ireland's best-educated and proper-tied classes. They have made a choice to live and work abroad and reserve the option of returning home. In between are the disaffected adventurers and at least some of the lottery winners or opportunists, who are representative of an increasingly disillusioned Irish middle and lower-middle classes. They see themselves as having made a circumscribed choice, exchanging the exigencies of life in Ireland for the uncertainties of life in New York City. Whether they will settle or return home depends on several factors, including the prospects for legalization and economic trends in both the United States and Ireland.

Working Lives

As should be clear by now, the nature of contemporary Irish emigration is complex and multidimensional. The greatest gulf in terms of life chances and experience of migration, is that between the groups of immigrants at the two ends of the migratory continuum, that is, between the illegal aliens and the elite *eirepreneurs.* The experience of the illegals is particularly interesting and worthy of further exploration.

A useful distinction to employ in exploring the work destinations of Irish immigrants in New York City is that between "invisible" immigrants and "gap fillers."[21] Legal Irish immigrants with appropriate skills and qualifications form part of the transnational professional elite found in the core metropolises of the world. As members of this mobile elite, Irish professionals, or *eirepreneurs*, are not necessarily perceived (nor do they perceive themselves) as immigrants or foreign workers. Rather, they are often so well integrated that distinctions between them and their American colleagues—at least in the workplace—are practically invisible. As one of them has remarked, "Given that Irish business practices were consistent with American practices and that we spoke a common language, co-workers tended not to be conscious of our Irishness. Ethnicity was a nonissue, sometimes, to the point of frustration as you didn't get the opportunity to play the 'green card' in dealings with clients."[22]

The majority of Irish immigrants in New York City in the 1980s, however, were not legally resident high-flyers but undocumented workers destined to become gap fillers in the city's economy. Conservative estimates put the number of illegals in the United States during the decade at about 40,000, while immigrant activists have suggested that the real number was closer to 200,000.[23] The true figure is probably closer to the lower estimate, and has probably declined further in the wake of the various visa programs.

As has been the pattern in Europe, metropolitan centers throughout the United States, in particular, New York City and Los Angeles, have experienced sectoral and occupational shortages that are generally dealt with by employing foreigners, either lawfully or unlawfully.[24] The three main employment sectors in which Irish illegals work in New York City are the construction industry, the restaurant and bar trades, and child care and home help in private homes. A tendency to operate (albeit to varying degrees) in the informal economy is a characteristic of all three employment sectors. The term "informal economy" is generally reserved for the production and sale of goods and services that are in themselves legal, but that are produced and sold outside of the regulatory apparatus governing health, safety, tax, minimum wage laws, and other standards.[25]

The construction industry in New York, for example, has seen a steady expansion in the past few decades. According to New York State Department of Labor statistics, New York City had more than 10,000 registered construction firms in 1988. The average number of workers in these firms is 11, with 80 percent of all firms employing fewer than 10 workers. A major trend in this sector (as in many other industrial sectors) is a decline in unionized employment and a parallel expansion in informal, "off-the-books" job opportunities that are increasingly being taken up by new immigrants.

Construction work in the city is organized on a two-tiered system, with one sector of the industry operating in the formal economy and the other in the informal economy. Construction outfits working on commercial buildings in downtown Manhattan and on public contract projects, such as maintenance of the subway system, tend to be unionized and highly regulated. In Manhattan, for example, construction union locals, which are ethnically controlled, jostle for control of new construction jobs. By prior arrangement, Irish-run locals operate on the west side of the city, while Italian-run locals operate on the east side. In contrast, commercial and residential alterations and renovations are almost the exclusive preserve of independent contractors or subcontractors who rely to a great extent on nonunion labor. Many of these firms are unlicensed and carry out construction work without the necessary permits. Since they already work outside the regulatory apparatus, they are more likely than the larger licensed operators to hire undocumented aliens. It is the savings from tax and social security obligations that gives these companies their edge and that has contributed to their proliferation.

The majority of Irish men who came to work illegally in the United States in the mid-1980s found work in the booming construction sector. Not all ended up in the informal sector, however. Those with skills in short supply and with good union contacts gained access to the unionized jobs in the formal sector. At the other extreme, those with limited contacts and limited skills (the "JFK carpenters" whose credentials materialize rather dubiously at the point of arrival) generally work for small contractors or set up on their own. These workers are confined within the informal economy. Crucial for both groups of workers are their ethnic contacts, which allow them to gain entry into the labor market. Most independent contractors, construction union agents, and proprietors of bars and restaurants in the ethnic Irish enclave are first-generation immigrants who came to the United States in the 1950s and early 1960s. Lacking formal education and skills, they went into the construction industry or the bar trade. There the successful ones worked their way up in the union hierarchy or set up their own contracting or bar or restaurant businesses. They are therefore, the "gatekeepers" who control access to jobs in the key sectors of the construction industry and the bar or restaurant trade, and on whom the illegals are most dependent. The second- and third-generation Irish are much less likely to be involved in these areas of work, having had the opportunity to acquire the college education denied their parents or grandparents.

Because of their illegal status, new Irish workers in these sectors of employment are all subject to excessive surveillance, exploitation, and control.

It has been the practice for unionized companies to hire Irish illegals on the basis of a recommendation from a union agent or broker. The prospective employee will be asked to produce some documentation such as a social security card, but the authenticity of the documentation (which is almost always false) is not questioned. There is an implicit rather than explicit acknowledgment of the illegal status of the employee. This is important because unionized companies are highly regulated and must conform to the letter of the law.

An industrious broker can use his position to displace other immigrant workers with hand-picked workers from his own ethnic group, as one beneficiary explains:

> Peter had been a construction worker in both Ireland and England before coming to the States. He got work with a subsidiary of a major construction company which has a big contract with the Transport Authority. Peter was initially the only Irishman on the construction crews, which were made up of immigrants from Antigua, Trinidad, Jamaica, Spain, Italy, and Portugal. A vacancy came up and Peter got Michael, a mutual friend, onto his construction crew. More workers were needed and the foreman asked if there was anyone else Peter could recommend. He phoned some lads in Philadelphia, and they came up and joined another crew. The amount of work increased and extra help was hired. Another Irish guy and myself were taken on. Within 10 months, nearly 20 of the 80 men on the crews we worked with were Irish, most having got their jobs through Peter.[26]

Once ensconced in a job on a construction site (or in a bar or restaurant), the Irish immigrants becomes part of an occupational matrix that is itself tightly woven into the larger Irish ethnic community in the city. News of jobs travels largely through word of mouth, so it is incumbent on the immigrant to extend his or her network of contacts. Ethnic contacts and ties must be cultivated because of the exigencies of survival and the structure of job opportunity in the illegal immigrant market. As one disillusioned immigrant from an east coast county explained: "I didn't understand the meaning of the word 'clannish' until I came out here. I could have starved on the street here before someone from the West of Ireland would come to my aid. I have been unemployed for a total of about six months during a period of three years here. It wasn't that there was no work going, it was just that I didn't have good enough contacts to get from one job straight onto the next."[27]

As is the case with all immigrant groups, the Irish illegals make maximum use of the ethnic network to improve their position. They move beyond the obvious first-order contacts—such as close relatives and friends—to make use of second-order contacts: key brokers in the different employment sectors, who are ultimately more influential in the community at large. The fact that they are without documentation, however, limits their advancement and confines them to work in the ethnic enclave.

Illegality intensifies dependence on patrons and power brokers in the established Irish community. As undocumented workers, the Irish are dependent on employers who won't ask awkward questions. Hence they gravitate toward Irish contractors and the Irish-owned bars and restaurants. Conditions of employment are dictated by the employer, and the employees find they have little option but to comply. For example, work on construction sites that is physically demanding is often tightly controlled:

> The foreman would stand over us, and it really got on my nerves. The work was complicated but I really resented the constant supervision . . . when the whistle blows you start working. When the coffee break comes you don't sit down because you are on company time. The foreman stands over you and shouts. . . . I think for most of the guys its a case of leaving your brain at home when you leave in the morning.[28]

In Ireland the lads show up on the construction site 5 minutes late; here the workers are there half an hour before they are supposed to start. Coffee breaks are taken standing up.[29]

Other workers are denied any sense of security or continuity in the job:

Membership of a [construction] union does not confer a right to work. . . . It is always up to the company to decide whether or not you will work. They hire on a day-to-day basis.[30]

My boss [in the bar] has everything [figured out to his advantage]. I have been with him for seven or eight months. Everyday I call up to see if I am due in. That's the way the boss likes it. You call up and you are told if you are working that day, and the next day the same again.[31]

The desire to be retained in employment often entails greater risk-taking on the job. Not only are construction jobs dangerous, but the Irish are more willing than others to volunteer for the dangerous tasks:

Irish guys work hard, they take a lot of chances I think because they are afraid of losing their jobs. They will push harder to make a name for themselves so that they don't get laid off. But sometimes they push so hard they end up getting injured and having to stay off work for weeks at a time. They'll take the chance on dangerous work, not because they are crazy but because they want to be kept on. The Irish guy goes home each evening and worries if he is going to be back at work tomorrow.[32]

The work ethic is thus positively and negatively reinforced: people work hard because of the monetary rewards but also out of fear of losing their jobs.

Undocumented construction workers may be paid at a lower rate than other unionized and nonunionized workers in the city, although they are all doing the same tasks. It should be pointed out, however, that Irish immigrants generally fare much better than all other illegal immigrants. For example, undocumented Dominican workers working in construction in New York City tend to be concentrated in small firms, in nonunion jobs. Their earnings are 40 percent less than those of documented Dominican workers. Men averaged $150 per week in 1988.[33] In contrast, even the lowest-paid Irish construction worker (in the same year) earned twice that amount per week. Those who did not pay taxes could take home even more. Indeed, when compared with other white but non-English speaking ethnic groups, the Irish still do better, because of the extent of the ethnic contacts they can draw on in the Irish enclaves and their superior ability to bargain for a higher rate of pay.

Immigrants in the informal sector do not constitute a homogeneous group. They are stratified according to race, ethnicity, skills, and experience, as well as legal status, and that stratification determines to a great extent their labor market experience. This explains why Irish immigrants—with good English, a high level of skill, and close ties to Irish American power brokers in the workplace—tend to do better in the migrant labor market than both their

European and Central American counterparts, both of whom have access to a much smaller pool of affluent employers. Interestingly, it has recently emerged that London-based Irish subcontractors in the construction sector are increasingly turning toward Bosnian refugees in a bid to cut their labor costs by half. Polish and Bulgarian immigrants are also being hired at lower rates of pay than, and in preference to, Irish laborers.[34] This suggests that overall there is a lower level of ethnic solidarity operating among the Irish in London that among their counterparts in New York, a fact attested to by many of the immigrants interviewed in this study.

Most of the Irish women who came to New York City in the 1980s took up employment in private homes looking after children and the elderly. The high incidence of dual-career families and the increased emphasis on home rather than institutionalized health care in the United States, has created a demand for labor in this sector.[35] Nannies and home companions work long hours for poor remuneration and are often subject to tight control and surveillance at work.

> I took a job with an Orthodox Jewish family in Manhattan, but it was a very bad experience. I was supposed to work from 6 a.m. until 8 p.m., taking care of three children. There were two of everything in the kitchen—kosher and nonkosher. It was a real culture shock for me to see all these different cups and saucers, meat, cloths and dairy cloths. I was living off the kitchen in a tiny room and in addition to minding the children, I was expected to scrub floors and clean the cooker, all for $140 per week.[36]

Since home and work are often located in the same place, there is little scope for maintaining an independent existence. If a woman loses her job, she frequently loses her home too, often at short notice. "Eventually things just blew up. I told them it was best if I left for my sake and the sake of the kids. I went up to see my friend and cool off for a while. When I got back to the apartment at 11:30 pm I found my suitcases packed and in the hall. They hadn't even paid me my weeks wages and they obviously didn't care what happened to me."[37] Women's work contrasts quite starkly with men's work. A construction worker has his day's work finished by late afternoon and generally has his weekends free. He earns up to twice what a woman worker earns in half the time. Thus he has more money to spend and more leisure time in which to spend it. Irish women must take on at least two jobs (thus eroding their free time) to earn an income comparable with that of men. This indicates a grave inequality in the position of men and women in the illegal immigrant work force.

New Irish and First-Generation Irish Immigrants

For the new Irish who occupy gap filler jobs in the informal economy, relationships with older first-generation Irish immigrants (that is, those who emigrated in the 1950s and 1960s and whose work or homes are based in traditional ethnic neighborhoods) tend to be highly pragmatic, rooted as they are in the "cut and thrust" of the immigrant labor market. Living and working in close proximity to each other makes for an often uneasy coexistence. Given that the supply of labor frequently exceeds demand, and that the majority of those seeking work in the ethnic enclaves of New York City are illegal, it is not surprising that employer–employee relations are characterized by patterns of paternalism and clientelism. Employment conditions are variable and often exploitative, a fact that strains ethnic loyalty among these two groups.

Among the new Irish, the illegals have tended to settle in the traditional immigrant neighborhoods of the Bronx and Queens, while the legally documented have settled in neighborhoods that are less ethnically homogeneous. Illegal immigrants rely to a great extent on ethnic networks into which they can be absorbed relatively quickly. The established ethnic communities in these neighborhoods offer work and leisure opportunities, and in addition, the psychological assurance of safety in numbers. Legal immigrants, in contrast, are not reliant on such networks because of their ease of access to occupational and other institutional affiliations. Hence, they live in neighborhoods that are not identifiably Irish, and they mix socially with people from a wide range of backgrounds.

The Irish population in the traditional ethnic neighborhoods of the Bronx and Queens has been severely depleted in recent years by the flight to the outer

County Kerry native Joan Dineen and other 1950s immigrants found work in Stouffer's and Schrafft's, both restaurant chains with a reputation for hiring Irish women. This photograph was taken in Stouffer's, Pershing Square (42nd Street), in 1958, but such service sector employment was so easy to find in New York that waitress work was an ethnic niche even for the 1980s undocumented Irish. (Photograph © Charles Harbutt, Actuality, Inc.)

suburbs. Those who were not upwardly mobile or who were too old to leave remained behind to weather the problems of inner-city decline. The inflow of new Irish in the 1980s heralded a virtual renaissance for these neighborhoods, which offered the new arrivals an ethnic Irish ambience, reasonable rental rates, and proximity to the city where most of them work. A variety of Irish businesses ranging from bars and diners to bakeries, import stores, and Irish delis once more flourish in these neighborhoods. Irish accents are heard on the street, and Irish children attend the local schools. Gaelic sports have been revived, while many Irish American County associations, which were all but defunct, have been reestablished. There has also been a resurgence of Irish festivals and cultural events. Once more these neighborhoods have taken on the characteristics of "urban villages," which include concentrated networks and organizations among residents of similar ethnicity, strong kinship ties, and a primary dependence on local institutions and personal connections to obtain jobs.[38]

The attitude of older first generation immigrants toward the new arrivals is one of ambivalence. On the one hand, they dissociate themselves from the new Irish who are frequently labeled "rude and arrogant." On the other hand, they acknowledge that the arrival of a new generation of Irish immigrants has helped revitalize and regenerate New York City's Irish ethnic neighborhoods. What emerges in these neighborhoods is a symbiotic relationship between the two groups. The older immigrants provide jobs that the illegals need and that they probably could not get elsewhere without documentation. In turn, the new Irish strengthen the white constituency in neighborhoods that are increasingly populated by black, Hispanic, and Asian immigrants. Their mutual relationship then is primarily based on instrumentalism. As one immigrant summed up, "We're using them, and they're using us."

Sharing the same workplaces and neighborhoods brings the intraethnic cultural and value differences into sharp relief. One local priest working in the Bronx puts it succinctly: "People don't mix easily outside of their own social group. The older Irish tend to be more family oriented, better established and more upwardly mobile. The younger, single people are into a totally different lifestyle. Bars are their cultural center, and they tend to close in on themselves."[39] This cultural and social distance is an indicator of a fragmentation of Irish ethnic culture, along age and social status lines. While the new Irish immigrants and their predecessors have forged alliances in the labor market and in the political sphere, culturally, there has been much less coalescence. The new Irish immigrant's sense of ethnic identity is framed, after all, within a dialectic that involves the contradictory influences of Irish American ethnicity, American culture and contemporary Irish culture. As one commentator notes: "Increasingly, we [the Irish] are no longer the product of the cultural tradition of any one nation in the way that generations who went before us were. More and more of us have lived our lives in more than one place."[40]

Irish illegals in New York City see themselves primarily as transients and are more oriented toward Ireland than toward either the ethnic community or the host society. At the same time, their lifestyles reflect the influence of all three social contexts. Identification with the home culture is maintained through their high levels of media consumption. National and local papers are imported and sold widely in the new Irish community. Tapes of sports events and Irish current affairs programs are regularly screened in the bars, and for special events live transmissions by satellite are arranged. Telephones charges are relatively cheap, and most immigrants phone home on a regular basis. This elaborate communications network enables the immigrant community to continue to identify instantaneously with national and international events and issues from a distance. They can experience sports events live. They can view tapes of current affairs programs dealing with contentious issues. They can read analysis of current events in the national Irish, local Irish, and local New York press. In short, the psychological distance from home is minimized by the range of mass media available to them through the neighborhood bars.

At the heart of these transnational communication systems lies a paradox. On the one hand, they tend to disrupt existing forms of national identification (for example, through the Americanization or Anglicization of Irish culture). On the other hand, they also offer opportunities for new forms of bonding and solidarity and new ways of forging cultural communities. It has been found among South Asian families in West London, for example, that the circulation and consumption of ethnically specific information and entertainment on video serves to construct and maintain cross-national "electronic communities" of geographically dispersed people who would otherwise lose their ties with tradition and its active perpetuation.[41] It seems that the modern communications revolution has profoundly affected the subjective experience of migration: "The Moroccan construction worker in Amsterdam can every night listen to Rabat's broadcasting services and has no difficulty in buying pirated cassettes of his country's favorite singers. The illegal alien . . . Thai bartender in a Tokyo suburb shows his Thai comrades karaoke video tapes just made in Bangkok. The Filipina maid in Hong Kong phones her sister in Manila and sends money electronically to her mother in Cebu."[42]

Legal documentation such as passports, immigrant visas, green cards, and false social security cards are less a testament of any given individual's allegiance to a particular nation-state and more a claim for participation in a labor market. For Irish immigrants living in New York, and especially those living in the twilight zone imposed by illegality, New York may be the workplace but home is still home. Despite the geographical distance from home, the psychological identification with Ireland and the international Irish community is maintained through the ready availability of transnational cultural goods.

This is not to say that Irish immigrants do not engage with their immediate environments in New York. In constructing their own cultural identity, the new immigrants also draw on the experience of living and working in New York City. While they may attend Gaelic hurling and football matches and occasional county dances—organized by the Irish ethnic organizations in New York City—the kind of music they will listen to is distinctly contemporary rather than traditional. New York City has witnessed the proliferation of a range of popular Irish bands that play rock and roll, or rock variations on traditional or Celtic themes, a hybrid derived from traditional Irish music and American rock and roll. As Susan McKeown, a singer with The Chanting House, recently told an Irish journalist: "It's music that the older generation of traditional people don't like because it ignores classic rules. But it's not like we're trying to kill it. . . . We just want to carry it on, open it up to a wider audience and bring it into the world music sphere."[43]

More and more Irish bars are catering to the tastes of the younger clienteles, by providing rock bands in their bars at night. Soccer and skiing are both popular leisure-time pursuits among the new Irish immigrants. Soccer is primarily an urban sport in Ireland, Britain, and Continental Europe, and its popularity among the new Irish in New York represents the penetration of urban values into contemporary Irish culture. The unprecedented numbers who supported the Irish national soccer team in their 1994 World Cup games in New York/New Jersey and Orlando, testifies to the intense loyalty of the Irish ethnic community abroad.

The celebration of ethnicity in the new Irish community is conflated with a celebration of youth, and this distinguishes this recent group from the generation of Irish immigrants who came to New York City in the 1950s and 1960s. Indeed, one Irish commentator has argued that for many young Irish people today, America (rather than Ireland or the ethnic Irish community) is their cultural and spiritual homeland.[44] In generating their own cultural identity the new Irish draw on several sources—Irish American culture, contemporary Irish culture, and international youth culture (which originates largely in the United States). As such, the new Irish community is potentially subversive of the ethnic culture, in that ethnic traditions (such as Irish dancing, the Irish language, and even Gaelic games) may no longer form part of every Irish immigrant's cultural repertoire. At the same time, the cultural crossover that is taking place creates new opportunities for the communication of Irish culture to a wider, nonethnic audience. For example, the new Irish rock groups that have emerged in recent years play not only at venues in the ethnic neighborhoods but also to a wider nonethnic audience in the trendy bars and cafes of Greenwich Village and the Lower East Side. In addition, a range of artistic initiatives ranging from Irish film festivals to theatrical ventures have brought Irish arts to a wider audience beyond the confines of the ethnic Irish community.[45] In practice, Irish American culture is going off in many different directions—some traditional and some innovative. This serves to highlight the plurality rather than homogeneity of the Irish ethnic group, broadly defined.

Irish Americans and the Issue of Legalization

Apart from their close economic ties with first-generation Irish immigrants, the new Irish also formed links with Irish Americans to launch a political challenge to U.S. immigration law. Irish Americans have been crucial to the new Irish, and the illegals in particular, in terms of political mobilization.[46] The Irish Immigration Reform Movement (IIRM) founded in 1987 to lobby on behalf of the illegals, sought the help of this powerful political constituency, whose extensive resources offered the possibility of a successful campaign for legalization. In the early days of operation the IIRM relied heavily on facilities provided by ethnic Irish organizations in New York City. The United Irish Counties Association (the umbrella group for all county associations in New York) donated an office and telephone line in the summer of 1987. Venues for holding meetings (and fund-raisers) were donated by prominent members of the Irish American community. Many Irish Americans became actively involved in the movement, often acting in an advisory capacity and using their contacts in a variety of American institutions, including the media, to highlight the plight of the illegal Irish.

Prominent clergymen, county association presidents, and businessmen, among others, were asked to join a panel of advisers to the nascent organization. They served to lend legitimacy to the organization, and to present it as a broad coalition of Irish interests. The IIRM quickly developed linkages with influential groups like the Ancient Order of Hibernians (AOH), the Irish American Labor Coalition (IALC), and the Brehon Law Society. The creation of a united front on immigration reform was achieved with the establishment of the Irish Immigration Working Committee (IIWC) under the auspices of the Irish Consulate in New York City. This committee gave formal status to the informal linkages already in place between the IIRM, the AOH, the IALC, and Catholic Charities of the Archdiocese of New York. The IIWC coordinated the lobbying efforts of the Irish community for a series of immigration reform bills that were introduced into the House of Representatives and the Senate between 1987 and 1990. Every time there was a hearing on the bill a deputation from the IIWC would go to Washington, D.C., to lobby politicians to vote in favor of the bill. The various Irish organizations backed up the lobbying efforts with mailouts to Irish American voters urging them to lobby their congressional representatives to vote for legislative reform.

Effectively, the IIRM was able to draw on a preexisting network of Irish American organizations that offered financial resources, organizational skills, and local political contacts, all crucial to the emergent organization. The Irish

American community was appealed to as a 'conscience constituency' of relatively affluent, middle-class people who could provide necessary resources but did not themselves stand to gain directly from success in the accomplishment of the movement's goals.[47]

Why did the various organizations in the Irish American community rally around the IIRM? Recent research suggests that the attenuation of ethnic differences among whites in the United States has seriously weakened traditional Irish ethnicity both in terms of social allocation and social solidarity. However, *ethnic identity*—a person's subjective orientation toward his or her origins—remains a salient feature in American society.[48] The realization among Irish Americans that a new generation of Irish immigrants was arriving in the United States to work without documentation, activated their ethnic identity. For a significant number, this reactivation served as a catalyst for ethnic solidarity.

Following the classic ethnic solidarity model, Irish Americans in conjunction with the new Irish activists, mobilized themselves to bring about a partial resolution to the Irish illegal problem. This problem is a much less contentious one than the issue of northern Ireland. (The latter tends to be politically divisive, resulting in a fragmentation rather than a coalescence of Irish American opinion.) In reopening Irish immigration to the United States, The Irish American community stood to strengthen itself numerically, culturally, and politically. In the late 1980s Irish American activists found themselves with a cause that could unite their constituent bodies and create the potential for the revitalization of the Irish lobby as a force among other powerful ethnic groups.[49]

Since the mid-1980s, a two-tiered flow of emigration from Ireland to the United States has emerged and is likely to persist into the next century, ebbing and flowing in line with trends in both economies. Given the high level of interest generated by the lottery visa programs, it can be assumed that many successful applicants will be drawn from the ranks of the highly skilled who possess good educational credentials.[50] (These are the applicants most likely to secure the job offers that must accompany the application for a Morrison visa). In the meantime, there will be a continuing (if declining) demand for unskilled workers in the informal labor market, where many of the jobs are off the books and therefore officially nonexistent. The informal sector will continue to recruit from a cheap, pliable pool of undocumented labor.

Many of the new Irish who came to New York in the 1980s and became part of the city's undocumented labor force have revitalized the ethnic enclaves of the Irish American community. They have breathed new life into these aging neighborhoods through their provision and consumption of a variety of ethnic goods and services. Thus they have performed an important economic function.

They have also performed a significant political function in that they provided the Irish American community with a cause around which to rally its considerable resources. Culturally, the new Irish are different from the generations that went before them. While they have much in common with contemporary generations of Irish Americans, they also remain different from them. The new Irish constitute a new dimension in the multidimensional patterning that makes up the Irish American mosaic. What new and distinctive patterns that mosaic will yield remains to be seen.

Rebecca S. Miller

CHAPTER 19

Irish Traditional and Popular Music in New York City

IDENTITY AND SOCIAL CHANGE,

1930–1975

T HE ROLE of traditional music, dance, and song in the lives of Irish immigrants in America and particularly in New York can be viewed as an indicator of ever-changing ethnic pride and community identity. Surviving years of social change and upheaval—ranging from religious persecution in Ireland to mass immigration to America and elsewhere—these vital expressions of an ancient folk culture have maintained a foothold in communities throughout Ireland and America.

The popularity of traditional Irish performing arts in New York City has waxed and waned over the course of the last century. Ranging from the early 1900s, when Irish traditional musicians were routinely bestowed the honorary title of "professor," to the 1950s when the music was, for the most part, ignored, to its "revival" in the early 1970s, the changing attitude toward Irish folk culture in general can be directly correlated to prevailing social, political, and economic forces within New York's Irish community. Further, the mercurial public sentiment toward Irish traditional culture is indicative of evolving perceptions of ethnic pride and self-identity among New York City's Irish immigrant community.

As immigrants establish themselves in a new country, their old culture appears to be replaced by "a new one, shaped by the distinctive experiences of life in America . . . and a new identity created." Completely discarding ethnicity, is, however, difficult because of the "unavailability of a simple 'American' identity." To some extent, "ethnic identities have taken over some of the task in self-definition."[1] Such is the case of the immigrant Irish. Despite the varying degrees of assimilation of different generations of immigrants to twentieth-century America, an inherent sense of "Irishness" has steadfastly been maintained. This self-identification has varied in orientation and intensity over the years, depending on the certain realities of assimilation into the mainstream, class affiliation and an eye toward upward mobility, and the changing image of the Irish community as projected to both itself and to the general public. The tension between maintaining a core identity of ethnicity while simultaneously adapting to the dominant culture can be measured and evaluated, in part, through the examination of social and artistic activities—in this case, the practice and popularity of traditional Irish music versus the more commercial Irish and Irish American musics by successive waves of Irish immigrants between 1930 and 1975.

The Music

The traditional instrumental music of Ireland originated centuries ago primarily as accompaniment for dancing. Today, the music is played more often in concert settings and in informal *seisúns* (sessions) as well as for *ceilis* (group folk dancing) in both community and familial contexts. Like most folk arts, the music has been passed down from the elder to the younger generation as an oral tradition. Playing style and repertoire are learned through listening and imitation, tunes are composed more or less anonymously, and the music is, on the whole, crafted through a communal process.

Among the most commonly found instruments in the tradition are the tin whistle, wooden flute, fiddle, and uilleann pipes (small, elbow-driven bagpipes), as well as the concertina, button accordion, mandolin, and tenor banjo. Rhythmic accompaniment is most commonly provided by piano, bodhran (a hand-held frame drum) or guitar, and more recently, by the bouzouki or cittern.

Traditional music is primarily melodic with a subtle but propelling rhythmic pulse. Because of this reliance on an often intricate melody line, harmonic accompaniment is a relatively new development in the course of the centuries-old history of traditional Irish music. Countermelodies and harmonies are uncommon. Dance tunes span a range of rhythmic meters and tempi—from sprightly reels, polkas, and jigs to slower, syncopated hornpipes and propulsive slipjigs and slides, to stately marches and evocative slow airs or laments.[2]

Traditionally, playing styles in Ireland have varied from region to region, as have tune repertoires. Before the advent of modern technology, style was generally transmitted from player to player; in recent decades, however, tape recorders and modern music have dramatically altered this process of dissemination.

By comparison, popular Irish and Irish American music are somewhat less clearly definable, given the vast array of styles over different eras.[3] In general, Irish and Irish American popular musics in the twentieth century have included such instruments as big band horn and reed sections, amplified guitar and bass, and piano or (more recently) synthesizer keyboards, as well as drums and other instruments commonly found in mainstream popular music. Unlike traditional Irish music, performances of Irish and Irish American musics are largely oriented to songs, rather than instrumental dance tunes without words. Harmonic and rhythmic accompaniment play a prominent role in popular music, and melody lines are, on the whole, simpler than traditional instrumental dance tunes.

The difference between Irish traditional and popular music is sometimes difficult to discern, and the lines between the two often blur, particularly as technology and media affect expressive culture on all levels. Traditional musicians have been recorded by large and small labels since the early years of the recording industry, and today, traditional music is disseminated in large part by the media. Popular Irish musicians, particularly Irish American showbands, excel at a variety of contemporary songs, including country and western songs, but they also play traditional set and *ceili* dance music on instruments such as the fiddle, accordion, guitar, and drums.

The tension between the preservation of the older traditional ways and the development of newer styles of Irish cultural expression has been particularly evident throughout the second half of the twentieth century as various waves of Irish immigrants established new lives in the United States. As a result of increased mobility and technology over the years, popular American culture has permeated Irish ethnic identity both in Ireland and in the United States, resulting in hybridized genres of music and dance. Paralleling American popular trends and often short lived, these performative genres have been and continue to be, indicative of an evolving Irish social identity, particularly with regard to Irish immigrant culture in America.

Irish Traditional Music in America to 1935

The mid-1800s saw the arrival of massive numbers of Irish who came to America to escape the devastating effects of the Irish potato blight. Unlike the earlier Scots-Irish immigrants who settled in rural areas throughout the east coast, the newly arrived famine Irish moved to America's cities: New York, Chicago, Boston, Philadelphia, and New Orleans.[4] In general, the Irish language and other aspects of traditional Irish culture did not survive the transition from a rural, agrarian-based life to an urban American lifestyle. Irish traditional music, however, proved surprisingly resilient, and master fiddlers, pipers, accordionists, flutists, and others found work in the vaudeville circuits, dance halls, pubs, and other venues. Moreover, unlike those who remained in Ireland, traditional musicians during these years were greeted in America with great respect throughout the immigrant community.[5] Support for Irish music and dance was so strong that in 1892 the "Golden Age of Irish Music" was formally ushered in with the completion of New York City's Celtic Hall, a major venue for Irish music and dance located at 446 West 54th Street in Manhattan.[6] Built with funds raised from the immigrant Irish and Irish American community, Celtic Hall served as "the Mecca for the best class of Irish sociables and gatherings for many years."[7]

By the early 1900s, New York City had become a focal point for Irish music when record companies reacted to the market potential of the "Golden Age" and began producing hundreds of 78 rpm recordings. Between 1900 and 1940, many outstanding Irish traditional musicians, most of whom lived or had passed through New York City, were recorded by such major companies as Columbia and Victor, as well as by smaller, ethnic music labels. These recordings were widely listened to by the Irish both in America and in Ireland and today provide invaluable documentation of the playing of such legendary musicians as fiddlers Michael Coleman, Paddy Killoran, and James Morrison; button accordionist John Kimmel; uilleann piper Patsy Touhey; and others.[8]

During the first three decades of the twentieth century, the "Golden Age of Irish Music" in New York was fueled by the arrival of hundreds of thousands of immigrants. Most of these newcomers hailed from the northern and western regions of Ireland, where traditional music and dance were often part of everyday life and among the only forms of entertainment available. Mary O'Beirne, who emigrated from Killavil, County Sligo, in 1930, married the late fiddler James "Lad" O'Beirne, also from Killavil. Like many immigrants during this era, the O'Beirnes brought a social aesthetic that revolved largely around traditional music and dance: "We danced a lot in Ireland. There was always house parties and we'd get up and do the four-hand reel. . . . On a Sunday evening, everybody knew that there was always music at the Coleman's Crossroads. So people would come from Gorteen, Bunninadden, Tubbercurry, all the townlands. And boys and girls would ride the bicycles and just stop there and the next thing you'd know, there'd be music right at the Crossroads."[9]

With a growing immigrant audience, Irish American societies flourished in New York. These organizations catered to their audiences by sponsoring regular *ceili* dances and other activities. The larger societies presented gala concerts featuring some of the master musicians in the United States at the time. Those musicians selected to record early 78s benefited from this enthusiasm and traveled from city to city to play in variety shows and in concert. Fiddler Michael Coleman occasionally took his family with him, as recalled by his daughter, Mary Coleman Hannon:

> My father was a beautiful dancer. Besides playing violin, he danced and played together. I have a picture of him dancing and playing in Chicago on the stage. . . .
> And, he traveled a lot. Maybe 1928, 1929, we went to Philadelphia, my mother and

my father and myself. I was about ten years old, I guess, and they had a beautiful, beautiful big concert for him. We went on the train and [when] we got off the train, they had all kinds of banners. Oh, I was so proud of my father! "Welcome Michael Coleman to Philadelphia!" And I thought, "Oh, isn't this great!" And we went in and the stage was gorgeous. . . . But everybody was tearing themselves apart looking at him. And I'm saying "That's my father!"[10]

The Golden Age of Irish Music in New York during the 1920s served as both an ingroup affirmation of Irish traditional culture as well as a positive display of Irish self-identity to the general public. For immigrant musicians, there were regular house *seisúns,* some of which would, years later, become legendary gatherings of the finest players at the time. Mary Coleman Hannon remembers always seeing a violin in her father's hand: "I just took it for granted. . . . I figured everybody kind of did the same thing. There was music in everybody's house; and my home was like that when I grew up, there were always musicians. Lad O'Beirne and James Morrison and Paddy Killoran. . . . But it was absolutely beautiful. I remember I'd go out in the morning and hear all the neighbors talk—'Did you hear all that music last night?' And I'd be kind of embarrassed, you know, because they'd all be playing until 3:00 am [in] their sessions."[11]

Membership in such Irish immigrant societies "enabled the individual to express feelings and kinship that helped to offset the isolation so often induced by immigration into the impersonal settings of urban districts."[12] Just as the network of fraternal and religious institutions served the immigrant community, so did the many informal associations made among traditional musicians at the regular *seisúns* and *ceilis.* These activities united certain sectors of New York's immigrant Irish community during the prewar years, offering them the opportunity to play music as part of a larger group as well as providing secure venues where they could meet, exchange information about housing and jobs, and socialize.

The Golden Age of Irish Music in New York peaked in the 1920s. By the early 1930s, a dramatic decrease in Irish immigration occurred as a result of the Depression and later, World War II.[13] These considerations, along with a wartime shellac ban, curtailed the recording industry's interest in ethnic music in general. By 1945 the "Irish" series disappeared altogether from active catalog lists.[14] Lacking a fresh infusion of immigrants to maintain interest, the popularity of Irish traditional music in America began a steady decline.

A similar rejection of Irish traditional music had already been taking place in Ireland in the 1930s. In its stead, popular music from England and America appealed to growing numbers, particularly those in urban areas, as well as elsewhere in the country. One of the reasons for Irish traditional music's demise during these years was its growing association with rural poverty. According to Jack Coen, a flute player who was born in 1925 near Woodford, County Galway, dance halls began catering less to traditional *ceili* dances and more often to the popular dance standards—foxtrots, quicksteps, and the like—from outside of Ireland: "Irish traditional music was something that they figured . . . was associated with the poor, the poor people. And they didn't want to be associated for that reason. Everybody wanted to associate with the rich and they want to be, do what they did, in the big dance halls; and then the brass band section, they all wanted to be associated with that."[15]

With this conflict between basic community social traditions and an evolving class consciousness came a movement away from traditional music and dance to the popular ballroom dance music of America and Europe. What had once been creative, essentially communal social activities of music making and dance were now becoming commodified and in the process, exclusionary by nature. "Things were changing as I was growing up and [traditional music] 'twas going out. Even to the point that in the smaller little town halls right around through the country, they used to up the price so high that the poor people couldn't afford to go to the dance. So they retreated back to some farmer's house and they played their traditional Irish music and they danced the old traditional sets."[16]

Fueling this interest in modern music and dance was the growing influence of radio in Ireland. Although the government-owned Radio Telefis Eireann (RTE) was founded in 1929, it did not broadcast traditional Irish music until 1933, when the Ballinakill *Ceili* Band was presented. Daniel Collins, a fiddler and president of Shanachie Records, believes that such neglect was intentional: "The government, not understanding the music themselves, felt that this kind of music was a . . . manifestation of being a very primitive, backward people. . . . The government has always felt that people, that the elite people in Ireland sort of always had been ashamed of the regular ordinary—that's my opinion—of the regular, ordinary people."[17]

Although traditional Irish music did not die out altogether, it increasingly took a back seat to popular ballroom dance music. Local bands that had once played *ceili* music now heard the sounds of early big band music and many adapted their instrumentation to approximate the new sound. Forward-looking traditional musicians expanded their marketability by learning "modern" instruments such as the saxophone and piano accordion. Martin Mulhaire, a button accordionist who now lives in Flushing, Queens, recalls his father's band from Eyrecourt, County Galway during the 1930s: "He had a band at that time, which was unusual, I guess, out in the middle of the country. He had a *ceili* band, and he had, what he called, a modern band which did waltzes and what was popular music in them days. The songs I remember from back then were like Frank Sinatra, Bing Crosby. . . . They would do whatever was popular anyway in them days in the band. In them days, it was just drums, if there was a piano in the place, they would use piano. Fiddles and flutes were the dominant instruments. Later on, they got a saxophone player."[18]

Traditional flutist Jack Coen lived in the same part of Galway and remembers the Mulhaires' band well: "I saw [Martin Mulhaire] in Ireland, singing in his father's band when he was about eight years old. His father had a dance band, well, he played everything that was needed for people's entertainment or amusement. . . . If they needed *ceili* music, they played that. Or if you needed the other stuff, they played that."[19]

In addition to the local bands that played both *ceili* and popular music, the trend toward the modern, non-Irish musical styles in Ireland spawned a number of American-style dance bands that during the 1940s traveled and performed outside of their towns but primarily within their home county. Performing in dance halls for weddings, dinners, and other social functions, these bands were often quite formal: the players wore tuxedos and sat while they played, reading music off charts mounted on music stands—a far cry from Irish traditional music that was learned by ear and played in a more relaxed, communal style.

Irish big band instrumentation typically included piano, drums, piano accordion, violin, and a variety of wind instruments (trumpet, saxophone, clarinet). Musical repertoire included a mix of popular Irish songs, some traditional instrumental music for *ceili* dancing, and big band selections learned via the radio waves: the BBC from England and, in the late 1940s, via the American Armed Forces Network broadcast from Germany. Demand for these semilocal bands was high and jobs were plentiful.

Many dance bands modeled themselves after the more prominent big bands that traveled throughout Ireland. The most popular of these ensembles was the Mick Delahunty Orchestra, a 12-piece group that formed in 1943 and played a different venue every night of the week, often seven nights in a row. Brendan Ward, a native of Foxford, County Mayo, who later immigrated to New York, joined the Mick Delahunty Orchestra in 1952. He remembers that Ireland danced up a storm during these years: "In fact, the dances in Ireland in those years were, generally from nine until three or two in the morning, ten until three. Some parts of the country . . . we played from ten until six. And in summertime, the sun would be brilliantly shining in the window in the morning and we were still playing."[20]

Brendan Ward's contributions to the Mick Delahunty Orchestra as music arranger and instrumentalist were considerable for it was ultimately his arrangements that gave Delahunty's orchestra its trademark sound. The orchestra had been playing "stock music"—standards from the big band era such as "In The Mood" and "American Patrol." But it was Ward who captured the Glenn Miller sound and adapted it to Irish popular songs.

> Nobody [in Ireland] seemed to know how to write, to get that sound that Miller got. . . . And the moment I heard it, I knew exactly how he was getting it. He was using a lead clarinet on top playing the melody . . . and a tenor saxophone one octave below, playing the same melody. In between there were three instruments playing very close harmony.
>
> And I started to write for Mick, not Miller stuff now, but Irish music . . . That's one thing that Mick became very famous for even after I left him. He

was able to play Moore's melodies, "Love's Roses," "Believe Me If All Those Endearing Young Charms," etc. . . . It's very easy to understand, even a person who is not a musician can clearly hear the melody there. One problem, I think, that there was with the American music . . . was that you didn't hear a melody, and the average man on the street has to hear a melody, particularly an Irish person has to hear a melody.[21]

Ward's arrangements proved to be on target, as noted in a 1959 article in New York's *Irish Echo* about an early Mick Delahunty performance: "With a stroke of sheer genius, his orchestra opened up with a simple, old-time waltz. beautifully played, with emphasis on the melody. The kind of familiar, well-loved lyrics [the audience] could sing as they danced."[22]

What Ward and Mick Delahunty's orchestra succeeded in doing was to create and popularize a hybrid genre of music. Familiar Irish songs (popular, not necessarily traditional) were recontextualized in the contemporary style of American big band music. As local dance bands catered to the developing dual interests of their audience for *ceili* dances as well as the popular dance standards, Delahunty's music went one step further and offered a similar parallel using *popular* Irish (as opposed to traditional) and contemporary American music. In this regard, Delahunty's orchestra offered a cultural bridge between the familiar and the new, a statement of modern Irishness within the larger context of developing popular culture.

Shortages of consumer goods and rising unemployment marked the years in Ireland just after World War II.[23] Small farms and large families forced the young Irish to seek work elsewhere, but with little industry in Ireland, jobs were scarce, leaving many with little choice but to emigrate. The increase in immigration during the latter half of the 1940s was notable: between 1941 and 1945, only 1,059 Irish came to the United States whereas 26,444 arrived between 1946 and 1950.[24]

Immigration to the United States further increased when Congress passed the Immigration and Nationality Act of 1952 (McCarran-Walter Act) allowing, among other things, unrestricted immigration from the Western Hemisphere and a stated preference for those with relatives who were American citizens. Thus favoring Irish immigrants, this bill opened the doors wide to a surge of new arrivals, and 48,362 Irish arrived in the United States between 1951 and 1960.

A number of traditional musicians arrived in New York City during the early years of this renewed immigration in the late 1940s. Indeed, an advertisement placed in the *Irish Echo* on November 12, 1949, invites membership in the "Emerald Musical Society, Inc. (A Benevolent Society)": "The Emerald Musical Society, Inc. is composed of Irish Musicians who have played Irish Music professionally all their lives. The Society was formed with the intention of providing needy assistance to our members when emergencys [*sic*] exist. . . . It is these men, whom we credit with keeping the traditional Irish Music alive. . . . We have in the past year admitted to membership a number of Irish Musicians recently arrived from Ireland. We hope the arrivals will continue to join our group and welcome them to work side by side with us."[25]

Like many immigrant groups, the newly arrived Irish of this era were able to join established immigrant institutions; in the case of traditional musicians, there were, aside from the Emerald Music Society, many Irish American county societies, the Gaelic League, and several traditional music clubs that sponsored *seisúns*. Through these organizations, some of the newly arrived traditional musicians found opportunities to socialize and meet others with similar interests. Once connected, there were private house parties and *seisúns* that took place on a regular basis.

In the late 1940s it was possible to find employment as a traditional musician in New York. Once a job was obtained, however, it often offered a less than satisfactory lifestyle. Tom Doherty, for example, emigrated from his native Mountcharles, County Donegal, in 1948. He recalls being offered—and subsequently turning down—a job playing traditional music on his melodeon (a single-row button accordion) in a pub on Closson Avenue in Brooklyn: "I was hired right away to play for Friday night, Saturday night, and Sunday night. My brother-in-law says 'No, you've got to get a job. . . . Because you're finished in the saloon at 4:00 am and [then] you'd go home and you're up again at 11:00 am.' He says, 'Where you gonna go when you get up again except [back] to the saloon and then to play there that night again.' He says 'It's no good.' So I took his advice and I'm not sorry that I did!"[26]

Paddy Reynolds, a fiddler from Ballinamuck, County Longford, also immigrated to New York in 1948. Like Doherty, he was offered a job playing traditional music.

> My first job I ever had in this country playing music was in the cabaret. . . . I was walking by, I was only a greenhorn, when I heard Irish music. I walked in, stood at the bar, and I was homesick as hell, and I was almost in tears. And there was the lousiest fiddler I'd ever heard in my life on the stage. . . . She came down . . . and I turned around and I complimented, I says "Nice music. You play nice music. My name is Paddy Reynolds." "Oh, Paddy Reynolds. Where are you from?" She had a husky voice; she liked her whiskey. And I said, "I'm from Co. Longford." "I'm from Tipperary meself." And we got talking and well, she says to me, "Do you play music?" And I said, "A little bit, on the fiddle." "Do you have it with you?" . . . and I got out the fiddle and I went up on the stage and I played that night. And that night I was employed for Friday, Saturday, and Sunday night, in Brooklyn, in Plunket's Cabaret. Incidentally, that's where I met my darling.[27]

Venues featuring both Irish traditional and popular music were plentiful in New York City during these years. They included large dance halls that had been catering to New York's Irish immigrant community since the 1920s and halls that were routinely rented by Irish societies for dinner dances and other occasions. A glance through issues of New York's *Irish Echo* during these years lists dozens of dance halls where Irish American dances took place throughout the week.

Irish American dances, in general, were sponsored by an array of Irish American societies and county associations. Most of the dances warranted some mention in the Irish weekly newspapers, and larger dances might garner a preview write-up complete with lists of committee members and organizers. If newsworthy (often made so if the reporter happened to attend the event), the larger dances would be written up in the following week's paper, along with who attended, the inevitable success of the event, and, of course, who provided the music.

The dance music at these events reflected a split allegiance to both Irish and American cultures. The late Louis Quinn, a native of County Armagh who came to New York in 1936, led "The Shamrock Minstrels," an ensemble specializing in both traditional Irish music and the popular foxtrots, quicksteps, and other American standards of the day. His band often featured three saxophonists, a banjo player, two fiddlers, a button accordionist, two trumpeters, a trombonist, a pianist, and a drummer. The traditional instrumentalists in "The Shamrock Minstrels" often learned the modern music, but not necessarily vice versa: "Well, the American music was in demand and so was the Irish music. That's why I got so many jobs at that time. . . . I leaned a bit towards the Irish dancing and these guys with all the modern numbers, they wouldn't get two jobs with that crowd because they didn't know enough of the traditional music, you know. So they'd come to me to get the jobs. And when I got called, I definitely would have to play the popular music and that's why I got some of these other fellows in here because they were very good."[28]

Pickup bands were also put together specifically for a job. Fiddler Paddy Reynolds recalls being hired for jobs in New York's dance halls as part of the traditional component of an otherwise popular ensemble. "You'd get jobs . . . usually two-, three-, and four-piece band jobs and one half of that band would be able to play American and the other half would play Irish. Now, the accompanist—and that was all pianos in those days—was always a professional who knew how to back up Irish music in all its forms as well as American music. So they used to dance set dancing. They used to dance the Stack of Barley, Varsovienna, old-time waltzes. . . . You always got the music to suit the blend of the people that would be there."[29]

By the 1950s, a distinctive popular musical aesthetic had solidified in New York's Irish community. Borrowing from a similar hybridized musical style developed simultaneously in Ireland and in the United States in the years before World War II, this new form took into account both repertoire as well as playing style and placed new demands on musicians. While always maintaining a definitive sense of "Irishness," the preferred dance music was moving away from the inclusion of traditional instruments and more toward a bona fide big band sound with increasing emphasis on brass and reed instruments. Irish musicians in New York attempted to adapt, often with mixed results. Paddy Noonan, a commercial Irish American musician and owner of Rego Records, is critical of the semiprofessional Irish musicians who played in New York City's dance halls at that time:

> The standard of music in Ireland was way ahead of what was happening here. All the ballrooms throughout Ireland featured big bands. You must realize that the [musicians at these New York] dances were people who were bus drivers, they were subway trainmen.... On the weekend, they were trying to play music ... And when the big immigration [started], people had been used to listening to big bands in Ireland all through the war years—Glen Miller, huge stuff. In fact, some of the big American bands used to tour Ireland. And a lot of [the immigrants], when they came over here, were surprised to hear such a different standard of music.[30]

Instrumentation and repertoire were undergoing similar changes. Whereas Irish American bands in the 1930s and 1940s moved with ease between traditional Irish dance tunes and popular American standards, now they played a larger percentage of modern music, often on traditional instruments. Brendan Ward, the former arranger and instrumentalist with Mick Delahunty's Orchestra, immigrated to New York in 1955. He recalls his reaction to hearing American music played on traditional instruments and vice versa. "You don't play a 'Darktown Strutter's Ball' on a button-keyed accordion. It just doesn't sound right.... And, by the same token, you cannot play [the *ceili* dance] 'The Stack of Barley' on the tenor saxophone.... It is not the sound that one would look for with the tenor saxophone. And a lot of recordings had been made around those years with the Irish music with the tenor saxophone with a very bad, bad vibrato, a very wide vibrato, and it just doesn't sound right."[31]

Finally, a distinctive Irish American band style was emerging with an emphasis on texture and arrangement. Dorothy Hayden, a longtime Irish radio host in New York City, inherited her radio position from her father, James A. Hayden. On his program, he played largely traditional Irish music in addition to popular Irish songs during his 13-year tenure on WARD. When his daughter took over as radio host after his death in 1943, she played less traditional music and catered instead to her audience's changing tastes. "Because you got the best songs coming out and the best singers and the best voices and everybody was in tune and they kept together, you know? ... And the music was arranged and it was great songs. [Popular singer] Carmel Quinn, she came in about '54 ... with the songs we were all singing. Real Irish songs, we would say ... the [traditional musicians] used to start together and finish together, you understand? There was no variation and no color to it. Music played continuously for two hours drives some people crazy."[32]

Thus as socializing patterns changed among the Irish immigrants in the United States, so did the rhythms and melodies to which they danced. This compromise—American arrangements, textures, and rhythms combined with a popular Irish repertoire—was thus both a creative response to the pressures of cultural adaptation and an important beacon of ethnic identity for the Irish as they adjusted to life in the new country.

All Roads Lead to the City Center Ballroom

Amidst the dozens of Irish dance halls in New York City during the 1950s, City Center in Manhattan stood out. Opening its doors on September 15, 1956, City Center would become the premier Irish dance hall in New York City and, arguably, in the United States. Under the shrewd direction of County Kerry native Bill Fuller, City Center developed its reputation by its unique combination of big band music by Brendan Ward and his 12-piece "All Star" Orchestra; shorter sets of Irish *ceili* dance music and old-time waltzes by piano accordionist Paddy Noonan; and guest appearances by Irish entertainers, country and western bands, and later, in the early 1960s, Irish showbands. Local talent was also spotlighted in talent and dance competitions.

In its heyday, up to 2,000 people reportedly would pack City Center on a Saturday night. In general, the audiences were the newly arrived Irish immigrants and, to a lesser extent, Irish Americans. Most hailed from rural Ireland and had danced to big band music in Ireland's dance halls before immigration.

City Center's immense success was due to a number of factors, some of which were fortuitous coincidences of time and place, others strategically developed by Bill Fuller. Aside from attracting an instant—and growing—audience, City Center, at West 55th Street between Sixth and Seventh avenues, was centrally and ideally located at the hub of several subway lines connecting Queens, Brooklyn, and the Bronx to Manhattan. Thus, City Center was an easy and safe trip for immigrants who tended to live in Irish enclaves in these boroughs. In addition, City Center's location in fashionable midtown Manhattan lent an air of sophistication and more importantly, a sense of integration—at least physically—with mainstream New York City nightlife and culture.

Moreover, City Center, like other New York Irish dance halls, offered an essential hub for socializing, dancing, and finding romance and spouses. In what was to many new immigrants from rural Ireland an often harsh and impersonal city, City Center offered a sort of haven. Accordionist Paddy Noonan recalled, "We're a people that like to stick together. City Center, you'd go there on a Friday night, you'd probably meet seven or eight people that you knew from home, that came out that week. City Center, if you lived in Cleveland, on a long weekend, you'd pile into a car and drive to New York. People from Boston would come down. Because they'd meet 100 people that they knew in Ireland. . . . It was a meeting place . . . You wouldn't feel at home any place else."[33] Martin Mulhaire, who was hired by Bill Fuller in 1958 to play the Irish *ceili* dance sets on the button accordion at City Center, remembers the dance hall scene vividly:

"They came mostly to meet people . . . [It] was typical to dancing in Ireland where there was not very much emphasis on drinking, even though you could get a drink at the bar, a sandwich, but people just came and stood around the floor, girls and boys together, and the dances were called out and they just danced all night long. They danced 'The Stack of Barley,' old-time waltzes, all that. They would dance to all the new songs as well: foxtrots, quicksteps, slow waltzes, slow foxtrots, words that have gone by the wayside."[34]

And dance they did. On a typical weekend evening, Brendan Ward's orchestra played the popular American dance standards and Ward's unique Americanized Irish songs polished during his tenure with Mick Delahunty's orchestra. With continental and Latin music also in demand, Ward led his 12-piece orchestra through Strauss waltzes, rumbas, cha-chas, and tangos. After a 40-minute set, the big band would take a break, and an accordionist, pianist, and drummer would take the stage and play a 20-minute set of old-time Irish waltzes, an occasional continental waltz such as "The Blue Danube," and popular Irish songs. After Brendan Ward's orchestra returned for another 40-minute set, the Irish accordionist would follow with 20 more minutes of *ceili* dance music—traditional set pieces, jigs, and reels, depending on the dance. Brendan Ward recalls the popularity of these Irish traditional sets, most often played by Paddy Noonan on the piano accordion: "It was an Irish ballroom and [Bill Fuller] was catering to Irish people, 100% Irish people, who wanted . . . the Irish music. A certain percentage of them did. I must say that whatever Paddy played, they did enjoy. He could play 'The Siege of Ennis,' maybe one in the night. I think he couldn't have done two in one night, they might get tired of it, but they would do one dance in one night, which would take about 15 minutes."[35]

Paddy Noonan's sets did indeed offer his audiences a chance to dance *ceili* or group figure dances. Yet these sets were, in effect, a watered-down version of traditional music and dance. *Ceili* dance itself succeeded the more traditional and regionally based set dancing. With few exceptions, set dancing did not survive the transition to America, in part because of the rapid popularization of the less localized and more uniform style of *ceili* dancing, as it came to be called. In general, *ceili* dances were standardized and notated around the turn of the century, thus are less reflective of a specific community or regional style.

Paddy Noonan played jigs, reels, and set pieces for his 20-minute *ceili* sets at City Center. These tunes were played in a different style from that of traditional Irish music—largely unadorned (as opposed to highly ornamented) and propulsively rhythmic, as opposed to maintaining a subtle inner pulse and swing.[36] In addition, Noonan played the piano accordion—a more contemporary cousin to the button accordion—and an instrument not commonly found in Irish traditional music; rather, it is most often used in commercial Irish music. The resultant Irish dance and music offered by City Center followed a standardized and semitraditional style, a compromise gesture toward Ireland's folk culture and the more palatable, commercial culture preferred by Irish America.

Another reason behind City Center's alternating sets of American music and Irish *ceili* music was the union requirement that bands play for no more than 40 minutes, followed by a strictly enforced 20-minute break.[37] A smaller band was thus ideal for keeping the audience in the dance hall by offering nonstop music throughout the evening. By all accounts, City Center's audiences were pleased with this dual offering of music and the dance hall was packed virtually every weekend.

City Center—and other New York City Irish dance halls in the 1950s—offered more *ceili* dance music than did the dance halls in Ireland. Aside from the nostalgia and homesickness inherent in the immigrant experience, the dual offerings of New York's Irish dance halls served the all-important purpose of providing a bridge between the traditional culture the Irish immigrants had left behind and the new American lifestyle they encountered. Mainstream American culture was attractive in its sophistication and associations with commercialized glamour. Nevertheless, the Irish ethnic affiliation was strong and deeply rooted. In effect, City Center borrowed from both Irish and American social and musical aesthetics and created a comfortable compromise.

The Irish dance hall and big band era was also the big dollar era. Issues of the *Irish Echo* and the *Irish Advocate* in the late 1950s contain ads for "Irish and American dancing" at the larger dance halls and detail the group featured that week. In contrast, a typical issue included only occasional (and much smaller) advertisements for a traditional *ceili* dance sponsored by the Gaelic League or by an Irish American society. Matty Connolly, who immigrated to the United States from County Monaghan in 1960, is an All-Ireland uilleann pipe champion and an electric bass player. He was frequently hired to play popular music and rarely, if ever, traditional music. "The dollar sign. There was more money to be made playing the other type of music than there was playing traditional music. And for that reason, I was playing mainly showband music those years. And any piping I done was just a tune with my mom and myself, just for our own enjoyment."[38]

New York's Irish immigrant community, thus, was abandoning whatever vestiges of folk culture its members had known prior to immigration. The most visible and public displays of traditional culture—music and dance—were relegated to private house *seisúns* and the occasional *ceili*, events that were, in general, removed from the Irish immigrant mainstream. This aesthetic would extend into the late 1950s and early 1960s as one style of popular Irish music was replaced by a new one.

Showband Music

The late 1950s in Ireland saw the meteoric rise in popularity of a new wave of popular music, loosely termed "showband music." With television not arriving in Ireland until the end of 1961, radio was the sole source for the new sounds of popular music: rock 'n roll, "skiffle," and country and western, all of which emanated from England and America via the BBC, Radio Luxembourg, and the American Armed Forces Network broadcast from Germany. Showbands performed covers of these popular styles plus standard *ceili* dance tunes and popular Irish songs. In doing so, traveling showbands served to personify the faceless performers heard on the radio. Simultaneously, a revived Irish economy put money into the pockets of teenagers, and a renewed optimism sent them out in droves to the dance halls.

And *ceili* dancing it was not. Rock 'n roll spread throughout Ireland, largely replacing big band music as the popular music genre of the day. With strong rhythm sections and an emphasis on guitars and brass, showbands offered stylized (and provocative) showmanship, matching stage costumes (mohair suits were especially popular), a versatile repertoire, and an occasional comedy act. By the early 1960s the showband era was in full swing, and Ireland's roads were crisscrossed by scores of groups in their buses heading to gigs. Their destinations were the newly built ballrooms that dotted the countryside and cities.[39]

Of the many showbands that got their start between 1958 and 1965, the Royal Showband, with lead singer Brendan Bowyer of County Waterford, was the most famous. Bowyer's stage presence was modeled after Elvis Presley and he became to Ireland, in fact, what Presley was to the rest of the Western world. Bowyer caused girls to faint and the Royal Showband quickly spawned dozens of imitators. Bowyer recalls that, in no time, showbands became big business with the larger groups earning unheard of amounts of money: "People started building ballrooms. It could happen on a crossroads! It was amazing. There were parts of County Mayo, for example, small towns that wouldn't have a population of 1500 or 2000 and there'd be 3000 at the dance, you know, because they'd drive for miles."[40]

The showband scene coincided with the rise in popularity of early British rock bands, notably the Beatles, who in 1962 opened for the Royal Showband at the Liverpool Empire Theatre. But showbands were essentially copycat bands. This, explains Bowyer, was in part the reason why the Royal Showband remained the most famous band in Ireland while the Beatles become the most famous in the world: "The lesson we should have learned from the Beatles was that we should have gotten away and started to do our own stuff. We were making so much money doing everybody else's stuff and were so overwhelmed with our success that we neglected to look farther [than] that."[41]

Brendan Bowyer and the Royal Showband first toured the United States in 1960 during the Lenten season. In New York City, they performed at City Center in dance halls packed with recent Irish emigrants. Their style, sound, and success inspired the formation of several local showbands and the craze quickly took off in New York. Martin Mulhaire and Matty Connolly, for example, both traditional Irish musicians, pooled their talents and formed the six-piece Majestic Showband in December, 1963. The instrumentation included drums, tenor saxophone/clarinet, rhythm and lead guitars, bass guitar, and vocalists.

Hired in 1963 by the newly opened Red Mill on Jerome Avenue in the Bronx, the Majestic Showband played three nights a week from 9:00 p.m. to 1:00 a.m. for the next 10 years. According to Matty Connolly, their popularity stemmed from their variety and approach to the music. "A showband is a band that does a little bit of everybody's music . . . light rock, country music, Irish music, a little bit of Irish traditional, they dip into everbody's pot and this is what seemed to go at that particular time. . . . The term showband really means, I guess, to give a good presence like you're on stage. That you're just not up there just playing an instrument, but in addition to doing that you're having a reasonably good time. And you're supposed to act and look the part."[42]

Like the groups of the big band era, Irish showbands also incorporated a traditional Irish element into their performances. In the Majestic Showband, Martin Mulhaire played mostly electric guitar and a little bit of button accordion for the old-time waltzes, largely "out of necessity because . . . everybody had to have an accordion in a band, or you got no work." Mulhaire recalls that other than that, the differences between the big bands and the showbands were notable: "Showbands . . . stood up and they wore uniforms and they were more alive looking on a stage than the old fashioned [big] bands. [Big bands] sat down in front of music stands and they read sheet music and they never looked at the people. But the showband scene, you stood up and played from memory and it was a more fun thing to watch than to participate in."[43]

Like the big bands, Irish showbands offered their audiences a popular and contemporary sound, yet uniquely Irish. Again, the showband era satisfied New York's Irish community with a musical expression that was quintessentially theirs, while also sounding and appearing closer to the music of the mainstream.

In 1965 Congress passed the Immigration and Nationality Act amendment, which in effect cut off the steady stream of Irish immigrants to America. With no new audiences of young, unattached immigrants in search of a night life, the dance halls closed, one by one, and the showband era ended. As in Ireland, the dance halls gave way to bars and discos, and with television beaming pop stars directly into living rooms, the showband's role as copycat was no longer fresh and became redundant.

A myriad of reasons explains the general abandonment of Irish traditional culture in New York during the 1950s. One of the most commonly stated rationales is that many Irish immigrants—particularly those from the larger towns in Ireland—were simply not exposed much to traditional music before immigration. As discussed earlier, the main socializing forces were found in the dance hall scene where contemporary European and American music had become the rage. This trend was further enhanced by the growing influence of radio and, into the 1940s, by American film. As traditional music fell into disuse, the only association that many Irish had were its negative stereotypes. Depending on the region of Ireland from which they came, many Irish immigrants were thus aware only of what they perceived to be shameful and loaded images and were ignorant of the positive role that traditional music had and could play in community self-identity and expression. For example, Daniel Collins traveled to Ireland at age 12 in 1950 to compete in the Fleadh Ceoil na Eireann (the annual Irish traditional music competitions). He recalls that there were few outstanding Irish-born traditional players but plenty of overt hostility toward the music in general.

> I'm in this little town, Abbeyfeale, Mountcollins, County Limerick, my mother's village . . . and there were a bunch of people at this dance who were relatives of mine also . . . And we were going to play a few tunes, you know. . . . An uproar broke out, a bloody goddamn uproar broke out. And they opened the doors up, the double doors, and they threw them out, bing! We would have been thrown out if my relatives weren't there [because] we were playing Irish music.
>
> The fight was about, needless to say, we're going to stop Teresa Brewer playing "Put Another Nickel in the Nickelodeon," we've got some Americans here that are going to perform some Irish music. The place went into an uproar. You'd think that we had gone into a church and peed, like, on the main aisle. Something as bad as that. It was worse. That we had desecrated, you know, we had, like, insulted the mass.[44]

A more subtle form of this antagonism came to the United States with the surge of immigrants in the 1950s. Flutist Jack Coen worked for several years as a bartender at City Center and every weekend observed his fellow immigrants dancing to modern music to the neglect of traditional. According to Coen, the traditional music scene in New York had so deteriorated that he was forced to put his flute away for several years after he immigrated in 1949.

> They used to call it the "diddely-diddely music." That's why I hate that word. It's poisonous. It's a slur on Irish traditional music, because this is what the progressive Irish people, or people who thought they were progressive back in those days, this is what they called it.[45]

> A lot of people didn't even want to be associated with us Irish people! They thought it was degrading, or I don't know what you'd call it. They thought it was Rocky Mountain music that should be left where we got it and not be brought from there at all. That's strange, isn't it? But that was the way it was in those days.[46]

Similarly, Tommy Makem, who, along with the Clancy Brothers, brought Irish folk song to international prominence, remembers his audience's attitude in the late 1950s toward singing traditional, as opposed to popular, Irish songs: "When we started out, we refused to sing for Irish audiences because they would all be into Bing Crosby, 'Danny Boy,' things like that. That's what they were being fed by the radio programs at the time. . . . They figured this was all there was to it. They had left Ireland and sort of looked down on Irish music. You were a peasant if you sang that kind of thing. These people were trying to drag themselves up by their boot straps and you know, be ultra-respectable. It wasn't what we were about."[47]

Commercial musicians, promoters, and others active in the Irish popular music scene had a somewhat different bias. Piano accordionist Paddy Noonan remembers some of the traditional music in New York during the 1950s was "rough": "They were what they called 'tenement house disturbers.' You had people playing violins that were out of tune. You had pianos that were always out of tune. . . . You had bad music, you had terrible music. . . . Some of the stuff that they're passing as Irish music and playing is a bit primitive. . . . in the quality of the recording, the quality of playing, quality of accompaniment. . . . they're an embarrassment."[48]

Dorothy Hayden cites an alleged lack of professionalism owing to alcoholism on the part of some traditional Irish musicians—a stereotype that ultimately worked to the traditional musicians' disadvantage. In contrast, the drinking habits and professional behavior of ensembles and individuals specializing in hybridized Irish American music were less harshly judged and thus seen as more appropriate for venues such as City Center and as guests on Hayden's long-running radio program: the traditional musicians "kind of kept to themselves a little. . . . You wouldn't even hire [them]. You know what I mean, because you didn't know if [they were] going to be sober or whatever. People wanted to know why was I making a fuss over this Paddy Noonan. . . . because he was dedicated to it. You knew [when] his band came in and the band was clean and dressed and presentable and you know what I mean. And they were sober and industrious."[49]

More important, the association of traditional Irish music with poverty or the lower class came into conflict with the "American dream" harbored by many immigrants during these years. The 1950s and 1960s were eras of strong unions and relatively high salaries and offered the opportunity for upward mobility on the part of the working and middle class. The choice of social activity thus had to fit the prevailing American ideal, and ballroom music and dance were appropriate public displays. This trend, recalls Dorothy Hayden, was also manifested in the quest for material gain. "Any of the girls that were [here] in the 50s . . . they'd stay home and their homes would be much more beautiful than their mothers'. . . . You see, they have, there's two cars in every garage, there's wall-to-wall. It was important to get all you can get."[50] The prevailing American political issues of the day were also at odds with ethnic traditional culture. The McCarthy hearings in the early 1950s gave rise to a strongly pro-American sentiment, especially toward immigrant groups in the States. The implicit corollary—an unspoken but extant condemnation of ethnic diversity—pervaded American society.

In the Irish community, this sense of outsider status was reinforced throughout the 1950s and into the 1960s by the media in both subtle and overt ways. The *Irish Advocate*, for example, ran an advertisement on October 8, 1960, issued by J. Edgar Hoover, director of the Federal Bureau of Investigation in which readers were urged to "Fight COMMUNISM and Preserve AMERICA." One of the ways this could be done was to "Inform yourself. Know your country—its history, tradition, and heritage."[51] By implication, the celebration of one's *native* history, tradition, and heritage might thus have been construed as anti-American. Put another way, it is possible that it may have been simpler for the majority of Irish immigrants to celebrate aspects of American lifestyle and, by necessity, ignore elements of their native culture in an effort to quietly assimilate.

For some, the mainstream movement away from overt celebrations of traditional Irish culture was also an unconscious response to a legacy of longtime political and social forces in Ireland. Martin Mulhaire, the son and grandson of traditional instrumentalists in Eyrecourt, County Galway, came to the United States in 1958 when he was on tour with the Tulla *Ceili* Band. He opted to remain in New York and for a time, filled in as the accordionist in Bill Fuller's City Center. After several years, however, Mulhaire put aside the button accordion in favor of the electric guitar and played popular showband music almost exclusively. In Mulhaire's opinion, the lack of public interest in Irish traditional music was a result, in part, of years of British political oppression:

> That goes back deep into our heritage of British occupation. When the British came to Ireland, they tried to destroy everything that was Irish and what they couldn't destroy, they tried to make you feel ashamed of. They abolished the language, you weren't allowed to fly green flags, you weren't allowed to play music. The music was played, but it was played sort of underground. And that feeling has persisted I'd say, even to this day, to a point where most Irish musicians are really ashamed of their music because they were made to feel that way. It wasn't mainstream. . . . Along with that came a kind of reserve where they kept it to themselves and they didn't play for other people or they felt ashamed to play for other people.
>
> Having come from this suppression of Irish music, then come to another country, I guess they felt that it was time to put that behind them or put it away. They kept it in the back of the minds and all that, but they didn't come over to demonstrate their Irishness. They came over to blend in, to become part of American society, which they did. They adapted to American ways, to American music, to American customs. They still had a love for Irish music, but it wasn't in the forefront.[52]

And there were the personal considerations. For some musicians, immigration caused homesickness, which was soothed by playing traditional music; for others, such as Mulhaire, it only served to exacerbate:

> There were strong ties, and the sound of the accordion, it made me melancholy. I was looking for something else to put my time into, so I more or less left the accordion to one side and started playing the guitar more. Because I found it brought me more happiness than the accordion did. The accordion just reminded me of what I had left. I was trying to make a new life.

Traditional music seemed to fit in better over there than it did here. . . . It was transported here and it sounded more foreign here. It didn't sound foreign in Ireland.[53]

In a discussion of performance contexts for Irish traditional and commercial or hybrid musics, Mick Moloney writes that "the more public the context, the more commercial, theatrical and/or hybridized the genres of Irish music that would characteristically be performed. The more private or controlled environment, the more conducive it is to the performance of the older, more traditional forms of music."[54] With the mainstream Irish opting for American and Irish American hybrid music genres, the traditional instrumental music scene throughout the 1950s was quiet and restricted largely to private or semipublic venues in Irish neighborhoods, as well as *ceili* dances organized by Irish groups. Fiddler Andy McGann was born in 1928 in West Harlem. He recalls that as the 1950s wore on, New York City public venues for traditional Irish music became increasingly rare. He played "mostly at these *ceili*s, Gaelic League *ceili*s, the *Feis* and various house parties, or music sessions. There was a music club going on at the time, once a month. These were about the only occasions where traditional music was played. It was mostly sessions, session music."[55]

House sessions were the most private venue for traditional music during these years. Unlike *ceili* dances and the dance hall scene, house sessions focused primarily on strictly traditional instrumental music and less on dance. Some of these sessions have become legendary:

> Fiddler Paddy Reynolds: [James] "Lad" O'Beirne and Andy McGann, and I, and Gerry Wallace and later on Felix Dolan, . . . we used to get together in the homes for session in the Bronx, that's were I used to live . . . 138th Street and Cypress Avenue . . . which was 100% Irish there in those days. . . . There was plenty of music and the neighbors loved it. In the summertime, they'd all be sitting with the windows opened and listening to us. In those days, there was no air conditioning; there was only fans in the windows. And the fans used to blow out exhaust and they'd blow out everything, including the music.[56]

> James O'Beirne Jr.: The sessions of music in our home in the South Bronx, in our apartment, were impromptu . . . and they were generally on Saturday night. There might be 10 or 12 or 15 musicians there. And . . . there were occasions where they went on all night actually til dawn. I remember on a number of occasions, my mother would shove all the musicians off to church in the morning . . . and she would make a big breakfast and they would all come back, have a good breakfast, and play again.[57]

> Fiddler/pianist Maureen Glynn Connolly: The music was all around me because we used to go to a lot of house parties back then even when I was very small and there was always Irish music and stepdancers. I started dancing before I actually started taking lessons because I saw it in front of me. The music was constantly going.[58]

Semipublic sessions also were held on a regular basis in a number of halls and clubs in New York's Irish neighborhoods. In the years just after World War

II, for example, fiddler James "Lad" O'Beirne organized "The Irish Music and Social Club of Greater New York" at the Vasa Temple in the South Bronx. Attracting upward of 70 traditional musicians, these monthly sessions proved immensely popular for young and old musician alike. Similarly, in 1956 the Irish Musicians Association, Inc., was established by musicians Louis E. Quinn of New York, Frank Thornton of Chicago, and Ed Reavy of Philadelphia "to promote and preserve our heritage."[59] Branches of the association were located throughout the New York metropolitan area, each named after a famous traditional musician (the Patsy Touhey Branch in Brooklyn, the Paddy Killoran Branch in Manhattan, the Louis E. Quinn Branch in Long Island, and so on).[60]

In all, Irish music associations and clubs and the sessions they sponsored served several important functions. First, they offered opportunities for traditional musicians to connect with others during an era in which the traditional arts went largely publicly uncelebrated by the majority of Irish. Second, the music associations and clubs, with their often formal—and indeed "incorporated"—infrastructure, put a legitimizing modern twist on what had been for centuries familial and community traditions, one that had eschewed organization and relied on spontaneity. By erecting a formal structure around the essentially informal practice of traditional music, these associations created an aura of modernity by pointing to membership, goals, hierarchy, and financial support. Sessions thus offered a new community context for what was perceived as a dying tradition.[61] They also encouraged and preserved a folk-rooted identity among the older musicians and, perhaps most important, they offered a sense of continuity and traditionally based Irish identity for children of the musicians.

Other venues for Irish traditional music were the weekly Gaelic League *ceili* dances that took place in each borough of New York City beginning in 1940. Established in Ireland in 1893 with the aim of "keeping alive the traditions of Ireland," the Gaelic League focused primarily on the teaching and practice of the Irish language and dance as well as Irish history and, secondarily, the music. Accused from time to time of elitism in their approach to Irish culture, members of the Gaelic League in New York City eagerly advertised their regular *ceilis* and encouraged participation by all members of the community. The Gaelic League did, however, place a certain amount of emphasis on the importance of associating Irish traditional culture with respectful appearance and behavior. Dr. Frank Holt, the former president of the New Jersey Gaelic League, attended Gaelic League *ceilis* since the 1940s: "You went well dressed. You'd dress in a tie and a shirt and a suit and the girls would dress in a dress. We did not come from well-to-do families, but we dressed properly . . . We had a couple in the Bronx Gaelic League who were assigned the job of when a stranger would come in to the hall, you'd pay particular attention to them to make them feel welcomed. And very frequently . . . we'd break up a couple who enjoy dancing together and put them with a couple who've never danced before."[62]

The Gaelic League had their pick of the finest of New York's traditional musicians to play at *ceilis* and the standard of music at these events, by all accounts, was very high. According to Dr. Frank Holt, musicians received little if any payment for their services, but "they had a skill, a knowledge, and wanted to put it to use."[63]

Like the Gaelic League, the United Irish Counties Association also offered a venue for Irish folk arts in New York via the annual *Feis* (festival). Beginning in 1932, the *Feis* was a day of competitions in traditional Irish music, song, dance, language, and a variety of other cultural expressions such as Irish costumes, elocution, and recitation. During its heyday, thousands of Irish and Irish American children competed in the *Feis* and the winners proudly walked off with gleaming medals.

The *Feis* served as an opportunity for New York's Irish community to meet and socialize in the name of Irish culture. Held outdoors on the grounds of Iona College, Fordham University, or Hunter College, the *Feis* also sought to encourage Irish American children to learn various aspects of "the culture of the Gael." In doing so, promoters of the *Feis* saw the event as a "great force in the promotion of juvenile decency."[64] The *Feis'* objectives also expanded as needed to incorporate issues of timely political concern: "Time and distance has [*sic*] not lessened the love and interest of the United Irish Counties Association for the motherland. We have a permanent Anti-Partition Committee which has campaigned and will continue to campaign by every means at its disposal, to hasten the departure of England's Army of Occupation from the Counties of Antrim, Armagh, Down, Derry, Fermanagh, and Tyrone and for the establishment of a thirty-two county Irish Republic for the Irish Nation."[65]

And lest the American public interpret such a display of proud Irish culture as overly nationalistic in tenor (and thus anti-American), the program booklet hastens to add that "love of Ireland has not diminished the loyalty of the people of Irish birth and descent in the United States. They stand shoulder to shoulder with all loyal Americans in combating the evil forces that seek to destroy our freedom—our religion—our homes. The Irish have always answered America's call. They will always respond promptly."[66] The *Feis* served as a significant display of Irish ethnicity both to New York's Irish community and to the general public. By 1955, it expanded its goals to also include the fostering of pluralism in America. The program booklet outlines this in rhetoric characteristic of the era: "Many contemporary sociologists in America see the New York Irish *Feis* as a great unifying force in the U.S. They feel that its cultural program is a rare and valuable gift from Ireland to America. . . . Being intended for all Americans, irrespective of their national origin, color, or creed, the *Feis* is an instrument which sows seeds of good will not only in New York but across the U.S."[67]

Writing in the 1955 *Feis* program booklet, Judge James J. Comerford, the chairman of the United Irish Counties *Feis*, dates the beginning of the event to 918 B.C. and portrays it as "a direct descendant in modern times of the Ancient

Feis of Tara": "It is a historical fact, long established, that the early Irish over the centuries B.C. had often been in contact with the Ancient East and that on the civilization and cultural levels of the period, Ireland was highly developed and advanced. The *Feis* of Tara, therefore, is not to be looked upon as a figment of the imagination."[68]

The association of the New York Irish *Feis* with events held centuries earlier can be viewed in terms of Eric Hobsbawm's theory of "invented traditions," whereby events and rituals are created with reference to a largely fictitious or mythological past. From this historical precedent, Hobsbawm writes, traditions are created "not because old ways are no longer available or viable, but because

In a City Hall ceremony, Mayor William O'Dwyer accepts the subway poster announcing the seventeenth annual *Feis* of the United Irish Counties Association, to be held on the grounds of Fordham University in June 1949. The *Feis* was a one-day affair that, by the 1940s, drew 15,000 spectators for 975 amateurs in seventy-five competitive events, including voice, choir, solo instruments, bands, step and figure dancing, Irish language, storytelling, recitation, essay, design, and athletics. Next to the St. Patrick's Day parade, the UICA *Feis* was the biggest and most visible Irish event in New York City for fifty years. Left to right: Joseph F. McLoughlin, Tommy Ayres, Mayor William O'Dwyer, Consul General of Ireland Garth Healy, and James J. Comerford. (McLoughlin, from County Galway, was cochairman of the *Feis*; Ayres, from County Clare, was president of the UICA; O'Dwyer was a native of County Mayo; and Comerford, later chairman of the St. Patrick's Day Parade Committee, was from County Kilkenny.) (From the collection of Rita McLoughlin FitzPatrick.)

they are deliberately not used or adapted."[69] Such is the case with New York's Irish community in the 1950s. The *Feis* was foremost a display of Irishness and ethnic pride as well as an attempt to re-create a tradition that sought to publicly acknowledge and validate Irish folk arts. Yet the *Feis* undermined these goals as it was a one-day celebration based on a claimed historical construct, rather than a celebration of the reality of everyday practice of folk arts in New York's Irish community.

Moreover, the *Feis* sought to equate folk arts with high arts. In some instances, the required pieces for the instrumental competitions were classical selections in addition to classical arrangements of Irish tunes. Maureen Glynn Connolly, a fiddler and pianist born in Brooklyn in 1950, remembers learning pieces by Bach as well as arranged Irish tunes to compete at the *Feis* in the late 1950s and early 1960s. There were also Western classical categories for the violin, harp, and voice.[70] Finally, infrequent recognition, if any, was afforded the master practitioners of Irish music in the community, even though many of them labored for hours on the day of the *Feis*, playing music for the dance competitions. As fiddler Brian Conway noted: "It just didn't seem to be important to the people who were running the *Feis*es who it was that was playing for the dancers and it was a shame. And obviously the attitude of the people who were making the decisions with respect to the dancing was that you really didn't need much more than a machine to do it. And it's a real shame that it came to that because there, in later years, the musicians didn't become important."[71]

Other criticism focused on the *Feis* as reveling in symbolism rather than in reality, thereby neglecting traditional musicians. Fiddler/pianist Maureen Glynn Connolly said that "trophies, the competitiveness itself, is what has become so horrendous. The trophies are as tall as the ceiling here and they cost a fortune. And unfortunately, the [*Feis* organizers] had to blame the musician for what's happened. You know, they did the same thing to Mozart. They worked him to death and gave him a few shillings and the man came up with all this beautiful music. The same thing, blame the artist all the time."[72]

By focusing one day a year on the antiquity and grandeur of Irish arts, history, and culture, the *Feis* sought to re-create Irish folk arts in a manner more palatable to the prevailing aesthetics of the Irish community. To this end, the *Feis* attempted to legitimize the practice of Irish traditional culture in a modern, urban context. And while the *Feis* did indeed encourage children to learn to play instruments, speak the Irish language, and dance Irish steps, its competitive format laid more emphasis on individual accomplishment, rather than on the communal component of traditional music.

The *Feis*, then, can be seen as another manifestation of conflicted self-identity on the part of New York's Irish community during the 1950s. While attempting to paint a picture of continuity with a proud cultural past, the *Feis* successfully reinforced a strong sense of ethnicity among the immigrant Irish and Irish

Americans in New York. However, the result was a mixed message that in the end did little to allay the Irish community's ambivalence toward its folk culture.

The Revival and Beyond

A resurgence of interest in Irish traditional music had its beginnings in the late 1960s as a result of the confluence of a number of cultural and social developments both in the United States and in Ireland. Most influential was the international attention brought to Irish music by the Clancy Brothers and Tommy Makem with their gutsy renditions of Irish folk songs. Accompanying themselves on guitar and banjo, the Clancy Brothers and Tommy Makem sang traditional ballads in a manner that invited audience participation and was thus well in keeping with the communal spirit of the 1960s. Their success worldwide served as an affirmation of the cultural significance of traditional Irish song to both Irish immigrants and to Irish Americans.

In New York, this revival of interest in Irish traditional music was furthered by the Irish immigrant community, which in turn, directly benefited from it. Irish Americans who had been introduced to Irish song by the Clancy Brothers and Tommy Makem now turned their attention to the older masters of instrumental music. In addition, music *seisúns* began anew in New York City pubs and concerts of traditional bands from Ireland—Planxty, the Bothy Band, the Boys of the Lough, and the Chieftains, for example—were presented in both mainstream and Irish venues. Eventually, many of these venues began featuring the older traditional instrumentalists in New York.

The 1960s also saw the physical dissolution of many Irish neighborhoods throughout the boroughs of New York City. As the demographics of these neighborhoods changed, Irish families increasingly moved to the suburbs in Long Island, Westchester, and other metropolitan areas. For a number of Irish and Irish Americans in New York during the 1960s and 1970s, the loss of immediate physical community, combined with the outside recognition of Irish traditional culture, encouraged a reevaluation of heritage and community.

Furthermore, unlike earlier generations of Irish immigrants, those who came to the United States in the 1940s and 1950s were able to retain closer ties with Ireland via affordable transatlantic flights. As a consequence, Irish-born parents could renew an interest in their heritage and inspire the same in their children. The sense of importance of ethnicity thus rekindled, the late 1960s and early 1970s saw an unprecedented number of Irish American youngsters flocking to one of several New York schools for Irish traditional step dance or music. In New York's most popular schools—John Glynn's in Brooklyn (taken over after his death in 1971 by his daughter Maureen) and the late County Limerick fiddler Martin Mulvihill's in the Bronx—literally thousands of students learned to play music on a variety of instruments. Traditional musicians who had come over to the States some years earlier also sent their children to study at a school or with another master player in the community in addition to informally teaching the music at home sessions. Maureen Doherty, for example, was prodded into music lessons by her melodeon-playing father, Tom Doherty: "My dad came to me one day and asked me if I wanted to play the accordion. And I said, 'No way, Dad I don't want to do that!' He says, 'Come on, please?' He says there's a girl down the street named Maureen Glynn who is just taking over teaching a music school. Irish traditional music school. So he said, 'Why don't you take up the tin whistle or something? Just try it for awhile?' So I said, 'I don't know.' So he says 'The kids down the street are doing it. Why don't you do it?'"[73]

An additional factor in the revival of Irish music in New York was the increasing and positive attention paid by mainstream media. Through the 1960s, Irish traditional musicians and dancers were featured from time to time on the nationally televised Ed Sullivan Show: the McNiff School of Irish Stepdancers, Louis Quinn & The Quinnettes, the Clancy Brothers and Tommy Makem, and others. By the early to mid-1970s, Irish traditional bands from Ireland toured the United States and attracted press attention as well as a growing general audiences of folk music aficionados. In 1976 the enormous popularity of the television series *Roots* offered mainstream respect for ethnic culture and history in general. These positive portrayals of ethnicity from outside the community served to affirm the importance of heritage and folk culture, and for the Irish, this outside approval legitimized the performance of traditional music.

Since the early years of this century, both popular and traditional musics have existed side by side in New York's Irish and Irish American communities, with popular music typically attracting larger audiences. As with other immigrant groups in the United States, the presence of both musical styles over many years indicates a duality of cultural orientation among the Irish immigrant population. The popular musical styles—notably Irish big band and Irish showband musics—have retained an inherent and uniquely "Irish" sensibility and flavor. In this regard also, the hybridization of Irish social music can be attributed to its audience's developing bicultural identity.

The evolution of Irish cultural identity in the United States is clearly dependent on circumstances of the era. Immigrants who came over prior to World War II exhibited stronger ties to Irish folk culture—and specifically to Irish traditional music—than those who arrived after the war. Part of this was due, no doubt, to the increasing postwar influence of the mainstream music and recording industries, as well as to the mass media. As these industries became stronger, popular music, both mainstream American and Irish and Irish American, benefited from widespread dissemination and marketing practices.

In general, since Irish and Irish American popular musics are aimed at audience approval, they have had, by and large a performance and commercial orientation. Thus perceived by Irish immigrant audiences as a commodity, they have historically resonated with an aura of progressive, modern lifestyles. To varying degrees, these musics rely on "star" or "entertainer" imagery, while audiences play an essentially passive role in the creation of the music itself, although an active role in its consumption.[74] On the other hand, Irish traditional music, has until recently been an essentially creative process open to all members of the community and not limited by a need for a passive audience. Created through active and communal participation, traditional Irish music has remained more of a localized entity in comparison with Irish and Irish American popular musics.[75] That traditional and modern Irish musics have waxed and waned in popularity in direct proportion to each other over the years suggests changing immigrant attitudes toward self-expression and group identity. As button accordionist Martin Mulhaire reflects, all immigrants live between two worlds: "Once you leave your native country and go someplace else, you're split between both countries I think for the rest of your life. There's always a loyalty in both directions. . . . Because you left your family and traditions and that stays with you. But you've also made a life of your own and so that's a big part of your life too."[76]

Over the years, Irish popular musical genres have come and gone in New York's immigrant community, one pop style easily replacing another.[77] That traditional Irish music has survived in New York's Irish communities despite periods of unpopularity points to its inherent vitality as both an art form and as an important symbolic component of Irish immigrant culture. In general, Irish music—both popular or traditional—continues to serve as an extremely visible vehicle for changing group identity. This social cohesion has evolved with each subsequent wave of Irish immigrants throughout the twentieth century; for most, what is retained is a core sense of Irishness. It is precisely this enduring sense of ethnicity that underscores how Irish expressive culture, particularly the music, serves both as an indicator of social change and as a strategy of cultural adaptation and negotiation.

CHAPTER 20

The Heart's Speech No Longer Stifled

NEW YORK IRISH WRITING

SINCE THE 1960s

Yet a word ancient mother,
You need crouch there no longer on the cold ground with
forehead between your knees,
O you need not sit there veil'd in your old white hair so dishevel'd,
For know you the one you mourn is not in that grave,
It was an illusion, the son you love was not really dead,
The Lord is not dead, he is risen again young and strong in
another country,
Even while you wept there by your fallen harp by the grave,
What you wept for was translated, pass'd from the grave,
The winds favor'd and the sea sail'd it,
And now with rosy and new blood,
Moves to-day in a new country.
　　　　　　　　—Walt Whitman, "Old Ireland" (1861)

IN HIS memoir *The Village of Longing,* Irish writer George O'Brien recalls what the emigrant County Waterford villagers back on holiday from England meant to his "seven going on twelve"-year-old self: "And as for those gin-swilling, vowel-devouring peacocks in their British chain-store plumage, they became my archetypes of doubleness, embodiments of home's foreignness and the allure of the far away, specialists in longing and in longing mollified. Welcome aliens. Metropolitans. Brothers to whom in doubleness I felt my own life obscurely but enlargingly twinned."[1] This view of ethnic otherness not as destructive alienation but as creative expansion of possibility—ethnicity not as crippling, but as liberating doubleness—has been much in evidence in Irish American writing since the 1960s.

This liberating doubleness can be stylistic as well as thematic. It can be a freedom to use language experimentally, creatively, in flights and gripes of tours de force. As the ghost of James Joyce tells Seamus Heaney: "The English language belongs to us. . . . it's time to swim / out on your own and fill the element / with signatures on your own frequency, / echo soundings, searches, probes, allurements." A good figure for this is Finley Peter Dunne's unabashed appropriation, when he invented "Mr. Dooley" in the 1890s, of the brogue as a medium both for realistic rendering of the common life of working-class Irish Americans and for inspired riffs of linguistic fancy.[2]

Now, in the overall history of ethnic American literature, including Irish, such confident, positive voices have not dominated the discourse. There has always been a type of ethnic writing that appears to have been spurred by anger and bitterness at the perceived oppressions, distortions, and injustices of the author's own ethnic culture. Often these are first novels by young writers who feel the need to exorcise aspects of their own upbringing and family life that they find disturbing or embarrassing. Sometimes these books are funny, sometimes not so funny, but, because of the skewed perspective they embody, they almost never last. This is the kind of novel that the immature Danny O'Neill thinks about writing when in the middle of James T. Farrell's *Studs Lonigan* trilogy he vows that "some day he would drive this neighborhood and all his memories of it out of his consciousness with a book."[3] This is a kind of book, I hasten to add, that Farrell himself never wrote.

One New York example, though, is Mary Gordon's first novel, *Final Payments* (1978). Here the movement is from a caricatured constriction to an exaggerated escape into the open air. The protagonist is the daughter of a widowed college professor, rendered an invalid by a series of strokes. Electing to nurse her father at home, Isabel Moore has been a virtual prisoner in her own house in Queens for 11 years, until her father's death releases her. The situation is made even more extreme by the further dimension of sexual guilt. Professor Moore's first stroke came just after he discovered 19-year-old Isabel in bed with his prize student. The governing perception of all the main characters is similarly slanted. Isabel is surrounded by a collection of stereotypes. Her father is an intolerant Catholic conservative who makes William F. Buckley Jr. look like Dorothy Day: "In history, his sympathies were with the Royalists in the French Revolution, the South in the Civil War, the Russian czar, the Spanish fascists." The Moores' former housekeeper Margaret Casey is a hateful, whining spinster who uses her self-indulgent piousness as a club. Professor Moore's best friend is a mawkish, alcoholic priest who retards Isabel's growth with his childish appeals that she return to "normal." Isabel describes her Queens neighborhood as full of "working-class Irish who are always defending something, probably something indefensible—the virginity of Mary, the C.I.A.— which is why their parties always end in fights."[4] There is no scrap of sympathetic community here, only embarrassing nets to be escaped. And escape Isabel does—to a rash sexual encounter, a reactionary self-immolation as Margaret Casey's servant, and a final movement up and out toward a new and stable life. *Final Payments* is a collection of clever stereotypes, and the largely enthusiastic early response of many New York critics illustrates the truth of a remark Calvin Trillin made in a *New Yorker* piece about the St. Patrick's Day parade: "A lot of New Yorkers who think of themselves as people of unshakeable tolerance take a sort of easement when it comes to the Irish."[5]

One could have hoped that maturity would bring wisdom, but when Mary Gordon returned again to the Irish in her 1989 novel *The Other Side,* her distorted perspective was even more pronounced. This unremittingly bleak story of the MacNamara family's cheerless odyssey in Ireland and America uses the familiar convention of the matriarch's death to bring four generations together in one house. Once again, the book features stereotyping negative generalities about working-class Irish Catholics. For example, the narrator describes the late 1950s as "the age when students were polite, the students of working-class parents who worshipped teachers as the incarnation of the intellectual life they despised and feared." But now Catholicism, and especially the charismatic movement, is even more contemptuously bashed: Ellen and John MacNamara's daughter Theresa "is one of those people who stand in churches where there are still highly colored leftover statues of the Virgin," people who "feel moved to stand and cry out, 'Praise the Lord' as if they had just been given the good news of their salvation from a wild-eyed preacher holding in his hands his oversized and rusty hat. They stand together in these churches built with bingo money or with dollars that parishioners thrust in the basket, dollars sealed in numbered envelopes recorded by the pastor for his records and the IRS. They stand together in these churches crying 'Praise the Lord,' 'Amen,' 'I hear it, brother.' If they are teenagers they sing and play the tambourine."

Moreover, Gordon's antipathy now also extends to the Irish back in Ireland. After visiting his grandparents' homeland, Dan MacNamara delivers an appalling, dismissive judgment: "But for him, the country was a sign: they could never be happy, any of them, coming from people like the Irish. Unhappiness was bred into the bone, a message in the blood, a code of weakness. The sickle-cell anemia of the Irish: they had to thwart joy in their lives. You saw it everywhere in Irish history; they wouldn't allow themselves to prosper. They didn't believe in prosperity."[6] Sadly, nothing in this mean-spirited book, nor in Gordon's interviews since its publication, suggests that we are meant to see her blanket indictment of a people as anything other than a realistic assessment. She perceives Irishness as a genetic defect and a cultural curse, an unqualified burden to be escaped and overcome.[7]

Fortunately, Gordon's is now an atypical voice, as Irish American writing marked by eager condemnation of the ethnic dimension of experience has given way to writing that features a fuller, more balanced rendering of ethnicity. In this transformation, the decade of the 1960s, so great a watershed for American culture in general, was crucial here as well. Shaping events for Irish America in those turbulent times included the Second Vatican Council, the civil rights and sexual revolutions, the ascendancy and tragedies of the Kennedy clan, the breakup of Irish ethnic ghettoes and the old Catholic fortress identity, upward social and economic mobility, and the related move to the suburbs. This change and energy are reflected in the perspective of liberating doubleness that characterizes much Irish American literature since the 1960s.

A clarifying contrast in this context is provided by the Australian Irish and their literature. In the knowledgeable view of Oliver MacDonagh, the key historical difference "is that the Irish were a founding people in Australia and maintained their position in the new society, more or less, for almost a century and a half," whereas in America, "the Catholic Irish at least entered a firmly stratified society, an already elaborated class structure and an established economy," and "they were doomed to slotting into the bottom layers, or even layer, of the hierarchy of occupations."[8] Moreover, in Irish Australian writing the sense of ethnicity as liberating doubleness is consistently observable all along the way—from the beginnings of Australian literature in the 1890s (to which the Irish contributed a great deal), to the earliest fictional masterworks, Joseph Furphy's *Such Is Life* (1903) and Henry Handel Richardson's *The Fortunes of Richard Mahony* (1917–29), to the richness and assurance of contemporary writers such as Thomas Keneally.[9]

By the 1990s, of course, the American Irish as a group have been out of the bottom social layers for several generations, and in no place have they been more successful than New York. As poet Terence Winch puts it in one of his songs: "We worked on the subways, we ran the saloons, / We built all the bridges, we played all the tunes, / We put out the fires and controlled city hall, / We started with nothing and wound up with it all."[10] Thus, it makes sense that among the strongest of the positive new Irish ethnic voices are those of several New Yorkers.

This chapter considers self-images of ethnicity in New York Irish writing since the 1960s. It begins with a brief look at poetry and autobiography, followed by a survey of the wealth of recent fiction by, among others, Maureen Howard, Jimmy Breslin, Jack Dunphy, J. P. Donleavy, Thomas McGonigle, Alice McDermott, Tom Grimes, Anna Quindlen, Thomas E. Kennedy, and Elizabeth Cullinan.

Poems that engage and clarify issues of ethnicity have been written by many New Yorkers of Irish background over the years, from Shaemus O'Sheel ("They Went Forth to Battle but They Always Fell") and Marianne Moore ("Spenser's Ireland") to Alan Dugan, Robert Kelly, and Joan Murray.[11] Two recent collections stand out, however, as books of poems in which Irish ethnicity is a large concern throughout. John Montague, a major voice in contemporary poetry, was born in New York and raised in Ireland, and has carried on a literary relationship with both countries. His American strain has been organized into a collection of prose and verse, *Born in Brooklyn* (1991), and it contains some of the finest poems anyone has written on ethnic themes. Among these are "A Graveyard in Queens," "flower encumbered / avenues of the dead; / Greek, Puerto-Rican, / Italian Irish— / (our true Catholic / world, a graveyard)," where "far from / our supposed home," at his uncle's grave, he hears "the creak / of a ghostly fiddle / filter through / American earth / the slow pride / of a lament."; "The Cage," a sad lyric about Montague's father, "the least happy / man I have known," a toll-taker in the Clark Street subway station, whose "face / retained the pallor / of those who work underground," "And yet picked himself / up, most mornings, / to march down the street / extending his smile"; and "A Muddy Cup," "my mother's memories / of America; / a muddy cup / she refused to drink", "but kept / wrinkling her nose / in souvenir of".[12]

The second collection is *Irish Musicians/American Friends* (1985), by Terence Winch, the New York son of Irish immigrant parents. Winch's poems are deceptively spare and conversational, with deft line breaks and titles that spring from unlikely places inside the poems to focus attention and create resonance. They capture memorably the two worlds of his title: that of Irish American music in the 1950s and 1960s to which he was introduced by his father, a musician who played dances and weddings all over New York, and that of the Irish neighborhood in the Bronx where the Winch family grew up. From "Rockaway for the Day" to "The Catskills" to "Home in the Bronx," these poems are invested with the spirit of place ("six families of Puerto Ricans had moved / into nineteen fifteen Daly Avenue the Mitchells' / building") and the power of naming ("Frank Pearson Bob Hines / and Mona Geelan's nephew Richard) / (whose going away party me and my brother / and P. J. and my father played for) / were all killed in Vietnam").[13]

There are memorable portraits from both worlds: Winch's father's best friend and musician partner "The Great P. J." Conway; Joe Garvey the hypocrite, "who would seduce girls with villainous / relish then afterwards kneel down / and say the rosary"; fiddler Brendan Mulvihill, who "fills your head / with dreams of music / and with memories of events / that never happened"; and the tight-fisted Conlons who would only give their tenants "fifty degrees in the winter / and no hot water." A fine example is Winch's quiet tribute to "My Father," who was "a natural pacifist,"

> and when I got reclassified One A
> and asked him what I should do after enumerating
> my options one night when we were eating supper
> back in sixty eight   he thought about it painfully
> for about ten minutes during which time
> I didn't say a word
> and then he said "go to jail" which was a very hard thing
> for him to say (17)

And there are also "these two old guys I used to see / when I was a kid and spent my summers / in Rockaway, which was known as The Irish Riviera":

> one of them played the fiddle   the other played
> the accordion   and I think one of them wore
> a top hat   they just wandered in and out of bars
> playing for drinks   they were like bums
> but I still remember how fine they sounded (36)

Two poems further along, "my brother Jesse whose name is really James" tells the speaker that their names were "Mike and Ike / and that they were in the great tradition of Irish street singers." Winch and his brother have carried on that tradition as well, in their Irish band "Celtic Thunder," and in songs of New York and family history that Winch writes and the band performs, such as "When New York Was Irish" and "The Best Years of Our Lives."

New York Irish writing has also been rich in autobiography. There is no lovelier memoir of any time and place than William Gibson's *A Mass for the Dead* (1968), the lyrical, vivid rendering of growing up in Highbridge in the 1920s, the son of "my cheerful demon and mother," named "Florence Agnes, for bloom and purity," herself born "late in the eighties, in a house on Broadway and 35th Street," one of the 19 children of "Mary Kane, who at 15 had run away from a convent school to marry a song-and-dance man named Dennis Dore," and who ended her days "in the thick of Negro life" in a corner tenement at Eighth Avenue and 139th Street in a flat that was "the ancestral rock" in "the flow of my childhood" for her grandson.[14] In the late 1960s and 1970s, worthwhile Irish American memoirs with New York materials included Frank Conroy's *Stop-Time*, Francis Hackett's *American Rainbow*, Horace Gregory's *The House on Jefferson Street*, and Dennis Smith's *Report from Engine Co. 82*.[15]

In this category, Maureen Howard's *Facts of Life* (1978) is a landmark document in Irish American literary self-definition, not least because of the balance between her sense of her parents' cultural shortcomings and her clearly articulated love and admiration for them. Equally memorable are the evocative images through which she presents the world of her upbringing and education. One such recurrent image is a description of stepping off a Manhattan curb as a figure for life as all promise. Howard's final expression of this figure ends the book:

> I am walking up lower Madison Avenue in an old straw hat, circa 1918. Yes, always the heightening. The last golden hour of the day. Everything is clear: the rose marble of the Morgan Library, mahogany bushes, tulips on the verge. Soon to marry, I am twenty-three years old in a blue suit, size eight. Natural time. I hardly touch ground the last blocks to Grand Central, but come triumphantly to rest alone on Forty-second Street, on the edge of evening. I am beginning. My life is beginning which cannot be true.

That last qualifying clause marks *Facts of Life* as realistic. Nevertheless, the image is powerful and telling, and the book makes it clear that her life has had this quality of promise. Though she now declares that "I've finally learned not to want things I cannot have," there is nothing of cynicism or bitterness in her tone.[16]

In fact, Howard's later fiction opens out adventurously in style, and her tolerant, forgiving, comic vision expands along with it. There is a significant difference between the painful break into a measure of freedom of the late-blooming Mary Agnes Keely in *Bridgeport Bus* (1965) and the sharp, satiric eye and forthright confidence, even in the face of dangerous heart disease, of novelist Margaret Flood in *Expensive Habits* (1986).[17] Indeed, a similar progression is observable between the early and later fiction of many New York Irish writers who began in the 1960s and earlier 1970s. I would argue that in many cases their later work contains a more positive evocation of the spirit of place, a deepening sense of the value of ethnic doubleness, and a presentation of characters who find their voices, articulate their troubles and needs, and move toward the light of resolution and change for the better.

Jimmy Breslin's *World without End, Amen* (1973) presents Dermot Davey, a tortured, alcoholic young cop from Queens whose sensitivity and promise as a child have been thwarted by a broken home, a repressive parochial school experience, and a marriage without communication, and whose inarticulate rage and frustration drive him helplessly toward disaster.[18] By contrast, Breslin's *Table Money* (1986), also set in Queens in the early 1970s, depicts a similar struggle with alcoholism and deadening macho values of Vietnam veteran and tunnel-digging "sandhog," Owney Morrison. But now, there are resources available, most importantly Owney's wife Dolores, presented as a figure of courage and strength who breaks through the barriers to communicate and help her husband change.[19]

Joe Flaherty's *Fogarty & Co.* (1973) is a rollicking, satiric depiction of the three-day pilgrimage through his native Flatbush of Shamus Fogarty, who casts a jaundiced eye at both his ethnic upbringing and his Manhattan success as an artist. He hasn't a good word to say about either, but responsibility for his son and humor help bring him through. Along the way, the hilarious scene of his attempted reconciliation with the church in his old parish is a classic in the genre of *recherche du* Catholic upbringing *perdu*.[20] But there is much less laughter and more balanced understanding in Flaherty's *Tin Wife* of 1983, a sensitive novel about the New York police and the Brooklyn Irish in which a thoughtful cop's transformation from idealist to bigot is presented as plausibly rooted in his dangerous job. Moreover, the Brooklyn scenes where Eddie and Sissy Sullivan meet, marry, and raise their children are much warmer and evocative of a welcoming spirit of place than the Brooklyn of the earlier novel, and, as in the Breslin book, the wife here is a strong, resourceful character, who speaks her mind and fights effectively for her family after her husband's death.[21]

One can also contrast the minimal resolving communication (in a shared saloon brawl) in Pete Hamill's *The Gift* (1973) and the broad-brush, sensationalized sexual situation in *Flesh and Blood* (1977) with the more tangible, realistic initiations into a larger world of the Brooklyn boy in *Loving Women* (1989).[22] Or the greater depth of understanding of human relations in Dennis Smith's *Steely Blue* (1984) as compared with *The Final Fire* (1975).[23] Or Ellen Currie's early short stories, which detail the initiation of young women into troubling adult mysteries (a disturbingly eccentric teacher in "On the Mountain Stands a Lady" and a neighborhood suicide in "O Lovely Appearance of Death"), and the frank, ebullient, offbeat independence of fashion stylist Kitty O'Carolan in her novel *Available Light* (1986).[24]

Finally, from the older generation, Jack Dunphy's novels of the 1980s provide a solid example of Irish American fiction opening out into an accepting, positive, liberating vision of ethnic doubleness. Unexpected—given the bleakness of vision in *John Fury*, his first novel (1946)—have been the warmth and vitality of *First Wine* (1982) and *The Murderous McLaughlins* (1988), the two books in which Dunphy returns to his childhood for a second, more tolerant and appreciative look.[25] (Though set in Philadelphia, these novels are a part of the contemporary New York literary corpus, I would argue, as Dunphy has been a New Yorker for decades.) One of the best ethnic novels of the past decade, *The Murderous McLaughlins* illustrates well the immigrant/ethnic experience seen not as exile and alienation but as challenge and transformation into a confident assumption of identity. The story of the developing relationship between an eight-year-old boy and his grandmother from Galway, this book ends with a lyrical summation of this perspective. When the boy hears that his grandmother has died, he slips out of bed before dawn and goes over to the neighborhood swimming pool, "where I waited until the sun rose. When the swimmies opened I swam in the blue water as if it was the sea, or Galway Bay. For she had taught me to love many waters, and to feel at home everywhere, the world being her country, as it is mine."[26]

In a much darker thematic area, New York Irish writers have rung some of the most affecting recent changes on the powerful, often related subjects of madness and drink. These vestigial elements from the nineteenth-century legacy of the Irish American urban underclass received pioneering treatment in the "black humor" of J. P. Donleavy's *The Ginger Man* (1955).[27] In the character of Sebastian Balfe Dangerfield, a World War II veteran on the G. I. Bill in Dublin, blarney and charm mask boozy, manipulative cruelty and a frightening amorality. There has been brilliant short fiction written in this genre, perhaps because the emotional intensity of this material is better suited to the short form. An early example is the mordant, chilling deadpan of Donleavy's "A Fairy Tale of New York" (1961), which updates and parodies the nineteenth-century crossing narrative in its rendering of the return of Cornelius Christian to New York City with the body of his Irish wife, who has died on board ship. Like the famine immigrants, Christian runs a gauntlet of crass, money-grubbing American sharpers, including the oily undertaker, Mr. Vine, who misinterprets Christian's shocked, stalled emotions as rational calm, and offers him a job in "this profession": "There's a place for you here, remember that."[28]

Literary evocations of alcoholic degeneration sometimes mine the Irish American vein of wild linguistic exuberance to dark, entropic extremes. Notable here are John F. Murray's two *New Yorker* stories from the late 1970s, "O'Phelan's Daemonium" and "O'Phelan Drinking," which trace the movements of narrator John O'Phelan, "both a psycho and a drunk,"[29] from a botched suicide attempt on eastern Long Island to a private hospital near Boston, to "St. Justin's" Alcoholic Rehabilitation Unit in Manhattan, from which he is ejected for drinking once again. Both stories begin with "My brother, hateful Martin O'Phelan," hateful because of his persistent, fruitless attempts to stop John's helpless 16-year degenerative plunge: "And what do you [Martin] know of losing a family, of divorce, of losing a second wife (died), losing a third wife (we split), losing jobs, going broke, owing the banks, drinking and losing weekends, losing days at work horizontal in bed at home with the electric blanket . . . and a plastic tumbler on the night table beside the bed full of good old Gordon's eighty-proof vodka."[30] The memory of two shakily happy weeks with his three children on Nantucket in the midst of O'Phelan's sorrowful progress punctuates this heart-breaking narrative, which is as searing a self-scrutiny of a life tangled in manic depression and alcoholism as Robert Lowell's *Life Studies*.

T. Coraghessan Boyle has two 1989 stories somewhat in the same vein. In "The Miracle at Ballinspittle," New Yorker Davey McGahee, on an impulsive, drunken holiday in Ireland, finds himself the lightning rod for a miraculous visitation of his sins of drunkenness, gluttony, and debauchery, which come raining down on him in the Irish village where crowds are already gathering in hopes of observing reported movements by a statue of the Virgin Mary. The sky rains ordinary sins—barrels of beer, sides of beef, and representations of every girl after whom Davey has ever lusted—and Irish Catholic guilt is transformed into his apotheosis as "the Saint of the Common Sinner," "for who hasn't lusted after women or man or drunk his booze and laid to rest whole herds to feed his greedy gullet?"[31]

"The Miracle" is a lighthearted satiric exorcism, but wholly serious and moving is the portrait of a lost alcoholic seen through his own and his son's eyes in "If the River Was Whiskey." This wrenching short narrative is told alternately by a boy and his father in the context of a lakeside vacation gone sour, in which the father's far-gone alcoholism finally dawns on both. The story is a progression of ever more painful images: from the boy's memory of his father's drunken guitar rendition of the old folk tune, "If the River Was Whiskey," to the mother's last-ditch, hopeless pronouncement: "Get used to it, he's a drunk, your father's a drunk," to the fishing trip during which the boy really sees his wheezing, hungover father: "With his beard and long hair and with the crumpled suffering look on his face, he was the picture of the crucified Christ Tiller had contemplated a hundred times at church." And the last image is the most haunting. "Beyond drunk" and fallen into a despairing, fitful sleep, the father has a dream in which "all of a sudden they were going down, the boat sucked out from under them, the water icy and black, beating in on them as if it were alive. Tiller called out to him. He saw his son's face, saw him going down, and there was nothing he could do."[32]

There is no more powerful evocation in contemporary short fiction of madness and its family legacy than Frank Conroy's 1984 story, "Midair," in which middle-aged Sean Kennedy traces his adult instability back to a terrifying childhood afternoon, since blocked from his memory, when his insane father held him suspended out a fifth-floor window. Since that buried trauma, "He lives as if he did not have a past, and so there is a great deal about himself of which he is not aware. He is entirely ignorant of his lack of awareness, and believes himself to be in full control of his existence." Though punctuated with moments of near enlightenment, Sean's life is a kind of sleepwalk through early marriage, the births of his two children, first writing projects, jobs, divorce, and remarriage. He sees through a glass darkly, only dimly perceiving that there is a mystery at his core into which he cannot penetrate. One day Sean, now in his late 40s, gets stuck in an elevator between the sixty-third and sixty-fourth floors with a young stranger who resembles his son. When the elevator falls a few feet, the boy is terrified, but Sean is able to calm him by holding his head gently and speaking calmly: "I know we are safe, and if you focus on me *you* will know we are safe." The elevator starts up again, and all is well. That night, "as he lies in bed waiting for sleep," Sean finally remembers "the day in 1942 when his father showed up unexpectedly, took him home from school, washed the windows, and carried him out on the windowsill. He remembers looking down at the cracks in the sidewalk. Here, in the darkness, he can see the cracks in the sidewalk from more than 40 years ago. He feels no fear—only a sense of astonishment."[33]

Conroy writes with a clarity and perfect pitch that amount to a kind of super-realism, to use the analogy from painting, and the intensity generated in "Midair" is breathtaking. The buried emotional life of Irish Americans, their "inarticulate speech of the heart" in musician/lyricist Van Morrison's phrase,[34] has been a major theme in this ethnic literature back through James T. Farrell to the nineteenth century.[35] Moreover, work in the early 1980s on Irish Americans in therapy by Monica McGoldrick and others describes the persistence of "Irish indirectness and difficulty in dealing with feelings at the moment."[36] And yet, Conroy's fine story embodies the progression that I see in recent Irish American fiction from New York and elsewhere—a movement from stifling emotional stasis to release into communication and understanding.[37]

Another unique document in this liberating movement is Thomas McGonigle's *Going to Patchogue* (1992), the extended stream-of-consciousness narration of "Tom McGonigle's" journey from his Lower East Side apartment to his home-town of Patchogue, Long Island, and back. This one-day pilgrimage frames a richly layered meditation, encrusted with memories and might-have-beens, the scope of which is the narrator's life to date and his wanderings through the world, including experiences in Dublin, Sofia, Istanbul, Helsinki, and Venice. An example of Ignatian "composition of place" with a vengeance, the novel is a collage of conversations, recollections, Suffolk County folk tales, newspaper clippings, town-meeting minutes, photographs, Long Island Railroad time-tables, handwritten notes. The challenge throughout is "how to hold all of these items in my hands," and the aim is description, definition, understanding, both personal and cultural.[38] Nearing age 40 and considering suicide, the narrator seeks directing self-knowledge. Child of a family that made the typical move of the late 1940s and 1950s from Brooklyn out to "the Island," he also aims to diagnose suburbia as a failed Promised Land. That diagnosis is vividly embodied in the voices of customers in the Patchogue bars who spew anti-Semitic, anti-intellectual, and anti–African American vitriol that reveals white flight as a prime motive for their migration out of the city. McGonigle's is the most forthright rendering of such voices since James T. Farrell's *Studs Lonigan* in 1935, and he provides an important though disturbing piece of the postwar suburban story.

The harshness of the narrator's confrontation with his communal and personal demons is redeemed by two elements: the Rabelaisian comic vision informing the novel, and the boldness and intelligence of the voice that drives the narrative. This flawed pilgrim soul is neither mad nor alcoholic. Nor is he a straw character like one of Mary Gordon's, created to ridicule or apologize for Irishness. "Tom McGonigle" has a relentlessly questioning consciousness, courageously persistent in the hard work of psychological and cultural critique.

Throughout his difficult journey, the narrator scrutinizes with admirable directness the ghosts that continue to haunt him: his mother, his father, his first love, high school friends and fellow townspeople, and most of all, himself. He is the novelist uncomfortably aware of his lack of adherence to conventions: "Here we are pages later and not a single character has made the scene; there has been no conflict laid into the story, there is no motor installed in the locomotive of plot, no sex to grease the wheels of the pages. Still sitting" (30). He is the failed, bewildered lover of his high school sweetheart Melinda: "Each person is given one love story. Usually it doesn't coincide with another love story" (194). He is the restless but reluctant traveler in search of meanings from Patchogue to the world and back, who comes to realize that "I don't have to travel to Patchogue to be there. I am always in Patchogue" (42), and who decides to keep on living, despite—or perhaps because of—the inconclusive nature of his findings so far: "I am not ready, please, just yet. I have places to go. I must be getting myself to Patchogue" (57).

The novel's ending is plausibly anticlimactic: "It is all so painful. To have gone away and not stayed. To have failed, again . . . to have brought nothing back from this journey, not even the ash of some exotic adventure." And yet,

"Tom" has come through psychologically intact: "Myself has come back. I am in the City. I have gone to Patchogue. I have been in Patchogue. I have come back from Patchogue" (212). Moreover, he has delivered salutary indictments of the persistent xenophobia and complacency of his own and the world's suburban subcultures; as, for example, in a late, arresting image of tourists, "drift[ing] to Venice for a final appearance before heading back to their empty northern hovels, their American suburbs, hurrying in fact because the new season is already underway on the television, brunch is being missed and hey, what about the World Series?" (209). *Going to Patchogue* provides a compelling figure for American as well as Irish American migratory rootlessness, one that is grounded by a voice of honesty and moral outrage. At the realistic conclusion of this often surreal narrative, two mysteries remain intact: the imaginative and meditative variousness of an individual consciousness and the dark swervings of communal thought into prejudice and hatred.[39]

Much of the fiction so far discussed has been concerned with family matters, and it is certainly true that domestic fiction is a significant strength of Irish American writing in our time. Willa Cather's placement of Katherine Mansfield's New Zealand stories in 1936 also describes the achievement of many Irish Americans:

> I doubt whether any contemporary writer has made one feel more keenly the many kinds of personal relations which exist in an everyday "happy family" who are merely going on living their daily lives, with no crises or shocks or bewildering complications to try them. Yet every individual in that house-hold (even the children) is clinging passionately to his individual soul, is in terror of losing it in the general family flavour. As in most families, the mere struggle to have anything of one's own, to be one's self at all, creates an element of strain which keeps everybody almost at the breaking-point. . . .
>
> Katherine Mansfield's peculiar gift lay in her interpretation of these secret accords and antipathies which lie hidden under our everyday behaviour, and which more than any outward events make our lives happy or unhappy.[40]

Many younger New York Irish writers—first or second novelists whose books have appeared in the later 1980s and early 1990s—also carry on with the thematic focus on everyday life in families. In addition, much of this fiction published over the past few years illustrates both the persistence of ethnicity and the phenomenon of ethnicity as liberating doubleness. These contemporary New York voices are newly authoritative. The younger writers have learned from the previous generation the value of their sort of experience—and ethnicity is part of it. It is largely a middle-class and lower-middle-class suburban experience, often focused on childhood in the 1960s, and many of these writers are themselves first-generation college graduates. Helping to bring this experience into American literature is one of the most valuable accomplishments of New York Irish writers. There is an expansion of boundaries and an awakening here that is very much worthy of note.

A sure evocation of lower-middle-class suburban Long Island in the early 1960s is Alice McDermott's *That Night* (1987), the story of Rick and Sheryl, high school sweethearts who are separated abruptly when Sheryl becomes pregnant. The narrator is a young woman who recalls her childhood observation of "that night" when the tenuous bonds of suburban community broke down as Rick and his "hood" friends enter Sheryl's house by force to try to rescue her. The neighborhood men beat them back in a shocking eruption of violence. (Sheryl has already been sent to an aunt in Ohio.) "That night" focuses for the narrator the "vague and persistent notion, a premonition or memory of possible if not impending doom," that she sees as just beneath the surface of those "bedroom communities, incubators, where the neat patterns of the streets, the fenced and leveled yards, the stop signs and traffic lights and soothing repetition of similar homes all helped to convey a sense of order and security and snug predictability." Their fathers all have "iron crosses and silver swastikas, tarnished medals marked with bright red guns" in their attics, and most families have grandparents "who remained in embattled city apartments or dilapidated houses buzzed by highways."[41] McDermott conveys loss of place and community with quiet authority.

To my mind, however, the book's strongest element is the narrator's sense of Sheryl's coming into knowledge of love and death. Sheryl's revelation is the product of her father's sudden death, her doomed romance with Rick, and other "sources," which the narrator lists as "the love songs of the Shirelles and Shangri-las, the auto accident/undying love poems printed in odd spaces in her teen magazines, the old-fashioned, heaven-saturated Catholicism of her [Polish] grandmother" (78). McDermott presents the revelations that come to this ordinary 16-year-old with uncondescending, respectful attention.

McDermott's next novel, *At Weddings and Wakes* (1992), is much more explicitly ethnic in its focus. It involves the four daughters of Irish immigrants who met on the boat coming over: "He said he was from Kildare, she wrote, and I said Cork by way of Mallow."[42] The heart of these lives and the novel is the top-floor Brooklyn apartment, weighted down with family history, where three of the "Towne girls" still live with "Momma," their mother's sister, who married their father after their mother's death. The salient events in the present are the courtship and marriage of middle-aged May Towne, a former nun, and her sudden death four days after the wedding. But the past is never far from the consciousness of these people, and family happenings all the way back to immigration come up again and again. Memory is the coin of this six-room realm, and the narrative is a subtle weave of past and present, seen mostly through the eyes of the three children of Lucy Dailey, the third Towne daughter. There is a hushed timelessness about this novel. Outside events make few impressions upon the Townes, for whom emotional life within the family is paramount. Cather on Mansfield is a perfect gloss for McDermott's work, and virtually the only historical reference in *At Weddings and Wakes* is to John F.

Kennedy's assassination, reported on the cover of *Life* magazine. (Kennedy is linked to Ireland's Charles Stewart Parnell in a heated discussion at May's wedding reception: "Women were the trouble with all of them," 201).

The novel opens with an extended description of the trip between the Daileys' Long Island home and Lucy's old neighborhood in Brooklyn. The journey, "twice a week in every week of summer," begins at the Daileys, front door—"the white, eight-panel door that served as backdrop for every Easter, First Holy Communion, confirmation, and graduation photo in the family album" (3)—and ends in front of the bakery on the old Brooklyn street with the dispensation of just-bought bread ("the kind of bread," declares Lucy to her children, "that Christ ate at the Last Supper,") after which, "her pace slowed just that much to tell them that she was home after all and as happy—she allowed them to walk a few paces ahead of her—as she'd ever be" (14). Marked by scrupulous, loving detail and framed by Christian symbols, this odyssey by way of two buses and two subway lines is an opening antiphon to the variety and richness of city life.

Indeed, McDermott's book is full of set pieces in which close observation and lyrical style combine to celebrate the urban everyday. Here, for example, is her rendering of the cinder-block schoolyard incinerator as microcosm:

> Here was burned every botched effort of the day, torn sheets of loose-leaf and crumbled bits of construction paper, cracked erasers, broken pens, paper air-planes, the rough caricatures and pierced, initialed hearts that had been ripped from notebooks by quickeyed teachers pacing the aisles. Here, too, the opened Sunday envelopes went, the junk mail, the dated parish bulletins, the scented notes from home that explained yesterday's absence or warned of tomorrow's, crumpled tissues (some stained with lipstick), pencil sharpenings—all turned out of the round steel wastebaskets that the two janitors collected at the end of each day. There were flowers, too, on some occasions, barely wilted flowers from the altar or flattened muddied ones from the small cemetery behind the church. And palm fronds, once a year, blessed and dried and made obsolete on each new Palm Sunday. (117–18)

As in *That Night*, McDermott brings a discriminating, respectful eye to the presentation of character and motive in ordinary life. The crucial example of this is Momma's austere crankiness and the fatalism that prompts her to say of her husband, "The only thing I ever held against him was that he made me believe the worst was over" (151). These are traced to, and understood in terms of, her experience of arrival in this country just weeks before her sister died, leaving a newborn baby and three older girls under six, for whom Momma had shouldered immediate responsibility: "She had a sense—she would have it all her life—that she'd been left off in these rooms as abruptly as the darkness at her window fell away from the light" (138). Moreover, Momma's ingrained contrariness ("this need to disagree, to raise her voice in utter disagreement, came on her like hunger"), is explained as her husband came to understand it:

"he had discovered it too, had discovered in himself her own need to object, to stand stubbornly against something. He had discovered in a life so easily shifted, battered, turned about, this overwhelming need to be, in impersonal argument if nothing else, immovable" (144). McDermott is eloquent here. She gets just right the emotional fulcrum on which this family moves. Another of the incisive yet compassionate justifications of motive is the presentation of the bond between "May's mailman" Fred and his widowed mother as the plausible product of her life of unremitting labor as a housekeeper to sustain them both and send him to Catholic schools. Fred's slightly embarrassed sense of himself as "a bachelor son, an Irish mother's loyal boy" (130) completes the picture of a thoughtful, sensitive man. There are no caricatures here, but solid, fully realized characterizations. The writing reminds me of James T. Farrell's fiction about Irish American working-class life, in particular his five O'Neill-O'Flaherty novels, and of a favorite Farrell epigraph from Spinoza: "Not to weep, not to laugh, but to understand."[43]

The final chapter of *At Weddings and Wakes* describes the beginning of the Daileys' summer vacation on the day after May and Fred's wedding. Poised just before the news of May's death, which is about to be delivered as the novel ends, are climactic revelations that come to Lucy Dailey and her husband. Lucy realizes why her husband gets them a different cottage every summer: "The family had no history here, no memory of another time—no walls marked off with the children's heights, no windowsills or countertops to remind her of how much they had grown." Coming from a home where family history is all but encompassing, Lucy suddenly appreciates her husband's gift: "It was as if he stopped time for them two weeks out of every year, cut them off from both the past and the future so that they had only this present in a brand new place, . . . when the past and the future grew still enough to let you notice it. He did that for her. This man she'd married." Similarly, Lucy's husband comes to an appreciative judgment about the Townes. Realizing that "he was suited to his wife's family, although they often wore him thin," he thinks first, "perhaps it was the challenge to distract them from their mournfulness and anger," but he moves on to a further reflection that constitutes a major revelation of this novel: "But there was something they gave him, too, with all their ghosts, something he couldn't deny: they provided his ordinary day, his daily routine of office, home, cocktails, dinner, homework, baths, and twenty minutes of the evening news, with an undercurrent—it was like the low music that now played on the kitchen radio—that served as some constant acknowledgment of the lives of the dead."[44] Mr. Dailey is in the tradition of William Kennedy's Francis Phelan in *Ironweed* and James Joyce's Gabriel Conroy in "The Dead," men who come to understand the presentness of the past, and whose capacity for mercy and compassion expands with that knowledge.

A Stone of the Heart (1990) is the first novel by Tom Grimes, born in New York City in 1954 and raised in Queens. The opening line sets the time and the crucial events, both familial and cultural: "The day my father was arrested, Roger Maris hit his sixty-first home run." The narrator is the 14-year-old son of a disintegrating Irish and Italian family in Queens. Michael McManus's father is a petty conman with alcoholic tendencies, stuck mostly through his own fault in a dead-end clerical job. Like Joyce's Farrington in "Counterparts," he takes it all out on his family. The situation is made bleaker by the fact that younger son Rudy seldom speaks and may be autistic. Grimes's title is from Yeats's "Easter 1916," but the situation echoes Farrell's O'Neill-O'Flaherty novels, with the tension between parents, the sensitive son's love of baseball, and even the father's job working for a freight-forwarding company.

Young Michael's weapons are humor, exile (to the movies and the television screen), and baseball, which provides the metaphor and means for the acceptance that he achieves in the minimally hopeful conclusion. While at the Yankees' game preceding the one in which Maris breaks the record (Roger goes 0 for 4), Michael communicates with his brother and gently crazy grandfather and experiences what "began to feel like a clamorous peace." "Please, don't blame us," says Michael's mother, and the boy's real victory is in his not doing so. When his father is shamefully arrested on their doorstep and when Maris breaks Ruth's record, Michael rejects "the idea of constants," and sees clearly that "the best I felt we could hope for in a world in which the illusion of order is untenable is someone who is willing to assume responsibility for us, and a capacity for forgiveness beyond our largest hopes."[45] Grimes's writing is spare, restrained. The affirmation here is in his having brought to these ordinary, even threadbare materials the shaping gift of narrative art.

Another novel of a job-troubled Irish New Yorker with a resolution that is curved hopefully is T. Glen Coughlin's *The Hero of New York* (1985).[46] Here the namesake is a 21-year police veteran who is suspended from the force pending investigation into his overzealous reaction to the storming of his Brooklyn precinct by angry Hasidim demanding better protection. The perspective here on lower-middle-class family life in Long Island is that of the cop's son, 19-year-old Charlie Patterson, a community-college dropout with problems of his own. Charlie fends bravely and with some success with his suddenly house-bound and drinking father, his devoutly Catholic mother, and his snotty 13-year-old sister. We come to care about this family because Coughlin presents them in brisk, lively prose and with a sense for the texture of everyday life. Moreover, Charlie's dawning appreciation of his father's tough job and his recognition of how much he is like the old man make for a plausibly positive ending.

Set one year later than Tom Grimes's novel and also keyed to a historical event (Scott Carpenter's orbiting of the earth on May 24, 1962) is Thomas Mallon's *Aurora 7*, published in 1991. (The name of the novel is that of Carpenter's mission.) Here the setting is middle-class Westchester, and the protagonist is 11-year-old Gregory Noonan, son of a World War II veteran and midlevel advertising sales executive, and grandson of Noonans from Hell's Kitchen. Recently, inexplicably estranged from his puzzled father, Gregory sleepwalks through the day of the Aurora mission, skipping school after lunch, taking a train to Grand Central, and narrowly missing being hit by a speeding taxi. Ultimately, he comes face to face with his distraught father in the Grand Central crowd, in a scene of equally puzzling but convincing reconciliation.

The progress through this day of large and small events and resolutions in several other lives is also tracked. These include Gregory's parents, his teacher, the cab driver who nearly hits the boy, a young priest having doubts about celibacy, and a smug, egocentric novelist (seemingly modeled on Mary McCarthy) who steps off the curb to pull Gregory from the path of the speeding taxi. The mixing of events and fates here is deftly accomplished. Mallon's voice is precise yet engaged, he is lightly ironic and compassionate at once, and this novel achieves a genuine sense of mystery. The Noonans and others in it take their Catholicism seriously. Gregory is nearing confirmation and one theme throughout is the disjunction between the Baltimore Catechism and lived experience. This is, of course, familiar territory in Irish American fiction, but Mallon's treatment is fresh and impressive in its thoughtfulness. *Aurora 7* describes a pilgrimage. At the end, "whatever [Gregory had] had to do, he'd done, and he'd come through," and this novel earns its concluding, open-ended and provocative meditation on free will and mercy and God's plan on earth.[47]

Anna Quindlen's first novel, *Object Lessons* (1991), also contributes detail to the familiar pattern of recent New York Irish fiction. Set in the early 1960s, it is an adolescent coming-of-age story that also explores the misalliance that lurks just below the surface of suburban life for returning G.I.s and first-time home owners, many of them newly middle class. As in many of these books, one message involves the loss of the older urban/ethnic community. John Scanlan is an intimidating patriarch, a figure out of the old Irish urban neighborhood life who has made millions in religious artifacts, from communion wafers to vestments, and who now concentrates on exerting control over his children's lives. Perspective on this frightening figure comes from the novel's three main narrative voices: John's only independent son, Tommy, Tommy's wife Connie, a double outsider because of her Italian background, and their 13-year-old daughter Maggie, whose many awakenings over the course of one summer are the novel's major events.

The "object lessons" of the title are the didactic points of emphasis that the various people influencing Maggie, especially her grandfather, are trying to drive home. Her own stubborn impositions of meaning (along with the more urgent battle for independence waged by her parents) make for the novel's tensions and revelations. This struggle centers on John Scanlan's attempt to move his son Tommy's family into an imposing house three doors down from his own stone fortress, and the novel's emphasis on houses as defining social status, ethnicity, and power relationships puts *Object Lessons* squarely in the tradition of Irish

American classics such as Brendan Gill's *The Trouble of One House* (1950) and Elizabeth Cullinan's *House of Gold* (1970). Connie Mazza Scanlan grew up in a tiny house on the grounds of the cemetery tended by her immigrant father, and she and Tommy now live in a modest home, too small for their growing family and about to be encroached upon by a new development of semi slab tract houses. (The start of this new construction sets the theme of this "time of changes" on the novel's opening page.)

Quindlen also introduces a suburban variation on the dominant ethnic theme of the passing of the old ways with the death of the patriarch, and a crucial set of events for all concerned is the last illness, death, wake, and funeral of John Scanlan. Throughout, the local colors of both Westchester and the Bronx are credibly painted. The Scanlans learn and grow from their various object lessons, and this book belongs in the group of delineations of ethnicity as liberating rather than crippling that marks so much New York Irish writing in recent years. Particularly heartening, and resonant in the context of examining the emergence of strong, new narrative voices, is the revelation that comes to Maggie on the last page. Recalling her walk down the aisle as her cousin's maid of honor the day before, Maggie realizes that "she had heard another voice, telling her to lift her chin, to keep her shoulders square, to walk slowly. And suddenly it had come to her, as she was dancing with her father, the stars of darkness exploding inside her closed lids, that the voice she was hearing was her own, for the first time in her life."[48]

In its focus on house and home, the weight of family history, and the difficulties of communicating emotion, Thomas E. Kennedy's *Crossing Borders* (1990) is also squarely in the mainstream of Irish American fiction, and it, too, is a novel of breakthrough into enlightenment and change for the better. Jack Sugrue is 40, working in a public relations job that he enjoys less and less, and stuck in a marriage that is coming apart. He drinks too much and is prone to romantic daydreaming about his mildly freewheeling youth in the 1960s. The novel is framed by the house in the suburbs that Sugrue is allowing to fall down around him: "On the driveway and terrace, unswept drifts of cut grass decomposed and sprouted spontaneously as new grass, rooted in its own decay. Inside, leaking faucets wore green splotches into the scarred porcelain. Ash-white mold ate into the corners of woodwork window frames. Lightbulbs burnt out and went unchanged. The evenings grew dim." But when the novel ends, the house has become the homeground where Sugrue will make his stand for his family and his life: "He would just stay here. That's all. He would stay here, and he would be here when she returned. And she would have to deal with him. . . . The children were his, too, his family. She could not just take them from him. She could not just leave. She was his wife. She had made promises." Moreover, the still decaying house has been transfigured as well: "He looked around the once grand, decrepit living room, at the knotty pine ceiling, at the gummy spider webs in the corners of the moldings, the dust clumps, the blisters of peeling paint, and as the snores rose up from the base of his throat, he heard himself murmur, *Lord, I love the beauty of thy house, the place where thy glory dwells.*"[49]

This is a New York commuting story of coming in from Bayside through "the shabby landscape of north Queens' shops, garages, restaurants, delis, taco stands, burger stands, Dunkin' Doughnuts stands" (39), and over the 59th Street Bridge into Manhattan and work and the promise of change. Nostalgic for "the New York of the fifties, the forties," Sugrue recognizes "those years of calm, of grace," as "a false dream, a misinterpretation of the present" (39), and yet he also sees the city as "the only home he knew," and "the place of his boyhood, the place where his dreams took place" (41). The bridge is one of many borders that the protagonist crosses in this novel that is, like Mallon's *Aurora 7*, a pilgrimage with an authentic spiritual dimension. To escape the decay and stasis of the present life that his crumbling suburban house represents at the novel's outset, Jack Sugrue must break several taboos. He begins by grimly drinking to excess almost every night, and then starts an affair marked by sexual abandon and roughness approaching violence with a fellow worker, Cindy Beeman.

Meanwhile, Sugrue's wife has become increasingly exasperated by his lack of connection with their family world. The pragmatic daughter of a financially successful German American father, she sees Sugrue's downward slide as related to his ethnic history: "She had seen the crummy little house they lived in. Typical Irish. All those kids in a crummy little house that was falling apart. They didn't even *see* the flaws, the dirt, the mismatched furniture. (Never marry and Irishman, Angela)" (46). On the other hand, Sugrue remembers his family with a mixture of compassion and gratitude. His father had revealed that "your mother and I haven't had relations in twenty-two years. . . . They told her another baby'd kill her. And that was the end of it" (134). That renunciation also echoes in later years, in the "pale torture" of Sugrue's inability to share feelings with his widowed mother: "He could not cry. He could not—he knew from experience—fling open his heart. It would only frighten her" (101). Sadly, only after his mother's death is he "able to begin to reform the connection with her. Only in death could he love her unconditionally again, only when she could no longer be hurt by his love or he by hers, only when he no longer had to suffer the torment of their failure to connect in life" (109).

And yet, although his parents' stifled emotional life is a frightening admonitory model for Sugrue, he also appreciates their great gift of stability: "All those years of thirst, drinking tap water for the passion. They had been loyal to their fate. And it had been important to him and to his brothers, he knew that. The glue of their rituals, their self-control. He knew them. They were there. Always. You always got a fair deal from them, and you knew they would always be there for you. . . . A single, stable base from which to address the world" (135). In addition, Sugrue sees his father as a man whose "warmth and humor still lived in Sugrue's heart, still warmed him" (5). This was "a grown man who knelt beside his bed each night and bowed his face into his palms," and the son cherishes his father's legacy of kindness and faith and love: "But beneath it all, he had the certainty in his eyes. The certainty of a man who has God, a certainty that had warmed Sugrue's childhood, had blessed his eyes, each time they looked into the eyes of his father" (199–200). Throughout the excesses of drink and his affair with Cindy, Sugrue keeps coming back to this legacy. He loves his children as his father had loved him, and he finds himself "seeking prayers" in an old grade school book. Significantly, the prayer he finds asks for a voice: "Teach me to pronounce the judgements of thy mouth" (144).

Ultimately, Jack Sugrue does break his silence in the novel's climactic scene. Discovered in adultery, he is faced at the breakfast table with his wife's decision to take the children away to her parents' house. He breaks a final + boo, crosses the last, crucial border, by standing up and shouting: "He took a   sion. They must see this. They must know. That it was not for lack of love   r of passion or for fear of pain. He slammed the flat of his hand down onto the table. The cups jumped in their saucers. And he bellowed out: *'I do not want this to happen to us!*,'" Moreover, in finding his voice, Sugrue's mind "flashed with thoughts of his own father and mother, the stillness in which they had lived, survived, the stand-off they had survived, dead now, gone, all of them, as his lungs heaved for air and his heart banged against the wall of his chest" (190). Thomas Kennedy's is a strong, courageous voice, a liberating voice grounded in understanding of his culture's strengths and limits both. His is an honest voice on sex, drink, love for one's family, and the struggle for articulation. He speaks without contempt or ridicule for his people's limitations, and the reward of listening to him is considered, deliberate insight into ethnic life in New York. We hear the heart's speech no longer stifled.

The career to date of Elizabeth Cullinan, one of the finest contemporary Irish American writers, is exemplary and paradigmatic, and thus provides an appropriate conclusion to this chapter. Cullinan began with *House of Gold* (1970), a remarkable first novel containing a definitive portrait of a powerful, controlling Irish American matriarch and the fortress house that embodies her fierce hold on respectability.[50] At the end of this benchmark critique of potentially destructive aspects of Irish American domestic life, there is only minimal hopeful resolution, in the persons of the ne'er-do-well son, whose failure has absolved him of the weight of family responsibility, and the two teen-aged granddaughters, whose skeptical perspective bodes well for their generation. However, in her more recent fiction, Cullinan has explored the lives of female protagonists from Irish backgrounds who have landed sanely on their feet in the wider New York world.

Indeed, the Cullinan narrative voice has become that of one of those skeptical granddaughters grown into a reasonably assured and independent adulthood. It is a voice of clarity and perspective, balanced between then and now, the ethnic and the worldly, and better able to judge self and others because of the doubleness. One example is Louise Gallagher, who emerges in three stories in the collection *Yellow Roses* (1977) as happy in her work and having achieved a measure of equilibrium between her Bronx upbringing and her present life as a single woman in Manhattan.[51] She describes herself as "five feet six inches, one hundred and eight pounds . . .—of Irish-American Roman Catholic." At one time daunted by her lover's New England Scots background, Louise has changed: "All that had given Louise a feeling of being beyond the pale that it took years to get over; when she did, she discovered she liked being beyond the pale, and she got a kick out of rubbing it in."[52] Similarly, Ann Clarke, the protagonist of the story "A Good Loser" (1977) and Cullinan's second novel, *A Change of Scene* (1982), brings useful perspective to a comparison of Dublin and New York, of Irish and Irish Americans, based on her experiences as a student at Trinity College and a returning tourist ten years later.[53]

A typical Cullinan short story follows this pattern: incisively observed encounters and emotional consequences build in seemingly casual movement to climactic generalizations so appropriate and valid as to be immediately recognizable as wisdom. In "Life After Death," a series of minor events punctuate in desultory fashion a day in the life of a young New Yorker. These include picking up a check at the Catholic college where she does part-time work in admissions, attending evening Mass at a city Dominican church, and passing one of President Kennedy's sisters on Lexington Avenue. This conjunction somehow causes the narrator to reflect that "There's no such thing as the whole truth with respect to the living, which is why history appeals to me. I like the finality. . . . The reasons I love Mass are somewhat the same. During those twenty or so minutes, I feel my own past to be not quite coherent but capable of eventually proving to be that. And if my life, like every other, contains elements of the outrageous, that ceremony of death and transfiguration is a means of reckoning with the outrageousness, as work and study are means of reckoning with time."[54] In "The Perfect Crime," the memory of a little boy who has died of cancer and the physical resemblance between the natural gas delivery man and Picasso lead Nora Barrett, self-described as a woman "fatally attracted to the random," to "the signature of the master," a sense of life's underlying mystery: "Resemblances, contrasts, contradictions, coincidence, anomaly, incongruity, ambiguity—the spirit that moves the world has these wonderful resources with which to confound us. We live at the mercy of that spirit, and the spirit lets us live, by and large, in ignorance."[55] In "The Sum and Substance," surgery prompts a young woman to understand the body's primacy; hers is a revelation of *thisness*, like something out of Duns Scotus. She sees—and feels—that "The body took the blows. Nothing was lost on it. Blows to flesh and bone, to the senses, the faculties—the body took them and felt them more deeply than mind or spirit possibly could. Cuts, bruises, infection, disease, shock, sorrow—the body grasped them all at once and forever. The body had its own insight, its own learning."[56] And in "A Good Loser," an awkward reunion in Dublin between New Yorker Ann Clarke and her former lover and his wife ends with Ann playing the part of the "good loser." Her farewell pose, "a pathetic picture, standing there alone in front of that awful house," her drab and tacky summer rental, again prompts generalizing wisdom of swiftness and clarity: "but I wasn't as pathetic as I looked. Nor were the Cronins, as they slammed and locked their car doors, so very safe. For with all the resources it has to command, happiness remains a shaky fortress. Sorrow is the stronghold."[57]

A good piece with which to end this train of thought and this chapter is Cullinan's story "Commuting," in which the narrator travels from a life in Manhattan to a university job in her old neighborhood in the Bronx. The result is a paradigm of chosen migration and a metaphor for ethnic consciousness in our time. Released from her teaching stint in the music department of an unnamed college (probably Fordham), the narrator "sailed back through the campus and out the main gate, into a daunting scene of urban decay—though I remember those surroundings as comfortable, middle class New York." This first contrast sets others in motion. The "blue jeans and t-shirts" of the street crowd remind her that "when I was in school we wore real uniforms—navy serge jumpers and boleros over tan shirts," and that hers were 'my sisters, castoffs, which came to me already worn at the elbow, were also too big at the waist." A "plainly dressed" mother and child, "the mother in a shapeless green pants suit, the little girl in a white blouse with a gray skirt that was too long," remind the narrator of her own relationship with her mother: "like that mother and child we were each other's world, and our world was under a constant threat. It came to me then with a shock—she'd disguised the hard fact that now struck me as obvious—we were poor."

She runs an urban gauntlet of propositions for sex and stolen goods to the express bus stop for Manhattan, and measures the past against the present all the way: "My grandmother boasted of having grown up near the Boulevard, and when I was young its solid brick and Art Deco style still stood for a certain fashionable respectability. Now the street is choked with derelict buildings, desperate lives." One "point of stability," the Boulevard Grand Hotel, reminds her of her sister's wedding reception there, the scene of a tenuous reconciliation in her parents' troubled marriage. Once on the bus, the narrator experiences the legendary commute, moving "over the Harlem River Bridge and onto upper Fifth Avenue," and here the complex spirit of place again triggers comparison, this time among three different groups of migrants in the same place—nineteenth-century burghers, turn of the century Irish immigrants, and contemporary African Americans. After a few blocks, with night falling, "the streets began to throb with the menace and exuberance that the very name Harlem brings to mind. What was it like at the turn of the century when my father was born there? He himself tells a tenement idyll of hardship and happiness that, passing through Harlem, I found it easy to picture. Some of the houses are as beautiful as any on the east side of New York, the proportions as noble, the facades as full of ornamental masonry." She has a quick imaginative flash: "I felt as if I might walk into some splendid, wrecked brownstone and find my father with his parents and his brothers and sisters, having their supper or sitting together by lamplight in some small room." Here the richness of context does not lead to nostalgia, but instead to a deeper realism: "Surely something was wrong even then. Only deep-seatedness would explain the persistence of his need to ruin himself and us, his readiness to punish and be punished over and over. 'Be careful!' I wanted to warn that phantom family. 'Watch what you do and say! My life is in your hands!'"

The bus comes down Fifth Avenue, "where for several blocks, shabby public housing still alternated with beautiful broken buildings; then at Central Park the city made its fresh start." Past Mt. Sinai Hospital and the Metropolitan Museum, "I began collecting my things; the next stop was mine." And the story ends with its valuable revelation: "Riding that last half-mile, my head swam with relief, my heart sang—they do every week, as this realization comes over me: I've reenacted, in spirit, the journey that has given my life its substance and shape, color and brightness. I've escaped!"[58]

This gem of a story embodies the central theme of ethnicity as liberating doubleness. "Commuting" has the particular New York connotation of movement between the outer boroughs and Manhattan. Sometimes, to be sure, that movement is depicted as oscillation between the solid yet parochial ethnic neighborhood and the liberating, promise-filled center of "the city," and in a sense, this does describe an aspect of the pattern of immigration from rural Europe to urban America, from outlying farm to inner city, from constricting provincial community to the freedom of an individual's urban life. However, this stark dichotomy is unfairly slanted and simplistic when used by critics who judge ethnic consciousness as necessarily narrow and unsophisticated. And this is not what writers such as Cullinan, Kennedy, McDermott, and others treated in this essay are saying. Their work tells us instead that the doubleness of ethnic consciousness is enriching and clarifying, that the debate cannot really be resolved, and that a refusal to decide between the poles of ethnic community and cosmopolitan individuality can mark the beginning of a rich, varied life. The middle, straddling position, having something to compare everything with—therein lies a valuable source of energy and understanding. The ethnic has come from some place—a different culture with its world view and mores—that still provides meaningful context. And this place hasn't been repudiated, hasn't been thrown out. It's around a corner in the old neighborhood. It's in church, where the symbolic power of religious experience that so impresses children is sometimes still there for adults, only with more meaning added to the mystery. It's in connections established with the old country through music, literature, dance, language study, travel back.

For this message of enriching, liberating doubleness, Cullinan's central metaphor is appropriate. Commuting means literally going back and forth daily between two parts of a life, and it is of course central to the experience of many New Yorkers, ethnic and otherwise. Cullinan's story reverses the usual rhythm of urban American commuting in that her narrator travels from a life in the city to a job in the old neighborhood, and yet the richness of comparative contexts is still the point. Everything that she sees during the commute she sees twice, and thus more clearly—as the Irish girl from the Bronx that she was, and the New Yorker that she is now. The story ends "I've escaped!" which expresses the relief of someone who has moved successfully to a larger world. But the penultimate sentence is equally important: "I've reenacted, in spirit, the journey that has given my life its substance and shape, color and brightness." This is not a repudiation of the ethnic world, but an expression of the value of belonging to two worlds. "Commuting" between them is a figure for the persistence and value of ethnicity in our time.

Conclusion

WRITING A history of an ethnic group is a complicated task. It requires an understanding of the great adjustment that takes place in a new environment under the pressures created by such factors as politics, culture, work, and residence. And New York, with its millions of inhabitants and numerous racial and ethnic groups, is a particularly complicated setting for such a history. In a sense, it presents the historian with too much information, which, however, is not easily secured or understood.

As the preceding chapters make clear, Irish life in New York is particularly difficult to sum up. In the words of the late Dennis Clark, "Almost anything you can say about [Irish Americans] is both true or false." Simple conclusions about the largest Irish community in the United States, living in the nation's biggest and most complex city, can only be even more tenuous. Nonetheless, this book manages to provide considerable insight into New York's Irish and ethnic history. Specifically focused on the Irish and covering the colonial period to the present, it offers a point of departure for comparing the history of the New York Irish to the experiences of Irish Americans in other cities. It also reveals what research has been and is being done on this group, what level ethnic research has reached in general, what methodologies can be used to study and write about ethnic history, and what further avenues of inquiry might be explored. It is in every sense a beginning book that will, its contributors hope, encourage scholars to pursue this line of study.

The New York Irish and Irish Americans in Other Cities

Although there are many possible points of comparison between the New York Irish and their fellow Irish in Boston, Chicago, and elsewhere, the scholarship on the New York Irish summarized by Leo Hershkowitz, Hasia Diner, Lawrence McCaffrey, Christopher McNickle, and David Reimers, as well as studies of the Irish in other parts of America, focus largely on four principal dimensions of Irish American experience: the struggle to earn a living, participation in politics, fights for the homeland, and roles in the Catholic Church.

Americans have long celebrated their country's opportunities for rags to riches success, but for the hundreds of thousands of Irish migrants fleeing persistent, grinding rural poverty, collapsing trades and industries, or even famine, simple survival seemed a lofty enough aspiration. Most of them achieved little more than that. Most refugees from the Great Famine of the 1840s, Hasia Diner points out, barely eked out an existence toiling at the city's worst jobs and living in its worst neighborhoods. The later immigrants left a very different postfamine Ireland better educated and more disciplined, but were only marginally more successful economically in America than their Famine predecessors. As late as 1890, Lawrence McCaffrey points out, nearly 30 percent of New York's Irish men were laborers. For most of the twentieth century, it seems, Irish immigrants lagged far behind native-born Americans of native parents, and even some other immigrants, in occupational status and income. Even today, thousands of Irish immigrants suffer from the constraints of illegal status and are stuck in dead-end construction or child-care jobs. It is clear, then, that many, perhaps most, Irish immigrants never advanced far beyond the bottom of New York's economic hierarchy.[1]

American-born generations in New York have apparently been more successful. Christopher McNickle, citing Suzanne Model's studies, points out that the second-generation Irish in New York had pulled more or less even with the city's whites of native parentage in terms of occupational status and income by 1940. Model's data, he notes, reveals that the American-born Irish made particularly significant gains between 1910 and 1940. Furthermore, David Reimers suggests that though pockets of Irish American poverty have persisted to the present, the incomes and status of self-identified Irish men and women in New York compare favorably with almost all other ancestry groups.

But how did the occupational achievements of the New York Irish compare with the Irish elsewhere? A generation of scholarship in the 1960s and 1970s appeared to establish that the farther west Irish men and women moved the greater their chances for economic success. Based largely on a contrast of Irish mobility in Californian cities such as San Francisco and Los Angeles with their painfully slow upward mobility in Boston, this geographic rule, a frontier thesis for Irishmen, oversimplifies the pattern of opportunity available to the Irish in America and obscures its critical causes. The Boston Irish suffered severely from the chronic weakness of that city's economy and the social rigidity imposed by an entrenched Yankee Protestant elite. California Irishmen, in contrast, profited from a dynamic economy and the absence of a well-established and hostile ruling class. Whereas in Boston the Irish became the principal focus of nativist hostility, in San Francisco they helped deflect such anger onto Asian immigrants and thus enjoyed the broader privileges of whiteness in a city acutely conscious of white supremacy. It was not where Irishmen landed on the map, then, west or east, so much as the mix of economic and social conditions that structured the opportunities they found.[2]

Such conditions appeared favorable for the Irish as well as for other groups in New York. The city's sustained growth and rapid turnover in elites encouraged upward mobility. Irishmen may have also levered their progress upward in New York as on the west coast by helping to fix the status of other non-white groups on the bottom. It is difficult to assemble accurate comparable data, but from an examination of census statistics from the 1850s, 1900, and 1980 it appears that the occupational status of the New York Irish—especially given the larger number of immigrants among them—compares favorably with the economic achievements of the Irish in other cities and states over the past century and a half.[3]

Curiously, however, there seems a special sense of sadness and loss, a sense of displacement among today's New York Irish, a feeling that they were once powerful and visible and now are not. Such a sense of loss troubles Irish men and women all across the country, but in New York it seems to have a special edge, a peculiar bitterness. Both McNickle and Reimers note Daniel Patrick Moynihan's quotation over 30 years ago in *Beyond the Melting Pot*: "They [the Irish] felt it was their town. It is no longer and they know it. That is one of the things bothering them." A restaurant owner in the Norwood section of the Bronx stated it more succinctly recently: "They say it's not our city anymore." While Irishmen elsewhere in America might also resent their displacement, nowhere else in America did the Irish seem to fall from positions of such great power and notoriety, and eventually so completely out of sight, as in New York.[4]

As both McCaffrey and McNickle suggest, the emergence of the Irish as leaders of Tammany and the club's rise to the apogee of its power under Charlie Murphy best symbolized Irish power at the turn of the century. Murphy extended Tammany's power from City Hall to the State House in Albany and eventually into the national councils of the Democratic Party. Hidden away upstairs at Delmonico's, issuing orders through a host of lieutenants to a seemingly vast organization, the respectable, but hard-nosed and taciturn "Mr. Murphy" seemed the very image of Irish power in New York. As McNickle argues, if New York was Irish at the turn of the century, then it may have been because Mr. Murphy made it so.[5]

Some might date the fall of Irish power to Murphy's death in 1924. Mayor Jimmy Walker understood well what Murphy's passing meant to the "organization": "The brains of Tammany hall are buried in Calvary Cemetery," he lamented after Murphy's death. McNickle points out that the heavy-handed, clumsy corruption of Murphy's successors set Tammany and Irish Democratic power up for a fall to Fiorello La Guardia; La Guardia's victory was clearly another marker in the Irish political descent. In 1945 an Irishman, an Irish immigrant no less, William O'Dwyer, succeeded La Guardia, but, as David Reimers argues, there would be no revival of Irish power in New York. By the 1960s the Irish had ceased to be a recognizable and powerful bloc in the city's politics.[6]

Whether the Irish rose higher and fell faster and lower than Celts in any other city would be hard to determine, but the course of Irish politics in New York was unique. In Philadelphia, the Irish never really ruled, or at least not for very long. The old WASP-run GOP machine held on tenaciously until 1951 when blue blood Democratic reformers—not Irish regular Democrats—toppled it and reaped many of the rewards of power. San Francisco's Irish, divided along class lines and between reform Democrats and an independent labor party, lost control of the city by the early twentieth century and never regained it. In Boston, on the other hand, the Irish gained almost total control of the city's politics by the early twentieth century and have only recently yielded the mayoralty to another group. In Chicago the Irish were important players among many competing groups until the 1930s, when they finally achieved dominance in the city and held it for many decades thereafter. In Pittsburgh, where a WASP Republican machine had dominated until the 1920s, the New Deal raised the city's Irish Democrats from bit players to leaders in the city's politics for many years.

Perhaps the most important force shaping the singular course of Irish politics in New York was the changing ethnic composition of the city and the resulting shifting balance of power among the city's many different nationalities and races. In the nineteenth century the Germans were numerous enough to have been potent ethnic rivals of the Irish. The Germans, rich in useful skills and confident of the achievements of their culture, however, did not need politics to lever their upward economic climb or earn them respect as the Irish did; they thus had little of the Irish burning ambition for political power. The Germans were also seriously divided by regional origin, political ideology, class, and religion. They were not a major threat, then, to Irish political ambitions. In the twentieth century, however, millions of new migrants poured into New York from all over the world and the rural South. Among the largest of the new groups, Christopher McNickle notes, were the Italians and Jews. By 1930 more than one million first- and second-generation Italians and close to two million Jews lived in New York and made up at least two-fifths of the city's population. In no other great city in the nation were Italians and Jews as numerous or as large a proportion of the population. The Italians and Jews had very different cultures, were often suspicious of one another, and were both divided internally; they nonetheless posed a significant challenge to the Irish in New York. As early as 1929 the *Irish World* worried openly that "we see all around us, the people of other races forging ahead."[7]

Irish politicians in other cities did not face this same mix of groups. In Boston the new groups—the Italians, the Jews, and others—would never be as numerous as in New York; the Irish could always control the city if they remained united and often even if they did not. The antagonism between the Boston Yankees and Irish, kept alive by real Yankee disdain for the Celts and the needs of Irish politicians to maintain group solidarity, continued to shape Irish politics into the middle of the twentieth century. In Chicago the Irish faced hosts of newcomers as well, but poverty (and the obstacles posed by race prejudice for African Americans) hindered the mobilization of the two largest new groups there, the Poles and Southern blacks, and severe mutual antagonism made their mutual alliance unlikely. Still, the Irish in Chicago were also luckier than the their fellow Celts in New York. Anton Cermak, the Czech ethnic who built the new multiethnic Chicago machine, was killed, delivering the organization into the hands of Pat Nash and Ed Kelly, just in time for those Irish bosses to profit from New Deal patronage. Some Irish organizations in New York, such as Ed Flynn's in the Bronx, reaped rewards from the New Deal and the national Democratic triumph, but Tammany—out of power and suspected by FDR—did not. New York's Irish politicians also had the misfortune to confront in Fiorello La Guardia an extremely talented and personable reform opponent who proved extraordinarily popular among their Jewish and Italian rivals, as well as among many other groups.[8]

The final ouster of the Irish from power in New York would not come until after World War II. Irish Democrats in many cities after the war confronted challenges from increasing African American populations or ambitious second-generation Italian or Polish ethnics. The mix of groups and evolution of politics in New York, however, was, as David Reimers reveals, characteristically complicated. In the 1950s reform "amateur" Democrats, largely Jewish and WASP, sought to wrest control of the Democratic party from the Irish and other Democratic regulars. In the 1960s a coalition of Jewish and WASP liberals, allied with African Americans and other minorities, rallied behind John Lindsay and took over City Hall. Conservative opposition to the Lindsay coalition formed behind Jewish regular Democrats or Italian Republicans and Democrats. By the time Beame and Koch ushered in the "Jewish era" in New York politics in the 1970s and David Dinkins raised the possibility of an African American one in 1989, the Irish had finally disappeared as an independent and powerful bloc in the city's politics.[9]

The peculiar political history of the Irish in New York may not only have given them a special sense of loss; it may have also made them more politically and religiously conservative than their Celtic counterparts in other American cities. In nineteenth-century New York, business leaders were always an important part of the city's Democratic coalition, and, indeed, as McCaffrey points out, after the Tweed Ring scandals, a group of wealthy merchants, manufacturers, bankers, and lawyers—the "Swallowtail Democrats"—took control of the party and dominated it for nearly 15 years. In some other cities Irish Americans had to fight their way to power through Whig or Republican business and social elites, but the New York Irish were often political partners with one faction or other of the city's economic and social establishment. As they began to rise to power in the party in the late nineteenth century, McCaffrey suggests, Irish leaders were acutely conscious of the need to placate the business community and build cross-class coalitions to maintain both the party's domination of the city and their control of the party. "Honest John" Kelly's reign as Tammany chieftain illustrates this conservatism well. Eager for business support, Kelly endorsed tax and budget cuts and mobilized the Hall's forces to crush Henry George's labor campaign in 1886. Later Tammany leaders, such as Richard Croker and Charlie Murphy, tangled with a host of "reformers" or radicals from Seth Low and John Purroy Mitchel to William Randolph Hearst and Morris Hillquit.[10]

If power or access to it made the New York Irish especially conservative in the nineteenth and early twentieth century, then their fighting retreat in the face of challenges by new groups may have pushed them even further to the right later. Irish fears for their declining power, exacerbated by Depression anxieties, McNickle argues, appeared to make them especially receptive to Father Coughlin's ethnocentric extremism and anti-Semitism in the 1930s. Pushed by Jewish and WASP reform Democrats, New York's Irish also appeared to move out of the Democratic Party earlier than their fellow Celts in Boston or Chicago. Kevin Phillips has traced steadily increasing votes for Republican candidates among Irish New Yorkers in the 1950s and 1960s, far larger than Irish Republican totals in other cities. Two Irish Catholics, Kieran O'Doherty and J. Daniel Mahoney, founded the Conservative Party in New York in 1961 and some observers, David Reimers reports, have even claimed that a majority of the New York City Irish voted for Goldwater in 1964.[11]

It is important, however, not to overstress Irish conservatism in New York or anywhere else. Irishmen also were vitally involved in antebellum labor reform and in the fashioning of a working-class republican radicalism in New York and other cities. After the Civil War, Irish men and women were at the forefront of working-class reform; indeed, they were critical to the upsurge of republican labor radicalism all across the country in the 1880s. Irishmen in New York and elsewhere probably became more conservative after the 1890s. Nevertheless, New York City Irish Tammany men, and Irish Democrats in Boston, Chicago, Cleveland, and other cities, helped forge an urban liberalism in the 1910s that would come to full fruition in the Democratic Party of the 1930s and 1940s.[12]

How then to judge Irish political ideology? Radicals, conservatives, modest liberals? It is hard to say for sure. This is, in part, because there were so many conflicting voices within the Irish community. It is also, perhaps, as Moynihan and others have suggested, because the Irish have seemed the consummate pragmatic politicians, convinced by experiences in Ireland and America that gaining and holding power, not determining how to use it, is the fundamental problem in politics.[13]

Yet it may also be because it is difficult to find appropriate standards of radicalism, liberalism, or conservatism to measure them against. Despite enduring desperate poverty and participating actively in hosts of labor struggles, few Irishmen in New York or elsewhere embraced socialism or communism. Indeed, in twentieth-century New York and other American cities they often emerged as virulent opponents of socialism (a notable exception in New York was Mike Quill of the Transport Workers Union). Since American historians have long been preoccupied with the problem of socialism's failure in America, the Irish have appeared to be conservatives despite their support for working-class republicanism or urban liberalism. Yet socialism has been only a marginal force in American politics—albeit more important in New York than in other parts of the country. It is not clear then how useful a standard it is for measuring ideology along the narrow spectrum of American political opinion.

On the other hand, the narrowness of that spectrum is precisely the point many historians have argued. Working-class republicanism and urban liberalism, such historians contend, were too limited, too conservative to effect substantial change; they were a diffusion of anger and energy that might have been more profitably channeled into a real overhaul of the American political and social systems. David Roediger has recently argued, for example, that racist presuppositions and biases fundamentally flawed Irish American working-class republicanism.[14]

New York's importance as a communications center, as well as its huge Irish population and wealth, made the city a unique force in the Irish American nationalist movement. As Dennis Clark has suggested, New York could rightly claim to be the "overseas capital" of Irish nationalism. Rebel exiles from MacNeven, Emmet, and Sampson, to Meagher, Mitchel, and O'Mahony, to Rossa and Devoy, flocked to the city, and most settled there while they plotted to free their homeland. Major conclaves of nationalists—from Repeal meetings in the early 1840s, to the mass rallies of the Fenians at Jones's Wood in Yorkville in the 1860s, and the great Madison Square Garden gatherings during and after World War I—were usually held in New York. Most of the important nationalist movements were also headquartered in the city: the Young Ireland's "Directory" met in New York in the 1840s; the Moffat Hotel in Union Square was the Fenian "capital" in the 1860s; Ford's *Irish World* was the headquarters of radical nationalism in the early 1880s; John Devoy directed the Clan na Gael and spun many conspiracies from his hotel room on the Lower East Side through most of the turn-of-the-century period; and the central offices of the Friends of Irish

Freedom, organized to press for Irish independence after the Easter Rebellion, were there as well. Of course, nationalism flourished in other cities. Boston was a stronghold of conservative nationalists in the early 1880s, for example, and Chicago a powerful influence in both the Clan na Gael and the Land League through the rest of the decade. Still, New York has remained more or less the epicenter of Irish nationalism for almost 200 years. Irish American nationalism no longer has as broad a cross-generational or cross-class appeal in New York or elsewhere as it did before the creation of the Free State or the declaration of the Republic. Nevertheless, because New York continues to be America's communications center and also draws a disproportionately large number of the Irish who emigrate to the United States, it still is at the forefront of the Irish American nationalist movement.[15]

The New York Irish may have been important to the nationalist movement in America, but they did not all speak with one voice. They and Irish nationalists around America disagreed about how the nationalist war should be waged and what kind of Ireland they wished to see emerge after victory. By the 1880s those disagreements had crystallized into three distinct nationalist ideologies: constitutional nationalism, dedicated to working through the British political system for home rule; "physical force," or militant nationalism, committed to violent revolution to make Ireland a republic but not to change its economic system; and radical nationalism endorsing a variety of tactics to work an economic as well as political transformation of the old country. There was no clear regional cast to the support for these clashing visions in America. Rather, conflicts usually occurred within American cities; in communities as disparate as Denver, Worcester (Massachusetts), and Pittsburgh, as well as New York, all three nationalist ideologies won support and vied for local control of the movement. Class, generation, even gender and place of origin in Ireland—not region of residence in America—were generally the most important determinants of who would support which of these nationalist ideologies. There were some regional differences, but they were of degree, not kind: in Denver, Boston, and Worcester, middle-class constitutionalists tended to dominate local movements; in places like Chicago and Butte, Montana, physical force nationalists usually ruled; and in many mining towns and some small New England mill cities the radical nationalists were especially powerful. Through the 1890s and 1910s economic radicalism grew weaker and all but disappeared in most cities, including New York. Some radicals reappeared in the 1910s in places like New York or Butte, Montana, where there were strong local socialist movements, but these radical groups were usually tiny or ephemeral bands.[16]

In contrast to the fuzziness of regional differences in the Irish American nationalist movement, some historians have argued that regional divisions are very important to understanding the history of American Catholicism. They have suggested that Catholic America has long been divided into a conservative "core," centered in the East Coast dioceses, where Catholics are numerous and powerful and thus have had little need to adapt their church to American culture, and a liberal Midwest and Western periphery, where Catholics are fewer in number and have had to work hard to accommodate themselves to more powerful neighbors. Such an explanation may oversimplify complexity within both the core and the periphery. Where a diocese was located may not have been so important in shaping its leader's opinions on religious issues as the conditions of its environment. In late-nineteenth-century New York there were few incentives for Catholic bishops to adjust their thinking on religious questions. Democrats dominated the city after the Civil War and became increasingly dependent on Catholic voters through the early twentieth century. They thus had no interest in harassing the church about parochial education or forcing it to make any other adjustments in its religious positions; indeed, Tammany Democrats sought to help the church with subsidies for its charitable institutions. After Tammany's collapse and after the Irish fought their stubborn rear guard action to preserve influence and power, the issues they contested with liberal Jews or WASPs were sometimes religious or moral, as well as economic and political. Such fights may have hardened their cultural as well as their political and economic conservatism.

In any case, whether because of such conditions or simply from personal inclination, McCaffrey, McNickle, and Reimers point out that New York's Irish Catholic bishops usually aligned with Catholic conservatives in the battles within the church and between church members and outsiders over Catholicism's role in America. Parochial education was an important issue in these battles, and New York's bishops were outspoken in their commitment to a separate Catholic system. Leo Hershkowitz tells how Archbishop Hughes waged a celebrated battle to win public funds for his schools in the early 1840s; defeat in that battle only hardened his resolve to build a separate Catholic system. In the 1880s and 1890s the fight within the American church over parochial education escalated to public debate. Michael Corrigan of New York, who had emerged as a spokesman for the conservatives, adamantly opposed the efforts of liberals like Archbishop John Ireland of St. Paul to explore new options of accommodation with the public schools. Not all New Yorkers, not even all of New York's Irish clergymen, agreed with their conservative leaders. Edward McGlynn and many of his associates in the "Academia," a loosely knit group of liberal priests within the New York diocese, were committed to "americanizing" the church and they therefore opposed parochial education. By 1900 a Vatican crackdown had routed the liberals, but their suspicion of parochial education may have had some effect on Catholic schooling in the archdiocese. By 1898 only one-third of New York's Catholic students were in parochial schools, and in 1900 only a little more than half of New York's parishes had schools. That proportion was higher than the percentages in some big city dioceses like Boston or San Francisco, about the same as in Philadelphia, and substantially lower than the proportion in Chicago. Nevertheless, by the middle

of the twentieth century, as McNickle and Reimers suggest, no bishop and no
diocese in the country seemed more fully committed to theological orthodoxy,
political conservatism, and the building up of the ghetto church than Francis
Cardinal Spellman and his Archdiocese of New York.[17]

The New York Irish and the Future of Irish American and Ethnic Research

A great deal of research is now being done on this and other aspects of Irish and
ethnic experience in New York. Nevertheless, unexplored avenues still abound.
For example, the Irish have often been pictured as victims of or combatants in
ethnic conflict in New York, Boston, Philadelphia, and elsewhere, yet little has
been written about cooperative intergroup relations. Irish—black contacts, in
particular, have been examined in the context of hostility. Graham Hodges
offers a different perspective in his study of the Sixth Ward. In New York's
polyglot neighborhoods, where the daily routine of life brought people of
different backgrounds together, cooperation as well as conflict was evident.
Historians have only begun to focus on cooperation as part of the spectrum of
ethnic relations. Most notably in their book on Ybor City, George Pozzetta and
Gary Mormino revealed the long-term cooperative contacts between Italian,
Cuban, and Spanish immigrants.[18] Yet the Irish experience reveals an even
earlier example, and there are others as well. In the midst of racial tensions and
violence, many Irish and black New Yorkers were able to live together peacefully. The dynamics of that relationship for the Irish and blacks, as well as
between the Irish and other groups, must be further analyzed. In a multiethnic,
competitive society in which conflict continues to be the norm, an understanding of the basis for cooperative living takes on a special importance.

In a different context, John Kuo Wei Tchen looks at Irish-Chinese relations
and images through the life of Quimbo Appo, a Chinese immigrant who married
an Irish woman. The little-known contact between these two groups, occurring
in the Sixth Ward as well as the Fourth, also involved both cooperation and
conflict. In this chapter, which further discusses Irish-black contacts, Tchen's
analysis of stereotypes and the Irish, Chinese, and black place in New York's
ethnic hierarchy indicates a new way of looking at group relations. Irish
performers were able to manipulate stereotypes to their group's advantage. Irish
entry into a white Euro-American group foreshadowed the race-based ethnic
alliances that have developed in the mid to late twentieth century. The process
of changing ethnic images and the evolution of group coalitions is a timely topic
that speaks to the New York and America of today. It is a topic that has not been
fully researched but nonetheless can provide useful insights into the dynamics
of a multiethnic, multiracial society in regard to conflict, cooperation, intermarriage, mobility, pluralist politics, and images of oneself and others. Especially for the Irish, with a greater proportion of women than men emigrating to
America, it is important to consider intermarriage. To do so would open up a

topic that has not received the attention it deserves. Furthermore, Irish family life over a number of generations remains largely unexplored.[19]

Hodges and Tchen are not the only contributors to this volume who suggest a new focus and further research. Residential mobility is covered well in Robert Snyder's and Marion Casey's papers. Snyder's work brings the process of neighborhood succession to the present and comments on the forces that shaped and changed the community. Although neighborhood ethnic succession is not a new concept, Snyder is able to provide a long-term view and a needed personal and contemporary emphasis through his use of oral history. His analysis, in a sense, is the story of all New York neighborhoods that have undergone transition. The longing for the old community, the attachment to place, relations between incoming and outgoing groups, and the pull of suburbia all form parts of his narrative, as they do in the history of many changing communities. His survey of the neighborhood over time, noting earlier ethnic relations, provides a good prototype for understanding the long-term dynamics of community cohesion and transition. Casey's study of Irish residential mobility suggests a new and intriguing way of looking at this process. Previously, historians focused on an increase in income through a better job to explain upward residential mobility. A rise in class or occupational status often brought with it a move to a better neighborhood. But at least for the Irish it did not always happen this way. In this detailed study of Irish residential choices, another pattern emerges. The opening up of new neighborhoods and Irish strategies to make them affordable created a horizontal mobility. Irish New Yorkers were able to move into better housing with more neighborhood amenities without an accompanying rise in income or class levels. Moving into the suburbs or buying a home did not necessarily indicate social mobility. It was a move that exhibited a rise in the standard of living but not class. Low-income New Yorkers have always designed various strategies (for example, taking in boarders) to be able to afford their housing. But Casey takes this mode of living a step further to understand how it was used to disperse a working-class ethnic population throughout the city and beyond and into better neighborhoods.

New housing and transportation lines, which developed almost simultaneously in early-twentieth-century New York, were the factors spurring this movement. Apartments in better neighborhoods became accessible and available. How much of this was a particularly New York Irish response awaits further research. Other groups may have used or are using the same strategies to secure footholds in upscale communities. If that is the case, then the theories must be revised that tie residential mobility strictly to class and occupation and suggest an ethnic succession that brought newer groups into a neighborhood as older groups, now wealthier, moved to better areas.

Snyder and Casey also raise the issue of the suburbanization of the Irish. Although dealing well with the suburbs in terms of residential mobility, historians must address the ethnic Irish and Catholic religious culture that formed in those new areas. Snyder speaks of "maintaining an ethnic identity in suburban towns far removed from city neighborhoods" and of an ethnic identity that "will have to be constantly recreated if it is to endure." What type of community emerged and what forms ethnicity took need further exploration.

Irish religious behavior gets a new look in Colleen McDannell's essay. Focusing on parish fairs, she makes a convincing case for the diversity of Irish-Catholic religiosity. Breaking from the usual stereotypes, McDannell provides a more textured analysis of Irish religious practices and places her focus on the lay people rather than on the clerics. She also discusses the way in which Irish Catholics through their fairs fit into the American consumer culture, their relations with Protestants, and the role of women in the parish fairs as contrasted to the male-run St. Patrick's Day parades. As her conclusions make clear, much more work needs to be done on the nuances of group behavior. Although the subject has been broached in a few cases—for example, in Robert Orsi's work on Italian religious behavior, and Andrew Heinze's on Jews and American consumerism—the intertwining of religious culture, consumerism, and attitudes toward other religions and gender illustrates the interconnections possible in a detailed and wide-ranging analysis and the elements in Irish American religious history that need further research.[20]

The chapters dealing with Irish nationalism, by David Brundage and by Joe Doyle, also develop new insights into Irish attitudes. Brundage discusses the period between two peaks of Irish nationalistic activity. Concentrating on the leadership element, he looks particularly at attitudes toward the Catholic Church, socialism, and class and gender issues. Noting a divergence of views on these topics between the 1890s nationalists and those of the preceding period, Brundage explains how these changing opinions affected and defined the nationalist organizations and movement. Particularly interesting, and a good tie-in with Doyle's study, is his discussion on women in the movement and women's rights. Doyle offers an intriguing look at a longshoremen's strike against British ships in 1920 that was precipitated by Irish American women nationalists and involved the joining together of Irish and black stevedores. Reflecting both the role of women in the movement and the possibilities for interracial cooperation, his analysis, like others in this book, sheds light on neglected aspects of Irish and New York history and offers a new perspective by combining issues extending from intergroup relations to union activity to gender roles. Both analyses also reveal the impact of Old World issues on American ethnic groups, a much-discussed topic that still is relevant today for the Irish and others.

Irish American politicians, especially those involved in Tammany, have also been a much covered topic. After Steven Erie's and Christopher McNickle's books, it is easy to ask whether anything more needs to be said about Irish politicos.[21] Yet John McClymer offers a different approach through his comparison of the careers of John Purroy Mitchel and Al Smith. Mitchel, the consummate assimilationist, and Smith, tied closely to his ethnicity, indicated the ways in which the Irish (and presumably other ethnic groups) could become part of America's political life. The impact of each on progressivism and on the development of urban liberalism in New York is also noted. Different views on Americanism, reform, and ethnicity revealed different political styles and results. That successful Irish politicians could reflect totally opposite views and styles indicates the variety of attitudes found in any ethnic community's leadership. This chapter fits in with a reevaluation of ethnic leadership and identity evident in Victor Greene's 1987 book.[22]

Other topics that have previously received much attention are Irish workers and entrepreneurs, unions, ethnic organizations, and involvement in major national events (in this case, the Civil War). Each of the chapters on these subjects provides either a different perspective or new information. William Devlin's study, for example, depicts the role of the Irish in the burgeoning clothing industry. Famine-era immigrants included skilled artisans and businessmen who were able to enter into and succeed within this industry. Devlin presents a first-time in-depth look at the Irish presence in such industries as hatting. In a close analysis of New York's garment industry, the author describes ethnic entrepreneurship, succession, the workings of this industry, and Irish consumerism ("dressing like an American was an indispensable part of becoming one"). His narrative offers a ready comparison to other ethnic entrepreneurial studies and indicates the research still needed on the Irish to add nuance to commonly held notions of their place in the city's economic structure.

John McKivigan and Thomas Robertson concentrate on Irish workers and union activity, noting the shift of most of these workers from radicalism to conservatism within the labor movement. Although focusing on unions, they also include information on ethnic succession, New York politics, ethnic employment concentrations, the role of the Catholic church in workers' issues, and socialism. There is also an interesting discussion on the Irish control of union leadership positions during a period when there was an ethnic shift in the city's workers, a situation that later occurs among other ethnic groups as well. The Irish clearly had a significant impact on the city's labor movement, and it continued beyond their period of dominance.

John Ridge's essay on Irish county societies reverses the tendency to view ethnic communities as inexorably moving from local identifications to national ones. He studies the continuation of regional or county loyalties. Noting that a number of these societies appeared long after the peak immigration years and continue to the present, Ridge suggests that historians' declarations of the end of these local feelings, once a national ethnic sense emerged, were premature. He carefully relates the flowering of these societies, their role in the ethnic community, and in Ireland. While maintained by immigration over the years, their very persistence indicates the multifaceted nature of ethnic identity. Furthermore, Ridge reveals a migration network from various counties to specific New York neighborhoods that was first noted by Carol Groneman: a chain migration that needs more detailed study but appears similar to previous in-depth work on Italians, Norwegians, Slovaks, and Germans in New York and other parts of the United States.[23]

Edward Spann's study of the Irish during the Civil War seemingly treats a subject that has already received significant attention. Yet he brings something new to the discussion by focusing on the impact of the war specifically on the Irish community: on recruiting, Irish participation in the war, acceptance, political attachments, community institutions, and identity.

A persistence of Irish identity is, of course, also related to a sense of a unique culture and language. Kenneth Nilsen on the Irish language, Rebecca Miller on Irish music, and Charles Fanning on literature discuss the cultural aspects of identity. Nilsen describes the strength and retention of Gaelic in nineteenth-century New York and the efforts to maintain the language. Language maintenance for other groups as well is a topic that has not always received the attention it deserves but remains important in a nation where "English only" has become the war-cry of modern nativists.[24] Miller's study of popular and traditional Irish music and dance traces the perseverance of this art form "as an indicator of ever-changing ethnic pride and community identity." And as the interest in their traditional music shows, that identity has remained strong. Miller reveals the interplay between assimilating to the new culture and retaining elements of the old, the feelings of embarrassment for traditional music along with pride in the Old World musical tradition. She ties in the changing attitudes to the political and cultural milieu in the United States and offers one of the few analyses on ethnic music—a topic that also deserves scholarly attention but has of yet received little. Fanning's study of Irish American literature since the 1960s reveals the same duality. Considering a number of works, he looks at the persistence of a concern with ethnicity, family, and community and the value of each even to those who have moved beyond the ethnic world. Further works should consider the impact of this ethnic music and literature on American culture and the interplay between the two.[25]

A continuing stream of Irish immigrants, beginning in the colonial era and continuing virtually uninterrupted into the 1990s, has been a factor in maintaining the Old World culture and identity. Joyce Goodfriend discusses the disparate origins of this ethnic community by studying its component parts—Gaelic Irish, Scots-Irish, Anglo-Irish, and German-Irish. She concludes that the Irish and specifically the Anglo-Irish (mostly Anglicans) represented important groups in colonial New York. The Gaelic Irish (Catholics), while present among the colonial Irish, were a minority and one that historians have largely neglected. A sense of some ethnic cohesion was evident among the city's Irish initially but began to fade as religion and class fragmented the group.

The most recent Irish immigration also reveals fragmentation. Many Irish come to the city as illegal immigrants, and try to make use of existing ethnic networks. But these immigrants represent a culture and lifestyle somewhat different from present-day Irish Americans, and as Mary Corcoran relates there is tension within the ethnic group. But the reasons for emigrating, from the colonial to the contemporary periods, remain similar, and the impact on a sense of identity in both eras is strong. For example, some old Irish neighborhoods, businesses, cultural activities, and organizations, such as the county associations that Ridge discusses, have experienced a resurgence with the recent immigration. Who are the new Irish immigrants to New York, why did they come to the United States, what jobs do they take, and what is their place within the established Irish community, are the questions Corcoran seeks to answer. These are questions for other new arrivals as well. Their fit into and impact on already established ethnic communities and cultures are relatively unexplored. Yet, group comparisons would be useful. The recent Russian Jewish immigration and its effect on fading Jewish neighborhoods and American Jewish culture in general would make an interesting comparison to the Irish.[26]

While Goodfriend and Corcoran write about the Irish community in its very early years and present time, respectively, Paul Gilje discusses the transformation of that community before the Famine exodus. Fragmenting in the manner Goodfriend noted, the Irish split along religious and class lines. The group that emerged and defined the Irish community for decades was Catholic and working class. As Gilje states, middle-class Irish efforts to shape the Irish group into a nonsectarian and broadly based body did not succeed. The Irish splintering reveals the intragroup friction evident as well among other New York ethnics in a later period. Although not as severe, splits in the Jewish and Italian communities showed a similar class-based antagonism. In Gilje's narrative, we get a close look at these early nineteenth-century working-class Irish immigrants—their neighborhoods, occupations, organizations, and politics—and the developing cohesion of their community. The violence based on class, ethnic, religious and work frustrations, and rivalries, that erupted frequently also indicated the drawing together of the lower-class Irish Catholics. A sense of identity emerged, as Gilje contends, through "a mixture of class awareness and ethnicity."

An identity with a specific ethnicity and class also brought with it stereotyping of their group from others. Nativists often attacked the Irish because of their ethnic, religious, and class identities. The attacks sometimes revolved around the diseases the Irish immigrant supposedly brought into the United States. Using the discussion on disease to look at immigration practices regarding illness, Alan Kraut also offers an expansive discussion of immigration policy, health, nativism, and the Irish. What Kraut calls the "medicalization of prejudice" applied to many groups over the years and is still evident today. The nature of this medically related prejudice and its impact on the group attacked, and on immigration policy, are topics that have not been well researched until recently for any ethnic group. Although historians have made these connections before, they could delve even deeper into these topics.

Whatever the topic, it is clear that the Irish had a significant impact on ethnicity, New York, and American life. Walter Walsh provides one new aspect of this influence in regard to the first court cases involving the free exercise of religion in early-nineteenth-century New York. Looking at the "ethnocultural . . . construction of law," he discusses particularly the role of William Sampson, a Protestant and United Irish exile, in arguing this concept, and in supporting "religious and cultural equality." Once again the fragmentation of the Irish community along religious and class lines is noted as the Irish republican vision of a broad and egalitarian Irish community faded.

Combined with the overviews, the chapters in this volume provide as comprehensive a history of the New York Irish as is now available. They suggest as well the topics that need further research. As such, the book offers historians and others a study that should be the starting point for writing a definitive history of the Irish in New York. That book will have to inform readers of the importance of the Irish to the study of ethnicity and New York. The beginning of this discussion was one of the aims of this collection.

The Irish, one of the first immigrant groups to be analytically studied, and a group that has been in the United States long enough to see the full process of assimilation at work, is also part of the new immigration to America in the 1990s. It is therefore a key group in America's ethnic mosaic, one that encompasses all the elements needed to understand the differences and similarities between earlier immigrant migration, adjustment, and assimilation and the behaviors of today's arrivals. Its history also sheds considerable light on such issues as intergroup relations, stereotyping, the development of an Euro-American identity, the impact of a new migration on those of the group already settled, neighborhood succession, mobility, and gender roles. Furthermore, the Irish, as a group that challenged the cultural hegemony of the majority of Americans in the nineteenth century, provide a good comparative example through which to understand the friction evident today as the sources of immigration have shifted to non-European countries.

Finally, the Irish experience raises the questions of how and in what ways an ethnic group is shaped by and shapes its environment. Comparative studies between the Irish in various cities can answer the first question, but the New York experience, owing to the size of the city and the Irish population, and the continuing Irish migration into the present, must be part of the analysis. The role the Irish played in shaping their environment raises a key issue in understanding American ethnicity and its impact. One might well ask what New York would have been like without the Irish. Their impact on politics, neighborhood development and residential patterns, industry, unions, and culture, as well as on other groups, is evident. New York's development, from neighborhoods to businesses, was largely due to the multitudes of immigrants it received. And the Irish were a major part of the immigrant influx. Understanding the role of ethnicity in American life means also understanding its role in shaping urban society. The Irish were not the only ethnic group to play such a role, of course, but their longevity in the city, along with other factors, makes them an important group to consider in assessing the impact of ethnicity on New York, not to mention the entire nature of ethnicity in the history of this country.

Statistical Tables

TABLE A.1. Irish-born Population, New York City, by Decade, 1860–1990

	Borough										Total Irish-born New York City
Year	Manhattan	Percent of total	Brooklyn	Percent of total	Bronx	Percent of total	Queens	Percent of total	Staten Island	Percent of total	
1860	203,740		56,710		—		—		—		—
1870	201,999		78,220		—		—		—		—
1880	198,595		78,814		—		—		—		—
1890	190,418		84,738		—		—		—		—
1900	166,066	60.4	83,400	30.3	12,820	4.7	7,958	2.9	4,858	1.8	275,102
1910	151,061	59.8	70,654	28.0	18,269	7.3	8,671	3.4	4,017	1.6	252,672
1920	116,749	57.4	56,660	27.9	18,679	9.2	10,618	5.2	3,744	1.8	203,450
1930	96,861	43.9	53,571	24.3	38,816	17.6	27,139	12.3	4,244	1.9	220,631
1940	68,996	37.9	39,689	21.8	42,709	23.5	26,953	14.8	3,479	1.9	181,826
1950	49,073	33.9	29,717	20.5	38,004	26.2	25,277	17.5	2,737	1.9	144,808
1960	—		—		—		—		—		114,008
1970	13,623	19.8	11,085	16.1	23,525	34.2	19,176	27.9	1,369	2.0	68,778
1980	7,260	17.6	6,572	15.9	12,559	30.5	13,590	32.9	1,333	3.2	41,354
1990	4,255	13.7	4,307	13.9	9,720	31.4	11,828	38.2	897	2.9	31,007

Sources: U.S. Census Bureau Reports, 1860–1980; Public Use Sample (New York, N.Y., 1990).

— Not available.

Note: From the middle of the nineteenth century to the consolidation of the five boroughs into the City of New York in 1898, the Irish-born population was remarkably stable as the large Irish-born population of the famine year was replaced by a steady stream of new arrivals. After 1900, during World War I, and more noticeably after the early 1930s, Irish immigration to the United States was substantially reduced, never again to approach the earlier levels. By 1990 the Bronx and Queens contained the majority of the now greatly reduced Irish-born population of the city. Many of these were recent arrivals from the increased Irish immigration of the 1980s.

Table A.2. Irish-born, Manhattan and Annexed District, 1855, 1865, 1875, by Ward

Ward	Area of Manhattan and Annexed District	1855		1865		1875	
		Total population	Irish-born population and percent of total	Total population	Irish-born population and percent of total	Total population	Irish-born population and percent of total
1st	Battery	13,486	6,207 (46.0)	9,852	4,080 (41.4)	14,298	5,025 (35.1)
2nd	South and East of City Hall	3,249	1,164 (35.8)	1,194	426 (35.7)	1,012	312 (30.8)
3rd	South and West of City Hall	7,909	2,283 (28.9)	3,367	1,179 (35.0)	2,874	740 (25.7)
4th	Near East River and Brooklyn Bridge	22,895	10,446 (45.6)	17,352	6,605 (38.1)	20,828	6,681 (32.1)
5th	Tribeca S. of Canal, nr. Hudson River	21,617	4,866 (22.5)	18,205	4,430 (24.3)	15,951	4,380 (27.5)
6th	North of City Hall, South of Canal	25,562	10,845 (42.4)	19,754	7,211 (36.5)	19,861	5,304 (26.7)
7th	East River and South of East Broadway	34,422	11,777 (34.0)	36,962	11,645 (31.5)	45,636	12,400 (27.2)
8th	So Ho, between Canal & Houston	34,052	7,210 (21.2)	30,098	5,133 (17.1)	32,465	5,313 (16.4)
9th	Greenwich Village	39,982	7,909 (19.7)	38,504	6,348 (16.5)	49,403	8,259 (16.7)
10th	East of the Bowery, North of Division	26,378	3,442 (13.0)	31,537	3,139 (10.0)	41,747	2,435 (5.8)
11th	South of East 14th near East River	52,979	9,291 (17.5)	58,953	7,178 (12.2)	63,855	5,578 (8.7)
12th	Northern Manhattan above 86th St.	17,656	5,831 (33.0)	28,259	5,967 (21.1)	60,510	11,492 (19.0)
13th	Near East River between Grand and Houston	26,597	4,965 (18.7)	26,388	4,259 (16.1)	34,013	4,207 (12.4)

Ward	Location	1855 Total	1855 Irish-born	1865 Total	1865 Irish-born	1875 Total	1875 Irish-born
14th	Near Old St. Patrick's Cathedral	24,754	8,961 (36.2)	23,382	7,322 (31.3)	26,453	7,102 (26.8)
15th	Washington Square	24,046	6,285 (26.1)	25,572	6,041 (23.6)	25,529	4,027 (15.8)
16th	Between 6th Ave. and Hudson River, 14th and 26th	39,823	11,572 (39.0)	41,972	10,196 (24.2)	48,235	10,434 (21.6)
17th	East of 4th Ave., South of East 14th	59,548	14,815 (24.9)	79,563	12,007 (15.1)	101,075	9,672 (9.6)
18th	North of E. 14th between 5th Ave. and East River	39,509	14,666 (37.1)	47,613	15,050 (31.6)	61,195	16,993 (27.8)
19th	East of 6th Ave. between 40th and 86th	17,866	6,320 (35.4)	39,945	10,309 (25.8)	118,727	25,153 (21.1)
20th	West Side between 26th and 40th	47,055	12,853 (27.3)	61,884	14,722 (23.8)	79,764	15,977 (20.0)
21st	East of 6th Ave. between East 26th and East 40th	27,914	8,287 (29.7)	38,669	10,502 (27.2)	58,831	16,275 (27.7)
22nd	West of Central Park, South of 86th St.	22,605	5,740 (25.4)	47,361	7,585 (16.0)	83,420	16,057 (19.2)
23rd	Southern Bronx, West of Bronx River	—	—	—	—	24,320	2,850 (11.7)
24th	North Bronx, West of Bronx River, North of Highbridge	—	—	—	—	11,874	2,418 (20.4)
Total		622,924	175,735 (28.2)	726,386	161,334 (22.2)	1,041,886	199,084 (19.1)

Sources: Census for the State of New York for 1855 (Albany, 1857), 110; *Census for the State of New York for 1865* (Albany, 1867), 130; *Census for the State of New York for 1875* (Albany, 1877), 37.

Note: Although the total number of Irish-born in Manhattan increased, the proportion of Irish-born in the more rapidly increasing total population dropped by an average of 10.1 percent. The Manhattan Irish were certainly less concentrated than ever before, nevertheless two East Side wards between East 14th Street and East 42nd Street recorded a modest increase of about 2 percent. This was accomplished despite a near doubling of the total population for this East Side district. Several long-established Irish neighborhoods continued to hold on as Irish enclaves despite experiencing declines. These included the lower Manhattan wards south of old St. Patrick's Cathedral: the First through Seventh and the Fourteenth wards. Overall the Irish were to be found throughout Manhattan in large numbers with the exception of the lower East Side.

TABLE A.3. Irish-born, Brooklyn and Kings County, 1855, 1865, 1875, by Town or Ward

Ward or town	Area of Kings County	1855		1865		1875	
		Total population	Irish-born population and percent of total	Total population	Irish-born population and percent of total	Total population	Irish-born population and percent of total
Ward							
1st	Brooklyn Heights	6,441	2,227 (35.2)	6,128	1,835 (29.9)	16,084	3,442 (21.4)
2nd	Fulton Ferry	8,383	2,967 (35.4)	8,760	2,890 (33.0)	8,850	2,705 (30.5)
3rd	South Brooklyn Heights	8,900	1,964 (22.1)	8,890	1,751 (19.7)	15,809	2,120 (13.4)
4th	Downtown	12,282	2,440 (19.9)	11,506	1,878 (16.3)	12,616	1,889 (15.0)
5th	Irishtown, East of Navy Yard	16,352	5,629 (34.4)	17,820	5,658 (31.8)	18,591	5,229 (29.7)
6th	Cobble Hill	18,490	6,463 (35.0)	26,407	7,717 (29.2)	34,072	9,500 (27.9)
7th	Southeast of Navy Yard	12,523	6,471 (51.7)	15,968	3,104 (19.4)	26,488	4,525 (17.1)
8th	Park Slope to 60th St.	5,318	1,717 (32.3)	9,829	1,938 (19.7)	12,127	2,375 (19.6)
9th	Northeast of Prospect Park	9,133	2,449 (26.8)	23,443	3,102 (13.2)	13,643	3,757 (27.5)
10th	Gowanus	21,749	6,690 (30.8)	28,668	6,121 (21.4)	24,866	6,106 (24.6)
11th	Fort Greene Southwest	22,213	4,985 (22.4)	18,242	3,462 (19.0)	21,629	4,020 (18.6)
12th	Red Hook	6,990	3,332 (47.7)	13,085	4,914 (37.6)	17,525	5,349 (30.5)
13th	Central Williamsburg	14,044	2,036 (14.5)	17,791	1,753 (9.9)	19,547	1,686 (8.6)
14th	North Williamsburg	12,414	4,314 (34.8)	15,425	3,770 (24.4)	23,925	5,277 (22.1)
15th	Northeast Williamsburg	6,559	870 (13.3)	11,449	1,024 (8.9)	21,255	1,650 (7.8)
16th	Southeast Williamsburg	15,350	846 (5.5)	24,379	835 (3.4)	39,206	910 (2.3)

	1855		1865		1875	
	Total	Irish	Total	Irish	Total	Irish
17th	5,508	966 (17.5)	10,234	1,828 (17.9)	23,998	3,754 (15.6)
18th	2,601	387 (14.9)	6,319	674 (10.7)	17,459	1,541 (8.8)
19th	—	—	8,055	961 (11.9)	21,908	1,797 (8.2)
20th	—	—	13,980	1,928 (13.8)	21,430	2,876 (13.4)
21st	—	—	—	—	24,834	2,956 (11.9)
22nd	—	—	—	—	17,736	2,346 (13.2)
23rd	—	—	—	—	10,005	972 (9.7)
24th	—	—	—	—	5,799	1,045 (18.0)
25th	—	—	—	—	13,081	1,052 (8.0)
Subtotal Brooklyn	205,250	56,753 (27.7)	296,378	57,143 (19.3)	482,493	78,880 (16.4)
Town						
Flatbush	3,280	1,150 (35.1)	2,778	528 (19.0)	6,940	1,966 (28.3)
Flatlands	1,578	241 (15.3)	1,904	231 (12.1)	2,651	252 (9.5)
Gravesend	1,256	208 (16.6)	1,627	314 (19.3)	2,180	358 (16.4)
New Lots	2,261	229 (10.1)	5,009	389 (7.7)	11,047	866 (7.8)
New Utrecht	2,730	727 (26.6)	3,394	839 (24.7)	3,843	747 (19.4)
Total Kings County	216,355	59,308 (27.4)	311,090	59,444 (19.1)	509,154	83,069 (16.3)

Sources: Census for the State of New York for 1855 (Albany, 1857), 103; *Census for the State of New York for 1865* (Albany, 1867), 116; *Census for the State of New York for 1875* (Albany, 1877), 36.

Note: The proportion of Irish to the total population in Brooklyn and Manhattan in 1855 was almost identical (Brooklyn, 27.7%; Manhattan, 28.2%). Like Manhattan's Irish, the Brooklyn Irish were especially concentrated in several wards and it was in the Seventh Ward, adjacent to the Navy Yard on the Southeast and centering on St. Patrick's Church on Kent Avenue, that the greatest proportion of Irish (51.7%) was to be found in either of the two boroughs. The overall decline by 1875 in Brooklyn was slightly greater than in Manhattan (11.3% compared to 10.1%) with only one ward (the ninth) showing a proportional increase, although very slight. A dramatic change occurred in the seventh Ward where more than a 34% drop-off took place. The newly added wards of the Eastern District contained relatively few Irish and like the lower East Side became the principal residence of the German community.

Table A.4. Irish-born, Queens County, 1855, 1865, 1875, by Town or Ward

Town or ward	Area	1855		1865		1875	
		Total population	Irish-born population and percent of total	Total population	Irish-born population and percent of total	Total population	Irish-born population and percent of total
Flushing	Modern Queens County	7,970	1,660 (20.8)	10,813	1,865 (17.3)	15,357	1,940 (12.6)
Jamaica		5,632	746 (13.3)	6,777	697 (10.3)	10,614	999 (9.4)
Newtown		4,694	1,402 (29.9)	13,891	2,528 (18.2)	8,983	600 (6.7)
Long Island City							
1st Ward		—	—	—	—	4,638	1,393 (30.0)
2nd Ward		—	—	—	—	1,977	577 (29.1)
3rd Ward		—	—	—	—	2,113	342 (16.2)
4th Ward		—	—	—	—	4,713	503 (10.7)
5th Ward		—	—	—	—	2,146	444 (20.7)
Hempstead	Modern Nassau County	10,477	547 (5.2)	11,764	451 (3.8)	14,792	597 (4.0)
North Hempstead		9,446	486 (5.2)	5,335	715 (13.4)	7,217	814 (11.3)
Oyster Bay		8,046	858 (10.7)	9,417	1,045 (11.1)	11,461	1,261 (11.0)
Total	Old Queens County	46,266	5,699 (12.3)	57,999	7,301 (12.6)	84,011	9,470 (11.3)

Sources: Census for the State of New York for 1855 (Albany, 1857), 131; *Census for the State of New York for 1865* (Albany, 1867), 151; *Census for the State of New York for 1875* (Albany, 1877), 40–44.

— Not available.

Note: The county of Queens included modern Nassau County in this period. The modern confines of Queens County are almost the same, however, as the towns of Flushing, Jamaica, Newtown, and later Long Island City combined. A small portion of western Hempstead was included in the modern county of Queens in 1898, but for practical purposes the combination of the aforementioned towns gives us the basis for comparison with the modern entity. In 1855 the Irish-born constituted 20.8 percent of the Queens population. Although by 1875 this figure had dropped to 13.5 percent, the loss was less than in either Manhattan or Brooklyn. The western portion of the county adjacent to the East River, especially in the vicinity of Calvary Cemetery, had the heaviest concentration of Irish-born and when Long Island City was formed in this part of Queens, the Irish-born accounted for 30 percent of the inhabitants.

TABLE A.5. Irish-born, Staten Island, 1855, 1865, 1875, by Area

Area	1855		1865		1875	
	Total population	Irish-born population and percent of total	Total population	Irish-born population and percent of total	Total population	Irish-born population and percent of total
Castleton	8,252	673 (8.2)	7,683	1,853 (24.1)	10,957	2,326 (21.2)
Middletown	—	—	6,866	1,376 (20.0)	8,332	1,195 (14.3)
Northfield	4,187	549 (13.1)	5,201	451 (8.7)	6,619	635 (9.6)
Southfield	5,449	1,540 (28.3)	4,407	1,250 (28.4)	4,426	950 (21.5)
Westfield	3,501	332 (9.5)	4,052	352 (8.7)	4,862	337 (6.9)
Total	21,389	3,144 (14.7)	28,209	5,282 (18.7)	35,196	5,443 (15.5)

Sources: Census for the State of New York for 1855 (Albany, 1857), 138; *Census for the State of New York for 1865* (Albany, 1867), 151; *Census for the State of New York for 1875* (Albany, 1877), 41.

— Not available.

Note: During this period the Irish-born population of Staten Island was close in size to that of Queens, and like Queens it was largely rural except for a few towns. Although the Irish community was much smaller than that of Manhattan and Brooklyn, it represented 15 percent of the general population. Several Irish population centers on the island formed even larger proportions of the population; most of these were located close to the ferry, the north shore and St. Peter's Church. In contrast to all the other future boroughs the Irish-born proportion to the general population remained constant.

Table A.6. Irish Stock, Manhattan, Annexed District and Brooklyn (Kings County), 1890, by Ward

Ward	Area and annexed district	Total population	Irish stock	Percentage Irish stock	Percentage Irish stock under age 15
Manhattan					
1st	Battery	11,122	5,911	53.0	20.3
2nd	South and East of City Hall	923	381	41.2	4.7
3rd	South and West of City Hall	3,765	1,568	41.6	10.4
4th	East River and Brooklyn Bridge	17,869	8,267	46.2	14.2
5th	Tribeca	12,385	6,363	51.3	23.4
6th	North of City Hall	23,119	4,508	19.4	14.1
7th	East River and South of East Broadway	57,366	21,818	38.0	19.7
8th	SoHo	31,220	9,625	30.8	18.4
9th	Greenwich Village	54,425	18,293	33.6	20.7
10th	East of Bowery and North of East Broadway	57,596	2,173	3.7	12.1
11th	South of East 14th St. near East River	75,426	6,668	8.8	16.2
12th	Yorkville and East Side	245,046	58,721	23.9	21.3
13th	Near East River between Grand and Houston	45,884	5,396	11.7	16.4
14th	Near Old St. Patrick's Cathedral	28,094	7,258	25.8	17.5
15th	Washington Square	25,399	4,655	18.3	11.6
16th	West of 5th Ave. to Hudson River, North of 14th St.	49,134	17,601	35.8	18.2
17th	East of 4th Ave., South of East 14th St.	103,158	10,815	10.4	15.3
18th	North of East 14th St. between 5th Ave. and East River	63,270	23,373	36.9	17.9
19th	East of Central Park and South of Yorkville	234,846	61,858	26.3	20.5
20th	Hell's Kitchen and West Side	84,327	28,922	34.2	22.4
21st	East of 5th Ave. to East River East 30s and 40s	63,019	26,606	42.2	17.1
22nd	West of Central Park, Upper West Side	153,877	51,605	33.5	20.5
23rd	South Bronx, West of Bronx River	53,948	19,571	19.5	22.8
24th	North Bronx, West of Bronx River	20,137	6,389	31.7	21.2
Total		1,515,301	399,348	26.3	19.8
Brooklyn and Kings County					
1st	Brooklyn Heights	20,040	6,806	33.9	15.1
2nd	Fulton Ferry	8,986	4,213	46.8	21.3
3rd	S. Brooklyn Heights	18,754	4,087	21.7	18.6
4th	Downtown	12,324	3,650	29.6	11.9

Table A.6. Irish Stock, Manhattan, Annexed District and Brooklyn (Kings County), 1890, by Ward (*Continued*)

Ward	Area and annexed district	Total population	Irish stock	Percentage Irish stock	Percentage Irish stock under age 15
5th	Irishtown	20,175	9,914	49.1	20.7
6th	Cobble Hill	37,693	16,986	45.0	23.1
7th	Southeast of Navy Yard	35,726	10,285	28.7	20.1
8th	Park Slope	31,239	9,401	30.0	25.1
9th	Northeast of Prospect Park	17,690	8,228	46.4	23.4
10th	Gowanus	34,031	14,150	41.5	21.0
11th	Fort Greene	22,693	7,354	32.4	18.0
12th	Red Hook	27,368	12,656	46.2	25.7
13th	Central Williamsburg	21,628	3,882	17.9	15.3
14th	North Williamsburg	27,246	9,660	35.4	23.5
15th	Northeast Williamsburg	27,630	4,229	15.3	17.9
16th	Southeast Williamsburg	45,720	1,633	3.5	20.6
17th	Greenpoint	41,424	12,442	30.0	24.4
18th	Bushwick	74,960	6,876	9.1	23.6
19th	East Bushwick	36,244	5,407	14.9	19.5
20th	Fort Greene Southeast	24,136	5,764	23.8	13.4
21st	Bedford	50,118	8,652	17.2	23.0
22nd	Park Slope-Greenwood	50,250	10,646	21.1	17.1
23rd	Bedford-Stuyvesant	29,348	3,940	13.4	12.3
24th	Crown Heights	16,771	5,588	33.1	29.0
25th	Brownsville	44,638	6,315	14.1	20.4
26th	East New York	29,505	3,628	12.3	25.1
Total		806,343	196,372	24.3	21.2

Source: Department of the Interior, Census Office, *Vital Statistics of New York City and Brooklyn, U.S. Census Office, Eleventh Census* (Washington, D.C., 1894), 234–36, 242–44.

Note: At almost 600,000, the Irish stock (offspring of an Irish mother, that is, born in Ireland or elsewhere of an Irish mother) of New York and Brooklyn constituted the largest Irish settlement in the world. The share of the Irish in the total population of each city continued to be very similar (New York, 26.3%; Brooklyn, 24.3%). The percentage of the Irish population under 15 years of age in the two cities was also similar, but Brooklyn now had a slight edge (21.2% to 19.8%). This probably reflects the movement of families out of increasingly urbanized Manhattan into areas of recent industrial growth in Brooklyn. Some of the wards with the highest percentages of "under 15s" were in newly developed areas away from the downtown core. The beginning of the exodus of the Irish out of the downtown districts of lower Manhattan is evident from the decline in the position of the Irish in the Sixth Ward. The lower percentages of "under 15s" in the downtown districts foretell a change in the position of the Irish in the entire area.

Table A.7. Percentage of Irish-born Naturalizations, New York City, 1910–1930

	Borough					Totals	
Year	Manhattan	Brooklyn	Bronx	Queens	Staten Island	Irish-born,[a] New York City	All foreign-born, New York City
1910	57.6	71.2	67.6	72.9	72.7	63.0	44.4
1920	53.9	66.1	70.8	73.3	70.5	60.0	40.5
1930	52.9	63.4	76.8	69.9	70.1	59.2	54.4

Source: U.S. Department of Commerce, Bureau of the Census, *Fifteenth Census of the United States: 1930, Population,* 2 (Washington, D.C., 1933), 472–75.

[a]For 1930, figure includes those born in the Irish Free State and in Northern Ireland.

Note: The Irish exceeded the average percentage for all the foreign-born for naturalizations. The immigrant wave of the 1920s brought the Irish proportion down only slightly. Manhattan as the main center for recent and single immigrants had the lowest percentage of Irish-born who had become citizens.

Table A.8. Percentage of Irish-born Population, New York City, 1930, by Year of Emigration and Borough

	Borough					Total	
Date of emigration	Manhattan	Brooklyn	Bronx	Queens	Staten Island	Irish-born[a] New York City (%)	Irish-born as percent of total foreign-born, New York City
1900 or earlier	28.6	39.2	29.0	40.3	11.1	72,808 (33.0)	22.3
1901–10	19.4	16.1	18.3	18.7	44.9	40,376 (18.3)	29.0
1911–14	7.3	6.1	7.5	7.7	16.5	15,665 (7.1)	13.0
1915–19	4.0	3.1	3.5	3.5	6.3	7,943 (3.6)	4.8
1920–24	12.0	10.2	12.5	9.5	3.1	24,931 (11.3)	16.1
1925–30	23.7	19.1	23.8	15.1	7.0	46,994 (21.3)	11.1
Unknown	5.0	6.2	5.4	5.2	11.1	11,914 (5.4)	3.7

Source: U.S. Department of Commerce, Bureau of the Census, *Fifteenth Census of the United States: 1930, Population,* 2 (Washington, D.C., 1933), 543.

[a]For all tables derived from the 1930 Census, "Irish-born" includes those born in the Irish Free State and in Northern Ireland.

Note: The large emigration from Ireland in the 1920s put the Irish well ahead of the average for all foreign-born immigrants who had come to the city since 1920, although a large proportion of the Irish were older immigrants in Brooklyn, Queens, and Staten Island. Manhattan and the Bronx had above average shares of the recent immigrants. Queens was not at this point a mecca for recent immigrants, while Staten Island had only 7 percent of the recent arrivals.

Table A.9. Family Size by Foreign-born Group, New York City, 1930

Country of origin	Single-person households	Total foreign-born families	Median family size	Children under age 10 as a percent of the total families				
				None	1	2	3	4 or more
Ireland	7,351	75,135	3.43	69.6	14.1	8.8	4.7	2.8
Germany	10,506	92,954	2.74	79.4	14.6	4.7	1.0	0.3
Italy	10,094	201,170	4.47	47.6	20.8	16.2	9.2	6.1
England	2,932	28,159	2.93	71.7	17.8	7.8	2.0	0.7
Scotland	865	11,428	3.22	68.2	18.5	9.2	3.0	1.1
Norway	983	12,301	3.29	62.1	22.7	11.0	3.1	1.1
Russia	5,196	195,113	4.05	56.5	26.1	13.9	2.9	0.6
Poland	3,934	98,289	4.08	55.7	25.2	14.0	3.9	1.2

Sources: U.S. Department of Commerce, Bureau of the Census, *Special Report on Foreign-born Whites* (Washington, D.C., 1933), 133–35, 178, 186; U.S. Department of Commerce, Bureau of the Census, *Special Report on White Families by Country of Birth of the Head, Fifteenth Census: 1930* (Washington, D.C., 1933), 185.

Note: The Irish family was behind the median size of the southern and eastern Europeans but ahead of northern and western European groups. As one of the older immigrant ethnic groups, the Irish had one of the greatest proportions of families without any children. Nevertheless, they came next to the Italian group, at 7.5 percent of the total with families having three children or more.

Table A.10. Percentage of Gainfully Employed Workers in Foreign-born Families, New York City, 1930

Country of origin	Total foreign-born families	Gainfully employed workers per family, as a percentage of total group				
		None	1	2	3	4 or more
Ireland	75,135	5.9	48.2	23.8	12.8	9.4
Germany	92,954	8.0	54.0	25.1	9.3	4.0
Italy	201,170	2.5	54.6	20.6	12.4	9.9
England	28,159	5.4	59.0	23.1	8.5	4.0
Scotland	11,428	3.8	53.5	24.6	11.6	6.5
Norway	12,301	3.0	60.1	22.5	9.6	4.8
Russia	195,113	2.9	55.6	20.9	12.4	8.3
Poland	98,289	3.3	54.6	21.3	12.5	8.4

Source: U.S. Department of Commerce, Bureau of the Census, *Fifteenth Census of the United States: 1930, Population*, 2 (Washington, D.C., 1933), 93.

Note: The number of workers in a family reflects not only the current conditions of employment in an immigrant family but also the median age of the immigrants. The Irish, like the Germans, tended to be older than Italians as a consequence of a larger proportion of the former groups who were immigrants before 1900. This factor probably accounts for the relatively high percentage of families without a single worker. The Irish formed the largest group of two or more workers in a family at 46 percent of the total.

Table A.11. Percentage of Foreign-born Home Ownership, New York City, 1930, by Borough, Value, and Monthly Rental (Nonfarm Homes)

Country of origin	Borough					Percentage of group's total population, New York City
	Manhattan	Brooklyn	Bronx	Queens	Staten Island	
Ireland	1.9	35.2	17.4	51.5	58.9	21.5
Germany	2.7	34.8	16.3	50.4	61.0	28.3
Italy	2.3	35.2	23.9	47.7	60.1	26.8
England	1.8	24.7	9.3	42.5	52.4	20.4
Scotland	1.7	19.2	12.2	36.6	45.2	19.5
Norway	1.9	25.3	16.6	64.4	64.1	31.2
Russia	1.7	24.6	5.6	42.6	52.5	16.1
Poland	1.2	22.7	5.3	51.4	63.1	15.7
	Value					
	Less than $1,500	$1,500– $2,999	$3,000– $4,999	$5,000– $7,499	$7,500– $9,999	More than $10,000
Ireland	0.3	0.9	4.7	21.1	24.0	49.0
Germany	0.4	0.9	4.9	22.4	23.9	48.9
Italy	0.5	1.0	5.3	20.9	20.6	51.7
England	0.6	1.3	5.2	24.0	23.9	44.9
Scotland	0.5	1.1	5.0	25.5	27.1	40.7
Norway	0.3	1.0	5.8	26.9	26.8	39.1
Russia	0.2	0.3	1.7	10.8	15.4	71.5
Poland	0.3	0.6	4.0	16.1	17.7	61.4
	Monthly rental					
	Less than $15	$15–$29	$30–$49	$50–$99	More than $100	
Ireland	2.0	22.0	43.6	29.1	3.3	
Germany	2.2	20.1	41.3	29.1	6.9	
Italy	4.0	41.0	38.6	15.3	1.1	
England	1.1	11.6	33.6	44.2	9.4	
Scotland	1.0	13.1	42.8	37.5	5.5	
Norway	1.0	9.7	39.5	47.0	2.8	
Russia	1.8	11.8	34.2	46.1	6.1	
Poland	5.2	24.3	34.5	31.8	3.4	

Source: U. S. Department of Commerce, Bureau of the Census, *Special Report on Foreign-born Whites* (Washington, D.C., 1933), 133–135, 161–64.

Note: The percentage of home ownership for the Irish-born was about midway between the other European groups. The Norwegians led the others with 31.2 per cent home ownership, while the eastern Europeans, more recent immigrants, were at the bottom at about 16 percent. Home ownership in Manhattan was very small for all the immigrant groups and increased dramatically in Brooklyn, Queens, and Staten Island. Irish home ownership was actually higher than any of the other groups in Brooklyn, but because a large number of Irish were Manhattan residents the overall percentage in the city was not high. The value of Irish homes was in the higher middle range, and all were well represented in values in excess of $10,000. Monthly rentals stood squarely in the middle.

Table A.12. Number of Persons Claiming Single or Multiple Irish Ancestry, New York City, 1980

	Ancestry		
Borough	Single (Irish only)	Multiple (Irish plus other)	Ratio of single ancestry to multiple ancestry
Manhattan	51,603	63,190	0.82
Brooklyn	74,180	74,210	1.00
Bronx	56,673	31,995	1.77
Queens	106,982	112,330	0.95
Staten Island	28,163	48,447	0.58
Total, New York City	317,601	330,132	0.96

Source: Socioeconomic Profiles: A Portrait of New York City's Community Districts from 1980 and 1990 (New York, N.Y., 1993), 63.

Note: The ratio of single to multiple Irish ancestry generally indicates the relative "age" of an Irish community in each borough. The higher the ratio of single to multiple indicates the relative closeness to the immigrant generation, which is presumed to be less mixed with other ethnic groups. The Bronx clearly leads in this category, while Staten Island's Irish community has more remote connections to the immigrant generation.

Table A.13. Number of Persons Claiming Irish Ancestry, New York City, 1980 and 1990

	Year			
Borough	1980	1990	Net change	Percent change
Manhattan	114,793	108,963	-5,830	-5.1
Brooklyn	148,390	114,041	-34,349	-23.1
Bronx	88,628	64,969	-23,659	-26.7
Queens	219,312	175,124	-44,188	-20.1
Staten Island	76,610	72,749	-3,861	-5.0
Total, New York City	647,733	535,846	-111,887	-17.3

Source: Socioeconomic Profiles: A Portrait of New York City's Community Districts from 1980 and 1990 (New York, N.Y., 1993), 14, 20, 27, 33.

Note: New York City's population of Irish ancestry continues to decline. Between 1980 and 1990 the overall loss was 17.3 percent and was even higher in Brooklyn (23.1%) and the Bronx (26.7%).

Table A.14. Irish-born Population, New York City, 1990, by Year of Emigration

Date of Emigration	Native of Republic of Ireland	Native of Northern Ireland	Total Irish-born population, New York City	Percent of total 1990 Irish-born population, New York City
Before 1950	10,345	589	10,934	35.3
1950–59	5,779	224	6,003	19.4
1960–64	3,268	23	3,291	10.6
1965–69	1,156	20	1,176	3.8
1970–74	935	17	952	3.1
1975–79	805	22	827	2.7
1980–81	662	79	741	2.4
1982–84	1,437	50	1,487	4.8
1985–86	2,387	71	2,458	7.9
1987–90	3,079	59	3,138	10.1
Total	29,853	1,154	31,007	100.0

Source: Foreign-born Population of NYC by Birthplace and Year of Arrival, 1990 Census Public Use Sample (New York, N.Y., 1993).

Note: The relatively small numbers of Irish-born settling in the city since 1965 are evident from the analysis of the Irish population by year of emigration. The figures have risen slightly thanks to a few legislative actions by Congress aimed at mitigating the unfavorable immigration laws toward the Irish, but they are still just a trickle compared with many other ethnic groups continuing to come to the city. Almost 55 percent of the Irish-born arrived before 1960.

APPENDIX 2
Maps

Notes to Maps

The maps on the following eight pages display historical and demographic information on the Irish population in New York City.

The maps of the five boroughs of New York City (Maps 1–5) reflect those neighborhoods and parishes which are, or once were, Irish. The maps are impressionistic and include both the nineteenth and twentieth centuries. The goal was to chart the geography of Irish New York as it is reflected in contemporary folk memory.

Data for the 1890 map (Map 6) reflects the Irish stock population of 24 wards of Manhattan and the annexed district of the Bronx, plus 26 wards in Brooklyn and Kings county, drawn from *Vital Statistics of New York City and Brooklyn, U.S. Census Office, Eleventh Census* (Washington, D.C.: Government Printing Office, 1894).

Data on the Irish-born population in 1920 (Map 7) was compiled by Sanitary District for the Federal Census and published in Walter Laidlaw, *Statistical Sources for the Demographic Studies of Greater New York* (NY: New York City 1920 Census Committee, Inc., 1922). The data used to create the 1920 map was total number of Irish-born in each sanitary district. The Sanitary Districts were used as the basis for Tract numbering in later censuses, and represent 1,627 neighborhoods. The data used to create the 1970 map (Map 8) was total number of Irish-born in each census tract, provided in a computer-generated list drawn from the Federal Census by the New York City Department of City Planning.

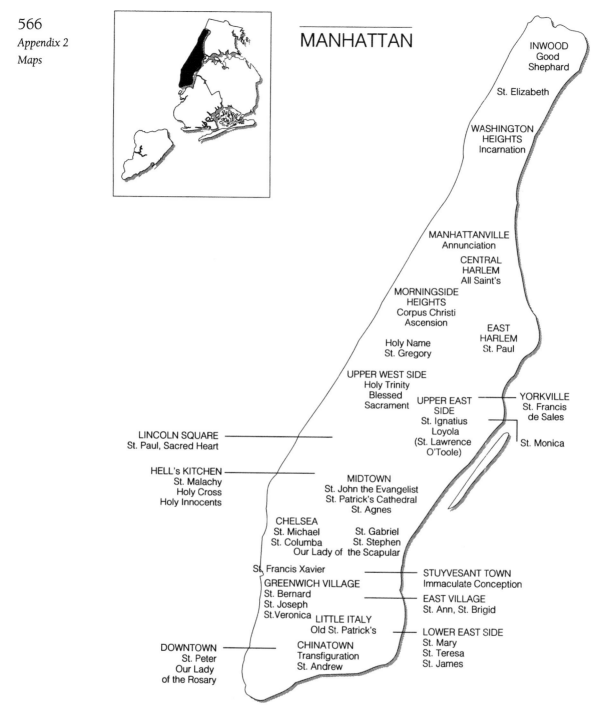

MANHATTAN

INWOOD
Good
Shephard

St. Elizabeth

WASHINGTON
HEIGHTS
Incarnation

MANHATTANVILLE
Annunciation

CENTRAL
HARLEM
All Saint's

MORNINGSIDE
HEIGHTS
Corpus Christi
Ascension

EAST
HARLEM
St. Paul

Holy Name
St. Gregory

UPPER WEST SIDE
Holy Trinity
Blessed
Sacrament

UPPER EAST
SIDE
St. Ignatius
Loyola
(St. Lawrence
O'Toole)

YORKVILLE
St. Francis
de Sales

St. Monica

LINCOLN SQUARE
St. Paul, Sacred Heart

HELL's KITCHEN
St. Malachy
Holy Cross
Holy Innocents

MIDTOWN
St. John the Evangelist
St. Patrick's Cathedral
St. Agnes

CHELSEA
St. Michael
St. Columba
Our Lady of the Scapular

St. Gabriel
St. Stephen

St. Francis Xavier

GREENWICH VILLAGE
St. Bernard
St. Joseph
St.Veronica

STUYVESANT TOWN
Immaculate Conception

EAST VILLAGE
St. Ann, St. Brigid

LITTLE ITALY
Old St. Patrick's

LOWER EAST SIDE
St. Mary
St. Teresa
St. James

DOWNTOWN
St. Peter
Our Lady
of the Rosary

CHINATOWN
Transfiguration
St. Andrew

 Map 1.

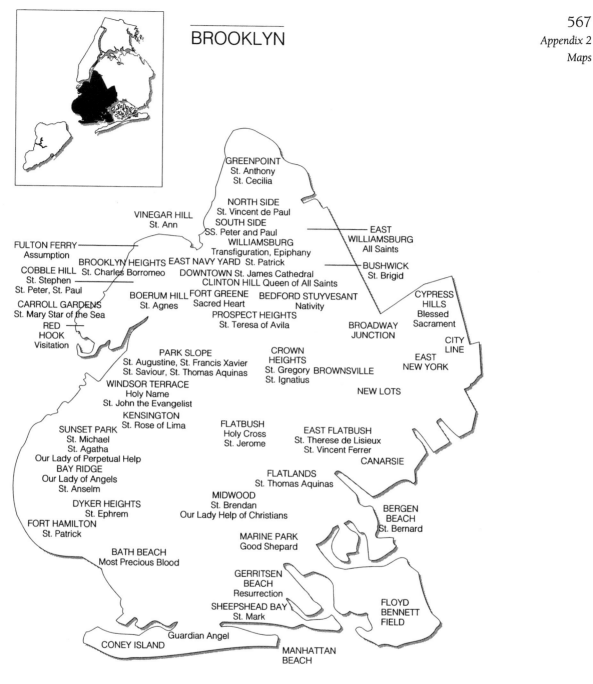

BROOKLYN

GREENPOINT
St. Anthony
St. Cecilia

NORTH SIDE
St. Vincent de Paul
VINEGAR HILL   SOUTH SIDE
St. Ann   SS. Peter and Paul   EAST
WILLIAMSBURG   WILLIAMSBURG
FULTON FERRY   Transfiguration, Epiphany   All Saints
Assumption   BROOKLYN HEIGHTS EAST NAVY YARD St. Patrick
COBBLE HILL St. Charles Borromeo DOWNTOWN St. James Cathedral   BUSHWICK
St. Stephen   CLINTON HILL Queen of All Saints   St. Brigid
St. Peter, St. Paul
BOERUM HILL FORT GREENE   BEDFORD STUYVESANT   CYPRESS
CARROLL GARDENS   St. Agnes   Sacred Heart   Nativity   HILLS
St. Mary Star of the Sea   PROSPECT HEIGHTS   Blessed
RED   St. Teresa of Avila   Sacrament
HOOK   BROADWAY   CITY
Visitation   JUNCTION   LINE
PARK SLOPE   CROWN   EAST
St. Augustine, St. Francis Xavier   HEIGHTS   NEW YORK
St. Saviour, St. Thomas Aquinas   St. Gregory BROWNSVILLE
WINDSOR TERRACE   St. Ignatius
Holy Name   NEW LOTS
St. John the Evangelist
KENSINGTON
St. Rose of Lima   FLATBUSH
SUNSET PARK   Holy Cross   EAST FLATBUSH
St. Michael   St. Jerome   St. Therese de Lisieux
St. Agatha   St. Vincent Ferrer
Our Lady of Perpetual Help   CANARSIE
BAY RIDGE   FLATLANDS
Our Lady of Angels   St. Thomas Aquinas
St. Anselm
DYKER HEIGHTS   MIDWOOD   BERGEN
St. Ephrem   St. Brendan   BEACH
FORT HAMILTON   Our Lady Help of Christians   St. Bernard
St. Patrick
MARINE PARK
BATH BEACH   Good Shepard
Most Precious Blood
GERRITSEN   FLOYD
BEACH   BENNETT
Resurrection   FIELD
SHEEPSHEAD BAY
St. Mark
Guardian Angel
CONEY ISLAND   MANHATTAN
BEACH

Map 2.

THE BRONX

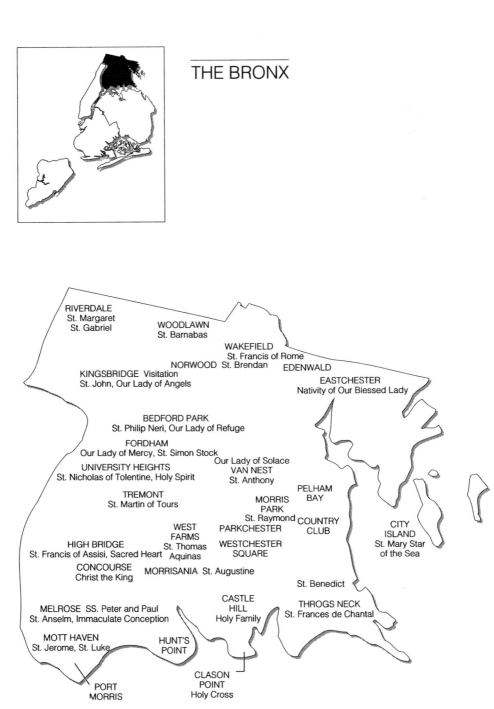

RIVERDALE
St. Margaret
St. Gabriel

WOODLAWN
St. Barnabas

WAKEFIELD
St. Francis of Rome

NORWOOD St. Brendan
KINGSBRIDGE Visitation
St. John, Our Lady of Angels

EDENWALD

EASTCHESTER
Nativity of Our Blessed Lady

BEDFORD PARK
St. Philip Neri, Our Lady of Refuge

FORDHAM
Our Lady of Mercy, St. Simon Stock
Our Lady of Solace
UNIVERSITY HEIGHTS
St. Nicholas of Tolentine, Holy Spirit

VAN NEST
St. Anthony

TREMONT
St. Martin of Tours

PELHAM
BAY

MORRIS
PARK
St. Raymond COUNTRY
CLUB

WEST
FARMS
St. Thomas
Aquinas

PARKCHESTER

CITY
ISLAND
St. Mary Star
of the Sea

HIGH BRIDGE
St. Francis of Assisi, Sacred Heart

WESTCHESTER
SQUARE

CONCOURSE
Christ the King

MORRISANIA St. Augustine

St. Benedict

MELROSE SS. Peter and Paul
St. Anselm, Immaculate Conception

CASTLE
HILL
Holy Family

THROGS NECK
St. Frances de Chantal

MOTT HAVEN
St. Jerome, St. Luke

HUNT'S
POINT

PORT
MORRIS

CLASON
POINT
Holy Cross

Map 3.

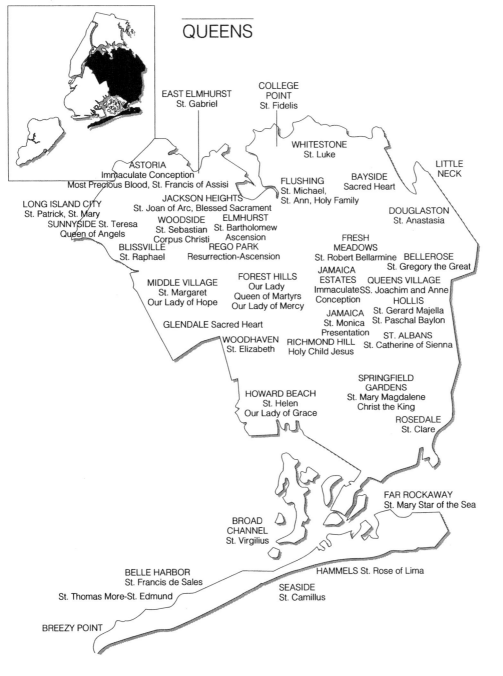

QUEENS

EAST ELMHURST
St. Gabriel

COLLEGE
POINT
St. Fidelis

WHITESTONE
St. Luke

LITTLE
NECK

ASTORIA
Immaculate Conception
Most Precious Blood, St. Francis of Assisi

BAYSIDE
Sacred Heart

FLUSHING
St. Michael,
St. Ann, Holy Family

JACKSON HEIGHTS
St. Joan of Arc, Blessed Sacrament

DOUGLASTON
St. Anastasia

LONG ISLAND CITY
St. Patrick, St. Mary

SUNNYSIDE St. Teresa
Queen of Angels

WOODSIDE
St. Sebastian
Corpus Christi

ELMHURST
St. Bartholomew
Ascension

FRESH
MEADOWS
St. Robert Bellarmine

BELLEROSE
St. Gregory the Great

BLISSVILLE
St. Raphael

REGO PARK
Resurrection-Ascension

JAMAICA
ESTATES
Immaculate
Conception

QUEENS VILLAGE
SS. Joachim and Anne

MIDDLE VILLAGE
St. Margaret
Our Lady of Hope

FOREST HILLS
Our Lady
Queen of Martyrs
Our Lady of Mercy

HOLLIS
St. Gerard Majella
St. Paschal Baylon

JAMAICA
St. Monica
Presentation

ST. ALBANS
St. Catherine of Sienna

GLENDALE Sacred Heart

WOODHAVEN
St. Elizabeth

RICHMOND HILL
Holy Child Jesus

SPRINGFIELD
GARDENS
St. Mary Magdalene
Christ the King

HOWARD BEACH
St. Helen
Our Lady of Grace

ROSEDALE
St. Clare

FAR ROCKAWAY
St. Mary Star of the Sea

BROAD
CHANNEL
St. Virgilius

BELLE HARBOR
St. Francis de Sales

St. Thomas More-St. Edmund

HAMMELS St. Rose of Lima

SEASIDE
St. Camillus

BREEZY POINT

Map 4.

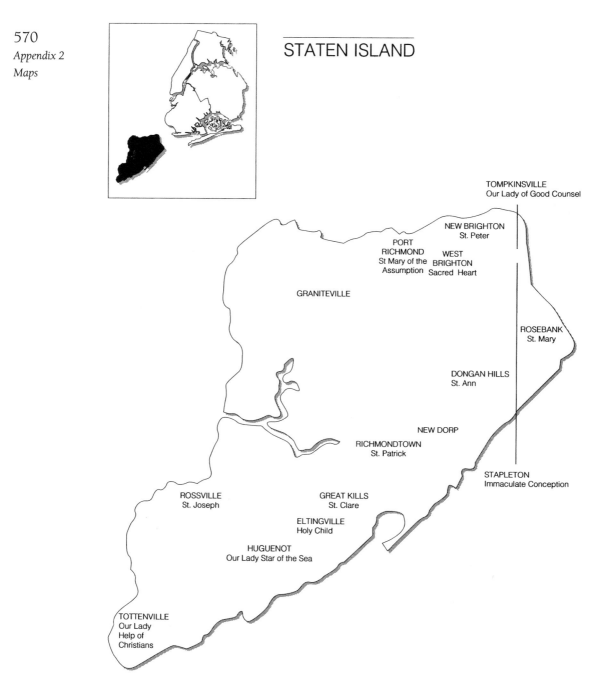

STATEN ISLAND

TOMPKINSVILLE
Our Lady of Good Counsel

NEW BRIGHTON
St. Peter

PORT
RICHMOND
St Mary of the
Assumption

WEST
BRIGHTON
Sacred Heart

GRANITEVILLE

ROSEBANK
St. Mary

DONGAN HILLS
St. Ann

NEW DORP

RICHMONDTOWN
St. Patrick

STAPLETON
Immaculate Conception

ROSSVILLE
St. Joseph

GREAT KILLS
St. Clare

ELTINGVILLE
Holy Child

HUGUENOT
Our Lady Star of the Sea

TOTTENVILLE
Our Lady
Help of
Christians

Map 5.

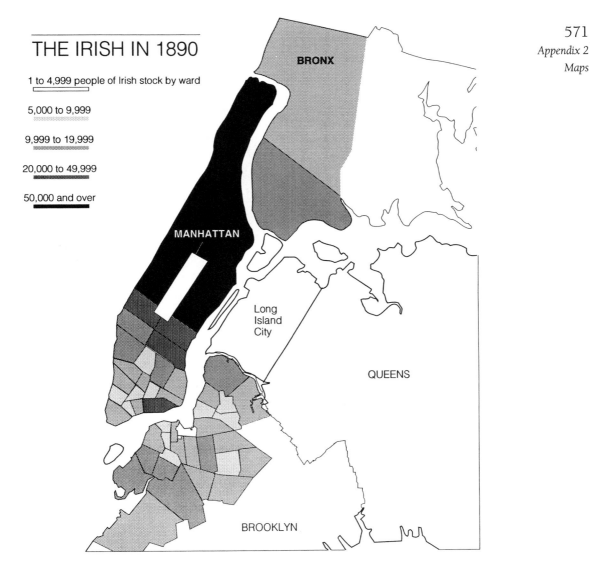

THE IRISH IN 1890

1 to 4,999 people of Irish stock by ward

5,000 to 9,999

9,999 to 19,999

20,000 to 49,999

50,000 and over

BRONX

MANHATTAN

Long
Island
City

QUEENS

BROOKLYN

Map 6.

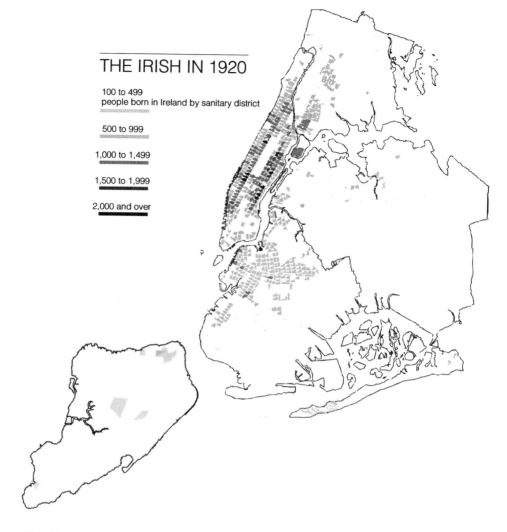

THE IRISH IN 1920

100 to 499
people born in Ireland by sanitary district

500 to 999

1,000 to 1,499

1,500 to 1,999

2,000 and over

Map 7.

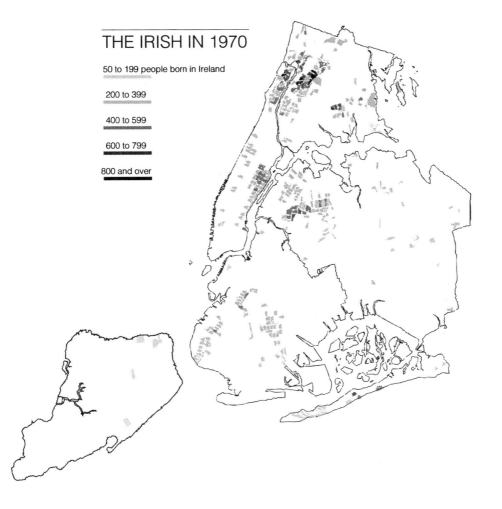

THE IRISH IN 1970

50 to 199 people born in Ireland

200 to 399

400 to 599

600 to 799

800 and over

Map 8.

Notes

INTRODUCTION

1. Richard Dorson, "Folklore from Kerry," *Journal of American Folklore* 66 (1953): 41–42.

2. Miller estimates that 50,000 to 100,000 Irish men and women left their homes for America in the seventeenth century and another 250,000 to 400,000 in the eighteenth. The numbers of Irish "exiles" increased enormously in the early nineteenth century. Between 1845 and 1855, more than 2.1 million fled Ireland for other countries and about 1.5 million entered the United States. Irish migration never reached such proportions again, but it continued to flow steadily through the nineteenth century and occasionally experienced large bursts in the twentieth. Meanwhile, new generations of Irish were born in America. By 1980, more than 10 million people in the United States claimed purely Irish ancestry and more than 40 million claimed to be predominately Irish. Cormac O'Grada, *The Great Irish Famine* (London, 1989), 14–15; Kerby Miller, *Emigrants and Exiles: Ireland and the Irish Exodus to North America* (New York, 1985), 137.

3. Irish migration to the city began to pick up in the 1820s and 1830s but became a tidal wave of refugees from the Famine disaster in the 1840s and 1850s. Between 1845 and 1855, New York's population grew from 371,223 to 629,904 (Brooklyn's rose from about 78,000 to 205,250). In the same period, the Irish population in New York City rose from 96,581 to 175,735 and in Brooklyn from 22,342 to 56,753. The Irish continued to arrive in New York as elsewhere after the end of the Famine. Indeed, the number of the Irish born in the city continued to rise until the late nineteenth century. By 1980, 900,000 persons in the New York metropolitan area claimed only Irish ancestry and nearly 1.5 million claimed predominately Irish roots. Ira Rosenwaike, *Population History of New*

York City (Syracuse, N.Y., 1972), 51, 54, 70. U.S. Bureau of the Census, *Census of Population, 1980: General Social and Economic Characteristics*, pt. 34, pp. 119, 127–28.

4. On the numbers of Irish immigrants see Rosenwaike, *Population History of New York City*, 42, 67–74. By 1860, Richard Stott points out, 60 percent of the nation's imports and a third of its exports were passing through the New York port, and the city had emerged as a major manufacturing center. Manufacturing changed, he asserts, in the antebellum era, largely because of the growing supply of cheap labor and rising real estate costs, as big plants moved out and small labor-intensive manufacturers became the norm. Stott argues that the early nineteenth century witnessed the development of a new working-class culture in New York City, which was unlike the native artisanal culture but "drew upon old world culture during the formative period of the 1840s and 1850s." Saloons, for example, borrowed "much" from Irish rural places, and the Irish contributed to the making of the working-class theater, the rise of prizefighting, and even New York speech. On the economy and working-class culture see Richard Stott, *Workers in the Metropolis: Class, Ethnicity, and Youth in Antebellum New York City* (Ithaca, N.Y., 1989), 9, 17–18, 216, 224–30, 259, 268. On contemporary speech in New York, see *New York Times*, Feb. 24, 1993. On the contribution of the Irish to a broader American, urban popular culture see Nathan Glazer and Daniel Patrick Moynihan, *Beyond the Melting Pot: The Negroes, Puerto Ricans, Jews, Italians and Irish of New York City* (Cambridge, Mass., 1970), 246; and Robert Snyder, *Voice of the City: Vaudeville and Popular Culture in New York* (New York, 1989). Stanley Nadel notes that New York City attracted more urban skilled German immigrants than Midwestern cities, which "contained fewer Irish laborers competing for unskilled jobs and . . . attracted large numbers of Germans from rural districts, immigrants who went to those cities hoping to work there only long enough to save toward the ownership of midwestern farms. Germans provided their proportionate share of unskilled laborers in . . . Baltimore, Chicago, Cincinnati, and St. Louis . . . and far more than their share of unskilled workers in less industrialized cities from Syracuse to Milwaukee . . . [Un]skilled Germans tended to seek employment where the Irish didn't already dominate the unskilled labor markets—that is by moving west away from the heavily Irish coastal cities." Stanley Nadel, *Little Germany: Ethnicity, Religion and Class in New York City* (Urbana, Ill., 1990), 64. In 1841 James Gordon Bennett decried the "scheming, tricky, intriguing French influence" in the New York church, as opposed to the "honest, straightforward, open, manly Irish Catholic influence." Vincent Lannie, *Public Money and Parochial Education: Bishop Hughes, Governor Seward and the New York School Controversy* (Cleveland, 1968), 199. Jay Dolan notes that, to the French clergy "who could still vividly recall the upheavals of the French Revolution, . . . wide eyed republicanism was not a healthful sign and they continually sought to tame it. Their model of Catholicism was clearly alien to the American republican movement and evidenced no influence at all from the Catholic enlightenment; it was a traditional European model of Roman Catholicism grounded in a monarchical view of authority, moral rigorism, elaborate devotionalism and an exaggerated loyalty to the Papacy." Jay Dolan, *The American Catholic Experience: A History from Colonial Times to the Present* (New York, 1983), 120. Dolan (pp. 101–24) also notes, however, the strong strain of republican openness among the American-born in the early church. On the machine in New York see Amy Bridges, *A City in the Republic: Antebellum New York and the Origins of Machine Politics* (Ithaca, N.Y., 1984), 7–8. Plunkitt's quotation appears in Oscar Handlin, ed., *Immigration as a Factor in American History* (Englewood Cliffs, N.J., 1959), 128. On corruption and mismanagement in recent years in New York City, see Christopher McNickle, *To Be Mayor of New York: Ethnic*

Politics in New York City (New York, 1993), 239–40, 288–90. On the Irish and their influence on working-class ideology see chapter 12 of this volume.

5. Robert Ernst, *Immigrants in New York City, 1825–1963* (New York, 1979), table 10, p. 189. See chapter 11 herein for 1882 figures and chapter 18 for a discussion of recent Irish migration to New York. See Rosenwaike, *Population History of New York City*, table 37, p. 89, for the growing proportion of the New York Irish among all Irish immigrants in the United States. In 1930, 17 percent of the Irish immigrants who arrived in the United States before 1901 lived in New York City, but 30 percent who came between 1915 and 1919, 32 percent who arrived in 1920 to 1924, and 42.9 percent who arrived 1925 to 1930 lived in New York City. *Census of Population, 1980*, pt. 15, p. 70; pt. 23, p. 57. David Doyle discusses the increasing concentration of Irish foreign-born in Northeastern cities in the late nineteenth century, after the relative dispersal of Irish immigrants earlier in the century, in "The Irish as Urban Pioneers in the United States, 1850 to 1870," *Journal of American Ethnic History* 10, nos. 1, 2 (1990–91): 53–54.

6. David Hammack, *Power and Society: Greater New York at the Turn of the Century* (New York, 1987), 109–81; Ralph M. Goldman, *Search for Consensus: The Story of the Democratic Party* (Philadelphia, 1979), 89–119; Gerald Fogarty, *The Vatican and the American Hierarchy* (Wilmington, 1985), 10 (on McCloskey), chap. vii (on Mundelein and O'Connell); James J. Hennessy S.J., *American Catholics: A History of the Roman Catholic Community in the United States* (New York, 1981), 204–307.

7. James Paul Rodechko, *Patrick Ford and His Search for America: A Case Study of Irish American Journalism, 1870–1913* (New York, 1976), 48–49. The *Irish American* had a circulation of 35,000 in 1882 and 25,000 in 1907, the *Irish Nation* had a circulation of about 6,000 in 1882, and the *Gaelic American* upward of 14,000 in 1970. John Tebbel, *History of Book Publishing in the United States* (New York, 1972), 1: 262–64, 523–30; 2: 17–18, 24, 183, 545–48. See also Mick Moloney, "Irish Ethnic Recordings and the Irish American Imagination," in *Ethnic Recordings in America: A Neglected Heritage* (Washington, D.C., 1982), 90–95; Lawrence McCullough, "An Historical Sketch of Traditional Irish Music in the United States," *Folklore Forum* 7 (July 1974): 185–86; *Irish Voice*, Feb. 9, 1993.

8. Thomas Sowell, *Ethnic America: A History* (New York, 1981), 37–38; Joel Perlman, *Ethnic Differences: Schooling and Social Structure among the Irish, Italians, Jews and Blacks in an American City, 1880–1935* (New York, 1988), 56–59. Perlman cities high school graduation rates for second-generation Irish, Germans, and Russians (largely Jews) counted in the 1960 census who would have reached age fifteen in the years 1901 to 1910. The comparative statistics are as follows: Irish 23.5 percent, Russians 29.6 percent, Germans 14.9 percent. The median educational level in New York State for persons over age twenty five claiming pure Irish ancestry in 1980 was 12.6; for those claiming English ancestry it was 12.6; for those claiming French ancestry it was 12.3; for those claiming German ancestry it was 12.4; for those claiming Italian ancestry it was 12.2; and for those claiming Polish ancestry it was 12.4. A higher proportion of Irish males had graduated from high school than any other pure ancestral group recorded, and a higher proportion of females than all but the English. *Census of Population, 1980*, pt. 34, p. 205. See also Andrew Greeley, *The American Catholic: A Social Portrait* (New York, 1977); Greeley, "The Success and Assimilation of Irish Protestants and Catholics in the United States," *Social Science Research* 72, no. 4 (1988): 229–35; and Greeley, *Ethnicity, Denomination and Inequality* (New York, 1976). On the disadvantageous effect of government work and slow Irish mobility see Moynihan and Glazer, *Beyond the Melting Pot*, 254; Steven Erie, *Rainbow's End: Irish Americans and the Dilemmas of Urban Machine Politics, 1840–1985* (Berkeley, Calif., 1988), 88–89. Suzanne Model,

"The Ethnic Niche and the Structure of Opportunity: Immigrants and Minorities in New York City," in Michael Katz, ed., *The Underclass Debate: Views from History* (Princeton, N.J., 1992), 172–74. Median incomes for families and proportions of males in managerial and professional occupations for persons in New York State claiming pure ancestry in 1980 were as follows: English $20,307 and 29.5 percent, French $17,992 and 20.1 percent; German $21,963 and 26.2 percent; Irish $23,323 and 27.8 percent; Italian $21,498 and 21.1 percent; Polish $22,181 and 26.8 percent. *Census of Population, 1980*, pt. 34, p. 210.

9. Donald Akenson, *The Irish Diaspora: A Primer* (New York, 1993); Thomas Sowell, *Race and Culture: A World View* (New York, 1994), 160.

10. Peter Quinn, *Banished Children of Eve* (New York, 1994).

11. On church attendance, Jay Dolan, *The Immigrant Church: New York's Irish and German Catholics, 1815–1865* (Baltimore, 1975), 55–58; Kerby Miller, "Class, Culture and Immigrant Group Identity in the United States: The Case of Irish American Ethnicity," in Virginia Yans McLaughlin, ed., *Immigration Reconsidered: History, Sociology and Politics* (New York, 1990), 96–129; S. J. Connolly, *Priests and People in Pre Famine Ireland, 1780–1845* (New York, 1982). On riots and lay conflict, Patrick Carey, "The Laity's Understanding of the Trustee System, 1785–1855," in Timothy Walch, ed., *Early American Catholicism, 1634–1820* (New York, 1988), 361. For the church's successful negotiation of an American identity at the turn of the century see Charles Shannabruch, *Chicago's Catholics: The Evolution of an American Identity* (Notre Dame, Ind., 1981); Leslie Tentler, *Seasons of Grace: A History of the Archdiocese of Detroit* (Detroit, 1990); Ellen Skerret, "The Catholic Dimension," in Lawrence McCaffrey, ed., *The Irish in Chicago* (Urbana, Ill., 1989), 22–60; Edward Kantowicz, *Corporation Sole: Cardinal Mundelein and Chicago Catholicism* (Notre Dame, Ind., 1983); James M. O'Toole and Robert E. Sullivan, eds., *Catholic Boston: Studies in Religion and Community, 1870–1970* (Boston, 1985). For an overall study of the transformation of Catholic spiritual life to reflect the American environment, see Jay Dolan, *Catholic Revivalism: The American Experience, 1830–1900* (Notre Dame, Ind., 1978); and Joseph Chinnici, *Living Stones: The History and Structure of Catholic Spiritual Life in the United States* (New York, 1989), 91–156. The quotation appears in Hugh McLeod, "Catholicism and the New York Irish, 1880 to 1910," in Jim Obelkevich et. al., eds., *Disciplines of Faith: Studies in Religion, Politics and Patriarchy* (New York, 1987), 350. Knights of Columbus figures are from James E. Foley, *Knights of Columbus in the State of New York, 1891–1968* (New York, 1968); and Christopher Kauffman, *Faith and Fraternalism: The History of the Knights of Columbus, 1882–1982* (New York, 1982), 77, 98–104. According to McLeod, the "survival strategy" the church "implicitly endorsed" included "hard work, independence, strict standards of decent behavior and subordination of individual desires to the apparent needs of the family. At the neighborhood and parish level it included an ethos of mutual support and solidarity and various forms of collective action in defence of sectional interests." Moloney, "Irish Ethnic Recordings," 93; McCullough, "An Historical Sketch," 184–85; Richard Alba, *Ethnic Identity: The Transformation of White America* (New Haven, 1990), 290–318; Moynihan and Glazer, *Beyond the Melting Pot*, xxiii–xxiv; Mary C. Waters, *Ethnic Options: Choosing Identities in America* (Berkeley, Calif., 1990), 147–68. See also Richard Alba, ed., *Ethnicity and Race: Toward the Twenty-First Century* (New York, 1988); and Stanley Lieberson and Mary C. Waters, *From Many Strands: Ethnic and Racial Groups in Contemporary America* (New York, 1988). For the development of other pan ethnic identities see Yen Le Spiritu, *Asian American Pan Ethnicity: Bridging Institutions and Identities* (Philadelphia, 1992); Richard Trottier,

"Charters of Pan Ethnic Identity: American Indians and Immigrant Asian Americans," in Charles Keyes, ed., *Ethnic Change* (Seattle, 1986), 272–331.

12. Ernst, *Immigrant Life in New York City, 1825–1863,* 67; Leo Lourdeaux, *Italian and Irish Filmmakers in America: Ford, Capra, Coppola and Scorcese* (Philadelphia, 1990), 46–56; John J. Appel, "From Shanties to Lace Curtains: The Irish Image in *Puck*, 1876 to 1910," *Comparative Studies in Society and History* 13, no. 4 (1981): 365–75; Dale Knobel, *Paddy and the Republic: Ethnicity and Nationality in Antebellum America* (Middletown, Conn., 1986), 94.

13. "Abie's Irish Rose" ran from 1922 to 1927 on Broadway. In 1928 it was made into a film. Charles Musser, "Ethnicity, Role Playing and American Film Comedy: From Chinese Laundry to Whoopee, 1894–1930," in Lester Friedman, ed., *Unspeakable Images: Ethnicity and the American Cinema* (Urbana, Ill., 1991), 58; Joseph M. Curran, *Hibernian Green on the Silver Screen: The Irish and American Movies* (Westport, Conn., 1989), 36. A surprising hint of the persistence of a darker stereotype of the Irish can be seen in the *New York Times*, Mar. 17, 1993: a story about apes and Irish identity on the op ed page was accompanied by matching silhouettes of a young Irishman and an ape. Shades of Thomas Nast!

14. U.S. Bureau of the Census, *Census of Population, 1980: General Social and Economic Characteristics*, pt. 34, pp. 119, 127–28. On the controversy over gays in the St. Patrick's Day parade see *New York Times*, Jan. 27, 1993; Feb. 27, 1993; Oct. 29, 1992; Mar. 18, 1993; Mar. 21, 1993. Also *Washington Blade*, Mar. 5, 1993; *Stonewall News*, Mar. 1993. There is also some tentative evidence that the rate of outmarriage among the Irish may have stopped rising and even declined slightly. Robert McCaa, "Ethnic Intermarriage and Gender in New York City," *Journal of Interdisciplinary History* xxiv, no. 2 (1993): 221.

15. David M. Emmons, *The Butte Irish: Class and Ethnicity in An American Mining Town, 1875–1925* (Urbana, Ill., 1989); Brian C. Mitchell, *The Paddy Camps: The Irish of Lowell, 1821–1861* (Urbana, Ill., 1988); McCaffrey, ed., *The Irish in Chicago*; R. A. Burchell, *The San Francisco Irish: 1848–1880* (Berkeley, Calif., 1980); Dennis Clark, *The Irish in Philadelphia: Ten Generations of Urban Experience* (Philadelphia, 1973); Jo Ellen Vinyard, *The Irish on the Urban Frontier: Detroit, 1850–1880* (New York, 1976); Victor Walsh, "'Across the Big Wather': Irish Community Life in Pittsburgh" (Ph.D. diss., University of Pittsburgh, 1983); Margaret Connor Harrigan, "'Their Own Kind': Family and Community Life in Albany New York, 1850–1915" (Ph.D. diss., Harvard University, 1975); Vincent Power, "'Invisible Immigrants': The Pioneer Irish of Worcester, Massachusetts, 1826–1860" (Ph.D. diss., Clark University, 1976); Timothy J. Meagher, "'The Lord is Not Dead': The Irish American Community in Worcester, Massachusetts in the Turn of the Century Era, 1880 to 1920" (Ph.D. diss., Brown University, 1982). See also Seamus Mettress, *The Irish American Experience: A Guide to the Literature* (Washington, D.C., 1981); David Doyle, "The Regional Bibliography of Irish America, 1880 to 1930: A Review and Addendum," *Irish Historical Studies* 23, no. 91 (1983).

Part I Overview: THE IRISH AND THE EMERGING CITY
(Hershkowitz)

1. Cecil Woodham-Smith, *The Great Hunger* (New York, 1962), 52; Ira Rosenwaike, *Population History of New York City* (Syracuse, N.Y., 1972), 27, 42.

2. Edmund O'Callaghan, ed., *Documents Relative to the Colonial History of the State of New York* (Albany, 1858), 3: 213, 415; 4: 781.

3. Ibid., 4: 1187; Goodfriend, chap. 1.

4. Kerby A. Miller, *Emigrants and Exiles* (New York, 1985), 137–38.

5. William Barrett, *The Old Merchants of New York City* (New York, 1885), 3: 131; Virginia Harrington, *The New York Merchant on the Eve of the Revolution* (New York, 1935), 175; John A. Stevens, *Colonial Records of the New York Chamber of Commerce 1768–1784* (New York, 1867), 19–26.

6. Barrett, *Old Merchants*, 3: 131–32.

7. Ibid., 249–50. See also Michael O'Brien, *In Old New York* (New York, 1928), passim for the names and careers of many individuals in many trades and professions; and Richard C. Murphy and Lawrence J. Mannion, *The History of the Friendly Sons of Saint Patrick in the City of New York, 1784–1955* (New York, 1962), 20–32.

8. William B. Willcox, *The American Rebellion* (New Haven, 1954), 110, 111, 514; Thomas H. Maginnis, *The Irish Contribution to America's Independence* (Philadelphia, 1913), 99, 135–40.

9. O'Callaghan, *Documents*, 8: 813; *The Colden Papers, 1765–1775* (New York, 1923), 7: 188.

10. Willcox, *The American Rebellion*, 110.

11. Richard B. Morris, *John Jay, The Making of a Revolution, 1745–1780* (New York, 1975), 15; William H. Bennett, *Catholic Footsteps in Old New York* (New York, 1909), 450; Murphy and Mannion, *Friendly Sons*, 17, 20.

12. Sidney Pomerantz, *New York, An American City, 1783–1803* (New York, 1939), 264–67.

13. Henry M. Field, *The Irish Confederation and the Rebellion of 1798* (New York, 1851), 326.

14. Jerome Mushkat, *Tammany* (Syracuse, 1971), 65–66.

15. Leo Hershkowitz, "The Native American Democratic Association in New York City, 1835–1836," *New-York Historical Society Quarterly* (Jan. 1962): 51–54; Mushkat, *Tammany*, 162.

16. Leo Hershkowitz, "Politics in New York City, 1834–1840" (Ph.D. diss., New York University, 1960), 325–27.

17. Paul A. Gilje, *The Road to Mobocracy* (Chapel Hill, 1987), 132–135; Louis D. Scisco, *Political Nativism in New York State* (New York, 1901), 34; Mushkat, *Tammany*, 222.

18. *An American Citizen, A Rejoinder to the Replies from England, etc. . . . Lamentable Occurrences at the Astor Place Opera House* (New York, 1849), 76–78, et passim; Richard Moody, *The Astor Place Riot* (Bloomington, 1958), passim; Allan Nevins and Milton H. Thomas, eds., *The Diary of George Templeton Strong* (New York, 1952), 4: 269, 295.

19. Ann K. Bradley, *History of the Irish in America* (Secaucus, N.J., 1986), 41; W. T. Brough, unpublished manuscript, "A Tour of the United States," in the author's collection, p. 11.

20. Robert Ernst, *Immigrant Life in New York City, 1825–1863* (New York, 1949), 5, 6, 187; Robert G. Albion, *The Rise of New York Port, 1815–1860* (New York, 1939), 336–41.

21. Albion, *Rise of New York Port*, 340–41, 349–50; *Program and Songs of Mr. Brough's Musical Lecture on the United States of America* (Dublin, 1847), 3–4; Thomas Addis Emmet, *Incidents of My Life* (New York, 1911), 138–40.

22. Albion, *Rise of New York Port*, 57–58.

23. Ernst, *Immigrant Life*, 193; Terry Coleman, *Going to America* (New York, 1972), 31–32, et passim; Woodham-Smith, *The Great Hunger*, 252.

24. Ernst, *Immigrant Life*, 65, 125, 164; Bradley, *History of the Irish*, 46; Murphy and Mannion, *Friendly Sons*, 255; Blunt's *Strangers Guide to the City of New York* (New York, 1817), 182, 183.

25. Ernst, *Immigrant Life*, 67.

26. Francis G. Fairchild, *The Clubs of New York* (New York, 1873), 19; Ernst, *Immigrant Life*, 100, 104–5; Joseph G. Rayback, *A History of American Labor* (New York, 1974), 80, 85.

27. It was also seemingly true in 1800, when there were 14 members of the Common Council, as well as in intervening years. David Valentine, *Manual of the Corporation of the City of New York, 1844–1845* (New York, 1844), 139, 159–60 (hereafter referred to as "*M.C.C.*"); Barrett, *Old Merchants*, 2: 251.

28. Howard B. Rock, *Artisans of the New Republic* (New York, 1979), 226. See also Graham R. Hodges, *New York City Cartmen, 1667–1850* (New York, 1986), 112, 123, 136, 170. By 1811, he reports, 20 percent of all cartmen were Irish. With little trade union activity in Ireland, many immigrants, including John Commerford, one of the founders of the 1828–29 Workingmen's party, became active participants in such activity. See also, Ernst, *Immigrant Life*, 100–103; Rayback, *History of American Labor*, 26, 85.

29. Ernst, *Immigrant Life*, 73–75, 76–77.

30. Jay P. Dolan, *The Immigrant Church . . . 1815–1865* (Baltimore, 1975), 29.

31. Ibid., 33. See also p. 35.

32. On the "nymphs," see Timothy Gilfoyle, *City of Eros: New York City, Prostitution and the Commercialization of Sex, 1790–1920* (New York, 1992), 58, 65. On the medical and other details, see *Alms House Reports, 1849* (New York, 1850), 28, 34, 109; Ernst, 54–55, 200; Robert S. Pickett, *House of Refuge* (Syracuse, 1969), 5; Dolan, *The Immigrant Church*, 37, 39; *Alms House Reports, 1850* (New York, 1851), 21, 28; John T. Nagle, *Suicide in New York City Ending December, 1880* (Cambridge, Mass., 1882), 2, 8.

33. Ernst, *Immigrant Life*, 52–55; Pickett, *House of Refuge*, 5.

34. Ernst, *Immigrant Life*, 37–39, 193, 197.

35. Ibid., 11; Florence E. Gibson, *The Attitudes of the New York Irish toward State and National Affairs, 1848–1892* (New York, 1951), 27–28.

36. See Ernst, *Immigrant Life*, 89, 93; David Longworth, *American Almanac, New York Register and City Directory* (New York, 1831), 404. See also advertisement in the *Irish Shield*, Aug. 1829, 1: 313.

37. *M.C.C.*, 1860, 404–6.

38. Charles H. Haswell, *Reminiscences of an Octogenarian* (New York, 1896), 379.

39. Henry B. Fearon, *Sketches of America* (London, 1818), 32.

40. Ernst, *Immigrant Life*, 86, 87.

41. *M.C.C.*, 1847, 283, 284–85, 286–88; *M.C.C.*, 1860, 399–401; Ernst, *Immigrant Life*, 86.

42. *M.C.C.*, 1860, 405–6; Ernst, *Immigrant Life*, 86, 87, 95.

43. *Irish Shield*, Aug. 1829, 313.

44. *Dictionary of American Biography*, 16: 283–84.

45. William L. Joyce, *Editors and Ethnicity, A History of the Irish American Press 1848–1883* (New York, 1976), 49–52; John P. O'Connor, "*The Shamrock*, The First Irish-American Newspaper," *New York Irish History* (1989), 4: 4–5.

46. Ernst, *Immigrant Life*, 144; Fairchild, *Clubs of New York*, 51, 81.

47. Mantle Fielding, *Dictionary of American Painters, Sculptors and Engravers* (New York, 1965), 183, 196, 265.

48. George C. D. Odell, ed., *Annals of the New York State* (New York, 1928), 3: 655–56; Nevins and Thomas, *Diary*, 1: 98; Ernst, *Immigrant Life*, 148.

49. Henry D. Stone, *Personal Recollections of the Drama* (Albany, 1873), 51, 52, 108–110.

50. Ibid., 260–61.

51. Ibid., 204–5, Bradley, *History of the Irish*, 120; Coleman, *Going to America*, 187; Nat Fleisher and Sam Andres, *A Pictorial History of Boxing* (New York, 1975), 40–41.

52. *M.C.C., 1844*, 198–200, 188–92; *M.C.C., 1860*, 276–79.

53. Edward K. Spann, *The New Metropolis: New York City, 1840–1857* (New York, 1981), 504; Ernst, *Immigrant Life*, 163–64; *M.C.C., 1855*, 120–47.

54. *M.C.C., 1858*, 127, 164; J. Frank Kiernan, *Reminiscences of the Old Fire Laddies* (New York, 1885), 403–5, 482–83, 529–30.

55. *The New York Annual Register, 1830* (New York, 1830), 253; *M.C.C., 1847*, 323; *M.C.C., 1849*, 60–61; *M.C.C., 1860*, 100,112–13.

56. It should be mentioned that although leadership in the Reformation Society was of the Establishment, it appeared to be very concerned with the sufferings of families as they tried to adjust to a new environment. The House of Refuge managed by the society took under its care large numbers of poor Irish. The same would be true for other social organizations.

57. Gibson, *Attitudes of the New York Irish*, 83.

58. Charles Lyell, *Travels in North America in the Years 1841–2* (New York, 1845), 182; Nevins and Thomas, *Diary*, 2: 371.

59. Bennett, *Catholic Footsteps*, 458; Dolan, *The Immigrant Church*, 11; John M. Farley, *History of St. Patrick's Cathedral* (New York, 1908), 5: 15; Ira Rosenwaike, *Population History* 16, 27.

60. Dolan, *The Immigrant Church*, 50–51.

61. Ibid., 57.

62. John T. Ridge, "The Hidden Gaeltacht in Old New York," *New York Irish History*, 6 (1991–92): 13–17.

63. Farley, *History of St. Patrick's*, 15, 62, 65, 71. For additional information about school attendance and funding, see Thomas Boese, *Public Education in the City of New York* (New York, 1869), 98, 102. Farley, *History of St. Patrick's*, 67.

64. Boese, *Public Education*, 98; Farley, *History of St. Patrick's*, 70; Diane Ravitch, *The Great School Wars, New York City, 1805–1973* (New York, 1974), 8–9.

65. *New-York Annual Register, 1830* (New York, 1830), 193.

66. Henry B. Fearon, *Sketches of America* (London, 1818), 39.

67. Farley, *History of St. Patrick's*, 86.

68. Ravitch, *Great School Wars*, 34–35.

69. Bradley, *History of the Irish*, 36.

70. Ravitch, *Great School Wars*, 36.

71. *New-York As It Is* (New York, 1839), 57, 119.

72. Ravitch, *Great School Wars*, 37.

73. Joyce, *Editors and Ethnicity*, 24–25; Arthur Hertzberg, *The Jew in America* (New York, 1989), 106; Mushkat, *Tammany*, 3–4; Rosenwaike, *Population History*, 36, 54; Charles P. Connor, "Archbishop Hughes and the Question of Ireland," *New York Irish History* 4 (1989), 6–10. Hone thought the *Truth Teller* "celebrated for nothing but the lowest scurility and abuse." Nevins and Thomas, *Diary*, 1: 327.

74. Farley, *History of St. Patrick's*, 88; Ravitch, *Great School Wars*, 33–76; Nevins and Thomas, *Diary*, 2: 660.

75. Farley, *History of St. Patrick's*, 88; Ravitch, *Great School Wars*, 33–76; Connor, "Archbishop Hughes and the Question of Ireland."

76. The quotations are from Gibson, *Attitudes of the New York Irish*, 66, 142. See also 67.

77. Ibid., 90.

Chapter 1: THE IRISH IN COLONIAL NEW YORK CITY (Goodfriend)

1. On the history of the term "Scots-Irish" see Maldwyn A. Jones, "Scotch-Irish" in Stephan Thernstrom, ed., *Harvard Encyclopedia of American Ethnic Groups*, 895–96; and Roger Daniels, *Coming to America: A History of Immigration and Ethnicity in American Life* (New York, 1990), 79–80. Bernard Bailyn, *Voyagers to the West: A Passage in the Peopling of America on the Eve of the Revolution* (New York, 1986), ignores Ireland as a source of British immigration to America.

2. John D. Crimmins, *St. Patrick's Day: Its Celebration in New York and Other American Places, 1737–1845* (New York, 1902); John D. Crimmins, *Irish-American Historical Miscellany. Relating Largely to New York City and Vicinity, Together with Much Interesting Material Relative to Other Parts of the Country* (New York, 1905); Michael J. O'Brien, *In Old New York. The Irish Dead in Trinity and St. Paul's Churchyards* (New York, 1928); Richard J. Purcell, "Irish Contribution to Colonial New York," *Studies: An Irish Quarterly Review of Letters, Philosophy, and Science* 29 (1940): 591–604, 30 (1941): 107–20; Richard David Doyle, "The Pre-Revolutionary Irish in New York (1643–1775)" (Ph.D. diss., St. Louis University, 1932).

3. The perennial focus of New York's colonial historians on the interaction of the English and the Dutch may have led to the neglect of smaller groups such as the Irish and Germans.

4. Kerby A. Miller, *Emigrants and Exiles: Ireland and the Irish Exodus to North America* (New York, 1985), 137–67; J. C. Beckett, *Protestant Dissent in Ireland 1687–1780* (London, 1948).

5. For a review of the debate, with references to the key articles, see Maldwyn A. Jones, "The Scotch-Irish in British America," in Bernard Bailyn and Philip D. Morgan, eds., *Strangers within the Realm: Cultural Margins of the First British Empire* (Chapel Hill, N.C., and London, 1991), 284–313. See also Thomas Purvis, "The National Origins of New Yorkers in 1790," *New York History* 67 (1986): 133–53.

6. Thomas M. Truxes, *Irish-American Trade, 1660–1783* (Cambridge, 1988); David Noel Doyle, *Ireland, Irishmen, and Revolutionary America, 1760–1820* (Dublin, 1981); Audrey Lockhart, *Some Aspects of Emigration from Ireland to the North American Colonies between 1660 and 1775* (New York, 1976); R. J. Dickson, *Ulster Emigration to Colonial America 1718–1775* (London, 1966).

7. Carl Bridenbaugh, ed., "Patrick M'Robert's Tour through Part of the North Provinces of America," *Pennsylvania Magazine of History and Biography* 59 (1935): 146. "Roughly a fifth of the indentured servants landed from Ireland found employment in the colonial seaports, although urban demand for indentures began to decline in the decade before 1775." Truxes, *Irish-American Trade*, 144.

8. Rita S. Gottesman, comp., *The Arts and Crafts in New York, 1726–1776: Advertisments and News Items from New York City Newspapers*, in *Collections* of the New-York Historical Society for the Year 1936 [hereafter CNYHS], 188; Truxes, *Irish-American Trade*, 141–42.

9. Marianne S. Wokeck, "German and Irish Immigration to Colonial Philadelphia," *Proceedings of the American Philosophical Society* 133 (1989): 128–43; Marianne S. Wokeck, "Irish Immigration to the Delaware Valley before the American Revolution,"

unpublished paper, 1988. I am grateful to Professor Wokeck for allowing me to see her work before publication.

10. For a more extended discussion of ships arriving from Ireland in the first third of the eighteenth century, see Joyce D. Goodfriend, *Before the Melting Pot: Society and Culture in Colonial New York City, 1664–1730* (Princeton, N.J., 1992), 146–48.

11. This figure is based on ships listed in Lockhart, *Emigration from Ireland;* Dickson, *Ulster Emigration;* and New York newspapers.

12. David Colden to William Cockburn, Aug. 12, 1773, Cadwallader Colden Papers, "The Letters and Papers of Cadwallader Colden, Volume 7," CNYHS, 1923, 188.

13. John Watts to [Gen. Robert] Monckton, New York, May 30, 1774, *Collections of the Massachusetts Historical Society*, 4th ser., 10 (Boston, 1871): 711.

14. Bridenbaugh, ed., "Patrick M'Robert's Tour," 146.

15. Cited in Wokeck, "Irish Immigration to the Delaware Valley," 30.

16. A. Roger Ekirch, "Bound for America: A Profile of British Convicts Transported to the Colonies, 1718–1775," *William and Mary Quarterly* 3d ser., 42 (1985): 184–200; Miller, *Emigrants and Exiles*, 144; Truxes, *Irish-American Trade*, 128.

17. Will of Thomas Scurlock, 1747, CNYHS, 1895, 116.

18. John Pell, "The Saga of Will Gilliland," *New York History* 13 (1932): 399–403; and Elizabeth Marting, "Footnote to the Revolution: The Tribulations of William Gilliland," *New-York Historical Society Quarterly* 30 (1946): 234–53; Dickson, *Ulster Emigration*, 174.

19. *New-York Mercury*, Nov. 5, 1761.

20. *Rivington's New York Gazeteer*, Mar. 17, 1774.

21. "Robert Neilson to Jeremiah Smith, Maddybenny, 18th June, 1764," Massachusetts Historical Society, *Proceedings* 51 (1917–18): 338. This reference comes from Virginia D. Harrington, *The New York Merchant on the Eve of the Revolution* (New York, 1935), 189.

22. Will of David Young, 1769, CNYHS, 1898, 284.

23. Truxes, *Irish-American Trade*, 113.

24. Biographical information on New York's Irish merchants has been taken from Truxes, *Irish-American Trade;* John Austin Stevens Jr., *Colonial Records of the New York Chamber of Commerce 1768–1784 with Historical and Biographical Sketches* (New York, 1971; originally published 1867); and Richard C. Murphy and Lawrence J. Mannion, *The History of the Society of the Friendly Sons of Saint Patrick in the City of New York, 1784–1955* (New York, 1962).

25. Michael J. O'Brien, *Hercules Mulligan: Confidential Correspondent of General Washington* (New York, 1937), 18, 19, 38, 42; *Rivington's New York Gazeteer*, Mar. 10, 1774.

26. Murphy and Mannion, *Friendly Sons*, 92–93; David C. Humphrey, *From King's College to Columbia University 1746–1800* (New York, 1976), 32, 123, 134–35; *Dictionary of American Biography*, s. v. Robert Harpur, Joseph Murray; Will of John Wilson, 1749, CNYHS, 1895, 236.

27. Alfred Lawrence Lorenz, *Hugh Gaine: A Colonial Printer-Editor's Odyssey to Loyalism* (Carbondale and Edwardsville, Ill., 1972).

28. Gottesman, *Arts and Crafts*, 244, 256, 297, 330, 357; Will of Jeremiah Field, 1762, CNYHS, 1897, 194.

29. Gottesman, *Arts and Crafts*, 302–3. See also Will of Thomas Valentine, 1773, CNYHS, 1899, 157–58.

30. Gary B. Nash, *The Urban Crucible: Social Change, Political Consciousness, and the Origins of the American Revolution* (Cambridge, Mass., 1979), 239–40.

31. Will of Michael Dunn, 1758, CNYHS, 1896, 419–20. See also Will of Charles Burns, 1757, CNYHS, 1896, 182; and Will of John Moorehead, 1762, CNYHS, 1897, 226.

32. On the bounties see Nash, *The Urban Crucible*, 244. On occupations, "Muster Rolls of New York Provincial Troops, 1755–1764," CNYHS, 1891, 112–19, 132–35, 162–67, 170–75, 206–13, 292–309, 338–47, 374–79; Murphy and Mannion, *Friendly Sons*, 25; and Stevens, *Chamber of Commerce*, 157–58.

33. "Muster Rolls of New York Provincial Troops."

34. Graham Russell Hodges, *New York City Cartmen, 1667–1850* (New York and London, 1986), 43.

35. Newspaper advertisements for runaway servants are the major source for documenting the experiences of New York City's Irish servants.

36. "At the New Theatre in Chapel-Street . . . will be presented a Comedy, call'd The COMMITTEE OR The Faithful IRISHMAN. The Part of TEAGUE, to be performe'd by Mr. Hallam," advertisement from *The New-York Mercury*, Apr. 26, 1762, in "Old New York and Trinity Church," CNYHS, 1870, 182–83. "This day is published by Hodge and Shober . . . *The Irish Widow* in Two Acts." *Rivington's New-York Gazeteer*, Apr. 29, 1773. For background on Irish stock characters in English plays, see J. O. Bartley, *Teague, Shenkin and Sawney. Being an Historical Study of the Earliest Irish, Welsh and Scottish Characters in English Plays* (Cork, 1954).

37. "Brigadier Hunter's Answers to Queries relating to New-York" (London, Aug. 11, 1720), in E. B. O'Callaghan, ed., *Documents Relative to the Colonial History of the State of New York*, 15 vols. (Albany, 1856–87), 5: 556.

38. Will of James Cochran, 1759, CNYHS, 1896, 332–33; O'Brien, *Hercules Mulligan*, 16: *New-York Mercury*, Dec. 3, 1764.

39. Lorenz, *Hugh Gaine*; Truxes, *Irish-American Trade*, 115; Will of Alexander Wallace, 1772, CNYHS, 1899, 75.

40. Gottesman, *Arts and Crafts*, 244, 256, 282, 297, 330, 357; Will of Hugh Kennedy Hoy, 1768, CNYHS, 1898, 140; Miller, *Emigrants and Exiles*, 150; Will of Charles Burns, 1757, CNYHS, 1896, 182; Will of Jeremiah Field, 1762, CNYHS, 1897, 194.

41. Miller, *Emigrants and Exiles*, 137–68.

42. *New-York Post Boy*, Oct. 27, 1746.

43. Zenger's *New-York Weekly Journal*, May 28, 1750.

44. Quoted in "The Genealogical Record of Rev. Ebenezer Pemberton . . . ," *New York Genealogical and Biographical Record* 54 (1923): 224.

45. "Petition of the Presbyterians of N.Y. to the King," Mar. 18, 1766, in E. B. O'Callaghan, ed., *The Documentary History of the State of New York*, 4 vols. (Albany, 1850–51), 3: 497.

46. Samuel Miller, *Memoirs of the Rev. John Rodgers, D.D.* (New York, 1813), 147. Rodgers himself was of Scots-Irish descent, his parents having emigrated from Londonderry to Boston in 1721. William B. Sprague, *Annals of the American Pulpit* (New York, 1868), 3: 154.

47. Shepherd Knapp, *A History of the Brick Presbyterian Church in the City of New York* (New York, 1909), 32.

48. Dorothy Ganfield Fowler, *A City Church: The First Presbyterian Church in the City of New York, 1716–1976* (New York, 1981), 5.

49. Humphrey, *King's College*, 123.

50. Sessions Minutes, 1765–1808, First Presbyterian Church of New York City, Mss., (microfilm). Gilliland's name is followed by that of Elizabeth Gilliland (his

wife), Charity Gilliland (his sister), and Mary Gilliland, presumably another family member.

51. Murphy and Mannion, *Friendly Sons*, 25, 26, 59.

52. Will of John Neilson, 1762, CNYHS, 1897, 184–85.

53. James G. Leyburn, *The Scotch-Irish: A Social History* (Chapel Hill, N.C., 1962), 243–45; Jones, "The Scotch-Irish in British America," 298. Presbyterians from the north of Ireland formed the largest proportion of Philadelphia's Irish merchant community between 1731 and 1775. Truxes, *Irish-American Trade*, 118.

54. Miller, *Emigrants and Exiles*, 137; Miller (p. 150) also states that members of the Church of Ireland constituted one-fourth of Protestant emigrants.

55. Lorenz, *Hugh Gaine*, 16.

56. Miller, *Emigrants and Exiles*, 151–52.

57. Doyle, *Ireland, Irishmen, and Revolutionary America*, 37–39; Julian Gwyn, *The Enterprising Admiral: The Personal Fortune of Admiral Sir Peter Warren* (Montreal and London, 1974).

58. See note 26.

59. Edward P. Alexander, *A Revolutionary Conservative: James Duane of New York* (New York, 1938), 3–8.

60. Stevens, *Chamber of Commerce*, 165; Truxes, *Irish-American Trade*, 113.

61. Miller, *Emigrants and Exiles*, 150; O'Brien, *Hercules Mulligan*, 35, 140; Murphy and Mannion, *Friendly Sons*, 25, 26, 123, 125; Stevens, *Chamber of Commerce*, 157–58.

62. Frank Baker, *From Wesley to Asbury: Studies in Early American Methodism* (Durham, N.C., 1976); William Crook, *Ireland and the Centenary of American Methodism* (London and Dublin, 1866).

63. Miller, *Emigrants and Exiles*, 137; David Noel Doyle, "The Irish in North America, 1776–1845," in W. E. Vaughan, ed., *A New History of Ireland*. (Oxford, 1989), 5: 693.

64. John Tracy Ellis, *Catholics in Colonial America* (Baltimore, 1965); and Jay P. Dolan, *The American Catholic Experience: A History from Colonial Times to the Present* (Garden City, N.Y., 1985), 69–97. Kerby Miller stresses the assimilation of Catholics in the American colonies. Miller, *Emigrants and Exiles*, 147.

65. After 1691, anti-Catholic sentiment was embodied in New York laws prohibiting Roman Catholics from worshipping and voting. For a convenient digest of New York's laws pertaining to Catholics see Francis X. Curran, *Catholics in Colonial Law* (Chicago, 1963). See also Mary Augustina Ray, *American Opinion of Roman Catholicism in the Eighteenth Century* (New York, 1936).

66. *Marriages from 1639 to 1801 in the Reformed Dutch Church, New York* (New York, 1940).

67. Sally Schwartz, *"A Mixed Multitude": The Struggle for Toleration in Colonial Pennsylvania* (New York and London, 1987), 152.

68. Ellis, *Catholics in Colonial America*, 369.

69. "Earl of Bellomont to the Lords of Trade" (New York, Oct. 28, 1700), *Documents Relative to . . . New York*, 4: 770–71. At the turn of the eighteenth century, New York politics were deeply factionalized. Governor Bellomont sided with the Leislerians, who were known for their vehement anti-Catholicism.

70. T. J. Davis, *A Rumor of Revolt: The "Great Negro Plot" in Colonial New York* (New York, 1985), 165–66; 233–35. In 1741 a series of suspicious fires and thefts in New York City unleashed a wave of mass panic in which scores of African slaves were unjustly accused of conspiracy to burn down the city and kill its white residents. Irish soldiers of

the British garrison were among those brought in for questioning during the investigation of the "conspiracy."

71. Cadwallader Colden to Daniel Horsmanden, Coldengham, July 29, 1742, in "The Letters and Papers of Cadwallader Colden, Volume 8, Additional Letters and Papers 1715–1748," CNYHS, 1934, 288–89.

72. Andrew Burnaby, *Travels through the Middle Settlements in North-America in the Years 1759 and 1760*, 2d ed. (London, 1775, Ithaca, N.Y., 1960); 79.

73. I. N. Phelps Stokes, *The Iconography of Manhattan Island, 1498–1909*, 6 vols. (New York, 1928), 4: 909. Richard Pointer states that there were "closet Catholics" in New York City before the Revolution. Richard W. Pointer, *Protestant Pluralism and the New York Experience; A Study of Eighteenth-Century Religious Diversity* (Bloomington and Indianapolis, 1988), 67.

74. Sally Schwartz, *"A Mixed Multitude,"* 104, 333.

75. Ellis, *Catholics in Colonial America*, 375–76.

76. Davis, *A Rumor of Revolt*, 12, 274n. 1. Crimmins, *St. Patrick's Day*, 25, dates the earliest celebration as 1762.

77. Crimmins, *St. Patrick's Day*, 26–27.

78. Michael F. Funchion, ed., *Irish American Voluntary Organizations* (Westport, Conn., 1983), 49–50.

79. Crimmins, *St. Patrick's Day*, 27–29.

80. Stokes, *Iconography*, 4: 818.

81. "P. V. Schaack to Henry Van Schaack, New-York, Friday, 27 Jan'y, 1769," in Henry C. Van Schaack, *The Life of Peter Van Schaack, LL.D., Embracing Selections from his Correspondence and Other Writings, During the American Revolution and His Exile in England* (New York, 1842), 11.

82. Thomas Smith (1734–1795) was the brother of noted lawyer and historian William Smith Jr., a major figure in New York politics in this era. James McLachlan, *Princetonians, 1748–1768: A Biographical Dictionary* (Princeton, N.J., 1976), 122–25.

83. *Whereas a Report Prevails in this City . . . New-York, January 23, 1769.* Broadside (Evans #11433). For another contemporary reference to the "Men of Straw," see *Card (A) Jack Hathaway and Tom Bowling, return Their Service to Messrs. Axe and Hammer . . . January 18, 1769.* Broadside (Evans #11199).

84. *The Irishmen's Petition, to the Honorable C-mm-ssi-n-rs of Excise, & C. . . .* Broadside (New York, 1769) (Evans #11485). On the identification of Lawrence Sweeney, see O'Brien, *Hercules Mulligan*, 28–29.

85. Though concerned with a later period, Donald H. Akenson, *Small Differences: Irish Catholics and Irish Protestants, 1815–1922: An International Perspective* (Kingston, 1988), offers valuable insights into the contrasting worlds of Irish Catholics and Protestants.

86. *Remarkable Experiences in the Life of Elizabeth Ashbridge. A True Account (Written Mostly by Herself)* (1927), 11–12.

87. See, for example, the advertisements for William Bowen and William Ashton. *New-York Mercury*, June 27, 1757; July 18, 1763.

88. Carl Bridenbaugh, ed., *Gentleman's Progress: The Itinerarium of Dr. Alexander Hamilton, 1744* (Chapel Hill, 1948), 82–83. On his trip to Albany, Hamilton claimed to have identified another Irishman masquerading as a Scot. "I soon found by his howl in singing the Black Jock . . . that he was a genuine Teague" (*Gentleman's Progress*, 70–71.)

This essay is dedicated to my mother, the bravest and strongest person I know. Funding was generously provided by Harvard Law School's Mark de Wolfe Howe Fund for Research into Legal History and Civil Liberties. Special thanks go to my teacher Morton J. Horwitz, to my magpie friend John O'Connor, and to my intrepid guide Katherine A. Dickason, great-great-granddaughter of both William Sampson and Theobald Wolfe Tone. As always, my greatest debt is to my constant inspiration and keenest critic, Anita Ramasastry.

1. "An Act to Prevent persons from returning to His Majesty's Dominions, who have been, or shall be transported, banished, or exiled, on Account of the present Rebellion, and to prohibit them from passing into any Country at War with His Majesty," 38 Geo. III, chap. 78 (Ir. 1798).

As a group, there is a vast and widely scattered body of information on the exiles of 1798 in both manuscript and printed form, including much from their own pens. All the United Irish leaders, including the New York City exiles, have lengthy chapters devoted individually to them in Richard Robert Madden, *The United Irishmen, Their Lives and Times,* 2d ser. (London, 1842–46). In the 1840s, Madden visited New York City to gather information for this biographical series and he mentions the situation of their survivors, who contributed much of his material. The Irish Jacobins are usually discussed in Irish American histories, such as Henry M. Field, *The Irish Confederates, and the Rebellion of 1798* (New York, 1851); Thomas D'Arcy McGee, *A History of the Irish Settlers in North America* (New York, 1852); Richard C. Murphy and Laurence T. Mannion, *The History of the Friendly Sons of Saint Patrick in the City of New York, 1784–1955* (New York, 1962). They occupy an important place in the history of radical immigrant influences in the United States. See, for example, Richard J. Twomey, *Jacobins and Jeffersonians: Anglo-American Radicalism in the United States, 1790–1820* (New York, 1989). They are also covered in standard biographical dictionaries, including the *Dictionary of National Biography* and the *Dictionary of American Biography,* and in standard histories of the United Irish movement.

For biographical detail on Sampson, see Madden, "Memoir of William Sampson," in *United Irishmen,* 2: 335–88; Maxwell Bloomfield, "William Sampson and the Codification Movement," in *American Lawyers in a Changing Society* (Cambridge, Mass., 1976); Maxwell Bloomfield, "William Sampson and the Codifiers: The Roots of American Legal Reform," *American Journal of Legal History* 11 (1967), 234; Paul O'Higgins, "William Sampson (1764–1836)," *Dublin University Law Review* 2 (1971), 45; Edward J. McGuire, "William Sampson," *Journal of the American Irish Historical Society* 15 (1916): 343; Charles Currier Beale, *William Sampson—Lawyer and Stenographer* (Boston, 1907); Irving Browne, "William Sampson," *Green Bag* 8 (1896): 313; and Walter J. Walsh, "Redefining Radicalism: A Historical Perspective," *George Washington Law Review* 59 (1991): 636.

For biographical detail on Emmet, see Madden, "Memoir of Thomas Addis Emmet," in *United Irishmen,* 2: 1–208; Thomas Addis Emmet, *Memoir of Thomas Addis and Robert Emmet* (New York, 1915) (by his grandson); Thomas P. Robinson, "The Life of Thomas Addis Emmet" (Ph.D. diss., New York University, 1955); and Charles Glidden Haines, *Memoir of Thomas Addis Emmet* (New York, 1829).

For biographical detail on MacNeven, see Madden, "Memoir of William James MacNeven," in *United Irishmen,* 2: 209–88; Myles D. Wyndham, "William James MacNeven and Early Laboratory Instruction in the United States," *Ambix* 17 (1970): 143; D. Reilly, "An Irish-American Chemist: William James MacNeven," *Chymia* 2

(1949): 17; Deasmumhan O Raghallaigh, "William James MacNeven," *Studies* 30 (1944): 247. Thus far Chambers has almost eluded the biographer. "John Chambers—Printer and United Irishman," *The Irish Book*, Vol. 1 (1964), 1.

2. The Supreme Court decision is *Employment Division v. Smith*, 494 U.S. 872 (1990); the Congressional response is the Religious Freedom Restoration Act, Pub. L. No. 103–141, s.3(a), 107 Stat. 1488 (1993) (to be codified at 42 U.S.C. s.2000bb). For the resulting scholarly controversy concerning *People v. Philips* (1813) see Michael W. McConnell, "The Origins and Historical Understanding of Free Exercise of Religion," *Harvard Law Review* 103 (1990): 1410, 1410–12, 1504–6; Michael W. McConnell, "Free Exercise Revisionism and the Smith Decision," *University of Chicago Law Review* 57 (1990): 1109, 1147–48; Gerard V. Bradley, "Beguiled: Free Exercise Exemptions and the Siren Song of Liberalism," *Hofstra Law Review* 20 (1991): 245, 289–92; Mark Tushnet, "The Rhetoric of Free Exercise Discourse," *Brigham Young University Law Review* (1993): 117, 123–27.

3. Simon Butler, *A Digest of the Popery Laws* (Dublin, 1792); Denys Scully, *Statement of the Penal Laws affecting Roman Catholics*, 3 parts (Dublin, 1812–13); William Sampson, "Irish Penal Code Abridged," in *The Catholic Question in America . . .* (New York, 1813, 1974; revised to avoid seditious libel prosecution, Dublin, 1814); H. B. Parnell, *History of the Penal Laws against the Irish Catholics*, 4th ed. (London, 1825). Recent works include S. J. Connolly, *Religion, Law and Power* (Cambridge, 1992); Joel Berlatsky, "Roots of Conflict in Ireland: Colonial Attitudes in the Age of the Penal Laws," *Eire-Ireland* 18 (1983): 40; Margaret Wall, *The Penal Laws, 1691–1760* (Dundalk, 1961); R. E. Burns, "The Irish Penal Code and Some of Its Historians," *Review of Politics* 21 (1959): 276.

4. For a notable exception to the traditional American jurisprudential understanding of religion as a private pact between believer and creator, see Robert M. Cover, "The Supreme Court 1982 Term—Foreword: Nomos and Narrative," *Harvard Law Review* 97 (1983): 4. Cover portrays free exercise problems in terms of sharp cultural conflict.

5. State of New York, *The Colonial Laws of New York* (New York, 1894–96), 1: 248; J. Pratt, *Religion, Politics and Diversity: The Church-State Theme in New York History* (New York, 1967), 38–40.

6. E. B. O'Callaghan and B. Fernow, eds., *Documents Relating to the Colonial History of the State of New York* (New York, 1853–87), 3: 689; Pratt, *Religion, Politics and Diversity*, 39.

7. Hugh Hastings, ed., *Ecclesiastical Records of the State of New York* (Albany, 1901), 2: 1012, 1367–69; E. J. Maguire, "An Historical Sketch of the Relations of Church and State in New York," *Historical Records and Studies* 2 (1908) (United States Catholic Historical Society): 109, 113–15; James H. Dohan, "Our State Constitutions and Religious Liberty," *American Catholic Quarterly Review* 40 (1915): 295; William Harper Bennett, *Catholic Footsteps in Old New York* (New York, 1909), 215; Leo Raymond Ryan, *Old St. Peter's* (New York, 1935), 10–14; John Gilmary Shea, *History of the Catholic Church in the United States* (1886–92), 1: 356–57; James R. Bayley, *A Brief Sketch of the Early History of the Catholic Church on the Island of New York* (New York, 1870), 39–41; Gustavus Myers, *A History of Bigotry in the United States* (New York, 1945), 94–96; Sydney E. Ahlstrom, *A Religious History of the American People* (New York, 1975), 1: 414–15.

8. Ray Allen Billington, *The Protestant Crusade: A Study of the Origins of American Nativism* (New York, 1938), 1–19; Ahlstrom, *Religious History*, 1: 88, 104, 158–59,

403–17, 666–81. This view was shared by John Jay, first chief justice of the United States. Pratt, *Religion, Politics, and Diversity*, 84–85.

9. See, for example, John Locke, *A Letter Concerning Toleration* (London, 1689).

10. See, for example, Sanford H. Cobb, *The Rise of Religious Liberty in America* (New York, 1968), 362–98; McConnell, "Origins and Historical Understanding," 1424–25.

11. Billington, *Protestant Crusade*, 22–23; Myers, *History of Bigotry*, 94–96; Gordon S. Wood, *The Radicalism of the American Revolution* (New York, 1991).

12. N.Y. Const. of 1777, arts. 25 & 38, B. Poore, ed., *Federal and State Constitutions, Colonial Charters, and Other Organic Laws of the United States*, 2, 2d ed. (1878); McConnell, "Origins and Historical Understanding," 1436–37. Congregationalist establishments continued in New England until 1834.

13. *Journals of the Provincial Congress, Provincial Convention, Committee of Safety and Council of Safety of the State of New York* (1842), 1: 844; see also Charles Z. Lincoln, *The Constitutional History of New York* (New York, 1906), 541–45; Pratt, *Religion, Politics and Diversity*, 81–90.

14. Billington, *Protestant Crusade*, 21; Morton Borden, *Jews, Turks, and Infidels* (1984), 13–14; Pratt, *Religion, Politics, and Diversity*, 107–8.

15. Cobb, *Rise of Religious Liberty*, 301–61; T. Curry, *The First Freedoms: Church and State in America to the Passage of the First Amendment* (1986), 62–73.

16. Ryan, *Old St. Peter's*, 96–98; Jay P. Dolan, *The Immigrant Church . . . 1815–1865* (Baltimore, 1975), 2, 11–13; Thomas Adams, Harold M. Lewis, and Theodore T. McCrosky, *Regional Survey of New York and Its Environs* (New York, 1929), 2: 71.

17. Kerby A. Miller, *Emigrants and Exiles* (New York, 1985), 178–90.

18. *Argus*, Mar. 20, 25, 1799; *People v. O' Brien*, New York Court of General Sessions, Apr. 16, 1802 (New York City Municipal Archives and Record Center); New York City Common Council, *Minutes . . . 1784–1831*, (1917–30), 3: 228; *Evening Post*, Mar. 15, 1804. See also Paul A. Gilje, *Road to Mobocracy* (Chapel Hill, N.C., 1987), 129–30, 206–11; John D. Crimmins, *St. Patrick's Day: Its Celebration in New York and Other American Places, 1737–1845 . . .* (New York, 1902), 298–303; John Ridge, *The St. Patrick's Day Parade* (New York, 1988), 7.

19. For more on Cooper, see William H. Bennett, "Francis Cooper: New York's First Catholic Legislator," *Historical Records and Studies* 12 (1918): 29.

20. Dolan, *Immigrant Church*, 54–58.

21. *American Citizen*, Feb. 12, 1806; Ryan, *Old St. Peter's*, 83–86; John M. Farley, *History of St. Patrick's Cathedral* (New York, 1908), 37–40; Bayley, *Brief Sketch*, 53; Myers, *History of Bigotry*, 111.

22. Brian McDermott, ed., *The Irish Catholic Petition of 1805* (Dublin, 1993).

23. Gilje, *Road to Mobocracy*, 125–33.

24. Rufus King to Timothy Pickering, Sept. 13, 1798, King Papers, vol. 52, New-York Historical Society.

25. King to Pickering, June 14, 1798, King Papers, Box 7, New-York Historical Society. The notorious alien and sedition laws were designed to exclude United Irish and French radicals. See James Morton Smith, *The Alien and Sedition Laws and American Civil Liberties* (Ithaca, N.Y., 1956), 23–24; Billington, *Protestant Crusade*, 23–24.

26. Rufus King to Duke of Portland, Sept. 13, 1798, King Papers, vol. 52, New-York Historical Society.

27. The story is told in Robert Ernst, *Rufus King* (Chapel Hill, N.C., 1968), 261–64, 302–4, 349–51; E. H. Brush, *Rufus King and his Times* (New York, 1926), 75–76, 95;

Emmet, *Memoir of Thomas Addis and Robert Emmet,* 1: 410–20 (with a facsimile reprint of Emmet's broadsheet).

28. Quoted in Emmet, *Memoir of Thomas Addis and Robert Emmet,* 415.

29. Rufus King to Theodore Sedgwick, Mar. 21, 1799, Sedgwick Papers, Box D, Massachusetts Historical Society.

30. *American Citizen,* Apr. 1, 10, 1807.

31. William to Grace Sampson, Apr. 27, 1807, private collection of Katherine A. Dickason.

32. *American Citizen,* Apr. 28, 1807.

33. William to Grace Sampson, July 4, 1807, private collection of Katherine A. Dickason.

34. Rufus King to Christopher Gore, May 15, 1816, King Papers, New-York Historical Society.

35. *People v. Philips,* Mar. 3, 5, 8, and June 8, 9, 14 (New York Court of General Sessions, 1813). The *Philips* decision is reported in William Sampson, *The Catholic Question in America. . . . Whether a Roman Catholic Clergyman Be in Any Case Compellable to Disclose the Secrets of Auricular Confession. Decided at the Court of General Sessions, in the City of New-York. . . . With the Arguments of Counsel, and the Unanimous Opinion of the Court, Delivered by the Mayor, with his Reasons in Support of that Opinion* (New York, 1813, 1974; revised to avoid seditious libel prosecution, Dublin, 1814). Unless otherwise indicated, the history that follows is drawn from Sampson's work. Partial abstracts or extracts are *Port Folio* magazine, Dec. 1813, 599; *Western Law Journal* 1 (1844): 109; *Southwestern Law Journal* 1 (1844): 90; Anson Phelps Stokes, *Church and State in the United States* (New York, 1950), 1: 838–50; "Privileged Communications to Clergymen," *Catholic Lawyer* 1 (1955): 199.

36. Sampson, *Catholic Question,* 199. See also "Court of General Sessions Minutes Book," Mar. 3, 5, 8, 1813, Municipal Archives of the City of New York (henceforth MARC); "New York City Police Court Register of Felonies," Feb. 10, 1813, MARC; *Port Folio,* Dec. 1813, 599; McConnell, "Origins and Historical Understanding," 1410–12, 1504–6; Ryan, *Old St. Peter's,* 111–15; Myers, *History of Bigotry,* 118–22.

37. Sampson, *Catholic Question,* 9. For more on Kohlmann, see Wilfrid Parsons, "Reverend Anthony Kohlmann, S.J. (1771–1824)," *Catholic Historical Review* 4 (1918): 38; Thomas F. Meehan, "Anthony Kohlmann," *Catholic Encyclopedia* (1910), 8: 686.

38. In the Jeffersonian era, there was no strict separation of powers; the mayor acted as chief magistrate. Charles P. Daly, *A Historical Sketch of the Judicial Tribunals of New York from 1623–1846* (New York, 1855); Howard B. Rock, *Artisans in the New Republic* (New York, 1984), 28. This changed with the mayorality of Stephen Allen shortly before President Jackson came to power. Paul O. Weinbaum, *Mobs and Demagogues* (Ann Arbor, Mich., 1979), 112; Gilje, *Road to Mobocracy,* 269–70.

39. Sampson, *Catholic Question,* 9.

40. Petition of the Trustees of St. Peter's Church to New York District Attorney, Apr. 19, 1813 (quoting Article 38 of the state constitution), reprinted in Sampson, *Catholic Question,* 52–54. For the turbulent history of trusteeism—the lay ownership of church property and the consequent shift in power from hierarchy to congregation—see Peter Guilday, "Trusteeism," *Historical Records & Studies* 18 (1929): 7; Patrick J. Dignan, *A History of the Legal Incorporation of Catholic Church Property in the United States, 1784–1932* (New York 1935); Farley, *History of St. Patrick's,* 4–17, 32, 74–82; Ryan, *Old St. Peter's,* 44–56, 132–56, 184–208; Shea, *History of the Catholic Church,* 2: 324; Billington, *Protestant Crusade,* 38–41, 292–300.

41. Sampson, *Catholic Question,* 13, 42–51.

42. Hence the recent political controversy over the U.S. Supreme Court's *Smith* decision culminating in Congress's passage of the Religious Freedom Restoration Act.

43. Sampson, *Catholic Question*, 52–95.

44. Sampson described his practice as a radical United Irish lawyer in his preface to William Henry Curran, *Life of the Right Honourable John Philpot Curran* (New York, 1820). He defended Archibold Hamilton Rowan, Reverend William Jackson, William Orr, the proprietors of the *Northern Star* (including Samuel Neilson), and Peter Finerty (the printer of the *Press*) all against sweeping English common law charges of treason, sedition, and seditious libel.

45. Sampson, *Memoirs* (1807 ed.), 19.

46. For example, in addition to the first free exercise case, Sampson defended the first strikers in New York to be prosecuted for a conspiracy to raise their wages. Curiously, his adversary was Emmet. William Sampson, *Trial of the Journeymen Cordwainers of the City of New-York; for a Conspiracy to Raise their Wages . . .* (New York, 1810), reprinted in Yates' Select Cases (New York, 1811), 1: 142; N.Y. Common L. Rep., 7 (New York, 1884), 153. Partial reprints are John R. Commons et al., eds., *A Documentary History of American Industrial Society* (1910), 3: 251; Wheeler's Criminal Cases, (New York, 1851), 2: 262; and American State Trials (St. Louis, Mo., 1914–36), 3: 576. Sampson also argued numerous other issues of religious freedom, free speech, and equality, often for indigent Irish and African clients. His instrumental legal philosophy is best expressed in William Sampson, *Sampson's Discourse, and Correspondence with Various Learned Jurists, upon the History of the Law* (Pishey Thompson, ed., Washington, D.C., 1826). See generally Walsh, "Redefining Radicalism"; cf. Walter J. Walsh, "Poor People and the Law," in *One Million Poor?*, Stanislaus Kennedy, ed. (Dublin, 1981). For a more recent Irish American cause lawyer, see Paul O'Dwyer, *Counsel for the Defense: The Autobiography of Paul O'Dwyer* (New York, 1979).

47. See Martin Burke, "Piecing Together a Shattered Past: The Historical Writings of the United Irish Exiles in America," in David Dickson, Daire Keogh, and Kevin Whelan, eds., *The United Irishmen* (Dublin, 1993), 297; Martin Burke, "The Politics and Poetics of Nationalist Historiography," in Cecil Barfoot, ed., *The Politics of Literature and the Literature of Politics* (Amsterdam, forthcoming). For other perspectives on United Irish historiography, see Nancy J. Curtin, *The United Irishmen* (Oxford, 1994), 20–21, 184–85; Mary Helen Thuente, *The Harp Re-strung* (Syracuse, N.Y., 1994), 1–46.

48. *Butler v. Moore* (Irish Chancery 1802), discussed in Leonard MacNally, *The Rules of Evidence on Pleas of the Crown* (London, 1804), 1: 253–55.

49. Sampson, *Catholic Question*, at 55–56, 68. In the paragraphs that follow in the text, subsequent quotations from this source refer to Sampson's pages 59, 64; 76, 65; 70–71; 70–71, 67; 72, 81, 65, 87, 66, 84; 80, 85; 92; 85, 93–95.

50. The Jeffersonian push for immigrant votes is recounted in Rock, *Artisans*, 26–27, 38, 83, 98, 144.

51. Ibid., 107–8.

52. Sampson, *Catholic Question*, 108–9, 114.

53. N.Y. Rev. Stat. 1828, pt. 3, chap. 7, tit. 3, sec. 72. See also Michael James Callahan, "Historical Inquiry into the Priest-Penitent Privilege," *Jurist* 36 (1976): 328; "Privileged Communications to Clergymen," *Catholic Lawyer* 1 (1955): 199.

54. The earliest federal free exercise decision also involved Roman Catholics. *Permoli v. Municipality No. 1*, 44 U.S. (3 Howard) 588 (1845). Subsequent cases tell their own story: Mormons, Jews, Jehovah's Witnesses, Amish, Hare Krishnas, Muslims, Native Americans, Santerria, and so on. See generally R. Laurence Moore, *Religious Outsiders and the Making of Americans* (New York, 1986). The federal First Amendment was not formally extended to regulate state action until 1940.

55. John P. O'Connor, "*The Shamrock* of New York, The First Irish-American Newspaper," *New York Irish History* 4 (1989): 4.

56. Sampson, "Irish Penal Code Abridged," in *Catholic Question.*

57. Anthony Kohlmann, S.J., "A True Exposition of the Doctrine of the Catholic Church, Touching the Sacrament of Penance, with the Grounds on Which This Doctrine Is Founded," in Sampson, *Catholic Question,* i–cxii. See also Charles Wharton, *A Short Answer to a True Exposition of the Doctrine of the Catholic Church Touching the Sacrament of Penance* (New York, 1813), rebutted by Simon F. O'Gallagher, *A Brief Reply to a Short Answer to a True Exposition of the Doctrine of the Catholic Church Touching the Sacrament of Penance* (New York, 1815). Shea, *History of the Catholic Church,* 3: 167. For an account of later theological battles against nativists, see Billington, *Protestant Crusade,* 41–68.

58. Sampson, *Catholic Question,* "Preface," 3.

59. Sampson ranked with William Drennan as the penman of the United Irishmen. He published almost forty books and pamphlets, including many radical political tracts, political satires, and reports of political trials, as well as frequent contributions to the periodical press, including the United Irish newspapers the *Northern Star* and the *Press,* both of which he defended after their suppression.

His views on the place of the 1798 Rebellion in Irish history emerge most directly from [William Sampson], *Advice to the Rich* (Belfast, 1796; Dublin, 1796); William Sampson, *An Appeal from William Sampson* (Dublin, 1798); *Memoirs of William Sampson* (New York, 1807, 1826; Leesburg, Va., 1817; London, 1832); William Sampson, *The Catholic Question in America* (New York, 1813, 1974; Dublin, 1814); William Sampson, "Introduction," to Curran, *Life of the Right Honourable John Philpot Curran;* William Sampson, "Conclusion," to William Cooke Taylor and William Sampson, *History of Ireland* (New York, 1833, 1841).

Sampson also expressed his thoughts on law and politics in several outwardly whimsical but deeply serious satires. These include [William Sampson], *A Faithful Report of the Trial of Hurdy Gurdy* (Belfast, 1794, several eds.; Dublin, 1794; New York, 1806, 1807); [William Sampson and Thomas Russell], *Review of the Lion of Old England; or the Democracy Confounded* (Belfast, 1794); [William Sampson], *Trial of Capt. Henry Whitby . . . Also . . . Capt. George Crimp, for Piracy and Manstealing* (New York, 1812).

Sampson saw the courtroom as an arena for political struggle. He was one of the earliest court reporters, frequently recording treason and sedition cases that he argued alongside John Philpot Curran. His reports include [William Ridgeway and William Sampson], *Report of the Trial of Archibold Hamilton Rowan . . . for the distribution of a libel* ([Archibold Hamilton Rowan, ed.,] Dublin, 1794; London, 1794; New York, 1794); [William Sampson], *A Faithful Report of the Trial of the Proprietors of the Northern Star . . . for the Insertion of a Publication by the Irish Jacobins of Belfast* (Belfast, 1794); [William Sampson], *A Faithful Report of the Second Trial of the Proprietors of the Northern Star . . . for the Insertion of the Society of United Irishmen's Address to the Volunteers of Ireland* (Belfast, 1795); William Sampson, *The Trial of the Rev. William Jackson . . . for High Treason* (Dublin, 1795); [William Sampson], *A Brief Account of the Trial of William Orr* (Dublin, 1797); [William Sampson], *Commissioners of the Alms-House vs. Alexander Whistelo, a Black Man* (New York 1808, 1897); [William Sampson], *The Trial of Amos Broad and his Wife . . . for Beating Betty, a Slave* (New York, 1809); William Sampson, *Trial of the Journeymen Cordwainers of the City of New-York; for a Conspiracy to Raise Their Wages* (New York, 1810); Sampson, *Catholic Question;* William Sampson, *Is a Whale a Fish? An Accurate Report of the Case of James Maurice against Samuel Judd* (New York, 1819).

Sampson's radical codification argument is contained in his *Trial of the Journeymen Cordwainers;* and William Sampson, *An Anniversary Discourse Delivered before the*

Historical Society of New-York . . . Showing the Origin, Progress, Antiquities, Curiosities, and Nature of the Common Law (New York, 1824); Pishey Thompson, ed., *Sampson's Discourse, and Correspondence with Various Learned Jurists, upon the History of the Law* (Washington, D.C., 1826).

It is also noteworthy that Sampson published in Dublin, with his own introduction, his correspondence with James Fenimore Cooper's uncle, who settled much of upstate New York. William Cooper, *A Guide in the Wilderness or the History of the First Settlements in the Western Counties of New York with Useful Instructions to Future Settlers* (William Sampson, ed., Dublin, 1810; Rochester, N.Y., 1897; Cooperstown, N.Y., 1936, 1949).

60. William James MacNeven, ed., *Pieces of Irish History, Illustrative of the Conditions of the Catholics . . .* (New York, 1807). Emmet's contribution is entitled "Towards a History of Ireland." See also, William James MacNeven, "Report of Dr. Macneven in Relation to Mr. Emmet's Monument," reprinted as appendix to Taylor and Sampson, *History of Ireland*, 2: 351.

61. William Tone, ed., *Life of Theobold Wolfe Tone*, 2 vols. (Washington, D.C., 1826) (Wolfe Tone's autobiography).

62. Marianne Elliott, *Wolfe Tone: Prophet of Irish Independence* (New Haven, 1989).

63. Miller, *Emigrants and Exiles*, 193–279; Robert Ernst, *Immigrant Life in New York City, 1825–1863* (New York, 1949).

64. *People v. Moore* (New York City Court of General Sessions, 1824), Wheeler's Criminal Cases, III, 82, Am. State Trials, XIII, 189 (the prosecution against the Protestant Irish); *People v. M'Evoy*, Wheeler's Criminal Cases, III, 414, Am. State Trials, XIII, 209 (the prosecution against the Catholic Irish). In addition to the court report and newspaper stories, a contemporary account is *An Unbiased Irishman, Orangeism Exposed, with a Refutation of the Charges, and c., Brought against the Irish Nation, by Lawyer David Graham, of New-York, in His Defense of the Orangemen, Tried in this City, on the Thirteenth and Fourteenth Days of September, 1824, for Assault and Battery on a Poor Irishman, on the Twelfth Day of July, 1824* (New York, 1824). See also Emmet, *Memoir of Thomas Addis and Robert Emmet*, 1: 464–65; Gilje, *Road to Mobocracy*, 133–38; Sean Wilentz, *Chants Democratic: New York City and the Rise of the American Working Class, 1788–1850* (New York, 1986), 85.

65. *People v. Moore*, 84.

66. *People v. Moore; People v. M'Evoy*. Some of Sampson's historiographical reflections are in Taylor and Sampson, *History of Ireland*, 289–307. For the paradoxes of that period's nationalist historiography, see Jacqueline R. Hill, "Popery and Protestantism, Civil and Religious Liberty: Disputed Lessons of Irish History, 1690–1812," *Past and Present* 118 (1988): 96; Francis G. James, "Historiography and the Irish Constitutional Revolution of 1782," *Eire-Ireland* 18 (1983); Donal MacCartney, "The Writing of History in Ireland, 1800–1830," *Irish Historical Studies* 10 (1957): 347.

67. *People v. Moore*, 99.

68. *People v. M'Evoy*, 430–31.

69. Ibid., 432–33.

70. *Irish Shield and Monthly Milesian*, Feb. 1829, 68, and Mar. 1829, 101; William James MacNeven, "The Friends of Ireland," *Truth Teller*, July 1830; [Catherine MacNeven], "William James MacNeven," in Madden, *The United Irishmen*, 2: 227–28. For accounts of the Irish Emigrant Society, see Richard J. Purcell, "The Irish Emigrant Society of New York," *Studies* 27 (1938): 583; Thomas F. Meehan, "New York's First Irish Emigrant Society," *Historical Records and Studies* 6 (1912): 202. Thomas O'Connor (later O'Conor) co-edited *The Shamrock* with Edward Gillespy and was the father of Charles O'Conor.

71. Thomas Wyse, *Historical Sketch of the Late Catholic Association of Ireland*, vol. 1 (London, 1829), 310–21.

72. The funeral is described in Emmet, *Memoir of Thomas Addis and Robert Emmet*, vol. 1.

73. See MacNeven, "Report of Dr. MacNeven in relation to Mr. Emmet's Monument," reprinted as appendix to Taylor and Sampson, *History of Ireland*, 351. See also Emmet, *Memoir of Thomas Addis and Robert Emmet*, vol. 1.

74. *Irish Shield and Monthly Milesian*, Apr. 1829, 189–90.

75. William Sampson to Gulian Verplanck, Apr. 17, 1827, Verplanck Papers, New-York Historical Society; Grace Sampson to Catherine Sampson Tone, June 1, 1828, private collection of Katherine A. Dickason.

76. Miller, *Emigrants and Exiles*, 263–79.

77. See, for example, the several reports in the *Irish Shield and Monthly Milesian*, Mar. 23, 1831.

78. [Henry Darley], *A Full and Accurate Report of the Trial for Riot before the Mayor's Court of Philadelphia, . . . Arising out of A Protestant Procession on the 12th of July, and in which the Contending Parties were Protestants and Roman Catholics* (Philadelphia, 1831), 54, 57.

79. Quoted in Madden, *United Irishmen*, 2: 377; Francis Joseph Bigger, *William Orr* (Dublin, 1906), 70–73.

80. For the shift in mood from Jeffersonian-Federalist to Jacksonian-Whig politics, see Lee Benson, *The Concept of Jacksonian Democracy: New York as a Test Case* (New York, 1969); Dixon Ryan Fox, *The Decline of Aristocracy in the Politics of New York, 1801–1840* (New York, 1965); Richard P. McCormick, *The Second American Party System: Party Formation in the Jacksonian Era* (Chapel Hill, N.C., 1966).

81. See William James MacNeven, "Doctor MacNeven's Letter", *Commercial Advertiser*, Apr. 1, 1934.

82. See Sampson's letter in defense of MacNeven, *Morning Courier*, Apr. 9, 1834.

83. See *Commercial Advertiser*, Apr. 2, 5, 7, 1834 (numerous Whig claims to Irish vote including listing 150 Irish supporters of MacNeven and summoning them to meeting); *Morning Courier*, Apr. 8, 9, 15, 1834 (Whig publication of Sampson's letter to the adopted citizens); *Evening Post*, Apr. 7, 12, 17, 1834 (Jacksonian attacks on Mac-Neven and defense of "combustible" Irish rioters).

84. See, for example, *Evening Post*, Apr. 17, 1834 (acknowledging Jacksonian Irish majority, but accusing Whigs of attracting foreign French, Scotch, German, Spanish and Italian vote).

85. *Morning Courier*, Oct. 29, 30, and Nov. 4, 1834 (speeches describing Emmet, MacNeven, and Sampson as defenders of freedom, "Vinegar Hill" to the natives of Ireland, and the plight of an honest Irishman with Whig sympathies); *New York Times*, Oct. 31 and Nov. 5, 1834 (various appeals to the Irish Democrats).

86. See, for example, *New York Times*, Oct. 31, 1834 (claiming that Sampson's "monstrous alliance" with Rufus King's son was an affront to Irishmen).

87. The election returns are printed in *New York Commercial Advertiser*, Nov. 10, 1834; *Morning Courier*, Nov. 11, 1834. Sampson won in the First through Third, Fifth, and Fifteenth Wards; he was defeated in the Fourth Ward and the Sixth through Fourteenth Wards.

88. For the peculiar synergy between abolitionism and Hibernophobia, see Tyler Ambinder, *Nativism and Slavery; the Northern Know-Nothings and the Politics of the 1850s* (New York, 1992).

89. The most detailed account is Weinbaum, *Mobs and Demagogues* 1–10, 13–14. See also Gilje, *Road to Mobocracy*, 138–42.

90. Billington, *Protestant Crusade*; Ryan, *Old St. Peter's*, 172–73; Myers, *History of Bigotry*, 140–218; Wilentz, *Chants Democratic*, 266–69; Ahlstrom, *Religious History*, 1: 666–81.

91. On New York politics during the Bank War, see Sean Wilentz, *Chants Democratic*, 230–44. The conventional economic wisdom has been that the MacNeven-Sampson position was correct. Walter Buckingham Smith, *Economic Aspects of the Second Bank of the United States* (New York, 1969); Ralph C. H. Catterall, *The Second Bank of the United States* (Chicago, 1968). For the opposing view see Peter Temin, *The Jacksonian Economy* (New York, 1969).

92. Benson, *Jacksonian Democracy*.

93. For the Puritan analogy between the Irish and the Native Americans see James Muldoon, "The Indian as Irishman," *Essex Institute Historical Collections* 111 (1975): 267. For the ethnic basis of anti-Catholic persecution in Ireland see Joel Berlatsky, "Roots of Conflict in Ireland: Colonial Attitudes in the Age of the Penal Laws," *Eire-Ireland* 18 (1983): 40.

Chapter 3: BEFORE THE GREAT MIGRATION (Gilje)

1. Dennis J. Clark, "The Philadelphia Irish: Persistent Presence," in Allen F. Davis and Mark H. Haller, eds., *The Peoples of Philadelphia: A History of Ethnic Groups and Lower-Class Life, 1790–1940* (Philadelphia, 1973), 135–54; Oscar Handlin, *Boston's Immigrants: A Study in Acculturation*, rev. ed. (New York, 1975); Oliver MacDonagh, "The Irish Famine Emigration to the United States," in *Perspectives in American History* 10 (1976): 357–446; John Francis Maguire, *The Irish in America* (London, 1868); Kerby A. Miller, *Emigrants and Exiles: Ireland and the Irish Exodus to North America* (New York, 1985); Carl Wittke, *The Irish in America* (Baton Rouge, La., 1956).

2. William Forbes Adams, *Ireland and Irish Emigration to the New World from 1815 to the Famine* (New York, 1967; orig. pub. New Haven, 1932); William J. Bromwell, *History of Immigration to the United States . . .* (New York, 1856); David Noel Doyle, *Ireland, Irishmen and Revolutionary America, 1760–1820* (Dublin, 1981); House of Commons, *Third Report: Emigration from the United Kingdom, 1827* (London, 1827); MacDonagh, "Irish Famine Emigration," 393–96; Cormac O'Grada, "Across the Briny Ocean: Some Thoughts on Irish Emigration to America, 1800–1850," in T. M. Devine and David Dickson, eds., *Ireland and Scotland, 1600–1850: Parallels and Contrasts in Economic and Social Development* (Edinburgh, 1983), 118–30; Gearoid O'Tuathaigh, *Ireland before the Famine, 1798–1848* (Dublin, 1979).

3. Brian C. Mitchell, *The Paddy Camps: The Irish of Lowell, 1821–1861* (Urbana, Ill., 1988); Sam Bass Warner Jr., *The Private City: Philadelphia in Three Periods of Its Growth* (Philadelphia, 1968), 49–157; Michael Feldberg, *The Philadelphia Riots of 1844: A Study of Ethnic Conflict* (Westport, Conn., 1975). On population see Shamrock Society of New York, *Hints to Emigrants from Europe, Who Intend to Make a Permanent Residence in the United States* (New York, 1816), 28; Ira Rosenwaike, *Population History of New York City* (Syracuse, N.Y., 1972), 14–54.

For other studies of New York Irish in this period see Jay P. Dolan, *The Immigrant Church: New York's Irish and German Catholics, 1815–1865* (Baltimore, 1975); Robert Ernst, *Immigrant Life in New York City, 1825–1863* (New York, 1949); Paul A. Gilje, *The Road to Mobocracy: Popular Disorder in New York City, 1763–1834* (Chapel Hill, N.C., 1987), 121–42; Richard B. Stott, *Workers in the Metropolis: Class, Ethnicity, and Youth in Antebellum New York City* (Ithaca, N.Y., 1990); John D. Crimmins, *St. Patrick's Day:*

Its Celebration in New York and Other Places, 1737–1845 (New York, 1902), 44–54, 108–9, 145–57, 174–77, 190–200. For political émigrés see Richard J. Twomey, *Jacobins and Jeffersonians: Anglo-American Radicalism in the United States, 1790–1820* (New York, 1989); and Doyle, *Ireland, Irishmen and Revolutionary America.*

4. Shamrock Society, *Hints to Emigrants.* See also Richard J. Purcell, "The Irish Emigrant Society of New York," *Studies: An Irish Quarterly Review* 27 (1938): 583–99.

5. For example see *Truth Teller*, Mar. 20, 1830; Mar. 19, 26; July 9, 1831; Mar. 23, July 7, 1832; Mar. 23, 30, 1833.

6. Leo Raymond Ryan, *Old St. Peter's: The Mother Church of Catholic New York (1785–1935)* (New York, 1935); John Gilmary Shea, ed., *The Catholic Churches of New York City . . .* (New York, 1878), 587–95; John Talbot Smith, *The Catholic Church in New York: A History of the New York Diocese from its Establishment in 1808 to the Present Time,* 1 (New York, 1905).

7. Gilje, *Road to Mobocracy,* 130–33.

8. *People v. French,* Apr. 5, 1820, Supreme Court, Police Court, Cases (henceforth SCPC-Cases), District Attorney Papers (henceforth DA Papers), Municipal Archives of the City of New York (henceforth MARC). For a general discussion of the selling of pews see Shea, *The Catholic Churches,* 594, 603; and Dolan, *Immigrant Church,* 51–52.

9. Ray Allen Billington, *The Protestant Crusade, 1800–1869: A Study of the Origins of American Nativism* (New York, 1938).

10. Rev. John M. Farley, *History of St. Patrick's Cathedral* (New York, 1908); Shea, *Catholic Churches,* 602–3.

11. Dolan, *Immigrant Church,* 45–67.

12. The first issue of the *Shamrock* appeared Dec. 15, 1810, and contained a prospectus. Orangism was attacked in the next issue on Dec. 22, 1810. An article on Catholic emancipation appeared on Jan. 15, 1811. After these dates these themes were constantly repeated. On immigration see *Shamrock*, Jan. 27, 1816, and the lists republished in the *Recorder* 3 (1926): 2–19. Also *Shamrock*, Jan. 15, 1811 and Mar. 23, 1811. For an editorial in support of emigration to the United States and for the settlement of immigrants onto the frontier see *Shamrock*, July 5, 1816.

13. *Shamrock*, Aug. 16, 1817.

14. See, for example, *Truth Teller*, June 25, July 30, Aug. 6, Nov. 5, 12, 26, Dec. 17, 24, 31, 1825; Jan. 7, 1826.

15. *Truth Teller*, July 9, 1825, and July 6, 13, 20, 1833.

16. Gilje, *Road to Mobocracy,* 127–28, 142, 161. See also Carol Groneman Pernicone, "The 'Bloody Ould Sixth': A Social Analysis of a New York City Working-Class Community in the Mid-Nineteenth Century" (Ph.D. diss., University of Rochester, 1973).

17. A word about methodology is necessary here. The records do not indicate nativity. The researcher is thus left to guess the ethnic origins of individuals on the basis of names alone. Even with the most sophisticated techniques this unscientific method leaves something to be desired. I examined various records listing residents and noted those that appeared the most Irish. If I erred, the error is on the side of excluding some individuals whose ethnic status based upon the name is uncertain. The idea here was not to locate every Irish American in the city, but to identify those streets and areas where there were concentrations of Irish. Thus I may not have included a John Smith who was Irish and I may have included an Englishman with the improbable name Patrick O'Roarke. But such errors are likely to be minimal and the general trends sustained. To help identify Irish neighborhoods I used the New York City Jury and Census List (henceforth Jury List), 1819, Wards 1, 2, 4–10, MARC, and New York City Tax Assessment Records, Wards 7 and 10 for 1800, 1810, 1820, 1830, and 1840, MARC. For a discussion

on the use of names in establishing ethnic identity see Forrest McDonald and Ellen Shapiro, "The Ethnic Origins of the American People, 1790," *William and Mary Quarterly,* 3d ser., 37 (1980): 179–99; and Thomas L. Purvis, "The National Origins of New Yorkers in 1790," *New York History* 67 (1986): 133–53.

18. For a different view of this weavers' community see Jacob D. Wheeler, *Trial of John Moore, John Mullen, and Henry Bush . . .* (New York, 1824).

19. Report of George Cumming and others to Board of Health, Sept. 20, 1819, File Papers of the Common Council (henceforth File Papers), MARC. A detailed analysis of the sixth ward is provided by Pernicone, "'Bloody Ould Sixth'."

20. To get a sense of the crowded living conditions and thinness of walls see [William Coleman], *Report of the Trial of Levi Weeks, on the Indictment for the Murder of Guliema Sands* (New York, 1800); John H. Griscom, *The Sanitary Conditions of the Laboring Population of New York* (New York, 1845); and Ladies of the Mission, *The Old Brewery and the New Mission House at the Five Points* (1854; New York, 1970). See also Elizabeth Blackmar, *Manhattan for Rent, 1785–1850* (Ithaca, N.Y., 1989), 68–71, 101–3, 122–23, 208–9; and Ernst, *Immigrant Life,* 48–60.

21. Jury List, 1819, Sixth Ward, MARC. See also Pernicone, "'Bloody Ould Sixth'," 24; Ernst, *Immigrant Life,* 61–98.

22. Petition of Licensed Cartmen, June 1, 1818, File Papers, MARC.

23. Graham Russell Hodges, *New York City Cartmen, 1667–1850* (New York, 1986), 136–37, 152.

24. Gilje, *Road to Mobocracy,* 137–38.

25. *Gazette,* July 7, 1826; *Commercial Advertiser,* Aug. 14, 1832; *Morning Courier,* July 13, 1830; *People v. O'Brian,* Sept. 10, 1832, New York Court of General Sessions (henceforth Sessions), DA Papers, MARC; *Vandewater v. McGlone,* Aug., 30, 1826, SCPC-Cases, DA Papers, MARC.

26. "Letter of John Doyle to His Wife, Fanny, January 25, 1818," *Journal of the American Irish Historical Society* 2 (1913): 201–4; Richard C. O'Connor, "John T. Doyle," *Journal of the American Irish Historical Society* 11 (1912): 141–42.

27. *People v. Martin,* Sessions, Aug. 14, 1833, DA Papers, MARC.

28. The grocery remains a difficult institution to study. For brief comments on groceries see Stott, *Workers in the Metropolis,* 210; Dolan, *Immigrant Church,* 53; and Ernst, *Immigrant Life,* 86–87. Much of this paragraph derives from my reading of archival material on New York City. Some sample descriptions of Irish groceries can be found in *Seek v. Rooney et al.* (July 5, 1818), *People v. Martin et al.* (Aug. 14, 1833, Sessions), and *People v. McDermot, et al.* (Jan. 15, 1807), all in SCPC-Cases, DA Papers, MARC. See also *The British Mechanic's and Labourer's Hand Book and Travel Guide to the United States* (London, 1840), 269–70.

29. I randomly selected May 1810. There were a total of 107 bail bonds that month. Thirty-five had clearly identifiable Irish names. Fourteen of these had bail bonds sworn out by grocers, and almost all of them had Irish names. Of the remaining 72, some of whom may have been Irish with names not ethnically distinct, 21 grocers pledged bonds. Of those 21 grocers, 5 had distinctly Irish names. When I did a quick check on random samples of bail bonds from 1800 and 1820, these proportions remained roughly the same. Supreme Court, Police Court, Bonds, DA Papers, MARC.

30. MacDonagh, "Irish Famine Emigration," 393–96.

31. Although the alien population of any given ward is not identical with the Irish American population, the majority of immigrants in this period were from Ireland, and these numbers reflect the general pattern of male–female ratios that would be found among the immigrant Irish. Jury List, 1819, Fourth and Sixth Ward, MARC.

32. Jury List, 1819, Sixth Ward, MARC.

33. Society for the Encouragement of Faithful Domestic Servants, *Third Annual Report* (New York, 1828), esp. 23. See also Ernst, *Immigrant Life*, 66–69; Christine Stansell, *City of Women: Sex and Class in New York, 1789–1860* (New York, 1986), 155–68.

34. Paul A. Gilje, "Infant Abandonment in Early Nineteenth-Century New York City: Three Cases," *Signs* 8 (1983): 586–87.

35. Petition of Mary Erwin, Oct. 1, 1810, File Papers, MARC.

36. *Dougherty v. Odell et al.*, Nov. 16, 1824, SCPC-Cases, DA Papers, MARC.

37. *Yates v. Doyle*, Feb. 16, 1827, SCPC-Cases, DA Papers, MARC.

38. Alfred F. Young, *The Democratic Republicans of New York: The Origins, 1763–1797* (Chapel Hill, N.C., 1967), 476–95.

39. *New York Evening Post*, Apr., June, 1807. See also Thomas E. V. Smith, *Political Parties and Their Places of Meeting in New York City* (New York, 1893), 10.

40. Crimmins, *St. Patrick's Day*, 309–10.

41. *New York Evening Post*, Apr. 5, 1816; *Shamrock*, May 4, 1816. See also *New York Evening Post*, Sept. 26, 1816.

42. Jerome Mushkat, *Tammany: The Evolution of a Political Machine, 1789–1865* (Syracuse, 1971), 58.

43. Thomas Addis Emmet, M.D., *Incidents of My Life: Professional—Literary—Social, with Services in the Cause of Ireland* (New York, 1911; Thomas Addis Emmet, M.D., *Memoir of Thomas Addis and Robert Emmet with Their Ancestors and Immediate Family* (New York, 1915); *An Unbiased Irishman, Orangism Exposed with a Refutation of the Charges Brought against the Irish Nation, by Lawyer David Graham, of New York, in Defense of the Orangemen* (New York, 1824); *New York Evening Post*, Mar. 1, 1825.

44. *British Mechanic's and Labourer's Hand Book*, 127–28; Mushkat, *Tammany*, 56–157; Gustavus Myers, *The History of Tammany Hall*, 2d ed. (New York, 1917), 60–139.

45. Quotations from *New York Evening Post*, Apr. 9 and 11, 1834. For detailed citation and discussion see Gilje, *Road to Mobocracy*, 138–42.

46. Gilje, *Road to Mobocracy*.

47. *New York Evening Post*, Oct. 27, 1832.

48. Ibid., Nov. 1, 1814.

49. *Morning Courier*, July 13, 1830. See also *New York Evening Post*, Jan. 15, 1827.

50. Adams, *Ireland and Irish Immigration*, 22–31; Doyle, *Ireland, Irishmen and Revolutionary America*; Peter Way, "Shovel and Shamrock: Irish Workers and Labor Violence in the Digging of the Chesapeake and Ohio Canal," *Labor History* 31 (1989): 489–517; M. R. Beames, "The Ribbon Societies: Lower-Class Nationalism in Pre-Famine Ireland," *Past and Present* 97 (1982): 128–43; Beames, "Rural Conflict in Pre-Famine Ireland: Peasant Assassination in Tipperary, 1837–1847," *Past and Present* 81 (1978): 75–91; Tom Garvin, "Defenders, Ribbonmen and Others: Underground Political Networks in Pre-Famine Ireland," *Past and Present* 96 (1982): 135–55; David Fitzpatrick, "Class, Family and Rural Unrest in Nineteenth-Century Ireland," in P. J. Drudy, ed., *Ireland: Land, Politics and People* (Cambridge, 1982), 37–71; Joseph J. Lee, "Patterns of Rural Unrest in Nineteenth-Century Ireland: A Preliminary Survey," in L. M. Cullen and F. Furet, eds., *Ireland and France, 17th - 20th Centuries: Toward a Comparative Study of Rural History* (Paris, 1980), 223–37; Patrick O'Donnell, *The Irish Faction Fighters of the 19th Century* (Dublin, 1975).

51. James F. Richardson, *The New York Police: Colonial Times to 1901* (New York, 1970), 23–81; Gilje, *Road to Mobocracy*, 265–82.

52. Gilje, *Road to Mobocracy*, 130–38.

53. *Statesman*, June 2, 1829.

54. Quote in *Hall v. Dougherty*, Aug. 15, 1832, SCPC-Cases, DA Papers, MARC. See also Gilje, *Road to Mobocracy*, 227–32.

55. Quote in *People v. Cromer et al.*, Apr. 11, 1828, Sessions Records, DA Papers, MARC. For a general treatment and more citations see Gilje, *Road to Mobocracy*, 222–24.

56. *People v. Martin et al.*, Aug. 14, 1833, Sessions Records, DA Papers, MARC. See also Gilje, *Road to Mobocracy*, 245–46.

57. For a full discussion of this violence see Gilje, *Road to Mobocracy*, 123–70.

58. *Gazette*, July 7, 1826.

59. Gilje, *Road to Mobocracy*, 133–35.

Part II Overview: THE ERA OF THE GREAT MIGRATION
(Diner)

1. Quoted in George W. Potter, *To the Golden Door: The Story of the Irish in Ireland and America* (Boston, 1960), 180.

2. Robert Ernst, *Immigrant Life in New York City: 1825–1863* (New York, 1949), 15, 18, 20.

3. Bayrd Still, *Mirror for Gotham: New York as Seen by Contemporaries from Dutch Days to the Present* (New York, 1956), 78.

4. David M. Schneider and Albert Deutsch, *The History of Public Welfare in New York State, 1867–1940* (Chicago, 1941), 8.

5. Adrian Cook, *The Armies of the Streets: The New York City Draft Riots of 1863* (Lexington, Ky., 1974), 13.

6. Amy Bridges, *A City in the Republic: Antebellum New York and the Origins of Machine Politics* (Cambridge, 1984), 7; Jerome Mushkat, *Tammany: The Evolution of a Political Machine: 1789–1865* (Syracuse, N.Y., 1971), 367; Roy v. Peel, *The Political Clubs of New York City* (Port Washington, N.Y., 1935).

7. Florence E. Gibson, *The Attitude of the New York Irish toward State and National Affairs, 1848–1892* (New York, 1951), 71.

8. Diane Ravitch, *The Great School Wars: New York City, 1805–1973: A History of the Public Schools as Battlefields of Social Change* (New York, 1974), 80; Gibson, *Attitude of New York Irish*, 27, 72–74; Edward K. Spann, *The New Metropolis: New York City, 1840–1857* (New York, 1981), 55.

9. Quoted in Kerby A. Miller, *Emigrants and Exiles: Ireland and the Irish Exodus to North America* (New York, 1985), 26–107; L. M. Cullen, "Population Growth and Diet, 1600–1850," in J. M. Goldstrom and L. A. Clarkson, eds., *Irish Population, Economy, and Society: Essays in Honour of the Late K. H. Connell* (Oxford, 1981), 89–112.

10. Miller, *Emigrants and Exiles*, 26–101.

11. Robert Dudley Edwards and T. Desmond Williams, eds., *The Great Famine: Studies in Irish History, 1845–1852* (Dublin, 1956); Cecil Woodham-Smith, *The Great Hunger* (London, 1962).

12. James S. Donnelly, "Land and the People of Cork" (Ph.D. diss., Harvard University, 1970), 151–52.

13. Quoted in Miller, *Emigrants and Exiles*, 285.

14. Ibid., 293.

15. Hasia Diner, *Erin's Daughters in America: Irish Immigrant Women in the Nineteenth Century* (Baltimore, 1988), 5–14.

16. Ibid., 30–42.

17. The concentration of the Irish in cities like New York versus those dispersed around the country in smaller communities and in rural areas has become a subject of some debate among historians. The usual picture of the Irish as resource-poor immigrants trapped in cities has been challenged by Donald H. Akenson in such provocative studies as *The Irish in Ontario: A Study in Rural History* (Kingston and Montreal, 1984); *Being Had: Historians, Evidence, and the Irish in North America* (Port Credit, Ont., 1985); and *Small Differences: Irish Catholics and Irish Protestants, 1815–1922: An International Perspective* (Kingston and Montreal, 1988).

18. Cormac O'Grada, "Irish Emigration to the United States in the Nineteenth Century," in David N. Doyle and Owen D. Edwards, eds., *America and Ireland: 1776–1976: The American Identity and the Irish Connection* (Westport, Conn., 1980), 93–103.

19. Ernst, *Immigrant Life*, 188.

20. Spann, *New Metropolis*, appendix 3; Robert G. Albion, *The Rise of New York Port (1815–1860)* (New York, 1939), 338.

21. Spann, *New Metropolis*, 24.

22. Gibson, *Attitude of the New York Irish*, 17; Richard C. Murphy and Lawrence J. Mannion, *The History of the Society of the Friendly Sons of St. Patrick in the City of New York, 1784–1955* (New York, 1962), 273; Bridges, *A City in the Republic*, 40.

23. Richard H. Leach, "The Impact of Immigration upon New York, 1840–1860," *New York History* 31, no. 1 (1950): 15–30.

24. Ira Rosenwaike, *Population History of New York City* (Syracuse, N.Y., 1972), 41; Dennis Clark, *Hibernia America: The Irish and Regional Cultures* (New York, 1986), 56; Cook, *Armies of the Street*, 3.

25. Steven P. Erie, *Rainbow's End: Irish-Americans and the Dilemmas of Urban Machine Politics, 1840–1985* (Berkeley, Calif., 1988), 18; Stephen Byrne, *Irish Emigration to the United States: What It Has Been and What It Is* (New York, 1873), 162.

26. Erie, *Rainbow's End*, 26.

27. Quoted in Miller, *Emigrants and Exiles*, 318.

28. Rosenwaike, *Population History of New York*, 51, 79.

29. Ernst, *Immigrant Life*, 39; Cook, *Armies of the Street*, 13.

30. Selma Berrol, "Who Went to School In Mid-Nineteenth Century New York? An Essay in the New Urban History," in Irwin Yellowitz, ed., *Essays in the History of New York City: A Memorial to Sidney Pomerantz* (Port Washington, N.Y., 1978), 43–60.

31. Clark, *Hibernia America*, 52; Ernst, *Immigrant Life*, 39, 43; Bridges, *A City in the Republic*, 43.

32. Murphy and Mannion, *Society of the Friendly Sons*.

33. Jeremiah O'Donovan, *A Brief Account of the Author's Interview with His Countrymen, and the Parts of the Emerald Isle Whence They Emigrated* (Pittsburgh, 1864), 155. See also, John D. Crimmins, *Irish-American Historical Miscellany: Relating Largely to New York City and Vicinity, Together with Much Interesting Material Relative to Other Parts of the Country* (New York, 1905).

34. Ravitch, *The Great School Wars*.

35. Diner, *Erin's Daughters*, 97.

36. Berrol, "Who Went to School," 53.

37. Diner, *Erin's Daughters*, 70–105; Carol Groneman, "'She Earns as a Child—She Pays as a Man': Women Workers in a Mid-Nineteenth Century New York Community,"

in Richard L. Ehrlich, ed., *Immigrants in Industrial America, 1850–1920* (Charlottesville, Va., 1977), 33–46; Ernst, *Immigrant Life,* 66, 68, 85.

38. Ernst, *Immigrant Life,* 69, 71, 73,77,78; Graham Russell Hodges, *New York City Cartmen, 1667–1850* (New York, 1986), 170; Albon P. Man, "Labor Competition and the New York Draft Riots of 1863,"*Journal of Negro History* 36, no. 4 (1951): 376; Iver Bernstein, *The New York City Draft Riots: Their Significance for American Society and Politics in the Age of the Civil War* (New York, 1990), 5, 79, 114; Diane Lindstrom, "Economic Structure, Demographic Change, and Income Inequality in Antebellum New York," in John Hull Mollenkopf, ed., *Power, Culture, and Place: Essays on New York City* (New York, 1988), 14; Spann, *New Metropolis,* 27, 349; Bridges, *City in the Republic,* 55, 99.

39. Ernst, *Immigrant Life,* 105, 107.

40. Ibid., 85–89.

41. Leo Hershkowitz, *Tweed's New York: Another Look* (Garden City, N.Y., 1977), 114.

42. Hodges, *New York City Cartmen,* 170; Spann, *New Metropolis,* 349.

43. Louis Dow Scisco, *Political Nativism in New York State* (New York, 1901), 39.

44. Wilbur C. Miller, *Cops and Bobbies: Police Authority in New York and London, 1830–1870* (Chicago, 1973), 30; James F. Richardson, *The New York Police: Colonial Times to 1901* (New York, 1970), 51, 134; Alexander B. Callow, *The Tweed Ring* (New York, 1966), 64; Robert Ernst, *Immigrant Life,* 163.

45. Callow, *Tweed Ring,* 66.

46. Cook, *Armies of the Street,* 43.

47. Miller, *Cops and Bobbies,* 156.

48. Cook, *Armies of the Street,* 21, 24, 29; Bernstein, *New York City Draft Riots;* Spann, *New Metropolis,* 393; Richardson, *New York Police,* 166; Michael A. Gordon, *The Orange Riots: Irish Political Violence in New York City, 1870 and 1871* (Ithaca, N.Y. 1993).

49. Miller, *Cops and Bobbies,* 154.

50. Eric Foner, "Class, Ethnicity, and Radicalism in the Gilded Age: The Land League and Irish America," *Marxist Perspectives* 1, no. 2 (1978): 7.

51. Ernst, *Immigrant Life,* 105, 107.

52. Bridges, *City in the Republic,* 99–100.

53. John T. Ridge, *The St. Patrick's Day Parade in New York* (New York, 1988), 19; Bernstein, *The New York City Draft Riots,* 5, 112, 114.

54. Foner, "Class, Ethnicity, and Radicalism," 7; Gibson, *Attitude of the New York Irish,* 270–75.

55. Quoted in Ray Allen Billington, *The Protestant Crusade: A Study of the Origins of American Nativism* (New York, 1938), 323; For statistics on Irish inmates of the New York Almshouse, see Gibson, *Attitude of the New York Irish,* 16.

56. Quoted in Cook, *Armies of the Street,* 10.

57. Diner, *Erin's Daughters,* 135.

58. Ernst, *Immigrant Life,* 53–58; Clark, *Hibernia America,* 52; John H.Griscom, *The Sanitary Condition of the Laboring Population of New York* (New York, 1845), 19.

59. Ray Allen Billington, *Protestant Crusade,* 266, 306–9; Scisco, *Political Nativism,* 39, 48, 64, 203, 210; Hershkowitz, *Tweed's New York,* 40, 46; Mushkat, *Tammany,* 352; Gibson, *Attitude of the New York Irish,* 123; Michael Gordon, *The Orange Riots: Irish Political Violence in New York City, 1870 and 1871* (Ithaca, N.Y., 1993).

60. As yet little research has been done on the nature of Irish-German relations and the topic is sorely in need of analysis.

61. Man, "Labor Competition," 375–405; Bernstein, *New York City Draft Riots.*

62. Arnold Schrier, *Ireland and the American Emigration, 1850–1900* (New York, 1958), 24.

63. Peel, *Political Clubs of New York City,* 37; Bridges, *City in the Republic,* 100.

64. Lee H. Benson, *The Concept of Jacksonian Democracy: New York as a Test Case* (Princeton, N.J., 1961), 187–90; Gibson, *Attitudes of the New York Irish,* 58; Murphy and Mannion, *Society of the Friendly Sons,* 316.

65. Spann, *New Metropolis,* 360.

66. Mushkat, *Tammany,* 367.

67. Callow, *Tweed Ring,* 65.

68. Seymour J. Mandelbaum, *Boss Tweed's New York* (New York, 1965), 82; quoted in Clark, *Hibernia America,* 56.

69. Erie, *Rainbow's End,* 39; Crimmins, *Irish-American Miscellany,* 419.

70. John Gilmary Shea, *The Catholic Churches of New York City* (New York, 1878), 564–66.

71. Billington, *Protestant Crusade,* 33; Jay P. Dolan, *The Immigrant Church: New York's Irish and German Catholics, 1815–1865* (Baltimore, 1975), 9, 100–112, 130, 132.

72. Dolan, *Immigrant Church,* 13.

73. Ibid., 56; Hasia Diner, *Erin's Daughters,* 135.

74. Dolan, *Immigrant Church,* 45–67.

75. The classic articulation of this position is Will Herberg, *Protestant, Catholic, Jew: An Essay in American Religious Sociology* (Garden City, N.Y., 1955).

76. Clark, *Hibernia America.*

77. Ridge, *St. Patrick's Day Parade.*

78. George W. Potter, *To the Golden Door: The Story of the Irish in Ireland and America* (Boston, 1860), 471.

79. Cook, *Armies of the Street,* 21, 24.

80. Gibson, *Attitudes of the New York Irish,* 20.

81. See, for example, Murphy and Mannion, *Society of the Friendly Sons,* 287, 316, 320.

Chapter 4: "DESIRABLE COMPANIONS AND LOVERS" (Hodges)

1. George Foster, *New York by Gaslight* (New York, 1850), 56–57.

2. For classic examples see Robert Ernst, *Immigrant Life in New York City: 1825–1863* (New York, 1949), 105, 173; Carl Wittke, *The Irish in America* (Baton Rouge, La., 1956), 125–35; Florence E. Gibson, *The Attitudes of the New York Irish Toward State and National Affairs, 1848–1892* (New York, 1951); Carl N. Degler, "Labor in the Economy and Politics of New York City, 1850–1860" (Ph.D. diss., Columbia University, 1952); Phyllis F. Field, *The Politics of Race in New York: The Struggle for Black Suffrage in the Civil War Era* (Ithaca, N.Y., 1982). For popular histories that accept the presence of racial lore see Herbert Asbury, *Gangs of New York* (New York, 1927), 3–15; and Alvin F. Harlow, *Old Bowery Days* (New York, 1931), 180–82.

3. David Roediger, *The Wages of Whiteness: Race and the Making of the American Working Class* (London, 1991), 133–67, esp. 140–43, and "Labor in White Skin," in Roediger, *Towards the Abolition of Whiteness* (London, 1994), 21–39; Barbara Jeanne Fields, "Slavery, Race, and Ideology in the United States of America," *New Left Review* 181 (1990): 95–118.

4. Amy Bridges, "Becoming American," in Ira Katznelson and Aristide R. Zolberg, eds., *Working-Class Formation: Nineteenth-Century Patterns in Western Europe and the United States* (Princeton, N.J., 1986), 195.

5. For this view see Carol Groneman, "Working-Class Immigrant Women in Mid-Nineteenth Century New York: The Irish Women's Experience," *Journal of Urban History* 4 (1978): 255–71; Sean Wilentz, *Chants Democratic: New York City and the Rise of the American Working Class, 1788–1850* (New York, 1984); Christine Stansell, *City of Women: Sex and Class in New York: 1789–1860* (New York, 1986); Peter George Buckley, "To the Opera House: Culture and Society in New York City, 1820–1860" (Ph.D. diss., State University of New York at Stony Brook, 1984), 5–6, and Iver Bernstein, *The New York City Draft Riots: Their Significance for American Society and Politics in the Age of the Civil War* (New York, 1990), 23–24, 31–40. On pursuers of the American dream see Stuart Blumin, *The Emergence of the Middle Class Social Experience in the American City, 1760–1800* (New York, 1989), 230–257; Richard B. Stott, *Workers in the Metropolis: Class, Ethnicity, and Youth in Antebellum New York City* (Ithaca, N.Y., 1990), 237–42, 252.

6. George Walker, *The Afro-American in New York City, 1827–1860* (New York, 1993), 50.

7. Degler, "Labor in the Economy," 140–41 and Lawrence Costello, "The New York City Labor Movement, 1861–1873" (Ph.D. diss., Columbia University, 1967), 130–33. For black advising whites see Walker, *The Afro-American in New York City,* 51.

8. Carol Groneman, "The 'Bloudy Ould Sixth,' A Social Analysis of a Mid-Nineteenth-Century Working-Class Community" (Ph.D. diss., University of Rochester, 1973), 61.

9. Foster, *New York by Gaslight,* 56. On Cartmen's Ward see Graham Russell Hodges, *New York City Cartmen, 1667–1850* (New York, 1986); for percentages see Groneman, "'Bloody Ould Sixth,'" 23–24; and Elizabeth Blackmar, *Manhattan for Rent, 1785–1850* (Ithaca, N.Y., 1989), 68–71, 93.

10. Ernst, *Immigrant Life,* 214–17. For an updating see Stott, *Workers in the Metropolis,* 92. For transformation of crafts see Wilentz, *Chants Democratic.* For black artisans see Shane White, *Somewhat More Independent: The End of Slavery in New York City, 1790–1810* (Athens, Ga., 1991), 158; and Walker, *The Afro-American in New York City,* 40–65. On paucity of blacks in manufacturing see Stott, *Workers in the Metropolis,* 92. On "communitas" see Victor Turner, *Structure and Anti-Structure* (Chicago, 1969), 131–32.

11. Ernst, *Immigrant Life in New York,* 38–42; Groneman, "'Bloody Ould Sixth,'" 35.

12. For the importance of laborers in crafts in transition see David Montgomery, *The Fall of the House of Labor* (New York, 1987), 58–62. For union movement see Wilentz, *Chants Democratic,* 250–51; and Stott, *Workers in the Metropolis,* 58–61.

13. Degler, "Labor in the Economy," 19–23, 40–53; Amy Bridges, *A City in the Republic: Antebellum New York and the Origins of Machine Politics* (New York, 1984), 99–100.

14. Groneman, "'Bloody Ould Sixth,'" 100, 155, 164; Stott, *Workers in the Metropolis,* 196–97, 204.

15. For businesses see *Doggett's New York City Street Directory for 1851 . . .* (New York, 1851). For tabulation see Edward K. Spann, *The New Metropolis: New York City, 1840–1857* (New York, 1981), 343.

16. On boardinghouses see Blackmar, *Manhattan for Rent,* 122–26; for a classic description of boardinghouses see Thomas B. Gunn, *The Physiology of New York Boarding-Houses* (New York, 1857).

17. *Rode's New York City Directory for 1850–1851* (New York, 1850), appendixes; James D. McCabe, *Lights and Shadows of the Great City* (New York, 1872), 401, 412–21. For career of the Five Points Mission see Carol Smith-Rosenberg, *Religion and the Rise of the American City: The New York Mission Society, 1812–1870* (Ithaca, N.Y., 1971), 225–44.

18. Blackmar, *Manhattan for Rent*, 93; Groneman, "'Bloudy Ould Sixth,'" 23–8.

19. Foster, *New York by Gaslight*, 52–63. For comment on pornography see Stansell, *City of Women*, 174–75. On historical descendants of Five Points see Eileen Southern, *The Music of Black Americans: A History* (New York, 1971), 120–22

20. For the texture of community life in lower wards see Kenneth A. Scherzer, *The Unbounded Community: Neighborhood Life and Social Structure in New York City, 1830–1875* (Durham, N.C., 1992), 211–13; and Paul A. Gilje, *The Road to Mobocracy: Popular Disorder in New York City, 1763–1834* (Chapel Hill, N.C., 1987), 160–61.

21. For Orange Street see *Doggett's New York City Street Directory for 1851* (New York, 1851), 260. For other examples see Anthony Street, 15–17; Centre Street, 94; Cross Street, 121–22; and Mott Street, 264–66.

22. For Washington see 1850 Manuscript Census, Sixth Ward, National Archives Microfilm, 101; for Downey 1860 Manuscript Census, Sixth Ward, Second District, 167. For street conversation see John D. Vose, Esq., *Seven Nights in Gotham* (New York, 1852), 78. For comment on blacks in white homes, see White, *Somewhat More Independent*, 172–76.

23. Robert S. Pickett, *House of Refuge, Origins of Juvenile Reform in New York State, 1815–1857* (Syracuse, N.Y., 1969). For apprentices see "Apprentices File," Common Council Papers, Reel 81, New York Municipal Archives.

24. John H. Griscom, *The Sanitary Condition of the Laboring Population of New York with Suggestions for Its Improvement* (New York, 1845), 18. For an accounting of the dismal statistics of Irish and black lives see Leonard Curry, *The Free Black in Urban America, 1800–1850* (Chicago, 1981), 40–41, 53–54, 73, 79.

25. Kenneth Scott, compiler, "Coroner's Reports for New York City, 1823–1842," Collections of the New York Genealogical and Biographical Society, 12 (New York, 1989). For death rates see John Duffy, *A History of Public Health in New York City, 1625–1866* (New York, 1966), 536–37. For children see "Book of Indentures of the Association for the Benefit of the Colored Orphan Asylum, vol. 1 (1835–66), Mss., New-York Historical Society (N-YHS); J. D. B. De Bow, compiler, *Mortality Statistics of the Seventh Census of the United States, 1850 . . .* (Washington, 1855), 161–63, 171–87. For missionary efforts see Smith-Rosenberg, *Religion and the Rise of the American City*, 240.

26. For number of murders see David T. Valentine, ed., *Manual of the Common Council of New-York 1854* (New York, 1854), 332. For image of Five Points in Literature see Adrienne Siegel, *The Image of the American City in Popular Literature 1820–1870* (Port Washington, N.Y., 1981). For a good study of gang culture see Eliott J. Gorn, "Good-Bye Boys, I Die A True American: Homicide, Nativism, and Working Class Culture in Antebellum New York City," *Journal of American History* 74 (1987): 388–411.

27. Gilje, *The Road to Mobocracy*, 138–39, 152.

28. Ibid., 166–68. For reports see *New York Commercial Advertiser*, July 10–12, 1834. For composition of mobs see Leonard L. Richards, *"Gentlemen of Property and Standing": Anti-Abolition Mobs in Jacksonian America* (New York, 1970), 141–45. For Irish as targets see Harlow, *Old Bowery Days*, 294–300.

29. *Commercial Advertiser*, June 22–25, 1835; *New York American*, June 22–25, 1835; *New York Sun*, June 22–25, 1835. For arrests see "Watch Returns, June 22–25, 1834," New York Municipal Archives, Reel 22.

30. *Diamond,* 2 (July 1840): 19.

31. *Irish-American,* Nov. 11, 1849; Buckley, "To the Opera House," 5–7; Bernstein, *New York City Draft Riots,* 334–38. On the Dead Rabbit Riots see Asbury, *Gangs of New York,* 112–18.

32. "William H. Bell Diary," Jan. 8, 1851, N-YHS; cf. n. 25.

33. *Political Bulletin and Miscellaneous Repository,* May 10, 1810, and Jan. 2, Feb. 16, 1811; *Diamond,* 2, (July 1840). See the *Irish-American,* Aug. 10, 1849, for opposition to slavery; Aug. 21, 1850, for a description of Douglass and approval of colonization. On the comparison of slavery and the Irish condition see Philip S. Foner and Herbert Shapiro, eds., *Northern Labor and Antislavery: A Documentary History* (Westport, Conn., 1994).

34. For the fullest coverage of black struggles over the vote see Walker, *Afro-Americans in New York City,* 188–211; and Field, *Politics of Race.* For number of voters see *Census of the State of New York for 1845 . . .* (Albany, 1846). See also Jerome Mushkat, *The Reconstruction of the New York Democracy, 1861–1874* (Rutherford, N.J., 1981), 70, 120–37.

35. Minutes of the Common Council of the City of New York, 1784–1831, 22 vols. (New York, 1930), 15: 406, 429–30, 467, 492.

36. For general comments see Stott, *Workers in the Metropolis,* 235–38; Bridges, *A City in the Republic,* 132. For transformation of government see Jon C. Teaford, *The Municipal Revolution* (Baltimore, 1975). For specific occupations see Hodges, *New York City Cartmen,* chap. 7; James F. Richardson, *The New York Police: Colonial Times to 1901* (New York, 1970). For firemen see Stott, *Workers in the Metropolis,* 242–43. For appointive office see *The City Election Handbook Votes for Mayor from 1834 to 1863* (New York, 1864).

37. For Loco-Foco effect of Democrats and party attitudes on blacks see Jerome Mushkat, *Tammany: The Evolution of a Political Machine, 1789–1865* (Syracuse, N.Y., 1971), 158–67, 231–33; Wilentz, *Chants Democratic,* 193–96.

38. [Thomas Mooney], *Mooney's Nine Years in America in a Series of Letters* (Dublin, 1850), 152–54. Similar sentiments can be found in Isaac Lyon, *Memoirs of an Old Cartman* (Newark, 1872).

39. Compare *Superintendant of Carts License Book,* New York Municipal Archives and Records Center (MARC), J-40-A with Ernst, *Immigrant Life,* 217; and Groneman, "'Bloudy Ould Sixth,'" 100, 115, 118.

40. For discussions on integrating carting see Hodges, *New York City Cartman.* For Fernando Wood see Stott, *Workers in the Metropolis,* 226. For 1900 figures see George E. Haynes, *The Negro at Work in New York City: A Study in Economic Progress* (New York, 1912), 69–72. For porters see Mooney, *Nine Years,* 85–87.

41. For policeman see "William H. Bell Diary," 1850–51, N-YHS. For licenses see "List of Licensed Pawnbrokers in City of New York, 1823–41"; "Licensed Dealers in Second-Hand Articles"; "List of Carts Licensed to Keepers of Junk"; "Licensed Dealers in Second-Hand Articles, 1842–1860," all in MARC, J-40-A. For number on Orange Street see David T. Valentine, ed., *Manual of the Common Council for the City of New York, 1854* (New York, 1854), 330–32. For anti-Semitic descriptions of junk dealers and intelligence offices see [George Foster], *New York in Slices by an Experienced Carver* (New York, 1849), 30–32, 37.

42. For comments see Mooney, *Nine Years,* 81. For counts of various occupations see *Wilson's Business Directory of New York City* (New York, 1860), 229–34.

43. The classic on butchers is Thomas F. Devoe, *The Market Book* (New York, 1861). For good articulation of their culture, see also Gorn, "Good-Bye Boys, I Die A True American"; and Wilentz, *Chants Democratic,* 137–39.

44. See *People v. Alexander Davis*, Sept. 14, 1842, Box MDA 411, and *People v. Samuel Daily*, Sept. 11, 1842, Box MDA 427, both in District Attorney Indictment Papers, MARC. I am grateful to Michael Kaplan for this reference.

45. For comments on grocers see Luc Sante, *Low Life: Lures and Snares of Old New York* (New York, 1991), 105–6. For reform efforts see Blackmar, *Manhattan for Rent*, 136, for 1836; and Spann, *The New Metropolis*, 373, for 1856.

46. For Irish keepers see *Wilson's Business Directory*, 26–32. For blacks see 1860 Manuscript Census, Sixth Ward, Fourth District, 114.

47. For attitudes about manual laborers and domestics see Jonathan Glickstein, *Concepts of Free Labor in Antebellum America* (New Haven, Conn., 1991), 175–77, 237. For ethnophobia and racial attitudes see Dale T. Knobel, *Paddy and the New Republic: Ethnicity and Nationality in Antebellum America* (Middletown, Conn., 1986).

48. Blackmar, *Manhattan for Rent*, 57–62, 116–20, 311–13; Stansell, *City of Women*, 156–68; Glickstein, *Concepts of Free Labor*, 175–77, 424.

49. Blackmar, *Manhattan for Rent*, 119–20; Stansell, *City of Women*, 161–63; Hasia R. Diner, *Erin's Daughters in America: Irish Immigrant Women in the Nineteenth Century* (Baltimore, Md., 1983), 93; Mooney, *Nine Years*, 87.

50. *Wilson's Business Directory of New York City* (New York, 1860), 478–81.

51. For antebellum patterns of black family see Scherzer, *Unbounded Community*, 117–19; Walker, *Afro-Americans in New York City*, 10. For Irish women and marriage see Diner, *Erin's Daughters*, 7–13, 52–58, 77, 92.

52. Diner, *Erin's Daughters*, 94–96. For black and Irish nurses see *Wilson's Business Directory for 1860*.

53. For Irish see Diner, *Erin's Daughters*, 110. For blacks see Mary Thompson, *Sketches of the Colored Old Folks Home* (New York, 1851).

54. Timothy Gilfoyle, *City of Eros: New York City, Prostitution, and the Commercialization of Sex, 1790–1920* (New York, 1992), 36–42; Marilyn Wood Hill, *Their Sisters, Keepers: Prostitution in New York City, 1830–1870* (Berkeley, Calif., 1993), 55–58, 352n., 70, 71, 190–91.

55. See " Bell Diary." For a good assortment of terms see Vose, *Seven Nights*, 32–3. For comments see Irvin Lewis Allen, *The City in Slang* (New York, 1993), 21–23, 57–71, 149–77. For cant names see Harlow, *Old Bowery Days*, 180.

56. For hot corn see *Life in New York In Doors and Out of Doors, Illustrated with Forty Engravings by the late William Burns* (New York, 1851); Solon Robinson, *Hot Corn* (New York, 1855); Foster, *New York by Gaslight*, 122. For "dancing for eels" see Vose, *Seven Nights*, 88; and Devoe, *The Market Book*, 344–45. For legends see Asbury, *Gangs of New York*, 7–8.

57. The quotation is from Charles Dickens, *American Notes for General Circulation* (London, 1842). For humming see Ned Buntline (pseud. of E. Z. C. Judson), *The G'Hals of New York: A Novel* (New York, 1850), 7. Whitman quoted in Graham Hodges, "Muscle and Pluck, Walt Whitman's Working Class Ties," *Seaport Magazine*, 26, no. 1 (1992).

58. Gilfoyle, *City of Eros*, 38–46; Foster, *New York by Gaslight*, 74–76; McCabe, *Lights and Shadows*, 596–600. For the Diving Bell see Vose, *Seven Nights*, 85–88. For tameness of Juba and Peter Williams see Robert C. Toll, *Blacking Up: The Minstrel Show in Nineteenth-Century America* (New York, 1974), 43.

59. For the descriptions in this paragraph see *The Old Brewery and the New Mission House at the Five Points by Ladies of the Mission* (New York, 1854), 33, 45. For comments on interracial love see Asbury, *The Gangs of New York*, 21–25. Updated in

Sante, *Low Life,* and in Eric Lott, *Love and Theft: Blackface Minstrelsy and the American Working Class* (New York, 1993), 47.

60. For marriage between ethnic groups see Groneman, "'Bloudy Ould Sixth,'" 70–73. For interracial children see cases 1973, 2097, 2496, 2701, and 2996 in House of Refuge Papers, New York State Library, Albany.

61. For 1850 interracial couples see Manuscript Census for 1850, National Archives Microfilm, Sixth Ward, 36, 37, 76 (John and Francis Hall), 101, 153, 162, 163.

62. For Sanders, DePoyster, and Francis see Manuscript Census for 1860, Sixth Ward, Second District, 213. For others see First District, 16; Second District, 80, 158, 160; Fourth District, 116.

63. See entries for Moses Roper, Frederick Hill, Manuel Gilbert, Sylvester White, Perry Cooper, Henry Willis, Frederick Mingo, Joseph Armstrong, Daniel Young, and Benjamin Hosley, Manuscript Census of 1870, Sixth Ward of New York City, National Archives Microfilm, 54, 56, 80. A few couples appear in popular novels of the 1850s. See, for example, Robinson, *Hot Corn,* 71, 94–97; and Harriet E. Wilson, *Our Nig; or, Sketches from the Life of a Free Black* (1859; New York, 1983).

64. Commentary on interracial marriages in the urban north is scanty, but see the useful comments, in a different context, in James O. Horton, *Free People of Color: Inside the African American Community* (Washington, D.C., 1993), 175.

65. Ibid., chap. 8.

66. It is striking how few residents of the Sixth Ward were involved in the Draft Riots of 1863. For the residences of those killed, injured, and arrested see Adrian Cook, *The Armies of the Streets: The New York City Draft Riots of 1863* (Lexington, Ky., 1974), 213–16; and Bernstein, *New York City Draft Riots,* 28, 31–36.

Chapter 5: QUIMBO APPO'S FEAR OF FENIANS (Tchen)

I would like to thank Tim Meagher, Joe Doyle, Judy Susman, and Marion Casey for helpful comments on this manuscript. An earlier version of this essay, entitled "Other's Others: Anglo-Irish-Chinese Relations in New York City," was presented at the Organization of American Historians annual conference in Chicago, Apr. 2, 1992.

1. "'Devil' Appo's Son, Thought Dead, Is Alive," *New York World,* June 24, 1912. Appo, Quimbo, Case File, 456, Certificate of Insanity, State of New York—Matteawan State Hospital, New York State Archives, Albany, 3, 4, 5, 6, 9, hereafter referred to as "patient notes." The reference to Boxers is about an antiforeign movement during 1900 in northern China. For insights on how the Boxer Rebellion related to overseas Chinese see Shih-shan Henry Tsai, *China and the Overseas Chinese in the United States, 1868–1911* (Fayetteville, Ark., 1983).

2. Appo, patient notes, cover sheet.

3. Letter from Reverend E. W. Syle, *The Spirit of Missions* (Sept. 1854): 323–28. For the experience of the Chinese opera troupe, see John Kuo Wei Tchen, "New York before Chinatown: Orientalism, Identity Formation, and Political Culture in the American Metropolis, 1784–1882," (Ph.D. diss., New York University, 1992), 79–86.

4. Syle, *The Spirit of Missions,* 323–28; "Autobiography of George Appo," Society for the Prevention of Crime Papers, Rare Books and Manuscript Library, Columbia University, 1. Dan Czitrom and Timothy Gilfoyle generously shared their information about George Appo's autobiography with me. Professor Gilfoyle is currently working on a biography of George Washington Appo. On events involving Zhusan (Chusan) Island see John King Fairbanks, *Trade and Diplomacy on the China Coast: The Opening of the Treaty*

Ports, 1842–1854 (Cambridge, Mass., 1964), 58, 59, 81, 82, 90, 94, 121, 135n., 156, 286, 333. Speaking several dialects of Chinese with some fluency, Gutzlaff took two unauthorized trips into the Chinese countryside in 1831 and 1832. He published his diary as Charles Gutzlaff, *The Journal of Two Voyages along the Coast of China, in 1831 and 1832* (New York, 1833). He also published *Sketch of Chinese History, Ancient and Modern* (New York, 1834). For background on Gutzlaff, see Clifton Jackson Phillips, *Protestant America and the Pagan World: The First Half Century of the American Board of Commissioners for Foreign Missions, 1810–1860* (Cambridge, Mass., 1969), 178, 183–85.

5. Syle, *The Spirit of Missions*, 323–28; *Tribune*, Oct. 23, 1876; Arthur Bonner, "The Chinese in New York, 1800–1950" (unpublished manuscript, author's copy), 4: 4.

6. *New York Times*, Dec. 26, 1856.

7. Louis Beck, *New York's Chinatown* (New York, 1898), 8–9.

8. *New York Times*, Dec. 26, 1856; Robert Greenhalgh Albion, *The Rise of the Port of New York* (Boston, 1984), 201; Kenneth Scott Latourette, *This History of Early Relations between the United States and China, 1784–1844* (New Haven, 1917), 76–77.

9. Syle, *The Spirit of Missions*, 339–43.

10. *New York Times*, Dec. 26, 1856.

11. John Kuo Wei Tchen, "New York Chinese: The Nineteenth Century Pre-Chinatown Settlement," *Chinese America History and Perspectives* (1990): 160–68. According to Carol Groneman (Pernicone), a well-paid police officer in New York City received $600 per year in the early 1850s. Carole Groneman Pernicone, "'The Bloody Ould Sixth': A Social Analysis of a New York City Working-Class Community in the Mid-Nineteenth Century" (Ph.D. diss., University of Rochester, 1973), 113.

12. *Yankee Notions*, 7, no. 3 (1858).

13. "Pacific Railroad Complete (comic)," *Harper's Weekly*, 1869, 384.

14. *Harper's*, Oct. 1857; "The Result of Immigration from China," *Yankee Notions*, 7, no. 3 (1858); W. A. Rogers, "A Wedding in the Chinese Quarter, Mott Street, New York," and accompanying article, "Our Chinese Colony," *Harper's*, Nov. 22, 1890.

15. Pernicone, "'Bloody Ould Sixth,'" 71, 72, 73; Hasia R. Diner, *Erin's Daughters in America: Irish Immigrant Women in the Nineteenth Century* (Baltimore, 1983), 31, 28–29, 36; Ira Rosenwaike, *Population History of New York City* (Syracuse, 1972), 42, 75. In 1855 the total male and female population of Irish in New York City was 175,735. According to Diner, 10 of 18 were women, meaning there were 97,633 women. Using Pernicone's calculations of "Ever-Married Women" of 59–82 percent for different age groups, 97,633 non-Irish multiplied times the 4.7 percent intermarriage rate yields 2,707–3,762 Irish women who married non-Irish men. "Celebrating Chinese New Year. Visiting and Indulging in Luxuries—Waiting to Name a Baby," *New York Tribune*, Feb. 15, 1885.

16. Pernicone, "'Bloody Ould Sixth,'" 148; Tchen, "New York before Chinatown," 123–36.

17. Robert Ernst, *Immigrant Life in New York City, 1825–1863* (New York, 1949), 41, 67; Shane White, *Somewhat More Independent: The End of Slavery in New York City, 1770–1810* (Athens, Ga., 1991), 159–66, 168–69, 174–79; *New York Evening Day Book*, May 11, 1858, cited by Kerby Miller, "Green over Black: The Origins of Irish-American Racism, 1800–1863" (unpublished paper, 1969), 72. I thank professor Miller for sharing a copy of his insightful paper with me.

18. Tchen, "New York Chinese," 161, 162,

19. Ibid., 165, 172; Marshall and Jane Stearns, *Jazz Dance: The Story of American Vernacular Dance* (New York, 1968).

20. *Harper's*, Oct. 21, 1871, Suppl., 997–98.

21. George Templeton Strong, *The Diaries of George Templeton Strong*, ed. Allen Nevins and Milton Halsey Thomas (New York, 1962), 1: 348.

22. *Yankee Notions*, 7, no. 3 (1858).

23. "John Chinaman in New York" (1870), in Samuel Langhorne Clemens, *The Complete Humorous Sketches and Tales of Mark Twain*, ed. Carles Neider (Garden City, N.Y., 1961), 134–35.

24. Pernicone, "'Bloody Ould Sixth,'" 110.

25. Miller, "Green over Black," 30.

26. "Hibernian Celestial," *Yankee Notions*, 3, no. 4 (1854); "How the Chinaman Might Gain Favor," *Harper's*, Apr. 12, 1879; Allen's Jewell Five Cent Plug, trade card (Wong Ching Foo Collection, New York); and "Patsy O'Wang: An Irish Farce with a Chinese Mix-Up" (Chicago, 1895).

27. Lewis Perry Curtis, *Apes and Angels: The Irishman in Victorian Caricature* (Washington D. C., 1971); and Mary Cowling, *The Artists as Anthropologists* (Cambridge, 1989).

28. *Harper's*, Feb. 18, 1871.

29. *Puck*, Mar. 12, 1880.

30. Tchen, "New York before Chinatown," 405–8.

31. White, *Somewhat More Independent*, 14; and Elizabeth Blackmar, *Manhattan for Rent, 1785–1850* (Ithaca, 1989), 99, 101.

32. Beck, *New York's Chinatown*, 9–10. The term "Caliban" originated in Shakespeare's *The Tempest* and became a commonly used term in the nineteenth century. On the racial usage of the term with regard to the Irish see Curtis, *Apes and Angels*, 2, 4–5, 20, 22, 29. See also Roberto Fernandez Retamar, *Caliban and Other Essays* (Minneapolis, 1989), 3–55.

33. Beck, *New York's Chinatown*, 10–11.

34. Ibid., 9; "Return of Quimbo Appo," New York Supreme Court, 1–18, New York County Clerk's Office; *Herald*, Mar. 9, 10, and Apr. 11, 1859; *Tribune*, Mar. 9, 18, and Apr. 12, 1859; *Times*, Mar. 9, 10, and Apr. 12, 1859.

35. "Return of Quimbo Appo," 18–19.

36. Ibid., 18–19.

37. Ibid., 20–35.

38. *Brother Jonathan*, July 2, Nov. 19, 1859, and Mar. 3, 1860; *National Police Gazette*, May 14, 1859; *Herald*, Feb. 22, 1860.

39. "Return of Quimbo Appo," 1–12, 13.

40. Ibid., 20.

41. Ibid., 25, 26. We know from Hasia Diner's work that domestic violence in Irish households and drinking were not simply fabricated and stereotypic Irish issues. Diner, *Erin's Daughters*, 113–14. Diner has also noted a high rate of domestic violence, usually in the form of wife-beating, but she has added that Irish women rarely submitted passively. She cites one story of a woman using a flatiron in a parallel manner to what happened to Appo (pp. 56–57).

42. For discussions on nineteenth-century anxieties about urban social chaos and moral order see Karen Halttunen, *Confidence Men and Painted Women: A Study of Middle-Class Culture in America, 1830–1870* (New Haven, 1982); John F. Kasson, *Rudeness and Civility: Manners in Nineteenth-Century Urban America* (New York, 1990); and Paul Boyer, *Urban Masses and Moral Order in America, 1820–1920* (Cambridge, Mass., 1978).

43. Tchen, "New York before Chinatown," 432–64.

44. The best single account of the anti-Chinese movement in California is Alexander Saxton, *The Indispensable Enemy: Labor and the Anti-Chinese Movement in California* (Berkeley, Calif., 1971). For a classic Protestant (and anti-Irish) account see Mary Roberts Coolidge, *Chinese Immigration* (New York, 1909).

45. On this point, I agree with Michael Rogin's critique of Werner Sollors'dualistic concept of "descent" and "ascent." Michael Rogin, "Making America Home: Racial Masquerade and Ethnic Assimilation in the Transition to Talking Pictures," *Journal of American History*, 79, no. 3 (1992): 1053.

46. Iver Bernstein, *The New York Draft Riots: Their Significance for American Society and Politics in the Age of the Civil War* (New York, 1990), 34, 299, 131n., and 132; *New York Herald*, July 16, 1863; *New York Evening Express*, July 15, 1863.

47. Miller, "Green over Black," 36.

48. Ibid., 37–38; see also Albon P. Man Jr., "Labor Competition and the New York Draft Riots of 1863," *Journal of Negro History*, 36, no. 4 (1951): 95, 89n.

49. On North Adams and Belleville, see Tchen, "New York before Chinatown," 299–326, 461; and *Frank Leslie's*, Mar. 27, 1880.

50. Ping Chiu, *Chinese Labor in California, 1850–1880* (Madison, Wis., 1963); Saxton, *Indispensable Enemy*, 143–56; Miller, "Green over Black," 37, 40–41.

51. Miller, "Green over Black," 72; *Day Book*, May 11, 1858.

52. Sidney Kaplan, "The Miscegenation Issue in the Election of 1864," *Journal of Negro History* 24, no. 3, (1949): 277–80, 283; David Roediger, *The Wages of Whiteness* (New York, 1991), 155–56.

53. Kaplan, "Miscegenation," 284–85, 336.

54. Ibid., 281–82.

55. Ibid., 331–32; *London Morning Herald*, Nov. 1, Dec. 6, 1864.

56. Kaplan, "Miscegenation," 299; *National Anti-Slavery Standard*, Mar. 5, 1864.

57. Rogin, "Making America Home," 1050.

58. Richard Moody, *Ned Harrigan: From Corlear's Hook to Herald Square* (Chicago, 1980), 5, 170; Robert Toll, *Blacking Up: The Minstrel Show in Nineteenth Century America* (New York, 1974), 177–79.

59. Jean H. Baker, *Affairs of Party* (Ithaca, N.Y., 1983), 212–60; Alexander Saxton, *The Rise and Fall of the White Republic: Class Politics and Mass Culture in Nineteenth Century America* (New York, 1991), 165–82.

60. Tchen, "New York before Chinatown," 417–22. For two examples, see Scene 7, "The Mulligan Silver Wedding," (1881) Harrigan manuscripts, Rare Books Room, New York Public Library, Box 18, no. 47; and Act 2, "The O'Reagans," (1886) Harrigan manuscripts, Rare Books Room, New York Public Library, Box 20, no. 53.

61. Chuck Connors, *Bowery Life*, introduction and ed. Frederick A. Wilson (New York, 1904). See also "New York's Chinatown," King's Booklet, 1904.

62. Introduction to Connors, *Bowery Life*, no pagination; and Gerald Carson, "George Washington Connors," Manhattan Album, *Seaport Magazine*, Jan. 1987. This is a different role from the "racial masquerade" that Rogin writes about.

63. Edward Said, *Orientalism* (New York, 1979).

64. With regard to Irish mobility through westward migration, Timothy Sarbaugh has argued that the San Francisco Irish enjoyed relatively little discrimination and attributes this phenomenon to the lack of "an established elite capable, by virtue of prior arrival and control of local resources, of ascribing inferior places to subsequent immigrants." He does not deal with the relationship between Irish upward mobility and their role in the anti-Chinese movement. Timothy Sarbaugh, "Exiles of Confidence: The Irish

American Community of San Francisco, 1880–1920," in *From Paddy to Studs: Irish American Communities in Turn of the Century Era, 1880–1920*, ed. Timothy Meagher (Westport, Conn., 1986), 161–79. R. A. Burchell does make a brief acknowledgement of this dynamic in the concluding section of his book, yet the focus of his study is on the Irish and not the interrelations of the two groups. R. A. Burchell, *The San Francisco Irish, 1848–1880* (Berkeley, Calif., 1980), 180–81. A far more resonant understanding of intercultural dynamics in San Francisco during this time period can be gleaned from the Irish male lead triumphing over the Eurasian real estate mogul in the silent film "Old San Francisco," directed by Alan Crosland (Warner Brothers, 1927). For a discussion of this film see Rogin, *Making America Home*, 1056; and James Moy, *Marginal Sights: Staging the Chinese in America* (Iowa City, forthcoming), unpaginated prepublication copy, chap. 6.

65. Miller, "Green over Black," 47, 72.

66. Richard Williams, *Hierarchical Structures and Social Value: The Creation of Black and Irish Identities in the United States* (New York, 1991). Michael Rogin makes a similar point using different terms in his provocative essay "Racial Masquerade in Talking Pictures." Earlier versions of this essay were presented and written before I read his piece.

67. New York Irish success did not necessarily mean a simple identification with mainstream Anglo-Protestant society. They were not so easily accepted, nor did they necessarily want to "move uptown" in the way Scotch-Irish may have. Harrigan expressed this tension with the immensely popular "Cordelia's Aspirations" and "Dan's Tribulations," Moody, *Ned Harrigan*, 135–39.

68. For examples of the images of relationships between Irish women and Chinese men see "A man's a man for all o'that," postcard, postmarked 1907 (Wong Ching Foo Collection, N. Y.) and Edward W. Townsend, *A Daughter of the Tenements* (New York, 1900). For an excellent discussion on the phenomenon of transgressing established social boundaries see Peter Stallybrass and Allon White, *The Politics and Poetics of Transgression* (London, 1986).

69. Bonner, "Chinese in New York," 4:14; *Herald*, Dec. 26, 1869.

70. *Tribune*, Oct. 23, 1876; and *World*, Oct. 22, 1876, cited by Bonner, "Chinese in New York," 4: 16–17.

71. For more on the Bret Harte poem, see Tchen, "New York before Chinatown," 367–82.

72. *Herald*, Oct. 22, 29, 1876; *Times*, Oct. 21, 23, 25, 1876; *Tribune*, Oct. 21, 23, 25, 1876; *World*, Oct. 21, 22, 1876, and June 29, 1912.

73. *Times*, Oct. 21, 23, 25, 1876; *Herald*, Oct. 22, 1876; *Tribune*, Oct. 21, 23, 25, 1876; *World*, June 29, 1912.

74. Elaine Showalter, *The Female Malady: Women, Madness and English Culture, 1830–1980* (New York, 1985), 37, 75.

75. Quimbo Appo, Sing Sing Inmate Admission Register (B0143–80), New York State Archives, Dec. 22, 1876, 14: 161. I would like to thank Timothy Gilfoyle for providing me with this information.

76. Appo, patient notes, Jan. 1, June 10, 1879; Feb. 26, 1880; Mar. 30, 1885. Also Jonathan D. Spence, *The Question of Hu* (New York, 1989).

77. Appo, patient notes, Jan. 1, 1882.

78. See Paul C. P. Siu, *The Chinese Laundryman: A Study of Social Isolation*, introduction and ed. John Kuo Wei Tchen (New York, 1987), xxxi–xxxiii, 119, 226, 294, 301.

This chapter was written with the support of an interpretive research grant from the National Endowment for the Humanities and is based in part on themes developed in Alan M. Kraut's *Silent Travelers: Germs, Genes, and the "Immigrant Menace "* (New York, 1994).

1. *New York Times*, Jan. 2, 1892.

2. The author has discussed this gap in the historiography in several articles. See Alan M. Kraut, "Silent Strangers: Germs, Genes and Nativism in John Higham's *Strangers in the Land*," *American Jewish History* 76 (Dec. 1986):142–58; "Silent Travelers: Germs, Genes, and American Efficiency," *Social Science History* 12 (Winter 1988): 377–94; and "Healers and Strangers, Immigrant Attitudes toward the Physician in America—A Relationship in Historical Perspective," *Journal of the American Medical Association* 263 (Apr. 4, 1990): 1807–11.

3. Charles R. Rosenberg, *The Cholera Years, The United States in 1832, 1849 and 1866* (1962; Chicago, 1987).

4. John Duffy, *A History of Public Health in New York City, 1625–1866* (New York, 1968), 86.

5. Friedrich Kapp, *Immigration and the Commissioners of Emigration* (1870; New York, 1969), 20, 21.

6. Kate H. Claghorn, "The Foreign Immigrant in New York City," *United States Industrial Commission Reports* (Washington, D.C., 1901), 15:464.

7. *The Eighth Federal Census of the United States: 1860* (Washington, D.C., 1863), 609.

8. Anti-Catholicism is analyzed in John Higham's classic study of nativism, *Strangers in the Land* (New Brunswick, N.J., 1955). Antebellum anti-Catholicism is described most vividly in Ray Allen Billington, *The Protestant Crusade, 1800–1860, A Study of the Origins of American Nativism* (New York, 1938). Also, Dale T. Knobel, *Paddy and the Republic: Ethnicity and Nationality in Antebellum America* (Middletown, Conn., 1986).

9. *New York City Reports of Hospital Physicians and Other Documents in Relation to the Epidemic Cholera of 1832*, ed. Dudley Atkins (New York, 1832), 14–15.

10. *Niles' Register*, 42 (July 21, 1832): 372.

11. Gardiner Spring, *A Sermon Preached August 3, 1832, A Day Set Apart in the City of New-York for Public Fasting, Humiliation and Prayer* . . . (New York, 1832). Also cited by Rosenberg, *Cholera Years*, 44.

12. These varied religious responses are documented in Rosenberg, *Cholera Years*, 43–45.

13. Knobel, *Paddy and the Republic*, 56–57.

14. Timothy Dwight, *Travels in New England and New York* (New Haven, 1822), 3, 375.

15. Samuel F. B. Morse, *Imminent Dangers to the Free Institutions of the United States through Foreign Immigration* (1835; New York, 1969), 13.

16. *New York Times*, Oct. 15, 1851. Also cited in Terry Coleman, *Going to America* (Garden City, N.Y., 1973), 72.

17. Terry Coleman, *Going to America*, 74.

18. Ibid., 75–76.

19. Stanley Joel Reiser, *Medicine and the Reign of Technology* (Cambridge, 1978), 1–44.

20. Coleman, *Going to America,* 75.

21. Rosenberg, *The Cholera Years,* 135, n.5.

22. Kapp, *Immigration and the Commissioners of Emigration,* 105–24.

23. Samuel Busey, *Immigration: Its Evils and Consequences* (1856; New York, 1969), 125.

24. Robert Ernst, *Immigrant Life in New York City, 1825–1863* (1949; New York, 1965), 54.

25. Gerald N. Grob, *Mental Institutions in America, Social Policy to 1875* (New York, 1973), 153–56; and Grob, *Mental Illness and American Society, 1875–1940* (Princeton, N.J., 1983), 37–38.

26. Ernst, *Immigrant Life,* 54–55. The quotation is on p. 54.

27. Gerald Grob, *Mental Illness,* 169–70.

28. Ernst, *Immigrant Life,* 55.

29. Ibid.

30. Hasia Diner argues that Irish males in Ireland suffered the effects of mother-domination more than females. Emigrating males pined for home and mother and suffered higher rates of schizophrenia, while the females "made the decision to leave with a relatively light heart." Diner, *Erin's Daughters in America, Irish Immigrant Women in the Nineteenth Century* (Baltimore, 1983), 19.

31. Diner, *Erin's Daughters,* 110–11.

32. Grob, *Mental Institutions,* 230–35.

33. David J. Rothman, *The Discovery of the Asylum, Social Order and Disorder in the New Republic,* rev. ed. (1971; Boston, 1990), 285.

34. Grob, *Mental Institutions,* 236–41.

35. John Higham, *Strangers in the Land, Patterns of American Nativism, 1860–1925* (New Brunswick, N.J., 1955), 11. Dale Knobel makes the distinction between race and ethnicity in antebellum culture, but he , too, argues for a protean stereotype of the Irish, in Dale T. Knobel, *Paddy and the Republic, Ethnicity and Nationality in Antebellum America* (Middletown, Conn., 1986), xvii.

36. Knobel, *Paddy and the Republic,* 68–103.

37. "A Scene from Irish Life," *Harper's Monthly* 3(1851):833.

38. Orson S. Fowler and Lorenzo Fowler, *New Illustrated Self-Instructor in Phrenology and Physiology* (New York, 1859), 43–45, 55–56.

39. F. Edmund Hogan, S.J., *The Irish People, Their Height, Form, and Strength* (Dublin, 1899), 7, 12, 64. See also Janet A. Nolan, *Ourselves Alone, Women's Emigration from Ireland, 1885–1920* (Lexington, Ky., 1989), 9–10.

40. Kerby Miller, "Class, Culture, and Immigrant Group Identity in the United States: The Case of Irish-American Ethnicity," in Virginia Yans-McLaughlin, ed., *Immigration Reconsidered, History, Sociology, and Politics* (New York, 1990), 110–11. See also Kerby A. Miller, *Emigrants and Exiles, Ireland and the Irish Exodus to North America* (New York, 1985). The author heartily agrees with those critics who have denounced the frequent and careless use of the term social control ever since publication of Francis F. Piven and Richard A. Cloward's *Regulating the Poor* (New York, 1971). There is little new or worthy of note about the observation that throughout history, those who have held positions of power and authority have sought to use the material and cultural resources available to them to sustain and defend their position and to maintain quiescent the claims of those less wealthy or influential than themselves even as they engage in acts of altruism. That is the spirit in which I have used the term to describe William MacNeven's intentions and those of the Catholic Church with regard to Irish immigrants. Unfortunately, many of the new social historians have all but defined every

genre of social interaction among economic, racial, gender, and ethnic groups as the effort of one to assert social control over the other for only the most pernicious of motives. Often these scholars trace the origins of inclinations to exert social control to an underlying desire to preserve a social order supporting industrial capitalism's growth. I do not see such dark, covert motives at work in this analysis. For an iconoclastic view of social control theory, see some of the essays in Walter I. Trattner, *Social Welfare or Social Control? Some Historical Reflections on "Regulating the Poor"* (Knoxville, Tenn., 1983); and Willard Gaylin, Ira Glasser, Steven Marcus, and David Rothman, *Doing Good: The Limits of Benevolence* (New York, 1971). For a view of the problem from across the Atlantic, see F. M. L. Thompson, "Social Control in Victorian Britain," *Economic History Review* 34 (May, 1981): 189–209.

41. Patrick Logan, *Irish Country Cures* (Dublin, 1972), 1.

42. Miller, "Class, Culture and Immigrant Group Identity," 111–13. For a full discussion of Dr. William MacNeven as an Irish leader, see Victor R. Greene, *American Immigrant Leaders, 1800–1910, Marginality and Identity* (Baltimore, 1987), 25–29.

43. See the reference to MacNeven in the autobiography of Thomas Addis Emmet's grandson, Thomas Addis Emmet Jr., *Incidents of My Life* (New York, 1911), 65ff.

44. George Potter, *To the Golden Door* (New York, 1960), 208–9.

45. Marvin R. O'Connell, "The Roman Catholic Tradition since 1545," in Ronald L. Numbers and Darrel W. Amundsen, eds., *Caring and Curing, Health and Medicine in the Western Religious Traditions* (New York, 1986), 108–45.

46. Joseph and Helen McCadden, *Father Varela: Torch Bearer from Cuba* (New York, 1969), 165–67.

47. *New York Herald*, Aug. 8, 1849.

48. A Letter from the Right Reverend John Dubois, D.D., Bishop of New York, to Rev.———, Secretary of the Association for the Propagation of the Faith, Lyons, Mar. 16, 1830, in United States Catholic Historical Society, *Historical Records and Studies* (New York, 1907), 5:228.

49. Pastoral letter of Bishop John Dubois, 1834, as quoted by Jay Dolan, *The Immigrant Church, New York's Irish and German Catholics, 1815–1865* (Baltimore, 1975), 130.

50. All studies of hospitals in the nineteenth century mention the difficulties that Roman Catholic clergy had serving their flock and protecting the ill from Protestant conversion. See Morris J. Vogel, *The Invention of the Modern Hospital, Boston 1870–1930* (Chicago, 1980), 127–28; and Charles E. Rosenberg, *The Care of Strangers, The Rise of America's Hospital System* (New York, 1987).

51. An excellent sociological discussion of this issue, which remains a matter of significance for religious groups in spiritually heterogeneous societies can be found in William A. Glaser, *Social Settings and Medical Organization, A Cross-National Study of the Hospital* (New York, 1970), 33–35.

52. *Freeman's Journal and Catholic Register*, Feb. 20, 1847.

53. Ibid., Feb. 5, 1848.

54. Roman Catholics were not the only religious group concerned with other religions proselytizing their flock. By 1847 there were 50,000 Jews living in the United States, 16,000 of them in New York. Before the Civil War, Jews built their own hospitals to serve ritual needs and to prevent both Protestant and Catholic overtures of conversion reaching their sick and dying co-religionists. Cincinnati Jews were first, opening the Jewish Hospital in 1850. In 1855, Jews' Hospital, later renamed Mt. Sinai, was opened in New York City with the help of a $20,000 bequest from Judah Touro of New Orleans. The only study of the Jewish hospital in the United States is Daniel Ethan Bridge, "The

Rise and Development of the Jewish Hospital in America, 1850–1894" (unpublished Rabbinic Ordination thesis, Hebrew Union College, 1985). See also Joseph Hirsh and Beka Doherty, *The First Hundred Years of Mount Sinai Hospital of New York, 1852–1952* (New York, 1952).

55. *First Annual Report of Saint Vincent's Hospital under the Charge of the Sisters of Charity for the Year Ending January First, 1859*, 4. The best history of St. Vincent's Hospital is Sister Marie De Lourdes Walsh, *With a Great Heart, The Story of St. Vincent's Hospital and Medical Center of New York, 1849–1964* (New York, 1965).

56. Carlan Kraman, "Women Religious in Health Care: The Early Years," in Ursula Stepsis and Dolores Liptak, eds., *Pioneer Healers: The History of Women Religious in American Health Care* (New York, 1989), 22–23.

57. Historian Marvin R. O'Connell claims that "the sisters and their institutions of healing clearly gave priority to cure of soul over cure of body. They acted out of no mere humanitarian impulse, but out of the conviction that performing the corporal works of mercy was a primary means of securing salvation for those who performed them, as well as an occasion of supernatural grace to those for whom they were performed." Thus O'Connell views the bravery of the nuns in the face of disease as an aspect of their own religious odysseys. O'Connell, "The Roman Catholic Tradition since 1545," 137.

58. A useful treatment of the creation of the first Roman Catholic hospital in St. Louis is Ann Kathryn Webster, "The Impact of Catholic Hospitals in St. Louis" (Ph.D. diss., Saint Louis University, 1968).

59. *Fifty-First Annual Report of the St. Vincent's Hospital of the City of New York for the Year 1900* (New York, 1901), 8.

60. Ibid., 22.

61. *Freeman's Journal and Catholic Register*, Jan. 26, 1850.

62. *First Annual Report of St. Vincent's Hospital*, 4.

63. Ibid., 5.

64. *Fifty-First Annual Report of the St. Vincent's Hospital. . . 1900*, 22.

65. Aaron I. Abell, *American Catholicism and Social Action: A Search for Social Justice, 1865–1950* (Garden City, N.Y., 1960), 36.

66. Charles E. Rosenberg, "Disease and Social Order in America: Perceptions and Expectations," *Millbank Quarterly* 64 (1986): 35. Also, Rosenberg, "Afterword, 1987," in *The Cholera Years*, 238, and "Deconstructing Disease," in *Reviews in American History* 14 (Mar. 1986): 110–15. For an extended discussion of the subject, see Peter Wright and Andrew Treacher, eds., *The Problem of Medical Knowledge: Examining the Social Construction of Medicine* (Edinburgh, 1982).

67. Susan Sontag, *Illness as Metaphor* (New York, 1977), and *AIDS and Its Metaphors* (New York, 1988). On AIDS and the Haitians see Elizabeth Fee and Daniel M. Fox, eds., *AIDS, The Burdens of History* (Berkeley, Calif., 1988), passim; and Gerald Oppenheimer, "Causes, Cases and Cohorts: The Role of Epidemiology and the Historical Construction of AIDS," in Fee and Fox, eds., *AIDS, The Making of a Chronic Disease*, (Berkeley, Calif., 1992), 59–60.

Chapter 7: SHREWD IRISHMEN (Devlin)

1. "Portraits of the People," *New York Atlas*, Nov. 21, 1852; "New York," 211:216, R. G. Dun & Co. Collection, Baker Library, Harvard Graduate School of Business Administration (hereafter Dun, state, volume, and page).

2. Robert Ernst, *Immigrant Life in New York, 1825–1863* (New York, 1963), 215.

3. For good recent studies of seamstresses, many of whom were Irish immigrants, see Carol Groneman Pernicone, "'The Bloody Ould Sixth': A Social Analysis of a New York City Working-Class Community in the Mid-Nineteenth Century," (Ph.D. diss., University of Rochester, 1973), 139–79, and "She Earns as a Child—She Pays as a Man," in *Immigrants in Industrial America, 1850–1920* (Charlottesville, Va., 1977), 33–46; and Christine Stansell, *City of Women: Race, Sex and Class in New York, 1789–1860* (Chicago, 1982), 105–55.

4. William Forbes Adams, *Ireland and Irish Emigration to the New World from 1815 to the Famine* (New Haven, Yale University Press, 1932), 54; J. E. Bicheno, *Ireland and Its Economy* (London, 1830), 37; "Old Clothes Dealers in England," *Clothier and Furnisher*, (Sept. 1884), 45.

5. W. P. Ryan, *The Irish Labor Movement* (Dublin, 1919), 64–68.

6. Kerby Miller, *Emigrants and Exiles* (New York, 1986), 35; "Nine Tailors Make a Man," *Clothier and Hatter*, Apr. 1880, 4.

7. Adams, *Ireland and Irish Emigration*, 55–63.

8. Robert Crowe, *Reminiscences of the Octogenarian Tailor* (New York, 1903), 32; Egal Feldman, *Fit for Men* (Washington, D.C., 1960), 95; George O'Brien, *The Economic History of Ireland from the Union to the Famine* (Dublin, 1920), 395.

9. New York City Directories, 1786–1855; *Clothier and Hatter*, June 23, 1874 and Sept. 30, 1876; "Portraits of the People," *New York Atlas*, Dec. 3, 1848; New York State Census of 1855, Population Schedules, New York County. In Wards One to Six, Twelve, and Fourteen, 27 Irish-born tailors were found to have unrelated servants as part of their households, and not as boarders.

10. Joseph Kennedy, "Population of the United States in 1860," in U.S. Census Bureau, *Eighth Census of the United States, 1860*, xxii; U.S. Department of Commerce, *The Men's Factory-Made Clothing Industry*, Miscellaneous Series no. 34 (Washington, D.C., 1916), 16–17.

11. New York State Census of 1855, Population Schedules, Wards One–Six, Twelve, Fourteen and Election District One of Ward Nine.

12. For overviews of the development of the clothing industry during this period see Feldman, *Fit for Men*; Harry A. Cobrin, *The Men's Clothing Industry: Colonial through Modern Times* (New York, 1970); Richard B. Stott, *Workers in the Metropolis: Class, Ethnicity and Youth in Antebellum New York City* (Ithaca, N.Y., 1990) 7–67; Jesse A. Pope, *The Clothing Industry in New York* (New York, 1905); Sean Wilentz, *Chants Democratic: New York City and the Rise of the American Working Class* (New York, 1984), 107–40.

13. *Clothier and Furnisher*, Sept. 1883, 14; Crowe, *Reminiscences*, 20; James Dawson Burn, *Three Years among the Working Classes in the United States during the War* (London, 1865), 18.

14. U.S. Census Bureau, "Nationality in Manufacturing Industries," 1880 U.S. Census of Manufactures, 1:xxxvi; Ernst, *Immigrant Life*, 215; Pernicone, "'Bloody Ould Sixth,'" 105.

15. "The Press and the Rights of Labor," letter to the editor, *New York Tribune*, July 29, 1850; Charles Updegraff, *The Story of Two Famous Hatters* (New York, 1926), 6.

16. Feldman, *Fit for Men*, 113; *New York Times*, Nov. 10, 1861; U.S. Census Bureau, *Eighth Census, 1860*, Census of Industry, New York County.

17. Children of Thomas J. and Ellen Devlin, the former a clerk at Devlin & Co., in New York City Vital Records, in Municipal Archives; Dun, "New York," 209:26; Daniel Edward Ryan, "The Master Art," *Clothier and Furnisher*, Mar. 1883, 9.

18. United States Industrial Commission, *Reports of the Industrial Commission on Immigration* (Washington, D.C., 1901), 15:324; Jesse Pope, *The Clothing Industry in New York* (New York, 1905), 27.

19. Iver Bernstein, *The New York City Draft Riots* (New York, 1990), 80; *Clothier and Furnisher*, Sept. 1883, 14.

20. Dun, "New York," 209:36.

21. "The Commercial Revolution: Our Savings Banks," *New York Herald*, Oct. 25 and 31, 1857.

22. "The Press and the Rights of Labor," *New York Herald*, July 29, 1850; "Mass Meeting of Tailors in the Park," *New York Herald*, Aug. 5, 1850; Ernst, *Immigrant Life*, 101–2; Jean Hurley, "The Irish in the Early Labor Movement, 1820–1862" (Master's thesis, Columbia University, 1963), 105–15.

23. Crowe, *Reminiscences*, 26; "Labor and Wages," *New York Times*, May 2, 1876.

24. *Biographical Directory of the American Congress, 1774–1971* (Washington, D.C., 1971), 1341.

25. Bernstein, *Draft Riots*, 24–25, 245–46; "The Great Strike," *New York Herald*, June 22, 1872; June 21, 1872; *New York Times*, Aug. 14, 1877; "Agitation of Labor Questions," *New York Times*, July 4, 1882; "A Reception to Davitt," *New York Times*, July 6, 1882; *Irish World*, July 15, 1882; Dun, "New York," 404:1000.

26. Dun, "New York," 198:130, 196; Pope, *New York Clothing Industry*, 27.

27. "Daniel Edward Ryan," *Clothier and Hatter*, May 1880, 30; *Clothier and Furnisher*, Apr. 1912; "The Dreary Dress Suit," *Clothing-Furnishing Gazette*, May 1885, 30; Cobrin, *Men's Clothing Industry*, 61.

28. Daniel E. Ryan, "The Master Art," *Clothier and Furnisher*, Mar. 1883, 9–10; *American Cutter and Tailor*, 1881–82, at New York Public Library.

29. Dun, "New York," 214:546, and 212:383; Updegraff, *Two Famous Hatters*, 8.

30. *Gibson's Monthly Review of the Clothing and Furnishing Trades* (July 1882): 36; Dun, "New York," 211:260.

31. U.S. Census Bureau figures quoted in Stott, *Workers in the Metropolis*, 11; Burn, *Three Years among the Working Classes*, 15–16; Dun, "New York," 209:96; John Ridge, "County Colonies in the United States," *IE, a Supplement to the Irish Echo*, 65th Anniversary Issue, Sept. 1993, 29–30.

32. Wilentz, *Chants Democratic*, 113; "The Pioneers: Charles Knox," *Clothier and Hatter* (Sept. 29, 1877); Updegraff, *Two Famous Hatters*, 19, 22, 33–34, 53.

33. New York City Directories, 1820–1892; "Old Clothes Dealers in England," *Clothier and Furnisher*, Sept. 1884, 45; Dun, "New York," 209:77, 198:140, 173.

34. Dun, "New York," 209:6, 211:260.

35. Feldman, *Fit for Men*, 30.

36. Dun, "New York," 211:216, 213:440–41, 395:137; Obituary of Patrick Rogers, *Irish-American*, July 16, 1864.

37. Leary: *Boyd's Tax Book*, 1856–57, at New York Public Library; and Dun, "New York," 228:423; Corbett: Obituary, *Danbury* (Conn.)*Evening News*, Jan. 10, 1890; Fox: Dun, "New York," 209:75; McEvoys: Dun, "New York," 209:79.

38. Obituaries of Daniel Devlin: *New York Herald*, Feb. 23, 1867, and *Irish-American*, Mar. 2, 1867; display window: *Clothier and Furnisher*, Oct. 1883; business references in Robert Curtis Ogden Papers, Library of Congress.

39. *Hunt's Merchants' Magazine*, no. 20 (1849): 116; New York State Census of 1855, schedules of manufactures; *Clothier and Hatter*, Aug. 31, 1877; advertisements in *New York Times*, Dec. 17, 1876 and Dec. 10, 1877); obituary of William Devlin, *New Orleans Times-Picayune*, July 28, 1892.

40. Edwin Freedley, *Leading Pursuits and Leading Men* (Philadelphia, 1856), 133–34; *The Metropolis of To-Day* (New York, 1888), 320–21; "The Tailors' Strike," *New York Herald*, Aug. 9, 1850; Dun, "New York," 198:196, 365:123, 203:632.

41. Diary, Journals and papers related to *Jonathan Ogden v. Jeremiah Devlin*, New York Superior Court, in Robert Curtis Ogden Papers, Library of Congress; Court papers related to *Getty v. Devlin*, in New York Public Library; "Devlin & Co. Fail," *New York Times*, Jan. 16, 1897; "Claim of Daniel Devlin estate," in "Board of Audit," *New York Times*, Aug. 27, 1868.

42. "Clothier and Hatter Portraits No. 1: One of the Pioneers," *Clothier and Hatter*, Sept. 29, 1877, 14; *Clothier and Hatter*, Nov. 1878; Updegraff, *Two Famous Hatters*; Ralph Blume, City Historian of Norwalk, Conn., interview Sept. 1991.

43. "Arthur Leary Is Dead," *New York Times*, Feb. 24, 1893; Updegraff, *Story of Two Hatters*, 36; entry on Edward Fox, in New York Trade Agency Reports, p. 5, in New-York Historical Society; Dun, "New York," 209:2, 404:1000.

44. John Burke, *Reminiscences*, unpublished mss. in New-York Historical Society; New York City Directories, 1870–1892; *Brooklyn Eagle* quoted in *Clothier and Furnisher*, Nov. 1884.

45. Ernst, *Immigrant Life in New York*, 215–16; U.S. Department of Commerce, *Men's Factory-Made Clothing Industry*, 16–17.

46. Pope, *Clothing Industry in New York*, 45–78.

47. U.S. Census Bureau, *Eighth Census, 1860*, Census of Industry, New York County; Pope, *Clothing Industry in New York*, 303; "The Hebrews of Today," *Clothier and Furnisher*, Mar. 1887; Stephen Steinberg, *The Ethnic Myth: Race, Ethnicity and Class in America* (New York, 1981), 99–102; U.S. Industrial Commission, *Reports on Immigration*, 324.

48. Roger Waldinger, *Through the Eye of the Needle* (New York, 1986), 13–47.

49. Oscar Handlin, *Boston's Immigrants, 1790–1880* (New York, 1975), 75–87.

50. Wilentz, *Chants Democratic*, 29–35, 107–29.

51. Margaret Christman and Claudia Kidwell, *Suiting Everyone: The Democratization of Clothing in America* (Washington, D.C., 1974); Obituary of James Leary, *New York Herald*, Jan. 18, 1862.

52. New York State Census of 1855, quoted in Ernst, *Immigrant Life in New York*, 215; and in Stott, *Workers in the Metropolis*, 92; William H. Bennett, *A Chronological History of the Emigrant Industrial Savings Bank* (privately printed, New York, 1931), 1–8.

Chapter 8: UNION GREEN (Spann)

1. [Charles Graham Halpine], *The Life and Adventures, Songs, Services, and Speeches of Private Miles O'Reilly* (New York, 1864), 159; Benjamin A. Gould, *Investigations into the Military and Anthropological Statistics of American Soldiers* (New York, 1869), 27.

2. Madeleine Hook Rice, *American Catholic Opinion in the Slavery Controversy* (New York, 1944), 102–4; Florence E. Gibson, *The Attitudes of the New York Irish toward State and National Affairs, 1848–1892* (New York, 1951), 117; Robert Ernst, *Immigrant Life in New York City, 1825–1863* (New York, 1949), 152–53.

3. *Freeman's Journal*, Sept. 22, Oct. 6, 1860, and Apr. 20, 1861; *Irish-American*, Feb. 14, 1861. For John Mitchel, see Rice, *American Catholic Opinion*, 105–6; and *Freeman's Journal*, Nov. 1, 1862.

4. *Irish-American*, Mar. 14, 21, 1857; Mar. 22, 1858; Mar. 26, Nov. 26, Dec. 10, 1859; Oct. 5, 1861. Also see the occasional military affairs column of the *Irish-American* during the late 1850s.

5. Ibid., June 22, 1861. Stewart Sifakis, *Who Was Who in the Civil War* (New York, 1988), 143–44.

6. *Irish-American*, Jan. 12, Feb. 2, Mar. 2, Apr. 27, June 22, 1861; Ernest A. McKay, *The Civil War and New York City* (Syracuse, N.Y., 1990), 57.

7. Benjamin J. Blied, *Catholicism and the Civil War* (Milwaukee, 1945), 73. *Freeman's Journal*, Apr. 27, Aug. 31, 1861; Apr. 19, 1862. Office of the Postmaster-General to James McMaster, Mar. 7, Apr. 8, 1862, McMaster Papers, Notre Dame University.

8. *New York Times* [henceforth, *Times*], May 1, 1861. Also Archbishop John Hughes to Thurlow Weed, Apr. 21, 1861, Hughes Papers, New-York Historical Society.

9. Archbishop John Hughes to Bishop Lynch of South Carolina, public letter in *Times*, Sept. 4, 1861; Letter to James A. McMaster, June 6, 1861, McMaster Papers, Notre Dame University.

10. A. Milburn Petty, "History of the 37th Regiment, New York Volunteers," *Journal of the American Irish Historical Society* 31 (1937): 101–23; *Irish-American*, Apr. 10, 27, May 11, 25, June 1, 15, 1861.

11. *Irish-American*, Apr. 27, 1861; John Hughes, public letter to the *New York Herald* in *Complete Works of Most Rev. John Hughes*, ed. Lawrence Kehoe (New York, 1866), 2:545–46.

12. John R. G. Hassard, *Life of Most Rev. John Hughes* (New York, 1866), 482. The New York Association for Improving the Condition of the Poor estimated that unemployment in 1861 was "at least 25 per cent greater" than in any year since the panic year, 1857. *Annual Report* (New York, 1861), 17.

13. George W. Smith and Charles Judah, *Life in the North during the Civil War* (Albuquerque, 1966), 47; *Freeman's Journal*, May 11, 1861; Benjamin Brown French, *Witness to the Young Republic: A Yankee Journal, 1828–1870*, ed. Donald B. Cole and John J. McDonough (Hanover, N.H., 1989), 356; James P. McIvor to Colonel W. T. Sherman, n.d., McIvor Papers, New-York Historical Society.

14. *Freeman's Journal*, May 11, 1861; *Irish-American*, July 20, Aug. 2, 1861; *Times*, July 23, 24, 26, 1861; William D. Griffin, *The Irish in America, 1550–1972* (Dobbs Ferry, N.Y., 1973), 78–80.

15. Richard C. Murphy and Lawrence J. Mannion, *The History of the Friendly Sons of Saint Patrick in the City of New York, 1784–1955* (New York, 1962), 305–12; *Irish American*, May 4, 11, 1861.

16. Captain D. P. Conyngham, *The Irish Brigade and Its Campaign* (London, n.d.), 25–27; *Times*, Aug. 30, 1861; *Irish-American*, Nov. 9, 16, 1861, and Jan. 25, Feb. 15, Mar. 1, 1862.

17. *Times*, Nov. 3, 10, 1861; New York *Weekly Caucasian*, Dec. 21, 1861; New York City Board of Councilmen, *Proceedings* 87 (1862–63): 106–9, 370–71.

18. *Times*, July 28, 1861; *Irish-American*, Aug. 10, 31, 1861.

19. John C. O'Gallaghan, *History of the Irish Brigade in the Service of France* (repr.: Shannon, 1969), vii; *Freeman's Journal*, Oct. 27, Nov. 10, 17, 1860.

20. *Irish-American*, June 20, July 13, Sept. 14, 1861, and Mar. 7, 1863; Hassard, *Hughes*, 443.

21. Michael Cavanagh, *Memoir of General Thomas Francis Meagher* (Worcester, Mass., 1872); Thomas S. Lonergan, "General Thomas Francis Meagher," *Journal of the American Irish Historical Society* 12 (1912–13): 111–26.

22. *Times*, July 26, 1861; William L. Burton, *Melting Pot Soldiers: The Union's Ethnic Regiments* (Ames, Iowa, 1988), 125; Maria Lydig Daly, *Diary of a Union Lady, 1861–1865*, ed. Harold Earl Hammond (New York, 1962), 101, 136.

23. *Irish-American*, Aug. 2, 10, 17, Sept. 14, 1861; Lonergan, *Meagher*, 118–23. General T. F. Meagher, "Letters," *Journal of the American Irish Historical Society* 30 (1932): 83–87; Daly, *Diary*, 42, 60–63; Gould, *Investigations*, 182; W. Corby, *Memoirs of Chaplain Life* (Chicago, 1893), 31. The two standard histories of the Brigade are Conyngham, *Irish Brigade*, an enthusiastic contemporary account; and Paul Jones, *The Irish Brigade* (Washington-New York, 1960), a generally reliable narrative.

24. *Times*, Oct. 26, Nov. 9, 1861; *Irish-American*, Oct. 26, Nov. 2, 1861; Conyngham, *Irish Brigade*, 25–27; Daly, *Diary*, 42, 60–63.

25. *Irish-American*, Nov. 16, 1861.

26. Ibid., Nov. 16, 23, 1861; *Times*, Nov. 9, 19, 1861; Cavanagh, *Meagher*, 427.

27. *Irish-American*, July 20, Aug. 2, Dec. 21, 1861.

28. Along with Corby, *Memoir*, see David Power Conyngham, "The Soldiers of the Cross," typescript book, Notre Dame University, 107–11, and 149. Also Roxana Molency to Father William Corby, Aug. 23, 1862; and Account Book, William Corby Papers, Notre Dame University.

29. Corby, *Memoir*, 31; *Times*, July 26, 1862; *Irish-American*, Aug. 16, 1862; Conyngham, *Irish Brigade*, 119, 280, 301.

30. *Irish-American*, July 26, Aug. 2, 9, 16, 1862; *Times*, July 26, Aug. 17, 1862.

31. *Times*, Aug. 18, 19, Sept. 26, 1862.

32. *Irish-American*, Aug. 23, 30, Sept. 6, 13, 27, Oct. 11, 25, Nov. 15, 1862, and Jan. 31, 1863; *Times*, Aug. 19, 23, Sept. 15, 1862; Documents of the National War Committee (1862), New-York Historical Society. New York Board of Aldermen, *Proceedings*, 85 (1862): 100.

33. *Irish-American*, Sept. 27, Oct. 11, 25, Nov. 25, 1862; *Times*, Sept. 25, 1862; Michael Corcoran to J. B. Kirkes, Nov. 30, 1862, Corcoran Papers, New-York Historical Society.

34. *Times*, Sept. 20, 21, 1862; *Irish-American*, Oct. 11, 1862; John M. Priest, *Antietam* (Shippensburg, Pa., 1989), 159–60, 180, 216.

35. John F. Maguire, *The Irish American* (New York, 1968), 552.

36. Ella Lonn, *Foreigners in the Union Army* (Baton Rouge, 1951), 511–12; Burton, *Melting Pot*, 125; "The Sixty-ninth Regiments at Fredericksburg," *Journal of the American Irish Historical Society* 15(1916): 190–200.

37. *Irish-American*, Dec. 27, 1862; Conyngham, *Irish Brigade*, 170, 302.

38. Daly, *Diary*, 129–32; *Freeman's Journal*, Apr. 27, 1861, and June 28, 1862; Ellen Ryan Jolly, *Nuns of the Battlefield* (Providence, R.I., 1930), 20–21, 208, 213, 219, 222; Sister Mary Denis Maher, *To Bind Up the Wounds: Catholic Sister Nurses in the U.S. Civil War* (Westport, Conn., 1989), 73, 79–80; Hassard, *Hughes*, 442.

39. *Irish-American*, June 25, July 2, 1864; Conyngham, *Soldiers of the Cross*, 235–42; New York City Board of Councilmen, *Proceedings* 88(1862–63): 369.

40. Hassard, *Hughes*, 493; Paul Jacoby, *Catholic Child Care in Nineteenth Century New York* (repr.: New York, 1974), 126–27; Jay P. Dolan, *The Immigrant Church: New York's Irish and German Catholics, 1815–1865* (Baltimore, 1975), 136–38. Also *Irish-American*, Mar. 9, 1861; Nov. 15, Dec. 13, 1862; Feb. 28, Apr. 14, 28, June 6, Oct. 10. Nov. 14, 1863.

41. *New York Tribune*, Mar. 23, 1863; Hasia R. Diner, *Erin's Daughters in America: Irish Immigrant Women in the Nineteenth Century* (Baltimore, 1983), 78,

180n.14; Daly, *Diary,* 222, 283–84, 317, 323; James J. Kenneally, *The History of American Catholic Women* (New York, 1990), 83; *Times,* Dec. 14, 1864.

42. *Times,* Jan. 17, Mar. 18, 1863; *Freeman's Journal,* Jan. 31, 1863; *New York Tribune,* Mar. 18, 1863.

43. Jones, *Irish Brigade,* 132; J. Cutler Andrews, *The North Reports the Civil War* (Pittsburgh, 1983), 284, 301, 328; Conyngham, *Irish Brigade,* 200; New York *Weekly Day-Book,* Jan. 23, 1863; and Mar. 25, 1865; *Irish-American,* Apr. 18, May 23, 30, June 27, 1863, and July 2, 1864; *Times,* May 14, 24, 1863; Lonn, *Foreigners,* 525–26.

44. *Irish-American,* Nov. 8, 1862, and Jan. 17, July 4, 1863; *Times,* Oct. 9, 1862; *Weekly Day-Book,* Jan. 23, 1863; G. B. B. to James McMaster, May 31, 1864, McMaster Papers, Notre Dame University; Rice, *American Catholic Opinion,* 125.

45. Emerson David Fite, *Social and Industrial Conditions in the North during the Civil War* (repr.: New York, 1963), 189, 197; James F. Richardson, *The New York Police* (New York, 1970), 131–32; Gibson, *Attitudes,* 143–44; Philip S. Paludan, *A People's Contest* (New York, 1988), 181–83; *New York Tribune,* Mar. 25, 1863; *Weekly Caucasian,* Mar. 28, 1863; New York Association for Improving the Condition of the Poor, *Twenty-Second Annual Report* (New York, 1865), 24.

46. Paludan, *A People's Contest,* 190; Hughes, *Complete Works,* ed. Lawrence Kehoe (New York, 1866), 2:546; Gibson, *Attitudes,* 150–52; *Freeman's Journal,* July 18, 1863; *Irish-American,* July 18, 1863.

47. There are several studies of the Draft Riots: James McCague, *The Second Rebellion* (New York, 1968); Adrian Cook, *The Armies of the Streets* (Lexington, Ky., 1974); and Iver Bernstein, *The New York City Draft Riots* (New York, 1990).

48. *Times,* July 14, 15, 16, 17, 29. 1863; *Freeman's Journal,* July 18, 1863.

49. *Irish-American,* July 25, 1863. Iver Bernstein contends that the riots were an "insurrection" and "communal uprising" important for their "illumination, like a flash of lightning, of a darkened historical landscape." (Bernstein, *New York City Draft Riots,* vii, 3–6). This exaggeration of the illuminating value of lightning typifies the author's basic contention. Although the riots certainly did express the feelings of many people in the summer of 1863, they constituted a special incident that only partly represented the wartime situation and the relation of the Irish to the war.

50. *Irish-American,* Aug. 8, 1863; McKay, *Civil War,* 207–8. *Times,* July 17, 28, 1863; George Templeton Strong, *Diary,* ed. Allan Nevins and Milton Halsey Thomas (New York, 1952), 3:336, 342 and 352; New York Association for Improving the Condition of the Poor, *Annual Report* (New York, 1864), 35.

51. Sifarkus, *Who Was Who,* 144; Daly, *Diary,* 270–71; *Times,* Aug. 28, 1862, and Jan. 25, 1863; Resolution of Mourning, 170th Regiment, McIvor Papers, New-York Historical Society.

52. William Hanchett, *Irish: Charles G. Halpine in Civil War America* (Syracuse, 1970). Also, John D. Hayes and Doris D. Maquire, "Charles Graham Halpine," *New-York Historical Society Quarterly* 51 (1967), 326–44; *Irish-American,* Dec. 19, 1863; Halpine, *Miles O'Reilly,* 150.

53. Hanchett, *Irish,* 71, 91; Halpine, *Miles O'Reilly,* 55, 60. 115, 177–79, 213, 236; *Irish-American,* Mar. 11, May 13, 1865.

54. Conyngham, *Irish Brigade,* 210–12; *Irish-American,* Jan. 16, 23, 1864.

55. Jones, *Irish Brigade,* 216–19; Conyngham, *Irish Brigade,* 216–17; Hanchett, *Irish,* 103–4. The manuscript of the poem is in the Charles G. Halpine Papers, New-York Historical Society.

56. *Irish-American,* July 2, Sept. 3, 1864; Conyngham, *Irish Brigade,* 234–35; Sifakis, *Who Was Who,* 358.

57. Gibson, *Attitude*, 169–70; *Times*, Oct. 9, 1864; *Irish-American*, Oct. 15, 1864.

58. *Times*, July 1, 1865; New York Board of Councilmen, *Proceedings* 88 (1862–63): 29, and 93(1864): 117, 166, 236.

59. Wallis G. Sharrow, "Northern Catholic Intellectuals and the Coming of the Civil War," *New-York Historical Society Quarterly* 58 (1974): 43–56; Phyllis F. Field, *The Politics of Race in New York* (Ithaca, N.Y., 1982), 133–35; Hassard, *Hughes*, 437.

60. *Times*, Mar. 7, 1863; *Irish-American*, July 30, 1864; Daly, *Diary*, 305–13; Harold E. Hammond, *A Commoner's Judge: The Life and Times of Charles Patrick Daly* (Boston, 1954), 173–85; Strong, *Diary*, 3: 462.

61. *Times*, Apr. 3, Aug. 10, 1864; Gibson, *Attitudes*, 169; Jerome K. Mushkat, *The Reconstruction of the New York Democracy* (Rutherford, N.J., 1981), 40–42.

62. *Times*, Nov. 4, 9, 20, 1864; *Freeman's Journal*, Nov. 19, 26, 1864. Although the strong Irish support for McClellan did reflect Copperhead leanings, it also included support for the war, since McClellan himself publicly favored continuing military action for the restoration of the Union; the critical difference between him and Lincoln was not over the war but Lincoln's identification with Emancipation and racial equality.

63. *Freeman's Journal*, Apr. 22, 1865; *Irish-American*, Apr. 22, 29, 1865.

64. Ibid., June 3, 17, July 15, 22, 29, 1865; *Times*, July 3, 4, 6, 1865.

65. Meagher, *Letters*, 86; Lonergan, *Meagher*, 124–25.

66. Carl Wittke, *The Irish in America* (Baton Rouge, 1956), 153–55; Edward Wakin, *Enter the Irish-American* (New York, 1976), 141–42; *Irish-American*, Jan. 7, 28, Feb. 24, Apr. 1, 8, 22, 29, June 17, 1865; Miller, *Emigrants and Exiles*, 336; "The Fenian Invasion of Canada, 1866," *Journal of the American Irish Historical Society* 23 (1924): 193–203.

67. *Times*, Mar. 18, 1865; Dale J. Knobel, *Paddy and the Republic* (Middletown, Conn., 1986), 171–76; Jones, *Irish Brigade*, 255.

Part III Overview: FORGING FORWARD AND LOOKING BACK
(McCaffrey)

1. Janet Ann Nolan, in *Ourselves Alone: Female Emigration from Ireland, 1825–1920* (Lexington, Ky., 1989), argues that Ireland's postfamine economic and social climate had a more adverse affect on women than men, encouraging them to emigrate to the United States, where employment and marriage prospects were more promising. This same position can be found in Grace Neville, "'She Never Then After That Forgot Him': Irishwomen and Emigration to the United States in Irish Folklore," *Mid-America* 74 (Oct. 1992): 271–89.

2. The two best studies of American nativism are by Ray Allen Billington, *The Protestant Crusade, 1800–1860* (Chicago, 1964); and John Higham, *Strangers in the Land: Patterns of American Nativism, 1860–1925* (New York, 1965).

3. Kevin O'Neill, *Family and Farm in Pre-Famine Ireland: The Parish of Killashandra* (Madison, 1984), using a parish in County Cavan, presents a portrait of life in Ireland during 1780–1845. Postfamine changes in agrarian Ireland are discussed in Barbara Lewis Solow, *The Land Question and the Irish Economy, 1870–1903* (Cambridge, 1971), 89–120; Joseph Lee, *The Modernization of Irish Society, 1848–1918* (Dublin, 1973), 36–64; James S. Donnelly Jr., *The Land and the People of Nineteenth-Century Cork* (London, 1975), 219–50; and Samuel Clark, *Social Origins of the Land War* (Princeton, 1979), 107–219.

4. Patrick Blessing, "The Irish," in Stephan Thernstrom, ed., *The Harvard Encyclopedia of American Ethnic Groups* (Cambridge, Mass., 1980), 529. Arnold Schrier, *Ireland and the American Emigration, 1850–1900* (Minneapolis, 1958), 22, states that 94 out of

every 100 people in Ireland before the age of 40 could read and write in 1900. Since the overwhelming majority of emigrants were young, it is reasonable to assume that almost all were literate.

5. During his 1835 sojourn in Ireland, that famous French traveler, Alexis de Tocqueville, was most impressed with the religious faith and devotion of the people, contrasting them with the indifference he viewed in other countries, including his own. *Alexis de Tocqueville's Journey in Ireland, July–August, 1835,* transl. and ed. Emmet Larkin (Washington, D.C., 1990), 11–12.

6. Problems in prefamine Irish Catholicism are the focus of S. J. Connolly, *Priests and People in Pre-Famine Ireland, 1780–1845* (New York, 1982); and David W. Miller, "Irish Catholicism and the Great Famine," *Journal of Social Studies* 9 (Sept. 1975): 81–98. Patrick Corish in *The Irish Catholic Experience* (Wilmington, Del., 1985), 151–91, discusses reforms in prefamine Irish Catholicism, distinguishing between situations in various parts of the country.

7. For a detailed analysis of Cullen's impact on Irish Catholicism see Emmet Larkin, "The Devotional Revolution in Ireland," *The Historical Dimensions of Irish Catholicism* (Washington, D.C., 1984), 57–88; *The Making of the Roman Catholic Church in Ireland, 1850–1860* (Chapel Hill, 1980); and *The Consolidation of the Roman Catholic Church in Ireland, 1860–1870* (Chapel Hill, 1987).

8. On the role of religion in shaping Irish nationality see Patrick O'Farrell, *Ireland's English Question* (New York, 1971), 76–99; and Lawrence J. McCaffrey, "Irish Nationalism and Irish Catholicism: A Study in Cultural Identity," *Church History* 42 (Dec. 1973): 524–34.

9. For a thorough and highly readable study of the Irish journey to America by sail and by steam, and the emigrants' difficulties in Liverpool, on board ship, and upon arrival in New York see Terry Coleman, *Going to America* (Baltimore, 1987).

10. Boston and Jersey City, at 22.7 and 21.5 percent, respectively, had higher percentages of Irish immigrants than New York; and Albany at 19.1 and New Haven at 18.9 were ahead of Brooklyn. U.S. Census Office, *Ninth Census, 1870* (Washington, D.C., 1872), 1: table 8, 386–91. Cited in Steven P. Erie, *Rainbow's End: Irish-Americans and the Dilemmas of Urban Politics, 1840–1985* (Berkeley, Calif., 1988), 18.

11. Anthony Gronowicz, "Labor's Decline within New York City's Democratic Party from 1844 to 1884," in William Pencak, Selma Berrol, and Randall M. Miller, eds., *Immigration to New York* (Philadelphia, 1991), 16.

12. John S. Billings, *Vital Statistics of New York and Brooklyn* (Washington, D.C., 1894), tables 5 and 80, 6, 238–41. Cited in David C. Hammack, *Power and Society: Greater New York at the Turn of the Century* (New York, 1982), 213.

13. The Greater New York Charter created a city of five boroughs: Manhattan, Brooklyn, the Bronx, Queens, and Staten Island.

14. Hugh McLeod, "Catholicism and the New York Irish, 1880–1910," in Jim Obelkevich, Lyndal Roper, and Raphael Samuel, eds., *Disciplines of Faith: Studies in Religion, Politics, and Patriarchy* (New York, 1987), 337–38.

15. The unskilled character of New York Irish labor from 1880 to 1890 is discussed in Hammack, *Power and Society,* 66, 84, 86. In 1900, 25 percent of Irish males in Manhattan and the Bronx were unskilled workers, 75 percent were unskilled, semiskilled, and skilled manual laborers. See Hugh McLeod, "Catholicism and the New York Irish," 338.

16. For my comments on the employment and married lives of Irish American women I have relied on Hasia Diner, *Erin's Daughters in America: Irish Immigrant Women in the Nineteenth Century* (Baltimore, 1983).

17. Seymour J. Mandelbaum, *Boss Tweed's New York* (Chicago, 1990), details the social conditions that prevailed in New York's working-class neighborhoods in the early 1870s. Gangs are a topic in Richard O'Connor, *Hell's Kitchen* (New York, 1958). He discusses social problems, turbulence, and tribulations in perhaps the toughest New York Irish neighborhood. Germans shared Hell's Kitchen with the Irish and often married them. Many of the Hell's Kitchen Irish fought with the Fighting 69th (165th infantry) in World War I. Three were Congressional Medal of Honor winners. Father Francis P. Duffy, pastor of Holy Cross parish, was their chaplain.

18. Iver Bernstein, *New York City Draft Riots: Their Significance for American Society in the Age of the Civil War* (New York, 1990); and Michael A. Gordon, *The Orange Riots: Irish Political Violence in New York City, 1870 and 1871* (Ithaca, 1993). Bernstein and Gordon emphasize Irish riots as a proletarian protest against Anglo-American Protestant elites and indicate they have significance for future working-class movements. Both may be exaggerating the political sophistication and class consciousness of a people not far removed from Famine Ireland.

19. Hammack, *Power and Society*, 144, 287, 315, and 317, describes anti-Catholicism among New York elites during the period under discussion in this overview. Bernstein and Gordon, *The Orange Riots*, focus on upper- and middle-class New York anti-Catholicism. Anti-Irish caricatures are described and analyzed in John J. and Selma Appel, *The Distorted Image*, New York, Anti-Defamation League of B'nai B'rith, a slide collection with comments containing examples of negative newspaper and periodical cartoons of Irish Americans.

20. McLeod, "Catholicism and the New York Irish," 344–49 argues that although Catholicism alleviated the misery of poverty, it was not an opiate for the New York Irish. Quite often the very poor were so demoralized that they turned away from religion and sought escape in sin and vice. He attributes the strength of Catholicism among the New York Irish to an ethnic loyalty to the faith, respect for the clergy, and a realization that their religion encouraged moral discipline and values contributing to social mobility and respectability.

21. In the 1860s probably about 40 percent of New York Catholics attended mass on Sunday. See Jay Dolan, *The Immigrant Church: New York's Irish and German Catholics, 1815–1865* (Baltimore, 1975), 56–57. Dolan also discusses the religious ignorance and indifference of many early Irish Catholic immigrants. McLeod, "Catholicism and the New York Irish," 38, says that in 1900 some 90 percent of the New York Irish were Catholic, and 90 percent of them were parish affiliated. He emphasizes the devotionalism of the New York Irish and suggests that their attendance at mass in 1902 probably exceeded the general 50 percent figure for all New York Catholics.

22. Irish responses to parochial and public school education in New York and their role as educators are discussed in Howard Ralph Weisz, *Irish-American and Italian-American Educational Views and Activities, 1870–1900: A Comparison* (New York, 1976).

23. Jay Dolan, *The American Catholic Experience* (New York, 1985), 326.

24. The social and economic views of the American Catholic hierarchy are the subject of James Edmund Roohan, *American Catholics and the Social Question, 1865–1900* (New York, 1976).

25. Robert Emmet Curran, *Michael Augustine Corrigan and the Shaping of Conservative Catholicism in America, 1878–1902* (New York, 1978), 385–86. It was not until Monsignor John A. Ryan in *A Living Wage: Its Ethical and Economic Aspects* (New York, 1906), and *Distributive Justice: The Right and Wrong of Our Present Distribution of Wealth* (New York, 1916), and later as Head of the National Catholic Welfare Conference,

authoring a social justice agenda for the American hierarchy, that papal encyclicals were given an American relevance. Garry Wills, in *Bare Ruined Choirs* (New York, 1972), 38–56, shows how papal encyclicals on social issues were actually more conservative than many Catholic liberals believed them to be and had to be reinterpreted for a meaningful social justice message in the urban-industrial world.

26. For information on conflicts within the hierarchy over labor, Americanism, and other issues see Roohan, *American Catholics*; Henry J. Browne, *The Catholic Church and the Knights of Labor* (New York, 1976); Marvin O'Connell, *John Ireland and the American Catholic Church* (St. Paul, 1988); Robert Emmett Curran, *Michael Augustine Corrigan and the Shaping of Conservative Catholicism in America, 1878–1902*; Gerald P. Fogarty, *The Vatican and the American Hierarchy from 1870 to 1965* (Wilmington, Del., 1985); and Robert D. Cross, *The Emergence of Liberal Catholicism in America* (Cambridge, Mass., 1958).

27. According to Fergus O'Ferrall, *Catholic Emancipation: Daniel O'Connell and the Birth of Irish Democracy, 1820–1830* (Dublin, 1985), 277, O'Connell and Andrew Jackson deserve shared credit for putting political democracy into action.

28. Erie, *Rainbow's End*, 61, 62–63, 89–90, 241–42, 246.

29. Kelly's time as Tammany boss is discussed in Alfred Connable and Edward Silberfarb, *Tigers of Tammany: Nine Men Who Ruled New York* (New York, 1967), 173–96.

30. Connable and Silberfarb, 197–230. Croker's career is clearly the model for the main character in Ramona Stewart's *Casey* (Boston, 1968). It offers an interesting fictional insight into Irish New York from Tweed through Croker.

31. Hammack, *Power and Society*, 110–45, discusses Swallow Tail influences in New York politics. On the limitations of Tammany's power see Martin Shefter, "The Electoral Foundations of the Political Machine; New York City, 1884–1897," in Joel H. Silbey, Allan G. Bogue, and William H. Flanigan, eds., *The History of American Political Behavior* (Princeton, 1978), 263–79.

32. Bocock's complaints are contained in "The Irish Conquest of Our Cities," *Forum* 17 (1894). Roosevelt described first-generation Irish Catholics in the Assembly as "low, venal, corrupt and unintelligent brutes." This quotation is cited by Gronowicz, "Labor's Decline," 16. It is taken from Elting Morrison, ed., *The Letters of Theodore Roosevelt* (Cambridge, Mass., 1951), 2: 1470.

33. Gronowicz, "Labor's Decline," 18.

34. Daniel Czitrom, "Underworlds and Underdogs: Big Tim Sullivan and Metropolitan Politics in New York, 1889–1913," *Journal of American History* 78 (Sept. 1991): 536–58.

35. For a diary-explained day in the life of Plunkitt see William L. Riordan, *Plunkitt of Tammany Hall* (New York, 1963), 91–93.

36. For book length treatments of Fenianism see R. V. Comerford, *The Fenians in Context: Irish Politics and Society* (Atlantic Highlands, N.J., 1985); William D'Arcy, *The Fenian Movement in the United States, 1858–1886* (Washington, D.C., 1947); Maurice Harmon, ed., *Fenians and Fenianism* (Seattle, 1970); and T. W. Moody, ed., *The Fenian Movement* (Cork, 1968). Thomas Flanagan's novel, *The Tenants of Time* (New York, 1988), presents interesting and perceptive Fenian portraits in Ireland and America.

37. Thomas N. Brown, in "The Origins and Character of Irish-American Nationalism," *The Review of Politics* 58 (July, 1956): 327–58, emphasizes the respectability quest of late nineteenth-century Irish American nationalism.

38. Joseph Edward Cuddy, in *Irish-America and National Isolationism, 1914–1920* (New York, 1976), shows how Irish American nationalism offended American Protestant

nativism. Francis M. Carroll, *American Opinion and the Irish Question, 1910–1923* (New York, 1978), is a comprehensive study of American reactions to the 1912–14 home rule crisis, the Easter Week Rebellion, and the Anglo-Irish and Civil wars.

39. On the life and opinions of Patrick Ford see James Paul Rodechko, *Patrick Ford and His Search for America: A Case Study of Irish-American Journalism, 1870–1913* (New York, 1976).

40. The New York origins of the New Departure are discussed in Thomas N. Brown, *Irish-American Nationalism, 1870–1890* (Philadelphia, 1966), 85–98. T. W. Moody, *Davitt and Irish Revolution, 1847–1882* (Oxford, 1981), is the best biographical study of Davitt.

41. For studies of the land war see Paul Bew, *Land and the National Question in Ireland, 1858–82* (Dublin, 1978); Samuel Clark, *Social Origins of the Land War* (Princeton, 1979); Charles Townshend, *Political Violence in Ireland: Government and Resistance Since 1848* (New York, 1983); and W. E. Vaughn, *Landlords and Tenants in Ireland, 1848–1904* (Dublin, 1984).

42. Maureen Murphy, "*The Gael:* 1881–1904," *An Gael* (Spring 1984): 20–22. Professor Murphy permitted me to examine *The Gael* in her personal library.

43. "Racial" connotations in British anti-Irish Catholic prejudice is the theme of L. P. Curtis Jr., *Anglo-Saxons and Celts: A Case Study of Anti-Irish Prejudice in Victorian England* (Bridgeport, Conn., 1968); and Richard Ned Lebow, *White Britain and Black Ireland: The Influence of Stereotypes on Colonial Policy* (Philadelphia, 1976). British Anglo-Saxon depictions of the Neanderthal, ape-like Irish influenced American academic, journalist, and public opinion. For cartoon depictions of simian-featured Irish brutes see John J. and Selma Appel, *The Distorted Image.* Negative Irish portraits in American literature are the subject of Stephen Garrett Bolger, *The Irish Character in American Fiction, 1830–1860* (New York, 1976). The subject is also discussed in Charles Fanning, *The Irish Voice in America: Irish-American Fiction from the 1760s to the 1980s* (Lexington, Ky., 1990).

44. Fanning, *The Irish Voice in America*, 167–76.

45. Robert Emmet Curran, "The McGlynn Affair and the Shaping of the New Conservatism in American Catholicism," *Catholic Historical Review* 66 (Apr. 1980): 184–204. Roohan, *American Catholics*, 332–83.

46. For a description and analysis of the 1886 contest for mayor see Brown, *Irish-American Nationalism*, 147–51.

47. The intrusion of Irish nationalism into American politics is treated in ibid., 153–77; and Joseph Patrick O'Grady, *Irish-Americans and Anglo-American Relations, 1880–1888* (New York, 1976).

48. David Montgomery, "The Irish and the American Labor Movement," in David Noel Doyle and Owen Dudley Edwards, eds., *America and Ireland, 1776–1976: The American Identity and the Irish Connection* (Westport, Conn., 1980), 206.

49. Michael Gordon, "Irish Immigrant Culture and the Labor Boycott in New York City, 1880–1886," in Richard L. Ehrlich, ed., *Immigrants in Industrial America, 1850–1920* (Charlottesville, Va., 1977), 111–22. The word "boycott" originated in an 1880 application of a Land League shunning strategy suggested by Charles Stewart Parnell to those who worked on a County Mayo estate managed by a Captain Charles Cunningham Boycott. Irish immigrant nationalists who fought in the Anglo-Irish War (1919–21) and the Irish Civil War (1922–23) were even more radical than those of the late nineteenth century. According to Joshua Freeman, they cooperated with Communists in the creation of the New York Transport Workers Union. See Joshua B. Freeman, "Catholics, Communists, and Republicans: Irish Workers and the Organization of the Transport Workers Union," in

Michael H. Frisch and Daniel J. Walkowitz, eds., *Working Class America: Essays on Labor, Community, and American Society* (Urbana, Ill., 1983), 256–83.

50. Erie, *Rainbow's End*, 50. Herbert Hill claims that before 1930 Irish and Jewish leaders in the American Federation of Labor protected white ethnics at the expense of African, Asian, and Hispanic Americans. See his "Race and Ethnicity in Organized Labor: The Historical Sources for Resistance to Affirmative Action," in Winston A. Van Horne and Thomas V. Tonneson, eds., *Ethnicity and the Work Force* (Madison, 1985).

51. The revitalization of Tammany is the theme of Shefter, "Electoral Foundations of the Political Machine," 281–98. Shefter gives much of the credit of example to Purroy, but Czitrom's essay on Sullivan, "Underworlds and Underdogs," shows that "Big Tim" also deserves a great deal.

52. Nancy Joan Weiss, *Charles Francis Murphy, 1858–1924: Respectability and Responsibility in Tammany Politics* (Northampton, Mass., 1968); and Connable and Silberfarb, *Tigers of Tammany*, 231–68.

53. Erie, *Rainbow's End*, 1–106. For other discussions of Tammany's resistance to significant social and economic change consult Hammack, *Power and Society*, 109–81; and William V. Shannon, *The American Irish* (New York, 1963), 66–85.

54. For defenses of Irish political machines as inclusive see Joseph Huthmacher, "Urban Liberalism and the Age of Reform," *Mississippi Valley Historical Review* 49 (1962): 231–41; John B. Buenker, *Urban Liberalism and Progressive Reform* (New York, 1973); Robert Dahl, *Who Governs? Democracy and Power in an American City* (New Haven, 1961); and Elmer E. Cornwell, "Bosses, Machines, and Ethnic Groups," *Annals* 353 (May 1964): 27–39.

55. For a detailed examination of intellectual activities at St. Joseph's Seminary and the Modernist issue in the church see R. Scott Appleby, *"Church and Age Unite!": The Modernist Impulse in American Catholicism* (Notre Dame, 1992); and Dolan, *The American Catholic Experience*, 304–20.

56. Hammack, *Power and Society*, tables 3-7, 85. Although the social mobility of the New York Irish was slower than in some Midwest and West Coast cities, in 1880 it was second best to Baltimore in the East. But the situation in Brooklyn was worse than any major American urban center except Jersey City. See JoEllen McNergney Vinyard, *The Irish on the Urban Frontier: Detroit 1850–1880* (New York, 1976), table IX, 315–16. For information on the Irish labor force involved in building the Brooklyn Bridge see David McCullough, *The Great Bridge* (New York, 1972).

57. For a fictional description of the dark side of Irish tenement life in the 1890s see James W. Sullivan, *Tenement Tales of New York* (New York, 1895).

58. Brown, *Irish-American Nationalism*, 57.

59. Ralph Weisz discusses tensions between the Irish and Italians in *Irish-American and Italian American Educational Views and Activities*. See also Mary Elizabeth Brown, "'The Adoption of the Tactics of the Enemy': The Care of Italian Immigrant Youth in the Archdiocese of New York During the Progressive Era," in *Immigration to New York*, 109–25. Ronald H. Bayor, *Neighbors in Conflict: The Irish, Germans, Jews, and Italians of New York City, 1929–1941* (Baltimore, 1978), describes how the Great Depression inflamed old ethnic and religious antagonism in New York, greatly intensifying Irish anti-Semitism.

60. Hammack, *Power and Society*, tables 3–7, 85.

61. Already in 1870, according to the census, 17 percent of all contractors in the United States were born in Ireland, which was three times as many Englishmen or Germans. Montgomery, "The Irish and the American Labor Movement," 211.

62. Hammack, *Power and Society*, table 3–1, 67.

63. Blessing, "The Irish," 532.

64. Weisz, *Educational Views*, table 1, 83.

65. Diner, *Erin's Daughters in America*, 120–38.

66. The subject of the disproportionately large number of Irish and German players in the early days of professional baseball is treated in Stephen A. Reiss, *Touching Base: Professional Baseball and American Culture in the Progressive Era* (Westport, Conn., 1980), 184–87. In *The Bill James Historical Baseball Abstract* (New York, 1986), 8–59, the author credits the Irish with baseball predominance from 1870 to 1900, especially in the 1890s; as does Peter C. Bjarkman in "Forgotten Americans and the National Pastime: Literature on Baseball's Ethnic, Racial, and Religious Diversity," *Multi-Cultural Review* 1 (Apr. 1992): 46–48. For baseball lineups I referred to *The Baseball Encyclopedia: The Complete and Official Records of Major League Baseball* (New York, 1976).

67. John McCabe, *George M. Cohan: The Man Who Owned Broadway* (New York, 1973), 22, 67. The Irish in vaudeville get some attention in Robert W. Snyder, *The Voice of the City: Vaudeville and Popular Culture in New York* (New York, 1989).

68. Maureen Murphy, "Irish-American Theatre," in Maxine Schwartz Seller, ed., *Ethnic Theatre in the United States* (Westport, Conn., 1983), 221–35, is an interesting and informative brief study of Irish American theater.

69. For my comments on songs of and about the Irish I am indebted to William H. A. Williams's "From Lost Land to Emerald Isle: Ireland and the Irish in American Sheet Music, 1800–1920," *Eire-Ireland* 26 (Spring 1991): 19–45.

70. Ibid., 45.

71. In the film, *Yankee Doodle Dandy*, President Franklin D. Roosevelt (actor Captain Jack Young) tells Cohan (actor James Cagney), "That's one thing I've always admired about you Irish-Americans. You carry your love of country like a flag, right out in the open. It's a great quality." Joseph M. Curran, *Hibernian Green on the Silver Screen: The Irish and American Movies* (Westport, Conn., 1989), 87.

72. In a well-written, comprehensive, and informative study of the background of Irish immigrants and their American experience Kerby A. Miller, *Emigrants and Exiles: Ireland and the Irish Exodus to North America* (New York, 1985) concludes that the fatalistic and communalistic features of Catholic and Gaelic psychology handicapped the Irish in the United States. In individualistic, capitalistic, and competitive America they felt themselves aliens, exiles from the land of their birth. Nationalism was a cry of anguish and a search for revenge against a Britain that forced their exodus. Miller's main source of information for the immigrant's state of mind is letters that they sent back to Ireland. The problem with this evidence is that it is only partial. Many immigrants did not write home. Those who were least successful probably were the ones who sent complaints home to parents and siblings. And most people writing to fathers, mothers, sisters, brothers, and friends from a long distance are bound to say something sentimental about former homes. Another problem with Miller's thesis is the difficulty in determining degrees of alienation. Did the Irish feel any more uncomfortable in urban industrial America than other ethnics, African Americans from the South, Anglo-Protestant migrants from the country, or even those who had lived in the cities for generations and watched their Irish conquest? We do know that in comparison with other immigrants from Europe the Irish were one of the least likely to return home. Donald Harman Akenson in *The Irish Diaspora: A Primer* (Toronto, 1993), examines the Irish immigrant experience in New Zealand, Australia, South Africa, the British Empire, Britain, Canada, and the United States and decides that Catholic and other Old World influences had no real effect on their occupational and social mobility. His evidence, together with what

he gleans from other scholars, shows that educational and skill limitations, not religion, might have temporarily delayed Irish Catholic immigrant progress, but very quickly they caught up to British and Irish Protestants wherever they went. Akenson also says that he cannot detect any unusual feelings of exile or alienation among various branches of the Irish diaspora.

Chapter 9: GOING TO THE LADIES' FAIR (McDannell)

I would like to thank Lauren Blough, Marion Casey, Richard Ouellette, the New York Irish History Roundtable, and the priests of the Manhattan parishes who all helped make this essay possible.

1. According to Jay Dolan in *The American Catholic Experience* (New York, 1985), 143 f., the Irish accounted for less that 50 percent of the Catholic population in 1900, but 62 percent of the bishops were Irish. Most major urban centers had Irish bishops. Sociologist Andrew Greeley describes the Irish "church" in *That Most Distressful Nation: The Taming of the American Irish* (Chicago, 1972), 62–94, and Irish-American Catholicism in most of his novels. See also Ellen Horgan Biddle, "The American Catholic Irish Family," in Charles H. Mindel and Robert W. Habernstein, eds., *Ethnic Families in America: Patterns and Variations* (New York, 1976), 89–123. Perhaps the most popular current novelist exploring Irish American spirituality is Mary Gordon. On music, see Thomas Day, *Why Catholics Can't Sing: The Culture of Catholicism and the Triumph of Bad Taste* (New York, 1991).

2. Perry Miller, *The New England Mind* (New York, 1939); Amanda Porterfield, *Female Piety in Puritan New England: The Emergence of Religious Humanism* (New York, 1992). Porterfield's contribution to Puritan studies is only one among many fine monographs. The diversity of the field may be captured by citing David D. Hall's popular culture analysis, *World's of Wonder, Days of Judgment: Popular Religious Belief in Early New England* (Cambridge, Mass., 1989); Edmund Leites's psychohistorical analysis of English Puritans, *The Puritan Conscience and Modern Sexuality* (New Haven, 1986); and Sacavan Bercovitch's literary analysis, *The Puritan Origins of the American Self* (New Haven, 1975).

3. Leslie Woodcock Tentler, "On the Margins: The State of American Catholic History," *American Quarterly* 45 (1993): 104–27. Major studies on ethnicity and religion were published during the late 1960s and 1970s. They include Rudolf J. Vecoli, "Prelates and Peasants: Italian Immigrants and the Catholic Church," *Journal of Social History* 2 (Spring 1969): 217–68; Jay P. Dolan, *The Immigrant Church: New York's Irish and German Catholics, 1815–1865* (Notre Dame, Ind., 1975), which is based on a 1971 dissertation; Randall Miller and T. D. Marzik, *Immigrants and Religion in Urban America* (Philadelphia, 1977); Timothy L. Smith, "Religion and Ethnicity in America," *American Historical Review* 83 (1978): 1155–85; and Paul Wrobel, *Our Way: Family, Parish, and Neighborhood in a Polish-American Community* (Notre Dame, 1979). Recent research includes Robert A. Orsi, *The Madonna of 115th Street: Faith and Community in Italian Harlem, 1880–1950* (New Haven, 1985); Timothy J. Meagher, ed., *Urban American Catholicism* (New York, 1988); John Joseph Parot, *Polish Catholics in Chicago, 1850–1920* (De Kalb, Ill., 1981); and my own articles, "True Men As We Need Them: Catholicism and the Irish Male," *American Studies* 27 (1986): 19–36, and "'The Devil was the First Protestant': Gender and Intolerance in Irish Catholic Fiction," *U.S. Catholic Historian* 8 (1986): 19–36. Dolores Liptak, *Immigrants and Their Church* (New York, 1989), provides a summary of secondary sources.

4. James S. Olson, *Catholic Immigrants in America* (Chicago, 1987), 28.

5. By 1860 the archdiocese of New York had the largest Catholic population of any diocese in the country, but very little has been written about it, leaving the scholar to work from primary sources. Dolan's *Immigrant Church* is an excellent critical study of the 1815–65 period. Nineteenth-century descriptions may be found in John Gilmary Shea, *The Catholic Churches of New York City*, 2 vols. (New York, 1878); and John Talbot Smith, *The Catholic Church in New York* (New York, 1908). Robert Emmet Curran, *Michael Augustine Corrigan and the Shaping of Conservative Catholicism in America, 1878–1902* (New York, 1978), deals with the McGlynn controversy but has little on parish life. For a more social history orientation, see Hugh McLeod, "Catholicism and the New York Irish 1880–1910," in Jim Obelkevich et al., eds., *Disciplines of Faith: Studies in Religion, Politics and Patriarchy* (London, 1987), 337–50; Florence D. Cohalan, *A Popular History of the Archdiocese of New York* (Yonkers, 1983); James F. Donnelly, "Catholic New Yorkers and the New York Socialists, 1870–1920" (Ph.D. diss., New York University, 1982); and Joseph J. Casino, "From Sanctuary to Involvement: A History of the Catholic Parish in the Northeast," in Jay P. Dolan, ed., *The American Catholic Parish* (Mahwah, N.J., 1987).

6. Beverly Gordon, "Playing at Being Powerless: New England Ladies' Fairs, 1830–1930," *Massachusetts Review* 27 (1986): 147.

7. Mary A. Livermore, *My Story of the War* (New York, 1972), 410–57. See also Sylvia G. L. Dannett, ed., *Noble Women of the North* (New York, 1959), 276–80; and Harold Earl Hammond, ed., *Diary of a Union Lady, 1861–1865* (New York, 1962), 278–87. On women and fund-raising see Lori D. Ginzberg, *Women and the Work of Benevolence: Morality, Politics, and Class in the Nineteenth-Century United States* (New Haven, 1990). On world's fairs, see Robert W. Rydell, *All the World's a Fair: Visions of Empire at American International Expositions, 1876–1916* (Chicago, 1984).

8. *New York Weekly Register and Catholic Diary*, Dec. 6, 1834.

9. *Metropolitan Record*, Dec. 17, 1859: "Those who remember the fair at the Crystal Palace will not neglect the opportunity of visiting the one now going on [at the Academy of Music for Catholic charities]." On the Crystal Palace and the trade fair as the chief vehicle for the display of manufactured goods before the advent of the department store, see Miles Orvell, *The Real Thing: Imitation and Authenticity in American Culture, 1880–1940* (Chapel Hill, N.C., 1989), 25–27.

10. Ginzberg, *Women and the Work of Benevolence*, 168.

11. On the American Institute Fair, see *New York Times*, Oct. 23, Nov. 4, and Nov. 7, 1878. On the Dairy Fair, *New York Times*, Nov. 25, 1878.

12. "Methodist Church Fair," *New York Times*, Dec. 14, 1878; and "Some Hints for Charity Fairs," *Harper's Bazaar* 12 (1879): 790 f.

13. Since the practice of Catholicism was strictly controlled by the British, fund-raising before the nineteenth century was informal. See Patrick Corish, *The Irish Catholic Experience: A Historical Survey* (Wilmington, Del., 1985), 106–70; and Sean J. Connolly, *Priests and People in Pre-Famine Ireland, 1780–1845* (New York, 1982), 94 f. Pre-Reformation English parishes raised money from wills, church dinners, and periodic collections. Pew rents did not become popular until the sixteenth century. See Francis Aidan Gasquet, *Parish Life in Mediaeval England* (New York, 1907), 127–33.

14. Emmet Larkin, "Economic Growth, Capital Investment, and the Roman Catholic Church in Nineteenth-Century Ireland," in *The Historical Dimensions of Irish Catholicism* (Washington, D.C., 1984), 27. On church building in nineteenth-century Ireland see Desmond Keenan, *The Catholic Church in Nineteenth Century Ireland: A Sociological Study* (Totowa, N.J., 1983), 115–25. Michael McCarthy mentions that one

bazaar raised £30,000 for the Cathedral of Armagh, *Priests and People in Ireland* (London, 1906), 17.

15. Gordon, "Playing at Being Powerless," 160, quoting *The Gentlewoman's Magazine*.

16. *Catholic Herald*, Apr. 19, 1879. This issue of the *Catholic Herald* also mentions that St. Ann's Charity Fair will be held in Ferrero's Assembly Rooms, Apr. 19, 1879. See also "Grand Fair in Tammany Hall," *New York Tablet*, Oct. 24, 1868.

17. *Centennial Anniversary, Church of St. James, 1827–1927* (privately printed, no pagination).

18. "Persuasion and Argument," *Journal of the Fair for St. Patrick's Cathedral*, found at St. Teresa's Church, New York City. "Regiment of Soldiers," *Journal of St. James Fair* (privately printed in 1886).

19. Occupational information is from *Trow's New York City Directory* for the year ending May 1, 1879.

20. *The Catholic Herald*, Dec. 20, 1879.

21. (Cathedral) *Journal of the Fair for St. Patrick's Cathedral*; (St. James) *Journal of St. James Fair*; (St. Agnes) *Catholic Herald*, Dec. 20, 1879; (St. Lawrence) *Catholic Herald*, May 10, 1879.

22. (St. Francis Xavier) *Catholic Herald*, Dec. 6, 1879. (St. Lawrence) *Catholic Herald*, May 10, 1879. The *Catholic Herald* reported on Nov. 2, 1878, "After entering by the main entrance [of the Cathedral] on Fifth Avenue, the first exhibit that meets the eye is the historical little lamb that Mary had, now grown to a good old age, but still showing the gentle care of its mistress in the well-combed wool and pink ribbons which adorn its neck, enclosed in a wooden cage. Mary has shown her loyalty to the church by offering it for sale."

23. *Journal of the Fair for St. Patrick's Cathedral.*

24. (St. Lawrence) *Catholic Herald*, May 10, 1879; (St. James) *Journal of St. James Fair*; (Cathedral) *Journal of the Fair for St. Patrick's Cathedral*; (St. Francis Xavier) *Catholic Herald*, Dec. 6, 1879; (St. Gabriel) *Catholic Herald*, Oct. 25, 1879; (St. Teresa) *Catholic Herald*, Oct. 25, 1879.

25. On Dec. 11, 1869, St. Anthony of Padua's church had a fair reported in the *New York Tablet*. Although St. Anthony's would eventually become an Italian parish, at this point the women who ran the fair were Irish-surnamed. Half of the men involved were Italian and the other half Irish. While religious goods were exhibited, there were no goods of either Italian or Irish origins. Likewise, St. Alphonsus, a German and Irish parish, had major fairs in 1876, 1880, 1882, and 1886. An unusual New York parish, St. Alphonsus, displayed both German and "Irish" flags and blessed a statue of St. Patrick in 1873, but still had a separate First Communion service for German speaking children as late as 1881. See Francis X. Murphy, *The Centennial History of Saint Alphonsus Parish* (New York City, 1947).

26. (St. Teresa) *Catholic Herald*, Oct. 25, 1879; (St. Lawrence) *Catholic Herald*, May 10, 1879.

27. (St. Francis Xavier) *Catholic Herald*, Dec. 18, 1880; (St. Lawrence) *Catholic Herald*, May 10, 1879; (Cathedral) *Journal of the Fair for St. Patrick's Cathedral*; (St. Agnes) *Catholic Herald*, Dec. 20, 1879; (St. Bernard) *Catholic Herald*, Nov. 28, 1880.

28. *New York Times*, Nov. 13, 1878.

29. *Catholic Herald*, Nov. 16, 1878.

30. (St. Rose) *Catholic Herald*, May 7, 1879; (St. Bridget's) *Catholic Herald*, Dec. 13, 1879; (St. Alphonsus) Francis X. Murphy, *The Centennial History of Saint Alphonsus Parish*, 30–35.

31. (St. Bernard) *Catholic Herald*, Feb. 8, 1879. (Holy Cross) *Catholic Herald*, Dec. 7, 1878.

32. Richard L. Burtsell Diary, Nov. 14, 1875.

33. These statistics have been gathered from *Guide to Vital Statistics in the City of New York, Borough of Manhattan, Churches* (New York, 1942).

34. *Catholic News*, Oct. 4, 1899.

35. In 1923, in an essay entitled the "Splendor of External Worship," St. Agnes's pastor John Chidwick wrote: "Religion must follow in the footsteps of the works of God and by appealing to man's senses as well as to the faculties of his soul, lift him up to his Maker in body and soul." For Father Chidwick, the Protestant reformers had "humiliated Christ to exalt themselves and robbed the house of God to embellish their own palaces." As cited in *The Golden Jubilee of Saint Agnes' Parish, New York City, 1873–1923* (New York, 1923).

36. Dolan, *Immigrant Church*, 263.

37. Henry J. Browne, *The Parish of Saint Michael, 1857–1957* (New York, 1957), 36.

38. In 1870 there were 27 Manhattan parishes sponsoring parochial schools as separate from "select" or private schools. Catholic education was divided by sex, with nuns teaching girls and young boys and Brothers (or more rarely priests) teaching older boys. In New York, 15 schools (56% of all parochial schools) were staffed by Sisters of Charity; 12 schools (44%) employed the Brothers of the Christian School. By 1890, there were 49 parishes with such schools. Twenty-three schools (47%) were staffed by Sisters of Charity, and 15 schools (31%) employed the Brothers of the Christian Schools. The rest of the schools (1% in 1870 and 24% by 1890) were staffed by a variety of religious orders, often of the same national origins as the parishioners.

39. St. James' Home was founded in 1878 and run by the Sisters of Charity. In 1883 a fair was held to pay off the debt the sisters had incurred when they made alterations to their building and heating. *Centennial Anniversary, Church of Saint James, 1827–1927* .

40. St. Paul the Apostle, *Calendar*, May 1892, 15 (Paulist Archives, Washington, D.C.). Henry A. Brann (pastor of St. Ann's) to Archbishop John M. Farley, Oct. 2, 1905. Father Brann was writing on behalf of a Mrs. Borden who wanted to have Franciscan nuns start a day nursery in her neighborhood, for which she would provide funds (New York Archdiocesan Archives).

41. J. H. McMahon to Cardinal John M. Farley, Nov. 29, 1904 (Archdiocese of New York Archives).

42. "New York City Church Debts," *Christian Advocate*, Jan. 31, 1878.

43. St. Paul's *Calendar* for the year 1894. In 1885 St. Francis Xavier parish calendar noted that "the seats are all free except at 8, 9 and 11. There are, however, some free seats provided at every Mass." Free seating for adults was at the 5:00, 5:30, 6:00, 6:30, 7:00, and 7:30 morning masses.

44. The church used both the English (Bridget) and Irish (Brigid) spelling. *Souvenir of the Consecration Year of St. Bridget Church, 1849–1889* (New York, 1889), 40.

45. Ibid., 31.

46. Church of St. James, New York City, 1890 Financial Record.

47. On the connection between piety, consumerism, and Victorian domesticity, see Colleen McDannell, *The Christian Home in Victorian America, 1840–1900* (Bloomington, Ind., 1986); and Andrew R. Heinze, *Adapting to Abundance: Jewish Immigrants, Mass Consumption, and the Search for American Identity* (New York, 1990).

48. Father Henry Brann, "The Theology of the Fair," *Journal of the Fair for St. Patrick's Cathedral.*

49. *St. Paul's Monthly Calendar*, Sept. 1891, 7.

50. *Journal of St. James Fair.*

51. *Centennial Anniversary, Church of Saint James.*

52. McDannell, *The Christian Home in Victorian America*, 42.

53. On St. Therese see Barbara Corrado Pope, "A Heroine without Heroics: The Little Flower of Jesus and Her Times," *Church History* 57 (1986): 46–60. On devotion to St. Jude see Robert A. Orsi, "'He Keeps Me Going': Women's Devotion to Saint Jude Thaddeus and the Dialectics of Gender in American Catholicism, 1929–1965," in Thomas Kselman, ed., *Belief in History: Innovative Approaches to European and American Religion* (Notre Dame, Ind., 1991), 137–169.

54. Hasia R. Diner, *Erin's Daughters in America* (Baltimore, 1983), 140.

55. Statistics assembled from the "Mission Chronicle" in the Paulist Archives. The Paulists divided their missions between men, women, and children. The priests counted the number of people going to confession and communion. Sometimes they also counted the numbers of unmarried men or women.

56. "Mission Chronicle," Holy Innocents, Dec. 9–23, 1888 (Paulist Archives).

57. In the Jan. 31, 1887, weekly meeting notes of the St. Vincent de Paul Society, the secretary notes that the "investigating committee" on poor families gave funding to "Mary Ryan husb + 4," "Eliza Murphy husb + 2," and "Mrs. Collins family of 5 persons" (Minutes at St. Teresa's Church, Manhattan).

58. This discussion of St. Patrick's Day parades is based on Timothy J. Meagher, "Why Should We Care for a Little Trouble or a Walk in the Mud: St Patrick's Day and Columbus Day Parades in Worcester, Massachusetts, 1845–1915," *New England Quarterly* 58 (1985): 5–26; Colleen McDannell, "True Men As We Need Them: Catholicism and the Irish Male," *American Studies* 27 (1986): 19–36; and Sallie A. Marston, "Public Rituals and Community Power: St. Patrick's Day Parades in Lowell, Massachusetts, 1841–1874," *Political Geography Quarterly* 8 (1989): 255–69.

59. Henry J. Brown, *St. Ann's on East Twelfth Street, New York City, 1852–1952* (New York, 1952), 38.

Chapter 10: THE IRISH LANGUAGE IN NEW YORK (Nilsen)

I would like to express my gratitude to the New York Irish History Roundtable and the Irish American Cultural Institute for grants in support of the research for this paper.

1. Allan Nevins and Milton Halsey Thomas, eds., *The Diary of George Templeton Strong* (New York, 1952), 348. The Irishmen were apparently Michael Dugan and John Dougherty. For mention of the accident, see *Irish-American*, July 18, 1857, 3, and *New York Daily Times*, July 7, 1857, 5.

2. D. N. Doyle, *Irish Americans, Native Rights and National Empires: The Structure, Attitudes and Division of the Catholic Minority in the Decade of Expansion, 1890–1901* (New York, 1976), 32n. 63. Doyle estimates that from 1851 to 1855 approximately 28 percent of all emigrants were Irish-speaking. Kerby A. Miller estimates that 27.1 percent of Irish emigrants between 1851 and 1855 were Irish-speaking; see *Emigrants and Exiles* (New York, 1988), 580. John Ridge also gives an estimate of 28 percent in a paper given to the New York Irish Teachers' Association in 1983.

3. D. Doyle, quoted by Stiofán Ó hAnnracháin, in *Go Meiriceá Siar* (Baile Átha Cliath, 1979), 10.

4. Garrett Fitzgerald, "Estimates for Baronies of Minimum Level of Irish-speaking amongst Successive Decennial Cohorts: 1771–1781 to 1861–1871," *Proceedings of the Royal Irish Academy* 84, C, no. 3 (1984): 118.

5. See, for instance, O'Brien's *A Hidden Phase of American History* (New York, 1919),159–60, 259, and *Pioneer Irish in New England* (New York, 1937), 39, 46, 237.

6. Quoted from the *Irish World* in *Irish Book Lover* 18 (1930): 29. See also R. R. Madden, *Ireland in '98: Sketches of the Principal Men of the Time*, ed. J. B. Daly (London, 1888), 367. Madden received this information from MacNeven's daughter.

7. The Irish inscription on the Emmet monument is now (1993) nearly illegible. O'Donovan Rossa gives the text in his book *Rossa's Recollections* (New York, 1898; reprinted Shannon, 1972), 400: "Do mhiannaig se ard-mhathas chum tir a bhraith [*sic*]; Do thug se clu, a's fuair se molah a dtir a bhais," for which he gives the translation: "He contemplated great good for the land of his birth. He shed lustre, and received commendation in the land of his decease." Michael J. O'Brien credits Bishop John England of Charleston, S.C., with being the composer of the Gaelic text. See O'Brien, *In Old New York: The Irish Dead in Trinity and St. Paul's Churchyards* (New York, 1928), 99.

8. The Irish text, which was beautifully executed in the Gaelic character and composed by John O'Mahony, is still perfectly legible. It reads:

> Do thogbhadh an liag-so
>   Le saethar
> A chomh-dhuthchasach agas a g-clann
>   Ag sior-chuimhniughadh
>   Ar
> UILLIAM-SHEAMAS MAC NEIMHINN,
>   Do rugadh in Eirinn
> Ar an dara la deag d'an Mharta
>   1763;
>   D'eag is an g-cathair-so
> Ar an d-treas la ar fhichead d'an Mhitheamh
>   1841.

9. Seán Ó Lúing, *O Donnabháin Rosa* (Baile Átha Cliath, 1979), 2: 200.

10. See R. Ó Foghludha, *Pádraig Phiarais Cúndún 1777–1857* (Baile Átha Cliath, 1932); and B. Ó Buachalla, "Litreacha Phádraig Phiarais Cúndún," in Ó hAnnracháin, *Go Meiriceá Siar*, 31–37. The New York Public Library has a photostat of Condon's manuscript made in 1930. The copy is bound and on the flyleaf is the following note: "Gift of Miss S. Carty, 211 Berkeley Place, Brooklyn, N.Y. Dec. 1930." The current location of the original manuscript is unknown.

11. Rossa, *Recollections*, 391–400. Rossa gives the lament "Baas Donal A Barra" in Irish with an English translation on pp. 393–95.

12. Liam Ó Buachalla, *Journal of the Cork Historical and Archaeological Society* 67, no. 205 (1962): 33. On Ó Dreada and O'Flyn, see Breandán Ó Conchúir, *Scríobhaithe Chorcaí 1700–1850* (Baile Átha Cliath, 1982), 61–63, 69–78, 234–35.

13. Seán Ó Dreada died in 1840, and presumably the family decided to come to America after that. See Ó Conchúir, *Scríobhaithe Chorcaí*, 61–63, and 97 for a photographic reproduction of a page from one of Ó Dreada's manuscripts.

14. Jeremiah O'Donovan, *A Brief Account . . .* (Pittsburgh, 1864), 165. On the Draddys, see also Séamus Ó Casaide, "Seán Ó Dreada: Irish Scribe and Sculptor," *Irish Book Lover* 22 (1934): 15; and Liam Ó Buachalla, "Some Unique Gravestone Inscriptions," *Journal of the Cork Historical and Archaeological Society* 67 (1962): 33. O'Donovan makes only a few passing references to the Irish language in the New York area. These include his use of Irish with fellow passengers while traveling up the Hudson River from New York City to Albany (101) and his meeting with Michael Burke, of whom

he writes: "Mr. Burke . . . teaches in the Orphan Asylum in Brooklyn, which is indisputably a meritorious and laudable vocation. Mr. Burke is both a scholar and poet, and composes in the Irish language admirably" (155–56).

At least a few of Burke's poems found their way into print, including "The Irish Language," in *Irish-American* (Oct. 10, 1857); laments in English and Irish for Reverend M. Coughlan, President of St. Joseph's College, Bardstown, Kentucky, who was a classmate of Burke's in Esker, County Galway, in *Irish-American*, Oct. 26, 1878; and an Irish poem on the Night of the Big Wind that appeared posthumously in the February and March 1884 issues of *An Gaodhal*.

15. Reverend M. B. Buckley, *Diary of a Tour in America*, edited by his sister Kate Buckley (Dublin, 1889), 280. Buckley also mentions meeting a Kerrywoman in the hospital on Blackwell's Island in New York Harbor "who spoke no language but Irish" (21).

16. Miller, *Emigrants and Exiles*, 22, 297, 298.

17. Richard J. Purcell "The New York Commissioners of Emigration," *Studies* 37 (Mar. 1948): 33, reprinted from the *Tipperary Vindicator*, Apr. 29, 1848.

18. Figure given by William D. Griffin, *The Book of Irish Americans* (New York, 1990), 38.

19. Laws of New York, Seventy-first Session, chap. 219. An Act for the Protection of Immigrants Arriving in the State of New York, passed Apr. 11, 1848.

20. Quoted by David Doyle, "Inimircigh Nua agus Meiriceá Tionsclaíoch 1870–1910," in Ó hAnnracháin, *Go Meiriceá Siar*, 172.

21. See Ó hAnnracháin, *Go Meiriceá Siar*, 10.

22. Miller, *Emigrants and Exiles*, 298.

23. In John T. Ridge, "The Hidden Gaeltacht in Old New York," *New York Irish History* (Journal of the New York Irish History Roundtable), 6 (1992).

24. On the use of the Irish language in Ireland by Protestant evangelical groups see numerous articles by Pádraig de Brún in recent volumes of *Éigse* and the *Journal of the Kerry Archaeological and Historical Society*. I am grateful to Professor Peter Toner for the reference to the use of Irish in New Brunswick, Canada.

25. *American and Foreign Christian Union* 1, no. 4 (1850): 183.

26. I would like to thank the staff of the Presbyterian Historical Society, Philadelphia, for providing me with a photostat copy of McNulty's report.

27. In the "Answers to Correspondents" column, the editor responded to ROD-ERICK DHU of Darten, New York: "A celtic paper, that is one printed in the ancient Irish language has never been published in this country. Several papers have from time to time made specialities of Gaelic departments giving selections and their translations. The only attempt made to introduce it into the public schools was by the school trustees of a ward in New York City without result, of course."

28. For other references to Irish-speaking native New Yorkers, see Ridge, "The Hidden Gaeltacht."

29. See T. F. O'Sullivan, *The Young Irelanders* (Tralee, 1944), appendix II, 658.

30. One of the manuscripts O'Mahony used is now Boston College Irish Manuscript No. 5 written by William Sheehan of Coolivote, Cork, in 1753. The manuscript has several notations in the hand of S[eán] O M[athghamhna] (=John O'Mahony). In the 1850s it belonged to Michael Sheehan of New York. Another of the Keating manuscripts O'Mahony used was loaned to him by a Mrs. James O'Dwyer of New York.

31. After 739 pages of English translation and notes, O'Mahony's edition concludes with the following words: Ar na chrīchnūghadh i g-cathair Brūcluinne, lāimh re h-Eborach Nuadh, le Seāghan mac Dhomhnaill, mhic Thomāis Oig na bh-Foradh Ui Mhath-

ghamhna, ō Choill Bheithne, lāimh re Sliabh Grott ris a rāidhter an Ghaillte Mhor aniu, ar an t-ochtmhadh lā dēg de mhi Iuil, is an m-bliadhain d'aeis an Tighearna 1857 (English translation is completed in the city of Brooklyn, near New York, by John, son of Daniel, son of Thomas Oge. [Thomas Oge's nickname, Na Bh-Foradh, can be translated in many ways.] O'Mahony, from Kilbeheny, near Slieve Grot, which is called the Galty more today, on the eighteenth day of July in the year of the Lord, 1857.)

32. William Smith O'Brien took up the study of Irish in his later years and attained a certain level of proficiency in the language. He also copied a number of Irish manuscripts, among them National Library of Ireland manuscript G313.

33. This contemporary account leaves out a salient point given in the obituary of P. J. Meehan, *Irish-American*, Apr. 28, 1906, 1: "The desire to revive the national language was no new fad even then with him for, as far back as 1857, he had the work in view, and as there was no Gaelic type in this country wherewith to begin the publication of a Gaelic Department in the *Irish-American*, he sent to London and had the dies and matrices made that were necessary to cast a font of type in this city."

34. The New York Irish type predated the Boston set by more than 20 years. On the Boston Gaelic type, which dates from 1879, see George E. Ryan, "The Philo-Celtic Society of Boston," *Bulletin of the Eire Society of Boston* 31, no. 3 (1972).

35. See *Irish-American*, Dec. 6, 1884, 4, which states that Colonel Michael Doheny had charge of the Gaelic Department.

36. Four of O'Mahony's Irish manuscripts are now in the National Library of Ireland (Mss. G 640–43). See Pádraig de Brún, *Lámhscríbhinní Gaeilge: Treoirliosta* (Dublin, 1988), 6–7. One of these, a copy of Keating's *History*, was used by O'Mahony when he was working on his translation. It was written by Seághan Ó Duibhidhir (John O'Dwyer) of Fethard, County Tipperary, in 1837 and belonged to Mrs. James O'Dwyer of New York, who may well have been the wife of the owner of the Daisy, a pub on Duane Street. For a partial description of these four manuscripts see S. Ó Casaide, "Seán Ó Mathghamhna's Irish MSS.," *Irish Book Lover* 18 (1930): 80–84.

37. *Daily News*, Aug. 5, 1857, quoted in *Irish-American*, Aug. 15, 1857.

38. "The Flag of the Irish Brigade," *Irish-American*, Dec. 7, 1861, 1.

39. Captain W. L. D. O'Grady in *New York at Gettysburg*, ed. William Fox (Albany, 1902), 2: 511. Quoted by Ella Lonn, *Foreigners in the Union Army and Navy* (New York, 1969), 120. I am grateful to Marion Truslow for these references.

40. Quoted by T. W. Moody in *The Fenian Movement* (Cork, 1968), 108.

41. Several books had been printed in Irish using roman characters with dots over the consonants to show aspiration. See, for instance, Father Jonathan Furlong's *Compánach an Chríosdaigh/The Christian's Companion* and his *The Irish Primer*, both of which use roman letters and express vowel length with the usual acute accent. Both of these books were published in Dublin in 1842, and a copy of each can be found in the New York Public Library.

42. In a letter to the *Irish World* (Dec. 28, 1872), written from "Reno, Pa.," William Russell discusses his involvement as Gaelic editor of the *Irish-American*.

43. One exception to this was in the Mar. 15, 1879, issue when a translation of Robert Emmet's "Speech in the Dock" by P. J. O'Daly of Boston was printed in the Irish character in the calligraphy of Charles Sprague. Ford continued to advertise for sale copies of the Irish translation of the speech for the next five years!

44. John Ridge, "The Gaelic Revival in 19th Century New York," *New York Irish [History]* (Journal of the New York Irish History Roundtable) 1 (1986): 6. See also letter by GAEL (Michael Logan) to *Irish World* (Mar. 8, 1873) announcing the formation of an Irish class. Note that Irish was being taught at this time at the University of Notre Dame,

Indiana, by Brother John Fleming, a native of Gort, County Galway (*Irish World*, Sept. 9, 1871, May 10, 1873; and Sept. 6, 1873). As mentioned earlier, the Ossianic Society of New York organized Irish classes around 1860–61.

45. See Fionnuala Uí Fhlanagáin, *Mícheál Ó Lócháin agus an Gaodhal* (Baile Átha Cliath, 1990), 11; and *Irish-American*, Nov. 30, 1878, 8.

46. See *Irish-American*, June–Dec. 1878.

47. See *Irish-American*, July 6 and 13, 1878.

48. Magner worked especially with manuscripts that were subsequently bought by the University of Wisconsin. See Cornelius G. Buttimer, *Catalogue of Irish Manuscripts in the University of Wisconsin-Madison* (Dublin, 1989); and Kenneth E. Nilsen, "Mícheál Ó Broin agus Lámhscríbhinní Gaeilge Ollscoil Wisconsin," *Celtica* 22 (1991): 116–18.

49. See Tomás de Bhaldraithe, "Uilliam H. Mac Giolla Iosa-Foclóirí," in Ó hAnnracháin, *Go Meiriceá Siar*, 154–58.

50. On O'Beirn, see Breandán Ó Conaire, "Pádraig Ó Beirn: Fear a D'fhill," in Ó hAnnracháin, *Go Meiriceá Siar*, 111–124.

51. See Hyde's *Mise Agus An Connradh* (Baile Átha Cliath, 1937), 40.

Chapter 11: IRISH COUNTY SOCIETIES IN NEW YORK (Ridge)

1. John T. Ridge, *Erin's Sons in America: The Ancient Order of Hibernians* (New York, 1986), 17. The independent beneficial societies appear to have been swamped by the rapid growth of the AOH and were probably absorbed as individual divisions.

2. John T. Ridge, *The St. Patrick's Day Parade in New York* (New York, 1988), 28–29. At midcentury certain trades like quarrying and stevedoring were Irish monopolies and their associations consisted of both labor unions and Irish fraternal societies.

3. Robert Ernst, *Immigrant Life in New York City 1825–1863* (New York, 1979), 39–40.

4. Jay P. Dolan, *The Immigrant Church: New York's Irish and German Catholics, 1815–1865* (Baltimore, 1975), 39–40.

5. According to John Devoy, the noted Fenian, O'Donovan Rossa tried to capitalize on county and regional loyalty from his old country neighbors and ran (unsuccessfully) for the state senate against Boss Tweed in 1872, against the advice of friends and acquaintances. "But he knew better than his friends and counted on the Corkmen, whose families, reinforced by Kerrymen, formed the bulk of the population on the Lower East Side of New York at that time, especially the old Fourth and Seventh Wards, which made up the Senatorial District." See John Devoy, *Recollections of an Irish Rebel* (New York, 1929), 328.

6. Concentrations of Kerry people could be found in both the First Ward (the Battery District) and on the East River, where it could once be said (about the area around St. James Roman Catholic Church near the Manhattan Bridge) that "nearly every one who knows anything about the city of New York is aware that the Fourth Ward, and particularly that portion of it close to the East River front, is a favorable spot for Kerry men and their descendents." In addition to the Kerry and Cork settlements in Manhattan, a number of other counties established a noticeable presence in the city in the nineteenth century. The Sixth Ward, the area north of City Hall and east of Chatham Street and the Bowery, "was for many years a Tipperary and Longford colony." The area north of the Manhattan Bridge along the East River, known as the Seventh Ward, was also called the "Cork Ward" in city politics because of its large Cork contingent, especially on Monroe Street, nicknamed "Cork Row." Just to the north of the Cork

colony, north of Grand Street and south of Rivington Street near the East River, was a place where Tyrone men were "most numerous." Separated from the Tyrone men by the old German colony of the East Side was Mackrelville, north of 10th and south of 14th Street, where Cavan men were most numerous. Limerick people were numerous north of this, between 14th and 23rd streets in the "Gas House District" on the East Side, followed by Tipperary as far north as 59th Street. The West Side of Manhattan had its Irish county neighborhoods, too, but to a less noticeable extent than on the East Side because "the diversity of business pursuits has been destructive of the divisional county lines." Below 14th Street the most numerous were from the north of Ireland: Derry, Donegal, and Antrim, the last county in largest numbers around Jackson Square. Meath, Mayo, and Leitrim were said to be numerous further north on the West Side. See "Some Old County Divisions," *Hibernian Magazine* (New York and Seneca Falls), 1, no. 6 (1896): 142–43.

7. The county societies were perhaps one of the few Irish organizations able to entice exiles back to Manhattan. Accounts of county association social affairs in the late nineteenth and early twentieth centuries frequently made mention of such visitors from outside of Manhattan and nearby cities. Tipperary's summer excursion in 1887, for example, was long anticipated as a "grand annual event" looked forward to by exiles living many miles outside of New York as an opportunity to meet, if only for one day, and to "renew those memories about the happy days they enjoyed in the land of their birth" (*Irish World*, May 7, 1887). The Cork ball in 1901 attracted attendees from as far away as Hartford, Bridgeport, New Haven, Albany, Syracuse, Buffalo, Rochester, and Canada (*Irish-American*, Jan. 19, 1901).

8. A tradition claims that a Cavan Society was founded in the city in 1848. No confirmation of this could be found in contemporary Catholic and Irish American newspapers. According to the *Irish World*, Apr. 25, 1896, the current Cavan Society was founded in 1866.

9. Sligo was still a minor port of embarkation for Irish emigrants at midcentury. This factor undoubtedly contributed to the especially high population loss in the period 1841–51 when the county population dropped sharply, from 180,886 to 128,515 (or 29%). Only Mayo, Roscommon, and Monaghan had a greater population loss for this period. See W. C. Vaughan and A. J Fitzpatrick, eds., *Irish Historical Studies, Population 1821–1871* (Dublin, 1978), 5–26.

10. A list of 25 members of the arrangements committee with their respective addresses accompanied an ad of the Sligo Association in the *Irish-American*, Dec. 9, 1850. Ten of the committee could be traced with certainty through the city directories for the years 1850–51, 1851–52, and 1852–53. The livelihoods of these 10 individuals were as follows: cabinetmaker, shoemaker, liquors, upholsterer, carpenter, porter (house proprietor), clerk, wines, ship carpenter, and grocer.

11. *Irish-American*, Aug. 10, 1850.

12. One of the early gangs of New York was called the Kerryonians, its members presumably natives of County Kerry. It was formed in a Sixth Ward grocery store on Centre Street near Worth Street. It was "a small gang which seldom roamed beyond Center Street and did little fighting; its members devoted themselves exclusively to hating the English." See Herbert Asbury, *The Gangs of New York* (New York, 1928), 21. There is no known connection between this group and the Kerry Society that existed in Manhattan in the 1850s.

13. Strictly speaking, the Athlone Guild of Friendship, which prospered from the early 1850s until well into the 1880s, was a town rather than a county society. It was composed of tradesmen and businessmen and for many years was headed by

John Savage, the Fenian leader, historian, journalist, and publisher. Most of the members seem to have been former residents of the town. One of them was prominent musician Patrick Sarsfield Gilmore, who conducted his world-famous band at the musical programs of the society. The possibility also exists that most Irish lower-class social activities were not reported at all in the newspapers.

14. Ridge, *Erin's Sons in America*, 28. Although kept at arm's length by the church at the time, the AOH organized a system of individual units called divisions, which were often geographically based and frequently equivalent to parish boundaries. Most divisions were regulated by the county board and prevented from taking members from the area of others. Other divisions were recruited from a particular trade or occupation, such as firemen or construction workers.

15. An interesting letter appeared in the *Irish World*, June 23, 1877, over the pseudonym "Smith O'Brien." Addressed to "some gentlemen who are in the habit of getting up picnics every summer, and who could give some practical assistance to the Irish national movement," the writer challenged the county societies, particularly the Mayo Young Men's Association, to turn over the proceeds of the day to the Skirmishing Fund, an effort to provide the funds to carry out a guerrilla-type war for Irish liberation. There is no evidence to suggest the idea was taken up by any of the county societies.

16. The last half of the 1870s witnessed a dramatic downturn in the economy, followed in 1880 by a healthy turnaround. See *Duns Review*, July, 1976, 41.

17. Immigration from Ireland fell to less than 20,000 a year in the period 1876 to 1879, the lowest numbers since Famine times. Spurred by the agricultural distress in Ireland and the improving American economy Irish immigration surged to 71,000 in 1880 and remained well above an average 50,000 a year to 1893. See Department of Commerce, Census Bureau, *A Century of Population Growth* (Washington, D.C, 1958), 105–6.

18. *Irish-American*, Apr. 2, 1881. Several other county societies had similar appeals signed by individuals representing various parts of the home county.

19. Many of the county societies that began in the early 1880s—such as Meath, Limerick, Waterford, Antrim, Tyrone, Kilkenny, Longford, Queens (Laois), and Sligo— were dead within a few years, but some of the large counties prospered, notably, Tipperary, Kerry, Cork, Mayo, and Galway. A few others managed to limp along. A new wave of reorganization began as early as 1886. New county societies then appeared: Dublin (1886), Sligo (1887), Clare (1888), Carlow (1890), Antrim (1890), Westmeath (1890), Armagh (1893), Louth (1893), Kildare (1895), and Wicklow (1896). Defunct societies also returned to the active list, such as Queens (Laois), Limerick, Waterford, Tyrone, and Longford, all of which formed strong organizations between 1889 and 1891. This second wave of county organizations proved to be longer lasting than the first, and most of the present-day Irish county organizations trace their origin to this period.

20. *Irish World*, Sept. 13, 1890; Jan. 10, 1891; and Mar. 10, 1894. There were still several strong Irish county societies in Brooklyn up to World War I. The last survivors were the Antrim men of Greenpoint, which became defunct in the early 1930s, and the Donegal Association, which merged with two Manhattan-based Donegal groups in 1939. James H. McLaughlin, *A History of the Donegal Association Inc. of New York, 1939–1981* (New York, 1983), 5.

21. *Irish World*, Nov. 15, 1890; Dec. 13, 1890; and Jan. 31, 1891. Several other American cities also organized Irish county societies. The earliest one seems to have been the Sligo Society of Boston, "the parent society of the Irish County Clubs in Boston," which was founded in 1895 (*Irish Advocate*, Mar. 10, 1910, and Apr. 9, 1910). In the first decade of this century Boston had a number of active associations, including

Kerry, Galway, and Cork. Philadelphia had an active county movement, especially from the northern counties like Donegal, Derry, and Antrim. Yonkers had two Irish county societies in 1909: Waterford, which supplied the city with a very large number of immigrants, and Kerry (*Irish Advocate*, Feb. 8, 1908). Other major centers of Irish population had one or two societies such as San Francisco's Knights of St. Finnbarr (Cork) and a Cork society in St. Louis (*Irish Advocate*, Feb. 27, 1904). On the Mayomen of Chicago, the first county association in that city, see also *Irish Advocate*, Sept. 5, 1908.

22. *Irish World*, Feb. 28, 1891; Mar. 21, 1891; Apr. 11, 1891; Mar. 21, 1894; and Jan. 4, 1896.

23. *Counties Mayo, Kildare, Cork, Galway, Limerick, Sligo Associations vs. Henrietta Brown as Executrix of the Last Will and Testament of William F. Brown, Deceased, and the Irish Palace Building Association*, Supreme Court, County of New York, Mar. 18, 1908. Irish Palace Building Association funds were donated to the American Irish Historical Society for the purchase of their present building on Fifth Avenue. Only within the past 15 years did the Palace Association finally disband.

24. *Irish World*, May 27, 1899. After the turn of the century the United Irish Societies appears to have gradually become an AOH-dominated society.

25. Vaughan and Fitzpatrick, *Irish Historical Statistics: Population, 1821–1971* (Dublin, 1978), 15–16; and *Irish Nation*, May 6 to July 29, 1882, "Arrivals from Ireland."

26. Donegal immigrants overwhelmingly headed for Philadelphia and other towns in Pennsylvania, while Mayo sent large numbers of its immigrants to Ohio (Cleveland) and to Chicago. Antrim sent many of its immigrants to Pennsylvania, but fewer to Philadelphia than Donegal. Other counties sent most of their immigrants to New York City, with Longford (64%), Dublin (60%), and Westmeath (56%) showing an especially high preference in this regard.

27. *Irish Nation*, May 6 to July 29, 1882, "Arrivals from Ireland." Since destinations in the arrivals column indicate only about a dozen destinations inside today's geographical New York City that were not either Manhattan or Brooklyn, there are insufficient data to determine any settlement pattern for Irish immigrants in the other three boroughs.

28. The New York Board G.A.A., *The New York Irish* (New York, 1976), 105–20. It is possible some of the other old teams were composed primarily of members from one county. The use of patriotic names may have been a way to disguise sectionality in the 1890s.

29. Sports writers in the New York Irish weeklies made their living from provoking controversy, and their reviews of games often stirred heated protests from the offended counties. Liam O'Shea (a nom de plume for Martin J. Hurley) in the *Irish Advocate* was a strong advocate of county teams changing their names back to the Emmets, the Tones, and other such names that had been in use before the turn of the century. A typical response came in a letter from J. M. Griffin, a spokesman for the Kerrymen: "A word of warning, Mr. Liam, the sooner you stop nosing into the doings of the Kerrymen the better. They never were, or never will be, the first to wage a fight, but once roused they can fight; and strange, they always manage to come out top dog. A little of the recent history of the G.A.A. matters in New York will prove that they stand alone, uninterfering, and on kindly terms with all; they want to be treated similarly. They know who their enemies are, and they are watchful of men who, for personal purposes, would break the power of the Kerrymen in the morning, and some of them are individuals that have Mr. Liam O'Shea's flattering unction laid weekly to their souls. But the Kerrymen want no fulsome flattery; far less do they want ruffianly and insulting criticism."

30. *Irish Advocate*, July 2, 1904. J. M. Griffin, an officer of the Kerry Men's Association, argued in a letter to the editor that the bad experience of the Irish Palace fiasco had been the reason why some counties had been reluctant to join the ICAU. He stated that if the rights of each county could be guaranteed, a united Irish counties organization would at last be completed (*Irish Advocate*, Sept. 9, 1918).

31. Many good players immigrated to America and quickly joined their county team. The Dublin Football Club was organized in late 1913 from "old time members of the Kickhams, Geraldines, Parnells, Keatings, Faughs, Grocers, Commercials and others." Some of these were Dublin teams. Longford advertised some recent arrivals from Ireland in 1908, including "Tommy Quinn, one of Ireland's greatest goal keepers; another player who is familiarly known all over the County Longford as the Rabbit Morgan, whom many of his old admirers will be glad to see" (*Irish Advocate*, Mar. 14, 1908).

32. On the purchase price see *Irish Advocate*, June 12, 1909; and on the split see ibid., May 15, 1909.

33. Michael F. Funchion, "United Irish Counties Association of New York (UICA)," in Michael Funchion, ed., *Irish American Voluntary Organizations* (Westport, Conn., 1983), 266–70.

34. The *Irish Advocate* frequently carried obituaries of members of Irish county organizations in its pre–World War I issues. An examination of this paper between 1904 and 1914 indicates that practically all of the deceased members were Irish-born.

35. *Irish-American*, Mar. 6 and Aug. 4, 1883.

36. See *Irish Advocate*, Apr. 16, 1910, "Nineteen-twentieths of the Members are Native-born Corkmen," 18.

37. *Irish-American*, June 2, 1883. The original Derry Society became defunct and was succeeded by a Derry Men's and Derry Ladies Society in the early 1890s. See *Irish World*, Mar. 18 and Jan. 14, 1893.

38. The Gaelic Society and the Philo-Celtic Society were an interesting cross of educational, social, musical, and dramatic societies. They had a large number of middle-class American-born Irish who were anxious to promote an Irish cultural rebirth.

39. Irish Land League, *Annual Report of the Secretary*, 1882, 26–32. There were many ladies' branches of the Land League throughout the northeastern United States.

40. Any Irish organization that combined women and men at this time would in effect be creating a social mix of many married men with single young women. As Frank Pilkington of the Kings (Offaly) County Hurling Team observed in a letter to the *Irish Advocate*, Feb. 12, 1910, "We want all Kings Co. men to join the club; we would be only too glad to let the Kings Co. girls join, too. We did admit 2 or 3 with disastrous results to our club, instead of the women promising to love, honor and obey, etc., it has come to pass that the men have to do the obeying so much so that we have lost some of our best players, as their wives won't let them hurl, consequently we have to bar women. It's useless for them to apply for membership, as none but fat or crippled players will be allowed to associate with them in the club and (God knows there will be no temptation)."

41. Although the dances of the county societies were primarily attended by single young people, there was a difference between the men's and ladies' dances in terms of the percentage of married couples participating. At the Longford Ladies' dance (*Irish Advocate*, Mar. 19, 1910) only 7 percent of the 125 couples in the "grand march" were listed as married (Mr. and Mrs.), whereas at the Longford Men's dance (Dec. 14, 1912) 12 of the 55 couples, or 22 percent, were married. Similar results can be seen for the Kildare Men (Nov. 8, 1908), where 24 percent of the 42 couples in the grand march were married, whereas only 3 percent of the 37 couples in the Kildare Ladies (Feb. 14, 1908) were married. Some county societies were decidedly "old" in composition. The Corkmen's

Mutual Aid Association claimed "about 300 members" in 1910, of whom "there are about 75% of them over the 40-year mark." This was so even though only new members between 18 and 45 were acceptable (*Irish Advocate*, Nov. 12, 1910).

42. *Irish Advocate*, Feb. 5, 1910. The county ladies societies were consequently very dependent on a steady flow of young immigrants to replace those who were getting married. World War I cut off immigration from Ireland almost completely and as a consequence only nine of the ladies' societies survived by 1923: Cavan, Kilkenny, Offaly, Cork, Tipperary, Kerry, Galway, Sligo, and Roscommon. See "Are Irish County Ladies' Societies Dying Out?" in the *Irish Advocate*, Dec. 22, 1923.

43. *Irish Advocate*, Apr. 23 and July 16, 1910, and Sept. 13, 1912; and Financial Secretary's book of the Sligo Men's Association for 1912. Sligo was still paying at the old $5 rate in 1922, but Donegal increased their rate to $10 a month in 1913. Normal monthly dues amounted to 25¢ a month, although the Cork Men's P. & B. charged 30¢ (*Irish Advocate*, Nov. 12, 1910) and Donegal increased its dues to 50¢ when they raised their rate of benefits. Tipperary had dispensed $14,000 for deceased members, $4,500 for their wives, and $7,500 in sick benefits in the 30-year period to 1911 (see *Irish Advocate*, Mar. 18, 1911). In 1913 the Cork Men's Mutual Aid Society, a breakaway group from the old association, paid $6 per week for 13 weeks to its sick members. It also gave a $100 member's death benefit and a death benefit for the wife of a member of $75.

44. Membership figures were only rarely mentioned in the Irish American press. Figures were given for the following: Cavan, 230 members (*Irish-American*, Apr. 1, 1883); Kerry, 150 (*Irish-American*, July 29, 1882); Wexford, 200+ (*Irish-American*, July 29, 1882); Tipperary, 250 (*Irish-American*, June 30, 1883); Roscommon, 100 (*Irish World*, Apr. 11, 1891); Tyrone, 20 for 1891: McElroy, *Red Bricks and Green Bushes or the Story of the County Tyrone Society* [New York, n.d.], 10); Corkmen's Mutual, 250 (*Irish Advocate*, Nov. 19, 1910); Kilkenny, 258 (June 19, 1909); Waterford, 100 (*Irish World*, Sept. 20, 1890); Cork, 500 (*Irish Advocate*, June 19, 1909); Sligo, 125 (Financial Secretary's Book, Sligo Men's S. & B. Association, 1909); Cork, 600 (*Irish Advocate*, Apr. 16, 1910); Queens, 150 (*Irish Advocate*, Feb. 22, 1913).

45. Corkmen's Mutual Aid Society, corporate dissolution papers, Supreme Court County of New York, 1917. The Corkmen's Mutual Aid Society's members were concentrated between 42nd and 96th streets, where 49 of the 107 Manhattan members lived. Twenty-three lived south of 14th Street and 14 between 14th and 42nd. The remainder lived north of 96th Street. The financial records of the Sligo Association between 1909 and 1914 also reveal a small percentage of members residing outside of Manhattan.

46. Whenever a home address for an officer appeared in the Irish American press, it was almost without exception a Manhattan address. In a list of corresponding secretaries for 32 men's and ladies' county organizations only one (in the Bronx) resided outside of Manhattan (*Irish Advocate*, Feb. 5, 1910).

47. Caroline Ware, *Greenwich Village* (Boston, 1935), 204–5. The Clare colony stretched along the waterfront from the vicinity of West 14th Street south to what is today modern Tribeca and SoHo.

48. Ibid., 204.

49. The employment of 43 Manhattan members of the Corkmen's Mutual Aid Society who could be traced using the city directories from 1914 to 1917 was as follows: 12 laborers, 4 clerks, 3 porters, 2 conductors, 2 prison guards, 2 foremen, 2 saloon keepers. One of each of the following employments were also listed: bartender, printer, stoker, boarding house (proprietor), motorman, inspector, lawyer, carpenter, steward, caulker,

water piper, teamster, badges, plumber, and horseshoer. The directories had a reputation for not listing laborers, and presumably many of those not found were in this category.

50. Author's interview with Monsignor James Brew of the Clare Association, May 11, 1978; James Mulvihill of the Kerrymen's Association, Feb. 6, 1992; and William J. Cunningham of the Donegal Association, Mar. 11, 1992. See also *Irish Advocate*, Apr. 11, 1911.

51. Banquet speakers sometimes alluded to how their immigrant members were employed. "Kerrymen are in every line of business in New York; they can be found in all the professions and there is quite a number of them in the City, State and Federal service. In the New York Police Department alone, there are at least 500 Kerrymen, of which four are Police Captains and a score of Lieutenants, Sergeants, etc." (*Irish Advocate*, Mar. 2, 1912). The Corkmen's P. & B. was proud "of its lawyers, of its doctors, of its policemen, firemen and letter carriers and Plebians" (*Irish Advocate*, Nov. 12, 1910).

52. *Irish Advocate*, Nov. 19, 1910. At the championship match at Celtic Park, which had one of the largest crowds ever seen at the grounds, Hearst had the honor of throwing out the football to the Kerry and Kilkenny teams. Mitchel was at one time president of the United Irish League of New York City, the political arm of John Redmond and the Irish Parliamentary party. See *Irish Advocate*, Jan. 27, 1913.

53. Buckley's trip back to Kerry in 1913 was the local equivalent of a royal visit. He was welcomed with a elaborate celebration in the Parish of Tuogh, where the local pipers' band escorted him through the streets of the village playing "See, the Conquering Hero Comes." A children's choir entertained with "The Exile's Return," and the locals hung on "The Big Chief's" every word. Suitably honored but also suitably cornered, they got Buckley to promise he would raise the money to build their new parish hall with the aid of the New York Kerrymen.

54. William J. Crowley, president for several terms of the Clare Men's Association, was a successful businessman in the Clare stronghold on the Lower West Side. In addition to his liquor stores, he was the owner of the Huron Cigar Company, which employed 200 hands. The Clare organization endorsed his candidacies for alderman, and although he lost he did quite well for a Republican in such an overwhelmingly Democratic district, losing by only a 3 to 2 margin (*Brooklyn Eagle Almanac*, 1912; also *Irish Advocate*, Nov. 4, 1911, and Oct. 25, 1913). James J. Hagan of the Longford Association was a regularly featured speaker at various county functions with a reputation as a capable master of ceremonies. He made an unsuccessful bid for county clerk of Manhattan as a Democrat in 1909 but lost to a fusion candidate 169,015 to 135,573 (*Brooklyn Eagle Almanac*, 1910, 555).

55. *Irish World*, Mar. 25, 1899. The Mayomen unveiled a statue in January 1896 of Nally who had died almost six years before. See also *Hibernian Monthly Magazine*, Dec., 1896, 888.

56. *Gaelic American*, Nov. 14, 1905.

57. *Irish Advocate*, Sept. 3, 1910.

58. James McElroy, *Red Bricks and Green Bushes*, 12. In 1910, however, Tyrone occupied a box along with 10 other counties at the Carnegie Hall reception for John Redmond, leader of the Irish Parliamentary party and joined in the resolution that stated "We indorse (*sic*) most sincerely that splendid body of unselfish workers the Irish Parliamentary Party" (*Irish Advocate*, Oct. 8, 1910).

59. *Irish Advocate*, Jan. 13, 1912. Thomas Rock was involved in the Roscommon organization as early as 1891. Such prominent Irish nationalists as Harry Boland, Count Plunkett, and Father Michael O'Flanagan became members after 1919, if only in name.

60. *Irish Advocate*, Feb. 11, 1911, and Jan. 13, 1912.

61. *Irish Advocate*, Aug. 24, 1918. The deaths of many county members were recounted on a weekly basis as the American army joined the last big push in France. Father Duffy thought that members of the Irish county associations made the best members of the 69th Regiment. As far back as the Civil War some units of the 69th were probably recruited in part from immigrants from a particular county. See John T. Ridge, *Sligo in New York—The Irish from Co. Sligo 1849–1991* (New York, 1991), 16.

62. Author's Interview with Michael J. Flannery, past president of the United Irish Counties Association, Mar. 6, 1982.

63. Funchion, "United Irish Counties Association," 269.

Chapter 12: THE IRISH AMERICAN WORKER IN TRANSITION, 1877–1914 (McKivigan and Robertson)

1. Edward K. Spann, *The New York Metropolis: New York City, 1840–1857* (New York, 1981), 440–41; Thomas Kessner, *The Golden Door: Italian and Jewish Immigrant Mobility in New York City, 1880–1915* (New York, 1977), 48; Dirk Hoerder, ed., *The Immigrant Labor Press in North America, 1840s–1970s: An Annotated Bibliography*, 3 vols., *Volume 3: Migrants from Southern and Western Europe* (Westport, Conn., 1987), 25; Graham Russell Hodges, *New York City Cartmen, 1677–1850* (New York, 1986), 136–37; Sean Wilentz, *Chants Democratic: New York City and the Rise of the American Working Class, 1788–1850* (New York, 1984), 118–19; Iver Bernstein, *The New York City Draft Riots: Their Significance for American Society and Politics in the Age of the Civil War* (New York, 1990), 112, 238. In a survey of five other industrial cities and towns, Theodore Hershberg and his colleagues noted a similar grouping of Irish Americans in unskilled jobs in the first half of the nineteenth century. Theodore Hershberg et al., "Occupation and Ethnicity in Five Nineteenth-Century Cities: A Collaborative Inquiry," *Historical Methods Newsletter* 7 (June 1974): 197–220.

2. Kerby A. Miller, *Emigrants and Exiles: Ireland and the Irish Exodus to North America* (New York, 1985), 521.

3. Steven P. Erie, *Rainbow's End: Irish-Americans and the Dilemma of Urban Political Machine Politics, 1840–1985* (Berkeley, Calif., 1988), 26, 49, 61; Thomas Henderson, *Tammany Hall and the New Immigrants: The Progressive Years* (New York, 1976), 72.

4. David Bensman, *The Practice of Solidarity: American Hat Finishers in the Nineteenth Century* (Urbana, Ill., 1985), 118; Erie, *Rainbow's End*, 49; Bernstein, *New York City Draft Riots*, 112, 238. Irish Americans were noticeably absent in the metal trades of most other cities. See Hershberg et al., "Occupation and Ethnicity," 199; David N. Doyle, "Unestablished Irishmen: New Immigrants in Industrial America, 1870–1910," in Dirk Hoerder, ed., *American Labor and Immigration History, 1877–1920s: Recent European Studies* (Urbana, Ill., 1983), 194–97.

5. Gerald Grob, *Workers and Utopia: A Study of Ideological Conflict in the American Labor Movement, 1865–1900* (Evanston, Ill., 1961), 34–59; Bruce Laurie, *Artisans into Workers: Labor in Nineteenth-Century America* (New York, 1989), 79–91, 142.

6. Grob, *Workers and Utopia*, 37.

7. David Montgomery, "The Irish and the American Labor Movement," in David Noel Doyle and Owen Dudley Edwards, eds., *America and Ireland, 1776–1976: The*

American Identity and the Irish Connection (Westport, Conn., 1976), 214–15; Doyle, "Unestablished Irishmen," 217–19.

8. David Montgomery, "The Irish Influence in the American Labor Movement," (Hibernian Lecture, Notre Dame, Ind., 1984), 2; John R. Commons, *Races and Immigrants in America*, rev. ed. (New York, 1930), 153–54; Gary M. Fink, ed., *Biographical Dictionary of American Labor Leaders* (Westport, Conn., 1974), 583–84 (hereafter cited as *BDALL*); Warren Van Tine, *The Making of the Labor Union Bureaucrat: Union Leadership in the United States, 1870–1920* (Amherst, Mass., 1973), 62–63; Robert D. Cross, *The Emergence of Liberal Catholicism in America* (Cambridge, Mass., 1958), 188; Erie, *Rainbow's End*, 50; Hoerder, *Immigrant Press*, 257.

9. Miller, *Emigrants and Exiles*, 499–500; Bernstein, *New York City Draft Riots*, 238, 243–48; Erie, *Rainbow's End*, 49; Fink, *BDALL*, 583–84; Irwin Yellowitz, "Eight Hours and the Bricklayers' Strike of 1868 in New York City," in Irwin Yellowitz, ed. *Essays in the History of New York City: A Memorial to Sidney Pomerantz* (Port Washington, N.Y., 1978), 78–79, 84–85; Montgomery, "The Irish and the American Labor Movement," 210; Michael Gordon, "Studies in Irish and Irish-American Thought and Behavior in Gilded Age New York City" (Ph.D. diss., University of Rochester, 1977), 467–68;

10. Bernstein, *New York City Draft Riots*, 243–57.

11. Samuel Bernstein, *The First International in America* (New York, 1962), 246–48, 290–92; Thomas R. Brooks, *The Road to Dignity: A Century of Conflict* (New York, 1981), 19–20, 31–33; Walter Galenson, *The United Brotherhood of Carpenters: The First Hundred Years* (Cambridge, Mass., 1983), 22–26, 33–34, 86–88; Fink, *BDALL*, 380–81; Larry Grossman, "Who Is the Father of Labor Day?" *Labor History* 14 (Fall 1973): 612–13; Mark Erlich, "Peter J. McGuire's Trade Unionism: Socialism of a Trades Union Kind?" *Labor History* 24 (Spring 1983): 165–97; Michael Kazin and Steven J. Ross, "America's Labor Day: The Dilemma of a Workers' Celebration," *Journal of American History* 78 (Mar. 1992): 1297, 1299–1302; Gordon, "Studies in Irish and Irish American Thought and Behavior," 487.

12. Leon Fink, *Workingmen's Democracy: The Knights of Labor and American Politics* (Urbana, Ill., 1983), xii, 4; Martin Segal, *The Rise of the United Association: National Unionism in the Pipe Trades, 1884–1924* (Cambridge, Mass., 1970), 20–21; Laurie, *Artisans into Workers*, 148–51; Erie, *Rainbow's End*, 49; Leon Fink, "The Uses of Political Power: Toward a Theory of the Labor Movement in the Era of the Knights of Labor," in Michael H. Frisch and Daniel J. Walkowitz, eds., *Working-Class America: Essays on Labor, Community, and American Society*, (Urbana, Ill., 1983), 104–5, 111–15; Montgomery, "Irish and the American Labor Movement," 216.

13. For example, Joseph A. Mullaney headed the Salamander Association. *Journal of the Knights of Labor*, July 3, 1890; Fink, *BDALL*, 261–62.

14. *Journal of United Labor*, Sept. 10, 1886, and Feb. 26, 1887; *Journal of the Knights of Labor*, July 3, 1890; Montgomery, "Irish and the American Labor Movement," 215–16; Gordon, "Studies in Irish and Irish American Thought and Behavior," 502, 525.

15. As quoted in Fink, *Workingmen's Democracy*, 11.

16. In the *Irish World*, Ford also defended the Irish Catholic immigrants from attacks by Protestant nativist critics and occasionally twitted the local Catholic prelates for their opulent living and indifference to the cause of Irish independence. Ford also condemned the leaders of both the city's Democratic and Republican parties as interested solely in the spoils of office and sometimes backed third-party groups such as the Greenback-Labor Party. Florence E. Gibson, *The Attitudes of the New York Irish toward State and National Affairs, 1848–1892* (New York, 1951), 305–7, 321–22; James P.

Rodechko, "An Irish-American Journalist and Catholicism: Patrick Ford of the *Irish World*," *Church History* 39 (Dec. 1970): 524–29; William Leonard Joyce, "Editors and Ethnicity: A History of the Irish-American Press, 1848–1883" (Ph.D. diss., University of Michigan, 1974), 155.

17. A key figure in this agitation was John Devoy, an exiled Fenian who had spent the 1870s working as a journalist for a number of New York City dailies. From 1881 to 1885, Devoy operated his own paper, the *Irish Nation*, and rallied the city's Irish population behind the Land League. Together with Irish radical Michael Davitt, Devoy persuaded Clan na Gael militants to support the economic program of Parnell's "New Departure" campaign. Patrick Ford's *Irish World* also enlisted in this movement. Peter A. Quinn, "John Devoy: Recollections of an Irish Rebel," *American Irish Historical Society Recorder* 40 (1979): 27–28; James Reidy, "John Devoy," *Journal of the Irish American Historical Society* 27 (1928): 419; Joyce, "Editors and Ethnicity," 165–66; Rodechko, "An Irish American Journalist," 532–33; William D'Arcy, "The Fenian Movement in the United States,: 1858–1886" (Ph.D. diss., Catholic University of America, 1947), 398–401, 407.

18. Tammany boss 'Honest' John Kelly and other Tammany members received Parnell in 1880 and also set up the "Tammany Hall Irish Relief Fund." Eric Foner, "Class, Ethnicity, and Radicalism in the Gilded Age: The Land League and Irish-America," in Eric Foner, ed., *Politics and Ideology in the Age of the Civil War* (New York, 1980), 157, 164–66, 177; James J. Green, "American Catholics and the Irish Land League, 1879–1882," *Catholic Historical Review* 35 (Apr., 1949): 27.

19. Peter A. Speek, "The Single Tax and the Labor Movement," in *Bulletin of the University of Wisconsin*, Economics and Political Science Series 8 (Oct. 1917), 57–61; A. D. Vinton, "The History of Boycotting," *Magazine of Western History* 5 (Dec. 1886): 212; Bensman, *The Practice of Solidarity*, 118, 123–24; Miller, *Emigrants and Exiles*, 549; Michael A. Gordon, "The Labor Boycott in New York City, 1800–1886," *Labor History* 16 (Spring 1975):185–86; Michael A. Gordon, "Irish Immigrant Culture and the Labor Boycott in New York City, 1880–1886," in Richard L. Erlich, ed., *Immigrants in Industrial America, 1850–1920*, (Charlottesville, Va., 1977), 114, 118.

20. *New York Times*, July 16, 1882, as quoted in Gordon, "Studies in Irish and Irish American Thought and Behavior," 549; Gordon, "Irish Immigrant Culture," 111–12; Montgomery, "Irish and the American Labor Movement," 213–14.

21. *New York Times*, Apr. 7, 1889, as quoted in Gordon, "Irish Immigrant Culture," 117.

22. As quoted in Gordon, "The Labor Boycott," 198; David Scobey, "Boycotting the Political Factory: Labor Radicalism and the New York City Mayoral Election of 1884 [*sic*]," *Radical History Review* 28–30 (1984), 282, 287–95; Gordon, "Studies in Irish and Irish-American Thought and Behavior, 457, 461–65.

23. Scobey, "Boycotting the Political Factory," 288–89; Kazin and Ross, "America's Labor Day," 1299–1300; Speek, "The Single Tax and the Labor Movement," 91; Louis F. Post and Fred C. Leubuscher, *Henry George's 1886 Campaign: An Account of the George–Hewett Campaign in the New York Municipal Election of 1886*, rev. ed. (New York, 1961), 6, 16–17; Gordon, "Irish Immigrant Culture," 117; Gordon, "Studies in Irish and Irish-American Thought and Behavior," 577.

24. [New York] *Boycotter*, July 10, 1886; see also *Irish World*, June 17, 1882; Bernstein, *New York City Draft Riots*, 243–48; Gordon, "Studies in Irish and Irish-American Thought and Behavior," 467–68, 558, 583–84.

25. One careful study calculates that 87,685 Irish-born voters were eligible to vote in New York City in 1880, and that of those listed as native born, 42.5 percent were all

or part Irish in ancestry. Erie, *Rainbow's End*, 51; Gibson, *Attitudes of the New York Irish*, 321–22.

26. During this period, the Fenian exile and New York City editor, Jeremiah O'Donovan Rossa bitterly remarked: "We Irish of New York are American politicians before we are Irish, or anything else." As quoted in Erie, *Rainbow's End*, 50. See also Theodore J. Lowi, *At the Pleasure of the Mayor: Patronage and Power in New York City, 1898–1958* (London, 1964), 34–35; Henderson, *Tammany Hall and the New Immigrant*, 87; Miller, *Emigrants and Exiles*, 496; Joyce, "Editors and Ethnicity," 151.

27. Much of its "patronage" was diverted from the city payroll to jobs with politically connected and frequently Irish American contractors. While these private contractors certainly became wealthy, there is little evidence that this indirect form of patronage did much to raise the economic status of other Irish Americans in their employ. Erie, *Rainbow's End*, 56–57, 60–63.

28. Robert Blissert, T. B. McGuire, Jeremiah Murphy, and other Irish Americans also campaigned actively for longshoreman Roger Burke, a labor candidate for state assembly in 1882. One notable exception to the movement away from political action after 1882 was the Typographers Local 6, headed by John R. O'Donnell, which endorsed Grover Cleveland because of their opposition to Blaine's running mate, William W. Reid, managing editor of the *New York Tribune*, which the union was boycotting. While Local 6 frequently claimed to have provided Cleveland with his narrow margin over Blaine in New York City, giving him the White House, the real beneficiary turned out to be Tammany Hall, not labor. George A. Stevens, *New York Typographical Union No. 6: Study of a Modern Trade Union and Its Predecessors* (Albany, 1913), 386–92, 657–58; Gordon, "Labor Boycott," 200–201, and "Studies in Irish and Irish American Thought and Behavior," 491–92, 556–60.

29. New York State Bureau of Labor Statistics, *Fourth Annual Report* (Albany, 1886), 713; Bensman, *The Practice of Solidarity*, 118; Stevens, *New York Typographical Union No. 6*, 388–92; Gordon, "Labor Boycott," 184.

30. [New York], *Boycotter*, Jan. 31, Oct. 31, 1885; [New York] *John Swinton's Paper*, May 11, 1884, May 9 and July 11, 1886; New York Bureau of Labor Statistics, *Fourth Annual Report*, 744; Speek, "The Single Tax and the Labor Movement" 56–57; Gordon, "Studies in Irish and Irish American Thought and Behavior," 551–59, 571–77.

31. New York *Irish World*, Nov. 4, 1882; Neil Betten, *Catholic Activism and the Industrial Worker* (Gainesville, Fla., 1976), 7–8; James Dombrowski, *The Early Days of Christian Socialism in America* (New York, 1936), 35–49; Miller, *Emigrants and Exiles*, 442; Hoerder, *Immigrant Labor Press*, 257–58.

32. The CLU-organized "labor conference" on August 5, 1886, which created the Independent Labor Party, was attended by 402 delegates, representing 165 labor organizations, including the Socialist Labor Party. Speek, "The Single Tax and the Labor Movement," 63.

33. It also seems that, with the exception of Peter McGuire, the leadership of the SLP had few Irish Americans. Howard H. Quint, *The Forging of American Socialism: Origins of the Modern Movement* (Columbia, S.C., 1953), 37–38.

34. Post and Leubuscher, *Henry George's 1886 Campaign*, 133; Robert Emmett Curran, S. J., "The McGlynn Affair and the Shaping of the New Conservatism in American Catholicism, 1886–1894," *Catholic Historical Review* 66 (1980): 187; David Saposs, "The Catholic Church and the Labor Movement, *Modern Monthly* (June 1933): 294–95.

35. [New York] *John Swinton's Paper*, Oct. 24, 1886; Post and Leubuscher, *Henry George's 1886 Campaign*, 132; Speek, "Single Tax and the Labor Movement," 90–91, 101–3, 105.

36. Powderly actively participated in the George campaign because, he argued, "the nomination of Henry George by the laboring men of New York was a solemn protest against the manner in which the rights of the many were ruthlessly trampled under foot by the ringsters of the party in power." *Journal of United Labor*, Nov. 25, 1886; Terence Powderly, *Thirty Years of Labor, 1859 to 1889* (Columbus, Ohio, 1890), 288, 293–94.

37. Rodechko, "An Irish American Journalist," 533.

38. Post and Leubuscher, *Henry George's 1886 Campaign*, 168.

39. Martin Shefter, "The Electoral Foundations of the Political Machine" in Joel Sibley, Allen Bogue, and William Flannigan, eds., *The History of American Political Behavior* (Princeton, N.J., 1978), 287–92; Scobey, "Boycotting the Politics Factory," 303–17.

40. The original Central Committee had been McMackin, McGlynn, and Professor David B. Scott, but Scott declined because of illness and was replaced by Redpath. It is interesting that Daniel DeLeon was chairman of the platform committee. DeLeon, who would later be prominent in the Socialist Labor Party, was a strong George supporter, even compromising his position at Columbia University in order to set up Henry George Clubs and give speeches on the candidate's behalf. DeLeon would survive the Socialist Labor Party and United Labor Party split by staying with the George camp. DeLeon would later totally embrace socialism and try to downplay his involvement with the George campaign. see, L. Glen Seretan, *Daniel DeLeon, The Odyssey of an American Marxist* (Cambridge, Mass., 1979), 24–28; Post and Leubuscher, *Henry George's Campaign*, 177. See also Charles A. Barker, *Henry George* (New York, 1955), 485; Speek, "The Single Tax and the Labor Movement," 91.

41. J. H. M. Laslett, "Haymarket, Henry George, and the Labor Upsurge in Britain and America during the Late 1880s," *International Labor and Working Class History* 29 (Spring 1986), 77; Post and Leubuscher, *Henry George's 1886 Campaign*, 171–77; Quint, *Forging of American Socialism*, 43.

42. In one letter in the *New York Tribune*, Oct. 28, 1886, Preston stated flatly that George's "principles are unsound and unsafe and contrary to the teachings of the church." Also see Post and Leubuscher, *Henry George's 1886 Campaign*, 132; Betten, *Catholic Activism and the Industrial Worker*, 7–8; Speek, "Single Tax and the Labor Movement," 90–91, 101–3, 105.

43. Quint, *Forging American Socialism*, 46; Speek, "Single Tax and the Labor Movement," 101–5.

44. [New York] *John Swinton's Paper*, May 8, and June 26, 1887; John L. Thomas, *Alternative America: Henry George, Edward Bellamy, Henry Demarest Lloyd and the Adversary Tradition* (Cambridge, Mass., 1983), 231–32; Laslett, "Haymarket, Henry George, and the Labor Upsurge," 77–78.

45. Curran, "The McGlynn Affair," 184–94; Foner, "The Land League and Irish-America," 187–88; Speek, "The Single Tax and the Labor Movement," 103–4, 147–48.

46. [New York] *John Swinton's Paper*, July 3, 1887, also May 29, 1887; [New York] *Journal of United Labor*, Mar. 10, 1888; Henry Browne, *Catholic Church and the Knights of Labor* (New York, [1949] 1976), 284–85, 292, 307–9.

47. In his appeal to have his excommunication lifted, McGlynn had received support from liberal Catholics outside New York City, such as James Cardinal Gibbons. Betten, *Catholic Activism and the Industrial Worker*, 7–8; Dombrowski, *The Early Days of Christian Socialism*, 46–49; Curran, "The McGlynn Affair," 199–203.

48. *Knights of Labor and the Federation: Mass Meeting of Wage-Earners at Cooper Union, New York* (n.p., 1890), 1–6; *Journal of the Knights of Labor*, July 3, 1890; Harold Coffin Syrett, *The City of Brooklyn, 1865–1898: A Political History* (New York, 1944), 241–42; Joshua B. Freeman, *In Transit: The Transport Workers Union in New York City,*

1933–1966 (New York, 1989), 16–17; James J. McGinley, *Labor Relations in the New York Rapid Transit Systems, 1904–1944* (New York, 1949), 259; Segal, *Rise of the United Association*, 24–27, 48; Grob, *Workers and Utopia*, 128–32; Patricia Ann Cooper, "From Hand Craft to Mass Production: Men, Women and Work Culture in American Cigar Factories, 1900–1915," (Ph.D. diss., University of Maryland, 1981), 3–5.

49. *Journal of United Labor*, Oct. 15 and Dec. 31, 1887; Irwin Yellowitz, *Labor and the Progressive Movement in New York State, 1897–1916* (Ithaca, N.Y., 1965), 22–23, 27–28, 186–87; David Montgomery, *The Fall of the House of Labor: The Workplace, the State, and American Labor Activism, 1865–1925* (Cambridge, Mass., 1987), 105–6; Gary M. Fink, ed., *Labor Unions* (Westport, Conn., 1977), 37–39, and *BDALL*, 520–21; Grob, *Workers and Utopia*, 128–32, 136; Stevens, *New York Typographical Union No. 6*, 392–93, 399–401.

50. Elizabeth Bogen, *Immigration in New York* (New York, 1987), 6–7; Melvyn Dubofsky, "Organized Labor and the Immigrant in New York City, 1900–1918," *Labor History* 2 (Spring 1961): 183.

51. One special category of Irish American immigrants to note were the large numbers of single women leaving their island homeland throughout the century and entering the work force in New York City and elsewhere. Scholars have long noted the unusual pattern of large numbers of unmarried Irish women who immigrated alone to the United States. The availability of jobs in domestic service and the willingness of Irish American women to accept those positions made this migration economically feasible. Although studies have found that Irish American women preferred work as domestics, many in New York City also entered the needle trades and other industries. Hasia R. Diner, *Erin's Daughters in America: Irish Immigrant Women in the Nineteenth Century* (Baltimore, 1983), 30–42; Commons, *Races and Immigrants*, 122–23; Doyle, "Unestablished Irishmen," 193–220.

52. Ronald L. Filippelli, *Labor Conflict in the United States: An Encyclopedia* (New York, 1990), 351–52; John Bodnar, *The Transplanted: A History of Immigrants in Urban America* (Bloomington, Ind., 1985), 79–80; Stephen Steinberg, *The Ethnic Myth: Race, Ethnicity, and Class in America* (Boston, 1981), 151–66; Ronald H. Bayor, *Neighbors in Conflict: The Irish, Germans, Jews, and Italians of New York City, 1929–1941* (Baltimore, 1978), 4, 22; Kessner, *Golden Door*, 58–59; Diner, *Erin's Daughters*, 70–105; Montgomery, "Irish and the American Labor Movement," 24, 298.

53. Philip Taft, *Organized Labor in American History* (New York, 1964), 203–5, 209–11; Freeman, *In Transit*, 16–17; Bayor, *Neighbors in Conflict*, 22–23; Diner, *Erin's Daughters*, 97–98; McGinley, *Labor Relations in the New York Rapid Transit System*, 258; Montgomery, "Irish and the American Labor Movement," 212, 214.

54. Stephan Thernstrom noted that Boston's Irish at the turn of the century were marginally middle class, having jobs in the clerical and sales forces or the city bureaucracy, not the professions or business. Miller, *Emigrants and Exiles*, 500–501; Henderson, *Tammany Hall and the New Immigrant*, 82; Timothy J. Meagher, ed., *From Paddy to Studs: Irish American Communities in the Turn of the Century Era, 1880 to 1920* (Westport, Conn., 1986), 8–9; Diner, *Erin's Daughters*, 70–105; Commons, *Races and Immigrants*, 205; Edwin Gabler, *American Telegrapher: A Social History, 1860–1890* (New York, 1988), 119–21, 123; Erie, *Rainbow's End*, 62; Hoerder, *Immigrant Press*, 257; Gordon, "Studies in Irish and Irish-American Thought and Behavior," 467; Montgomery, "Irish and the American Labor Movement," 211.

55. Commons, *Races and Immigrants*, 204; Henderson, *Tammany Hall and the New Immigrants*, 72–76; Montgomery, "Irish and the American Labor Movement," 207; Doyle, "Unestablished Irishmen," 194–96.

56. Tammany regained much of the support it lost during the 1886 mayoral campaign by imitating the strategy of its chief rival, the George campaign. Local assembly district organizations were created, which, according to historian Martin Shefter, entered into the social life of their members, "conducting excursions and clambakes, and involving the wives and children in [their] activities." The Associated Tammany Societies, organized in 1888, consolidated the local assembly district organizations under Tammany control, just as the CLU helped organize the trade unions for George. Shefter, "Electoral Foundations of the Political Machine," 290–91.

57. Ford complained editorially that the "Irish instinctively are Protectionists" but remained "a cabled annex to the Democratic party" because of the group's "superstitious allegiance to party management." Patrick Ford, "The Irish Vote in the Pending Presidential Election," *North American Review* 147 (Aug. 1888): 186, 189. See also *Irish World*, Nov. 4, 1893; *Irish-American*, Sept. 23, 1895; Richard L. McCormick, *From Realignment to Reform: Political Change in New York State, 1893–1910* (Ithaca, N.Y., 1979), 94–95; Gwendolyn Mink, *Old Labor and New Immigrants in American Political Development: Union, Party, and State, 1875–1920* (Ithaca, N.Y., 1986), 129, 136–37, 153–54; Henderson, *Tammany Hall and the New Immigrant*, 84–85; Rodechko, "An Irish American Journalist," 531, 536–37.

58. Yellowitz, *Labor and the Progressive Movement*, 171–77.

59. Erie, *Rainbow's End*, 90–91.

60. Historians have noted that this job structure placed the Irish in a highly precarious position when the Great Depression hit. Economic stringencies caused layoffs on the city payrolls, and many Irish American families did not recover economically until the Second World War. Charles W. Cheape, *Moving the Masses: Urban Public Transit in New York, Boston, and Philadelphia, 1880–1912* (Cambridge, Mass., 1980), 80, 87–89; Melvyn Dubofsky, *When Workers Organize: New York City in the Progressive Era* (Amherst, Mass., 1968), 21; McGinley, *Labor Relations in the New York Rapid Transit System*, 519–20; Bayor, *Neighbors in Conflict*, 24–25; Erie, *Rainbow's End*, 67–69, 89–91; Diner, *Erin's Daughters*, 96–98; Lowi, *At the Pleasure of the Mayor*, 33, 45; Henderson, *Tammany Hall and the New Immigrants*, 86–87, 90.

61. Yellowitz, *Labor and the Progressive Movement*, 169; Mink, *Old Labor and the New Immigrant*, 146–47, 152–54; Henderson, "Tammany Hall and the New Immigrants," 78–79.

62. Yellowitz, *Labor and the Progressive Movement*, 2–3, 30–33, 100–101, 115, 126, 166.

63. New York *Irish-American*, Feb. 4, 1895; see also Jan. 21, 1895, and July 1, 1888; Betten, *Catholic Activism*, 5; Henderson, *Tammany Hall and the New Immigrant*, 81–82, 86–87; Curran, "The McGlynn Affair," 196–97; Aaron I. Abell, "American Catholic Reaction to Industrial Conflict: The Arbitral Process, 1885–1900," *Catholic Historical Review* 41 (Jan. 1956), 391–93, 399.

64. *Irish World*, Sept. 9, 1893; Jan. 5, 19, 26, Feb. 9, 23, 1895. Also Betten, *Catholic Activism*, 3; Rodechko, "An Irish American Journalist," 533, 535, 537–38.

65. In Buffalo, St. Louis, and elsewhere, the Roman Catholic Church's antisocialist program led priests to guide workers in forming Catholic labor groups when radicals controlled the local unions. No instance of such religious-inspired dual unionism occurred among the Irish Catholic–dominated trades of New York City. Patrick Ford's *Irish World* also argued that a Catholic could not in good conscience belong to an organization guided by socialist or anarchist views. See *Irish World*, Sept. 9, 1893; Jan. 5, 19, 26, and Feb. 9, 23, 1895. Also *Weekly People*, Apr. 9, 1910, and Mar. 9, and Aug. 3, 1912; Philip S. Foner, *History of the Labor Movement in the United States*, 5 vols. (New

York, 1947–80), 3:112–15; Betten, *Catholic Activism,* 3, 10–13, 15; Meagher, *From Paddy to Studs,* 23; Bayor, *Neighbors in Conflict,* 4; Cross, *Emergence of Liberal Catholicism,* 188; Aaron I, Abell, "The Reception of Leo XIII's Labor Encyclical in America, 1891–1919," *Review of Politics* 7 (Oct. 1945): 164–70; Grob, *Workers and Utopia,* 165–66; Curran, "The McGlynn Affair," 196–203; Saposs, "The Catholic Church and the Labor Movement," 227–28, 229–30; Rodechko, "An Irish American Journalist," 533, 535, 537–38.

66. As quoted in Betten, *Catholic Activism,* 16.

67. Reidy, "John Devoy," 420; Quinn, "John Devoy," 28–29; D'Arcy, "Fenian Movement," 407–8; Gordon, "Studies in Irish and Irish American Thought and Behavior," 485–86.

68. For example, Ford's *Irish World* devoted less attention to labor issues and more to events in Ireland. See Carl Wittke, *The Irish in America* (Baton Rouge, La., 1956), 212. Also Henderson, *Tammany Hall and the New Immigrant,* 80–81; Meagher, *From Paddy to Studs,* 10–112; Miller, *Emigrants and Exiles,* 538–42, 548–50; Reidy, "John Devoy," 420–21; Quinn, "John Devoy," 31–32; Rodechko, "An Irish American Journalist," 538–39; Joyce, "Editors and Ethnicity," 164–65.

69. As quoted in Charles Leinenweber, "The Class and Ethnic Bases of New York City Socialism, 1904–1915," *Labor History* 22 (1981): 47; see also Gary Marks and Matthew Burbank, "Immigrant Support for the American Socialist Party, 1912 and 1920," *Social Science History* 14 (Fall 1990): 178–81, 186; Miller, *Emigrants and Exiles,* 551.

70. Quint, *Forging American Socialism,* 150–53.

71. For the ethnicity of the SLP membership see Hubert Perrier, "Socialist and the Working Class in New York, 1890–96," in Hoerder, ed., *American Labor and Immigration History,* 121–22; also Quint, *Forging American Socialism,* 153–60.

72. Milton Cantor, *The Divided Left: American Radicalism, 1900–1975* (New York, 1978), 19; Perrier, "Socialist and Working Class," 126.

73. The New York City-born son of emigrants from County Mayo, Cassiday was an officer of Local 6 of the Typographical Workers Union. In his 1909 mayoral campaign, Cassiday declared that "the greatest purpose to which a man can put his brain, his strength and his life is to battle for the abolition of the existing industrial slavery of the wealthy producers." Perhaps on account of the presence of Hearst in this election Cassidy did poorly in working-class Irish wards. Finally, in 1921 the Socialists elected Cassidy to a term as a New York City alderman. Edward F. Cassiday to Eugene V. Debs, Nov. 5, 1921, Eugene V. Debs Papers, Reel 4, frame 55.

74. Born to an expatriate Irish working-class family in Edinburgh, Connolly became a socialist before immigrating to the United States in 1903. Although he initially sided with the SLP, and later backed candidates of Debs's Socialist Party, including Cassiday, Connolly tried to maintain a more independent position with the ISF. Connolly launched the monthly periodical the *Harp,* with the help of Donegal immigrant JEC Donnelly as its publisher and financial "angel." According to one historian, the *Harp* was "designed to attract members of the Irish Community into an American working class movement. . . . Connolly's desire [was] to make socialist inroads into a well-established ethnic community by manipulating the political culture of Irish-America." Austen Morgan, *James Connolly: A Political Biography* (New York, 1988), 68–69.

75. [New York] *Harp* 1 (Jan. 1908): 9, 1 (June 1908): 6, 1 (Aug. 1908): 6, 2 (Oct. 1909): 3.

76. [New York] *Harp* 2 (Jan. 1909): 3. Connolly also advised Irish American voters that "as the Democratic party is going down to an unhonored grave because of its inability to grasp the problems of our time, shall we Irish Workers suffer ourselves to be

dragged to social perdition with it?" [New York] *Harp* 1 (May 1908): 6. See also 1 (Sept. 1908): 6, 2 (Feb. 1909): 62, (Apr. 1909): 6.

77. In 1910, the discouraged Connolly relocated the *Harp* to Dublin and died there six years later in the Easter Week Uprising. Morgan, *James Connolly*, 69–70; C. Desmond Greaves, *The Life and Times of James Connolly* (London, 1961), 214–20; Ruth D. Edwards, *James Connolly* (Dublin, 1961), 55–65; Kieran Allen, *The Politics of James Connolly* (London, 1990), 57–82.

78. O'Reilly left the labor movement for a time in the 1890s to become an industrial education teacher for women at the Asacog Settlement House in Brooklyn. This later developed into the Manhattan Trade School for Girls. She later represented the WTUL in the investigation of safety practices in the garment industry after the Triangle Shirt Waist Company fire in 1911. Mary J. Bularzik, "The Bonds of Belonging: Leonora O'Reilly and Social Reform," *Labor History* 24 (Winter 1983): 60–83; James J. Kenneally, *Women and American Trade Unions* (St. Albans, Vt., 1978), 58–60, 68–69; Nancy Schrom Dye, *As Equals and as Sisters: Feminism, the Labor Movement, and the Women's Trade Union League of New York* (Columbia, Mo., 1980), 26–27, 31, 34–35, 128; Mari Jo Buhle, *Women and American Socialism, 1870–1920* (Urbana, Ill., 1983), 189, 199–200, 226. Another Irish American leader of the WTUL in New York in this period was Maud O'Farrell Swartz. Edward James et al., *Notable American Women, 1607–1950: A Biographical Dictionary*, 3 vols. (Cambridge, Mass., 1971), 3:413–15.

79. Melvyn Dubofsky, "Success and Failure of Socialism in New York City, 1900–1918: A Case Study," *Labor History* 9 (Fall 1968): 361–65; Mink, *Old Labor and New Immigrants*, 201–2.

80. There was significant Irish American support of the Western Federation of Miners (WFM), the precursor to the IWW. The first president of the WFM was Irish immigrant Ed Boyce. See David Saposs, *Left Wing Unionism: A Study of Radical Policies and Tactics* (New York, 1926), 152; James Weinstein, *The Decline of Socialism in America, 1912–1925* (New Brunswick, N.J., 1967), 14–15; Foner, "Irish Land League," 199–200.

81. New York *Weekly People*, Dec. 10, 24, 31, 1910, and Jan. 7, 14, 21, 28, 1911; Horace B. Davis, *Shoes: The Workers and the Industry* (New York, 1940), 171–72, 194–98; Matthew Josephson, *Union House, Union Bar: The History of the Hotel and Restaurant Employees and Bartenders International Union, AFL-CIO* (New York, 1956), 97–98; Saposs, *Left Wing Unionism*, 153; Julian Jaffe, *Crusade against Radicalism: New York during the Red Scare, 1914–1924* (Port Washington, N.Y., 1972), 26–27.

82. One notable exception to the dearth of New York Irish support of the IWW is Elizabeth Gurley Flynn. Flynn was introduced to radical politics by her father, Thomas Flynn, an associate of James Connolly, who organized a radical club in Harlem. Elizabeth joined an IWW mixed local as a young high school student in 1906. More intrigued with the IWW than with her school work, Flynn left school and became active as an organizer and speaker for the Wobblies throughout the United States. Flynn played a prominent role in the IWW free speech and assembly struggles in Montana and Washington State, as well as in the textile strikes in Lawrence, Massachusetts, in 1912 and the silk strike in Paterson, New Jersey, in 1913. A forceful and effective speaker, Flynn was described as "Irish all over, with the Celt inner grey-blue eyes and almost black hair and in the way she clenches her small hands into fists when she's speaking." Melvyn Dubofsky, *We Shall Be All: A History of the IWW, The Industrial Workers of the World* (New York, 1969), 180–81; Rosalyn Fraad Baxandall, *Words on Fire: The Life and Writing of Elizabeth Gurley Flynn* (New Brunswick, N.J., 1987), 7; Buhle, *Women and Socialism*, 202–3, 288.

83. *Weekly People*, Aug. 31, 1912; David Brody, *The Butcher Workmen: A Study of Unionization* (Cambridge, Mass., 1964), 67–71; Foner, *History of the Labor Movement*, 3: 112; Segal, *Rise of the United Association*, 24–27, 48; Freeman, *In Transit*, 16–17; Montgomery, "The Irish and the American Labor Movement," 206.

84. One significant exception was the International Association of Machinists. See Mark Perlman, *The Machinists: A New Study in American Trade Unionism* (Cambridge, Mass., 1961), 19–22, 36; also Fink, *BDALL*, 85, 261, 276; Van Tine, *Labor Union Bureaucrat*, 135–37; Foner, *History of American Labor*, 3: 153–60; Montgomery, "Irish and the American Labor Movement," 206–7.

85. Harold Seidman, *Labor Czars: A History of Labor Racketeering* (New York, 1938), 11–26, 68–93; Montgomery, *Fall of the House of Labor*, 298; Foner, *History of the Labor Movement*, 3:140; Fink, *BDALL*, 263–64; Van Tine, *Labor Union Bureaucrat*, 146–48, 175–77; Taft, *Organized Labor*, 209–11; Segal, *Rise of the United Association*, 104–7.

86. Brooks, *Road to Dignity*, 54–55; Galenson, *United Brotherhood of Carpenters*, 108–10; Fink, *BDALL*, 85; Erlich, "Peter J. McGuire's Trade Unionism," 190–93.

87. Frank Duffy, *Some Facts in the Controversy between the United Brotherhood of Carpenters and Joiners of America and the Amalgamated Wood Workers International Union* (n.p., 1903), 5, 11; Galenson, *United Brotherhood of Carpenters*, 123–24; Charles A. Madison, *American Labor Leaders: Personalities and Forces in the Labor Movement* (New York, 1950), 140–42.

88. Mink, *Old Labor and New Immigrants*, 165–66; Robert Asher, "Union Nativism and the Immigrant Response," *Labor History*, 330, 336; Dubofsky, *When Workers Organize*, 76, and "Organized Labor and the Immigrant," 185–90.

89. For example, the International Association of Machinists, led by James O'Connell, abolished their all-white membership requirement in 1895 but admitted no blacks until the 1940s. See Perlman, *The Machinists*, 17. See also Walter Galenson, *Rival Unionism in the United States* (New York, 1940), 37; Dubofsky, *When Workers Organize*, 120–21; Taft, *Organized Labor*, 189; Segal, *United Association*, 48; Herman D. Bloch, "Labor and the Negro, 1866–1910," *Journal of Negro History* 50 (July 1965): 175–84.

90. Jesse Thomas Carpenter, *Competition and Collective Bargaining in the Needle Trades, 1910–1967* (Ithaca, N.Y., 1972), 1, 6; Dubofsky, "Organized Labor and the Immigrant," 186–87.

91. Charles Elbert Zaretz, *The Amalgamated Clothing Workers of America: A Study in Progressive Trades-Unionism* (New York, 1934), 49–51, 106–10; James O'Neal, *A History of the Amalgamated Ladies' Garment Cutters' Union, Local 10* (New York, 1927), 12–19, 44–49, 93–95; Irving Bernstein, *Turbulent Years: A History of the American Worker, 1933–1941* (Boston, 1971), 66–75; Mink, *Old Labor and New Immigrants*, 201–2; Madison, *American Labor Leaders*, 335–38, 341; Van Tine, *Labor Union Bureaucrat*, 109, 157; Fink, *BDALL*, 485; Van Tine, *Labor Unions*, 57–61, 117–20; Dubofsky, "Organized Labor and the Immigrant," 186–87, 191–92.

92. A. T. Lane, *Solidarity or Survival: American Labor and European Immigrants, 1830–1924* (New York, 1987), 202–3; Zaretz, *Amalgamated Clothing Workers*, 67; Jaffe, *Crusade against Radicalism*, 29–32; Foner, *History of the Labor Movement*, 3: 261; Dubofsky, "Organized Labor and the Immigrant," 192–97, 201.

93. Jaffe, *Crusade against Radicalism*, 30–31, 34; Mink, *Old Labor and New Immigrants*, 257–58; Montgomery, *Fall of the House of Labor*, 356–85; Meagher, *From Paddy to Studs*, 26–27; Yellowitz, *Labor and the Progressive Movement*, 246–47.

94. David M. Emmons, *The Butte Irish: Class and Ethnicity in an American Mining Town, 1875–1925* (Urbana, Ill., 1989); Dennis J. Clark, *The Irish in Philadelphia: Ten*

Generations of Urban Experience (Philadelphia, 1974), passim; Jo Ellen Vinyard, *The Irish on the Urban Frontier: Detroit, 1850–1880* (New York, 1976); Michael Kazin, "Barons of Labor: The San Francisco Building Trades, 1896–1922" (Ph.D. diss., Stanford University, 1982), 573–78; Foner, "Class, Ethnicity and Radicalism," 20–44; Montgomery, "The Irish and the American Labor Movement," 205–18; Marks and Burbank, "Immigrant Support for the American Socialist Party," 186–87; Doyle, "Unestablished Irishmen," 193–96.

Chapter 13: "IN TIME OF PEACE, PREPARE FOR WAR" (Brundage)

I would like to thank Timothy J. Meagher and three anonymous reviewers for their helpful comments on earlier versions of this essay. I would also like to thank Angela M. Carter, Dennis Clark, Joe Doyle, and Joshua Freeman for directing me toward important sources.

1. Ernest Gellner, *Nations and Nationalism* (Ithaca, N.Y., 1983), 101–9. For the Land League era, see Thomas N. Brown, *Irish-American Nationalism, 1870–1890* (Philadelphia, 1966); Eric Foner, "Class, Ethnicity, and Radicalism in the Gilded Age: The Land League and Irish-America," in his *Politics and Ideology in the Age of the Civil War* (New York, 1980), 150–200. For the 1916–21 period, see F. M. Carroll, *American Opinion and the Irish Question, 1910–23: A Study in Opinion and Policy* (New York, 1978); Alan J. Ward, *Ireland and Anglo-American Relations, 1899–1921* (London, 1969); and chapter 14 in this volume.

2. Tom Garvin, *Nationalist Revolutionaries in Ireland, 1858–1928* (New York, 1987), 124–25, 172–73.

3. T. W. Moody, "The New Departure in Irish Politics, 1878–9," in H. A. Cronne, T. W. Moody, and D. B. Quinn, eds., *Essays in British and Irish History in Honour of James Eadre Todd* (London, 1949), 303–33; T. W. Moody, *Davitt and Irish Revolution, 1846–82* (New York, 1981), xv–xvii, 221–327; D. George Boyce, *Nationalism in Ireland* (London, 1982), 192–227; Tom Garvin, *The Evolution of Irish Nationalist Politics* (Dublin, 1981), 69–84; Brown, *Irish-American Nationalism,* 85–98; Foner, "Class, Ethnicity, and Radicalism," 154–58. Jeremiah O'Donovan Rossa, New York's second most famous Fenian exile, vehemently opposed the New Departure, but he was far less influential than Devoy.

4. Florence Gibson, *The Attitudes of the New York Irish toward State and National Affairs, 1848–1892* (New York, 1951), 273–75, 303–8; Brown, *Irish American Nationalism,* 108; Foner, "Class, Ethnicity, and Radicalism," 170–77.

5. Gibson, *Attitudes of the New York Irish,* 326–27; Foner, "Class, Ethnicity, and Radicalism," 177–79; Michael A. Gordon, "The Labor Boycott in New York City, 1880–1886," *Labor History* 16 (1975): 194–98; Stephen P. Erie, *Rainbow's End: Irish-Americans and the Dilemmas of Urban Machine Politics, 1840–1985* (Berkeley, Calif., 1988), 50.

6. Foner, "Class, Ethnicity, and Radicalism," 187–89, 193; Robert Emmett Curran, S.J., "The McGlynn Affair and the Shaping of the New Conservatism in American Catholicism, 1886–1894," *Catholic Historical Review* 66 (1980): 185–86.

7. John L. Thomas, *Alternative America: Henry George, Edward Bellamy, Henry Demarest Lloyd and the Adversary Tradition* (Cambridge, Mass., 1983), 175–81, 220–27; Gibson, *Attitudes of the New York Irish,* 396–98; Foner, "Class, Ethnicity, and Radicalism," 184–86, 198; Curran, "The McGlynn Affair," 186–88.

8. Jane McL. Côté, *Fanny and Anna Parnell: Ireland's Patriot Sisters* (New York, 1991), 134–40; Denver *Labor Enquirer,* Aug. 11, 1883; Curran, "The McGlynn Affair,"

191–92; Peter A. Speek, *The Single Tax and the Labor Movement* (Madison, Wis., 1917), 101–4. Hasia Diner, *Erin's Daughters in America: Irish Immigrant Women in the Nineteenth Century* (Baltimore, 1983), 128, disputes the importance of the Ladies Land League for Irish American women, but for some vital local branches in America and for the organization's tremendous significance in Ireland, see David Brundage, "Irish Land and American Workers: Class and Ethnicity in Denver, Colorado," in Dirk Hoerder, ed., *"Struggle a Hard Battle": Essays on Working-Class Immigrants* (DeKalb, Ill., 1986), 56–57; Timothy J. Meagher, "Sweet Good Mothers and Young Women Out in the World: The Roles of Irish American Women in Late Nineteenth and Early Twentieth Century Worcester, Massachusetts," *U.S. Catholic Historian* 5 (1986): 326–27; Joseph Lee, *The Modernisation of Irish Society, 1848–1918* (Dublin, 1973), 93–94.

9. *Irish World,* Jan. 5, 1884; James P. Rodechko, *Patrick Ford and His Search for America: A Case Study of Irish-American Journalism* (New York, 1976), 166–68; Elizabeth Gurley Flynn, *The Rebel Girl: An Autobiography* (New York, 1973), 42–43.

10. Garvin, *Evolution,* 84–88; Foner, "Class, Ethnicity, and Radicalism," 189–92; Brown, *Irish-American Nationalism,* 153–77.

11. Carroll, *American Opinion,* 7; Peter J. Sammon, "The History of the Irish National Federation of America" (Master's thesis, Catholic University of America, 1951); Thomas Addis Emmet, *Incidents of My Life* (New York, 1911), 281–89; Boyce, *Nationalism,* 259–62; Garvin, *Evolution,* 84–88.

12. Carroll, *American Opinion,* 7–8; Ward, *Ireland and Anglo-American Relations,* 12–21.

13. J. J. Lee, *Ireland, 1912–1985: Politics and Society* (New York, 1989), 15; Rodechko, *Patrick Ford,* 168–82.

14. Alan Himber, ed., *The Letters of John Quinn to William Butler Yeats* (Ann Arbor, Mich., 1983), 78. See also B. L. Reid, *The Man from New York: John Quinn and His Friends* (New York, 1968).

15. United Irish League of America, *Proceedings of the Second National Convention, 1904,* 48; John Hutchinson, *The Dynamics of Cultural Nationalism: The Gaelic Revival and the Creation of the Irish Nation State* (Boston, 1987), 152; Bourke Cockran to Moreton Frewen, July 30, 1915, William Bourke Cockran Papers, New York Public Library; James McGurrin, *Bourke Cockran: A Free Lance in American Politics* (New York, 1948), 220.

16. Bourke Cockran to Moreton Frewen, May 19, 1914, Cockran Papers; Carroll, *American Opinion,* 23–24.

17. Emmet, *Incidents,* 301; Richard C. Murphy and Lawrence J. Mannion, *The History of the Society of the Friendly Sons of Saint Patrick in the City of New York, 1784 to 1955* (New York, 1962), 348; John Redmond to Bourke Cockran, Mar. 31, 1900, John D. Crimmins to Bourke Cockran, Nov. 21, 1901, and William Redmond to Bourke Cockran, Mar. 1902, Cockran Papers. For a fine discussion of middle-class Irish American nationalism in these years see Kerby A. Miller, *Emigrants and Exiles: Ireland and the Irish Exodus to North America* (New York, 1985), 541–48. See also Dennis Clark's discussion of UILA president Michael J. Ryan in his *Erin's Heirs: Irish Bonds of Community* (Lexington, Ky., 1991), 157–70.

18. Charles Leinenweber, "Socialists in the Streets: The New York City Socialist Party in Working Class Neighborhoods, 1908–1918," *Science and Society* 41 (1977): 152–71; Melvyn Dubofsky, *When Workers Organize: New York City in the Progressive Era* (Amherst, Mass., 1968).

19. John Laslett, *Labor and the Left: A Study of Socialist and Radical Influences in the American Labor Movement, 1881–1924* (New York, 1970), 54–97, 241–86; Leinen-

weber, "Socialists in the Streets," 152–53; Carl Reeve and Ann Barton Reeve, *James Connolly and the United States: The Road to the 1916 Irish Rebellion* (Atlantic Highlands, N.J., 1978), 27–28; William O'Dwyer, interview, 81–85, Oral History Collection, Columbia University.

20. Rodechko, *Patrick Ford*, 108–17; Henry F. Bedford, *Socialism and the Workers in Massachusetts, 1886–1912* (Amherst, Mass., 1966), 190; Reid, *Man from New York*, 285; Carroll, *American Opinion*, 40.

21. Graham Adams Jr., *Age of Industrial Violence, 1910–1915* (New York, 1966), 115–16; J. J. Huthmacher, "Charles Evans Hughes and Charles Francis Murphy: The Metamorphosis of Progressivism," *New York History* 46 (1965): 25–40.

22. UILA, *Proceedings of the Second National Convention, 1904*, 47–48, 50–51, 80–82.

23. Cliona Murphy, *The Women's Suffrage Movement and Irish Society in the Early Twentieth Century* (New York, 1989), 172–78; Carroll, *American Opinion*, 16; *New York Times*, May 5, 1912.

24. Bourke Cockran to Moreton Frewen, Mar. 25, 1914, and Dr. Gertrude B. Kelly to Bourke Cockran, Oct. 2, 1914, Cockran Papers.

25. John Devoy, *Recollections of an Irish Rebel* (New York, 1929; reprint ed., Shannon, Ireland, 1969), 392–96, 416–22; Ward, *Ireland and Anglo-American Relations*, 8–10, 24–29; Carroll, *American Opinion*, 6–9, 26–36.

26. Garvin, *Nationalist Revolutionaries*, 172; William O'Brien and Desmond Ryan, eds., *Devoy's Post Bag, 1871–1928*, 2 vols. (Dublin, 1948), 2: 482–83. A similar situation existed in the separatist movement in Ireland. The women's organization, Cumann na mBan, played an important role in the revolutionary challenge to British rule, but this role was carefully defined and limited by men. See Margaret Ward, *Unmanageable Revolutionaries: Women and Irish Nationalism* (London, 1983), 88–107.

27. Dr. Gertrude B. Kelly to Bourke Cockran, Oct. 2, 1914, Cockran Papers; Diner, *Erin's Daughters*, 25; Carroll, *American Opinion*, 267.

28. This paralleled the situation in Ireland. See Garvin, *Nationalist Revolutionaries*, 51, who argues that because separatists drew support from an unstable coalition of agrarian radicals, urban workers, and the Catholic lower middle class, they avoided developing any social program that would divide these groups.

29. Adams, *Age of Industrial Violence*, 115–18.

30. Emmet Larkin, "The Devotional Revolution in Ireland, 1850–75," *American Historical Review* 77 (1972): 625–52; Sheridan Gilley, "The Catholic Church and Revolution," in D. G. Boyce, ed., *The Revolution in Ireland, 1879–1923* (London, 1988), 157–72.

31. Anthony M. Brogan to Bourke Cockran, Jan. 6, 1915, Cockran Papers; Joseph Edward Cuddy, *Irish-America and National Isolationism, 1914–1920* (New York, 1976), 44–47; John Patrick Buckley, *The New York Irish: Their View of American Foreign Policy, 1914–1921* (New York, 1976).

Part IV Overview: WHEN NEW YORK WAS IRISH, AND AFTER
(McNickle)

1. Edward M. Levine, *The Irish and Irish Politicians: A Study of Cultural and Social Alienation* (Notre Dame, Ind., 1966), 35–37, 45, 78; Nathan Glazer and Daniel Moynihan, *Beyond the Melting Pot: The Negroes, Puerto Ricans, Jews, Italians and Irish of New*

York City, 2d ed. (Cambridge, Mass., 1970), 221–30; William Riordan, *Plunkitt of Tammany Hall* (New York, 1963); Steven P. Erie, *Rainbow's End: Irish Americans and the Dilemmas of Urban Machine Politics, 1840–1985* (Berkeley, Calif., 1988), 1–17.

2. Morton Keller, *Affairs of State* (Cambridge, Mass., 1977), 239; Gustavus Myers, *The History of Tammany Hall* (New York, 1971), 283; Terry Nichols Clark, "The Irish Ethic and the Spirit of Patronage," *Ethnicity* 2 (1975), 305–59; Riordan, *Plunkitt*, 25–29, 90–98.

3. Myers, *Tammany Hall*, 278–79; Glazer and Moynihan, *Beyond the Melting Pot*, 218; William V. Shannon, *The American Irish: A Political and Social Portrait* (New York, 1963), 78.

4. Nancy Joan Weiss, *Charles Francis Murphy, 1858–1924* (Northampton, Mass., 1968); J. Joseph Huthmacher, "Charles Evans Hughes and Charles F. Murphy, The Metamorphosis of Progressivism," *New York History* 46 (Jan. 1965), 28; Robert Wesser, *A Response to Progressivism: The Democratic Party and New York Politics, 1902–1918* (New York, 1986), 11–12.

5. Ira Rosenwaike, *Population History of New York* (Syracuse, N.Y., 1972), appendices.

6. Chris McNickle, *To Be Mayor of New York: Ethnic Politics in the City* (New York, 1993), 20–32, 48.

7. Weiss, *Charles Francis Murphy*, 28; Wesser, *A Response to Progressivism*, 23.

8. Moses Rischin, *The Promised City: New York's Jews, 1870–1914* (Cambridge, Mass., 1962), 42–44; Melvyn Dubofsky, *When Workers Organize: New York City in the Progressive Era* (Amherst, Mass., 1968), 16–18; Melvyn Dubofsky, "Success and Failure of Socialism in New York City, 1900–1918: A Case Study," *Labor History* 9 (1968), 365; Irving Howe, *Socialism and America* (New York, 1977), 8.

9. Huthmacher, "Charles Evans Hughes and Charles Francis Murphy," 29; J. Joseph Huthmacher, *Senator Robert F. Wagner and the Rise of Urban Liberalism* (New York, 1968), 28–37; Weiss, *Charles Francis Murphy*, 45–49, 88; Wesser, *A Response to Progressivism*, 27–30.

10. Erie, *Rainbow's End*; McNickle, *To Be Mayor of New York*, 20–40.

11. Shannon, *The American Irish*, 201–33; Roger Biles, *Big City Boss in Depression and War: Mayor Edward J. Kelly of Chicago* (DeKalb, Ill., 1984).

12. Edwin R. Lewinson, *John Purroy Mitchel: The Boy Mayor of New York* (New York, 1965); Jacob A. Friedman, *The Impeachment of Governor William Sulzer* (New York, 1939).

13. Rischin, *The Promised City*; Irving Howe, *World of Our Fathers: The Journey of the East European Jews to America and the Life They Found and Made* (New York, 1976); Arthur Goren, *New York Jews and the Quest for Community: The Kehillah Experiment, 1908–1922* (New York, 1970); Thomas Kessner, *The Golden Door: Italian and Jewish Immigrant Mobility in New York City, 1880–1915* (New York, 1977); Luciano J. Iorizzo and Salvatore Mondello, *The Italian Americans* (Boston, 1980), 76–91, 188–92; David Burner, *The Politics of Provincialism: The Democratic Party in Transition, 1918–1932* (Cambridge, Mass., 1986), 74–75.

14. Andrew M. Greeley, *The Irish Americans: The Rise to Money and Power* (New York, 1981) 8, 138. Greeley points out that the national figures may not precisely reflect the conditions in New York, but the large number of Irish in New York implies that they must have participated in the upward mobility reflected across the country. Suzanne Model, "The Ethnic Niche and the Structure of Opportunity: Immigrants and Minorities

in New York City," in Michael Katz, ed., *The Underclass Debate: Views From History*, (Princeton, N.J., 1992), 172–74.

15. Shannon, *The American Irish*, 86; Kerby Miller, *Emigrants and Exiles: Ireland and the Irish Exodus to North America* (New York, 1985), 496.

16. Arthur M. Schlesinger Jr., *Robert Kennedy and His Times* (New York, 1978), 3–15.

17. Shannon, *The American Irish*, 337, 431–32; *New York Times*, Jan. 18, Mar. 9, 1961, and June 19, 1978.

18. Charles Fanning, *The Irish Voice in America: Irish-American Fiction from the 1760s to the 1980s* (Lexington, Ky., 1990), 1–3.

19. Fanning, *The Irish Voice in America*, 238–40.

20. Charles Scribner III, "Introduction," to F. Scott Fitzgerald, *The Great Gatsby* (New York, 1986).

21. Malcolm Crowley, *The Literary Situation* (New York, 1958), 153, quoted in Shannon, *The American Irish*, 234; Robert E. Rhodes, "F. Scott Fitzgerald: All My Fathers," 45, in Daniel J. Casey and Robert E. Rhodes, eds., *Irish-American Fiction: Essays in Criticism* (New York, 1979).

22. Miller, *Emigrants and Exiles*, 493; Rhodes, "F. Scott Fitzgerald: All My Fathers," 31.

23. Shannon, *The American Irish*, 244.

24. Ibid., 245; Joseph Browne, "John O'Hara and Tom McHale: How Green Is Their Valley," 132, in Daniel J. Casey and Robert E. Rhodes, eds. *Irish American Fiction*.

25. Fanning, *The Irish Voice in America*, 293–311; Barry O'Connell, "The Lost World of James T. Farrell's Short Stories," 53–70, in Daniel J. Casey and Robert E. Rhodes, eds., *Irish American Fiction*.

26. Shannon, *The American Irish*, 278.

27. Diane Ravitch, *The Great School Wars, New York City, 1805–1973* (New York, 1974), 219–33.

28. Jay Dolan, *The Immigrant Church: New York's Irish and German Catholics, 1815–1865*, (Baltimore, 1975), 103; Ravitch, *The Great School Wars*, 33–76.

29. John Cooney, *The American Pope: The Life and Times of Francis Cardinal Spellman* (New York, 1984), 176–85; William O'Dwyer, *Beyond the Golden Door* (New York, 1987), 312.

30. Cooney, *The American Pope*, 79; Miller, *Emigrants and Exiles*, 530.

31. John Patrick Buckley, *The New York Irish: Their View of American Foreign Policy, 1914–1921* (New York, 1976), 6–7; R. F. Foster, *Modern Ireland: 1600–1972* (London, 1988), 359.

32. Foster, *Modern Ireland*, 359–60; Miller, *Emigrants and Exiles*, 494–95; Lawrence J. McCaffrey, "Introduction," in Lawrence J. McCaffrey, ed., *Irish Nationalism and the American Contribution* (New York, 1976), iv; Thomas N. Brown, *Irish American Nationalism, 1870–1890* (Philadelphia, 1966), 20–24.

33. Foster, *Modern Ireland*, 431–61; Alan J. Ward, "America and the Irish Problem, 1899–1921," in McCaffrey, ed., *Irish Nationalism and the American Contribution* for Relief in Ireland. See Francis M. Carroll's invaluable history of the era, *American Opinion and the Irish Question, 1910–1923* (New York, 1978).

34. Buckley, *The New York Irish*, 36.

35. Ibid., 189–90.

36. Joseph O'Grady, "The Irish," in Joseph O'Grady, ed., *The Immigrants' Influence on Woodrow Wilson's Peace Policies* (Lexington, Ky., 1967), 59, cited in

Buckley, *The New York Irish*, 194; see also 207, 212, 221. Also Burner, *The Politics of Provincialism*, 58.

37. Foster, *Modern Ireland*, 360; Ward, "America and the Irish Problem, 1899–1921"; Carl Wittke, *The Irish in America* (Baton Rouge, La., 1956), 273–85.

38. Foster, *Modern Ireland*, 360.

39. George Walsh, *Gentleman Jimmy Walker: Mayor of the Jazz Age* (New York, 1974), 52, 67, 79–80, 165–66.

40. Walsh, *Gentleman Jimmy Walker*; Matthew and Hannah Josephson, *Al Smith: Hero of the Cities* (Boston, Mifflin, 1969), 444; Burner, *The Politics of Provincialism*, 179–216; William E. Leuchtenburg, *The Perils of Prosperity, 1914–1932* (Chicago, 1958), 225–40.

41. Theodore Lowi, *At the Pleasure of the Mayor: Patronage and Power in New York City, 1898–1958* (London, 1964), 38; Thomas Kessner, *Fiorello H. LaGuardia and the Making of Modern New York* (New York, 1989), 245–57; Edward J. Flynn, *You're the Boss* (New York, 1947), 73, 144; McNickle, *To Be Mayor of New York*, 37–45.

42. Alan Brinkley, *Voices of Protest* (New York, 1982), 82–83, 93, 266–73; Ronald Bayor, *Neighbors in Conflict: The Irish, Germans, Jews, and Italians of New York City, 1929–1941* (Baltimore, 1978), 87–104.

43. Bayor, *Neighbors in Conflict*, 87, 150–62; Cooney, *The American Pope*, 41; Howe, *World of Our Fathers*, 326–30.

44. Bayor, *Neighbors in Conflict*, 87–107.

45. Charles Barnes, *The Longshoreman* (New York, 1915), 5–7.

46. Bayor, *Neighbors in Conflict*, 109–14.

47. McNickle, *To Be Mayor of New York*, 55–56.

Chapter 14: STRIKING FOR IRELAND ON THE NEW YORK DOCKS (Doyle)

1. Unpublished interviews by the author with Thomas W. "Teddy" Gleason, Feb. 11, 1983, and Nov. 9, 1992. Mr. Gleason, president of the International Longshoremen's Union, 1963–87, was 19 years old in 1920 and a longshoreman on the West Side docks. In a speech he gave on January 7, 1983, Gleason recalled the MacSwiney strike as one of the proudest moments of his life.

2. Fanny Parnell proposed the Ladies Land League to Michael Davitt and set it in motion with an open letter to the *Irish World*, initially as a means to resuscitate the flagging fund-raising efforts of the American Land League. It was hoped that friendly competition from a parallel women's organization would spur the men to start contributing again, which indeed proved to be the case.

3. Ladies Land League branches were established in Denver, Boston, Buffalo; Pawtucket, Rhode Island; Carbondale, Pennsylvania; Jersey City, Hoboken, Montclair and Paterson, New Jersey; and in Fall River and Gloucester, Massachusetts. The Ladies League of Scranton, Pennsylvania, remitted $1,000 for the No Rent Campaign in July 1881. Three Ladies Land League branches were organized in Philadelphia.

4. *Irish World*, May 14, July 16, and July 23, 1881; Feb. 25, 1882.

5. The Ladies Land League was somewhat fragmented on ideological lines. According to Jane Côté in *Fanny and Anna Parnell: Ireland's Patriot Sisters* (New York, 1990), Fanny Parnell, directing operations of the American arm of the league, maneuvered Ellen Ford out of the organization for supporting the *Irish World* and Henry George program of nationalizing land and commiting acts of violence against the property of landlords

threatening eviction. At the same time, Anna Parnell's memoirs criticize the Land League as a "great sham" for being preoccupied with paying rent to landlords threatening to evict their tenants.

6. *Irish World,* Jan. 29, 1881, 2.

7. Margaret Ward, *Unmanageable Revolutionaries: Women and Irish Nationalism* (London, 1983), 39.

8. Hasia Diner, *Erin's Daughters in America: Irish Immigrant Women in the Nineteenth Century* (Baltimore, 1983), chapt. 7: "Irish Men/Irish Women: The World View from the Nineteenth Century."

9. AOH historian John Ridge has documented nineteenth-century AOH ladies' auxiliaries and short-lived women's auxiliaries to the Irish county organizations. Most of them lasted only a few years, sprouting up as contemporaries of the Ladies Land League, or organized themselves in the 1880s as Parnell's home rule movement reached its peak, but failed with the collapse of the Parnellite movement.

10. Dirk Hoerder, *Immigrant Labor Press in North America, 1840s–1970s,* vol. 3, (Westport, Conn., 1987); Diner, *Erin's Daughters,* 143.

11. Joan of Arc was frequently chronicled in the pages of the *Irish World* because her canonization was being processed at the time by the Vatican, and because "English intriguers" were instrumental in her martyrdom.

12. "The Suffrage Not a Natural Right," *Irish World,* June 9, 1894; "Another Piteous Wail from the Land of English-Made Famines," ibid., Oct. 4, 1890; "Sister Mary Catherine: Miss Drexel's Life Consecrated to the Service of the Indian and Negro Races," ibid., Feb. 1991.

13. Helena Maloney was also a cofounder (with James and Delia Larkin) of the Irish Women Workers Union in 1911. Leah Levenson and Jerry H. Natterstad, *Hanna Sheehy-Skeffington, Irish Feminist* (Syracuse, N.Y., 1986).

14. *Irish World,* Nov. 12, 1914, 5.

15. Leonora O'Reilly enlisted support from Frank P. Walsh, whom she had known from her work as head of the Wage Earners' Suffrage League, and Thomas Rock of the New York City Central Trades Council, who was a public supporter of the Women's Trade Union League, which O'Reilly headed for many years.

16. *Bulletin of the Irish Progressive League,* no. 4, Sept. 1919, 4. References in this chapter to the Irish Progressive League are drawn in part from notes taken by Professor David Brundage (and shared with the author) from documents in the Peter Golden Papers in the National Library in Dublin, which include a number of Helen Merriam Golden's papers.

Bernard Ferguson, in an unpublished interview with the author on May 25, 1984, recalled that as an 18-year-old college student he took one of these classes in public speaking from Jeremiah O'Leary, at the 85th Street Turn Verein Hall in Yorkville. Ferguson remembered the class as a cross section of Irish American New Yorkers: housewives, house painters, and trolley car conductors. Each new person joining the class was brought forward to address the class, with O'Leary's coaching. The other students heckled the neophyte and grilled her or him on points of Irish history, trying to reproduce the difficulties the new soapboxer would encounter on the streets. At the outdoor meetings, Ferguson recalled substantial heckling from New Yorkers who considered the soapboxers disloyal to the recent Allied war effort. Ferguson added that such hecklers would have been further aggrieved had they known that the standard operating procedure for Irish street speakers was to borrow the ladders that served as their speaking platforms from the closest German delicatessen.

17. Between 1917 and 1922 Dr. William J. Maloney authored a series of highly influential articles making the case for Irish sovereignty; wrote a satire of England's manipulation of American public opinion, *The Reconquest of America*, which sold an estimated 750,000 copies; bankrolled (with Joseph McGarrity) the Women Pickets' Washington campaign; and founded the American Commission on Conditions in Ireland and the American Committee

18. Patrick McCartan, *With de Valera in America* (New York, 1932), 175.

19. Thomas K. Corless, born in Dublin, was son of the restauranteur who had pioneered the Corless oyster beds in Galway. *Irish World*, July 3, 1920, 12. The *New York Times*, Apr. 3, 1920, 2, refers to the meeting in Gertrude Corless's 8th Avenue apartment.

20. The Irish Progressive League was founded in the autumn of 1917. An intriguing letter to the editor dated October 27, 1917, in the Helen Golden Papers of Dublin's National Library, claims as its founders, Peter and Helen Golden, Nora Connolly, Padraic and Mary Colum, and calls them "the firebrands of the late lamented American Truth Society," which Jeremiah O'Leary founded in 1912. See also Mary Colum, *Life and the Dream* (New York, 1947).

21. "Irish Americans and Woodrow Wilson and Self-Determination," *Newsletter of the American Catholic Historical Society*, vol. 74, Sept. 1963.

22. Tim Pat Coogan, *Michael Collins* (London, 1991), 92.

23. *The Globe and Commercial Advertiser*, Apr. 3, 1920.

24. Hattie McGinnis, for example, a "gold star mother," from Frockville, Pennsylvania, told reporters: "Self-determination, bah! That's for my boy who gave his life fighting for the self-determination of small nations." *Washington Evening Star*, Apr. 9, 1920.

25. *Irish World*, June 16, 1917, 3.

26. O'Reilly headed the Wage Earners Suffrage League from 1911 to 1912 and had been invited by Paul to join the executive committee of the National Women's Party. Inez Hayes Irwin, *The Story of Alice Paul and the National Women's Party* (Fairfax, Va., 1964).

27. *New York Times*, Apr. 3, 1920, 1.

28. Unlike the women suffragists, the Irish pickets were treated well in jail. Mary Galvin, for example, who refused bail for three days, reported not only that she and her fellow Women Pickets received kind treatment from jailers and prisoners alike, but the food was to her liking: "Piles of Irish potatoes were offered us, besides Hungarian goulash and New England dinners." *Washington Evening Star*, Apr. 6, 1920.

29. Newsreels of the women pickets' campaign were shown in movie houses nationwide. McCartan, *With de Valera*, 180.

30. *New York Tribune*, Apr. 6, 1920. Mollie Carroll told reporters her upbringing wedded her to the cause of Irish freedom; her mother, especially, had been active in Ireland in the independence struggle. *New York Times*, Apr. 3 and 7, 1920. Carroll was a member of the Irish Progressive League. Golden Papers, Minutes, Nov. 30, 1917.

31. *New York Times*, Apr. 7, 1920. The American public seemed to approve of the picketing campaign, to judge from mail received at Hotel Lafayette headquarters, including the following telegram: "Five liberty bonds in National Bank, Omaha, Nebraska, belonging to undersigned horny-handed son of toil to assist in defraying expenses of the righteous campaign to forestall the plan of the English government to massacre Irish people. Hold the fort until our Nebraska women arrive. [signed] J. H. Howard."

32. *Irish World*, June 1920. One Woman Picket managed to get onto the floor of the House. She shouted: "Cowards! We Don't Want Your Sympathy, but Freedom for Ireland." *Washington Evening Star*, June 1, 1920.

33. The *Irish World* lionized the Women Pickets, running editorial cartoons paying tribute to them on its front page, and an appeal for funds on its back page.

34. *New York Times*, Feb. 17, 1934.

35. Jeremiah O'Leary, *My Political Trial and Experiences* (New York, 1919).

36. David Brundage, "The 1920 New York Dockers' Boycott: Class, Gender, Race and Irish-American Nationalism" (paper given at Organization of American Historians meeting, Chicago, Ill., Apr. 1992), 6.

37. To give an example of the IPL's combative organizational style: when the U.S. Post Office banned the *Irish Press* (published in Philadelphia by Dr. Patrick McCartan and Joseph McGarrity), the women of the IPL started selling it at the doors of Catholic churches on Sundays after mass. As the men of the IPL took on other tasks in the nationalist struggle, the IPL's women members, who had been coequals from its founding, assumed command of the organization, with Margaret Hickey and Helen Golden directing its operations in 1920.

38. The Women Pickets by and large supported de Valera. The Women Pickets affiliated with the IPL firmly, but Gertrude Corless and the more conciliatory picket women did so less firmly. Circular letter to New York newspapers, Aug. 10, 1920, Golden Papers. The IPL was expelled from the Friends of Irish Freedom on July 24. Maloney, McCartan, McGarrity, Frank P. Walsh, IRB men Liam Mellows and Harry Boland, Robert Ford, and James O'Mara, director of the bond drive for the Irish republic, sided with de Valera.

39. Francis M. Carroll, "Friends of Irish Freedom," in Michael F. Funchion, ed., *Irish American Voluntary Organizations* (Westport, Conn., 1983).

40. Golden Papers, Minutes, IPL meeting, July 26, 1920.

41. *Irish World*, July 10, 17, 24, 31, 1920.

42. Reports of the size of such crowds need to be treated skeptically. Art Shields, whose career as a New York reporter began in 1910, recalled in his memoirs the common practice of reporters to pool news stories, and then rewrite the facts, adding dramatic embellishments. Reporters called it "piping the news," that is, piping gas into the facts. See Shields, *My Shaping Up Years* (New York, 1983), 54–57.

43. *New York Times*, July 1, 1920.

44. A number of the Women Pickets handed out circulars to the crowd protesting Jim Larkin's imprisonment in Dannemora for antiwar activities. Leonora O'Reilly, Kathleen O'Brennan, Kathleen Sheehan and Dr. Kelly were ardent campaigners on Larkin's behalf and members of the Women's Larkin Committee. Peter Golden to Congressmen and Senators, Apr. 18, 1918, Golden Papers.

45. Frank Murphy, *Daniel Mannix: Archbishop of Melbourne, 1917–1963* (Melbourne, 1972).

46. *Irish World*, Aug. 21, 1920.

47. A benefit the Celtic Players performed in August 1920 for the Friends of Freedom for India (a cause to which Dr. Kelly and Leonora O'Reilly were deeply committed) and a note in the Golden Papers indicate the company was politically aligned with the Irish Progressive League.

48. *New York Call*, Aug. 28, 1920.

49. Charles P. Larrowe, *Shape-Up and Hiring Hall, A Comparison of Hiring Methods and Labor Relations on the New York and Seattle Waterfronts* (Berkeley, Calif., 1955.) Commenting on the 1919 strike by New York longshoremen, the *Nation* Magazine described them, along with Illinois miners, San Francisco and Seattle stevedores, Pittsburgh steel workers, and British railroad workers, as participants in a worldwide, post–World War I "revolt of the rank and file" who had defied their union officials and

shown "authority cannot any longer be imposed from above, it comes automatically from below." Jeremy Brecher, *Strike!* (San Francisco, 1972), 101.

50. John Ridge notes that it is widely believed that several Manhattan chapters of the AOH were almost exclusively made of longshoremen. Ridge to author, personal communication, June 6, 1995.

51. *Irish World*, May 29, 1920; *Sun and New York Herald*, Aug. 28, 1920.

52. Iver Bernstein, *The New York City Draft Riots: Their Significance for American Society and Politics in the Age of the Civil War* (New York, 1990).

53. Maud Russell, *Men along the Shore* (New York, 1966); Larrowe, *Shape-Up and Hiring Hall*.

54. The October 1920 issue of *World's Work* also makes note of the fact that the African American longshoremen struck in solidarity with the Irish longshoremen.

55. Robert Hill, ed., *The Marcus Garvey and Universal Negro Improvement Association Papers* (Berkeley, Calif., 1983), lxxv.

56. *New York Tribune*, Aug. 28, 1920, 1. Thomas Milligan of the Marine, Firemen, Oilers and Watertenders Union, and Thomas Rock of the Rammers and Pavers Union also played instrumental roles in laying the groundwork for the August 27th strike.

57. *New York World*, Aug. 28, 1920, 3.

58. Frank P. Walsh was a tremendous force in the Irish community. He was part of the delegation sent by the Third Irish Race Convention to lobby for Ireland at the Versailles Peace Conference. He had cleared the Women Pickets of the criminal charges accumulated against them during the Washington campaign. He was a staunch friend of Leonora O'Reilly from labor and suffrage battles. He was joint chairman, with William Howard Taft, of the War Labor Board. And he had presided over the federal Commission on Industrial Relations in June 1914 when they interviewed Chelsea longshoremen about their murderously dangerous working conditions, an experience that permanently affected Walsh's view of labor relations.

59. *New York Times*, Aug. 28, 1920. Another member of the audience, S. N. Ghose, said that he had "never witnessed such enthusiasm before in America. . . . Last night's meeting convinced me that we can secure more by actions than by political manipulation. . . . We pray that you live long [enough] to see the downfall of the English imperialism and the dismemberment of the British empire." S. N. Ghose, National Organizer, Friends of Freedom for India, to Frank P. Walsh, Aug. 29, 1920, Walsh Papers, Manuscript collection, New York Public Library.

60. *New York Call*, Aug. 28, 1920.

61. *New York Times*, Aug. 28, 1920.

62. New York City Directory, 1920. Mrs. George Warner was expelled from the Friends of Irish Freedom in July, allegedly for breaking up the FOIF meeting (she denied the charge.) For lack of an identifying middle initial, the other 23 women who marched on the ships on August 27 cannot be traced.

In answer to the question, "Were these women drawn into the movement through cultural activities?" the opposite seems to be true of the Cumann na mBan members. Months after it was formed in 1914 the Cumann na mBan suffered a split, because Dr. Kelly's faction would not permit a banquet to be organized to raise funds. Dr. Kelly considered "feasting" inappropriate while Irish citizens were being persecuted by British soldiers. The Irish Progressive League, while receptive to banquets, songs, and poetry in their public meetings, was first and foremost a political organization, eager to make common cause with American socialists. IPL members were deeply influenced by the writings of James Connolly.

63. IPL Minutes, Mar. 21, 1921, Papers of Eithne Golden Sax.

64. Personal papers of Eithne Golden Sax; unpublished interview with Eithne Sax, May 30, 1993.

65. *New York Times*, Aug. 29, 1920.

66. *New York American*, Aug. 29, 1920.

67. *New York World*, Aug. 26, 1920.

68. *Sun and New York Herald*, Aug. 30, 1920. "MacSwiney Now in Last Weak Stages," *New York World*, Sept. 5, 1920; "MacSwiney Is at Death's Door," *Sun*, Sept. 12, 1920.

69. Hill, UNIA Papers, 1: 13.

70. David Brundage, "Dockers' Boycott," 12. Harold Gates, a waterfront teamster who grew up on the West Side of Manhattan, asserted in an interview with the author in March 1980 that the decades of corruption on the New York waterfront documented by the New York–New Jersey Waterfront Crime Commission stemmed from long-time longshore president (1927–51) Joseph Ryan's undercutting of the MacSwiney strike. Gates alleged that Ryan built a power base among second-generation Irish Americans in the union whom he led across the MacSwiney picket lines that the first-generation Irish longshoremen were honoring.

71. *New York American*, Sept. 12, 1920. The women pickets made up signs for the women with such slogans as "Brothers, if you scab Ireland, you scab our race" and "Ireland's Liberty, Our Liberty, Liberty for Mankind. Let British Ships Rot." Golden Papers, Folder 6. See also Brundage, "Dockers' Boycott, "11.

72. "Decision of Colored Longshoremen Engaged in the Breaking of the Irish Patriotic Strike," Sept. 13, 1920, Golden Papers.

73. *Sun and New York Herald*, Aug. 31, 1920, 12; Sept. 12, 1920, 22.

74. *New York Times*, Sept. 3, 1920.

75. *Irish World*, Sept. 11, 1920, 12.

76. *Papers of the Women's Trade Union League and Its Principal Leaders*, Reel 2, Leonora O'Reilly Papers.

77. Golden Papers, *I.P.L. Bulletin*, Sept. 1919, 4.

78. *New York Tribune*, Nov. 1, 1920; *New York Times*, Nov. 1, 1920.

79. *New York Times*, Jan. 3, 1923, 4; *Times*, Sept. 11, 1925.

Chapter 15: OF "MORNIN' GLORIES" AND "FINE OLD OAKS" (McClymer)

1. Edwin R. Lewinson, *John Purroy Mitchel: The Boy Mayor of New York* (New York, 1965) is the standard biography. See pp. 248–57 for an account of Mitchel's military service and fatal last flight.

2. Oswald Garrison Villard, "John Purroy Mitchell," *Nation* 107, no. 36 (1918): 36; Julian Street, "New York's Fighting Mayor: Shall Tammany Stay Out or Come Back?" *Collier's Weekly* 59 (Aug. 25, 1917): 46. It is quite possible the unnamed "political prognosticator" was Theodore Roosevelt.

3. See "Why the Fighting Mayor of New York Is Thought to Be of Presidential Caliber," *Current Opinion* 63 (Oct. 17, 1917): 238–39.

4. Villard, "John Purroy Mitchel," 36.

5. See Oscar Handlin, *Al Smith and His America* (Boston, 1958), 71–78. Smith's own account is in his *Up to Now: An Autobiography* (Garden City, N.Y., 1929), 153–60. See also Nancy Joan Weiss, *Charles Francis Murphy, 1858–1924* (Northampton, Mass., 1968).

6. Willaim L. Riordan, *Plunkitt Of Tammany Hall: A Series of Very Plain Talks on Very Practical Politics* (1905; New York, 1963), 17, 19.

7. Riordan, *Plunkitt of Tammany Hall,* 19.

8. The election of 1897 was the first one after the linking of the five boroughs to form "Greater" New York. Mitchel's plurality in 1913 was upward of 121,000.

9. See, for example, "Tammany's Waterloo," *Literary Digest* 47 (Nov. 15, 1913): 927–29; "Significance of the Elections," *Outlook* 105 (Nov. 15, 1913): 567–69; "Murphy, The Terrible Ogre of American Politics," *Current Opinion* 55 (Dec. 1913): 403–4; P. M. Michelson, "With Murphy at Waterloo," *Harper's Weekly* 58 (Dec. 6, 1913): 18–20; S. Brooks, "Was Tammany Really Destroyed?" *Harper's Weekly* 58 (Dec. 27, 1913): 8–9; B. J. Hendrick, "Twilight of Tammany Hall," *World's Work* 27 (Feb. 1914): 432–40; "Final Blow at Tammany Hall," *World's Work* 33 (Feb. 1917): 355. See also "Imperturbable Murphy," *Literary Digest* 48 (Jan. 3, 1914): 34–35.

10. Diane Ravitch, *The Great School Wars: New York City, 1805–1973* (New York, 1974), 227. See also Augustus Cerillo Jr., "The Reform of Municipal Government in New York City: From Seth Low to John Purroy Mitchel," *New-York Historical Society Quarterly* 57 (Jan. 1973), 51–71.

11. Villard, "John Purroy Mitchel," 36. Theodore Roosevelt's endorsement was published in *Collier's Weekly* 59, (Aug. 1917): 6; William Hard, "The New York Mayoralty Campaign," *New Republic* 12 (Oct. 6, 1917): 270, and 12 (Oct. 13, 1917): 294. For similar statements see, for example, Charles A. Beard, "John Purroy Mitchel," *Survey* 40 (July 13, 1918): 437, and "John Purroy Mitchel: His Chief Contributions to City Government," *Survey* 40 (Aug. 3, 1918): 505 ff., a series of commemorative tributes by Mitchel appointees.

12. Howard Lee McBain, "Editorial: John Purroy Mitchel," *National Municipal Review* 7 (Sept. 1918): 506. The most fulsome contemporary version of this view of Mitchel's career is Emanie N. Sachs, "Being Human: A Great Mayor and What Happened to Him," *Century Magazine* 3 (Feb. 1926): 385–98.

13. Smith, *Up to Now,* 156.

14. Cleveland Rogers, *Robert Moses* (New York, 1952), 19; Oswald Garrison Villard, "The New York Mayoralty Election," *Nation* 105 (Oct. 25, 1917): 448. For Moses' role in the Mitchel administration and for the circumstances surrounding his recruitment by Smith see Robert A. Caro, *The Power Broker: Robert Moses and the Fall of New York* (New York, 1975), 70–96.

15. A carefully modulated version of the Plunkitt thesis informs the only full-scale scholarly biography of Mitchel, Lewinson's, *John Purroy Mitchel;* and, via Lewinson, other scholarly treatments of Mitchel's administration such as Ravitch, *The Great School Wars,* 219–29; and Robert Caro, *The Power Broker,* 70–86. Many scholars tend to ignore Mitchel. The most notable recent example, perhaps, is Thomas Kessner, *Fiorello H. La Guardia and the Making of Modern New York* (New York, 1989). Kessner mentions Mitchel only twice, both times in passing, and misspells his name (as Mitchell) each time, in a 700-page study of New York City mayoral politics in the first half of the twentieth century.

16. Tocqueville is equally critical of "men of letters" who have never taken part in public affairs and are "always inclined to find general causes" for everything. *The Recollections of Alexis de Tocqueville,* trans. Alexander Teixeira de Mattos (New York, 1896), as excerpted in Jan Goldstein and John W. Boyer, eds., *University of Chicago Readings in Western Civilization* (Chicago, 1988), 8: 228.

17. See Lewinson, *John Purroy Mitchel,* 17–30, 36. Ellison had served as John Purroy Mitchel's father's attorney in 1895 when political opponents unsuccessfully attempted to remove him as fire marshall. He had been the executor of Mitchel's uncle Henry's estate in 1903.

18. William Dillon, *Life of John Mitchel*, 2 vols. (1888).

19. Smith, *Up to Now*, 3–68; Norman Hapgood and Henry Moskowitz, *Up from the City Streets: Alfred E. Smith: A Biographical Study in Contemporary Politics* (New York, 1927), 3–54; Handlin, *Al Smith and His America*, 6–26; Riordan, *Plunkitt of Tammany Hall*, 7–10.

20. See the full-length portrait in Street, "New York's Fighting Mayor," 7. Also Sachs, "Being Human," 386, 390.

21. Street, "New York's Fighting Mayor," 39.

22. Riordan, *Plunkitt of Tammany Hall*, 50, 52.

23. Hapgood and Moskowitz, *Up from the City Streets*, 75.

24. Quoted in Sachs, "Being Human," 395. Hearst had supported Mitchel in 1913 but broke with him shortly after the Fusion administration took office. The ostensible reason was a disagreement over the expansion of the subways, but Mitchel's unwillingness to consult with Hearst on policy questions in general was in all likelihood a more important factor. See Lewinson, *John Purroy Mitchel*, 213. Oswald Garrison Villard, in his obituary of Mitchel, commented somewhat obliquely that "the evil genius of American journalism, William R. Hearst, was early alienated from Mr. Mitchel, for reasons entirely creditable to the latter." Villard, "John Purroy Mitchel," 37.

25. *New York Evening Journal*, Oct. 18, 1917, as reprinted in Lewinson, *John Purroy Mitchel*, 237.

26. *New York Evening Journal*, Oct. 18, 1917, as quoted in Lewinson, *John Purroy Mitchel*, 238. For "the Little Brother to the Rich" nickname see Sachs, "Being Human," 397.

27. Villard, "John Purroy Mitchel," 37.

28. Street, "New York's Fighting Mayor," 39–41.

29. For Mitchel's own account, see J. P. Mitchel, "What We Have Done For New York," *Independent* 82 (May 10, 1915): 237–39. Other positive accounts include "Trained Social Workers Take Charge of New York City Government," *Survey* 31 (Jan. 10, 1914): 430–32; "New York City's Government by Experts," *Review of Reviews* 49 (Feb. 1914): 171–78; "Efficiency and the City," *Independent* 80 (Nov. 30, 1914): 327–28; "Businesslike Mayor," *Outlook* 113 (May 10, 1916): 52; H. S. Gilbertson, "Municipal Revolution under Mayor Mitchel," *Review of Reviews* 56 (Sept. 1917): 300–303; and G. Harvey, "Mayor Mitchel and His Work," *North American Review* 206 (Aug. 1917): 261–70. Favorable accounts of the Municipal Research Bureau, chief source of experts for the Fusion administration, include William H. Allen, "Training Men and Women for Public Service," *Annals of the American Academy* 41 (May 1912): 307–12; and J. P. Heaton, "School for Mayors," *Survey* 27 (Dec. 9, 1912): 1340–41.

30. See John A. Kingsbury, "Municipal Welfare Work as Exemplified in New York's Treatment of Dependent Children," *National Conference of Social Work Proceedings* (1917), 371–79.

31. It is possible that Kingsbury chose Doherty, a Catholic who had been raised in a church-run orphanage, to lead the investigation as a way of heading off Catholic opposition.

32. Lewinson, *John Purroy Mitchel*, 178. Emanie Sachs's version of this story is similar: "Fellow-churchmen begged him to fight from inside and not from outside [the church]. His right wing said, 'Oh, well, if you want to compromise. . . .' Whereupon Mitchel flared: 'I won't compromise. I have to keep my self-respect. I won't let them dictate to me. I can't do it their way.'" Sachs, "Being Human," 394.

33. Eda Amberg and William H. Allen, *Civic Lessons from Mayor Mitchel's Defeat* (New York, 1921), 24–26.

34. *New York Times*, Nov. 20, and Dec. 4, 1915.

35. Ibid., Nov. 20, 1915.

36. Amberg and Allen, *Civic Lessons*, 24, 26. For Allen's career see ibid., 78–80.

37. Father William B. Farrell, *A Public Scandal* (New York, 1916), *Charity for Revenue* (New York, 1916), and *Priest-Baiting in 1916* (New York, 1916); Amberg and Allen, *Civic Lessons*, 24.

38. *New York Times*, May 19, 1916. A good account of the entire controversy is Lewinson, *John Purroy Mitchel*, 180–88. According to Emanie Sachs, "Friends begged Mitchel to see Cardinal Farley" before making the wiretap records available to the grand jury. "An appointment was to be arranged. But instead of asking for it with proper respect, one of Mitchel's secretaries telephoned the cardinal's office thus: 'The cardinal wants to see Mayor Mitchel. What time shall we make it?'" The reply was that "'His Eminence does not want to see the mayor.' For cardinals do not 'want to see' mayors. Mayors ask to see them." "Being Human," 394.

39. *New York Times*, May 24, 1916. See also "Mayor Mitchel's Charges of Criminal Conspiracy against a Group of Roman Catholic Ecclesiasts," *Current Opinion* 61 (July 1916): 39–40; "Mayor Mitchel and the Children," *Outlook* 113 (July 5, 1916): 525–26; and Winthrop D. Lane, "Mayor Mitchel Takes the Stand: A Further Chapter in the Story of the Children's Institutions of New York," *Survey* 36 (June 3, 1916): 263–65.

40. Quoted in Lewinson, *John Purroy Mitchel*, 187.

41. "The Mayor and His Church," *Nation* 102 (June 1, 1916): 585, 586; Villard, "The New York Mayoralty Election," 448; Street, "New York's Fighting Mayor," 42, 44. See also "Mayor Mitchel and His Church," *Literary Digest* 52 (June 3, 1916): 1621–22.

42. Street, "New York's Fighting Mayor," 42; Winthrop D. Lane, "Mothered by The City," *Survey* 39 (Jan. 19, 1918): 435–39. See also "Mayor Mitchel Sustained," *Outlook* 113 (June 14, 1916): 342–43; "Mayor Mitchel and His Church," *Literary Digest* 52 (June 3, 1916), 1621–22.

43. *New York Times*, May 24, 1916, contains the details of the fracas at the Thompson hearings.

44. Sachs, "Being Human," 394.

45. Smith, *Up to Now*, 38–42; Hapgood and Moskowitz, *Up from the City Streets*, 31–32. Hapgood and Moskowitz cite Smith himself as their source for this story.

46. Hapgood and Moskowitz, *Up from the City Streets*, 32–33. Smith also noted the link between his acting and the parish's need to support the orphanage. *Up to Now*, 41.

47. See *Fusion's Platform: A Promise, Backed by Achievements, That Will Be Fulfilled* (New York, 1917). According to Lewinson, "pay as you go" was initially imposed upon the administration as a condition for managing a city bond issue by a coalition of bankers in 1914. Mitchel complained that "the worst features of the transaction from the city's point of view were the conditions imposed as to the new policy of financing public improvements." However, pay as you go soon became an article of Fusion faith. Lewinson, *John Purroy Mitchel*, 126–27.

48. Undated *New York Evening Post* story reprinted in *School and Society* 7 (May 11, 1918): 560.

49. For a full account see Ravitch, *The Great School Wars*, 195–230. The most influential contemporary account of the Gary Plan was Randolph Bourne, *The Gary Schools* (Boston, 1916). William A. Wirt, the originator of the plan had been a student of John Dewey's, and Dewey himself endorsed his ideas in 1915. See John and Evelyn Dewey, *Schools of Tomorrow* (New York, 1915). A convenient means of following the Gary Plan controversy in New York is in the pages of the progressive education journal *School and Society*, which reprinted official reports, newspaper editorials, and public statements by the principals in addition to reporting developments.

50. John Dewey, "Public Education on Trial," *New Republic* 13 (Dec. 29, 1917): 246. Also *New York Times*, June 7, 1915; *School and Society* 1 (Apr. 10, 1915): 525–26.

51. Ravitch, *The Great School Wars*, 205. Prendergast's own account is William A. Prendergast, "Why New York City Needs a New School Plan," *Review of Reviews* 52 (Nov. 1915): 584–88. Enthusiastic early appraisals of the Fusion plan include Winthrop D. Lane, "From Gary to New York City: A Demonstration in Better and Cheaper Schools," *Survey* 33 (Mar. 6, 1915): 628–30; "Gary School System Moves East," *World's Work* 30 (Aug. 1915): 391; and William G. Willcox, "The Principle of the Gary Plan and Its Application to New York," *American City* 14 (Jan. 1916): 6–10. Willcox became president of the New York Board of Education the month this article appeared.

52. *New York Times*, Feb. 8, 1916; Churchill quoted in Lewinson, *John Purroy Mitchel*, 160.

53. Roosevelt quoted in Amberg and Allen, *Civic Lessons*, 15. For Fusion's failure to campaign for the plan in the affected neighborhoods, see Ravitch, *The Great School Wars*, 214.

54. Roosevelt quoted in Amberg and Allen, *Civic Lessons*, 15; B. R. Buckingham, *Report to the Superintendent of Schools of New York City* (1916) as excerpted in *School and Society* 3 (Feb. 12, 1916): 245–47.

55. The most outspoken proponent of the Gary Plan for New York and the loudest critic of the Buckingham Report was Howard W. Nudd. See his "The Buckingham Tests of the Gary Schools in New York City," *School and Society* 3 (Apr. 8, 1916): 529–32. See also J. S. Taylor, "Report on the Gary Experiment in New York City," *Education Review* 51 (Jan. 1916): 8–28, and the editorial in the *Journal of Education*, Nov. 15, 1917. Abraham Flexner and Frank P. Bachman, *The Gary Schools: A General Account* (New York, 1918). A recent account is *Children of The Mill: Schooling and Society in Gary, Indiana, 1906–1960* (Bloomington, Ind., 1990).

56. W. H. Maxwell, *Annual Report of the New York City Superintendent of Schools (1916)* as excerpted in *School and Society* 3 (Apr. 29, 1916): 638–39. The quotation appears on p. 639. See also "Superintendent Maxwell's Annual Report," *Education Review* 52 (June 1916): 102–6.

57. *New York Times*, Oct. 5, 1917. For Hillquit's opposition see Zosa Szajkowski, *Jews, Wars, and Communism*, (New York, 1972), 1: 143. This account of the riots comes from Amberg and Allen, *Civic Lessons*, 15–20. See also the account in Ravitch, *The Great School Wars*, 224–26.

58. Dewey, "Public Education on Trial," 246.

59. See Handlin, *Al Smith and His America*; J. Joseph Huchmacher, *Senator Robert F. Wagner and the Rise of Urban Liberalism* (New York, 1968); John D. Buenker, *Urban Liberalism and Progressive Reform* (New York, 1963); Caro, *The Power Broker*; Elisabeth J. Perry, *Belle Moskowitz: Feminine Politics and the Exercise of Power in the Age of Alfred E. Smith* (New York, 1992).

60. "Hearst, Tammany, Mitchel, and America," *Literary Digest* 55 (Oct. 13, 1917): 11–13; "The Nation's Eyes on New York," *Nation* 105 (Oct. 11, 1917): 389; McBain, "Editorial: John Purroy Mitchel," 506. See also L. B. Stowe, "New York Mayoralty Campaign: Why It Is a National Issue," *Outlook* 117 (Oct. 31, 1917): 332–33; and "National Aspects of the Mayoralty Contest in New York City," *Current Opinion* 63 (Nov. 1917): 292–94.

61. Most accounts of the rise of urban liberalism in New York follow Oscar Handlin's lead and emphasize Smith's willingness to learn from Belle Moskowitz, Robert Moses, and their colleagues. His contribution was political savvyness, especially an ability to communicate with the ethnic voters on New York. See, for example, Irving Howe, *World of Our Fathers: The Journey of the East European Jews to America and the Life They Found and Made* (New York, 1976), esp. 385–91. Less emphasized is how much of their earlier reform beliefs the experts had to unlearn. See, however, Caro, *The Power Broker*, 71–88, for a detailed

account of how Robert Moses came to appreciate the perils of hitching his wagon to Mitchel's star.

62. Quoted in William Hard, "The New York Mayoralty Campaign, I: Sizing up Mitchel's Opponents," *New Republic* 12 (Oct. 6, 1917): 272. This pledge to rid the city of "outside" experts was Hylan's most important campaign promise. It was also the earliest theme sounded in his campaign to win the Democrat nomination. As early as January 1917 he was denouncing "the inefficient 'efficiency engineers and so-called experts' now running New York City" and complaining that many "have been drafted from other parts of the country by the promise of large salaries to be mulcted from the taxpayers." Quoted in Lewinson, *John Purroy Mitchel*, 224.

63. *Brooklyn Eagle*, Jan. 23, 1918, as quoted in Caro, *The Power Broker*, 84; "Only Democrats Need Apply," *Survey* 39 (Jan. 19, 1918): 451. For details concerning firings of experts and reformers in the city's Department of Public Charities see "Winding Up the Fusion Administration," *Survey* 39 (Mar. 2, 1918): 604–5.

64. This is the burden of his *Civic Lessons from Mayor Mitchel's Defeat*, which carried on its cover the blurb, "Why every democratically governed people can find encouragement rather than discouragement in New York City's vote against Fusion Reform in 1917." A similar view of Mitchel is Frederic C. Howe's. He had been on the committee that called on Mitchel to run in 1913. "As mayor," Howe believed, "Mr. Mitchel drifted away from his early [reform] militancy, he lost interest in the things he had stood for, and alienated the great mass of the people who had previously supported him." The *Confessions of a Reformer* (1925; New York, 1967), 245.

65. Hylan took 48.9 percent of the vote in 1917 in a four-way race. Fusion could only win if it picked up all of the Republican and Socialist vote in 1921.

66. Handlin, *Al Smith and His America*, 82.

67. See Julian F. Jaffe, *Crusade against Radicalism: New York during the Red Scare, 1914–1924* (Port Washington, 1972); Lawrence H. Chamberlain, *Loyalty and Legislative Action: A Survey of Activity by the New York State Legislature, 1919–1949* (Ithaca, N.Y., 1951); John F. McClymer, *War and Welfare: Social Engineering in America, 1890–1925* (Westport, Conn., 1980), 75–78, 192–215. The (Lusk) Joint Committee Investigating Seditious Activities published a four-volume report, *Revolutionary Radicalism: Its History, Purpose, and Tactics with an Exposition of the Steps Being Taken and Required to Curb It* (Albany, N.Y., 1920).

68. Mitchel quoted in Lewinson, *John Purroy Mitchel*, 230. See also Fusion's platform as reprinted in Amberg and Allen, *Civic Lessons*, 69.

69. Karl de Schweinitz, "Tammany by Default," *Survey* 39 (Nov. 17, 1917): 162.

70. See Amberg and Allen, *Civic Lessons*, 27–29. The Root quotation appears on p. 27.

71. *New York Times*, Sept. 22, 1917; Hillquit quoted in Szajkowski, *Jews, Wars, and Communism*, 1:143.

72. See Amberg and Allen, *Civic Lessons*, 28; DeSchweinitz, "Tammany by Default," 163. This is also Lewinson's conclusion, *John Purroy Mitchel*, 231ff.

73. Hard, "The New York Mayoralty Campaign I," 271, 272.

74. Villard, "The New York Mayoralty Election," 449. Some Mitchel supporters did oppose his use of the patriotism issue on principle. The *New York World*, for example, urged the mayor to "stick to the issue" of Tammany versus reform. Quoted in Lewinson, *John Purroy Mitchel*, 232.

75. See, for example, the obituary notice by Charles A. Beard, then affiliated with the Bureau of Municipal Research. "It must be said, too, that he early saw the menace of German militarism in American life, warned his countrymen against it, sought to

prepare for the coming storm, and then gave his all to the cause in which he believed." "John Purroy Mitchel," *Survey* 40 (July 13, 1918): 437.

76. De Schweinitz, "Tammany by Default," 163, 164.

77. For Mitchel's month of training at Plattsburg in the summers of 1915 and 1916 see Lewinson, *John Purroy Mitchel*, 190–94.

78. De Schweinitz, "Tammany by Default," 163.

79. Villard, "The New York Mayoralty Election," 449. William Hard attributed Mitchel's crackdown on "the Friends of Irish Freedom," despite Fusion's rhetorical commitment to "free speech," to his commitment to "government." He was willing to allow labor to denounce capital and capital to denounce labor, but "it is of the essence of government to ensure the continuance of government." Since the Irish nationalists attacked the U.S. government's alliance with Britain, and since Mitchel saw the alliance as vital to U.S. survival, he was "stirred to action." Hard, "Mayor Mitchel's Record," in Part II of his "The New York Mayoralty Campaign," 291.

80. Plunkitt claimed "Tammany's the most patriotic organization on earth" and cited as proof positive its annual Fourth of July celebration. Five thousand of the party faithful crammed the Hall each Fourth and listened to the reading of the Declaration of Independence and then to hours of patriotic oratory, even though each knew that in the basement were a hundred cases of champagne and two hundred kegs of beer "ready to flow when the signal is given." "Just think of five thousand men sittin' in the hottest place on earth for four long hours, with parched lips and gnawing stomachs, and knowin' all the time that the delights of the oasis in the desert were only two flights downstairs! Ah, that is the highest kind of patriotism, the patriotism of long sufferin' and endurance." Riordan, *Plunkitt of Tammany Hall*, 69–70.

81. See Kessner, *Fiorello H. La Guardia*, 57–58. The Murphy quotation appears on p. 57. A fuller account is Arthur Mann, *La Guardia: A Fighter against His Times* (Philadephia, 1960), 94–99.

82. The classic accounts are Stanley Coban, "A Study in Nativism: The American Red Scare of 1919–20," *Political Science Quarterly* 79 (Mar. 1964): 55–75; Robert K. Murray, *Red Scare: A Study in National Hysteria, 1919–1920* (New York, 1964); and William Preston Jr., *Aliens and Dissenters: Federal Suppression of Radicals, 1903–1933* (New York, 1963), 88–237.

83. Concurrent Resolution Authorizing the Investigation of Seditious Activities, reprinted in the Committee's report, *Revolutionary Radicalism*. Secondary accounts of the Lusk Committee include Julian F. Jaffe, *Crusade against Radicalism*; and Lawrence H. Chamberlain, *Loyalty and Legislative Action*. See also McClymer, *War and Welfare*, 192–215.

84. *New York Times*, June 13, 22, 24, 1919. For the committee's own account of its raids, see *Revolutionary Radicalism*, 1: 20–24.

85. *New York Times*, May 7, 1919.

86. Chamberlain estimated that the committee sometimes functioned with a staff exceeding 1,000. See *Loyalty and Legislative Action*, 13. For the participation of New York City police, see the *New York Times* account of the raid on the Russian People's House, Aug. 16, 1919. For Smith's acquiescence in the extra term for the supreme court, see ibid., July 10, 1919.

87. *New York Times*, June 21, 13, 1919.

88. Reprinted in *Progressive Democracy: Addresses and State Papers of Alfred E. Smith* (New York, 1928), 271.

89. Reprinted in *Progressive Democracy*, 273; ibid., 272, 273.

90. Reprinted in *Progressive Democracy*, 277, 278–79. Progressive Democracy was a campaign document and it is significant that Smith chose to include his 1920 annual

message, his statement against the expulsion of the Socialist assembly members, and his vetoes messages for all four Lusk Laws in his collection of his "addresses and state papers."

91. *New York Times*, Dec. 17, 1922. For the actual repeal, see ibid., May 27, 1923.

Chapter 16: "FROM THE EAST SIDE TO THE SEASIDE" (Casey)

I want to thank David Reimers, the late Dennis Clark, Edward Cortese and Patrick Mullins for their very helpful comments on drafts of this essay.

1. The number was 165,211 (53%) of a total of 311,638; this figure does not include foreign stock for Northern Ireland. See table P.1 in U.S. Bureau of the Census, *U.S. Censuses of Population and Housing: 1960 Census Tracts*, Final Report PHC(1)-104, Part 1 (Washington, D.C., 1962). This chapter does not deal with Staten Island, because its Irish population was negligible for the time period under discussion. The Irish stock of the borough remained constant at 2 percent of the city's Irish population from 1910 to 1960.

2. This loss is typical for the city's total population during the period. For example, Manhattan "lost 170,821 of its residents between 1930 and 1938, and this shifting of population represents a trend that is likely to continue as a result of the development of cheap transportation to the suburbs." Federal Writers' Project, *The WPA Guide to New York City* (New York, 1982, originally published 1939), 53.

3. For a discussion of the period 1950–80, see Morton D. Winsberg, "The Suburbanization of the Irish in Boston, Chicago and New York," in *Éire-Ireland* 21, no. 3, (1986): 90–104, esp. the diagram on p. 96. Italian migration within the metropolitan area shows a similar pattern. See Ira Rosenwaike, *Population History of New York City* (Syracuse, New York, 1972), 167.

4. For the most recent discussions of Italian and Jewish migration, see the essays by Donna Gabaccia and Deborah Dash Moore in David Ward and Olivier Zunz, eds., *The Landscape of Modernity: Essays on New York City, 1900–1940* (New York, 1992).

5. "Many entrepreneurs recognized that the opportunities for fast profit in real estate multiplied with the development of mass transit." Kenneth T. Jackson, *Crabgrass Frontier: The Suburbanization of the United States* (New York, 1985), 124. By one 1929 estimate, "an elevated line . . . will approximately double neighboring land prices while a subway will multiply them from four to twelve times." R. L. Duffus, *New York Times*, Sept. 22, 1929, quoted in Edwin H. Spengler, "Land Values in New York in Relation to Transit Facilities," *Studies in History, Economics and Public Law* (Columbia University), 333 (1930): 17.

6. Crimmins' father began the family firm in the 1850s when he obtained street and sewer contracts during the breakup of Manhattan's large middle East Side estates. The Crimmins firm was also involved in the construction of the first elevated railroads. See Edward J. McGuire, "A Memoir of John D. Crimmins," *Journal of the American Irish Historical Society* 17 (1918): 20. For Crimmins' real estate transactions on the Upper West Side see *The Diary of John D. Crimmins from 1878–1917* (privately printed, 1925), 11, 18, 20, 25, 28, passim. A copy of this diary is in the collection of the American Irish Historical Society. See also The Real Estate Record Association (RERA), *A History of Real Estate, Building and Architecture in New York City during the Last Quarter Century* (1898; New York, 1967), 90, 96, 134; and Rosa Pringle, "The Irish in Business, Banking and Industry," TD, 1938, Box 3579, Folder 5, 17, *WPA Historical Records Survey: Federal Writers Project*, "Irish in New York," Department of Records and Information Services, Municipal Archives, New York.

7. For example, a 25 by 102.2-foot lot he purchased between 72nd and 73rd Streets, just west of Central Park, in 1879 for $10,000 (with a $5,000 mortgage), he resold two years later for $23,000 (same mortgage). See RERA, *Real Estate, Building and Architecture*, 90–91.

8. Likewise, the prominent Irish American auctioneer Joseph P. Day, as a 25-year-old real estate broker, got a successful start in business by buying and selling "to a great extent on the West Side around Central Park." See RERA, *Real Estate, Building and Architecture*, 194; and Pringle, "The Irish in Business," 24.

9. RERA, *Real Estate, Building and Architecture*, 305; also McGuire, "A Memoir," 20. Another member of the West End Association was the real estate agent and broker John F. Doyle (1837–1911). Doyle, like Crimmins, was the son of an Irish immigrant, and both men were members of the Friendly Sons of St. Patrick and the American Irish Historical Society. Doyle served three terms as president of the Real Estate Board of Brokers. Of him it was written, "he was a survivor of the old days, when the real estate business was regarded as an honorable business which was not to be made a field for the exploitation of speculators or the exhibition of chicanery. He kept faithful to these standards always." See necrology by Edward J. McGuire in the *Journal of the American Irish Historical Society*, 11 (1912): 197.

10. Fox had already purchased lots in the area, valued at $27,930 (5% of total sale), in the Jumel auction of 1882. See RERA, *Real Estate, Building and Architecture*, 145–49 for a list of purchasers in the Morgenthau sale and 134–41 for the Jumel sale. This latter is particularly interesting because four Irish women are listed as purchasers of six lots, totaling in land value $7,245: Ellen Barry ($930), Catharine Kelly ($2,250), Ellen O'Hare (2 lots, $2,115), and Margaret Quinlin (2 lots, $1,950).

11. This chapter does not discuss those parts of New Jersey that fall in the metropolitan area, but a similar relationship between municipal improvements and real estate development occurred there. For example, Myles Tierney (1841–1921) was a contractor with extended interests in transportation and public utilities who operated in Jersey City, Bayonne, Hoboken, and Weehawken. Before the turn of the century, he built "hundreds of small dwellings and flats in both Jersey City and Hoboken," and later he served on the original New York Tenement House Commission. *Journal of the American Irish Historical Society*, 19–20 (1920–21): 215–20.

12. "After the enactment of the Greater New York Charter, Mr. Dunn organized the Bureau of Street Openings in the Boroughs of Brooklyn and Queens." See Friendly Sons of St. Patrick, "Memorials of Deceased Members," *Necrology* (New York, 1923–25), 7–14.

13. Degnon, the son of Irish immigrants, was raised on a farm in Ohio. He formed the Degnon Construction Company there in 1895 but moved the business to New York City in 1897. By 1910, the company's volume of business was valued at "nearly $6,000,000 a year" and it employed 4,000 men and 20 engineers. See *National Encyclopedia of American Biography* (New York, 1917), 14:122. See also Degnon's obituary in the *New York Times*, Apr. 23, 1925, 21.

14. See ads in the *Irish Advocate* placed by Thomas V. Dowling, May 7, 1910, and by the Carrollton Realty Co., June 4, 1910.

15. *Crimmins Diary*, 536, 549, 568, 571.

16. *New York Times*, Aug. 29, 1926; see full-page advertisement in the Real Estate section, 4. The firm's late president, Bryan L. Kennelly, was said to have "made all of the important lot auction sales on Long Island." Like the Crimmins Construction Company, the Kennelly Corporation began with the breakup of Manhattan's large estates. See Kennelly's obituary, *New York Times*, Dec. 29, 1923, 13; and *Necrology*, 59.

17. The geographic mobility experience of the Irish was less ethnic than that of the Jews. Deborah Dash Moore claims that in New York City "the general process of suburban development in the growth of the outer city received a special twist: the bonds of ethnicity supported ethnically separate construction industries catering to an ethnically distinct housing market." See *At Home in America: Second Generation New York Jews* (New York, 1981), 16, 39.

18. Such as John D. Crimmins, Michael J. Degnon, John F. Doyle, John P. Dunn, Bryan L. Kennelly, Bernard J. Noonan, and John Stratton O'Leary. The Catholic Club was an important networking institution for many of these men.

19. For a chronological list of parishes by foundation dates see Reverend John K. Sharp, comp., *Priests and Parishes of the Diocese of Brooklyn, 1820–1944* (New York, 1944), 177–217; and *A Guide to Vital Statistics in the City of New York, Borough of the Bronx: Churches* (New York, 1942), 6–9. For institution dates and histories of local Knights of Columbus councils, see James E. Foley and Nicholas Virgadamo, *The Knights of Columbus in the State of New York, 1891–1968* (New York, 1968).

20. For a discussion of ethnic population pressures on housing and settlement patterns in New York City at the turn of the century see Rosenwaike, *Population History*, 82–85.

21. U.S. Congress, Senate, *Report of the Immigration (Dillingham) Commission*, 61st Cong., 2d sess., 1911, S. Doc. 338, serial no. 5665, 4.

22. Between 1900 and 1930 the trend for second- and third-generation ethnics, age 25 and over, was outward movement from the city. See Rosenwaike, *Population History*, 99. In 1920, however, Manhattan was still an attraction for second-generation Irish and Italians, while Germans preferred Queens and Brooklyn, and the Bronx attracted Jews. By 1930 there was a sharp increase in the percentage of second-generation Irish choosing Queens, and the Bronx was also more popular. See Walter Laidlaw, ed. and comp., *Statistical Sources for Demographic Studies of Greater New York, 1920* (New York, 1922), table 6, xxiv–xxv, and Walter Laidlaw, ed. and comp., *Population of the City of New York, 1890–1930* (New York, 1932), table 59.

It was only after World War II that the Irish pattern began to resemble that of the Jews, with young married couples moving into modern middle-class complexes like Parkchester in the Bronx and Stuyvesant Town in Manhattan. Dorothy Hayden and John Cudahy, interview by author, Mar. 2, 1992, tape recording, Middle Village, Queens, N.Y. Also Thomas Ward, interview by author, Apr. 5, 1992, Chicago, Ill.

Boston's second-generation Irish also migrated out of old neighborhoods between 1900 and 1920. See Robert A. Woods and Albert J. Kennedy, *The Zone of Emergence: Observations of the Lower Middle and Upper Working Class Communities of Boston, 1905–1914* (Cambridge, Mass., 1962; repr., Cambridge, Mass., 1969), 133.

23. For more details on changes in housing design and land use, see Richard Plunz, *A History of Housing in New York City: Dwelling Type and Social Change in the American Metropolis* (New York, 1990), pp. 122–63.

24. "Raise in Living Standard Cause of Cost in Building," *Bronx Real Estate and Building News*, 1, no. 9 (1927): 2.

25. Richard O'Connor, *Hell's Kitchen: The Roaring Days of New York's Wild West Side* (New York, 1958), 187–88.

26. Chelsea and Hell's Kitchen are very likely exceptions in the New York experience because of the employment draws of the docks and railroads on the West Side. These made for a relatively stable, multigenerational, working-class Irish American population. But the emigrants from Ireland in the late 1920s did not seek out such employment and therefore had no need to settle in the outdated buildings of this area.

27. Ronald H. Bayor, *Neighbors in Conflict: The Irish, Germans, Jews, and Italians of New York City, 1929–1941* 2d ed. (Urbana, Ill., 1988), 152. It remained one of the stablest Irish areas in the city through 1960, actually increasing in the number of Irish-born residents with each decade. An examination of two sample tracts, 261 and 262, in Incarnation parish showed 1,130 Irish immigrants in 1920, 1,592 in 1950, and 2,148 in 1960.

28. The WPA observed that the Irish moved from east of Second Avenue, between Houston and 23rd Streets, to Amsterdam and Columbus Avenues on the West Side "shortly after the Slocum Disaster (15 June 1904)." A. Fitzpatrick, "The Irish in Various Industries, Professions, Etc.," TD, 1938, Box 3579, Folder 5, 2, *Federal Writers Project*, "Irish in New York."

29. Indeed, northern Manhattan and parts of the Bronx between the two world wars were both primary and secondary areas of settlement for the New York Irish. Manhattan's continuing attraction for immigrant Irish may also indicate lower income levels than the Jews, for example. Bayor, *Neighbors in Conflict*, 152–55, found that in general Washington Heights Catholics (that is, the Irish) lived in lower-middle-class sections and in housing that was less superior than that chosen by the Jews in the area. In the South Bronx, the Irish tended to be working class, too.

30. After 1960 an entirely different set of conditions prevailed in the city and a lot of Irish movement out of the neighborhoods described in this chapter resulted from "white flight." It is conceivable that before 1960 race was sometimes a contributing factor to Irish migration (for example, in response to riots in Harlem during the Depression), but there is not enough conclusive evidence at this time.

31. For a comparative example, Incarnation parish was established at 171st Street and St. Nicholas Avenue in 1911 and within six years had a congregation of 3,000. "Father Mahoney Dead: Washington Heights Pastor Built Up Large Parish," *New York Times*, Apr. 16, 1917.

32. Reverend Thomas F. X. Walsh, "A Study of the Increased Wages and the Increased Leisure of the Working Class, in a Catholic Parish, in Upper Manhattan" (Master's thesis, Columbia University, 1920), 2, 3, 11. A similar phenomenon was affecting the Irish of Hell's Kitchen, where rents for railroad flats on 10th Avenue rose to $20 a month after the war. See O'Connor, *Hell's Kitchen*, 193–94.

33. Walsh, "Increased Wages," 37. Even for working people, the standard of living seems to have been inclined towards the middle class, reflecting the growing impact of consumerism. For example, Walsh claimed that "in nearly every home in the Parish, some sort of musical instrument has been installed, victrolas and player pianos, especially, and records ranging from those of the highest price to the type sold in the 5&10 Cent Stores." Ibid., 22.

34. Marie Walsh, letter to the author, Feb. 29, 1992.

35. Charlie and Maureen Mooney, interview by author, Mar. 18, 1992, tape recording, Greenlawn, Long Island, N.Y. St. Gabriel's was an old Irish parish on the middle East Side. The impact of the tunnel is best illustrated by figures from a sample tract in the parish: in 1920, Tract 78 had 1,597 Irish immigrants; in 1940, there were 220 Irish-born heads of families; and in 1950, 169 Irish immigrants. It is ironic to note that while the tunnel pushed Irish parishioners up the East Side, the altar, pews, statues and pastor of St. Gabriel's migrated to Riverdale in the Bronx, where a new St. Gabriel's Church was built in 1939. The Murphys, an Irish American family whose wealth came from construction, were instrumental in getting the parish established there. Ibid., and Geraldine Murphy Walsh and Frank Murphy, interview by author, Mar. 30, 1992, Riverdale, Bronx, N.Y. A similar displacement for the Irish occurred when the blocks

around Lincoln Square on the West Side were razed during the 1950s for a new cultural arts center.

36. Joshua B. Freeman, *In Transit: The Transport Workers Union in New York City, 1933–1966* (New York, 1989), 26–27.

37. Charlie and Maureen Mooney, interview, Mar. 18, 1992.

38. Dorothy Hayden and John Cudahy, interview, Mar. 2, 1992. In 1899 John D. Crimmins had transferred title to property in Woolsey Point to the Astoria Light, Heat and Power Company. *Crimmins Diary*, Jan. 21, 1899, 101. Guinness had a brewery in Long Island City and was importing Irish barley for its operations. *Irish Echo*, Sept. 23, 1950, 9, advertisement.

39. Maureen Griffin Mooney's father was a clerk for Reeves in the late 1920s, and Dorothy Hayden's father began working for Butler's in 1907, eventually becoming a manager. John Traynor, from Virginia, County Cavan, joined his sister in Woodside when he emigrated in 1925. Eight months later he was hired as a manager for the A&P and, although he was assigned to a number of stores, he always worked in the neighborhoods surrounding Woodside in Queens. Catherine Traynor Gregory, telephone interview by author, July 27, 1992. "To keep his overhead low, [Butler] staffed his stores with just two, or at the most three, young clerks, and to keep his overhead even lower, he hired only young Irishmen—many of whom he would buttonhole as they came down the gangplank—who were eager and hungry and would work hard for small wages." Stephen Birmingham, *Real Lace: America's Irish Rich* (New York, 1973), 78.

40. Ibid., 75–85. "Butler's remarkable success came from two sources, the profits of his grocery stores, and real estate operations in which he was particularly shrewd. . . . The extent of his real estate transactions may be estimated by the fact that in 1929 he auctioned off four million dollars worth of property." Pringle, *Federal Writers Project*, "Irish in New York," 33.

41. In 1911 James Reeves renamed the business upon the death of his brother Daniel. *Irish Echo*, Oct. 10, 1957, 1. Also, Harold F. Hamill, "James Reeves and Eugene F. Kinkead," TD, 1938, Box 3579, Folder 5: "Occupations and Locations," *Federal Writers Project*, "Irish in New York." Reeves operated several grocery stores along Columbus Avenue on Manhattan's Upper West Side, which was very Irish at the time, and bought 25 stores on Long Island in 1927. *New York Times*, Jan. 15, 1927, 22; Sept. 9, 1928, 29; and Aug. 8, 1929, 3.

42. "The Feminine Touch in Realty Appraisals," *New York Times*, Oct. 29, 1926, X, 22.

43. Dorothy Hayden continued to live in this apartment after her marriage until she moved to Queens in the 1950s. Dorothy Hayden and John Cudahy, interview, Mar. 2, 1992. When James Hayden married Delia Brennan in 1916, they first moved to Brooklyn where James had an uncle. Dorothy Hayden said that her mother "hated it, they lived for a year in Brooklyn, because her sister and her cousins and all the fun was in Manhattan."

44. Mary Gilrane Flynn and Vincent Flynn, interview by author, Mar. 30, 1992, Throggs Neck, Bronx, N.Y.

45. "Catherine Kennedy" is a pseudonym for the woman interviewed on Apr. 22, 1974, for the New York Immigrant Labor History Collection (Herbert Gutman), Tamiment Institute Library and Wagner Labor Archives, New York University, Drawer 4, Tapes 12–14. A typed summary of this oral history by Scott Ware (especially pp. 4–5) was used in the preparation of this chapter.

46. Agnes Campbell Sinclair, interview by author, Mar. 22, 1992, tape recording, Wantagh, N.Y. Many of the Irish men who worked for Socony (formerly Standard Oil of

New York) commuted from St. Teresa's parish by trolley to Long Island City. The area encompassed by the parish was variously called the Ninth Ward, Prospect Heights, or Crown Heights. Jack Devaney, "The Religious Orders of St. Teresa's," in the 1984 newsletter of the St. Teresa of Avila Alumni Association (Brooklyn, N.Y.).

47. John T. Ridge, *The Flatbush Irish* (New York, 1983), 13.

48. Charlie and Maureen Mooney, interview, Mar. 18, 1992.

49. Maurice Forge, quoted in Freeman, *In Transit*, 31.

50. Eileen O'Rourke Simpson, letter to author, Apr. 9, 1992. In Boston c. 1936 boarders in Irish apartments paid $20 a week for their room, meals, and laundry. Ide O'Carroll, *Models for Movers: Irish Women's Emigration to America* (Dublin, 1990), 38.

51. Mary Higgins Clark, "My Wild Irish Mother," *Woman's Day*, May 9, 1989, 112.

52. In exchange for this, they received a four-room flat. Agnes Campbell Sinclair, interview, Mar. 22, 1992. In Betty Smith's famous book about an Irish American family, *A Tree Grows in Brooklyn* (New York, 1943, 1947), Katie Nolan works as the janitor in their Williamsburg building on the eve of the first world war while her husband Johnny works as a singing waiter.

53. Eileen O'Rourke Simpson, letter, Apr. 9, 1992.

54. Hugh O'Rourke Jr., telephone interview by author, Mar. 8, 1992.

55. Charlie and Maureen Mooney, interview, Mar. 18, 1992.

56. For example, in 1914 John Fitzgerald's hotel, "on the Boulevard, near Rockaway Park," was said to be "the Mecca for Yorkville folk visiting Rockaway." "Social Notes," *Irish Advocate*, Sept. 5, 1914, 4.

57. The old summer spot, Keansburg on the Atlantic Heights in New Jersey, was only accessible by ferry from Manhattan. Workingmen had to wait for the tides, which cut hours off their weekend and made weeknights impractical. Dorothy Hayden and John Cudahy, interview, Mar. 2, 1992.

58. Ibid.

59. Ibid. The tenants were not exclusively Irish.

60. Immigrants settling on the Rockaway peninsula from the 1880s led to the development of an "Irishtown," which was only demolished under urban renewal efforts during the 1960s. Bruce L. Weiser, "Hammels, Rockaway (1900–1976): A Case Study of Ethnic Change and Urban Renewal" (Master's thesis, Queens College, CUNY, 1976), 6. The southern area of Hammels eventually became known as "Slum Town." However, St. Rose of Lima in Hammels continued as an Irish parish; according to Census Tract 942–942.01, the number of Irish immigrants living there increased from 69 in 1920 to 245 in 1950 and 850 in 1960. In the early 1960s, the Rockaway Irish moved further west on the peninsula to Breezy Point, where they formed a cooperative community of bungalows on 415 acres. Ibid., 12.

61. Nora Joyce, an immigrant from the Aran Islands, recalled her ambition to own a house in Boston: "We were three years married and living on top of a store and I said, ' . . . we're going to buy a house.'. . . . [In] thirty-eight we bought a house; a three family house, down at Fields Corner. I knew how to save. I knew bargains and my uncles and aunts had houses. Paying rent, you don't get nothing out of it. . . . I said I'd rather live on a cup of tea and have my own place." O'Carroll, *Models for Movers*, 38–39.

62. William O'Dwyer, *Beyond the Golden Door*, ed. Paul O'Dwyer (New York, 1987), 119–120.

63. Francis P. Vardy, interview by author, July 6, 1992, New York City. Likewise, Michael Lennon, a plumbing contractor from County Sligo, purchased a two-story, attached row house in St. Teresa's parish in Brooklyn in 1924 after living in a series of apartments in the neighborhood. He heard about it from a business acquaintance who

lived next door. He was able to afford the house because he had lucrative work installing colored bathrooms in the Eastern Parkway apartment houses during the 1920s. Although his occupation did not change, economic good times helped improve the family's standard of living. Margaret Lennon Kennedy, interview by author, Mar. 25, 1992, New York City.

64. According to Plunz, *A History of Housing*, 131, such incidents illustrate the "geographical stratification of the city's population based on ethnic and economic characteristics." He gives as an example Jackson Heights' (Queens) policy against "Catholics, Jews or dogs." But in general the Irish rarely encountered discrimination in housing in New York during this period.

The Murphys were in a Yorkville townhouse they had built until 1911, then briefly in Babylon on Long Island and in Montclair in New Jersey. Geraldine Murphy Walsh and Frank Murphy, interview, Mar. 30, 1992. Riverdale had a nineteenth century "Irish-town," inhabited by servants and gardeners who worked on about 25 local estates. These Irish were largely responsible for the establishment of St. Margaret of Cortona parish in 1887, which was the church Frank Murphy and his family attended when they first moved to Riverdale.

65. This is not to imply in any way that there were no obstacles to class advancement in the traditional sense. Steven Erie, for example, argues that municipal employment that was dependent upon political connections restricted mobility for the Irish. See *Rainbow's End: Irish-Americans and the Dilemmas of Urban Machine Politics, 1840–1985* (Berkeley, Calif., 1988), 89–90. However, this chapter only focuses on the interaction between geography and social mobility among the New York Irish.

66. Dorothy Hayden and John Cudahy, interview, Mar. 2, 1992. Because the amount of cash available for a downpayment was minimal, multiple mortgages were common. The first mortgage was typically with a relative, or with the seller (today this is called a purchase money mortgage). To make up any shortfall, a second mortgage was often with the attorney who closed the sale, and a third might be with a mortgage broker. Mr. Donohue held the Cudahy's third mortgage, but he had first call; John Cudahy believes their agreement was for 10 years, with 6 percent interest on the principal due every six months.

67. Thomas Ward, interview, Apr. 5, 1992.

68. Stephan Thernstrom argues this for nineteenth-century Newburyport Irish-born home owners; he calls it "low-level social mobility." Quotation from Thernstrom, "Class and Mobility in a Nineteenth Century City," in Robert Gutman and David Popenoe, eds., *Neighborhood, City, and Metropolis: An Integrated Reader in Urban Sociology* (New York, 1970), 361, 366.

69. Charlie and Maureen Mooney, interview, Mar. 18, 1992.

70. According to Gunther Barth, the apartment offered New Yorkers a new concept of "home"; see *City People: The Rise of Modern City Culture in Nineteenth Century America* (New York, 1980), 48. There is a need to analyze some of the fiction that has been written about the New York Irish community for its unique perspective on the meaning of "house" and "home"; see, for example, the novels of Elizabeth Cullinan, Alice McDermott, and Anna Quindlen.

71. "All Roads Lead to Massapequa Park, the Transportation City" (c. 1929), brochure, "Massapequa" vertical file, Long Island Studies Institute, Hofstra University.

72. Clark, "My Wild Irish Mother," 110.

73. *Irish Advocate*, Sept. 15, 1914, 2, advertisement. Another real estate agent, T. Flynn, placed a similar ad with the lure: "I will teach you the business and pay you well while learning." *Irish Advocate*, Oct. 10, 1914, 5, advertisement.

74. "Thousands of Young Irishmen Lose Their Vocations; Successful Real Estate Operator Defines How Real Money Can Be Made," *Irish Advocate*, Feb. 19, 1916.

75. Despite his lucrative career, Gleeson followed the typical pattern of his contemporaries: when he married Miss Nellie Nolan (former president of the Carlow Ladies Association) in St. Gabriel's Church on East 37th Street in 1914, the couple did not migrate to Hempstead (where he was selling lots) but took up residence in Inwood, "at Pleasant View apartment house, No. 601 West 190th Street." *Irish Advocate*, Feb. 19, 1916, and Jan. 31, 1914, 2. Gleeson took an active interest in Irish social and sporting events and presumably wanted to remain within the community.

76. Dorothy Hayden and John Cudahy, interview, Mar. 2, 1992. John Cudahy got his start in the business in 1945 when he took a course in real estate that was offered by the Knights of Columbus; the $90 fee was put up for him by Jack Gleason, proprietor of the Keeper Hill Bar in the Bronx. Twenty-nine years earlier, real estate man Daniel Gleeson had lamented, "Too bad that influential Irishmen in the city didn't some time or other start an association which would acquaint our young men with the advantages to be derived from certain positions or to keep them in touch with berths that would compensate them, besides having them 'hewers of wood and drawers of water.'" *Irish Advocate*, Feb. 19, 1916.

77. Dorothy Hayden and John Cudahy, interview, Mar. 2, 1992. Jimmy Lavin later bought apartment houses on the East Side of Manhattan and in Jackson Heights. Forty years earlier, Thomas Daly was the well-known builder of "Daly's Homes" in Elmhurst and Corona. See "Irishman's Sad Mishap at Corona, Long Island," *Irish Advocate*, Jan. 31, 1914, 6.

78. "Of all the working women in your city [New York] the Irish maid is considered the 'easiest mark' as a subject for installment plan book agents, real estate men, and peddlers of religious articles. . . . Bluntly tell Mary to leave real estate severely alone unless she is going to build her home on the ground she buys. For a start, tell her to open a savings account in a regular savings bank and to keep her money there. It will bring her 4% and she can get her 'dough' when she needs it." *Irish Advocate*, Jan. 10, 1914, 2.

79. For their first day of business in 1927, the city auctioneer Joseph P. Day (see note 8) lent them his largest tent. "Massapequa Park 25th Anniversary Annual Report" (1956), brochure, "Massapequa" vertical file, Long Island Studies Institute, Hofstra University. Brady was 31 years old, Cryan 26, and Colleran 36 when they purchased a mile long by half-mile-wide tract of land in Massapequa Park for a $167,000 first mortgage and $214,000 second mortgage. "Long Island Mayor Accused of Fraud," *New York Times*, Oct. 6, 1936, 15.

80. "Massapequa Park 25th Anniversary Annual Report" and "All Roads Lead to Massapequa Park, the Transportation City," brochure (Hofstra University, c. 1929)

81. Paul O'Dwyer, telephone interview by author, July 13, 1992; "50,000 Present at New Flying Field Opening," *Nassau Daily Review*, May 13, 1929; "Hangar at Massapequa Park," *New York Times*, Apr. 27, 1930, XII, 1. Fitzmaurice gained fame for the first east-west transatlantic crossing, in "the first heavier-than-air ship to reach North America from Europe." D. J. Hickey and J. E. Doherty, *A Dictionary of Irish History, 1800–1980* (Dublin, 1980), 173–74, and "Massapequa Park 25th Anniversary Annual Report."

82. "Officials Face Court Today in Larceny Count," *Nassau Daily Review*, Oct. 6, 1936. Apparently this was not a novel concept. Marie Walsh recalled being told "about a fine old mansion in the woods [at Edenwald in the Bronx] used by Irish real estate developers around World War I to entertain prospective buyers. They arranged excursions

from downtown by subway to White Plains Road, about two miles to the west, and brought people to the house by horse and carriage—where elaborate parties were held. It was said to be an impressive sight, particularly at night, all lit up. (They may have been agents rather than developers, working through the county organizations.)" Marie Walsh, letter, Feb. 29, 1992.

83. Fitzpatrick dropped charges when he received a quit-claim deed to the property. The firm's lawyer stated that Fitzpatrick's original deed "was but one of more than 4,000 negotiated by the corporation." *Nassau Daily Review*, Oct. 6, 1936; *New York Times*, Oct. 6, 1936, Apr. 7, 1937, and Aug. 26, 1937. In the long memory of the New York Irish community, the urban folklore on this incident says that "all the lots were under water." Paul O'Dwyer, telephone interview, July 13, 1992.

84. "Money Coming to Restore a Lived-In Art Form in the Bronx," *New York Times* Aug. 20, 1976. Also *New York Times*, Oct. 11, 1930, XI, 11, and Dec. 9, 1943, 27. Bernard Noonan began his real estate career in Yonkers and Manhattan before building in the Bronx during the 1920s boom. "Noonan was responsible for the erection of several noteworthy apartment houses, including Bernard Court, Rose Terrace, Noonan Towers, Maryknoll Terrace, Wynne Terrace, and Summit Lodge." See Donald G. Sullivan and Brian J. Danforth, *Bronx Art Deco Architecture: An Exposition* (New York, 1976), 5; a copy is in the collection of the Bronx County Historical Society.

85. The pool also contained a replica of an Irish Round Tower. Sullivan and Danforth, *Bronx Art Deco Architecture*, 5 (illustration).

86. Charlie and Maureen Mooney, interview, Mar. 18, 1992; Dorothy Hayden and John Cudahy, interview, Mar. 2, 1992. In Census Tract 211, which includes Noonan Plaza, there were 85 Irish immigrants in 1920, 603 in 1950, and 1,337 in 1960. It is ironic that to non-Irish observers, "sights such as . . . the vast Noonan Plaza apartments . . . told the visitor that the area was largely inhabited by the sons of Erin." Lloyd Ultan, *The Beautiful Bronx, 1920–1950* (New York, 1979), 13–14. Oddly enough, no one in the Irish community seems to recall Bernard Noonan, even though his funeral was from Sacred Heart Church in 1943.

87. Patricia O'Connor, "John Stratton O'Leary and the O'Leary Flats," *New York Irish History* (Journal of the New York Irish History Roundtable), 4 (1989): 36–38. Also, *Bronx Real Estate and Building News* 4, no. 4 (1930): 24; and O'Leary's obituary, *New York Times*, Sept. 25, 1942.

88. Margaret Sullivan, letter to the author, Apr. 10, 1992. Margaret Sullivan's husband was working for the Corn Exchange Bank at the time they moved to the Bronx.

89. Mary Gilrane Flynn and Vincent Flynn, interview, Mar. 30, 1992. Vincent Flynn was a policeman at the time. In 1954, Kitty Davey's father, from County Kerry, took a superintendent's position in an O'Leary building on Beach Avenue and moved his family down from a Kerry area of Woodlawn in the North Bronx. They had heard about O'Leary's Flats from friends and relatives. Kitty Davey, letter to author, Apr. 24, 1992. Census Tract 218 in the O'Leary's Flats neighborhood shows an increase in the number of Irish-born, from 99 in 1920 to 555 in 1950, to 1,234 in 1960.

90. Celtic Park is also typical of the changes in New York City housing after 1900 when "the private production of housing shifted to larger and larger scales. The small-scale lot-by-lot development of the nineteenth century lapsed as the economic milieu changed. The modern development corporation emerged, involving private investment. These corporations managed all of the activity related to the production of a new generation of middle-class housing, from real estate acquisition to design and construction, to rental and maintenance." Plunz, *A History of Housing*, 130.

The only other example resembling Celtic Park was the construction of Parkchester in the East Bronx between 1939 and 1941 by the Metropolitan Life Insurance Company. It was built on land once occupied by the Catholic Protectory, a large and well-known orphanage, which was also adjacent to O'Leary's Flats. "Most of those who moved into this instant neighborhood [Parkchester] were Irish, and from the beginning the community was close-knit." Ultan, *The Beautiful Bronx,* 45.

91. *New York Times,* June 28, 1931, XI & XII, 10. Celtic Park's attendance figures declined not because of location but because of the competition between the Irish American Athletic Club (IAAC) (which promoted track and field events, bicycle and handball tournaments, and Irish football and hurling) and the Gaelic Athletic Association (GAA) of New York (which just promoted Gaelic games). While the war did have an impact on attendance, the big crisis did not occur until the mid-1920s when the IAAC declined and the GAA gained ascendancy in Irish athletic circles, most probably because of the arrival of thousands of new Irish immigrants. By 1928, GAA games were ensconced in Innisfail (now Gaelic) Park at 240th Street and Broadway in the Bronx, and Celtic Park's days as a playing field were numbered. Also "The New York GAA, 1914–1976" in *The New York Irish: American Bicentennial Commemorative Issue, The New York GAA Board* (Dublin, 1976), 6–11.

92. Federal Housing Administration, *Four Decades of Housing with a Limited Dividend Corporation* (Washington, D.C., 1939), 58. "The Regional Plan Association has found that Greater New York's center of population is in Queens and only a block or two from Celtic Park. If the Company completes the development of this property, it will have provided some 900 homes almost exactly at the city's present center of population." *Annual Report of the City and Suburban Homes Company* (New York, 1932), 14.

93. *New York Times,* Oct. 18, 1931, XI, 2, and *Annual Report of the City and Suburban Homes Company,* 12. While there is no way to quantify the extent of Irish occupation of Celtic Park Apartments until the 1940 census schedules are opened, the general impression is that Celtic Park had a lot of Irish tenants. Dorothy Hayden and John Cudahy, interview, Mar. 2, 1992.

94. *New York Times,* Aug. 30, 1931, XI, 2.

95. "The Worlds of Woodside," *Newsday,* Nov. 9, 1989; *New York Times,* Oct. 18, 1931, XI, 2; "Woodside Rages Over Influx of Illegal Aliens," *New York Times,* June 14, 1979. See also *Woodside* (New York, 1978); a copy of this can be found in the vertical files of the Municipal Research and Reference Library, New York City, and contains a 1939 map of ethnic distribution in the area, showing the Irish dominance. An examination of Census Tract 235 shows 71 natives of Ireland in 1920, 606 in 1950, and 1,399 by 1960. Woodside, even more than Washington Heights/Inwood, retained an Irish presence throughout this century.

96. In contrast, Jewish preference for urban "proximity" was manifested in their housing of choice—garden style and perimeter block apartment houses in the outer boroughs (especially the Bronx), many of them built as labor cooperative ventures. See Moore, *At Home in America,* 36.

97. James T. Farrell, *Bernard Clare* (New York, 1946), 147, 150.

98. It is possible, although unexplored in this chapter, that other ethnic groups in the city were affected by this phenomenon too.

99. Howard Chudacoff speculated whether "horizontal movement reflect[ed] social and economic aspirations of importance equal to or greater than occupational patterns." See "A New Look at Ethnic Neighborhoods: Residential Dispersion and the Concept of Visibility in a Medium-Sized City," *Journal of American History* 60, no. 1 (1973): 92.

Interestingly, Andrew Greeley describes the lower-middle-class contentment of some Chicago Irish parishes in the 1930s and 1940s, where they lived in "moderate suburban comfort." Andrew M. Greeley, *That Most Distressful Nation: The Taming of the American Irish* (Chicago, 1972), 181–86.

In the nineteenth-century city, "mobile people thriving on the opportunities of the modern city as well as suffering the social insecurities that made up-and-down movement possible, sought to buttress their newly gained position through the kind of housing they rented." Barth, *City People*, 47.

On the other hand, Ellen Skerrett posits a more traditional view: that by 1920 Irish economic advancement correlates with suburban progression ("into apartment house districts and bungalow belts"); that in this movement, middle-class Chicago Irish "preferred to live as outsiders in largely Protestant areas rather than to remain in heavily Catholic ethnic neighborhoods"; and, yet, they identified themselves with strong Catholic parishes in these new areas. See Ellen Skerrett, "The Development of Identity Among Irish Americans in Chicago, 1880–1920," in Timothy J. Meagher, ed., *From Paddy to Studs: Irish-American Communities in the Turn of the Century Era, 1880–1920* (Westport, Conn., 1986), 119, 134.

Part V   Overview: AN END AND A BEGINNING (Reimers)

1. Nathan Glazer and Daniel P. Moynihan, *Beyond the Melting Pot: The Negroes, Puerto Ricans, Jews, Italians and Irish of New York City* (Cambridge, 1963), 217.

2. Deborah Dash Moore, *At Home: Second Generation New York Jews* (New York, 1981), 95–96. For changes in Irish participation see Chris McNickle, *To Be Mayor of New York: Ethnic Politics in the City* (New York, 1993); Theodore Lowi, *At the Pleasure of the Mayor: Patronage and Power in New York City, 1898–1958* (New York, 1964).

3. *New York Times*, Mar. 18, June 13, 1947.

4. Data drawn from *Annual Reports* and *Statistical Yearbooks* of the Immigration and Naturalization Service.

5. P. J. Drudy, "Irish Population Change and Emigration since Independence," in P. J. Drudy, ed., *The Irish in America: Emigration, Assimilation and Impact* (New York, 1985), 73–78.

6. Dept. of City Planning, *The Newest New Yorkers: An Analysis of Immigration into New York City During the 1980s* (New York, 1992), 52.

7. Morrison visas were named after Representative Bruce Morrison of Connecticut who was the House leader in shaping the 1990 immigration act. The visas were determined by lottery.

8. U.S. Bureau of the Census, *New York, 1980*, vol. 1, chap. C, pt. 34, Selected Ancestry Groups, table 60.

9. Summary Tape File 1, New York City, 1990 census data.

10. Morton D. Winsberg, "The Suburbanization of the Irish in Boston, Chicago and New York," *Eire-Ireland* 21 (Fall 1986): 94, 98, 101. I am indebted to Marion Casey for bringing my attention to this article. Census data are from Summary Tape File 1, New York City, New York Metropolitan Area, 1990 Census.

11. See T. J. English, *The Westies: Inside the Hell's Kitchen Irish Mob* (New York, 1990); *New York Times*, Sept. 28, 1992; *Irish Voice*, Oct. 6, 1992.

12. *New York Times*, Feb. 12, 1991.

13. U.S. Bureau of the Census, *Census of Population and Housing, 1980*, NY-NJ SMSA, table P-8 and Summary Tape File 1, New York City, 1990 census data.

14. John Cooney, *The American Pope: The Life and Times of Francis Cardinal Spellman* (New York, 1984), 102.

15. Joshua Freeman, *In Transit: The Transport Workers Union in New York City, 1933–1966* (New York, 1989), 26–29. See ibid. for a discussion of transport workers and *Irish Voice*, Nov. 12, 1991.

16. Winsberg, "Suburbanization of the Irish," 97; Andrew Greeley, *The Irish Americans: The Rise to Money and Power* (New York, 1981), 137–38; U.S. Bureau of the Census, 1980, *General Social and Economic Characteristics, New York*, vol. 1, chap. C, pt. 34, tables 108–14. See also Dennis Clark, "The Irish in the American Economy," Drudy, *The Irish in America*, 242–45.

17. See United Irish Counties Community Action Bureau, *The Needs of the American-Irish Community in the City of New York* (New York, 1975).

18. *New York Times*, Nov. 28, 1993.

19. Warren Moscow, *What Have You Done for Me Lately? The Ins and Outs of New York City Politics* (Englewood Cliffs, N.J., 1967), 119. An especially good account of patronage is Lowi, *At the Pleasure of the Mayor*.

20. Thomas Kessner, *Fiorello H. La Guardia and the Making of Modern New York* (New York, 1989), esp. 287–89.

21. McNickle, *To Be Mayor of New York*, 66–67. O'Dwyer's story is told in William O'Dwyer, *Beyond the Golden Door* (New York, 1987), and McNickle, *To Be Mayor of New York*, 54–57, 82–84. A critical view of O'Dwyer's connection to criminals is George Walsh, *Public Enemies: The Mayor, the Mob, and the Crime That Was* (New York, 1980).

22. McNickle, *To Be Mayor of New York*, 91, 102–8. The discussion of Wagner is based heavily on McNickle's excellent book.

23. *New York Times*, Aug. 1, 1986.

24. McNickle, *To Be Mayor of New York*, 113–23.

25. Ibid., 149–52, 169. On De Sapio see Warren Moscow, *The Last of the Big-Time Bosses: The Life and Times of Carmine De Sapio and the Rise and Fall of Tammany Hall* (New York, 1971).

26. Lindsay polled only 40 percent of the Irish vote. About 22 percent went to Buckley. William Buckley, *The Unmaking of a Mayor* (New York, 1966), 333.

27. *New York Times*, Mar. 17, 1988; Mar. 15, 1990.

28. Dennis Clark, *Hibernia America: The Irish and Regional Cultures* (Westport, Conn., 1986), 66.

29. Ibid.; McNickle, *To Be Mayor of New York*, 122.

30. Moscow, *What Have You Done . . .* , 121.

31. Cooney, *The American Pope*, 217–20.

32. Moscow, *What Have You Done . . .* , 120–22.

33. McNickle, *To Be Mayor of New York*, 208.

34. Buckley, *The Unmaking of a Mayor*, 333.

35. Charles Green and Basil Wilson, *The Struggle for Black Empowerment in New York City: Beyond the Politics of Pigmentation* (New York, 1989), 22.

36. David Abbott et al., *Politics, Police and Race: The New York City Referendum on Civilian Review* (New York, 1969), 22–23.

37. See Mayor's Commission on Black New Yorkers, *Report* (New York, 1988).

38. *New York Times*, Oct. 18, 1992.

39. Ibid., Mar. 20, 1983.

40. Patrick Fenton, "In Brooklyn, Irish Quit the Democrats," *New York Times*, Oct. 16, 1984.

41. *New York Times*, Sept. 13, Nov. 9, 1989; Nov. 4, 1993.

42. *Irish Echo*, Dec. 11–17, 1991.

43. Steven Erie, *Rainbow's End: Irish-Americans and the Dilemmas of Urban Machine Politics, 1940–1985* (Berkeley, Calif., 1988), 142–44, 161–65, 171–76.

44. For a critical but comprehensive view of Spellman, see Cooney, *The American Pope*. The discussion below is based on Cooney's account.

45. Clark, *Hibernia America*, 66. For a defense of McCarthy see Charles F. Connolly, "Food for Thought and Action," *Irish Echo*, May 11, 1957.

46. Glazer and Moynihan, *Beyond the Melting Pot*, 2d ed., lvii.

47. For O'Connor and Koch see John Cardinal O'Connor and Mayor Edward I. Koch, *His Eminence and Hizzoner: A Candid Exchange* (New York, 1989).

48. *New York Times*, Sept. 20, Sept. 22, 1991.

49. Ibid., Jan. 6, Jan. 9, 1983.

50. Daily News, *New York's New World*, special reprint (1990), 40.

51. Monsignor George A. Kelly, *The Battle for the American Church* (Garden City, N.Y. 1979), 454–55.

52. Data based on the *Official Catholic Directory*.

53. *New York Times*, June 10, Sept. 26, 1992.

54. Ibid., Mar. 8, 1985.

55. Ibid., June 7, 1986. Greeley's results can be found in several books, including *The American Catholic: A Social Portrait* (New York, 1977); *American Catholics since the Council: An Unauthorized Report* (Chicago, 1985).

56. Greeley, *American Catholics since the Council*, 57–58.

57. United Irish Counties Community Action Bureau, *The Needs . . .* , 36, 54.

58. *Irish Voice*, Mar. 16, 1991.

59. Information furnished by Ruth Doyle of the archdiocese's Pastoral Research Office.

60. *New York Times*, Oct. 3, 1986.

61. Ibid., Mar. 6, 1987.

62. *New York Times*, Mar. 13, 17, 1991.

63. *Irish Echo*, Sept. 25–Oct. 1, 1991, and Oct. 30–Nov. 5, 1991; *Irish Voice*, Oct. 29, 1991.

64. *Irish Echo*, Jan. 22–29, 1992. Some Irish also associated ILGO with a demonstration staged by another gay rights group, Act Up, in St. Patrick's Cathedral in 1989. *New York Times*, Feb. 19, 1992.

65. See, for example, the letter to the *Irish Echo* in the Jan. 22–29, 1992 issue. Paul O'Dwyer's criticism of the parade organizers can be found in *New York Times*, Nov. 13, 1992.

66. *New York Times*, Jan. 10, 25, 1992; *Irish Voice*, Jan. 7, 21, and Feb. 4, 1992.

67. *New York Times*, Mar. 17, 18, 1992; Mar. 18, 1994.

68. *New York Times*, Mar. 18, 1972.

69. See, for example, the coverage of the twentieth testimonial dinner in *Irish People*, Jan. 25, 1992. The dinner drew a crowd of 900 and featured many prominent Irish American New Yorkers and non-Irish sympathizers.

70. See *New York Times*, Aug. 30, 1972; Dec. 16, 1975; Sept. 24, 1979; May 2, 1982.

71. Ibid., Mar., 18, 1983; Mar. 8, 1984.

72. *Irish Echo*, Mar. 12, 19, 1983.

73. *New York Times*, Mar. 4, 1983,

74. Clark, *Hibernia America*, 67.

75. *New York Times*, Aug. 14, 1984.

76. Ibid., Dec. 13, 1991, and Jan. 16, Feb. 20, 1992; *Irish Echo*, Oct. 23–29, 1991.

77. *Irish Echo*, Oct. 23–29, 1991.

78. *New York Times*, Mar. 18, 1990; *Irish Voice*, Feb. 18, 1992.

79. *Irish Echo*, Jan. 8–14, 1992.

80. *New York Times*, Mar. 18, 1983.

81. Ibid., Dec. 7, 1972.

82. Ibid., Aug. 1, 1986.

83. In addition to Corcoran's study, see Linda Dowling Almeida's survey in *Irish Voice*, Mar. 16, 1991, and her published analysis, "'And they still haven't found what they're looking for': A survey of the New Irish in New York City" in Patrick O'Sullivan, ed., *Patterns of Migration*, vol. 1 of *The Irish World Wide: History, Heritage, Identity* (England: Leicester University Press, 1992).

84. *Irish Echo*, May 28, 1988.

85. While attendance at football games at Gaelic Park in the Bronx grew during the 1980s, the future of the park, which needed renovation, became the center of a dispute between the newcomers and older Irish New Yorkers. See *New York Times*, Oct. 12, 1990, and Feb. 11, 1991; *Irish Echo*, Jan. 15–21, 1992.

86. *Irish Echo*, May 21, 1988; *New York Times*, Oct. 12, 1991. The new immigration act is covered in David M. Reimers, *Still the Golden Door: The Third World Comes to America*, 2d ed. (New York, 1992), chap. 8.

87. *New York Times*, Sept. 11, 1992.

88. For coverage of the nearly frantic efforts to win Morrison visas in the fall of 1991, see the *Irish Echo* and the *Irish Voice*. The *Voice*, in its Oct. 22, 1991 issue, called it "Visa Frenzy!," while the *Echo* headlined "Morrison Mania" in its Oct. 16–22, 1991 issue. Some 17 million applications for 40,000 slots poured in on the Merrifield, Va., post office.

Chapter 17: THE NEIGHBORHOOD CHANGED (Snyder)

This chapter could not have been written without the help of many past and present residents of Washington Heights and Inwood who shared their memories with me. Whether or not they are cited in this chapter, they have my gratitude. I first examined the recent history of northern Manhattan while researching the press and crime in contemporary New York at the Freedom Forum Media Studies Center at Columbia University, where Bruce Cronin was my research assistant. I thank both the center and Bruce for their generous assistance. Finally, special thanks to Thomas Bender, James W. Carey, Peter Eisenstadt, Clara Hemphill, William Murphy, and Jim Sleeper for reading drafts of this essay.

1. For the invasion formula, see the reference to Paul Cressey cited in Ronald H. Bayor, "The Neighborhood Invasion Pattern," in Ronald H. Bayor, ed., *Neighborhoods in Urban America* (Port Washington, N.Y., 1982), 86.

2. Sally Engle Merry, *Urban Danger: Life in a Neighborhood of Strangers* (Philadelphia, 1981), 14, 217–21, 237–43. The quotation is from pp. 242–43.

3. Ira Katznelson, *City Trenches: Urban Politics and the Patterning of Class in the United States* (Philadelphia, 1981), 14, 217–21, 237–43.

4. Ibid., 75–77; Lee A. Lendt, "A Social History of Washington Heights, New York City," Columbia–Washington Heights Community Mental Health Project (New York, 1960), 11–13, 58–59; interview with Leo Shanley, New York City, 1990; interview with Sister Veronica, New York City, 1992.

5. Katznelson, *City Trenches*, 79; *The WPA Guide to New York City* (New York, 1939; reprinted 1982), 293–306.

6. On the neighborhood's class composition see Katznelson, *City Trenches*, 79–86; on population see Ronald H. Bayor, *Neighbors in Conflict: The Irish, Germans, Jews and Italians of New York City, 1919–1941* (Baltimore, 1978), 152.

7. Interviews with Charles and Norene Walck, Dumont, New Jersey, 1990; Kathleen O'Halloran, New York City, 1990; and Buddy McGee, New York City, 1990.

8. Interview with McGee, 1990. Gaelic Park went through several name changes before acquiring its present name in the 1950s. On the dances at Innisfail Hall, see interview with Nora Goodwin, New York City, 1991.

9. Interviews with McGee, 1990; Mrs. Walck, 1990.

10. Bayor, *Neighbors in Conflict*, 87–104, 152–55. Also interviews with Michael Cohn, 1990, and Paul O'Dwyer, 1992.

11. Bayor, *Neighbors in Conflict*, 87–108, 155–56.

12. Interviews with Walck, 1990, and O'Dwyer, 1992.

13. Bayor, *Neighbors in Conflict*, 156–57; also Lendt, "A Social History of Washington Heights," 75–77.

14. Robert Lee, "Upper Manhattan: A Community Study of Washington Heights" (paper prepared for Protestant Council of the City of New York, 1954), 17.

15. Author's conversations with residents of Washington Heights and Inwood.

16. This estimate is based on the calculation that the ratio of native-born to foreign-born Irish was, at the least, consistent with the ratio of native to foreign-born for all whites in the neighborhood. U.S. Bureau of Census, *United States Census of Population, 1950*. vol. 3; Census Tract Statistics, chap. 37 (Washington, D.C., 1952), 98–100.

17. Interview with Mr. Walck, 1990.

18. Interviews with Mr. and Mrs. Walck, 1990.

19. Interviews with McGee, 1990, and O'Halloran, 1990.

20. Interview with McGee, 1990.

21. Interview with O'Halloran, 1990; also see Rudy Garcia, "Luching," *Heights-Inwood*, Mar. 11, 1981, 3.

22. Calculations for her sections of Inwood derived from tracts 253 and 261 from the 1950 U.S. census and tracts 307 and 303 from the 1960 U.S. census.

23. Interview with O'Halloran, 1990.

24. "Washington Heights Project," report attached to Aug. 16, 1957 letter from Maurice H. Greenhill, M.D. to Mayor Robert F. Wagner, Wagner Subject Files, Box 160, juvenile delinquency folder—1957, 3.

25. Lee, "Upper Manhattan," 9.

26. "Juvenile Delinquency in Critical Areas," 1957, Wagner Papers, Box 163, 1957 folder; "Perspectives on Delinquency Prevention," submitted by Deputy Mayor Harry Epstein, Wagner Papers, Box 159, 1955 juvenile delinquency folder; "976,936 Added to Youth Board Appropriation; Agency to Open 4 New Areas, Extend 4 Old Ones," in *Youth Board News*, June 1955, 1, in Wagner Papers, Box 48, January–June 1955 folder; "Washington Heights Project" report.

27. Interview with Mrs. Walck, 1990.

28. Lee, "Upper Manhattan," 7, 17. The quotation is from p. 17.

29. The park as a flashpoint between Irish and Jewish youths is based on an interview with Cohn, 1990, and "Washington Heights Project" report. On the events of the night, see "Youth, 15, Killed in Park Stabbing," *New York Times*, July 31, 1957, 46; and "Polio-crippled Boy Slain, Pal Knifed in Park; 25 Held" in *New York Post*, July 31, 1957, 2. Also see Irwin D. Davidson and Richard Gehman, *The Jury Is Still Out* (New York, 1959), 2–3.

30. See "Youth, 15, Killed . . . ," *New York Times*, July 31, 1957, 46; and "Polio-crippled Boy . . . " in *New York Post*, July 31, 1957, 2. Press accounts made much of the fact that Farmer had once suffered from polio, creating the image of a disabled victim unable to flee his attackers. However, the judge in the subsequent murder trial, Judge Irwin D.

Davidson, determined that Farmer suffered no residual ill effects from his polio and that it was not a factor in the incident. See Davidson and Gehman, *The Jury Is Still Out*, 2–3.

31. See "Cops Guard Gang-War District . . . ," *New York Post*, Aug. 1, 1957, 3. The *Post* reported that both McShane and Farmer were members of the Jesters. However, the *Times* reported that while McShane was a member, Farmer was not. See "Boy Is Badly Hurt in 3D Gang Battle," *New York Times*, Aug. 2, 1957, 38.

32. I thank Professor Joshua B. Freeman of the Department of History, Columbia University, and Assistant Dean Eric Schneider of the College of Arts and Sciences, University of Pennsylvania, for discussing with me their research and the relationships between gangs, turf, and identity. Dean Schneider's work on crime and gangs in post–World War II New York will illuminate further the kinds of issues raised by the Farmer case. For an ethnographic analysis of interracial relations in gangs, see Jay MacLeod, *Ain't No Makin' It: Levelled Aspirations in a Low-Income Neighborhood* (Boulder, Colo., 1987), 35–39, 44.

33. See "4 Youths Convicted in Boy's Murder; 3 Others Cleared," *New York Times*, Apr. 16, 1958, 1; and "4 Slayers of Boy Get Stiff Terms; Judge Indicts Public for Apathy," *New York Times*, May 29, 1958, 1.

34. See "Washington Heights Inquiry," a press release dated Aug. 15, 1957, Wagner Subject Files, Box 165, juvenile delinquency–Mental Health Board folder.

35. Interview with Mrs. Walck, 1990.

36. Lendt, "A Social History of Washington Heights," 87, 93.

37. *United States Census of Population and Housing: 1950: Census Tracts: Final Report PHC (1)-104, Part 1* (Washington, D.C., 1962), 130–32.

38. Interviews with O'Halloran, 1990; McGee, 1990.

39. Jim Carroll, *The Basketball Diaries* (New York, 1978, 1987). For the quotation see p. 17, and also 11–12, 23–24, 152.

40. See *1970 Census of Population and Housing Census Tracts: New York, New York Standard Metropolitan Statistical Area: Part 1: PHC (1)-145, New York, New York* (Washington, D.C., 1972), P314-P317.

41. Crime rates calculated from *Uniform Crime Reports for the United States, Annual Reports* (Washington, D.C., 1965–88), supplemented by data from the New York City Police Department on the 34th Precinct for the years 1970–90 and the City as a whole for 1988 and 1989. Special thanks to Bruce Cronin for his help in this exercise. In 1978, the southern border of the 34th Precinct, which covers Washington Heights and Inwood, was expanded to 155th Street. This added to the precinct an area that contained streets whose crime rates were higher than those of the northern and western sections of the Heights and Inwood.

42. For an extended discussion of these issues and their theoretical ramifications for urban politics, see Katznelson, *City Trenches*, 89–189.

43. On the Dominican immigration to New York City, see David B. Bray, "The Dominican Exodus: Origins, Problems, Solutions," passim, in Barry B. Levine, ed., *The Caribbean Exodus* (New York, 1987); and Patricia R. Pessar, "The Dominicans: Women in the Household and the Garment Industry," passim, in Nancy Foner, ed., *New Immigrants in New York* (New York, 1987). Interviews with Rafael Lantigua, M.D., Columbia Presbyterian Medical Center, and Moises Perez, executive director, Alianza Dominicana in New York, 1990, impressed upon me the general failure to appreciate both the Dominicans' contribution to the New York City labor force and their suffering due to crime. The unacknowledged similarities between the Dominicans and the Irish is based on an interview with Monsignor Thomas Leonard, New York City, 1990.

44. Interview with Barry Dunleavey, New York City, 1990.

45. On neighborhood politics and its larger implications in Washington Heights and Inwood, see Katznelson, *City Trenches*, 126–30, 132–34, 179–81. For a general discussion of relations between older white ethnic groups, political machines, the demands of people of color, and the programs of the Great Society, see Frances Fox Piven, "The Great Society as Political Strategy" and "The Urban Crisis," in Richard A. Cloward and Frances Fox Piven, *The Politics of Turmoil: Essays on Poverty, Race and the Urban Crisis* (New York, 1974), esp. 274–84 and 320–24.

46. On the concentration of black and Latino children in public schools compared with Irish and Jewish children who were more likely to be in private or parochial schools, see Katznelson, *City Trenches*, 129.

47. Interview with Tom Mullany, New York City, 1990.

48. Interview with McGee, 1990. Also "Fear of Violence, Locked Doors Mark Inwood Bar Scene," *Heights-Inwood*, July 25, 1974, 2.

49. "Fear of Violence . . . ," *Heights-Inwood*, July 25, 1974, 2.

50. Interview with O'Halloran, 1990.

51. "Police Response to Task Force Report Washington Heights-Inwood," Sept. 27, 1978, vertical file, New York City Municipal Archives.

52. Interview with Cathy Finnerty, New York City, 1990.

53. Interview with McGee, 1990.

54. Interview with Mullany, 1990.

55. Interview with Cohn, 1990.

56. Interview with Eileen Quinn, New York City, 1990.

57. Steven M. Lowenstein, *Frankfurt on the Hudson: The German-Jewish Community of Washington Heights, 1933–1983, Its Structure and Culture* (Detroit, 1989), 212–16.

58. See Katznelson, *City Trenches*, 103, 244–45. Katznelson, using a block survey of northern Manhattan, calculates that in 1972 approximately 93.2 percent of the Irish in the neighborhood were in the manual and nonmanual working class; for Jews, the corresponding figure was 62 percent. In the categories "petit bourgeois," "professional," and "manager," the Jews numbered 19.7, 9.9, and 4.2 percent, respectively. The Irish numbered 1.6 percent among the petit bourgeois, and none among professionals and managers.

59. *1980 Census of Population and Housing Census Tracts: New York, New York, New Jersey Standard Metropolitan Statistical Area: PHC80-2–260: Section 1* (Washington, D.C., 1983), table P-8, P620–P621.

60. Figures calculated by comparing the average Irish percentage of the population in 1960 census tracts 253, 261, 291,293, 295, and 303 with the average of Irish percentage of the population in 1980 census tracts 291, 293, 295, and 303. Tracts 253 and 261 were omitted from the 1980 calculation because by then they had small Irish populations. See 1980 census, P620–P621.

61. See 1980 U.S. census table P-8, "Ancestry of Persons: 1980," P620–P621. Also interview with Karen Ramos, New York City, 1992.

62. On the Dominican presence in the drug trade, see Terry Williams, *The Cocaine Kids: The Inside Story of a Teenage Drug Ring* (New York, 1989), 51–53, also 21–25, 88. On middle-class crack users see "Crack, Bane of Inner City, Is Now Gripping Suburbs," *New York Times*, Oct. 1, 1989, 1.

63. See "Alcoholism: H-I Study," *Heights-Inwood News*, May 6, 1981, 3.

64. According to New York City Police Department Statistics, in 1990, the 34th Precinct, with a population of 198,192 suffered 103 murders. In the same period, the entire city, with a population of 7,322,564 suffered 2,262 murders. The citywide total

was inflated by the killing of 87 people in an act of arson at the Happyland social club. Depending on whether the Happyland death toll is included, the citywide murder rate is just over or just under 30 per 100,000 inhabitants.

65. See Beth S. Rosenthal and David Rubel, "A Community in Transition: State of Current Resources and Needs," (paper prepared for Northern Manhattan Improvement Corporation, New York, 1989), passim.

66. See "In 26 Tongues, Common Complaints," *New York Times*, Aug. 20, 1989, 34.

67. Interview with Mrs. Walck, 1990.

68. For useful discussions of these changes, see John Mollenkopf and Manuel Castells, eds., *Dual City: Restructuring New York* (New York, 1991), passim.

69. Interview with O'Halloran, 1990.

70. Interviews with Sister Elizabeth Tierney, New York City, 1992, and Quinn, 1990.

71. Interview with McGee, 1990.

72. For the racial and ethnic composition of the neighborhood, derived from the 1980 census, see "Washington Heights at a Glance," *New York Newsday*, July 18, 1982, 18. For the quotation, see Goodwin.

73. See the poem, "Whatever You Say Say Nothing," in Seamus Heaney, *Poems: 1965–1975* (New York, 1984), 212–15.

74. Jim Dwyer, "Crime Is Biased against the City," *New York Newsday*, Jan. 15, 1992, 2.

75. Ibid.

76. On the Ortiz service, see "Inwood Angry at Murder of Storekeeper," *New York Newsday*, May 15, 1989, 25; on the O'Brian case, see "Dispatch Crime Beat," *Uptown Dispatch*, Aug. 7–16, 1989, 9. The point about the elderly Irish invited to Dominican weddings is based on an interview with Monsignor Leonard, 1990.

77. Merry, *Urban Danger*, 243.

78. Comments about the privatization of Irish life are based on telephone interviews with O'Dwyer, 1992; and John Finucane, Pearl River, New York, 1992. On the relative absence of painful consequences for ethnic identity among white Americans see Mary C. Waters, *Ethnic Options: Choosing Identities in America* (Berkeley, Calif., 1990), 147–68.

79. On the increasingly emotional and psychological dimension of Irish ethnicity, see interview with O'Dwyer, 1992.

Chapter 18: EMIGRANTS, *EIREPRENEURS*, AND OPPORTUNISTS (Corcoran)

This chapter draws on Corcoran, *Irish Illegals: Transients between Two Societies* (Westport, Conn., 1993), a book based on my doctoral research. The research was partly supported by a grant from the Wenner-Gren Foundation for Anthropological Research, New York City.

1. Brendan Walsh, *Emigration: An Economist's Perspective* (Dublin, 1988), 4.

2. Irish America is a somewhat difficult term to define because of the multidimensionality and diversity of Irish American life. In this chapter I am referring for the most part to the Irish American community still living and working in New York City's ethnic Irish neighborhoods or enclaves, and to those who still maintain strong social and economic ties with the old neighborhoods. These Irish Americans are

generally first generation immigrants who have not fully assimilated into main-stream American life.

3. Benedict Anderson, "Exodus," *Cultural Inquiry* (Winter 1994): 327.

4. National Economic and Social Council (NESC), *The Economic and Social Implications of Emigration* (Dublin, 1991), 52–54.

5. Interview with undocumented Irish immigrant, New York City, Dec. 5, 1988.

6. Interview with undocumented Irish immigrant, New York City, May 14, 1988.

7. Interview with undocumented Irish immigrant, New York City, Mar. 3, 1988.

8. Interview with undocumented Irish immigrant, New York City, Mar. 14, 1988.

9. Edna Bonacich, "A Theory of Middlemen Minorities," *American Sociological Review* 38 (Oct. 1973): 583–94.

10. Interview with undocumented Irish immigrant, New York City, Jan. 14, 1988.

11. Interview with undocumented Irish immigrant, New York City, Feb. 1, 1988.

12. James Morrissey, "The Eirepreneurs," *Irish Independent,* July 9, 1988.

13. Brendan Walsh, *Ireland's Changing Demographic Structure* (Dublin, 1989), 16.

14. NESC, . . . *Implications of Emigration,* 86–87. Ibid., 9.

15. Gerard Hanlon, "The Emigration of Irish Accountants: Economic Restructuring and Producer Services in the Periphery," *Irish Journal of Sociology* 1, no. 1 (1991): 52–65.

16. Personal communication from an Irish stockbroker who spent five years working for Merrill Lynch in New York City.

17. Gerard Hanlon, "Emigration of Irish Accountants."

18. Interview with Patricia O'Callaghan, director of Project Irish Outreach, May 10, 1990. According to O'Callaghan, Donnelly visa holders are "passive" immigrants in the sense that they very often know no one in New York City and have skills that do not transfer easily. In contrast, she characterized illegals as "active" immigrants who generally have contacts that enable them to secure accommodation and jobs.

19. For a discussion of Ireland's culture of emigration see Corcoran, *Irish Illegals,* 47–53.

20. This information was obtained from an American embassy official in Dublin at a seminar, "Immigration in the United States Today," sponsored by the United States Information Service, Dec. 6, 1989.

21. W. R. Bohning, "Integration and Immigration Pressures in Western Europe," *International Labor Review* 130, no. 4. (1991): 445–58.

22. Personal communication from an Irish stockbroker who spent five years working for Merrill Lynch in New York City.

23. Consular officials at the Department of Foreign Affairs in Dublin provided the figure of 40,000. Immigrant activists and church sources have offered estimates in the range of 136,000 to more than 200,000. See discussion in Padraig Yeates, "A New Breed of Irish Emigrant," *Irish Times,* June 16, 1988. The United States Catholic Conference provided a figure of 44,000 in "Undocumented Irish in the U.S.," *Migration and Refugee Services Staff Report* (Washington, D.C., 1988).

24. Saskia Sassen, "New York City's Informal Economy" (paper presented at the Second Symposium on the Informal Sector, Johns Hopkins University, Oct. 1986).

25. Saskia Sassen, "The Informal Economy," in J. H. Mollenkopf and M. Castells, eds., *Dual City: Restructuring New York* (New York, 1991), 79–101.

26. Interview with undocumented Irish immigrant, New York City, Oct. 19, 1987.

27. Interview with undocumented Irish immigrant, New York City, Feb. 1, 1988.

28. Interview with undocumented Irish immigrant, New York City, May 14, 1988.

29. Interview with undocumented Irish immigrant, New York City, Oct. 28, 1987.

30. Interview with undocumented Irish immigrant, New York City, Feb. 1, 1988.

31. Interview with undocumented Irish immigrant, New York City, Feb. 1, 1988.

32. Interview with undocumented Irish immigrant, New York City, Mar. 14, 1988.

33. Patricia Pessar, "Dominican Workers in the U.S. Labor Market" (paper presented at the Center for Immigration and Population Studies Seminar, "New Immigrants and Economic Restructuring," New York City, May 6, 1988).

34. "Refugees for 'Slave Labor,'" *Irish Post,* July 9, 1994.

35. See, for example, Janet G. Hunt and Larry L. Hunt, "The Dualities of Careers and Families: New Integrations or New Polarizations," in A. S. Skolnick and J. S. Skolnick, eds., *Family in Transition* (Boston, 1994); 275–89; and N. Glazer, "The Decommodificaiton of Health Care in the United States" (paper presented at the Socialist Scholars Conference, New York City, Apr. 1987).

36. Interview with undocumented Irish immigrant, New York City, June 18, 1988.

37. Ibid.

38. William Yancey, Eugene Ericksen, and Richard Juliani, "Emergent Ethnicity: A Review and Reformulation," *American Sociological Review* 41, no. 3 (1976): 391–403; Michael Young and Peter Willmott, *Family and Kinship in East London* (London, 1957).

39. Interview with a local priest, St. Brendan's Parish, Bronx, May 3, 1988.

40. Helena Sheehan, "Irish Identity Is Only Part of What We Are," *Irish Times,* Nov. 29, 1991.

41. Ien Ang, "Culture and Communication: Toward an Ethnographic Critique of Transnational Media Systems," *European Journal of Communication* 5, nos. 2–3 (1990).

42. Anderson, "Exodus," 314–27.

43. Susan McKeown was quoted by Helena Mulkerns, "Not So Green in the Big Apple," *Irish Times,* Jan. 19, 1994.

44. Fintan O'Toole, "Some of Our Emigrants Are Happy to Go," *Irish Times,* Sept. 14, 1989.

45. Personal communication from Mary Doran, Doran Film Distribution, Dublin, Aug. 9, 1994. See also Helena Mulkerns, "Not So Green."

46. In terms of political mobilization, the Irish Americans who proved most important to the new Irish community were, in general, a rather different constituency from those they encountered in the labor market. Irish Americans who became actively involved in the legalization campaign were drawn primarily from the ranks of the upwardly mobile who have left the ethnic enclaves behind and who are integrated into mainstream American society. In particular, the IIRM drew on the support of institutional leaders from a variety of influential Irish American interest groups.

47. John M. McCarthy and Meyer N. Zald, "Resource Mobilization and Social Movements," *American Journal of Sociology* 82, no. 6 (1977): 1212–41.

48. Richard Alba, *Ethnic Identity: The Transformation of White America* (New Haven, 1990), 16–17, 25.

49. Other ethnic groups in the New York City area engaged in similar organizing strategies on behalf of their undocumented immigrants. The Polish and Slavic Center runs the biggest social services program for East Europeans in the New York City area. In 1987, led by clergy and community leaders, they successfully lobbied Congress for the legalization of thousands of Polish illegal immigrants who faced deportation. The American Committee for Italian Immigration founded in 1952 has also lobbied Congress to secure higher immigration quotas for Italians seeking entry to the United States.

50. The Morrison visa program was launched in October 1991. As the October 14 deadline for receipt of applications approached, the American embassy in Dublin fielded more than 15,000 inquiries about the program. Three agencies offering visa services in Dublin reported brisk business, with some of their clients submitting up to 1,000 applications to

increase their chances of selection. (This practice was later disallowed in the subsequent lotteries). On the weekend before Monday, October 14, thousands of Irish illegals resident in the United States converged on the designated post office in Virginia to mail multiple applications. The *Irish Voice* newspaper in New York handled 100,000 such applications for its readers. The interest in the Morrison visa program was reminiscent of the Donnelly visa program inaugurated five years earlier. That program had been so well publicized, and strategic mailing of multiple applications used so successfully, that Irish applicants won 41 percent of the 40,000 NP-5 visas allotted to residents of 36 countries in the period 1987–90.

Chapter 19: IRISH TRADITIONAL AND POPULAR MUSIC IN NEW YORK CITY (Miller)

1. Nathan Glazer and Daniel P. Moynihan *Beyond the Melting Pot: The Negroes, Puerto Ricans, Jews, Italians, and Irish of New York City*, 2d ed. (Cambridge, Mass., 1970), xxxiii.

2. For detailed information on Irish traditional music, see Brendan Breathnach, *Folk Music and Dances of Ireland* (Dublin, 1980).

3. The distinction made here between Irish popular music and Irish American popular music is based on country of origin rather than on style or form. "Irish popular music" thus refers to that popular genre created in Ireland, whereas "Irish American popular music" refers to that created in America by Irish immigrants or by Irish Americans. The earliest known recording of Irish traditional music in the United States was made by the Edison Company (New York) in 1899 of uilleann piper James C. McAuliffe. The recording features four tunes: "Minstrel Boy," "Miss McCloud's Reel," "Donnybrook Fair," and "A Stack of Barley." For more information on these early Irish recordings, see Richard K. Spottswood, *Ethnic Music on Records, A Discography of Ethnic Recordings Produced in the United States, 1893–1942*, vol. 5 (Urbana, Ill., 1990).

4. Irish traditional music arrived in America with the original Irish immigrants who settled in rural areas up and down the East Coast during the late seventeenth century. These immigrants were for the most part descendants of Presbyterian Scots who, a century earlier, had been relocated from Scotland to assist in the colonization of northeastern Ireland by the English. The musical tradition they brought to America was non-Celtic and more closely related to a Lowland Scottish style. See Lawrence E. McCullough, "An Historical Sketch of Traditional Irish Music in the U.S.," *Folklore Forum* 7, no. 3 (1974): 178.

5. McCullough, "Historical Sketch," 180–81.

6. *Trow's New York City Directory for the Year Ending July 1st, 1896*, 230.

7. For an exceptional record of this period of immigrant Irish musical culture in the United States, see two books by Capt. Francis O'Neill: *Irish Folk Music—A Fascinating Hobby* and *Irish Minstrels and Musicians*. Published in 1910, these books discuss in frequently peculiar detail and with great pride the many figures in Irish music in the Chicago area during the time. (Both reprinted Darby, Pa., 1973).

8. For further information on early Irish 78s see Michael Moloney, "Irish Ethnic Recordings and the Irish-American Imagination," in *Ethnic Recordings in America: A Neglected Heritage* (Washington, D.C., 1982), 84–101; and Phillippe Varlet's liner notes to "From Galway to Dublin: Early Recordings of Irish Traditional Music," *Rounder Records*, 1993, 1087.

9. Videotaped interview with Mary O'Beirne, Woodside, N.Y., Nov. 18, 1990, conducted for the video documentary *From Shore to Shore: Irish Traditional Music in New York City* (Cherry Lane Productions, 1993), hereafter cited (FSTS).

10. Videotaped interview with Mary Coleman Hannon, Woodside, N.Y., Nov. 18, 1990 (FSTS).

11. Ibid.

12. Dennis Clark, *Erin's Heirs: Irish Bonds of Community* (Lexington, Ky., 1991), 50.

13. The U.S. Immigration and Naturalization Service's Annual Report indicates that 210,024 Irish immigrated between 1921 and 1930, whereas only 10,973 came between 1931 and 1940. *U.S. INS Annual Report, 1986* (Washington, D.C.).

14. Lawrence E. McCullough, "Historical Sketch," 185.

15. Taped interview with Jack Coen, Bronx, N.Y., Mar. 7, 1992.

16. Ibid.

17. Taped interview with Daniel Collins, Newton, N.J., Mar. 24, 1992.

18. Taped interview with Martin Mulhaire, Flushing, N.Y., Oct. 4, 1985.

19. Interview with Jack Coen, Mar. 17, 1992.

20. Taped interview with Brendan Ward, New York City, Mar. 13, 1992.

21. Ibid.

22. Ann Daly, "Mick Delahunty," *Irish Echo*, Feb. 7, 1959.

23. The headlines of the *Irish Echo*, Sept. 30, 1944, indicate that 14,687 Irish workers lost their jobs "after five years of war work."

24. Census Bureau, *Historical Statistics of the United States* (Washington, D.C., 1960), 56, as cited in McCullough.

25. *Irish Echo*, Nov. 12, 1949, 3.

26. Patrick Mullins' videotaped interview with Tom Doherty, Bay Ridge, Brooklyn, N.Y., Feb. 24, 1989 (FSTS).

27. Taped interview with Paddy Reynolds, Staten Island, New York, Mar. 20, 1992.

28. Taped interview with Louis Quinn, Flushing, N.Y., Oct. 24, 1990.

29. Interview with Paddy Reynolds, Mar. 20, 1992.

30. Taped interview with Paddy Noonan, Garden City, N.Y., Feb. 27, 1992.

31. Interview with Brendan Ward, Mar. 13, 1992.

32. Taped interview with Dorothy Hayden, Rego Park, N.Y., Mar. 4, 1992.

33. Interview with Paddy Noonan, Feb. 27, 1992.

34. Taped interview with Martin Mulhaire, Flushing, N.Y., Oct. 4, 1986.

35. Interview with Brendan Ward, Mar. 13, 1992.

36. In the liner notes to the recording "St. Patrick's Day Celebration," Mick Moloney writes that this style of playing was popularized by the Gallowglass Ceili Band, a hybrid Irish ensemble that had its heyday in the early 1950s. Playing during the radio and recording era, the Gallowglass Ceili Band incorporated nontraditional instruments such as the saxophone and drum set and became a model for a commercialized style of Irish instrumental music. Legacy Records, AAD CK48694, 1992.

37. The Musicians' Union in New York City (American Federation of Musicians, Local 802) kept a tight rein on both musicians and dance hall owners in the 1940s and 1950s. Aside from stage time on and time off rules, Local 802 established additional regulations that directly affected immigrant musicians during these years: one had to be a union member in order to work in union halls and most of the halls were, in fact, unionized; to be eligible to join the union, one had to be a resident of the United States for six months; and if a union hall hired a foreign band (for example, a visiting group from Ireland), an equal number of union musicians had to be hired ("stand-ins") for the evening, whether or not they actually played.

When asked about this last regulation, fiddler Paddy Reynolds comments: "Many a night I brought my fiddle and sat down and never played a tune all night, but got paid the same as they did. . . . That was the good thing about the union." When asked if he got bored during the course of such an evening, Reynolds says, "No, goddamnit! When I got that check, it cured everything! Are you kidding? When we'd get our check, we'd go somewhere else and enjoy a good *seisún*!" (Taped interview by author).

38. Taped interview with Matty Connolly, Richmond Hill, N.Y., June 12, 1988.

39. Many of the ballrooms built during the late 1950s and early 1960s were part of several chains owned and operated by a handful of entrepreneurs. The first and one of the largest chains was owned by brothers Albert and Jim Reynolds. Their first dance hall, Cloudland, opened in 1957 in Roosky, County Roscommon. At the height of the showband era, the Reynolds' empire would include 14 ballrooms that could accommodate audiences from 2000 to 4000. Thirty-five years later in 1992, Albert Reynolds was elected Ireland's *Taoiseach* (prime minister). For more on the showband era in Ireland see Vincent Power, *Send 'Em Home Sweatin'* (Dublin, 1990).

40. Taped interview with Brendan Bowyer, Massapequa Park, N.Y., July 29, 1992.

41. Ibid.

42. Interview with Matty Connolly, June 12, 1988.

43. Taped interview with Martin Mulhaire, Flushing, N.Y. May 10, 1988.

44. Interview with Daniel Collins, Mar. 24, 1992.

45. Interview with Jack Coen, Mar. 7, 1992.

46. Interview with Jack Coen, from Lori Jane Kaplan, "The Lark on the Strand: A Study of a Traditional Irish Flute Player and His Music" (Master's thesis, Western Kentucky University, 1979).

47. Taped interview with Tommy Makem, New York City, Apr. 4, 1992.

48. Interview with Paddy Noonan, Feb. 27, 1992.

49. Interview with Dorothy Hayden, Mar. 4, 1992.

50. Ibid.

51. *Irish Advocate,* Oct. 8, 1960, 6.

52. Taped interview with Martin Mulhaire, Flushing, N.Y., Oct. 4, 1986.

53. Taped interview with Martin Mulhaire, Flushing, N.Y., May 10, 1988.

54. Michael Moloney, "Irish Music in America: Continuity and Change, A dissertation in Folklore and Folklife" (Ph.D. diss., University of Pennsylvania, 1992), 323.

55. Videotaped interview with Andy McGann, Woodside, N.Y., Nov. 18, 1990 (FSTS).

56. Patrick Mullins' videotaped interview with Paddy Reynolds, Staten Island, N.Y., Feb. 24, 1989 (FSTS).

57. Videotaped interview with James O'Beirne Jr., Woodside, N.Y., Nov. 18, 1990 (FSTS).

58. Taped interview with Maureen Glynn Connolly, New York City, Mar. 23, 1992.

59. Mary C. McElwain, "Irish Musicians Association, Inc., Musical Highlights," *Irish Echo*, Sept. 28, 1963, 6.

60. The Irish Musicians Association, Inc., was modeled after its counterpart organization in Ireland, Comhaltas Ceoltóiri Éireann, which was established in 1951. Comhaltas' mission was to "promote, nurture, and perpetuate the playing of Irish traditional music and the accompanying song and dances of Ireland." Branches of Comhaltas formed throughout Ireland, offering sessions and music lessons with the intent of reviving traditional instrumental music. Comhaltas's largest presentation every year is the Fleadh Ceoil na Éireann, a summer event consisting of music competitions for all ages and instruments and informal, nonstop music sessions. Comhaltas branches also opened in countries with large immigrant Irish populations, and eventually the Irish Musicians Association in the United States became Comhaltas Ceoltóiri Éireann affiliates as well.

61. Arising from these sessions was the formation in 1958 of the New York Ceili Band, a now legendary ensemble of the finest practitioners of Irish traditional music in New York at the time. Featuring fiddlers Andy McGann, Paddy Reynolds, and Larry Redican, Paddy O'Brien on button accordion, Felix Dolan on piano, Gerry Wallace on piccolo, Jack Coen and Mike Dorney on flutes, and an occasional drummer, the New York Ceili Band was one of the most polished groups of its kind. The band quickly developed a strong following and was in high demand for ceili dances throughout New York. In 1960, the New York Ceili Band became the first American-based ceili band to compete in the annual Fleadh Ceoil na Éireann. After recording an undistributed 78 record, the group fizzled the following year owing to the lack of an audience and general disinterest on the part of the public.

62. Telephone interview with Dr. Frank Holt, Jersey City, N.J., June 29, 1992.

63. Ibid.

64. *Irish Echo*, May 11, 1957.

65. Notes from the 23rd Annual United Irish Counties Association *Feis* program booklet, May 29, 1955.

66. Ibid.

67. James J. Comerford, Chairman, UICA *Feis*, program notes, May 29, 1955.

68. Ibid.

69. Eric Hobsbawm and Terence Ranger, eds., *The Invention of Tradition* (Cambridge, 1983), 2–8.

70. Interview with Maureen Glynn Connolly, New York City, Mar. 23, 1992.

71. Brian Conway, "The Feis and Teaching the Tradition," a panel discussion that was part of the exhibition "Keeping the Tradition Alive: A History of Irish Music and Dance in New York City," sponsored by the New York Irish History Roundtable at the Museum of the City of New York, Mar. 9, 1991.

72. Maureen Glynn Connolly, "The Feis and Teaching The Tradition," panel discussion for "Keeping The Tradition Alive: A History of Irish Music and Dance in New York City," Mar. 9, 1991.

73. Videotaped interview with Maureen Doherty Macken, Bayside, N.Y., Dec. 27, 1990 (FSTS).

74. Irish and Irish American pub songs—specifically, ballads and rebel songs—are an exception to the passive consumption of popular music by both Irish and Irish American audiences. Most of these songs have known composers (as opposed to traditional music where the tunes are anonymously written) and are introduced to audiences by a performer (rather than via communal participation). Over the years, however, many pub songs have become familiar to audiences everywhere and have taken on a life of their own. Their performance in public venues more often than not engages the audience through unison singing with the performer.

75. Just as Irish popular pub songs in recent years have invited group participation, so, too, has the nature of traditional Irish music changed, given its expanding market in both Ireland and the United States. The enormous increase throughout the 1980s in the number of professional traditional music ensembles and individuals points to the continual evolution of Irish traditional music and its role in the music industry.

76. Taped interview with Martin Mulhaire, Flushing, N.Y., May 10, 1988.

77. Just as Irish big band music gave way to Irish showband music, the current hybridized form of Irish music is Celtic rock, with bands such as Black 47 and Celtic Cross, which are in high demand among young Irish immigrants and Irish Americans.

1. George O'Brien, *The Village of Longing and Dancehall Days* (New York, 1988), 59.

2. Seamus Heaney, *Station Island* (New York, 1985), 93–94. For the pieces in which "Mr. Dooley" recreates his Chicago Irish community, see Finley Peter Dunne, *Mr. Dooley and the Chicago Irish: The Autobiography of a Nineteenth-Century Ethnic Group,* ed. Charles Fanning (Washington, D.C., 1987).

3. James T. Farrell, *Studs Lonigan: A Trilogy* (1935; Urbana, Ill., 1993), 453.

4. Mary Gordon, *Final Payments* (New York, 1978), 4, 15.

5. Calvin Trillin, "American Chronicles: Democracy in Action," *New Yorker,* Mar. 21, 1988, 89.

6. Mary Gordon, *The Other Side* (New York, 1989), 50, 160, 183–84.

7. A subsequent autobiographical piece by Mary Gordon helps to explain her animosity toward the Irish part of her background. This memoir describes a lonely child's fear of her Jansenist Irish immigrant grandmother and the devastating loss of her Jewish father. When Mary's mother moved herself and her daughter back into the grandmother's house, what seemed to the child a shocking betrayal was added to her grief. See "The Important Houses," *New Yorker,* Sept. 28, 1992, 34–45.

8. Oliver MacDonagh, "Emigration from Ireland to Australia: An Overview," in Colm Kiernan, ed., *Australia and Ireland 1788–1988, Bicentenary Essays,* (Dublin, 1986), 133–34.

9. Contributors to the burst of Australian literary activity in the 1890s included poets and journalists Christopher Brennan, Victor Daley, John Farrell, Bernard O'Dowd, John O'Hara, and Roderick Quinn. Among subsequent writers who have described Australian Irish life are Eleanor Dark, Ruth Park, Gavin Casey, Xavier Herbert, Frank Hardy, Barry Oakley, Desmond O'Grady, Laurie Clancy, Vincent Buckley, D'Arcy Niland, Gerald Murnane, Barbara Hanrahan, David Ireland, and Peter Carey.

10. Terence Winch, "When New York Was Irish," performed by "Celtic Thunder" on *The Light of Other Days* (CSIF 1086, Green Linnet Recording Co., 1988). See also *Celtic Thunder* (GLCD 1029, Green Linnet Recording Co., 1981).

11. See a fine anthology full of provocative juxtapositions: David Lampe, ed., *The Legend of Being Irish: A Collection of Irish-American Poetry* (Fredonia, N.Y., 1989).

12. John Montague, *Born in Brooklyn* (Fredonia, N.Y., 1991), 16–17, 41, 64.

13. Terence Winch, *Irish Musicians / American Friends* (Minneapolis, 1985).

14. William Gibson, *A Mass for the Dead* (New York, 1968), 11, 87.

15. Frank Conroy, *Stop-Time* (New York, 1967); Francis Hackett, *American Rainbow* (New York, 1971); Horace Gregory, *The House on Jefferson Street: A Cycle of Memories* (New York, 1971); Dennis Smith, *Report from Engine Co. 82* (New York, 1972).

16. Maureen Howard, *Facts of Life* (Boston, 1978), 174, 182.

17. Maureen Howard, *Bridgeport Bus* (New York, 1965); *Expensive Habits* (New York, 1986).

18. Jimmy Breslin, *World without End, Amen* (New York, 1973).

19. Jimmy Breslin, *Table Money* (New York, 1986).

20. Joe Flaherty, *Fogarty & Co.* (New York, 1973).

21. Joe Flaherty, *Tin Wife* (New York, 1983).

22. Pete Hamill, *The Gift* (New York, 1973); *Flesh and Blood* (New York, 1977); *Loving Women, A Novel of the Fifties* (New York, 1989).

23. Dennis Smith, *Steely Blue* (New York, 1984); *The Final Fire* (New York, 1975).

24. Ellen Currie, "On the Mountain Stands a Lady," *Accent* 17, no. 4 (1957): 202–16; "Lovely Appearance of Death," *Dial* 1, no. 1 (1959), 88–124; *Available Light* (New York, 1986).

25. Jack Dunphy, *John Fury: A Novel in Four Parts* (1946; New York, 1976); *First Wine* (Baton Rouge, 1982); *The Murderous McLaughlins* (New York, 1988).

26. Dunphy, *The Murderous McLaughlins*, 234.

27. J. P. Donleavy, *The Ginger Man* (Paris, 1955). Donleavy has also published a book detailing the inspiration, writing, and struggles over censorship concerning this novel. See J. P. Donleavy, *The History of "The Ginger Man"* (Boston, 1994).

28. J. P. Donleavy, "A Fairy Tale of New York," in Daniel J. Casey and Robert E. Rhodes, eds., *Modern Irish-American Fiction: A Reader* (Syracuse, 1989), 147–64. This collection also contains New York stories by Betty Smith, John O'Hara, Joseph Dever, Maureen Howard, Jimmy Breslin, Mary Gordon, Pete Hamill, Joe Flaherty, and Elizabeth Cullinan.

29. John F. Murray, "O'Phelan Drinking," *New Yorker*, Oct. 3, 1977, 42.

30. John F. Murray, "O'Phelan's Daemonium," *New Yorker*, May 24, 1976, 35.

31. T. Coraghessan Boyle, "The Miracle at Ballinspittle," in *If the River Was Whiskey* (New York, 1990), 185.

32. T. Coraghessan Boyle, "If the River Was Whiskey," in *If the River Was Whiskey*, 217, 222, 224.

33. Frank Conroy, "Midair," in *Midair* (New York, 1985), 12, 27, 28.

34. Van Morrison, *Inarticulate Speech of the Heart* (9–23802–1, Warner Brothers Records, 1983).

35. See Charles Fanning, *The Irish Voice in America: Irish-American Fiction from the 1760s to the 1980s* (Lexington, Ky., 1990).

36. Monica McGoldrick, "Irish Families," in Monica McGoldrick and John K. Pearce, eds., *Ethnicity and Family Therapy* (New York, 1982), 335.

37. This movement also occurs in another Conroy story in the same collection, "Gossip," in which the narrator is a young writer similarly blocked: "He did not deny pain's existence, but only its power over him. (In this he was of course mistaken.) He was twenty-eight, intelligent, and ignorant of the forces that moved him." Again, the narrator arrives, after experiences that have not quite yielded enlightenment, at middle age and a measure of clarity: "What mattered was that everyone was connected in a web, that pain was part of that web, and yet, despite it, people loved one another." *Midair*, 89–90, 121.

38. Thomas McGonigle, *Going to Patchogue* (Elmwood Park, Ill., 1992), 34.

39. Compare another painful chronicle of migration from the city to Long Island (in this case, Mineola) in the two novels of Michael Stephens, *Season at Coole* (1972; Elmwood Park, Ill., 1984) and *The Brooklyn Book of the Dead* (Elmwood Park, Ill., 1994).

40. Willa Cather, "Katherine Mansfield," in *Stories, Poems, and Other Writings*, ed. Sharon O'Brien (New York, 1992), 877–78.

41. Alice McDermott, *That Night* (1987; New York, 1988), 107, 163, 164.

42. Alice McDermott, *At Weddings and Wakes* (New York, 1992), 165.

43. Farrell's largely autobiographical pentalogy is as follows: *A World I Never Made* (1936), *No Star Is Lost* (1938), *Father and Son* (1940), *My Days of Anger* (1943), and *The Face of Time* (1953), all published in New York.

44. McDermott, *At Weddings and Wakes*, 206–7, 211.

45. Tom Grimes, *A Stone of the Heart* (New York, 1990), 1, 121, 129–30.

46. T. Glen Coughlin, *The Hero of New York* (New York, 1985).

47. Thomas Mallon, *Aurora 7* (New York, 1991), 235.

48. Anna Quindlen, *Object Lessons* (New York, 1991), 262.

49. Thomas E. Kennedy, *Crossing Borders* (Wichita, Kan., 1990), 3, 206.

50 Elizabeth Cullinan, *House of Gold* (Boston, 1970). One year later, Cullinan published her first collection of stories, *The Time of Adam* (Boston, 1971).

51. Elizabeth Cullinan, "Yellow Roses," "An Accident," "A Foregone Conclusion," in *Yellow Roses* (New York, 1977), 62–98.

52. Cullinan, "An Accident," in *Yellow Roses,* 76.

53. Elizabeth Cullinan, "A Good Loser," *New Yorker,* Aug. 15, 1977, 32–44; *A Change of Scene* (New York, 1982).

54. Elizabeth Cullinan, "Life After Death," in *Yellow Roses,* 178.

55. Elizabeth Cullinan, "The Perfect Crime," in *Yellow Roses,* 143.

56. Elizabeth Cullinan, "The Sum and Substance," in *Yellow Roses,* 38.

57. Elizabeth Cullinan, "A Good Loser," *New Yorker,* Aug. 15, 1977, 44.

58. Elizabeth Cullinan, "Commuting," *Irish Literary Supplement* 2, no. 1 (1983), 34–35.

CONCLUSION

1. Robert Ernst, *Immigrant Life in New York City, 1825–1863* (1949; New York, 1979), 66–68; David Hammack, *Power and Society: Greater New York at the Turn of the Century* (New York, 1982), 83; Jeff Kisseloff, *You Must Remember This: An Oral History of Manhattan from the 1890s to World War II* (New York, 1989), 550, 551, 553.

2. Timothy J. Meagher, "Introduction," in Meagher, ed., *From Paddy to Studs: Irish American Communities in the Turn of the Century Era, 1880 to 1920* (Westport, Conn., 1986) 5–7, 9; Martin J. Towey, "Kerry Patch Revisited: Irish Americans in St. Louis in the Turn of the Century Era," in Meagher, ed., *From Paddy to Studs,* 139–57; Timothy Sarbaugh, "Exiles of Confidence: The Irish American Community of San Francisco, 1880 to 1920," in Meagher, ed., *From Paddy to Studs,* 161–79; William Shannon, *The American Irish: A Political and Social Portrait* (New York, 1974), 86–94, 183–200; John Higham, "Another Look at Nativism," *Catholic Historical Review* 44, no. 2 (1958): 155–58; James Walsh, "The Irish in the New America: 'Way out West," in David N. Doyle and Owen Dudley Edwards, eds., *America and Ireland, 1776–1976: The American Identity and the Irish Connection* (Westport, Conn., 1976), 165–77; Moses Rischin, "Immigration, Migration and Minorities in California: A Reassessment," *Pacific Historical Review* 41, no. 1, (1973) 81. See also Dennis Clark, *Hibernia America: The Irish and Regional Cultures* (New York, 1986), and *The Irish in Philadelphia: Ten Generations of Urban Experience* (Philadelphia, 1973); R. A. Burchell, *The San Francisco Irish: 1848–1880* (Berkeley, Calif., 1980); Jo Ellen Vinyard, *The Irish on the Urban Frontier: Detroit, 1850–1880* (New York, 1976).

3. Hammack, *Power and Society,* on economy, 31–58, and on elites, 65–79; Richard Stott, *Workers in the Metropolis: Class, Ethnicity, and Youth in Antebellum New York City* (Ithaca, N.Y., 1989), 7–29; Thomas Kessner, *The Golden Door: Italian and Jewish Immigrant Mobility in New York City, 1880–1915* (New York, 1977), 165–71; Frederick Jaher, *The Rich, The Wellborn, and the Powerful: Elites and Upper Classes in History* (Urbana, Ill., 1973), on New York, 156–57, 169–70, 189–93, 203–5, 231–33, 245–64, and 275–81; on Boston, 15–125; on Chicago, 453–554; and on Los Angeles, 581–659. It is difficult to get accurate comparative statistics for the early period. Kathleen Conzen lists data suggesting that the proportion of Irish who were white-collar workers was about twice as large in New York in 1855 as in Boston in 1850, about the same proportion as

in Milwaukee in 1850, but a smaller percentage than in St. Louis and Detroit in 1850. She found, however, a larger proportion of skilled workers among the Irish in New York than in any of the other four cities for those years, and a smaller proportion of unskilled Irish than in the other cities. Kathleen Conzen, *Immigrant Milwaukee: Accommodation and Community in a Frontier City* (Cambridge, Mass., 1976), 73. The table below of Irish foreign stock (immigrants and second-generation Irish) males should give a rough idea of the relative success of Irish men in New York and Brooklyn compared to their Celtic counterparts in other cities in 1900. The percentages are of the proportion of Irish foreign stock males in the labor force in each city:

Occupation	San Francisco (%)	Chicago (%)	New York (%)	Brooklyn (%)	Boston (%)
I	2.4	1.9	1.6	1.6	1.5
II	6.4	5.1	4.4	5.8	4.4
III	11.6	13.9	13.1	13.0	10.4
IV	14.8	19.1	17.4	16.3	21.2
Total	25,742	75,695	141,607	78,682	58,122

Source: U.S. Bureau of the Census, *Special Report: Occupations, 1900,* 516–23, 642–54, 712–14, 722–25, 496–99.

Note: I-Selected professional occupations (architects, clergymen, engineers, journalists, lawyers, dentists, physicians, teachers and professors); II-selected proprietors and managerial occupations (manufacturers, bankers and brokers, officials of banks, merchants, and dealers); III-selected clerical occupations (bookkeepers, clerks and copyists, commercial travelers, salesmen, stenographers, foremen, and overseers); and IV-laborers.

The table below shows the percentage of persons in professional and managerial occupations for men and women claiming only Irish ancestry in New York State, Illinois, and Massachusetts and for families headed by a person claiming only Irish ancestry in those states.

	Males (%)	Females (%)	Families' median income (1980 U.S. dollars)
NY	27.8	26.4	23,323
IL	24.6	23.2	24,760
MA	28.5	26.8	23,131

Source: Census of Population, 1980, pt. 12, 24, 132; pt. 15, 145, 148; pt. 39, 207–8, 210–11.

4. Daniel Patrick Moynihan and Nathan Glazer, *Beyond the Melting Pot: The Negroes, Puerto Ricans, Jews, Italians and Irish of New York City* (Cambridge, Mass., 1970), 217; *New York Times,* Jan. 17, 1993.

5. Moynihan and Glazer, *Beyond the Melting Pot,* 217–87, quotation on 217; William D'Arcy, *The Fenian Movement in the United States, 1858–1886,* (New York, 1947), 124; Charles C. Alexander, *John McGraw* (New York, 1988). Other signs of Irish power included the church. The New York Archdiocese in 1908 boasted 317 churches, 186 chapels, and about 1.2 million Catholics. Reverend Monsignor Florence D. Cohalan, *A Popular History of the Archdiocese of New York* (Yonkers, N.Y., 1983), 194–95. See also Nancy Joan Weiss, *Charles Francis Murphy, 1858–1924: Respectability and Tammany Politics* (Northhampton, Mass., 1968), 43–99; Christopher McNickle, *To Be Mayor of New York: Ethnic Politics in the City,* (New York, 1993), 12, 20–28. Nationalist crusades also swept and reswept the city in this era. On Land League frenzy, for example, see *Irish World,* Feb. 5, 12, 1881.

6. Weiss, *Charles Francis Murphy*, 86; McNickle, *To Be Mayor*, 32–179; Ronald H. Bayor, *Neighbors in Conflict: The Irish, Germans, Jews and Italians of New York City, 1929–1941* (Baltimore, 1978), 30–56; Arthur Mann, *LaGuardia Comes to Power, 1933* (Philadelphia, 1965); Moynihan and Glazer, *Beyond the Melting Pot*, 263.

7. Stanley Nadel, *Little Germany: Ethnicity, Religion and Class in New York City*, (Urbana, Ill., 1990), 29–46, 62–103, 137–62; Ira Rosenwaike, *Population History of New York City* (Syracuse, N.Y., 1972), 167; Deborah Dash Moore, *At Home: Second Generation New York Jews* (New York, 1981), 7. Quotation in Bayor, *Neighbors in Conflict*, 6.

8. Steven Erie, *Rainbow's End: Irish Americans and the Dilemma of Urban Machine Politics, 1840 to 1985* (Berkeley, Calif., 1988), 75–76, 180; Jack Beatty, *The Rascal King: The Life and Times of James Michael Curley, 1874–1958* (Reading, Mass., 1992); Alec Barbrook, *God Save the Commonwealth: An Electoral History of Massachusetts* (Amherst, Mass., 1973), 15–58; Geoffrey Blodgett, "Yankee Leadership in a Divided City, 1860–1890," Paul Kleppner, "From Party to Factions," and Charles Trout, "Curley of Boston: The Search for Irish Legitimacy," in Ronald Formisano and Constance Burns, eds., *Boston, 1700–1980: The Evolution of Urban Politics* (Westport, Conn., 1984); Harold Gosnell, *Machine Politics: Chicago Model* (1937; New York, 1968); John Allswang, *A House for All Peoples* (Lexington, Ky., 1971); Gerald Gamm, *The Making of New Deal Democrats: Voting Behavior and Realignment in Boston, 1920–1940* (Chicago, 1989); Bruce Stave, *The New Deal and the Last Hurrah: Pittsburgh Machine Politics* (Pittsburgh, 1970); Michael Funchion, "The Political and Nationalist Dimension," in Lawrence McCaffrey, ed., *The Irish in Chicago* (Urbana, Ill., 1987), 81–91; Edward C. Banfield, *Big City Politics: A Comparative Guide to the Political Systems of Atlanta, Boston, Detroit, El Paso, Los Angeles, Miami, Philadelphia, St. Louis and Seattle* (New York, 1965).

9. McNickle, *To Be Mayor*, 75–271; Moynihan and Glazer, *Beyond the Melting Pot*, lvii–lxxvi; Asher Arain, Arthur S. Goldberg, John H. Mollenkopf, and Edward T. Ragowsky, *Changing New York City Politics* (New York, 1990).

10. Amy Bridges, *The City in the Republic: Antebellum New York and the Origins of Machine Politics* (Ithaca, N.Y., 1984), 19, 126–30, 141; Hammack, *Power and Society*, 109–57, esp. 131; Erie, *Rainbow's End*, 49–51; McNickle, *To Be Mayor*, 1–28.

11. Bayor, *Neighbors in Conflict*, 87–108; Kevin Phillips, *Emerging Republican Majority* (New Rochelle, N.Y., 1969), 155–68; McNickle, *To Be Mayor*, 176, 186–87, 201; Moynihan and Glazer, *Beyond the Melting Pot*, xliii–lxxvi, 270; Donald J. Crosby, *God, Church and Flag: Senator Joseph R. McCarthy and the Catholic Church, 1950–1957* (Chapel Hill, N.C., 1974), 231–32. In 1984, for example, Irish Catholics in Massachusetts voted 56 to 43 percent for Mondale, but in New York State the Irish Catholic vote was 68 to 32 percent for Reagan. Carolyn Smith, ed., *The 84 Vote* (New York, 1984), 225, 227.

12. Bridges, *City in the Republic*, 110–11, 152. See also Sean Wilentz, *Chants Democratic: New York City and the Rise of the American Working Class, 1788 to 1850* (New York, 1978); Martin Shefter, "The Electoral Foundations of the Political Machine: 1884–1897," in Joel Sibley, Allen Bogue, and William Flanigan, eds., *The History of American Political Behavior* (Princeton, N.J., 1978), 289; Robert F. Wesser, *A Response to Progressivism: The Democratic Party and New York Politics, 1902–1918* (New York, 1986), 135–227; Weiss, *Charles Francis Murphy*, 69–90; McNickle, *To Be Mayor*, 1–40.

13. Weiss, *Charles Francis Murphy*, 98–99; Moynihan and Glazer, *Beyond the Melting Pot*, 224–25, 229; Thomas N. Brown, *Irish American Nationalism, 1870 to 1890* (Philadelphia, 1966), 133–34, 181.

14. Leon Fink, "American Labor History," in Eric Foner, ed., *The New American History* (Philadelphia, 1990), 233–50; Richard Oestreicher, "Urban Working Class Political Behavior and Theories of American Electoral Politics, 1870 to 1940," *Journal of*

American History 74, no. 4 (Mar. 1988): 1257–86; Sean Wilentz, "Against Exceptionalism: Class Consciousness and the American Labor Movement, 1790 to 1920," *International Labor and Working Class History* 26 (1984); John Patrick Diggins, "Comrades and Citizens," *American Historical Review* 90, no. 5 (1985): 619–39; James Weinstein, *The Decline of Socialism in America, 1912–1925* (New York, 1967), 149–54, 324–39; John H. M. Laslett and Seymour Martin Lipset, *Failures of a Dream? Essays in the History of American Socialism* (Berkeley, Calif., 1974); David P. Roediger, *The Wages of Whiteness: Race and the Making of the American Working Class* (New York, 1991), 133–63; Kerby Miller, "Class, Culture, and Immigrant Group Identity in the United States: The Case of Irish American Ethnicity," in Virginia McLaughlin, ed., *Immigration Reconsidered: History, Sociology and Politics* (New York, 1990), 96–129.

15. Ernst, *Immigrant Life in New York*, 123–24; William D'Arcy, *The Fenian Movement in the United States, 1858–1886* (New York, 1947), 2, 124; Kerby Miller, *Emigrants and Exiles: Ireland and the Irish Exodus to North America* (New York, 1985), 308–12, 334–35; 538–44; Thomas N. Brown, *Irish American Nationalism, 1870 to 1890* (Philadelphia, 1966), 34; Charles Callan Tansill, *America and the Fight for Irish Freedom, 1866–1922* (New York, 1957); Frank M. Carroll, *American Opinion and the Irish Question, 1910–1923* (New York, 1978); Patrick J. Buckley, *The New York Irish: Their View of American Foreign Policy, 1914–1921* (New York, 1976).

16. Victor Walsh, "'A Fanatic Heart: The Cause of Irish American Nationalism in Pittsburgh during the Gilded Age," *Journal of Social History* 15 (Winter 1981): 187–203; Eric Foner, "Class, Ethnicity and Radicalism in the Gilded Age: The Land League and Irish America," *Marxist Perspectives* 1, no. 2 (1978): 6–55; Michael Funchion, "The Political and Nationalist Dimensions," in Lawrence McCaffrey, ed., *The Irish in Chicago* (Urbana, Ill., 1987); David Emmons, *The Butte Irish: Class and Ethnicity in an American Mining Town, 1875–1925* (Urbana, Ill., 1989); Timothy J. Meagher, "Irish, American, Catholic: Irish American Identity in Worcester, Massachusetts, 1880 to 1920," in Meagher, ed., *From Paddy to Studs*; Brown, *Irish American Nationalism*; Tansill, *America and the Fight for Irish Freedom*; Buckley, *The New York Irish*; David Brundage, "Irish Land and American Workers: Class and Ethnicity in Denver, Colorado," in Dirk Hoerder, ed., *Struggle a Hard Battle: Essays on Working Class Immigrants* (De Kalb, Ill., 1986).

17. Christopher Kauffman in conversation with the author. See also Thomas T. McAvoy, *The Great Crisis in American Catholic History* (Chicago, 1957); Timothy J. Meagher, "'Irish All the Time': Ethnic Consciousness among the Irish in Worcester, Massachusetts, 1880–1905," *Journal of Social History* 19 (Winter 1985); Vincent Lannie, *Public Money and Parochial Education: Bishop Hughes, Governor Seward, and the New York School Controversy* (Cleveland, 1968), 245–58; Robert Emmet Curran, *Michael Augustine Corrigan and the Shaping of Conservative Catholicism in America* (New York, 1978). See also Jay Dolan, *The American Catholic Experience: A History from Colonial Times to the Present* (New York, 1983), 262–93, on regional differences in parochial schools see 282, and on the proportion of Catholic students in New York parochial schools see 275. In 1901 the proportions of parishes with parochial schools and proportions of parochial students of the total diocesan Catholic populations in the following dioceses were as follows: San Francisco, 39 percent of parishes and 5.7 percent of total population; Boston, 41 percent of parishes and 6.5 percent of population; Philadelphia, 51.8 percent of parishes and 10.2 percent of population; New York, 53 percent of parishes and 3.4 percent of population; Chicago, 73 percent of parishes and 7.8 percent of population. *The Catholic Directory, Almanac and Clergy List Quarterly, 1901* (Milwaukee, 1901), 48, 115, 135, 169.

18. Gary R. Mormino and George E. Pozzetta, *The Immigrant World of Ybor City: Italians and Their Neighbors in Tampa, 1885–1985* (Urbana, Ill., 1987).

19. On Irish women and family life during the immigrant generation see Hasia Diner, *Erin's Daughters in America: Irish Immigrant Women in the Nineteenth Century* (Baltimore, Md., 1983). On intermarriage see Robert McCaa, "Ethnic Intermarriage and Gender in New York City," *Journal of Interdisciplinary History* 24, no. 2 (1993): 221.

20. Robert Orsi, *The Madonna of 115th Street: Faith and Community in Italian Harlem, 1880–1950* (New Haven, 1985); Andrew R. Heinze, *Adapting to Abundance: Jewish Immigrants, Mass Consumption, and the Search for American Identity* (New York, 1990).

21. Erie, *Rainbow's End*, McNickle, *To Be Mayor of New York*.

22. Victor R. Greene, *American Immigrant Leaders, 1800–1910: Marginality and Identity* (Baltimore, 1987).

23. Carol Groneman, "Working-Class Immigrant Women in Mid-Nineteenth Century New York: The Irish Woman's Perpective," *Journal of Urban History* 4 (1978): 255–71; Donna Gabaccia, *From Italy to Elizabeth Street* (Albany, N.Y., 1983); Jon Gjerde, *From Peasants to Farmers: The Migration from Balestrand, Norway to the Upper Middle West* (Cambridge, Mass., 1985); June Granatir Alexander, "Staying Together: Chain Migration and Patterns of Slovak Settlement in Pittsburgh Prior to World War I," *Journal of American Ethnic History* 1 (Fall 1981): 56–83; Walter D. Kamphoefner, *The Westfalians: From Germany to Missouri* (Princeton, N.J., 1987).

24. For a pioneering study see Joshua A. Fishman and Vladimir Nahirny et al., *Language Loyalty in the United States: The Maintenance and Perpetuation of Non-English Mother Tongues by American Ethnic and Religious Groups* (The Hague, 1966).

25. On Jews see Charles Allan Madison, *Jewish Publishing in America: The Impact of Jewish Writing on American Culture* (New York, 1976).

26. See, for example, Annelise Orleck, "The Soviet Jews: Life in Brighton Beach, Brooklyn," in Nancy Foner, ed., *New Immigrants in New York* (New York, 1987): 273–304.

Select Bibliography

PRIMARY SOURCES

Archives

Archives of the Archdiocese of New York, Yonkers, New York
Archives of the Archdiocese of Brooklyn, Douglaston, New York
Archives of the Sisters of Charity, Mount St. Vincent, Riverdale, New York
Archives of the Sisters of Mercy, New York Province, Dobbs Ferry, New York
Archives of the Sisters of Mercy, Brooklyn Province, Brooklyn, New York
Archives of the Carmelite Friars, Middletown, New York
Archives of the Irish Brigade, Sixty-ninth Regiment Armory, New York City
Archives of the Transport Workers Union of America, New York City

Collections of Papers

American Irish Historical Society, New York City
  American Irish Historical Society Records
  Catholic Club of Greater New York Records
  Friends of Irish Freedom Records
  The Guild of Catholic Lawyers Records
  Society of the Friendly Sons of St. Patrick Records
  Daniel F. Cohalan Papers
  Reverend Donald M. O'Callaghan Papers

Butler Library, Columbia University, New York City
  Oral History Research Office:
    William O'Dwyer (1950)
    Paul O'Dwyer (1962)
    James A. Farley (1957)
    Edward J. Flynn (1950)
  Rare Book and Manuscript Library:
    Kilroe Collection
    Mitchel and Purroy Family Papers
Catholic University of America, Washington, D.C.
  Archbishop John Hughes Papers
  Papers of the Fenian Brotherhood
  Richard J. Purcell Papers
Iona College, New Rochelle, New York
  Michael J. O'Brien Papers
Irish American Center of Nassau, Suffolk and Queens, Mineola, New York
  New York Gaelic Society Library
Municipal Archives and Records Center, New York City
  Fiorello H. La Guardia Papers
  William O'Dwyer Papers
National Library of Ireland, Dublin, Ireland
  John Devoy Papers
  Jeremiah O'Donovan Rossa Papers
National Museum of American History, Smithsonian Institution, Washington, D.C.
  John D. Crimmins Collection
New-York Historical Society, New York City
  Devlin and Company Papers
  John Burke Papers
Manuscript and Archives Division, New York Public Library, New York City
  William Bourke Cockran Papers
  Charles Patrick Daly Papers
  Henry George Papers
  Jane Verner Mitchel Papers
  John Quinn Collection
St. John's University, Jamaica, New York
  Paul O'Dwyer Papers
Tamiment Institute/Robert F. Wagner Labor Archives, New York University, New York
  City
  Michael J. Quill Councilmanic Papers

Newspapers (All available on microfilm at the New York Public Library, unless otherwise noted.)

Shamrock, or *Hibernian Chronicle,* New York, N.Y.: E. Gillespy (weekly), vol. 1, no. 1 (12/15/1810) to vol. 3, no. 26 (6/5/1813).
Shamrock, New York, N.Y.: E. Gillespy and T. O'Connor (weekly), vol. 1, no. 1 (6/18/ 1814) to vol. 1, no. 23 (1/28/1815). Suspended publication 1/28/1815; resumed new series vol. 1, no. 1 (9/2/1815). Suspended (8/17/1816); resumed (12/2/1816) to vol. 2, no. 33 (8/16/1817).

Irish-American, New York, N.Y.: Lynch, Cole and Company (weekly), vol. 1, no. 1 (8/12/1849) until ceased 1915 (?). Scattered issues missing 1849–1903, 1906–1914; single issue 1915.

Irish-American Advance, New York, N.Y.: Michael B. Ryan (weekly), vol. 1, no. 1 (3/12/1832).

The Irish News, New York, N.Y.: Thomas F. Meagher (weekly), vol. 1, no. 1 (4/12/1856) to 1861 (?). Microfilm begins 1858.

The Irish People, New York, N.Y.: Michael J. O'Leary and Company (weekly), no. 1 (1/20/1866) to no. 399 (9/13/1873). Microfilm of one issue only, 1867.

The Irish Citizen, New York, N.Y.: John Mitchel, editor (weekly), vol. 1, no. 1 (10/19/1867) to vol. 5, no. 38 (7/27/1872). Scattered issues missing, 1867–1868.

The Irish World, New York, N.Y.: Irish World Publishing Company (weekly), vol. 1, no. 1 (9/10/1870) to vol. 9, no. 16 (12/14/1878). Renamed *The Irish World and American Industrial Liberator*, New York, N.Y.: Irish World and American Industrial Liberator Company (weekly), vol. 9, no. 17 (12/21/1878) to vol. 82, no. 4, 242 (12/15/1951). Renamed *The Irish World and American Industrial Liberator and the Gaelic American*, New York, N.Y. (weekly), vol. 82, no. 4243 (12/22/1951) to 1984.

The Irish Nation, New York, New York: John Devoy (weekly) 1881–85 (?). Various issues mutilated.

The Gaelic American, New York, N.Y.: Gaelic American Publishing Co. (weekly), vol. 1, no. 1 (9/19/1903) to vol. 48, no. 3459 (12/15/1951).

Irish Echo, New York: Charles F. Connolly/Patrick Grimes (weekly), vol. 1 (1928) to present (Microfilm 1935, 1938–40, 1944–45, 1949–52, 1954, 1956–88, 1990–91).

The Irish Voice, New York, N.Y.: Niall O'Dowd, vol. 1, no. 1 (12/1987) to present (not microfilmed).

Select Secondary Sources

Albion, Robert G. *The Rise of New York Port, 1815–1860*. New York: 1939.

Allen, Oliver. *New York: A History of the World's Most Exhilarating-Challenging City*. New York: Addison Wesley, 1990.

Bayor, Ronald H. *Neighbors in Conflict: The Irish, Germans, Jews, and Italians of New York City, 1929–1941*. 2d ed. Urbana: University of Illinois Press, 1988.

Bellush, Jewel and Netzer, Dick, eds. *Urban Politics New York Style*. Armonk, N.Y.: M. E. Sharpe, 1990.

Bennett, William H. *Catholic Footsteps in Old New York*. New York: Schwartz, Kirwin and Fauss, 1909.

Bernstein, Iver. *The New York City Draft Riots: Their Significance for American Society and Politics in the Age of the Civil War*. New York: Oxford University Press, 1990.

Billington, Ray Allen. *The Protestant Crusade: A Study of the Origins of American Nativism*. New York: Macmillan, 1938.

Bradley, Ann K. *History of the Irish in America*. Secaucus: 1986.

Bridges, Amy. *A City in the Republic: Antebellum New York and the Origins of Machine Politics*. Cambridge: Cambridge University Press, 1984.

Brinkley, Alan. *Voices of Protest: Huey Long, Father Coughlin and the Great Depression* New York: Vintage Books, 1983.

Brown, Thomas. *Irish American Nationalism, 1870–1890*. Philadelphia: J. B. Lippincott, 1966.

Buckley, John P. *The New York Irish: Their View of American Foreign Policy, 1914–1921.* New York: Arno Press, 1976.

Callow, Alexander B. *The Tweed Ring.* New York: Oxford University Press, 1966.

Carroll, Francis M. *American Opinion and the Irish Question, 1910–1923.* Dublin: Gill and MacMillan, 1978.

Casey, Daniel and Rhodes, Robert E., eds. *Irish American Fiction: Essays in Criticism.* New York: AMS Press, 1979.

Clark, Dennis. *Hibernia America: The Irish and Regional Cultures.* Westport, Conn.: Greenwood Press, 1986.

Cooney, John. *The American Pope: The Life and Times of Francis Cardinal Spellman.* New York: Time Books, 1984.

Curran, Robert Emmet. *Michael Augustine Corrigan and the Shaping of Conservative Catholicism in America, 1878–1902.* New York: Arno Press, 1978.

Czitrom, Daniel. "Underworlds and Underdogs: Big Tim Sullivan and Metropolitan Politics in New York, 1889–1913." *Journal of American History* 78 (Sept. 1991): 536–58.

Diner, Hasia. *Erin's Daughters in America: Irish Immigrant Women in the Nineteenth Century.* Baltimore: Johns Hopkins University Press, 1983.

Dolan, Jay. *Catholic Revivalism: The American Experience, 1830–1900.* Notre Dame, Ind.: University of Notre Dame Press, 1978.

Dolan, Jay P. *The Immigrant Church, New York's Irish and German Catholics, 1815–1965.* Baltimore, 1975.

Donnelly, James F. "Catholic New York and New York Socialists, 1870–1920." Ph.D. diss., New York University, 1982.

Doyle, David N. *Ireland, Irishmen, and Revolutionary America, 1760–1820.* Dublin: Mercier Press, 1981.

Dubofsky, Melvyn. *When Workers Organize: New York City in the Progressive Era.* Amherst: Univeristy of Massachusetts Press, 1968.

Erie, Stephen P. *Rainbow's End: Irish Americans and the Dilemmas of Urban Machine Politics, 1840–1985.* Berkeley: University of California Press, 1988.

Ernst, Robert. *Immigrant Life in New York City, 1825–1863.* New York, King's Crown Press, 1949; reprint, Syracuse, N.Y.: Syracuse University Press, 1994.

Fanning, Charles. *The Irish Voice in America: Irish American Fiction from the 1760s to the 1980s.* Lexington, Ky.: University of Kentucky Press, 1990.

Farley, Reverend John M. *The New York Police: Colonial Times to 1901.* New York: 1970.

Fitzgerald, Maureen. "The Perils of 'Passion and Poverty': Women Religious and the Care of Single Women in New York City, 1845–1890." *U.S. Catholic Historian* 10, nos. 1–2 (1990): 45–58.

Foner, Eric. "Class, Ethnicity, and Radicalism in the Gilded Age: The Land League and Irish America." *Marxist Perspectives* 1, no. 2 (1978): 6–55.

Freeman, Joshua. *In Transit: The Transport Workers Union in New York City, 1933–1966.* New York: Oxford University Press, 1989.

Gibson, Florence E. *The Attitudes of the New York Irish Toward State and National Affairs, 1848–1892.* New York: Columbia University Press, 1951.

Gilje, Paul A. *The Road to Mobocracy.* Chapel Hill, N.C.: University of North Carolina Press, 1987.

Glazer, Nathan and Moynihan, Daniel P. *Beyond the Melting Pot: The Negroes, Puerto Ricans, Jews, Italians and Irish of New York City.* Cambridge, 1963, MIT Press, 1970.

Goodfriend, Joyce D. *Before the Melting Pot: Society and Culture in Colonial New York City 1664–1730*. Princeton, N.J.: Princeton University Press, 1992.

Gordon, Michael. "Irish Immigrant Culture and the Labor Boycott in New York City, 1880–1886." In Richard L. Ehrlich, ed., *Immigrants in Industrial America, 1850–1920*. Charlottesville: University of Virginia Press, 1977.

Gordon, Michael. *The Orange Riots: Irish Political Violence in New York City, 1870 and 1871*. Ithaca, N.Y.: Cornell University Press, 1993.

Groneman, Carol. "'She Earns as a Child—She Pays as a Man': Women Workers in a Mid-Nineteenth Century New York City Community." In Milton Cantor and Bruce Laurie, eds., *Class, Sex and the Woman Worker*. Westport, Conn.: Greenwood Press, 1977.

Hammack, David. *Power and Society: Greater New York at the Turn of the Century*. New York: Columbia University Press, 1982.

Henderson, Thomas. *Tammany Hall and the New Immigrants: The Progressive Years*. New York: Arno Press, 1976.

Hershkowitz, Leo. *Tweed's New York: Another Look*. Garden City, N.Y.: Doubleday, 1977.

Joyce, William L. *Editors and Ethnicity: A History of the Irish-American Press 1848–1883*. New York: Arno Press, 1976.

Lowi, Theodore J. *At the Pleasure of the Mayor: Patronage and Power in New York City, 1898–1958*. New York: Free Press, 1964.

Mandelbaum, Seymour J. *Boss Tweed's New York*. New York: John Wiley and Sons, 1965.

Mann, Arthur. *LaGuardia: A Fighter against His Times, 1882–1933*. Chicago: University of Chicago Press, 1959.

Mann, Arthur. *LaGuardia Comes To Power 1933*. Philadelphia: J. B. Lippincott, 1965.

McLeod, Hugh. "Catholicism and the New York Irish." In Jim Obelkevich, Lynda Roper, and Ralph Samuel, eds., *Disciplines of Faith: Studies in Religion, Politics and Patriarchy*. New York: Routledge, Keegan and Paul, 1987.

McNickle, Chris. *To Be Mayor of New York: Ethnic Politics in the City*. New York: Columbia University Press, 1993.

Miller, Kerby A. *Emigrants and Exiles: Ireland and the Irish Exodus to North America*. New York: Oxford University Press, 1985.

Miller, Wilbur R. *Cops and Bobbies: Police Authority in New York and London, 1830–1870*. Chicago: University of Chicago Press, 1973.

Model, Suzanne. "The Ethnic Niche and the Structure of Opportunity: Immigrants and Minorities in New York City." In Michael Katz, ed., *The Underclass Debate: Views from History*. Princeton, N.J.: Princeton University Press, 1992.

Mollenkopf, John H. and Manuel Castells, eds. *Dual City: Restructuring New York*. New York: Russell Sage, 1991.

Morris, Charles R. *The Cost of Good Intentions: New York City and the Liberal Experiment*. New York: W. W. Norton, 1980.

Moscow, Warren. *What Have You Done for Me Lately? The Ins and Outs of New York City Politics*. Englewood Cliffs, N.J.: Prentice Hall, 1967.

Murphy, Richard C. and Mannion, Lawrence J. *The History of the Society of the Friendly Sons of Saint Patrick in the City of New York, 1784–1955*. New York: J. C. Dillon, 1962.

Mushkat, Jerome. *Tammany: The Evolution of a Political Machine: 1789–1865*. Syracuse, N.Y.: Syracuse University Press, 1971.

Nolan, Janet Ann. *Ourselves Alone: Female Emigration from Ireland, 1825–1920*. Lexington, Ky.: University of Kentucky Press, 1989.

O'Brien, Michael. *In Old New York: The Irish Dead in Trinity and St. Paul's Church-yards.* New York: American Irish Historical Society, 1928.

O'Connor, John Cardinal and Koch, Edward I. *His Eminence and Hizzoner: A Candid Exchange.* New York: William Morrow, 1989.

O'Connor, Richard. *Hell's Kitchen: The Roaring Days of New York's Wild West Side.* Philadelphia: J. B. Lippincott, 1958.

O'Dwyer, William. *Beyond the Golden Door.* New York: St. John's University Press, 1987.

Pomerantz, Sidney. *New York, An American City 1783–1803.* New York: Columbia University Press, 1939.

Ravitch, Diane. *The Great School Wars: New York City, 1805–1973: A History of the Public Schools as Battlefields of Social Change.* New York: Basic Books, 1974.

Reid, B. L. *The Man From New York: John Quinn and His Friends.* New York: Oxford University Press, 1968.

Richardson, James F. *The New York Police: Colonial Times to 1901.* New York: Oxford University Press, 1970.

Riordan, William. *Plunkitt of Tammany Hall.* New York: Dutton, 1963.

Rodechko, James Paul. *Patrick Ford and His Search for America: A Case Study of Irish American Journalism, 1870–1913.* New York: Arno Press, 1976.

Rosenwaike, Ira. *Population History of New York City.* Syracuse, N.Y.: Syracuse University Press, 1972.

Scisco, Louis P. *Political Nativism in New York State.* New York: Columbia University Press, 1901.

Shefter, Martin. "The Electoral Foundations of the Political Machine: New York City, 1884–1897." In Joel Sibley, Allan C. Bogue, and William Flannigan, eds., *The History of American Electoral Behavior.* Princeton, N.J.: Princeton University Press, 1978.

Sleeper, Jim. *The Closest of Strangers: Liberalism and the Politics of Race in New York.* New York: W. W. Norton, 1990.

Snyder, Robert. *The Voice of the City: Vaudeville and Popular Culture in New York.* New York: Oxford University Press, 1989.

Spann, Edward K. *The New Metropolis: New York City, 1840–1857.* New York: Columbia University Press, 1981.

Starr, Roger. *The Rise and Fall of New York City.* New York: Basic Books, 1985.

Tansill, Charles C. *America and the Fight for Irish Freedom, 1866–1922.* New York: Devin-Adair, 1957.

Truxes, Thomas M. *Irish-American Trade, 1660–1783.* Cambridge: Cambridge University Press, 1988.

Weiss, Nancy J. *Charles Francis Murphy, 1858–1924.* Northhampton, Mass.: Smith College, 1968.

Wesser, Robert. *A Response to Progressivism: The Democratic Party and New York Politics, 1902–1918.* New York: New York University Press, 1986.

Williams, William H. A. "From Lost Land to Emerald Isle: Ireland and the Irish in American Sheet Music, 1800 to 1920." *Eire—Ireland* 26 (Spring 1991): 19–45.

Wittke, Carl. *The Irish in America.* Baton Rouge: Louisiana State University Press, 1956.

For further sources see

Shea, Ann M. and Marion R. Casey. *The Irish Experience in New York City: A Select Bibliography.* New York: New York Irish History Roundtable, 1995. Distributed by Syracuse University Press.

JOHN T. RIDGE is the author of *The History of the Ancient Order of Hibernians and the Ladies' Auxiliary of Brooklyn* (1985), *Erin's Sons in America: The Ancient Order of Hibernians* (1986), *The St. Patrick's Day Parade in New York* (1988), *The Flatbush Irish* (1990), and *Sligo in New York: The Irish from Co. Sligo, 1849–1991* (1991), in addition to many articles. He was one of the founders of the New York Irish History Roundtable and served as its president (1985–86) and vice president for local history (1994–96).

THOMAS J. ROBERTSON is instructor of history and philosophy at Allegany Community College, Cumberland, Maryland. He is currently completing his dissertation entitled "Because There Is No Coal: The Struggle for Social, Economic and Political Stabilization in the Bituminous Coal Industry, 1920–1934," at West Virginia University. He is the author and coauthor of several articles on the coal industry and coal communities and is at present working on several projects dealing with community studies and working-class history in the Western Maryland region.

ROBERT W. SNYDER is a writer and historian with a special interest in the history of New York City and is currently managing editor of *Media Studies Journal* at the Freedom Forum Media Studies Center at Columbia University. He is the author of *The Voice of the City: Vaudeville and Popular Culture in New York* (1989) and coauthor, with Rebecca Zurier, of *Metropolitan Lives* (forthcoming), a study of the Ashcan School artists and turn-of-the century New York. He is also completing a book on the folklore and oral history of New York City transit workers.

EDWARD K. SPANN is professor of history at Indiana State University. He has authored four books, two of which relate to his chapter on the New York Irish, *Ideals and Politics: New York Intellectuals and American Liberalism, 1820–1880* (1972) and *The New Metropolis: New York City, 1840–1857* (1983). Two more recent books are *Brotherly Tomorrows: Movements for Cooperative Society in America, 1820–1920* (1989) and *Hopedale: From Commune to Company Town, 1840–1920* (1992). Among even more recent and as yet unpublished works is a projected book on New York City and the North Atlantic world during the Civil War era.

JOHN KUO WEI TCHEN is associate professor in the Department of Urban Studies at Queens College, the director of the Asian/American Center at Queens College (CUNY), and a cofounder of the New York Chinatown History Project (1980), now called the Museum of Chinese in the Americas. A version of this essay will appear in his forthcoming book *New York before Chinatown: The Racialization of Public Culture in the American Metropolis, 1784–1882*.

WALTER J. WALSH is associate professor in the School of Law, Seton Hall University, where he teaches legal history and legal philosophy. He has also taught at the University of Chicago and at the Central European University in Budapest, Hungary. Born in Dublin, he trained as a lawyer in Ireland, where he was also a director of the Free Legal Advice Centers. He is completing his S.J.D. at Harvard University and writing a jurisprudential biography on the life and thought of William Sampson (1764–1836).

Index

Abie's Irish Rose (play), 7, 579n13
Abolitionist movement, 100–101, 115, 193–94, 203. *See also* Slavery
Abortion, 430, 432
Abyssinian Baptist Church, 112
"Academia," 541
Acquitania (ship), 366
Act of Union of 1800, 27
actors. *See* Theater
Act Up, 684n64
Adams, John, 53
Adelaide (ship), 130
"Adhbhar ár m-Bróin" (O'Beirn), 271
Advertising, in clothing industry, 186
Affirmative action, 427
AFL. *See* American Federation of Labor
African Americans, 6, 83, 100–101, 105, 107–24, 114, 131, 134, 145–46, 227, 229, 422, 423, 542, 603–08n; affirmative action and, 427; American Women Pickets and, 357, 366–67, 370–71, 544; Chinese "superiority" to, 150; Civil War and, 193–94, 203–5, 207; co-existence with Irish, 108–9, 112–13; Irish intermarriage with, 19, 107, 123–24, 130, 140–42, 607–08n59, 608n60, 608n61, 608n64; labor movement and, 100–101, 302, 318, 654n89; neighborhoods of, 110–12; occupations of, 116–21, 139–40; in the police department, 427–28; politics and, 116–17, 426, 537; suffrage for, 15, 132; theatrical performers' ridicule of, 143, 145; in Washington Heights/Inwood neighborhood, 444, 445–49, 450, 452, 456, 458, 459, 688n46. *See also* Race riots; Slavery
African Mission, 244
Ahearn, John F., 378
AIDS, 168, 430, 431, 616n67
Aid to Families with Dependent Children, 423
Alamo, attack on, 16
Albany, New York, 624n10
Alcoholism, 72, 160, 220–21; as a subject in literature by Irish American writers, 515–17; in Washington Heights/Inwood neighborhood, 456
Ale and Porter Brewers Association, 304
Alger, Horatio, 139
Alien and sedition laws, 70, 590n26
Alienist, The (Carr), 7
Allen, Stephen, 591n39
Allen, William H., 382, 389
Alley Cats (gang), 444–45
All Saints' Parish (Manhattan), 413
Alms House, 21, 99
Alvarez, Luis, 448
Amalgamated Association of Street Railway Employees, 317
Amalgamated Carpenters, 304
Amalgamated Clothing Workers, 316, 318
Amalgamated Trades and Labor Union (ATLU), 304, 306
Amalgamated Woodworkers International Union, 318
Ambrose, James (Yankee Sullivan), 25

American and Foreign Christian Union, 257
American Armed Forces Network, 487, 495
American Association for the Recognition of
the Irish Republic, 321, 360, 372
American Bible Society, 257
American Bond and Mortgage Company, 400
American Can Company, 408
American Citizen, 52, 53
American Colonization Society, 116
American Commission on Conditions in Ire-
land, 372
American Commission on Irish Inde-
pendence, 351, 368
American Committee for Italian Immigra-
tion, 691n49
American Federation of Labor (AFL), 227,
304, 311, 316, 317, 318–19, 332, 628n50;
Catholic Church and, 314; politics and,
308
American Federation of Musicians, Local
802, 693–94n37
American Institute Exhibition, 237
American Irish Historical Society, 641n23
American Irish Society, 21
American Labor Party, 424
American Land League. *See* Irish National
Land League of America
American Legion, 393
American Longshoremen's Union, 367
American Protective Association, 312
American Protestant Society, 30–31, 257
American Protestant Union, 16
American Rainbow (Hackett), 513
American Revolution, 50
American Women Pickets for the Enforce-
ment of America's War Aims, 351,
357–73, 544, 660–65n; arrests of members,
362, 662n28; British embassy protest of,
361–62; Marcus Garvey's support of, 367,
370–71; original purpose of, 360
Amityville, New York, 399
Amsterdams (gang), 443
Ancient and Most Benevolent Order of the
Friendly Brothers of St. Patrick, 45
Ancient Order of Hibernians (AOH), 281, 282,
442, 458, 639n1, 640n14; gay participation
in parade and, 433; immigration legaliza-
tion and, 478; Irish nationalism and, 360; la-
dies auxiliaries of, 359, 661n9; Molly
Maguire episode and, 279; reasons for suc-
cess of, 278; Woodrow Wilson and, 351
Anderson, Isaac, 76
An Gaodhal, 268, 272. *See also* The Gael
Anglican Church, 42–43, 50
Anglo-Irish, 42–43, 546
Anglo-Irish War, 224, 225, 351, 627n49
Anti-Catholicism, 50–52. *See also* Nativism
Antietam, Battle of, 200–201
Anti-Poverty Society, 310, 323
Antrim, County, 287, 288t, 289t, 434f,
639n6, 641n26
Antrim Men, 640n20
AOH. *See* Ancient Order of Hibernians
A&P (Atlantic and Pacific Tea Company), 403
Appo, Catherine Fitzpatrick, 127, 134–38,
148

Appo, George Washington, 126, 127, 148,
608n4
Appo, Quimbo, 146, 147, 542, 608n1,
610n41; background of, 126–28; signifi-
cance of story, 148–52; trial of, 134–38
Appointment in Samarra (O'Hara), 346
Appomattox surrender, 208
The Arcade, 123
Ardree Company, 413
Armagh, County, 288t, 289t
Arrah-na-Pogue (Boucicault), 232
Artists, 24
Asbestos Workers, 317
Ashbridge, Elizabeth, 46
Asian Americans, 6, 535. *See also* Chinese
Asquith, Herbert, 330, 359
Assing, Bridget, 128
Assing, William, 128
Associated Tammany Societies, 651n56
Association for the Improvement of the Con-
ditions of the Poor, 381
Association of the Friends of Ireland, 64
Astor, William B., 187
Astoria (Queens), 399, 400, 403
Astoria Light, Heat and Power Company, 403
Astor Place Theatre Riot, 17, 97, 116
Athletics. *See* Sports
Athlone Guild of Friendship, 639–40n13
Atif, Joseph, 459
Atlantic Dock (Brooklyn), 96
Atlas, 169, 183
ATLU. *See* Amalgamated Trades and Labor
Union
At Weddings and Wakes (McDermott),
520–22
Augustus Street riot, 82, 83
Aurora 7 (Mallon), 523–24, 526
Australian Irish, 511
Available Light (Currie), 515
Ayres, Tommy, 503f

Back-Lane Parliament (Catholic Convention
of 1793), 164
Bacock, Paul, 223
Bagenal, Philip, 324–25
Bail bonds, 77, 598n29
Baker, Jean, 147
Baker, John, 123
Baker, Julia, 123
Ballinakill *Ceili* Band, 486
Baltic (ship), 364–44, 368
Baltimore, Maryland, 628n56
Baltimore Council, 244
Bamber, James, 16
Bamber, John, 16
Banished Children of Eve, (Quinn), 6
Banks, 344
Bank War, 596n91
Barden, Graham, 348
Barnes, James, 136
Barnswell, George, 20
Barry, Daniel, 255
Barrys (sports team), 290
Bartlett, Caleb, 23
Baseball, 231, 404f, 629n66
Basketball Diaries, The (Carroll), 449–50

Bayley, Richard, 166
Bay Ridge (Brooklyn), 399, 400, 422
BBC, 487, 495
Beame, Abraham, 537
Beard, Charles A., 670n75
Beatles, 495
Beautiful and the Damned, The (Fitzgerald),
    346
Beck, Louis, 127–28, 134–35
Bedlow's Island, 155
Beirne, Frank, 433
Belfast, County Antrim, Ireland, 40–41, 351
Bell, James W., 306
Bell, William H., 116, 118
Bellamy, Carol, 426
Bellevue Hospital, 21, 159, 165
Bellomont, Earl of, 44, 586n69
Belton, Maria, 26
Benevolent associations, 71–72, 94, 104. *See
    also* Irish county societies
Bennett, James Gordon, 164, 576n4
Bennett, William, 375, 391
Bergen County, New Jersey, 395, 421
"Best Years of Our Lives, The" (Winch), 513
Beyond the Melting Pot (Moynihan), 8
Bierne, Deborah, 360
Big bands, 487–88, 490–91, 496
Birch, Leroy, 448
Birth control, 432
Black Ball shipping line, 18
Blacklists, 305
Blacks. *See* African Americans
Blakes and the Flanagans, The (Sadlier), 23
Blissert, Robert, 178–79, 188, 304, 306, 312,
    323, 648n28
Bloody Sunday, 434
BMT East River subway tunnel, 399, 403
Boarders, 406, 407–8, 677n50
Boardinghouse trade, 22, 109, 120; African
    Americans and, 111, 604n16; languages
    spoken in, 253
Board of Aldermen, 27
Board of Commissioners of Emigration, 91
Board of Councilmen, 27
Board of Estimate, 424
Boer War, 315, 350
Boland, Harry, 368, 644n59, 663n38
Bolshevik revolution, 393
Bonfire of the Vanities (Wolfe), 7
Booksellers, 23
Boot and Shoe Workers' International Union,
    311, 316
Born in Brooklyn (Montague), 512
Boru (pen name), 267
Bosnian refugees, 473
Boston, Massachusetts, 4, 92, 534–35,
    624n10; clothing industry in, 191; Irish
    county societies in, 640–41n21; Irish na-
    tionalism and, 540; parochial schools in,
    541, 701n17; politics in, 341, 536, 537;
    residential patterns in, 674n22
Boston system of clothing manufacturing,
    191
Bothy Band, 505
Boucicault, Dion, 25, 232
Bourke, Ulick, 268

Bowery Boys, 143
Bowery Life (Connors), 144
Bowery Theater, 111
Bowyer, Brendan, 495
Boxing, 25, 231
Boyce, Ed, 653n80
Boycott, Charles Cunningham, 627n49
Boycotts, 227, 305–6, 307, 627n49
Boyle, James, 23
Boyle, T. Coraghessan, 516–17
Boyne, Battle of, 61–62, 65, 82
Boys of the Lough, 505
Bradley, Sr. M. Prudentia, 202
Brady, Cryan and Colleran, 411–12,
    679–80n79–83
Brady, Hugh, 41
Brady, James T., 207
Brady, John F., 228
Brady, John R., 27
Brady, Michael J., 411–12, 679n79
Braham, David, 232
Braisted, William, 180
Brann, Fr. Henry, 246
Brass Workers, 306
Brattan, William, 7
Bread-and-butter immigrants, 463–64, 468
Breezy Point (Queens), 677n60
Brehon Law Society, 478
Brennan, Christopher, 696n9
Brennan, Joseph P., 298
Breslin, Howard, 347
Breslin, Jimmy, 7, 424, 511, 514
Brice, John, 26
Bricklayers' Union, 307, 317
Brick Presbyterian Church, 41–42
Bridgeport Bus (Howard), 514
Bridget Loves Bernie (television program), 7
*Brief Account of the Author's Interview with
    His Countrymen, A* (O'Donovan), 255
Britain. *See* Great Britain
British army, Irish regiments in, 12, 14,
    37–38, 45
Brody, J.P., 26
Bronx, New York: Greater New York Char-
    ter and, 624n13; Irish-born naturalizations
    in, 564t; Irish-born population in, 555t;
    new Irish immigrants in, 474–75;
    occupations/employment opportunities
    in, 404; residential patterns in, 231, 395,
    396, 397, 398, 399, 400, 401, 402, 408,
    413, 414, 422, 674n22, 675n29. *See also*
    South Bronx
Brooke, Charlotte, 262
Brooklyn, New York, 624n10, 628n56; cloth-
    ing industry in, 189; Greater New York
    Charter and, 217, 624n13; Irish ancestry
    represented in, 567t; Irish-born naturaliza-
    tions in, 564t; Irish-born population in,
    93, 555t, 558–59t, 564t; Irish county popu-
    lations represented in, 286, 287, 288t,
    289t; Irish county societies in, 283, 296,
    640n20; Irish stock in, 562–63t; residen-
    tial patterns in, 231, 395, 396, 399, 400,
    402t, 408, 414, 422, 674n22
The Brooklyn Book of the Dead (Stephens),
    697n39

Brooklyn Bridge, 229, 628n56
Brooklyn Bridge (television program), 7
Brooklyn Dodgers, 231
Brooklyn Eagle, 188
Brooks, Philip, 39
Brooks Brothers, 179, 182, 184, 190
Brothels, 112, 122
Brotherhood of Butcher Workmen, 317
Brothers (religious), 219–20, 231, 244, 343f
Brothers of the Christian School, 633n38
Brown, Rebecca, 128
Brown, William, 128
Brown Derby campaign, 377
Browne, Porter Emerson, 390
Browning, King, 179, 190
Brownsville (Brooklyn), 399
Brunt, Robert, 76
Buckingham, Burdette R., 387
Buckingham Report, 669n55
Buckley, Charles, 419, 426, 430f
Buckley, Denis, 298, 644n53
Buckley, James, 426
Buckley, Michael B., 255
Buckley, Vincent, 696n9
Buckley, William F., Jr., 2, 426, 427, 683n26
Bulgarian immigrants, 473
Bull, 359
Bull Moose Party, 340
Bull Run, Battle of, 196, 197
Bureau of City Revenue, 26
Bureau of Municipal Research, 382, 388–89
Bureau of Street Openings, 398
Burke, Joseph, 25
Burke, Fr. Joseph, 28, 257
Burke, Michael, 635–36n14
Burke, Roger, 648n28
Burke, Thomas, 15
Burn, James Dawson, 181
Burnaby, Andrew, 44
Burns, Charles, 41
Burr, Aaron, 52
Burtsell, Fr. Richard L., 28, 240, 243
Busey, Samuel, 159
Business, 13, 22–23, 94, 192, 230, 342–43.
    See also Financial industry; Grocery
    stores; Merchants; Real estate developers
Butchers, 116–17, 118–19
Butler, Alban, 23
Butler, James, 403–4, 676n39–40
Butt, Isaac, 224
Butte, Montana, 540
Butterfield 8 (O'Hara), 346
Byrne, Jane, 324, 429
Byrne, Stephen, 93

"Cage, The" (Montague), 512
California, 534–35. *See also specific regions of*
Call, 370
Callaghan, Henry, 23
Callahan, John, 181
Calvary Cemetery (Queens), 290, 299, 413
Calvert family, 49, 50
Calyo, Nicolino, 10f
Campbell, Annie, 238
Cannon, Anthony. *See* Hart, Tony
Cardinal Hayes High School (Bronx), 431

Carey, Hugh, 426, 435, 436
Carey, Matthew, 65–66
Carey, Peter, 696n9
Carlow, County, 288t, 289t
Carlow Ladies Association, 679n75
Carlow Men's Society, 295
Carmelites, Irish, 404f
Carnarvon, Earl, 272
Carr, Caleb, 7
Carrigan, Andrew, 192
Carroll Club, 24
Carroll, Jim, 449–50
Carroll, John, 22
Carroll, Matthew, 73
Carroll, Michael, 354f
Carroll, Mollie, 362, 662n30
Carroll, Thomas, 40
Carroll Hall Democrats, 31
Carson, James, 37
Carters, 20, 40, 76, 97, 581n28; African
    American, 116–18, 606n40
Cartman's Ward, 108
Casement, Roger, 333
Casey (Stewart), 626n30
Casey, Gavin, 696n9
Casey, James, 180, 182
Cassiday, Edward F., 316, 652n73
Castle Garden, 92, 158, 216
Cather, Willa, 519, 520
Catholic Charities, 478
Catholic Church, 3, 102–4, 348–49, 429–33;
    American identity negotiated by, 578n11;
    bishops, ethnic background of, 630n1;
    debts of, 244–45; early growth of, 28–29,
    52, 103; Irish independence movement
    and, 350; Irish nationalism and, 324–25,
    326–27, 332–33; labor movement and,
    221, 308–9, 310, 314, 626n26, 651–52n65;
    medical care and, 164–67, 613n8, 614n40,
    615n50; new Irish immigrants and, 438;
    parishes, 218, 243–44, 399, 674n19; pew
    and seat rentals in, 28, 245, 597n8,
    631n13; plate collections, 245; politics
    and, 338, 429–31; poverty and, 221,
    625n20; real estate development and, 399;
    socialism and, 314, 651–52n65; *Truth
    Teller* and, 74. *See also* Catholics; *and
    names of religious orders*
Catholic Club, 674n18
Catholic Herald, 241
Catholic Orphanage (Brooklyn), 202
Catholic Protectory (Bronx), 220f, 681n90
Catholic Question in America (Sampson), 60
Catholic Review, 282, 314
Catholics, 5, 11–12, 13, 14–17, 28, 35, 43–44,
    46, 50–52, 70–73, 103–4, 219–22, 226, 228,
    230, 419, 540–42, 625n21; Ancient Order
    of Hibernians and, 278; book publishing
    and, 4, 23; devotional revolution and,
    215–16, 218–19; disease and, 156–57;
    French, 253, 576n4; funeral masses and,
    245; Greenwich Village riot and, 61–64,
    79, 81–83; home rule movement and, 350;
    Irish Brigade and, 199; Italian, 342, 431;
    John Purroy Mitchel and, 377, 380–84; par-
    tition of Ireland and, 245; compared with

Puritans, 234–35; Alfred E. Smith and, 384–85; social work and, 99, 219–22. *See also* Catholic Church; Free exercise of religion; *and name of religious order*
Catholic schools. *See* Parochial schools
Catholic Total Abstinence Union, 220
Catholic University, 244
"Catskills, The" (Winch), 512
"Cause of Our Sorrow, The" (O'Beirn), 271
Cavanagh, Michael, 259, 264, 266
Cavan, County, 288t, 289t, 639n6
Cavan Society, 639n8, 643n44
Ceannt, Eamonn, 361
Ceili music and dances, 482, 483, 485, 487, 488, 492, 493, 494, 500, 501–2
Celtic (ship), 366, 370
Celtic Hall, 484
Celtic Magazine, 272
Celtic Monthly, 272
Celtic Park (Queens), 290, 291, 413, 644n52, 681n91
Celtic Park Apartments, 413–14, 680–81n90, 681n92–93
Celtic Players, 365, 368, 663n47
Celtic rock, 695n77
Censuses: 1850, 91; 1855, 130, 172, 175; 1880, 93; 1890, 302; 1960, 449; 1970, 450; 1980, 423; 1990, 421. *See also* Population
Centennial Exhibition of 1876, 237
Central Federated Union (CFU), 311, 317, 318–19. *See also* Central Labor Union
Central Labor Union (CLU), 178, 306, 307, 308, 309, 311, 323, 324, 648n32, 651n56. *See also* Central Federated Union
Central Park, 399, 401
Century Club, 24
Cermak, Anton, 341, 537
CFU. *See* Central Federated Union
Chamber of Commerce, 20
Chambers, John, 49, 53, 63, 64, 68, 588n1
Change of Scene, A (Cullinan), 528
Chanting House, 477
Charities, State Board of, 381–82
Charlton, John, 13, 39
Chelsea (Manhattan), 217, 333f, 399, 674n26
Chicago, Illinois, 4, 341; immigrants in, 641n26; Irish county societies in, 641n21; Irish nationalism and, 540; Irish traditional music in, 692n7; parochial schools in, 541, 701n17; politics in, 428–29, 536, 537
Chichesters (gang), 114
Chicken Soup (television program), 7
Chidwick, John, 633n35
Chieftains, 505
Children's Aid Society, 202, 220f
Children's Law, 220f
Child's restaurant, 404
Chinatown (Manhattan), 128, 129
Chinese, 105, 125–52, 542, 608–12n; in clothing industry, 190; criminalization of, 138–48; disease and, 167; intermarriage with, 128–30, 609n15; Irish-Chinese mix-ups, 131–32, 133f; occupations of, 139–40; theatrical performers' ridicule of, 142–45
Chinese Exclusion Laws, 125, 147, 151

Cholera, 21, 100, 154, 155–56, 157–58, 159, 164–65, 166
Cholera Years, The (Rosenberg), 154
Christ Church (Manhattan), 243
Christian Brothers, 231
Christian Companion, The (Furlong), 637n41
Christian Front, 353–72, 443
Christian Mobilizers, 354, 443
Churchill, Thomas W., 386, 388
Church of England. *See* Anglican Church
Church of Ireland, 42
City and Suburban Homes Company, 413–14
City Center Ballroom (Manhattan), 437, 492–94, 495, 499
Civilian Review Board, 427
Civil rights movement, 427
Civil service, 229, 313, 424
Civil War, American, 33, 100, 106, 193–209, 546, 619–23n; Catholic soldiers and, 199; fairs in support of, 236, 237; effect on Irish language activity due to, 263–64, 265; Irish losses in, 200–201; labor movement and, 203–4; medical care in, 201–2; miscegenation issue and, 142; orphans of, 202; support for Confederacy in, 194. *See also* Draft Riots
Clancy, George, 177, 188
Clancy, John, 26
Clancy, Laurie, 696n9
Clancy, Lawrence, 26
Clancy Brothers, 497, 505, 506
Clan na Gael, 225, 281, 282, 284, 305, 315, 331–33, 334, 363, 539, 647n17; Catholic Church and, 332–33; in Chicago, 540; founding of, 223–24; Irish county societies and, 299; purpose of, 349; social class and, 332; Tammany Hall and, 226; Transport Workers Union and, 354f; women in, 331–32
Clare, County, 288t, 289t
Clare Men's Association, 295, 296, 299, 644n54
Clark, Dennis, 533, 539
Clarke, Thomas, 299
Clary, Mrs. William, 238
Classical and Mathematical Bookstand, 23
Cleery, Thomas, 26
Clemens, Samuel, 131–32
Cleveland, Grover, 273, 310, 648n28
Clinton, DeWitt, 2, 15, 28, 62, 63, 64; *People v. Philips* and, 54, 59–60; Test Oath and, 52
Clinton, George, 15
Clinton, Henry, 14
Cloch an Chúinne (pen name), 266
Clossey, Samuel, 13, 39
Clothier & Furnisher Magazine, 174, 177, 185, 186, 190
Clothing industry, 169–92, 545, 616–19n; entrepreneurship in, 179–81; family system in, 177; health hazards in, 176; intracommunal patronage and, 180, 185; journeymen in, 176–77; labor movement in, 177–79; lack of security in, 176; mass production and, 173, 174; niche markets in, 181; production seasons in, 175; subdivision of labor in, 175. *See also* Secondhand dealers

Cloudland (Roosky, County Roscommon), 694n39
CLU. *See* Central Labor Union
Cochran, James, 40
Cockran, William Bourke, 325, 327, 328, 330, 334
Coen, Jack, 485–87, 497, 695n61
Cohalan, Daniel Florence, 331, 349, 350, 363, 368
Cohan, George M., 2, 232, 233
Cohn, Michael, 455
Colden, Cadwallader, 44
Colden, David, 37
Coleman, Andrew, 120
Coleman, Michael, 484–85
Colleen Bawn, The (Boucicault), 25, 232
Colleran, Peter F., 411–12, 679n79
Colles, Christopher, 13
Collier's Weekly, 374, 383
Colligan, Patrick, 188
Collins, Daniel, 486, 497
Collins, Jerome J., 223
Collins, John, 24
Colonial era, 11–14, 35–47, 583–87n; occupations in, 38–41; politics in, 45–46
Colored Home, 244
Colum, Mary, 359, 363, 373, 662n20
Colum, Padraic, 359, 363, 662n20
Columbia College, 20
Columbia records, 484
Comerford, James J., 502–3, 503f
Comhaltas Ceoltoiri Eireann, 694n60
Commercial Advertiser, 114, 115
Commerford, John, 19, 581n28
Committee or The Faithful Irishman, The (theatrical production), 40
Common Council, 97
Common School System, 26
Communism, 353–54, 429, 498–99, 539, 627–28n49. *See also* Red Scares; Socialism
Communist Party, 353
"Commuting" (Cullinan), 529–31
Compánach an Chríosdaigh (Furlong), 637n41
Concanen, Richard Luke, Bishop, 28
Condon, Patrick. *See* Cúndún, Pádraig Phiarais
Conelly, P., 26
Connaught (province), Ireland, 286, 288t, 289t
Connolly, James, 316, 322, 328, 652n74, 652n76, 653n77, 664n62; Catholic Church and, 332–33; home rule movement and, 332
Connolly, John, 29
Connolly, Matty, 494, 495–96
Connolly, Maureen Glynn, 500, 504, 505, 506
Connolly, Nora, 360, 662n20
Connolly, Richard, 279
Connors, Chuck, 143, 144–45, 152
Conroy, Frank, 513, 517, 697n37
Conscription Act, 204
Conservative Party, 427, 538
Construction workers, 302f, 424, 469–72, 473
Consumerism, 675n33
Consumption, 21, 157. *See also* Tuberculosis

Convicts, 37
Conway, Brian, 504
Cooke, Terrence J., Cardinal, 430, 435–36
Cooper, Francis, 14, 51–52
Cooper, Miles, 43
Cooperative Shirtmakers, 304
Coote, Richard, 12
Copperheads, 207–8, 623n62
Corbitt, Patrick, 183, 192
Corby, Fr. William, 198, 199
Corcoran, Michael, 194, 196, 197, 198, 200, 204, 205, 209
Corcoran, Tommy, 344
Corcoran Legion, 200
Cork, County, 288t, 289t, 638–39n6
Corkmen's Association (Shandon Club), 279
Corkmen's Mutual Aid Association, 296, 642–43n41, 643n43, 643n44, 643n45, 643–44n49
Corkmen's Patriotic and Benevolent Society, 285, 643n43, 644n51
Corless, Gertrude, 361, 363, 371, 372–73, 659n19, 660n38
Corless, Thomas K., 659n19
Corrigan, Jeremiah, 184
Corrigan, Luke, 184
Corrigan, Michael Augustine, Archbishop, 221, 226, 228, 271, 309, 310, 314, 541
Cosby, Grace, 43
Cosby, William, 43
Cosgrove, Joanna, 113
Costello, John, 304
Coughlin, Fr. Charles E., 353, 443, 538
Coughlin, T. Glen, 523
"Counterparts" (Joyce), 523
County Democrats, 223
Courier & Enquirer, 16
Le Courrier des États-Unis, 253
Cow Bay, 123
Cowley, Malcolm, 345
Crady, Timothy, 15
Crawford, Elizabeth Ann, 25
Cricket, 290–91
Crime; in Washington Heights/Inwood neighborhood, 440–41, 450–51, 452–53, 456–57, 687n41
Crimean War, 194
Crimmins, John D., 35, 192, 328, 329, 398, 399, 672n6, 674n18, 676n38
Crimmins, Thomas, 255
Croker, Richard, 222–23, 228, 313, 538, 626n30
Croly, David Goodman, 141–42, 151
Crossing Borders (Kennedy), 525–27
Croton Water Aqueduct, 26–27, 93, 400
Crowe, Helen, 369
Crowe, Robert, 174, 178, 188
Crowley, William J., 644n54
Crowley, William J., Association, 298
Crown, Michael, 119
Cryan, Frank, 411–12, 679n79
Cudahy, John, 409, 411, 678n66, 679n76
Cúirt a' Mheadhon Oidhche, 264
Cullen, Paul, Cardinal, 215–16, 218
Cullinan, Elizabeth, 511, 525, 527–31, 678n70

Cumann na mBan, 359–60, 361, 363, 368, 372, 373, 657n26, 664n62
Cunard Line, 369–70
Cúndún, Pádraig Phiarais, 254–55, 262
Cunningham, Nora, 238
Cunningham, Waddell, 38–39
Curley, James Michael, 341
Curran, Eileen, 360, 365, 367, 368, 369
Curran, John Philpot, 56, 593n59
Currie, Ellen, 515
Custodial work, 406–7, 677n52
Custom House, 27
Custom tailoring, 176–77
Custom Tailors Benevolent and Protective Union, 178
Cuthbert, Joseph, 53
Cutters, 174, 175, 176, 179. *See also* Clothing industry

Dáil Éireann, 363, 372
Daily, Samuel, 119
Daily News, 263, 378
Dairy Fair, 237
Daley, Richard J., 341, 347, 428–29
Daley, Victor, 696n9
Daly, Charles P., 20, 24, 196, 198, 202, 207
Daly, Maria, 198, 199, 201, 202
Daly, P.J., 268
Daly, Thomas, 679n77
Dance bands, 487
Dance halls, 122–23, 418f, 489–90
Dancing, Irish, 293f, 493, 503f
Dark, Eleanor, 696n9
Darrah, J. Neil, 282
Darrow, Clarence, 56
Daugherty, Michael, 41
Daugherty, Daniel, 208
Davis, Alexander, 119
Davitt, Michael, 178, 224, 226, 272, 307, 323, 324, 325, 332, 647n17, 660n2
Dawson, James, 174
Day, Joseph P., 673n8, 679n79
"Dead, The" (Joyce), 522
Dead Rabbits Riots, 97, 114, 116
Deane, Elkanah, 39
Deane, Nesbett, 39
Dearie, John, 432
Death. *See* Mortality rates
Debs, Eugene V., 315–16, 652n73
Degnon, Michael J., 398–99, 673n13, 674n18
Degnon Realty and Terminal Improvement Company, 399
Delahunty, Mike, 487–88, 491, 493
DeLeon, Daniel, 315, 649n40
DeLeon, Leonci, 448
Democratic Party, 15, 66, 78–79, 80, 101–2, 104, 223, 338–41, 424, 426–27, 428, 535–36, 537; African Americans and, 117; Catholics and, 31, 541; Civil War and, 193, 206–8, 209; factions of, 31, 223, 226, 227, 538, 626n31; defection from, 426–27, 428, 538; Irish language and, 257; labor movement and, 306–7, 312–14, 317, 319–20; miscegenation issue and, 142; John Purroy Mitchel and, 388–89; parochial school issue and, 31

Denison, John, 132
Denman, William, 31
Denver, Colorado, 540
DePoyster, Bridget, 123
DePoyster, John, 123
Depressions, economic, 95. *See also* Great Depression
Derry, County, 287, 288t, 289t, 639n6
Derry Society, 293, 642n37
De Sapio, Carmine, 425–26
de Schweinitz, Karl, 390, 391, 392
D'Eshinville, Charles, 73
Deutsche Schnellpost, 253
de Valera, Eamon, 351, 360, 363, 364, 368–69, 372, 404f, 663n38
Devitt, John, 306
Devlin, Daniel, 184–87, 191, 192, 208. *See also* Devlin & Co.
Devlin &Co., 181, 183–87, 184f, 188. *See also* Devlin, Daniel
Devlin, Mrs. Jeremiah, 238
Devlin, John, 179
Devotional revolution, 216, 218, 332
Devoy, John, 4, 105, 223–24, 225, 226, 265, 299, 315, 323, 331, 332, 349, 539, 647n17, 655n3; American Women Pickets and, 363, 368; Bourke Cockran alliance with, 334
Dewey, John, 385, 388, 668n49
Diamond, 116
Dickens, Charles, 20, 112, 123
Dignity (homosexual religious group), 432–33
Dillon, Christopher, 22
Dillon, Gregory, 256
Dillon, Fr. J.M., 199
Dillon, John, 283, 330
Dillon, John L., 22
Dineen, Joan, 474f
Diner, Hasia, 106, 129, 358
Dinkins, David, 426, 428, 431, 433, 436, 537
Disaffected adventurers, 464–65, 468
Discount pricing, in clothing industry, 185
Disease, 21, 100, 106, 114, 153–68, 217–218, 547, 613–16n; African Americans and, 114; germ theory of, 154; nativism and, 154, 155, 161–62, 167–68; quarantines and, 155, 158; reasons for prevalence in Irish, 155–56. *See also* Medical care
District Assembly 49, 304, 306, 311, 315
The Diving Bell, 123
Divorce, 432
Dockworkers' union, 303
Doheny, Michael, 223, 259, 260–62, 263–64, 266, 267, 274
Doherty, Joseph, 436
Doherty, Maureen, 506
Doherty, Tom, 489, 506
Doherty, William J., 381–82, 667n31
Dolan, Felix, 695n61
Dolan, Jay, 106
Domestic service, 77–78, 93, 95, 96, 101, 120–121, 217; African Americans in, 109, 120–21; new Irish immigrants in, 473; real estate and, 679n78; residential patterns and, 404
Dominican immigrants, 190, 422, 439, 453–45, 455, 456, 459, 687n43; drug problem

Dominican immigrants (*continued*)
and, 457, 688n62; illegal immigrants
among, 472; lack of communication with,
441; similarities to Irish, 451–52
Donahue, Michael, 433
Donegal Association, 282, 283, 297, 640n20,
643n43
Donegal, County, 287, 288t, 289t, 639n6,
641n26
Donegal Hill (Brooklyn), 405
Donegal Relief Fund, 278
Dongan, Thomas, 12
Donleavy, J.P., 511, 515–16
Donnelly, Joseph, 177
Donnelly, Rosanna, 182
Donnelly, Terence, 192
Donnelly visas, 462, 467–68, 690n18, 692n50
Doody, Patrick, 306
Dooley, John, 368
Doris, Cornelius, 176
Dorney, Mike, 695n61
Dosai, Singmer, 130
Dougherty, Dennis, 82
Dougherty, William, 180
Dougherty, Betsy, 78
Douglass, Frederick, 116, 606n33
Dowd, Mary, 238
Down, County, 287, 288t, 289t
Down Men, County, 293
Downey, Moses, 113
Doyle, Bridget, 78
Doyle, John, 17, 76
Doyle, John F., 673n9, 674n18
Doyle, Richard, 35
Draddy, Daniel, 255
Draddy, John (Seán Ó Dreada), 255
Draft Riots, 26, 31, 97, 100–101, 108, 115,
116, 123, 134, 139, 206, 218, 367, 608n66;
description of, 204–5; significance of,
622n49
Dramatic shipping line, 18
Driscoll, James A., 228–29
Drugs, 456–57, 688n62
Duane, Anthony, 43
Duane, James, 13
Dublin, County Dublin, Ireland, 11, 41,
288t, 289t, 351, 641n26
Dublin Football Club, 642n31
Dublinmen, 292–93
Dubois, John, Bishop, 29–30, 165
Duffy, Ellen, 165
Duffy, Fr. Francis P., 2, 228–29, 625n17
Duffy, Frank, 317–18
Dugan, Alan, 511
Dun, R.G., & Co., 176, 177, 179, 180, 181,
185, 188, 189, 191
Dunleavey, Barry, 452
Dunn, Msgr. John J., 382
Dunn, John P., 398, 673n12, 674n18
Dunn, Maggie, 238
Dunn, Michael, 39
Dunn, Thomas, 39
Dunne, Finley Peter, 509
Dunphy, Jack, 511, 515
Durkheim, Emile, 145
Dutch Reformed Church, 43

Dwight, Timothy, 156–57
Dwyer, Jim, 7
Dwyer, John Hamburg, 25
Dyckman Houses (Inwood), 449, 454

Eagles (gang), 444–45
Easter Rising, 224, 225, 298, 327, 331, 334,
357, 373, 540; Roger Casement and, 333;
influence on Irish Progressive League, 363;
Irish World interest in, 359; reaction to,
350
Eccentric Engineers, 306
Eco d'Italia, 253
Eddy, Thomas, 29
Edenwald (Bronx), 403, 679n82
Edgar, William, 13
Edison Company, 692n3
Edson, Franklin, 282
Ed Sullivan Show, 506
Education. 336f, 342, 343f, 348, 424; ethnic
comparisons, 577n8; in Ireland, 215. *See
also* Parochial schools; Schools
Egyptian Dragons (gang), 446–48
Eighth Ward (Manhattan), 75
Eighty-fourth Regiment, 98f
Eighty-eighth Regiment, 198, 265
"Eirepreneurs," 466–67, 468, 469
Eisenhower, Dwight David, 427
Election riots of 1834, 16
Elevated railways, 229, 397, 398, 400
Ellis Island (immigration station), 153, 216
Ellison, William B., 378, 666n17
Elmhurst (Queens), 399
Elm Park Festival, 243
Irish, Dr. Elwood, 136
Emancipation Proclamation, 100, 203
Emerald, 267
Emerald Musical Society, Inc., 488–89
Emerald societies, 437
Emerson, Mrs. K., 240
Emigrant Industrial Savings Bank, 92f, 104,
177, 186, 342
Emigrants and Exiles (Miller), 233
Emigrant Landing Depot, 158
Emmet, Robert, 56, 325, 637n43
Emmet, Thomas Addis, 15, 20, 48–49, 53,
61, 63, 66, 68, 164, 539, 588n1; Greenwich
Village riot and, 62, 79; monument to,
64–65, 254, 635n7; *People* v. *Philips* and,
56; William Sampson versus, 592n47
Emmet, Dr. Thomas Addis, 325, 328, 329
Emmets (sports team), 290
Employment. *See* Occupations
Employment Division v. *Smith*, 589n3,
592n43
England, John, 635n7
English immigrants: education of, 577n8;
family size and, 565t; gainful employment
and, 565t; income of, 578n8
Entrepreneurship, in clothing industry,
179–81
Erie, Steven, 544, 678n65
Erie Canal, 59
Erie Railroad, 96
Erin Guard, 194

Erin's Daughters in America (Diner), 106
Erwin, Mary, 78
Essay on Elocution (Dwyer), 25
Estevez, Carlos, 459
Ethnic identity, 479, 543–44
Ethnicity, 6–7, 578–79n11; in literature, 508–9, 511–12, 519–22, 525
Ethnic succession, 397, 543
European Common Market, 420
European Union, 466
Evening Journal, 380
Evening Star, 16, 24
Exile, 23
Expensive Habits (Howard), 514

Facts of Life (Howard), 513–14
"Fairy Tale of New York, A" (Donleavy), 515–16
Fallon, Malachi, 19
Family size, 565t
The Famine, 11, 61, 67, 70, 89–90, 214, 534, 575n3; Catholic society affected by, 215; Irish-speakers increased by, 254, 256; labor movement and, 301
Fanning, Charles, 345
Farley, James, 212f
Farley, John M., Cardinal, 228, 244, 314
Farley, Terence, 27
Farley, Thomas M., 313
Farmer, Michael, 446–48, 686n30, 687n31
Farmer-Labor Party, 369
Farrell, Herman D., 426
Farrell, James T., 345, 347, 509, 517, 518, 522, 523; *Bernard Clare*, 415
Farrell, John, 696n9
Farrell, Fr. William B., 382–83
Fearon, Henry, 29
Federalist, 50
Federalists, 14–15, 16, 53, 78–79, 222, 595n80
Feis, United Irish Counties Association, 503f, 502–5
Felon's Track, The (Doheny), 260
Feminism, 430. *See also* Women
Fenian Brotherhood, 6, 105, 194, 265, 305, 322–23, 539, 626n36; Quimbo Appo's fears of, 125, 151; Catholic Church and, 332; Civil War and, 209; Clan na Gael influenced by, 331; hostility toward, 223–24; John O'Mahony and, 264
Ferguson, Bernard, 661n16
Ferguson, D.F., 277
Fermanagh, County, 288t, 289t
Fermanagh Republican Guards, 278
Ferrell, Frank, 306
Ferriter Manuscript 33, 264
Fiction. *See* Literature, by Irish American authors
Field, Jeremiah, 39, 41
Field, John, 41
Fifth Avenue Coach Company, 403, 409
Fighting 69th. *See* Sixty-ninth Regiment
Final Fire, The (Smith), 515
Final Payments (Gordon), 509–10
Financial industry, 344–45
Finerty, John F., 329
Finerty, Peter, 592n45

Finland (ship), 366–67
Finnegan, Patrick, 299
Finnegan, Tim, 6
Finnerty, Cathy, 454
Fire Department, 26, 105, 419, 427, 437
First Ward (Manhattan), 94, 638n6
First Wine (Dunphy), 515
Fitch, Drake, 75
Fitzgerald, F. Scott, 345–46, 347
FitzGerald, Garret, 436
Fitzgerald, Fr. Thomas, 271
Fitzmaurice, James J., 412, 679n81
Fitzpatrick, Michael, 412, 680n83
Five Points (Manhattan), 6, 20, 74–75, 99, 217; African Americans in, 112–13, 114, 122–23, 130; flash talk in, 122. *See also* Sixth Ward; House of Industry
Flack, John, 22
Flaherty, Joe, 514
Flanagan, Fr. [Lawrence D.], 363
Flanigan, Horace C., 344
Flannery, Michael, 435–36, 435f
Flatbush (Brooklyn), 400, 401, 405
Fleadh Ceoil na Eireann, 497, 694n60, 695n61
Fleishman, Joel, 7
Flesh and Blood (Hamill), 515
Fletcher, Mary F., 135–38
Fletcher, Patrick, 136
Flexner, Abraham, 386, 387
Floral Park (Queens), 399
Flushing (Queens), 399
Flynn, Edward, 353, 419, 426, 537
Flynn, Elizabeth Gurley, 325, 328, 653n82
Flynn, Mary Gilrane, 405
Flynn, Thomas, 325, 653n82
Flynn, Vincent, 413, 680n89
Fogarty & Co. (Flaherty), 514
FOIF. *See* Friends of Irish Freedom
Folliot, George, 39
Football, Gaelic, 287–90, 291, 418f
Ford, Ellen A., 293, 358, 660–61n5
Ford, Patrick, 4, 224, 225, 226, 229, 332, 539; American Women Pickets and, 358–59; Irish language and, 267–68; Irish nationalism and, 323, 324, 326; labor movement and, 305, 308, 312, 314, 323, 329, 646–47n16, 651n57, 651n65, 652n68; Land League and, 315
Ford, Robert, 359, 663n38
Ford, Thomas, 306
Fordham University (St. John's College), 231, 343f, 503f
Fordham (Bronx), 398, 400, 401, 404f, 422
Fordham Property Owners' Association, 398
Foreign Conspiracy against the Liberties of the United States, 67
Forest Hills (Queens), 399
Forrest, Edwin, 17
Fort Clinton (Manhattan), 216
Fort Sumter, South Carolina, 194
Fort Tyron Park (Manhattan), 441
Fortunes of Richard Mahony, The (Richardson), 511
Forty Thieves (gang), 114
Fosdick, Raymond B., 386

Foster, George G., 99, 107, 108, 112, 118, 122–23
Fourteenth Ward (Manhattan), 94
Fourth Ward (Manhattan), 23, 75, 77, 94, 217, 638n6; Chinese in, 129; Irish county societies in, 276
Fowler, Lorenzo, 162
Fowler, Orson, 162
Fox, Edward, 181, 183, 185, 187–88
Fox, Patrick, 398, 673n10
Fox, Richard, 144
Francis, John, 123
Francis, Susan, 123
Franciscan Brothers of Brooklyn, 343f
Franklin, John W., 307
Franks, Jacob, 41
Fredericksburg, Battle of, 201
Free exercise of religion, 49–61, 68–69, 548, 586n65; earliest decision pertaining to, 592n54; Hibernocentric history of, 50–53; *People* v. *Philips* and, 53–61, 589n3, 591n36
Freeman's Journal, 23, 31, 194, 196, 201, 204, 208
Freighthandlers strike, 305
French immigrants, 253; Catholicism of, 576n4; education of, 577n8; income of, 578n8
French and Indian War, 37–38, 39
French Lines, 367
Frewen, Moreton, 327
Friendly Sons of St. Patrick, 13, 71, 72, 91, 94, 186, 275, 277, 351; Civil War and, 196
Friends of Freedom for India, 663n47
Friends of Irish Freedom (FOIF), 333f, 334, 351, 539–40; American Women Pickets and, 360, 363, 368, 372; Irish Progressive League expulsion from, 663n38; John Purroy Mitchel and, 671n79
Fugitive Slave Act, 110, 123
Fuller, Bill, 492, 493, 499
Furlong, Fr. Jonathan, 637n41
Furman, Gabriel, 15
Furphy, Joseph, 511
Fusion administration, 313, 424; John Purroy Mitchel and, 375, 381, 382, 385–88, 389, 390, 391–92; school system and, 385–88
Fusion Flashlight, 390

GAA. *See* Gaelic Athletic Association
The Gael, 225, 258, 269f
Gaelic. *See* Irish language
Gaelic American, 4, 224, 349, 363; American Women Pickets and, 372; Irish nationalism and, 331; Land League and, 315; sports and, 290; World War I and, 350
Gaelic Athletic Association (GAA), 225, 292, 331, 641n28, 641n29, 681n91
Gaelic Irish, 43, 546
Gaelic Journal, 272
Gaelic League, 273, 293, 331, 489, 494, 501–2
Gaelic Park (Bronx), 418f, 442, 685n85, 686n8
Gaelic Revival, 269f, 293f
Gaelic Society, 273, 642n38
Gaelic Union of Dublin, 272
Gaine, Hugh, 13, 39, 40, 42

Gallagher, James, 38
Gallagher, James, 113
Gallagher, Mary, 113
Gallaher, Rev. Dr. H.M., 283
Gallowglass *Ceili* Band, 693n36
Gallowglasses, in St. Patrick's Day Parade, 86f
Galvin, Mary, 662n28
Galway, County, 288t, 289t
Galway Society, 281
Gangs, 218, 446–48, 450; African Americans and, 114, 116; in Washington Heights/Inwood neighborhood, 443, 444–45, 687n32
Garden City, New York, 399
Garment strike (1910), 329, 332
Garrick, David, 40
Garrick, Patrick, 22
Garvey, Marcus, 367, 370–71
Garvin, Tom, 322
Gary Plan, 348, 385–88, 668n49, 669n51, 669n55
Gas House district, 217, 399, 639n6
Gay Men's Health Crisis, 2
Gay Rights movement, 7, 430, 431, 432–33, 684n64. *See also* Irish Lesbian and Gay Organization
Gazette, 83
Gellner, Ernest, 321
General Society of Mechanics and Tradesmen, 20
General Trades Union, 19
Gentleman's Magazine, 37
Geographic mobility. *See* Residential patterns
George, Henry, 226, 227, 307–10, 312, 330, 363, 538, 649n36, 649n42, 651n56, 660–61n5; Catholic Church and, 308–9, 326, 332; Irish nationalism and, 323, 324, 325, 326; mayoral campaign of, 324; Edward McGlynn's suspension and, 271
George, Lloyd, 364, 367
George Washington Bridge (Manhattan), 441, 456
German Irish, 43, 546
German Jews, 340, 345; in clothing industry, 190; in Washington Heights/Inwood neighborhood, 443, 455
German immigrants, 18, 91, 97, 99, 100, 216–17, 253; African Americans and, 124; baseball and, 629n66; in clothing industry, 175, 177, 189, 190, 191; education of, 577n8; family size and, 565t; gainful employment and, 565t; home ownership and, 566t; income of, 578n8; labor movement and, 99, 100; medical care for, 166; mental illness in, 161; mobility of, 276; occupations of, 10f, 22, 118, 230, 576n4; politics and, 102, 391, 424, 536; residential patterns of, 674n22; Alfred E. Smith and, 392
Ghent, Treaty of, 61
Ghose, S.N., 664n59
Giants (baseball team), 2, 231
Gibbons, James, Cardinal, 221–22, 314, 649n47
Gibson, William, 513
Gift, The (Hamill), 514–15
Gilfoyle, Timothy, 122

Gill, Brendan, 525
Gillespy, Edward, 60, 73
Gilliland, William, 37, 42
Gilmore, Margaret, 371
Gilmore, Patrick Sarsfield, 640n13
Gilmour, Richard, 324
Ginger Man, The (Donleavy), 515
Giuliani, Rudolph, 428, 433
Gladstone, William E., 224
Gleason, Jack, 679n76
Gleason, Teddy, 366, 657–58n1
Gleeson, Daniel, 410–11, 679n75, 679n76
Glengariff Construction Company, 413
Globe & Emerald, 23
Glynn, John, 505
Goff, John W., 332, 368
Going to Patchogue (McGonigle), 517–19
Golden, Helen, 363, 365, 368, 369, 371, 373,
    662n20, 663n37
Golden, Peter, 363, 369, 662n20
Goldwater, Barry, 427, 538
Gompers, Samuel, 311, 319, 332
Gonne, Maud, 359, 373
"Good Loser, A" (Cullinan), 528–29
Good Shepherd Parish (Manhattan), 441,
    442, 444, 445, 449, 456, 458
Goodwin, Nora, 458
Gophers (gang), 218
Gordon, Mary, 509–10, 518, 696n7
Gorillas (gang), 218
"Gossip" (Conroy), 697n37
Gotham City Cutters, 318
Grace, William R., 212f, 307
Grammar of the Irish Language (Joyce), 270
Grammar School 14 (Manhattan), 93–94, 95
Grand Council of United Emerald Societies,
    437
Grand Fair of the Roman Catholic Churches
    (St. Patrick's Cathedral Fair), 241–42, 242f
Grant, Ulysses S., 206, 223, 271
Gratton, Henry, 14
Gravesend (Brooklyn), 399
"Graveyard in Queens, A" (Montague), 512
Great Britain, 224–25, 443; American
    Women Pickets and, 361–62; Great Fam-
    ine and, 89–90; immigration to, 466; Irish
    county societies and, 285; Irish Home
    Rule politics in, 326; Irish music affected
    by, 499; partition of Ireland by, 351; poli-
    cies towards Ireland, 214–15, 224–25,
    333–34, 434; racial connotations in anti-
    Irish prejudice, 627n43; union movement
    in, 303
Great Depression, 337, 352–55, 406, 407,
    420, 424, 628n59, 651n60
Greater New York Charter, 217, 624n13
Great Gatsby, The (Fitzgerald), 345–46
Great Hunger. *See* The Famine
Great Neck, New York, 399
Greeley, Horace, 17, 149, 205
Greenback-Labor Party, 99, 323, 646n16
Green Dragon, 115
Greene, Victor, 545
Greenpoint (Brooklyn), 400
Greenwich Village (Manhattan), 329, 399
Greenwich Village riot, 61–64, 79, 81–83

Greg, Cunningham and Company, 13, 38–39
Greg, Thomas, 38
Gregory, Horace, 513
Gregory, Lady [Augusta], 359, 365
Gregory XVI, Pope, 33
Griffin, J.M., 642n30
Grimes, Tom, 511, 522–23
Grob, Gerald, 154
Grocery stores, 10f, 22, 76–77, 109, 119–20,
    403–4, 598n28, 598n29, 676n39–41
Groneman, Carol, 129, 545
Guinness, 403, 676n38
Gunther, G. Godfrey, 208
Gutzlaff, Karl, 127

Hackett, Francis, 513
Hagan, James J., 644n54
Hagan, James J., Association, 298
Haitian immigrants, 168, 616n67
Halpine, Charles Graham, 205–6, 207
Haltigan, James, 272
Hamilton, Alexander, 52
Hamilton, Dr. Alexander, 46, 587n88
Hammels, Rockaway (Queens), 408, 677n60
Hamill, Pete, 7, 514–15
Hanan, J.C., 297
Hand, Edward, 14
Handlin, Oscar, 389, 669n61
Hanford, Catharine, 273
Hanley, Catherine, 182
Hanlon, Ned, 231
Hannon, Mary Coleman, 484–85
Hanrahan, Barbara, 696n9
Hapgood, Norman, 379, 384
Harbutt, Charles, 474f
Hard, William, 376, 391, 671n79
Hardiman, [James], 262
Hardy, Frank, 696n9
Harlem (Manhattan), 442, 445, 449, 675n30
Harlem Bridge, 400
Harlem Railroad, 93
Harmon National Real Estate Corporation,
    405
Harp, 316, 652n74, 653n77
Harper, James, 30
Harper's Weekly, 129, 131, 132, 133, 162, 218
Harpur, Robert, 39, 42
Harrigan, Edward, 143–45, 232, 612n67
Hart, Tony, 143, 232
Harte, Bret, 148, 150
Haskins, Mattie, Shamrock Imports, 422
Hat Corporation of America, 187
Hatters, 169–92. *See also* Clothing industry
Haverty, Geraldine M., 269f
Haverty, P.M., 261
Hawley, Hughson, 302f
Hayden, Delia Brennan, 405, 408, 676n43
Hayden, Dorothy, 405, 491, 498, 676n43
Hayden, James A., 491, 676n43
Haymarket Square bombing, 310
Hays, William, 12
Healy, Garth, 503f
Healy, Jeremiah, 285
Healy, Paul, 75
Healy, Timothy, 297, 317
Heaney, Seamus, 458, 509

Hearst, William Randolph, 298, 313, 380, 390, 538, 644n52, 667n24
Heck, Barbara, 43
Heenan, John J., 25
Heeney, Cornelius, 20
Heffernan, M.J., 266
Heights-Inwood, 452, 453
Heinze, Andrew, 544
Hell's Kitchen (Manhattan), 6, 217, 218, 399, 422, 625n17, 674n26, 675n32
Hennessy, Patrick, 271
Henratty, Margaret F., 25
Herbert, Xavier, 696n9
Heron, Brian, 437
Hero of New York, The (Coughlin), 523
Herron, David, 37
Hewitt, Abram S., 226, 309
Hibernian Hall, 98f, 196f
Hibernian Provident Society, 71, 79
Hibernian Universal Benevolent Society, 72
Hibernia Trust Company, 344
Hickey, John, 39
Hickey, Margaret, 363, 368, 663n37
Higgins, Nora, 406, 410
Higham, John, 161–62
Highbinders, 52, 72–73
High Bridge, 400
Highbridge (Bronx), 400, 403, 680n86
Highbridge Park (Manhattan), 441, 446–47
Hill, John, 39
Hillquit, Morris, 375, 387, 390, 391, 538
Hills, Richard, 448
Hispanic immigrants, 422, 423; Catholic Church and, 431, 432; in Washington Heights/Inwood neighborhood, 444, 445–49, 450, 451, 452, 458–59, 688n46. *See also specific ethnic groups*
History of Ireland (Keating), 261
History of Ireland (Plowden), 62
History of Ireland (Taylor), 60
Hitler, Adolf, 443
Hoare, Frank, 459
Hobsbawm, Eric, 503–4
Hodges, Graham, 40
Hogan, Michael, 19
Hog-Eye (stage caricature), 143–44
Hoguet, Henry, 192
Holt, Frank, 501–2
Holy Cross Parish (Manhattan), 229, 242–43
Holy Family Parish (Bronx), 407, 409
Holy Ground (Manhattan), 21
Holy Innocents Parish (Manhattan), 248
Holy Name Parish (Manhattan), 238, 243, 402
Holy Trinity Parish (Manhattan), 405
"Home in the Bronx" (Winch), 512
Home ownership, 408–10, 566t
Home Rule movement, Irish, 321, 325, 326–31, 349–50; Catholic Church and, 326–27; criticism of, 331; Irish county societies and, 299; social class and, 327–28; socialism and, 327–29; women and, 330; World War I and, 333
Home Rule Party, 225
Homosexuals. *See* Gay Rights movement
Hone, Philip, 16, 19, 24, 27, 31

Hoover, J. Edgar, 499
Horticultural Society, 20
Horton, Charles, 448
Horton, James O., 124
Hose Company No. 42, 26
Hotel Workers Industrial Union, 316
House of Gold (Cullinan), 525, 527–28
House of Industry, Five Points, 112, 114, 165
House of Refreshment, 19
House of Refuge, 113, 123, 582n56
House on Jefferson Street, The (Gregory), 513
Housing, 400–401, 543
Howard, Maureen, 511, 513–14
Hoy, Hugh Kennedy, 41
Hoy, Zerviah, 41
Hoyt, John, 75
Hu, John, 151
Hudson River Railroad, 93
Hughes, Charles Evans, 340
Hughes, John, Archbishop, 20, 21, 28, 33, 166, 429; Civil War and, 195, 197, 199, 200, 201, 202, 204, 207; in medical care movement, 164–65; parochial schools and, 30–32, 68, 95, 103, 348, 541; philosophy of, 103
Hughes, Sr. Mary Angela, 166
Hughes, Tracy P., 200

Humanae Vitae (papal encyclical), 432
Hunter, David, 205
Hunter, Robert, 40
Hunts Point (Bronx), 399
Hurley, Martin J. (Liam O'Shea), 641n29
Hurling (sport), 287–90, 418
Huron Cigar Company, 644n54
Huston, John, 128
Huston, Margaret, 128
Hyde, Douglas, 271, 273
Hylan, John Francis ("Red Mike"), 364; John Purroy Mitchel and, 375, 387, 388–89, 390, 391, 392, 670n62, 670n65; Red Scare and, 393

IACL. *See* Irish American Labor Coalition
Iasachta, Eamon Mac Giolla, 267
ICAU. *See* Irish Counties Athletic Union
Iceman Cometh, The (O'Neill), 347
"If the River Was Whiskey" (Boyle), 516–17
IIRM. *See* Irish Immigration Reform Movement
IIWC. *See* Irish Immigration Working Committee
ILGO. *See* Irish Lesbian and Gay Organization
Illegal immigrants, Irish, 4, 420–21, 438, 462–63, 546–47, 691n49; 1950s immigrants and, 473–74, 476; occupations of, 468–73
Illiteracy rates. *See* Literacy rates
Illness. *See* Disease
ILP. *See* Independent Labor party
Immigrant Church, The (Dolan), 106
Immigration, 11–12, 17–19, 36–41, 70–72, 75–76, 90–93, 213–14, 216–17, 420–17, 640n17; alienation and, 629–30n72; Irish county of origin and, 288–89t; Irish

county societies and, 280, 643n42; laws protecting newcomers, 256; music and, 488–89, 497; quotas on, 420–21. *See also* Illegal immigrants; New Irish immigrants

Immigration Act of 1965, 462

Immigration Act of 1990, 421, 462

Immigration and Nationality Act of 1952, 488

Immigration Reform and Control Act of 1986, 421, 438, 462

Imminent Dangers to the Free Institutions of the United States through Foreign Immigration, 67

Impellitteri, Vincent, 425

Incarnation Parish (Manhattan), 444, 449, 450, 451, 456, 675n27, 675n31

Income, 421, 423–24, 578n8

Indentured servants, 36, 37, 38, 40, 583n7

Independent Labor Party (ILP), 227, 308–9, 312–13, 648n32

IND subway line, 441

Industrial Workers of the World (IWW), 316–17, 319, 328, 393, 653n82

INFA. *See* Irish National Federation of America

"Informal economy," Irish in, 469–73

Ingham, Charles C., 24

Innisfail Park. *See* Gaelic Park

Institute for the Protection of Catholic Children, 186

Institution for the Deaf and Dumb, 27

Interboro Rapid Transit (IRT), 354f, 403, 423

Interborough Row (Bronx), 403

Intermarriage, 438; Irish-African American, 19, 107, 123–24, 130, 140–42, 607–08n59, 608n60, 608n61, 608n64; Irish-Chinese, 128–30, 609n15; Irish-Jewish, 7

International Association of Machinists, 654n84, 654n89

International Brotherhood of Stationary Firemen, 317. *See also* Timothy Healy

International Convention of the Negro Peoples of the World, 367

International Ladies Garment Workers Union, 318

International Longshoremen's Association, 367, 370

International Socialist Review, 314

International Workingmen's Association, 306

Invented traditions, 503–4

Inwood (Manhattan), 422, 424, 439–60, 685–89n; crime in, 440–41, 450–51, 452–53, 456–57, 687n41; drug problem in, 456–57; gangs in, 443, 444–45, 687n32; residential patterns in, 401, 402, 679n75

Inwood Park (Manhattan), 441

IPL. *See* Irish Progressive League

IPP. *See* Irish Parliamentary Party

IRA. *See* Irish Republican Army

Ireland: British policy in, 214–15, 350; Civil War in, 351, 627n49; devotional revolution in, 215–16; education in, 215; emigration from northern 40–41; Irish language preservation in, 268; Land War in, 224, 279–81; marriage in, 90, 216; partition of, 351; post-Famine social changes, 90, 216;

trade with in colonial era, 13. *See also* specific counties

Ireland, David, 696n9

Ireland, John, Archbishop, 221–22, 541

Irish Advocate, 399, 410, 411, 498–99; Irish county societies and, 293, 295, 642n34; music advertisements and, 494; sports and, 291

Irish Ambassador, The (play), 24–25

Irish-American, 4, 115, 181, 295, 349; Civil War and, 194, 195, 197, 200, 203, 204, 205, 206, 207, 208, 209; founding of, 27; Irish county societies and, 277, 280, 281, 282, 283; Irish language in, 225, 258, 259–60, 261–64, 265–66, 267, 268–69, 270, 271, 272, 273; Irish nationalism and, 323; labor movement and, 99, 308, 314; slavery and, 33, 116; sports and, 290

Irish-American Almanac, 270

Irish American Athletic Club (IAAC), 291, 413, 681n91

Irish American Labor Coalition (IACL), 478

Irish Americans (sports team), 290

Irish Arts Center, 437

Irish Brigade, 186–87, 199–203, 206, 207, 208, 265, 621n23. *See also* Sixty-ninth Regiment

Irish Brigade Committee, 198

Irish Citizen, 33, 378

Irish Confederation of America, 281–83

Irish Counties Athletic Union (ICAU), 291–92, 298, 299, 642n30. *See also* United Irish Counties

Irish Counties Campaign Committee, 298

Irish county societies, 275–300, 293f, 545, 638–45n; age of members, 642–43n41; categories of, 278; Irish Confederation of America and, 281–83; Irish land war and, 279–81; New Irish immigrants and, 475; occupations of members of, 297–98, 639n10, 643–44n49, 644n51; origins of, 275–79; politics and, 298; reorganization of, 283–85; sick and death benefits provided by, 295; sports and, 287–92, 641n28, 641n29, 642n31; women and, 294, 643n42, 642n40–41, 661n9

Irish County Societies of Brooklyn, Federation of, 283

Irish Dancing, 293f, 493, 503f

Irish Echo, 434, 435, 436–37; Michael Flannery supported by, 436; music and, 488, 490, 494

Irish Emigrant Association, 19

Irish Emigrant Society, 19, 92f, 94, 104, 256, 594n70. *See also* Emigrant Industrial Savings Bank

Irish Free State, 321, 357, 373, 540

Irish Immigration Reform Movement (IIRM), 438, 478–79, 691n46

Irish Immigration Working Committee (IIWC), 478

Irish in America, The (Maguire), 201

Irish Institute, 430f

Irish language, 4, 225, 252–74, 546, 634–38n; in church services, 28; classes in, 263, 268, 270–71, 637–38n44; Irish speakers,

Irish language (*continued*)
265, 405; journals in, 272; politics and, 257, 272; societies, 268–70; type style used for, 261, 266, 637n34
Irish Legion, 206, 208–9
Irish Lesbian and Gay Organization (ILGO), 433, 684n64
"Irishmen's Petition, The" (O'Connor, et al.), 46
Irish Minstrelsy (Hardiman), 262
Irish Music and Social Club of Greater New York, 501
Irish Musicians/American Friends (Winch), 512–13
Irish Musicians Association, Inc., 501, 694n60
Irish Nation, 4, 286t, 288t, 289t, 641n27
Irish National Federation of America (INFA), 325, 326, 327–28, 329
Irish National Grenadiers, 194
Irish nationalism, 16, 27, 32–33, 104–05, 222, 223–26, 227, 305, 321–34, 349–51, 433–37, 539–40, 544, 655–57n; Catholic Church and, 324–25, 326–27, 332–33; Irish-Americans and, 349–51; Irish county societies and, 299; Irish Republicanism and, 48–50, 64–69; labor movement and, 314–15, 323, 328–29, 366; Noraid and, 434–35, 435f; *The Shamrock* and, 23; women and, 359–60. *See also* Home Rule movement, Irish; and American Women Pickets for the Enforcement of America's War Aims
Irish National Land League, 224, 323, 627n49; Irish county societies and, 279, 280, 281; labor movement and, 307; strife in, 325. *See also* Ladies Land League
Irish National Land League of America, 224, 225, 226, 321, 322, 323, 333, 540; boycotts and, 627n49; labor movement and, 305, 315, 647n17. *See also* Ladies Land League
Irish National League, 325, 358
Irish News, 198, 278
Irish Northern Aid Committee. *See* Noraid
Irish Palace Building Association, 284–85, 292, 641n23, 642n30
Irish Parliament, 14
Irish Parliamentary Party (IPP), 224–25, 298, 299, 325, 334; attacks on, 331; millionaire committee and, 328; United Irish League of America and, 326
Irish People, 265–67
Irish People, 434–35, 436
Irish Poor Law of 1838, 18
Irish Press, 663n37
Irish Primer, The (Furlong), 637n41
Irish Progressive League (IPL), 360, 361, 363, 365, 368, 371, 372, 373, 663n37–38; James Connolly's influence on, 664n62; founding of, 662n20
Irish Race Conventions, 367
Irish Republican Army (IRA), 434–36, 435f
Irish Republican Brotherhood, 223, 225, 299, 331
Irish Republicanism, 48–50, 66, 71; abandoning of ideals of, 68; original mean-

ing of, 69; transformation in meaning of, 61
Irish republicanism. *See* Irish nationalism
Irish Revolutionary Brotherhood Centre for Connaught, 299
Irish Rifles. *See* Seventy-fifth Regiment
Irish Shield, 23, 65
Irish Socialist Federation (ISF), 316, 328, 652n74
Irish Town. *See* Navy Yard (Brooklyn)
Irishtown. *See* Seaside (Queens)
Irish Voice, 438
Irish Volunteers, 284, 285, 331, 359
Irish Widow, The (Garrick), 40
Irish Women's Council. *See* Cumann na mBan
Irish Women Workers Union, 661n13
Irish World, 4, 254, 293, 537, 539; American Women Pickets and, 361, 368, 663n33; anti-Semitism and, 229; founding of, 224; Irish county societies and, 284; Irish language in, 258, 267–68; Irish nationalism and, 323, 324–25, 326; Joan of Arc in, 661n11; labor movement and, 99, 305, 308, 323, 329, 646–47n16, 652n68; Ladies Land League and, 660–61n5; Land League and, 315; Orange-Green Riot (1871) and, 98f; women and, 358–59
Irish Zouaves, 198
Ironweed (Kennedy), 522
IRT. *See* Interboro Rapid Transit
Irving and Moore Literacy Association, 24
Irving Hall Democrats, 223
Irwin, Rea, 390
ISF. *See* Irish Socialist Federation
Isham Park (Manhattan), 441
Italian immigrants, 217, 229, 341–42, 353, 431, 547, 628n59; 1920 dock strike, 370; in clothing industry, 190; in construction industry, 470; disease and, 167; education of, 577n8; family size and, 565t; gainful employment and, 565t; Great Depression and, 352; home ownership and, 566t; illegal immigrants and, 691n49; income of, 578n8; newspapers for, 253; politics and, 339, 341, 353, 424, 426, 427, 536–37; residential patterns of, 397, 674n22
Ivy Green Tavern, 19
IWW. *See* Industrial Workers of the World

Jackson, Andrew, 66–67, 626n27
Jackson, William, 592n45
Jackson Heights (Queens), 678n64
Jacobins, 53, 588–89n2
Jamaica (Queens), 399
James II, King, 62
Janitors. *See* Custodial work
Jarvis, Edward, 159
Jay, John, 14, 50–51, 590n9
Jefferson, Thomas, 15, 49, 53
Jeffersonians, 14–15, 66, 78–79
Jersey City, New Jersey, 92, 624n10, 628n56, 643n11
Jesters (gang), 447
Jesuits, 231

Jews, 341–42, 419, 541, 547; anti-Semitism, 167, 229, 353–54, 628n59; in clothing industry, 182, 189, 190, 191; education and, 31, 348; free exercise of religion and, 51; income of, 423, 675n29; intermarriage with, 7; labor movement and, 316, 318–19, 628n50; medical care and, 615–16n54; politics and, 339–41, 353, 424, 426, 427, 536–37, 538; residential patterns of, 397, 412–13, 422, 674n17, 674n22, 675n29, 681n96; in Washington Heights/Inwood neighborhood, 441, 442–44, 450, 455–56, 458, 688n46, 688n58. *See also* German Jews; Russian Jews

"JFK carpenters," 470
Joan of Arc, 661n11
Jogues, Isaac, 2, 12
John Fury (Dunphy), 515
Johnson, Andrew, 186
Johnson, Lyndon, 429
Johnson, Samuel, 42
Johnson, William, 14
John Taylor (ship), 130
Joint Committee to Investigate Seditious Activities, 393, 670n67, 670n83
Journeyman Tailors' Union of America, 178, 303
Joyce, James, 509, 522, 523
Joyce, Nora, 677n61
Joyce, P.W., 270
Juba (dancer), 123

Kane, Sarah, 238
Kapp, Friedrich, 155
Kean, John, 384
Keansburg, New Jersey, 677n57
Kearns, B.F., 398
Kearny, Denis, 143
Keating, Geoffrey, 261
Keating, James, 53–54
Keenan, Mike, 7
Kefauver, Estes, 424–25
Kelley, Eugene, 328
Kelly, Austin, 190
Kelly, Ed, 537
Kelly, Eugene, 283
Kelly, Gertrude B., 330, 332; American Women Pickets and, 359–60, 361, 362, 363, 365, 368, 369, 371, 372, 373, 663n44, 664n62
Kelly, Helen G., 369
Kelly, Hugh, 26, 192
Kelly, "Honest" John, 26, 102, 212f, 222–23, 228, 307, 338, 538, 647n18
Kelly, Martin, 354f
Kelly, Michael, 365, 368
Kelly, Pat, 7
Kelly, Patrick, 203, 206
Kelly, Raymond, 7, 428
Kelly, Robert, 511
Kelly, Thomas, 24
Keneally, Thomas, 511
Kenedy, P.J., 4, 258
Kennedy, Catherine, 405, 676n45
Kennedy, Daniel, 180

Kennedy, John, 317
Kennedy, John F., 347, 427, 430f, 520–21
Kennedy, Joseph, 344
Kennedy, Robert F., 426
Kennedy, Thomas E., 511, 525–27, 530
Kennedy, William, 522
Kennelly, Bryan L., 398, 673n16, 674n18
Kennelly Corporation, 399, 673n16
Keogh, Martin J., 328
Keppler, Johannes, 133, 145
Kerrigan, James, 192
Kerry, County, 287, 288t, 289t, 638n6
Kerry Men's Association, 276, 278, 639n12, 642n30
Kerrymen's Patriotic and Benevolent Society, 280–81
Kerryonians (gang), 114, 639n12
Kevney, Margaret, 26
Kickhams (Tipperary football team), 290
Kildare, County, 288t, 289t
Kilkenny, County, 288t, 289t
Kilkenny football team, 290
Killoran, Paddy, 484, 485, 501
Kimmel, John, 484
King, Rufus, 52–53, 67, 79, 595n86
Kingsbridge (Bronx), 400, 401
Kingsbury, John A., 381–82, 667n31
Kings County (Brooklyn), 558–59t, 562–63t
Kings (Offaly) County (Ireland), 288t, 289t, 294, 642n40
Kipp and Brown, 22
Kip's Bay (Manhattan), 399
Knicks (basketball team), 7
Knights of Columbus, 6, 250, 314, 351, 399, 674n19, 679n76
Knights of Labor, 227, 306, 308, 314, 367; Catholic Church and, 221; decline of, 310–11; District Assembly 49 and, 315; Irish nationalism and, 323, 324; philosophy and character of, 304
Knights of St. Crispin, 139
Knights of St. Finnbarr, 641n21
Knights of Tara (Meath Association), 279, 295
Know-Nothing movement, 33, 67, 100
Knox, Charles, 175, 180, 181–82, 185, 186–87, 192
Knox, Edward, 186–87
Knox Building, 183
Knox Hats, 187, 187f, 188, 189
Koch, Edward, 428, 431, 537
Koch, Robert, 154
Kohlmann, Fr. Anthony, 54–61, 62
Korean immigrants, 431
Korean War, 411
Kortright and Company, 39
Kossuth, Louis, 259

Labor Day, 304
Laborers, 40, 95, 98–99, 217, 302f, 301–2; "informal economy" and, 469–73; semiskilled, 20, 109, 229, 624n15; skilled, 20, 97, 109, 229, 624n15; unskilled, 20, 91, 94, 97, 203, 229, 303, 624n15
Laborers United Benevolent Society, 99

Labor movement, 19, 96, 98–100, 221, 227, 301–320, 354–55, 545, 628n50, 649-55n; Catholic Church and, 221, 314, 626n26; Chinese and, 139–40; Civil War and, 203–4; in clothing industry, 177–79; Archbishop Corrigan's views on, 221; Irish competition with New Immigrants in, 311–12, 318; Irish nationalism and, 314–15, 323, 328–29, 366; politics and, 306–10, 312–14, 315–16, 319–20, 538. *See also* Strikes; Boycotts; Unions

Ladies auxiliaries, Ancient Order of Hibernians', 359, 661n9

Ladies' fairs, Catholic, 234–51, 544, 630–34n; compared with Protestant fairs, 239, 247, 249; gender role reversal at, 237–38; goods sold at, 239–41, 632n25; money raised at, 241–43, 631–32n14; popularity contests at, 241; refreshments at, 239

Ladies Land League, 293, 324, 358, 642n39, 655n8, 660n2, 660n3, 660–61n5, 661n9

LaFayette, Marquis de, 62

La Guardia, Fiorello, 353, 392, 419, 424, 443, 536, 537

Lament of the Irish Emigrant, 18

Land League. *See* Irish National Land League

Landlordism, 222, 224–25, 227

Lane, Winthrop, 669n51

Laois, County. *See* Queens County (Ireland)

Lapin, James, 181

Larkin, Delia, 661n13

Larkin, James, 328, 329, 661n13, 663n44

Larue, Lewis, 73

Latinos. *See* Hispanic immigrants

Laundry work, 139, 152

Lavin, Jimmy, 411, 679n77

Leary, James, 172, 181, 183, 187, 192

Leary, James, & Co., 22

Lee, Robert E., 208

Lehan, Cornelius, 329

Lehman, Herbert, 353

Leinster (province), Ireland, 286, 287, 288t, 289t

Leisler's Rebellion, 50

Leitrim, County, 288t, 289t, 639n6

Leitrim Men, 298

Lendt, Lee A., 448–49

Lennon, James, 297

Lennon, Michael, 677n63

Leo, Patrick J., 257

Leonard, Msgr. Thomas, 451

Leonard, William, 177

Leo XIII, Pope, 221, 310, 314

Let Go of Yesterday (Breslin), 347

Lexington Opera House, 368

Leyburn, James, 42

Liberal Party, 326, 350

"Life After Death" (Cullinan), 528

Life and Adventures, Songs, Services and Speeches of Private Miles O'Reilly, The (Halpine), 205

Life Studies (Lowell), 516

Lightfoot, Richard, 39

Limerick, County, 288t, 289t, 639n6

Limerick Guards, 278

Limerick Men's Patriotic and Benevolent Association, 292, 295

Lincoln, Abraham, 193, 203, 207, 208, 209

Lincoln Center (Manhattan), 402

Lincoln Square (Manhattan), 676n35

Lindsay, John V., 426, 427, 429, 452, 537, 683n26

Lister, Joseph, 154

Literacy rates, 215, 230f, 623–24n4; in Irish language, 255, 259

Literary Digest, 388

Literature by Irish American authors, 345–47, 508–31, 546, 678n70, 700–698n; alcoholism as a subject in, 515–17; compared with Australian Irish writing, 511; theme of ethnic identity in, 508–9, 511–12, 519–22, 525

Liverpool Empire Theatre, 495

Lives of the Saints (Butler), 23

Llúid, Seán, 267

Locke, John, 49, 50, 51

Loco-Foco movement, 117, 606n37

Logan, Michael J., 225, 268, 269f, 270

Logan, Patrick, 268

Longáin, Michael Mac Pheadair Ui; 262

Long Day's Journey into Night, A (O'Neill), 347

Longford Association, 644n54

Longford, County, 287, 288t, 289t, 638n6, 641n26

Long Island, Battle of, 14

Long Island, New York, 398, 414, 421

Long Island City (Queens), 400, 403

Long Island Railroad, 407

Longshoremen, 98f, 108, 203–4, 297. *See also* American Women Pickets for the Enforcement of America's War Aims

Longshoremen's Union Protective Association, 367

Loughlin, John, Bishop, 343f

Louis, Joe, 231

Louis XIV, King, 43

Louth, County, 288t, 289t

Loving Women (Hamill), 515

Low, Seth, 538

Lowell, Robert, 516

Lusk, Clayton Riley, 389, 393–94, 670n67, 670n83

Lusk Laws, 393–94

Lyell, Charles, 27

Lynch, Dominick, 19-20, 72

Lynch, Dominick, Jr., 22

Lynch, Edward, 115

Lynch, James, 73, 367

Lynch, Patrick, 27

Lyric Hall (Manhattan), 237

McAleer, Fr. M., 271

McAleer, Martin, 23

McAuliffe, James C., 692n3

McBain, Howard Lee, 376, 388, 389

McCabe, John, 23

McCadden, Henry, 22

McCafferty, Paddy, 204

McCaffrey, Ann, 23

McCaffrey, Hugh, 22-23

McCaffrey, John Thomas, 213–14, 215, 216, 233
McCarran-Walter Act. *See* Immigration and Nationality Act of 1952
McCartan, Patrick, 368, 663n37
McCarthy, Charles, 27, 203
McCarthy, Dennis, 64
McCarthy, John, 448
McCarthy, Joseph, 426–27, 429, 498
McClellan, George B., 200, 208, 313, 623n62
McCloskey, John, Cardinal, 103, 219, 221, 240
McComb, John, 56
McCormack, John, 232
McCormick, Daniel, 42
McCready, B.W., 113
Mac Cruitín, Aindrias, 267
McCunn, John, 20
MacCurtain, Tomas, 360
McDaniel, Edward, 113
McDermott, Alice, 511, 520–22, 530, 678n70
McDermott, John, 22
MacDonagh, Oliver, 511
McDonnell, James Francis, 422–23
McFarland, Stephen, 298
McGann, Andy, 500, 695n61
McGarrity, Joseph, 331, 662n17, 663n37
McGee, Buddy, 442, 444, 454, 458
McGee, Thomas D'Arcy, 21
McGlone, Bridget, 78
McGlynn, Fr. Edward, 226, 240, 332, 349, 541, 649n40; excommunication of, 310, 649n47; Irish Confederation of America and, 282; Irish language and, 254; Irish nationalism and, 323, 324–25, 326; labor movement and, 309, 310; suspension of, 271, 310
McGoldrick, Monica, 517
McGonigle, Thomas, 511, 517–19
McGowan, Terence, 75
McGraw, John J., 2, 231
MacGuire, Carney, 46
McGuire, Peter J., 303, 304, 311, 317–18, 323, 648n33
McGuire, Robert J., 423
McGuire, Thomas B., 304–5, 311, 648n28
McGunnigle, Bill, 231
MacHale, John, Archbishop, 262, 270
McHugh, James, 41
McHugh, John, 303
Mack, Connie (Cornelius A. McGillicuddy), 231
McKeen, Joseph, 25
McKeon, John, 20, 27, 208
McKeown, Susan, 477
MacKnight, Patrick, 42
Mackrelville (Manhattan), 639n6
McLees, William H., 270
McLoughlin, Joseph F., 503f
McMackin, James, 306
McMackin, John, 309, 649n40
McMahon, J.H., 244
McManus, James R., 422
McMaster, James, 194
McNaire, William, 304
McNally, Francis, 25

McNamara, George, 257
MacNeill, Eoin, 359
McNeill, George, 323
MacNeven, William James, 15, 49, 53, 64–66, 539, 588n1, 614n40; Association of the Friends of Ireland and, 64; Democratic politics and, 66, 595n83, 596n91; early years of, 163–64; Irish language and, 254; medical care provided by, 163–64; monument to, 65, 254, 265; political vision of, 61, 63, 67, 68; Society for Civil and Religious Liberties and, 64
McNiff School of Irish Stepdancers, 506
McNulty, Michael, 257
McQuaid, Bernard, Bishop, 221–22
Macready, William, 17
McRobert, Patrick, 36, 37
McShane, Roger, 446–47, 687n31
MacSwiney, Mary, 360
MacSwiney, Muriel, 360, 372
MacSwiney, Terence, 357, 365, 366, 367–69, 370, 371–72, 665n70
McWhorter, Mary, 359, 360, 373
Madden, Owney, 2
Madison, James, 15, 49, 59
Magner, Daniel, 270, 638n84
Maguire, John F., 201
Maher, James P., 178
Mahon, Peter J., 428
Mahon, William D., 317
Mahoney, J. Daniel, 538
Mahoney, Jeremiah, 26
Majestic Showband, 495–96
Makem, Tommy, 497–98, 505, 506
Makemie, Francis, 12
Mallon, Edward, 174
Mallon, Thomas, 523–24, 526
Malone, Dudley Field, 369, 370
Maloney, Helena, 359, 661n13
Maloney, William J., 360, 361, 362, 662n17, 663n38
Manhattan, New York, 445; clothing industry in, 189; Greater New York Charter and, 217, 624n13; Irish ancestry represented in, 567t; Irish-born naturalizations in, 564t; Irish-born population in, 555t, 556–57t, 564t; Irish county populations represented in, 286, 287, 289t; Irish county societies in, 276–77, 296; Irish stock in, 562–63t; occupations/employment opportunities in, 403, 404; residential patterns in, 94, 231, 395, 396, 397–98, 399–400, 401–2, 407, 422, 674n22, 675n29. *See also specific neighborhood names*
Manhattan Bridge, 400
Manhattan College, 231, 343f
Mannix, Daniel, Archbishop, 357, 363–66, 367, 369, 370
Mansfield, Katherine, 519, 520
Manufacturers Hanover Trust, 344
Marcy, William L., 16, 32
Marine, Firemen, Oilers and Watertenders Union, 367
Marine Hospital, 155
Mariners, 39–40

Markievicz, Constance, 359, 373
Marks, Levi, 113
Marsh, Eleanor Taylor, 371
Martin, John, 32
Maryland, 43
Mason, Jackie, 7
Mason, William, 360
Mason Bill, 361
Massapequa Park, New York, 411–12, 679n79, 680n83
Mass for the Dead, A (Gibson), 513
Masterson, Thomas, 304
Mathew, Fr. Theobald, 116, 220
Fr. Mathew Total Abstinence and Benevolent Society, 279
Matthews, David, 13
Matthews, Henry, 113
Mauretania (ship), 370
Maxwell, William Henry, 386–87
May Day (1919) bomb scare, 393
Mayo, Ann, 22
Mayo, County, 287, 288t, 639n6, 639n9, 641n26
Mayo Young Men's Association, 299, 640n15, 644n55
Meagher, Thomas Francis, 32, 200, 201, 203, 204, 205, 209, 539; attitude towards Democratic party, 206–7; background of, 197–98
Meagher, Mrs. Thomas Francis, 198
Meath Association (Knights of Tara), 279, 295
Meath, County, 288t, 289t, 639n6
Meath Football Club, 278
Medical care, 106, 153–68, 547, 613–16n; Catholic Church and, 164–67, 201–2, 613n8, 614n40, 615n50; nativism and, 154, 155, 161–62, 167–68. *See also* Disease
Meehan, Patrick J., 4, 267, 637n33
Mehan, Denis, 75
Mehan, Patrick, 75
Melendez, George, 448
Melgola. *See* John O'Mahony
Mellows, Liam, 368, 660n38
Melodies (Moore), 232, 262, 270
Melrose (Bronx), 400
Memoirs (Sampson), 60
Mental illness, 159–61, 217, 614n30; in literature, 517
Merchants, 13, 38–39, 584n24, 586n53
Merriman, Brian, 267
Methodists, 43
Metropolitan Record, 208
Mexican War, 16–17
Michels, Stanley E., 458
"Midair" (Conroy), 517
Middle class, 402, 408; amenities in housing, 397, 400–1, 408–9, 412–13, 414; character of pre-Famine community, 71–72, 73, 74, 79, 80, 547; Great Depression and, 352; Irish county societies and, 278; Irish nationalism and, 656n17; labor movement and, 303, 650n54
Military. *See* Irish Brigade, Irish Legion, Sixty-ninth Regiment, *and specific wars or unit names*
Militia of Christ for Social Service (Social Service Commission), 314

Miller, Glenn, 487
Miller, Kerby, 2, 43, 233
Miller, Perry, 234–35
Miller, Samuel, 41
Miller, Wilbur, 97
Milligan, Thomas, 664n56
Minstrel shows, 143
"Miracle at Ballinspittle, The" (Boyle), 516
Miscegenation, 141–42. *See also* Intermarriage
Miscegenation: The Theory of the Blending of the Races, 141–42
Mission of the Immaculate Virgin (Staten Island), 220f
Mitchel, James, 378
Mitchel, John, 32–33, 105, 194, 378, 539
Mitchel, John Purroy, 298, 329, 341, 348, 374–94, 538, 544, 644n52, 665–72n; background of, 378; Catholics and, 377, 380–384; Gary Plan and, 385–88; loses reelection, 375, 388–92; rejection of Irish heritage by, 379–81
Mitchels (sports team), 290
Mixed assemblies, 304–5
Mix-up, Irish-Chinese, 131–32, 133f
Model, Suzanne, 534
Moleneaux, Joseph, 20
Molly Maguires, 279, 354
Moloney, Mick, 500
Monaghan, County, 288t, 289t, 639n9
Monaghan Men's Society of New York, County, 293f
Mondale, Walter, 700n11
Montague, John, 511–12
Montgomery, Richard, 14
Mooney, Charlie, 403
Mooney, Maureen Griffin, 406, 407, 410, 676n39
Mooney, R.J., 199
Mooney, Thomas, 117, 121
Moon Gaffney (Sylvester), 347
Moore, Annie, 153–54
Moore, Henry, 45
Moore, Marguerite, 358, 362
Moore, Marianne, 511
Moore, Thomas, 232, 262, 270
Moore, William, 123
Moore, William J., 400
Moore, Winnifred, 123
Moran, Mrs. Owen, 238
Morgan, Rabbit, 642n31
Mormino, Gary, 542
Morris, Harriet, 113
Morrisania (Bronx), 400
Morrison, Bruce, 462, 682n7
Morrison, James, 484, 485
Morrison, Van, 517
Morrison visas, 438, 467, 682n7, 685n88, 691–92n50
Morrissey, John, 25, 223
Morse, Samuel F.B., 16, 67, 157
Mortality rates, 21, 155; of African Americans, 114, 605n25
Mortgages, 409, 678n66
Moses, Robert, 376, 385, 388, 669n61
Moskowitz, Belle, 388, 669n61
Moskowitz, Henry, 379, 384, 388

Mott Haven (Bronx), 400, 422
Mount Saint Vincent College, 231
Mount Sinai Hospital, 615n54
Moynihan, Daniel Patrick, 8, 347, 419, 420, 426, 435, 436, 535, 539
"Muddy Cup, A" (Montague), 512
Mugavero, Frank, 430
Mulcahey, Jack, 6
Mulhaire, Martin, 486–87, 492–93, 495–96, 499–500, 507
Mullaly, John, 208
Mullaney, Joseph A., 317
Mullaney, William, 26
Mullany, Tom, 452–53, 455
Mulligan, Dan (character), 143
Mulligan, Hercules, 39, 43
Mulligan, Hugh, 40
Mullins, Denis, 404f
Mulqueen, Michael J., 398
Mulvihill, Martin, 505
Municipal Research Bureau, 667n29
Munster (province), Ireland, 286, 288t, 289t
Murderous McLaughlins, The (Dunphy), 515
Murnane, Gerald, 696n9
Murphy, Catherine, 26
Murphy, Charles Francis, 2, 227–28, 313, 339–40, 341, 538; death of, 535–36; Alfred E. Smith and, 4, 375, 392; woman's suffrage and, 329
Murphy, Frank, 409
Murphy, Henry C., 27
Murphy, James, & Co., 22
Murphy, Jeremiah, 305, 648n28
Murphy, Mary, 23
Murphy, Matthew, 208
Murphy, Patrick, 315
Murphy, Thomas, 22, 419
Murphy Brothers, 409
Murray, George E., 304
Murray, James, 177
Murray, Jas. E., 268
Murray, Joan, 511
Murray, John, Jr., 29
Murray, John F., 516
Murray, John K., 182
Murray, Joseph, 39, 43
Murray, Thomas A., 317
Music, 25, 232, 437, 438, 481–507, 546, 692–95n; big band, 487–88, 490–91, 496; at City Center, 492–94; instrumentation, 482–83, 486, 487, 490, 491, 496; musicians' union, 693n37; New Irish immigrants and, 477; popular, 483 (defined), 488, 489–91, 692n3; showband, 494–96; songs, 232, 491, 497, 502, 505, 695n74–75; traditional. See Traditional music
"My Father" (Winch), 512

Nadler, Jerrold, 422
Nagle, David, 257
Nally, P.W., 299, 644n55
Nanjing, Treaty of, 127
Napoleonic Wars, 11, 18
Nash, Pat, 537
Nassau County, New York, 395, 411, 414, 421–22

Nast, Thomas, 133, 142, 145, 162, 218
Nation, 21, 263, 376, 383, 388, 391
National bank, 66, 67
National Defense League, 393
Nationalism. See Irish nationalism
National Municipal Review, 376, 388
National Repeal Association, 32
National Republicans. See Whigs
National Review, 426
National Steamship Line and Atlantic Transport Company, 367
Native Americans Democratic Association, 16
Nativism, 16–17, 30, 80, 88–89, 102, 352; African Americans and, 116–17; anti-radicalism and, 393; behind 1834 riot, 67; Highbinders (gang), 52, 72–73; effect on Irish American writers, 345; Irish nationalism and, 224, 226; literature and, 345; medical prejudice and, 154, 155, 161–62, 167–68; "Paddies" and, 51. See also Know-Nothing movement
Naturalizations, Irish-born, 564t
Navy Yard (Brooklyn), 93, 336f, 400
Nearing, Scott, 392
Negro Burying Ground, 108
Neilson, Robert, 38
Neilson, Samuel, 53, 592n45
Neilson, William, 38
Nelden Corporation, 412
Nevada (ship), 153
New Beef Steak and Oyster House, 39
New Deal, 536, 537
New Departure, 224, 225, 323, 325, 330, 332, 647n17, 655n3
New Haven, Connecticut, 624n10
New Illustrated Self-Instructor in Phrenology and Physiology (Fowler), 162
New Immigrants Unit, in Police Department, 438
New Irish immigrants, 421, 432, 438, 461–80, 546–47, 689–92n; campaign for legalization and, 478–80; 1950s immigrants and, 473–78; statistics on, 461–62, 463t; types of, 463–68. See also Illegal immigrants, Irish
New Jersey, 257, 421, 673n11. See also specific regions of
New Law (Tenement House Law of 1901), 400
New Lots (Brooklyn), 399
Newman, John Henry, Cardinal, 228
Newman, Lesing, 130
New Republic, 376, 391
Newspapers, 4, 23–24, 73–74, 104; American Women Pickets and, 362; foreign language, 253; journalism as an occupation, 229; labor movement and, 99; shift to lower-class values in, 73–74; slavery and, 116. See also specific publications
New York American, 368, 370, 380
New York Catholic Library Association, 24
New York Ceili Band, 695n61
New York City Lunatic Asylum, 21, 88, 159, 160, 161
New York Constitutional Convention, 15

New York Cutters' and Tailors' Association, 179

New Yorker, 510, 516

New Yorker Staats-Zeitung, 253

New York Evening Day Book, 130, 140, 141

New York Evening Post, 78–79, 383, 385

New York Herald, 24, 149, 164, 223, 271

New-York Historical Society, 20

New York Irish History, 437

New York Irish History Roundtable, 437

New York Journal of Commerce, 132

New-York Mercury, 39, 45

New York Metropolitan Fair, 237

New York Post, 447

New York Review, 228–29

New York's Chinatown, An Historical Presentation of Its People and Places (Beck), 127–28

New York Sun, 115, 357

New York Times, 24, 102, 108, 115, 130, 157, 200, 241, 284, 423; American Women Pickets and, 361, 364, 365, 368–69, 370; Quimbo Appo and, 127, 128, 149; on the clothing industry, 175, 178

New York Tribune, 17, 24, 32, 129, 149, 205, 370

New York University, 20

New York Women's Trade Union League, 316

New York World, 141, 370

Niblo's Saloon (Niblo's Garden), 236

Niland, D'Arcy, 696n9

Niles, Hezekiah, 156

Niles Weekly Register, 156

1950s immigrants, 411, 420, 473–78, 474f

'98 Club. _See_ Wexford Men

Ninth Ward (Manhattan), 75

Ninth Ward (Brooklyn), 677n46

Noah, Mordecai, 16

Noonan, Bernard J., 412, 674n18, 680n84, 680n86

Noonan, Paddy, 491, 492, 493, 498

Noonan Plaza (Bronx), 412–13, 414, 680n86

Noraid, 434–36, 435f

Norman Monarch (ship), 367

Norris, Thomas, 264, 273–74

Northern Ireland, conflict in, 433–36, 479; Joseph Doherty's deportation to, 436; reactions to hunger strikes in, 434f, 435

Northern Star, 592n45, 593n59

Norwegian immigrants, 565t, 566t

Norwood (Bronx), 422

NP-5 visa program. _See_ Donnelly visas

Nudd, Howard W., 669n55

Nugent, Robert, 204

Nuns, 219–20, 230–31, 244, 616n57. _See also_ specific orders; Women

Nursing, 121

NYPD Blue (television program), 7

Oakley, Barry, 696n9

O'Beirn, Patrick, 271

O'Beirne, James "Lad", 484, 485, 500, 501

O'Beirne, Mary, 484

Object Lessons (Quindlen), 524–25

O'Brennan, Kathleen, 361, 371, 663n44

O'Brian, Charlotte, 459

O'Brien, Charlotte Grace, 256–57

O'Brien, George, 508

O'Brien, Henry, 204

O'Brien, Jimmy "The Famous", 223

O'Brien, Michael J., xi, 35

O'Brien, Paddy, 695n61

O'Brien, William, 313

O'Brien, William P., 419

O'Brien, William Smith, 32–33, 261, 283, 325, 637n32, 640n15

O'Bryan, Blaney, 46

O'Byrne, Feagh McHugh, 266

Occupations, 10f, 19–27, 38–41, 75–78, 94–98, 217, 229–31, 302f, 342, 423–24, 534–35, 576n4; of African Americans, 109, 116–22, 139–40; of Chinese, 139–40; Irish county societies and, 297–98, 639n10, 643–44n49, 644n51; of ladies' fairs participants, 238; of New Irish immigrants, 468–73; residential patterns and, 403–7. _See also specific work_; Business

O'Connell, Daniel, 31, 32, 33, 52, 60, 64, 65, 86f, 216, 222, 241, 253, 626n27

O'Connell, James, 654n89

O'Connell Brothers [John O'Connell], 10f

O'Connor, George Washington. _See_ Connors, Chuck

O'Connor, John, 430–31, 433

O'Connor, Michael, 280

O'Connor, Patrick, 46

O'Connor, Thomas, 53, 64, 594n70

O'Conor, Charles, 20, 24, 27, 594n70

Octoroon, The (Boucicault), 25

O'Daly, Angus, 266

O'Daly, John, 262, 263, 264

O'Daly, P.J., 637n43

Ó Daoir, Séamas (James O'Dwyer), 260

O'Doherty, Kieran, 538

O'Donnell, John "Kerry", 418f

O'Donnell, John R., 648n28

O'Donnell, M.J., 25

O'Donohue, Joseph J., 308

O'Donovan, Jeremiah, 94, 255, 635–36n14

O'Donovan Rossa, Mary J., 331

O'Donovan Rossa, Jeremiah 105, 255, 331, 539, 648n26; Irish language and, 258, 272, 274; New Departure and, 655n3; senate race of, 638n5

O'Dowd, Bernard, 696n9

O'Dowd, The (Boucicault), 232

Ó Dreada, Seán (John Draddy), 255

O'Dwyer, James (Séamas Ó Daoir), 260

O'Dwyer, Paul, 423, 428, 430f, 443

O'Dwyer, William, 328–29, 355, 408, 419, 423, 424–25, 503f, 536

Offaly, County. _See_ Kings County (Ireland)

O'Flaherty, Edward, 298

O'Flaherty, Mary, 329

O'Flanagan, Fr. Michael, 644n59

O'Flyn, Denis, 255

O'Gorman, Richard, 202, 208

O'Grada, Cormac, 2

O'Grady, Desmond, 696n9

O'Grady, Joseph, 350

O'Grady, W.L.D., 265

O'Halloran, Kathleen, 445, 453, 458

O'Hara, Frank, 2
O'Hara, John, 346–65, 696n9
O'Hara, William P., 179
Ohio, 641n26
O'Keeffe, David, 264–65, 269, 270
O'Kelly, Aloysius, 269f
Olcott, Chauncy, 232
Old Brewery. *See* House of Industry, Five Points
Old Countryman, 23
Old Established Ready Made Coffin Warehouse, 22
"Old Ireland" (Whitman), 508
O'Leary, Jeremiah, 359, 360, 363, 371, 661n16
O'Leary, John Stratton, 413, 674n18
O'Leary's Flats (Bronx), 413, 414, 680n89
O'Lenihan, Michael J., 258–59
"O Lovely Appearance of Death" (Currie), 515
Olympic (ship), 366, 370
O'Mahony, John, 6, 105, 223, 539; Irish language and, 259, 260–62, 263–64, 265–67, 274, 635n8, 636n30, 636–37n31, 637n36; pen name of, 266
O'Mara, James, 663n38
Ó Miodhacháin, Tomás, 267
O'Neil, Bernard S., 201
O'Neill, Eugene, 347
O'Neill, Hugh, 192
O'Neill, Paul, 7
"On the Mountain Stands a Lady" (Currie), 515
Opdyke, George, 186
Operative Masons, 99
"O'Phelan Drinking" (Murray), 516
"O'Phelan's Daemonium" (Murray), 516
Opium trade, 127, 146
Opportunity structures, 190
Orange lodges, 81, 98f
Orangemen, 15, 65
Orange Riots, 97, 98f, 100, 218, 625n18, 625n19. *See also* Greenwich Village riot
Order of the Star Spangled Banner, 100
Order of United Irishmen. *See* Sligo Young Men's Association
O'Reilly, Father Bernard, 199, 202
O'Reilly, Leonora, 316, 657; American Women Pickets and, 360, 362, 363, 661n15, 662n26, 663n44
O'Reilly, Miles (character), 205–6
Organisation for Economic Co-operation and Development (OECD), 461
O'Rourke, Catherine, 26
O'Rourke, Hugh, 406–7
Orphanages, 29, 220f, 244; John Purroy Mitchel and, 381–84
Orr, John S., 100
Orr, John W., 24
Orr, William, 592n45
Orsi, Robert, 544
Ortiz, Israel, 459
O'Shea, Liam (Martin J. Hurley), 641n29
O'Sheel, Shaemus, 511
Ossianic Society, 264, 273
O'Sullivan, John, 17

Other Side, The (Gordon), 510
"Our Gaelic Department" (newspaper column), 261–64
Our Lady of Lourdes Parish (Manhattan), 243
Our Lady of Victory School (Brooklyn), 268
Outline of a New System of Physiognomy (Redfield), 162

Paddies (straw effigies), 51
Painter's Union, 306
Palmer, A. Mitchel, 389
Palmer, Gilbert, 113
Palmer, Sean, 1
Palmer Raids, 389
Panic of 1837, 67
Panic of 1873, 188
Pannonia (ship), 366, 370
Papal encyclicals, 625–26n25. *See also* specific encyclicals
Paper Handlers Union, 297
Paradise Square (Manhattan), 112
Parente, Robert, 457
Parchester (Bronx), 674n22, 681n90
Park, Ruth, 696n9
Park Theatre (Manhattan), 24
Parlor Mob (gang), 218
Parnell, Anna, 324, 358
Parnell, Charles Stewart, 222, 224–25, 305, 322, 358, 521, 647n17; boycotts and, 627n49; fall of, 314, 325
Parnell, Delia, 358
Parnell, Fanny, 324, 358, 660n2, 660–61n5
Parochial schools, 20–32, 68, 95, 103, 219, 244, 348, 429, 541–42, 633n38, 701n17; closing of, 431; in Washington Heights/Inwood neighborhood, 452. *See also* Education; Schools
Parsons, Daniel, 100
Parsons, Ralph L., 161
Pascendi Dominici Gregis (papal encyclical), 228
Pasteur, Louis, 154
Patrolmen's Benevolent Association (PBA), 427
Paul, Alice, 361–62, 373
Paulists, 245, 634n55
Paul VI, Pope, 430
Pay-as-you-go policy, 385, 668n47
Pearse, Padraic, 365, 373
Pemberton, Catherine, 41
Pemberton, Ebenezer, 41
Penal Laws, 50, 60, 589n4
Peninsula Campaign, 200
Penn, William, 44, 49
Pennsylvania, 43, 44, 641n26. *See also* specific regions in
Pennsylvania Railroad terminal, 399
Pentecostals, 451
People v. *Philips*, 53–61, 589n3, 591n36
Perez, Reverend, 446
"Perfect Crime, The" (Cullinan), 528
Permoli v. *Municipality No. 1*, 592n54
Phelan, John J., Jr., 423
Philadelphia, Pennsylvania, 44, 536; immigrants in, 641n26; Irish county societies in, 641n21; parochial schools in, 541, 701n17

Philadelphia Athletics, 231
Philbin, Eugene A., 383
Philips, Daniel, 54
Philips, Mary, 54
Phillips, Kevin, 538
Philo-Celtic societies, 268–70, 273, 293, 642n38
Phoenix, 264–65
Phrenology, 162
Physicians, 39, 155–68
Physiognomy, 133, 145, 162
Pickering, Timothy, 52
Pieces of Irish History (MacNeven and Emmet), 61
Pilkington, Frank, 642n40
Pillson, Robert, 41, 43
Pinckney, Charles, 64
Pittsburgh, Pennsylvania, 536, 540
Pius VII, Pope, 28
Pius IX, Pope, 215
Pius X, Pope, 228–29
Pius XI, Pope, 353
Planxty, 505
Playboy of the Western World, The (Synge), 226
Plete, Anaste, 113
Pleurisy, 114
Plowden, Francis, 62
Plug Uglies (gang), 114
Plunkett, George, Count, 644n59
Plunkitt, George Washington, 3, 223; John Purroy Mitchel and, 375, 376, 377, 378–79, 381, 666n15, 671n80
Pneumonia, 114
Poetry, 511–13; in the Irish language, 259–60, 271
Poets and Poetry of Munster (O'Daly), 262, 264
Polish immigrants, 473; family size and, 565t; gainful employment and, 565t; home ownership and, 566t; illegal immigrants, 691n49; income of, 578n8; politics and, 537
Police Department, 26, 81–82, 97, 105, 352, 419, 427–28, 644n51; brutality charges and, 427; New Immigrants Unit in, 438; in popular culture, 7; 25th Precinct station, 230f; in Washington Heights/Inwood neighborhood, 444, 453–54
Police Gazette, 144
Political Bulletin and Miscellaneous Repository, 116
Political patronage, 117, 313, 338
Politics, 3, 45–46, 78–81, 96–97, 101–2, 222–23, 338–41, 424–31, 535–39; African Americans and, 116–17, 426, 537; Catholics and, 541; Great Depression and, 352–53; Irish language used in, 257, 272; Irish county societies and, 298–99; labor movement and, 306–10, 312–14, 315–16, 319–20, 538; United Irish Republicanism and, 64–68. *See also specific political parties*
Poole, Big Bill, 25
Pope, Jesse, 176, 179
Pope Day, 51

Popularity contests, at Catholic Fairs, 241
Popular music, 483, 488, 489–91, 692n3. *See also* Music
Population: African Americans in, 110; comparision of Ireland and United States, 286–87; in early 20th century, 339; Germans in, 216–17; Irish ancestry of, 396t, 567t; Irish-born by county (New York), 396t, 556–563t; Irish-born by decade, 555t; Irish-born by specific census tract, 675n27, 675n35, 677n60, 680n86, 680n89, 681n95; Irish-born of Washington Heights/Inwood neighborhood, 442, 675n27; Irish-born by year of emigration, 564t, 568t; of Irish speakers, 254; in mid nineteenth century, 91, 92–93, 94; in late nineteenth century, 302; in the 20th century, 420, 421; at the turn of the century, 216–17. *See also* Censuses
Porterfield, Amanda, 235
Porterhouses, 119, 120
Potatoes, 89–90, 163
Poverty, 20, 74–75, 88, 94, 99–100, 217–18, 221, 423–24; African Americans and, 114; Catholic Church and, 221, 625n20; in Washington Heights/Inwood neighborhood, 457
Powderly, Terence V., 304, 310, 311, 649n36
Power, Tyrone, 24–25
Pozzetta, George, 542
Prendergast, William A., 385–86
Presbyterians, 12–13, 35, 41–42, 61–64, 586n53
Presley, Elvis, 495
Press. *See* Newspapers
Press, 592n45, 593n59
Preston, Thomas S., 308, 649n42
Priest Baiting in 1916 (Farrell), 382
Priests, 219–20, 230; Irish language spoken by, 257, 271. *See also specific orders*
Progress and Poverty (George), 308, 324
Progressive Painters, 304
Progressivism, 377, 671–72n90
Prohibition, 352
Property Owners' Association, 398
Prospect Park (Brooklyn), 400
Prostitution, 21, 109, 112, 121–22
Protestant Council of the City of New York, 443, 446
Protestants, 11–12, 15–17, 19, 46, 70–72, 218; Chinese and, 132–33; disease/medical care and, 156, 165–66, 615n50; disestablishment of churches in Ireland, 214; Greenwich Village riot and, 61–64, 79, 81–83; Home Rule movement and, 350; Irish, 5, 36, 41–43, 46, 98f; Irish language used by, 257, 636n24; Irish nationalism and, 327; ladies' fairs and, 247; John Purroy Mitchel and, 383, 384; Orange lodges of, 81, 98f; parochial schools and, 29–32, 68; partition and, 351; Public School Society and, 25–26, 29–30, 31, 89. *See also* United Irish
Public Scandal, Charity for Revenue, A (Farrell), 382
Public School No. 5, 30
Public schools. *See* Schools

Public School Society, 25, 29–30, 31–32, 89
Public sector employment. *See* Civil service
Puck, 133
Puerto Rican Immigrants, 431, 445–48
Punch, 133, 163
Purcell, Richard, 35
Puritans, compared with Irish American
  Catholics, 234–35
Purroy, Henry, 227, 378

Quakers, 36, 42
Quarantine Hospital, 166
Quarantines, 155, 158
Quarrymen's United Protective Society, 99
Queensboro Bridge, 400
Queens (Laois) County, 288t, 289t, 640n19;
  cricket team, 290–291
Queens County, New York, 400, 422;
  Greater New York Charter and, 624n13;
  Irish ancestry represented in, 567t; Irish-
  born naturalizations in, 564t; Irish-born
  population in, 555t, 560t, 564t; New Irish
  immigrants in, 474–75; occupations/em-
  ployment opportunities in, 403; residen-
  tial patterns in, 395, 396, 399, 400, 401,
  402t, 408, 414, 674n22
Queens-Midtown Tunnel, 401–2, 403,
  675n35
Quill, Michael J., 2, 354–55, 423, 539
Quindlen, Anna, 7, 511, 524–25, 678n70
Quinn, Carmel, 491
Quinn, Eileen, 455, 458
Quinn, James, 304
Quinn, John, 322, 326–27, 328, 329, 332
Quinn, Louis, 490, 501, 506
Quinn, Peter, 6
Quinn, Roderick, 696n9
Quinn, Tommy, 642n31

Race riots, 114–15. *See also* Draft Riots
Racism, 105–6, 107. *See also* Nativism
Radio Luxembourg, 495
Radio Telefis Eireann (RTE), 486
Raffles at Catholic fairs, 239, 247
Ragged Dick (Alger), 139
Railroad workers, 139
Railway Express Company, 403
Ramage, John, 24
Rams (gang), 444
Randall, Thomas, 40, 43
Rand School for Social Science, 393
Rangers (hockey team), 7
Rayill, Brian, 453
Rayill, James, 453
Reagan, Ronald, 700n11
Real estate developers, 397–99, 410–14,
  679–80n82
Reavy, Ed, 501
Rebellion of 1798, 14, 15, 48, 51, 53, 61, 62;
  legacy of, 68–69; William Sampson's
  views on, 60–61, 593n59. *See also* United
  Irish
Reconquest of America, The (Maloney),
  662n17
Reconstruction Amendments, 116
Redfield, James, 162

Red Mill (Bronx dance hall), 496
Redican, Larry, 695n61
Redmond, John, 299, 325, 326, 328, 349,
  644n52, 644n58; support for British in
  World War I, 333–34; woman's suffrage
  and, 330
Redpath, James, 282, 309, 649n40
Red Scares, 377, 393–94, 426–427, 670n67,
  671n82
Red Star Line, 18, 366
Reeves, Daniel, 403–4
Reeves, James, 404, 676n41
Reform. *See* Mitchel, John Purroy; Smith, Al-
  fred E.
Reformation Society, 582n56
Regan, Ann, 23
Regan, Henry, 182
Rego Records, 491
Reid, William W., 648n28
Reidy, David, 255
Reilly, Columba, O.S.F., 343f
Reilly, John, 398
Reilly, Mary, 238
Religious freedom. *See* Free exercise of
  religion
Religious Freedom (Liberty) Restoration Act,
  589n3, 592n43
Reliques (Brooke), 262
Repeal Party, 31, 105
Report from Engine Co. 82 (Smith), 513
Republican Party, 222, 424, 426–27, 536,
  537; African Americans and, 132, 139;
  Civil War and, 193, 207, 208, 209;
  increasing support for, 538; Jews and, 340;
  labor movement and, 312–13; miscegena-
  tion issue and, 142; slavery issue and, 33;
  switch of allegiance to, 426–27
Rerum Novarum (papal encyclical), 221, 314
Residential patterns, 276, 343, 395–415,
  421–22, 672–82n.; Catholic parishes and,
  399; ethnic succession in, 397, 543; home
  ownership and, 408–10, 566t; housing and,
  400–401, 543; Irish-born by county (New
  York), 396t, 556–63t, 638–39n6; occupa-
  tions/employment opportunities and,
  403–7; real estate developers and, 397–99,
  410–14, 679–80n82
Restaurant/bar trades, 470, 474f
Revolutionary War, 13–14
Reynolds, Albert, 694n39
Reynolds, Paddy, 489, 490, 500, 693–94n37,
  695n61
Rhodes, Robert E., 345–46
Rhodes Gang, 218
Ribbon societies, 81
Richardson, Henry Handel, 511
Richmond (Staten Island), 396, 402t
Richmond Enquirer, 378
Rieder, Jonathan, 6
Riker, Richard, 62–63
Riley, Pat, 7
Riordan, William L., 375
Riots. *See specific names*
Riverdale (Bronx), 409, 418f, 678n64, 675n35
Rivington's New-York Gazeteer, 38
Roach, John, 192

Roach, Thomas, 13, 43

Roach Guards, 114

Rock, Thomas, 299, 644n59, 664n56

Rockaway Beach, (Queens), 400, 407–8, 677n60. *See also* Seaside; Hammels

"Rockaway for the Day" (Winch), 512

Rockefeller Foundation, 386, 387

Rockland County, New York, 395, 421, 455

Rock 'n roll, 495

Rodgers, John, 41

Roediger, David, 539

Rogers, Patrick L. , 22, 169–70, 183, 185, 187, 191, 192

Roman Catholic Church. *See* Catholic Church

Roman Catholic Female Orphan Asylum, 27

Roman Catholic Orphan Asylum, 27

Rooney, John, 426

Roosevelt, Franklin D., 344, 352–53, 426, 537

Roosevelt, Theodore, 223, 309, 326, 340, 374–75, 376, 386, 389, 666n11

Root, Elihu, 390

Roscommon, County, 287, 288t, 289t, 639n9

Roscommon Society, 299, 644n59

Rosenberg, Charles, 154, 158, 167

Rowan, Archibold Hamilton, 592n45

Rowland, John T., 259

Royal Showband, 495

Runners, 256

Russell, Thomas O'Neill, 270

Russian Jews, 217, 546; in clothing industry, 189, 190

Russian immigrants; education of, 577n8; family size and, 565t; gainful employment and, 565t; home ownership and, 566t

Ryan, Daniel Edward, 176, 179, 191

Ryan, James, 23

Ryan, Joseph, 366, 665n70

Ryan, Redmond, 24

Ryan, William Fitz, 426

Sachs, Emanie N., 379, 384

Sadlier, Denis, 4, 23

Sadlier, James, 23

Sadlier, Mary Ann, 23

Safeway, 404

Said, Edward, 145

St. Agnes' Parish (Manhattan), 237, 239, 241, 243, 246

St. Alphonsus' Parish (Manhattan), 242, 632n25

St. Andrew's Parish (Manhattan), 111

St. Ann's Parish (Manhattan), 237, 239, 244

St. Anthony of Padua (Manhattan), 237, 238, 632n25

St. Augustine's Parish (Bronx), 243

St. Bernard's Parish (Manhattan), 238, 241, 242

St. Brigid's Parish (Manhattan), 242, 245, 250

St. Cecilia's Parish (Manhattan), 241

St. Columba's Parish (Manhattan), 28, 257, 333f

St. Francis College, 231, 343f

St. Francis Hospital, 166

St. Francis Xavier Parish (Manhattan), 237, 238, 239, 240, 241, 433

St. Gabriel's Parish (Manhattan), 240, 403, 675n33

St. Gregory the Great Parish (Manhattan), 402–3, 675n33

St. James' Dramatic Society, 384

St. James' Home, 244, 633n39

St. James' Parish (Manhattan), 28, 238, 239, 245, 247, 384, 638n6

St. James' Union, 384

St. John Nam Parish (Bronx), 431

St. John's College (Fordham), 231, 343f

St. Joseph's Seminary (Dunwoodie), 228

St. Jude's Parish (Manhattan), 445

St. Lawrence's Parish (Manhattan), 237, 239, 240, 241

St. Louis, Missouri, 641n21

St. Luke's Parish (Bronx), 406–7, 413

St. Margaret of Cortona Parish (Bronx), 678n64

St. Mary's Parish (Manhattan), 30

St. Michael's Parish (Manhattan), 244

St. Patrick's Cathedral, Old (Manhattan), 28, 196f

St. Patrick's Cathedral, 219, 237, 239, 240, 241–42, 242f

St. Patrick's Charity School (Manhattan), 29, 30

St. Patrick's Day, 51, 65

St. Patrick's Day parade, 72, 86f, 419–20, 503f; Michael Flannery and, 435f, 435–36; gay participation issue and, 7, 433; Irish county societies and, 283; Irish republicanism supported in, 333f, 437; labor movement and, 99; ladies' fairs compared with, 236, 249–50, 634n58; significance of, 104; Calvin Trillin on, 510

St. Patrick's Mutual Alliance, 279

St. Patrick's School (Brooklyn), 336f

St. Paul's (Episcopal) Church (Manhattan), 65

St. Paul the Apostle Parish (Manhattan), 244, 246

St. Peter's Parish (Manhattan), 28, 29, 52, 54, 72–73, 237

St. Philip's African Episcopal Church, 112, 114

St. Rose of Lima Parish (Manhattan), 242, 442

St. Rose of Lima Parish (Queens), 677n60

St. Simon Stock Parish (Bronx), 404f

St. Stephen's Parish (Manhattan), 226, 271, 310

St. Teresa of Avila Parish (Brooklyn), 400, 405, 414, 677n46, 677n63

St. Teresa of Avila Parish (Manhattan), 237, 240, 241, 243, 248

St. Vincent de Paul Society, 99, 220, 244, 248

St. Vincent Ferrer Parish (Manhattan), 237, 238

St. Vincent's Hospital (Manhattan), 20, 166–67, 201

St. Vincent's Nursery (Brooklyn), 220f

Salamander Association of Boiler and Pipe Covers, 304

Saloon keepers. *See* Taverns

Sampson, William, 15, 48–49, 53, 55f, 63, 64–66, 68, 164, 302f, 539, 548, 588n1; Association of the Friends of Ireland and, 64; beliefs on law and politics, 593–94n59; famous cases of, 592n45, 592n47; Greenwich Village riot and, 62, 79; Rufus King

and, 595n86; *People* v. *Philips* and, 54–61, 591n36; Society for Civil and Religious Liberties and, 64
Sanchez, Ben, 130
Sanders, Mary, 123
Sanders, Stephen, 123
Sands Point, New York, 399
San Francisco, California, 534–35, 536, 541, 611–12n64; Irish county societies in, 641n21; parochial schools in, 701n17
Sanger, Margaret Higgins, 2
Sanitary Commission fair, 236
Savage, John, 640n13
School No. 5, 25
School No. 11, 25
School No. 17, 25
Schools, 25–26, 68, 89, 95; African Americans and, 112; Bible reading controversy in, 88–89; Gary Plan and, 348, 385–88, 668n49, 669n51, 669n55; John Purroy Mitchel and, 385–88; pay-as-you-go policy in, 385, 668n47; prayer in, 431. *See also* Education; Parochial schools
Schrafft's restaurants, 404, 474f
Schwencke Land and Improvement Company, 410–11
Scots-Irish, 192, 546; in colonial era, 35, 41–42, 583n1; family size and, 565t; gainful employment and, 565t; home ownership and, 566t; music and, 692n3
Scott, David B., 649n40
Scurlock, Thomas, 37
Seaside, Rockaway (Queens), 408, 677n60
Season at Coole (Stephens), 697n39
Secondhand dealers, 22–23, 182, 188
Second Ward (Manhattan), 94
Seisúns, 482, 485, 489, 505
Self-Instruction in Irish (O'Daly), 264
Selkridge, J.F., 370
Semiskilled labor. *See* Laborers
Senate Special Investigating Committee on Organized Crime, 424–25
Seton, Elizabeth Ann, 29, 166
Seventh Ward (Manhattan), 75, 94, 276, 638n6
Seventy-fifth Regiment, 195, 196
Seward, William H., 30, 31, 32
Sewing machines, 185, 189
Shamrock (gunboat), 203
Shamrock, or Hibernian Chronicle (newspaper), 23, 60, 73–74, 79, 597n12
Shamrock Friendly Association, 15, 19, 71–72
Shamrock Minstrels, The, 490
Shamrocks (gang), 443
Shanachie Records, 486
Shandon Club (Corkmen's Association), 279
Shanley, Leo, 441
Shannon, Joseph, 27
Shannon, William, 344
Shaughraun, The (Boucicault), 232
Sheehan, Kathleen, 363, 369, 663n44
Sheehy-Skeffington, Hannah, 360, 361, 362, 363
Shefter, George, 651n56
Shirt Tails (gang), 114
Shoemakers union, 304

Showband music, 494–96
Simpson, Eileen O'Rourke, 406, 407
Sinclair, Agnes Campbell, 405, 406
Single-tax movement, 226, 308, 323, 324, 330, 363
Sinn Fein, 225, 331, 333f, 361
Sinn Fein Society of New York, 299
Sisters. *See* Nuns
Sisters of Charity, 20, 29, 164, 166, 167, 201, 202, 231, 633n38
Sisters of Mercy, 99, 103, 201, 220f, 336f
Sisters of the Poor St. Francis, 166
Siu, Paul, 152
Six Months in a Convent, 16
Sixth Ward (Manhattan), 23, 66–67, 75, 76, 77, 79, 80, 94, 111f, 638n6; African Americans in, 107–24, 542; Chinese in, 129, 130; 1834 Riot, 80; Kerryonians (gang) and, 639n12; George B. McClellan and, 208; police in, 26; Tammany Hall and, 80. *See also* Five Points
Sixth Ward Hotel, 22
Sixty-ninth Regiment, 194–95, 196, 197, 198–99, 202, 206, 229, 265, 365, 368, 625n17, 645n61. *See also* Irish Brigade; Irish Zouaves
Sixty-third Regiment, 198, 200–201
Skeffington, Harry J., 311
Skiing, 477
Skilled labor. *See* Laborers
Skirmishing Fund, 640n15
Slave revolts, 13
Slavery, 13, 32–33, 116, 145, 194, 378, 586–87n70. *See also* Abolitionist movement
Sligo, County, 288t, 289t, 639n9
Sligo Young Men's Association, 277–78, 297, 639n10, 643n43, 643n44, 643n45
Sligo Society of Boston, 640n21
Slocum Disaster, 675n28
Sloughter, Henry, 50
SLP. *See* Socialist Labor Party
Smallpox, 157
Smith, Alfred E., 4, 212f, 228, 339, 340, 341, 377–79, 381, 388, 389, 544, 669n61, 671n86; American Women Pickets and, 372; background of, 378–79; as Board of Alderman president, 375, 376; Catholicism of, 384–85; as defender of civil liberties, 390; as governor, 392–94; presidential campaign of, 352; Red scare and, 393–94; St. James' Dramatic Society and, 384–85; socialism and, 392, 671–72n90
Smith, Betty, 677n52
Smith, Dennis, 513, 515
Smith, Robert, 38
Smith, Thomas, 45–46, 587n82
Smith, William, Jr, 587n82
Smyth, J.P., 271
Soccer, 477
Social class, 71–74, 79, 80, 94–95, 412; Irish county societies and, 278, 297; Irish nationalism and, 327–28, 332; labor movement and, 303; social mobility and, 396–97, 406, 407, 409, 410, 415, 678n65. *See also* Middle class; Working class
Social control, 614–15n40

Social Democrat Party, 304. *See also* Socialist Labor Party

Socialism, 221, 225, 226, 539; Catholic Church and, 314, 651–52n65; Irish nationalism and, 327–29; labor movement and, 315–16, 318, 319; Alfred E. Smith and, 392, 671–72n90. *See also* Communism; *individual socialist parties*

Socialist Labor Party (SLP), 227, 304, 308, 309–10, 315, 648n33

Socialist Party of America, 315–16, 328, 340, 390

Social Service Commission (Militia of Christ for Social Service), 314

Society for Civil and Religious Liberties, 64

Society for the Encouragement of Faithful Domestic Servants, 19, 120

Society for the Preservation of the Irish Language, 268, 270

Society for the Reformation of Juvenile Delinquents, 27

Society of St. Tammany, 88. *See also* Tammany Hall

Socony, 405, 676–77n46

Songs. *See* Music

Sons of Erin, 24

South Africa, 350

South Bronx, New York, 400, 405, 406, 407, 409, 413, 500, 501, 675n29

Southern Citizen, 378

Soviet Mission, 393

Sowell, Thomas, 5

Spanish Civil War, 443

Spellman, Francis, Cardinal, 2, 4, 349, 419–20, 431, 542; loss of power by, 429–30; Joseph McCarthy supported by, 427, 429; parochial school funding and, 429

"Spenser's Ireland" (Moore), 511

Sports, 7, 231, 438, 629n66; Irish county societies and, 287–92, 641n28, 641n29, 642n31; New Irish immigrants and, 477. *See also specific sports*

Sprague, Charles, 637n43

Spread the Light Clubs, 305. *See also* Irish National Land League of America

Squeeze Gut Alley (Manhattan), 123

"Stanzas for Kossuth" (WBR), 259

Stars of Erin (sports team), 290

State Board of Charities, 381–82

State Charities Aid Association, 381

Staten Island, New York, 672n1; Greater New York Charter and, 624n13; Irish ancestry represented in, 567t; Irish-born naturalizations in, 564t; Irish-born population in, 555t, 561t, 564t

Stationary Engineers Union, 297

Steely Blue (Smith), 515

Steffens, Lincoln, 3

Stephens, James, 260

Stephens, Michael, 697n39

Stevenson, Adlai, 425, 427

Stewart, Alexander T., 192

Stewart, Ramona, 626n30

Stock market crash of 1929, 352

Stone of the Heart, A (Grimes), 522–23

Stop-Time (Conroy), 513

Stouffer's restaurants, 404, 474f

Straus, Oscar, 340

Street, Julian, 374, 381, 383

Streetcars, 397

Stret, Julian, 379

Strikes, 96, 99, 100; Chinese and, 139–40; clothing industry, 177; criticism of, 314; Erie Railroad, 96; freighthandlers, 305; garment workers, 329, 332; longshoremen, 108, 203–4; William Sampson's defense of, 592n47; shoe industry, 316. *See also* American Women Pickets for the Enforcement of America's War Aims

Strong, Charles H., 382

Strong, George Templeton, 17, 19, 131, 204–5, 252–53, 274

Studs Lonigan (Farrell), 345, 347, 509, 518

Stuyvesant Town (Manhattan), 674n22

Subterranean, 17

Suburbanization, 396, 672n3

Suburbs, 403, 421, 440, 543–44

Subway system, 229, 400, 441

Such Is Life (Furphy), 511

Sue, Ah, 130

Suffolk County, New York, 421–22

Suffrage; African American, 15, 116, 132; woman's, 329–31, 359, 361–62

Suicide, 21

Sullivan, Margaret, 413

Sullivan, Mary L., 369

Sullivan, "Big" Tim, 223, 227

Sullivan, Yankee (James Ambrose), 25

Sulzer, William, 341

"Sum and Substance, The" (Cullinan), 528

Sun, 370

Sunburst, 267

Sunnyside (Queens), 400, 403

Sunset Park (Brooklyn), 400

Superintendent. *See* Custodial work

Survey magazine, 383, 389, 390, 391

Sutter's Mill, California, 127

Swallow Tail Democrats, 223, 226, 227, 538, 626n31

Sweeney, David, 19

Sweeney, Lawrence, 46

Sweeney, Timothy, 2

Sweeney's Shambles (Manhattan), 20, 21

Sweeny, Peter B., 24, 27

Sweet, Orr & Co., 179

Swimming Bath, 123

Swinton, John, 310

Syle, Edward, 126–27

Sylvester, Harry, 347

Synge, John Millington, 226, 365

Table Money (Breslin), 424, 514

Taft, William Howard, 326, 664n58

Tailor and Cutter magazine, 179

Tailors, 169–92. *See also* Clothing industry

Tammany Hall, 2, 3, 4, 15, 19, 33, 79–80, 88, 102, 218, 226–228, 237, 338–41, 424, 425–26, 535–36, 537, 538; Catholics and, 541; as defender of civil liberties, 377, 390; Carmine De Sapio and, 425–26; Irish National Land League of America and, 305; Irish nationalism and, 324; labor move-

ment and, 307, 308–9, 312–14, 316, 319–20, 651n56; John Purroy Mitchel and, 381, 385–87, 389, 391–92, 671n80; parochial schools and, 30; Red Scare and, 393–94; refusal to nominate Thomas Addis Emmet, 79; resistance to change, 628n53; revitalization of, 628n51; Alfred E. Smith and, 379, 392–94; Washington Heights/Inwood neighborhood and, 443
Tammany Hall Irish Relief Fund, 647n18
Tammany Tiger, 212f
Tap dancing, 131
Taverns, 39, 109, 122, 230
Taylor, William Cooke, 60
Teachers, 95, 105, 121, 230–31, 313, 419; John Purroy Mitchel and, 385–86
Tea merchants, 128
Temperance movement, 220–21. *See also* Mathew, Fr., Total Abstinence and Benevolent Society
Templeton, Oliver, 43
Templeton and Stewart, 43
Tenant Leagues, 305. *See also* Irish National Land League of America
Tender Is the Night (Fitzgerald), 346
Test Oath, 51–52
That Night (McDermott), 520, 521
Theater, 24–25, 231–33, 347, 629n68; Chinese ridiculed in, 142–45. *See also* Vaudeville
"They Went Forth to Battle but They Always Fell" (O'Sheel), 511
Third Avenue Railway, 403, 423
This Side of Paradise (Fitzgerald), 346
Thomas Davis Club, 24
Thomas Francis Meaghers (sports team), 290
Thompson, Acheson, 39
Thompson, George, 120
Thompson, George P., 383, 384
Thompson, James, 39
Thornton, Frank, 501
Tierney, Elizabeth, 458
Tierney, Myles, 673n11
Tiffany and Company, 199
Times (London), 102
Tin Wife (Flaherty), 514
Tipperary, County, 288t, 289t, 638n6, 639n6; football team (Kickhams), 290
Tipperary Society, 281, 639n7, 643n43
Tobin, John F., 316
Tocqueville, Alexis de, 215, 377, 624n5, 666n16
Toll, Robert, 143
Tombs, 109, 112, 121
Tone, Theobold Wolfe, 61
Tone, William, 61
Tories, 66
Touhey, Patsy, 484, 501
Toumey, John, 26
Townsend, Edward, 148
Trade assemblies, 304
Trade unions. *See* Unions
Traditional music, Irish, 4, 437, 482–92, 496–505, 546; declining interest in, 496–500; defined of, 482–83; earliest known recording of, 692n3; employment

in, 489; "golden age" of, 484–85; Irish Musicians Association and, 501, 694n60; New York Ceili Band and, 695n61; revival of, 505–7. *See also* Ceili music and dances
Transactions of the Ossianic Society (O'Daly), 262
Transfiguration Parish (Manhattan), 28, 73, 111, 129, 238
Transit workers, 403, 406, 423
Transport Workers Union, 2, 354f, 355, 423, 539, 627–28n49
Transportation, 397, 421, 543. *See also types of transportation*
Traynor, John, 676n39
Traynor, Thomas, 53
Tree Grows in Brooklyn, A (Smith), 677n52
Tremont (Bronx), 403
Triangle Shirt Waist Company fire, 653n78
Trillin, Calvin, 510
Trinity (Episcopal) Church (Manhattan), 42–43
Trouble of One House, The (Gill), 525
Trow's City Directory, 179, 181, 188
Truman, Harry S., 425
Trusteeism, 591n41
"Truthful James" (Hart), 148
Truth Teller, 23, 31, 74
Tuberculosis, 114, 167, 217. *See also* Consumption
Tulla *Ceili* Band, 499
Turner, Victor, 109
Tweed, William M. ("Boss"), 102, 207, 638n5
Tweed Ring, 222, 307, 538
Type style, for Irish language text, 261, 266, 637n34
Typhoid fever, 100
Typhus, 21, 100, 113, 155
Typists, 121
Typographers Local 6, 648n28
Tyrone, County, 287, 288t, 289t, 639n6
Tyrone Men, 299

UGWA. *See* United Garment Workers of America
UHT. *See* United Hebrew Trades
UIC. *See* United Irish Counties
UILA. *See* United Irish League of America
ULP. *See* United Labor Party
Ulster (province), Ireland, 13, 35, 41, 286, 287, 288t, 289t
Ultramontanism, 216, 219
Union Club, 24
Unions, 105, 221, 303–4, 317–20, 354–55, 545, 639n2; African Americans and, 109; Catholic Church and, 221; changes in leadership, 317–18; construction, 469–70; Irish nationalism and, 323; New Immigrants and, 311–12, 318; politics and, 312, 316; Alfred E. Smith administration and, 392–93. *See also* Labor movement
United Brotherhood of Carpenters and Joiners, 303, 304, 317–18
United Garment Workers of America (UGWA), 316, 318
United Hatters, 178
United Hebrew Trades (UHT), 318–19

United Irish, 49, 62, 63, 66, 71; exiles, 48–50, 61, 67, 68, 588n2; free exercise of religion and, 52–53; *People* v. *Philips* and, 57–58, 59; Republicanism and, 64–68
United Irish Counties (UIC), 284, 291, 292. *See also* Irish Counties Athletic Union
United Irish Counties Associations (UICA), 420, 478, 502, 503f. *See also* Feis, United Irish Counties Association
United Irish Counties Association, 284
United Irish League, 325
United Irish League of America (UILA), 298, 315, 325–26, 327, 329–30, 331, 333–34, 363, 644n52
United Irishman, 225, 258, 272, 273
United Irish Societies, 285, 641n24
United Labor Party (ULP), 227, 309–10
United Nations, 428
United Negro Improvement Association, 370–71
Unskilled labor. *See* Laborers
Up from the City Streets (Hapgood & Moskowitz), 384
Urban liberalism, 388, 669n61

Vaik, Francis, 282
Vale, Gilbert, 115, 116
Vallentine, Thomas, 39
Van Buren, Martin, 64
Van Buren, William, 166–67
van Schaack, Peter, 45
Vardy, Frank, 408–9
Varela, Fr. Felix, 164
Vatican II, 429, 432, 511
Vaudeville, 231, 629n67
Veronica, Sr., 441
Versailles, Treaty of, 426
Victor records, 484
Vietnam War, 427, 429, 451
Village of Longing, The (O'Brien), 508
Villard, Oswald Garrison, 374, 375, 376, 380, 383, 391, 392, 667n24
Vincentians, 231
Visa lotteries. *See* Donnelly visas; Morrison visas
Voluntary organizations. *See* Benevolent associations
Volunteers of Ireland, 14
Vose, John D., 113
Voting. *See* Suffrage

Waddell, Robert Ross, 13, 40
Wages of whiteness, 107, 117
Wagner, Robert F. (1877–1953), 212f, 228, 340, 388, 389
Wagner, Robert F. (1910–1991), 425–26
Waiters, 108
Waitresses, 404, 474f. *See also* Restaurant/bar trades
Wakefield Park (Bronx), 291–92
Wakeman, George, 141–42
Walck, Charles, 444
Walck, Norene, 442, 443, 444, 446, 448, 457
Walker, James J., 340, 352, 353, 394, 424, 535–36
Wall, William Guy, 24, 33

Wallace, Alexander, 13
Wallace, Gerry, 695n61
Wallace, Hugh, 13, 39, 43
Wallander, Arthur, 419
Walsh, Frank P., 351, 368, 661n15, 663n38, 664n58
Walsh, Geraldine Murphy, 409, 675n35, 678n64
Walsh, Marie, 403, 679n82
Walsh, Michael, 17, 117
Walsh, Thomas P., 26
Ward, Benjamin, 428
Ward, Brendan, 487–88, 491, 492, 493
Ward, George, 409–10
Ward Line, 367
Ward School No. 8, 26
Warner, Margaret, 363, 369
War of 1812, 53, 64
Warren, Peter, 43
Washerwomen, 121
Washington, Adelaide, 113
Washington, George, 14, 24
Washington, George (African American), 113
Washington, Harold, 429
Washington Engine Company No. 20, 26
Washington Heights (Manhattan), 439–60, 685–89n; crime in, 440–41, 450–51, 452–53, 456–57, 687n41; drug problem in, 456–57; gangs in, 443, 444–45, 687n32; murder rate in, 456–57, 688–88n64; residential patterns in, 399, 401, 402, 414, 675n27, 675n31
Washington Star, 361
Waterford, County, 288t, 289t
Watts, John, 37
WBR (pen name), 259
Webb, James W., 16
Weber, John B., 153
Webster, Daniel, 64
Weekly Day-Book, 203
Weiss, Ted, 422
Welfare democracy, 319
Welsh immigrants, 253
Welsh language, 253
Wesley, John, 43
Westchester County, New York, 395, 421
West End Association, 398
Western Federation of Miners (WFM), 328, 653n80
Westies (gang), 422
Westmeath, County, 287, 288t, 289t, 641n26
Westmeath Men, 298
Wexford, County, 288t, 289t
Wexford Men, 279, 281, 292, 298
"When New York Was Irish" (Winch), 395, 513
Whigs, 16, 66, 67, 80, 101–2, 222, 595n80, 595n83; African Americans and, 117, 132; parochial school issue and, 31
White flight, 675n30
White Star Line, 363, 369, 370
Whitman, Charles Seymour, 382
Whitman, Walt, 122, 508
Wicklow, County, 288t, 289t
Wilkinson, Joseph, 303, 304
Willcox, William G., 669n51

William of Orange, King, 61, 65
Williams, Barney, 24
Williams, Bert, 144
Williams, C.F., 136
Williams, Deborah, 123
Williams, Lizzie, 148
Williams, Peter (dance hall owner), 112, 122–23
Williams, Peter (seaman), 123
Williams, Roger, 49
Williamsburg (Brooklyn), 400
Williamsburg Bridge, 398, 400
Wilson, John, 39
Wilson, Woodrow, 319, 326, 350–51, 359, 360, 361, 426
Wilson's Business Directory, 188, 260
Winch, Terence, 395, 511, 512–13
Wobblies. *See* Industrial Workers of the World
Wold, Emma, 371
Wolfe, Tom, 7
Wolfe Tones (sports team), 290
Women, 7, 93, 219, 230–31, 324; African American, 120–22; Ancient Order of Hibernians and, 359, 661n9; Augustus Street riot and, 83; Catholicism and, 219, 429; "ethnic cleansing" and, 147; female-headed households, 121; feminism and, 430; Irish county societies and, 293–95, 642n40–41, 643n42, 661n9; Irish nationalism and, 324, 329–32, 359–60; labor movement and, 313, 316, 650n51; mental illness in, 160–61; as New Irish immigrants, 473; occupations of, 77–78, 95, 96, 109, 120–22, 182, 217, 230–31, 238, 336f, 404–5, 473, 474f; ordination issue and, 432; Religious orders of., 219–20, 230–31, 244, 336f, 383–84, 625n57; residential patterns and, 404–5, 407–8, 415; role in ladies' fairs, 237–38, 248–49; suffrage for,

329–31, 359, 361–62. *See also* American Women Pickets for the Enforcement of America's War Aims; Nuns
Women's Municipal League, 391
Wood, Fernando, 26, 118
Woods, Arthur, 392
Woodside (Queens), 400, 401, 403, 422, 681n95
Worcester, Massachusetts, 540
Work House, 21
Working class, 547, 576n4; Irish county societies and, 297; labor movement and, 303; in Washington Heights/Inwood neighborhood, 688n58. *See also* Social class
Workingmen's Party, 19, 117, 143, 303
Workingmen's Petition, 117
Workingmen's Political League of New York City, 313
Workingmen's Union, 304
Working Women's Protective Union, 202
World War I, 224, 229, 333–34, 359; pro-German support and, 350–51, 390–91
World War II, 354, 355, 441, 443
World without End, Amen (Breslin), 514

Yankee Kitchen (Manhattan), 123
Yankee Notions, 129, 131, 132, 147
Yankees (baseball team), 7, 231
Yates, Ann, 78
Yeats, William Butler, 327, 365
Yellow Roses (Cullinan), 528
Yorkville (Manhattan), 399, 677n56, 678n64
Young, Arthur, 163
Young, David, 38
Young, Hamilton, 40
Young Ireland, 31, 32, 105, 223, 259, 260–61, 321, 539
Youngs, James, 137
Youth culture, 477

Library of Congress Cataloging-in-Publication Data

The New York Irish / edited by Ronald H. Bayor and Timothy J. Meagher.
   p.   cm.
   Includes bibliographical references (p.) and index.
   ISBN 0-8018-5199-8 (alk. paper)
   1. Irish Americans—New York (N.Y.)—History.   2. New York (N.Y.)—Ethnic
Relations.   3. New York (N.Y.)—History.   I. Bayor, Ronald H., 1944– .
II. Meagher, Timothy J.
F128.9.16N49   1995
974.7´1—dc20   95-20319

ISBN 0-8018-5764-3 (pbk.)